ADMINISTRATIVE LAW

Text and Materials

ADMINISTRATIVE LAW

Text and Materials

FIFTH EDITION

Mark Elliott
Jason N. E. Varuhas

OXFORD
UNIVERSITY PRESS

OXFORD

UNIVERSITY PRESS

Great Clarendon Street, Oxford, OX2 6DP,
United Kingdom

Oxford University Press is a department of the University of Oxford.
It furthers the University's objective of excellence in research, scholarship,
and education by publishing worldwide. Oxford is a registered trade mark of
Oxford University Press in the UK and in certain other countries

© Professor Mark Elliott, Dr Jason Varuhas, and Mr Martin Matthews 2017

The moral rights of the authors have been asserted

Third edition 2005
Fourth edition 2011
Fifth edition 2017

Impression: 1

Published in the United States of America by Oxford University Press
198 Madison Avenue, New York, NY 10016, United States of America

British Library Cataloguing-in-Publication Data
Data available

Library of Congress Control Number: 2016948895

ISBN 978-0-19-871946-5

Printed in Great Britain by
Bell & Bain Ltd, Glasgow

PREFACE

In the three decades since its first edition was published, this book—like English administrative law itself—has undergone many changes. The first two editions, published in 1983 and 1989 and written by Sir Jack Beatson and Martin Matthews, took the form of casebooks in which excerpts from cases and other materials were accompanied by concise but always penetrating commentary. The third and fourth editions, published in 2005 and 2011, were written by Mark Elliott, with Sir Jack Beatson and Martin Matthews serving as consultant editors. The third edition amounted to a fundamental rewrite of the book—a step that was necessary in the light of the 16-year period that had elapsed since the publication of the previous edition, and which involved transforming the book from a casebook into a text and materials book.

This fifth edition forms a further milestone in the evolution of the book. It is the first edition to be produced under the joint authorship of Mark Elliott and Jason Varuhas. While the book remains a text and materials book, the excerpts from cases and the literature that we have included are generally shorter and the text relatively more extensive. At a time when so much information is available online, the value of a book such as this lies in providing students with a sound conceptual framework and source of analysis that they can deploy when navigating the cases and other materials. We have endeavoured in producing this edition not only to supply precisely such a framework and analysis but to challenge readers to think critically about the law. We have also striven to present matters in an objective fashion that enables students to make up their own minds about difficult and contentious issues of theory and policy.

New to this edition

Every chapter in this edition has been thoroughly updated, and many chapters have been substantially rewritten. In particular, chapter 15, on the liability of public authorities, has been rewritten largely from scratch. It now focuses on a more select range of issues, encouraging readers to engage with those matters in greater and more critical depth. Parts of chapter 8, which deals with substantive judicial review, have been fundamentally recast in the light of recent Supreme Court judgments concerning the relationship between the *Wednesbury* reasonableness and proportionality doctrines and the likely future trajectory of this bellwether area of administrative law.

The chapter on jurisdiction now takes account of the key Supreme Court decisions in *R (Cart)* v. *Upper Tribunal* [2011] UKSC 28, [2012] 1 AC 663 (which is addressed too in the chapters on tribunals and restrictions on remedies) and *R (Jones)* v. *First-tier Tribunal* [2013] UKSC 19, [2013] 2 AC 48. The same Court's path-breaking judgment in *Braganza* v. *BP Shipping Ltd* [2015] UKSC 17, [2015] 1 WLR 1661 is examined in the chapter on the scope of public law principles, which also includes a new discussion of the public law–private law distinction.

Chapter 5, concerning retention of discretion, discusses recent developments in the law on delegation of decision-making power, including the Supreme Court decision in *R (Bourgass)* v. *Secretary of State for Justice* [2015] UKSC 54, [2015] 3 WLR 457. In the same chapter we identify and examine a sea change in the judicial approach to policy which today, far from being considered a threat to discretionary decision-making, is often seen by the courts as a tool for disciplining the exercise of administrative discretion so that it conforms to rule-law-values in certainty, consistency, and openness. Such considerations are, of course, also in play in respect of legitimate expectations; in the chapter dealing with that area, we identify a number of emergent trends and chart a series of crucial recent developments, noting, in particular, the Court of Appeal's important judgment in *R (Patel)* v. *General Medical Council* [2013] EWCA Civ 327, [2013] 1 WLR 2801. Chapter 7 has been thoroughly updated and includes a new discussion of the interaction between the longstanding principle that statutory powers must be exercised consistently with statutory purposes, and newer doctrines requiring adoption of rights-consistent interpretations of legislation. Chapter 10, on procedural fairness, takes account of a number of important recent decisions including that of the Supreme Court in *R (Osborn)* v. *Parole Board* [2013] UKSC 61, [2014] AC 1115, and a new section has been added on the fast-developing jurisprudence on the law of consultation.

Meanwhile, chapter 13, on the judicial review procedure, charts the increasingly significant impact of human rights claims on core features of the judicial review procedure, and the pressure such claims have placed on (what remains of) the procedural distinction between public and private law. Our examination of restrictions on remedies in chapter 14 takes account of new limitations introduced following recent government consultations on judicial review that were animated by concerns about the volume of judicial review challenges being brought and the abuse of judicial review for political ends. In particular, we examine and consider the likely implications of the statutory 'no difference' principle inserted into the Senior Courts Act 1981 by s 84 of the Criminal Justice and Courts Act 2015. The section of chapter 14 that deals with the law of standing has been substantially rewritten, not least in order to take account of the Supreme Court's landmark judgments in *AXA General Insurance Ltd* v. *The Lord Advocate* [2011] UKSC 46, [2012] 1 AC 868 and *Walton* v. *Scottish Ministers* [2012] UKSC 44, [2013] PTSR 51. Chapter 12 notes a series of interesting developments in the law governing stays of proceedings and injunctions in judicial review proceedings.

The chapters dealing with administrative justice mechanisms—ombudsmen, tribunals, and inquiries—have also been thoroughly updated and, in places, rewritten to take account of developments in those areas, including recent and proposed changes to various public sector ombudsmen systems, and the enhanced role now played by the Upper Tribunal in immigration-related matters.

Acknowledgements

We are grateful to all at Oxford University Press who have been involved in the production of this new edition. Special thanks, however, go to Carol Barber, for whose efficiency and helpfulness we are immensely grateful, and to Philip Moore, to whom we are indebted for his meticulous attention to detail in respect of the proofs. Finally, we wish to record our thanks to our families for their love and support—in particular, in Jason's case to his mother, Nicola, and in Mark's case to his wife, Vicky, and their daughter, Maisie.

Mark Elliott, Cambridge
Jason Varuhas, Melbourne
July 2016

ACKNOWLEDGEMENTS

Grateful acknowledgment is made to all the authors and publishers of copyright material which appears in this book, and in particular to the following for permission to reprint material from the sources indicated:

Contains public sector information licensed under the Open Government Licence v1.0 (http://www.nationalarchives.gov.uk/doc/open-government-licence/open-government-licence.htm).

Crown Copyright material reproduced with the permission of the Controller, HMSO (under the terms of the Click Use licence).

Cambridge Law Journal for extracts from: TRS Allan, 'Human Rights and Judicial Review: A Critique of 'Due Deference' (2006) CLJ 671; Paul Craig, 'Ultra Vires and the Foundations of Judicial Review' (1998) CLJ 63 and Bruce Harris, 'Judicial Review, Justiciability and the Prerogative of Mercy' (2003) CLJ 631.

Cambridge University Press and the authors for extracts from D. Feldman, 'Error of Law and Flawed Administrative Acts' (2014) CLJ, 275; Carol Harlow and Richard Rawlings, Law and Administration (1997) and Mary Seneviratne, Ombudsmen: Public Services and Administrative Justice (2002) from the Law in Context series, reproduced with permission.

Canadian Bar Foundation for extract from John Willis, 'Delegatus Non Potest Delegare' (1943) 21 Canadian Bar Review 257.

Harry Arthurs for extract from HW Arthurs, 'Rethinking Administrative Law: A Slightly Dicey Business' (1979) 17 Osgoode Hall Law Journal 1.

Hart Publishing Ltd for extracts from M Elliott, The Constitutional Foundations of Judicial Review (2001) and M Hunt, 'Constitutionalism and the Contractualisation of Government in the United Kingdom' in M Taggart (ed), The Province of Administrative Law (1997). Used by permission of Bloomsbury Publishing Plc.

Incorporated Council of Law Reporting for England and Wales: extracts from the Law Reports: Appeal Cases (AC), Chancery Division (Ch), King's Bench Division (KB), Queen's Bench Division (QB), and Weekly Law Reports (WLR).

LexisNexis for extracts from All England Law Reports [All ER]. Reproduced by permission of RELX (UK) Limited, trading as LexisNexis.

New Zealand Law Review and Nicky Taggart for extract from M Taggart, 'Proportionality, Deference, Wednesbury' [2008] NZ L Rev 423.

Oxford University Press for extracts from DJ Galligan, 'Procedural Fairness' in Peter Birks (ed), The Frontiers of Liability, Volume 1 (1994); Jeffery Jowell, 'The Rule of Law Today' in Jeffery Jowell, Dawn Oliver and Colm O'Cinneide (eds), The Changing Constitution (2007); M. Beloff, 'Time, Time, Time, It's on my side, yes it is', Christopher Forsyth, 'The Metaphysic of Nullity: Invalidity, Conceptual Reasoning and the Rule of Law', Sir John Laws 'Wednesbury' and S. Sedley, 'The Crown and Its Own Courts' in Christopher Forsyth and Ivan Hare (eds), The Golden Metwand and the Crooked Cord: Essays in Public Law in Honour of Sir William Wade QC (1998) and Soren Schønberg, Legitimate Expectations in Administrative Law (2000).

Oxford University Press Journals for extract from Oxford Journal of Legal Studies: TRS Allan, 'Procedural Fairness and the Duty of Respect' (1998) 18 OJLS 497. Permission conveyed through Copyright Clearence Center.

Sweet & Maxwell Ltd for extracts from European Human Rights Reports [EHRR] and from Public Law: Drewry, 'Judicial Inquiries and Public Reassurance' [1996] PL 368; Freedland, 'The Rule Against Delegation and the Carltona Doctrine in an Agency Context' [1996] PL 19; Irvine, 'Judges and Decision Makers' [1996] PL 67; Oliver, 'Functions of a Public Nature under the Human Rights Act' [2004] PL 329; Olowofoyeku, 'The Nemo Judex Rule: The Case Against Automatic Disqualification' [2000] PL 456 and Schiemann, Locus Standi [1990] PL 342 reproduced with permission of THOMSON REUTERS (PROFESSIONAL) UK LIMITED via PLSclear.

Thomas, Robert for extracts from 'Immigration Judicial Reviews' (UK Constitutional Law Blog, September 2013).

Thomson Reuters for extract from Commonwealth Law Reports [CLR], New South Wales v. Bardolph (1934) 52 CLR 455. Reproduced with permission of Thomson Reuters (Professional) Australia Limited, www.thomsonreuters.com.au.

Every effort has been made to trace and contact the copyright holders but this has not been possible in all cases. If notified, the publisher will undertake to rectify any errors or omissions at the earliest opportunity.

OUTLINE CONTENTS

19   Ombudsmen

DETAILED CONTENTS

2 Jurisdiction

3 The Status of Unlawful Administrative Action

4 The Scope of Public Law Principles

5 Retention of Discretion

6 Legitimate Expectations

7   Abuse of Discretion I

8   Abuse of Discretion II

9   Bias, Impartiality, and Independence

10 Procedural Fairness

11 Giving Reasons for Decisions

12 Remedies

15 Liability of Public Authorities

17 Inquiries

18   Statutory Tribunals

TABLE OF CASES

*Page references in **bold** indicate that the item is given particular prominence in the text.*

TABLE OF STATUTES

*Page references in **bold** indicate that the item is given particular prominence in the text.*

TABLE OF STATUTORY INSTRUMENTS

*Page references in **bold** indicate that the item is given particular prominence in the text.*

TABLE OF EUROPEAN UNION LEGISLATION AND INTERNATIONAL TREATIES AND CONVENTIONS

*Page references in **bold** indicate that the item is given particular prominence in the text.*

LIST OF ABBREVIATIONS

AC	Law Reports, Appeal Cases
Admin LR	Administrative Law Reports
All ER	All England Law Reports
ALR	Australian Law Reports
App Cas	Law Reports, Appeal Cases
BMLR	Butterworths Medico-Legal Reports
CBNS	Common Bench Reports, New Series
Ch	Law Reports, Chancery Division
CJEU	Court of Justice of the European Union
CLJ	*Cambridge Law Journal*
CLP	*Current Legal Problems*
CLR	Commonwealth Law Reports
CMLR	Common Market Law Reports
CPR	Civil Procedure Rules
Crim LR	*Criminal Law Review*
DLR	Dominion Law Reports
EC	European Community
ECHR	European Convention on Human Rights
ECtHR	European Court of Human Rights
Ed CR	Education Case Reports
EHRLR	*European Human Rights Law Review*
EHRR	European Human Rights Reports
EMLR	Entertainment and Media Law Reports
Env LR	Environmental Law Reports
EU	European Union
Eu LR	European Law Reports
EWCA Civ	[Neutral citation for Court of Appeal (Civil Division) decisions]
EWHC	[Neutral citation for High Court decisions]
EWHC (Admin)	[Neutral citation for Administrative Court decisions]
Ex	Exchequer Reports
Fed LR	Federal Law Reports
FLR	Family Law Reports
FSR	Fleet Street Reports
HC	House of Commons papers
HL	House of Lords papers
HLC	Clark & Finnelly's House of Lords Reports New Series

HLR	Housing Law Reports
HRA	Human Rights Act 1998
ICR	Industrial Cases Reports
ILJ	*Industrial Law Journal*
INLR	Immigration and Nationality Law Reports
IRLR	Industrial Relations Law Reports
JCHR	Parliamentary Joint Committee on Human Rights
JPL	*Journal of Planning and Environment Law*
JR	*Judicial Review*
Jur Rev	*Juridical Review*
KB	Law Reports, King's Bench
Law Com	Law Commission papers
Ld Raym	Lord Raymond's King's Bench and Common Pleas Reports
LGR	Local Government Reports
LQR	*Law Quarterly Review*
LR HL	Law Reports, English & Irish Appeals
LS	*Legal Studies*
LSG	*Law Society Gazette*
LT	Law Times Reports
MLR	*Modern Law Review*
NILQ	*Northern Ireland Legal Quarterly*
NZ L Rev	*New Zealand Law Review*
NZLR	New Zealand Law Reports
OJLS	*Oxford Journal of Legal Studies*
P	Law Reports, Probate
Parl Aff	*Parliamentary Affairs*
P & CR	Property and Compensation Reports
PL	*Public Law*
Pub Admin	*Public Administration*
QB	Law Reports, Queen's Bench
RSC	Rules of the Supreme Court
S Ct	Supreme Court Reporter
SIAC	*Special Immigration Appeals Commission*
SJLB	*Solicitors' Journal Law Brief*
SR (NSW)	New South Wales State Reports
Stat L Rev	*Statute Law Review*
Stra	Strange's King's Bench Reports

TLJ	*Torts Law Journal*
TR	Taxation Reports
UBCLR	*University of British Columbia Law Review*
U Chi LR	*University of Chicago Law Review*
UKHL	[Neutral citation for House of Lords decisions]
UKHRR	United Kingdom Human Rights Reports
UKPC	[Neutral citation for Privy Council decisions]
UKSC	[Neutral citation for United Kingdom Supreme Court decisions]
UTLJ	*University of Toronto Law Journal*
VR	Victorian Reports
Web JCLI	*Web Journal of Current Legal Issues*
WLR	Weekly Law Reports

1 INTRODUCTORY MATTERS

1.1 Administrative law

To many, if not all, readers of this book, *private law* will be a familiar notion. Private law refers to such branches of the law as contract and tort, and is concerned principally with the duties and obligations which individuals owe to one another. Now, it is, of course, possible for government and other public bodies to enter into contracts and to engage in conduct which may be tortious; when they do, they are, quite rightly, in general regulated by the same body of private law as citizens. However, it is clear that, in addition to doing things, such as breaching contracts and carelessly causing injury, that can readily be dealt with by private law, government and public bodies commit a wide range of acts that cannot meaningfully be so regulated. Consider, for instance, the position of an individual whose house is to be compulsorily purchased and demolished by government to make way for a new airport, or an asylum seeker who is told that he must leave the country. Many of the issues which arise in such circumstances cannot adequately be regulated by private law. Does the government, in the first place, possess the legal power to order the purchase and destruction of the house? Would it make a difference if the government had decided to site the airport in a particular location for self-serving party political reasons—eg to create jobs in a nearby marginal constituency? Should the asylum seeker have been given an opportunity—and, if so, what sort of opportunity—to plead his case before the decision to deport him was taken? Can the asylum seeker be deported to a particular country if there is evidence to suggest that he would be treated inhumanely or tortured upon arrival there? Questions such as these are peculiarly relevant to the type of powers exercised by government and public bodies, and a separate body of law to regulate the exercise of such powers—*administrative law*—is therefore required.

1.2 How is good administration to be secured?

There can be little doubt that the central purpose of administrative law is to promote good administration. For example, administrative bodies should act efficiently and honestly to promote the public good; they should listen to individuals likely to be affected by their decisions, taking their views into account; and they should operate in a fair, transparent, and unbiased fashion, seeking always to serve the public interest while, at the same time, respecting the rights of individuals.

However, while it is uncontroversial that administrative law's central purpose is to secure good government along these lines, the same cannot be said of the methodology by which that objective is to be secured. For instance, should *courts* bear primary responsibility for ensuring good administrative conduct, or can this better be secured in some other way? And is it appropriate to borrow from the private law model of adjudication, under which courts seek to resolve disputes after they have arisen, so that administrative law operates retrospectively to correct misuses of public power? Or should administrative law be regarded as a template of good practice which primarily exists not to punish or correct misuses of power, but to promote an environment within which such misuses are, in the first place, rare? Differing answers to these questions are supplied by the 'red light' and 'green light' models of administrative law.

1.2.1 Red light theory

The red light view—like its green light counterpart, to which we turn shortly—comprises a number of different threads, and is elaborated at length by Harlow and Rawlings, *Law and Administration* (Cambridge 2009), ch 1. They identify a strand of literature (at 23) which holds that the 'primary function of administrative law should be to control excesses of state power' and to subject exercises of such power 'to the rule of law courts'. They cite the following passage from Wade and Forsyth's *Administrative Law* (Oxford 2004) at 4–5 (which also appears in the most recent edition, published in 2014, at 4–5) as a paradigm example of this red light tradition:

> A first approximation to a definition of administrative law is to say that it is the law relating to the control of governmental power. This, at any rate, is the heart of the subject, as viewed by most lawyers. The governmental power in question is not that of Parliament: Parliament as the legislature is sovereign and, subject to one exception [concerning European Union law], is beyond legal control. The powers of all other public authorities are subordinated to the law, just as much in the case of the Crown and Ministers as in the case of local authorities and other public bodies. All such subordinate powers have two inherent characteristics. First, they are all subject to legal limitations; there is no such thing as absolute or unfettered administrative power. Secondly, and consequentially, it is always possible for any power to be abused. Even where Parliament enacts that a Minister may make such an order as he thinks fit for a certain purpose, the court may still invalidate the order if it infringes one of the many judge-made rules. And the court will invalidate it, *a fortiori*, if it infringes the limits which Parliament itself has ordained.
>
> The primary purpose of administrative law, therefore, is to keep the powers of the government within their legal bounds, so as to protect the citizen against their abuse. The powerful engines of authority must be prevented from running amok. 'Abuse', it should be made clear, carries no necessary innuendo of malice or bad faith. Government departments may misunderstand their legal position as easily as may other people, and the law which they have to administer is frequently complex and uncertain. Abuse is therefore inevitable, and it is all the more necessary that the law should provide means to check it ...
>
> As well as power there is duty. It is also the concern of administrative law to see that public authorities can be compelled to perform their duties if they make default ... The law provides compulsory remedies for such situations, thus dealing with the negative as well as the positive side of maladministration.

This passage exhibits two features which are characteristic of the red light model: it is the *courts* which are centrally charged with securing good administration, while the emphasis is on administrative law as a *control* upon government—an external fetter upon the freedom of public authorities, a corrective to be invoked when power is abused. Within this tradition, courts and public authorities are ultimately regarded as combatants, the former invoking the weapon of administrative law against the latter as part of an ongoing fight against the abuse of governmental power.

1.2.2 Green light theory

A different approach is commended by green light theory, the following explanation of which is taken from an earlier edition of Harlow and Rawlings (London 1997) at 67–74:

[We turn now to] an alternative tradition, which we have called 'green light' theory. In using this metaphor, we do not wish to suggest that green light theorists favour unrestricted or arbitrary action by the state. What one person sees as control of arbitrary power may, however, be experienced by another as a brake on progress … Where red light theorists favour judicial control of executive power, green light theorists are inclined to pin their hopes on the political process …

New accounts of administrative law … began to appear in England. These were *administration centred*—the role of administrative law was not to act as a counterweight to the interventionist state but to facilitate legitimate government action—and *collectivist* in character, advancing the claim to promote the public interest or common good …

Because they see their own function as the resolution of disputes and because they see the administrative function from outside, lawyers traditionally emphasise external control through adjudication. To the lawyer, law is the policeman; it operates as an external control, often retrospectively. But a main concern of many green light writers was to *minimise* the influence of courts. Courts, with their legalistic values, were seen as obstacles to progress, and the control which they emphasise as unrepresentative and undemocratic. To emphasise this crucial point, in green light theory, decision-making by an elite judiciary, imbued with a legalistic, rights-based ideology and eccentric vision of the 'public interest'—Griffith's phrase [see *The Politics of the Judiciary* (London 1991) at 274–300]—was never a plausible counter to authoritarianism.

If, as green light theorists maintain, the courts' influence should be minimized, how *should* good administration be pursued? We return to the explanation of Harlow and Rawlings (*op cit* at 75–8):

Griffith set out his personal creed in 'The Political Constitution' [(1979) 42 *MLR* 1]. Dismissing the recently fashionable constitutional device of a Bill of Rights, justiciable and enforceable in the courts to enshrine and protect individual 'rights', Griffith argued for the collectivist view of 'rights' as group interests or 'claims' to be evaluated through the political process. Griffith emphasised the need for access to information, open government, a free and powerful press, and ultimately expressed faith in decentralisation through local government and a strengthened Parliament. On the other hand, he prescribed a reduced role for the judiciary and a diminution in the amount of discretionary power at its disposal. Policy-making and accountability, in short, are political functions …

If the model of law is to be abandoned, then many feel that something other than the traditional model of government must take its place. Few administrative lawyers—or, indeed, citizens—would wish to set sail in a barque as frail as that of ministerial responsibility. Because it revealed the inadequacies of ministerial responsibility, Crichel Down is often described as the beginning of modern administrative law. Very briefly, Crichel Down had been acquired before World War II by the Air Ministry as a bombing range. Subsequently, when no longer required for these purposes, it was transferred to the Ministry of Agriculture. Later, a dispute arose when the Ministry, wishing to dispose of the land, tried to let it as a single unit to a new tenant instead of allowing its original owners to buy it back. Fierce objections from the latter forced a public inquiry, which established the responsibility of civil servants both for the policy and also for its execution. Controversially, the Minister, Sir Thomas Dugdale, resigned ...

Crichel Down exposed a world of administrative policy and decision-making apparently immune from political and parliamentary controls. In Griffith's phrase, 'the fundamental defect revealed was not a failure in the constitutional relations of those involved nor the policy decisions nor even the length of the struggle [the complainant] had to wage. It was in the method and therefore in the mental processes of the officials' [(1955) 18 *MLR* 557 at 569]. But content to rely on 'that personal integrity which is so much more than an absence of corruption', Griffith concluded that the civil service must be left to put its own house in order. Here we find the characteristic reliance of green light theorists on political and administrative institutions. For those who were less trusting, yet did not wish to tip the balance too far in the direction of judicial control, the challenge was to provide alternatives. In the aftermath of Crichel Down, this was to become a major preoccupation of administrative lawyers ...

[The authors noted that they had used the word 'control' without stopping to consider its meaning, and continued:] Control can be symbolic or real; it can mean to check, restrain or govern. Griffith and Street [*Principles of Administrative Law* (London 1973) at 24] clearly sense latent ambiguities. They say: 'A great deal turns on the meaning which is attached to the word "controls". Banks control a river; a driver controls his car. The influence of a parent over a child may be greater than the power of a prison guard over a convict.' If we try applying these metaphors to the administrative process, we will see that the 'controls' are direct and internal rather than indirect and external. To extend our metaphors, a river bank may be inspected by an officer of the catchment board (today more probably the official of a privatised water authority) to see that it is in good repair; a policeman may stop the driver and caution him for speeding; a health visitor may advise the child's parents to exert a different kind of influence ... These are all controls, but they are external ...

... Obviously, however, the first control of administrative activity is *internal:* hierarchical and supervisory. Consider the doctrine of individual ministerial responsibility central to the argument over Crichel Down. One function of the doctrine is to provide internal control because the Minister must, as head of his department, supervise the activities of his subordinates by establishing policies and checking the way in which they are implemented. The doctrine also provides for external control through responsibility to Parliament, but this is envisaged as a last resort. And Griffith hints at the superiority of internal control when he prescribes as a remedy for Crichel Down 'more "red tape" not less'.

A second distinction is between *prospective* and *retrospective* control. Judicial review of administrative action is primarily retrospective, although it can possess a prospective element if the administration accepts that judicial precedent establishes the limits of its future conduct. Legislation is primarily prospective. Like the banks of the river, legislation controls administrative activity by prescribing its limits. When an administrator asks, 'May I do X?', the lawyer replies 'if the law permits'. He knows where to find the law: statutes, regulations, precedent etc, and he knows how to rank it when it has been found. Lawyers like to assume that administrators approach the law in the same way ...

Generally speaking, [however,] neither administrators nor politicians seek their mandate in law but in policy; they are, in other words, policy-orientated. Administrators see law positively as a set of pegs on which to hang policies; viewed negatively, the law may be a series of hurdles to be jumped before policy can be implemented, in which sense it acts as a control …

As prevention is proverbially better than cure, so fire-watching can be seen as more 'efficient' than fire-fighting … [For this reason,] the notion of legislative control has widened. Rule-making has developed into a primary technique for control of bureaucracies. And … the trend of post-war public administration generally has been to put in place controls which are internal and prospective.

Alongside the new internal controls we find new fire-watchers added. The Council on Tribunals [now the Administrative Justice and Tribunals Council] was installed in the 1960s essentially to carry out fire-watching functions; the ombudsmen [see ch 19] were primarily used for fire-fighting. There is an irony here, in that the introduction of this new, external machinery for control had been heavily promoted by lawyers. Yet the agencies, although external, were often only semi-autonomous. In consequence, the developments were frequently misunderstood by lawyers who, using the courts as their paradigm, doubted the independence and integrity of the new institutions. Again, because they lacked some of the compulsive attributes of law, relying on negotiation rather than command/control, they were often described as 'toothless watch-dogs'.

This extract captures the essence of the green light view, and the way in which it contrasts with its red light counterpart. The former downplays the role of the judiciary as an agency which exerts external control over administrative bodies, and instead prefers to place greater trust in the political process—not only through the somewhat fragile doctrine of ministerial accountability, but also by means of more robust techniques of internal administrative regulation. This, in turn, re-characterizes administrative law itself: it shifts from being an external restriction upon state power which is largely concerned with righting wrongs occasioned by maladministration, and is instead conceived of as a framework which facilitates good government by providing a template of good practice, and practical mechanisms which permit the administration to regulate itself.

QUESTIONS

- Is the red light or green light theory preferable in your view?
- Why?

1.2.3 Why is theory important?

The red and green light theories are presented here as polar opposites in order that their differences might be drawn out. In reality, most administrative systems reflect aspects of both traditions, relying upon a combination of external, court-based control, and internal regulation of the administrative process. Harlow and Rawlings (London 1997) at 127 acknowledge that reality lies somewhere between the pure red and green light models, in an 'amber light theory' which recognizes both the '"fire-watching" and "fire-fighting" functions of administrative law, finding solutions outside as well as inside courts'. Indeed, notwithstanding Harlow and Rawlings' characterization of Wade and Forsyth's approach in red light terms, the latter (*Administrative Law* (Oxford 2014) at 6–7) recognize that judicial intervention does not have to be cast in wholly combative terms, observing that the judge-made body of administrative law may serve as a template of best practice for administrators. The role of the courts thus transcends that which is ascribed to them by red light theory: in the words of Sir John Donaldson MR in *R* v. *Lancashire County Council, ex parte Huddleston* [1986] 2 All ER 941 at 945, 'a new relationship [has emerged] between the courts and those who derive their authority from the public law, one of partnership based on a common aim, namely the maintenance of the highest standards of public administration'.

While the position is therefore more complex than choosing *either* a red *or* green light approach, this discourse remains useful because it forces us to confront fundamental questions about the purpose of administrative law. This is valuable not only in relation to big picture issues such as the respective roles of judicial and other mechanisms, but also because it provides a theoretical framework in which to address more specific issues. For instance, to the extent that we are prepared to concede judicial oversight of the administration, should courts confine themselves to resolving disputes which have *already* arisen, or should they act pre-emptively, seeking to clarify the extent of administrators' powers even if no specific dispute has yet occurred? We explore this issue at 14.5.4, where we consider what role is, and should be, played by 'advisory declarations'; here, we simply observe that reliance upon theory is imperative if coherent answers are to be supplied to this question and many others like it.

1.3 The changing face of judicial review

In light of the foregoing, it will come as no surprise that English law adopts a combination of judicial intervention and other approaches in an attempt to ensure good administrative practice. In chs 17–19, we consider methods of regulating government action—such as ombudsmen, inquiries, and tribunals—which are not court-based. We begin, however, with judicial review, the principal court-based mechanism by which the legality of public authorities' actions may be addressed.

1.3.1 The scope and intensity of review

One of the dominant themes which will be apparent throughout this book is that judicial review has changed rapidly in recent years. For instance, as we explain in ch 4, the scope of judicial review has expanded radically, now extending well beyond the sphere of statutory powers to include diverse forms of 'public' power in response to the changing architecture of government. Not only has judicial review grown wider in scope; its intensity has also increased. It is, however, central to received perceptions of judicial review that courts may not interfere with exercises of discretion merely because they disagree with the decision or action in question; instead, courts intervene only if some specific fault can be established—for example if the decision was reached procedurally unfairly. Such judicial recognition of the so-called distinction between appeal and review has fundamentally shaped judicial review, and requires further explanation.

Sometimes, legislation specifically states that if an individual is not content with a particular administrative decision or act, then a right of *appeal* lies to a tribunal, court, or

Minister. The general principle is that bodies with appellate jurisdiction can make up their own mind about the merits, substituting their view for that of the original decision-maker. The central question for appellate bodies, therefore, is whether they think the original decision was right or not. Where legislation does not provide for appeal, the decision will still be open to *judicial review* (unless this is specifically excluded). Reviewing courts, however, are concerned with the *legality* of the decision, not with its *correctness* or *merits*; intervention is therefore possible only if the administrator has exceeded the legal limits of its powers. Those limits are considered in detail elsewhere in this book, and we will not attempt to summarize them here. For the time being, the key point is that review has traditionally been understood in much narrower terms than appeal, as Laws J explained in *R v. Somerset County Council, ex parte Fewings* [1995] 1 All ER 513 at 515:

> [I]n most cases, the judicial review court is not concerned with the merits of the decision under review. The court does not ask itself the question, 'Is this decision right or wrong?' Far less does the judge ask himself whether he himself would have arrived at the decision in question … [T]he task of the court, and the judgment at which it arrives, have nothing to do with the question, 'Which view is the better one?'

A number of reasons underlie the courts' willingness to accept these limits upon judicial review. Appellate bodies can afford to adopt a bold approach because they are specifically given the power to reopen issues on appeal, whereas the power of reviewing courts, as we will see later, is not explicitly conferred; rather, it depends upon a constitutional assumption. In the light of this, reviewing courts confine themselves to questions of legality and avoid substituting their view for that of the decision-maker on the merits in order to avoid usurping the powers of the latter. Indeed, at the most fundamental level, the appeal/review distinction is keyed into the doctrine of parliamentary sovereignty: if the sovereign legislature has given power to a particular administrative body from which it has created no right of appeal then, the argument goes, the courts have no business interfering with the body's decisions (other than by making sure that it has acted lawfully). For these reasons, the courts have traditionally accepted the appeal/review distinction, confining themselves to questions of legality—which, in practice, led to a focus on the *procedure* by which decisions are made, and a tendency to eschew scrutiny of their *content*, for fear that this might lead to consideration of the merits.

QUESTION

- Are courts right to display reticence when asked to review the content, or merits, of administrative decisions?

In recent years, however, this line has become increasingly difficult to maintain. In a variety of contexts, the intensity of judicial review has increased, and the distinction between appeal and review has come under pressure. We will see this phenomenon time and again in this book—from the expansive approach to jurisdictional review (ch 2) which all but eliminates the distinction between appeal and review as far as questions of law are concerned, to the adoption of principles such as substantive legitimate expectation (ch 6) and proportionality (ch 8) which require the courts to look at the content of administrative decisions more closely than they have traditionally. Because we consider these developments in detail in subsequent chapters, it would be fruitless to attempt to summarize them here. It is important, however, to bear in mind the traditional distinction between appeal and review—and the rationale upon which it is based—when considering these developments, since this provides us with a useful benchmark by which to measure the development of judicial review, and to evaluate its legitimacy.

1.3.2 Why is judicial review expanding?

Possible reasons for the growing prominence of judicial review were addressed by Lord Mustill in his dissenting speech in *R* v. *Secretary of State for the Home Department, ex parte Fire Brigades Union* [1995] 2 AC 513. The case concerned a challenge to the Home Secretary's refusal to exercise his discretion under s 171(1) of the Criminal Justice Act 1988 to bring into force a new scheme for compensating victims of crime. The majority concluded that, by introducing an alternative (cheaper) scheme and indicating that the statutory scheme would not be brought into force, the Home Secretary had acted unlawfully by breaching the duty (held to be implicit in s 171(1)) to keep under active consideration the implementation of the statutory compensation scheme. Lord Mustill, however, was against judicial intervention, arguing that, since the case essentially concerned legislation not yet in force, the matter was one which should have been resolved by Parliament and the executive. In advancing this argument, his Lordship (at 567) made the following comments about the development of judicial review:

> It is a feature of the peculiarly British conception of the separation of powers that Parliament, the executive and the courts have each their distinct and largely exclusive domain. Parliament has a legally unchallengeable right to make whatever laws it thinks right. The executive carries on the administration of the country in accordance with the powers conferred on it by law. The courts interpret the laws, and see that they are obeyed. This requires the courts on occasion to step into the territory which belongs to the executive, to verify not only that the powers asserted accord with the substantive law created by Parliament but also that the manner in which they are exercised conforms with the standards of fairness which Parliament must have intended. Concurrently with this judicial function Parliament has its own special means of ensuring that the executive, in the exercise of delegated functions, performs in a way which Parliament finds appropriate. Ideally, it is these latter methods which should be used to check executive errors and excesses; for it is the task of Parliament and the executive in tandem, not of the courts, to govern the country. In recent years, however, the employment in practice of these specifically Parliamentary remedies has on occasion been perceived as falling short, and sometimes well short, of what was needed to bring the performance of the executive into line with the law, and with the minimum standards of fairness implicit in every Parliamentary delegation of a decision-making function. To avoid a vacuum in which the citizen would be left without protection against a misuse of executive powers the courts have had no option but to occupy the dead ground in a manner, and in areas of public life, which could not have been foreseen 30 years ago. For myself, I am quite satisfied that this unprecedented judicial role has been greatly to the public benefit. Nevertheless, it has its risks, of which the courts are well aware. As the judges themselves constantly remark, it is not they who are appointed to administer the country. Absent a written constitution much sensitivity is required of the parliamentarian, administrator and judge if the delicate balance of the unwritten rules evolved (I believe successfully) in recent years is not to be disturbed, and all the recent advances undone.

> **QUESTIONS**
> - What sort of 'sensitivity' might Lord Mustill have had in mind?
> - How, in practical terms, can the three branches of government display such sensitivity?

These comments reveal an important tension in our administrative order. On the one hand, Lord Mustill reminds us that the desirability of expanding judicial review must always be tested by asking whether (or to what extent) the subject-matter of the administrative act is one upon which judges may legitimately adjudicate (on which see chs 4 and 8). On the other hand, political accountability to Parliament is no panacea, bearing in mind the limits of the doctrine of ministerial accountability. Hence, as Lord Mustill puts it, the courts—by developing their powers of judicial review—have stepped in to fill the 'dead ground'.

This account should not, however, be accepted unquestioningly. After all, judicial review and ministerial accountability to some extent offer *complementary*, not *alternative*, mechanisms for ensuring good administration. Whereas the latter is focused largely upon broad issues such as the wisdom of policy choices made by the executive and the management of government departments, the former provides an apparatus whereby individuals may pursue specific grievances concerning legality against administrative bodies. In truth, the growth of judicial review must be located in a wider setting, prominent features of which are the increasing trend to resort to litigation (in both public and private law spheres) and the associated rise of a rights-based culture which emphasizes the entitlements of the individual *vis-à-vis* the state. The most obvious evidence of this trend in the United Kingdom lies in the enactment of the Human Rights Act 1998, the impact of which on administrative law will be seen throughout this book. Understood in this broader perspective, judicial review's evolution is the product of a complex web of political and philosophical changes concerning the state, the individual, and their relationship with one another.

1.3.3 Is (more) judicial review a good thing?

The expansion of judicial review is not universally welcomed: green light theorists, for instance, remind us that extensive judicial regulation of the administrative process is by no means the only way in which good government might be pursued. Scepticism about judicial review is stimulated by a broad range of concerns—some pragmatic, others ideological.

The court-oriented model of administrative justice, which places judicial review centre-stage, is closely associated with a conception of the rule of law which emphasizes the primacy of 'ordinary law' administered by courts of general jurisdiction. This view—prominently advanced in Dicey's *Introduction to the Study of the Law of the Constitution*, first published in 1885—is antagonistic to the idea of a separate body of administrative law applied by specialized tribunals. Dicey therefore condemned France's *droit administrative*—its separate body of administrative law. Arthurs (1979) 17 *Osgoode Hall LJ* 1, in common with many commentators, strongly disputes Dicey's account. Many of Arthurs' concerns are practical in nature. For example, he observes (at 25) that, in addition to courts, there are many other agencies which might play a role in overseeing the administration, such as ombudsmen, the legislature, and tribunals, all of which are 'more likely than the courts to address the substance, rather than the technicalities, of discretion abused'. Rather than leaving everything to the courts, Arthurs prefers a pluralistic approach which recognizes that some regulatory tasks can more appropriately be performed by other institutions. Informed, at least in part, by a functional perspective—according to which the 'legal-administrative response' should be shaped by the demands of particular contexts, leading to the emergence of 'largely autonomous systems in various sectors of administrative activity' (at 29)—Arthurs concludes (at 43–5) that judicial review should play a decidedly modest role:

> [It is necessary] to distinguish Law—'Rule of' variety [meaning Dicey's 'ordinary law', applied by traditional courts]—from law—administrative variety—in the conviction that the latter, much more than the former, is capable of vindicating essential democratic values in a modern state. It is true that some [of my] proposals, such as the considerable restraint on judicial review, may be seen as potentially depriving aggrieved individuals of recourse, but this is to assess the proposals only in terms of pathology.
>
> Constructive measures to enhance the original quality of decisions will not result in perfection, but they will, in the aggregate, ensure greater justice for more people than could possibly benefit from any system of judicial review. Such measures would include clearer statements of legislative purpose, better defined and more open procedures to ensure participation, more careful training of administrative decision-makers, systems of internal appeal, and external, but largely nonjudicial, accountability.
>
> In matters of policy formulation and institutional design, the legislature should clearly have, and periodically utter, the last word. Assessments of administrative professionalism and performance (including excessive zeal and sloth) should be confided to higher administrative bodies, and ultimately to authorities who are politically accountable. Remedies for patent injustice and violations of administrative law should be sought from a senior administrative tribunal or, in its absence, an ombudsman.
>
> What, then, of judicial review? I suggest that the focus of judicial review should shift to more authentic concerns from its present preoccupation with commanding adherence to 'ordinary' law, often couched in the spurious language of 'jurisdiction' and 'error of law' and analogies to traditional court practices misdescribed as 'natural justice'. There are three main functions for judicial review: ensuring that tribunals (and other bodies) perform tasks of the sort generically confided in them, protecting transcendent constitutional values, and enforcing fidelity to the distinctive 'law' of the tribunal …
>
> … [T]here is no reason why [judges] should not give full recognition to the distinctive legal systems which have emerged in various tribunals, no reason why they should not abandon the effort to evaluate these distinctive systems according to the inappropriate criteria of 'ordinary' law. If they did so, they would not merely be acknowledging the reality of pluralism, which seems always to have been an important feature of the English legal system. They would, as well, be promoting the development of an authentic, indigenous administrative law, which is the citizen's best protection against abuse.

Scepticism about judicial review stems not only from practical concerns, such as those of Arthurs. Some writers also object to judicial review—or to an expansive form of review, at any rate—on ideological grounds. Griffith's doubts about judicial review reflect his wider concerns about judicial power. In *The Politics of the Judiciary* (London 1997), he argues that judges cannot be politically neutral because they are forced to make political choices that are inevitably affected by the rather narrow social, educational, and ethnic backgrounds from which the judiciary is presently drawn. In the public law sphere, this leads Griffith to declare himself 'very strongly against any further judicialisation of the administrative process' ((1979) 42 *MLR* 1 at 19).

Indeed, not all judges are comfortable with the scope of the role that courts play today in the public law sphere. For instance, in his 2011 FA Mann Lecture—delivered shortly before he took up his post as a Justice of the Supreme Court—Lord Sumption argued that

> decisions of the courts on the abuse of discretionary powers are based, far more often than the courts have admitted, on a judgment about what it is thought right for Parliament to wish to do. Such judgments are by their nature political. By this I do not mean that the judges who decided them were politically partisan, but simply that they were dealing with matters (namely the merits of policy decisions) which in a democracy are the proper function of Parliament and of ministers answerable to Parliament and the electorate.

He suggests that

> [p]art of the problem has been that the judiciary and the executive are looking at the issue from different ends of the telescope. The judiciary's instincts are moulded by their experience of individual cases, many of which have involved profound human tragedies to which no judge could be indifferent. By comparison, politicians, policy-makers and electors are primarily concerned by the problem viewed impersonally and *en masse*. But it clear that there is also a serious difference of sentiment between the political community and the judiciary. In *R* v. *Secretary of State for Social Security, ex parte Council for the Welfare of Immigrants* [[1997] 1 WLR 275] a majority of the Court of Appeal found it impossible to believe that Parliament could have intended to authorise the removal of all social security entitlements from asylum seekers who failed to claim asylum upon entry into the United Kingdom. They therefore quashed regulations which had that effect. Parliament evidently did not agree. It immediately passed fresh legislation authorising such regulations in [clear] terms. Some might say that this was a vindication of the proper role of the Courts. They were not prepared to allow a harsh policy to be followed by the executive on such an issue until Parliament had authorised it in unmistakable terms. But another possible conclusion is that the Court of Appeal's view that Parliament could not have intended such a thing always was unrealistic. It ignored the political background to the legislation and underrated the level of Parliamentary concern about the effect of the UK's relatively generous level of social provision in drawing asylum-seekers across Europe to our shores.

Sumption's lecture was subjected to forensic and excoriating criticism by Sir Stephen Sedley, one of his generation's pre-eminent public law judges, in an article in the *London Review of Books* (23 February 2012). Responding to Sumption's contention that the question of the proper extent of judicial review 'has never troubled practitioners, and rarely features in the judgments of the courts', Sedley says that it is 'as difficult to know where to begin answering [Sumption's] assertions as it is to know what they are based on'. He goes on to suggest that Sumption's thesis is undermined by insensitivity to the distinct constitutional roles of the legislature and the executive, and to the courts' markedly different remits in respect of those two branches:

> Like a good many other public law practitioners, academics and judges, I have spent my working life thinking about and dealing with little else. But one thing we have not done is to conflate government and legislature, as Sumption does in order to suggest that both ought to be

equally immunised by their democratic credentials from judicial oversight. The courts go to considerable lengths to respect the constitutional supremacy of Parliament; Sumption gives no serious instances to the contrary. It is the executive—the departments of state over which ministers preside, along with quangos and local government—which is subject to public law controls. That is because executive government exercises public powers which are created or recognised by law and have legal limits that it is the courts' constitutional task to patrol. When I argued the leading case of *M* v. *Home Office* in the Court of Appeal [[1992] QB 270] (the case went on to the House of Lords [[1994] 1 AC 377], which confirmed the liability of ministers for contempt of court in the discharge of their offices), I proposed a formulation which Lord Justice Nolan adopted in his judgment and which has been accepted as correct by our unreflective and atheoretical profession: 'The proper constitutional relationship of the executive with the courts is that the courts will respect all acts of the executive within its lawful province, and that the executive will respect all decisions of the courts as to what its lawful province is.'

The striking disagreement that this exchange between Sedley and Sumption illustrates is emblematic of a deep fissure within public law itself, which ultimately turns upon differing understandings of what the UK's three foundational constitutional principles—the sovereignty of Parliament, the rule of law, and the separation of powers—mean, and how they interact with and operate upon one another. The repercussions of this disagreement for administrative law should be obvious, not least because—as we will see throughout this book—it goes to the heart of the questions about the grounds upon and the extent to which judicial review ought to lie in respect of executive action.

1.4 The constitutional basis of judicial review

It is implicit in what has just been said that there must be a relationship between the position that one takes in relation to the sort of big picture constitutional questions already referred to and what role courts can properly play in scrutinizing administrative action. Disagreement about what this role is is thus—to some extent, at least—a function of an underlying controversy about how, in the first place, we are to rationalize in constitutional terms the very existence of the courts' judicial review jurisdiction. In the absence of a sovereign constitutional text, the starting point is inevitably the constitutional principles referred to in the previous paragraph. In this section, then, we examine the debate about the constitutional foundations of judicial review. As we will see, that debate evidences sharp disagreement about the nature and interaction of the fundamental principles that form the constitutional bedrock of judicial review.

1.4.1 The *ultra vires* doctrine

Understood in its traditional form, the *ultra vires* doctrine—the 'central principle of administrative law', according to Wade and Forsyth, *Administrative Law* (Oxford 2014) at 27—may be stated with disarming simplicity. Courts may intervene whenever a decision-maker acts '*ultra vires*', meaning 'beyond the powers' conferred by legislation. Meanwhile, *intra vires* administrative acts—being within the power granted by legislation to the decision-maker—are lawful and unimpeachable. Thus, in reviewing governmental action, courts are merely doing Parliament's bidding by enforcing the limits upon power which are found (expressly or impliedly) in statute. *Prima facie*, this theory provides a powerful justification for the exercise of supervisory jurisdiction, as Baxter, *Administrative Law* (Cape Town 1984) at 303, explains:

> [T]he logic behind the doctrine provides an *inherent* rationale for judicial review ... The self-justification of the ultra vires doctrine is that its application consists of nothing other than *an application of the law itself,* and the law of Parliament to boot.

This logic is particularly compelling in a legal system, like that of the United Kingdom, which embraces the principle of parliamentary sovereignty, for if judicial review can be characterized simply as the implementation of legally unimpeachable legislation, the courts find themselves on ground that is constitutionally rock solid.

But examined more closely, the *ultra vires* doctrine is highly problematic. Although there certainly are situations in which the courts enforce limits upon statutory power which bear a clear relation to the words or policy of the statute—Forsyth and Elliott [2003] *PL* 286 at 299–303 point to *Lloyd* v. *McMahon* [1987] AC 625, *R* v. *Secretary of State for the Home Department, ex parte Venables* [1998] AC 407, and *Padfield* v. *Minister of Agriculture, Fisheries and Food* [1968] AC 997 as leading examples of this phenomenon—there are many others in which the courts enforce principles of good administration which bear no obvious relation to the statute. Laws [1995] *PL* 72 at 78–9 comments that

> [i]n the elaboration of [principles of judicial review] the courts have imposed and enforced judicially created standards of public behaviour ... [T]heir existence cannot be derived from the simple requirement that public bodies must be kept to the limits of their authority given by Parliament. Neither deductive logic nor the canons of ordinary language ... can attribute them to that ideal, since ... in principle their roots have grown from another seed altogether ... They are, categorically, judicial creations. They owe neither their existence nor their acceptance to the will of the legislature. They have nothing to do with the intention of Parliament ...

Laws therefore concludes that the *ultra vires* doctrine is a 'fig-leaf' which simply covers the 'true origins' of judicial review, while Woolf [1995] *PL* 57 at 66 makes the same point by means of a different metaphor, characterizing the doctrine as a 'fairy tale'. Similarly, Forsyth [1996] *CLJ* 122 at 136 remarks that '[n]o-one is so innocent as to suppose that judicial creativity does not form the grounds of judicial review'. The shortcomings of *ultra vires* do not, however, end there, as the following excerpt indicates.

Craig, 'Ultra Vires and the Foundations of Judicial Review' [1998] *CLJ* 63

[T]he orthodox justification for the controls which exist on discretion makes little if any sense when we consider the development of these controls across time. The constraints which exist on the exercise of discretionary power are not static. Existing constraints evolve and new types of control are added to the judicial armoury. Changes in judicial attitudes towards fundamental rights, the acceptance of legitimate expectations, and the possible inclusion of proportionality as a head of review in its own right are but three examples of this process. These developments cannot plausibly be explained by reference to legislative intent. Let us imagine that, for example, the UK courts were to decide in 1998 that proportionality was an independent head of review. Can it plausibly be maintained that this is to be justified by reference to changes in legislative intent which occurred at this time? Would the legislature in some manner have indicated that it intended a new generalised head of review in 1998 which had not existed hitherto? The question only has to be posed for the answer to be self-evident ...

A further problem with the ultra vires doctrine is that it is beset by internal tensions. These are most apparent in the context of statutory provisions which seek to exclude the courts from judicial review through the presence of preclusive or finality clauses [see at 14.6]. If the rationale for judicial review is that the courts are thereby implementing legislative intent this leads to difficulty where the legislature has stated in clear terms that it does not wish the courts to intervene with the decisions made by the agency. As is well known such clauses have not in fact served to exclude judicial review. The courts have used a number of interpretative techniques to limit the effect of such clauses, most notably in *Anisminic* v. *Foreign Compensation Commission* [1969] 2 AC 147 [see at 14.6.2] where their Lordships held that the relevant provision did not serve to protect decisions which were nullities.

Various attempts can and have been made to square such decisions with the orthodox ultra vires principle. It might be argued that Parliament really did not intend such clauses to cover decisions which could otherwise be rendered null. It might alternatively be contended that Parliament acquiesced in the actual decision reached by the courts in the instant case. It might further be argued that in the future Parliament would know that any such clause would be interpreted in this manner and that it signalled its consent in this respect by its willingness to include such clauses in legislation while being fully cognisant of their limited legal effect.

While such arguments can be made they are susceptible to two complementary objections, one substantive, the other formal.

In substantive terms, arguments of this nature should not be allowed to conceal the reality of what the legislature was attempting to achieve, nor should it be allowed to mask the judicial response. Such clauses were clearly designed to exclude the courts. This might be for a 'legitimate' reason, in the sense that the legislature was merely trying to signify that it preferred the view of a specialist agency to that of the reviewing court. It might be for a more 'dubious' reason, as where the legislature was merely seeking to immunise the decisions of a Minister from any challenge. We should be equally honest about the nature of the courts' response. Although it is capable of being reconciled with orthodoxy in the above manner, the reality is that the courts were reaching their decision by drawing upon a constitutional principle independent of Parliamentary intent. The essence of this principle was that access to judicial review, and the protections which it provides, should be safeguarded by the courts, and that any legislative attempt to block such access should be given the most restrictive reading possible, irrespective of whether this truly accorded with legislative intent or not.

The other objection to the arguments made above is more formal in nature. Even if one believes that the decisions in this area can be reconciled with ultra vires orthodoxy this reconciliation is only bought at a price. The price in this instance is the straining of the ultra vires doctrine itself. The malleability of the doctrine allows it to be formally stretched in the above manner. Yet the more contrived the search for the legitimation of legislative intent, the more strained and implausible does the whole ultra vires doctrine become ...

For all its difficulties it is at least plausible to think of the ultra vires principle as being the basis for judicial review in relation to those bodies which derive their power from statute. The courts have, however, expanded the principles of judicial review to cover institutions which are not public bodies in the traditional sense of the term, in circumstances where these bodies do not derive their power from statute or the prerogative [see at 4.3]. This trend has been more marked as of late because of reforms in the law of remedies. It would none the less be mistaken to think of this as a recent development. The courts have applied public law, or analogous principles to such bodies for a very considerable period of time, irrespective of whether this was in the context of an action for judicial review as such. Trade associations, trade unions and corporations with *de facto* monopoly power have, for example, been subject to some of the same principles as are applied to public bodies *stricto sensu*.

It is difficult to apply the ultra vires principle to such bodies without substantially altering its meaning. These bodies do not derive their power from statute and therefore judicial control cannot be rationalised through the idea that the courts are delineating the boundaries of Parliament's intent. The very language of ultra vires can only be preserved by transforming it so as to render the principles of judicial review of generalised application to those institutions which wield a certain degree of power; these principles are then read into the articles of association or other governing document under which the body operates. While this step can be taken it serves to transform the ultra vires doctrine. It can no longer be regarded as the vehicle through which the courts effectuate the will of Parliament. It becomes rather a juristic device through which those private or quasi-public bodies are subject to the controls which the courts believe should operate on those who possess a certain type of power.

QUESTIONS

- Do you find these criticisms of the *ultra vires* doctrine convincing?
- How powerful is the point that judicial review now extends beyond statutory power?
- Must review of the exercise of statutory and non-statutory powers rest on the same constitutional foundation?

1.4.2 The common law theory

In light of the problems highlighted earlier, there is broad agreement that the *ultra vires* doctrine, understood in its traditional form, is unsatisfactory. So what should replace it? Oliver [1987] *PL* 543, concerned particularly with the last of the issues mentioned by Craig, noted the increasing prominence of bodies performing public functions but not created by statute or exercising statutory powers. Since judicial review of such bodies plainly cannot be justified by reference to the *ultra vires* doctrine, Oliver proposed that the fiction of parliamentary intention should be dispensed with, and that we should instead acknowledge that the principles of good administration are judicial creations that form part of the common law.

Oliver's influential paper laid the foundation for what is now known as the common law theory of judicial review, which Craig [1999] *PL* 428 at 429 explains in the following terms:

It is ... self-evident that the enabling legislation must be considered when determining the ambit of a [statutory] body's powers. This is not, however, the same thing as saying that the heads of review, their meaning or the intensity with which they are applied can be justified by legislative intent. The central issue is therefore how far these relevant legal rules and their application can satisfactorily be explained by reference to legislative intent. Proponents of the common law model argue that the principles of judicial review are in reality developed by the courts. They are the creations of the common law. The legislature will rarely provide any indications as to the content and limits of what constitutes judicial review. When legislation is passed the courts will impose controls which constitute judicial review which they believe are normatively justified on the grounds of justice, the rule of law, etc. They will therefore decide on the appropriate procedural and substantive principles of judicial review which should apply to statutory and non-statutory bodies alike. Agency action which infringes these principles will be unlawful. If the omnipotent Parliament does not like these controls then it is open to it to make this unequivocally clear. If it does so then the courts will then adhere to such dictates. If Parliament does manifest a specific intent as to the grounds of review the courts will also obey this, in just the same way as they will obey such intent in other areas where the primary obligations themselves are the creations of the common law. There is, in this sense, nothing odd or strange about a set of principles derived from the common law, which are then supplemented or complemented by specific legislative intent if and when this is to be found. This is indeed the paradigm in areas such as contract, tort, restitution, and trusts.

The common law theory successfully resolves many of the problems encountered by the *ultra vires* doctrine. The implausible assumption lying at the heart of the latter—that the principles of judicial review are somehow intended, yet never actually articulated, by Parliament—is replaced with open acknowledgement that the judiciary has largely created such principles, just as common law principles of tort, contract, and so on have been fashioned by judges. Hence the justification for enforcing the principles of review lies not in Parliament's wish that they should be enforced, but in the fact that such principles are desirable in a normative sense, since their application helps to secure good government. This approach helpfully clears the way for open discussion of the principles of judicial review applied by the courts: judges can no longer hide behind the 'fig-leaf' of supposed parliamentary intention, and must instead be willing to defend the principles of administrative law for whose development they are acknowledged to be responsible. Not only is this more coherent and more believable than the account furnished by the *ultra vires* doctrine: its transparency also rightly and constructively exposes administrative law to the same critical scrutiny as other judge-made bodies of common law.

The common law model can also comfortably accommodate the changing content of administrative law—*eg* the emergence of new principles of review—which, as Craig notes above, cannot plausibly be explained away, as the *ultra vires* doctrine would have it, on the basis of changing legislative intention. The common law theory simply acknowledges that the nature and level of judicial control of the administration varies over time, as circumstances change.

It has, however, been doubted by some commentators whether the common law theory resolves all of the criticisms made of the *ultra vires* doctrine. One of those criticisms is that *ultra vires* is a highly formal doctrine which is devoid of any real content. As Laws (in Supperstone and Goudie (eds), *Judicial Review* (London 1997) at 52) puts it:

[The *ultra vires* doctrine has] nothing to say as to what the court will *count* as a want of power in the deciding body; and so of itself it illuminates nothing. It amounts to no more than a tautology, viz that the court will strike down what it chooses to strike down.

However, Allan [2002] *CLJ* 87 at 100 suggests that the specific principles of good administration are themselves so general as to be almost meaningless—meaning that the common law model is susceptible to the same criticism in this respect as *ultra vires*. (The meaning of the term 'jurisdiction', which Allan uses in the following passage, is explored in ch 2.)

Could the ultra vires defenders not bring their own similar charges [of indeterminacy] against the common law school? Is not their reliance upon such open-ended categories [of judicial review] as 'procedural impropriety', 'illegality' and 'irrationality' [as set out by Lord Diplock in *Council of Civil Service Unions* v. *Minister for the Civil Service* [1985] AC 374 at 410], in stressing the basis of the court's jurisdiction in the common law, not quite as futile and self-serving as the ultra vires defenders' invocation of legislative intent? Does anyone really imagine that such labels do more than announce the *conclusions* of legal analysis—an analysis that must focus on all the pertinent details of the particular case, including the statute that confers the administrative power?

If it is true, as is claimed [by critics of *ultra vires*], that enabling legislation will often afford 'scant guidance' about which considerations are properly relevant to the exercise of discretion and which are not, it is equally true that no sensible conclusions could be drawn without close attention to the statutory scheme. As Elliott [in Forsyth (ed), *Judicial Review and the Constitution* (Oxford 2000) at 350–1] observes, it is the enabling statute that inevitably defines the 'jurisdiction' of the public agency, in the narrow sense of its proper sphere of action. (And this is so even if it is also true that it may be controversial whether any particular statutory requirement should be treated as a jurisdictional condition.) And he is also right to insist that the other grounds of review—those that determine the agency's jurisdiction in its broader sense—cannot be applied without regard to legislative intention, even if such intention must be collected from a sense of the overall statutory scheme or purpose. Legislative intention—at least in the broad sense that the courts must be faithful to the statutory scheme as a whole—is plainly relevant to the *application* of the various grounds of review, even if it is thought irrelevant to their abstract formulation and intellectual defence.

This passage underlines two related points. First, it reminds us that although the *ultra vires* doctrine is problematic in that it views parliamentary intention as a panacea which can explain judicial review in its entirety, it is wrong to overlook the fact that such intention is part—albeit not the whole—of the explanation. There are clearly some circumstances in which what a reviewing court does is influenced, directly or otherwise, by the language of the relevant statute. Second, what of those circumstances in which the relationship between judicial review and the legislation is tenuous or non-existent? Plainly, legislative intention cannot furnish the explanation here: but it does not necessarily follow that the common law theory can. As Allan points out, it is all very well to invoke concepts such as fairness and reasonableness, and to argue that their normative weight justifies their application via judicial review. Such concepts, however, are undeniably vague: one person's conception of fairness might differ quite radically from another's.

1.4.3 Must judicial review be related to legislative intention?

These points notwithstanding, the common law theory is, in many respects, a significant improvement upon the *ultra vires* doctrine. Nevertheless, some writers have argued that, while the *ultra vires* doctrine, as traditionally understood, is indefensible, recognition of some form of relationship between parliamentary intention and judicial review remains essential. This has led them to develop a modified version of the *ultra vires* theory. The nature of that theory is considered in what follows; first, however, it is necessary to consider why the relationship between legislative intention and review is considered so important by the *ultra vires* school. Forsyth and Elliott [2003] *PL* 286 at 288–9 advance two reasons. The first relates to practical considerations concerning ouster clauses and collateral challenge, matters which we consider in chs 14 and 3 respectively. For the time being, we focus on the second strand of the argument which favours the retention of some form of *ultra vires* theory. The essence of this part of the argument is that the courts' supervisory jurisdiction and the sovereignty of Parliament can *only* be reconciled by means of (some version of) the *ultra vires* doctrine. Forsyth [1996] *CLJ* 122 at 133–4 explains the reasoning behind this proposition as follows:

> Suppose that a Minister in the apparent exercise of a statutory power to make regulations, makes certain regulations which are clearly so vague that their meaning cannot be determined with sufficient certainty. Classic [*ultra vires*] theory tells us that Parliament never intends to grant the power to make vague regulations—this seems an entirely reasonable and realistic intention to impute to Parliament—and thus the vague regulations are *ultra vires* and void; there would be no difficulty in the court striking down the regulations. But [within the common law model] classic theory has been abandoned: the grounds of review [including that which requires regulations to be clear, not vague] derive, not from the implied intent of the legislature, but from the common law. It follows that although the regulations are *intra vires* the Minister's powers, they are none the less invalid because they are vague.
>
> The analytical difficulty is this: what an all powerful Parliament does not prohibit, it must authorise either expressly or impliedly. Likewise if Parliament grants a power to a Minister, that Minister either acts within those powers or outside those powers. There is no grey area between authorisation and the denial of power. Thus, if the making of vague regulations is within the powers granted by a sovereign Parliament, on what basis may the courts challenge Parliament's will and hold that the regulations are invalid? If Parliament has authorised vague regulations, those regulations cannot be challenged without challenging Parliament's authority to authorise such regulations ...
>
> The upshot of this is that ... one is led inevitably to the conclusion that to abandon *ultra vires* is to challenge the supremacy of Parliament.

This argument reduces to the proposition that when statutory power is conferred, everything which is done in reliance upon that grant of power is actually either done within the scope of the power (and is therefore lawful) or outside the scope of the power (and is therefore unlawful). It must be one thing or the other; and while courts can strike down acts in the latter category, they cannot, if Parliament is sovereign, strike down administrative acts in the former, since Parliament has authorized them. Therefore, the argument runs, only an *ultra vires* doctrine will do: the courts are only constitutionally able to upset administrative action which lies outside the power conferred by Parliament, and have no business imposing common law restrictions on discretionary power which bear no relation to the scope of the power actually conferred by Parliament. To do so may involve removing from administrators power which Parliament conferred, thereby setting the courts and the legislature on a collision course.

QUESTION

- Is Forsyth's analysis of any relevance to judicial review of the exercise of *non-statutory* powers?

This analysis has been attacked on a number of grounds, three of which merit particular attention. First, the conclusion itself has been challenged by a number of writers, Endicott (2003) 53 *UTLJ* 201 and Laws supplying especially detailed critiques. The latter, writing in Supperstone, Goudie, and Walker (eds), *Judicial Review* (London 2005) at 97, says that

> Forsyth's reasoning as to the 'analytical consequences' of the abandonment of *ultra vires* is unsound. It is simply not correct to assert that 'there is no grey area between authorisation and prohibition' ... It is, as a matter of logic, quite possible for Parliament neither to authorise nor to prohibit a particular act. Such a situation would arise where, as regards a particular issue, Parliament has expressed no intention one way or the other.
>
> The fact that Parliament is all powerful does not affect this conclusion. The sovereignty of Parliament means that, through expressions of intent in statutory form, Parliament can lay down any rule it chooses. It is, however, simply a *non sequitur* to say that therefore every legal rule must be derived (whether expressly or impliedly) from such expressions of intent.

On this view, Parliament might not have any intention at all about whether certain limits—*eg* a duty to act fairly—ought to exist in relation to a given power. This legislative vacuum can be filled by common law principles of fairness: no risk arises of contradicting Parliament because it has no relevant intention capable of contradiction. However, this assumption that Parliament is neutral about some or all of the conditions which attach to the exercise of discretionary power does not fit comfortably with broader ideas about the relationship between legislation and the rule of law. Although it is widely accepted that Parliament is sovereign, and can therefore, at least in theory, do as it pleases, the reality is that a high level of protection is conferred upon the rule of law by means of statutory interpretation. Leading examples of this technique are furnished by *Anisminic Ltd* v. *Foreign Compensation Commission* [1969] 2 AC 147 and *R (Evans)* v. *Attorney-General* [2015] UKSC 21, [2015] AC 1787, in which the House of Lords and the Supreme Court respectively went to considerable lengths to find interpretations of statutory provisions which were consistent with fundamental constitutional principles.

In neither of these cases did the courts doubt the sovereignty of Parliament; instead, they invoked the widely-held assumption that, as Lord Steyn put it in *R* v. *Secretary of State for the Home Department, ex parte Pierson* [1998] AC 539 at 587, 'Parliament does not legislate in a vacuum. Parliament legislates for a European liberal democracy founded on the principles and traditions of the common law. And the courts may approach legislation on this initial presumption.' It is the use of such presumptions which allows Allan [1985] *CLJ* 111 at 112 to conclude that the British constitution 'possesses its own harmony, in which the protection of individual liberties can coexist with recognition of the ultimate supremacy of the democratic will of Parliament'. Laws' suggestion that we should suppose Parliament to be agnostic about the principles of administrative justice, relying upon the courts *unilaterally* to impose standards of good administration, chafes awkwardly against the well-established tradition to which Allan refers, and which rightly advances a vision of the constitution within which courts, administrators, and the legislature are *collectively* engaged in the co-operative endeavour of promoting good governance.

The second criticism levelled at the defence of *ultra vires* focuses upon its consequences. Craig [1999] *PL* 428 at 433–4 writes that if the logic of the argument is extrapolated, then surprising—indeed absurd—results are produced. For example, Craig says that, on

Forsyth's analysis, if Parliament passes a statute which gives power to a particular public body, then we would not be

> entitled to impose any limits on the way in which that power is exercised unless we can find justification in terms of legislative intent. If therefore we wish to argue that the public body should be subject to rules of [for example] contractual, tortious or restitutionary liability then the requisite legislative intent must be found. There may be some specific legislative intent that we can point to, but this will often be absent, since Parliament will not have the necessary expertise, time, etc, to manifest a specific intent on the matter. So we have to fall back on some general legislative intent … If no such intent can be found then the existence and applications of such principles [of civil liability] cannot be justified. If we are satisfied that the requisite intent can be found then we can and must say that the 'central principle' of this area of the law is legislative intent. We must, moreover, say this notwithstanding the fact that the principles of civil liability which are thus applied to public bodies have a normative force of their own which warrants their application to public bodies and to private parties where there is no relevant background statute.

This analysis is largely correct. On Forsyth's view, any limits upon statutory power must somehow be related to the statutory scheme. It therefore would, as Craig suggests, be necessary to find some sort of legislative intention to the effect that the principles of civil liability should restrict the decision-maker's power, if such principles are to be operative. However, Craig's implicit assertion that this is ultimately absurd, because it is inconsistent with the fact that the principles of civil liability have a 'normative force of their own', conflates two separate issues—*viz* the *existence* and *application* of those principles. It is self-evident that they have largely been authored by judges; no one disputes the fact that the judiciary is responsible for their *existence*. Correctly understood, Forsyth's argument is simply that when such principles are applied to—and are therefore restrictive of—statutory power, some legislative permission to this effect must exist if the *application* of the principles of civil liability is not to cut across the scheme laid down by the sovereign legislature. This argument denies neither the normative force nor the judicial authorship of those principles.

Craig goes further, arguing (at 434–5) that if Forsyth's analysis is pressed to its ultimate conclusion, then much of private law would have to be justified by reference to parliamentary intention. For example, employment law is founded upon the common law of contract, but some aspects of it are regulated by statute (*eg* minimum wage legislation). Craig suggests that, on Forsyth's logic, once Parliament has passed legislation dealing with some aspects of the employment relationship, *all* of employment law must be characterized as the express or implied creation of Parliament, even though we know that much of it was created by judges using the traditional common law method. 'If this is true,' says Craig, 'then writers in areas as diverse as labour law, company law, commercial law and tax will have a good deal of re-writing to do.' However, Forsyth's argument relates only to circumstances in which Parliament has conferred a *power* upon a public body to do a certain thing, the limits of which must, he says, somehow be determined by reference to the statute. This is of no relevance whatever to areas such as employment law which regulate the *liberty* of private parties to enter into contracts and so on. When employers and employees relate to one another, they are not exercising a statutory power the limits of which must be determined by reference to the statute which created it, but are instead exercising their freedom to do as they please, subject to any relevant legal rules. Those legal rules may be created by the common law, by legislation, or by both.

The third, and strongest, criticism of the *ultra vires* school is advanced by Allan, although we should begin by noting that, in common with Dyzenhaus (see Forsyth (ed), *Judicial Review and the Constitution* (Oxford 2000) at 153–4), Allan [2002] *CLJ* 87 at 90 accepts the logic of the argument that judicial review may be reconciled with parliamentary sovereignty *only* through some form of *ultra vires* doctrine (the 'modified' version of the theory to which he refers is explained later):

> Despite their protestations to the contrary, the common law theorists cannot reasonably object to *ultra vires*, in its very modest 'modified' version, while continuing to accept absolute parliamentary supremacy. In that sense Christopher Forsyth was right to maintain that 'weak' critics of *ultra vires*—those who do not explicitly challenge the sovereignty of Parliament—are 'whether they intend it or not … transmuted into "strong" critics' [who do challenge the supremacy of Parliament]. In so far as the common law basis for judicial review is offered as a viable and genuine alternative to legislative intent, broadly understood, it entails at least a limited qualification of legislative power.

Allan therefore attacks not the *logic* of *ultra vires*, but rather the *premise* that—according to *ultra vires* theory—renders that logic pertinent. Allan's position reduces to the view that the *ultra vires* doctrine would be imperative *if* Parliament were sovereign—but that Parliament is *not* sovereign. This is an entirely logical position: *ultra vires*, as it is usually understood, only makes sense if Parliament is sovereign, since its purpose is to reconcile judicial review and legislative supremacy. If Parliament is not sovereign, then *ultra vires* becomes unnecessary; more precisely (see Elliott (1999) 115 *LQR* 119), if the principles of administrative justice are constitutional fundamentals which, perhaps along with other values such as substantive human rights, form a higher-order of law which constrains Parliament, then parliamentary intention—and therefore *ultra vires*, as traditionally understood—becomes irrelevant. On this view, discretionary power is subject to the principles of administrative justice not because Parliament so intends, but because those principles are fundamentals which will *always* apply, irrespective of legislative intention. This would amount to a constitutional, rather than an interpretive, doctrine of *ultra vires*: decision-makers would lack statutory authority to breach the principles of judicial review not because Parliament had chosen to withhold such power, but because it was, in the first place, constitutionally unable to confer such power.

All of this begs the question whether Allan is right to say that interference with the principles of good administration lies outwith Parliament's authority: are they, in other words, constitutional fundamentals which bind even Parliament itself? If they are, then Parliament is not sovereign—meaning that Allan's claim is a bold one. It is undeniable that the ground appears to be shifting: certain judges have for some time extrajudicially questioned the traditional view of legislative supremacy (see, eg Laws [1995] *PL* 72; Woolf [1995] *PL* 57), and such doubts have now found expression—albeit in *obiter dicta*—from the bench itself. For instance, in *R (Jackson) v. Attorney-General* [2005] UKHL 56, [2006] 1 AC 262, three of the nine Law Lords questioned whether Parliament can still be said to be sovereign in the orthodox sense, and—notably for present purposes—Lord Steyn (at [102]) and Baroness Hale (at [159]) questioned Parliament's constitutional capacity to abolish judicial review or to place areas of governmental activity beyond its reach. However, while they are significant barometers of judicial opinion, such views were tentatively expressed and do not anyway go as far as Allan's assertion that Parliament is wholly incapable of modifying or disapplying particular principles of review.

QUESTIONS

- If Parliament is sovereign, must some form of *ultra vires* doctrine be retained?
- Conversely, if Parliament is not sovereign, is the *ultra vires* doctrine necessarily irrelevant?

1.4.4 The modified *ultra vires* theory

We saw earlier that the traditional *ultra vires* theory is riddled with problems. This led to the articulation of a 'modified *ultra vires* theory'. It is based upon what might be called constitutional interpretation, and draws heavily upon the tradition, described earlier and epitomized by the celebrated *Anisminic* decision, under which the courts approach statutory texts on the assumption that Parliament legislates consistently with a tradition of respect for fundamental constitutional values. That is a category which undoubtedly includes the principles that are vindicated through judicial review, and the characterization of those principles as the fruit of a process of constitutional interpretation is therefore unproblematic. This theme is developed in the following extract.

Elliott, *The Constitutional Foundations of Judicial Review* (Oxford 2001)

Just as the courts' construction of legislation dealing with, say, personal liberty is rationalised in terms of a legislative endeavour that is fundamentally shaped by constitutional principle, so the courts' approach to legislation which creates discretionary powers may be conceptualised as an interpretative process which is normatively premised on those values which make up the rule of law.

Consequently, when Parliament enacts legislation which (typically) confers wide discretionary power and which makes no explicit reference to the controls which should regulate the exercise of the power, the courts are constitutionally entitled—and constitutionally right—to assume that it was Parliament's intention to legislate in conformity with the rule of law principle. This means that Parliament is properly to be regarded as having conferred upon the decision-maker only such power as is consistent with that principle. It follows from this that, in the absence of very clear contrary provision, Parliament must be taken to withhold from decision-makers the power to treat individuals in a manner which offends the rule of law: for this reason, the competence to act unfairly and unreasonably should be assumed to be absent from any parliamentary grant. However, the task of transforming this general intention—that the executive should respect the rule of law—into detailed, legally enforceable rules of fairness and rationality is clearly a matter for the courts, through the incremental methodology of the forensic process. Parliament thus leaves it to the judges to set the precise limits of administrative competence. It is, therefore, the simple and plausible assumption—which is widely made in other contexts—that Parliament intends to legislate in conformity with the rule of law which bridges the apparent gulf between legislative silence and the developed body of administrative law which today regulates the use of executive discretion.

Hence, on this view, there is a relationship between parliamentary legislation and the grounds of review. However, whereas the traditional ultra vires principle conceptualises the relationship as direct in nature, the present approach maintains that the relationship exists in indirect form. While the details of the principles of review are not attributed to parliamentary intention, the judicially-created principles of good administration are applied consistently with Parliament's general intention that the discretionary power which it confers should be limited in accordance with the requirements of the rule of law. Thus it is possible to acknowledge the role of judicial creativity while ensuring that the limits which the judges impose on administrators can be reconciled with the intention of Parliament.

... [O]nce legislation which creates discretionary power is located within its proper constitutional context, it becomes clear that the rule of law must operate to limit and control the exercise of that power. Since the rule of law is a pervasive constitutional principle which shapes both the environment within which Parliament legislates and the context within which statutes are interpreted, the courts rightly impute to Parliament an intention that the rule of law should be upheld. In this manner the courts' vindication of the rule of law is of a piece with Parliament's will, and judicial review comes to rest on a secure constitutional foundation which acknowledges both its normative roots and its relationship with legislative intention.

... [T]here is nothing in this approach which denies that those constitutional principles to which judicial review gives effect possess an inherent normative value which exists independently of legislative intention. Indeed, one of the purposes of the modified theory is to permit open acknowledgement of the intrinsic worth of the principles on which administrative law is founded. Holding that Parliament's intention is consistent with respect for those constitutional principles does not, therefore, rob them of their autonomous normative resonance. Rather, it simply recognises that the constitutional order itself locates the legislature and the legislation which it passes within a framework which is founded on the rule of law, and which therefore attributes to the legislature an intention to act consistently with that principle. Far from denying the inherent normative worth of constitutional principles, such an approach recognises the pervasiveness of the values on which the constitution is founded, such that judicial vindication of the rule of law through judicial review is seen to fulfil, rather than conflict with, the endeavours of the legislature.

Supporters of the modified *ultra vires* theory claim that it overcomes the failings of its traditional counterpart, while preserving what they contend to be the all-important link between the principles of review and the enabling legislation. Most significantly, the modified version of the *ultra vires* doctrine jettisons the implausible assumption that Parliament directly intends the myriad principles of judicial review, openly acknowledging that those principles are normatively rooted, being developed by judges seeking to give meaning to the rule of law within, and subject to, specific statutory frameworks. The modified theory is also able to account for the evolution, over time, of administrative law, since it is self-evident that judges will draw upon contemporary notions of constitutionalism and the rule of law in developing the principles of administrative justice.

An obvious criticism of the modified *ultra vires* doctrine is that it is weakened by its reliance upon the rule of law, because of the vagueness of that concept. However, while it is undeniable that, like the principles of good administration championed by common law theorists, the content of the rule of law—as it relates to administrative justice, as in all other contexts—is a matter of considerable debate (see, *inter alios*, Allan, *Constitutional Justice* (Oxford 2001) and Craig [2003] *PL* 92), the modified *ultra vires* theory, unlike its traditional counterpart, allows that debate to take place in the open, rather than attempting to conceal it behind an unconvincing façade of implied legislative intention.

1.4.5 Conclusion

Although some writers (notably Allan [2002] *CLJ* 87) regard the debate about the constitutional foundations of judicial review as largely sterile, Craig [2003] *PL* 92 at 93 denies that it is an

exercise in arid formalism. It is substantive and principled, and would be so regarded in any legal system, civil or common law. It speaks to the respective powers of courts and legislature in a constitutional democracy. It reflects contending views as to the autonomy of courts when developing judicial review. It encapsulates differing views about the relationship between the rule of law and Parliament.

Indeed, while considerable disagreements remain, the debate has clarified much. The traditional *ultra vires* doctrine is widely regarded as untenable; the role of judicial creativity in the development of the modern law of judicial review is openly acknowledged; and it is accepted on all sides that the principles of administrative justice are rooted in the constitutional bedrock of the rule of law. The principal disagreement is about the role, if any, to be ascribed to legislation. Does this difference of opinion matter? Yes. If proponents of the modified *ultra vires* doctrine are to be believed, then that theory is key to the legitimacy of judicial review because, they contend, only an interpretative model can be truly consistent with parliamentary sovereignty. Moreover, the two models reflect very different views of the relationship between courts, administrators, and the legislature. The common law model envisages the pursuit of administrative justice as the sole preserve of the courts, with principles of good administration unilaterally imposed by the judiciary upon administrators, independently of legislative intention. In contrast, the modified *ultra vires* doctrine presents administrative law as a co-operative endeavour, in which shared and pervasive constitutional values are given concrete meaning and effect by the judicial branch. Properly understood, then, the *ultra vires* debate is much more than a discussion about how judicial review should be justified: it is a debate about the very nature of the British constitution, and of the courts' role within it.

1.5 Administrative power in the modern constitution

When considering administrative power—the proper use of which is, as we have seen, administrative law's central concern—we tend to think principally of the familiar model of central government: of Ministers of the Crown and their officials exercising powers conferred upon them by statute (or occasionally the royal prerogative) taking decisions for which they are legally accountable to the courts and politically accountable to Parliament. In fact, administrative power in the United Kingdom is wielded by an increasing diversity of institutions in a growing variety of ways.

1.5.1 Devolution

Following referendums, the Scotland Act 1998, the Government of Wales Act 1998 (now largely superseded by the Government of Wales Act 2006), and the Northern Ireland Act 1998 established new seats of government in Edinburgh, Cardiff, and Belfast, devolving different amounts of legislative and administrative power to them. In this section, we highlight the main features of the devolution systems to the extent that they illuminate changes in the locus of administrative power in the UK. Before we do so, we mention two preliminary matters.

First, the devolution arrangements do not extend to England. The UK Parliament and the UK government therefore legislate for and administer England, albeit that the position in relation to England is developing. The Cities and Local Government Devolution Act 2016 provides for the 'devolution' of administrative powers by central government to 'combined authorities'—consortia of local authorities under the leadership of an elected mayor. Meanwhile, steps were taken in 2015 to acknowledge the fact that, to some extent, the UK Parliament functions, in some situations, as England's *de facto* Parliament. The Standing Orders of the House of Commons were thus amended in order to ensure that legislation affecting only England must secure the approval of a majority of MPs representing English constituencies, as well as a majority of all MPs.

Second, the devolution settlement is not static. The scheme applicable in Wales was revamped and extended through the passage of the Government of Wales Act 2006, and—if legislation that is before Parliament at the time of writing is enacted—will shortly be further altered and developed, while the Scotland Act 2012 and the Scotland Act 2016—the latter enacted in the aftermath of the independence referendum that was held in Scotland in 2014—significantly augmented the Scottish devolution settlement. The Northern Ireland settlement has also been adjusted (in relatively modest ways) including by legislation. The Assembly and Executive Reform (Assembly Opposition) Act (Northern Ireland) 2016, enacted by the Northern Ireland Assembly itself, provides for the establishment of an official opposition within the Assembly. In these ways, devolution is responsive to changing circumstances and attitudes within relevant parts of the UK—albeit that concerns have been raised that infinite responsiveness risks, at best, a disordered approach to the territorial constitution and, at worst, an ongoing erosion of the ties that bind the four countries of the UK together.

1.5.2 The powers and nature of the devolved institutions

In all three of the devolved systems, power is divided between a legislative branch (the Scottish Parliament; the National Assembly for Wales, colloquially known as the Welsh Assembly; and the Northern Ireland Assembly) and an executive (the Scottish government; the Welsh Assembly government; and the Northern Ireland executive). The UK Parliament has not relinquished its power to legislate on devolved issues, and so (at least in theory) remains sovereign—albeit that the Scotland Act 2016 states that the Scottish Parliament and government 'are a permanent part of the United Kingdom's constitutional arrange-ments', and 'declare[s]' that they cannot be abolished absent the consent of the Scottish people manifested in a referendum. In contrast, none of the devolved legislatures has unlimited power: none can therefore lay any claim to being sovereign in the sense that the Westminster Parliament is said to be. Thus, although the Scottish Parliament and the Northern Ireland Assembly enjoy general legislative competence, this is subject to certain exceptions (Northern Ireland Act, ss 5–8; Scotland Act, ss 28–30). This means that they have a general power to legislate on any matter save those which are excluded from the devolu-tion arrangements. Such matters include the alteration of certain pieces of UK legislation (such as the Human Rights Act 1998) and certain policy areas (*eg* defence and interna-tional relations). The Scottish Parliament and the Northern Ireland Assembly are also not authorized to make laws that contravene European Union law or certain provisions of the European Convention on Human Rights.

The position in Wales is different. Whereas the Scottish and Northern Ireland legislatures can, on matters within their devolved competence, repeal and amend UK legislation as it applies to Scotland and Northern Ireland, enacting fresh legislation if they wish, no such power existed in Wales before the Government of Wales Act 2006 took effect. The Welsh Assembly now can do such things, but rather than having general legislative power subject to exceptions, the Assembly only has law-making authority over specific matters listed in the Government of Wales Act 2006, sch 5. The upshot is that the Welsh Assembly's powers are more limited than those of its counterparts in Belfast and Edinburgh. However, legisla-tion introduced into the UK Parliament in 2016, but which had not completed its passage through Parliament at the time of writing, will, if enacted, invest the Welsh Assembly with general legislative competence—thereby bringing the architecture of Welsh devolution into line with the models that apply in Scotland and Northern Ireland—albeit subject to signifi-cant restrictions.

Just as legislative power has been ascribed to the devolved legislatures, so administra-tive power is now exercised by the devolved executive branches. Such power is acquired from two sources. First, the devolved legislatures can themselves confer upon the respective executives discretionary powers and delegated law-making powers (on which see ch 16) to the extent that the legislatures are empowered by the devolution legislation to do so. Second, the devolved executives exercise in relation to devolved matters the administrative powers that would previously have been exercised for Scotland, Wales, and Northern Ireland by UK Ministers.

1.5.3 Political and legal accountability

Just as members of the UK government are drawn from the Westminster Parliament, so members of the devolved administrations are drawn from the respective devolved legis-latures. And just as the work of central government departments is scrutinized by the Westminster Parliament—by means of parliamentary questions, select committees, and so on—so the devolved administrations are answerable to the corresponding devolved legislatures.

However, the voting systems used in elections to all three devolved legislatures are different from that which applies to the Westminster Parliament. Although it did not do so in the 2010 UK general election, the system currently used at Westminster generally delivers an overall majority for one party. In contrast, the devolved voting systems are less likely to do so. This increases the probability of coalition or minority government. Indeed, the Northern Ireland Act *requires* coalition government in Northern Ireland in order to ensure that the executive is perceived to have legitimacy by both the Unionist and Republican communities (who disagree sharply on whether Northern Ireland should remain part of the UK). The fact that coalition or minority government is commonplace in Scotland, Wales, and Northern Ireland does not preclude the operation of the normal processes of political accountability, whereby executive policies and decisions are subjected to critical scrutiny by legislative members, just as the outcome of the 2010 UK general election did not prevent such processes from continuing at Westminster. However, the absence of a single governing party with an overall majority inevitably impacts upon the dynamics within the legislature, including those which condition how the legislature holds the executive to account. In particular, minority administrations which are reliant upon issue-by-issue and bill-by-bill support from other political parties are inevitably required to govern in a manner that is, other things being equal, relatively consensual.

Exercises of legislative and administrative power by the devolved institutions are subject to judicial review. The former proposition is noteworthy: because, as already noted, the devolved legislatures, unlike their counterpart at Westminster, have limited powers, the possibility arises that their enactments, or parts thereof, may be struck down as *ultra vires*. Indeed, not only can courts scrutinize legislation and administrative acts once they have been taken: there is also the possibility, albeit a rarely used one, of pre-emptive judicial consideration of the legality of both legislation (under s 33 of the Scotland Act 1998, s 112 of the Government of Wales Act 2006, and s 11 of the Northern Ireland Act 1998) and administrative acts (under sch 6 of the Scotland Act, sch 10 of the Northern Ireland Act, and sch 9 of the Government of Wales Act).

QUESTIONS
- Do you agree that courts should be able to issue opinions on the legality of proposed actions by devolved institutions?
- What difficulties might courts encounter when faced with such hypothetical issues?

1.5.4 Local government

Although devolution is a recent and stark example of the dispersal of administrative (and legislative) power, it would be wholly wrong to suppose that, prior to devolution, administrative authority was concentrated solely in central government. No attempt will be made here to list all the powers possessed by the institutions of local government, but it should be noted that they wield substantial administrative powers in certain fields (planning and licensing being prime examples), including legislative powers to enact byelaws (a form of secondary legislation).

The Local Government Act 1972 is the foundation of the contemporary system of local government. It envisaged a two-tier structure. Each metropolitan area had a metropolitan county council, but was also subdivided into districts, each with a metropolitan district council. Similarly, non-metropolitan areas were divided into counties, each with a county council, but also subdivided into districts, each with a district council; a similar structure applied in Wales. Meanwhile, London was divided into a number of boroughs, each with its own council, but there was also a city-wide authority, the Greater London Council. The organization of local government has changed somewhat since 1972.

Five main developments should be noted. First, the Greater London Council and metropolitan county councils were abolished by the Local Government Act 1985, and many of their functions transferred to London borough councils and metropolitan district councils. Second, the unitary model has been extended to many non-metropolitan areas in which unitary authorities perform the functions that would otherwise be performed by both county and district councils. The decision whether to retain the two-tier structure or shift to a unitary authority is ultimately taken by central government. Third, two-tier government has been reintroduced in London: the Greater London Authority Act 1999 created a new, city-wide Greater London Authority, comprising an elected mayor and elected members of a new Assembly. Fourth, the Local Government (Wales) Act 1994 replaced two-tier government with unitary authorities in Wales. Fifth, as noted earlier, the Cities and Local Government Devolution Act 2016 provides for the 'devolution' of powers from central government to 'combined authorities'—that is, groups of local authorities under the leadership of an elected mayor.

This is evident not only from the structural changes just described, but also from striking reforms concerning the role and operation of local government. As to the former, a radical change in emphasis—partly influenced by ideological considerations about the role and scale of the 'state', partly motivated by more prosaic concerns about efficiency—was effected by the Conservative government in the 1980s. Under reforms that it introduced, local authorities were, in relation to certain matters, transformed from service providers to service commissioners, with many services being performed not by local councils themselves but by private sector service providers operating under contractual arrangements with councils.

The attitude of central government to local government tends to ebb and flow over time. By the mid-2000s, local government had become subject to a straightjacket of centrally imposed targets and inspections—so much so that, in some respects at least, local government could without much exaggeration be considered a vehicle for the delivery of central government programmes. In recent years, however, the pendulum has begun to swing in the other direction; 'localism' being much in vogue. For instance, in 2011 the UK Parliament enacted the Localism Act, which resulted in some (modest) extensions to local authorities' powers, while the Cities and Local Government Devolution Act 2016, mentioned above, forms the latest element of central government's localism agenda.

It is apparent from the sketch set out above that local government—in contrast to the devolved governance arrangements in Scotland, Wales, and Northern Ireland—finds itself in a constitutionally fragile position. Indeed, it—like many other spheres within the public sector—is in an almost perpetual state of reform as both the architecture of local government and the balance of power between it and central government shifts by reference to the agenda of the latter. However, while, as a result, the role and powers of local government ebb and flow over time, the key point for present purposes is that it is, and will remain, a significant site of administrative authority.

1.5.5 Agencies and the private sector

Over the course of recent decades, the role of government in Britain has been radically reconceived as a result of three interrelated innovations introduced by the Thatcher administration
and pursued with varying degrees of enthusiasm by its successors. These changes reflect a
critical view of the role of the state, and a willingness to question whether in-house provision
by government is necessarily the best way of delivering services.

First, the landscape of the 'state' has been transformed by the *privatization programme*
instituted, and prosecuted with particular zeal, in the 1980s by the Thatcher government.
Functions which had been performed by the state—most notably the provision of utilities
such as electricity, water, and gas—were henceforth to be discharged by the private sector
(albeit subject to state regulation). These changes were radical, and represented an entirely
new view of the function of government; in particular, they reflected a vision of 'smaller'
government, and the notion that many things traditionally done by the state were not government functions, properly so-called.

The other two key changes in this sphere were different in type, but no less radical. The
contracting out of service provision and the introduction of *executive agencies* represented a
new approach to the discharge of those functions which, within the new landscape, remained
government functions. As we will see, these two developments are related, and share some
common features; let us begin, however, with contracting out.

It has always been the case that government—central and local—has had to enter into
contracts with the private sector in order to procure goods and so on. For instance, in discharging its functions with respect to the penal system, central government must purchase
supplies for the purpose of building and maintaining prisons. However, within the traditional
model, the function itself—in our example, the running of prisons—is discharged directly
by government. Contrary to this tradition, contracting out involves fulfilling government
functions by engaging private sector organizations: within this model, therefore, the government function of running prisons may be (and, in some instances, is) discharged by means
of contractual arrangements with private sector security firms which are engaged to operate
particular institutions.

The legal framework for contracting out is found in Part II of the Deregulation and
Contracting Out Act 1994. The effect of s 69 is that Ministers may make provision for private
sector organizations to exercise their statutory functions. Similar arrangements are made
by s 70 in respect of functions of local authorities. By s 72, acts and omissions of the private
sector body 'shall be treated for all purposes as done or omitted to be done' by the Minister,
office-holder, or local authority, as the case may be. Contracting out raises a number of legal
and constitutional questions (on which see generally Auby [2007] *PL* 40). In particular, while
the 1994 Act appears to preserve the ultimate responsibility of government, two problems
arise. First, there is a question mark over the extent to which Ministers can be held politically accountable for the actions of private sector bodies. Freedland [1995] *PL* 21 at 26 writes
that he is

apprehensive that the effect of providing that public duties may be entrusted on a day-to-day basis
to private contractors cannot fail to be the erosion of the responsibilities of the state to its citizens
at quite a fundamental level. The state comes to look more like the sleeping trustee and less and
less like the active trustee for the public good.

On the other hand, as Craig, *Administrative Law* (Oxford 2012) at 116, notes, 'it can be argued that these very contracts, like the framework documents used in agency creation [discussed below], sharpen accountability by defining goals, setting targets and monitoring performance'. The second issue concerns legal accountability. Existing case law shows that courts are reluctant to subject contracted-out service providers to judicial review, and that such providers are also unlikely to be bound by the terms of the Human Rights Act 1998. This creates a risk that the use of contractual arrangements may defeat the protections to which individuals are usually entitled under public law; although the contracting-out public authority remains subject to public law, this may be of little practical utility where the complaint relates to the conduct of the private sector body. These issues are fully considered in ch 4.

Like contracting out, the introduction of executive agencies represented a major change in the way in which government functions are discharged: Oliver and Drewry, *Public Service Reforms: Issues of Accountability and Public Law* (London 1996) at 39 suggest that it might 'well be regarded as "a revolution in Whitehall"'. Agencies which exist outside the departmental structure of central government are hardly an innovation. However, a new breed of such bodies was ushered in following a report, *Improving Management in Government: The Next Steps*, commissioned by the then Prime Minister and published in 1988. The report concluded that many of the administrative tasks carried out by central government departments could be performed more efficiently by separate agencies; Ministers and civil servants would concentrate on policy strategy and formulation, while agencies, headed by chief executives, would implement policy and deliver services. Drewry (1994) 47 *Parl Aff* 583 at 589 explains that the Next Steps programme is premised on 'institutionalising the crucial but elusive distinction between ministerial support and policy functions on the one hand (performed by … civil servants, working in close proximity to ministers) and executive or service delivery functions on the other'. (It is, however, clear that some agencies *do* have responsibility for policy or at least what is referred to in HM Treasury/Office of Public Services Reform, *Better Government Services: Executive Agencies in the 21st Century* (2002) (hereinafter the 'Treasury Review') at 10, as 'operational/process policy' (*eg* the Prison Service).) In that Review, the then government said that '[t]he agency model has been a success', transforming 'the landscape of government and the responsiveness and effectiveness of services' delivered by it. A number of reasons for this have been identified (at 17–18), including agencies' 'clarity and focus on specified tasks', their 'culture of delivery', and their 'accountability and openness'.

Executive agencies presently handle matters as diverse as child support and benefits payments, the running of the royal parks, and the maintenance of highways. The appropriateness of 'hiving off' functions to agencies was considered by the Treasury Review (at 16):

> In the majority of situations, executive services within departments are not highly politically sensitive and it is neither realistic nor appropriate for Ministers to take personal responsibility for the day-to-day running of the function. In this case an agency will be the best solution. The agency model is sufficiently flexible and accountable to make it the best choice for delivering most central government services.

However, the Review went on to note that some executive functions continue to be 'delivered internally within departments'. It suggested that the hiving-off of certain functions to agencies would be inappropriate because of the political sensitivity of the work involved or the difficulty in separating policy and operational matters. This raises the question of the relationship between departments and agencies—a matter considered by Freedland [1994] *PL* 86 at 88:

> When an executive agency is created by separation from its parent department, the relationship between the two is governed by a so-called Framework Document, which defines the functions and roles of the agency, and the procedures whereby the department will set and monitor the performance targets for the agency. Although it is asserted that the framework documents are not strictly speaking contracts, it is increasingly accepted that they are contracts in every sense but the technical one, so much is the nature of these arrangements like that of the contracts whereby activities are contracted out to the private sector.

It is evident, therefore, that framework documents can permit Ministers to hold agencies and chief executives to account, by making provision for appropriate oversight in terms of performance, service delivery, the attainment of targets, and so on. However, the Treasury Review highlighted some concerns in this regard. It noted (at 28) that framework documents need to be regularly reviewed in order to ensure that the governance of agencies and their relationships with departments are appropriate to contemporary circumstances. More generally, the Review found (at 10) that '[s]ome agencies have ... become disconnected from their departments', giving rise to a 'gulf between policy and delivery'. In light of this, the Review reconsidered how departments and agencies should relate to one another, concluding that a rigid distinction between policy and operations is problematic because questions of effective delivery of services must feed into the departmental policy-making process. The Review therefore recommended (at 25–30) closer co-operation and better communication between agencies and departments. The Cabinet Office's *Executive Agencies: A Guide for Departments* (2006) sets out best practice in relation to such matters.

In constitutional terms, the growing role of agencies poses challenges to the operation of the principles of ministerial accountability and responsibility. For instance, Agency Chief Executives (ACEs) can be required to give evidence to parliamentary select committees— but where does this leave *ministerial* accountability or responsibility? Addressing this point, Drewry (in Jowell and Oliver, *The Changing Constitution* (Oxford 2007) at 199) writes:

> In recent years, governments have sought to address the tricky problem of how to maintain some credibility for the classical doctrine of ministerial responsibility ... by claiming ... that there is a clear distinction between *responsibility* ([which lies in respect of] the job one is charged with doing) and *accountability* (the duty to explain, or render an account of what has or has not been done). Thus, in the present context, ACEs are *responsible* for the operational performance of their agencies (and liable to shoulder the blame when things go wrong); ministers are *responsible* for the policy framework within which agencies operate and—in accordance with the rules of ministerial responsibility—*account to* Parliament and the electorate both for that policy and for matters that fall within the responsibility of the ACE.

The difficulty, of course, is that the distinction between policy and operations—and, therefore, between matters for which ACEs and Ministers are accountable/responsible (on which see further Oliver and Drewry, *Public Service Reforms: Issues of Accountability and Public Law* (London 1996) at 6–13)—is far from clear; it is, consequently, open to manipulation by Ministers wishing to evade responsibility for failures in areas in which agencies are involved.

1.6 Concluding remarks

The location and nature of administrative power in the UK are increasingly diverse. Such power is today wielded by central and local government, by government agencies and devolved administrations, and by resort to novel contractual arrangements. These changes pose considerable challenges to administrative law, as it seeks to ensure that the enormous administrative powers wielded today are exercised lawfully and fairly. In the remainder of this book, we explore the principles applied to this end by courts of law, as well as extra-judicial methods of promoting good administration and dealing with abuses of power.

FURTHER RESOURCES

Allan, 'Constitutional Dialogue and the Justification of Judicial Review' (2003) 23 *OJLS* 563

Craig, 'The Common Law, Shared Power and Judicial Review' (2004) 24 *OJLS* 237

Elliott, *The Constitutional Foundations of Judicial Review* (Oxford 2000)

Forsyth (ed), *Judicial Review and the Constitution* (Oxford 2000)

Freedland, 'Government by Contract Re-examined: Some Functional Issues' in Craig and Rawlings (eds), *Law and Administration in Europe* (Oxford 2003)

2 JURISDICTION

2.1 Introduction

2.1.1 What is 'jurisdiction'?

All administrative power is limited by (i) the express terms of the statute which confers it, (ii) the implied terms of that statute, and (iii) general principles such as natural justice and reasonableness. (We know, from ch 1, that *ultra vires* theorists consider that there is no distinction between (ii) and (iii).) Decision-makers act lawfully only so long as they do not transgress these limits on their powers. The central concern of the courts, on judicial review, is to identify whether the decision-maker has acted (or is proposing to act) beyond those limits. In this sense, all of judicial review is about jurisdiction: is the action under scrutiny within or outside the powers of the decision-maker? Provided that the decision-maker remains within the limits of his jurisdiction, or power, the courts have no business interfering: if, however, the decision-maker exceeds his jurisdiction, the courts have every right to strike down the resulting decision.

Assume, for example, that immigration legislation confers upon the Home Secretary a discretionary power to detain 'illegal entrants'. Adopting the most likely construction of this statutory power, it may be reformulated in the following manner: *if* the person concerned is an illegal entrant, *then* the Home Secretary may decide whether to detain him. Faced with such a power, it is probable that a Home Secretary would, in individual cases, address two major issues. *May* the power be exercised in respect of the individual in question? If so, *should* the power be exercised in respect of that person?

The answer to the first question depends upon whether the individual concerned is an illegal entrant. If not, then it is clear that the person cannot be detained under this power. The person's status as an illegal entrant is a jurisdictional condition: only if it is met is it possible for the Home Secretary lawfully to proceed. The defining characteristic of jurisdictional matters is that they cannot conclusively be determined by the decision-maker. Of course the Home Secretary must himself try to work out whether the person is an illegal entrant—he has to do this in order to deduce whether he can go on to consider detaining him—but the Home Secretary's decision on the jurisdictional matter is not conclusive: because it represents a limitation upon his power, he cannot be the final judge of it. It follows that, if the person concerned is not shown to be an illegal entrant to the satisfaction of the reviewing court, then any purported exercise of the discretion to detain him will be struck down: there was no power to act because a jurisdictional condition was not met. Characterizing a particular question as jurisdictional is therefore highly significant because such questions have only one lawful answer: the answer favoured by the reviewing court.

What if the Home Secretary decides (correctly) that the person concerned *is* an illegal entrant? He then moves on to address the second issue mentioned: given that the power *may* be exercised in respect of that person, *should* he exercise it? Such questions are sometimes said to go to 'the merits of the case' or to the 'discretion of the decision-maker'. In other words, they are not jurisdictional questions *per se*. In our example, whether a given illegal entrant should be detained is the very issue which Parliament intended the Home Secretary to determine: that is why, after all, it gave the power to him. It is therefore for the Home Secretary to exercise his judgement in deciding whether to detain any particular illegal entrant; the court's view as to whether a particular illegal entrant should be detained is not determinative.

So: 'jurisdictional questions' must be answered correctly, in the view of the reviewing court; 'merits questions', meanwhile, are for the decision-maker. However, the picture is, in fact, more complicated. Even if the decision-maker correctly decides that the person under consideration is an illegal entrant, such that the power *may* be exercised in relation to him, it is wrong to suppose that the decision-maker, at that point, clears a single jurisdictional hurdle which gives him access to discretion that is otherwise unlimited. The decision-maker has cleared *a* jurisdictional hurdle: after all, if the person had not been an illegal entrant, that would have been the end of the matter. However, once the decision-maker clears *that* hurdle, the decision-maker must still remain within the scope of his power. Even after the decision-maker has correctly decided the initial jurisdictional issue ('is this person an illegal entrant?') and has begun to address the 'merits question' ('should this person be detained?'), his power remains limited: issues will therefore arise *in the course of answering the merits question itself* which, if incorrectly determined, will send the decision-maker outside his jurisdiction.

To illustrate this point, let us return to our example and assume that the Home Secretary is deciding whether to detain someone who is an illegal entrant. Let us also assume that the person concerned approaches the Home Secretary and asks for an opportunity to present his case—that is, to put arguments before the Home Secretary as to why he should not be detained (*eg* that he is not a risk to national security, or that he has dependant relatives whom he must look after). Must the Home Secretary grant him such an opportunity—a 'hearing'—or not? Although the ultimate question ('should this person be detained?') is a 'merits question', and therefore for the Home Secretary, this specific question ('must this person be given a hearing?') is a jurisdictional one. As we will see in ch 10, administrative law prescribes the circumstances in which individuals must be given a hearing: the duty to comply with what are known as the principles of natural justice therefore represents a limit on the Home Secretary's power. Ultimately, then, whether the illegal entrant must be given a hearing is a matter that the court can decide for itself: if the Home Secretary incorrectly decides that no hearing should be afforded, the court can simply strike down the decision.

The example can be varied. Assume that the person concerned has attracted public attention (*eg* because he has expressed controversial and unpopular views on some matter of current interest) such that public opinion strongly favours his detention. May the Home Secretary take this consideration into account when deciding whether to detain the individual concerned? As with our first example, although the ultimate question ('should this person be detained?') is for the Home Secretary, this specific question ('may public opinion be taken into account?') is a jurisdictional one. As we shall see in ch 7, whether any particular factor may be taken into account by a decision-maker is regarded as a jurisdictional issue: either it may or may not be taken into account, and it is ultimately for the court to decide into which of those categories any particular factor falls.

This takes us back to the (disarmingly) simple proposition with which we began this chapter: that 'all of judicial review is about jurisdiction'. The one and only ground upon which the courts may intervene is that the decision-maker has 'acted *ultra vires*' or 'exceeded the limits of his power' or has 'exceeded his jurisdiction' (all three expressions mean the same thing). However, a practical distinction may be drawn, which reflects the way in which we tend to think about jurisdictional issues. As is apparent from our earlier example of the Home Secretary's power to detain illegal entrants, most statutory powers can be expressed in the terms:

(i)   *If* [a particular condition is met, or a particular state of affairs exists (*eg* that the person concerned is an 'illegal entrant')],

(ii)   *then* [the decision-maker may exercise discretion by choosing whether to, say, carry out some prescribed activity (*eg* detaining that person)].

This sort of formulation reflects the two-stage analysis which decision-makers, faced with a statutory power, will tend to adopt:

(i)   *May* it be exercised? (a jurisdictional question)

(ii)   If so, *should* it be exercised? (a merits question)

When the decision-maker addresses the first matter, he enjoys no discretion: either the power can or cannot be exercised in the circumstances of the particular case. This is a jurisdictional matter pure and simple. In contrast, when the decision-maker addresses the second question, it is ultimately for him to answer it; however, in the course of doing so, he will have to confront a number of subsidiary matters, such as whether a fair hearing must be given, whether certain information may be taken into account, and so on. These are jurisdictional questions which, if answered incorrectly, will cause him to exceed his power, and thereby to act unlawfully, just as though he had, at the first stage, erroneously concluded that he had the power to act. It follows that, in answering the ultimate question—in our example, 'should this person be detained?'—the decision-maker must clear a number of hurdles. Some of these, typically because they are explicit in the statute, naturally fall into the first part of our '*if ... then*' formulation. It is jurisdictional questions of this type with which we are centrally concerned in this chapter. Others, typically because they are not explicit in the statute, tend to arise as sub-issues once the decision-maker has moved on to address the second question (given that the power *may* be exercised, *should* it be exercised?); such jurisdictional limits derive from general principles of administrative law such as natural justice and reasonableness, and are discussed in later chapters.

2.1.2 Distinguishing jurisdictional and non-jurisdictional matters

So far, we have seen that whether something falls into the 'jurisdictional' or 'merits' question has significant consequences. How, then, do we decide into which category a given matter should be placed? There is, unfortunately but perhaps not unsurprisingly, no simple answer to this question. Indeed, much of this chapter is devoted to addressing it. It is true that some situations are straightforward. Our example, for instance, is relatively simple: 'The Home Secretary may detain illegal entrants.' Working on the assumption that Parliament must have specified the category of persons capable of detention under this power for a reason—*viz* to ensure that the power can be used *only* in respect of such persons—it is fairly uncontroversial that a particular individual's status as an illegal entrant should be regarded as a jurisdictional limit upon the Home Secretary's detention power.

However, if we modify the example slightly, then the 'jurisdictional or merits?' question becomes more difficult. Assume now that our imaginary statutory power provides that 'The Home Secretary may detain dangerous illegal entrants.' Is dangerousness a jurisdictional matter? Did Parliament intend that the Home Secretary should merely be able to choose which people, out of a group of people who are 'dangerous illegal entrants', should be detained? If so, then we should treat dangerousness as a jurisdictional matter—something of which the court must ultimately be satisfied. Or did Parliament—perhaps because it felt that determining 'dangerousness' is a more impressionistic enterprise than deciding whether someone is an 'illegal entrant'—intend that the Home Secretary should decide which 'illegal entrants' are dangerous (and whether he should detain any of them)? If so, then we should not treat dangerousness as a jurisdictional matter; instead, it should be regarded as a 'merits question' because, on this view, the dangerousness of a particular illegal entrant is a matter for the Home Secretary to decide.

These questions do not invite simple answers, although we explain later in this chapter that there are some general principles that can be applied in analysing such issues. For the time being, we merely note that the location of the line between factors upon which the decision-maker's jurisdiction depends and matters which are regarded as ultimately for the decision-maker is crucial, because it determines the scope of the relevant power. The greater the number of factors which are regarded as jurisdictional, the smaller the decision-maker's discretion. If this approach is carried too far, then that discretion vanishes: everything becomes a question of jurisdiction over which the reviewing court has the final word. There are, however, risks in the other direction, too. If jurisdictional limits are drawn too loosely, thereby making (nearly) everything a question for the decision-maker to determine on the merits, then it effectively becomes a law unto itself: it can decide the scope and limits of its own powers, and there is no (adequate) opportunity for objectively checking that the decision-maker is acting in accordance with the terms of the statute which, in the first place, conferred power upon him. This raises serious problems with respect to the rule of law.

Nevertheless, a very limited view of what matters should be counted as jurisdictional was famously championed by Gordon in a series of articles (see (1929) 45 *LQR* 459; (1931) 47 *LQR* 386 and 557; (1960) 1 *UBCLR* 185; (1966) 82 *LQR* 263 and 515). He argued that questions of jurisdiction depend on the nature of the facts into which a decision-maker has to enquire, not on the truth or falsity of those facts. On this view, returning once again to our example of a power to detain illegal entrants, the Home Secretary would be permitted conclusively to decide that someone was an illegal entrant *even if they were not actually an illegal entrant*. Any error which the Home Secretary made (*eg* by deciding that the person was a US citizen when in fact he was a UK citizen) in determining whether the person was an illegal entrant would be an error *within* jurisdiction. On this approach, judicial intervention on jurisdictional grounds would be confined to circumstances in which the

Home Secretary formulated the question incorrectly (*eg* by asking whether the person was an 'undesirable character' rather than an 'illegal entrant').

Although this formalism may purchase certainty, by avoiding the need to make fine distinctions between jurisdictional and non-jurisdictional matters, it almost eviscerates jurisdictional control, in effect permitting the decision-maker to determine the extent of its own powers. In fact, such an approach is not adopted by English law, which, as we explain later, characterizes a wide range of issues as jurisdictional, thus giving reviewing courts extensive powers in this context, and departing radically from the limited model of jurisdictional review advanced by Gordon.

2.2 Errors of law

2.2.1 Introduction

In considering the courts' approach to questions of jurisdiction, we need to distinguish between a number of issues which can be illustrated by reference to our example of a power to detain illegal entrants. We have already seen that the power of the decision-maker arises only if the individual is, in the first place, an 'illegal entrant'. The existence of an illegal entrant is therefore a jurisdictional requirement: it is something upon which the decision-maker's power depends. But what does this mean? The analysis of whether a particular individual is an illegal entrant can be broken down into at least three stages:

(i) Some meaning must be attributed to the statutory term 'illegal entrant'. Most issues of this nature are characterized as *questions of law*.

(ii) The decision-maker must make certain findings of fact about the individual concerned: for instance, in what circumstances did he enter the United Kingdom? These are *questions of fact*.

(iii) The decision-maker must apply these findings of fact to the legal definition of 'illegal entrant', in order to determine whether the person concerned is or is not an illegal entrant over whom relevant statutory powers of detention may be exercised. This involves *questions of both fact and law*.

Are all of these issues jurisdictional? Can the court substitute its opinion in relation to all of these matters?

Before addressing these questions, we need to note that underlying this area which resounds with argument couched in *conceptual* language is a *policy* debate about how best to draw the line between judicial supervision and agency autonomy. This is clear from the following remarks of Farina (1989) 89 *Columbia Law Review* 452 at 452–3:

> Assume ... that Congress enacts legislation which establishes a system of rights and responsibilities for 'employees' and creates an agency to administer that system. Should the court or the agency decide whether the critical statutory term 'employees' encompasses persons who would be considered independent contractors under the common law, or workers who are foremen and so, at least arguably, part of management? To determine 'what the law is' in the context of

an actual controversy that turns on a question of statutory meaning is the quintessential judicial function. At the same time, however, such questions are so bound up with successful administration of the regulatory scheme that it may seem only sensible to give principal interpretive responsibility to the 'expert' agency that lives with the statute constantly. And if this challenge of mediating between principle and practicality were not difficult enough, there are other pieces to the puzzle. At times, the consequence of adopting one interpretation of the statute over another is to subject an individual to civil or criminal penalties for her past behavior. Fundamental fairness to someone threatened with sanctions might require that the decisive legal standard be interpreted by a decision maker whose life tenure and salary protection promote impartiality, objectivity and insulation from political pressure. Finally, the legislature that enacted the statute may have had an intention about apportioning interpretive responsibility between court and agency. Determining how to 'retrieve' such an intention after the fact and deciding whether, once retrieved, it is dispositive, present additional complications.

QUESTIONS

- Are the criteria suggested by Farina helpful?
- What factors do you think should be taken into account in identifying the dividing line between jurisdictional and non-jurisdictional matters?

2.2.2 Jurisdictional and non-jurisdictional errors of law

Until comparatively recently, some errors of law were regarded as jurisdictional, while others were not. A decision-maker could make a 'non-jurisdictional error of law' while remaining within jurisdiction; only a 'jurisdictional error of law' would take it outside jurisdiction. The point was explained in the following terms by Denning LJ in *R* v. *Northumberland Compensation Appeal Tribunal, ex parte Shaw* [1952] 1 KB 338 at 346:

No one has ever doubted that the Court of King's Bench can intervene to prevent a statutory tribunal from exceeding the jurisdiction which Parliament has conferred on it; but it is quite another thing to say that the King's Bench can intervene when a tribunal makes a mistake of law. A tribunal may often decide a point of law wrongly whilst keeping well within its jurisdiction.

There are, however, two difficulties with this approach. First, if a decision-maker is able to make a particular error of law while remaining within jurisdiction then, in the absence of a right of appeal, the error will stand: the decision-maker's conclusion is final, and the reviewing court cannot intervene. Different decision-makers may therefore attach different meanings to the same legal provision, with the result that the scheme laid down in the relevant legislation is interpreted and operated in different ways. Such diversity in legal meaning might be considered inimical to the rule-of-law requirement of legal certainty.

Second, the distinction between jurisdictional and non-jurisdictional questions was notoriously difficult to draw. It was said to turn upon matters which were 'collateral' to the jurisdiction of the decision-maker—and upon which its jurisdiction therefore depended— and matters which the decision-maker itself was empowered to decide. Although it was generally held that such matters were to be resolved by recourse to the relevant legislation, in practice the statute was likely to provide little guidance. This gave rise to the strong impression that the courts manipulated the distinction for instrumental purposes, choosing to find that a particular issue was jurisdictional if they wanted to intervene, and non-jurisdictional if they did not.

We will see, in the following section, that the problematic distinction between jurisdictional and non-jurisdictional errors of law is now almost completely redundant. First, however, we should note one other issue. We have, thus far, assumed that jurisdictional errors of law were reviewable but that non-jurisdictional errors were not. However, some non-jurisdictional errors of law were reviewable under the doctrine of error on the face of the record, which Denning LJ revived in *R* v. *Northumberland Compensation Appeal Tribunal, ex parte Shaw* [1952] 1 KB 338. The effect was to permit any error of law disclosed on the face of the record of the proceedings to be quashed, irrespective of whether it was categorized as a jurisdictional error. This provided the courts with a useful tool by which to expand the scope of review for error of law, free from the restrictions which would otherwise have been imposed by the distinction between jurisdictional and non-jurisdictional errors of law. However, the contemporary irrelevance of that distinction in practice, to which we now turn, has made the doctrine of error on the face of the record largely, if not wholly, superfluous.

2.2.3 The *Anisminic* decision

The decision of the House of Lords in *Anisminic* is one of the most celebrated cases in modern administrative law for two (intimately connected) reasons. First, it demonstrated an extremely robust judicial approach to a statutory provision which seemed to exclude the courts' supervisory jurisdiction; this aspect of the case is considered at 14.6.2. Second, this bold interpretation of the statute was facilitated by the underlying view of jurisdiction adopted by their Lordships: although they did not actually abolish the distinction between jurisdictional and non-jurisdictional errors of law, they laid the foundation for such a step to be taken. It is this aspect of the case which is of present interest.

Anisminic Ltd v. Foreign Compensation Commission [1969] 2 AC 147
House of Lords

The claimant, an English company, had owned property in Egypt worth about £4.4m which the Egyptian authorities sequestrated in 1956. In 1957 the claimant sold the property to TEDO, an Egyptian organization, for £0.5m. By a treaty between the United Arab Republic and the United Kingdom, £27.5m was paid over to the latter as compensation for property confiscated in 1956 and the claimant sought to participate in this fund by applying to the Foreign Compensation Commission. The Commission's provisional determination was that the claimant had failed to establish a claim under the Foreign Compensation (Egypt) (Determination and Registration of Claims) Order 1962 on the ground that its successor in title was a non-British national and consequently it did not comply with the terms of Article 4(1)(b)(ii) of the Order (which is set out in the excerpt from Lord Reid's speech which follows). The claimant sought a declaration that the provisional determination was a nullity, contending that the Commission had misconstrued the Order. The Commission denied this and also contended that the court was precluded from considering whether the determination was a nullity because of the presence of an ouster clause in the Foreign Compensation Act 1950; on which see 14.6.2.

Lord Reid

... It has sometimes been said that it is only where a tribunal acts without jurisdiction that its decision is a nullity. But in such cases the word 'jurisdiction' has been used in a very wide sense, and I have come to the conclusion that it is better not to use the term except in the narrow and original sense of the tribunal being entitled to enter on the inquiry in question. But there are many cases where, although the tribunal had jurisdiction to enter on the inquiry, it has done or failed to do something in the course of the inquiry which is of such a nature that its decision is a nullity. It may have given its decision in bad faith. It may have made a decision which it had no power to make. It may have failed in the course of the inquiry to comply with the requirements of natural justice. It may in perfect good faith have misconstrued the provisions giving it power to act so that it failed to deal with the question remitted to it and decided some question which was not remitted to it. It may have refused to take into account something which it was required to take into account. Or it may have based its decision on some matter which, under the provisions setting it up, it had no right to take into account. I do not intend this list to be exhaustive. But if it decides a question remitted to it for decision without committing any of these errors it is as much entitled to decide that question wrongly as it is to decide it rightly. I understand that some confusion has been caused by my having said in *Reg. v. Governor of Brixton Prison, Ex parte Armah* [1968] A.C. 192, 234 that if a tribunal has jurisdiction to go right it has jurisdiction to go wrong. So it has, if one uses 'jurisdiction' in the narrow original sense. If it is entitled to enter on the inquiry and does not do any of those things which I have mentioned in the course of the proceedings, then its decision is equally valid whether it is right or wrong subject only to the power of the court in certain circumstances to correct an error of law. I think that, if these views are correct, the only case cited which was plainly wrongly decided is *Davies v. Price* [1958] 1 W.L.R. 434. But in a number of other cases some of the grounds of judgment are questionable.

I can now turn to the provisions of the Order under which the commission acted, and to the way in which the commission reached their decision. It was said in the Court of Appeal that publication of their reasons was unnecessary and perhaps undesirable. Whether or not they could have been required to publish their reasons, I dissent emphatically from the view that publication may have been undesirable. In my view, the commission acted with complete propriety, as one would expect looking to its membership.

The meaning of the important parts of this Order is extremely difficult to discover, and, in my view, a main cause of this is the deplorable modern drafting practice of compressing to the point of obscurity provisions which would not be difficult to understand if written out at rather greater length.

The effect of the Order was to confer legal rights on persons who might previously have hoped or expected that in allocating any sums available discretion would be exercised in their favour. We are concerned in this case with article 4 of the Order and more particularly with paragraph (1) *(b)* (ii) of that article. Article 4 is as follows:

'(1) The Commission shall treat a claim under this Part of the Order as established if the applicant satisfies them of the following matters:— *(a)* that his application relates to property in Egypt which is referred to in Annex E; *(b)* if the property is referred to in paragraph (1) (a) or paragraph (2) of Annex E—(i) that the applicant is the person referred to in paragraph (1) *(a)* or in paragraph (2), as the case may be, is the owner of the property or is the successor in title of such person; and (ii) that the person referred to as aforesaid and any person who became successor in title of such person on or before February 28, 1959, were British nationals on October 31, 1956, and February 28, 1959; *(c)* if the property is referred to in paragraph (1) *(b)* of Annex E—(i) that the applicant was the owner on October 31, 1956, or, at the option of the applicant, on the date of the sale of the property at any time before February 28, 1959, by the Government of the United Arab Republic under the provisions of Egyptian Proclamation No. 5 of November 1, 1956, or is the successor in title of such owner; and (ii) that the owner on October 31, 1956, or on the date of such sale, as the case may be, and any person who became successor in title of such owner on or before February 28, 1959, were British nationals on October 31, 1956, and February 28, 1959 ...'

The task of the commission was to receive claims and to determine the rights of each applicant. It is enacted that they shall treat a claim as established if the applicant satisfies them of certain matters. About the first there is no difficulty: the appellants' application does relate to property in Egypt referred to in Annex E. But then the difficulty begins.

Annex E originally only included properties which had been sold during the sequestration, so the person mentioned in Annex E as the owner is the person who owned the property before that sale, and his claim is a claim for compensation for having been deprived of that property. Normally he will be the applicant. But there is also provision for an application by a 'successor in title.' The first difficulty is to determine what is meant by 'successor in title.' Before the Order was made the position was that former owners whose property had been sold during the sequestration had no title to anything. They had no title to the property because it had been sold. And they had no title to compensation. All they had was a hope or expectation that they might receive some compensation. They had no legal rights at all. It is now common ground that 'successor in title' cannot mean the person who obtained a title to the property which formerly belonged to the applicant. The person who acquired the property from the sequestrator was generally an Egyptian and he could have no ground for claiming compensation. So 'successor in title' must refer to some person who somehow succeeded to the original owner as the person now having the original owner's hope or expectation of receiving compensation. The obvious case would be where the original owner had died. But for the moment I shall leave that problem.

The main difficulty in this case springs from the fact that the draftsman did not state separately what conditions have to be satisfied (1) where the applicant is the original owner and (2) where the applicant claims as the successor in title of the original owner. It is clear that where the applicant is the original owner he must prove that he was a British national on the dates stated. And it is equally clear that where the applicant claims as being the original owner's successor in title he must prove that both he and the original owner were British nationals on those dates, subject to later provisions in the article about persons who had died or had been born within the relevant period. What is left in obscurity is whether the provisions with regard to successors in title have any application at all in cases where the applicant is himself the original owner. If this provision had been split up as it should have been, and the conditions, to be satisfied where the original owner is the applicant had been set out, there could have been no such obscurity.

This is the crucial question in this case. It appears from the commission's reasons that they construed this provision as requiring them to inquire, when the applicant is himself the original owner, whether he had a successor in title. So they made that inquiry in this case and held that T.E.D.O. was the applicant's successor in title. As T.E.D.O. was not a British national they rejected the appellants' claim. But if, on a true construction of the Order, a claimant who is an original owner does not have to prove anything about successors in title, then the commission made an inquiry which the Order did not empower them to make, and they based their decision on a matter which they had no right to take into account. If one uses the word 'jurisdiction' in its wider sense, they went beyond their jurisdiction in considering this matter. It was argued that the whole matter of construing the Order was something remitted to the commission for their decision. I cannot accept that argument. I find nothing in the Order to support it. The Order requires the commission to consider whether they are satisfied with regard to the prescribed matters. That is all they have to do. It cannot be for the commission to determine the limits of its powers. Of course if one party submits to a tribunal that its powers are wider than in fact they are, then the tribunal must deal with that submission. But if they reach a wrong conclusion as to the width of their powers, the court must be able to correct that—not because the tribunal has made an error of law, but because as a result of making an error of law they have dealt with and based their decision on a matter with which, on a true construction of their powers, they had no right to deal. If they base their decision on some matter which is not prescribed for their adjudication, they are doing something which they have no right to do and, if the view which I expressed earlier is right, their decision is a nullity. So the question is whether on a true construction of the Order the applicants did or did not have to prove anything with regard to successors in title. If the commission were entitled to enter on the inquiry whether the applicants had a successor in title, then their decision as to whether T.E.D.O. was their successor in title would I think be unassailable whether it was right or wrong: it would be a decision on a matter remitted to them for their decision. The question I have to consider is not whether they made a wrong decision but whether they inquired into and decided a matter which they had no right to consider.

... In themselves the words 'successor in title' are, in my opinion, inappropriate in the circumstances of this Order to denote any person while the original owner is still in existence, and I think it most improbable that they were ever intended to denote any such person. There is no necessity to stretch them to cover any such person. I would therefore hold that the words 'and any person who became successor in title to such person' in article 4 (1) *(b)* (ii) have no application to a case where the applicant is the original owner. It follows that the commission rejected the appellants' claim on a ground which they had no right to take into account and that their decision was a nullity. I would allow this appeal.

Lord Pearce

... Lack of jurisdiction may arise in various ways. There may be an absence of those formalities or things which are conditions precedent to the tribunal having any jurisdiction to embark on an inquiry. Or the tribunal may at the end make an order that it has no jurisdiction to make. Or in the intervening stage, while engaged on a proper inquiry, the tribunal may depart from the rules of natural justice; or it may ask itself the wrong questions; or it may take into account matters which it was not directed to take into account. Thereby it would step outside its jurisdiction. It would turn its inquiry into something not directed by Parliament and fail to make the inquiry which Parliament did direct. Any of these things would cause its purported decision to be a nullity ...

Lord Wilberforce

... I must first say something as to the legal framework of this appeal: for though, in my opinion, the solution of this case is to be looked for in the thickets of subsidiary legislation, it is useful to be clear as to the general character of the argument. I do not think that it is difficult to describe this and I shall endeavour to do so, initially at least, in non-technical terms, avoiding for the moment such words as 'jurisdiction,' 'error' and 'nullity' which create many problems.

The Foreign Compensation Commission is one of many tribunals set up to deal with matters of a specialised character, in the interest of economy, speed, and expertise. It has acquired a unique status, since it alone has been excepted from the provisions of section 11 of the Tribunals and Inquiries Act, 1958. It is now well established that specialised tribunals may, depending on their nature and on the subject-matter, have the power to decide questions of law, and the position may be reached, as the result of statutory provision, that even if they make what the courts might regard as decisions wrong in law, these are to stand. The Foreign Compensation Commission is certainly within this category; its functions are predominantly judicial; it is a permanent body, composed of lawyers, with a learned chairman, and there is every ground, having regard to the number and the complexity of the cases with which it must deal, for giving a wide measure of finality to its decisions …

In every case, whatever the character of a tribunal, however wide the range of questions remitted to it, however great the permissible margin of mistake, the essential point remains that the tribunal has a derived authority, derived, that is, from statute: at some point, and to be found from a consideration of the legislation, the field within which it operates is marked out and limited. There is always an area, narrow or wide, which is the tribunal's area; a residual area, wide or narrow, in which the legislature has previously expressed its will and into which the tribunal may not enter. Equally, though this is not something that arises in the present case, there are certain fundamental assumptions, which without explicit restatement in every case, necessarily underlie the remission of power to decide such as (I do not attempt more than a general reference, since the strength and shade of these matters will depend upon the nature of the tribunal and the kind of question it has to decide) the requirement that a decision must be made in accordance with principles of natural justice and good faith. The principle that failure to fulfil these assumptions may be equivalent to a departure from the remitted area must be taken to follow from the decision of this House in *Ridge v. Baldwin* [1964] A.C. 40. Although, in theory perhaps, it may be possible for Parliament to set up a tribunal which has full and autonomous powers to fix its own area of operation, that has, so far, not been done in this country. The question, what is the tribunal's proper area, is one which it has always been permissible to ask and to answer, and it must follow that examination of its extent is not precluded by a clause conferring conclusiveness, finality, or unquestionability upon its decisions …

The separate but complementary responsibilities of court and tribunal were very clearly stated by Lord Esher M.R. in *Reg. v. Commissioners for Special Purposes of the Income Tax* (1888) 21 Q.B.D. 313, 319, in these words:
'When an inferior court or tribunal or body, which has to exercise the power of deciding facts, is first established by Act of Parliament, the legislature has to consider what powers it will give that tribunal or body. It may in effect say that, if a certain state of facts exists and is shown to such tribunal or body before it proceeds to do certain things, it shall have jurisdiction to do such things, but not otherwise. There it is not for them conclusively to decide whether that state of facts exists, and, if they exercise the jurisdiction without its existence, what they do may be questioned, and it will be held that they have acted without jurisdiction.'

That the ascertainment of the proper limits of the tribunal's power of decision is a task for the court was stated by Farwell LJ in *Rex. v. Shoreditch Assessment Committee, Ex parte Morgan* [1910] 2 K.B. 859, 880 in language which, though perhaps vulnerable to logical analysis, has proved its value as guidance to the courts:

> 'Subjection in this respect to the High Court is a necessary and inseparable incident for all tribunals of limited jurisdiction; for the existence of the limit necessitates an authority to determine and enforce it: it is a contradiction in terms to create a tribunal with limited jurisdiction and unlimited power to determine such limit at its own will and pleasure—such a tribunal would be autocratic, not limited—and it is immaterial whether the decision of the inferior tribunal on the question of the existence or non-existence of its own jurisdictions is founded on law or fact.'

[Although Lord Wilberforce did not set it out in his speech, it is worth noting that this passage is immediately preceded by the following: 'No tribunal of inferior jurisdiction can by its own decision finally decide on the question of the existence or extent of such jurisdiction: such question is always subject to review by the High Court, which does not permit the inferior tribunal either to usurp a jurisdiction which it does not possess, whether at all or to the extent claimed, or to refuse to exercise a jurisdiction which it has and ought to exercise.']

[Lord Wilberforce went on to cite the words of Denning LJ set out at the beginning of 2.2.2, and continued:] These passages at least answer one of the respondents' main arguments, to some extent accepted by the members of the Court of Appeal, which is that *because* the commission has (admittedly) been given power, indeed required, to decide some questions of law, arising out of the construction of the relevant Order in Council, it must necessarily have power to decide those questions which relate to the delimitation of its powers; or conversely that if the court has power to review the latter, it must also have power to review the former. But the one does not follow from the other: there is no reason why the Order in Council should not (as a matter of construction to be decided by the court) limit the tribunal's powers and at the same time (by the same process of construction) confer upon the tribunal power, in the exercise of its permitted task, to decide other questions of law, including questions of construction of the Order. I shall endeavour to show that this is what the Order has done.

The extent of the interpretatory power conferred upon the tribunal may sometimes be difficult to ascertain and argument may be possible whether this or that question of construction has been left to the tribunal, that is, is within the tribunal's field, or whether, because it pertains to the delimitation of the tribunal's area by the legislature, it is reserved for decision by the courts. Sometimes it will be possible to form a conclusion from the form and subject-matter of the legislation. In one case it may be seen that the legislature, while stating general objectives, is prepared to concede a wide area to the authority it establishes: this will often be the case where the decision involves a degree of policy-making rather than fact-finding, especially if the authority is a department of government or the Minister at its head. I think that we have reached a stage in our administrative law when we can view this question quite objectively, without any necessary predisposition towards one that questions of law, or questions of construction, are necessarily for the courts. In the kind of case I have mentioned there is no need to make this assumption. In another type of case it may be apparent that Parliament is itself directly and closely concerned with the definition and delimitation of certain matters of comparative detail and has marked by its language the intention that these shall accurately be observed ... The present case ..., as examination of the relevant Order in Council will show, is clearly of the latter category.

> I do not think it desirable to discuss further in detail the many decisions in the reports in this field. But two points may perhaps be made. First, the cases in which a tribunal has been held to have passed outside its proper limits are not limited to those in which it had no power to enter upon its inquiry or its jurisdiction, or has not satisfied a condition precedent. Certainly such cases exist (for example *Ex parte Bradlaugh* (1878) 3 Q.B.D. 509) but they do not exhaust the principle. A tribunal may quite properly validly enter upon its task and in the course of carrying it out may make a decision which is invalid—not merely erroneous. This may be described as 'asking the wrong question' or 'applying the wrong test'— expressions not wholly satisfactory since they do not, in themselves, distinguish between doing something which is not in the tribunal's area and doing something wrong within that area—a crucial distinction which the court has to make. Cases held to be of the former kind (whether, on their facts, correctly or not does not affect the principle) are *Estate and Trust Agencies (1927) Ltd v. Singapore Improvement Trust* [1937] A.C. 898, 915–917; *Seereelall Jhuggroo v. Central Arbitration and Control Board* [1953] A.C. 151, 161 ... *Reg. v. Fulham, Hammersmith and Kensington Rent Tribunal, Ex parte Hierowski* [1953] 2 Q.B. 147. The present case, in my opinion, and it is at this point that I respectfully differ from the Court of Appeal, is of this kind.

Lord Wilberforce went on to agree with Lord Reid's analysis of the statutory provisions and was in favour of allowing the appeal. Lords Morris and Pearson delivered speeches in favour of dismissing the appeal. Appeal allowed.

Three issues should be noted about this landmark case. First, a *broad concept of jurisdiction* was recognized, such that a decision-maker may commit a jurisdictional error either by embarking upon an unauthorized inquiry or, once having begun its decision-making process, by exercising its powers in an unauthorized manner, for example by breaching the rules of natural justice. This is particularly clear from the extract from Lord Pearce's speech.

Second, the concept of jurisdiction which was embraced in *Anisminic* was central to *the impact of the 'ouster clause'*. The clause in the Foreign Compensation Act which prevented 'any court of law' from calling into question the Commission's 'determination' appeared to preclude judicial review. However, the House of Lords concluded that a determination made outwith jurisdiction was not a 'determination' in the statutory sense: it was merely an invalid attempt to reach a determination. When this interpretation of the ouster clause was linked to their Lordships' view of jurisdiction, it became clear that the impact of the ouster clause would be minimal. (In fact it only precluded review on the peculiar ground of non-jurisdictional error of law on the face of the record, all other grounds being jurisdictional and therefore unaffected by the ouster.)

The third major point which emerges from *Anisminic* concerns the concept of *jurisdictional error of law*. As the earlier extract shows, the claimant's complaint was that the Commission had made such an error by misconstruing the Foreign Compensation (Egypt) (Determination and Registration of Claims) Order 1962, leading it to conclude erroneously that the claimant was ineligible for compensation. The majority adopted a robust approach to errors of law, holding that the provision which the Commission had misinterpreted was a factor upon which its jurisdiction depended. This meant that the Commission's interpretation of the term was not conclusive: because, according to the House of Lords, Parliament had intended the term in question to delimit the Commission's power, it would be nonsensical to suggest that the Commission could itself authoritatively determine its meaning. *Anisminic* did not, however, render *all* errors of law jurisdictional. For instance, Lord Wilberforce concluded that a decision-maker might be permitted to decide some questions of law conclusively for itself, while other statutory provisions may constitute jurisdictional limits the interpretation of which is for the decision-maker in the first instance but ultimately for the reviewing court. His Lordship acknowledged that it may be difficult to distinguish between these categories, but suggested that adequate guidance would often be found if not in the specific words of the legislation, then in its 'form and subject-matter'. Moreover, Lord Wilberforce considered it desirable that some questions of law should be left to the decision-making body, bearing in mind that it may possess legal expertise.

QUESTIONS

- Do you agree with Lord Wilberforce? Should some questions of law be capable of being conclusively determined by the decision-maker?
- If so, can you suggest any more specific criteria which should inform the distinction between matters of law lying within the jurisdiction of the decision-maker, and those upon which its jurisdiction depends (and which are therefore ultimately open to interpretation by the reviewing court)?

2.2.4 The general principle: errors of law as jurisdictional errors

In the years following *Anisminic*, the courts struggled to understand precisely what its implications were. In particular, there was disagreement about whether the concept of non-jurisdictional error of law survived, a proposition which is usefully illustrated by *Pearlman* v. *Keepers and Governors of Harrow School* [1979] QB 56. A County Court judge decided that a tenant who installed central heating in a house which he held on a long lease had not carried out a 'structural alteration' and was not therefore eligible for certain benefits under the Leasehold Reform Act 1967. The tenant argued that the judge had misinterpreted the term 'structural alteration' and that this mistake of law constituted a jurisdictional error. Geoffrey Lane LJ, dissenting, strongly disagreed with this contention. In a passage which was later endorsed by the Privy Council in *South East Asia Fire Bricks Sdn Bhd* v. *Non-Metallic Mineral Products Manufacturing Employees Union* [1981] AC 363, he said (at 76):

> I am, I fear, unable to see how that determination, assuming it to be an erroneous determination, can properly be said to be a determination which he was not entitled to make. The judge is considering the words in the [legislation] which he ought to consider. He is not embarking on some unauthorised or extraneous or irrelevant exercise. All he has done is to come to what appears to this court to be a wrong conclusion upon a difficult question. It seems to me that, if this judge is acting outside his jurisdiction, so then is every judge who comes to a wrong decision on a point of law. Accordingly, I take the view that no form of [quashing order] is available to the tenant.

The two majority judges held that a jurisdictional error had been committed, but they each reached this conclusion by distinct processes of reasoning. Eveleigh LJ agreed with Geoffrey Lane LJ that a distinction remained between jurisdictional and non-jurisdictional errors of law, but—demonstrating the instability of that distinction—concluded, unlike Geoffrey Lane LJ, that the error in this case fell into the former category. Meanwhile, Lord Denning MR, at 69–70, concluded, more radically, that the error of law in question was jurisdictional in nature because there was no longer any such thing as a non-jurisdictional error of law:

> [T]he distinction between an error which entails absence of jurisdiction—and an error made within the jurisdiction—is very fine. So fine indeed that it is rapidly being eroded. Take this very case. When the judge held that the installation of a full central heating system was not a 'structural alteration ... or addition' we all think—all three of us—that he went wrong in point of law. He misconstrued those words. That error can be described on the one hand as an error which went to his jurisdiction. In this way: if he had held that it was a 'structural alteration ... or addition' he would have had jurisdiction to go on and determine the various matters set out in [the legislation]. By holding that it was not a 'structural alteration ... or addition' he deprived himself of jurisdiction to determine those matters. On the other hand, his error can equally well be described as an error made by him within his jurisdiction. It can plausibly be said that he had jurisdiction to inquire into the meaning of the words 'structural alteration ... or addition'; and that his wrong interpretation of them was only an error within his jurisdiction, and not an error taking him outside it.
> That illustration could be repeated in nearly all these cases. So fine is the distinction that in truth the High Court has a choice before it whether to interfere with an inferior court on a point of law. If it chooses to interfere, it can formulate its decision in the words: 'The court below had

no jurisdiction to decide this point wrongly as it did.' If it does not choose to interfere, it can say: 'The court had jurisdiction to decide it wrongly, and did so.' Softly be it stated, but that is the reason for the difference between the decision of the Court of Appeal in *Anisminic Ltd.* v. *Foreign Compensation Commission* [1968] 2 Q.B. 862 and the House of Lords [1969] 2 A.C. 147.

I would suggest that this distinction should now be discarded. The High Court has, and should have, jurisdiction to control the proceedings of inferior courts and tribunals by way of judicial review. When they go wrong in law, the High Court should have power to put them right. Not only in the instant case to do justice to the complainant. But also so as to secure that all courts and tribunals, when faced with the same point of law, should decide it in the same way. It is intolerable that a citizen's rights in point of law should depend on which judge tries his case, or in which court it is heard. The way to get things right is to hold thus: no court or tribunal has any jurisdiction to make an error of law on which the decision of the case depends. If it makes such an error, it goes outside its jurisdiction and [a quashing order] will lie to correct it. In this case the finding—that the installation of a central heating system was not a 'structural alteration'—was an error on which the jurisdiction of the county court depended: and, because of that error, the judge was quite wrong to dismiss the application outright. He ought to have found that the installation was an 'improvement' …, and gone on to determine the other matters referred to in [the legislation].

Lord Denning's dissatisfaction with the distinction between jurisdictional and non-jurisdictional errors of law rested upon two distinct foundations. First, he considered that the distinction could not be drawn in any principled fashion, and that in reality the courts manipulated it for instrumental purposes. Second, he felt that consistency required that the same meaning be attributed to legal provisions by all decision-makers and that, to this end, the High Court should be able to furnish *conclusive* interpretations of legislation.

QUESTIONS

- Which of the three judges in *Pearlman* do you agree with?
- Do you find Lord Denning's arguments in favour of treating all errors of law as jurisdictional convincing?

Some clarity was brought to this situation by the remarks of Lord Diplock in *Re Racal Communications Ltd* [1981] AC 374 and *O'Reilly* v. *Mackman* [1983] 2 AC 237 (see at 2.2.7); in the latter, he suggested that, as a general principle, all errors of law should be regarded as jurisdictional. These matters were considered further by Lord Browne-Wilkinson in *R* v. *Lord President of the Privy Council, ex parte Page* [1993] AC 682 at 701–2:

In my judgment the decision in *Anisminic Ltd.* v. *Foreign Compensation Commission* [1969] 2 A.C. 147 rendered obsolete the distinction between errors of law on the face of the record and other errors of law by extending the doctrine of ultra vires. Thenceforward it was to be taken that Parliament had only conferred the decision-making power on the basis that it was to be exercised on the correct legal basis: a misdirection in law in making the decision therefore rendered the decision ultra vires … [I]n my judgment the decision of this House in *O'Reilly* v. *Mackman* [1983] 2 A.C. 237 establishes the law in the sense that I have stated. Lord Diplock, with whose speech all the other members of the committee agreed, said, at p. 278, that the decision in *Anisminic*:

'has liberated English public law from the fetters that the courts had theretofore imposed upon themselves so far as determinations of inferior courts and statutory tribunals were concerned, by drawing esoteric distinctions between errors of law committed by such tribunals that went to their jurisdiction, and errors of law committed by them within their jurisdiction. The break-through that the *Anisminic* case made was the recognition by the majority of this House that if a tribunal whose jurisdiction was limited by statute or subordinate legislation mistook the law applicable to the facts as it had found them, it must have asked itself the wrong question, ie, one into which it was not empowered to inquire and so had no jurisdiction to determine. Its purported 'determination,' not being 'a determination' within the meaning of the empowering legislation, was accordingly a nullity.'

Therefore, I agree with [counsel for the claimant] that in general any error of law made by an administrative tribunal or inferior court in reaching its decision can be quashed for error of law.

At this point I must notice an argument raised by Mr. Beloff for the university. He suggests that the recent decision of this House in *Reg.* v. *Independent Television Commission, ex parte T.S.W. Broadcasting Ltd.* [reported at [1996] EMLR 291], has thrown doubt on the proposition that all errors of law vitiate the decision. In my judgment this is a misreading of that authority. This House was asserting that the mere existence of a mistake of law made at some earlier stage does not vitiate the actual decision made: what must be shown is a relevant error of law, *ie*, an error in the actual making of the decision which affected the decision itself. This is demonstrated by Lord Templeman's quotation from the well known judgment of Lord Greene M.R. in *Associated Provincial Picture Houses Ltd.* v. *Wednesbury Corporation* [1948] 1 K.B. 223 (including the passage, at p. 229, 'a person entrusted with a discretion must, so to speak, direct himself properly in law') and the manner in which thereafter he applied those principles to the facts of the case before the House.

This case is highly significant because it recognizes as a general principle that errors of law are jurisdictional. It is not, however, a panacea. What counts as an error of law is not always clear; we will see later that the fact/law distinction is malleable, and may be used by courts to manipulate the extent of judicial supervision. Moreover, the basic proposition that only courts should be able conclusively to determine questions of law is not itself uncontroversial. For instance, Daly (2011) 74 *MLR* 694, 696–7 argues that

the default English rule, in favour of a standard of correctness [review in respect of questions of law], should be changed. Instead, where legislative intent and practical considerations so suggest, English courts should defer to administrative interpretations of law by applying a less exacting standard of review.

He goes on (at 697) to contend that, for two reasons, courts should be open to the possibility of departing from a correctness standard:

First, they may be required to do so. The legislature may intend that a body other than a court should render an interpretation of law, either generally or (more likely) in respect of a particular area of regulation. If a court is obliged to give effect to legislative intent (as manifested in a statute as interpreted by the usual means of construction), then it may have to defer to a delegated decision-maker's interpretation of law. Secondly, the delegated decision-maker may have greater institutional competence than a reviewing court. Taken together, the expertise of the delegated decision-maker, the complexity of a particular question, the accountability or democratic legitimacy of the delegated decision-maker, and the level of participation permitted in the decision-making process may place a reviewing court in a vastly inferior position to a delegated decision-maker. Indeed, this set of what might be called 'practical justifications' for curial deference may also be reasons why the legislature intended to delegate decision-making power in the first place. So, not only might a reviewing court find itself at a disadvantage in practical terms, but its obligation to give effect to legislative intent may reinforce its lack of institutional competence.

Daly thus argues (at 699) that rigid adherence to a correctness standard may frustrate legislative intent, and casts doubts on the sort of arguments advanced by Lord Denning MR in *Pearlman* in favour of such a standard, noting (at 706) that the decision-maker may have 'greater familiarity with the purposes of the statute and its underlying policies and principles than a reviewing court', such that '[t]he best answer to a question of law might come from a delegated decision-maker', and (at 709) that the ascription of differential meanings to legal provisions is not *per se* incompatible with the rule of law, provided that the law is 'sufficiently clear to be followed'. On this view, it would not offend the rule of law if, for example, different local authorities interpreted a given statutory provision differently, provided that the position in respect of each local authority was sufficiently clear.

QUESTION

- Should the default position be that questions of law fall to be answered by reviewing courts applying a reviewing standard?

2.2.5 Are *all* questions about the meaning of legal rules jurisdictional questions?

Characterizing errors of law as jurisdictional implies a hard-edged review whereby the court will substitute its view for that of the decision-maker. For example, in *Pascoe* v. *First Secretary of State* [2006] EWHC 2356 (Admin), [2007] 1 WLR 885, the evidence indicated that the decision-maker, which was empowered compulsorily to acquire land if it was, *inter alia*, 'under-used or ineffectively used', had proceeded on the basis that this meant *predominantly* under-used or ineffectively used. This, the Court said, constituted an impermissible watering-down of the statutory requirement: the decision-maker was not at liberty to adopt its own interpretation of the statute at odds with the court's, and had therefore committed an error of law which deprived it of jurisdiction.

That English courts can and do treat issues of law as jurisdictional questions to which there exists only one correct answer is therefore clear. This reflects a commitment to (a particular view of) the separation of powers doctrine, whereby questions of law are deemed ultimately to be questions for courts. However, that constitutional principle—to whose flexibility the British constitution is in any event testament—necessarily sits in relationship with other such principles and policy concerns. This, in turn, points away from an absolutist notion of the separation of powers that would exclude any scope for ascribing interpretive latitude to decision-makers, and creates a space in which considerations of policy can enter into play—about such matters as the relative importance of the generalist legal expertise of reviewing courts and the subject-specific expertise of a decision-maker who may have a particular degree of familiarity with the contested statutory provision. Indeed, much in this area ultimately turns upon perceptions of the relative institutional competence of reviewing courts and decision-makers when it comes to the interpretation of relevant statutory provisions. Whether a question is characterized as a jurisdictional question of law may therefore reflect judicial conclusions—that may or may not be explicitly articulated—about where the balance of such policy considerations falls in the given case, albeit that such considerations might well, in the first place, be examined through a lens of constitutional principle that produces the default assumption that questions of law are for courts.

Indeed, it is clear that the courts acknowledge that the *Page* principle articulated in that case is not and should not be an uncompromising one, such that in some situations questions about the meaning of legal terms will *not* be regarded as jurisdictional questions. There are two ways in which this position can be achieved, both of which have been leveraged by the courts. First, in 2.2.6–2.2.8, we examine a number of situations to which the general principle announced in *Page* does not appear to extend, such that questions of law fall to be characterized as non-jurisdictional questions, with the result that the reviewing court applies a standard other than correctness. Second, in 2.2.9, we consider the possibility of characterizing certain questions of statutory interpretation as questions of fact rather than questions of law, such that there is no possibility, in the first place, of the *Page* principle—which is concerned with the jurisdictional nature of questions of *law*—applying.

2.2.6 The *Page* case and the extent of the general principle

We have already seen that the general principle that questions of law are jurisdictional questions was established in *Page*. Paradoxically, however, the House of Lords declined to apply that general principle in *Page* itself.

R v. Lord President of the Privy Council, ex parte Page [1993] AC 682
House of Lords

The claimant was appointed to a lectureship at the University of Hull in 1966. His contract of employment provided that either party could terminate the appointment by giving three months' notice and was subject to the university statutes, which provided that lecturers had to retire at the age of 67. In addition, s 34(1) of the statutes stated that members of staff who, like the claimant, had been appointed to the retiring age could be removed 'for good cause', and s 34(3) provided that, subject to their terms of appointment, such individuals could not be removed save for good cause. The university purported to terminate the claimant's contract in 1988 on grounds not of good cause, but of redundancy. The claimant sought a declaration from the university visitor, whose role is explained below by Lord Browne-Wilkinson, that the dismissal was contrary to s 34 and therefore beyond the university's powers. The defendant, acting on behalf of the visitor, refused to grant such a declaration. The claimant sought judicial review, and the Divisional Court granted a declaration; however, the Court of Appeal decided that, while the visitor's decision was subject to judicial review, the university had not exceeded its powers in dismissing the claimant. The claimant appealed against the Court of Appeal's interpretation of the statutes; the university and the visitor cross-appealed against the Court of Appeal's decision that the visitor's decisions were subject to judicial review.

Lord Browne-Wilkinson

… It is established that, a university being an eleemosynary charitable foundation [that is, one 'founded for the purpose of distributing the founder's bounty': *Thomas* v. *University of Bradford* [1987] AC 795 at 827, *per* Lord Ackner], the visitor of the university has exclusive jurisdiction to decide disputes arising under the domestic law of the university. This is because the founder of such a body is entitled to reserve to himself or to a visitor whom he appoints the exclusive right to adjudicate upon the domestic laws which the founder has established for the regulation of his bounty. Even where the contractual rights of an individual (such as his contract of employment with the university) are in issue, if those contractual rights are themselves dependent upon rights arising under the regulating documents of the charity, the visitor has an exclusive jurisdiction over disputes relating to such employment …

Under the modern law, [a quashing order] normally lies to quash a decision for error of law. Therefore, the narrow issue in this case is whether, as Mr Page contends and the courts below have held, [a quashing order] lies against the visitor to quash his decision as being erroneous in point of law notwithstanding that the question of law arises under the domestic law of the university which the visitor has 'exclusive' jurisdiction to decide …

[Lord Browne-Wilkinson reviewed the authorities and continued:] In my judgment this review of the authorities demonstrates that for over 300 years the law has been clearly established that the visitor of an eleemosynary charity has an exclusive jurisdiction to determine what are the internal laws of the charity and the proper application of those laws to those within his jurisdiction. The court's inability to determine those matters is not limited to the period pending the visitor's determination but extends so as to prohibit any subsequent review by the court of the correctness of a decision made by the visitor acting within his jurisdiction and in accordance with the rules of natural justice. This inability of the court to intervene is founded on the fact that the applicable law is not the common law of England but a peculiar or domestic law of which the visitor is the sole judge. This special status of a visitor springs from the common law recognising the right of the founder to lay down such a special law subject to adjudication only by a special judge, the visitor …

[His Lordship considered general developments in the law of judicial review, in the terms set out at 2.2.4, and continued:] Although the general rule is that decisions affected by errors of law made by tribunals or inferior courts can be quashed, in my judgment there are two reasons why that rule does not apply in the case of visitors. First, as I have sought to explain, the constitutional basis of the courts' power to quash is that the decision of the inferior tribunal is unlawful on the grounds that it is ultra vires. In the ordinary case, the law applicable to a decision made by such a body is the general law of the land. Therefore, a tribunal or inferior court acts ultra vires if it reaches its conclusion on a basis erroneous under the general law. But the position of decisions made by a visitor is different. As the authorities which I have cited demonstrate, the visitor is applying not the general law of the land but a peculiar, domestic law of which he is the sole arbiter and of which the courts have no cognisance. If the visitor has power under the regulating documents to enter into the adjudication of the dispute (*ie*, is acting within his jurisdiction in the narrow sense) he cannot err in law in reaching this decision since the general law is not the applicable law. Therefore he cannot be acting ultra vires and unlawfully by applying his view of the domestic law in reaching his decision. The court has no jurisdiction either to say that he erred in his application of the general law (since the general law is not applicable to the decision) or to reach a contrary view as to the effect of the domestic law (since the visitor is the sole judge of such domestic law).

… Mr Burke [for the claimant] urged that the position of a visitor would be anomalous if he were immune from review on the ground of error of law. He submitted that the concept of a peculiar domestic law differing from the general law of the land was artificial since in practice the charter and statutes of a university are expressed in ordinary legal language and applied in accordance with the same principles as those applicable under the general law. He pointed to the important public role occupied by universities and submitted that it was wrong that they should be immune from the general law of the land: 'There must be no Alsatia in England where the King's writ does not run': *per* Scrutton L.J. in *Czarnikow v. Roth, Schmidt & Co.* [1922] 2 K.B. 478, 488. He further suggested that to permit review of a visitor's decision for error of law would not impair the effectiveness of the visitor's domestic jurisdiction.

I accept that the position of the visitor is anomalous, indeed unique. I further accept that where the visitor is, or is advised by, a lawyer the distinction between the peculiar domestic law he applies and the general law is artificial. But I do not regard these factors as justifying sweeping away the law which for so long has regulated the conduct of charitable corporations. There are internal disputes which are resolved by a visitor who is not a lawyer himself and has not taken legal advice. It is not only modern universities which have visitors: there are a substantial number of other long-established educational, ecclesiastical and eleemosynary bodies which have visitors. The advantages of having an informal system which produces a speedy, cheap and final answer to internal disputes has been repeatedly emphasized in the authorities, most recently by this House in *Thomas v. University of Bradford* [1987] A.C. 795: see *per* Lord Griffiths, at p. 825D; see also *Patel v. University of Bradford Senate* [1978] 1 W.L.R. 1488, 1499–1500. If it were to be held that judicial review for error of law lay against the visitor I fear that, as in the present case, finality would be lost not only in cases raising pure questions of law but also in cases where it would be urged in accordance with the *Wednesbury* principle (*Associated Provincial Picture Houses Ltd. v. Wednesbury Corporation* [1948] 1 K.B. 223) that the visitor had failed to take into account relevant matters or taken into account irrelevant matters or had reached an irrational conclusion. Although the visitor's position is anomalous, it provides a valuable machinery for resolving internal disputes which should not be lost.

I have therefore reached the conclusion that judicial review does not lie to impeach the decisions of a visitor taken within his jurisdiction (in the narrow sense) on questions of either fact or law. Judicial review does lie to the visitor in cases where he has acted outside his jurisdiction (in the narrow sense) or abused his powers or acted in breach of the rules of natural justice. Accordingly, in my judgment the Divisional Court had no jurisdiction to entertain the application for judicial review of the visitor's decision in this case.

Lord Slynn

… With deference to the contrary view of the majority of your Lordships, in my opinion if [a quashing order] can go to a particular tribunal it is available on all the grounds which have been judicially recognised. I can see no reasons in principle for limiting the availability of [quashing orders] to a patent excess of power (as where a visitor has decided something which was not within his remit) and excluding review on other grounds recognised by the law. If it is accepted, as I believe it should be accepted, that [a quashing order] goes not only for such an excess or abuse of power but also for a breach of the rules of natural justice there is even less reason in principle for excluding other established grounds. If therefore [a quashing order] is generally available for error of law not involving abuse of power (as … I consider that it is) then it should be available also in respect of a decision of a visitor.

Lords Keith and Griffiths agreed with Lord Browne-Wilkinson. Lord Mustill agreed with Lord Slynn, who concluded that although review could lie for error of law, no such error had occurred. Appeal dismissed.

Extracting general principles from Lord Browne-Wilkinson's speech in *Page* is not straightforward, since the precise basis on which he arrives at his conclusion is somewhat opaque. Two of the reasons he offers—the common law's respect for the founder's intention that the visitor should have exclusive authority to resolve disputes relating to the University's internal rules, and the consequent inapplicability of the *ultra vires* principle—are very particular to the case. They therefore do not suggest a broad exception to the general principle established in *Page*. Yet, as well as the fact that the visitor was applying a body of 'domestic' law, Lord Browne-Wilkinson was influenced by practical considerations, such as speed and cost—considerations that may apply much more generally, and which suggest that the principle that errors of law are jurisdictional may (at least exceptionally) yield in the face of practical considerations.

Two other sets of factors are arguably relevant to *Page*, although it is far from clear that they influenced Lord Browne-Wilkinson's thinking. First, the *constitutional* case for a high degree of judicial control in respect of questions of law was arguably weaker in *Page* than in the typical situation that involves an executive body exercising powers defined by statute. In the latter circumstances, the constitutional case in favour of judicial interventionism is arguably bolstered on rule-of-law and separation-of-powers grounds, there being a clear constitutional interest in seeing that administrative bodies remain within boundaries upon their powers set down in statute by the legislature. As we will see later, circumstances can and do arise that are less unusual than those that confronted the House of Lords in *Page*, but in which, as in *Page*, the constitutional case for close judicial control may be weaker.

Second, *Page* at least raises (without fully resolving) questions about the relevance of *institutional* considerations, given that the institutionally unusual position of the visitor was plainly a factor that bore upon Lord Browne-Wilkinson's reasoning. There are two aspects to this. It may be thought that the case for close judicial supervision is less compelling when a decision-maker enjoys a particular type of *institutional status*. This matter is thrown into sharp relief when the decision-maker is a court or a court-like body—a matter that we consider at 2.2.7. A distinct point is that a decision-maker may—either because or irrespective of its institutional status—in substance possess *institutional characteristics*, such as expertise, that warrant immunity from close judicial scrutiny on questions of law. The idea that a decision-maker's expertise may call for particular deference in relation to the exercise of its discretion in respect of merits questions is a well-established proposition (on which see further at 8.4). However, just because a decision-maker possesses expertise of that nature—*ie* expertise that is relevant to the sort of judgments that have to be made when *merits questions* are confronted—does not mean that the reviewing court will consider deference appropriate in respect of *questions of law*. For instance, in *Société Coopérative de Production SeaFrance SA v. Competition and Markets Authority* [2015] UKSC 75, [2015] Bus LR 1573, the exercise by the Competition and Markets Authority of certain of its powers was conditional upon there being a 'relevant merger situation'. Lord Sumption (with whom the other Justices agreed) said (at [31]):

[The legislation] requires the Authority to decide in the first instance whether such a situation has been created … But the test for determining what are the relevant 'activities' whose absorption by another enterprise founds the jurisdiction of the Authority is a question of law. It depends on the construction of the [legislation]. Of course, the process of construction must necessarily be informed by the purpose of these provisions, and to that extent the economic implications of different interpretations may be relevant. Moreover, once the test has been identified its application to particular facts may call for expert economic judgments by the tribunal of fact, in this case the Authority. But otherwise the Authority's expertise and the specialised nature of its functions do not clothe it with any wider power to determine its statutory jurisdiction than is enjoyed by other administrative decision-makers, and its conclusions on the point are entitled to no greater deference on a review or appeal.

2.2.7 The institutional status of the decision-maker

Lord Diplock's speech in *Re Racal Communications Ltd* [1981] AC 374 provides some support for the view that the institutional status of the decision-maker be relevant to determining whether it is to be accorded any discretion over questions of law. In fact, the point for which the case authoritatively stands is that there can be no question of the High Court (or a judge of the High Court acting in his judicial capacity) committing a jurisdictional error, so that there can be no question of judicial review of the High Court or High Court judges acting judicially. However, in arriving at that conclusion, Lord Diplock also considered (at 382–3) the question of jurisdictional error of law as it relates to institutions other than the High Court:

> [*Anisminic*] proceeds on the presumption that where Parliament confers on an administrative tribunal or authority, as distinct from a court of law, power to decide particular questions defined by the Act conferring the power, Parliament intends to confine that power to answering the question as it has been so defined: and if there has been any doubt as to what that question is, this is a matter for courts of law to resolve in fulfilment of their constitutional role as interpreters of the written law and expounders of the common law and rules of equity. So if the administrative tribunal or authority have asked themselves the wrong question and answered that, they have done something that the Act does not empower them to do and their decision is a nullity. Parliament can, of course, if it so desires, confer upon administrative tribunals or authorities power to decide questions of law as well as questions of fact or of administrative policy, but this requires clear words, for the presumption is that where a decision-making power is conferred on a tribunal or authority that is not a court of law, Parliament did not intend to do so. The break-through made by *Anisminic* [1969] 2 A.C. 147 was that, as respects administrative tribunals and authorities, the old distinction between errors of law that went to jurisdiction and errors of law that did not, was for practical purposes abolished. Any error of law that could be shown to have been made by them in the course of reaching their decision on matters of fact or of administrative policy would result in their having asked themselves the wrong question with the result that the decision they reached would be a nullity.

Lord Diplock drew a distinction between the position, set out in the excerpt above, in relation to administrative bodies (in which category he included tribunals: we consider later whether that characterization is appropriate today) and the position where legislation confers a decision-making function on a 'court of law'. In the latter situation, there is, he said (at 383), no presumption to the effect that

> Parliament did not intend to confer upon it power to decide questions of law as well as questions of fact. Whether it did or not and, in the case of inferior courts, what limits are imposed on the kinds of questions of law they are empowered to decide, depends upon the construction of the statute unencumbered by any such presumption. In the case of inferior courts where the decision of the court is made final and conclusive by the statute, this may involve the survival of those subtle distinctions formerly drawn between errors of law which go to jurisdiction and errors of law which do not that did so much to confuse English administrative law before *Anisminic* [1969] 2 A.C. 147; but upon any application for judicial review of a decision of an inferior court in a matter which involves, as so many do, interrelated questions of law, fact and degree the superior court conducting the review should not be astute to hold that Parliament did not intend the inferior court to have jurisdiction to decide for itself the meaning of ordinary words used in the statute to define the question which it has to decide.

Lord Diplock appeared to resile from the above position in the later case of *O'Reilly v. Mackman* [1983] 2 AC 237 at 278 (quoted by Lord Browne-Wilkinson in *Page*: see the extract at 2.2.4), in which he appeared to suggest that the distinction between jurisdictional and non-jurisdictional errors of law had become redundant generally, including in respect of inferior courts of law. It would, however, be wrong to attach too much weight to these remarks, which were made in passing. The position in relation to inferior courts of law is not, unfortunately, placed beyond doubt by *Page*. Lord Browne-Wilkinson's leading speech sent mixed signals in this regard. On the one hand, he relied upon Lord Diplock's comments in *O'Reilly* in which no distinction was made between courts of law and tribunals. On the other hand, in advancing a reason for recognizing the special position of visitors in addition to that set out in the excerpt from his speech at 2.2.4, Lord Browne-Wilkinson accepted (at 703) that it may sometimes be appropriate to acknowledge that an inferior court of law is capable of conclusively determining certain questions of law, thereby implicitly suggesting that the presumption that errors of law are jurisdictional may not apply to inferior courts.

Given that the case law does not put this matter beyond doubt, it is appropriate to ask whether it makes sense to distinguish between inferior courts of law and other decision-makers in the manner suggested by Lord Diplock in *Racal*. The constitutional principle of the separation of powers (whose application in this context is considered by Hare (in Forsyth and Hare (eds), *The Golden Metwand and the Crooked Cord* (Oxford 1998)) suggests that the willingness of reviewing courts to overturn others' conclusions on questions of law should be affected by the ability of the latter to determine such questions. However, this effectively reduces to an argument of relative institutional competence, and the difficulty with Lord Diplock's approach in *Racal* is that it wrongly takes institutional status to be a reliable indicator of expertise. In reality, an equation between those two things is unlikely to exist. For instance, situations will arise in which a 'court', such as a magistrates' court, may have little by way of legal expertise relative to the High Court exercising its judicial review jurisdiction. Meanwhile, bodies that are not called 'courts' may nevertheless be court-like in terms of their independence and legal expertise; this is generally true today of tribunals, for reasons considered briefly later in this section and in more detail in ch 18. Moreover, bodies that are court-like in neither form nor substance may nevertheless have a high degree of expertise by dint of their familiarity with and insight into the likely consequences of different interpretations of the relevant statutory provisions.

Some further light is cast on these matters—albeit, for reasons we explain later, somewhat obliquely—by *R (Cart) v. Upper Tribunal*. The case—and, in particular, the decision of the Supreme Court: [2011] UKSC 28, [2012] 1 AC 663—is considered further at 14.6.3 and 18.4.6. For the time being, it suffices to say that the key issue was whether the Upper Tribunal—a statutory body that is designated a 'superior court of record', hears appeals against first-instance tribunal decisions and has statutory power to hear certain categories of judicial review cases in place of the High Court—is susceptible to judicial review and, if so, on what grounds. The aspect of that issue which is pertinent for present purposes is whether, when a question of law falls to be determined by the Upper Tribunal, it is to be considered a jurisdictional question of law, such that any error can be corrected in the event of disagreement between the Tribunal and a reviewing court.

In engaging with these questions, both the Divisional Court ([2009] EWHC 3052 (Admin), [2010] PTSR 824) and the Court of Appeal ([2010] EWCA Civ 859, [2011] QB 120) declined to adopt a formalistic approach. Neither the fact that the body is known as a *tribunal* nor the fact that it is statutorily characterized as a 'superior *court* of record' was therefore determinative. In the Divisional Court, Laws LJ was impressed by characteristics of the Upper Tribunal—such as its independence, expertise, and position at the apex of the tribunals system—and by its (statutory) powers of judicial review. This led Laws LJ to the conclusion (at [94]) that the Upper Tribunal is 'an *alter ego* of the High Court', meaning that there was no good reason for subjecting the Upper Tribunal to the full width of the High Court's supervisory jurisdiction: the rule of law did not require this, because the Upper Tribunal itself 'constitutes an authoritative, impartial and independent judicial source for the interpretation and application of the relevant statutory texts'.

The Court of Appeal reached the same conclusion but by a different analytical route. Giving the judgment of the Court of Appeal, Sedley LJ highlighted (at [42]) the position of the Upper Tribunal as part of a 'newly coherent and comprehensive edifice designed, among other things, to complete the long process of divorcing administrative justice from departmental policy' by means of a largely self-contained, judicialized system of independent tribunals capable of hearing appeals against administrative decisions. This led him to the conclusion that the model of judicial review best suited to 'implement[ing] Parliament's intent in enacting the ... reforms [to the tribunals system of which the creation of the Upper Tribunal was a key component] is one which secures the boundaries of the system but does not invade it.' Against that background, the Court of Appeal took the view that, as far as the Upper Tribunal is concerned, the distinction between jurisdictional and non-jurisdictional errors of law should be resurrected:

> [36] It seems to us that there is a true jurisprudential difference between an error of law made in the course of an adjudication which a tribunal is authorised to conduct and the conducting of an adjudication without lawful authority. Both are justiciable before the UT if committed by the FTT [*ie* First-tier Tribunal], but if committed by the UT will go uncorrected unless judicial review lies. The same of course is true of errors of law within jurisdiction; but these, in our judgment, reside within the principle that a system of law, while it can guarantee to be fair, cannot guarantee to be infallible. Outright excess of jurisdiction by the UT and denial by it of fundamental justice, should they ever occur, are in a different class: they represent the doing by the UT of something that Parliament cannot possibly have authorised it to do.
>
> [37] Thus if for some reason the UT made an order giving a money judgment which it had no power to give, with the possibility of enforcement under its [statutory] powers, it would be inimical to the rule of law if the High Court could not step in, should the appellate system for some reason not do so. Similarly if a member of the UT were to sit when ineligible or disqualified by a pecuniary interest, or if the UT conducted a hearing so unfairly as to render its decision a nullity, the High Court ought to be able to quash the determination. We do not mean this list to be exhaustive but to be illustrative of the kind of error, rare as it will be, which would take the UT outside the range of its decision-making authority.

On the Court of Appeal's view, then, the Upper Tribunal would commit a jurisdictional error of law only exceptionally, since ascribing an interpretation to a statutory provision different from the interpretation preferred by the reviewing court would amount only to a non-jurisdictional error.

The Supreme Court ([2011] UKSC 28, [2012] 1 AC 663) was also satisfied that there were sound policy reasons for heavily circumscribing the scope for judicial review of the Upper Tribunal. However, it chose to do so other than by means of distinguishing between jurisdictional and non-jurisdictional errors of law; Lady Hale (at [40]) said that that distinction had been 'given its quietus by the majority in *Anisminic*' and that adopting the Court of Appeal's analysis would mean a 'return to some of the technicalities of the past'. Instead, the Supreme Court decided that the Upper Tribunal should be shielded from judicial review by means of reviewing courts refusing, on a discretionary basis, to hear cases against the Upper Tribunal in the absence of certain exceptional circumstances. (We explain what those circumstances are at 18.4.6.)

In one sense, then, the culmination of the *Cart* litigation suggests that the case has no place in a chapter on jurisdiction, given that the Supreme Court disparaged the Court of Appeal's attempt to leverage that concept in order to shape the extent of judicial review of the Upper Tribunal. However, the very fact that the case took such a turn in the Supreme Court is itself significant for two reasons. First, it amounts to an acknowledgement, at the highest judicial level, that there are at least some circumstances in which it is desirable, in normative terms, to escape the strictures of the *Page* principle. Second, however, the Supreme Court's decision in *Cart* demonstrates a preference for addressing this issue by sidelining, rather than engaging with and refining, the *Page* principle, the policy objective of limiting judicial review of the Upper Tribunal being realized through reliance upon judicial discretion rather than legal principle. The paradoxical picture painted by the Supreme Court's judgment in *Cart* is therefore one of judicial unease (at least in this context) with the *Page* principle coupled with judicial reluctance formally to disturb it.

QUESTION

- Which of the judicial approaches to the issue that arose in *Cart* do you consider to be preferable? In particular, if—in this context or in other contexts—the *Page* principle results in judicial review that is considered too extensive from a policy perspective, should the Court of Appeal's approach (involving the modification of the principle) or the Supreme Court's approach (involving explicit reliance upon policy considerations that are extrinsic to questions of jurisdiction) be preferred?

2.2.8 The nature of the statutory provision

We have so far seen very limited evidence of judicial preparedness to depart from (as distinct from circumventing) the principle that questions of law are jurisdictional matters. The following case, however, arguably does demonstrate such preparedness—albeit in only very limited circumstances and, even then, only ambivalently.

R v. Monopolies and Mergers Commission, ex parte South Yorkshire Transport [1993] 1 WLR 23
House of Lords

The first claimant was a company which provided public transport services in South Yorkshire, and was owned by the second claimant, South Yorkshire Passenger Transport Authority. When the first claimant acquired a number of bus companies operating in South Yorkshire, the Secretary of State for Trade and Industry, acting under s 64 of the Fair Trading Act 1973, referred the matter to the defendant Commission, which could investigate the matter if (*inter alia*) the area concerned was 'a substantial part of the United Kingdom'. The Commission considered that 'substantial' meant 'something real or important as distinct from something merely nominal', and that although the area in question comprised only 1.65 per cent of the total geographical area of the UK, the statutory requirement was met because of the important part which the region played in the 'economic development and growth, and cultural life of the country'. In light of this the Commission recommended that the first claimant should be required to divest itself of the acquisitions in question. The Secretary of State adopted the Commission's conclusions and recommendation. The claimants sought judicial review, arguing that the requirement that the matter concerned a 'substantial part' of the UK was a jurisdictional precondition, and that the Commission erred in its interpretation of the Act in this respect. They succeeded at first instance. Having appealed unsuccessfully to the Court of Appeal, the defendants appealed to the House of Lords.

Lord Mustill

... [N]o recourse need be made to dictionaries to establish that 'substantial' accommodates a wide range of meanings. At one extreme there is 'not trifling.' At the other, there is 'nearly complete,' as where someone says that he is in substantial agreement with what has just been said. In between, there exist many shades of meaning, drawing colour from their context. That the protean nature of the word has been reflected in the decided cases is, I believe, made quite clear by the judgment of Otton J. [at first instance], in which the authorities are so thoroughly discussed as to make it unnecessary to go through them again. It is sufficient to say that although I do not accept that 'substantial' can never mean 'more than de minimis', ... I am satisfied that in section 64(3) the word does indeed lie further up the spectrum than that. To say how far up is another matter. The courts have repeatedly warned against the dangers of taking an inherently imprecise word, and by redefining it thrusting on it a spurious degree of precision. I will try to avoid such an error. Nevertheless I am glad to adopt, as a means of giving a general indication of where the meaning of the word in section 64(3) lies within the range of possible meanings, the expression of Nourse L.J. [1992] 1 W.L.R. 291, 301g 'worthy of consideration for the purpose of the Act.' ...

Thus far, therefore, I accept the respondents' submission that if the commission proceeded when examining its jurisdiction on the basis that it was enough for the reference area to be more than trifling this was a radical misconception. At first sight it appears that this gives them a powerful case, for we find in the report that the commission calls up the idea of 'something more than merely nominal.' If this expression truly reflects the basis of the decision there is reason for the court to interfere. Whilst acknowledging the force of this argument, I have come to the conclusion that it gives too little weight to the reasoning of the commission as a whole ...

[Lord Mustill examined the commission's reasoning, concluding that they had applied an interpretation of the term 'substantial' which was in reality much closer to that suggested by Nourse LJ than might have been suggested by the words which the commission had used to describe the test they applied. He continued:] There remains however the question whether, even if the commission had placed the test in broadly the right part of the spectrum of possible meanings it nevertheless failed to apply the test correctly. Here, the contest is between three methods of approach. 1. An arithmetical proportion should be struck between the reference area of the United Kingdom as a whole, as regards surface area, population and volume of the economic activity with which the reference is concerned. If the proportion(s) are too low, the area does not qualify. 2. An assessment in absolute terms of the size and importance of the area, independent of proportions. 3. A mixture of the two kinds of criterion ...

[His Lordship assessed these competing approaches, concluding:] I would prefer to state that the part must be 'of such size, character and importance as to make it worth consideration for the purposes of the Act.' ...

Applying this test to the present case one will ask first whether any misdirection is established, and secondly whether the decision can be overturned on the facts. As to the first it is quite clear that the approach of the commission was in general accord with what I would propose. It is true that matters such as academic and sports activities, mentioned by the commission, are of marginal importance at the most, but I do not regard their inclusion in the list of features to which the commission paid regard as vitiating an appreciation of 'substantive' which was broadly correct. On the second question the parties are at odds as to the proper function of the courts. The respondents say that the two stages of the commission's inquiry involved wholly different tasks. Once the commission reached the stage of deciding on public interest and remedies it was exercising a broad judgment whose outcome could be overturned only on the ground of irrationality. The question of jurisdiction, by contrast, is a hard-edged question. There is no room for legitimate disagreement. Either the commission had jurisdiction or it had not. The fact that it is quite hard to discover the meaning of section 64(3) makes no difference. It does have a correct meaning, and one meaning alone; and once this is ascertained a correct application of it to the facts of the case will always yield the same answer. If the commission has reached a different answer it is wrong, and the court can and must intervene.

I agree with this argument in part, but only in part. Once the criterion for a judgment has been properly understood, the fact that it was formerly part of a range of possible criteria from which it was difficult to choose and on which opinions might legitimately differ becomes a matter of history. The judgment now proceeds unequivocally on the basis of the criterion as ascertained. So far, no room for controversy. But this clear-cut approach cannot be applied to every case, for the criterion so established may itself be so imprecise that different decision-makers, each acting rationally, might reach differing conclusions when applying it to the facts of a given case. In such a case the court is entitled to substitute its own opinion for that of the person to whom the decision has been entrusted only if the decision is so aberrant that it cannot be classed as rational: *Edwards v. Bairstow* [1956] A.C. 14. The present is such a case. Even after eliminating inappropriate senses of 'substantial' one is still left with a meaning broad enough to call for the exercise of judgment rather than an exact quantitative measurement. Approaching the matter in this light I am quite satisfied that there is no ground for interference by the court, since the conclusion at which the commission arrived was well within the permissible field of judgment. Indeed I would go further, and say that in my opinion it was right.

I would accordingly allow the appeal, and restore the decision of the Commissioners and the Secretary of State.

Lords Templeman, Goff, Lowry, and Slynn agreed with Lord Mustill. Appeal allowed.

Lord Mustill's comments are somewhat opaque. At one point in his speech he appears to suggest that the Commission was merely required to place the test 'in broadly the right part of the spectrum of possible meanings'. This implies that the *definition* of a jurisdictional statutory term may, in certain circumstances, be treated not as a hard-edged matter for the court, to which there is only one correct answer, but as a question capable of yielding a range of lawful answers, such that the decision-maker acts lawfully by choosing any of the answers within that range. We can call this a reasonableness, rather than a correctness, standard of review. However, in the penultimate paragraph of our excerpt, Lord Mustill appears to adopt a different view, suggesting that while the statutory term, being a jurisdictional one, can lawfully bear only one *definition* (*viz* that which is favoured by the reviewing court), that definition may be so vague that, in practice, its *application* may be difficult to review on a hard-edged basis. On this matter, see 2.3.2.

The first interpretation of Lord Mustill's comments implies a category of cases in which substitutionary review will not apply. Williams [2007] *PL* 793 agrees that such a category should exist, but goes much further than Lord Mustill appeared to so far as the extent of that category is concerned. Whereas Lord Mustill (on the first interpretation of his judgment) appears to envisage the reasonableness standard as an exceptional one to be adopted in a minority of cases, Williams contends that it should be the norm. On her view, substitutionary review should be limited to cases in which it is unarguable that the statutory term in question has only one correct meaning. In all other cases, she contends, it is meaningless to speak of an *error* of law—an error is only possible if there is an objectively correct answer—and so the courts should acknowledge that what they are reviewing is an exercise of interpretative discretion on the decision-maker's part, with the result that they should intervene only if an unreasonable interpretation has been adopted.

QUESTIONS

- Is the distinction which Lord Mustill appears to draw in the penultimate paragraph of our excerpt, between the definition of jurisdictional terms and their application to the facts, a helpful one?
- Is the process of judicial attribution of a fixed meaning to vague statutory terms a meaningful one, if (as envisaged by Lord Mustill) close judicial supervision of their application to the facts is impossible or inappropriate?

2.2.9 The scope of the 'question of law' category

If (as we have seen) the general principle is that questions of law are jurisdictional matters attracting correctness review and if (as we will see at 2.3–2.4) the same is not necessarily true of other types of questions (*ie* questions of fact and questions about the application of the facts to the law), then it follows that the distinction between things that do and things that do not count as questions of law is highly significant. This does not mean that the distinction between questions of law and other types of questions marks the boundary between jurisdictional and non-jurisdictional questions: questions of law, as already explained, are occasionally considered to be non-jurisdictional in nature, while other types of questions, as explained later in the chapter, can be jurisdictional. Nevertheless, the extent of the 'question of law' category is important because it traces the boundary between situations (involving questions of law) that will almost inevitably attract review on a correctness basis and those (involving other types of questions) in which there is a greater possibility of a less intrusive standard applying.

One of the supposed attractions of the dismantling of the distinction between jurisdictional and non-jurisdictional questions of law is that the distinction is unstable and malleable, the risk being that courts might decide how closely they wish to scrutinize a given matter and accordingly categorize the matter as a jurisdictional or non-jurisdictional question of law. Treating all (or nearly all) questions of law as jurisdictional removes the possibility of courts proceeding in such a way. However, the implicit assumption must be that while the distinction between jurisdictional and non-jurisdictional questions of law is problematic (and so must be done away with) the distinction between questions of law and other types of questions is more serviceable. But is the distinction between (jurisdictional) questions of law and (perhaps not necessarily jurisdictional) questions of fact really one that can be drawn easily, and which is less susceptible to the sort of manipulation that used to occur within the question of law category? If it were the case that every question about the meaning of a statutory provision were to be considered a question of law, then the answer to that question might be 'yes'. That might bring problems of its own—it might, for instance, be considered to result in too great a degree of judicial control and too little administrative discretion over interpretation—but it would at least yield certainty as to what counts as a question of law and hence certainty as to the reach of the *Page* principle. However, the following case casts doubt upon the stability of the distinction between questions of law and other types of questions, and raises the prospect of the instrumental use of that distinction so as to secure what is judicially considered to be a normatively desirable level of judicial intervention.

R (Jones) v. *First-tier Tribunal* [2013] UKSC 19, [2013] 2 AC 48
Supreme Court

Barry Hughes jumped into the path of an articulated lorry on a busy dual carriageway and succeeded in his apparent attempt to kill himself. The lorry swerved, hitting a vehicle being driven by Gareth Jones, who sustained very severe injuries. Jones sought compensation from the Criminal Injuries Compensation Authority (CICA), arguing that Hughes had inflicted upon him grievous bodily harm contrary to s 20 of the Offences Against the Person Act 1861. However, the CICA declined to award any compensation: it considered that no such offence had been committed, and that its power to award compensation in respect of 'crimes of violence' had not been triggered.

Jones appealed to the First-tier Tribunal (FTT), which upheld the CICA's decision, and then sought judicial review of the FTT's ruling. On the judicial review challenge, Jones failed at first instance but succeeded in the Court of Appeal, which held that the FTT had made an error of law by (the Court of Appeal thought) assuming that Hughes's actions *could not* amount to a crime of violence. (In fact, the FTT concluded that his actions *did not*, on the facts, amount to such a crime.) The matter then went to the Supreme Court.

Lord Hope gave the leading judgment. He held that while a s 20 offence is *necessarily* a crime of violence, the crucial issue, within the factual matrix of the case, was whether Hughes's conduct in the first place amounted to a s 20 offence, and, in particular, whether he had the relevant *mens rea*. Lord Hope held that whether a s 20 offence had been committed was a question of fact for the FTT to determine, and that its conclusion that no such offence had been committed was a conclusion that it had been entitled to reach. Although this conclusion is not particularly surprising, the factual matrix of the case provided the occasion for some significant remarks, by Lord Carnwath in particular, concerning the relationship between questions of law and questions of fact.

Lord Hope

[16] ... [I]t is for the tribunal which decides the case to consider whether the words 'a crime of violence' do or do not apply to the facts which have been proved. Built into that phrase, there are two questions that the tribunal must consider. The first is whether, having regard to the facts which have been proved, a criminal offence has been committed. The second is whether, having regard to the nature of the criminal act, the offence that was committed was a crime of violence. I agree with Lord Carnwath JSC for all the reasons he gives that it is primarily for the tribunals, not the appellate courts, to develop a consistent approach to these issues, bearing in mind that they are peculiarly well fitted to determine them. A pragmatic approach should be taken to the dividing line between law and fact, so that the expertise of tribunals at the first tier and that of the Upper Tribunal can be used to best effect. An appeal court should not venture too readily

into this area by classifying issues as issues of law which are really best left for determination by the specialist appellate tribunals....

Lord Carnwath

[41] Where, as here, the interpretation and application of a specialised statutory scheme has been entrusted by Parliament to the new tribunal system, an important function of the Upper Tribunal is to develop structured guidance on the use of expressions which are central to the scheme, and so as to reduce the risk of inconsistent results by different panels at the First-tier level.

[42] Promotion of such consistency was part of the thinking behind the recommendation of Sir Andrew Leggatt for the establishment of an appellate tribunal: *Tribunals for Users, One System, One Service* (March 2001), paras 6.9–6.26. It was adopted by the government in the 2004 White Paper, paras 7.14–7.21, which spoke of the role of the new appellate tier 'in achieving consistency in the application of the law'. ...

[43] ... [I]t was hoped that the Upper Tribunal might be permitted to interpret 'points of law' flexibly to include other points of principle or even factual judgment of general relevance to the specialised area in question. That might have seemed controversial. However, as an approach it was not out of line with the developing jurisprudence in the appellate courts. In *Moyna v Secretary of State for* Work *and Pensions* [2003] 1 WLR 1929, paras 20–28, Lord Hoffmann, in the leading speech, had considered the interpretation by the social security commissioners of the so-called 'cooking test' for welfare benefits. [The test, which governed entitlement to a particular benefit, asked whether the claimant was so severely disabled that he would be unable to cook a main meal if he had all the ingredients.] He rejected the submission that, because the words used were ordinary English words, it should be treated as a pure question of fact ...

[44] Commenting on the distinction between issues of law and fact, Lord Hoffmann said, at paras 26–27:

> '[26] It may seem rather odd to say that something is a question of fact when there is no dispute whatever over the facts and the question is whether they fall within some legal category. In his classic work on *Trial by Jury* (1956) Lord Devlin said, at p 61: "The questions of law which are for the judge fall into two categories: first, there are questions which cannot be correctly answered except by someone who is skilled in the law; secondly, there are questions of fact which lawyers have decided that judges can answer better than juries."
>
> [27] Likewise it may be said that there are two kinds of questions of fact: there are questions of fact; and there are questions of law as to which lawyers have decided that it would be inexpedient for an appellate tribunal to have to form an independent judgment. But the usage is well established and causes no difficulty as long as it is understood that the degree to which an appellate court will be willing to substitute its own judgment for that of the tribunal will vary with the nature of the question: see *In re Grayan Building Services Ltd* [1995] Ch 241, 254–255.'

[45] Lord Hoffmann took this line of thinking a stage further in *Lawson v Serco Ltd* [2006] ICR 250, where the issue was the application of the Employment Rights Act 1996 to 'peripatetic employments', involving substantial work outside the United Kingdom. He described this as 'a question of law, although involving judgment in the application of the law to the facts': para 24. Under the heading 'fact or law?', he said, at para 34:

> 'Like many such decisions, it does not involve any finding of primary facts (none of which appear to have been in dispute) but an evaluation of those facts to decide a question posed

by the interpretation which I have suggested should be given to section 94(1), namely that it applies to peripatetic employees who are based in Great Britain. Whether one characterizes this as a question of fact depends, as I pointed out in *Moyna v Secretary of State for Work and Pensions* [2003] 1 WLR 1929, upon whether as a matter of policy one thinks that it is a decision which an appellate body with jurisdiction limited to errors of law should be able to review. I would be reluctant, at least at this stage …, altogether to exclude a right of appeal. In my opinion, therefore, the question of whether, on given facts, a case falls within the territorial scope of section 94(1) should be treated as a question of law. On the other hand, it is a question of degree on which the decision of the primary fact-finder is entitled to considerable respect. In the present case I think not only that the tribunal was entitled to reach the conclusion which it did but also that it was right.'

[46] I discussed these developments in an article in 2009: 'Tribunal Justice—A New Start' [2009] PL 48, 63–64. Commenting on *Moyna* [2003] 1 WLR 1929, I said:

'The idea that the division between law and fact should come down to a matter of expediency might seem almost revolutionary. However, the passage did not attract any note of dissent or caution from the other members of the House. That it was intended to signal a new approach was confirmed in another recent case relating to a decision of an employment tribunal, *Lawson v Serco*.'

Of Lord Hoffmann's words in *Serco* itself, I said:

'Two important points emerge from this passage. First, it seems now to be authoritatively established that the division between law and fact in such classification cases is not purely objective, but must take account of factors of "expediency" or "policy". Those factors include the utility of an appeal, having regard to the development of the law in the particular field, and the relative competencies in that field of the tribunal of fact on the one hand, and the appellate court on the other. Secondly, even if such a question is classed as one of law, the view of the tribunal of fact must still be given weight. This clarifies the position as between an appellate court on the one hand and a first instance tribunal. But what if there is an intermediate appeal on law only to a specialist appellate tribunal? Logically, if expediency and the competency of the tribunal are relevant, the dividing line between law and fact may vary at each stage. Reverting to Hale LJ's comments in [*Cooke* v. *Secretary of State for Social Security* [2002] 3 All ER 279, paras 5–17], an expert appellate tribunal, such as the Social Security Commissioners, is peculiarly fitted to determine, or provide guidance, on categorisation issues within the social security scheme. Accordingly, such a tribunal, even though its jurisdiction is limited to "errors of law", should be permitted to venture more freely into the "grey area" separating fact from law, than an ordinary court. Arguably, "issues of law" in this context should be interpreted as extending to any issues of general principle affecting the specialist jurisdiction. In other words, expediency requires that, where Parliament has established such a specialist appellate tribunal in a particular field, its expertise should be used to best effect, to shape and direct the development of law and practice in that field.'

Baroness Hale and Lords Sumption and Walker agreed with the judgments of Lords Hope and Carnwath.

Five points should be noted about *Jones* and, in particular, Lord Carnwath's judgment. First, it acknowledges that the law–fact distinction can be manipulated in order to modulate the intensity of judicial review. Indeed, Lord Carnwath's approach suggests that the law–fact distinction has come to eclipse the distinction between jurisdictional and non-jurisdictional errors of law as the principal frontier in this area of judicial review. With the latter distinction largely spent thanks to *Page*, some of the heavy lifting now falls to be undertaken by the former.

Second, both Lord Hope and Lord Carnwath go beyond acknowledging the capacity of the law–fact distinction to modulate review: they endorse the manipulation of the distinction so as to ensure a normatively desirable degree of judicial intervention. Indeed, *Jones* arguably elevates the notion of malleability to a preposterous level by suggesting that a given matter can be *both* a question of law and question of fact. On this analysis, the Upper Tribunal might legitimately characterize something as a question of law (so as to enable it to intervene and secure a coherent approach within the tribunals system), whilst a regular court called upon to examine the Upper Tribunal's decision (as the Court of Appeal had to do in *Jones*) might characterize *the same matter* as a question of fact (so as to avoid over-interference by regular courts in the operation of the tribuals system). On this approach, 'law' and 'fact' serve as little more than conclusory labels signalling that, for other reasons, a particular degree of judicial intervention has been judged to be normatively warranted.

Third, *Jones* sits in an interesting relationship with *Cart* (considered at 2.2.7). In one respect, *Jones* might be considered a conceptualist counterpoint to *Cart*'s raw pragmatism: whereas in *Cart* the Supreme Court eschewed any engagement with questions about the extent of legal power, preferring instead to regulate the availability of judicial review on a discretionary basis, *Jones* does engage with jurisdictional questions. However, this contrast notwithstanding, *Jones* has something significant in common with *Cart*. Both cases implicitly accept that the *Page* principle may sometimes fail to produce normatively desirable outcomes and seek to address that perceived difficulty *other than* by revisiting the possibility of a category of non-jurisdictional questions of law. In *Cart* the Supreme Court, by holding that judicial review is unlikely to be available even if a jurisdictional error of law has been committed, leaves the *Page* principle untouched whilst rendering it largely irrelevant *vis-à-vis* the Upper Tribunal. *Jones*, while also not questioning the proposition that errors of law are jurisdictional, fixes upon the possibility of shrinking the *Page* principle's field of application by shifting the boundary between questions of law and fact.

Fourth, it might be thought that *Jones* is relevant only in respect of the tribunals system. However, in doctrinal terms, there is no reason why the scope of the 'question of law' category cannot be manipulated in other contexts—and, in normative terms, the factors that underpin Lord Carnwath's case for judicial deference to the Upper Tribunal could equally apply to other decision-makers with relevant expertise.

Fifth, and finally, any assessment of the approach commended in *Jones* must distinguish—and may take different positions in relation to—two matters. There is the question whether it is normatively desirable to modulate the extent of decision-makers' interpretive discretion in the light of such factors as the decision-makers' expertise. As we have seen, there are arguments for and against that. However, even if we think that the flexibility afforded by *Jones* is a good thing, it does not follow that the methodology promoted in *Jones*—which casts 'law' and 'fact' as artificial categories to be manipulated in order to secure the right level of judicial intervention—is also a good thing. Such an approach is no substitute for explicitly confronting any perceived shortcomings of the *Page* principle in a transparent and coherent way.

2.3 Applying statutory criteria to the facts

We have seen thus far that mistakes about the applicable law—provided that questions of statutory interpretation are, in the first place, characterized as questions of law—are likely to constitute jurisdictional errors; reviewing courts may therefore substitute judgment concerning the meaning of legal terms which demarcate the decision-maker's powers. But what if the dispute concerns not a pure question of law but what we will call an 'application question' concerning the way in which the decision-maker has applied the law to the facts? If legislation provides that some state of affairs—for example the making of a 'structural alteration' to a building—must exist before a particular power may be exercised, is the *existence in fact* of that state of affairs a jurisdictional matter of which the court must itself be satisfied?

2.3.1 A correctness standard

The answer to that question is—at least sometimes—'yes'. As Lord Goddard CJ put it in *R v. Fulham, Hammersmith and Kensington Rent Tribunal, ex parte Zerek* [1951] 2 KB 1 at 6:

> [I]f a certain state of facts has to exist before an inferior tribunal have jurisdiction, they can inquire into the facts in order to decide whether or not they have jurisdiction, but cannot give themselves jurisdiction by a wrong decision upon them; and this court may, by means of proceedings for [a quashing order], inquire into the correctness of the decision.

Does this mean that if, say, an immigration official is authorized to detain or deport 'illegal entrants', the power can be exercised in respect of someone who (according to the reviewing court's assessment of the evidence) actually *is* an illegal entrant as distinct from someone whom the official (wrongly) *thinks* to be an illegant entrant? That was the question that confronted the House of Lords in *Khawaja* v. *Secretary of State for the Home Department* [1984] AC 74, the matter having arisen because the appellants were said to have obtained leave to enter the UK by deceiving immigration officers at their ports of entry as to their marital status. The crucial legal issues were set out in the following terms by Lord Bridge (at 120):

> [T]he authorities from *Reg. v. Secretary of State for the Home Department, Ex parte Hussain* [1978] 1 W.L.R. 700 to *Reg. v. Secretary of State for the Home Department, Ex parte Zamir* [1980] A.C. 930 have consistently affirmed the principle that the decision of an immigration officer to detain and remove a person as an illegal entrant under these provisions can only be attacked successfully on the ground that there was no evidence on which the immigration officer could reasonably conclude that he was an illegal entrant.
>
> It will be seen at once that this principle gives to an executive officer subject, no doubt, in reaching his conclusions of fact, to a duty to act fairly, a draconian power of arrest and expulsion based upon his own decision of fact which, if there was any evidence to support it, cannot be examined by any judicial process until after it has been acted on and then in circumstances where the person removed, being unable to attend the hearing of his appeal, has no realistic prospect of

prosecuting it with success. It will be further observed that to justify the principle important words have to be read into paragraph 9 of Schedule 2 [to the Immigration Act 1971] by implication. [That provision says that where an illegal entrant is not given leave to enter or remain in the UK, an immigration officer may give directions for his removal. Meanwhile, para 16(2) of sch 2 authorized detention pending deportation under, *inter alia*, para 9.] [Paragraph 9,] on the face of the language used, authorises the removal of a person who is an illegal entrant. The courts have applied it as if it authorised the removal of a person whom an immigration officer on reasonable grounds believes to be an illegal entrant. The all important question is whether such an implication can be justified.

Lord Bridge went on (at 122–3) to answer that question in the negative:

My Lords, we should, I submit, regard with extreme jealousy any claim by the executive to imprison a citizen without trial and allow it only if it is clearly justified by the statutory language relied on. The fact that, in the case we are considering, detention is preliminary and incidental to expulsion from the country in my view strengthens rather than weakens the case for a robust exercise of the judicial function in safeguarding the citizen's rights.

So far as I know, no case before the decisions under the Act which we are presently considering has held imprisonment without trial by executive order to be justified by anything less than the plainest statutory language, with the sole exception of the majority decision of your Lordships' House in *Liversidge v. Anderson* [1942] A.C. 206. No one needs to be reminded of the now celebrated dissenting speech of Lord Atkin in that case, nor of his withering condemnation of the process of writing into the statutory language there under consideration the words which were necessary to sustain the decision of the majority. Lord Atkin's dissent now has the approval of your Lordships' House in *Reg. v. Inland Revenue Commissioners, Ex parte Rossminster Ltd* [1980] A.C. 952. A person who has entered the United Kingdom with leave and who is detained under Schedule 2 paragraph 16 (2) pending removal as an illegal entrant on the ground that he obtained leave to enter by fraud is entitled to challenge the action taken and proposed to be taken against him both by application for habeas corpus and by application for judicial review. On the view I take, paragraph 9 of Schedule 2 must be construed as meaning no more and no less than it says. There is no room for any implication qualifying the words 'illegal entrant'.

Lord Wilberforce (at 105) summarized as follows what he considered to be the correct approach:

1. The immigration authorities have the power and the duty to determine and to act upon the facts material for the detention as illegal entrants of persons prior to removal from the United Kingdom. 2. Any person whom the Secretary of State proposes to remove as an illegal entrant, and who is detained, may apply for a writ of habeas corpus or for judicial review. Upon such an application the Secretary of State or the immigration authorities if they seek to support the detention or removal (the burden being upon them) should depose to the grounds on which the decision to detain or remove was made, setting out essential factual evidence taken into account and exhibiting documents sufficiently fully to enable the courts to carry out their function or review. 3. The court's investigation of the facts is of a supervisory character and not by way of appeal … It should appraise the quality of the evidence and decide whether that justifies the conclusion reached—e.g. whether it justifies a conclusion that the applicant obtained permission to entry by fraud or deceit. An allegation that he has done so being of a serious character and involving issues

of personal liberty, requires a corresponding degree of satisfaction as to the evidence. If the court is not satisfied with any part of the evidence it may remit the matter for reconsideration or itself receive further evidence. It should quash the detention order where the evidence was not such as the authorities should have relied on or where the evidence received does not justify the decision reached or, of course, for any serious procedural irregularity.

2.3.2 Does a correctness standard *always* apply?

It is clear, then, that the courts can apply a correctness standard when examining how a decision-maker has answered an application question. However, it does not follow that the court will—or should—*always* adopt such an approach. Beatson (1984) 4 *OJLS* 22 at 26, for instance, cautions that compelling reasons for judicial deference may also arise in this context, including the risk that treating all questions of application as jurisdictional questions attracting a correctness standard of review risks overextending judicial supervision so as to 'defeat legislative intentions in allocating the implementation of a policy to an administrative body'. An alternative to the correctness standard is a reasonableness standard which, as Beatson puts it, would enable decision-makers to act lawfully provided that, in deciding whether the facts satisfy the relevant statutory criterion, they remain within a 'zone of "reasonable" conclusions'.

In fact, it is clear from the case law that, in relation to application questions, a reasonableness standard of review can, and sometimes does, apply. This raises two issues. First, how, conceptually and doctrinally, is the application of a reasonableness standard achieved? And, second, how do the courts decide which standard should be applied in a given case? We consider these two questions in turn.

As to the first matter, the default position is that jurisdictional questions attract correctness review. This suggests that the most obvious way of examining application questions other than on a correctness basis is to characterize such questions other than as jurisdictional. Such an approach was adopted in *R v. Hillingdon London Borough Council, ex parte Puhlhofer* [1986] AC 484. The question was whether the claimants were homeless and hence entitled, under the Housing (Homeless Persons) Act 1977, to accommodation—a question which turned on whether they already had 'accommodation' within the meaning of the Act. Giving the only reasoned speech, Lord Brightman said (at 517):

In this situation, Parliament plainly, and wisely, placed no qualifying adjective before the word 'accommodation' in ... the Act, and none is to be implied. The word 'appropriate' or 'reasonable' is not to be imported ... [The position is now somewhat different: s 175(3) of the Housing Act 1996 says that, 'A person shall not be treated as having accommodation unless it is accommodation which it would be reasonable for him to continue to occupy.' The meaning of this phrase has been the subject of considerable litigation, culminating in the House of Lords' decision in *Ali v. Birmingham City Council* [2009] UKHL 36 [2009] 1 WLR 1506.] What is properly to be regarded as accommodation is a question of fact to be decided by the local authority. There are no rules. Clearly some places in which a person might choose or be constrained to live could not properly be regarded as accommodation at all; it would be a misuse of language to describe Diogenes [who was said to have lived in a barrel] as having occupied accommodation within the meaning of the Act. What the local authority have to consider, in reaching a decision whether a person is homeless for the purposes of the Act, is whether he has what can properly be described as accommodation within the ordinary meaning of that word in the English language ...

Where the existence or non-existence of a fact is left to the judgment and discretion of a public body and that fact involves a broad spectrum ranging from the obvious to the debatable to the just conceivable, it is the duty of the court to leave the decision of that fact to the public body to whom Parliament has entrusted the decision-making power save in a case where it is obvious that the public body, consciously or unconsciously, are acting perversely.

The upshot of the reasoning adopted in *Puhlhofer* is that the statutory criterion relating to 'accommodation' was not characterized as a jurisdictional precondition: whether the claimants already had 'accommodation' was not a question which the decision-maker had to answer correctly (in the view of the court); rather, it was a matter that, subject to a requirement not to act perversely, was for the decision-maker to determine.

An alternative means of subjecting application questions to review other than on a correctness basis is demonstrated by *South Yorkshire Transport* (see 2.2.8). In that case, it will be recalled, judicial review of whether a jurisdictional statutory criterion was satisfied on the facts was limited by its ambiguity: whether the criterion was met was not a hard-edged question for the court; the decision-maker was free to apply it in any of a range of permissible ways. However, rather than, as in *Puhlhofer*, characterizing the statutory criterion as non-jurisdictional, the House of Lords in *South Yorkshire Transport* treated it as a jurisdictional condition, but one that was capable of diverse application. The judicial policy in the two cases is, however, the same—*viz* to permit judicial deference to the decision-maker's judgment on the question whether the statutory criterion is satisfied on the facts.

This leads on to the second of the two questions outlined earlier, namely, how do we distinguish between situations in which the reasonableness and correctness standards will apply? In normative terms, what falls to be decided here is the appropriateness, in constitutional and institutional terms, of (on the one hand) close judicial scrutiny of whether the relevant statutory criterion is satisfied and (on the other hand) the allocation of some degree of latitude to the decision-maker when it comes to determining whether the criterion is met. Reviewing courts thus have to decide on the optimum balance, or trade-off, between judicial control and administrative autonomy by determining how much, if any, deference to afford by means of deviating from a correctness standard. In this regard, the case law suggests that three considerations are particularly important.

The first concerns *the nature and normative importance of the matters that are at stake.* For instance, the fact that individual liberty was at stake in *Khawaja* made the more intrusive approach adopted in that case constitutionally appropriate. This is certainly a point that appeared to influence Lord Scarman in *Khawaja*, who, having referred to the 'reasonable grounds' test which *Zamir* appeared to endorse, said (at 109):

My Lords, in most cases I would defer to a recent decision of your Lordships' House on a question of construction, even if I thought it wrong. I do not do so in this context because for reasons which I shall develop I am convinced that the *Zamir* reasoning gave insufficient weight to the important—I would say fundamental—consideration that we are here concerned with, the scope of judicial review of a power which inevitably infringes the liberty of those subjected to it. This consideration, if it be good, outweighs, in my judgment, any difficulties in the administration of immigration control to which the application of the principle might give rise. The *Zamir* construction of paragraph 9 [of sch 2 to the Immigration Act 1971] deprives those subjected to the power of that degree of judicial protection which I think can be shown to have been the policy of our law to afford to persons with whose liberty the executive is seeking to interfere. It does therefore, in my view, tend to obstruct the proper development and application of the safeguards our law provides for the liberty of those within its jurisdiction.

Second, although, as we saw at 2.2.6, *the decision-maker's expertise* generally cuts little ice when it comes to questions of law: greater store is set by expertise in respect of application questions. For instance, in *Dowty Boulton Paul Ltd* v. *Wolverhampton Corporation (No 2)* [1976] Ch 13, it was contended (*inter alia*) that a local authority had erred by exercising powers to put certain of its land to a new use, on the ground that the statutory precondition that the land was 'not required' for the purpose for which it was originally acquired was not satisfied. Russell LJ held that the court should not make up its own mind on this matter, observing (at 26) that 'not required' meant 'not needed in the public interest of the locality' for the original purpose', a question raising 'matters of both degree and of comparative needs, as to which there can be no question but that the local authority is better qualified than the court to judge, assuming it to be acting bona fide and not upon a view that no reasonable local authority could possibly take'.

Third, *the nature of the statutory provision* itself—and, in particular, the extent to which it amounts to a hard-edged or objective criterion—is relevant to whether a correctness or a reasonableness standard of review applies, as the following case shows.

R (A) v. *Croydon London Borough Council* [2009] UKSC 8, [2009] 1 WLR 2557
Supreme Court

The claimants contended that the defendant local authorities were obliged by s 20(1) of the Children Act 1989 to provide them with accommodation. Section 20(1) provides that:

Every local authority shall provide accommodation for any child in need within their area who appears to them to require accommodation as a result of—

(a) there being no person who has parental responsibility for him;
(b) his being lost or having been abandoned; or
(c) the person who has been caring for him being prevented (whether or not permanently, and for whatever reason) from providing him with suitable accommodation or care.

The defendants, however, formed the view that neither claimant was a 'child' (which, according to s 105(1) of the 1989 Act, means 'a person under the age of 18'), and argued that this view was legally impregnable unless unreasonable. On the trial of preliminary issues, that argument was upheld at first instance ([2008] EWHC 1364 (Admin)) and the claimants' appeal was rejected by the Court of Appeal ([2008] EWCA Civ 1445). The claimants appealed to the Supreme Court.

Baroness Hale

[26] … The 1989 Act draws a clear and sensible distinction between different kinds of question. The question whether a child is 'in need' requires a number of different value judgments. What would be a reasonable standard of health or development for this particular child? How likely is he to achieve it? What services might bring that standard up to a reasonable level? What amounts to a significant impairment of health or development? How likely is that? What services might avoid it? Questions like this are sometimes decided by the courts in the course of care or other proceedings under the Act. Courts are quite used to deciding them upon the evidence for the purpose of deciding what order, if any, to make. But where the issue is not, what order should

the court make, but what service should the local authority provide, it is entirely reasonable to assume that Parliament intended such evaluative questions to be determined by the public authority, subject to the control of the courts on the ordinary principles of judicial review. Within the limits of fair process and '*Wednesbury* reasonableness' [on which see ch 8] there are no clear cut right or wrong answers.

[27] But the question whether a person is a 'child' is a different kind of question. There is a right or a wrong answer. It may be difficult to determine what that answer is. The decision-makers may have to do their best on the basis of less than perfect or conclusive evidence. But that is true of many questions of fact which regularly come before the courts. That does not prevent them from being questions for the courts rather than for other kinds of decision-makers.

[28] In section 20(1) a clear distinction is drawn between the question whether there is a 'child in need within their area' and the question whether it appears to the local authority that the child requires accommodation for one of the listed reasons. In section 17(10) a clear distinction is drawn between whether the person is a 'child' and whether that child is to be 'taken to be' in need within the meaning of the Act. 'Taken to be' imports an element of judgment, even an element of deeming in the case of a disabled child, which Parliament may well have intended to be left to the local authority rather than the courts.

[29] I reach those conclusions on the wording of the 1989 Act and without recourse to the additional argument ... that 'child' is a question of jurisdictional or precedent fact of which the ultimate arbiters are the courts rather than the public authorities involved ...

[31] This doctrine is not of recent origin or limited to powers relating to the liberty of the subject. But of course it still requires us to decide which questions are to be regarded as setting the limits to the jurisdiction of the public authority and which questions simply relate to the exercise of that jurisdiction. This too must be a question of statutory construction, although Wade and Forsyth on *Administrative* Law 9th ed (2004), p 257 suggest that 'As a general rule, limiting conditions stated in objective terms will be treated as jurisdictional'. It was for this reason that Ward LJ [in the Court of Appeal: [2008] EWCA Civ 1445] rejected the argument, for he regarded the threshold question in section 20 as the composite one of whether the person was a 'child in need'. This was not [in Ward LJ's view] a limiting condition stated in wholly objective terms so as to satisfy the Wade and Forsyth test ...

[32] However, as already explained, the Act does draw a distinction between a 'child' and a 'child in need' and even does so in terms which suggest that they are two different kinds of question. The word 'child' is undoubtedly defined in wholly objective terms (however hard it may be to decide upon the facts of the particular case). With a few limited extensions, it defines the outer boundaries of the jurisdiction of both courts and local authorities under the 1989 Act. This is an Act for and about children. If ever there were a jurisdictional fact, it might be thought, this is it.

The Supreme Court was unanimous in holding that the question whether a person is a child for the purposes of s 20(1) of the Children Act 1989 is one that can ultimately be determined by the court. This excerpt has not addressed a separate point which arose in this case, concerning the application of Article 6 ECHR: this aspect of the case is covered at 9.5.2.

Baroness Hale's analysis provides welcome clarification, subject to two caveats. First, it is not a panacea: whether a statutory criterion is objective enough to make the court the final arbiter is not itself a clear-cut question, and hard cases will doubtless continue to arise. Second, Baroness Hale's suggestion (at [29]) that her analysis of the legislative text is a separate matter from the application of the doctrine of precedent fact is somewhat mystifying, given that the purpose of the textual analysis is surely to determine whether a given criterion constitutes a precedent fact such that the court must be satisfied of its existence.

However, those remarks must be read in light of another passage in Baroness Hale's judgment (at [13]), where she explained that the putative distinction between the two issues had arisen because of how the case was argued and that they were, in any event, 'closely inter-related'.

Finally, it is important to bear in mind that the alternative approaches to application questions postulated earlier—*ie* correctness and reasonableness review—mark the ends of a spectrum rather than binary alternatives. In *R (Ali)* v. *Secretary of State for Justice* [2013] EWHC 72 (Admin), [2013] 1 WLR 3536 at [57], Beatson LJ said that even in relation to evaluative questions—which, as *Croydon* shows, may attract only reasonableness review— 'the line between a supervisory and an appellate jurisdiction may be almost non-existent'. In other words, there may be circumstances in which the reviewing court determines that, the evaluative nature of the criterion notwithstanding, something more than reasonableness review—albeit something that might fall short of outright correctness, or substitutionary, review—might be called for, the precise intensity of review being informed by a contextual assessment that might involve balancing against one another considerations pulling in opposing directions, as *Ali* itself illustrates. The case involved a challenge to the Secretary of State's decision that the claimants, whose criminal convictions had been reversed by the Court of Appeal, were not statutorily entitled to compensation. Beatson LJ observed (at [60]) that what was at stake was 'of high importance and significance, not only to the individual concerned, but also as a matter of public interest', and that 'the subject matter of the decision' involved matters lying 'close to the heart of the court's exercise of its criminal jurisdiction' and hence 'a task which it is well equipped to undertake'. Nevertheless, Beatson LJ concluded that a standard of review falling short of correctness was appropriate:

[62] Even where the court is as well equipped as the Secretary of State to deal with an issue, it must not lose sight of the fact that Parliament has assigned the primary decision-making function to a minister or another public body. ...

[63] In the present context, there is a particular factor which points against a substitutionary approach ... [I]n *In re McFarland* [2004] 1 WLR 1289, para 7[, Lord Bingham described] ... the question of whether and in what circumstances compensation should be paid to a person whose conviction has been set aside as 'difficult and sensitive'. The reasons he gave included, *inter alia*, the difficulty in distinguishing those who are the innocent victims of mistake or misidentification from those who are fortunate to have escaped their just deserts. He also referred to the 'interaction ... of judicial and executive activity' and the consequent need for each of these two branches of the state to recognise and respect the proper role of the other. The submissions on behalf of the claimants on this question [*ie* that a correctness standard should be adopted] would effectively reduce the role of the Secretary of State to a purely administrative one. They would eliminate virtually all the power of judgment which we have concluded [the relevant statutory provision] clearly confers on the Secretary of State and which it is appropriate for the executive branch of government to have.

QUESTION

- Do the cases considered here set out a sufficiently clear framework for determining the intensity with which courts should examine decision-makers' determinations as to whether a given statutory test is satisfied by the facts?

2.4 Supervision of the fact-finding process

We have seen that, where the court holds that a particular statutory criterion describes a state of affairs that is a jurisdictional condition, such that the court must be satisfied as to its existence, it is open to the court to examine the facts in order to decide for itself whether the condition is met.

It is convenient at this point to consider to what extent reviewing courts are able to go further than this in reviewing the fact-finding process. For example, if the court is satisfied that, on the facts, all relevant *jurisdictional conditions* are satisfied, may the court nevertheless overturn a decision because the decision-maker has exercised its discretion subject to an erroneous understanding of relevant facts in relation to a *non-jurisdictional matter*? It is accepted that decisions made on the basis of no admissible or relevant evidence may be set aside (see, *eg R v. Bedwellty Justices, ex parte Williams* [1997] AC 225 at 233); this means that a finding of fact by a decision-maker 'must be based upon some material that tends logically to show the existence of facts consistent with the finding and that the reasoning supportive of the finding, if it be disclosed, is not logically self-contradictory' (*per* Lord Diplock in *Mahon v. Air New Zealand Ltd* [1984] AC 808 at 821). Moreover, errors in relation to non-jurisdictional facts may lead decision-makers into other errors which are reviewable, such as the taking into account of irrelevant considerations (on which see 7.3). However, there is a case for more far-reaching powers of judicial review, as Forsyth and Dring (in Forsyth *et al* (eds), *Effective Judicial Review: A Cornerstone of Good Governance* (Oxford 2010) at 259–60) explain:

> Material mistakes of fact may be viewed as intrinsically unfair. In the absence of bad faith, it is reasonable and rational to assume that where there is a dispute between the decision-maker and the person affected, the individual tasked with resolving the dispute acts on the basis that he has understood the facts upon which the decision is based. Clearly there may be disagreements as to whose version of the facts is true, and this will be for the person hearing the dispute to decide. But where a factual finding which has an impact on the outcome is *objectively* shown to be mistaken, the process of fair dispute resolution can be seen to have failed. The outcome is no longer rooted in factual reality, putting the decision in the same category as one which is irrational, or is based on an irrelevant consideration, or is infected by bias. A material error of fact has the same effect on a decision as a mistake about the applicable law: the decision is rendered incorrect and unfairness results to one or both parties, or to the public interest generally. This analysis provides a compelling basis for concluding that material error of fact which causes unfairness should be viewed as an error of law in the same way that irrationality, bias, or a literal misdirection on the law, are.

QUESTIONS

- Do you agree with this argument?
- Should reviewing courts be able to intervene in the face of *any* error of fact?

The foundation of the modern law in this area is now found in the following case.

E v. *Secretary of State for the Home Department* [2004] EWCA Civ 49, [2004] QB 1044
Court of Appeal

An issue arose as to whether the (now defunct) Immigration Appeal Tribunal could take into account new evidence which had become available after the appellants' hearings but before the Tribunal had promulgated its decisions. The Tribunal refused to do so. The appellants appealed to the Court of Appeal. This extract is concerned only with the issue raised in the first sentence of our excerpt from the judgment. However, Carnwath LJ made it clear (at [42]) that the same principles would govern whether errors of fact can be challenged via judicial review. It follows that the criteria set out at [66], and reproduced in the following excerpt, are applicable in judicial review proceedings.

Carnwath LJ (giving the judgment of the Court)

[44] Can a decision reached on an incorrect basis of fact be challenged on an appeal limited to points of law? This apparently paradoxical question has a long history in academic discussion, but has never received a decisive answer from the courts ...

[45] The debate received new life following the affirmative answer given by Lord Slynn in *R v Criminal Injuries Compensation Board, Ex p A* [1999] 2 AC 330 ...

[46] One of the issues discussed in detail in argument [in *ex parte A*] was whether the decision could be quashed on the basis of a mistake, in relation to material which was or ought to have been within the knowledge of the decision maker: see pp 333–336. Lord Slynn thought it could. He said, at pp 344–345:

> 'Your Lordships have been asked to say that there is jurisdiction to quash the board's decision because that decision was reached on a material error of fact. Reference has been made to *Wade & Forsyth, Administrative Law,* 7th ed (1994), pp 316–318 in which it is said: "Mere factual mistake has become a ground of judicial review, described as 'misunderstanding or ignorance of an established and relevant fact', [*Secretary of State for Education and Science* v. *Tameside Metropolitan Borough Council* [1977] AC 1014, 1030], or acting 'upon an incorrect basis of fact' ... This ground of review has long been familiar in French law and it has been adopted by statute in Australia. It is no less needed in this country, since decisions based upon wrong facts are a cause of injustice which the courts should be able to remedy. If a 'wrong factual basis' doctrine should become established, it would apparently be a new branch of the ultra vires doctrine, analogous to finding facts based upon no evidence or acting upon a misapprehension of law." *De Smith, Woolf & Jowell, Judicial Review of Administrative Action,* 5th ed (1995), p 288: "The taking into account of a mistaken fact can just as easily be absorbed into a traditional legal ground of review by referring to the taking into account of an irrelevant consideration, or the failure to provide reasons that are adequate or intelligible, or the failure to base the decision on any evidence. In this limited context material error of fact has always been a recognised ground for judicial intervention." For my part, I would accept that there is jurisdiction to quash on that ground in this case'.

Carnwath LJ noted that these comments were obiter (Lord Slynn decided the case on a different ground—'unfairness'—which Carnwath LJ discusses below) but that Lord Slynn had repeated his views in *R (Alconbury Developments Ltd)* v. *Secretary of State for the Environment, Transport and the Regions* [2003] 2 AC 295 at [53]. Carnwath LJ then noted that differing judicial views have been expressed on this issue. He cited from Buxton LJ's judgment in *Wandsworth Borough Council* v. *A* [2000] 1 WLR 1246 at 1255–6, which endorsed the view in *Puhlhofer* (see 2.3.2) that the court should not intervene on issues of fact in the absence of perversity. By way of contrast, Carnwath LJ noted the comments of Lord Scarman in *Secretary of State for Education and Science* v. *Tameside Metropolitan Borough Council* [1977] AC 1014 at 1030 to the effect that judicial review lies on the ground of 'misunderstanding or ignorance of an established and relevant fact'. After considering various other authorities and academic commentaries, Carnwath LJ continued:

[61]...[T]he editors of the [fifth] edition of *de Smith, Woolf & Jowell, Judicial Review of Administrative Action* (unlike *Wade & Forsyth, Administrative Law*) are somewhat tentative as to whether this is a separate ground of review, at para 5–094:

'The taking into account of a mistaken fact can just as easily be absorbed into a traditional legal ground of review by referring to the taking into account of an irrelevant consideration, or the failure to provide reasons that are adequate or intelligible, or the failure to base the decision upon any evidence.'

[62] We are doubtful, however, whether those traditional grounds provide an adequate explanation of the cases. We take them in turn. (i) Failure to take account of a material consideration is only a ground for setting aside a decision, if the statute expressly or impliedly requires it to be taken into account: *In re Findlay* [1985] AC 318, 333–334, per Lord Scarman ... (ii) Reasons are no less 'adequate and intelligible', because they reveal that the decision-maker fell into error; indeed that is one of the purposes of requiring reasons. (iii) Finally, it may be impossible, or at least artificial, to say that there was a failure to base the decision on '*any* evidence' ... In most of these cases there is some evidential basis for the decision, even if part of the reasoning is flawed by mistake or misunderstanding.

[63] In our view, the *Criminal Injuries Compensation Board* case [1999] 2 AC 330 points the way to a separate ground of review, based on the principle of fairness. It is true that Lord Slynn distinguished between 'ignorance of fact' and 'unfairness' as grounds of review. However, we doubt if there is a real distinction. The decision turned, not on issues of fault or lack of fault on either side; it was sufficient that 'objectively' there was unfairness. On analysis, the 'unfairness' arose from the combination of five factors: (i) an erroneous impression created by a mistake as to, or ignorance of, a relevant fact (the availability of reliable evidence to support [the claimant's] case); (ii) the fact was 'established', in the sense that, if attention had been drawn to the point, the correct position could have been shown by objective and uncontentious evidence; (iii) the claimant could not fairly be held responsible for the error; (iv) although there was no duty on the [decision-maker] itself ... to do the claimant's work of proving her case, all the participants had a shared interest in co-operating to achieve the correct result; (v) the mistaken impression played a material part in the reasoning ...

[66] In our view, the time has now come to accept that a mistake of fact giving rise to unfairness is a separate head of challenge in an appeal on a point of law, at least in those statutory contexts where the parties share an interest in co-operating to achieve the correct result. Asylum law is undoubtedly such an area. Without seeking to lay down a precise code, the ordinary requirements for a finding of unfairness are apparent from the above analysis of the *Criminal Injuries Compensation Board* case. First, there must have been a mistake as to an existing fact, including a mistake as to the availability of evidence on a particular matter. Secondly, the fact or evidence must have been 'established', in the sense that it was uncontentious and objectively verifiable. Thirdly, the appellant (or his advisers) must not been have been responsible for the mistake. Fourthly, the mistake must have played a material (not necessarily decisive) part in the tribunal's reasoning.

In the subsequent case of *R (Iran)* v. *Secretary of State for the Home Department* [2005] EWCA Civ 982, [2005] Imm AR 535 at [29], the Court of Appeal drew together the following list of examples of judicially reviewable errors of fact which Carnwath LJ had mentioned in his judgment in *E*. It gives a useful flavour of the sort of things that may now be open to challenge.

(i) There was in fact contemporary documentary evidence of the injuries sustained by a claimant for compensation from the Criminal Injuries Compensation Board;

(ii) There was in fact, contrary to a Minister's belief, adequate school accommodation in a local education authority's area for the pupils to be educated;

(iii) The land in question had in fact once been part of the Green Belt;

(iv) The proposed building extension would in fact obstruct a particular aspect;

(v) The restructuring of a building was in fact viable;

(vi) A study by a local council did not in fact relate to the inclusion of a particular site within the Green Belt;

(vii) A critical witness was in fact a member of a totally different political party in Ethiopia to that which he was believed to support;

(viii) The appellant had in fact been tried and convicted in his absence in his home country and sentenced to ten years' imprisonment, a matter which cast an entirely new light on the risks he faced if he were returned there.

Two further points should be considered in relation to the criteria laid down in *E*. First, the reviewing court can only intervene if there has been a mistake of fact. But in order to establish that such a mistake has occurred, it will often be necessary to introduce fresh evidence. *When will a court admit such evidence?* According to *E*, the general principle is that such evidence should be admitted only when the following conditions, laid down by Denning LJ in *Ladd* v. *Marshall* [1954] 1 WLR 1489 at 1491, are met:

[F]irst, it must be shown that the evidence could not have been obtained with reasonable diligence for use at the trial [or hearing]; secondly, the evidence must be such that, if given, it would probably have an important influence on the result of the case, though it need not be decisive; thirdly, the evidence must be such as is presumably to be believed, or in other words, it must be apparently credible, though it need not be incontrovertible.

However, it was recognized in *E* (at [82]) that these criteria should constitute only a 'starting-point', and that 'there is a discretion to depart from them in exceptional circumstances'. For instance, in *R (SO (Eritrea))* v. *Barking and Dagenham London Borough Council* [2014] EWCA Civ 1486, the appellant appealed against an Upper Tribunal ruling that he was not who or the age he had claimed to be, and that the local authority therefore had no relevant statutory duty towards him. In order to demonstrate that the Upper Tribunal's decision was flawed by error of fact, the appellant sought, in proceedings before the Court of Apeal, to adduce DNA evidence confirming his identity. The Court permitted him to do so even though the first of the *Ladd* v. *Marshall* criteria was not satisfied because the evidence could have been obtained earlier. Elias LJ said (at [20]) that those criteria 'should not be rigorously applied in public law cases' and concluded (at [23]) that

[t]here is in cases of this kind a tension between the need for finality on the one hand and the need to ensure that there is no obvious injustice on the other, and no doubt the potential significance of the evidence will have an important bearing on how the court should strike the balance between those conflicting interests. But where the strength of the evidence is so overwhelming, it seems to me that it would be wrong to refuse to allow it to be admitted at this stage.

The second question prompted by *E* concerns the requirement that the fact in relation to which the alleged mistake has arisen must be *'uncontentious and objectively verifiable'*. As Craig [2004] *PL* 788 at 802–3 notes, in some cases there will be little doubt that this require-ment is met. For instance, in *R* v. *Criminal Injuries Compensation Board, ex parte A* [1999] 2 AC 330, the claimant said she had been raped, and sought compensation from a publicly-funded scheme. The decision-maker turned down her claim under the misapprehension that no medical evidence supporting it existed. In fact, a police doctor had examined the claimant and had written a report saying her injuries were consistent with her allegations. The fact at stake—that the report existed and said what it said—was uncontentious and verifiable. But some cases are not as clear-cut. It is unlikely, for instance, that (absent exceptional circum-stances) an uncontentious and verifiable error of fact can be established on the ground that a decision-maker believed witness X's version of events but should have believed witness Y's version. Similarly, an error of fact will be difficult to establish when the matter is significantly evaluative in nature. For example, in *Chalfont St Peter Parish Council* v. *Chiltern District Council* [2014] EWCA Civ 1393, it was argued that a planning authority's decision was viti-ated by error of fact because it had been mistaken as to the size of certain playing fields. It was held, however, that no uncontentious and verifiable error arose because, as Beatson LJ put it (at [105]):

> [W]hether a particular open space is a 'playing field' within [the meaning of the relevant policy] is a matter requiring the exercise of judgement … In some cases, for example, where the entirety of an open space is laid out for one or more sporting activities, determining the extent of the playing field or fields is likely to be a question of simple observation. But in cases where the area so laid out is to be part of a wider area including, for example, parkland, car-parking space, informal garden, or groups of trees, an evaluative exercise is needed.

However, as Beatson LJ went on (at [106]) to point out, this does not mean that '[t]he mere fact that the factual question under consideration is one requiring evaluation will … be fatal to establishing a mistake of fact'. For instance, in *A*, the medical report was itself an expert evaluation of the likely cause of the claimant's injuries—but, crucially, the alleged error of fact related not to the correctness or otherwise of the doctor's *evaluative conclusions* but to the *existence* of the report.

2.5 Subjective jurisdictional criteria

It is not uncommon for legislation to provide that a decision-maker may do something 'if he believes' or 'if he reasonably believes' that some state of affairs exists. The first of these formulations appears to turn what would otherwise have been a jurisdictional limit upon the decision-making power into an entirely subjective matter of opinion: the agency can act *if it thinks* that the jurisdictional criterion is satisfied. On this view, judicial review on jurisdic-tional grounds is all but eviscerated—there is nothing to review except the decision-maker's state of mind, since jurisdiction exists whenever he thinks it does.

Although the line of thinking outlined here has found favour in some cases (see, *eg Robinson* v. *Minister of Town and Country Planning* [1947] KB 702), the modern orthodoxy is to be found in cases such as *Commissioners of Customs and Excise* v. *Cure and Deeley*

Ltd [1962] 1 QB 340. The Finance (No 2) Act 1940, s 33(1), permitted the Commissioners to 'make regulations for any matter for which provision appears to be necessary for the purpose of giving effect to the provisions of this Part of this Act and of enabling them to discharge their functions thereunder'. The Commissioners duly purported to give themselves extraordinarily wide powers, which they exercised to the detriment of the claimant. In quashing the regulation made by the Commissioners, Sachs LJ (at 366–7) said:

> I reject the view that the words 'appear to them to be necessary' when used in a statute conferring powers on a competent authority, necessarily make that authority the sole judge of what are its powers as well as the sole judge of the way in which it can exercise such powers as it may have … To my mind a court is bound before reaching a decision on the question whether a regulation is intra vires to examine the nature, objects, and scheme of the piece of legislation as a whole, and in light of that examination to consider exactly what is the area over which powers are given by the section under which the competent authority is purporting to act.

According to this view, even when the legislation uses subjective language, there will still be objective jurisdictional criteria—to be ascertained by construing the statutory scheme as whole, if necessary—which limit the decision-maker's powers. Thus when legislation said that the Home Secretary could ban membership and support for organizations which he *believed* to be 'concerned in terrorism', it was held in *Lord Alton of Liverpool* v. *Secretary of State for the Home Department* [2008] EWCA Civ 443, [2008] 1 WLR 2341 that such a decision would be lawful only if a reasonable decision-maker could have concluded that the group was so concerned.

If the statute uses the term 'reasonably'—*eg* 'if the Minister reasonably believes'—then it is even easier for the court to ensure that objective jurisdictional criteria are enforced, since here the legislation itself acknowledges that there must exist evidence which makes the decision-maker's opinion reasonable. This obvious point famously evaded the House of Lords in *Liversidge* v. *Anderson* [1942] AC 206, concerning the Secretary of State's power, under regulation 18B of the Defence (General) Regulations 1939, to order detention if he had 'reasonable cause to believe' that such action was necessary for various stated security purposes. In spite of the objective language of the statute, which at the very least seemed to require the reviewing court to insist upon some evidence as justification for the Minister's belief, the House of Lords held that this was a matter for the Minister alone. As Lord Wright put it at 268: 'He must be reasonably satisfied before he acts, but it is still his decision and not the decision of anyone else.' The conclusion of the majority was the subject of a celebrated dissenting speech by Lord Atkin. Note, in particular, the following passages from his judgment (at 227 and 245):

> It is surely incapable of dispute that the words 'if A has X' constitute a condition the essence of which is the existence of X and the having of it by A. If it is a condition to a right (including a power) granted to A, whenever the right comes into dispute the tribunal whatever it may be that is charged with determining the dispute must ascertain whether the condition is fulfilled. In some cases the issue is one of fact, in others of both fact and law, but in all cases the words indicate an existing something the having of which can be ascertained. And the words do not mean and cannot mean 'if A thinks that he has.' 'If A has a broken ankle' does not mean and cannot mean 'if A thinks that he has a broken ankle.' 'If A has a right of way' does not mean and cannot mean 'if A thinks that he has a right of way.' 'Reasonable cause' for an action or a belief is just as much a positive fact capable of determination by a third party as is a broken ankle or a legal right. If

its meaning is the subject of dispute as to legal rights, then ordinarily the reasonableness of the cause, and even the existence of any cause is in our law to be determined by the judge and not by the tribunal of fact if the functions deciding law and fact are divided …

I know of only one authority which might justify the … construction [favoured by the majority]: '"When I use a word," Humpty Dumpty said in rather a scornful tone, "it means just what I choose it to mean, neither more nor less." "The question is," said Alice, "whether you can make words mean so many different things." "The question is," said Humpty Dumpty, "which is to be master—that's all."' ('Through the Looking Glass,' c. vi.) After all this long discussion the question is whether the words 'If a man has' can mean 'If a man thinks he has.' I am of opinion that they cannot, and that the case should be decided accordingly.

Lord Atkin's dissenting view is today regarded as the correct one (see, *eg Nakkuda Ali* v. *Jayaratne* [1951] AC 66 at 76–7; *Ahmed* v. *HM Treasury (No 1)* [2010] UKSC 5, [2010] 2 WLR 378 at [6], *per* Lord Hope). The majority view, in contrast, must be seen against the backdrop of war, and of a wider mid-twentieth century judicial reticence to hold the executive to account.

2.6 Non-compliance with statutory requirements

Finally, it is convenient at this point to consider in what circumstances a decision-maker's failure to comply with requirements laid down in the statute will deprive it of jurisdiction. The problem, as Lord Steyn explained in *R* v. *Soneji* [2005] UKHL 49, [2006] 1 AC 340 at [14], is that Parliament often 'casts its commands in imperative form without expressly spelling out the consequences of a failure to comply'. For instance, if Parliament says a particular step (*eg* consulting someone) 'must' be taken before a given decision is made, does failure to take that step deprive the decision-maker of jurisdiction, rendering the subsequent decision unlawful? The modern approach to this question (the seeds of which were sown by Lord Hailsham LC in *London and Clydeside Estates Ltd* v. *Aberdeen District Council* [1980] 1 WLR 182) is to acknowledge that the use of imperative language by Parliament does not necessarily mean that it intends non-compliance to deprive the decision-maker of jurisdiction. What, then, might lead a court to conclude that—words like 'must' and 'shall' notwithstanding—Parliament did not intend non-compliance to result in a lack of jurisdiction? The case law shows that three factors, in particular, are likely to influence the courts.

First, *the intention of Parliament* regarding the effect of non-compliance may be apparent from the structure of the relevant legislation. *Secretary of State for the Home Department* v. *E* [2007] UKHL 47, [2008] 1 AC 499 was concerned with the power of the Home Secretary to impose 'control orders' on suspected terrorists under the Prevention of Terrorism Act 2005. Such an order had been imposed on E, but the Home Secretary had failed to comply with s 8(2), which says that before a control order is created, the Minister 'must consult the chief officer of the police force about whether there is evidence available that could realistically be used for the purposes of a prosecution of the individual for an offence relating to terrorism' (the thinking being that the criminal justice system should be the first line of defence against the risk posed by suspected terrorists). The House of Lords held that Parliament had set out in s 2(1) of the Act the conditions precedent to the making of a control order, and that the location of the consultation requirement in a separate section indicated that Parliament had not intended it to constitute a jurisdictional precondition.

Second, the Court of Appeal emphasized in *R v. Immigration Appeal Tribunal, ex parte Jeyeanthan* [2000] 1 WLR 354 (which decision was endorsed by Lord Steyn, whose speech commanded the unqualified support of Lords Cooke and Clyde, in *Attorney General's Reference (No 3 of 1999)* [2001] 2 AC 91 at 117) the importance of considering *the consequences of non-compliance*. The more trivial those consequences, the less likely it is that Parliament intended non-compliance with the relevant statutory requirement to deprive the decision-maker of jurisdiction. Thus, in *Jeyeanthan*, the Court concluded that the Home Secretary's failure, in seeking leave to appeal against an asylum decision, to use the form prescribed by the relevant secondary legislation did not affect the validity of the ensuing appellate proceedings. Although the Court considered that the Home Secretary's failure to make a 'declaration of truth', as required by the legislation, meant that he had not substantially complied with the requirements as laid down, it concluded that this omission did not deprive the appellate tribunal of jurisdiction. Lord Woolf MR explained (at 366) that

> [i]f in these appeals you concentrate on what the Rules intend should be the just *consequence* of non-compliance with the statutory requirements as to the contents of an application for leave to appeal I would suggest the answer to these appeals is obvious. Neither [of the asylum seekers concerned in this case] have in any way been affected by the omission. It was as far as they were concerned a pure technicality. Other than to discipline the Secretary of State there could be no reason well after the event to treat his successful applications for leave as a nullity.

Third, the courts are also prepared to consider *the consequences that would follow if non-compliance were treated as fatal to legality*. For instance, in *Khakh v. Independent Safeguarding Authority* [2013] EWCA Civ 1341, the appellant, who had committed serious criminal offences, was 'listed', meaning that his name was added to the lists of people barred from certain activities involving children or vulnerable adults. However, the statutory requirement that he be notified that he would be listed had not been fulfilled. In holding that this did not undermine the legality of the listing decisions, Elias LJ said that

> the scheme is designed to protect children and vulnerable adults, and I cannot believe that Parliament can have intended that a failure by the judge should undermine that vital public objective. If the appellant were right, the judge's error would relieve a criminal from the consequences of listing even though that potentially puts children and/or vulnerable persons at risk

The approach adopted by the courts in this area means that it is not possible to say that failure to comply with a given statutory condition will always or will never deprive a decision-maker of jurisdiction: the legal effects attached to non-compliance turn, at least in large part, upon a contextual assessment of the consequences of non-compliance and/ or the implications that would follow if non-compliance were treated as fatal to legality. This highly pragmatic approach is difficult to account for in analytical terms, but presumably the position is that non-compliance is to be characterized as a jurisdictional error when significant injustice results and as a non-jurisdictional error otherwise. At least where the error involves misconstruction of the statute, this may be related to the view expounded in *Page* according to which non-material errors are not to be regarded as jurisdictional in nature.

2.7 Concluding remarks

Jurisdiction is a—if not *the*—pivotal concept in English administrative law. It is, however, as this chapter has shown, a concept that is far from straightforward. Indeed, the centrality ascribed by modern administrative law theory to the notion of jurisdiction itself forms part of the problem: the concept is pressed into service in a variety of ways, thus forcing it to assume a chameleonic character. Understood in its most expansive sense, the concept of jurisdiction lies at the root of every condition that applies to and constrains administrative authority. Viewed thus, every reviewable administrative error is a jurisdictional error, meaning that every chapter in this book that is concerned with the various grounds of judicial review is concerned with 'jurisdiction', such that this chapter has been concerned only with a subset of the things that can cause decision-makers to exceed their jurisdiction.

Why, then, single out the things addressed in this chapter as being particularly relevant to the idea of jurisdiction? The issues considered in this chapter have—at least until quite recently—tended to be approached by the courts through the lens of jurisdiction in a way that other matters have not. In particular, the extent of the courts' intervention in respect of questions of law and what we have called 'application questions' has traditionally tended to be modulated by leveraging the distinction between jurisdictional and non-jurisdictional errors. The concept (or at least the language) of jurisdiction has not played an equivalent role in relation to other grounds of judicial review: 'non-jurisdictional breaches of natural justice' and 'non-jurisdictional unreasonable decisions' are, for instance, concepts alien to English administrative law.

Perhaps paradoxically, however, we have seen in this chapter that—particularly in relation to questions of law—the jurisdictional lens has, in a sense, been discarded. Of course, the concept of jurisdiction remains pertinent in that the general principle is now that all errors of law are 'jurisdictional'. However, the concept of jurisdiction now does little, if any, work in this area: if all errors of law really are jurisdictional, then—unless courts wish to substitute judgement in respect of every question of law—some other mechanism must be found by which to delimit the extent of judicial intervention. The distinction between jurisdictional and non-jurisdictional errors of law has thus been replaced, at least to some extent, by other distinctions—for instance, between questions of law and fact, and between cases that, in exercise of their discretion, reviewing courts are and are not prepared to entertain—that have the capacity to modulate the relationship between the decision-maker and the reviewing court.

This serves to underline a fundamental truth about this area of administrative law—and, indeed, about administrative law more generally. The distinction between jurisdictional and non-jurisdictional errors of law reflected a judicial attempt to negotiate a pervasive and enduring dilemma concerning the allocation of authority between courts and decision-makers. To what extent should the reviewing court proceed on the basis that legislation has delimited the authority of the decision-maker, and that constitutional principle dictates that the court must see that the scope of that authority is not exceeded? And to what extent should the reviewing court be sensitive to the notion that the decision-maker—whether because the legislature so intended, or because of sound reasons of policy or constitutional principle—might or should itself play some role in shaping the contours of its authority? That these questions are policy-laden is a fact that is difficult to contest but which has often been obscured by the language and conceptual apparatus of 'jurisdiction'. In the light of this, the retreat from jurisdictional analysis might be viewed as a good thing if it clears the way for more direct and explicit judicial engagement with underlying issues of policy and principle. However, whether that possibility will be realized remains an open question. That is so not least because of the judicial willingness evidenced by the Supreme Court's decision in *Jones* to treat a porous boundary between questions of law and fact as the conceptualist successor to the now-spent distinction between jurisdictional and non-jurisdictional questions of law. Much has changed in this area over the last 50 years; but many of the underlying difficulties that have served to problematize this aspect of administrative law remain.

FURTHER RESOURCES

Allan, 'Doctrine and Theory in Administrative Law: An Elusive Quest for the Limits of Jurisdiction' [2003] *PL* 429

Beatson, 'The Scope of Judicial Review for Error of Law' (1984) 4 *OJLS* 22

Craig, 'Judicial Review, Appeal and Factual Error' [2004] *PL* 788

Daly, 'Deference on Questions of Law' (2011) 74 *MLR* 694

Endicott, 'Questions of Law' (1998) 114 *LQR* 292

Forsyth and Dring, 'The Final Frontier: The Emergence of Material Error of Fact as a Ground of Judicial Review' in Forsyth *et al* (eds), *Effective Judicial Review: A Cornerstone of Good Governance* (Oxford 2010)

Hare, 'The Separation of Powers and Judicial Review for Error of Law' in Forsyth and Hare (eds), *The Golden Metwand and the Crooked Cord* (Oxford 1998)

Gordon, 'The Relation of Facts to Jurisdiction' (1929) 45 *LQR* 458

Gordon, 'Jurisdictional Fact: An Answer' (1966) 82 *LQR* 515

Gould, '*Anisminic* and Jurisdictional Review' [1970] *PL* 358

Wilberg and Elliott, 'Deference on Questions of Law: A Survey of Taggart's Contribution and Themes in the Wider Literature' in Wilberg and Elliott (eds), *The Scope and Intensity of Substantive Review: Traversing Taggart's Rainbow* (Oxford 2015)

Williams, 'When is an Error Not an Error? Reform of Jurisdictional Review of Error of Law and Fact' [2007] *PL* 793

3 THE STATUS OF UNLAWFUL ADMINISTRATIVE ACTION

3.1 Void or voidable?

Administrative action may be unlawful for a variety of reasons. For example, the decision-maker may, as we saw in the last chapter, make a jurisdictional error of law by misinterpreting some statutory provision; it might act for an improper purpose (see ch 7) or under the (apparent) influence of bias (see ch 9); or it may act procedurally unfairly (see ch 10) or unreasonably (see ch 8). In all of these situations, the decision reached or action undertaken will be *unlawful*. But what does this mean? What is the status of such action? And what is the position of an individual in relation to whom an unlawful decision is taken: can he ignore it, because it is unlawful, or must he obey it until or unless it is set aside by a court?

At the root of these questions lies one fundamental issue: is unlawful administrative action void or voidable? In this chapter, we examine in some detail what those terms mean. However, to begin with, we adopt the following working definitions (which will be refined as the chapter progresses). If action is *voidable*, then it is to be regarded as perfectly valid unless and until it is set aside by a competent court; when it is set aside, it is quashed prospectively, meaning that it is treated as having existed until it was quashed. Therefore, if no competent person ever challenges the decision, it is for all practical purposes indistinguishable from a valid decision. However, if unlawful action is *void*, then it is invalid simply by virtue of its unlawfulness. It does not, in strict logic, need to be quashed, because as a matter of law it never existed in the first place: as is sometimes (redundantly) said, it is void '*ab initio*' (from the beginning).

3.1.1 The practical argument

The 'void or voidable?' question presents a difficult dilemma. Although the orthodox view is that unlawful administrative action should be regarded as void, rigid adherence to this view can cause great practical difficulties. In particular, it is often assumed that if a particular act is found to be void, all subsequent acts taken in reliance upon it will also be void. A 'domino effect' thus ensues: the failure of the first act causing all subsequent acts to fall—with potentially chaotic consequences.

Under the influence of these considerations (among others), Lord Denning concluded in *Director of Public Prosecutions* v. *Head* [1959] AC 83 that the unlawful action at stake in that case was voidable, not void. The defendant had been convicted under s 56(1)(a) of the Mental Deficiency Act 1913 of having sexual relations with a woman who, because of her mental condition, was under the care of an institution. However, the Secretary of State's orders concerning the institutionalization of the woman had been issued in the absence of certificates of 'mental deficiency' which fully complied with the relevant statutory requirements. The defendant argued that this made the original institutionalization order and all subsequent continuation orders void—and that he could not therefore have committed the offence because the woman was not legally under institutional care at the relevant time. Although the conviction was in fact quashed, this particular line of argument was strongly rejected by Lord Denning at 112 (who was in the minority in expressing this view; on the majority view, see Lord Irvine's remarks in the excerpt from the *Boddington* case at 3.1.2):

> The vital question to my mind is therefore: Was the original order absolutely void or was it only voidable? If the order had been outside the jurisdiction of the Secretary of State altogether, it would have been a nullity and void; see *The Case of the Marshalsea* (1612) 10 Co. Rep. 68b at 76a. But that is not this case. The most that appears here is that the Secretary of State—acting within his jurisdiction—exercised that jurisdiction erroneously. That makes his order voidable and not void. It is said that he made the order on no evidence or on insufficient materials. So be it. His error is a wrong exercise of a jurisdiction which he has, and not a usurpation of a jurisdiction which he has not; see *R v. Nat Bell Liquors Ltd* [1922] 2 A.C. 128 at 151 by Lord Sumner. If that error appears on the face of the record—as it is said to do here—it renders the order liable to be quashed ..., but it does not make it a nullity; see *Reg. v. Medical Appeal Tribunal, Ex parte Gilmore* [1957] 1 Q.B. 574 at 588 by Parker LJ. Unless and until it is so quashed, it is to be regarded as good. It is, moreover, sufficient to support all the continuation orders made on the faith of it. Even if the original order should be set aside, the continuation orders would remain good: for it is a general rule that when a voidable transaction is avoided, it does not invalidate intermediate transactions which were made on the basis that it was good; see *De Reneville* v. *De Reneville* [1948] P. 100 at 111–112 by Lord Greene MR, and *Reg.* v. *Algar* [1954] 1 Q.B. 279 at 287 by Lord Goddard CJ. I would uphold therefore the contention of the Attorney-General that, whatever the position of the original order, the continuation orders were good.

Lord Denning's rejection of the argument that the original order was void was clearly influenced by his concern that reaching such a conclusion would wreak administrative chaos: if the certificates fell, then the whole superstructure of administrative actions based upon those certificates would collapse too.

3.1.2 The theoretical argument

Lord Denning's views on voidness were also informed by his underlying theoretical perspective. He concluded that the Secretary of State had committed an error which appeared on the face of the record—an exceptional (and now practically defunct) species of error which, as we saw in ch 2, was characterized as an error *within* jurisdiction which was nevertheless reviewable. It is clear (as Wade (1967) 83 *LQR* 499 at 522 recognized) that if the error in *Head* was rightly characterized as non-jurisdictional, then it was acceptable for

Lord Denning to treat the decision as voidable. Today, however, the dominant view is that *any* reviewable error committed by a decision-maker will lead to an excess (in the broad sense) of 'jurisdiction' (or power). That, in turn, might be thought to imply that all unlawful administrative acts are void on account of their having never had any legal basis—a matter that is considered in the next case.

Boddington v. *British Transport Police* [1999] 2 AC 143

House of Lords

Byelaw 20 of the British Railways Board's Byelaws 1965 (made under s 67(1) of the Transport Act 1962) made it an offence to (*inter alia*) smoke on a train where 'no smoking' signs were 'exhibited in a conspicuous position'. A train operator, Network South Central, decided to prohibit smoking throughout all of its trains and displayed notices to that effect. The defendant, while in a carriage in which no smoking signs were prominently displayed, smoked a cigarette and refused to extinguish it upon being asked to do so. The defendant argued that byelaw 20 did not empower the train operator to adopt a policy of *completely* banning smoking; that its decision to post notices in every carriage was consequently *ultra vires*, and that he had therefore committed no offence because he had not smoked in a carriage in which a *valid* notice was displayed. These arguments were rejected by the stipendiary magistrate, and the defendant was convicted of an offence under byelaw 20; he appealed unsuccessfully to the Divisional Court, and thereafter to the House of Lords. The following extract is concerned only with the status of the 'no smoking' notices. Only if the notices were void, in the sense set out at the beginning of the chapter, could the defendant raise the matter by way of defence (or 'collaterally challenge' them—a term explored further at 3.4). For further extracts from this case, see 3.4.2 and 3.4.3.

Lord Irvine LC

… In *Director of Public Prosecutions* v. *Head* [1959] A.C. 83 [on which see 3.1.1] … Lord Denning, who was in the minority, was of the view that the order was valid as at the date of the alleged offence, so that the alleged offence was made out …, even although the order was voidable and therefore liable to be quashed … The majority, however, did not accept that the order was voidable rather than void, but in any event doubted that, even if it was to be characterised as voidable rather than void, a defendant could not raise the matter by way of defence. As Lord Somervell of Harrow put it, at p. 104: 'Is a man to be sent to prison on the basis that an order is a good order when the court knows it would be set aside if proper proceedings were taken? I doubt it.'

[After endorsing the majority view in *Head*, his Lordship continued:] In my judgment the views of the majority in [that case] have acquired still greater force in the light of the development of the basic principles of public law since [it] was decided. Lord Denning had dissented on the basis of the historic distinction between acts which were ultra vires ('outside the jurisdiction of the Secretary of State'), which he accepted were nullities and void, and errors of law on the face of the relevant record, which rendered the relevant instrument voidable rather than void. He felt able to assign the order in question to the latter category. But in 1969, the decision of your Lordships' House in *Anisminic Ltd.* v. *Foreign Compensation Commission* [1969] 2 A.C. 147 made obsolete the historic distinction between errors of law on the face of the record and other errors of law. It did so by extending the doctrine of ultra vires, so that any misdirection in law would render the relevant decision ultra vires and a nullity: see *Reg.* v. *Hull University Visitor, Ex parte Page* [1993] A.C. 682, 701–702, *per* Lord Browne-Wilkinson (with whom Lord Keith of Kinkel and Lord Griffiths agreed, at p 692), citing the speech of Lord Diplock in *O'Reilly* v. *Mackman* [1983] 2 A.C. 237, 278. Thus, today, the old distinction between void and voidable acts on which Lord Denning relied in *Director of Public Prosecutions* v. *Head* [1959] A.C. 83 no longer applies. This much is clear from *the Anisminic* case [1969] 2 A.C. 147 and these later authorities.

... [In *Anisminic,* Lord Reid] made it clear that all forms of public law challenge to a decision have the same effect, to render it a nullity: see especially p. 171B–F. (Also see pp 195–196, *per* Lord Pearce and p 207D–H, *per* Lord Wilberforce.) The decision of the Commission was wrong in law, and therefore a nullity, rather than a 'determination' within the protection of the ouster clause: see pp 170–171.

Thus the reservation of Lord Somervell in *Director of Public Prosecutions* v. *Head* [1959] A.C. 83, 104 (with which the majority allied themselves) whether the order of the Secretary of State could be described as voidable has been vindicated by subsequent developments. It is clear, in the light of *Anisminic* and the later authorities, that the Secretary of State's order in *Director of Public Prosecutions* v. *Head* would now certainly be regarded as a nullity (ie as void ab initio), even if it were to be analysed as an error of law on the face of the record. Equally, the order would be regarded as void ab initio if it had been made in bad faith, or as a result of the Secretary of State taking into account an irrelevant, or ignoring a relevant, consideration—that is, matters not appearing on the face of the record, but having to be established by evidence.

... In *Bugg* v. *Director of Public Prosecutions* [1993] Q.B. 473 the Divisional Court ... expressed the view, at p. 493, that 'except in the "flagrant" and "outrageous" case a statutory order, such as a byelaw, remains effective until it is quashed.' Three authorities were cited which were said to support this approach: *London & Clydeside Estates Ltd* v. *Aberdeen District Council* [1980] 1 W.L.R. 182, 189–190 in the speech of Lord Hailsham of St Marylebone LC; *Smith* v. *East Elloe Rural District Council* [1956] A.C. 736, 769–770, in the speech of Lord Radcliffe and *F Hoffmann-La Roche & Co AG* v. *Secretary of State for Trade and Industry* [1975] A.C. 295, 366, in the speech of Lord Diplock. This approach was then elevated by the Divisional Court into a rule that byelaws which are on their face invalid or are patently unreasonable (termed 'substantive' invalidity) may be called in question by way of defence in criminal proceedings, whereas byelaws which are invalid because of some defect in the procedure by which they came to be made (termed 'procedural' invalidity) may not be called in question in such proceedings, so that a person might be convicted of an offence under them even if the byelaws were later quashed in other proceedings.

Strong reservations about the decision of the Divisional Court in *Bugg* v. *Director of Public Prosecutions* [1993] Q.B. 473 have recently been expressed by this House in *R* v. *Wicks* [1998] A.C. 92. I have reached the conclusion that the time has come to hold that it was wrongly decided.

I am bound to say that I do not think that the three authorities to which I have referred support the position as stated in *Bugg's* case [1993] Q.B. 473. In my judgment Lord Diplock's speech in the *F Hoffmann-La Roche* case [1995] A.C. 295, when read as a whole, makes it clear that subordinate legislation which is quashed is deprived of any legal effect at all, and that is so whether the invalidity arises from defects appearing on its face or in the procedure adopted in its promulgation. Lord Diplock himself cited, at p 366, the speech of Lord Radcliffe in *Smith* v. *East Elloe Rural District Council* [1956] A.C. 736, 769–770 and regarded him as saying no more about the presumption of validity than he (Lord Diplock) was saying. I agree with that view.

... In my judgment the reasoning of the Divisional Court in *Bugg's* case, suggesting two classes of legal invalidity of subordinate legislation, is contrary both to the *Anisminic* case and the subsequent decisions of this House to which I have referred. The *Anisminic* decision established, contrary to previous thinking that there might be error of law within jurisdiction, that there was a single category of errors of law, all of which rendered a decision ultra vires. No distinction is to be drawn between a patent (or substantive) error of law or a latent (or procedural) error of law. An ultra vires act or subordinate legislation is unlawful simpliciter and, if the presumption in favour of its legality is overcome by a litigant before a court of competent jurisdiction, is of no legal effect whatsoever.

The Divisional Court in *Bugg's* case [1993] Q.B. 473 themselves drew attention to Lord Denning's dissenting speech in *Director of Public Prosecutions* v. *Head* and, whilst avowing that 'The distinction between orders which are void and voidable is now clearly not part of our law' identified his approach as interesting, because Lord Denning 'was drawing a distinction, as we are seeking to do, between different types of invalidity:' see p 496G. However, the distinction which Lord Denning drew is one which was made redundant by the decision in the *Anisminic* case, in which all categories of unlawfulness were treated as equivalent and as having the same effect ...

Lord Browne-Wilkinson

... The Lord Chancellor attaches importance to the consideration that an invalid bye-law is and always has been a nullity. The byelaw will necessarily have been found to be ultra vires; therefore it is said it is a nullity having no legal effect. I adhere to my view that the juristic basis of judicial review is the doctrine of ultra vires. But I am far from satisfied that an ultra vires act is incapable of having any legal consequence during the period between the doing of that act and the recognition of its invalidity by the court. During that period people will have regulated their lives on the basis that the act is valid. The subsequent recognition of its invalidity cannot rewrite history as to all the other matters done in the meantime in reliance on its validity. The status of an unlawful act during the period before it is quashed is a matter of great contention and of great difficulty ...

I prefer to express no view at this stage on those difficult points ...

Lord Slynn

... I consider that the result of allowing a collateral challenge in proceedings before courts of criminal jurisdiction can be reached without it being necessary in this case to say that if an act or byelaw is invalid it must be held to have been invalid from the outset for all purposes and that no lawful consequences can flow from it. This may be the logical result and will no doubt sometimes be the position but courts have had to grapple with the problem of reconciling the logical result with the reality that much have may have been done on the basis that an administrative act or a byelaw was valid. The unscrambling may produce more serious difficulties than the invalidity. The European Court of Justice has dealt with the problem by ruling that its declaration of invalidity should only operate for the benefit of the parties to the actual case or of those who had begun proceedings for a declaration of invalidity before the courts' judgment. In our jurisdiction the effect of invalidity may not be relied on if limitation periods have expired or if the court in its discretion refuses relief, albeit considering that the act is invalid. These situations are of course different from those where a court has pronounced subordinate legislation or an administrative act to be unlawful or where the presumption in favour of their legality has been overruled by a court of competent jurisdiction. But even in these cases I consider that the question whether the acts or byelaws are to be treated as having at no time had any effect in law is not one which has been fully explored and is not one on which it is necessary to rule in this appeal and I prefer to express no view upon it. The cases referred to in *Wade and Forsyth, Administrative Law* 7th ed. (1997), pp. 323–324, 342–344 lead the authors to the view that nullity is relative rather than an absolute concept (p. 343) and that 'void' is 'meaningless in any absolute sense. Its meaning is relative:' This may all be rather imprecise but the law in this area has developed in a pragmatic way on a case by case basis ...

Lord Steyn

... Leaving to one side the separate topic of judicial review of non-legal powers exercised by non statutory bodies, I see no reason to depart from the orthodox view that ultra vires is 'the central principle of administrative law' as *Wade and Forsyth, Administrative Law*, 7th ed., p. 41 described it. Lord Browne-Wilkinson observed in *Reg.* v. *Hull University Visitor, Ex parte Page* [1993] A.C. 682, 701:

'The fundamental principle [of judicial review] is that the courts will intervene to ensure that the powers of public decision-making bodies are exercised lawfully. In all cases ... this intervention ... is based on the proposition that such powers have been conferred on the decision-maker on the underlying assumption that the powers are to be exercised only within the jurisdiction conferred, in accordance with fair procedures and, in a *Wednesbury* sense ... reasonably. If the decision maker exercises his powers outside the jurisdiction conferred, in a manner which is procedurally irregular or is *Wednesbury* unreasonable, he is acting ultra vires his powers and therefore unlawfully. ...' [On '*Wednesbury* unreasonableness', see 8.2.1.]

This is the essential constitutional underpinning of the statute based part of our administrative law. Nevertheless, I accept the reality that an unlawful byelaw is a fact and that it may in certain circumstances have legal consequences. The best explanation that I have seen is by Dr. Forsyth who summarised the position as follows in 'The Metaphysic of Nullity, Invalidity, Conceptual Reasoning and the Rule of Law,' at p. 159 [on which see further at 3.3.2]:

'[I]t has been argued that unlawful administrative acts are void in law. But they clearly exist in fact and they often appear to be valid; and those unaware of their invalidity may take decisions and act on the assumption that these acts are valid. When this happens the validity of these later acts depends upon the legal powers of the second actor. *The crucial issue to be determined is whether that second actor has legal power to act validly notwithstanding the invalidity of the first act.* And it is determined by a[n] analysis of the law against the background of the familiar proposition that an unlawful act is void.' (Emphasis supplied.)

That seems to me a more accurate summary of the law as it has developed than the sweeping proposition in *Bugg's* case ...

Lord Hoffmann

... I have had the advantage of reading in draft the speeches of my noble and learned friends, Lord Irvine of Lairg L.C. and Lord Steyn. For the reasons they have given I, too, would dismiss the appeal.

QUESTION

- Explain how their Lordships' views as to the status of unlawful administrative action differed in *Boddington*. Which view, in your opinion, is preferable?

Certain differences of view notwithstanding, all of their Lordships in *Boddington* agreed (as we explain at 3.4) that the defendant could raise the alleged invalidity of the notices in his defence; all, therefore, appeared to subscribe to the view that unlawful administrative action is void rather than merely voidable since, if the notices had only been voidable, then they would have been valid unless or until they were quashed by a competent court.

3.1.3 Four more recent cases

Four post-*Boddington* decisions are worth noting. While the first three affirm the general view adopted in *Boddington*—that unlawful administrative acts are void—the fourth illustrates the preparedness of the courts, at least in certain circumstances, to circumvent or obscure the implications of that view.

McLaughlin v. *Cayman Islands* [2007] UKPC 50, [2007] 1 WLR 2839 concerned the unlawful dismissal in 1999 of a government officer in breach of natural justice and of relevant regulations. The Cayman Islands Court of Appeal held that he was entitled by way of relief only to damages, but the claimant argued that the dismissal was void and hence legally ineffective; that he had therefore remained an office-holder throughout; and that he should receive eight years' worth of salary arrears. The Privy Council had no hesitation in holding that the appeal court had erred. Lord Bingham, giving the Board's judgment, said (at [14]):

> It is a settled principle of law that if a public authority purports to dismiss the holder of a public office in excess of its powers, or in breach of natural justice, or unlawfully (categories which over-lap), the dismissal is, as between the public authority and the office-holder, null, void and without legal effect, at any rate once a court of competent jurisdiction so declares or orders. Thus the office-holder remains in office, entitled to the remuneration attaching to such office, so long as he remains ready, willing and able to render the service required of him, until his tenure of office is lawfully brought to an end by resignation or lawful dismissal.

The same view appeared to prevail in *Secretary of State for the Home Department* v. *JJ* [2007] UKHL 45, [2008] 1 AC 385 concerning a 'control order' imposed on a suspected terrorist under the Prevention of Terrorism Act 2005. The House of Lords concluded that the Secretary of State had exceeded his powers by doing that which the Act specifically forbade—*viz* impos-ing upon the claimant restrictions amounting to a deprivation of liberty within the meaning of Article 5 of the European Convention on Human Rights. The question then arose whether the order should be quashed or whether their Lordships should exercise their power under s 3(12)(c) of the Act to 'give directions to the Secretary of State for the revocation of the order or for the modification of the obligations it imposes'. The Minister wished the court to adopt the latter approach, so as to avoid any gap between the quashing of the original order and the making of a new, less draconian one, but a majority of the Law Lords held that the exercise of their s 3(12)(c) power was logically impossible. Lord Bingham (at [26]) endorsed the view of Richards J ([2006] EWHC 1623 (Admin) at [92]) that:

> A direction to revoke or to modify carries with it the implication that there is in existence an order which was lawfully made by the Secretary of State, but which has been found to be flawed for some reason. The short answer to the Secretary of State's submission that he should be directed to modify these orders is that since he had no power to make them in the first place, there is simply nothing to revoke.

A similar argument on behalf of the government was given equally short shrift by the Supreme Court in the *Ahmed* case. In *Ahmed* v. *HM Treasury (No 1)* [2010] UKSC 2, [2010] 2 AC 534, the Court held that certain administrative measures providing for the freezing of suspected terrorists' assets were *ultra vires*. The government then asked the Court to suspend the quashing of the measures so as to ensure that the assets would remain frozen until such time as emergency primary legislation could be enacted. In *Ahmed* v. *HM Treasury (No 2)* [2010] UKSC 5, [2010] 2 AC 534, that request was refused. Applying the same logic as that which the majority in *JJ* found compelling, Lord Phillips, giving the majority judgment in *Ahmed (No 2)*, said:

> [7] Mr Swift [counsel for HM Treasury] urged the court to suspend the operation of its judgment because of the effect that the suspension would have on the conduct of third parties. He submit-ted that the banks, in particular, would be unlikely to release frozen funds while the court's orders remained suspended. I comment that if suspension were to have this effect this would only be because the third parties wrongly believed that it affected their legal rights and obligations.

[8] The ends sought by Mr Swift might well be thought desirable, but I do not consider that they justify the means that he proposes. This court should not lend itself to a procedure that is designed to obfuscate the effect of its judgment. Accordingly, I would not suspend the operation of any part of the court's order.

On this analysis, suspending (or simply not issuing) a quashing order would serve merely to disguise legal reality, because the unlawful administrative order was, and always had been, void—a position that would obtain irrespective of any remedial steps taken (or not taken) by the Court.

Ahmed (No 2) and *JJ* are, however, difficult to square with the Supreme Court's decision in *Salvesen* v. *Riddell* [2013] UKSC 22, 2013 SC (UKSC) 236, in which it was held that the Scottish Parliament had exceeded its competence by enacting legislation that conflicted with the European Convention on Human Rights. In such circumstances, s 102 of the Scotland Act 1998 allows a court to make an order 'suspending the effect of the decision [that the legislation is outside devolved competence] for any period and on any conditions to allow the defect to be corrected'. The Court exercised this power so that the impugned legislation could remain applicable until fresh legislation could be enacted—which is exactly what the Treasury had asked the Supreme Court to do in *Ahmed (No 2)* in respect of regulations made outwith executive competence. Of course, there is an important difference between the two cases: in *Salvesen* there was a specific statutory power to suspend the effect of the court's decision, whereas in *Ahmed (No 2)* there was not. However, acknowledging this difference only gets us so far in trying to work out how the two cases relate to one another. After all, the very fact that remedies in judicial review are discretionary in itself demonstrates that courts can choose not to issue relief: the discrepancy between *Ahmed (No 2)* and *Salvesen* cannot therefore be explained away on the ground that legislation permitted the court to do something in the latter case which, in the absence of such legislation, it could not do in the former. Moreover, any attempt to distinguish *Salvesen* on the ground that the court had a specific statutory power to suspend the effect of its decision founders when account is taken of the fact that the existence of a comparable power in *JJ* did not persuade the House of Lords in that case to treat the *ultra vires* control order as anything other than void.

Where does this leave us? The weight of authority—including *Boddington, McLaughlin, JJ*, and *Ahmed (No 2)*—is consistent with the view that unlawful administrative and legislative action is void, and the better view is that *Salvesen* does not dislodge or cast doubt upon that established view. Indeed, that view was endorsed, in his dissenting judgment in *Ahmed (No 2)*, by Lord Hope—the impugned control orders, he said (at [18]), were '*ultra vires* and void from the moment that the Orders were made'—who went on to deliver the judgment of the Supreme Court in *Salvesen*. This suggests that *Salvesen* and *Ahmed (No 2)* fall to be distinguished in one of two ways.

The first possibility is that they can be distinguished on the same ground as that upon which the majority and minority views in *Ahmed (No 2)* itself can be distinguished. Lord Hope dissented in *Ahmed (No 2)* not because he thought the control orders were other than void, but because he considered that reasons of policy—including (at [22]) the 'national interest'—justified suspending relief. As to Lord Neuberger's concern that suspension would misrepresent the true legal position—the implication of suspension being that the existence or otherwise of a quashing order makes some legal difference—Lord Hope (at [24]) acknowledged this 'risk' but did not consider it to be a 'decisive factor in deciding where the balance of advantage lies'. This suggests that the Supreme Court in *Salvesen* did not place in doubt the legal principle for which *Ahmed (No 2)* and the other cases considered earlier stand; rather, the Court took the view that the 'balance of advantage' favoured the suspension of its decision—an exercise of remedial discretion that did nothing to breathe legal life into the *ultra vires* legislative provisions. There is, however, a second possibility—that s 102 of the Scotland Act 1998 modifies the default position, such that Scottish legislation that is *ultra vires* is, exceptionally, voidable rather than void. Precisely this analysis is advanced by Forsyth [2013] JR 360 at 377, although it does invite the question why the legislation in *JJ* was not also interpreted as modifying the default position.

QUESTION

- Forsyth (*op cit*) suggests that the inference that legislation displaces the default position regarding the voidness of unlawful administrative acts might more readily be drawn when the power in question is (as in *Salvesen*) a power to enact 'primary' legislation. Is this a defensible ground upon which to attempt to rationalize the different approaches adopted in *JJ* and *Salvesen*?

3.2 The nature of voidness

It is one thing to say that unlawful administrative action is 'void'. But exactly what does that mean? The beginnings of an answer to that question are implicit in what has already been said: if an administrative act is void, it can be treated as having never existed, such that (for instance) whether it is quashed makes no difference to the legal position. Indeed, the notion of collateral challenge—whereby courts that lack jurisdiction to quash unlawful administrative acts can simply ignore them—is premised upon this existential sense of voidness. It is not, however, the case that courts never take any account of unlawful administrative acts. It follows that if we are to adhere to the view that all such acts are void, that must mean something more subtle than that such acts are wholly and invariably treated as legally non-existent. In this section, we examine two respects in which the existence of unlawful acts may be judicially acknowledged.

3.2.1 The presumption of validity

The 'presumption of validity' refers to the fact that administrative acts are often assumed to be lawful and valid, even though some turn out to be unlawful. The presumption operates on two levels.

First, it is a descriptive phenomenon which reflects the fact that people will generally proceed on the basis that official action is valid. This aspect of the presumption of validity may, as noted at 3.1.3, have been leveraged by the Supreme Court in *Salvesen*, which proceeded on the assumption that by suspending its decision as to the unlawfulness of the legislative provisions in question, people would in general continue to treat those provisions as extant.

Second, the presumption of validity operates normatively in the sense that it can affect the outcome of judicial proceedings. Take, for instance, proceedings in which interim—or 'interlocutory'—injunctions are sought. *Hoffmann-La Roche and Co AG* v. *Secretary of State for Trade and Industry* [1975] AC 295 was concerned with a statutory instrument—a piece of delegated legislation—limiting the prices that the appellant could charge for certain drugs that it marketed. The appellant sought a declaration that the legislation was *ultra vires*. Meanwhile, pending a final judicial decision about the lawfulness of the statutory instrument, the Secretary of State sought an interim injunction restraining the appellant from charging prices higher than those specified in the legislation. The stakes were high, as Lord Reid noted (at 340):

> In the present case it is common ground that a long time—it may be years—will elapse before a decision can be given. During that period if an interim injunction is granted the appellants will only be able to make the charges permitted by the order. So if in the end the order is annulled that loss will be the difference between those charges and those which they could have made if the order had never been made. And they may not be able to recover any part of that loss from anyone. It is said that the loss might amount to £8m.

As to whether an interim injunction should be granted, the presumption of validity played a major role. Lord Reid said (at 341) that 'an order made under statutory authority is as much the law of the land as an Act of Parliament unless and until it has been found to be ultra vires'. It followed that it was for the appellant to show why an injunction requiring it to abide by the relevant order should not be issued. Lord Reid concluded (at 342) that because the appellants had 'completely failed to convince me that they have a strong *prima facie* case' the injunction in their favour should not be issued.

It may at first appear that adopting the presumption of validity implies that unlawful action is merely voidable. However, this does not follow. It is perfectly possible to assume, as a working hypothesis, that administrative action is valid, while at the same time accepting that, if it is found to be unlawful, then it is void. Of course, this means that action which was presumed to be lawful will turn out to be void, meaning that it was *always* unlawful. This, however, presents no difficulty: the presumption of validity is nothing more than an assumption, and assumptions can be, and sometimes are, wrong. It follows that the presumption of validity can be reconciled with the view that unlawful administrative action is void. This was recognized by Lord Hoffmann in *R* v. *Wicks* [1998] AC 92 at 115, who said that the presumption adopted in *Hoffmann-La Roche* was 'an evidential matter at the interlocutory stage'—a 'presumption [which] existed pending a final decision by the court' and which did not imply 'the sweeping proposition that subordinate legislation must be treated for all purposes as valid until set aside'.

3.2.2 The principle of legal relativity

In *Hoffmann-La Roche and Co AG* v. *Secretary of State for Trade and Industry* [1975] AC 295 at 365, Lord Diplock said:

> Under our legal system ... the courts as the judicial arm of government do not act on their own initiative. Their jurisdiction to determine that a statutory instrument is ultra vires does not arise until its validity is challenged in proceedings inter partes either brought by one party to enforce the law declared by the instrument against another party or brought by a party whose interests

are affected by the law so declared sufficiently directly to give him locus standi to initiate proceedings to challenge the validity of the instrument. Unless there is such challenge and, if there is, until it has been upheld by a judgment of the court, the validity of the statutory instrument and the legality of acts done pursuant to the law declared by it are presumed. It would, however, be inconsistent with the doctrine of ultra vires as it has been developed in English law as a means of controlling abuse of power by the executive arm of government if the judgment of a court in proceedings properly constituted that a statutory instrument was ultra vires were to have any lesser consequence in law than to render the instrument incapable of ever having had any legal effect upon the rights or duties of the parties to the proceedings (cf *Ridge v. Baldwin* [1964] A.C. 40). Although such a decision is directly binding only as between the parties to the proceedings in which it was made, the application of the doctrine of precedent has the consequence of enabling the benefit of it to accrue to all other persons whose legal rights have been interfered with in reliance on the law which the statutory instrument purported to declare ...

My Lords, I think it leads to confusion to use such terms as 'voidable,' 'voidable ab initio,' 'void' or 'a nullity' as descriptive of the legal status of subordinate legislation alleged to be ultra vires for patent or for latent defects, before its validity has been pronounced on by a court of competent jurisdiction. These are concepts developed in the private law of contract which are ill-adapted to the field of public law. All that can usefully be said is that the presumption that subordinate legislation is intra vires prevails in the absence of rebuttal, and that it cannot be rebutted except by a party to legal proceedings in a court of competent jurisdiction who has locus standi to challenge the validity of the subordinate legislation in question.

All locus standi on the part of anyone to rebut the presumption of validity may be taken away completely or may be limited in point of time or otherwise by the express terms of the Act of Parliament which conferred the subordinate legislative power, though the courts lean heavily against a construction of the Act which would have this effect (cf *Anisminic Ltd.* v. *Foreign Compensation Commission* [1969] 2 A.C. 147). Such was the case, however, in the view of the majority of this House in *Smith* v. *East Elloe Rural District Council* [1956] A.C. 736, at any rate as respects invalidity on the ground of latent defects, so the compulsory purchase order sought to be challenged in the action had legal effect notwithstanding its potential invalidity. Furthermore, apart from express provision in the governing statute, locus standi to challenge the validity of subordinate legislation may be restricted, under the court's inherent power to control its own procedure, to a particular category of persons affected by the subordinate legislation, and if none of these persons chooses to challenge it the presumption of validity prevails. Such was the case in *Durayappah* v. *Fernando* [1967] 2 A.C. 337 where on an appeal from Ceylon, although the Privy Council was of opinion that an order of the Minister was ultra vires owing to a latent defect in the procedure prior to its being made, they nevertheless treated it as having legal effect because the party who sought to challenge it had, in their view, no locus standi to do so.

This amounts to what Wade calls 'a general principle of legal relativity' ((1967) 83 *LQR* 499 at 512; see also (1968) 84 *LQR* 95)—a notion that Lord Carnwath endorsed in *R (New London College)* v. *Secretary of State for the Home Department* [2013] UKSC 51, [2013] 1 WLR 2358 at [45]–[46]. Like the presumption of validity, Wade's principle of legal relativity is built upon the insight that people (whether individuals or officials) are prone (for prudential, among other, reasons) to treat unlawful administrative action as lawful until and unless it is held to be unlawful by a court. However, the principle of legal relativity goes further by acknowledging that circumstances will arise in which there is no (longer any) prospect of a court so holding, such that little option remains but to treat the unlawful measure as a lawful one. This might be so, for instance, if an ouster clause precludes judicial review or if the time limit for seeking judicial review has expired. Where, for such reasons, there is no possibility of a successful judicial challenge, it follows, as Wade (1967) 83 *LQR* 499 at 512 puts it, that

> what was void must be treated as valid, being now by law unchallengeable. It is fallacious to suppose that an act can be effective in law only if it has always had some element of validity from the beginning. However destitute of legitimacy at its birth, it is legitimated when the law refuses to assist anyone who wants to bastardise it. What cannot be disputed has to be accepted.

Wade is not here suggesting that unlawful administrative acts are merely voidable. What he is acknowledging, however, is that voidness, at least when viewed from a practical rather than a theoretical perspective, is a relative concept. On this view, then, an unlawful act may fall to be treated as valid if all relevant opportunities to establish its unlawfulness have evaporated. Forsyth (in Forsyth and Hare (eds), *The Golden Metwand and the Crooked Cord* (Oxford 1998) at 143) pithily describes Wade's analysis by saying that, on it, unlawful acts are '*theoretically* void, yet *functionally* voidable' (our emphasis).

Our discussion so far in this section has proceeded on the basis that voidness may be relative in the sense that it is sometimes possible and sometimes impossible to establish the unlawfulness of an administrative act. Where it is impossible, the unlawful act, to adapt Forsyth's language, becomes functionally valid. However, voidness can be relative in other, more subtle ways, as Feldman [2014] *CLJ* 275 at 292–3 explains:

> [Administrative] [a]cts and orders, as a matter of law, are not simply either valid or void. They operate in and on an often complex web of legal relationships, and their effects depend crucially on the precise nature of the legal rights, powers and obligations of each actor towards each other or to the world. A person's legal rights and liabilities depend on the rules governing that person's relationships with other people, some of which apply to limited subject-matter, people, times or places. To say that something (such as a decision, or detention) is lawful or unlawful, valid or void, is to use a shorthand expression which expresses in general terms the effect of what may be a complicated network of rules and interests governing complex relationships. For example, requirements to notify and consult people, whether the public generally or particular groups or individuals, are particularly likely to be treated as central to the decision-making scheme. Nevertheless, people who are not prejudiced by failure to notify or consult, or who were notified or consulted, will not subsequently be able to challenge the decision or rule on the basis that someone else suffered prejudice through not being notified or consulted. To this extent, the effect of such a flaw is directional; courts will protect only those who are prejudiced, and may fashion remedies accordingly, for example by treating the scheme as generally effective except in relation to those who suffered through not being notified or consulted.

There is a fundamental difference between Wade's and Feldman's senses of relativity. Wade's is concerned with situations in which there is *no opportunity to have a court affirm the unlawfulness* of a flawed administrative act, such that the unlawful act falls to be treated *as if it were lawful*. In contrast, Feldman's argument is to the effect that *even an administrative act that has been held by a court to be legally flawed* may produce certain legal consequences, *its unlawfulness notwithstanding*. Feldman instances *Agricultural, Horticultural and Forestry Industry Training Board* v. *Aylesbury Mushrooms Ltd* [1972] 1 WLR 190, in which the Minister (in breach of a statutory requirement) failed to consult the defendant before making an administrative order. Donaldson J held (at 196) that, in these circumstances, the order had 'no application' to the defendant, but that it was otherwise valid.

This indicates that a given legal flaw might render an administrative act void from the perspective of one person but valid from the perspective of another. It is not, however, clear whether Donaldson J envisaged that the administrative order could—by virtue of some metaphysical sleight of hand—be simultaneously valid and invalid. An alternative—and perhaps more plausible—interpretation of the case is that the order was void, but that it might be rendered *de facto* valid through the use of remedial discretion; a court could, for instance, have refused to quash the order at the suit of any consulted party. (Remedial discretion is considered further in this context at 3.3.1.)

Feldman also points out that an administrative act might be legally flawed when examined from the perspective of public law but nevertheless capable of producing legal effects in private law. For instance, in *R (Lumba)* v. *Secretary of State for the Home Department* [2011] UKSC 12, [2012] 1 AC 245, the Supreme Court held that the claimants' detention was unlawful as a matter of *public law* because they had been detained in breach of the Home Secretary's published policy. (On that aspect of the case, see 5.3.3.) The question then arose whether this meant that the detention was also to be regarded as unlawful in *private law* such that it could found a claim for false imprisonment. On the facts, it was held the claimants had been falsely imprisoned. However, Lord Dyson (at [68]), advancing a view that also found expression in other judgments, said that

> the error must be one which is material in public law terms. It is not every breach of public law that is sufficient to give rise to a cause of action in false imprisonment. In the present context, the breach of public law must bear on and be relevant to the decision to detain. Thus, for example, a decision to detain made by an official of a different grade from that specified in a detention policy would not found a claim in false imprisonment. Nor too would a decision to detain a person under conditions different from those described in the policy. Errors of this kind do not bear on the decision to detain. They are not capable of affecting the decision to detain or not to detain.

Yet Lord Dyson did not consider this position to be incompatible with the view that administrative acts which are unlawful in public law terms are necessarily void. Indeed, in a powerful statement of principle he said (at [66]):

> A purported lawful authority to detain may be impugned either because the defendant acted in excess of jurisdiction (in the narrow sense of jurisdiction) or because such jurisdiction was wrongly exercised. *Anisminic Ltd* v. *Foreign Compensation Commission* [1969] 2 AC 147 established that both species of error render an executive act *ultra vires*, unlawful and a nullity. In the present context, there is in principle no difference between (i) a detention which is unlawful because there was no statutory power to detain and (ii) a detention which is unlawful because the decision to detain, although authorised by statute, was made in breach of a rule of public law. For example, if the decision to detain is unreasonable in the *Wednesbury* sense, it is unlawful and a nullity. The importance of *Anisminic* is that it established that there was a single category of errors of law, all of which rendered a decision ultra vires: see *Boddington* v. *British Transport Police* [1999] 2 AC 143, 158D–E.

How can we reconcile Lord Dyson's views that all unlawful administrative acts are 'a nullity' (*ie* void) and that some unlawful administrative acts are capable of supplying a basis for detention that, viewed from the perspective of the private law false imprisonment cause of action, is lawful? One possibility is that the conception of voidness adopted by Lord

Dyson is sufficiently subtle to enable unlawful administrative acts, in appropriate circumstances, to be taken account of and invested with legal consequences. This implies a version of legal relativity that exceeds Wade's, since it concedes the potential legal effects of unlawful acts *even if their unlawfulness has been judicially affirmed*. Another possibility, however, involves decoupling the normative and factual dimensions. Detention might be unlawful in public law terms, but the fact that detention occurred and was unvitiated by a subset of public law flaws might in itself be sufficient to serve as a lawful basis for detention when the matter is viewed through the private law prism of false imprisonment. This distinction between the normative and factual dimensions is leveraged by Forsyth's theory of second actor, which we examine at 3.3.2.

3.3 Accounting for the effect of unlawful administrative acts

Any attempt to develop a theoretical framework in this area must confront the empirical reality that unlawful acts sometimes produce legal consequences. In this section we examine a number of attempts to account for the effect of unlawful administrative acts. Such attempts fall into one of two broad categories: those that embrace the view that all unlawful administrative action is void and then seek to finesse the consequences of that position so as to enable such action to produce certain consequences notwithstanding its voidness; and those that reject the premise that unlawful administrative acts are necessarily void. The section concludes by exploring the divergent theoretical perspectives upon administrative law that underpin the different approaches that writers adopt to the status of unlawful administrative acts.

3.3.1 Judicial discretion

Remedies in judicial review proceedings are issued at the court's discretion. Persuading a court that administrative action is unlawful therefore does not guarantee that it will be quashed or that any other remedy will be issued. It follows that it is possible for a court to acknowledge that certain administrative action is unlawful and void, but to refuse to quash it in order (for instance) to avoid administrative chaos. This supplies a means by which to manage the practical effects of voidness without denying the fundamental equation between unlawfulness and voidness, albeit that such an approach leverages the relativity of voidness by relying upon people's propensity to treat unlawful but unquashed administrative acts as if they were lawful.

Craig, *Administrative Law* (London 2012) at 756–8, argues that the careful exercise of discretion is the best way in which to deal with the effects of voidness. Lord Slynn, in *R v. Governor of Brockhill Prison, ex parte Evans (No 2)* [2001] 2 AC 19 at 26–7, also considered that 'there may be situations in which it would be desirable, and in no way unjust, that the effect of judicial rulings should be prospective or limited to certain claimants' to avoid 'unscrambling transactions perhaps long since over and doing injustice to defendants'.

There are, however, two grounds on which reliance upon discretion in this sphere may be regarded as problematic. The first objection was powerfully articulated by Wade (1968) 84 *LQR* 95 at 113–15:

> The whole basis of civil liberty is that the acts of public authorities are white or black, lawful or unlawful, valid or void. A large area of grey, where no one could be sure of his rights, would be a dangerous innovation indeed …
>
> … There is serious danger in making the *ultra vires* principle … discretionary. Administrative inconvenience should not be allowed to distort the law.

Wade's position has obvious resonance from a rule of law perspective. But the rule of law argument can cut both ways. Take, for instance, *R (British Academy of Songwriters, Composers and Authors* v. *Secretary of State for Business, Innovation and Skills* [2015] EWHC 2041 (Admin). It had been held in earlier proceedings ([2015] EWHC 1723 (Admin)) that secondary legislation decriminalizing the copying for personal use of copyrighted material (*eg* music) was unlawful. Green J subsequently concluded that he should quash the legislation, ruling that the quashing order had prospective effect but leaving open the question as to the retrospective position. In framing his judgment thus, Green J was influenced (at [14]) by considerations of legal certainty—which is, of course, a core aspect of the rule of law. Thus he noted that 'very substantial numbers of persons commenced copying because they had become entitled in law to do so' and that they had 'perfectly reasonably changed their conduct and relied upon the new law as a justification so to do'.

A second objection is that remedial discretion may not necessarily be *effective* as a tool for managing the effects of invalidity because no amount of such discretion can alter the underlying legal position if the unlawful administrative act is void. Take, for instance, the *Ahmed* case, considered at 3.1.3. One of the reasons given by the Supreme Court for refusing to suspend the quashing orders it proposed to issue was that doing so would have an obfuscatory effect—an attempt to disguise the true legal position, namely that the unlawful delegated legislation was void and had never supplied a lawful basis for the freezing of the assets. Similar difficulties arise in respect of *British Academy of Songwriters, Composers and Authors*: if the secondary legislation removing criminal liability was void, the absence of a 'retrospective' quashing order would be irrelevant. Indeed, Green J went some way towards acknowledging this, albeit in two somewhat contradictory ways. He indicated (at [21]) that he was leaving open not only the question whether the unlawful secondary legislation should be retrospectively *quashed*, but also the question whether it was retrospectively *void* in the first place. Elsewhere (at [19]) he suggested that the unlawful secondary legislation may have generated a legitimate expectation (presumably to the effect that those engaging in the apparently decriminalized act would not be prosecuted). This amounts to an implicit acknowledgement of the limited capacity of remedial discretion, on its own, to permit circumvention of the implications of voidness.

QUESTION

- When, if at all, do you think it would be both desirable and effective for a court to utilize remedial discretion in seeking to manage the consequences of voidness?

3.3.2 The theory of the second actor

One of the principal sources of difficulty in this area is that an unlawful administrative act might not be recognized as such, and much might be done on the erroneous assumption that the act is perfectly lawful. As Forsyth (in Forsyth and Hare (eds), *The Golden Metwand and the Crooked Cord* (Oxford 1998) at 144) put it, 'unlawful acts which are undeniably non-existent *in law* do exist *in fact*. That factual existence may be perceived as legal existence; and individuals may understandably take decisions on that basis.' Assume, for instance, that delegated legislation appears to empower a Minister to grant licences. The legislation is unlawful, but no one realizes this until several thousand licences have been granted. In circumstances such as these, the consequences of treating not only the original administrative act (the delegated legislation) but all administrative acts taken under it (the licences) as void may range from mild inconvenience to profound chaos. For precisely that reason, in practice, the unlawfulness of the original act is not invariably considered to undermine the lawfulness of subsequent acts committed on the strength of it. As Maurice Kay LJ put it in *R (Shoesmith)* v. *Ofsted* [2011] EWCA Civ 642, [2011] IRLR 679 at [119]:

> It seems to me that there is an area, admittedly ill-defined …, in which the act of a public authority which is done in good faith on the reasonably assumed legal validity of the act of another public authority, is not ipso facto vitiated by a later finding that the earlier act of the other public authority was unlawful.

Against this background, Forsyth's 'theory of the second actor' seeks to explain how an unlawful administrative act can serve as a legal foundation for a valid subsequent act without denying the voidness of the original act. In the following excerpt Forsyth sets out the essence of the second actor theory—which has been referred to with approval in *Boddington* v. *British Transport Police* [1999] 2 AC 143; *D* v. *Home Office* [2005] EWCA Civ 38, [2006] 1 WLR 1003; and *White* v. *South Derbyshire District Council* [2012] EWHC 3495 (Admin), [2013] PTSR 536. (In the latter case, Singh J suggested (at [34]) that the second actor theory had in substance been applied, albeit prior to Forsyth's articulation of it, in *Percy* v. *Hall* [1997] QB 924, a case that we consider later.)

Forsyth, '"The Metaphysic of Nullity": Invalidity, Conceptual Reasoning and the Rule of Law' in Forsyth and Hare (eds), *The Golden Metwand and the Crooked Cord* (Oxford 1998)

The first step … is to investigate the ways in which undeniably void acts may have legal consequences. It is sometimes supposed that if an act is found to be void, then everything that flows from that act must also be void. The inconvenience and injustice that can readily flow from such attempted unscrambling of thoroughly scrambled eggs, is what drives some to believe that unlawful acts are not void.

But the law is not omnipotent; it cannot set everything right. Unlawful activity may (and does) have effects which cannot be rectified. Innocent third parties will have done all sorts of things that cannot be reversed or which it would be gravely unjust to reverse. For good or ill it is often impossible to return to the *status quo ante*. The law cannot wash away all signs of illegality.

Thus it is inevitable that there will be occasions on which an administrative act will be void, yet it will have legal consequences. Two important, though intimately linked, questions remain. What is the explanation for this state of affairs in terms of theory (rather than in terms of practical necessity) and how may it be determined, as a matter of law rather than judicial discretion, on what occasions void acts will have legal consequences?

The theoretical basis, it is submitted, is to be found in Hans Kelsen's *Pure Theory of Law* [see Kelsen (1934) 50 *LQR* 474]. This theory, it will be recalled, is built upon the distinction between the *Sein* (the Is) and the *Sollen* (the Ought), between the realm of things that are, ie facts or natural phenomena, and the realm of norms, including therein law. Now an administrative act, the writing of a decision letter in a planning appeal, say, is a fact. The piece of paper on which the letter is written coupled with the mental processes of the decision-maker that led up to it, are events from the realm of things that are, the *Sein*. But the meaning of that act—that certain development is permitted—is an element of the realm of norms, the *Sollen*.

Now a void act—say a decision letter written for an improper purpose—is not an act *in law* but it is and remains an act *in fact*—an event from the *Sein*. And events from the *Sein* often have an effect, directly or indirectly, in the realm of the *Sollen*. As Schiemann LJ said in *Percy* v. *Hall* [1996] 4 All ER 523 at 544, 'Manifestly in daily life the [*ultra vires* and void] enactment will have had an effect in the sense that people have regulated their conduct in light of it.' Where that conduct has legal consequences, that is, effects in the realm of the *Sollen*, those consequences flow from the legally non-existent unlawful act.

Put more precisely, the factual existence of a void act may serve as the basis for other decisions. For instance, an invalid administrative act (particular *seins* phenomenon) may, notwithstanding its non-existence in the *Sollen*, serve as the basis for another perfectly valid decision. Its factual existence, rather than its invalidity, is the cause of the subsequent act, but that act is valid since the legal existence of the first act is not a precondition for the second …

… [H]owever, [in other situations] it may be that the legal powers of the second actor depend upon the validity of the first act … In such cases the invalidity of the first act does involve the unravelling of later acts which rely on the first act's validity. However, the voidness of the first act does not determine whether the second act is valid. That depends upon the legal powers of the later actor. If the validity of the first act is a jurisdictional requirement for the valid exercise of the second actor's powers, then, if the first act is invalid, so is the second. Sometimes it will not be … and sometimes it will be …

The focus must thus—and this is the crucial conclusion—fall upon the second actor's legal powers.

Two contrasting cases are advanced by Forsyth to illustrate his argument. Both concern prosecutions (the second acts) to which earlier administrative acts (the first acts) were relevant. In the first case, *R* v. *Wicks* [1998] AC 92, a planning authority issued an enforcement notice, alleging that the defendant had breached planning control and requiring him to remove those parts of the building in question which exceeded a given height. The central question was whether prosecution could occur even if the enforcement notice was void. In considering this matter, Lord Hoffmann (at 117) said:

The question must depend entirely upon the construction of the statute under which the prosecution is brought. The statute may require the prosecution to prove that the act [*ie* the enforcement notice in this case] in question is not open to challenge on any ground available in public law … On the other hand, the statute may upon its true construction merely require an act which appears formally valid … In such a case, nothing but the formal validity of the act will be relevant.

Their Lordships concluded that all that was required in this case was an enforcement notice which *appeared to be valid*—that is, a notice which, on its face, complied with the requirements of the legislation under which it was issued; it would not matter if the notice was *actually void*. The second act—prosecution—could therefore take place even though the first act—the notice—was unlawful. According to the second actor theory, this conclusion is possible because the validity of the second act depends not upon the validity or otherwise of the first, but upon the way in which we construe the statutory power that authorizes the second act. In *Wicks*, the condition precedent to the valid exercise of the second power was something falling short of the actual validity of the first act.

Wicks may be contrasted with *Director of Public Prosecutions* v. *Head* [1959] AC 83 (see 3.1.1), in which the criminal liability of the defendant depended upon the validity of the order institutionalizing the alleged victim. The fact that the order was void meant that the defendant could not be successfully prosecuted for the offence. Here, then, is a situation where the second act can validly occur only if the first act is also legally valid. Once again, the crucial matter is the construction of the second actor's power: the reason for the different outcomes in *Wicks* and *Head* is that the second actor's power in the former case arose irrespective of the actual validity of the first act, whereas in the second case the second actor's power arose only if the first act was actually valid.

The second actor theory elegantly reconciles the voidness of unlawful administrative action with the fact that other actors will rely upon it, thereby imbuing it with a practical effect. However, it is necessary to consider how well the theory works in practice. In advancing the theory, Forsyth (*op cit* at 145–6) argues that an approach based on 'conceptual reasoning' is better than one based on discretion (see 3.3.1), because it is preferable that the status of administrative action can be determined—and therefore predicted—by the application of fixed rules. To this end, the second actor theory lays down a clear rule which says that the validity of subsequent acts is to be determined not by the exercise of judicial discretion, but by reference to the legal definition of the second actor's powers. But how are we to decide whether or not the second actor's powers are dependent upon a valid first act? If our analysis of subsequent actors' powers is based largely upon practical considerations, such as the amount of chaos which would result if their actions had to be undone, then it might be argued that this approach is, in reality, highly discretionary: our *legal* conclusion as to whether the second actor can act irrespective of the status of the first act is simply a tissue of pseudo-conceptualism behind which lurks what is in reality a *pragmatic* conclusion about the desirability of allowing the 'domino effect' to proceed unchecked.

Consider, for instance, *Percy* v. *Hall* [1997] QB 924, in which the Court of Appeal balked at the idea of holding that police constables could be liable for wrongful arrest in respect of arrests for breaches of byelaws which turned out to be *ultra vires*. Although (implicitly) consistent with the second actor theory, the conclusion reached in Simon Brown LJ's leading judgment that constables' powers of arrest should arise independently of the validity of byelaws was undoubtedly informed by policy considerations. A similar approach is evident in Schiemann LJ's judgment at 951–2:

> The policy questions which the law must address in this type of case are whether any and if so what remedy should be given to whom against whom in cases where persons have acted in reliance on what appears to be valid legislation. To approach these questions by rigidly applying to all circumstances a doctrine that the enactment which has been declared invalid was 'incapable

of ever having had any legal effect upon the rights or duties of the parties' seems to me, with all respect to the strong stream of authority in our law to that effect, needlessly to restrict the possible answers which policy might require.

This is not to suggest, however, that a principled approach cannot be adopted in this context. For instance, in concluding that prosecution was possible irrespective of the actual validity of the enforcement notice in *R v. Wicks* [1998] AC 92, Lord Hoffmann undertook a detailed analysis of the legislative policy and history, concluding that factors thereby established, such as the need for expediency in the planning context, militated against allowing defendants in criminal proceedings to raise questions about the validity of the notices with whose breach they are charged.

The decision of *R v. Central London County Court, ex parte London* [1999] QB 1260 also points towards the adoption of a principled approach. An interim court order was made, the effect of which was to permit an approved social worker to make an application to hospital managers for the compulsory treatment, under s 3 of the Mental Health Act 1983, of the claimant. Such an application was duly made; the hospital managers approved it, and the claimant was subjected to compulsory treatment. The claimant challenged the legality of that treatment by attacking (on grounds which are presently unimportant) the original court order. Although Stuart-Smith LJ, with whom Robert Walker and Henry LJJ agreed, concluded that the order was valid, he went on to consider what the position would be if he were wrong on that point. If the order was void, would that automatically render the compulsory treatment unlawful, too? Stuart-Smith LJ answered this question in the negative, offering two reasons for his conclusion that the powers of the second actors—the hospital managers—arose irrespective of whether the order was legally valid. First, his Lordship relied (at 1273–4) upon the general principle, laid down by Romer LJ in *Hadkinson v. Hadkinson* [1952] P 285 at 288 and approved by Lord Diplock in *Isaacs v. Robertson* [1985] AC 97 at 101, that '[i]t is the plain and unqualified obligation of every person against, or in respect of whom, an order is made by a court of competent jurisdiction, to obey it unless and until that order is discharged'. Second, and more specifically, Stuart-Smith LJ placed weight upon s 6 of the Mental Health Act 1983, the gist of which is that the *existence* of an application is sufficient to justify detention under (*inter alia*) s 3, and that hospital managers are under no obligation to look behind the application (*eg* at the validity of the court order upon which the applicant's authority to make the application is founded). In light of these factors, Stuart-Smith LJ concluded that the hospital managers' powers could validly be exercised even if the first act—the court order—was invalid as a matter of law.

Cases like *Wicks* and *London* show that there *are* criteria which can be deployed in a principled fashion in order to assist in the construction of the second actor's powers, and that judicial decision-making in this area does not necessarily reduce to the exercise of discretion. Judges may be guided by the language of the statutory scheme, its history and policy, and by more general principles. Of course, this is not to say that practical or policy considerations will not—or should not—play some role in this context. It is not improper for judges, as they seek to work out in what circumstances the second actor's powers do and do not arise, to take into account the consequences which would ensue if they concluded that those powers could be exercised only on the basis of a valid first act. Such considerations necessarily form part of the backdrop against which the legislation conferring power upon the second actor falls to be construed.

QUESTIONS

- Do you agree that the second actor theory is capable of principled application?
- What other principles may be used in order to inform our analysis of the circumstances in which the second actor's powers arise?

One further comment on the theory of the second actor is warranted. As noted earlier, its primary objective is to reconcile the fact (at least as Forsyth sees it) that unlawful administrative acts are void with the fact that such administrative acts are sometimes held by the courts to supply a foundation for (lawful) subsequent acts. The second actor theory attempts to resolve this paradox by means of a distinction between the *legal voidness* and the *factual existence* of the unlawful original act. However, it is not entirely clear that the distinction exists in the bright-line form that Forsyth assumes. After all, even if the original act is legally void, its *factual* existence may be *legally* relevant in the sense that it might serve as the *legal* basis for a lawful subsequent act. To this extent the second actor theory implicitly concedes that voidness is other than an absolute concept, and in that way it has at least something in common with the relative conception of voidness considered at 3.2.2.

3.3.3 The void/voidable distinction

We saw at 3.1.1 that practical concerns about the potentially chaotic consequence of treating all unlawful administrative acts as void contributed to Lord Denning's view in *Director of Public Prosecutions* v. *Head* [1959] AC 83 that some unlawful acts are merely voidable. He adopted a similar approach in *R* v. *Paddington Valuation Officer, ex parte Peachey Property Corporation Ltd* [1966] 1 QB 380. The applicant challenged the legality of a 'rating valuation list' that was to serve as a basis for determining how much local tax householders should pay (the amount of the tax payable being a function of the value of the property). If the list had been quashed, grave administrative difficulties would have arisen. But Lord Denning MR (with whom Danckwerts LJ agreed on this point) took the view that the court could decline to quash the valuation list pending the compilation (in a lawful manner) of a revised list. He said (at 402–3):

> By this solution, all chaos is avoided. The existing list will remain good until it is replaced by a new list: and then it will be quashed … But I think that then it must be quashed. You cannot have two lists in being at the same time.

Crucially, however, Lord Denning considered (at 402) that even after it had been quashed, 'everything done under the old list' would 'remain good'. This followed, he said, because the list was voidable rather than void, the general principle being that 'where a voidable transaction is avoided, it does not invalidate intermediate transactions which were made on the basis that it was good'. It was therefore central to Lord Denning's chaos-avoiding strategy that the legal flaw afflicting the valuation list rendered it not void but voidable.

The question arises whether it would be open to a judge today to do what Lord Denning did in *Peachey*. We noted earlier that the House of Lords' landmark decision in *Anisminic Ltd* v. *Foreign Compensation Commission* [1969] 2 AC 147 was regarded by Lord Irvine LC in *Boddington* v. *British Transport Police* [1999] 2 AC 143 as having swept away the distinction between legal flaws that do and do not cause a decision-maker to exceed jurisdiction. In the light of that, he said (at 158) that any attempt to draw a distinction between different types of invalidity could not survive *Anisminic*: '[A]ll categories of unlawfulness' are now to be treated as 'having the same effect'. We also noted earlier that Lord Dyson endorsed that view in *R (Lumba)* v. *Secretary of State for the Home Department* [2011] UKSC 12, [2012] 1 AC 245 at [66]. This suggests that there is no longer any possibility of invoking the void/voidable distinction in order to sustain an unlawful administrative act.

This situation arises because of the changes charted in ch 2 to the way in which the concept of jurisdiction is understood. If—as modern orthodoxy holds—all reviewable errors are, at some level of abstraction, errors of law, and if all errors of law are jurisdictional, and if all jurisdictional errors render administrative acts void, no room is left for a category of void-able acts. Every administrative act must be either lawful or void; no other possibility arises. Feldman [2014] *CLJ* 275 regrets the emergence of this modern orthodoxy, not least because it risks boxing the courts in when it comes to negotiating the practical consequences that unlawful administrative acts might have. He writes (at 276):

> Until the 1960s, judges had at their disposal a number of techniques for identifying those flawed decisions which were to have legal effects. They distinguished between issues of fact, which were within the decision-making power of officials unless an erroneous conclusion deprived the official of jurisdiction, and issues of law, which engaged the High Court's supervisory jurisdiction. They distinguished between errors of law which deprived an official of jurisdiction and those which did not; the latter were not subject to the High Court's supervisory jurisdiction unless they were apparent on the face of the record of the challenged decision. This allowed them to say that some erroneous or allegedly erroneous decisions were void (i.e. had never had legal effect) while others were voidable (i.e. valid and effective until successfully challenged). Such flexibility lay at the heart of administrative law. To some extent, it has been preserved. Judicial review of alleged errors of law is sometimes considered to be unnecessary or inappropriate. [Feldman cites *R v. Hull University Visitor, ex parte Page* [1993] AC 682 and *R v. Monopolies and Mergers Commission, ex parte South Yorkshire Transport Ltd* [1993] 1 WLR 23, on which see 2.2.6 and 2.2.8, for this proposition.]

Feldman (at 277–8) traces the erosion of the 'flexibility' referred to in the excerpt above to the House of Lords' decision in *Ridge* v. *Baldwin* [1964] AC 40 (on which see 10.2.1):

> It was established there that a breach of the common-law requirement for a fair hearing would usually make a decision void. After *Anisminic*, and particularly following the interpretation which the House [of Lords] put on *Anisminic* in *R. v Hull University Visitor, ex parte Page*, it became commonplace to treat a breach of any statutory or common-law requirement for administrative action as making it ultra vires, a term which is often confusingly treated as being synonymous with 'without jurisdiction', and as making the rule or decision 'void' or 'a nullity'. But the grounds for review are not all issues of law, except in the trivial sense that anything done in breach of a legal rule involves an error of law. *Anisminic* was a true, indeed paradigm, 'error of law': misinterpreting the statutory instruments which conferred power to act. By contrast, taking account of irrelevant considerations, acting with an improper purpose, reaching an unreasonable decision, and a fortiori reviewable errors of fact, are acts which courts treat as erroneous, but they are not 'errors of law', any more than a driver who negligently runs down a pedestrian commits an 'error of law'.

Feldman (at 278) goes on to argue that treating all reviewable errors as jurisdictional errors of law produces a number of undesirable consequences, including for the status of unlawful administrative acts:

> This deprives administrative lawyers of a useful tool for reaching sensible results, and it further reduces the law's coherence. By expanding the notion of 'error of law', we have deprived it of analytical coherence and usefulness. It debases the notion of 'error of law' to say that taking account of an irrelevant consideration, or acting when biased, or failing to allow a person a fair opportunity to put his or her case, is an error of law. They are simply examples of procedural steps which fail to meet legal requirements. At the same time, it has deprived the concept of 'jurisdiction' of any useful, analytical function. If any error deprives a body of jurisdiction, the notion of a 'jurisdictional error' is redundant. In addition, by undermining the technical distinction between 'void' and 'voidable' rules and decisions, it has deprived judges of a key tool for achieving sensible results.

In spite of this, argues Feldman (at 278), 'courts usually manage to get sensible results', including by treating voidness as as relative concept as outlined at 3.2.2. On Feldman's account, this enables courts to inject back into the law some of the flexibility that is removed by the jettisoning of the category of voidable administrative acts. Significantly, however, Feldman takes the view that this is second best because, on his view, '[a]s a matter of legal doctrine ... there are decisions which are neither valid (in the sense of being untouched by unlawfulness) nor void' but which are instead voidable.

3.3.4 Underlying perspectives

It is helpful at this point to step back from the details of the various perspectives on the status of unlawful administrative action that have been examined in this chapter. In order to understand the causes of the disagreement evidenced by the earlier discussion—and in order to facilitate evaluation of the various positions adopted—it is helpful to disaggregate two strands within the debate. The first is conceptual or metaphysical in nature. Put in its starkest terms, the disagreement is about whether unlawful administrative acts are necessarily void or whether they are (sometimes) voidable. Put less starkly, the question is whether such acts—whether or not characterized as void—have a form of legal existence that permits them to produce legal effects.

Perhaps surprisingly—given his views regarding the constitutional foundations of judicial review, on which see 1.4.2—Craig takes a particularly orthodox line here. While acknowledging that voidness is 'relative' in the sense that Wade uses that term, Craig argues (*Administrative Law* (Oxford 2012) at 749–50) that:

> The effect of finding that a decision is ultra vires is best approached from first principles. If the decision-maker had no power then the decision should have no effect. Translated into the *lingua franca* of our profession, we would say that such a decision was void ab initio, retrospectively null ... Where a jurisdictional error, abuse of discretion or failure to comply with natural justice has been proven, the court will regard the decision as being outside the power of the decision-maker.

Forsyth [2013] *JR* 360 at 368 adopts a similar position, arguing that 'the organising concept of administrative law is jurisdiction' and that 'an act made outside jurisdiction is legally non-existent or void' unless the legislation in question modifies that default position. Craig and Forsyth thus agree about the existential status of unlawful administrative acts: they do not legally exist. In contrast, Feldman [2014] *CLJ* 275 at 312 argues that even if—contrary to his normative preference—we embrace error of law, jurisdiction, and *ultra vires* as interlocking organizing concepts, the nullity, or ineffectiveness, of flawed administrative acts does not necessarily follow: '[T]he propositions that any error of law, broadly defined, makes a decision or rule ultra vires its maker, and that an ultra vires decision or rule is incapable of having any legal effect, are not logically linked.'

Viewed through a metaphysical lens, the positions adopted by Craig and Forsyth appear to align, and to be quite different from that of Feldman. We might rationalize this by reference to the debate about the constitutional foundations of judicial review. It is unsurprising that Forsyth, as a proponent of the *ultra vires* theory, takes the view that unlawful administrative acts are void, it being difficult to see how an act committed without any legal basis whatever could legally exist. However, if, like Feldman, one does not embrace *ultra vires* as the juristic basis of judicial review, it is easier to countenance an administrative act that is—as Feldman puts it (*op cit* at 282)—'touched by unlawfulness' but which might nevertheless legally exist. The unlawfulness might, for instance, arise from the infraction of some common law requirement pertaining to the exercise of administrative authority (the consequences of whose breach might be other than to render the offending act non-existent), rather than from (as on the *ultra vires* analysis) the absence of any statutory power to commit the act in the first place. How Craig's position relates to this analysis is, however, less clear, given his opposition to the *ultra vires* theory.

The second strand within the debate concerns not the metaphysical status of unlawful administrative acts but the methodology that courts ought to adopt in order to accommodate the fact that such acts sometimes do, and should, produce certain legal effects. Here, two distinct approaches can be discerned. Craig is alone in supporting remedial discretion as the means by which to deal with the practical imperatives that sometimes require unlawful administrative acts to be given effect. Forsyth and Feldman, in contrast, offer analyses that are conceptually rooted in legal reasoning as distinct from the exercise of discretion. The case for such an approach—in preference to one based on discretion—is made by Forsyth (in Bell, Elliott, Varuhas, and Murray (eds), *Public Law Adjudication in Common Law Systems: Process and Substance* (Oxford 2016) at 162) on the ground that 'the abandonment of doctrine and conceptual reasoning in favour of pragmatism and … discretion' not only risks 'deletrious uncertainty' but jeopardizes the 'legitimacy of the courts' themselves.

Feldman agrees with Forsyth that questions about the status of legally flawed administrative acts fall to be resolved by reference to the exercise of legal reasoning as distinct from discretion. Where they disagree is as to the nature of the legal reasoning that is entailed. As already noted, for Forsyth, the question is essentially one of statutory interpretation. In a 'second actor' scenario, does the legislation authorizing the subsequent act permit an unlawful prior act to trigger jurisdiction? Or, in a single act scenario (as in *Salvesen*) is the legislation authorizing the act exceptionally to be construed as providing that legally flawed acts are to be regarded as voidable rather than void? Feldman [2014] *CLJ* 275 at 312, however, adopts a much broader approach:

> Saying that a decision is ultra vires does not determine the effectiveness of the decision. That calls for a separate, normative judgment: is the error sufficiently significant to merit treating the decision as wholly ineffective? If any error makes a decision ultra vires, it is likely that many of them will not have a sufficiently serious impact on those subject to the decision to merit being treated as entirely ineffective.

For Feldman, then, questions about the legal status of unlawful administrative acts are ultimately *normative* questions that cannot be resolved (only) by recourse to statutory construction. Meanwhile, Feldman's resistance to any equivalence between unlawfulness and nullity opens up a conceptual space in which such normative issues can be addressed.

That said, Forsyth does not deny that normative considerations may be in play. For instance, as previously noted, he suggests (with reference *Salvesen*) that the Scotland Act 1998 might be read as modifying the default position, such that *ultra vires* provisions enacted by the Scottish Parliament would fall to be treated as merely voidable—a suggestion that might be taken to acknowledge the particular, albeit not unique, difficulties that can arise in respect of invalid 'primary' legislation, and hence of the normative arguments in favour of a different approach. For Forsyth, however, to the extent that normative issues must be confronted in this sphere, they must be refracted through the prism of statutory interpretation, the overarching question always being whether the administrative act in question is compatible with the statute—and, if not, whether the relevant statute (which might be the legislation authorizing either the flawed act or some subsequent but connected act) permits such unlawfulness to be overlooked.

Examined in this way, the debate about the status of unlawful administrative acts evidently has its roots in, even if it does not mirror, disagreement concerning the constitutional foundations of judicial review and the extent to which the notions of jurisdiction and error of law can and should serve as organizing concepts.

QUESTIONS

- Of the three analyses considered in this section—*ie* those advanced by Craig, Feldman, and Forsyth—which do you consider to be preferable?
- How does your answer to that question relate to the position you adopt in relation to the constitutional foundations of judicial review and jurisdiction?
- Why are these matters inevitably related?

3.4 Collateral challenge

3.4.1 Voidness and collateral challenge

The legality of administrative decisions and acts (including subordinate legislation) can be challenged directly, by means of judicial review. However, such questions of legality may also arise in other circumstances. For instance, the tenant of a council house who is sued in civil proceedings for failing to pay the rent, which the council says he owes, may wish to argue that the resolutions which the council adopted in order to raise his rent were *ultra vires* (see *Wandsworth London Borough Council* v. *Winder* [1985] AC 461, at 13.3.4). Or a passenger who is prosecuted for smoking on a train may want to assert in his defence that the administrative measures purporting to prohibit smoking are *ultra vires* (as in *Boddington* v. *British Transport Police* [1999] 2 AC 143). When they make these arguments, the tenant and the passenger are mounting *collateral challenges* to the relevant administrative acts: rather than attacking those acts *directly* via judicial review proceedings, they are questioning them *indirectly*, or collaterally, in civil or criminal proceedings.

If we think further about how collateral challenge works, we will see why it is intimately connected with the idea that unlawful administrative action is void, not merely voidable. Let us take as an example the *Boddington* case, the facts of which are set out at 3.1.2. The defendant's argument was that he could not have committed a criminal offence by falling foul of Network South Central's complete smoking ban because the train operator did not actually have the legal power necessary to institute such a ban. This reduces to the argument that the offence with which he was charged was *ultra vires*. It is obvious that the legality of the offence could be challenged by means of judicial review proceedings, and quashed if the reviewing court had found the offence to be *ultra vires*.

However, the defendant in *Boddington*—for reasons largely of convenience, as discussed at 3.4.2—elected not to institute such proceedings. Instead, he questioned the lawfulness of the offence collaterally, raising it in his defence in the criminal proceedings which were brought against him in a magistrates' court. If unlawful administrative action is merely voidable, it remains fully valid unless and until it is set aside by a court of competent jurisdiction; however, since the magistrates' court had no power to issue a quashing order, it would have been forced to treat the allegedly unlawful administrative action or subordinate legislation as valid unless a quashing order had been issued by the Administrative Court. The legality of administrative action would therefore be open to challenge *only* directly, by means of judicial review proceedings; collateral challenge would be impossible.

The picture changes radically, however, if the unlawful administrative act is regarded as void. In this scenario, the availability of a quashing order is not decisive. If, as in *Boddington*, the legality of administrative action or subordinate legislation is raised collaterally, it does not matter that the court concerned has no power to issue a quashing order. In strict logic, unlawful action does not need to be quashed: it is void *ab initio*, and therefore never legally existed. The court's conclusion that the act in question is unlawful and void is therefore enough to dispose of the matter. Thus, in a *Boddington*-type situation, it would be open to the magistrates' court to conclude that the offence was *ultra vires* and void: non-existent and incapable of being committed. The theory of voidness and the availability of collateral challenge therefore go hand in hand.

We should, however, enter two caveats. First, the fact that unlawful administrative acts can be collaterally challenged does not dispose of the debate considered earlier in this chapter about the legal status of such acts: voidness and collateral challenge go hand in hand in the sense that collateral challenge is only available *to the extent that* unlawful administrative acts are void. Second, it should not be inferred from the foregoing paragraph that quashing orders are redundant in respect of void administrative acts, not least because there are many practical reasons (considered at 12.5.1) why an individual may choose to seek a quashing order, rather than waiting to be prosecuted or sued and then pressing the logic of voidness through the medium of collateral challenge.

3.4.2 The importance of collateral challenge

Why is the availability of collateral challenge important? Why not require anyone who wishes to challenge executive action and subordinate legislation to do so in the Administrative Court (which, presumably, is able to bring far greater expertise than, say, magistrates' courts, to such questions)? A number of reasons, based upon both the rule of law and more practical considerations, make it imperative that administrative action can be challenged collaterally. They are set out in the following extract, in which Lord Steyn takes issue with earlier decisions which sought to restrict the availability of collateral challenge.

Boddington v. *British Transport Police* [1999] 2 AC 143
House of Lords

For the facts, see 3.1.2.

Lord Steyn

... It is a truth generally acknowledged among lawyers that the complexity of a civil or criminal case does not depend on the level of the hierarchy of courts where it is heard. On a given day a bench of magistrates may have to decide a more difficult case than an appeal being heard by the Appellate Committee of the House of Lords ... But in the last 10 years, in the wake of the expansion of judicial review and the resultant increase in the power of the Divisional Court, the idea has gained ascendancy that it is not part of the jurisdiction of a criminal court to determine issues regarding the validity of byelaws or administrative decisions even if the resolution of such issues could be determinative of the guilt or innocence of a defendant. Such a view was put forward by the Divisional Court in *Quietlynn* v. *Plymouth City Council* [1988] Q.B. 114 but that decision is explicable on the basis of the policy of the statute in question. In *Reg.* v. *Reading Crown Court, Ex parte Hutchinson* [1988] Q.B. 384 a differently constituted Divisional Court doubted the correctness of some of the general observations in the *Quietlynn* case. The leading decision suggestive of such a restriction on the jurisdiction of magistrates, and indeed of all criminal courts, is *Bugg* v. *Director of Public Prosecutions* [1993] Q.B. 473. In that case Woolf L.J., giving the judgment of the Divisional Court, distinguished in the context of byelaws between substantive and procedural validity and he held that while a criminal court may decide an issue as to substantive validity a question as to procedural validity is beyond its power. The decision of the Divisional Court [1997] C.O.D. 3 in the present case went significantly further. Auld L.J., sitting with Ebsworth J. and giving the reserved judgment of the Divisional Court, held that any issue of the validity of a byelaw or administrative action is beyond the jurisdiction of criminal courts ...

The reasons [given in *Bugg* by] Woolf L.J. [for restricting collateral challenge] can be grouped under two headings. First, there are his pragmatic reasons for thinking that a criminal court is not equipped to deal with the relevant issues. Woolf L.J. said that in cases of substantive invalidity of byelaws no evidence is required whereas in cases of procedural invalidity evidence is required. The fact that evidence is required, he said, may lead to different outcomes in different courts. He said that in cases of procedural invalidity the party interested in upholding a byelaw may well not be a party to the proceedings. Secondly, Woolf L.J. relied on the developments which have taken place in judicial review over the last 25 years. The principal ground of his reasoning was that, except in 'flagrant' and 'outrageous' cases, a byelaw remains effective until quashed ...

The pragmatic reasons given by Woolf L.J. need to be put in context. As Lord Hoffmann observed in *Reg.* v. *Wicks* [1998] A.C. 92, 116: 'the distinction between substantive and procedural invalidity appears to cut across the distinction between grounds of invalidity which require no extrinsic evidence and those which do.' An issue of substantive invalidity may involve daunting issues of fact, e.g. an issue as to unequal treatment of citizens in a pluralistic society or other forms of unreasonableness. In such a case the issues of law may also be complex. In contrast an issue of procedural invalidity of a byelaw may involve minimal evidence, e.g. simply the negative fact that an express duty to consult was breached. And the question of law may be straightforward. This aspect of the pragmatic case is not persuasive. It is true, as Woolf L.J. said, that on the evidence presented to them different magistrates' courts may come to different conclusions.

But this factor proves too much: it applies equally to substantive validity. In any event, although a criminal court cannot quash byelaws the Divisional Court can on appeal on a case stated from a decision of magistrates give a ruling which will in practice be followed by other magistrates' courts. Woolf L.J. added that the party with an interest in upholding the byelaws may not be before the court. But that is also true of cases of substantive invalidity. Moreover, in a criminal case the prosecution, backed by the resources of the state, will usually put forward the case for upholding the byelaws. I therefore regard the pragmatic case in favour of a rule that magistrates may not decide issues of procedural validity, even if the distinction can be satisfactorily drawn, as questionable.

There is also a formidable difficulty of categorisation created by *Bugg's* case [1993] Q.B. 473. A distinction between substantive and procedural invalidity will often be impossible or difficult to draw. Woolf L.J. recognised that there may be cases in a grey area, e.g. cases of bad faith: p. 500F. I fear that in reality the grey area covers a far greater terrain. In *Associated Provincial Picture Houses Ltd* v. *Wednesbury Corporation* [1948] 1 K.B. 223, 229, Lord Greene MR pointed out that different grounds of review 'run into one another.' A modern commentator has demonstrated the correctness of the proposition that grounds of judicial review have blurred edges and tend to overlap with comprehensive reference to leading cases: see *Fordham, Judicial Review Handbook*, 2nd ed, pp. 514–521. Thus the taking into account by a decision maker of extraneous considerations is variously treated as substantive or procedural. Moreover, even Woolf L.J.['s] categorisation of procedural invalidity is controversial. Wade and Forsyth rightly point out that contrary to normal terminology Woolf L.J. treated procedural invalidity as being not a matter of excess or abuse of power: Wade and Forsyth, *Administrative Law*, 7th ed., p. 323. Categorisation is an indispensable tool in the search for rationality and coherence in law. But the process of categorisation in accordance with *Bugg's* case which serves to carve out of the jurisdiction of criminal courts the power to decide on some issues pertinent to the guilt of a defendant, leads to a labyrinth of paths. It is nevertheless an inevitable consequence of *Bugg's* case that magistrates may have to rule on the satellite issue whether a particular challenge is substantive or procedural. That may involve hearing wide-ranging arguments. Even then there may be no clear cut answer. This is a factor militating against the pragmatic case on which Woolf L.J. relied in *Bugg's* case.

The problems of categorisation pose not only practical difficulties. As Lord Nicholls of Birkenhead explained in *Reg.* v. *Wicks* [1998] A.C. 92 they expose a fundamental problem. About the [distinction proposed] in *Bugg's* case [1993] Q.B. 473, 500, he said, at p 108:

> 'On this reasoning there is not only a boundary between the two different types of invalidity. There is also an imperative need for the boundary line to be fixed and crystal clear. There can be no room for an ambiguous grey area. On this reasoning the boundary is not merely concerned with identifying the proceedings in which, as a matter of procedure, the unlawfulness issue can best be raised. Rather, the boundary can represent the difference between committing a criminal offence and not committing a criminal offence. According to this reasoning, a decision on invalidity has sharply different consequences, so far as criminality is concerned, in the two types of case. Setting aside an impugned order for procedural invalidity, as distinct from substantive invalidity, has no effect on the criminality of earliest conduct. Despite a court decision that the order was not lawfully made, the defendant is still guilty of an offence, by reason of his prior conduct. Further, it would seem to follow that in the case of procedural invalidity, the defendant could be convicted even after the order is set aside as having been made unlawfully, so long as the non-compliance occurred before the order was set aside. In cases of substantive invalidity the citizen can take the risk and disobey the order. If he does so, and the order is later held to be invalid, he will be innocent of any offence. In case of procedural invalidity, the citizen is not permitted to take this risk, however clear the irregularity may be.'

I regard this reasoning as unanswerable. The rule of law requires a clear distinction to be made between what is lawful and what is unlawful. The distinction put forward in *Bugg's* case undermines this axiom of constitutional principle ...

[Lord Steyn then turned to Woolf LJ's principled justification for restricting collateral challenge. In doing so, his Lordship expressed the views set out in the excerpt from this case at 3.1.2, and continued:] [T]he decision in *Bugg's* case ... contemplates that, despite the invalidity of a byelaw and the fact that consistently with *Reg.* v. *Wicks* such invalidity may in a given case afford a defence to a charge, a magistrate[s'] court may not rule on the defence. Instead the magistrates may convict a defendant under the byelaw and punish him. That is an unacceptable consequence in a democracy based on the rule of law. It is true that *Bugg's* case allows the defendant to challenge the byelaw in judicial review proceedings. The defendant may, however, be out of time before he becomes aware of the existence of the byelaw. He may lack the resources to defend his interests in two courts. He may not be able to obtain legal aid for an application for leave to apply for judicial review. Leave to apply for judicial review may be refused. At a substantive hearing his scope for demanding examination of witnesses in the Divisional Court may be restricted. He may be denied a remedy on a discretionary basis. The possibility of judicial review will, therefore, in no way compensate him for the loss of *the right* to defend himself by a defensive challenge to the byelaw in cases where the invalidity of the byelaw might afford him with a defence to the charge. My Lords, with the utmost deference to eminent judges sitting in the Divisional Court I have to say the consequences of *Bugg's* case are too austere and indeed too authoritarian to be compatible with the traditions of the common law. In *Eshugbayi Eleko* v. *Government of Nigeria* [1931] A.C. 662, a habeas corpus case, Lord Atkin observed, at p. 670, that 'no member of the executive can interfere with the liberty or property of a British subject except on condition that he can support the legality of his action before a court of justice.' There is no reason why a defendant in a criminal trial should be in a worse position. And that seems to me to reflect the true spirit of the common law.

Lords Irvine LC, Browne-Wilkinson, Slynn, and Hoffmann were in agreement that it was open to the defendant to challenge collaterally the smoking ban under which he was charged; however, their Lordships were also unanimous that it lay within the train operating company's powers to adopt such a ban. The defendant's appeal against conviction was therefore dismissed.

Lord Steyn's argument can be resolved into three component elements. First, he considered that it would be unworkable to try to restrict collateral challenge, along the lines suggested by Woolf LJ in *Bugg*, by attempting to distinguish between procedural and substantive errors. Second, it would be wrong in principle to restrict collateral challenge: in the criminal context, such restriction would permit defendants to be convicted of offences which did not, in law, exist. And, third, it was naïve, for the practical reasons advanced in the closing paragraph of the extract above, to suppose that the possibility of directly challenging administrative action by means of judicial review was an adequate substitute for collateral challenge.

3.4.3 The limits of collateral challenge

In spite of the importance attached to collateral challenge in *Boddington*, that case did not guarantee its *universal* availability: while their Lordships cast off the restrictive approach adopted in earlier cases, they recognized that there will be circumstances in which administrative action cannot be challenged collaterally. However, as Lord Irvine LC explains in the following passage, this is a conclusion which the courts will reach only with reluctance.

Boddington v. *British Transport Police* [1999] 2 AC 143
House of Lords

For the facts, see 3.1.2.

Lord Irvine LC

… [I]n every case it will be necessary to examine the particular statutory context to determine whether a court hearing a criminal or civil case has jurisdiction to rule on a defence based upon arguments of invalidity of subordinate legislation or an administrative act under it. There are situations in which Parliament may legislate to preclude such challenges being made, in the interest, for example, of promoting certainty about the legitimacy of administrative acts on which the public may have to rely.

The recent decision of this House in *Reg.* v. *Wicks* [1998] A.C. 92 is an example of a particular context in which an administrative act triggering consequences for the purposes of the criminal law was held not to be capable of challenge in criminal proceedings, but only by other proceedings. The case concerned an enforcement notice issued by a local planning authority and served on the defendant under the then current version of section 87 of the Town and Country Planning Act 1971. The notice alleged a breach of planning control by the erection of a building and required its removal above a certain height. One month was allowed for compliance. The appellant appealed against the notice to the Secretary of State, under section 174 of the Town and Country Planning Act 1990, but the appeal was dismissed. The appellant still failed to comply with the notice and the local authority issued a summons alleging a breach of section 179(1) of the Act of 1990. In the criminal proceedings which ensued, the appellant sought to defend himself on the ground that the enforcement notice had been issued ultra vires, maintaining that the local planning authority had acted in bad faith and had been motivated by irrelevant considerations. The judge ruled that these contentions should have been made in proceedings for judicial review and that they could not be gone into in the criminal proceedings. The appellant then pleaded guilty and was convicted. This House upheld his conviction. Lord Hoffmann, in the leading speech, emphasised that the ability of a defendant to criminal proceedings to challenge the validity of an act done under statutory authority depended on the construction of the statute in question. This House held that the Town and Country Planning Act 1990 contained an elaborate code including provision for appeals against notices, and that on the proper construction of section 179(1) of the Act all that was required to be proved in the criminal proceedings was that the notice issued by the local planning authority was formally valid.

The decision of the Divisional Court in *Quietlynn Ltd* v. *Plymouth City Council* [1988] 1 Q.B. 114 is justified on similar grounds: see *Reg.* v. *Wicks* [1998] A.C. 92, 117–118, *per* Lord Hoffmann. There, a company was operating sex shops in Plymouth under transitional provisions which allowed them to do so until their application for a licence under the scheme introduced by the Local Government (Miscellaneous Provisions) Act 1982 had been 'determined.' The local authority refused the application. The company was then prosecuted for trading without a licence. It sought to allege that the local authority had failed to comply with certain procedural provisions and that its application had therefore not yet been determined within the meaning of the Act. The Divisional Court held as a matter of construction that the local authority's decision was a determination, whether or not it could be challenged by judicial review. In the particular statutory context, therefore, an act which might turn out for a different purpose to be a nullity (e.g. so as to require the local authority to hear the application again) was nevertheless a determination for the purpose of bringing the transitional period to an end.

However, in approaching the issue of statutory construction the courts proceed from a strong appreciation that ours is a country subject to the rule of law. This means that it is well recognised to be important for the maintenance of the rule of law and the preservation of liberty that individuals affected by legal measures promulgated by executive public bodies should have a fair opportunity to challenge these measures and to vindicate their rights in court proceedings. There is a strong presumption that Parliament will not legislate to prevent individuals from doing so: 'It is a principle not by any means to be whittled down that the subject's recourse to Her Majesty's courts for the determination of his rights is not to be excluded except by clear words:' *Pyx Granite Co Ltd* v. *Ministry of Housing and Local Government* [1960] A.C. 260, 286, *per* Viscount Simonds; cited by Lord Fraser of Tullybelton in *Wandsworth London Borough Council* v. *Winder* [1969] A.C. 461, 510 ...

The particular statutory schemes in question in *Reg.* v. *Wicks* [1998] A.C. 92 and in the *Quietlynn* case [1988] 1 Q.B. 114 did justify a construction which limited the rights of the defendant to call the legality of an administrative act into question. But in my judgment it was an important feature of both cases that they were concerned with administrative acts specifically directed at the defendants, where there had been clear and ample opportunity provided by the scheme of the relevant legislation for those defendants to challenge the legality of those acts, before being charged with an offence.

By contrast, where subordinate legislation (e.g. statutory instruments or byelaws) is promulgated which is of a general character in the sense that it is directed to the world at large, the first time an individual may be affected by that legislation is when he is charged with an offence under it: so also where a general provision is brought into effect by an administrative act, as in this case. A smoker might have made his first journey on the line on the same train as Mr. Boddington; have found that there was no carriage free of no smoking signs and have chosen to exercise what he believed to be his right to smoke on the train. Such an individual would have had no sensible opportunity to challenge the validity of the posting of the no smoking signs throughout the train until he was charged, as Mr. Boddington was, under byelaw 20. In my judgment in such a case the strong presumption must be that Parliament did not intend to deprive the smoker of an opportunity to defend himself in the criminal proceedings by asserting the alleged unlawfulness of the decision to post no smoking notices throughout the train. I can see nothing in section 67 of the Transport Act 1962 or the byelaws which could displace that presumption. It is clear from *Wandsworth London Borough Council* v. *Winder* [1985] A.C. 461 and *Reg.* v. *Wicks* [1998] A.C. 92, 116, *per* Lord Hoffmann that the development of a statutorily based procedure for judicial review proceedings does not of itself displace the presumption.

... Lord Nicholls of Birkenhead noted in *Reg.* v. *Wicks,* at pp. 106–107, that there may be cases where proceedings in the Divisional Court are more suitable and convenient for challenging a byelaw or administrative decision made under it than by way of defence in criminal proceedings in the magistrates' court or the Crown Court. Nonetheless Lord Nicholls held that 'the proper starting point' must be a presumption that 'an accused should be able to challenge, on any ground, the lawfulness of an order the breach of which constitutes his alleged criminal offence:' see p. 106. No doubt the factors listed by Lord Nicholls [*viz* the ability of the court in question to deal with the public law issues; the importance of preventing the avoidance of the procedural safeguards inherent in judicial review [see ch 13]; the fact that the public body whose decision is impugned may not be a party to criminal proceedings; the risk of inconsistent decisions in various criminal proceedings each dealing with the same administrative act] may, where the statutory context permits, be taken into account when construing any particular statute to determine Parliament's intention, but they will not usually be sufficient in themselves to support a construction of a statute which would preclude the right of a defendant to raise the legality of a byelaw or administrative action taken under it as a defence in other proceedings. This is because of the strength of the presumption against a construction which would prevent an individual being able to vindicate his rights in court proceedings in which he is involved. Nor do I think it right to belittle magistrates' courts: they sometimes have to decide very difficult legal questions and generally have the assistance of a legally qualified clerk to give them guidance on the law. . . . In my judgment only the clear language of a statute could take away the right of a defendant in criminal proceedings to challenge the lawfulness of a byelaw or administrative decision where his prosecution is premised on its validity.

Lord Irvine LC's analysis and the decisions in *Quietlynn* and *Wicks* upon which he relies demonstrate that collateral challenge may be legally prohibited by express or implied legislative provision. *DPP* v. *T* [2006] EWHC 728 (Admin), [2007] 1 WLR 209 is an example of a case in which the court was willing to find implied provision to that effect. The defendant had been made subject to an antisocial behaviour order (ASBO), the effect of which is to make it a criminal offence for the person concerned to engage, without lawful excuse, in conduct proscribed by the order. The defendant's ASBO was drafted in very broad terms—he was to refrain from acting 'in an anti-social manner in the City of Manchester'—and when charged with breaching it, he argued that it was so vague as to be void and thus unenforceable. The Administrative Court, however, held that he was not entitled to raise a collateral challenge: the ASBO was directed to the defendant; he knew of its existence; and he had a right of appeal against it.

QUESTIONS

- Can you think of any circumstances in which collateral challenge, although technically possible, would be pointless?
- For instance, could an individual unlawfully denied a trading licence and subsequently prosecuted for trading without a licence meaningfully raise in his defence the unlawfulness of the denial of a licence?

3.5 Concluding remarks

Like many aspects of administrative law, the status of unlawful administrative action is contested. However, while the disagreements that we have considered in this chapter are sometimes stark, it is noteworthy that, at least to some extent, they pertain not to what constitutes a desirable *outcome*—eg in terms of whether, for policy or pragmatic reasons, a given legally flawed administrative act should be accorded some degree of legal effect—but to the form of judicial *reasoning* that prefigures the reaching of the outcome. This may appear to lend an arid quality to the debate. Yet at its heart lie a series of interlocking disagreements about the nature of administrative law itself and about the framework within which adjudication ought to occur. Thus we have seen that roots of the contestations examined in this chapter run deep, engaging questions relating to the constitutional foundations of judicial review, the extent to which the notion of jurisdiction can and should serve as an organizing concept, and the relative merits of approaches to adjudication that are respectively premised upon judicial discretion and conceptual reasoning. In this way, the debate about the legal status of unlawful administrative acts serves as a lens through which much of the contested nature of administrative law can be appreciated.

The problems that arise in this area are thorny ones, and fine judgements must be, and are, made by the courts. Lying at the very core of the debate is a question about the nature of the tools to which courts should have recourse when addressing these inevitable complexities. As in so many other areas of administrative law, any successful attempt to infer a theory from— or to erect a scaffolding of theory around—judicial practice must reconcile the need to deliver outcomes that are normatively desirable and practically sensible with the conceptual apparatus that lends structure and intellectual coherence to administrative law. For reasons examined in the previous chapter, the concept of jurisdiction is now the centerpiece of that apparatus, and logic therefore dictates that unlawful administrative acts, being extra-jurisdictional, lack a legal foundation. From this it follows that such acts are void. And while that insight may not be the end of the matter—we have seen in this chapter that the devil is in the detail, and that voidness is at least to some extent a relative concept—it is nevertheless an essential starting-point when it comes to analysing the legal status of unlawful administrative action.

FURTHER RESOURCES

Feldman, 'Error of Law and Flawed Administrative Acts' [2014] *CLJ* 275

Forsyth, 'The Rock and the Sand: Jurisdiction and Remedial Discretion' [2013] *JR* 360

Forsyth, '"The Metaphysic of Nullity": Invalidity, Conceptual Reasoning and the Rule of Law' in Forsyth and Hare (eds), *The Golden Metwand and the Crooked Cord* (Oxford 1998)

Taggart, 'Rival Theories of Invalidity in Administrative Law: Some Practical and Theoretical Consequences' in Taggart (ed), *Judicial Review of Administrative Action in the 1980s* (Auckland 1986)

Wade, 'Unlawful Administrative Action: Void or Voidable? (Part I)' (1967) 83 *LQR* 499

Wade, 'Unlawful Administrative Action: Void or Voidable? (Part II)' (1968) 84 *LQR* 95

4 THE SCOPE OF PUBLIC LAW PRINCIPLES

4.1 Introduction

In subsequent chapters, we address the specific content of the principles of good administration that condition the exercise of many discretionary powers. We begin, however, by considering the reach of those principles. It seems intuitively right that, for instance, in exercising his powers of deportation, the Home Secretary should be required to respect public law principles of good decision-making such as fairness and rationality, as well as the human rights of the individual. But how far should the public law principles of good administration extend? What of the power to declare war? Should courts be able to scrutinize the exercise of that power for compliance with public law principles? And what about decisions made by non-governmental bodies, but which are of public significance? Should administrative law look beyond the state, as traditionally conceived? In determining the scope of the principles of public law, should we look to who holds the power, or to the nature of the power itself? Should privatizing an activity exempt it from the norms enforced via judicial review?

When we ask whether a given power is subject to judicial review, we in fact raise two questions. ('Judicial review' is used here simply to mean judicial scrutiny for compliance with the norms of public law. Whether that scrutiny must be by means of the special 'judicial review procedure' is a distinct question that we address at 13.3.) First, is it *amenable* in principle to judicial review? Traditionally, judicial review was essentially confined to discretionary powers granted by statute, but we will see that a new orthodoxy has now emerged, opening up to review a wider range of powers. Second, does the exercise of the power raise *justiciable* issues? The concept of justiciability requires courts to examine the subject-matter of the power and the issues raised by its exercise—and to determine, in light of such factors, the degree to which the matter is suitable for adjudication by a court.

4.2 Statutory powers

It is *usually* taken for granted that discretionary powers conferred by legislation are subject to judicial review. However, for two reasons, this does not *automatically* follow.

First, the exercise of some functions pursuant to statutory powers or duties may be regarded as insufficiently 'public' to attract judicial review (a position which, as we consider at 4.5, makes certain assumptions about the function of judicial review). This question arises most commonly when public bodies, using statutory powers, enter (or decline to enter) into or terminate contracts. Should such matters be amenable to judicial review? Bailey [2007] *PL* 444 identifies two approaches to this question in the case law. The first and, it seems, dominant, approach holds that the mere fact that a statutory power is being exercised is not enough to establish that judicial review applies: there must be some 'public law element'. So in *R* v. *Bolsover District Council, ex parte Pepper* [2001] BLGR 43, the Court declined to subject to judicial review the defendant local authority's refusal to sell land to the claimant. In the absence of a specific public law element, such as a failure to follow statutory procedural requirements, this was a private law matter. This approach, says Bailey, is unnecessarily complicated. The better analysis, he argues, is that of Elias J in *R (Molinaro)* v. *Kensington London Borough Council* [2001] EWHC 896 (Admin), [2002] BLGR 336, according to which the use of statutory power is treated as sufficient to render the matter a public law one, the only question then being whether a public law ground of challenge can be made out. The latter approach is preferable not least because it is analytically simpler: the question whether a particular function has a 'public law element' is, as we will see later in this chapter, a highly vexed one.

Second, even if the matter complained of is, in principle, susceptible to judicial review, the court must go on to ask whether the matter is justiciable: *ie*, whether it raises issues upon which it is appropriate for courts to adjudicate. This requires close judicial evaluation of the nature and subject-matter of the claim and statutory context, and judicial reasoning in this area is therefore heavily context-dependent. From this it follows that discretionary powers cannot, and should not, be placed into two watertight categories marked 'justiciable' and 'non-justiciable', where the former are subject to the full panoply of judicial review while the latter are wholly immune from it. Rather, modern judicial review recognizes that there exists a spectrum of justiciability, ranging from exercises of power which are completely excluded from review to matters which are subject to particularly rigorous judicial scrutiny. Between these poles, varying forms and levels of review may be appropriate: for instance, close judicial oversight of the fairness of the decision-making process may be appropriate, whereas scrutiny of the substance of the decision might not.

The case of *AXA General Insurance Ltd* v. *HM Advocate* [2011] UKSC 46, [2012] 1 AC 868 offers an interesting illustrative example of how contemporary administrative law approaches questions of 'justiciability', in the context of statutory powers. The case raised the novel issue of whether legislation passed by the Scottish Parliament was subject to judicial review on common law grounds, and if so, what approach the courts ought to take to reviewing such legislation. The Scottish Parliament was established by the Scotland Act 1998, passed by the UK Parliament, and its legislative powers are conferred by that statute; therefore, when the Scottish Parliament passes legislation it is exercising statutory powers.

The novelty of the issues raised by this case required the Court to approach it from first principles, and the decision therefore offers a valuable insight into the general framework of principle courts rely on in calibrating their approach to review of statutory powers in any given context.

The Supreme Court held legislation passed by the Scottish Parliament was subject to judicial review, consonant with a general judicial reluctance in contemporary administrative law to classify any particular power non-justiciable *per se*, given the courts' constitutional role in upholding the rule of law. The members of the Court reasoned that unlike the Westminster Parliament the Scottish Parliament is not a sovereign body that can make or unmake any law it wishes. Rather, it is a body to which power has been delegated pursuant to statute. A statutory body, by its nature, is a body of limited legal power; because its powers are defined they are necessarily confined and the body must work within those legal limits. Within the separation of powers it is for the courts to interpret and apply those limits, and the Scottish Parliament is therefore subject to the jurisdiction of the courts.

The 'much more important question' which faced the Court was 'what the grounds are, if any, on which [Scottish legislation] may be subjected to review' (at [47]). This was 'uncharted territory'—English courts have not previously reviewed legislation passed by a democratic legislature—and the matter had thus to be 'addressed as one of principle' (at [48]). The approach adopted by the Court reflects the contextual approach that is a hall-mark of contemporary judicial review. In an iconic statement of principle, Lord Reed said (at [142]):

> Judicial review under the common law is based upon an understanding of the respective con-stitutional responsibilities of public authorities and the courts. The constitutional function of the courts in the field of public law is to ensure, so far as they can, that public authorities respect the rule of law. The courts therefore have the responsibility of ensuring that the pub-lic authority in question does not misuse its powers or exceed their limits. The extent of the courts' responsibility in relation to a particular exercise of power by a public authority neces-sarily depends upon the particular circumstances, including the nature of the public authority in question, the type of power being exercised, the process by which it is exercised, and the extent to which the powers of the authority have limits or purposes which the courts can iden-tify and adjudicate upon.

Applying this contextual approach the members of the Court were agreed that in con-ducting judicial review of legislation passed by the Scottish legislature, the courts could only potentially intervene in the most exceptional circumstances. Reinforcing this, all (except Lord Mance (see [97])) considered rationality review was not open to the courts in this context. Lords Hope and Reed, in their lead judgments, placed emphasis on several contextual factors in settling on this limited approach. Importantly, these factors marked review of the legislature out from the paradigm context in which review principles are applied, namely review of statutory discretions by government officials, and thus war-ranted a different, far more restrained approach than would ordinarily be applied. Lord Reed placed particular emphasis on statutory context: the legislative powers conferred on the Scottish Parliament were very broad, reflecting that it was the UK Parliament's intent, in passing the Scotland Act, that the Scottish legislature have plenary power. Heavy emphasis was also placed on the Scottish legislature's democratic credentials; a democratically elected legislature is best placed to determine what lies in the polity's best interests, not the courts: '[T]he democratic process is liable to be subverted if, on a ques-tion of political or moral judgment, opponents of an Act achieve through the courts what they could not achieve through Parliament' (at [49]). Further, the courts would inevitably be illegitimately drawn into ordinary politics, contrary to the separation of powers, if they took to scrutinizing the substantive rationality of legislative measures. Also telling against a substantial judicial role was that the legislature was directly accountable to the electorate; the courts were not required to adopt an intensive approach to review, as the Scottish legislature is subject to other forms of accountability.

However, albeit the courts would adopt a restrained approach to review of legislative acts of the Scottish Parliament, the courts would not abdicate their primary function of upholding the rule of law and would intervene if necessary to uphold constitutional fundamentals. Lord Hope, observing that 'the rule of law enforced by the courts is the ultimate controlling factor on which our constitution is based', considered that legislation of an extreme kind, such as legislation purporting to 'abolish judicial review or to diminish the role of the courts in protecting the interests of the individual' would not be recognized as law (at [51]). Lord Reed, motivated by similar concerns, considered that the Scottish Parliament's legislative competence was subject to implied statutory limits: the UK Parliament, legislating for a liberal democracy founded on constitutional principles, would not have intended to empower the Scottish Parliament to act contrary to fundamental precepts of the rule of law or basic common law rights.

We see in *AXA* several core themes of contemporary judicial review of statutory powers. First, the courts are very reluctant to mark out particular statutory powers as altogether non-justiciable, given the fundamental judicial responsibility for upholding the rule of law and maintaining basic constitutional values. Second, consonant with a move from a rigid justiciable/non-justiciable dichotomy to a more subtle approach, how courts conduct review and on what grounds will vary with context and a range of factors. In the case of the Scottish legislature, that body's broadly framed powers, the political nature of its decisions, and strong democratic legitimacy all tell in favour of a restrained judicial approach, and strongly against judicial intervention on the basis of the substance of legislation. In other contexts, such as cases concerning exercise of narrowly framed statutory powers by unelected administrative officials, and which do not implicate open-ended questions of morality or high policy, the courts would not generally adopt such a restrained approach, and all grounds of review would be available in principle.

> **QUESTION**
> - While the move towards a more flexible approach has generally been seen as positive, what could be some drawbacks of such an approach?

4.3 Prerogative powers

4.3.1 The nature of prerogative power

Munro, *Studies in Constitutional Law* (London 1999) at 256, defines the prerogative as 'comprising those [legal] attributes belonging to the Crown which derive from common law, not statute, and which still survive'. Historically, the term 'prerogative' has usually been preceded by the epithet 'royal', but constitutional convention now dictates that the vast majority of prerogative powers are, in effect, exercised by government Ministers. Two preliminary matters should be noted.

First, those prerogatives which remain today do so because Parliament has not abolished or curtailed them. The dominant view (classically expounded by Lord Atkinson in *Attorney-General* v. *De Keyser's Royal Hotel Ltd* [1920] AC 508 at 539–40) is that the prerogative is placed in abeyance whenever legislation overlaps with it. In *R* v. *Secretary of State for the Home Department, ex parte Northumbria Police Authority* [1989] QB 26 at

44, Croom-Johnson LJ acknowledged that 'the Crown cannot act under the prerogative if to do so would be incompatible with statute'. However, in concluding in that case that no such incompatibility arose, so that the relevant prerogative and legislation could co-exist, their Lordships were clearly influenced by the fact that the former was being used for the public good, as they saw it, rather than (as in *De Keyser*) to attempt to undercut statutory safeguards beneficial to the public.

Second, there has been increasing recognition (see, *eg* Public Administration Select Committee, HC422, *Taming the Prerogative* (2003–04)) that prerogative powers are anachronistic. Such powers (unlike statutory powers) have not been democratically conferred on government; they are likely to be ill-defined; and, as a result, it is likely to be harder for Ministers to be held to account for their exercise, both politically and legally. Indeed, the government itself, in 2007, recognized the force of some of these arguments (see Cm 7170, *The Governance of Britain* (2007), ch 1). As a result, Part 1 of the Constitutional Reform and Governance Act 2010 shifted the government's powers to manage the civil service from a prerogative to a statutory basis. Meanwhile, Part 2 of the Act, although leaving intact the ministerial prerogative to conclude treaties on behalf of the United Kingdom, enables the House of Commons to veto exercise of that power. We also see increasing moves in the political sphere to bridle exercise of prerogative powers. For example, there is an emerging constitutional convention, the precise content and bounds of which are still developing, that before British troops are deployed, at least in major combat roles, the government must generally seek a debate in, and secure approval of, a majority of the House of Commons (Mills, *Parliamentary Approval for Military Action*, House of Commons Library Briefing Paper No 7166 (12 May 2015)).

These legal reforms and other developments notwithstanding, important prerogative powers—concerning, for example, deployment of the armed forces, granting of mercy, and governance of British overseas territories—remain. The question therefore arises whether, and if so on what terms, their exercise is susceptible to judicial review.

4.3.2 The amenability of the prerogative to judicial review

Although the courts traditionally refused to examine the exercise of prerogative powers, they have long been willing to adjudicate upon one aspect of the prerogative. Sir Edward Coke famously remarked in the *Case of Proclamations* (1611) 2 Co Rep 74 at 76 that 'the King hath no prerogative, but that which the law of the land allows him'. However, while welcome, such scrutiny of the prerogative was undeniably modest. Once the power in question was acknowledged to exist, such limited review left considerable scope for unchecked misuse.

Such concerns influenced the courts in a series of cases in the 1960s and 1970s—including *Chandler v. Director of Public Prosecutions* [1964] AC 763, *Laker Airways Ltd v. Department of Trade* [1977] QB 643, and *R v. Criminal Injuries Compensation Board, ex parte Lain* [1967] 2 QB 864—which evidenced growing judicial unease at the insulation of the prerogative from administrative law's increasingly exacting standards. That line of case law culminates in the seminal decision of the House of Lords in the so-called *GCHQ* case.

Council of Civil Service Unions v. *Minister for the Civil Service* [1985] AC 374
House of Lords

Article 4 of the Civil Service Order in Council 1982, promulgated under prerogative power, allowed the Minister for the Civil Service to make regulations concerning civil servants' employment conditions. The Minister issued an instruction under Article 4 to the effect that staff at Government Communications Headquarters (GCHQ) would no longer be permitted to belong to national trade unions. Trade union membership had been permitted since GCHQ's establishment in 1947 and there was a well-established practice of consultation at GCHQ about all important alterations to conditions of employment; however, no such consultation occurred in the instant case. The Council of Civil Service Unions and six members of staff sought judicial review, alleging a breach of the duty to act fairly and breach of legitimate expectations (on this aspect of the case see at 6.1.3). At first instance Glidewell J concluded that the instruction was unlawful, and issued a declaratory order to that effect. The Court of Appeal, however, allowed an appeal by the Minister. The claimants appealed to the House of Lords. One of the issues which their Lordships had to confront was whether the Minister's actions were amenable to review, given that the instruction was issued under powers conferred by prerogative.

Lord Diplock

… Judicial review … provides the means by which judicial control of administrative action is exercised. The subject matter of every judicial review is a decision made by some person (or body of persons) whom I will call the 'decision-maker' or else a refusal by him to make a decision.

To qualify as a subject for judicial review the decision must have consequences which affect some person (or body of persons) other than the decision-maker, although it may affect him too. It must affect such other person either: (a) by altering rights or obligations of that person which are enforceable by or against him in private law; or (b) by depriving him of some benefit or advantage which either (i) he had in the past been permitted by the decision-maker to enjoy and which he can legitimately expect to be permitted to continue to do until there has been communicated to him some rational grounds for withdrawing it on which he has been given an opportunity to comment; or (ii) he has received assurance from the decision-maker that it will not be withdrawn without giving him first an opportunity of advancing reasons for contending that they should not be withdrawn …

For a decision to be susceptible to judicial review the decision-maker must be empowered by public law (and not merely, as in arbitration, by agreement between private parties) to make decisions that, if validly made, will lead to administrative action or abstention from action by an authority endowed by law with executive powers, which have one or other of the consequences mentioned in the preceding paragraph. The ultimate source of the decision-making power is nearly always nowadays a statute or subordinate legislation made under the statute; but in the absence of any statute regulating the subject matter of the decision the source of the decision-making power may still be the common law itself, *ie,* that part of the common law that is given by lawyers the label of 'the prerogative.' Where this is the source of decision-making power, the power is confined to executive officers of central as distinct from local government and in constitutional practice is generally exercised by those holding ministerial rank …

My Lords, I intend no discourtesy to counsel when I say that, intellectual interest apart, in answering the question of law raised in this appeal, I have derived little practical assistance from learned and esoteric analyses of the precise legal nature, boundaries and historical origin of 'the prerogative,' or of what powers exercisable by executive officers acting on behalf of central government that are not shared by private citizens qualify for inclusion under this particular label. It does not, for instance, seem to me to matter whether today the right of the executive government that happens to be in power to dismiss without notice any member of the home civil service upon which perforce it must rely for the administration of its policies, and the correlative disability of the executive government that is in power to agree with a civil servant that his service should be on terms that did not make him subject to instant dismissal, should be ascribed to 'the prerogative' or merely to a consequence of the survival, for entirely different reasons, of a rule of constitutional law whose origin is to be found in the theory that those by whom the administration of the realm is carried on do so as personal servants of the monarch who can dismiss them at will, because the King can do no wrong.

Nevertheless, whatever label may be attached to them there have unquestionably survived into the present day a residue of miscellaneous fields of law in which the executive government retains decision-making powers that are not dependent upon any statutory authority but nevertheless have consequences on the private rights or legitimate expectations of other persons which would render the decision subject to judicial review if the power of the decision-maker to make them were statutory in origin. From matters so relatively minor as the grant of pardons to condemned criminals, of honours to the good and great, of corporate personality to deserving bodies of persons, and of bounty from moneys made available to the executive government by Parliament, they extend to matters so vital to the survival and welfare of the nation as the conduct of relations with foreign states and—what lies at the heart of the present case—the defence of the realm against potential enemies ...

My Lords, I see no reason why simply because a decision-making power is derived from a common law and not a statutory source, it should *for that reason only* be immune from judicial review.

Their Lordships all agreed that the exercise of prerogative power in question in this case could be judicially reviewed. However, bearing in mind the national security considerations that were in play, all five Law Lords declined to hold that the Minister had acted unlawfully.

It is clear from Lord Diplock's speech that judicial control of the prerogative was regarded as essential to the maintenance of the rule of law. Lord Roskill took a similar view, and was anxious that the courts' ability to protect individuals against abuse should not be curtailed by formal source-based considerations. Whether committed under statutory or prerogative authority, Lord Roskill said (at 417), 'the act in question is the act of the executive. To talk of that act as the act of the sovereign savours of the archaism of past centuries.'

In *GCHQ*, the Minister was exercising discretionary powers conferred by prerogative legislation (the 1982 Order in Council). Although the majority did not rely on this point, Lords Fraser and Brightman made more of it. While accepting that judicial review could in principle lie in the circumstances which applied in *GCHQ* (because, pursuant to a version of the *ultra vires* doctrine, conditions could be read into the prerogative legislation conferring power upon the Minister), they left open the question whether exercises of the prerogative itself could be reviewed. For example, can the legality of an Order in Council—as opposed to the legality of action purportedly taken under an Order in Council—be judicially reviewed? Precisely that question arose in the next case.

R (Bancoult) v. *Secretary of State for Foreign and Commonwealth Affairs (No 2)* [2008] UKHL 61, [2009] AC 453
House of Lords

In 1965, the Chagos Islands, part of the then British colony of Mauritius, were rendered a separate colony known as the British Indian Ocean Territory (BIOT). This was effected by the BIOT Order 1965, a statutory instrument made under the Colonial Boundaries Act 1895. The Order created the office of Commissioner of BIOT, authorizing him to 'make laws for the peace, order and good government of the territory'. This he purported to do by enacting the Immigration Ordinance 1971, which provided that no one could enter or remain in the territory without permission. The underlying purpose of the Ordinance was to provide a legal basis for exiling the whole of the Chagossian population pursuant to an agreement between the UK and US governments that the latter would be allowed to establish a military base on one of the islands, Diego Garcia. In 2000, the Divisional Court ([2001] QB 1067) found that the relevant part of the Immigration Ordinance was *ultra vires* the BIOT Order, holding that a provision facilitating the removal of the population could not be said to be in the interests of the peace, order, and good government of the territory. The government said it would not appeal against the Court's decision. However, in June 2004 the BIOT Order was revoked and the Crown in Council enacted prerogative legislation, known as the Constitution Order, s 9 of which reinstated the prohibitions on entry and residence which had been in place between 1971 and 2000. The claimants argued that s 9 was unlawful because the prerogative power of colonial governance was not broad enough in scope to permit the exiling of the population and that if, contrary to that argument, the enacting of population-exiling legislation was in principle possible, its enactment in the present circumstances had been irrational and in breach of legitimate expectations. The following excerpts are concerned only with the question whether the court could review the legality of an Order in Council.

Lord Hoffmann

[33] ... Mr Crow [for the Foreign Secretary] argued the courts had no power to review the validity of an Order in Council legislating for a colony [because, *inter alia*,] it was primary legislation having unquestionable validity comparable with that of an Act of Parliament ...

[34] It is true that a prerogative Order in Council is primary legislation in the sense that the legislative power of the Crown is original and not subordinate. It is classified as primary legislation for the purposes of the Human Rights Act 1998: see paragraph (f)(i) of the definition in section 21(1). That means that it cannot be overridden by Convention rights. The court can only make a declaration of incompatibility under section 4.

[35] But the fact that such Orders in Council in certain important respects resemble Acts of Parliament does not mean that they share all their characteristics. The principle of the sovereignty of Parliament, as it has been developed by the courts over the past 350 years, is founded upon the unique authority Parliament derives from its representative character. An exercise of the prerogative lacks this quality; although it may be legislative in character, it is still an exercise of power by the executive alone. Until the decision of this House in *Council of Civil Service Unions v. Minister for the Civil Service* [1985] AC 374, it may have been assumed that the exercise of prerogative powers was, as such, immune from judicial review. That objection being removed, I see no reason why prerogative legislation should not be subject to review on ordinary principles of legality, rationality and procedural impropriety in the same way as any other executive action. Mr Crow rightly pointed out that the *Council of Civil Service Unions* case was not concerned with the validity of a prerogative order but with an executive decision made pursuant to powers conferred by such an order. That is a ground upon which, if your Lordships were inclined to distinguish the case, it would be open to you to do so. But I see no reason for making such a distinction. On 21 February 2008 the Foreign Secretary told the House of Commons that, contrary to previous assurances, Diego Garcia had been used as a base for two extraordinary rendition flights in 2002 (Hansard (HC Debates), cols 547–548). There are allegations, which the US authorities have denied, that Diego Garcia or a ship in the waters around it have been used as a prison in which suspects have been tortured. The idea that such conduct on British territory, touching the honour of the United Kingdom, could be legitimated by executive fiat, is not something which I would find acceptable.

The other judges agreed with Lord Hoffmann that the legality of Orders in Council can be challenged via judicial review, although for the majority that conclusion was of little more than rhetorical significance. Lords Hoffmann, Rodger, and Carswell held that the colonial governance prerogative was a 'plenary' power that could be used for any purpose—a conclusion that effectively made it impossible for the claimants to succeed in their argument that the power did not extend to the enactment of population-exiling legislation. The starkest position was adopted by Lord Rodger, who although agreeing that in principle the legality of Orders in Council can be reviewed, said (at [109]) that the colonial governance prerogative was so broad as to be in practice 'equal in scope to the legislative power of Parliament'. For instance, it could, said Lord Rodger (at [98]), be used to enact legislation permitting torture (contrast the approach of the Supreme Court in *AXA General Insurance Ltd* v. *HM Advocate* [2011] UKSC 46, [2012] 1 AC 868 to a similarly broad legislative power, the Court being agreed that some basic limits must apply to protect important rights and constitutional values, even where the legislative power is exercised by a democratic body: see 4.2). The majority's willingness to characterize the power in such broad terms was informed by their refusal to accept that the Chagossians had a constitutional right of abode. Moreover, while the majority recognized that the colonial governance prerogative has traditionally been characterized as a power that can only be used for promoting 'peace, order and good government', they refused to inquire into whether those purposes were truly advanced by the Order in Council.

Contrast the majority's analysis with the following excerpt from Lord Mance's dissenting speech:

[157] [The] submission [that any right of abode that might have existed could be displaced by Order in Council] treats BIOT and the prerogative power to make constitutional or other laws relating to BIOT as if they related to nothing more than the bare land, and as if the people inhabiting BIOT were an insignificant inconvenience (a phrase which reflects the flavour of some of the government's internal memoranda in the 1960s), liable to be dispossessed at will for any reason that might seem good to the executive in the interests of the United Kingdom. Sir Sydney [Kentridge, for the Chagossians] accepts that in administering BIOT the Crown in Council was entitled to have regard to the interests of the United Kingdom and its territories generally, and was not confined to consideration of the benefits to BIOT alone. He also accepts that the United Kingdom could, in the defence interests of itself and its ally, require Chagossians resident in one part of the territory (Diego Garcia) to move to another part, and that there might be extreme circumstances of necessity (eg where a whole territory became unsafe for inhabitation, due to volcanic eruption or imminent threat of inundation) where the United Kingdom could by order in council require its evacuation. But enacting a constitution for a conquered or ceded colony which has the aim of depopulating the whole of a habitable territory in the interests of the United Kingdom or its allies is another matter. A colony, whether conquered, ceded or settled, consists, first and foremost, of people living in a territory, with links to a parent state. The Crown's 'constituent' power to introduce a constitution for a ceded territory is a power intended to enable the proper governance of the territory, at least among other things for the benefit of the people inhabiting it. A constitution which exiles a territory's inhabitants is a contradiction in terms. The absence of any precedent for the exercise of the royal prerogative to exclude the inhabitants of a colony from the colony is significant, although to my mind entirely unsurprising. Until the present case, no-one can have conceived of its exercise for such a purpose. Territories, such as Gibraltar or Malta, have been conquered or ceded with military purposes in mind, but never, so far as appears, has there been either an original purpose or a subsequent attempt

compulsorily to exclude their natural inhabitants. It may not have been necessary in the present case to use force to empty BIOT, but the logic of the government's position is that this too would have been permissible.

While conceiving of prerogative powers in very broad terms is most obviously likely to undercut claims that the extent of the power has been exceeded, it may also be fatal to claims that the power has been unlawfully exercised. The minority in *Bancoult* went on to conclude that if (as they thought it did not) the colonial governance prerogative in principle extended to the enactment of population-exiling legislation, its use for that purpose in the instant case was unlawful on grounds of irrationality (Lords Bingham and Mance could discern no good reason for the decision to exile the whole population) and breach of legitimate expectation (this aspect of the case is considered in ch 6). In contrast, the majority held that the exercise of the power disclosed no illegality—a conclusion that is unsurprising given their prepared-ness to characterize the power as a plenary one: the broader the power and the range of uses to which it can lawfully be put, the harder it will be for claimants to show that its exercise for any given purpose is irrational.

4.3.3 From form to substance: justiciability as the limiting factor

The extent to which the in-principle reviewability of the prerogative is of any practical sig-nificance is shaped by a further factor: the question of justiciability. In his speech in *GCHQ* [1985] AC 374 at 418, Lord Roskill, having concluded that the exercise of prerogative powers was reviewable in principle, said:

But I do not think that that right of challenge can be unqualified. It must, I think, depend upon the subject matter of the prerogative power which is exercised. Many examples were given during the argument of prerogative powers which as at present advised I do not think could properly be made the subject of judicial review. Prerogative powers such as those relating to the making of treaties, the defence of the realm, the prerogative of mercy, the grant of honours, the dissolution of Parliament and the appointment of ministers as well as others are not, I think susceptible to judi-cial review because their nature and subject matter are such as not to be amenable to the judicial process. The courts are not the place wherein to determine whether a treaty should be concluded or the armed forces disposed in a particular manner or Parliament dissolved on one date rather than another.

That approach reflects a highly limited conception of the courts' role in two senses. First, its focus is not on whether the specific questions raised by a given administrative act are beyond the courts' competence to answer; rather, it rules out judicial review of *any issue* arising from the exercise of particular prerogative powers. Second, Lord Roskill's view was not that judi-cial review should be less rigorous in such situations: he thought that there should be no judicial review *at all*.

Lord Roskill's approach gives rise to two questions. The first concerns the distinc-tion between a *subject-matter-based* and an *issue-based* conception of non-justiciabil-ity. Should courts (as Lord Roskill thought) decline to examine any exercise of a given power because it *may* raise non-justiciable questions, or should it decline to examine only those exercises of power that *do* raise such questions? The second question concerns the distinction between the concepts of *non-justiciability* and *deference*. When questions arise that are regarded by courts as less than normally suitable for judicial adjudication, should they hold such questions to be non-justiciable (such that they do not examine them at all) or should they subject them to a more limited or 'deferential' form of review?

As far as the first question is concerned (we return to the second at the end of this section), the better view is that the doctrine of non-justiciability is one of judicial self-restraint in the face of matters which are unsuitable for adjudication in the courts. It is therefore meaningless to classify particular *powers*—prerogative or otherwise—as non-justiciable; rather, the question is whether a given exercise of power raises an *issue* upon which courts are able to adjudicate. It is true that the use of some powers is unlikely to raise issues that are suitable for judicial review, and for that reason the exercise of some prerogative powers may in practice remain wholly or largely beyond the courts' purview. But it makes little sense to regard any power as *per se* non-justiciable. As Allan, *Constitutional Justice* (Oxford 2001) at 177, puts it, 'It is quite mistaken to seek to identify a field of executive power whose nature makes it unsuited to judicial review: the correct approach is always to examine the requirements of equality and procedural fairness, as they apply in the context of the decision-making process in question.' (Logically, the same should be true of the other principles of judicial review, too.)

The more subtle view preferred by Allan prevailed in *R v. Secretary of State for the Home Department, ex parte Bentley* [1994] QB 349. In 1952, the claimant's brother, Derek Bentley, was convicted of the murder of a police officer and sentenced to death. The Home Secretary refused to reprieve Bentley; he was therefore hanged. For many years the claimant campaigned for a posthumous pardon for her brother; in 1992 the Home Secretary reviewed the case, but ultimately refused to grant a pardon on the ground that the review had failed to establish Bentley's innocence. However, the Home Secretary had considered only the possibility of a 'free', or unconditional, pardon, and had failed to appreciate that other options— including a 'conditional' pardon, signifying the (retrospective, and so in the circumstances symbolic) substitution of the court-imposed penalty with some lesser penalty. Although declining to issue a formal remedy for the Minister's failure to give sufficient consideration to a conditional pardon, the Court concluded that it was competent to examine the issues given that the central question related to the scope of the Home Secretary's prerogative powers—a crisp legal question that was not rendered non-justiciable merely by the fact that it arose in relation to the prerogative of mercy. Following the Court's judgment, which invited the Minister to look at the matter again, the Home Secretary granted a limited pardon, which, in effect, acknowledged that the imposition of the death penalty had been inappropriate.

We find a similar approach in the recent Supreme Court decision in *R (Barclay) v. Secretary of State for Justice* [2014] UKSC 54, [2015] AC 276. In that case the Court considered the argument that UK courts lacked jurisdiction to hear a judicial review challenge to an Order in Council by which Royal Assent was given, on the advice of the UK executive, to a statute passed by the legislature of Sark, a Channel Island and UK Crown Dependency (the giving of Royal Assent being necessary for the statute to become law). The Court considered that it could not intervene in this case. The reasons included that the challenge had been made on human rights grounds: the Court considered it was more appropriate for challenges to the human rights compatibility of Sark legislation to be made in local courts on the basis of Sark's dedicated human

THE SCOPE OF PUBLIC LAW PRINCIPLES • 125

rights law (which was similar in nature to the Human Rights Act 1998 (HRA)), once the legislation had been passed, rather than preemptively by UK courts less familiar with local conditions and prior to the statute becoming law. However, the Court was very careful to state that its refusal to exercise its review powers *in this case* did not entail the proposition that such Orders were non-justiciable in general: '[T]he courts of the United Kingdom do have jurisdiction judicially to review an Order in Council which is made on the advice of the Government of the United Kingdom acting in whole or in part in the interests of the United Kingdom ... Nevertheless there are circumstances in which that jurisdiction should not be exercised. This is clearly one of them' (at [58]).

Although an issue-based, as opposed to a subject-matter based, approach to justiciability is now the dominant one, the rhetoric of the courts' judgments occasionally obscures this point. For instance, in *R* v. *Jones* [2006] UKHL 16, [2007] 1 AC 136 at [65], Lord Hoffmann said: '[T]he making of war and peace and the disposition of the armed forces has always been regarded as a discretionary power of the Crown into the exercise of which the courts will not inquire.' To similar effect, in *R (Abbasi)* v. *Secretary of State for Foreign and Commonwealth Affairs* [2002] EWCA Civ 1598, the Court referred to 'forbidden areas', which category included 'decisions affecting foreign policy'. But this language, which on its face implies the reinstatement of (at least part of) Lord Roskill's list of unreviewable prerogatives, is misleading. In *Abbasi*, the claimant, a British national held by the US government at Guantánamo Bay in Cuba, challenged the Foreign Secretary's refusal to make diplomatic representations on his behalf. That challenge was partly based on the contention that statements made by the British government had given rise to a legitimate expectation that representations would be made on behalf of people in the claimant's situation. The Court made it clear that it would not dictate to the Foreign Secretary what her policy regarding the making of representations should be, but it was perfectly happy to consider whether a legitimate expectation had arisen. (It had not.) In *R (Sandiford)* v. *Secretary of State for Foreign and Commonwealth Affairs* [2014] UKSC 44, [2014] 1 WLR 2697, which involved a challenge to a government decision not to pay the legal fees of a British national seeking to overturn their death sentence in Indonesia, Lords Carnwath and Mance said: '[T]here is no reason why a prerogative refusal to fund litigation should be immune from all judicial review. It does not raise any real issues of foreign policy' (at [65]). By implication this statement might be taken to suggest that a prerogative power which could be framed as generally concerned with matters of foreign policy may *per se* be 'immune' from judicial review. But the better reading of the statement is that exercise of prerogative powers is never immune from challenge; only that if a particular review challenge necessarily required the court to enter into the substance of high foreign policy matters this would militate against judicial intervention *in that case*. It is also worth noting that the Court indicated that the Minister's exercise or non-exercise of the power to fund a British national's litigation was in principle open to intensive substantive review on rationality and proportionality grounds; in turn signifying how far judicial review of the prerogative has developed. We would thus suggest that unhelpful references to 'forbidden areas' or 'immunities' notwithstanding, these cases, far from undermining the issue-based approach, serve to reinforce and apply it.

So if the modern approach is to treat certain issues—as opposed to entire powers—as non-justiciable, how do courts decide *which* issues those are? Harris commends the deployment of a number of criteria to guide this inquiry.

Harris, 'Judicial Review, Justiciability and the Prerogative of Mercy'
[2003] *CLJ* 631

A detailed appreciation of the subject matter of the executive decision-making … allows determination, from the point of view of the overall constitutional structure, of whether accountability is best facilitated by the courts, left to be effected by the legislature, or not expected at all.

… [This] invites reflection on aspects of the current operation of the doctrine of the separation of powers … Positive law ensuring the independence of the judiciary is a manifestation of the doctrine of the separation of powers … In determining justiciability in respect of an application for judicial review, the need for the assistance of the courts' independence may be taken into account. For example, where the executive decision requires the application of human rights norms, the independence of the courts from the majority will of the people may be highly relevant to determining the constitutional appropriateness of procedural accountability being through the courts.

The independence of the courts causes their own accountability to be the least overt of the three branches of government … The freedom which the courts enjoy from direct political accountability is a factor in some areas of executive decision-making involving elements of policy not being considered appropriate for judicial review. Possible areas of such non-justiciability include disposition of nuclear armaments [*Chandler* v. *Director of Public Prosecutions* [1964] AC 763], national security [*Chandler*], foreign relations [*R* v. *Secretary of State for Foreign and Commonwealth Affairs, ex parte Rees-Mogg* [1994] QB 552] and the distribution of scarce public resources [*R* v. *Cambridge Health Authority, ex parte B* [1995] 1 WLR 898], where society may wish review of the executive decision-making to be the responsibility of the more politically accountable legislature through ministerial responsibility.

… [However,] [t]he theoretical position that the courts should not review, and consequently not make policy decisions, does not correspond exactly with the practical needs of the community, or the way that the courts operate in reality. For example, the courts' development of the law of negligence has required the courts to make many policy decisions. Policy, to a greater or lesser degree, permeates most judicial decision-making. If one accepts the arguments against the courts making policy decisions, and yet acknowledges the practical necessity that the courts make some decisions with a policy element, the challenge is to formulate principles to assist in best determining those policy decisions which are capable of being justiciable and those which are not.

Finn [see 'The Justiciability of Administrative Decisions' (2002) 30 *Fed LR* 239 at 247] has commented on the need to distinguish between the decision-making of the public decision-maker being reviewed, which may be heavily policy laden, and the decision-making of the reviewing court, which need not necessarily be similarly policy laden. For example, judicial review on the natural justice ground of an alleged failure to give an applicant for a television station licence the right to be heard appropriately on its application, may not give rise to the need to consider any non-justiciable policy issues, even though the overall executive decision-making in respect of the allocation of television channels may be heavily policy laden and deserving of political, as different from judicial, accountability. The fact that an area of executive decision-making is heavily policy laden should not lead to the conclusion that particular decisions in that area are automatically non-justiciable. Political accountability through the executive and legislative branches, and judicial review through the courts, need not be mutually exclusive …

[A further] consideration is the suitability of the personnel, and methods of operation of the courts, to the particular decision-making which is expected of them. The necessarily limited qualities of the persons who perform the primary decision-making role in courts, namely the judges, and the procedures by which they operate, may also cause the subject matter of some disputes to be considered non-justiciable …

... [I]n some contexts, a judge's lack of expertise in relation to the subject matter of a dispute may make it difficult to achieve a quality of decision-making in which informed outside observers would have confidence. For example, if judicial review were to be sought of the exercise by the government of its prerogative power to break off diplomatic relations with a particular country, an executive argument would be likely to be made that a judge would not have the required expertise, or be capable of acquiring it during the trial, in order to decide the appropriate procedure and proportionality demanded by the executive decision. Similar concerns would be raised should judicial review be sought of the exercise of the prerogative to declare war. Both prerogatives are wide-ranging powers of the executive government which a reviewing court would find difficult to harness within concepts of legality, rationality and procedural propriety.

... [It is also necessary to consider the appropriateness] of the courts' processes to the determination required. Problems may flow from the fact that the courts are adversarial, participation of parties is limited, and the law of evidence may operate to constrain what is put before the court for consideration. Since the courts are not inquisitorial, they are largely dependent on the parties as to what is put before them by way of evidence and argument. The approach to evidence and argument has traditionally been conservative, with, for example, relatively little use of empirical evidence. The courts will often not have access to the breadth and depth of evidence, and spectrum of points of view, that are potentially available to the executive and legislature when they are involved in public decision-making. The executive and the legislature have the potential to listen to a wider range of people, and to bring a greater degree of direction and financial resource to the acquisition of thorough research and commentary that in many circumstances will allow better informed decision-making than can be provided by the courts. When the subject matter is policy-laden, such as in respect of the determination of issues to do with foreign affairs or the distribution of scarce resources, the courts, even if they had the requisite expertise, may not have presented to them appropriate ranges of relevant factual information to allow quality decisions to be made.

QUESTIONS

- A great deal of attention was given in *Bancoult* to the question whether, when exercising the prerogative power of colonial governance, the government was permitted to make only laws that were conducive to the peace, order, and good government of the territory concerned. Lord Rodger's view (at [109]) was that even if that was so, it would not be possible for a court to hold that legislation—even legislation exiling the entire population—did not so conduce: 'This is simply because such questions are not justiciable.' Do you agree?
- In the last paragraph of the excerpt Harris says that one important argument against courts considering difficult policy questions is that standard court procedures are not well suited to robust determination of such questions. What adaptations do you think could be made to ordinary adjudicative process to accommodate more policy-centred disputes?

Three points fall to be made by way of conclusion to our discussion of judicial review of the prerogative. First, although there are prerogative powers which, when exercised, are unlikely to raise justiciable issues, *there is no such thing as a non-justiciable prerogative power per se*. Rather, the question is always whether the particular ground of challenge invoked by the claimant raises justiciable issues given the factual matrix of the case. Second, while questions about justiciability are particularly common in relation to the use of pre-rogative powers—because of the nature of the 'high policy' issues that are still covered by the prerogative—*they can arise in relation to any form of power, including statutory power* (as we saw in the discussion of *AXA General Insurance Ltd* v. *HM Advocate* [2011] UKSC 46, [2012] 1 AC 868 in 4.2). Third, the matters which determine whether a particular issue is justiciable (*ie* subject to judicial review *at all*) are also relevant to the *intensity with which reviewable matters should be scrutinized by the courts*. It will be rare that a court can legiti-mately conclude that something is wholly immune from review on any ground: rather, the crunch question is, as Daly [2010] *PL* 160 at 173 puts it, whether judges should 'open their judicial review toolboxes fully' (rather than at all) on the given occasion. So, having considered the nature of the issues raised by a particular challenge to the exercise of a given power, a court might (very rarely) not be willing to review the matter at all (non-justici-able); review it only in a limited fashion, for example by asking whether the decision-maker has acted in bad faith or extremely unreasonably (deferential review); or review it rigor-ously (non-deferential, or high-intensity, review). Because questions about deference arise mainly in relation to what is called 'substantive review'—review of the content of decisions as opposed to the process by which they are made—we leave further discussion of it until we address that topic in ch 8.

4.4 The 'third source'

There are two conflicting views about what constitutes prerogative power: Blackstone (*Commentaries* (Oxford 1765), vol 1 at 239) restricted it to powers unique to govern-ment, whereas Dicey (*An Introduction to the Study of the Law of the Constitution* (London 1964) at 425) considered '[e]very act which the executive government can lawfully do without the authority of an Act of Parliament is done in virtue of ... [the] prerogative'. Although these views may seem starkly different, in that Blackstone's appears to confine governmental authority much more tightly, it is generally recognized that, alongside statu-tory and prerogative power, government has at its disposal so-called 'third source powers' (see generally Harris (1992) 108 *LQR* 626, (2007) 123 *LQR* 225, and (2010) 126 *LQR* 373). As Lord Sumption observed in *R (New London College Ltd)* v. *Secretary of State for the Home Department* [2013] UKSC 51, [2013] 1 WLR 2358 at [28]: 'It has long been recognised that the Crown possesses some general administrative powers to carry on the ordinary busi-ness of government which are not exercises of the royal prerogative and do not require statutory authority', albeit '[t]he extent of these powers and their exact juridical basis are controversial'.

While it has often been said that the Crown enjoys all of the capacities and powers of a natural person subject only to particular constraints imposed by law, Lord Sumption in *New London College* observed that 'it is open to question whether the analogy with a natu-ral person is really apt in the case of public or governmental action, as opposed to purely managerial acts of a kind that any natural person could do, such as making contracts, acquiring or disposing of property, hiring and firing staff and the like' (at [28]). In simi-lar vein, Carnwath LJ in *Shrewsbury and Atcham Borough Council* v. *Secretary of State for Communities and Local Government* [2008] EWCA Civ 148 at [48] endorsed the view that moves to extend third source powers beyond 'incidental powers' (such as the 'managerial acts' described by Lord Sumption) should be resisted in the interests of the rule of law; courts are naturally hesitant to recognize the existence of open-ended and substantial governmental powers not sourced in and confined by the express terms of statute, and outside the identifiable and circumscribed prerogative powers discussed in the previous section. Carnwath LJ also suggested that third source powers were bounded in a way that the ordinary powers and capacities of a natural person were not: third source powers could only be lawfully deployed 'for the public benefit' and in aid of 'identifiably "governmental" purposes'. Waller LJ tentatively shared this view. However, Richards LJ considered that any such 'limiting principle would have to be so wide as to be of no practical utility or would risk imposing an artificial and inappropriate restriction upon the work of government' (at [74]). Richards LJ has a point: a requirement to act for the 'public benefit' is rather open-ended. On the other hand, the executive government exists only to serve the public interest, and it would seem anomalous, therefore, if government could lawfully exploit its third source powers in ways inimical to that interest. While it is difficult to define what acting for the 'public benefit' involves in the abstract, there will be instances where it is clear that powers have not been exercised for the common good, for example where exercised for personal gain.

Thus, although the bounds and nature of third source powers are not well defined, the balance of authority suggests such powers are not sourced in statute or prerogative, are limited to incidental, ancillary, or managerial acts necessary for the carrying on of government business, and may only be used for pursuit of the public benefit.

The courts have confirmed that third source powers are amenable to review. In *Shrewsbury* Richards LJ observed, at [75]: '[S]uch powers cannot override the rights of others and, when exercised by government, are subject to judicial review on ordinary public law grounds', while 'such powers may be excluded expressly or impliedly by statute' or their exercise limited by statute (Carnwath LJ made similar observations at [45]). The Supreme Court, in *New London College*, indicated a further legal limit: absent specific statutory authority, government cannot adopt measures that are coercive in nature (at [29]). In addition, given the earlier discussion, it must be the case that purported exercises of third source power are reviewable on the basis that they must be exercised only for ancillary purposes, and in the public interest.

Several important points come out of these statements of principle. First, the capacity and powers of natural persons are not generally limited by public law duties, whereas third source powers are, further illustrating that an analogy between third source powers and the powers of natural persons is likely to mislead.

Second, we see in the foregoing dicta the outlines of a principle similar to that applied in the context of the prerogative: third source powers will be displaced to the extent statute covers the field. Whether this principle makes much difference to the managerial powers available to government is open to question, however. The Supreme Court, in *New London College*, was willing to recognize that statutes may impliedly confer upon government ancillary or managerial powers reasonably incidental to express statutory powers and duties, these powers being very similar in content and scope to third source powers.

Third, it is a welcome development that the courts have placed particular emphasis on the propositions that government cannot adopt coercive or rights-infringing measures absent specific statutory authority; rather such measures, given their potentially serious implications for individual liberty, ought to be the subject of democratic scrutiny and approval by Parliament, and as such, conferred by statute.

4.5 *De facto* powers

4.5.1 The *Datafin* case

The willingness of the courts to review prerogative and third source, as well as statutory, powers clearly represents a breakthrough in terms of judicial vindication of the rule of law, since there is no apparent reason why citizens ought to be unprotected from abuses of power merely because of the source of the power concerned. But how far can the logic of this argument be pressed? If individuals are vulnerable to the abuse of powers which derive neither from legislation nor the prerogative, should public law protect them?

R v. Panel on Take-overs and Mergers, ex parte Datafin plc [1987] QB 815
Court of Appeal

The claimant was bidding, in competition with Norton Opax plc, to take over a company. The claimant complained to the Panel on Takeovers and Mergers that Norton Opax had acted in concert with other parties and, thus, in breach of the Code promulgated by the Panel. The Panel, however, dismissed this complaint, and the claimant sought judicial review of its decision. At first instance permission to seek judicial review was refused, on the ground that the Panel was not amenable to judicial review. When the claimant renewed its application before the Court of Appeal, the central issue for the court was therefore whether the Panel's decisions could be subject to judicial review. The nature of the Panel's powers is apparent from the excerpt, below, from the judgment of Sir John Donaldson MR.

Sir John Donaldson MR

The Panel on Take-overs and Mergers is a truly remarkable body. Perched on the 20th floor of the Stock Exchange building in the City of London, both literally and metaphorically it oversees and regulates a very important part of the United Kingdom financial market. Yet it performs this function without visible means of legal support.

The panel is an unincorporated association without legal personality and, so far as can be seen, has only about twelve members ...

It has no statutory, prerogative or common law powers and it is not in contractual relationship with the financial market or with those who deal in that market. According to the introduction to the City Code on Take-overs and Mergers, which it promulgates: 'The code has not, and does not seek to have, the force of law, but those who wish to take advantage of the facilities of the securities markets in the United Kingdom should conduct themselves in matters relating to take-overs according to the code. Those who do not so conduct themselves cannot expect to enjoy those facilities and may find that they are withheld ...'

'Self-regulation' is an emotive term. It is also ambiguous. An individual who voluntarily regulates his life in accordance with stated principles, because he believes that this is morally right and also, perhaps, in his own long term interests, or a group of individuals who do so, are practising self-regulation. But it can mean something quite different. It can connote a system whereby a group of people, acting in concert, use their collective power to force themselves and others to comply with a code of conduct of their own devising. This is not necessarily morally wrong or contrary to the public interest, unlawful or even undesirable. But it is very different. The panel is a self-regulating body in the latter sense. Lacking any authority de jure, it exercises immense power de facto by devising, promulgating, amending and interpreting the City Code on Take-overs and Mergers, by waiving or modifying the application of the code in particular circumstances, by investigating and reporting upon alleged breaches of the code and by the application or threat of sanctions. These sanctions are no less effective because they are applied indirectly and lack a legally enforceable base …

As I have said, the panel is a truly remarkable body, performing its function without visible means of legal support. But the operative word is 'visible,' although perhaps I should have used the word 'direct.' Invisible or indirect support there is in abundance. Not only is a breach of the code, so found by the panel, ipso facto an act of misconduct by a member of the Stock Exchange, and the same may be true of other bodies represented on the panel, but the admission of shares to the Official List may be withheld in the event of such a breach. This is interesting and significant for listing of securities is a statutory function performed by the Stock Exchange in pursuance of the Stock Exchange (Listing) Regulations 1984 (SI 1984 No 716), enacted in implementation of EEC directives. And the matter does not stop there, because in December 1983 the Department of Trade and Industry made a statement explaining why the Licensed Dealers (Conduct of Business) Rules 1983 (SI 1983 No 585) contained no detailed provisions about take-overs. [The Master of the Rolls then went on to quote from the statement, in which the Department explained its intention to rely upon the Panel for the regulation of take-overs.]

The picture which emerges is clear. As an act of government it was decided that, in relation to take-overs, there should be a central self-regulatory body which would be supported and sustained by a periphery of statutory powers and penalties wherever non-statutory powers and penalties were insufficient or non-existent or where EEC requirements called for statutory provisions … The issue is thus whether the historic supervisory jurisdiction of the Queen's courts extends to such a body discharging such functions, including some which are quasi-judicial in their nature, as part of such a system.

[After referring to R v. Criminal Injuries Compensation Board, ex parte Lain [1967] 2 QB 864, the Master of the Rolls continued:] The Criminal Injuries Compensation Board, in the form which it then took, was an administrative novelty. Accordingly it would have been impossible to find a precedent for the exercise of the supervisory jurisdiction of the court which fitted the facts. Nevertheless the court not only asserted its jurisdiction, but further asserted that it was a jurisdiction which was adaptable thereafter. This process has since been taken further in O'Reilly v. Mackman [1983] 2 A.C. 237, 279 (per Lord Diplock) by deleting any requirement that the body should have a duty to act judicially; in Council of Civil Service Unions v. Minister for the Civil Service [1985] A.C. 374 by extending it to a person exercising purely prerogative power; and in Gillick v. West Norfolk and Wisbech Area Health Authority [1986] A.C. 112, where Lord Fraser of Tullybelton, at p 163F and Lord Scarman, at p 178F–H expressed the view obiter that judicial review would extend to guidance circulars issued by a department of state without any specific authority. In all the reports it is possible to find enumerations of factors giving rise to the jurisdiction, but it is a fatal error to regard the presence of all those factors as essential or as being exclusive of other factors. Possibly the only essential elements are what can be described as a public element, which can take many different forms, and the exclusion from the jurisdiction of bodies whose sole source of power is a consensual submission to its jurisdiction.

In fact, given its novelty, the panel fits surprisingly well into the format which this court had in mind in the Criminal Injuries Compensation Board case. It is without doubt performing a public duty and an important one. This is clear from the expressed willingness of the Secretary of State for Trade and Industry to limit legislation in the field of take-overs and mergers and to use the panel as the centrepiece of his regulation of that market. The rights of citizens are indirectly affected by its decisions, some, but by no means all of whom, may in a technical sense be said to have assented to this situation, eg the members of the Stock Exchange. At least in its determination of whether there has been a breach of the code, it has a duty to act judicially and it asserts that its raison d'être is to do equity between one shareholder and another. Its source of power is only partly based upon moral persuasion and the assent of institutions and their members, the bottom line being the statutory powers exercised by the Department of Trade and Industry and the Bank of England. In this context I should be very disappointed if the courts could not recognise the realities of executive power and allowed their vision to be clouded by the subtlety and sometimes complexity of the way in which it can be exerted ...

Lloyd LJ

... [Counsel for the Panel, Mr Alexander, argued that, for policy reasons, the Panel should be free from the constraints of judicial review. Lloyd LJ responded to that argument in the following terms:] On the policy level, I find myself unpersuaded. Mr. Alexander made much of the word 'self-regulating.' No doubt self-regulation has many advantages. But I was unable to see why the mere fact that a body is self-regulating makes it less appropriate for judicial review. Of course there will be many self-regulating bodies which are wholly inappropriate for judicial review. The committee of an ordinary club affords an obvious example. But the reason why a club is not subject to judicial review is not just because it is self-regulating. The panel wields enormous power. It has a giant's strength. The fact that it is self-regulating, which means, presumably, that it is not subject to regulation by others, and in particular the Department of Trade and Industry, makes it not less but more appropriate that it should be subject to judicial review by the courts.

It has been said that 'it is excellent to have a giant's strength, but it is tyrannous to use it like a giant.' Nobody suggests that there is any present danger of the panel abusing its power. But it is at least possible to imagine circumstances in which a ruling or decision of the panel might give rise to legitimate complaint. An obvious example would be if it reached a decision in flagrant breach of the rules of natural justice. It is no answer to say that there would be a right of appeal in such a case. For a complainant has no right to appeal where the decision is that there has been no breach of the code. Yet a complainant is just as much entitled to natural justice as the company against whom the complaint is made.

Nor is it any answer that a company coming to the market must take it as it finds it. The City is not a club which one can join or not at will. In that sense, the word 'self-regulation' may be misleading. The panel regulates not only itself, but all others who have no alternative but to come to the market in a case to which the code applies ... So long as there is a possibility, however remote, of the panel abusing its great powers, then it would be wrong for the courts to abdicate responsibility. The courts must remain ready, willing and able to hear a legitimate complaint in this as in any other field of our national life. I am not persuaded that this particular field is one in which the courts do not belong, or from which they should retire, on grounds of policy. And if the courts are to remain in the field, then it is clearly better, as a matter of policy, that legal proceedings should be in the realm of public law rather than private law, not only because they are quicker, but also because the requirement of leave [on which see 14.2] ... will exclude claims which are clearly unmeritorious ...

[Lloyd LJ then turned to counsel's other principal objection to judicial review of the Panel:] On the basis of [Lord Diplock's speech in *GCHQ* (see 4.3.2)], and other cases to which Mr. Alexander referred us, he argues (i) that the sole test whether the body of persons is subject to judicial review is the source of its power, and (ii) that there has been no case where that source has been other than legislation, including subordinate legislation, or the prerogative.

I do not agree that the source of the power is the sole test whether a body is subject to judicial review, nor do I so read Lord Diplock's speech. Of course the source of the power will often, perhaps usually, be decisive. If the source of power is a statute, or subordinate legislation under a statute, then clearly the body in question will be subject to judicial review. If, at the other end of the scale, the source of power is contractual, as in the case of private arbitration, then clearly the arbitrator is not subject to judicial review: see *R* v. *National Joint Council for the Craft of Dental Technicians (Disputes Committee), ex parte Neate* [1953] 1 Q.B. 704.

But in between these extremes there is an area in which it is helpful to look not just at the source of the power but at the nature of the power. If the body in question is exercising public law functions, or if the exercise of its functions have public law consequences, then that may, as Mr. Lever submitted, be sufficient to bring the body within the reach of judicial review. It may be said that to refer to 'public law' in this context is to beg the question. But I do not think it does. The essential distinction, which runs through all the cases to which we referred, is between a domestic or private tribunal on the one hand and a body of persons who are under some public duty on the other.

Nicholls LJ agreed with Sir John Donaldson MR and Lloyd LJ that the Panel was amenable to judicial review. However, all three judges also agreed that, on the facts, the Panel had not committed any error which should be set aside on judicial review.

The importance *of Datafin* is that it marks the first unequivocal judicial acknowledgement that the supervisory jurisdiction extends beyond the control of *legal* powers. The earlier excerpts raise a number of important issues which we consider in the following sections.

4.5.2 Defining the scope of judicial review

Datafin suggests that the outer boundary of judicial review is traced by some concept of 'publicness': Sir John Donaldson MR said that review is possible only if a 'public element' can be found, while Lloyd LJ required the body to be 'under some public duty'. But as Dyson LJ has observed, the 'public element' test 'is expressed in very general terms, and of itself provides no real guidance' (*Hampshire County Council* v. *Beer* [2003] EWCA Civ 1056, [2004] 1 WLR 233 at [14]). The true meaning of these concepts can be discerned only by reference to the factual matrices in which they have been deployed. In *Datafin* four features stand out. First, the Panel's immense power was emphasized by the judges. Second, the Master of the Rolls noted that, although not established in a legal sense, the Panel enjoyed abundant 'invisible or indirect [legal] support'. Third, he observed that the Panel's role within the regulatory system was attributable, to a large extent, to an 'act of government'. Finally, he considered that private law control would not be effective, but that it was 'unthinkable that ... the panel should go on its way cocooned from the attention of the courts in defence of the citizenry'. Ultimately, the Court felt that the Panel was serving an important governmental function, albeit that it happened not to be part of the structure of government in a formal or legal sense. Sir John Donaldson's suggestion that amenability turns simply on the existence of a 'public element' must therefore be viewed with some caution, since the reasoning in *Datafin* suggests a somewhat narrower approach—an impression which, as we explain in what follows, is confirmed by subsequent cases.

4.5.3 The limits of review and its underlying rationale

Datafin raises questions about what underlying rationale should inform decisions as to the reach of the supervisory jurisdiction—which, as Elliott [2012] *NZ L Rev* 75 has shown, is keyed into much broader questions about the purpose of judicial review itself. But given that the underlying rationale for judicial review is hotly contested, it is no surprise to find that the courts have struggled to identify and consistently apply a coherent test. The judgments in *Datafin* do not confront this matter head-on; however, at least three possible tests have emerged in the case law.

Abuse of power

There are numerous references in the judgments in *Datafin* to the considerable power wielded by the Panel; indeed, Lloyd LJ specifically mentioned the importance of correcting any abuses of such power. Dealing with the abuse of power has been presented as one of the key goals of public law in a number of cases (see, *eg Re Preston* [1985] AC 835 at 864–5; *R v. North and East Devon Health Authority, ex parte Coughlan* [2001] QB 213 at 242–3; *R (Nadarajah) v. Secretary of State for the Home Department* [2005] EWCA Civ 1363), while Laws [1997] *PL* 455 at 464 goes as far as to assert that preventing the abuse of power is the organizing concept upon which modern public law is founded. But while judicial review undoubtedly aims to prevent or correct abuses of power, such a criterion is surely too crude to serve as the guiding principle by which to rationalize the scope of judicial review. Unless all power which is liable to abuse, including purely private power, is to be brought within the courts' supervisory jurisdiction—a conclusion that is repudiated by the judgments in *Datafin* itself—then invoking abuse of power as the organizing concept merely begs the question, 'What *type* of power?'

Governmental power

Given the emphasis placed by Sir John Donaldson on the quasi-governmental character of the Takeover Panel, might the regulation of *governmental power* provide a more intelligible organizing principle? An affirmative answer to that question is an implicit premise in the following case.

R v. Disciplinary Committee of the Jockey Club, ex parte Aga Khan
[1993] 1 WLR 909
Court of Appeal

The claimant was a leading owner and breeder of racehorses. After one of his horses won a race in 1989, it was subjected to random urine testing and a prohibited substance was discovered. Although it was not alleged that the claimant was implicated, the horse was disqualified and the claimant deprived of the prize money for the race. That decision was taken by the Disciplinary Committee of the Jockey Club, the non-statutory body which regulates horse racing: all race meetings must be licensed by the Club and run according to its Rules of Racing, and all those involved in horse racing must be licensed by or registered with the Club. In 1978 the Royal Commission on Gambling described the Club as the 'supreme authority in British racing'. The claimant sought judicial review of the Club's decision. The Divisional Court, on the trial of a preliminary issue, held that the Club was not amenable to judicial review; the claimant therefore appealed to the Court of Appeal.

Sir Thomas Bingham MR

... The Jockey Club brings [its Rules] to bear in two main ways. First, and most importantly, it does so by contracts entered into with racecourse managements, owners, trainers and jockeys. The present case illustrates the routine practice. Thus the applicant when applying for registration as an owner (and, probably, when entering the filly for the race) and the trainer when seeking renewal of his trainer's licence each agreed to be bound in all respects by the Rules of Racing. All those seeking any licence or permit from the Jockey Club, on being registered with it, become similarly bound.

The Jockey Club cannot, of course, impose contractual conditions on those who do not seek any licence or permit from it and therefore do not enter into any contract with it. This is a class which includes members of the general public and also racecourse owners, owners, trainers and jockeys who, for whatever reason, do not choose to act under the Jockey Club rules. The Jockey Club's sanction here lies not in contract but in its domination of the market. While unrecognised meetings do occur in some parts of the country, they are insignificant. No serious racecourse management, owner, trainer or jockey can survive without the recognition or licence of the Jockey Club. There is in effect no alternative market in which those not accepted by the Jockey Club can find a place or to which racegoers may resort. Thus by means of the rules and its market domination the Jockey Club can effectively control not only those who agree to abide by its rules but also those—such as disqualified or excluded persons seeking to participate in racing activities in any capacity—who do not. For practical purposes the Jockey Club's writ runs in the British racing world, to the acknowledged benefit of British racing.

[After reviewing the authorities, the Master of the Rolls reached the following conclusion:] I have little hesitation in accepting the applicant's contention that the Jockey Club effectively regulates a significant national activity, exercising powers which affect the public and are exercised in the interest of the public. I am willing to accept that if the Jockey Club did not regulate this activity the government would probably be driven to create a public body to do so.

But the Jockey Club is not in its origin, its history, its constitution or (least of all) its membership a public body. While the grant of a royal charter was no doubt a mark of official approval, this did not in any way alter its essential nature, functions or standing. Statute provides for its representation on the Horseracing Betting Levy Board, no doubt as a body with an obvious interest in racing, but it has otherwise escaped mention in the statute book. It has not been woven into any system of governmental control of horse racing, perhaps because it has itself controlled horse racing so successfully that there has been no need for any such governmental system and such does not therefore exist. This has the result that while the Jockey Club's powers may be described as, in many ways, public they are in no sense governmental. The discretion conferred by s 31(6) of the [Senior Courts] Act 1981 to refuse the grant of leave or relief where the applicant has been guilty of delay which would be prejudicial to good administration can scarcely have been envisaged as applicable in a case such as this ...

Hoffmann LJ

The Jockey Club is an exclusive private club incorporated by royal charter which controls the racing industry. It does so by tradition, widespread acceptance and the contractual consent of almost all active participants in racing to the Jockey Club's Rules of Racing and the jurisdiction of its disciplinary committee. This control gives the Jockey Club considerable power over a section of the economy which is not only important in itself but supports another important economic activity, namely horse race betting. The question in this appeal is whether the power exercised by the Jockey Club brings its decisions into the realm of public law, so that they are amenable to judicial review. In my view it does not ...

R v. Panel on Take-overs and Mergers, ex parte Datafin plc [1987] Q.B. 815 shows that the absence of a formal public source of power, such as statute or prerogative, is not conclusive. Governmental power may be exercised *de facto* as well as *de jure*. But the power needs to be identified as governmental in nature ... [The Take-over Panel represents] a privatisation of the business of government itself. The same has been held to be true of the Advertising Standards Authority (*R. v. Advertising Standards Authority Ltd, Ex parte Insurance Service plc* (1989) 9 Tr. L.R. 169) and the Investment Management Regulatory Organisation (IMRO) (*Bank of Scotland v. Investment Management Regulatory Organisation Ltd* 1989 S.L.T. 432). Both are private bodies established by the industry but integrated into a system of statutory regulation. There is in my judgment nothing comparable in the position of the Jockey Club. It is true that it has been incorporated by royal charter, but this seems to me simply a mark of royal favour to racing. The Jockey Club nominates three members of the Horserace Betting Levy Board, but this is to represent the disparate private interests of the racing industry, which enjoys the benefit of the levy. There is nothing to suggest that, if the Jockey Club had not voluntarily assumed the regulation of racing, the government would feel obliged or inclined to set up a statutory body for the purpose. The reactions of successive governments to the proposals of, among others, the 1978 Royal Commission on Gambling (Cmnd 7200) and the 1991 Fourth Report of the House of Commons Home Affairs Committee on the Levy on Horserace Betting suggest a determination to leave racing firmly in the private sector.

Farquharson LJ agreed with Sir Thomas Bingham MR and Hoffmann LJ that the disciplinary committee's decision was not amenable to judicial review.

The governmental power criterion affords a less diffuse rationale than that offered by the notion of abuse of power. It also fits in with established ideas about the purpose of judicial review, which is traditionally thought of in terms of supervision of governmental authority—albeit that, post-*Datafin*, a less formalistic conception of 'government' obtains, reflecting modern developments such as the establishment of arm's-length agencies, the process of contracting out, and the growth of self-regulation (on which see 1.5.5).

However, using governmental power as the touchstone by which to delimit judicial review is not without difficulty. In particular, the application of a consistent test is difficult. For instance, while Sir Thomas Bingham MR appears to suggest in *Aga Khan* that there must be some *actual* government involvement (such that the non-statutory body is somehow interwoven into more formal regulatory mechanisms), others invoke the idea of *potential* involvement either by the government (see, *eg* the extract from Hoffmann LJ's judgment in *Aga Khan* earlier) or Parliament (see, *eg R v. Football Association Ltd, ex parte Football League Ltd* [1993] 2 All ER 833 at 848) by holding that the acid test of reviewability is whether, in the absence of the non-statutory body, the state would intervene to fill the gap. However, the difficulty of applying such a test is illustrated by the *Aga Khan* case. In the earlier excerpt, Sir Thomas Bingham MR opines that 'if the Jockey Club did not regulate this activity the government would probably be driven to create a public body to do so', yet Farquharson LJ ([1993] 1 WLR 909 at 930) reached the opposite conclusion, finding no grounds 'for supposing that, if the Jockey Club were dissolved, any governmental body would assume control of racing'—a view with which Hoffmann LJ's comments in the final paragraph of our earlier excerpt seem consistent. This divergence of opinion reflects the reality that there are as many views of what are properly governmental functions as there are political philosophies; this renders the test problematic as it is unlikely to foster consistency in judicial decision-making, while by requiring judges to offer their own opinions on what functions are properly governmental, such legal tests risk drawing judges into ordinary political debates. On the positive side, such approach does not make the scope of review depend on the happenstance of what functions government currently performs itself. One might argue that judges could instead look to the philosophy of the current executive or legislature as a more objective guide as to what is or is not a governmental function. However, it may be hard to demarcate the bounds of a particular government's ideology, and if one considers a particular function to be consonant with the current government's ideology, one may question why the government is not performing that function currently itself. Further, on such approach the scope of review will have a tidal quality, ebbing in and out over time according to the political disposition of the government or Parliament of the day.

QUESTIONS

- Should judges develop their own concept of what is sufficiently 'public' to merit oversight through judicial review, or should they be influenced by the prevailing political philosophy concerning the size and role of the state?
- Both options have their drawbacks, but which option do you consider to be 'least bad'?

Monopoly power

Campbell (2009) 125 *LQR* 491 argues that the best criterion for determining the scope of judicial review is that of 'monopoly power'. He contends that this can be used as an organizing concept which explains why judicial review lies in relation to statutory and prerogative powers—given that such powers generally enable state bodies, and *only* state bodies, to do things that could not otherwise be lawfully accomplished—and that the same concept is also capable of determining the extent to which *de facto* powers should be reviewable. The attraction of doing so, he argues (at 509), is that

[a]n individual who is subjected to an exercise of power that is not monopolistic, and who is of the view that he is not being treated morally in the relevant sense, can, if he is concerned so to be treated, choose to deal with another decision-making body. Such an alternate decision-making body will not necessarily treat the person in accordance with the principles of good administration, even if he wishes to be so treated. But there is at least some possibility that an alternate body or bodies may accord him such treatment.

Several other commentators (including Woolf [1986] *PL* 220, Borrie [1989] *PL* 552, Beloff (1995) 58 *MLR* 143, and Forsyth [1996] *CLJ* 122) have invoked monopoly power as a justification for review of certain *de facto* powers. Some judges, too, have taken the concept of monopoly into account: Roch J, in *R v. Disciplinary Committee of the Jockey Club, ex parte Massingberd-Mundy* [1993] 2 All ER 207 at 221, considered the existence of 'monopolistic or near monopolistic powers' to be salient to the question of amenability. But that is the exception, not the norm. In the later case of *R v. Football Association Ltd, ex parte Football League Ltd* [1993] 2 All ER 833 at 848, Rose J held that, even though the Football

Association exercised 'virtually monopolistic powers', it was not amenable to judicial review. The same approach was adopted in relation to the Jockey Club in *Aga Khan*.

This reluctance to scrutinize the use of the powers of the Jockey Club, and of analogous powers, is surprising in view of *Nagle* v. *Fielden* [1966] 2 QB 633, in which the claimant challenged the Jockey Club's refusal, solely on the ground of gender, to grant her a trainer's licence. Danckwerts LJ, at 650, considered that 'the courts have the right to protect the right of a person to work when it is being prevented by the dictatorial exercise of powers by a body which holds a monopoly'. Similarly, Lord Denning MR, at 645, using language which echoes that of the public law *Wednesbury* principle (on which see 8.2.1), thought that, '[i]f [the Jockey Club] make a rule which enables them to reject his application arbitrarily or capriciously, not reasonably, that rule is bad. It is against public policy.' Against this background, it might be expected that, as Simon Brown J put it in *R* v. *Jockey Club, ex parte RAM Racecourses Ltd* [1993] 2 All ER 225 at 246–7, cases like *Nagle* v. *Fielden*, 'had they arisen today and not some years ago, would have found a natural home in judicial review proceedings', the implication being that such matters should now attract the application of public law principles. However, Hoffmann LJ, in *Aga Khan* [1993] 1 WLR 909 at 932–3, disagreed, suggesting that there is 'an improvisatory air' about the approach in *Nagle*, which 'has probably not survived'. He opined:

> [T]he fact that the Jockey Club has power [is indisputable]. But the mere fact of power, even over a substantial area of economic activity, is not enough. In a mixed economy, power may be private as well as public. Private power may affect the public interest and the livelihoods of many individuals. But that does not subject it to the rules of public law. If control is needed, it must be found in the law of contract, the doctrine of restraint of trade, [legislation providing for the regulation of monopolies], [the relevant provisions of what is now the Treaty on the Functioning of the European Union] and all the other instruments available in law for curbing the excesses of private power.

However, as Black (1996) 59 *MLR* 24 notes (and as Hoffmann LJ himself accepted later in his judgment), the difficulty with this argument is that while these alternative methods of legal control may be suitable in respect of commercial monopolies, there are other monopoly powers—such as those of self-regulatory bodies—to which they are not so easily applicable.

Some outstanding problems with the monopoly concept remain, however. The most important is that it does not appear to be an account of *public* power, given it suggests that any concentration of power ought to be bounded by the principles of judicial review; therefore, rather than helping us to define public power, does the monopoly theory not entail a repudiation of that concept as the basis for delineating the bounds of review? Further, very few functions are performed exclusively by one entity, while even where multiple entities perform a particular function they may each nonetheless exercise immense power, suggesting the monopoly concept might draw the ambit of review too narrowly.

QUESTION

- Do you agree that the control of monopoly power is preferable to control of governmental power as the organizing principle by reference to which the scope of judicial review is determined?

4.5.4 Contractual arrangements

Thus far we have seen that the courts have limited their public law jurisdiction by recourse to the criterion of governmental power. It is now necessary to address the extent to which contractual arrangements may displace the courts' willingness to review.

Notwithstanding the discouraging dicta set out at 4.5.3, there are some oblique suggestions in Sir Thomas Bingham MR's judgment in *Aga Khan* [1993] 1 WLR 909 at 924 that there may be circumstances, where there is no contractual relationship between the claimant and the Jockey Club, in which the latter's decisions *can* be subjected to judicial review; Farquharson LJ (at 930) also suggested that judicial review might lie against the Club in some non-contractual settings. Similarly, Simon Brown J opined in *R v. Jockey Club, ex parte RAM Racecourses Ltd* [1993] 2 All ER 225 at 248 that the Jockey Club may be amenable to review when exercising 'quasi-licensing powers' over those with whom no contractual relationship exists—*eg* when deciding whether to allocate fixtures to a new racecourse. These dicta suggest that there may well be situations in which the powers of bodies such as the Jockey Club may be regarded as sufficiently 'public' or 'governmental' to attract judicial review, provided that there is no *contractual relationship* between the claimant and the defendant. Where such a relationship does exist, however, this may result in the matter being characterized as one purely of private law (although *cf* on this point the decision of the Privy Council in *Mercury Energy Ltd* v. *Electricity Corporation of New Zealand* [1994] 1 WLR 521). For instance, in *Aga Khan*, Sir Thomas Bingham MR said (at 924):

> I would accept that those who agree to be bound by the Rules of Racing have no effective alternative to doing so if they want to take part in racing in this country. It also seems likely to me that if, instead of Rules of Racing administered by the Jockey Club, there were a statutory code administered by a public body, the rights and obligations conferred and imposed by the code would probably approximate to those conferred and imposed by the Rules of Racing. But this does not, as it seems to me, alter the fact, however anomalous it may be, that the powers which the Jockey Club exercises over those who (like the applicant) agree to be bound by the Rules of Racing derive from the agreement of the parties and give rise to private rights on which effective action for a declaration, an injunction and damages can be based without resort to judicial review. It would in my opinion be contrary to sound and long-standing principle to extend the remedy of judicial review to such a case.

Against this background, two points should be noted.

First, the reluctance evidenced in *Aga Khan* to permit judicial review to encroach on existing contractual relationships raises questions regarding the reality of consent. Even if one accepts that it is not public law's function to regulate relationships which are based upon consent, the courts appear to be adopting an unusually two-dimensional view of that concept. Whereas in many situations—the relationship between employer and employee being perhaps the best example—the necessity of looking beneath the surface in order to determine whether there is a real consent is well-established, the courts seem unwilling to do so in the present context. Thus, even though Farquharson LJ recognized in *Aga Khan* (at 928) that those involved in horseracing have no choice but to submit to the Jockey Club's regulation, he still felt that there was an operative consent sufficient to displace the public law jurisdiction. This approach is disputed by many writers (*eg* Pannick [1992] *PL* 1 at 2–5), not least because when genuine consent is absent, this is precisely when abuse of power is most likely, and judicial protection most needed.

Second, the *Aga Khan* case does not establish that contract *invariably* displaces judi-cial review. The question is always whether the function in question is sufficiently pub-lic or governmental. Where the relationship between the claimant and the defendant is largely or exclusively contractual, this is indicative that the matter belongs to the private realm—but this is without prejudice to the possibility that certain contractual relation-ships may arise in relation to the performance of public functions. Consider, for instance, *R (Weaver)* v. *London and Quadrant Housing Trust* [2008] EWHC 1377 (Admin), [2009] EWCA Civ 587 and *R (McIntyre)* v. *Gentoo Group Ltd* [2010] EWHC 5 (Admin). In both cases, it was held that registered social landlords are amenable to judicial review when exercising contractual power under tenancy agreements. (This point was not argued in the Court of Appeal in *Weaver*, but Elias LJ (at [83]) indicated that he agreed with the Divisional Court's view that judicial review was available.) The allocation and manage-ment of publicly-subsidised housing, for which registered social landlords are responsible, was regarded as a public function—and contractual decisions taken in discharge of that function were thus amenable to judicial review. As John Howell QC (sitting as a Deputy High Court Judge) said in *McIntyre* at [26]:

> What makes public law applicable is that the decision was one taken in relation to the exercise of a public function. There is no additional requirement that the specific decision impugned has itself to have some other and further 'public law element' (whatever that might mean and involve).

This does not, however, mean that the existence of contractual power and the question whether the function is a governmental or public one are wholly independent consider-ations: the fact that a relationship is rooted in contract may affect the courts' preparedness to characterize the function as public or governmental in the first place.

Whereas *Aga Khan* indicates judicial reluctance to superimpose public law controls where a contractual relationship exists between the complainant and the body, a distinct issue arises where the contractual arrangements are between a body (*eg* a company or charity) and a pub-lic authority on whose behalf the former is delivering some service. Such arrangements are increasingly common: expenditure on contracted-out public services accounts for approxi-mately half of the £187 billion spent by the public sector on goods and services per annum, while approximately one-third of taxpayer money spent on public services goes to non-gov-ernmental agencies (National Audit Office, *Deciding Prices in Public Sector Markets* (2013) 4; HC810, *The Role of Major Contractors in the Delivery of Public Services* (2013) 10). These arrangements and their pervasiveness as a tool for delivery of public services and exercise of public power pose a potentially serious challenge to judicial review's capacity to effectively regulate the exercise of public power.

Hunt, 'Constitutionalism and the Contractualisation of Government in the United Kingdom' in Taggart (ed), *The Province of Administrative Law* (Oxford 1997)

In the United Kingdom, as in other liberal democracies, the last decade has been a period of quiet revolution in public administration. Successive governments elected on political platforms promising to 'roll back the state' have presided over changes in the mode of governance which have transformed the relation between public and private. In the United Kingdom the changes began in the most obvious way in the 1980s with the relatively straightforward transfer of public corporations to the private sector. Virtually all of the main utilities (telecommunications, water, electricity, gas, rail transport) are now in private ownership, subject in each case to a specific statutory regime of regulation.

In addition to privatisation in this most obvious sense, the reinvention of government has taken a variety of other forms. Activities previously subject to close administrative controls have been deregulated, and other activities formerly carried out directly by public bodies have been 'contracted out' to the private sector. Perhaps most dramatically of all, however, the techniques of public administration have been refashioned in the mould of the private commercial sector. Many of the responsibilities of central government departments have been transferred to executive agencies, whose relationship with its parent department is regulated by a Framework Document. 'Internal markets' have been introduced into the provision of the most fundamental of public services such as health and education, organised around a central separation between 'purchasers' and 'providers' of such services. Contract has replaced command and control as the paradigm of regulation. As public lawyers we must not shrink from recognising the significance of what has happened. In short, the state has been reconceived on the model of market ordering. Such a development obviously has the most profound implications for public law …

The retention of the source of the power as a factor in determining amenability to judicial review, and in particular the tendency evident in *Aga Khan* to assert that a decision-maker deriving power from contract cannot be amenable to the supervisory jurisdiction, has given rise to concern about the ability of public law to respond to the contractualisation of government. For if government chooses to constitute the delivery of a particular service by way of contractual arrangements with private bodies, there must be a very real danger that courts will treat such activity as being beyond the reach of public law, and regulated by the private law of contract only. As Freedland [see [1994] *PL* 86 at 102] puts it, the fear is of a total transfer of public activity into the private sphere and thereby into the realm of private rather than public law.

Such fears are apparently well founded. In *R* v. *Servite Houses, ex parte Goldsmith* (2001) 33 HLR 369, judicial review was sought of the decision of the defendant—a charity to which Wandsworth London Borough Council had, under s 26 of the National Assistance Act 1948, contracted out the provision of accommodation in discharge of its duty under s 21 of the same—to close the home in which the claimants resided. This breached promises given by the charity that (health permitting) the claimants could remain for life. Moses J held that public law obligations, such as fidelity to the legitimate expectations (see 6.1) to which the 'home for life' promises had arguably given rise, could not be enforced against Servite—a conclusion that, in the absence of any contractual remedies, left the claimants without any redress. His Lordship reasoned (at 389) that, for judicial review to lie, it must be possible to 'identify sufficient statutory penetration which goes beyond the statutory regulation of the manner in which the service is provided'. This was lacking because provisions such as s 26, permitting the contracting out of service provision, have the effect of 'disentangling' the service provider from the 'statutory embrace' of the public authority. 'It follows,' said Moses J, 'that not only is the relationship between Servite and Wandsworth governed solely by the terms of the contract between them, but the relationship between Servite and the [claimants] is solely a matter of private law.'

This reasoning is criticized by Craig (2002) 118 *LQR* 551 at 564–7, who argues that there is 'nothing in the logic of contracting out' which dictates that the service provider should be free from public law obligations. Moreover, the judge's conclusion that the contracting out power divorced Servite from Wandsworth's 'statutory embrace' is counterintuitive: provisions such as s 26 have the opposite effect, says Craig, 'explicitly and directly' telling us that public functions can be performed by private parties, thereby furnishing, if anything, a *greater* degree of statutory underpinning than that which was evident in *Datafin*. Despite such telling critiques there is no sign of a change of tack. For example, the High Court observed recently, in *R (Holmcroft Properties Ltd)* v. *KPMG* [2016] EWHC 323 at [44], that 'the fact that private arrangements are used to secure public law objectives does not bring those arrangements into the public domain sufficient to attract public law principles'. In that case the defendant, which was performing functions pursuant to private agreements, was held not to be subject to review despite being 'clearly "woven into" the regulatory function' of the Financial Conduct Authority (which is responsible for regulating financial services, and itself clearly exercises public power) and there being 'a clear public connection between [the defendant's] function and the regulatory duties carried out by the FCA' (at [39]–[40]). This illustrates how powerfully the presence of contractual relations weighs with courts in militating against extending the scope of review.

However, it is important to note that some writers are less critical of the judicial unwillingness to so extend review principles: they question whether extending judicial review is the right response to the phenomenon of contractualization. In the following extract, Aronson doubts the viability of the whole '*Datafin* project', arguing that judicial review is not necessarily the most appropriate device by which to ensure the responsible exercise of self-regulatory powers.

Aronson, 'A Public Lawyer's Response to Privatisation and Outsourcing' in Taggart (ed), *The Province of Administrative Law* (Oxford 1997)

Even if the power is classified as public, the level of review which *Datafin* provides is minimal, for two reasons. First, aside from review for breach of natural justice, the court [in *Datafin*] said that its remedies would be only declaratory, and only prospective. Secondly, whilst it offered the theoretical prospect of review where the regulatory body has misinterpreted its own rules, it particularly emphasised the unlikelihood of this ever occurring, given the court's deference to the body's expertise. Lord Donaldson [in *R* v. *Panel on Take-overs and Mergers, ex parte Guinness plc* [1990] 1 QB 146 at 159–60] subsequently emphasised this vagueness about the principles of administration which *Datafin* is meant to enforce, by saying that the court should perhaps fashion an 'innominate' ground of review for this sort of regulatory body, replacing 'formal categorisation' with review which would be 'more in the round than might otherwise be the case'. Indeed, what else could he say? … What is the point in supervising the way a body interprets rules which it can change without legal formality? The further a regulatory regime travels from the legal paradigm, the less relevant is judicial review as an accountability device.

In addition to the problems flowing from *Datafin's* own language, it is not much of an answer to the issues raised by privatisation and outsourcing. Judicial review of a regulator (where there is one) will quell very few of the non-economic (or social justice) anxieties posed by privatisation and outsourcing, particularly where (as in *Datafin*) the regulator is free to rewrite its rules. Judicial review of the service provider (where that is different from the regulator) is subject to all of the usual defects of judicial review generally, together with some peculiar to that area. The usual defects are familiar. Judicial review can occasionally remedy individual grievances, but rarely provides systemic relief. The decisions to litigate and to maintain the litigation can be happenstantial. Judicial review proceedings often pose no real threat to the respondent, which is usually free, on its redetermination of the substantive issue, to come to the same result but in a way which is impervious to judicial criticism. And however manipulable the demarcation line may be between a decision's merits and its legality, it is a line which judicial review continues to draw, with the result that the judge's role is substantially limited. Review in the wake of privatisation and outsourcing carries the additional problem that the complainant is typically conceived as a consumer with a consumer complaint, which is not the business of judicial review.

Aronson goes on to argue that the new architecture of government requires us to look beyond judicial review, to other solutions such as administrative tribunals, informal regulatory devices, and private law. Aronson's contribution to the debate is useful because it questions the notion that judicial review is a panacea, and reminds us that questions about judicial review's scope require us to grapple with the effectiveness of judicial oversight.

4.5.5 Judicial review beyond public law: The *Braganza* case

So far we have considered the scope of judicial review principles as they exist to control decisions and actions which are in some meaningful sense *public*. But similar principles, sourced in fields of law other than public law, may apply to decisions or actions which cannot be characterized as public.

It is not, for example, difficult to identify examples of concepts which resemble principles of public law in fields of private law, such as bias, which resembles the fiduciary no-conflicts duty in equity, or the *ultra vires* concept, which is also found in company law. Albeit there may be important differences in the way apparently similar concepts operate across different fields: see, *eg* Conaglen [2008] *PL* 58.

But in the recent, landmark decision of *Braganza* v. *BP Shipping Ltd* [2015] UKSC 17, [2015] 1 WLR 1661, the Supreme Court, in the context of a contract between private parties, not only deployed concepts identical to those in public law, but explicitly imported the relevant concepts from public law. This development is fascinating in itself. But it also has ramifications for our consideration of cases discussed earlier in which courts have been reluctant to allow judicial review principles to intrude upon contractual relations.

Contracts, like statutes, often confer decision-making powers and discretions. Typically such powers or discretions are held by one party to the contract, and may be exercised to affect the interests of the other party or both parties. It has generally been accepted that contractual powers or discretions are subject to legal norms not expressly provided for in the contract; however, the exact norms and their justification—and their interrelationship with public law norms—has long been a matter of contention.

In *Braganza*, the Supreme Court went a long way towards resolving these debates. In doing so the Court elaborated an approach to review of contractual discretions almost indistinguishable from the general approach to review of public powers. Lady Hale explained the justification for so bridling contractual decision-making powers (at [18]):

[T]he party who is charged with making decisions which affect the rights of both parties to the contract has a clear conflict of interest. That conflict is heightened where there is a significant imbalance of power between the contracting parties as there often will be in an employment contract. The courts have therefore sought to ensure that such contractual powers are not abused. They have done so by implying a term as to the manner in which such powers may be exercised,

> a term which may vary according to the terms of the contract and the context in which the decision-making power is given.

Lady Hale considered that because '[t]here is an obvious parallel between cases where a contract assigns a decision-making function to one of the parties and cases where a statute (or the royal prerogative) assigns a decision-making function to a public authority', the general approach to legal regulation of such decision-making powers should be broadly consonant across administrative law and contract law (at [19]).

So what principles ought to apply? While lower courts had been reluctant to explicitly draw upon public law principles, the reality was that '[t]here are signs ... that the contractual implied term is drawing closer and closer to the principles applicable in judicial review' (at [28]). Lady Hale observed that the constraints implied into discretions would depend on the terms and context of the particular contract. But as a general proposition contractual decision-making powers must be exercised lawfully, in good faith, consistently with contractual purpose, not characterized by arbitrariness, capriciousness or perversity, and the decision must abide by the two limbs of Lord Greene MR's classic statement of principle in *Associated Provincial Picture Houses Ltd v. Wednesbury Corporation* [1948] 1 KB 223: (i) irrelevant considerations must not be taken into account and obviously relevant considerations must be taken into account, and (ii) the decision must not be so unreasonable that no reasonable decision-maker could have come to it. Lady Hale emphasized that, as in judicial review, it is not for the court to substitute its own view for that of the decision-maker, but rather the court conducts a 'reviewing' function, and the principal focus will be on the decision-making process rather than the substance of the decision.

Many observations could be made about this fascinating decision, but we shall limit ourselves to three.

First, the alignment of the principles governing review of discretion under a private contract with principles developed in judicial review of public powers is striking. There is an alignment of concepts: the Court directly read public law principles into the law of contract. There were methodological similarities: the Court in *Braganza* implied the relevant principles into the terms of the contract, as courts imply the principles of good administration into the terms of statutes, at least on the *ultra vires* view. The justification given for recognizing these implied terms was very similar to a justification often given for judicial review: to protect against abuses of power. Further, a contextual approach was enunciated, similar to the contextual approach that characterizes contemporary judicial review (see 4.2); what principles apply and the intensity of review will vary according to many factors. Thus as Lord Neuberger concluded, commenting on Lady Hale's statements of principle, 'I consider that there is considerable force in the notion that this approach is, and at any rate should be, the same as the approach which domestic courts adopt to a decision of the executive' (at [103]).

Second, despite these striking similarities there are differences. The principles recognized in *Braganza*, while identical to those in judicial review, are principles *sourced* in *contract law*, not *judicial review or public law*. This has procedural ramifications—eg claims based on the *Braganza* principles, as contractual claims, could not be streamed via judicial review procedure—and remedial ramifications: the prerogative orders will not be available for breach of the *Braganza* principles. Rather, the relevant remedies will be contractual remedies such as declarations, injunctions, and damages.

Third, does the recognition, within contract law itself, of review-type principles reinforce or undermine the general judicial reluctance to recognize the applicability of *public law* principles of judicial review in cases such as *Aga Khan* [1993] 1 WLR 909, where one party to a contract seeks judicial review of the exercise of contractual powers by the other contracting party?

On the one hand, recognition of principles in contract law identical to judicial review principles as a constraint on exercise of contractual powers tends to undermine one of the core arguments against allowing judicial review of a body such as a jockey club, where it exercises contractual powers. That is, the argument that allowing judicial review of such powers would illegitimately cut across the intentions of the parties to the contract. But if contract law *itself* is willing to recognize that contractual powers are limited by principles identical to judicial review principles, then how could one maintain the argument against the applicability of the very same principles via judicial review? A response might be that the *Braganza* approach, based in contract, is one more respectful of the intentions of the parties to the contract, as the applicability of the contractual review principles and their content will be coloured by the intentions of the parties as expressed through the terms of the contract, while parties have the freedom to negotiate out of such principles. In contrast, review principles in public law will not be responsive, or as responsive, to the intentions of the parties, being standards external to the contract, drawn from public law and not sourced in contract law (but see *R (Holmcroft Properties Ltd) v. KPMG* [2016] EWHC 323 at [53]). However, it will in practice be very difficult for parties to oust the operation of the *Braganza* principles, given those standards will generally be assumed to apply 'in the absence of very clear language' to the contrary (*British Telecommunications plc v. Telefónica O2 UK Ltd* [2014] UKSC 42, [2014] Bus LR 765 at [37]).

On the other hand, one might argue that given the willingness of contract law itself to imply into contracts judicial review-like principles, the case for extending judicial review to cover at least some exercises of contractual power is now unnecessary, because contract law itself provides adequate alternative remedies (see, *eg Holmcroft* at [50]). Recall that Hoffmann LJ in *Aga Khan* had argued that any controls on contractual powers should be found in the law of contract; *Braganza* arguably fulfils the promise of Hoffmann LJ's dictum. Indeed, there may be advantages in bringing the claim as a contractual one, such as availability of more powerful remedies than are available in judicial review proceedings, such as damages. Of course, if the relevant contract explicitly ousts the *Braganza* standards then the claimant may be left without any remedy if public law standards are also inapplicable. But, as already explained, it would be an uncommon case where those standards were successfully ousted. Lastly, we should note that the *Braganza* principles will not aid a claimant who wishes to challenge the exercise of a contracted-out public power by a private firm. That is because, in general, only a party to a contract can sue for breach of the contract, and in the case of contracted-out services the relevant contract is one between the private provider and the public authority; the claimant is a third party without contractual rights.

4.5.6 Public law and private law: should there be a divide?

It is clear that the courts have found it difficult to delineate the proper scope of judicial review, and in particular to define and determine the metes and bounds of the concept of 'publicness'. For example, in *Hampshire County Council v. Beer* [2003] EWCA Civ 1056, [2004] 1 WLR 233 at [16], Dyson LJ observed that 'the question whether the decision of a body is amenable to judicial review requires a careful consideration of the nature of the power and function that has been exercised to see whether the decision has a sufficient public element, flavour or character to bring it within the purview of public law. It may be said with some justification that this criterion for amenability is very broad, not to say question-begging' (though he also noted progress in the case law towards identifying factors which made it more or less likely that a court would consider the 'publicness' criterion fulfilled).

One might consider that the difficulties experienced by the courts, and the concomitant inability of commentators to identify a workable and principled test to govern the concept of 'publicness', suggest that the problem does not lie in any failure on the part of courts or commentators. Rather, the difficulties and problems experienced may reflect that the distinction between 'public' and 'private' is not a sound basis for delineating application of judicial review principles. In other words, perhaps our starting point, that judicial review principles should be limited to decisions or acts with a 'public' element is wrong-headed, and we should cease trying to artificially limit application of those principles to the exercise of 'public' powers.

The difficulties associated with pinning down the concept of 'publicness' are particularly acute in the contemporary English context. Most arguments for treating public entities differently from private entities rely on the idea of 'the state' as in some way a unique entity which should be governed by a different set of rules from private entities. However, there is no such concept in English law, as Turpin and Tomkins record (*British Government and the Constitution* (Cambridge 2011) at 10–11):

> In Britain there is no legal entity called 'the state' in which powers are vested or to which allegiance or other duties are owed. The non-admission of the idea of the state helps to explain the tardy and partial development, in Britain, of a system of public law.

Furthermore, as we have seen, contemporary trends towards privatization and contracting-out, as well as the increased influence of market values of efficiency in public administration render the nature of public and private power increasingly indistinct, so that practically the distinction becomes impossible to draw. Similarly, we may observe a growing view—reflected in ideas such as corporate social responsibility—that private entities should not be free to greedily pursue their own interests but should be aware of the effects of their activities on, and be guided by the public good, in turn bringing private activity closer in nature to government activity, which is similarly associated traditionally with pursuit of the public interest. In the light of these sorts of developments Cane has observed that public and private spheres 'have become inextricably interwoven in a process better analogized to the scrambling of an egg than to the weaving of a two-stranded rope' ('Accountability and the Public/Private Distinction' in Bamforth and Leyland (eds), *Public Law in a Multi-Layered Constitution* (Oxford 2003) at 248). If public power is increasingly indistinguishable from private power and vice versa, how can we justify treating public and private exercises of power differently *per se*, and further, how could the concept of 'publicness' offer a sound and/or workable basis for a separate set of legal principles?

Even if we put to one side that public and private power are increasingly difficult to distinguish, power and its misuse and abuse have never been confined to the public sphere. For example, employers may exercise significant power over employees, landlords over tenants, large corporations over consumers. Given that the power of private entities may be just as significant, if not more significant, than that of government, Borrie observes the 'growing acceptance of a philosophy that *all* those who wield power should be accountable and should be subject to general principles of good administration'; 'the citizen is concerned that *all* power, public or private, should be conformable with liberty, fair dealing and good administration' ([1989] *PL* 552, 558–9).

Developments such as *Braganza* v. *BP Shipping Ltd* [2015] UKSC 17, [2015] 1 WLR 1661 (considered in the previous section) arguably reflect the growing influence of the philosophy Borrie describes; the Court in *Braganza* specifically justified recognition of judicial review-like principles in the law of contract on the basis that powers conferred on private persons or entities under contract could be abused. We see similar developments across other fields. For example, statute has created significant legal protections for employees *vis-à-vis* employers, and tenants *vis-à-vis* landlords, while there are now numerous consumer protection laws in place. Other fields such as competition law protect against private entities arrogating market power, while financial institutions such as banks are subject to elaborate regulatory schemes. Basic human rights in liberty, life, and the body have been protected against both public and private actors through longstanding fields such as the law of torts (see 15.3.1).

These examples reflect that it is not only public power that represents a threat to individual liberty and the public interest, and requires to be checked through legal constraints. But the examples just described also reinforce that we may not need to extend the scope of judicial review in order to ensure private power is properly checked. On the other hand, as *Braganza* shows, the principles developed in judicial review may provide an excellent model for the development of controls on private power in fields outside public law, such as the law of contract. Furthermore, that other tools, developed in other legal fields, may be effective in regulating private power, does not necessarily rule out application of judicial review norms in yet other contexts, where application of judicial review may be an effective and appropriate check on private power, and no other checks exist.

Perhaps the ultimate insight to come out of this discussion is that we need to avoid thinking in rigid categories. As Harlow and Rawlings argue, '[s]pecific situations call for thoughtful specific answers and not the mechanical application of the totemic word "public"' (*Law and Administration* (Cambridge 2009) at 21). Or, as Aronson argues, valuable responses to specific issues, whether characterized as involving 'public' or 'private' activities or entities might be derived from within public law or private law, or combine a mix of insights from both ('A Public Lawyer's Response to Privatisation and Outsourcing' in Taggart (ed), *The Province of Administrative Law* (Oxford 1997) at 51ff).

Thus, rather than resting the scope of review on whether a decision-maker is 'public' (hence subject to duties of considerate decision-making) or 'private' (so subject to no such duty), perhaps we should ask simply: to what extent (if any) should the relevant decision-maker be obligated to act considerately? If we find that a particular decision-maker should be required to act considerately we could then ask whether other controls, for example in contract, tort, or regulatory regimes, afford sufficient protection against abuse of power. If not, judicial review could be made available.

QUESTIONS

- Do you agree with the approach suggested in the last paragraph?
- What difficulties might this approach pose?

4.6 Section 6 of the Human Rights Act 1998

Thus far we have been concerned with the circumstances in which defendants may be fixed with an obligation to act consistently with the general public law principles of good decision-making. It remains to confront a closely allied question: which public bodies must respect individuals' human rights under the Human Rights Act 1998?

Human Rights Act 1998

6—(1) It is unlawful for a public authority to act in a way which is incompatible with a Convention right.

(2) Subsection (1) does not apply to an act if—

(a) as the result of one or more provisions of primary legislation, the authority could not have acted differently; or

(b) in the case of one or more provisions of, or made under, primary legislation which cannot be read or given effect in a way which is compatible with the Convention rights, the authority was acting so as to give effect to or enforce those provisions.

(3) In this section 'public authority' includes—

(a) a court or tribunal, and

(b) any person certain of whose functions are functions of a public nature, but does not include either House of Parliament or a person exercising functions in connection with proceedings in Parliament.

...

(5) In relation to a particular act, a person is not a public authority by virtue only of subsection (3)(b) if the nature of the act is private.

(6) 'An act' includes a failure to act but does not include a failure to—

(a) introduce in, or lay before, Parliament a proposal for legislation; or

(b) make any primary legislation or remedial order.

Although some writers (notably Wade (2000) 116 *LQR* 217) argue for full 'horizontal effect' of the HRA, such that all defendants—public or private—would be obliged to respect Convention rights, most commentators (see, *eg* Hunt [1998] *PL* 423 and Buxton (2000) 116 *LQR* 48) recognize that this would be inconsistent with the distinction between public authorities and others clearly envisaged by s 6 (even if Wade's approach may be a normatively attractive one). Consistently with this view, the current position is that Convention rights are directly enforceable only against public authorities. Meanwhile, private parties are bound by the HRA only where legislation governing their relations *inter se* must be interpreted compatibly with Convention rights (under HRA, s 3) or where principles of common law affecting their relationship have evolved so as to absorb human rights norms—a process which is most pronounced in relation to the action for misuse of private information, which has developed markedly under the influence of the Article 8 right to respect for private life (see *Campbell v. Mirror Group Newspapers Ltd* [2004] UKHL 22, [2004] 2 AC 457).

The scope of the s 6 duty to act compatibly with Convention rights is therefore crucial. Early decisions adopted a somewhat narrow approach, borrowing from the case law on amenability to judicial review and emphasizing institutional ('what is the defendant's relationship with the state?') over functional ('is this a public function?') criteria. For instance, in *Poplar Housing and Regeneration Community Association Ltd* v. *Donoghue* [2001] EWCA Civ 595, [2002] QB 48, the Court of Appeal, considering the 'public'/'private' distinction, stated (at [65]):

> What can make an act, which would otherwise be private, public is a feature or a combination of features which impose a public character or stamp on the act. Statutory authority for what is done can at least help to mark the act as being public; so can the extent of control over the function exercised by another body which is a public authority. The more closely the acts that could be of a private nature are enmeshed in the activities of a public body, the more likely they are to be public. However, the fact that the acts are supervised by a public regulatory body does not necessarily indicate that they are of a public nature.

A broader approach was commended in the important case of *Aston Cantlow and Wilmcote with Billesley Parochial Church Council* v. *Wallbank* [2003] UKHL 37, [2004] 1 AC 546. The defendants, as freehold owners of a farm constituting rectorial property, were liable to pay for all necessary repairs to the chancel of a parish church. When proceedings were brought under s 2(2) of the Chancel Repairs Act 1932, the defendants disputed their liability, arguing that the parochial church council (PCC) was obliged, by HRA, s 6, to act compatibly with Convention rights, and that the enforcement of chancel repair liability was inconsistent with Article 1 of Protocol 1. A central question before the House of Lords was whether the PCC constituted a public authority under s 6.

Their Lordships considered that s 6 recognized two types of public authorities, this distinction having ramifications for when each such authority would be bound to comply with the HRA.

'Core' public authorities are, pursuant to s 6(1), those entities which shall be bound to comply with the HRA in respect of everything they do. Lord Nicholls offered some guidance as to what sort of entity would fall into this category (at [7]):

> [T]he phrase 'a public authority' in section 6(1) is essentially a reference to a body whose nature is governmental in a broad sense of that expression ... The most obvious examples are government departments, local authorities, the police and the armed forces. Behind the instinctive classification of these organisations as bodies whose nature is governmental lie factors such as the possession of special powers, democratic accountability, public funding in whole or in part, an obligation to act only in the public interest, and a statutory constitution.

Lord Hope similarly considered that the wording of s 6(1) suggested that the court must look to the nature of the entity to determine whether it is a core public authority (at [41]):

> The word 'public' suggests that there [are] some persons which may be described as authorities that are nevertheless private and not public. The word 'authority' suggests that the person has regulatory or coercive powers given to it by statute or by the common law. The combination of these two words in the single unqualified phrase 'public authority' suggests that it is the nature of the person itself, not the functions which it may perform, that is determinative. Section 6(1) does not distinguish between public and private functions. It assumes that everything that a 'core' public authority does is a public function.

The second type was a 'hybrid' public authority. Pursuant to s 6(3)(b) such authorities are not bound to comply with the HRA in respect of everything they do. Such authorities perform a mixture of both public and private functions. When they are performing public functions, and only when they are performing public functions, they will be bound by the HRA. Lord Nicholls elaborated on the nature of such entities (at [9]–[10]):

> In a modern developed state governmental functions extend far beyond maintenance of law and order and defence of the realm. Further, the manner in which wide ranging governmental functions are discharged varies considerably. In the interests of efficiency and economy, and for other reasons, functions of a governmental nature are frequently discharged by non-governmental bodies. Sometimes this will be a consequence of privatisation, sometimes not. One obvious example is the running of prisons by commercial organisations. Another is the discharge of regulatory functions by organisations in the private sector, for instance, the Law Society. Section 6(3)(b) gathers this type of case into the embrace of section 6 by including within the phrase 'public authority' any person whose functions include 'functions of a public nature'. This extension of the expression 'public authority' does not apply to a person if the nature of the act in question is 'private'.

As Lord Hope stressed, whether an entity was a hybrid public authority could not be determined in the abstract. Rather, one had to inquire into whether the defendant's particular act or activities, that were in question in the proceedings, involved performance of a public function on a case-by-case basis. Equally, whether an act is a 'private act' under s 6(5), and not therefore regulated by the HRA, 'depends on the nature of the act which is in question in each case' (at [41]). This approach differs from that taken to determining whether a body is a 'core' public authority; in that case the court will look to the nature of the entity in the round, rather than focusing on specific acts or activities, to determine whether it is a public authority. Lord Nicholls offered some general guidance as to the nature of a public function (at [12]):

> Clearly there is no single test of universal application. There cannot be, given the diverse nature of governmental functions and the variety of means by which these functions are discharged today. Factors to be taken into account include the extent to which in carrying out the relevant function the body is publicly funded, or is exercising statutory powers, or is taking the place of central government or local authorities, or is providing a public service.

His Lordship added that while asking whether a function could be said to be governmental in nature would often be a useful guide in determining whether a function was 'public' or not for the purposes of s 6(3)(b), it was only a guide and not necessarily determinative: the word used in the statute was 'public' not 'governmental'.

Their Lordships emphasized that a cautious approach should be taken to designating an entity a core public authority. One reason was that this would have the significant ramification of binding the authority to observe human rights in respect of everything it did. A further reason was elaborated by Lord Nicholls (at [8]):

> One consequence of being a 'core' public authority, namely, an authority falling within section 6 without reference to section 6(3), is that the body in question does not itself enjoy Convention rights. It is difficult to see how a core public authority could ever claim to be a victim of an infringement of a Convention right. A core public authority seems inherently incapable of satisfying the

Convention description of a victim: 'any person, *non-governmental organisation* or group of individuals' (article 34, with emphasis added). Only victims of an unlawful act may bring proceedings under section 7 of the Human Rights Act, and the Convention description of a victim has been incorporated into the Act, by section 7(7). This feature, that a core public authority is incapable of having Convention rights of its own, is a matter to be borne in mind when considering whether or not a particular body is a core public authority. In itself this feature throws some light on how the expression 'public authority' should be understood and applied. It must always be relevant to consider whether Parliament can have intended that the body in question should have no Convention rights.

Unlike a core public authority, a 'hybrid' public authority, exercising both public functions and non-public functions, is not absolutely disabled from having Convention rights. A hybrid public authority is not a public authority in respect of an act of a private nature. Here again, as with section 6(1), this feature throws some light on the approach to be adopted when interpreting section 6(3)(b). Giving a generously wide scope to the expression 'public function' in section 6(3)(b) will further the statutory aim of promoting the observance of human rights values without depriving the bodies in question of the ability themselves to rely on Convention rights when necessary.

Applying these general principles their Lordships were in agreement that the PCC was not a core public authority, and all except Lord Scott considered that, in enforcing the chancel repair liability, the PCC was not performing a public function.

On the question of whether the PCC was a core public authority Lord Nicholls said (at [13]–[14]):

I do not think [PCCs] are 'core' public authorities. Historically the Church of England has discharged an important and influential role in the life of this country. As the established church it still has special links with central government. But the Church of England remains essentially a religious organisation. This is so even though some of the emanations of the church discharge functions which may qualify as governmental. Church schools and the conduct of marriage services are two instances. The legislative powers of the General Synod of the Church of England are another. This should not be regarded as infecting the Church of England as a whole, or its emanations in general, with the character of a governmental organisation.

As to parochial church councils, their constitution and functions lend no support to the view that they should be characterised as governmental organisations or, more precisely, in the language of the statute, public authorities ... [T]he essential role of a parochial church council is to provide a formal means, prescribed by the Church of England, whereby ex officio and elected members of the local church promote the mission of the Church and discharge financial responsibilities in respect of their own parish church, including responsibilities regarding maintenance of the fabric of the building. This smacks of a church body engaged in self-governance and promotion of its affairs. This is far removed from the type of body whose acts engage the responsibility of the state under the European Convention.

Lord Hope reasoned (at [59]–[63]):

[The PCC] plainly has nothing whatever to do with the process of either central or local government. It is not accountable to the general public for what it does. It receives no public funding, apart from occasional grants from English Heritage for the preservation of its historic buildings. In that respect it is in a position which is no different from that of any private individual. The statutory powers which it has been given by the Chancel Repairs Act 1932 are not exercisable

> against the public generally or any class or group of persons which forms part of it ... There is no Act of Parliament that purports to establish it as the Church of England ... It has regulatory functions within its own sphere, but it cannot be said to be part of government. The state has not surrendered or delegated any of its functions or powers to the Church. None of the functions that the Church of England performs would have to be performed in its place by the state if the Church were to abdicate its responsibility ... The relationship which the state has with the Church of England is one of recognition, not of the devolution to it of any of the powers or functions of government ... For these reasons I would hold that the PCC is not a 'core' public authority.

As to whether the PCC was nonetheless a hybrid public authority, performing a public function, Lord Nicholls said (at [16]):

> [I]t is not necessary to analyse each of the functions of a parochial church council and see if any of them is a public function. What matters is whether the particular act done by the plaintiff council of which complaint is made is a private act as contrasted with the discharge of a public function. The impugned act is enforcement of Mr and Mrs Wallbank's liability, as lay rectors, for the repair of the chancel of the church of St John the Baptist at Aston Cantlow. As I see it, the only respect in which there is any 'public' involvement is that parishioners have certain rights to attend church services and in respect of marriage and burial services. To that extent the state of repair of the church building may be said to affect rights of the public. But I do not think this suffices to characterise actions taken by the parochial church council for the repair of the church as 'public'. If a parochial church council enters into a contract with a builder for the repair of the chancel arch, that could hardly be described as a public act. Likewise when a parochial church council enforces, in accordance with the provisions of the Chancel Repairs Act 1932, a burdensome incident attached to the ownership of certain pieces of land: there is nothing particularly 'public' about this. This is no more a public act than is the enforcement of a restrictive covenant of which church land has the benefit.

Lord Hope placed emphasis on the 'nature of the obligation which the PCC is seeking to enforce. It is seeking to enforce a civil debt. The function which it is performing has nothing to do with the responsibilities which are owed to the public by the State. I would hold that section 6(5) applies, and that in relation to this act the PCC is not for the purposes of section 6(1) a public authority' (at [64]).

The Joint Committee on Human Rights (HL39/HC382, *The Meaning of 'Public Authority' under the Human Rights Act* (2003–04)) welcomed their Lordships' willingness in *Aston Cantlow* to balance a restrictive definition of 'core' public authorities with a wider and more flexible test for 'hybrid' bodies. Cane (2004) 120 *LQR* 41 at 45, in contrast, is more critical, observing that their Lordships failed 'to develop what is really needed to resolve the difficulties of s 6, namely a normative theory of the reach of human rights law'.

As with judicial review, particular difficulties arise when service provision is contracted out. Craig (2002) 118 *LQR* 551 at 556 argues that '[i]t is difficult to see why the nature of a function should alter if it is contracted out, rather than being performed in house [*ie* by a core public authority]. If it is a public function when undertaken in house, it should equally be so when contracted out.' However, as the next excerpt makes clear, not all functions performed by core public authorities are necessarily public functions—raising the possibility that their performance by contractors will not attract the application of the HRA.

Oliver, 'Functions of a Public Nature under the Human Rights Act'
[2004] *PL* 329

Public authorities are bound by s. 6 HRA to respect Convention rights in all that they do, even when performing acts of a private nature. Many activities of and functions exercised by standard (or core) public authorities such as local authorities and government departments are indisputably *not* activities or functions 'of a public nature'. If all the functions of all core public authorities were 'functions of a public nature', then there would have been no need to make the distinction in section 6 between public authorities and bodies certain of whose functions are of a public nature, for the Act could have applied quite simply to all exercises of functions of a public nature. Cleaning council offices [is] an example of an act or activity the nature of which is private. Managing car parking space would be another. Under HRA s. 6(1) standard public authorities exercising even private functions or activities are bound to respect Convention rights: the s. 6(1) duty does not depend on the classification of a function as of a public nature. However, the courts and commentators sometimes assume that the fact that a standard public authority is bound to respect Convention rights in all that it does means that all its functions are 'public functions' or 'functions of a public nature' when this is quite clearly not the case. In particular it is clear that not all decisions of standard public authorities are subject to judicial review.

When a standard public authority contracts or arranges informally with a private body for the latter to deliver certain services or do certain acts which the public authority itself or its employees have done in the past or might do, it follows that sometimes the activity contracted for with the private body will not be of a public nature and the private contractor will therefore not be under an obligation under s. 6 HRA to respect the Convention rights of those it deals with. An example would be where a local authority stops employing direct labour to maintain its parks and gardens and contracts the work out to self-employed gardeners or gardening contractors; or when it stops employing direct labour to clean the Town Hall and contracts with a private company for the cleaning to be done. Gardening, cleaning and managing a car park, it seems to me, are quite clearly acts the nature of which is private. If on the other hand the core public authority contracts with a private body … for the latter to exercise special statutory or common law authority, then the function will be of a public nature and the contractor will be under s. 6(3)(b) obligations.

It may of course seem unfair to the individual in receipt of services or the employee who is working for a private body rather than a public authority, that his or her Convention rights would have been respected if the activity had been done by the public authority itself and its direct labour force, but are not required to be respected by the private body to which the work is contracted out. But it was a deliberate policy in the Human Rights Act that there should be differences between the duties of public authorities and those of private bodies, unless the private body were exercising a function of a public nature, in which case the Act would have direct vertical effect.

Oliver's argument is a persuasive one, but it raises a difficult question. If some functions that can be performed by public authorities are not public in nature, such that those performing them on behalf of public authorities under contract will not be bound by the HRA, *how do we draw the line* between public functions (which attract the application of the HRA whoever performs them) and other functions (to which the HRA applies only when they are being performed by core public authorities)? That question was addressed in relation to contracting-out arrangements in the following case.

YL v. Birmingham City Council [2007] UKHL 27, [2008] 1 AC 95
House of Lords

The respondent local authority was required by the National Assistance Act 1948 (as amended) to arrange the provision of residential care and accommodation for the appellant, an 84-year-old Alzheimer's sufferer. The Council sought to discharge this duty by entering into a contract with the second respondent, Southern Cross Healthcare Ltd, in one of whose homes the appellant was duly accommodated, largely at public expense. When the company later sought to terminate the contract, the appellant, whose relatives had allegedly behaved inappropriately during visits, argued that the resulting eviction would infringe the right to respect for her home under Article 8 ECHR. This raised the question, with which this excerpt is concerned, whether Southern Cross was discharging a public function within the meaning of HRA, s 6(1), and was thus bound by Article 8.

Lord Mance

[110] ... Professor Dawn Oliver [in the article cited earlier] ... pertinently observes that it is a fallacy to regard all functions and activities of a core public authority as inherently public in nature. All such functions and activities are subject to the Convention, because the authority is a core public authority. It only becomes necessary to analyse their nature, if and when they are contracted out to a person who is not a core public authority. Some of them may then on analysis be private in nature. Reference to a core public authority performing a public function when providing care and accommodation is potentially confusing.

[111] How then is the provision of care and accommodation to be regarded? ...

[114] ... Neither the concept nor the extent of a function of a public nature is immutable in either national or European law ... The modern legislation distinguishes clearly between a local authority with a statutory duty to arrange care and accommodation and a private company providing services with which the local authority contracts on a commercial basis in order to fulfil the local authority's duty to arrange care and accommodation ...

[115] I do not regard the actual provision, as opposed to the arrangement, of care and accommodation for those unable to arrange it themselves as an inherently governmental function. The duty on a local authority under section 21 [of the 1948 Act] constitutes a safety net, conditional upon care and attention being 'not otherwise available'. In practice, this means that, if a person assessed as in need of care and accommodation has more than £21,000 capital and can arrange care and accommodation or (for example through relatives) make arrangements for it, then the local authority will not be further involved. In contrast with the position relating to the national health service, the default position is one in which the local authority is not involved. I can see no basis, and none was really suggested, on which a private care home could somehow be regarded as exercising functions of a public nature in providing care and accommodation for 'self-funders', those who or whose relatives could fund and make their own arrangements. The local authority's involvement is aimed at making arrangements (including funding) which put those in need in effectively the same position as those 'self-funders'. Once such arrangements are made, the actual provision of care and accommodation is a different matter, which, as the modern legislation recognises, does not need actually to be undertaken by the local authority and can take place in the private sector, as it does for those who or whose relatives are able to make arrangements including funding for themselves.

[116] In providing care and accommodation, Southern Cross acts as a private, profit-earning company. It is subject to close statutory regulation in the public interest. But so are many private occupations and businesses, with operations which may impact on members of the public in matters as diverse for example as life, health, privacy or financial well-being. Regulation by the State is no real pointer towards the person regulated being a state or governmental body or a

person with a function of a public nature, if anything perhaps even the contrary. The private and commercial motivation behind Southern Cross's operations does in contrast point against treating Southern Cross as a person with a function of a public nature. Some of the particular duties which it has been suggested would follow—a duty not to close the home without regard to the Convention right to a home of publicly funded residents, and perhaps even a duty to give priority to accepting such residents into the home—fit in my view uneasily with the ordinary private law freedom to carry on operations under agreed contractual terms, even accepting (as I would) that, if the Convention applied, a private care home would be able to invoke that freedom as a relevant factor under article 8(2).

[117] ... [If state- but not self-funded residents could invoke the HRA, this would introduce an] inherently questionable [distinction]. Care homes would be bound to be, and to make their staff, aware of the distinction between Human Rights Convention protected and other residents. If it came to an issue like closure of a wing of a home or relocation of some residents during works, there could be an incentive (it might be argued even a legal duty) to give priority to the wishes and demands of publicly funded residents. To distinguish between different residents in the same care home on the basis of their ability to make the relevant contractual arrangements necessary to gain entry to the home appears undesirable.

[123] ... I would hold that Southern Cross in providing care and accommodation for YL was not and is not exercising functions of a public nature within section 6(3)(b) of the Human Rights Act 1998 ...

Baroness Hale (dissenting)

[63] [I]t is common ground that 'functions of a public nature' include the exercise of the regulatory or coercive powers of the state. Thus, were a public authority to have power to delegate the task of regulating care homes to a private body, that regulation would be a function of a public nature. Again, it is common ground that privately run prisons perform functions of a public nature. In a similar category are private psychiatric hospitals when exercising their powers of compulsory detention under the Mental Health Act 1983: see R (A) v. Partnerships in Care Ltd [2002] 1 WLR 2610, 2619. This is so, even though the power to detain rests with the hospital managers rather than with a state body by whom it has been delegated.

[65] [Having quoted from paras 11 and 12 of Lord Nicholls's speech in Aston Cantlow (see earlier), Baroness Hale said:] While there cannot be a single litmus test of what is a function of a public nature, the underlying rationale must be that it is a task for which the public, in the shape of the state, have assumed responsibility, at public expense if need be, and in the public interest.

[66] One important factor is whether the state has assumed responsibility for seeing that this task is performed. In this case, there can be no doubt that the state has undertaken the responsibility of securing that the assessed community care needs of the people to whom section 21(1)(a) of the National Assistance Act 1948 applies are met. In the modern 'mixed economy of care', those needs may be met in a number of ways. But it is artificial and legalistic to draw a distinction between meeting those needs and the task of assessing and arranging them, when the state has assumed responsibility for seeing that both are done.

[67] Another important factor is the public interest in having that task undertaken. In a state which cares about the welfare of the most vulnerable members of the community, there is a strong public interest in having people who are unable to look after themselves, whether because of old age, infirmity, mental or physical disability or youth, looked after properly. They must be provided with the specialist care, including the health care, that they need even if they are unable to arrange or pay for it themselves. No-one can doubt that providing health care can be a public function, even though it can also be provided purely privately. This home was

providing health care by arrangement with the National Health Service as well as social care by arrangement with the local social services authority. It cannot be doubted that the provision of health care was a public function.

[68] Another important factor is public funding. Not everything for which the state pays is a public function. The supply of goods and ancillary services such as laundry to a care home may well not be a public function. But providing a service to individual members of the public at public expense is different. These are people for whom the public have assumed responsibility. There may be other residents in the home for whom the public have not assumed responsibility ...

[72] The fact that other people are free to make their own private arrangements does not prevent a function which is in fact performed for this person pursuant to statutory arrangements and at public expense from being a function of a public nature. People are free to provide their own transport rather than to use the publicly provided facilities. People are free to arrange their own health care rather than to use the National Health Service. Nor does the fact that people pay for or towards the service they receive necessarily prevent its provision being a function of a public nature. National Health Service dentistry is no less a function of a public nature because those patients who can afford to do so pay for it. I accept that not every function which is performed by a 'core' public authority is necessarily a 'function of a public nature'; but the fact that a function is or has been performed by a core public authority for the benefit of the public must, as Lord Nicholls pointed out in *Aston Cantlow* [2004] 1 AC 546, be a relevant consideration.

Lords Neuberger and Scott agreed with Lord Mance that Southern Cross was not performing a public function. Lord Bingham joined Baroness Hale in dissenting from that view.

The upshot of *YL* is that the provision of services pursuant to commercial contractual arrangements is generally unlikely to attract the application of the HRA, although it does not rule out the possibility. Much depends on the precise nature of the arrangements between the public body and the provider of the service. For instance, in *R (Weaver)* v. *London and Quadrant Housing Trust* [2009] EWCA Civ 587, [2010] 1 WLR 363, the defendant, a provider of low-cost social housing, was held subject to the HRA. One of the grounds on which *YL* was distinguished related to funding arrangements. Elias LJ noted that in *YL* Lord Neuberger had said (at [165]) that it is

easier to invoke public funding to support the notion that a service is a function of 'a public nature' where the funding effectively subsidises, in whole or in part, the cost of the service as a whole, rather than consisting of paying for the provision of that service to a specific person.

Whereas *YL* had fallen on the latter side of the line, the facts of *Weaver* fell on the former: social landlords receive block grants from state bodies as opposed to payments in respect of individuals.

But notwithstanding the fact that *YL* does not place all bodies outwith the formal structure of government beyond the reach of the HRA, its effect is undeniably restrictive. There are at least two major criticisms that can be made of the majority's approach.

First, the approach undermines Parliament's intentions in passing the HRA. The majority approach, with its heavy focus on the presence of contract, undermines Parliament's deliberate adoption of a 'functional' approach to defining publicness, and simultaneously rejection of a 'source-based' or 'institutional' approach. Parliament's adoption of a test that requires courts to be guided by the nature of the function being performed—*eg* is social care a public function?—rather than the source of powers—*eg* are powers sourced in statute or contract?—was motivated by the reality that much government business is now conducted through contract. The protection afforded to an individual's basic rights should not depend on the happenstance of whether government performs certain public functions itself or delegates the very same functions to a private entity via contract. The majority approach also arguably undermines the more general intentions underpinning the Act: the very purpose of the HRA is to afford strong protection to human rights; adopting a narrow approach to which entities may be bound by the Act cuts down the scope of protection. Surely the purpose underlying the Act suggests that at the very least in cases which are not clear-cut, such as *YL*, the courts ought to err on the side of an expansive view of the Act's scope. Further, the majority approach prioritizes preservation of private contractual arrangements over protection of human rights by largely insulating contractual arrangements from the application of human rights law. How is this to be reconciled with the idea that human rights are the most fundamental of rights? Should contract not bow to human rights?

Second, the majority approach fails to provide a coherent principle by reference to which these sorts of questions are to be resolved. Lord Mance says that there is nothing *inherently* governmental about providing care. But the truth is that there is nothing inherently governmental about *anything*. The notion of governmental, or public, function cannot be determined in the abstract. Instead, it must be determined by reference either to a normative theory of where the dividing line *should* lie between the public and private spheres—something which may be difficult to achieve given the fraught nature of the idea of 'publicness'—or by reference to empirical observations about what, *in fact*, is treated—in a given society at a given time—as falling within the responsibility of government. For that reason, the 'assumption of responsibility' test adopted by Baroness Hale in her dissenting speech is to be preferred. It echoes the following view of the Parliamentary Joint Committee on Human Rights (JCHR) (*op cit* at [140]):

> The key test of whether a function is public is whether it is one for which the government has taken responsibility in the public interest. For example, although the various activities involved in care for the sick may be performed by anyone, the State has chosen, through a comprehensive social programme, to provide healthcare to those who wish to receive healthcare from the State rather than privately. This programme is undertaken in the public interest to provide what the government considers to be an important social service. In our view, discharge of duties necessary for provision of the government programme of healthcare is a public function. Discharge of healthcare services, in itself, is not.

It followed, said the Committee (at [142]), that 'for a body to discharge a public function, it does not need to do so under direct statutory authority'. Sunkin [2004] *PL* 643 at 655–6 explains that this approach is

> programmatic rather than substantive ... Focusing as it does on government programmes this approach recognises that very few services are inherently public (caring for the sick or educating children can be provided by the state or by commercial or charitable organisations) and that views about what constitutes public functions can change over time.

The specific lacuna created by *YL* has been filled by s 145 of the Health and Social Care Act 2008 (see now: Care Act 2014, s 73), which provides that anyone providing accommodation together with nursing or personal care under relevant statutory powers is to be taken, in doing so, as performing functions of a public nature for the purpose of HRA, s 6(1). This means that even if the provider would otherwise not count as a public body, it will now count as such for these purposes. But the *YL* majority's approach otherwise represents the current position, the government having failed to take up the JCHR's suggestion (HC410/HL77, *The Meaning of Public Authority under the Human Rights Act* (2006–07) at [150]) that legislation of a more general nature should be enacted, making provision to the effect that 'a function of a public nature includes a function performed pursuant to a contract or other arrangement with a public authority which is under a duty to perform the function'. As such, while the gap in protection has been plugged in the nursing home context, similar gaps remain in other contexts: Choudhry [2013] *PL* 519.

QUESTIONS

- Do you agree that the approach adopted by Baroness Hale in *YL* is preferable to that adopted by Lord Mance?
- Does Baroness Hale's analysis risk drawing the range of functions covered by the HRA too widely?

A further question arises. How, if at all, may individuals' human rights be protected *vis-à-vis* contractors performing functions that do not, on the *YL* test, count as public? Two possibilities arise. First, some suggest that public bodies might insist, when entering into contracts with service providers, on terms requiring that the latter respect individuals' Convention rights. But, as Donnelly [2005] *PL* 785 points out, this would be problematic: not all public bodies might do so (leading to uneven safeguarding of rights), and individuals, not being parties to the relevant contracts, would be able to enforce their rights only in limited circumstances: see Contracts (Rights of Third Parties) Act 1999. Second, Lord Mance noted in *YL* at [118] that even if no contractual remedy is available, the individual will retain public law rights, including under the HRA, *vis-à-vis* the public authority that contracted out the service concerned. But this will often offer a remedy that is very much second best. Indeed, in *YL* itself, such a claim would not have availed the claimant: whether she was to be evicted from the particular home concerned was a matter within the control of the contractor, not the council, so it follows that only a human rights claim against the former could have got the claimant what she wanted.

4.7 Concluding remarks

Compared with the position which obtained 30 years ago, the scope of judicial review today is unrecognizable. No longer is the prerogative regarded as a discretionary power which may be exercised without regard to the principles of good administration. Misplaced judicial deference to the 'royal' prerogative has yielded to judicial recognition that it is now, in many respects, just another executive power (albeit that these developments are somewhat qualified by the House of Lords' decision in *Bancoult*). Similarly, the formalism of the past has given way to a new emphasis on substance as the courts' concern with the source of the power has been eclipsed by concerns as to justiciability. These developments in relation to the prerogative are mirrored in the courts' attitude to *de facto* powers. Here, too, matters of substance, rather than form, are now to the fore as the courts strive to avoid being deceived by what Sir John Donaldson, in *Datafin*, referred to as the new subtlety and complexity of executive power. The willingness of the courts to vindicate the rule of law in these new contexts is a positive development, but there are, as we have seen, a number of difficulties which remain fully to be resolved; contractualization poses particular problems for the scope of both judicial review and the HRA. Taken as a whole, however, the developments that are mapped in this chapter are to be welcomed. They evidence an increasingly mature system of administrative law which is concerned to ensure that public power, whatever its source, is used lawfully.

FURTHER RESOURCES

Campbell, 'The Nature of Power as Public in English Judicial Review' (2009) 68 *CLJ* 90

Craig, 'Contracting Out, the Human Rights Act and the Scope of Judicial Review' (2002) 118 *LQR* 551

Daintith, 'Contractual Discretion and Administrative Discretion: A Unified Analysis' (2005) 68 *MLR* 554

Daly, 'Justiciability and the 'Political Question' Doctrine' [2010] *PL* 160

Elliott, 'Judicial Review's Scope, Foundations and Purposes: Joining the Dots' [2012] *NZ L Rev* 75

Elliott and Perreau-Saussine, 'Pyrrhic Public Law: *Bancoult* and the Sources, Status and Content of Common Law Limitations on Prerogative Power' [2009] *PL* 697

Harris, 'Judicial Review, Justiciability and the Prerogative of Mercy' [2003] *CLJ* 631

Joint Committee on Human Rights, HL39/HC382, *The Meaning of 'Public Authority' under the Human Rights Act* (2003–04) http://www.publications.parliament.uk/pa/jt200304/jtselect/jtrights/39/3902.htm

Morgan, 'Against Judicial Review of Discretionary Contractual Powers' [2008] *LMCLQ* 230

Oliver, *Common Values and the Public/Private Divide* (London 1999)

Taggart (ed), *The Province of Administrative Law* (Oxford 1997)

Williams, 'A Fresh Perspective on Hybrid Public Authorities under the Human Rights Act: Private Contractors, Rights-Stripping and "Chameleonic" Horizontal Effect' [2011] *PL* 139

5 RETENTION OF DISCRETION

5.1 Introduction

This chapter is concerned with various principles of administrative law which require decision-makers to retain the discretion which they are granted. In general terms, the traditional concern of the law in this area has been to ensure that decision-making occurs in accordance with the scheme envisaged by Parliament, rather than in a manner which is distorted by limitations and practices superimposed upon the discretionary power by its holder.

More specifically, the traditional rules of administrative law developed in this context serve two distinct (but related) objectives. First, they require that decision-making is carried out by the specific agency to which the discretion was, in the first place, confided; the transfer or delegation of power to other agencies is therefore, in general, prohibited. Second, the law seeks to ensure that the agency has at its disposal the full discretion which was granted to it, and therefore precludes behaviour—such as the adoption of rigid policies—which has the effect of fettering or narrowing the discretion.

However, these orthodoxies have come under increasing pressure. This is especially so in relation to the rule against fettering of discretion, which now risks being turned on its head as the courts set about forging a new set of principles of administrative law designed to ensure discretions are appropriately bounded and fettered.

Further questions arise concerning the extent to which discretion may be limited by representations made by, or on behalf of, agencies as to how their discretionary powers will be exercised; these issues are addressed in ch 6.

5.2 Delegation of discretionary power

5.2.1 A presumption against delegation

Discretionary power may not, in general, be delegated. This notion is sometimes expressed through the maxim *delegatus non potest delegare*, meaning that the body to which power has been delegated by Parliament may not itself delegate that power. This principle of administrative law is not, however, an immovable rule; rather, it takes effect as a presumption. When interpreting a statutory scheme the courts therefore begin by assuming that Parliament intends the power in question to be exercised only by the decision-maker specified in the legislation, and the question then becomes whether anything in the scheme rebuts that presumption, expressly or by implication. Questions over the legality of delegation therefore typically require courts to closely analyse the relevant statutory scheme.

Some legislation expressly permits discretionary powers to be delegated (see, *eg* Local Government Act 1972, ss 101–102). However, the general policy that discretionary power should be exercised by its statutory holder means that such provisions tend to be narrowly construed. For instance, in *General Medical Council* v. *UK Dental Board* [1936] Ch 41, although the Dentists Act 1921 permitted the GMC to delegate functions to an executive committee, the Court held that this power of delegation did not extend to disciplinary functions. This reflects the fact (also illustrated by the following case) that the courts' willingness to find statutory permission for delegation and the importance of the function in question appear to be inversely related.

Barnard v. *National Dock Labour Board* [1953] 2 QB 18
Court of Appeal

The claimants appealed from a decision of McNair J dismissing their claim for a declaration that they had been wrongfully suspended and that, as their suspension had been carried out not by the local dock labour board but by the port manager, it was unlawful.

Denning LJ

... The second matter on which the men sought the ruling of the court was the question of procedure; whether they had been lawfully suspended; and this involved a consideration of the disciplinary powers of the board. Under the Dock Workers (Regulation of Employment) Scheme, 1947, the power to suspend a man is entrusted to the local dock labour board, which is composed of equal numbers of representatives of the workers and employers. In this case the board did not themselves suspend the men; the port manager did. The local board did not have anything to do with it; they did not see the report made by the employers; they did not investigate the matter; they did not make any decision upon it themselves; they left it all to the port manager. The suspension was not brought to their notice until after the appeal tribunal had given its decision.

It was urged on us that the local board had power to delegate their functions to the port manager on the ground that the power of suspension was an administrative and not a judicial function. It was suggested that the action of the local board in suspending men was similar in character to the action of an employer in dismissing him. I do not accept this view. Under the provisions of the scheme, so far from the board being in the position of an employer, the board are put in a judicial position between the men and the employers; they are to receive reports from the employers and investigate them; they have to inquire whether the man has been guilty of misconduct, such as failing to comply with a lawful order, or failing to comply with the provisions of the scheme; and if they find against him they can suspend him without pay, or can even dismiss him summarily. In those circumstances they are exercising a judicial function just as much as the tribunals which were considered by this court in the cornporters' case, *Abbott* v. *Sullivan* [1952] 1 K.B. 189, and in *Lee* v. *Showmen's Guild of Great Britain* [1952] 2 Q.B. 329, the only difference being that those were domestic tribunals, and this is a statutory one. The board, by their procedure, recognize that before they suspend a man they must give him notice of the charge and an opportunity of making an explanation. That is entirely consonant with the view that they exercise a judicial function and not an administrative one, and we should, I think, so hold.

While an administrative function can often be delegated, a judicial function rarely can be. No judicial tribunal can delegate its functions unless it is enabled to do so expressly or by necessary implication. In *Local Government Board* v. *Arlidge* [1915] A.C. 120, the power to delegate was given by necessary implication; but there is nothing in this scheme authorizing the board to delegate this function, and it cannot be implied. It was suggested that it would be impracticable for the board to sit as a board to decide all these cases; but I see nothing impracticable at all; they have only to fix their quorum at two members and arrange for two members, one from each side, employers and workers, to be responsible for a week at a time: probably each pair would only have to sit on one day during their week.

Singleton and Romer LJJ also delivered judgments in favour of allowing the appeal. The appeal was therefore allowed.

What lies at the root of this presumption against delegation? Most straightforwardly, *parliamentary intention*: if Parliament has specified that a particular agency should take the decision, then Parliament's will must prevail. Although this follows straightforwardly from the fact that Parliament is sovereign, there are richer normative reasons why the decision should be taken by the agency chosen by Parliament. In the first place, the decision-maker designated in the legislation is likely to have been chosen because of its *institutional ability* to take decisions in the area in question, due to the expertise of its personnel, its integration into a wider decision-making structure, or its ability to gain access to relevant information and expert advice. Moreover, the designated agency is most likely to be an *accountable* decision-maker: it may well be subject to a regime of political accountability and, in any event, its role in making decisions in the relevant area will be transparent, its specification in the legislation making it readily identifiable as the responsible agency.

5.2.2 Conflicting policies

However, while there are strong policy reasons for the existence of a presumption against delegation, these must be weighed against counterarguments which call for greater flexibility.

Willis, '*Delegatus Non Potest Delegare*' (1943) 21 *Canadian Bar Review* 257

The presumption that the person named was selected because of some aptitude peculiar to himself requires the authority named in the statute to use its own peculiar aptitude and forbids it to entrust its statutory discretion to another who may be less apt than it, unless it is clear from the circumstances that some reason other than its aptitude dictated the naming of it to exercise the discretion. Because, however, the courts will readily mould the literal words of a statute to such a construction as will best achieve its object; because they will, recognizing the facts of modern government, readily imply in an authority such powers as it would normally be expected to possess; because the presumption of deliberate selection, strong when applied to the case of a principal who appoints an agent or a testator who selects a trustee, wears thin when applied to a statute which authorizes some governmental authority, sometimes with a fictitious name such as 'Governor-in-Council' or 'Minister of Justice', to exercise a discretion which everyone, even the legislature, knows will in fact be exercised by an unknown underling in the employ of the authority, the *prima facie* rule of *delegatus non potest delegare* will readily give way, like the principles on which it rests, to slight indications of contrary intent.

What are these indications? The *prima facie* rule is displaced, of course, by a section in the statute which expressly permits the authority entrusted with a discretion to delegate it to another. In the absence of such a provision, how does the court decide whether the rule is or is not intended to apply; how does it decide whether to read in the word 'personally' or the words 'or any person authorized by it'? The language of the statute does not, *ex hypothesi*, help it; it is driven therefore to the scope and object of the statute. Is there anything in the nature of the authority to which the discretion is entrusted, in the situation in which the discretion is to be exercised, in the object which its exercise is expected to achieve to suggest that the legislature did not intend to confine the authority to the personal exercise of its discretion? This question is answered in practice by comparing the *prima facie* rule with the known practices or the apprehended needs of the authority in doing its work; the court inquires whether the policy-scheme of the statute is such as could not easily be realized unless the policy which requires that a discretion be exercised by the authority named thereto be displaced; it weighs the presumed desire of the legislature for the judgment of the authority it has named against the presumed desire of the legislature that the process of government shall go on in its accustomed and most effective manner and where there is a conflict between the two policies, it determines which under all the circumstances is the most important.

As Willis indicates, the over-rigid application of the non-delegation principle is liable to compromise the efficient conduct of government—and the policy objectives underlying the non-delegation principle apply with more or less force, depending on the context. It is therefore necessary to acknowledge that demands of expediency, pragmatism, and good administration may, and sometimes do, require that decision-making is devolved. As Willis observes, one way in which the courts are able to balance these conflicting policies is by *disapplying the non-delegation principle* where the context demands. A more subtle response, however, focuses on *the nature of delegation itself*: as we will see in the following sections, there are certain practices, such as consulting outside agencies and the devolution of decision-making within government departments, which are held to be wholly acceptable practices which do not constitute delegation at all. By manipulating the concept of delegation thus, the courts are able to remove what are regarded as legitimate modes of decision-making from the reach of the non-delegation principle.

5.2.3 The nature of delegation

Given that delegation is *prima facie* prohibited, it is crucial to work out the location of the dividing line between practices which are considered to involve delegation and other forms of administrative conduct which are regarded as acceptable. The most straightforward cases—such as *Barnard* v. *National Dock Labour Board* [1953] 2 QB 18 (see 5.2.1) and *Vine* v. *National Dock Labour Board* [1957] AC 488—are those in which the designated decision-maker purports simply to hand over its power to another institution. Such cases clearly involve delegation and therefore present little difficulty (albeit that, as seen earlier, the non-delegation presumption may be rebutted).

It is, however, possible for delegation to occur in more subtle ways; in such situations, the courts habitually look beyond the form of the decision-making practice, seeking instead to appreciate the reality of the situation. This can cut both ways. On the one hand, courts are alive to the fact that decision-making cannot—indeed, should not—occur within an institutional bubble. Practices such as consulting external bodies and utilizing expertise from outside the decision-making body are to be applauded, since they tend to increase the quality of decisions, allowing the designated agency to form rounder and better-informed views. There is, however, a distinction—sometimes a fine one—between seeking guidance from an external agency and placing so much weight on its opinion that it becomes, in substance if not in form, the true decision-maker.

It follows that superficially legitimate practices may conceal arrangements that amount to delegations of power. For example, where the designated decision-maker merely ratifies decisions taken by a delegate, the courts are quick to recognize that the former's involvement is purely formal, and that the decision is in substance that of the latter. This point was taken by Denning LJ in *Barnard* [1953] 2 QB 18 at 40:

> [I]t was suggested that even if the board could not delegate their functions, at any rate they could ratify the actions of the port manager; but if the board have no power to delegate their functions to the port manager, they can have no power to ratify what he has done. The effect of ratification is to make it equal to a prior command; but just as a prior command, in the shape of a delegation, would be useless, so also is a ratification.

On the other hand, if the defendant can show that they not only retain the formal power of final decision, but in practice exercise that power in a way that shows independent judgement, they cannot be accused of unlawful delegation. Thus under the Immigration Rules an applicant for a student visa must produce a 'Confirmation of Studies' (CAS) which is supplied by their sponsoring institution, such as a University. As part of the decision to issue a CAS a sponsoring institution must make certain judgements such as whether the individual has a bona fide intention to study. In *R (New London College Ltd)* v. *Secretary of State for the Home Department* [2013] UKSC 51, [2013] 1 WLR 2358, the Supreme Court rejected a claim that the Secretary of State had unlawfully delegated her powers to control entry into the country by conferring this role on sponsoring institutions. As a matter of law leave to enter or remain continued to be the responsibility of immigration officers and the Minister who retained the last word in each case by virtue of certain general grounds of refusal provided for in the Rules, such as that the Minister is not satisfied by the material used by the individual to obtain his offer for a course. But further and importantly, '[t]he evidence shows that a significant number of [student] migrants with a CAS are in fact refused leave to enter or remain on these grounds' (at [19]). As such, it could not be said that the grant of a CAS was tantamount to determining the application; rather, the CAS 'is strong but not conclusive evidence of some of the matters which are relevant upon the migrant's application for leave to enter or remain' (at [19]). The case demonstrates that the courts will look beyond the decision-maker's formal legal powers to the practical reality of the decision-making process.

We may contrast the *New London College* case with situations where the designated decision-maker effectively surrenders its power by allowing the opinion of some other actor or agency to capture its decision-making. Absent statutory authorization, such practice constitutes unlawful delegation.

Lavender and Sons Ltd v. *Minister of Housing and Local Government*
[1970] 1 WLR 1231
Queen's Bench Division

The claimant, a gravel extractor, purchased agricultural land, part of which was located in an area which, pursuant to government policy formulated on the basis of the Waters Report on sand and gravel extraction, was protected against such extraction and preserved instead for agriculture. Nevertheless, the claimant sought planning permission to extract gravel. The local planning authority consulted all interested parties including the Minister of Agriculture, who objected on agricultural grounds. The planning authority ultimately refused permission, prompting the claimant to appeal unsuccessfully to the Minister of Housing and Local Government. In explaining his decision, the Minister said that it was his policy to withhold permission in such cases 'unless the Minister of Agriculture is not opposed'; since the Minister of Agriculture had not withdrawn his objection, permission was denied. The claimant sought to have the decision of the Minister of Housing and Local Government quashed, arguing, *inter alia*, that he had unlawfully fettered his discretion by effectively giving a power of veto to the Minister of Agriculture.

Willis J

... It is common ground that the Minister must be open to persuasion that the land should not remain in the Waters reservation. How can his mind be open to persuasion, how can an applicant establish an 'exceptional case' in the face of an inflexible attitude by the Minister of Agriculture? That attitude was well known before the inquiry, it was maintained during the inquiry, and presumably thereafter. The inquiry was no doubt, in a sense, into the Minister of Agriculture's objection, since, apart from that objection, it might well have been that no inquiry would have been necessary, but I do not think that the Minister after the inquiry can be said in any real sense to have given genuine consideration to whether on planning (including agricultural) grounds this land could be worked. It seems to me that by adopting and applying his stated policy he has in effect inhibited himself from exercising a proper discretion (which would of course be guided by policy considerations) in any case where the Minister of Agriculture has made and maintained an objection to mineral working in an agricultural reservation. Everything else might point to the desirability of granting permission, but by applying and acting on his stated policy I think the Minister has fettered himself in such a way that in this case it was not he who made the decision for which Parliament made him responsible. It was the decision of the Minister of Agriculture not to waive his objection which was decisive in this case, and while that might properly prove to be the decisive factor for the Minister when taking into account all material considerations, it seems to me quite wrong for a policy to be applied which in reality eliminates all the material considerations save only the consideration, when that is the case, that the Minister of Agriculture objects. That means, as I think, that the Minister has by his stated policy delegated to the Minister of Agriculture the effective decision on any appeal within the agricultural reservations where the latter objects to the working ...

I am satisfied that the applicants should succeed. I think the Minister failed to exercise a proper or indeed any discretion by reason of the fetter which he imposed upon its exercise in acting solely in accordance with his stated policy; and further, that upon the true construction of the Minister's letter the decision to dismiss the appeal, while purporting to be that of the Minister, was in fact, and improperly, that of the Minister of Agriculture, Fisheries and Food.

An order to quash the decision of the Minister of Housing and Local Government was granted.

QUESTIONS

- How should the line be drawn between unlawful delegation and the legitimate involvement of other actors or agencies?
- Do the decisions in *New London College* and *Lavender* draw that line in the right place?

5.2.4 Departmental decision-making in central government

We have already seen that the general policy that discretionary powers must be exercised by the grantee falls to be balanced against the need for efficient government and expeditious decision-making. The tension between the objectives of the non-delegation principle and these other imperatives is especially acute in relation to decision-making in central government departments, for reasons made clear in our next excerpt. As a result the courts have been persuaded, in this context, to modify their usual approach.

Re Golden Chemical Products Ltd [1976] Ch 300
Chancery Division

Section 35 of the Companies Act 1967 empowered the Board of Trade, where it appeared expedient in the public interest, to present a petition for the winding up of a company. The functions of the Board of Trade were exercisable by the Secretary of State for Trade. Gill was a civil servant in the Department of Trade holding the office of Inspector of Companies. He presented a petition under s 35 in respect of Golden Chemical Products Ltd. As a preliminary issue, the court considered whether the power to present such a petition could be exercised by the Secretary of State acting through a departmental officer, rather than acting personally.

Brightman J

[Having found as fact that Gill had been 'entrusted by the Secretary of State for Trade with the power to make decisions under section 35', his Lordship continued:] Mr. Chadwick, for the Secretary of State, has formulated five propositions. (1) As a general rule a Minister is not required to exercise personally every power and discretion conferred upon him by statute. It is otherwise if there is a context in the statute which shows that the power is entrusted to the Minister personally. (2) As a general rule it is for the Minister or his appropriate officials to decide which of his officers shall exercise a particular power. (3) Unless the level at which the power is to be exercised appears from the statute, it is not for the courts to examine the level or to inquire whether a particular official entrusted with the power is the appropriate person to exercise that power. (4) As a general rule officers of a government department exercise powers incidental and appropriate to their functions. In the absence of a statutory requirement it is neither necessary nor usual for specific authority to be given orally or in writing in relation to a specific power. (5) Constitutionally there is no delegation by a Minister to his officers. When an officer exercises a power or discretion entrusted to him, constitutionally and legally that exercise is the act of the Minister.

Mr. Chadwick relies upon four cases, the earliest of which is *Carltona Ltd.* v. *Commissioners of Works* [1943] 2 All E.R. 560. Regulation 51(1) of the Defence (General) Regulations 1939, read with certain other enactments, provided that a competent authority, if it appeared to that authority necessary or expedient so to do, might requisition land. An assistant secretary of the Ministry of Works and Planning, which was the relevant department, signed a requisitioning notice. The notice was challenged by the proprietor of the land on the ground, among others, that the Commissioners of Works, wrongly assumed by the proprietor to be the competent authority, had not themselves personally brought their minds to bear on the exercise of the power. The argument, allowing for the necessary interpolation, was rejected. Lord Greene M.R. said, at p. 563:

'In the administration of government in this country the functions which are given to Ministers (and constitutionally properly given to Ministers because they are constitutionally responsible) are functions so multifarious that no Minister could ever personally attend to them. To take the example of the present case no doubt there have been thousands of requisitions in this country by individual ministries. It cannot be supposed that this regulation meant that, in each case, the Minister in person should direct his mind to the matter. The duties imposed upon Ministers and the powers given to Ministers are normally exercised under the authority of the Ministers by responsible officials of the department. Public business could not be carried on if that were not the case. Constitutionally, the decision of such an official is, of course, the decision of the Minister. The Minister is responsible. It is he who must answer before Parliament for anything that his officials have done under his authority, and, if for an important matter he selected an official of such junior standing that he could not be expected competently to perform the work, the Minister would have to answer for that in Parliament. The whole system of departmental organisation and administration is based on the view that Ministers, being responsible to Parliament, will see that important duties are committed to experienced officials. If they do not do that, Parliament is the place where complaint must be made against them.

In the present case the assistant secretary, a high official of the Ministry, was the person entrusted with the work of looking after this particular matter and the question, therefore, is, relating those facts to the argument with which I am dealing, did he direct his mind to the matters to which he was bound to direct it in order to act properly under the regulation?'

The other members of the Court agreed.

Brightman J concluded that the Carltona principle applied in the present case. Declaration accordingly.

The '*Carltona* principle', as it is known, raises a number of issues. The first concerns its *relationship with the non-delegation principle*. The traditional view is that the two principles can comfortably be reconciled. In *R* v. *Secretary of State for the Home Department, ex parte Oladehinde* [1991] 1 AC 254 at 284, Lord Donaldson MR said that, when the *Carltona* principle is in play, 'The civil servant acts not as the delegate, but as the *alter ego*, of the Secretary of State. "Devolution" may be a better word [than "delegation"]'. Similarly, in *R (Bourgass)* v. *Secretary of State for Justice* [2015] UKSC 54, [2015] 3 WLR 457 at [49], Lord Reed explained that 'a delegate would normally be understood as someone who exercises powers delegated to him in his own name', whereas 'a decision made on behalf of a minister by one of his officials is constitutionally the decision of the minister himself'. On this view, the non-delegation principle is never even engaged in *Carltona* situations, thanks to the application of the legal fiction that the exercise of the ministerial power by the official is deemed to be an exercise of power by the Minister himself. However, reliance upon legal fiction is rarely satisfactory: it masks the reality of the position, and inhibits attempts to rationalize and evaluate the law. A more realistic view was advanced by Lord Diplock in *Bushell* v. *Secretary of State for the Environment* [1981] AC 75 at 95. He said that '[d]iscretion in making administrative decisions is conferred upon a Minister not as an individual but as the holder of an office in which he will have available to him in arriving at his decision the collective knowledge, experience and expertise of all those who serve the Crown in the department of which, for the time being, he is the political head.' Freedland [1996] *PL* 19 at 22 applauds this approach: '[R]ather than seeing Parliament as indulging in a fiction that Ministers will normally exercise their discretions personally, it is preferable to see the draftsman as employing a notation or code whereby the entrusting of discretion to a government department is expressed by conferring that discretion upon the Minister concerned'.

Second, *how broad is the* Carltona *doctrine*: does it allow *any* power to be devolved to *any* departmental official? In the *Golden Chemical* case, it was argued that *Carltona* applied only to certain ministerial powers, and that it did not extend to powers expressed in personal terms (*eg* 'If it appears expedient to him, the Minister may …') unless their exercise, in a given case, would have no serious consequences for individuals' rights. However, Brightman J rejected this proposition, holding that it would be practically impossible to draw the distinction between delegable and non-delegable powers in a principled, consistent manner. Despite Brightman J's reservations it is increasingly common for courts to hold that it may be unlawful to delegate some powers to *certain* officials. In *Oladehinde* [1991] 1 AC 254 at 300, Lord Griffiths said that *Carltona* would only justify the exercise of ministerial power by an official of 'suitable seniority'. This view was echoed in *DPP* v. *Haw* [2007] EWHC 1931 (Admin), [2008] 1 WLR 379 at [29]. Lord Phillips MR said that the *Carltona* doctrine required 'further refinement', and that there was 'a case for saying … that the devolution of a minister's power should be subject to a requirement that the seniority of the official exercising a power should be of an appropriate level having regard to the nature of the power in question'. In *R (Hamill)* v. *Chelmsford Justices* [2014] EWHC 2799 (Admin), [2015] 1 WLR 1798, this view gained further traction: Aikens LJ said there 'must be some restriction on the degree of delegation to which this duty can be subject' (at [64]), and considered that the degree of delegation is subject to a requirement that the seniority of the official exercising the duty should be of an appropriate level having regard to the nature of the duty. In *Castle* v *DPP* [2014] EWHC 587, [2014] 1 WLR 4279 at [28], Pitchford LJ required any delegation to be to someone 'properly qualified to make the judgment'. Thus there is a consensus emerging around a general principle that ministerial powers may, pursuant to the *Carltona* doctrine, only be exercised by officials with appropriate seniority and qualifications to exercise those powers.

Further, the authorization of officials to perform particular ministerial functions must be consistent with ordinary review principles, including procedural fairness and rationality (*Bourgass* at [52]). Perhaps this provides one way of rationalizing the seniority principle: it would be irrational to authorize a very junior official to exercise great powers of state.

Importantly, where the relevant ministerial power is a statutory one, courts will closely analyse the statutory scheme to determine whether the power is one that may be exercised by officials other than the Minister according to the *Carltona* principle, and if so whether only certain classes of officials may be authorized to exercise the power on the Minister's behalf. Thus, in the recent Supreme Court case of *Bourgass*, Lord Reed, for the Court, observed: 'It is … possible that the performance of statutory ministerial functions by officials, or by particular officials, may be inconsistent with the intention of Parliament as evinced by the relevant provisions. In such circumstances, the operation of the *Carltona* principle will be impliedly excluded or limited' (at [52]). The case concerned certain powers conferred by the Prison Rules 1999, made under the Prisons Act 1952. Rule 45(1) provided for the prison governor to arrange for a prisoner to be placed in solitary confinement. Rule 45(2) provides that a prisoner shall not be placed in solitary for more than 72 hours without the Secretary of State for Justice's approval. The question before the Court was whether the governor or his officials could exercise the Minister's power under rule 45(2) pursuant to the *Carltona* doctrine. The Supreme Court held that he could not. One reason was that the governor has a very different relationship to the Minister than the Minister's relationship to departmental officials so that the governor could not be considered the Minister's alter ego (discussed further later). But even putting this to the side it was clear from the scheme of the Rules and the purpose of rule 45(2) specifically that it would be contrary to the intention underlying the relevant rules to apply the *Carltona* doctrine so as to allow the governor to exercise the Minister's power. Lord Reed said:

> [88] ... [I]t can in my opinion be inferred that rule 45(2) is intended to provide a safeguard for the prisoner: a safeguard which can only be meaningful if the function created by rule 45(2) is performed by an official from outside the prison. It makes sense that the governor should be able to act at his own hand initially, since decisions to remove a prisoner from association with other prisoners may need to be taken urgently. It also makes sense that the governor should be able, under rule 45(3), to arrange for the prisoner's resumption of association with other prisoners at any time, and, in particular, in response to any medical recommendation. Rule 45(2) however ensures that segregation does not continue for a prolonged period without the matter being considered not only by the governor but also by officials independent of the management of the prison. If, as counsel submitted, rule 45(2) was not intended to provide a safeguard, then the requirement to obtain the authority of the Secretary of State, before segregation can lawfully continue for more than 72 hours, would lack any rationale.
>
> [89] It follows that it is implicit in rule 45(2) that the decision of the Secretary of State cannot be taken on his behalf by the governor, or by some other officer of the prison in question. The *Carltona* principle cannot therefore apply to rule 45(2) so as to enable a governor or other prison officer to exercise the powers of the Secretary of State. It equally follows that the alternative argument advanced on behalf of the Secretary of State, that the expression 'the Secretary of State', in rule 45(2), implicitly includes the governor and other officers of the prison, must also be rejected ... [acceptance of this argument would] defeat the purpose of rule 45(2).
>
> [90] Any purported performance of the Secretary of State's function under rule 45(2) by a governor or other prison officer cannot therefore be treated as constituting performance by the Secretary of State.

Third, *what is the justification for the Carltona principle?* In the passage from Lord Greene's *Carltona* judgment quoted by Brightman J above, two justifications are advanced. On a *pragmatic* level, it is necessary to allow ministerial discretion to be exercised by officials, given the vast number of powers vested in Ministers. And, said Lord Greene, in *constitutional* terms it is acceptable for officials to exercise discretionary powers on Ministers' behalf because the former are answerable to the latter; in turn, Ministers are answerable to Parliament, through the doctrine of ministerial accountability, for the conduct of their departments. A chain of accountability therefore ensures that the exercise by officials of discretionary powers is subject to scrutiny. In *Bourgass* this was one of the principal reasons why the prison governor could not rely on the *Carltona* doctrine to exercise the Minister's power. Under the relevant Rules the governor held an independent statutory office and was personally conferred with a range of powers which the Minister could not direct or exercise himself, and which were clearly demarcated from the Minister's powers. As such the Minister could not be said to be constitutionally responsible or accountable for the governor's actions; the governor was responsible for his own actions, and those of his staff. Because there was no chain of accountability linking the governor and the Minister, it was impermissible for the governor to rely on the *Carltona* doctrine to purport to exercise the Minister's powers: there was no way the governor could be viewed as a mere servant or alter ego of the Minister, the relationship between the two bearing 'no resemblance to ... the relationship between the minister and his departmental officials' (at [72]).

It is important to observe that the expanding scope and scale of government activity since the Second World War means that the *practical* rationale for allowing officials to exercise ministerial powers is ever more pressing. In the recent case of *Castle*, Pitchford LJ observed that if the realities of government in 1943, when *Carltona* was decided, demanded recognition of the *Carltona* doctrine so as ensure the efficacy of public administration, then that rationale must be even stronger today given modern conditions 'in which administrati[ve] decisions and secondary legislation occur every second of the working day' (at [17]). On the other hand, these developments mean that the *constitutional* rationale for the *Carltona* doctrine has become far weaker over time, and concerns over accountability much stronger. On a general level, the efficacy of the doctrine of ministerial accountability is widely questioned (*eg* Scott [1996] *PL* 410). More specifically, the changing architecture of government means that the lines of accountability between Ministers and officials are becoming increasingly blurred, and there are increasing degrees of separation between Ministers and those officials who exercise powers in the Minister's name. As Freedland explains, these issues are particularly acute in relation to executive agencies (the role of which was explained at 1.5.5). (References to 'Next Steps' in the following two excerpts are to the name of the government programme under which agencies were first introduced.)

Freedland, 'The Rule against Delegation and the *Carltona* Doctrine in an Agency Context' [1996] *PL* 19

The setting up of these executive agencies has proceeded on the assumption that there has been no need to seek statutory authority to make their establishment lawful and valid ... [T]he basic constitutive act of separating off the agency within the parent department was not seen as creating or requiring the creation of a separate legal corporate entity, and was seen as lying within the inherent power of the Crown to organise the conduct of its business. Included within and inherent to that conception of the constitutional status of the new executive agencies was the view that there was no problem of unlawful or invalid delegation where a function assigned to the parent department was discharged by the agency. In particular, it seems to have been concluded that the *Carltona* principle extended to and protected the exercise by a civil servant acting within an executive agency of the department concerned, of a discretion conferred upon a Minister ...

The parent department retains, of course, a kind of responsibility for the decision-making which occurs at agency level. But the separation of the agency as a distinct centre of decision-making means that the departmental responsibility has been turned into a secondary and essentially supervisory one. The parent department has become in effect accountable for its supervision of the agency; moreover, that departmental accountability is, in a way which mirrors that of the agency, increasingly conceived of in financial terms—the primary role of the parent department tends to become that of accounting to the Cabinet and to Parliament for the efficiency and good financial management of the departmental operation as conducted through the subsidiary agencies ...

My argument about the non-delegation/*Carltona* doctrine [is] ... that if its history and current state are properly understood, it becomes clear that the application of the *Carltona* doctrine was heavily contingent upon a certain structure of civil service administration which assumed and depended upon a very active notion of ministerial responsibility to Parliament. The decline of that kind of constitutional practice has meant that the application of the non-delegation/*Carltona* doctrine now requires a very specific inquiry as to whether the decision-making structure within which a particular discretion is exercised is a sufficiently integrated and coherent one to sustain the conclusion that the discretion is being exercised in a meaningful sense by the person or body and within the decision-making framework which was intended and is appropriate.

These arguments notwithstanding it is now clear that the *Carltona* doctrine can be applied to the exercise of ministerial powers by executive agencies. In *R v. Secretary of State for Social Services, ex parte Sherwin* (1996) 32 BMLR 1, the question arose whether the Benefits Agency— which was an executive agency of the then Department for Social Security—could exercise a statutory power vested in the Secretary of State temporarily to suspend the payment of welfare benefits. The Court paid close attention to the 'framework document' that established the Agency and set out its relationship with the Department. In particular, the Court noted that the framework document specified that the Agency was to act in accordance with directions and policy guidance issued by the Secretary of State and that 'Ministers remain accountable to Parliament for the full range of their responsibilities'. Against that background, Latham J concluded that the Agency official who had exercised the ministerial power in question had lawfully acted 'as a civil servant within the Department of Social Security on the authority of the Secretary of State, in circumstances where the Secretary of State was answerable to Parliament'.

Sherwin has subsequently been relied upon, in *Castle [2014] EWHC 587, [2014] 1 WLR 4279*, to hold that officials in the Highways Agency may lawfully exercise the functions of the Secretary of State for Transport, specifically the Secretary of State's power to issue orders temporarily imposing speed restrictions on vehicles using particular roads. The touchstone for whether the *Carltona* doctrine applied was whether the Minister was accountable to Parliament for the Agency's responsibilities. As in *Sherwin* this led the judges in *Castle* to consider the relevant framework document for the Highways Agency. This document states that the duties of the Agency are to deliver departmental policy relating to certain road and traffic matters, that the Minister is accountable to Parliament for the Agency's areas of responsibility, and that the Agency Chief Executive is responsible to the Minister. Pitchford LJ needed no further convincing than these formal statements to reach the conclusion that 'the Highways Agency is the alter ego of the Department for Transport in the areas for which the Secretary of State accepts responsibility in Parliament, just as he does for the actions of civil servants housed under his departmental roof' (at [24]). It is worth noting that Pitchford LJ's judgment was very heavily influenced by the practical concern that if Ministerial powers could not be exercised by agencies, government would never get its business done.

In contrast, the other judge on the Court, Cranston J, albeit concurring in the result, was less focused on ensuring government could get its business done and somewhat more receptive to concerns raised by counsel over possible gaps in accountability as between Parliament, the Minister and agency officials. He readily acknowledged that issues of democratic accountability were squarely raised by the case, looking beyond the formal statements in the framework document to the reality of the relationships between the various institutions: '[I]t is unlikely the Secretary of State himself was aware of the details of this and many other similar orders made under his name' (at [43]). Cranston J also noted that there was no requirement to lay such orders before Parliament as is the case with regulations, which would have promoted direct democratic accountability. He did, however, observe the existence of certain controls which facilitated democratic accountability, including that the order had to be published in local newspapers; notified to various bodies; and certified, registered and published online by the Stationery Office, while questions could be raised over the order in Parliament in the ordinary way and judicial review of the order sought. He also noted the framework document, albeit he did not give it the same prominence in his own analysis as Pitchford LJ. While seemingly considering that these controls met accountability concerns raised by extending the *Carltona* doctrine to agency decision-making in this context, there were signs that Cranston J was not completely satisfied with his own conclusion: 'It may be that accountability in the making of this type of order could be improved. That however is a matter for Parliament' (at [44]).

It is apparent from *Sherwin* and *Castle* that whether agency officials can exercise ministerial powers turns upon an inquiry into the relationship between the department and the agency. That view was affirmed by the Supreme Court in *Bourgass*, in which counsel invited the Court to assume that the relationship between the Secretary of State for Justice and the governor of a prison was similar to that between the agency officials and Ministers in *Sherwin* and *Castle*, such that the *Carltona* doctrine ought to apply. However, Lord Reed, for the Court, empha-sized that such a relationship 'cannot ... be assumed' (at [52]). *Sherwin* and *Castle* could not be followed on the facts because there was no *evidence* before the Court to demonstrate that the Minister was accountable for the prison governor's activities (as we saw earlier, that the Minister was not responsible for the governor's activities was put beyond all doubt by the statutory scheme). However, perhaps regrettably, Lord Reed did not offer any guidance as to the nature and quality of evidence that would be required to establish such a link.

QUESTIONS

- How, if at all, are the concerns expressed by Freedland (earlier) met by the decisions in *Sherwin*, *Castle*, and *Bourgass*?
- Which of Pitchford LJ and Cranston J's approaches in *Castle* do you prefer?

May the *Carltona* principle operate to legitimize the devolution of power *within decision-making structures other than those of central government*? It is certainly the case that the tak-ing of decisions other than by the person named in the statute is sometimes lawful outwith the central government context. For instance, in *DPP v. Haw* [2007] EWHC 1931 (Admin), [2008] 1 WLR 379, it was held lawful for the Metropolitan Police Commissioner to allow another officer to exercise his power to attach conditions to a protest in the vicinity of Parliament. Similarly, in *Hamill* [2014] EWHC 2799 (Admin), [2015] 1 WLR 1798, the Court held that a statutory power conferred upon a Chief Constable of Police to determine whether a convicted sex offender should no longer be subject to certain notification obligations could be exercised by a detective superintendent on behalf of the relevant Chief Constable. But do these cases constitute applications of the *Carltona* doctrine (thus confirming its applicability beyond central government departments) or are they simply an application of the principle that delegation is lawful if the presumption against it is displaced by the statutory context? The following remarks of Lord Phillips MR in *Haw* (at [33]) suggest that the latter view is the correct one, but that the distinction is practically unimportant:

> Where powers are conferred on a minister by statute, the *Carltona* principle will apply to those powers unless the statute, expressly or by implication, provides to the contrary. Where a statutory power is conferred on an officer who is himself the creature of statute, whether that officer has the power to delegate must depend upon the interpretation of the relevant statute or statutes. Where the responsibilities of the office created by statute are such that delegation is inevitable, there will be an implied power to delegate. In such circumstances there will be a presumption, where additional statutory powers and duties are conferred, that there is a power to delegate unless the statute conferring them, expressly or by implication, provides to the contrary. Such a situation is, in practice, indistinguishable from one in which the *Carltona* principle applies.

This analysis was confirmed and applied in *Hamill*; the Court considering that it was inevitable that the relevant duty would be exercised by others 'given the weight of duties and powers that fall on chief constables in practice. There is nothing [in the Sexual Offences Act 2003] either expressly or by implication, that indicates that the duty ... cannot be delegated' (at [64]).

On the approach in *Haw*, the main difference between ministerial and non-ministerial powers is that whereas, in relation to the former, there is an automatic presumption that they can be exercised by persons in the department other than the Minister, such a pre-sumption will arise in relation to the latter only if it is unreasonable to expect the named power-holder personally to be involved in all exercises of the power concerned. But as Lord Phillips went on to say, that distinction is 'academic'. It seems to follow from this that whether we say the *Carltona* doctrine applies to non-ministerial powers or simply that the legislation conferring such powers may be interpreted as permitting delegation is a largely semantic matter. That is generally correct, but it should be recalled that the constitutional logic underpinning *Carltona* is that Ministers are (or at least are supposed to be) legally and politically responsible for those who are allowed to exercise power on their behalf. In *R (Chief Constable of West Midlands Police)* v. *Birmingham Justices* [2002] EWHC 1087 (Admin), Sedley LJ (at [9]) emphasized this point, indicating that his willingness to hold a Chief Constable's power to apply for an antisocial behaviour order to be delegable depended, *inter alia*, on the fact that the Chief Constable would remain ultimately responsible for its exercise. Key to ensuring that the Chief Constable remains responsible not only in theory but also in reality for official exercises of his powers is the principle articulated and emphasized in *Hamill*, that the degree to which powers may be delegated depends on the nature of the relevant power; the Court in *Hamill* considering that it was right that the power at issue should be exercised by an officer of the rank of superintendent or above. Among other things, this principle helps to ensure that those exercising very important powers in the name of the Chief Constable are not far removed from him in the police force's chain of accountability. It is to be hoped that the accountability principle underlying *Carltona* will be kept firmly in mind as courts in future cases consider whether non-ministerial powers should be delegable and to whom, whether or not the language of *Carltona* is employed.

Lastly, we note that statute may authorize a Minister to delegate his or her powers far beyond the bounds of central government or even agencies. For example, s 16(1) of the Localism Act 2011 provides that a Minister of the Crown may 'to such extent and subject to such conditions as that Minister thinks fit, delegate to a permitted authority any of the Minister's eligible functions'. Permitted authorities include county councils in England and district councils (s 20). Eligible functions include any functions which the Minister considers 'can appropriately be exercised by the permitted authority', while the only functions expressly designated as ineligible are those that 'consist of a power to make regulations or other instruments of a legislative character or a power to fix fees or charges' (s 16(2)). The power of delegation is thus a very wide one, and its exact boundaries are for the most part to be determined according to the Minister's view of what functions can appropriately be exercised by the relevant authority (as discussed at 5.2.1 one would expect a court to construe such a power of delegation narrowly, albeit set against this is the fact that it was clearly Parliament's intent to confer a wide power of delegation and allow the Minister flexibility in determining which functions are most appropriately delegated). The statute provides for some conditions for the delegation of functions, including that the permitted authority must agree to the delegation or any variation of it—albeit the Minister can revoke the delegation at any time without needing the authority's agreement—and that '[b]efore delegating a function ... the Minister of the Crown must consult such persons as the Minister considers appropriate' (s 16(3)–(5)).

QUESTIONS

- What concerns are raised by such a wide power of delegation?
- Do you think the conditions of delegation provided for in the legislation meet these concerns?

5.3 Discretion and policy

5.3.1 Distinguishing policies and rules

The *raison d'être* of discretionary power is that it permits decision-makers to respond appropriately to the demands of particular situations. However, for reasons which we explore in detail in what follows, it is often desirable or even necessary for decision-makers to exercise their discretion in line with a policy or a set of criteria. A tension therefore arises: to what extent may administrators legitimately structure their decision-making in this way, given that the very existence of discretionary power seems to demand an individualized, case-by-case mode of decision-making? As Galligan [1976] *PL* 332 at 332 explains, underlying this question is a deeper one about the nature of discretion itself:

> There is an idea buried deep in the hearts of various constitutional theorists and judges that 'to discipline administrative discretion by rule and rote is somehow to denature it' [Smith (1945) 23 *Public Administration* 23 at 30]. According to this idea, there is something about the nature of discretionary power which requires each decision to be made according to the circumstances of the particular situation, free from the constraints of preconceived policies as to the ends and goals to be achieved by such power. The circumstances of the situation will indicate the proper decision and policy choices must remain in the background. An alternative view is to recognise that discretion entails a power in the decision-maker to make policy choices, not just to deal with the individual case, but to develop a coherent and consistent set of guidelines which seek to achieve ends and goals within the scope of powers and which determine particular decisions.

We examine, later, the issues which underpin these distinct views about the relationship between discretion and policy. We begin, however, with the classic approach to this problem set out by Bankes LJ in *R* v. *Port of London Authority, ex parte Kynoch Ltd* [1919] 1 KB 176 at 184:

> There are on the one hand cases where a tribunal in the honest exercise of its discretion has adopted a policy, and, without refusing to hear an applicant, intimates to him what its policy is, and that after hearing him it will in accordance with its policy decide against him, unless there is something exceptional in his case. I think counsel for the applicants would admit that, if the policy has been adopted for reasons which the tribunal may legitimately entertain, no objection could be taken to such a course. On the other hand there are cases where a tribunal has passed a rule, or come to a determination, not to hear any application of a particular character by whomsoever made. There is a wide distinction to be drawn between these two classes.

This analysis is useful to the extent that it highlights the basic concerns which are at stake in this context. In particular, it emphasizes that the adoption of a policy, and thus of a more structured approach to decision-making, must ultimately be reconciled with the discretionary nature of the power: hence the distinction between a policy which is flexible enough to take account of the unusual or the exceptional, and a rule which is applied so rigidly as to eviscerate any genuine discretion. However, to the extent that it implies the existence of two wholly distinct categories of case, Bankes LJ's analysis is too simplistic. It is self-evident that, between the two extremes of unstructured discretion and immovable rules, there will exist a spectrum of policies of differing degrees of rigidity. It is, as we explain later, the courts' task to determine—taking account of such contextual factors as the nature of the decision-making function in question—whether a given policy, lying at a particular point on the continuum, is sufficiently flexible to be legitimate.

5.3.2 The legality of policy-oriented decision-making

In light of the conflicting views of discretion already considered, it is unsurprising that the case law in this area reveals diverging opinions on the extent to which it is legitimate for administrators to overlay their discretionary powers with policy. However, over time, and especially more recently, judges have evinced increasingly warm attitudes towards decision-making guided by formal statements of policy.

We find in some earlier decisions a restrictive view that adoption of policies by government to guide exercise of discretion was permissible but only on the basis that policy was to be one of many factors to be weighed in the decision-making process. For example, in *Stringer* v. *Minister of Housing and Local Government* [1970] 1 WLR 1281, the Court held that the Minister's adoption of a policy of discouraging development near a radio telescope, so as to avoid interference with the telescope's operation, and its invocation to reject an application to build houses near the telescope, was lawful. But the reason the adoption of such a policy survived legal challenge was that it was not a policy 'which [was] intended to be pursued to the disregard of other relevant considerations' (at 1297). The acceptability of the policy turned upon the fact that, as Cooke J put it (at 1298), it did not preclude the Minister from 'fairly judging all the issues which are relevant to each individual case as it comes up for decision'.

This approach is rather restrictive insofar as it significantly cuts down the role governmental policy may play in public decision-making; if policy guidance is only ever one factor to be weighed it will not provide much guidance at all as to how government will exercise discretions from one case to the next. The implications of this approach—also evident in other decisions: *eg Merchandise Transport Ltd* v. *British Transport Commission* [1962] 2 QB 173 and *Sagnata Investments Ltd* v. *Norwich Corporation* [1971] 2 QB 614—were explained in the following terms by Galligan, *op cit* at 349:

> The principle [adopted in cases such as *Stringer*] is that a predetermined policy is only one factor among all those that may be relevant. It was thought that by regarding a predetermined policy as merely one factor, consideration of the merits in each exercise of discretion was kept to a maximum. The corollary of this principle is that where a policy functions in such a way that the only question is 'should this policy apply to this situation,' a sufficient consideration of other relevant factors is excluded. Such a policy was thought to function invalidly as a rule. Nowhere was this corollary expressed more forcefully than by Lord Chief Justice Hewart in *R* v. *Rotherham Licensing Justices, ex parte Chapman* [[1939] 2 All ER 710]. Licensing justices had adopted a general rule not to grant more than two occasional liquor licences to the same applicant during a certain time, but they heard and considered all applications to determine whether an exception to the rule should be made, and from time to time exceptions were made. However the Court of Appeal considered that a general rule of this kind was an invalid fetter on the justices' discretion and an abdication of their duty to hear each case on its merits.

To restrict policies in this way is to go far beyond the principle in *Kynoch*. The implications of this more restrictive approach are that not only must an authority (a) direct itself to whether in the light of the particular situation a predetermined policy ought to be altered, but also (b) must refrain from regarding a policy as anything more than one factor amongst others to be taken into account. In other words a policy may not become a norm which, subject only to (a), determines the outcome of particular decisions.

QUESTIONS

- Is such a restrictive view of the role of policy justifiable?
- What are the advantages and disadvantages of such an approach?

As case law developed from the 1970s onwards, a more indulgent attitude towards policy-oriented decision-making emerged, sparked by the next decision.

British Oxygen Co Ltd v. *Minister of Technology* [1971] AC 610
House of Lords

Section 1(1) of the Industrial Development Act 1966 provided that the Board of Trade 'may make to any person carrying on a business in Great Britain a grant towards approved capital expenditure incurred by that person in providing new machinery or plant'. The Board adopted a policy of denying grants for any item of plant costing less than £25 and, in pursuance of that policy, rejected an application for a grant in respect of gas cylinders costing just under £20 each of which the claimant had, in the three years following the entry into force of the Act, purchased £4m worth. In proceedings for a declaration the court was required, *inter alia*, to determine whether the Board had properly exercised its discretion.

Lord Reid

... There are two general grounds on which the exercise of an unqualified discretion can be attacked. It must not be exercised in bad faith, and it must not be so unreasonably exercised as to show that there cannot have been any real or genuine exercise of the discretion. But, apart from that, if the Minister thinks that policy or good administration requires the operation of some limiting rule, I find nothing to stop him.

It was argued on the authority of *Rex* v. *Port of London Authority, Ex parte Kynoch Ltd.* [1919] 1 K.B. 176 that the Minister is not entitled to make a rule for himself as to how he will in future exercise his discretion. In that case Kynoch owned land adjoining the Thames and wished to construct a deep water wharf. For this they had to get the permission of the authority. Permission was refused on the ground that Parliament had charged the authority with the duty of providing such facilities. It appeared that before reaching their decision the authority had fully considered the case on its merits and in relation to the public interest. So their decision was upheld.

[After quoting the extract from Bankes LJ's judgment which is set out at 5.3.1, Lord Reid continued:] I see nothing wrong with that. But the circumstances in which discretions are exercised vary enormously and that passage cannot be applied literally in every case. The general rule is that anyone who has to exercise a statutory discretion must not 'shut his ears to an application' (to adapt from Bankes L.J. [see [1919] 1 KB 176 at 183]). I do not think there is any great difference between a policy and a rule. There may be cases where an officer or authority ought to listen to a substantial argument reasonably presented urging a change of policy. What the authority must not do is to refuse to listen at all. But a Ministry or large authority may have had to deal already with a multitude of similar applications and then they will almost certainly have evolved a policy so precise that it could well be called a rule. There can be no objection to that, provided the authority is always willing to listen to anyone with something new to say—of course I do not mean to say that there need be an oral hearing. In the present case the respondent's officers have carefully considered all that the appellants have had to say and I have no doubt that they will continue to do so ...

Viscount Dilhorne

... [T]he distinction between a policy decision and a rule may not be easy to draw. In this case it was not challenged that it was within the power of the Board to adopt a policy not to make a grant in respect of such an item. That policy might equally well be described as a rule. It was both reasonable and right that the Board should make known to those interested the policy it was going to follow. By doing so fruitless applications involving expense and expenditure of time might be avoided. The Board says that it has not refused to consider any application. It considered the appellants'. In these circumstances it is not necessary to decide in this case whether, if it had refused to consider an application on the ground that it related to an item costing less than £25, it would have acted wrongly.

I must confess that I feel some doubt whether the words used by Bankes L.J. in the passage cited above [see 5.3.1] are really applicable to a case of this kind. It seems somewhat pointless and a waste of time that the Board should have to consider applications which are bound as a result of its policy decision to fail. Representations could of course be made that the policy should be changed.

Lords Morris, Wilberforce, and Diplock agreed with Lord Reid.

The approach in *British Oxygen*, which has been consistently followed in subsequent case law, ascribes a generous role to policy, allowing it to become the norm upon which the decision-making process is founded, provided of course that the administrator is willing to make exceptions for unusual cases. The central principle is well summarized by Lord Kerr in *R (Gujra)* v. *CPS* [2012] UKSC 52, [2013] 1 AC 484 at [76]:

A person or agency who is exercising discretion as to how to use a statutory power may devise a policy to guide him in its use. He may formulate a policy or make a limiting rule as to the future exercise of his discretion, if he thinks that good administration requires it, provided that he listens to any applicant who has something new to say.

In seeking to determine whether this residual flexibility is present, and thus capable of legitimizing the decision-maker's policy-based approach, the courts are and ought to be more interested in substance than in form. Consequently, even if the decision-maker claims to be willing to depart from the policy in exceptional circumstances, the court may require evidence that this actually occurs in practice and, in the absence of such evidence, may draw the inference that the policy is operated over-rigidly (see, eg *R* v. *Warwickshire County Council, ex parte Collymore* [1995] ELR 217).

Although the willingness of the decision-maker to show flexibility in the face of the unusual is often the key factor *vis-à-vis* the legality of the policy, this criterion is not always determinative of the issue. For instance, in *Attorney-General ex rel Tilley* v. *Wandsworth London Borough Council* [1981] 1 WLR 854, a local authority resolved that families with young children who were intentionally homeless would not be assisted with alternative housing under the Children and Young Persons Act 1963. The Court of Appeal concluded that this policy admitted of no exceptions and was therefore over-rigid. Templeman LJ, however, went further (at 858); he was not 'persuaded that even a policy resolution hedged around with exceptions would be entirely free from attack. Dealing with children, the discretion and powers of any authority must depend entirely on the different circumstances of each child before them for consideration.' This suggests that there may be rare situations—delineated by factors such as the subject-matter of the discretion and the legislative framework within which the discretion subsists—where the need for detailed evaluation of the merits severely reduces the role which policy may legitimately play. It is likely, however, that these situations will be increasingly rare given the modern judicial disposition in favour of government adopting formal statements of policy, as discussed in the next section.

There may be situations where a decision-maker is required not only to keep their mind open to departing from policy, but is under a *legal duty* to depart from policy. In particular, it may be that following policy in a particular case would lead to a breach of the Human Rights Act 1998 (HRA). In such circumstances the decision-maker will be under a duty to depart from policy guidance in order to fulfil their legal duty to act compatibly with the rights under the Act: *R (BBC)* v. *Secretary of State for Justice* [2012] EWHC 13 (Admin), [2013] 1 WLR 964 at [81]–[82]. More generally, the law under the HRA reinforces the no-fettering principle where human rights are engaged. This is because human rights claims are individualized in nature and require, for example, that a proportionate balance be struck between the individual's rights and countervailing public interests *on the facts of that individual's case.* As such, blanket policies will, if decision-making pursuant to the policy touches upon human rights, almost always be susceptible to challenge on the basis of incompatibility with Convention rights: *eg S and Marper* v. *United Kingdom* (2008) 48 EHRR 1169; *R (GC)* v. *Commissioner of Police for the Metropolis* [2011] UKSC 21, [2011] 1 WLR 1230.

It seems that there may be situations, limited to certain statutory contexts, in which it is lawful to operate a policy which does not yield even in the face of exceptional circumstances (barring the presence of a human rights dimension). For instance, in *R (Nicholds)* v. *Security Industry Authority* [2006] EWHC 1792 (Admin), [2007] 1 WLR 2067, the defendant statutory body was empowered to grant licences to door supervisors. Pursuant to the requirement under the Private Security Industry Act 2001, s 7, to publish the criteria it would apply in making licensing decisions, the defendant adopted the position that people convicted of certain offences would be automatically disbarred from holding licences for two or five years (depending on the nature of the offence) from the end of their sentence. The claimants argued that any rule of automatic disbarment represented an unlawful fetter on the Authority's discretion. The Court rejected the argument (at [61], original emphasis):

> In most instances where a discretionary power is conferred it would be wrong for the decision-maker to frame a rule in absolute terms because to do so would defeat the statutory purpose. However, it seems to me that there are certain exceptional statutory contexts where a policy may lawfully exclude exceptions to the rule *because to allow exceptions would substantially undermine an important legislative aim which underpins the grant of discretionary power to the authority.*

Two factors led the Court to the conclusion that this was such a case. First, it was held that Parliament had 'deliberately ... conferred a rule-making power on the authority' by (as s 7(1) of the 2001 Act put it) requiring it to formulate and publish 'the criteria which it proposes to apply' when deciding whether to grant a licence. Taken alone, this would not be a convincing reason for concluding that the Authority should be allowed to make rules admitting of no exceptions: the Act refers only to *criteria* which the Authority *proposes* to apply, not to *rules* that it *must*, having announced them, enforce. But the judge identified a second reason (at [45]): that Parliament's purpose in passing the Act was to see 'that criminality would be driven out of door supervision'. This justified automatically barring people convicted of serious offences: any other approach would 'make a mockery of one of the crucial aims of the 2001 Act'. The judge was, however, careful to say that while he rejected the claimant's assertion that *any* automatic disbarment necessarily constituted an unlawful fetter, he might have been amenable to a more nuanced argument. He noted that some offences to which the Authority applied the automatic disbarment rule (*eg* owning a handgun without a licence—an offence that can be committed by simply forgetting to renew an existing licence) might not necessarily render someone unfit to work as a door supervisor: it might therefore be argued that the Authority should exercise discretion in relation to such an offence and that its inclusion within the automatic disbarment category was unlawful.

We find a similar approach in the immigration context in *R (Sayaniya)* v. *Upper Tribunal* [2016] EWCA Civ 85, [2016] 4 WLR 58. Under the Immigration Act 1971 the Minister may make rules to regulate the exercise of his discretion to grant or deny someone leave to enter or remain in the United Kingdom. Albeit these Immigration Rules are referred to as 'rules' they are not 'rules' in the traditional sense of having the status of statutory instruments such as regulations or Orders in Council. The question before the Court in *Sayaniya* was whether it was lawful for the Minister to make mandatory rules, in this case a rule mandating that a person be denied leave to remain where material facts had not been disclosed in their application. Beatson LJ, with whom the other judges agreed, approved of and followed the approach in *Nicholds*. That is, whether the no-fettering principle applies, and how it applies, 'has to reflect the statutory context' (at [22]). In this case a core aspect of the statutory context was the fact that while the Act explicitly contemplated the making of rules—which distinguished it from the relevant legislation considered in other cases in which the no-fettering principle had been held to apply including *British Oxygen* and *Tilley*—these were nonetheless not statutory instruments. But while they were not statutory instruments, (at [35])

> the Rules are different from and more than policy and 'have acquired a status akin to that of law' [quoting *Pankina* v. *Secretary of State for the Home Department* [2010] EWCA Civ 719, [2010] 3 WLR 526 at [15]–[17]] for particular purposes. That is not to say that the Secretary of State's power to formulate immigration rules is not a power to formulate policy. Because her exercise of the power is essentially an executive, not a legislative act, it is subject to the public law constraints appropriate to such acts. But that does mean that the non-fettering rule does not apply to such rules in the same way as it does to policies made in very different statutory contexts.

The nature of the rules as norms with a higher status than mere policy, and which are closer in nature to legal instruments such as regulations, meant that the Court would not impugn a rule simply on the basis it was mandatory, as it would a mere policy. It is, however, important to note that, similarly to the Court in *Nicholds*, Beatson LJ recalled that the Minister had a residual discretion to make a decision outside of the rules.

Beatson LJ had begun his analysis with the classic contrast between rules on the one hand, which are characteristically prescriptive and mandatory, and on the other, discretion, which is open-textured. As we noted earlier (5.3.1), there is in truth a spectrum between these polarities, and whether it is permissible to adopt a strict fetter on discretion, *ie* a prescriptive norm towards the 'rules' end of the spectrum, will depend on the decision-making context, including most importantly the statutory context. What Beatson LJ's judgment suggests is that in statutory contexts, such as those in play in *Sayaniya* and in *Nicholds*, where there is provision for the making of norms—which, while not in the nature of statutory instruments, are more than mere administrative policy—the administration may lawfully adopt mandatory policy prescriptions akin to rules (allied with a narrow residual discretion to deviate from those prescriptions). In stark contrast are cases such as *Tilley*, where Templeman LJ queried whether there was any scope at all for adoption of policies to guide decision-making; in other words, the relevant discretion ought to be relatively free of any policy constraints, whether mandatory or not. However, in most statutory contexts adoption of policies to guide decision-making is likely to be lawful so long as there is provision for deviation from that policy in a case that warrants deviation.

Lastly, we should note that there are some types of cases where the no-fettering principle has no applicability whatsoever. The paradigm case is that of exercise of common law powers (on which see further 4.3–4.4). In *R (Sandiford)* v. *Secretary of State for Foreign and Commonwealth Affairs* [2014] UKSC 44, [2014] 1 WLR 2697, Lord Sumption helpfully explained why this is so (at [82]–[83]):

> Since the decision in *Council of Civil Service Unions v Minister for the Civil Service* [1985] AC 374, the principles of public law applicable to the exercise of common law and statutory powers have in many respects been assimilated. But there remain inevitable differences arising from the distinct origins of these powers. One of them relates to the rule which precludes a decision-maker from fettering his own discretion. In *Elias v Secretary of State for Defence* [2006] 1 WLR 3213, the Court of Appeal held that the rule had no application to the exercise of common law powers. The decision concerned the rules of a scheme for compensating certain categories of British subject who had been interned by the Japanese during the Second World War. The scheme had no statutory basis. It was created under the common law powers of the Crown. Mummery LJ, at para 191 said:
>
> > 'The analogy with statutory discretion … is a false one. It is lawful to formulate a policy for the exercise of a discretionary power conferred by statute, but the person who falls within the statute cannot be completely debarred, as he continues to have a statutory right to be considered by the person entrusted with the discretion. No such consideration arises in the case of an ordinary common law power, as it is within the power of the decision-maker to decide on the extent to which the power is to be exercised in, for example, setting up a scheme. He can decide on broad and clear criteria and either that there are no exceptions to the criteria in the scheme or, if there are exceptions in the scheme, what they should be. If there are no exceptions the decision-maker is under no duty to make payments outside the parameters of the scheme.'
>
> The Court of Appeal in the present case were guided by this decision, which was plainly correct. A common law power is a mere power. It does not confer a discretion in the same sense that a statutory power confers a discretion. A statutory discretionary power carries with it a duty to exercise the discretion one way or the other and in doing so to take account of all relevant matters having regard to its scope. Ministers have common law powers to do many things, and if they choose to exercise such a power they must do so in accordance with ordinary public law principles, ie fairly, rationally and on a correct appreciation of the law. But there is no duty to exercise the power at all. There is no identifiable class of potential beneficiaries of the common law powers of the Crown in general, other than the public at large. There are no legal criteria analogous to those to be derived from an empowering Act, by which the decision whether to exercise a common law power or not can be assessed. It is up to ministers to decide whether to exercise them, and if so to what extent. It follows that the mere existence of a common law power to do something cannot give rise to any right to be considered, on the part of someone who might hypothetically benefit by it.

5.3.3 From the no-fettering rule to the law of policy: a sea change in the judicial approach to policy

Thus it is now clear that it is *in general* perfectly lawful for government to adopt policy provided that it allows for the exceptional case. However, in recent years courts have started to move beyond a merely *permissive* approach, allowing government to adopt policy if it so wishes, and developed a set of *prescriptive* legal rules to regulate the place of policy in public decision-making. In certain contexts at least the higher courts have prescribed a legal requirement that government *must* adopt policies to guide the exercise of public powers (these policies must generally allow for exceptional cases consonant with the case law discussed in the previous section), imposed various legal requirements that policies must fulfil, and erected a legal presumption that decision-makers must in general follow their policy unless they can show that they have good reasons for deviating from it. All of these developments have in general been motivated by rule-of-law concerns, such as promoting non-arbitrariness, certainty, consistency, and predictability in exercise of public power. In the light of these developments the type of traditional view espoused in cases such as *Stringer* has been stood on its head. It would not be an exaggeration to say that instead of speaking of a 'no-fettering rule' we should now speak of 'fettering rules' or the 'law of policy' more broadly.

In the last few years the courts, led by the Supreme Court, have increasingly required discretions to be exercised according to an established policy; in other words, the courts have *mandated* the adoption of policy as a matter of law. This requirement to have a policy has not yet been transformed into a general rule. Rather, the courts have progressed on a context-by-context basis. The common thread appears to be that policy will be lawfully required where powers touch on important interests as will be the case with surveillance or detention powers, for example. Thus, in *R (Lumba)* v. *Secretary of State for the Home Department* [2011] UKSC 12, [2012] 1 AC 245, Lord Dyson said (at [34]):

> The rule of law calls for a transparent statement by the executive of the circumstances in which the broad statutory criteria will be exercised. Just as arrest and surveillance powers need to be transparently identified through codes of practice and immigration powers need to be transparently identified through the immigration rules, so too the immigration detention powers need to be transparently identified through formulated policy statements.

The underlying concern in requiring a policy to be adopted is that otherwise there is a 'clear risk of arbitrariness' where broad discretions are conferred (at [33]); where important interests are at stake—such as privacy, liberty, or one's freedom to remain in the UK—discretions need to be circumscribed and the basis for their exercise clearly stated in policy, so as to protect against discretion being used to interfere with basic liberties on a whim. It is not surprising that it is in the context of important interests that the common law has developed these requirements. The requirements are inspired by the European Convention on Human Rights (and the jurisprudence generated by it), which of course protects the most basic of human interests. In *Lumba* itself Lord Dyson's statement quoted above followed a discussion of Convention requirements. In human rights law, for any interference with a human right to be capable of lawful justification, the interference must be 'in accordance with law' (see, *eg* Articles 8(2) and 10(2)). One of the core requirements of this legality principle is that 'the law must indicate with sufficient clarity the scope of any such discretion conferred on the competent authorities and the manner of its exercise' (*Gillan* v. *United Kingdom* (2010) 50 EHRR 45 at [77], quoted in *Lumba* at [32]). At common law also it has now been recognized that policy must be sufficiently clear and certain, and not misleading or inaccurate, so as to guard against arbitrariness and also because individuals and decision-makers rely on and form expectations on the basis of policy: *R (Gurung)* v. *Secretary of State for the Home Department* [2013] EWCA Civ 8, [2013] 1 WLR 2546 at [15]–[25]. Thus, the law under the HRA may itself require adoption of policies where human rights are engaged, but importantly the common law has also increasingly recognized such a requirement where basic interests are in play.

However, the common law requirement on administrators to have a policy has spread beyond cases with a human rights element, or which are closely analogous to human rights cases. *Nzolameso* v. *City of Westminster* [2015] UKSC 22, [2015] WLR (D) 165 concerned the lawfulness of local authorities accommodating homeless people a long way from the authority's own area, where the homeless person had previously been living. Local authorities have a statutory duty pursuant to the Housing Act 1996 and guidance under it to accommodate within their area so far as this is 'reasonably practicable', and if they cannot accommodate 'in borough' they must in general try to place the household as close as possible to where the person was previously living, albeit there are exceptions. One of the key determinants of whether it would be 'reasonably practicable' to house 'in borough' would of course be the number of houses available to the authority locally. In this case the defendant had made what the Supreme Court considered to be a woefully legally defective decision to house the claimant out of borough. Lady Hale, with whom the other members of the Court all agreed, set down guidance for local authorities to follow in their future decision-making in this context:

> [39] Ideally, each local authority should have, and keep up to date, a policy for procuring sufficient units of temporary accommodation to meet the anticipated demand during the coming year. That policy should, of course, reflect the authority's statutory obligations under both the 1996 Act and the Children Act 2004. It should be approved by the democratically accountable members of the council and, ideally, it should be made publicly available. Secondly, each local authority should have, and keep up to date, a policy for allocating those units to individual homeless households. Where there was an anticipated shortfall of 'in borough' units, that policy would explain the factors which would be taken into account in offering households those units, the factors which would be taken into account in offering units close to home, and if there was a shortage of such units, the factors which would make it suitable to accommodate a household further away. That policy too should be made publicly available.
>
> [40] This approach would have many advantages. It would enable homeless people, and the local agencies which advise them, to understand what to expect and what factors will be relevant to the decision. It would enable temporary letting teams to know how they should go about their business. It would enable reviewing officers to review the decisions made in individual cases by reference to those published policies and how they were applied in the particular case. It would enable reviewing officers to explain whether or not the individual decision met the authorities' obligations. It would enable applicants to challenge, not only the lawfulness of the individual decision, but also the lawfulness of the policies themselves.
>
> [41] Indeed, it would also enable a general challenge to those policies to be brought by way of judicial review. In some ways this might be preferable to a challenge by way of an individual appeal to a county court. But it may not always be practicable to mount a judicial review of an authority's policy, and an individual must be able to rely upon any point of law arising from the decision under appeal, including the legality of the policy which has been applied in her case.

As is clear from Lady Hale's guidance, in addition to a requirement in some contexts to adopt policies, the courts may also impose requirements which the policy must fulfil. We have already seen that one such requirement may be that the policy must be clear and accurate. Another significant requirement is that the policy be published. Such a requirement was enunciated in *Lumba* specifically in respect of policies governing immigration detention powers, which impact on the basic interest in liberty. But the requirement has since been extended to other contexts beyond those concerned with basic human rights, but which nonetheless concern some fairly important aspects of human well-being. For example, such a requirement was propounded in *Nzolameso*, in the context of housing the vulnerable, and also *R (Reilly)* v. *Secretary of State for Work and Pensions* [2013] UKSC 68, [2014] AC 453, where the Supreme Court held that the principle applied to 'administration of a scheme by which a person may be required to engage in unpaid work on pain of discontinuance of benefits' (at [65]); as the Court observed, the withdrawal of benefits 'may self-evidently cause significant misery and suffering' (at [64]). Albeit reliance on this principle has so far generally been limited to cases concerning basic aspects of well-being, the rationales given for it suggest it is likely to be of more general application. These rationales include that an individual liable to be affected by a policy should know the criteria to be applied so that he can make meaningful representations to the decision-maker before the decision is made. More generally, the courts have drawn an analogy with the constitutional imperative that statutes be made public (*eg Lumba* at [35], [37]–[38]). The more that policy is imbued with legal status and force the more it shall come to resemble generally applicable legal rules, such as those in statute or statutory instruments (*eg Lumba* at [36]). And it is a core aspect of the rule of law that such legal rules must be publicly available and known in advance so that individuals are able to plan their lives in accordance with them.

This brings us to perhaps the most important development over recent years, and which has had the effect of affording policy significant legal status and force. That is the emergence of a general legal principle that decision-makers must follow existing policy unless there are good reasons for departing from that policy. For many years there was confusion over the nature of this principle. It was often formulated as an aspect of the law of legitimate expectations: an individual had a legitimate expectation that policy should be followed (see 6.1.3). As previous editions of this book pointed out, this was problematic because it was difficult to see how legitimate expectations could have any application where the individual had no knowledge of the relevant policy (as would often be the case): how could they form expectations on the basis of a policy they never knew about? Yet we would still expect decision-makers to act consistently, applying their stated policies to cases before them regardless of the happenstance of whether the individual knew of the relevant policy or not. This confusion has now been definitively resolved by the Supreme Court. In *Mandalia* v. *Secretary of State for the Home Department* [2015] UKSC 59, [2015] 1 WLR 4546, Lord Wilson, with whom the other judges agreed, said (at [29]–[31]):

> In 2001, in *R (Saadi) v Secretary of State for the Home Department* [2001] EWCA Civ 1512, [2002] 1 WLR 356, Lord Phillips of Worth Matravers MR, giving the judgment of the Court of Appeal, said in para 7:
>
>> 'The lawful exercise of [statutory] powers can also be restricted, according to established principles of public law, by government policy and the legitimate expectation to which such a policy gives rise.'
>
> Since 2001, however, there has been some departure from the ascription of the legal effect of policy to the doctrine of legitimate expectation. Invocation of the doctrine is strained

in circumstances in which those who invoke it were, like Mr Mandalia, unaware of the policy until after the determination adverse to them was made; and also strained in circumstances in which reliance is placed on guidance issued by one public body to another, for example by the Department of the Environment to local planning authorities … So the applicant's right to the determination of his application in accordance with policy is now generally taken to flow from a principle, no doubt related to the doctrine of legitimate expectation but free-standing, which was best articulated by Laws LJ in *R (Nadarajah) v Secretary of State for the Home Department* [2005] EWCA Civ 1363, as follows:

'68 … Where a public authority has issued a promise or adopted a practice which represents how it proposes to act in a given area, the law will require the promise or practice to be honoured unless there is good reason not to do so. What is the principle behind this proposition? It is not far to seek. It is said to be grounded in fairness, and no doubt in general terms that is so. I would prefer to express it rather more broadly as a requirement of good administration, by which public bodies ought to deal straightforwardly and consistently with the public.'

Thus, in [*Lumba*] Lord Dyson said simply:

'35. The individual has a basic public law right to have his or her case considered under whatever policy the executive sees fit to adopt provided that the adopted policy is a lawful exercise of the discretion conferred by the statute.'

… But, in his judgment … Lord Dyson … articulated two qualifications. He had said:

'21 … it is a well established principle of public law that a policy should not be so rigid as to amount to a fetter on the discretion of decision-makers.'

… Lord Dyson had also said:

'26 … a decision-maker must follow his published policy … unless there are good reasons for not doing so.'

Thus there is now a clearly established general principle of administrative law that administrators must follow their policies, unless there are good reasons to depart from those policies. Administrative decisions are increasingly quashed on this basis: *eg R (O)* v. *Secretary of State for the Home Department* [2016] UKSC 19, [2016] 1 WLR 1717.

Evidently the law has come a long way from the 'no fettering' rule that, in cases like *Stringer*, afforded policy a role that was marginal at best. That rule remains relevant insofar as policies must in general not be so rigid that they admit of no exceptions. But overall the judges have aggressively developed the case law to ensure that discretions are subject to substantial constraints, based in formulated administrative policy, and thus in significant respects *fettered*.

Let us, by way of conclusion, reflect on the underlying motivations for these judicial moves towards ensuring that exercise of discretion is structured and legally constrained by publicly available policy. Such an approach is principally premised on rule-of-law values. If the basis on which public power is to be exercised is publicly stated in advance, this facilitates certainty and predictability in public administration. It also helps to guard against abuse or misuse of power, as power shall be constrained by the terms of policy, which are given legal force by the courts. Decision-making according to a common set of policies also facilitates consistency and efficiency in public administration, as a common set of decision criteria shall guide particular classes of decision. As suggested by Lady Hale's comments in *Nzolameso*, requiring government to adopt policy means that the courts can scrutinize that policy for consistency with judicial review norms of rationality, fairness, and legality. In turn the courts shall have far greater power to control the legality of administrative exercises of power on a *systemic* level than if the courts were limited to intervening only on the basis of individual exercises of discretion.

On the other hand, as Lord Walker observed in *R (Alvi)* v. *Secretary of State for the Home Department* [2012] UKSC 33, [2012] 1 WLR 2208 at [111], there is a tension between flexibility in decision-making on the one hand and predictability of outcome on the other: more of one means less of the other. One might argue that while some constraint and legal structuring of broad discretions is desirable, the recent developments discussed here have begun to strike the balance too far in favour of legal values. The result of imposing increasingly stringent legal fetters on discretion may be overly constrained public administration, so that administrators are less able to respond effectively and efficiently to changing facts and conditions, and to tailor solutions to individual cases—fearing that their justifications for deviating from policy may not stand up to scrutiny in court. In addition, exercising power within an increasingly elaborate web of formalized policy rules, guidance, circulars, etc may lead to more general delay, cost, inefficiency, ineffectiveness, and also complexity in public administration, ultimately to the detriment of the public interest and also possibly those affected by exercise of public powers. Consider the example of the Immigration Rules. Does it really help an ordinary citizen to understand how their case will be determined in advance where Rules comprise of over 400 paragraphs (with multiple sub-paragraphs to boot) and 26 appendices, framed in legalistic jargon, and which are supplemented by a miscellany of other guidance notes and circulars? Not surprisingly some judges have observed that 'the system is Byzantine and in some respects inaccessible' (*R (Sayaniya)* v. *Upper Tribunal* [2016] EWCA Civ 85, [2016] 4 WLR 58 at [20]). Further, policy may be changed frequently in the light of changing circumstances, undermining the greater certainty which adoption of policy is meant to facilitate. This has been the experience with the Immigration Rules; some judges observing that constant amendment, in addition to the number of different documents that have to be consulted to work out a given legal position, are real obstacles to achieving predictability, consistency, and trust in the immigration system (*Sayaniya* at [20]).

One response to these concerns might be to argue that balances need to be struck in particular contexts. Thus, perhaps we should be more willing to tolerate the increased inefficiency, delay, and formality that go with adoption of detailed policy where public powers touch on basic interests such as liberty. But of course, as we have seen, the trend seems to be towards legally requiring adoption of policy across a growing number of contexts beyond those concerned with basic rights, while the legal presumption that administrators must adhere to policy has already been generalized.

QUESTIONS

- Are recent developments in the law governing policy a welcome reinforcement and vindication of rule-of-law values or do they threaten a legal take-over of administrative discretion to the detriment of public administration and the public interest?
- If a contextual approach is taken, what sorts of factors do you think a court should take into account in deciding whether adoption of policy should be a mandatory requirement in a given context?

5.4 Concluding remarks

We have seen in this chapter how administrative law has traditionally given effect to the important policy that decision-makers upon whom discretionary powers are conferred should retain and exercise those powers. This policy has found expression in the specific principles which limit the ability of decision-makers to delegate or transfer their powers and to narrow their discretion by adopting policies and rules.

In each of these contexts, however, orthodoxies are under threat as countervailing policy concerns increasingly hold sway.

Thus the *Carltona* doctrine serves to ensure that the non-delegation doctrine is tempered by the need for efficient decision-making. However, concerns emerge over potential gaps in accountability as the scope of application of the *Carltona* doctrine continues to expand to meet the realities of the organization of modern government, with the consequence that there are increasing degrees of separation between Ministers and those officials who may lawfully exercise powers in the Minister's name.

In recent years there has been a sea change in the judicial approach to policy. While adoption of administrative policies to regulate the exercise of discretion was traditionally met with judicial scepticism, on the basis that it may unduly fetter the decision-maker's ability to respond to the facts of individual cases, the courts now view policy as a tool for disciplining exercise of administrative discretion so that it conforms to rule-of-law values in certainty, consistency, and openness. Decision-makers are now legally required to apply their policies unless they have good reasons for not doing so, while policies must conform to an increasing number of judicially articulated requirements. As such, we are witnessing a clear move away from the 'no-fettering rule' and towards 'fettering rules' or a 'law of policy'. In turn these developments raise concerns that the overall balance of the law has been struck too far in favour of rule-of-law values, and away from important administrative and public interests in flexible, responsive, and effective administrative decision-making.

FURTHER RESOURCES

Baldwin and Houghton, 'Circular Arguments: The Status and Legitimacy of Administrative Rules' [1986] *PL* 239

Dotan, 'Why Administrators Should be Bound by Their Policies' (1997) 17 *OJLS* 23

Freedland, 'Privatising *Carltona*: Part II of the Deregulation and Contracting Out Act 1994' [1995] *PL* 21

Freedland, 'The Rule against Delegation and the *Carltona* Doctrine in an Agency Context' [1996] *PL* 19

Galligan, 'The Nature and Function of Policy within Discretionary Power' [1976] *PL* 332

Hilson, 'Judicial Review, Policies and the Fettering of Discretion' [2002] *PL* 111

Jowell, 'Legal Control of Administrative Discretion' [1973] *PL* 178

6 LEGITIMATE EXPECTATIONS

In the previous chapter we considered how far the discretionary freedom of the decision-maker designated by statute may be constrained by delegation and the adoption of policies. This chapter concerns the extent to which a public authority's powers may be limited by representations as to how it will act. The central principle in this area of administrative law is that of legitimate expectation. We turn first to the application of that principle to lawfully created expectations, and then consider to what extent, if any, it may protect unlawfully generated expectations.

6.1 Lawfully created expectations

In *Council of Civil Service Unions* v. *Minister for the Civil Service* [1985] AC 374 at 408, Lord Diplock said that judicial review should lie when an individual is deprived of

> some benefit or advantage which either (i) he had in the past been permitted by the decision-maker to enjoy and which he can legitimately expect to be permitted to continue to do until there has been communicated to him some rational grounds for withdrawing it on which he has been given an opportunity to comment; or (ii) he has received assurance from the decision-maker will not be withdrawn without giving him first an opportunity of advancing reasons for contending that they should not be withdrawn.

This succinct explanation of the principle of legitimate expectation is a useful starting point, but it perhaps raises more questions than it answers. When, precisely, will the individual 'legitimately' expect the conferral of the benefit? What amounts to an 'assurance'? And can legitimate expectations be protected by more than the accordance to the expectation-holder of procedurally fair treatment, which is what Lord Diplock focuses on? We address these issues later, but begin with a more fundamental question about the underlying purpose of the legitimate expectation principle.

6.1.1 Why protect legitimate expectations?

At the heart of the doctrine of legitimate expectation lies a tension, familiar from the previous chapter, between the protection of administrative autonomy to pursue statutory goals and conflicting policy concerns which favour constraining administrative freedom of action. The importance of the former was underlined in the following terms by Laws LJ in *R (Niazi)* v. *Secretary of State for the Home Department* [2008] EWCA Civ 755 at [41]:

> Public authorities typically, and central government *par excellence*, enjoy wide discretions which it is their duty to exercise in the public interest. They have to decide the content and the pace of change. Often they must balance different, indeed opposing, interests across a wide spectrum. Generally they must be the masters of procedure as well as substance; and as such are generally entitled to keep their own counsel. All this is involved in what Sedley LJ described [in *R (BAPIO Action Ltd)* v. *Secretary of State for the Home Department* [2007] EWCA Civ 1139 at [43]] as the entitlement of central government to formulate and re-formulate policy. This entitlement—in truth, a duty—is ordinarily repugnant to any requirement to bow to another's will.

Against considerations of this nature, however, must be set other important concerns, as Forsyth [1988] *CLJ* 238 at 239 explains:

> The judicial motivation for seeking to protect [legitimate] expectations is plain: if the executive undertakes, expressly or by past practice, to behave in a particular way the subject expects that undertaking to be complied with. That is surely fundamental to good government and it would be monstrous if the executive could freely renege on its undertakings. Public trust in the government should not be left unprotected.

It is the tension between administrative autonomy to pursue whichever course of action best fulfils statutory public goals on the one hand, and on the other, interlocking interests such as those in legal certainty, individual fairness, and good administrative practice or 'fair dealing', which the modern concept of legitimate expectation is concerned to mediate. However, it is important at the outset to recognize that this tension is not straightforwardly one between individual interests (specifically the interests of the person in possession of the expectation) and public interests. For example, although the legal certainty afforded by holding authorities to their word is of importance to individuals as it allows them to order and plan their lives, there is also a *public* interest in legal certainty, since the community as a whole benefits from an environment in which its members are able to repose trust and confidence in their public institutions—a point which is developed in the following passage.

Schønberg, *Legitimate Expectations in Administrative Law* (Oxford 2000)

[A] public authority's freedom to take action in the public interest is limited to the extent that it causes harm to particular individuals. If a public authority has induced a person to rely upon its representations or conduct, realising that such reliance was a real possibility, it is under a *prima facie* duty to act in such a way that the reliance will not be detrimental to the representee. The authority must honour the expectations created by its representation or, at least, compensate the person affected for his reliance loss ...

... In a rapidly changing and increasingly uncertain world, law is something that operators should be able to, and to a large extent do, rely on. In administrative law, the importance of certainty is increased by wide-ranging discretionary powers being vested in public authorities. Individuals cannot easily predict how discretionary powers will be exercised because the provisions conferring such powers are linguistically indeterminate and because informal working rules and other constraints, of which individuals are not normally aware, affect their exercise in practice. Representations may create expectations as to the manner of, or criteria for, their exercise. Respect for these expectations therefore makes the exercise of discretion more predictable.

However, the importance of the rule of law does not stop here … First, the rule of law pre-supposes formal equality. That is, like cases must be treated alike by the correct and consistent application of law. Without formal equality law becomes arbitrary and thus unpredictable and uncertain. Second, the rule of law presupposes a certain measure of constancy in the law. The law should ensure that administrative action is based on a mix of short-term exigencies and more long-term considerations. Individual planning becomes difficult or impossible if law and policy are changed too often and too abruptly. Moreover, frequent changes may undermine individual rights by creating uncertainty about the boundaries of those rights. The legal protection of legit-imate expectations by administrative law is a way of giving expression to the requirements of predictability, formal equality, and constancy inherent in the rule of law …

… The rule of law justification for protection of legitimate expectations has a certain 'red light' quality [see 1.2.1 on the meaning of this term]. However, recognition of legitimate expectations is not only about fairness to the individual and control of administrative power, it is also a power-ful means to administrative efficacy. Administrative efficacy is an aspect of the wider notion of good administration, the enforcement of which is an important part of modern judicial review … [A]dministrative power is more likely to be perceived as legitimate authority if exercised in a way which respects legitimate expectations. Perceived legitimate authority is more efficacious because it encourages individuals to participate in decision-making processes, to co-operate with administrative initiatives, and to comply with administrative regulations. Greater compliance will in turn improve the administration's ability to solve co-ordination problems, and that may actu-ally make its exercise of authority more legitimate. The acceptance of principles of administrative law, which require authorities to respect legitimate expectations, is therefore not merely in the interests of individuals. It is, very much, in the interest of the administration itself.

QUESTIONS

- What does Schønberg mean when he says that the 'rule of law justification … has a certain 'red-light' quality'?
- Why does he argue that the justification for upholding legitimate expectations is wider than this?

Reflecting this thinking we see a multi-faceted justification for legitimate expectations emer-gent in the case law. For example, in *R (Niazi)* v. *Secretary of State for the Home Department* [2008] EWCA Civ 755, Laws LJ said (at [30]) that the law does not only recognize enforce-able legitimate expectations because of 'how harshly' deviation from an expectation 'bears on the individual' *but also* because good administration—specifically the idea that 'public bodies ought to deal straightforwardly and consistently with the public' (*R (Nadarajah)* v. *Secretary of State for the Home Department* [2005] EWCA Civ 1363 at [68] (Laws LJ))—'gener-ally requires that where a public authority has given a plain assurance, it should be held to it'.

6.1.2 Two variables: legitimacy and protection

In any situation which potentially engages the legitimate expectation principle, two key cri-teria will inevitably be in play: that of *legitimacy*, and that of the mode *of protection* which may be extended to expectations which satisfy the first criterion. It is important to be clear about the relationship between these two variables.

The criterion of *legitimacy* is crucial: the law is concerned not simply with what individuals *actually* expect in subjective terms, but only with what they are *entitled to* expect. As Lord Scarman explained in *Re Findlay* [1985] AC 318 at 338, the key question which the court must ask of the claimant is, '[W]hat was their *legitimate* expectation?' This matter is considered at 6.1.3.

Once the court has ascertained the existence of a legitimate expectation, it must go on to consider how (if at all) it should be *protected*. If the claimant merely expects that a particular procedure will be followed before certain action is taken, then the court will generally require adherence to such a procedure (see, *eg Attorney-General of Hong Kong* v. *Ng Yuen Shiu* [1983] 2 AC 629, an excerpt from which appears at 6.1.4). Hence there can be *procedural protection* of a *procedural legitimate expectation*. However, what if the claimant's expectation was not simply that he would (say) be *consulted before* having a benefit withdrawn, but that the benefit *would not* be withdrawn? There are three principal ways in which this issue may be analysed.

First, the court may determine that, while the claimant *actually* expected the ongoing conferral of the benefit (a *substantive* expectation), he was only *entitled* to expect a fair procedure (*eg* consultation or a hearing) before the taking of the decision whether to withdraw the benefit (a *procedural legitimate* expectation). In this manner the application of the criterion of legitimacy dictates that only procedural protection is appropriate, since procedurally fair treatment is all that the claimant was legitimately entitled to expect. (The decision in *R* v. *Secretary of State for the Home Department, ex parte Khan* [1984] 1 WLR 1337 is arguably an example of this approach.)

Second, the same result would be achieved if the court held that, while the claimant was entitled to expect the ongoing conferral of the benefit (a *substantive legitimate* expectation), the expectation should only be protected by requiring a fair *procedure* to be followed. This mode of analysis implies the possibility of *procedural protection* of a *substantive legitimate expectation*: it recognizes that, while the claimant was entitled to expect a substantive outcome, countervailing factors dictate that the court should only require the adoption of a fair procedure. This, in turn, reflects an underlying conclusion that the public interest in discretionary freedom, on the facts of the case, carries sufficient weight that the principle of legal certainty (which would tend to favour the substantive enforcement of the expectation) should yield.

Third, and finally, there are situations in which the individual expects—and is entitled to expect—a substantive outcome (a *substantive legitimate expectation*), and in which substantive protection is appropriate (so that the court requires the decision-maker to confer the benefit). This category—*substantive protection* of a *substantive legitimate expectation*—indicates judicial recognition that, in some contexts, the discretionary freedom of the decision-maker (which would favour retention of the decision-maker's ultimate substantive freedom to frustrate the expectation) must give way to the principle of legal certainty (see, *eg R* v. *North and East Devon Health Authority, ex parte Coughlan* [2001] QB 213, discussed at 6.1.5).

Thus, whenever individuals seek relief on the basis of expectations generated by public authorities, two matters are crucial. First, the court must assess what (if anything) they were legitimately entitled to expect. Second, the court must determine how (if at all) to protect the expectation; and, in addressing this issue, the court has to confront the relationship between the interests in discretionary freedom and legal certainty. This does not mean, however, that the issues of legitimacy and protection need be conceptualized as wholly distinct. In *R v. Ministry of Agriculture, Fisheries and Food, ex parte Hamble (Offshore) Fisheries Ltd* [1995] 2 All ER 714 at 732, Sedley J said that 'legitimate expectation is now in effect a term of art, reserved for expectations which are not only reasonable but which will be sustained by the court in the face of changes of policy'. This suggests that the expectation will only be legitimate if the court decides that it is worthy of protection; the distinct issues concerning the legitimacy of the expectation and whether (and, if so, how) it should be protected are thus presented as two sides of the same coin. Craig [1996] *CLJ* 289 at 303, however, is critical of such an approach, and argues that questions of legitimacy and protection should be kept distinct:

> On the one hand, [the approach which separates legitimacy and protection] comports better with reality. To be forced to conclude that the [claimant] ... never had any legitimate expectation ... [just because countervailing policy factors militate against its protection] does not fit with our intuition. Our natural reaction in such a case is that there was such an expectation which has been trumped by public interest considerations ...
>
> On the other hand, it is conceptually clearer. There are ... two values which are ultimately at stake in this type of case. Legal certainty is expressive of the individual's perspective; legality, as manifested through the non-fettering [or discretionary freedom] doctrine, captures the needs of the public body to develop policy. The approach favoured by Sedley J seeks to bring both of these within the phrase legitimate expectations itself: for the expectation to be legitimate it must not only be reasonable, but sustainable in the face of the need of the public body to change policy. The natural role of legitimate expectations is, however, to reflect the individual's perspective and the value of legal certainty. This is how it is employed in other contexts. It is, of course, true, as Sedley J points out, that legitimate expectations are not absolute. But this point is captured perfectly well by accepting that the public interest should allow the public body to resile from the expectation. It does not demand that the legality value should be incorporated within the phrase legitimate expectations itself.

QUESTIONS

- Contrast the notions of 'legitimacy' employed by Sedley J and Craig. Which approach do you consider to be the more satisfactory?
- Why?

6.1.3 Legitimacy: what is the claimant *entitled* to expect?

We note at the outset that it has often been difficult to predict when a court will find an expectation to be legitimate, the inquiry not being one governed by clear rules. For example, Lord Brown, dissenting in *Paponette v. Attorney General of Trinidad and Tobago* [2010] UKPC 32, [2012] 1 AC 1 at [61], quoted an academic article suggesting that the current law is more in the nature of 'a patchwork of possible elements to consider' rather than an organized system of rules, and 'little more than a mechanism to dispense palm-tree justice' (Watson (2010) 30 *LS* 633 at 651). As we shall see, some progress has been made towards pinning down and clarifying the criteria to be applied, though it is beyond doubt that the legitimacy inquiry remains one governed by fairly open-textured principles rather than concrete rules.

The nature and circumstances of the conduct or statement giving rise to the expectation

In the following case, the House of Lords considered the type of situations in which a legitimate expectation may arise.

Council of Civil Services Unions v. Minister for the Civil Service [1985] AC 374
House of Lords

For the facts, see 4.3.2. The present excerpt is concerned with whether the claimants had a legitimate expectation of consultation.

Lord Fraser

... Mr. Blom-Cooper [for the claimants] submitted that the Minister had a duty to consult the CCSU, on behalf of employees at GCHQ, before giving the instruction on 22 December 1983 for making an important change in their conditions of service. His main reason for so submitting was that the employees had a legitimate, or reasonable, expectation that there would be such prior consultation before any important change was made in their conditions.

It is clear that the employees did not have a legal right to prior consultation. The Order in Council confers no such right, and article 4 makes no reference at all to consultation. The Civil Service handbook (*Handbook for the new civil servant*, 1973 ed. as amended 1983) which explains the normal method of consultation through the departmental Whitley Council, does not suggest that there is any legal right to consultation; indeed it is careful to recognise that, in the operational field, considerations of urgency may make prior consultation impracticable. The Civil Service Pay and Conditions of Service Code expressly states:

> 'The following terms and conditions also apply to your appointment in the Civil Service. It should be understood, however, that in consequence of the constitutional position of the Crown, the Crown has the right to change its employees' conditions of service at any time, and that they hold their appointments at the pleasure of the Crown.'

But even where a person claiming some benefit or privilege has no legal right to it, as a matter of private law, he may have a legitimate expectation of receiving the benefit or privilege, and, if so, the courts will protect his expectation by judicial review as a matter of public law. This subject has been fully explained by my noble and learned friend, Lord Diplock, in *O'Reilly* v. *Mackman* [1983] 2 A.C. 237 and I need not repeat what he has so recently said. Legitimate, or reasonable, expectation may arise either from an express promise given on behalf of a public authority or from the existence of a regular practice which the claimant can reasonably expect to continue. Examples of the former type of expectation are *Reg.* v. *Liverpool Corporation, Ex parte Liverpool Taxi Fleet Operators' Association* [1972] 2 Q.B. 299 and *Attorney-General of Hong Kong* v. *Ng Yuen Shiu* [1983] 2 A.C. 629. (I agree with Lord Diplock's view, expressed in the speech in this appeal, that 'legitimate' is to be preferred to 'reasonable' in this context. I was responsible for using the word 'reasonable' for the reason explained in Ng *Yuen Shiu*, but it was intended only to be exegetical of 'legitimate'.) An example of the latter is *Reg.* v. *Board of Visitors of Hull Prison, Ex parte St. Germain* [1979] Q.B. 425 approved by this House in *O'Reilly*, at p. 274D. The submission on behalf of the appellants is that the present case is of the latter type. The test of that is whether the practice of prior consultation of the staff on significant changes in their conditions of service was so well established by 1983 that it would be unfair or inconsistent with good administration for the Government to depart from the practice in this case. Legitimate expectations such as are now under consideration will always relate to a benefit or privilege to which the claimant has no right in private law, and it may even be to one which conflicts with his private law rights. In the present case the evidence shows that, ever since GCHQ began in 1947, prior consultation has been the invariable rule when conditions of service were to be significantly altered. Accordingly in my opinion if there had been no question of national security involved, the appellants would have had a legitimate expectation that the Minister would consult them before issuing the instruction of 22 December 1983 ...

Lord Diplock

... To qualify as a subject for judicial review the decision must have consequences which affect some person (or body of persons) other than the decision-maker, although it may affect him too. It must affect such other person either:

(a) by altering rights or obligations of that person which are enforceable by or against him in private law; or
(b) by depriving him of some benefit or advantage which either (i) he had in the past been permitted by the decision-maker to enjoy and which he can legitimately expect to be permitted to continue to do until there has been communicated to him some rational grounds for withdrawing it on which he has been given an opportunity to comment; or (ii) he has received assurance from the decision-maker will not be withdrawn without giving him first an opportunity of advancing reasons for contending that they should not be withdrawn. (I prefer to continue to call the kind of expectation that qualifies a decision for inclusion in class (b) a 'legitimate expectation' rather than a 'reasonable expectation,' in order thereby to indicate that it has consequences to which effect will be given in public law, whereas an expectation or hope that some benefit or advantage would continue to be enjoyed, although it might well be entertained by a 'reasonable' man, would not necessarily have such consequences. The recent decision of this House in *In re Findlay* [1985] A.C. 318 presents an example of the latter kind of expectation. 'Reasonable' furthermore bears different meanings according to whether the context in which it is being used is that of private law or of public law. To eliminate confusion it is best avoided in the latter.) ...

Prima facie, therefore, civil servants employed at GCHQ who were members of national trade unions had, at best, in December 1983, a legitimate expectation that they would continue to enjoy the benefits of such membership and of representation by those trade unions in any consultations and negotiations with representatives of the management of that government department as to changes in any term of their employment. So, but again prima facie only, they were entitled, as a matter of public law under the head of 'procedural propriety,' before administrative action was taken on a decision to withdraw that benefit, to have communicated to the national trade unions by which they had theretofore been represented the reason for such withdrawal, and for such unions to be given an opportunity to comment on it.

Notwithstanding these conclusions about the claimants' legitimate expectations, Lords Fraser, Scarman, Diplock, Roskill, and Brightman were all of the opinion that national security considerations justified the Minister's failure to consult prior to the decision. The legality of the decision was therefore upheld on national security grounds. Appeal dismissed.

It is clear from this case that a legitimate expectation need not be generated by an express statement: an established practice may lead the claimant legitimately to expect that the same practice will be followed in the future. Thus consistent provision of a given *procedure* may trigger a legitimate expectation that that procedure will continue to be followed. But what if the past practice consists not in the provision of a given procedure, but in the conferral of a particular substantive benefit? Can a legitimate expectation arise in these circumstances, too? Laws LJ considered this question in *R (Niazi)* v. *Secretary of State for the Home Department* [2008] EWCA Civ 755. He indicated (at [43]–[46]) that a claimant is unlikely to be able to spell out of past practice a *substantive legitimate expectation* that the benefit will continue to be conferred, because, as he explained, such an expectation arises only if there is 'a specific undertaking, directed at a particular individual or group, by which the relevant policy's continuance is assured'. Further, as observed in *DM* v. *Secretary of State for the Home Department* [2014] CSIH 29, 2014 SC 635 at [25], 'Policy may be changed at any time, and a change might be rendered largely ineffective if it were still necessary to apply the policy that existed at an earlier date'; in other words, to recognize enforceable substantive expectations on the basis of a former practice or policy, since abandoned, would make too great an inroad into the executive's ability to respond to the changing demands of the public interest (see also *Niazi* at [34], [41], [43]).

However, in *Niazi*, Laws LJ said that it may be possible to spell out of consistent past conferral of a benefit a *procedural legitimate expectation* that it will not be withdrawn without consultation. Such an expectation arises, he said (at [49]), when there is

> an individual or group who in reason have substantial grounds to expect that the substance of the relevant policy will continue to ensure for their particular benefit: not necessarily for ever, but at least for a reasonable period, to provide a cushion against the change. In such a case the change cannot lawfully be made, certainly not made abruptly, unless the authority notify and consult.

It must also be the case that the impact on the claimant of a change in practice or policy is 'pressing and focussed' (at [58]). Laws LJ added that a case with these characteristics would be an 'exceptional case' and this category of legitimate expectation is one that is of 'narrow and specific compass' (at [58]–[59]). In Laws LJ's view the best exemplar of such a case is *R* v. *Inland Revenue Commissioners, ex parte Unilever plc* [1996] STC 681: the claimant was held to have a legitimate expectation of being notified before the Inland Revenue contradicted 20 years of past practice by refusing to accept the late submission of the claimant's applications for tax relief. As evidenced by Laws LJ's statements of principle the general trend in recent years has been towards a generally strict approach to recognizing legitimate expectations outside cases of express promises, representations, or undertakings as to future conduct, especially substantive expectations. It is notable in this regard that *Unilever* was explicitly classed as an exceptional case both by Laws LJ in *Niazi* and by the Court that decided it, and indeed the facts were unusually strong in that there had been a *consistent* pattern of conduct over a *long period* which was *individualized*. There are arguably several factors driving this increasingly strict approach outside cases of express promises or representations as to future conduct. First, there is the concern noted at the outset of this section that the doctrine of legitimate expectations has proven difficult to pin down, so that it has been difficult to predict in advance whether an expectation will arise. By focusing attention on cases involving promises the courts are able to place the case law on a more certain footing. Second, there is a concern that recognition of enforceable expectations on the basis of mere informal practices, which the administration may not have even consciously adopted, may unduly impede effective public administration. Third, a refocusing on promise cases has arguably followed from the recognition that certain classes of case not involving a promise, which have sometimes been analysed as legitimate expectation cases, are better analysed under distinct doctrines (see in particular the discussion of policy cases in the next section).

In *Secretary of State for the Home Department* v. *Rahman* [2011] EWCA Civ 814, Stanley Burnton LJ, with whom the other members of the Court agreed, argued (at [42]) that 'the concept of legitimate expectation is normally otiose in cases where there has been no representation, by words or conduct, by the public authority in question to the claimant seeking to rely on it'. What marks out promise cases from other cases is that a clear representation to a claimant positively induces the claimant to place trust in the official: *DM* at [18]. Note that these statements do not explicitly discriminate between procedural and substantive expectations. In other words, courts may be slow to recognize legitimate expectations, whether procedural or substantive, on the basis of practice, as opposed to promise. Albeit one would expect it to be easier, relatively, to establish a procedural expectation than a substantive one for reasons canvassed earlier, while it is worth noting that *Rahman* itself involved a claim of substantive expectations. Consonant with the dicta in *Rahman*, Laws LJ in *Niazi* considered promise cases to be the 'paradigm case' of legitimate expectations, and practice cases to be outliers. Similar views have been espoused in a series of decisions from Northern Ireland. In *Application by Charles Boyle for Judicial Review* [2016] NIQB 2 at [10]–[23], the Court considered that the number of cases, such as *Unilever*, where an applicant could establish a legitimate expectation based in past practice 'is vanishingly small'—judicial intervention outside promise cases is limited to cases where to change policy or practice absent consultation would be 'unconscionable' or 'outrageous'. In *Loreto Grammar School's Application* [2012] NICA 1 at [45], the Northern Irish Court of Appeal held that the doctrine of legitimate expectations should be 'narrowly construed' so as to protect against undue fettering of administrative discretion—the courts should 'lean against the finding of a fettering of discretion'—while acknowledging that the one type of case where a concern for administrative autonomy may have to give way is where there has been a clear, unequivocal representation to an individual: 'In such a situation the balance must be struck differently' (see similarly *Application by JR 47 for Judicial Review* [2013] NIQB 7 at [28]).

Apart from these more general statements the courts have developed the law to make it more difficult for a claimant to establish a legitimate expectation, whether procedural or substantive, on the basis of practice. Principally this has been effected by clarifying and reinforcing that certain prerequisites developed in promise cases also apply to practice cases. In particular, it has long been established that for a legitimate expectation to arise on the basis of a specific statement or representation, that statement must be 'clear, unambiguous and devoid of relevant qualification': *R* v. *Inland Revenue Commissioners, ex parte MFK Underwriting Agencies Ltd* [1990] 1 WLR 1545 at 1569. It is now clear that this requirement applies in practice cases, and it is equally clear that it will be very difficult for a claimant to prove the existence of a practice with such attributes. In a *promise* case the claimant will often be able to simply point to a written statement issued to them by an authority. In contrast, in a *practice* case the claimant will need to produce 'clear evidence' which shows that the 'practice was so unambiguous, so widespread, so well-established and so well-recognised as to carry with it a commitment to' a relevant group of persons of which the claimant is one: *R (Davies)* v. *Commissioners for Her Majesty's Revenue and Customs* [2011] UKSC 47, [2011] WLR 2625 at [49]. It also seems that the claimant will have to prove the practice is a 'settled' one (at [58]), which will make the claimant's task even more difficult as practices are likely to change regularly in response to changing circumstances. Where these tests have been applied in practice cases claimants have generally failed to establish a legitimate expectation (*eg DM* at [29]–[30]; *Davies* at [48]–[58]), reflecting Lord Wilson's observation in *Davies* that it will be more difficult to show a legitimate expectation on the basis of practice compared to written assurances (at [49]).

The evidential burden on the claimant would appear to be a heavy one; for example, in *Davies*, witness statements by expert tax advisors to the effect that they understood the Revenue to operate a particular practice were considered insufficient: the claimants needed 'evidence beyond the generalized, anecdotal understanding of their witnesses, however highly regarded' (at [51]). This in turn suggests the claimants may need to identify a 'paper trail' which provides an objective basis for tracing a particular practice, which will be very difficult given restraints on disclosure in judicial review proceedings (see ch 13.2.2), while even if one can show some semblance of an established practice it will be rather difficult to demonstrate the existence of a *sufficiently clear and unambiguous* practice on the basis of disparate documents, letters, and witness statements: see, *eg Davies* at [51]–[58].

Even in promise cases it may be difficult to demonstrate that the relevant representation is sufficiently clear and unequivocal. Consider the case of *R (Bancoult)* v. *Secretary of State for Foreign and Commonwealth Affairs (No 2)* [2008] UKHL 61, [2009] 1 AC 453 (the facts of which are set out at 4.3.2). After the Divisional Court ([2001] QB 1067) had held that prerogative legislation banishing the Chagos Islanders from their homeland was unlawful, the Foreign Secretary issued the following statement:

> I have decided to accept the court's ruling and the Government will not be appealing. The work we are doing on the feasibility of resettling the [islanders] now takes on a new importance. We started the feasibility work a year ago and are now well underway with phase two of the study. Furthermore, we will put in place a new Immigration Ordinance which will allow the [islanders] to return to the outer islands.

When, in spite of this undertaking, the government later reinstated the ban on the resettlement of the islands, the question arose whether the above statement had given rise to a legitimate expectation. Lords Bingham and Mance, in the minority, thought that it had. The former said (at [73]) that there had been

> a clear and unambiguous representation, devoid of relevant qualification, that (1) the Government would not be challenging the Divisional Court's decision that Mr Bancoult and his fellow Chagossians had been unlawfully excluded from the outer islands for nearly 30 years, (2) the Government would introduce a new Immigration Ordinance which would allow the Chagossians to return to the outer islands unless or until the United Kingdom's treaty obligations might at some later date forbid it, and (3) the Government would not persist in treating the Chagossians as it had reprehensibly done since 1971.

The majority, however, disagreed, holding that there had not been a clear and unambiguous representation. This apparently surprising conclusion appeared to rest on the willingness of the majority to treat the undertaking to permit return as contingent upon the outcome of the feasibility study—a conclusion which is hard to reconcile with the fact that the feasibility study was concerned with whether it would be financially viable for the UK government to undertake a resettlement programme, as distinct from the question whether the islanders should be permitted to return *at all*, under their own steam.

That the majority and minority split on whether the statement was sufficiently clear and unambiguous reflects that this legal test itself lacks clarity: different people are likely to subjectively disagree over whether a particular statement is sufficiently clear or not. It has thus not been unusual for appellate courts to split on this question; in addition to *Bancoult* see, for example, *Paponette* v. *Attorney General of Trinidad and Tobago* [2010] UKPC 32, [2012] 1 AC 1.

Despite the open-endedness of the *MFK Underwriting* test it should be noted that there is an identifiable trend in the case law towards a less strict approach to interpreting express assurances or statements than that adopted by the majority in *Bancoult*. Increasingly the courts ask how on a fair reading of the statement it would have been reasonably understood by those to whom it was made: *Paponette* at [30]; *R (Patel)* v. *GMC* [2013] EWCA Civ 327, [2013] 1 WLR 2801 at [44]–[49]. A focus on how the recipients of the promise, typically ordinary people without legal training, would have understood it tells against an overly formalistic, legalistic, or literal approach to interpreting the relevant statement. In other words, that a reasonable lay person reading the statement would consider it clear in its effect shall suffice even if a reasonable lawyer or judge reading the statement could detect some ambiguity.

It may also be necessary to examine the wider context or circumstances in which the relevant statement is made. In *MFK Underwriting*, for instance, the claimant was unable to establish a legitimate expectation arising from representations made by the Inland Revenue—in response to questions asked of it by the claimants—concerning how certain bonds would be taxed. Bingham LJ explained (at 1569–70) that

> it is necessary that the taxpayer should have put all his cards face upwards on the table. … [T]he taxpayer should indicate the use he intends to make of any ruling given. … [K]nowledge that a ruling is to be publicised in a large and important market could affect the person by whom and the level at which a problem is considered and, indeed, whether it is appropriate to give a ruling at all … The doctrine of legitimate expectation is rooted in fairness. But fairness is not a one-way street. It imports the notion of equitableness, or fair and open dealing, to which the authority is entitled as much as the citizen.

Contrast the case of *Patel*. In that case the claimant had, via written correspondence, clearly sought assurances from the General Medical Council that if he undertook certain medical courses these would be sufficient for the purpose of provisional registration with the Council. He had also gone back to the Council repeatedly to seek a clear answer to his question, and made his proposed course of action plain. These features of the case demonstrated the 'importance he attached to the information he was legitimately seeking' and that 'he was trying his utmost to provide a clear statement of his intentions and to obtain a clear unequivocal response to his question' (at [45]). These features made it more likely that the representation ultimately made by the Council, that the proposed medical courses would be acceptable for the purposes of registration, was one that would generate a legitimate expectation—and one was found to arise.

In *Rahman* we find, as in *MFK Underwriting*, an appeal to equitable notions of 'clean hands' or 'fair dealing'. The claimant sought to establish a legitimate expectation that he would continue to be dealt with under a now abandoned immigration policy. Among other reasons for rejecting the argument Stanley Burnton LJ considered that the claimant was disentitled from establishing a legitimate expectation as he had entered the country by deception and not sought to regularize his family's immigration status after his leave to remain had expired: 'His evasion or avoidance of immigration rules disqualifies him from establishing any legitimate expectation' (at [45]).

Lastly, we note that while statements made to the world at large are unlikely to generate legitimate expectations, and especially substantive expectations, the courts have acknowledged it is at least possible that they may: *eg MFK Underwriting* at 1569; *Attorney-General of*

Hong Kong v. *Ng Yeun Shiu* [1983] 2 AC 629, discussed at 6.1.4. What is important in such cases, and any case where a representation is made to a particular group, is that claimants invoking such statements are able to demonstrate that they fall within the class of people to whom the statement relates. In *R (Parents for Legal Action Ltd)* v. *Northumberland County Council* [2006] EWHC 1081 (Admin), the defendant adopted a resolution that, in order to inform consultation *with schools* concerning a proposed reorganization, it would commission an independent evaluation of certain matters following consultation with parents. The claimant—a group representing parents—argued that the council's failure to commission an independent evaluation in line with its resolution breached their legitimate expectations. However, Munby J held that the resolution was a decision made by the council 'purely for [its] own purposes', and could not be read as an undertaking to parents. As Munby J elaborates, 'a legitimate expectation arises, and arises only, in relation to some *benefit*, procedural or substantive, to a claimant and in relation to some promise made to him or at least *applying* to him' (emphasis in original).

Knowledge

Can the claimant have a legitimate expectation that he will be treated in a particular way if he was not aware of the public authority's statement or practice indicating how it intended to act? This question—which has been squarely confronted only fairly recently by English courts—divided the High Court of Australia in *Minister of State for Immigration and Ethnic Affairs* v. *Teoh* (1995) 183 CLR 273. The respondent sought to resist deportation from Australia on the ground that it would disrupt his family life by separating him from his wife and children. He successfully contended that the decision to deport was flawed because this matter had not been taken into consideration. In doing so, he relied in part upon Australia's ratification of the United Nations Convention on the Rights of the Child, Article 3.1 of which provides that 'in all actions concerning children ... the best interests of the child shall be a primary consideration'. The claimant argued that the act of ratification created a legitimate expectation that this practice would be followed. This argument was accepted by a majority of the judges. One of them, Toohey J, said:

> It is not necessary for a person in the position of the respondent to show that he was aware of the ratification of the Convention; legitimate expectation in this context does not depend upon the knowledge and state of mind of the individual concerned. The matter is to be assessed objectively, in terms of what expectation might reasonably be engendered by any undertaking that the authority in question has given, whether itself or, as in the present case, by the government of which it is a part. A subjective test is particularly inappropriate when the legitimate expectation is said to derive from something as general as the ratification of the Convention. For, by ratifying the Convention Australia has given a solemn undertaking to the world at large that it will: 'in all actions concerning children, whether undertaken by public or private social welfare institutions, courts of law, administrative authorities or legislative bodies' make 'the best interests of the child a primary consideration'.

However, McHugh J, in dissent, disagreed sharply:

> If a person does not have an expectation that he or she will enjoy a benefit or privilege or that a particular state of affairs will continue, no disappointment or injustice is suffered by that person if that benefit or privilege is discontinued. A person cannot lose an expectation that he or she does not hold.

Two questions arise. First, *should* English courts follow the majority in *Teoh* and accept that an individual can legitimately expect something they knew nothing about? And, second, *have* they done so? As to the first matter, on the one hand it may seem counter-intuitive—even 'comical', as McHugh J put it in *Teoh*—to hold that a claimant who has been denied a particular benefit or procedure has had his legitimate expectation frustrated in circumstances where he was unaware of the statement or practice in the first place. On the other hand, it may be unfair to make the protection afforded by the legitimate expect-ation doctrine wholly contingent upon the individual claimant's subjective knowledge. This point was taken by Sir Louis Blom-Cooper QC (sitting as a Deputy High Court Judge) in *R v. Secretary of State for Wales, ex parte Emery* [1996] 4 All ER 1 at 17, endorsing the following passage from *De Smith's Judicial Review of Administrative Action* (London 1995) at 426:

> The fact that the applicant is in the class to which the representation is directed but happens not to be aware of it should not, it is submitted, deprive him of the benefit of the representation. To do so would involve unfair discrimination between those who were and were not aware of the representation and would benefit the well-informed or well-advised. It would also encourage undesirable administrative practice by too readily relieving decision-makers of the normal con-sequences of their actions.

Doctrinally, there would be no great difficulty in uncoupling knowledge from legitimate expectation. Legitimate expectations are legal constructs and can be defined in whatever way is required to serve the law's goals. The question is therefore whether the law's goals suggest knowledge should be a prerequisite; the problem is that the law's goals are contested or at least multi-faceted. For example, if the principal goal of the law of legitimate expectations was to guard against individuals suffering detriments through reliance on representations made by authorities, then knowledge would logically be a prerequisite for recognition of a legitimate expectation: one could not possibly rely on a representation to one's detriment if one did not know of the representation. On the other hand, if the law's principal goal was to ensure that authorities adhered to standards of good administration, which include holding true to their word, then we might hold authorities to their representations even if nobody ever knew about the representations.

Indeed, through the 2000s the English courts accepted that knowledge was not an absolute prerequisite in a line of cases in which authorities had failed to apply their stated policies to the claimant's case: *eg R (Rashid)* v. *Secretary of State for the Home Department* [2005] EWCA Civ 744. The courts held that even though the particular claimant did not know of the relevant policies, this did not prevent a legitimate expectation arising; the relevant expectation was one that the authority would apply its policies unless there were good reasons for deviating from the relevant policy on the facts of the case. Evidently the courts were unwilling to countenance eccentric or unexplained deviations from policy given such deviations smack of arbitrariness. They thus reached for the tool of legitimate expectations. However, there remained some judicial unease about recognizing legitimate expectations in cases where the claimant had no knowledge of the policy that generated the legitimate expectation. For example, courts observed that this line of cases did not sit 'comfortably with the conventional concept of legitimate expectation' (*Rashid* at [26], [34]) and were 'not the usual legitimate expectation case' (*R (A)* v. *Secretary of State for the Home Department* [2006] EWHC 526 (Admin) at [30]).

As is discussed in more detail at 5.3.3 the Supreme Court has now held that there is a freestanding principle of public law that administrators must apply their policies consistently unless there are good reasons for departing from policy. In *R (Lumba)* v. *Secretary of State for the Home Department* [2011] UKSC 12, [2012] 1 AC 245, Lord Dyson stated as a general principle that '[t]he individual has a basic public law right to have his or her case considered under whatever policy the executive sees fit to adopt provided that the adopted policy is a lawful exercise of the discretion conferred by the statute' (at [35]). In the subsequent case of *Mandalia* v. *Secretary of State for the Home Department* [2015] UKSC 59, [2015] 1 WLR 4546, Lord Wilson observed that invocation of legitimate expectations is 'strained' where knowledge is absent, and confirmed that 'the applicant's right to the determination of his application in accordance with policy is now generally taken to flow from a principle, no doubt related to the doctrine of legitimate expectation *but free-standing*' (at [29]–[31] (emphasis added)).

Judicial recognition of this free-standing principle removes the motivation for courts to stretch the law of legitimate expectations to cover cases of administrative deviation from public policies where the claimant has no knowledge of the relevant policies.

Given the removal of what had been the principal motivation for recognizing legitimate expectations absent knowledge the courts have begun to hold that knowledge is now a prerequisite. Thus, in *DM*, Lord Drummond Young for the Court said (at [18]):

> For a case based on legitimate expectations to exist, it is essential that there should be an expectation based on a statement from government or another public authority: that is to say, the statement must cause the petitioner to look forward to something. The element of causation is critical. If there is no knowledge of the statement that element must logically be absent, and there can be no legitimate expectation.

The Court of Appeal in *Rahman* (at [42]–[43]) too indicated that it was wholly unlikely that a legitimate expectation could arise absent knowledge; the Court considering that its view was reinforced by the Supreme Court's decision in *Lumba* to decouple the policy cases from the doctrine of legitimate expectations. The Court in *Rahman* rejected a claim for legitimate expectation on the following basis (at [43]):

> None of the applicants knew of [the relevant policy] before its withdrawal. They cannot therefore show that they relied on it, quite apart from the question whether their reliance would have given rise to a legitimate expectation.

It seems the Supreme Court would be sympathetic to the stance taken in *DM* and *Rahman* given Lord Wilson's view in *Mandalia* that the law of legitimate expectations is 'strained' where knowledge is absent. However, we await an explicit clarification of the role of knowledge from the Supreme Court. In the meantime it seems knowledge shall play a central role in courts' assessments of the legitimacy of expectations.

QUESTION

- Do you agree that knowledge should play a determinative role in deciding whether an expectation is legitimate?

Detrimental reliance

When the courts were prepared to hold that *knowledge* of the material upon which a legitimate expectation is founded was not an absolute prerequisite, *detrimental reliance* upon such material could not invariably be insisted upon: reliance on something of which you are ignorant being impossible. On the other hand, as the analysis in *Rahman* indicates, as knowledge is increasingly viewed as a prerequisite this may signal a greater judicial focus on the subjective experience of the individual claimant in determining the legitimacy of an expectation, including whether they suffered detriment through their reliance on the representation.

There are certainly cases in which legitimate expectations have been held to arise in the absence of any proof of detrimental reliance (see, *eg Attorney-General of Hong Kong* v. *Ng Yeun Shiu* [1983] 2 AC 629, in which there was knowledge but no detrimental reliance), while the higher courts have said that reliance and detriment are not prerequisites: *R (Bibi)* v. *Newham London Borough Council* [2001] EWCA Civ 607, [2002] 1 WLR 237 at [26]–[32]; *R (Bancoult)* v. *Secretary of State for Foreign and Commonwealth Affairs (No 2)* [2008] UKHL 61, [2009] 1 AC 453 at [60].

However, detrimental reliance is far from irrelevant. In *R* v. *Secretary of State for Education and Employment, ex parte Begbie* [2000] 1 WLR 1115 at 1124, Peter Gibson LJ took the view that while detrimental reliance is not an absolute prerequisite, it will be relatively rare for a legitimate expectation to arise in the absence of such reliance:

> [I]t would be wrong to understate the significance of reliance in this area of the law. It is very much the exception, rather than the rule, that detrimental reliance will not be present when the court finds unfairness in the defeating of a legitimate expectation.

This raises two points. First, the existence of detrimental reliance may be *evidentially relevant*—it may assist a claimant in satisfying the court that he really did hold the expectation in question.

Second, if the existence of the expectation is accepted by the court, detrimental reliance may be relevant when it comes to determining whether it is lawful for the public authority to frustrate the expectation. This anticipates the discussion at 6.1.4 and 6.1.5 of how courts protect expectations, but it is convenient to deal with this point here. It is a relatively simple one: when courts determine whether it is lawful for a legitimate expectation to be denied, they are ultimately concerned with whether that would be unfair. Subject to an important qualification, it stands to reason that, other things being equal, denial of the expectation is likely to be more unfair—and thus is less likely to be lawful—if the claimant has relied upon it to his detriment.

Thus, in *R (Patel)* v. *GMC* [2013] EWCA Civ 327, [2013] 1 WLR 2801, Lord Dyson MR said: 'While detrimental reliance is not a condition precedent to the existence of a substantive legitimate expectation in public law, its presence may be an influential consideration in determining what weight should be given to the legitimate expectation when evaluating the balance of fairness' (at [84]). In *Patel* the claimant relied on an assurance from the General Medical Council that a particular course that he wished to take would be acceptable to the Council for the purposes of registration with the Council. In terms of detrimental reliance the Court took into account that the claimant had spent US$40,000 on the relevant course. But it also considered detriments beyond pecuniary losses including that the claimant had put considerable time and effort into completing the course; that he had to work part-time to fund the course, which meant he had little spare time; and that this imposed strains on him and his family. All in all the Court concluded 'detrimental reliance is present in abundance' and it was a short step to finding that the Council's frustration of its promise was not capable of lawful justification and thus unlawful (at [84]).

The implications of the representation

The following case highlights a number of the factors which courts take into account in determining what an individual may be *entitled* to expect of a public authority. It also sheds light generally on how the courts view the question of legitimacy and its relationship with the implications of protecting the expectation.

R v. Department of Education and Employment, ex parte Begbie [2000] 1 WLR 1115
Court of Appeal

The claimant—Heather Begbie, then aged nine—was offered a place in February 1997 at an independent school which educated students up to age 18 (an 'all through' school) under the state-run assisted places scheme (APS), which offered financial assistance to children whose circumstances would otherwise have inhibited them from attending a fee-paying school. The Labour Party, in opposition, had indicated its intention to abolish the APS, but undertook to continue to fund children already in the scheme. After the general election in May 1997, the Education (Schools) Act 1997 was passed, abolishing the scheme. Section 2 provided that children already in primary education under the scheme would be funded only until the end of their primary education, unless the Secretary of State, in his discretion, decided that a longer period of funding should apply. The discretion was not exercised in favour of the claimant. A quashing order was sought in respect of that decision on the ground (*inter alia*) that the claimant had a legitimate expectation that, in respect of children at 'all through' schools, funding would extend beyond the end of primary education. The grounds on which the claimant relied in attempting to establish such an expectation are set out in the first paragraph of the excerpt from Peter Gibson LJ's judgment. Maurice Kay J, at first instance, had dismissed the claim; the claimant appealed to the Court of Appeal.

Peter Gibson LJ

[51] Mr. Beloff [for the claimant] argues that the statements of prominent Labour Party politicians both in opposition and in office created a legitimate expectation that Heather would enjoy the benefit of the APS until conclusion of her education at The Leys. He relies in particular in relation to the pre-election period on the letters [stating that children already in the APS would continue to be funded] of the Leader of the Opposition on 1 November 1996 to Dr. Tillson [an interested parent], on 6 December 1996 to Mrs. Treadwell [an interested grandparent], and on 27 January 1997 to Mrs. Williams [an interested parent]; Mr. Trickett's letter of 27 February 1997 [written by an MP to the parent of a child at an 'all through' school under the APS, saying that funding would continue]; and the Kilfoyle letter [from the Shadow Minister for Schools, making a statement which said that funding would continue to age 13 in the case of children at schools which educated children to age 13]. And, in relation to the post-election period, the Prime Minister's 'Evening Standard' article [in which he said, 'No child currently at private school under the scheme or who has already got a place has lost out. They will be able to continue their

education'], the Teed letter [from the Education Secretary to an interested grandparent, Mrs Teed, saying that children with places at all through schools would receive funding to age 18] and the letter of 11 March 1998 from the Secretary of State to Mrs. Begbie [saying that the undertakings previously given, regarding 'all through' schools, would be met]. Mr. Beloff accepts that under the Act of 1997 the Secretary of State has a discretion and that he was entitled to formulate a policy on how the discretion would normally be exercised, but Mr. Beloff points to the fact that … the Secretary of State could admit further exceptions to the policy. Mr. Beloff submits that the Teed letter was a promise that those in the like circumstances to Heather would be allowed to keep their assisted places until the completion of their education, but that when the Secretary of State came to exercise his discretion in Heather's case, he reneged on that promise, consistent though that promise was with the other representations, thereby defeating legitimate expectations and that constituted an abuse of power which this court should not permit.

[52] Persuasively and skilfully though these submissions were advanced by Mr. Beloff, I am not able to accept them. No doubt statements such as those made by the Leader of the Opposition before May 1997 did give rise to an expectation that children already on the APS, from which group children at 'all through' schools were not excepted, would continue to receive support in their education until it was completed, and it may be that the clear and specific statement in the Teed letter did likewise, at any rate for a time. But the question for the court is whether those statements give rise to a legitimate expectation, in the sense of an expectation which will be protected by law.

[53] I do not think that they did. As Mr. Havers Q.C., appearing with Mr. Garnham for the Crown pointed out, the starting point must be the Act of 1997. It is common ground that any expectation must yield to the terms of the statute under which the Secretary of State is required to act. S. 2(1) limits the ability of a school to provide assisted places to the circumstances provided for in subsection (2). That subsection requires a child with an assisted place who is receiving primary education to cease to hold that place at the end of the year in which the child completes his or her primary education unless discretion is exercised by the Secretary of State under para. (b). That paragraph is plainly intended to cater for the exceptional case where, having regard to particular circumstances of a particular child, it is reasonable in the eyes of the Secretary of State to make an exception for the child. As Mr. Havers submitted, if the Teed letter promise is implemented, virtually all children receiving primary education at 'all through' schools would have to be allowed to keep their assisted places till the end of their secondary education. It is not in dispute that the Secretary of State is obliged to act in an even-handed manner and that if Heather were allowed to keep her assisted place, so must all others in the like circumstances. To treat the Secretary of State as bound to implement the promise in the Teed letter for all in Heather's position would plainly be outside the contemplation of the section, and contrary to what must have been intended by s. 2(2)(b).

[54] There are further difficulties in Mr. Beloff's way. His reliance on the pre-election statements founders on the fact that such statements were not made on behalf of a public authority. In *C.C.S.U. v. Minister for the Civil Service* [1985] A.C. 374, Lord Fraser (at p. 401) said of legitimate expectations which may be protected by judicial review as a matter of public law:

'Legitimate, or reasonable, expectation may arise either from an express promise given on behalf of a public authority or from the existence of a regular practice which the claimant can reasonably expect to continue.'

[55] An opposition spokesman, even the Leader of the Opposition, does not speak on behalf of a public authority. A further difficulty relates to the effect in law of a pre-election promise by politicians anxious to win the votes of electors. In *Bromley London Borough Council* v. *Greater London Council* [1983] 1 A.C. 768 Lord Diplock (at p. 829) said that elected representatives must not treat themselves as irrevocably bound to carry out pre-announced policies contained in

election manifestos. True it is, as Mr. Beloff pointed out, that Lord Diplock a little earlier on the same page recognised that an elected member 'ought' to give considerable weight, when deciding with the other elected members whether to implement policies put forward in a manifesto, to the factor that he received the support of the electors when he fought the election on the basis of the manifesto policies. But I do not read Lord Diplock as suggesting that the obligation in the word 'ought' was a legal one or giving rise to legal effects. No case has been shown to us of the court treating such a promise as of binding effect or otherwise as having legal consequences. There are good practical reasons why this should be so. As was explained on behalf of the Labour Party on 18 July 1997 in a letter to Mrs. Cutler [an interested parent]: 'Only once the new Government had full access to information on APS numbers and projected spending, was it possible to present more details on our policy of phasing out the APS.'

[56] It is obvious that a party in opposition will not know all the facts and ramifications of a promise until it achieves office. To hold that the pre-election promises bound a newly-elected government could well be inimical to good government. I intend no encouragement to politicians to be extravagant in their pre-election promises, but when a party elected into office fails to keep its election promises, the consequences should be political and not legal.

[57] Of the post-election statements to which Mr. Beloff points, the Prime Minister's words in the Evening Standard article must be read in their context. Most of the article was concerned with the honouring by the new government of the manifesto pledge to reduce the size of infant classes in state primary schools and the reallocation of money to achieve that. It was explained that the phasing out of the APS was funding that programme. Only in the short paragraph which I have quoted was there reference to the impact on children with existing assisted places. The words used are very general and in one sense are literally true because every child on an assisted place was allowed to continue at least for a while. But no reasonable informed reader of the article could believe that it was the announcement of a change of the policy in detailed form already promulgated. And there is Ms. Mackenzie's [an APS administrator in the Department for Education and Employment] evidence that it was not so intended. Nor is there evidence of any detrimental reliance by Heather's parents on the Prime Minister's words. On the contrary, they were, very reasonably, about this time trying to obtain, through their own M.P. as well as by other means, a clear and specific statement of what the Secretary of State was intending to do about those like Heather at 'all through' schools, but the indications from government were not encouraging. Indeed one Labour M.P., Mr. Ben Bradshaw, was complaining to the Secretary of State that the government's policy was not what the Prime Minister had promised before the election.

[58] The Teed letter does contain an unambiguous representation in terms applicable to a person in Heather's position:

[59] 'Where there was provision of an "all through" school and where there has been a clear promise of a place through to the age of 18, we have agreed to honour that promise.'

[60] But it was corrected some 5 weeks later by the letter from Mr. Wardle, acting on behalf of the Secretary of State, and there is no evidence that in the interim Heather's parents relied on the representation to change their position. Further there is no evidence that the Secretary of State intended to create a new category of children who would continue to keep their assisted places and there is clear evidence from Ms. Mackenzie that the Secretary of State in the Teed letter misstated by mistake what his own policy was.

[61] For my part I cannot accept that the mere fact that a clear and unequivocal statement such as that made in the Teed letter was made is enough to establish a legitimate expectation in accordance with that statement such that the expectation cannot be allowed to be defeated. All the circumstances must be considered. Where the court is satisfied that a mistake was made by the Minister or other person making the statement, the court should be slow to fix the public authority permanently with the consequences of that mistake. That is not to say that a promise made by mistake will never have legal consequences. It may be that a mistaken statement will,

even if subsequently sought to be corrected, give rise to a legitimate expectation, whether in the person to whom the statement is made or in others who learnt of it, for example where there has been detrimental reliance on the statement before it was corrected. The court must be alive to the possibility of such unfairness to the individual by the public authority in its conduct as to amount to an abuse of power. But that is not this case.

[62] As for the letter of 11 March 1998 from the Secretary of State to Mrs. Begbie, while she sought to extract from it what he was saying, on her own account it left her confused (and she is plainly of high intelligence) and the Secretary of State never confirmed her understanding of the letter. He promised to return to her on it, but when belatedly there was a clear decision, that ran counter to any expectation which she had arising from that letter. In short, the letter contained no clear representation and could never reasonably have been relied on; nor was it because of Mrs. Begbie's wholly justified attempts to obtain clarification. I have to say that the way the Secretary of State dealt with the proper concerns of parents like Mrs. Begbie reflects no credit whatsoever on him. But I cannot say that his statements gave rise to a legitimate expectation, still less that there was an abuse of power.

Laws and Sedley LJJ agreed that the claimant had failed to establish a legitimate expectation. Appeal dismissed.

A number of factors influenced the Court in reaching the conclusion that the claimant was not entitled to expect that pupils at 'all through' schools would be funded to age 18. As well as holding that this would be inconsistent with the statutory scheme—which, it was held, envisaged that APS funding should cease upon completion of primary education in all but exceptional circumstances—Peter Gibson LJ was concerned, more generally, with the consequences of permitting pre- and post-election statements to restrict the government's discretion. This suggests that, even if the criteria of legitimacy and protection are to some extent distinct, they are also to some extent related. The Court denied the *existence* of any legitimate expectation in this case partly because the *protection*, or enforcement, of the claimed expectation would have impacted substantially upon the government's discretionary freedom in this context. Similar reasoning applied in *R (Wheeler)* v. *Office of the Prime Minister* [2008] EWHC 1409 (Admin), in which Richards LJ, giving the judgment of the Court and refusing to accept that the claimant had a legitimate expectation that a referendum would be held concerning the ratification of the Lisbon Treaty, said that 'a promise to hold a referendum lies so deep in the macro-political field that the court should not enter the relevant area at all'. This, it was said, counted against recognizing a legitimate expectation in such circumstances in the first place.

6.1.4 Procedural protection

A court may protect an individual's expectation by requiring a fair procedure to be followed before the public authority makes the relevant decision. This mode of protection may result in the fulfilment of the claimant's legitimate expectation (if the claimant expected, or was only entitled to expect, procedural fairness); alternatively, it may be conferred in a situation where the court determines that, while the claimant reasonably expected a particular substantive outcome, competing demands based on the preservation of discretionary freedom dictate that the decision-maker, having considered the claimant's views in a procedurally fair manner, should be able to pursue a different course.

It is important to note the relationship between procedural protection of legitimate expectations and the duty to act fairly considered in ch 10. Both secure procedurally fair treatment for the individual. As we explain in ch 10, the duty to act fairly is flexible: its precise meaning turns on the context, so different situations will require different levels of fairness. The principle of legitimate expectation may well influence the precise level of fairness required in any given case—a point which Lord Denning MR recognized in *Schmidt v. Secretary of State for Home Affairs* [1969] 2 Ch 149 at 169. Rejecting the notion that the principles of natural justice applied only to 'judicial' as opposed to 'administrative' powers (on which see 10.2), Lord Denning said that

> an administrative body may, in a proper case, be bound to give a person who is affected by their decision an opportunity of making representations. It all depends on whether he has some right or interest, or, I would add, some legitimate expectation, of which it would not be fair to deprive him without hearing what he has to say.

For instance, the general context (taking account of the rights or interests of the claimant liable to be affected by the decision) may indicate that the claimant is entitled only to make written representations before a decision which affects him is taken. However, if the decision-maker has undertaken to give people in the claimant's situation an oral hearing (which is a more ample form of fairness) then such a hearing must be offered. It follows that the doctrine of legitimate expectation may entitle the claimant to be treated in a particular procedural way when—absent the expectation—*no such entitlement* would arise; or a legitimate expectation may entitle the claimant to a *more generous* form of procedural fairness than he would otherwise be entitled to. Albeit it is important to note that as the range of interests which are liable to trigger general duties of procedural fairness have expanded, and procedural protection under this general duty has become more ample over time (see ch 10), those classes of case where a claimant need resort to legitimate expectations to bolster procedural protection have narrowed.

The decision of the Privy Council in *Attorney-General of Hong Kong* v. *Ng Yuen Shiu* [1983] 2 AC 629 illustrates how legitimate expectations may bolster procedural protection beyond that which would otherwise be enjoyed. The Hong Kong government issued a statement saying that a certain category of illegal immigrants—into which the claimant fell—would be interviewed before any decision whether to deport them was taken. In the event, however, a decision to deport the claimant was taken *without* granting him an interview. The Privy Council assumed, without deciding, that the Hong Kong Court of Appeal had been right to conclude that the claimant had no free-standing right to a hearing, and focused on the question whether he had a legitimate expectation to be heard (by means of an interview). It held that he did. Giving the judgment of the Judicial Committee, Lord Fraser said (at 638) that the justification for holding the Hong Kong government to its undertaking

> is primarily that, when a public authority has promised to follow a certain procedure, it is in the interest of good administration that it should act fairly and should implement its promise, so long as implementation does not interfere with its statutory duty. The principle is also justified by the further consideration that, when the promise was made, the authority must have considered that it would be assisted in discharging its duty fairly by any representations from interested parties and as a general rule that is correct.

We similarly find strong procedural protection afforded by the doctrine of legitimate expectations in *R (Greenpeace Ltd) v. Secretary of State for Trade and Industry* [2007] EWHC 311 (Admin), [2007] Env LR 29. In 2003, the defendant Minister issued a 'white paper' containing the following passage (emphasis in original):

> This white paper does not contain proposals for building new nuclear power stations. However, we do not rule out the possibility that at some point in the future new nuclear build might be necessary if we are to meet our carbon targets. *Before any decision to proceed with the building of new nuclear power stations, there would need to be the fullest public consultation and the publication of a white paper setting out the Government's proposals.*

But in 2006 the Minister issued a consultation paper which said this:

> The [2003] White Paper left open the option of nuclear new build. Are there particular considerations that should apply to nuclear as the government re-examines the issues bearing on new build, including long-term liabilities and waste management? If so, what are these, and how should the government address them?

Following that consultation exercise, the government announced an in-principle decision that a new generation of nuclear power stations should be built. But the claimant argued that the 2006 consultation exercise failed to meet the undertaking in the 2003 white paper: the former sought consultees' views on *what the government should examine* when considering whether to build new nuclear stations, and did not—as the 2003 white paper seemed to promise—invite views on the *substantive issue whether new nuclear stations should be built.* The claimant thus complained that consultees had been misled as to the nature of the 2006 consultation exercise: far more effort would have been made to set out the case against nuclear energy if it had been appreciated that that exercise was supposed to constitute the 'fullest public consultation' promised in 2003. Sullivan J found for the claimant. A legitimate expectation had been generated by the 2003 white paper which had not been met by the 2006 consultation. A declaration was therefore granted to the effect that the in-principle decision concerning nuclear power was unlawful.

6.1.5 Substantive protection

The substantive protection of (necessarily substantive) legitimate expectations is a more controversial matter. Nonetheless, over the past 15 years substantive legitimate expectations have emerged as a staple of English administrative law, consonant with warmer attitudes to substantive review more generally (see ch 8). Procedural protection may potentially cause significant delay and expense to the decision-maker, but it does not ultimately reduce the scope of its discretion: it restricts *how* it makes decisions, but not *what* decisions it is entitled to make. In contrast, substantive protection impacts upon the range of options open to the decision-maker: the enforcement of substantive expectations may ultimately result in the removal of the public authority's discretion in cases where the court concludes that the only lawful option is for the expectation to be satisfied. This raises difficult constitutional questions about the respective roles of courts and decision-makers.

The extent to which judicial protection of substantive legitimate expectations risks usurping the executive's role turns on two key factors: the *circumstances* in which substantive legitimate expectations can arise in the first place, and the *latitude* which courts are prepared to grant public bodies in deciding whether the public interest justifies dashing a substantive expectation. Both of these points require discussion, but we begin this section with the foundational case on substantive legitimate expectation.

R v. North and East Devon Health Authority, ex parte Coughlan [2001] QB 213
Court of Appeal

The claimant was seriously injured in a road traffic accident in 1971, following which she became a long-term patient at Newcourt Hospital. In 1993 the defendant's predecessor, Exeter Health Authority, moved the claimant and several other residents to Mardon House, a new, purpose-built facility. The Newcourt residents consented to this because they had been assured that they would be able to remain at Mardon House 'for as long as they wished to stay there': it would be their 'home for life'. However, in 1998, the defendant resolved to close Mardon House, asserting that it had become 'prohibitively expensive' to run. The claimant argued (*inter alia*), successfully at first instance, that the 'home for life' promise gave rise to a substantive legitimate expectation which should be protected substantively. The Health Authority appealed.

Lord Woolf MR (giving the judgment of the Court)

[55] ... [I]t is necessary to begin by examining the court's role where what is in issue is a promise as to how it would behave in the future made by a public body when exercising a statutory function. In the past it would have been argued that the promise was to be ignored since it could not have any effect on how the public body exercised its judgment in what it thought was the public interest. Today such an argument would have no prospect of success ...

[56] What is still the subject of some controversy is the court's role when a member of the public, as a result of a promise or other conduct, has a legitimate expectation that he will be treated in one way and the public body wishes to treat him or her in a different way. Here the starting point has to be to ask what in the circumstances the member of the public could legitimately expect. In the words of Lord Scarman in *Re Findlay* [1985] AC 318 at p 338, 'But what was their *legitimate* expectation?' Where there is a dispute as to this, the dispute has to be determined by the court, as happened in *Findlay*. This can involve a detailed examination of the precise terms of the promise or representation made, the circumstances in which the promise was made and the nature of the statutory or other discretion.

[57] There are at least three possible outcomes. (a) The court may decide that the public authority is only required to bear in mind its previous policy or other representation, giving it the weight it thinks right, but no more, before deciding whether to change course. Here the court is confined to reviewing the decision on *Wednesbury* grounds. This has been held to be the effect of changes of policy in cases involving the early release of prisoners (see *Re Findlay* [1985] AC 318; *R v. Home Secretary ex parte Hargreaves* [1997] 1 WLR 906). (b) On the other hand the court may decide that the promise or practice induces a legitimate expectation of, for example, being consulted before a particular decision is taken. Here it is uncontentious that the court itself will require *the opportunity for consultation* to be given unless there is an overriding reason to resile from it (see *A-G for Hong Kong* v. *Ng Yuen Shiu* [1983] 2 AC 629) in which case the court will itself judge the adequacy of the reason advanced for the change of policy, taking into account what fairness requires. (c) Where the court considers that a lawful promise or practice has induced a legitimate expectation of a *benefit which is substantive*, not simply procedural, authority now establishes that here too the court will in a proper case decide whether to

frustrate the expectation is so unfair that to take a new and different course will amount to an abuse of power. Here, once the legitimacy of the expectation is established, the court will have the task of weighing the requirements of fairness against any overriding interest relied upon for the change of policy.

[58] The court having decided which of the categories is appropriate, the court's role in the case of the second and third categories is different from that in the first. In the case of the first, the court is restricted to reviewing the decision on conventional grounds. The test will be rationality and whether the public body has given proper weight to the implications of not fulfilling the promise. In the case of the second category the court's task is the conventional one of determining whether the decision was procedurally fair. In the case of the third, the court has when necessary to determine whether there is a sufficient overriding interest to justify a departure from what has been previously promised.

[59] In many cases the difficult task will be to decide into which category the decision should be allotted. In what is still a developing field of law, attention will have to be given to what it is in the first category of case which limits the applicant's legitimate expectation (in Lord Scarman's words in *Re Findlay*) to an expectation that whatever policy is in force at the time will be applied to him. As to the second and third categories, the difficulty of segregating the procedural from the substantive is illustrated by the line of cases arising out of decisions of justices not to commit a defendant to the Crown Court for sentence, or assurances given to a defendant by the court: here to resile from such a decision or assurance may involve the breach of legitimate expectation. (See *R v Reilly* [1985] 1 Cr. App. R (S) 273, 276; *R v Southampton Magistrates Court* [1994] Cr. App. R (S) 778, 781–2.) No attempt is made in those cases, rightly in our view, to draw the distinction. Nevertheless, most cases of an enforceable expectation of a substantive benefit (the third category) are likely in the nature of things to be cases where the expectation is confined to one person or a few people, giving the promise or representation the character of a contract. We recognise that the courts' role in relation to the third category is still controversial; but, as we hope to show, it is now clarified by authority.

[60] We consider that [counsel] are correct, as was the judge, in regarding the facts of this case as coming into the third category.

Having reached this conclusion, the Court carried out the balancing test, concluding that the financial arguments advanced by the Health Authority were insufficient to justify dashing the legitimate expectation. Appeal dismissed.

Coughlan was a highly significant decision for two main reasons. First, it established beyond doubt that courts would *recognize substantive legitimate expectations*. Second, it demonstrated judicial willingness to *protect such expectations rigorously*. Prior to *Coughlan*, there had been sharp disagreement over how courts should review government decisions to frustrate substantive expectations. Should the court, as Sedley J had suggested in *R v. Ministry of Agriculture Fisheries and Food, ex parte Hamble (Offshore) Fisheries Ltd* [1995] 2 All ER 714, adopt a rigorous approach, precluding frustration of substantive expectations unless itself satisfied that the public interest in doing so outweighs the unfairness likely to be thereby occasioned to the individual? Or was such a highly intensive form of review heretical, as Hirst LJ asserted in *R v. Secretary of State for the Home Department, ex parte Hargreaves* [1997] 1 WLR 906 at 921, such that decision-makers should be free to frustrate substantive expectations unless such action would be wholly unreasonable? The importance of the distinction between these two approaches is considerable: the *Hargreaves* reasonableness test gave decision-makers wide discretion to frustrate expectations, whereas the *Hamble Fisheries* approach gave the courts wide powers to protect such expectations.

Coughlan, at first glance, appears to lay this debate to rest. The Court of Appeal subjected the decision to close Mardon House to a form of high intensity review akin to that advocated in *Hamble Fisheries*. The judges weighed *for themselves* the financial arguments advanced by the Health Authority against the unfairness that closure would occasion to the claimant, concluding that the former were insufficient to outweigh the latter—and that closure was therefore unlawful. This form of review went well beyond the comparatively tame unreasonableness test advocated in *Hargreaves*, and is particularly striking given the case concerned decisions over distribution of scarce resources, which are, on any orthodox view, quintessentially for the executive branch. More generally, once a case is placed within Lord Woolf's category (c), it is for the court to decide 'whether the consequent frustration of the individual's expectation is so unfair as to be a misuse of the authority's power' (*Coughlan* at [82]). No wonder then that Sedley LJ has since pronounced that the description of his judgment in *Hamble* as 'heretical' has now been shown to have been 'mistaken': *R (Niazi)* v. *Secretary of State for the Home Department* [2008] EWCA Civ 755 at [69].

However, the way in which the Court approached its task in *Coughlan* raises concerns; specifically that there is a real risk of the distinction between appeal and review dissolving. Just how pressing these concerns are depends, however, on three further factors. We will see that, taken in combination, these factors make it at least *possible* for the doctrine of substantive legitimate expectation to operate in a way that properly acknowledges the respective constitutional responsibilities of the judicial and executive branches.

When will substantive legitimate expectations be recognized?

The first point, then, is that *the courts will recognize substantive legitimate expectations only in limited circumstances*. We have already looked (see 6.1.2) at the general criteria which determine whether a legitimate expectation arises. But it is important to note that particularly stringent criteria apply to substantive expectations. *Coughlan* is a case in point: it concerned an *individualized promise* rather than, say, a general statement of policy or general practice. In the earlier excerpt (at [59]), Lord Woolf emphasized that it was only in relation to specific undertakings that substantive expectations (at least of the type falling into his category (c)) were likely to arise. He did not explain why, but others have subsequently sought to do so. Sales [2006] JR 186 argues that the courts are correct to exercise greater caution before recognizing a substantive expectation. The need for such caution arises, he says, from the differential results that may follow from such recognition. Holding a public body bound to a procedural expectation does not ultimately detract from the range of policy choices open to it; but the same is not true if a public body is held to a substantive expectation, as *Coughlan* (in which the Health Authority had to keep Mardon House open) illustrates. This prompts Sales (at 189) to argue that

> where one is dealing with substantive legitimate expectations, the courts should focus very carefully on factors which affect the quality of the advance 'decision' taken by the public authority, and the appropriateness of treating that advance 'decision' as in some sense binding upon the public authority when taking an actual decision in a concrete case in the present. The more the public authority has had, at the advance stage, clearly in mind the particular ramifications of its representations or policy for the type of concrete decision which it eventually has to take and has

deliberately chosen a particular outcome, the more readily one would regard it is as legitimate for the courts (having regard to other considerations, including the general desirability of public authorities abiding by pre-declared policies) to treat the public authority as in some sense bound by that advance 'decision'. Conversely, the further away one is from that situation, the stronger the argument for retention of freedom of action for the public authority in the light of full information about current circumstances.

The logic of this argument suggests that substantive expectations will more commonly arise in relation to specific promises made to individuals or small groups, as opposed to generalized policy statements.

As the case law has developed it has come into alignment with Sales' preferred approach. In *R (Patel)* v. *GMC* [2013] EWCA Civ 327, [2013] 1 WLR 2801, the Court, following statements by Laws LJ in *Niazi* [2008] EWCA Civ 755, said that while 'in theory there may be no limit to the number of beneficiaries of a promise for the purpose of a substantive legitimate expectation, in reality it is likely to be small if the expectation is to be upheld because ... it is difficult to imagine a case in which government will be held legally bound by a representation or undertaking made generally or to a diverse class' (at [50]). The only circumstances where a representation to a large group might generate a legitimate expectation, however unlikely, is where the decision-maker, before issuing such a statement, has had a reasonable opportunity to evaluate the likely ramifications of making good on the promise concerned. But it is important to note that even if expectations are recognized in such circumstances, it will likely prove relatively easy for the decision-maker to justify defeating those expectations. As the Court added in *Patel*, 'the broader the class claiming the benefit of the expectation the more likely it is that the supervening public interest will be held to justify the change of position of which complaint is made' (at [50]). It is to the issue of justifications that we now turn.

What is the standard of review?

Since *Coughlan*, it has become clear that *not all substantive expectation cases will attract the high-intensity review adopted in that case*. Rather, the courts must ask, what is 'the appropriate standard of review' for the case before them: *Patel* at [60]. In other words, the intensity of review will vary depending on the particular circumstances of the case. As such, the courts have now moved beyond the 'categorical' approach espoused in *Coughlan*, to a 'sliding scale' approach. In the most significant decision on substantive legitimate expectations of recent years, *Patel*, the Court of Appeal (at [61]) endorsed and applied the following statement of principle from Laws LJ in *R* v. *Department of Education and Employment, ex parte Begbie* [2000] 1 WLR 1115 at 1130–1:

As it seems to me the first and third categories explained in *Coughlan* are not hermetically sealed. The facts of the case, viewed always in their statutory context, will steer the court to a more or less intrusive quality of review. In some cases a change of tack by a public authority, though unfair from the applicant's stance, may involve questions of general policy affecting the public at large or a significant section of it (including interests not represented before the court); here the judges may well be in no position to adjudicate save at most on a bare *Wednesbury* basis, without themselves donning the garb of policy-maker, which they cannot wear. The local government finance cases, such as *R v Secretary of State, Ex p Hammersmith* [1991] 1 AC 521, exemplify this. As Wade &

Forsyth observe (*Administrative Law*, 7th ed (1994), p 404): 'Ministers' decisions on important matters of policy are not on that account sacrosanct against the unreasonableness doctrine, though the court must take special care, for constitutional reasons, not to pass judgment on action which is essentially political.'

In other cases the act or omission complained of may take place on a much smaller stage, with far fewer players. Here, with respect, lies the importance of the fact in *Coughlan* that few individuals were affected by the promise in question. The case's facts may be discrete and limited, having no implications for an innominate class of persons. There may be no wide-ranging issues of general policy, or none with multi-layered effects, upon whose merits the court is asked to embark. The court may be able to envisage clearly and with sufficient certainty what the full consequences will be of any order it makes. In such a case the court's condemnation of what is done as an abuse of power, justifiable (or rather, falling to be relieved of its character as abusive) only if an overriding public interest is shown of which the court is the judge, offers no offence to the claims of democratic power.

There will of course be a multitude of cases falling within these extremes, or sharing the characteristics of one or other. The more the decision challenged lies in what may inelegantly be called the macro-political field, the less intrusive will be the court's supervision. More than this: in that field, true abuse of power is less likely to be found, since within it changes of policy, fuelled by broad conceptions of the public interest, may more readily be accepted as taking precedence over the interests of groups which enjoyed expectations generated by an earlier policy.

Thus the court will be called upon to place the case before them along the spectrum identified by Laws LJ, according to key features of the case. Where the matters raised by the case lie in the macro-political field the courts will adopt a light touch approach, only intervening if the authority has acted outrageously or with patent irrationality in frustrating the claimant's expectations. In other cases, for example where the expectation is of great significance to the individual and they would suffer terribly if it were frustrated, and where the number of persons affected by the ruling would be small and there are no considerations of high policy at stake, a more intrusive approach may be taken and the courts may require very strong justifications before allowing the expectation to be lawfully frustrated.

It is worth noting that, as the reader may have gathered, while the guidance offered by Laws LJ is helpful, it is also somewhat open-ended. Often cases can be framed in different ways, it not being clear which way is to be preferred. Consider *Coughlan*, in which a very intensive approach to review was adopted. One might criticize the Court of Appeal's approach on the basis that the case concerned policy questions over distribution of scarce resources so that a light touch or deferential approach to review ought to have been adopted. On the other hand, those who wish to defend the Court's approach may emphasize that the number of persons affected by the ruling was small and that what was at stake for those affected was of great significance. Perhaps the correct approach, given these conflicting concerns, would have been for a moderately intensive approach to be taken. But this does not exactly provide a great deal of guidance as to how the reviewing court should approach its task.

So far we have considered how courts should calibrate the intensity of review to be applied. Next we need to consider the general methodology that courts apply to assess the legality of frustration of a substantive legitimate expectation. It is increasingly clear that courts will apply a balancing approach, whereby the court examines whether countervailing public interest factors justify frustration of the legitimate expectation. In *Patel*, the Court endorsed the following approach adopted by the Privy Council in *Paponette* v. *Attorney General of Trinidad and* Tobago [2010] UKPC 32, [2012] 1 AC 1 at [36]–[37]:

> The critical question in this part of the case is whether there was a sufficient public interest to override the legitimate expectation to which the representations had given rise. This raises the further question as to the burden of proof in cases of frustration of a legitimate expectation.
>
> The initial burden lies on the applicant to prove the legitimacy of his expectation. This means that in a claim based on a promise, the applicant must prove the promise and that it was clear and unambiguous and devoid of relevant qualification. If he wishes to reinforce his case by saying that he relied on the promise to his detriment, then obviously he must prove that too. Once these elements have been proved by the applicant, however, the onus shifts to the authority to justify the frustration of the legitimate expectation. It is for the authority to identify any overriding interest on which it relies to justify the frustration of the expectation. It will then be a matter for the court to weigh the requirements of fairness against that interest.

This approach followed on from Laws LJ's obiter statements in *R (Nadarajah)* v. *Secretary of State for the Home Department* [2005] EWCA Civ 1363 at [68] that

> a public body's promise or practice as to future conduct may only be denied ... in circumstances where to do so is the public body's legal duty, or is otherwise, to use a now familiar vocabulary, a proportionate response (of which the court is the judge, or the last judge) having regard to a legitimate aim pursued by the public body in the public interest.

Thus the general method to be applied to test whether a substantive expectation may be lawfully frustrated is a balancing approach. As Laws LJ observed in *Nadarajah*, this is in essence a proportionality test (on which see further ch 8).

How does this balancing method marry up or interact with the sliding scale approach to the intensity of review elaborated by Laws LJ in *Begbie*? The answer is that the court must in every case scrutinize the claimed public interest justification put forward by the defendant, but the intensity of scrutiny that the court will apply will vary according to the factors identified by Laws LJ in *Begbie*.

Thus if the case is categorized as one within the macro-political field the courts will generally be willing to accept the balance struck by the administrative decision-maker, unless they consider the balance to be wholly unreasonable or outrageous. Put another way, they will not require much convincing before they will accept the defendant's justification for frustrating the expectation. While it is increasingly stated in substantive legitimate expectation cases that the court must decide for itself whether there is a sufficient overriding interest to justify a departure from what has previously been promised, the reality is that in cases in the macro-political field the courts do not decide the balance for themselves but exercise a secondary judgement over whether the balance struck by the decision-maker was wholly irrational. However, it is important to emphasize that even in this class of case, in which the court will be unlikely to impugn the decision, the defendant must put forward *some* justification for frustrating the expectation—it must have a reason. In *Paponette*, the Court rejected the proposition that it ought to infer that the defendant had a justification for frustrating the claimant's legitimate expectation from the bare fact the defendant had acted in breach of that expectation: 'So expressed this proposition would destroy the doctrine of substantive legitimate expectation altogether, since it would always be an answer to a claim that an act was in breach of a legitimate expectation that the act must have been in furtherance of an overriding public interest' (at [41]).

In contrast to cases raising matters in the macro-political field, for a case which falls at the other end of the spectrum, the courts will *themselves* weigh competing interests and *themselves* determine objectively where the balance lies between individual and public interests. The defendant will not only be required to put forward a justification for frustrating the expectation, but the purported justification will be subjected to searching judicial scrutiny and the court will form its own view of whether the justification holds water. In order to convince the court, the decision-maker may need to provide evidence to show that its public interest reasons for denying the legitimate expectation are grounded in fact rather than assertion. If the decision-maker is unable to produce such evidence then the court will likely infer that there is no good justification for frustrating the expectation.

In considering whether a particular decision to frustrate a legitimate expectation is justifiable or not, the courts will place weight on two factors in particular, which will operate to make it more or less likely that the courts will consider the frustration of the expectation lawfully justified.

The first is whether the decision-maker took the legitimate expectation into account in their decision-making and considered for themselves whether the detriment to the individual was outweighed by public interest considerations. First, if a decision-maker fails to consider the expectation, then the decision is liable to be impugned for failure to take into account a relevant consideration. Thus, in *Patel*, the General Medical Council's failure to consider how its change in policy would detrimentally affect those to whom the Council had given assurances based on a former policy provided a sufficient basis for the Court to quash the decision, without needing to engage in a balancing exercise. (See similarly *R (Bibi)* v. *Newnham LBC* [2001] EWCA Civ 607, [2002] 1 WLR 237 at [49], [51]; *Paponette* at [46]). Second, where the defendant has failed to weigh the unfairness to the claimant of frustrating their expectation against public interest goals, its decision to frustrate an expectation is less likely to be considered justifiable and afforded respect by a court, making judicial intervention more likely. Thus, in *Patel*, the Court said that while, in conducting the balancing exercise, it would usually afford the decisions of a specialist body such as the GMC 'a considerable degree of respect', in this case the GMC had offered no reasoning to explain key premises of its decision nor was there any serious consideration of how it might mitigate the impact of its change of policy on those in the claimant's position. These omissions made it more likely that the court would intervene on the basis that the defendant had failed to justify its decision to frustrate the claimant's expectations. As the Board observed in *Paponette* (at [42]), if reasons are not articulated by the decision-maker then it will be harder for the court to conclude that justifications exist for frustrating the expectation.

The second factor on which courts place weight when determining whether frustration of a legitimate expectation is justifiable, is the extent to which the defendant has adopted some measures which serve to mitigate the impact of its decision on those whose expectations are frustrated by it. For example, in *Patel*, the fact that the GMC had not put in place any 'mitigating measures' in changing policy, such as transitional provisions to lessen the impact of the change on those with legitimate expectations who would be negatively affected by the change, was one factor telling against lawful justification. Provision for measures such as a fair hearing or the making of transitional arrangements to 'cushion those who would otherwise be unfairly affected by a change of policy' (*Niazi* at [70]), operate to lessen the degree of prejudice to the claimant that calls to be justified; put another way, if a defendant adopts such measures it shall be easier for them to justify frustration of the expectation.

In the alternative it is possible that the court may make adoption of mitigating measures a condition precedent of upholding the defendant's decision as lawful. For example, in *Jones* v. *Environment Agency* [2005] EWHC 2270 (Admin), the claimant was held to have a substantive legitimate expectation that a licence would not be required for carrying out certain works. Ouseley J concluded that the legitimate expectation could lawfully be frustrated—the defendant could issue a notice requiring the removal of the works in order to compel the claimant to seek a licence—but only if at least a year's notice was given. In other circumstances, a court may require temporary continuation of promised benefits in order to allow the claimant a period of adjustment before the benefit is ultimately withdrawn.

In summary, there will be some cases in which the courts will take it upon themselves to strike the balance between individual and public interests and require very convincing justifications for frustration of a legitimate expectation, and some cases in which the courts will adopt the traditional *Wednesbury* standard, only intervening if the balance struck by the decision-maker was patently irrational. However, the majority of cases will fall somewhere in between. In such cases a decision to frustrate a substantive expectation will more likely than not be held lawful if the decision-maker has (i) taken the expectation into account as part of its decision-making process; (ii) reached a broadly reasonable conclusion concerning the balance between the public and private interests at stake (even if this is not the balance the court would have struck), backed by a statement of reasons; and (iii) taken some steps to mitigate the negative effects for the claimant of frustrating their legitimate expectation, or at least considered whether such steps are feasible.

What will the remedial outcome be?

It has not always been apparent that the remedial approach in legitimate expectation cases is guided by consistently applied principles. We would suggest that the remedial outcome in a substantive legitimate expectation case should turn upon a number of factors.

If the court concludes that the decision to frustrate the expectation is unlawful then it should generally follow that the decision will be quashed and the decision-maker will have no option but to respect the expectation by doing whatever was promised. This should most clearly be the outcome where the court has adopted an intensive approach to review and struck the balance itself, finding the decision unlawful. In such a case a finding that there is no justification for frustrating the expectation logically means that the expectation should be satisfied. Note that the burdens of such a finding may be limited as the court may hold that the expectation only has to be fulfilled *in the claimant's case*, even if it may be the case that there are other similarly placed individuals: *Patel* at [93]. However, where the case is one that falls at the macro-political end of the spectrum it is not obvious that the decision-maker should necessarily be required to fulfil the promise. In such a case the court would apply a *Wednesbury* standard of review, and a finding that the decision-maker had acted with patent irrationality would not exclude the possibility that given the opportunity to think again the decision-maker may be able to locate a not wholly irrational basis for frustrating the expectation. Further, given that the case will be one in the macro-political field, the issues raised will necessarily be ones far removed from the constitutional responsibilities of courts and ordinary judicial experience. This suggests that rather than the court compelling enforcement of the expectation it may be more appropriate for the court to require the decision-maker to reconsider his or her decision, ensuring that he or she takes the legitimate expectation into account and provides reasons for the ultimate decision. For an example of such an approach in action, see *R (Bibi)* v. *Newham LBC* [2001] EWCA Civ 607, [2002] 1 WLR 237 at [64]–[69].

We note that even in cases where the court itself strikes the balance and finds frustration of the expectation cannot be justified, relief on review is discretionary and the court may refuse to exercise its discretion to require actual fulfillment of the promise. For example, given the effluxion of time it may be that fulfillment of the promise is now practically impossible. In such a case the court may require the decision-maker to consider alternative means of satisfying the expectation, such as compensation.

If the court concludes that the legitimate expectation can lawfully be frustrated, but only if some condition precedent has been fulfilled (such as a year's notice, as in *Jones*), the court will quash the decision to frustrate the expectation while leaving open the possibility of the decision-maker frustrating it in the future once the relevant condition has been complied with.

6.2 Unlawfully created expectations

6.2.1 Introduction

We turn now to the problematic question of 'unlawfully created expectations'. We use this term to describe both expectations as to conduct which is *ultra vires* the agency concerned, and expectations as to conduct which, although *intra vires* the relevant agency, arise through representations issued by officials unauthorized to make them. As we explain later, a relatively recent House of Lords decision has signalled the potential for a change of approach in this area. However, it remains necessary to examine the older cases in order to understand the conflicting policy interests that are in play.

6.2.2 Fairness to the individual

The importance in this context of securing fairness for the individual appealed notably to Lord Denning. In a number of cases he sought to safeguard individuals by invoking the doctrine of estoppel, according to which, if a representation is made to an individual who then relies upon the accuracy of the statement to his detriment, it will generally be impermissible for the representor to derogate from the statement. This principle operates in a number of situations in private law, *eg* it can prevent the enforcement of contractual terms which one party has led another to believe will be waived (see *Central London Property Trust Ltd* v. *High Trees House Ltd* [1947] KB 130), while the doctrine of proprietary estoppel may permit an individual who has been promised an interest in land to enforce the promise if it has been detrimentally relied upon (see *Cobbe* v. *Yeoman's Row Management Ltd* [2008] UKHL 55, [2008] 1 WLR 1752; *Thorner* v. *Major* [2009] UKHL 18, [2009] 1 WLR 776). However, we will see later that it is open to debate whether estoppel is suited to the public law context. Such concerns did not, however, trouble Denning J in the following case.

Robertson v. *Minister of Pensions* [1949] 1 KB 227
King's Bench Division

The War Office originally had jurisdiction over all claims in respect of disability attributable to war service. By a Royal Warrant of 1940 the jurisdiction over claims in respect of service after 3 September 1939 was transferred to the Ministry of Pensions. In 1941 the appellant, a serving officer, wrote to the War Office regarding a disability of his which had resulted from an injury in December 1939. He received a reply stating, 'Your disability has been accepted as attributable to military service.' Relying on that statement, he did not obtain an independent medical opinion on his own behalf. The Minister of Pensions later decided that the disability was not attributable to war service but to an injury sustained in 1927. On appeal from a pensions tribunal:

Denning J

... The assurance was given to the appellant in these explicit words: 'Your disability has been accepted as attributable to military service.' That was, on the face of it, an authoritative decision intended to be binding and intended to be acted on. Even if the appellant had studied the Royal Warrant in every detail there would have been nothing to lead him to suppose that the decision was not authoritative. He might well presume that the army medical board was recognized by the Minister of Pensions for the purpose of certifying his disability to be attributable to military service under the Royal Warrant of June, 1940: and that their certificate of attributability was sufficient for the purpose of the warrant.

What then is the result in law? If this was a question between subjects, a person who gave such an assurance as that contained in the War Office letter would be held bound by it unless he could show that it was made under the influence of a mistake or induced by a misrepresentation or the like. No such defence is made here. There are many cases in the books which establish that an unequivocal acceptance of liability will be enforced if it is intended to be binding, intended to be acted on, and is in fact acted on ...

... Is the Minister of Pensions bound by the War Office letter? I think he is. The appellant thought, no doubt, that, as he was serving in the army, his claim to attributability would be dealt with by or through the War Office. So he wrote to the War Office. The War Office did not refer him to the Minister of Pensions. They assumed authority over the matter and assured the appellant that his disability had been accepted as attributable to military service. He was entitled to assume that they had consulted any other departments that might be concerned, such as the Ministry of Pensions, before they gave him the assurance. He was entitled to assume that the board of medical officers who examined him were recognized by the Minister of Pensions for the purpose of giving certificates as to attributability. Can it be seriously suggested that, having got that assurance, he was not entitled to rely on it? In my opinion if a government department in its dealings with a subject takes it upon itself to assume authority upon a matter with which he is concerned, he is entitled to rely upon it having the authority which it assumes. He does not know, and cannot be expected to know, the limits of its authority. The department itself is clearly bound, and as it is but an agent for the Crown, it binds the Crown also; and as the Crown is bound, so are the other departments, for they also are but agents of the Crown. The War Office letter therefore binds the Crown, and, through the Crown, it binds the Minister of Pensions. The function of the Minister of Pensions is to administer the Royal Warrant issued by the Crown, and he must so administer it as to honour all assurances given by or on behalf of the Crown.

In my opinion therefore the finding of the tribunal that the disability was not attributable to war service must be set aside.

Appeal allowed.

A similar approach was adopted in *Lever Finance Ltd* v. *Westminster (City) London Borough Council* [1971] 1 QB 222, in which the claimant was told by a planning officer that proposed changes to a housing development were not material, and that it was therefore unnecessary to obtain further planning consent. Lord Denning MR (with whose judgment Megaw LJ agreed) reasoned (at 230) that it was not later open to the planning authority to resile from the officer's statement, given that the latter had acted with 'ostensible authority'.

QUESTIONS

- What problems might attend the adoption of Lord Denning's approach?
- Should the existence of 'ostensible authority' depend on the behaviour of the party who assumes authority, or the behaviour of the party who is actually empowered to deal with the matter?

One further point should be noted about *Robertson*. Denning J's analysis was predicated on his view that, in appropriate circumstances, one government department's lack of authority should not prevent its undertaking from binding other departments. This, in turn, assumed that the two departments were legally distinct entities. If they had in fact merely been different emanations of a single legal entity, estoppel would have been beside the point: the War Office's letter would have bound the Ministry of Pensions not because the latter would have been estopped, but because the two bodies would legally have been one and the same entity. It is worth noting, therefore, that in *R (BAPIO Action Ltd)* v. *Secretary of State for the Home Department* [2008] UKHL 27, [2008] 1 AC 1003, Lord Rodger said (at [33]) that 'the executive power of the Crown is, in practice, exercised by a single body of ministers, making up Her Majesty's Government', such that an undertaking given by one Minister could generate a legitimate expectation concerning the exercise of powers falling within another Minister's remit. (Lord Mance implicitly accepted that view, although Lord Scott (at [27]–[28]) explicitly refuted it.)

6.2.3 Constitutionality and the public interest

Not everyone shared Lord Denning's enthusiasm for introducing estoppel into public law. For instance, in *Southend-on-Sea Corporation* v. *Hodgson (Wickford) Ltd* [1962] 1 QB 416, in which the Divisional Court refused to hold a public body bound by its official's unauthorized representation as to whether the claimant needed planning consent in order to put premises to a particular use, Lord Parker CJ (at 424) said that

> in a case of discretion there is a duty under the statute to exercise a free and unhindered discretion. There is a long line of cases to which we have not been specifically referred which lay down that a public authority cannot by contract fetter the exercise of its discretion. Similarly, as it seems to me, an estoppel cannot be raised to prevent or hinder the exercise of the discretion.

Against this background, the Court of Appeal, in *Western Fish Products Ltd* v. *Penwith District Council* [1981] 2 All ER 204, set out a very limited approach to estoppel in public law. The claimant purchased a disused factory and began building work, believing this to be permissible on the strength of a statement made to it by a representative of the local planning authority. When the Council later required the claimant to apply for planning permission and an established use certificate, neither of which were ultimately forthcoming, the claimant asserted that the Council was estopped by its representative's assurances from disputing the claimant's right to use the land in the way it desired. Giving the judgment of the Court of Appeal, Megaw LJ concluded that, properly interpreted, the representative's statement did nothing more than confirm the right to use the land as it had previously been used, and did not amount to a representation that the claimant could use it in the proposed way without securing planning permission. However, he continued (at 217):

> Even if we had been satisfied that the defendant council through their officers had represented to the plaintiffs that all they wanted to do on the ... site could be done because of the existing uses, planning permission being required only for new buildings and structures, and that they had acted to their detriment to the knowledge of the defendant council because of their representations, their claim would still have failed.

His Lordship then proceeded to articulate a highly restrictive approach to estoppel in public law. He considered *Lever Finance Ltd* v. *Westminster (City) London Borough Council* [1971] 1 QB 222, in which, as noted at 6.2.2, Lord Denning MR had taken a very broad view, saying (at 220–1):

> In our judgment [*Lever Finance*] is not an authority for the proposition that every representation made by a planning officer within his ostensible authority binds the planning authority which employs him. For an estoppel to arise there must be some evidence justifying the person dealing with the planning officer for thinking that what the officer said would bind the planning authority. Holding an office, however senior, cannot, in our judgment, be enough by itself. In the *Lever (Finance) Ltd* case there was evidence of a widespread practice amongst planning authorities of allowing their planning officers to make immaterial modifications to the plans produced when planning permission was given. Lever (Finance) Ltd's architect presumably knew of this practice and was entitled to assume that the practice had been authorised by the planning authorities in whose areas it was followed ... Whether anyone dealing with a planning officer can safely assume that the officer can bind his authority by anything he says must depend on all the circumstances. In the *Lever (Finance) Ltd* case ... [1970] 3 All ER 496, [1971] 1 QB 222 at 231 Lord Denning MR said: 'Any person dealing with them [*ie* officers of a planning authority] is entitled to assume that all necessary resolutions have been passed.' This statement was not necessary for the conclusion he had reached and purported to be an addendum. We consider it to be obiter; with all respect, it stated the law too widely.

It is clear from these remarks that *Western Fish* took a major step back from Lord Denning's broad approach to estoppel, heavily circumscribing the doctrine. As far as unauthorized representations were concerned, the lawfully designated decision-maker could be estopped by them only where the representee had good reason to believe that the representation had been issued with authority—a test which the Court of Appeal was at pains to emphasize would not be satisfied easily. This judicial reticence *vis-à-vis* estoppel in public law may be justified by two factors.

First, the *constitutional argument* holds that it is wrong in principle to recognize as binding decisions which are *ultra vires*. If an official issues an *ultra vires* statement which then prevents the proper decision-maker from reaching a different conclusion, the force of law is given to the official's unlawful representation. This, say Wade and Forsyth, *Administrative Law* (Oxford 2009) at 284, is fundamentally at odds with the *ultra vires* principle:

> If the force of law is given to a ruling from an official merely because it is wrong, the official who has no legal power is in effect substituted for the proper authority, which is forced to accept what it considered a bad decision. To legitimate ultra vires acts in this way cannot be a sound policy, being a negation of the fundamental canons of administrative law.

QUESTIONS

- Is it necessarily 'unconstitutional' to recognize estoppel in public law?
- Is it therefore 'unconstitutional' for a court to refuse to quash unlawful administrative action because, for example, the claimant lacks standing (on which see 14.7) or did not issue the claim for judicial review within the relevant time limit (on which see 14.4)?

Second, in his judgment in *Western Fish* at 219, Megaw LJ alluded to the *public interest argument*:

> The defendant council's officers, even when acting within the apparent scope of their authority, could not do what the [Town and Country Planning Act 1971] required the defendant council to do; and if their officers did or said anything which purported to determine in advance what the defendant council themselves would have to determine in pursuance of their statutory duties, they would not be inhibited from doing what they had to do. An estoppel cannot be raised to prevent the exercise of a statutory discretion or to prevent or excuse the performance of a statutory duty (see Spencer Bower and Turner on Estoppel by Representation (3rd Edn, 1977, p 141) and the cases there cited). The application of this principle can be illustrated on the facts of this case: under s 29 of the 1971 Act the defendant council as the planning authority had to determine applications for planning permission, and when doing so had to have regard to the provision of the development plan and 'to any other material considerations'. The plaintiffs made an application for planning permission to erect a tall chimney on the site. When considering this application the defendant council had to 'take into account any representations relating to that application' which were received by them following the publishing and posting of notices: see ss 26 and 29(2). This requirement was in the interests of the public generally. If any representations made by the defendant council's officers before the publication or posting of notices bound the council to act in a particular way, the statutory provision which gave the public opportunities of making representations would have been thwarted and the defendant council would have been dispensed from their statutory obligation of taking into account any representation made to them. The officers were appointed by the defendant council but the council's members were elected by the inhabitants of their area. Parliament by the 1971 Act entrusted the defendant council, acting through their elected members, not their officers, to perform various statutory duties. If their officers were allowed to determine that which Parliament had enacted the defendant council should determine there would be no need for elected members to consider planning applications. This cannot be. Under s 101(1) of the Local Government Act 1972 (which repealed s 4 of the 1971 Act, which re-enacted in an amended form s 64 of the Town and Country Planning Act 1968), a local authority may arrange for the discharge of any of their functions by an officer of the authority. This has to be done formally by the authority acting as such. In this case the defendant council issued standing orders authorising designated officers to perform specified functions including

those arising under ss 53 and 94 of the 1971 Act. Their officers had no authority to make any other determinations under the 1971 Act. We can see no reason why Mr de Savary, acting on behalf of the plaintiffs, and having available the advice of lawyers and architects, should have assumed, if he ever did, that [the official in question] could bind the defendant council generally by anything he wrote or said.

QUESTIONS

- Should the public interest argument *always* dictate that unauthorized representations may not bind the designated decision-maker?
- Can you think of any circumstances in which the public interest argument may carry little or no weight?

6.2.4 A new approach

In *R* v. *East Sussex County Council, ex parte Reprotech (Pebsham) Ltd* [2002] UKHL 8, [2003] 1 WLR 348, the House of Lords had occasion to consider whether the concept of estoppel should continue to play any role in planning law—and, by extension, public law generally. Lord Hoffmann, giving the only reasoned speech, reached the following conclusions:

[33] ... I think that it is unhelpful to introduce private law concepts of estoppel into planning law. As Lord Scarman pointed out in *Newbury District Council* v *Secretary of State for the Environment* [1981] AC 578, 616, estoppels bind individuals on the ground that it would be unconscionable for them to deny what they have represented or agreed. But these concepts of private law should not be extended into 'the public law of planning control, which binds everyone.' (See also Dyson J in *R* v *Leicester City Council, ex parte Powergen UK Ltd* [2000] JPL 629, 637.)

[34] There is of course an analogy between a private law estoppel and the public law concept of a legitimate expectation created by a public authority, the denial of which may amount to an abuse of power: see *R* v *North and East Devon Health Authority, ex parte Coughlan* [2001] QB 213. But it is no more than an analogy because remedies against public authorities also have to take into account the interests of the general public which the authority exists to promote. Public law can also take into account the hierarchy of individual rights which exist under the Human Rights Act 1998, so that, for example, the individual's right to a home is accorded a high degree of protection (see *Coughlan's* case at pp 254–255) while ordinary property rights are in general far more limited by considerations of public interest ...

[35] It is true that in early cases such as [*Wells* v. *Minister of Housing and Local Government* [1967] 1 WLR 1000] and *Lever Finance Ltd* v *Westminster (City) London Borough Council* [1971] 1 QB 222, Lord Denning MR used the language of estoppel in relation to planning law. At that time the public law concepts of abuse of power and legitimate expectation were very undeveloped and no doubt the analogy of estoppel seemed useful. In the *Western Fish* [case] the Court of Appeal tried its best to reconcile these invocations of estoppel with the general principle that a public authority cannot be estopped from exercising a statutory discretion or performing a public duty. But the results did not give universal satisfaction: see the comments of Dyson J in the *Powergen* case [2000] JPL 629, 638. It seems to me that in this area, public law has already absorbed whatever is useful from the moral values which underlie the private law concept of estoppel and the time has come for it to stand upon its own two feet.

On one view the distinction drawn between estoppel and legitimate expectations is overly stark, as are most attempts to distinguish public from private (see 4.5.6, 13.3). For example, estoppel by representation and legitimate expectations, at least where legitimate expectations are based on promises, have many common features, as Lord Hoffmann acknowledges when he observes that there are clear analogies between the two fields. But in addition some of the bases on which Lord Hoffmann distinguishes the two fields are arguably unconvincing. He lays especial emphasis on the fact that third party or public interests may be taken into account in deciding upon remedies in public law as a basis for distinguishing legitimate expectations from estoppel. Yet it is increasingly clear that in the context of equitable remedies too third party and public interests may play a significant and indeed determinative role in remedial decisions (*eg Coventry v. Lawrence* [2014] UKSC 13, [2014] 1 AC 822; *Dennis v. Ministry of Defence* [2003] EWHC 793, [2003] Env LR 34).

Nonetheless, as a matter of doctrine Lord Hoffmann's statements, even if obiter, send a clear signal that legitimate expectations and estoppel are different fields. This in turn paves the way in principle for a different approach to be taken to unlawful representations in the field of legitimate expectations from that taken traditionally in estoppel. Further, Lord Hoffmann's emphasis on the demands of the public interest paves the way for arguments that in some cases the public interest may well demand a degree of protection for unlawfully created expectations, and that the categorical proscription upon giving effect to *ultra vires* representations in equity is unsuited to the public law context, where a more flexible approach should prevail.

Thus, for example, Craig (1977) 93 *LQR* 398 at 420 argues that, provided an adequate mechanism exists for taking account of constitutional and public interest concerns raised by the question of whether to enforce an unauthorized representation, we can—with a clear conscience—dispense with what he calls the 'jurisdictional principle' (*ie* the rule, adopted in cases like *Western Fish*, that *ultra vires* representations are generally unenforceable):

> When the basis of the jurisdictional principle is scrutinised it is found to be wanting. The objective of preventing [unlawful] extension of power by public officials is obviously correct, but the operation of the doctrine in practice is misdirected. In the rare cases of intentional extension of power it strikes at the wrong person, the innocent representee, rather than the public official. In the more common case of careless, or inadvertent, extension of power any deterrent effect upon the public officer will be minimal. The unspoken hypothesis must be that whenever, *in fact*, the powers of the body are extended any hardship to the representee must be outweighed by the harm to the public, who are the beneficiaries of the *ultra vires* principle, were estoppel allowed to operate.
>
> ... [T]he complexity and diversity of situations in which representations occur does not permit of such a categorical answer. The balance of public and individual interest will produce different answers in areas as diverse as planning and licensing, social security and taxation, and even within each area. A doctrine with sufficient flexibility to recognise this diversity is needed. Whether it is introduced through the courts or through the legislature is a choice as to mechanism.

Precisely such a mechanism would appear to consist in the legitimate expectation doctrine, now clearly decoupled from estoppel. However, while subsequent decisions (*eg R (Wandsworth London Borough Council) v. Secretary of State for Transport, Local Government and the Regions* [2003] EWHC 622 (Admin), [2004] 1 P & CR 32 at [21]) accept that *Reprotech* firmly establishes the inapplicability of estoppel in planning law—and, by extension, public law generally—the courts have not enthusiastically seized the opportunity to adopt the flexible approach favoured by Craig to the protection of unlawfully created expectations.

It is true that there have been occasions on which judges appear to have countenanced a balancing test whereby the public interest in legality might be weighed against competing interests. For example, in *Henry Boot Homes Ltd* v. *Bassetlaw District Council* [2002] EWCA Civ 983 at [56], Keene LJ considered that it may be possible for a developer to enforce a legitimate expectation that the planning authority would waive planning conditions set under the statutory planning scheme; however, this would very much be the exception, not the norm:

> [Counsel] invited us to say that legitimate expectation could never operate so as to enable the developer to begin development validly and effectively in breach of condition. I am not prepared to adopt so absolute a proposition. It is possible that circumstances might arise where it was clear that there was no third party or public interest in the matter and a court might take the view that a legitimate expectation could then arise from the local planning authority's conduct or representations. But … one suspects that such cases will be very rare.

In order to explore more fully whether legitimate expectation theory may apply to unlawful representations—a proposition which appears counterintuitive: can *unlawfully* created expectations be *legitimate*?—it is helpful to distinguish the situations considered in the next two sections.

6.2.5 Representations issued by unauthorized officials

First, consider representations relating to acts and decisions which are *intra vires* the public body but *ultra vires* the official concerned. Although some judges—*eg* Dyson J in *R* v. *Leicester City Council, ex parte Powergen UK Ltd* (2000) 80 P & CR 176 at 186—have assumed that a lack of actual authority on the part of the official making the representation conclusively precludes a legitimate expectation from arising, others have taken a rather wider approach, as the following case indicates.

South Buckinghamshire District Council v. *Flanagan* [2002] EWCA Civ 690, [2002] 1 WLR 2601
Court of Appeal

The local authority initiated criminal proceedings in respect of the defendants' failure to comply with enforcement notices issued under the Town and Country Planning Act 1990. The solicitor instructed to represent the council was given authority, subject to certain conditions, to discontinue the prosecutions. In fact, at the hearing, the solicitor agreed to discontinue the prosecutions *and withdraw the enforcement notices*. When the council—which had not wanted to withdraw the notices—later sought to enforce them by seeking an injunction in the County Court, they were held to be estopped from doing so in light of the solicitor's (unauthorized) representation. The council successfully appealed, whereupon one of the defendants appealed, contending that the solicitor's representation gave rise to a legitimate expectation that no further enforcement of the notices would be attempted.

Keene LJ

[16] Before us Mr Lamming for the second defendant does not seek to uphold the order of the county court judge on the basis of an estoppel. He recognises that, in the light of the authorities,

estoppel by representation really no longer has any part to play in planning law. That was almost the position achieved after the Court of Appeal decision in *Western Fish Products Ltd* v *Penwith District Council* [1981] 2 All ER 204, there remaining only limited circumstances where a local planning authority would be bound by such a representation. This is because planning decisions are not simply matters of private interest, confined to the developer and the local planning authority, but involve the public interest also. One is here in the realm of public law. That has now been emphasised by the House of Lords decision in *R* v *East Sussex County Council, ex parte Reprotech (Pebsham) Limited* [2002] UKHL 8, where Lord Hoffmann, with whom the other members of the House agreed, said that

'it is unhelpful to introduce private law concepts of estoppel into planning law.' (para. 33)

Although he recognised the analogy between private law estoppel and the public law concept of a legitimate expectation created by a public authority, Lord Hoffmann pointed out that remedies against public authorities also have to take into account the interests of the general public (para 34). It is clear that the House saw the earlier cases where estoppel had been applied in planning law as an attempt to achieve justice at a time when the concepts of legitimate expectation and abuse of power had scarcely made their appearance in public law. Now that those concepts are recognised, there is no longer a place for the private law doctrine of estoppel in public law or for the attendant problems which it brings with it ...

[18] At the outset of his submissions on this aspect of the case, Mr Lamming conceded that a legitimate expectation based on a representation allegedly made on behalf of a public body can only arise if the person making the representation as to that body's future conduct has actual or ostensible authority to make it on its behalf. That would seem to be right. Legitimate expectation involves notions of fairness and unless the person making the representation has actual or ostensible authority to speak on behalf of the public body, there is no reason why the recipient of the representation should be allowed to hold the public body to the terms of the representation. He might subjectively have acquired the expectation, but it would not be a legitimate one, that is to say it would not be one to which he was entitled.

[19] Judge Parry [in the County Court] found that Mr Ikram [the solicitor] had 'actual or ostensible authority' to bind the Council to withdraw the enforcement notices and not to proceed save by way of new notices. Mr Lamming accepted, as he did before Harrison J. [on appeal from the County Court], that he could not seek to rely on any actual authority possessed by Mr Ikram ... The case for the second defendant therefore turns on the issue of whether or not Mr Ikram had the ostensible authority claimed ...

[20] The principal contention advanced by Mr Lamming was that, by appointing Mr Ikram to represent the local planning authority in the magistrates' court proceedings, the authority had represented that he had the authority to agree to a withdrawal of not just those proceedings but the enforcement notices themselves. Such a power fell, it was said, within the usual scope of a solicitor's authority to compromise proceedings. Reliance was placed on the decision in *Waugh* v *H.B. Clifford & Sons Ltd* [1982] Ch. 374, where it was held that a solicitor retained in civil proceedings had ostensible authority to compromise the suit provided that the compromise did not involve matters collateral to the action. Matters were only to be seen as collateral if they involved some extraneous subject matter. Therefore, where proceedings had been brought against the builders/vendors of houses for defects in the houses, it was within the ostensible authority of the defendants' solicitors to agree to the repurchase of the houses at a price reflecting their value in a proper condition. In the present case it was argued that the enforcement notices and their continuing validity could not be seen as collateral to the criminal prosecutions in the magistrates' court ...

[22] I return, therefore, to the submission based on the usual scope of a solicitor's authority to compromise proceedings. It has to be remembered that, as Harrison J. pointed out, an

enforcement notice is an important public document. It runs with the land, it is registrable, and it is enforceable against any subsequent owner or occupier of the land in question, so long as it has been registered. Moreover, for an enforcement notice to take effect may require a lengthy process to be undertaken: there are rights of appeal against it to the Secretary of State, which may result in a public inquiry; there are further rights of challenge on a point of law to the courts. So an enforcement notice which has become effective, as these two notices had, is a planning instrument of some significance. It enables the local planning authority to prosecute for a breach of it, as indeed had successfully happened in the past in respect of the 1980 enforcement notice in the present case. Once such a notice has become effective, it endures in principle for an indefinite period of time, unless the local planning authority decides to exercise its statutory power under section 173A of the 1990 Act to withdraw it.

[23] It is impossible to regard it as part of the usual authority of a solicitor, appointed to prosecute for a breach of the enforcement notice, to agree to a withdrawal of the underlying notice itself. That would be an action of great significance to the local planning authority, extending far beyond the issue of the particular breach of the notice for which the prosecution has been brought. The continuing validity and force of the underlying notice are not the subject matter of those proceedings in the magistrates' court but are truly extraneous to them. It would put local planning authorities, who exercise their powers in the public interest, at the mercy of every advocate instructed to prosecute for such a breach if they were to be held bound by an agreement or representation made by that advocate as to the future validity and force of an otherwise unimpeachable enforcement notice. I find myself in full agreement with Harrison J.'s conclusion that authority to withdraw the notices themselves goes beyond what could reasonably be regarded as normally incidental to the conduct of prosecuting for a breach.

Keene LJ, with whom Sumner J agreed, concluded that the solicitor's lack of ostensible authority to withdraw the enforcement notices precluded any legitimate expectation that the council would not take further proceedings in respect of those notices.

The significance of this decision turns on what is meant by 'ostensible authority' (on which see generally in this context Craig (1977) 93 *LQR* 398). It is a phenomenon borrowed from the law of agency, and arises where someone or some body represents, expressly or impliedly, that the person concerned has authority to deal with certain matters on their behalf (even though he may not): hence 'ostensible', rather than 'actual', authority. It was recognized by Diplock LJ in the context of company law in *Freeman and Lockyer* v. *Buckhurst Park Properties Ltd* [1964] 2 QB 480 at 504 that unauthorized representations may bind a body with *restricted powers* only in limited circumstances:

[S]ince the conferring of actual authority upon an agent is itself an act of the corporation, the capacity to do which is regulated by its constitution, the corporation cannot be estopped from denying that it has conferred upon a particular agent authority to do acts which by its constitution, it is incapable of delegating to that particular agent.

In the public law context, this suggests that, although representations issued with ostensible authority may bind the public body (as is clearly envisaged in *Flanagan*), such authority will only arise where (i) the representation relates to conduct which the public body itself could lawfully commit, (ii) it represents (expressly or impliedly) that the official has authority over the matter in question, and (iii) he could have been so authorized.

If these criteria are met, it is then necessary to consider the status of the official's representation. It is possible to envisage circumstances in which, although an official may not have been authorized as such by the public body for whom he works, his decisions on the matter in question are nevertheless not *ultra vires*. For instance, where conditions (i) to (iii) above are met, but where an official has been instructed not to deal with the matter in question, he is clearly not 'authorized' by the public body to do so in the sense that, as a matter of employment law, he may be guilty of a disciplinary offence or breach of contract; however, by dealing with the matter in question, the official is not acting *ultra vires* in a public law sense, because these is no statutory prohibition on his doing so. A public body in such circumstances may seek to argue that the internal prohibition upon the official's dealing with the matter in question should prevent the individual from relying upon the official's conduct as something capable of binding the public authority, in which case the individual may wish to invoke a legitimate expectation—based on the public body's express or implied representation (see point (ii))—that the official did have authority to deal with the matter (or, to use the old language, the individual may argue that the public body is estopped from invoking the internal prohibition upon the official). However, in strict logic, it is not clear that recourse to legitimate expectation (or estoppel) is necessary in such circumstances, bearing in mind that the official's conduct is not, in the public law sense, *ultra vires*.

Even where legislation restricts the capacity of an official to act in a given matter, *eg* by prescribing that authority must be conferred upon him *by recourse to some formal procedure*, it does not follow that failure to comply with such a statutory condition renders the official's conduct *ultra vires*. Whether this is so will turn upon whether (on the principles discussed at 2.6) compliance with the statutory procedural requirement is a precondition upon the official's acquisition of the relevant *vires*. Although, where the public body has not conferred the relevant power upon the official in the prescribed manner, the official may (as discussed earlier) be 'unauthorized' in one sense, this will not affect his *vires* in the public law sense if the statutory procedural requirement that is in play is not regarded as jurisdictional: there is, in this situation, no jurisdictional statutory prohibition on his exercising the power in question. Here, the analysis is the same as in the previous paragraph.

From these situations must be distinguished those in which there *is* some jurisdictional statutory prohibition—for example where the relevant power could have been conferred upon the official concerned, but only by means of some statutory procedure which is regarded as a condition precedent to the acquisition of *vires* by the official. Where such a procedure is not complied with, any purported decisions of the official will be *ultra vires*. Although, in this scenario, our three conditions for ostensible authority (set out earlier) are met, the fact that the official's decision is *ultra vires* presents a major difficulty, since, as we have already seen (in the analogous context of estoppel), it is widely held that allowing such *ultra vires* representations to bind public bodies would be constitutionally inappropriate. However, we conclude this section by noting that, on a policy level, it is important to remember that if the courts were to recognize legitimate expectations on the basis of *ultra vires* representations of the type presently under discussion, such representations would not, without more, bind the public body concerned. Rather, the court, having recognized the legitimate expectation, would simply acquire jurisdiction to decide whether the public interest (including the public interest in the principle of legality) outweighed, on the facts, the interests of the individual.

QUESTION

- Bearing this point in mind, should the courts be willing to recognize legitimate expectations on the strength of representations which are *ultra vires* the official concerned?

6.2.6 Representations concerning action which is *ultra vires* the agency

The courts have made it abundantly clear that the doctrine of legitimate expectation cannot operate so as to extend agencies' powers by rendering enforceable acts or decisions which are *ultra vires* the body itself: see, *eg R (Bibi)* v. *Newnham LBC* [2001] EWCA Civ 607, [2002] 1 WLR 237 at [46] and *R (Bloggs 61)* v. *Secretary of State for the Home Department* [2003] EWCA Civ 686, [2003] 1 WLR 2724 at [39].

While we will see later that there are plausible policy arguments against this orthodox position, we focus presently on a more immediate problem. Where the ECHR is in play, domestic law's mechanical characterization of the principle of legality as a trump card which closes the door to competing arguments of fairness to the individual could fall foul of the principle of proportionality. This point is illustrated by the decision of the European Court of Human Rights in *Stretch* v. *United Kingdom* (2004) 38 EHRR 12. The applicant purchased from a local authority a 22-year lease which obliged him to erect industrial buildings and apparently conferred an option to renew for a further 21 years. When renewal negotiations had reached an advanced stage, the local authority informed the applicant that the option could not be exercised because, *inter alia*, its statutory predecessor never had legal capacity to grant such an option. This argument met with grudging acceptance in the Court of Appeal (*Stretch* v. *West Dorset District Council* (1999) 77 P & CR 342), Peter Gibson LJ noting that it seems 'unjust' that public bodies which misconstrue their powers should be able to 'take advantage of their own errors to escape from the unlawful bargains that they have made'.

The ECtHR, however, was unwilling to accept as determinative the *ultra vires* nature of the representation. Without reference to that factor, the Court held that the applicant had acquired a legitimate expectation of exercising the option; that, for the purposes of Article 1, Protocol 1 ECHR, this could be characterized as attaching to the property rights arising under the lease; and that the local authority's conduct frustrated the expectation. The legal incapacity of the public body was considered only at the final stage of the analysis:

[38] The Government have emphasised in this case the doctrine of ultra vires which provides an important safeguard against abuse of power by local or statutory authorities acting beyond the competence given to them under domestic law. The Court does not dispute the purpose or use-fulness of this doctrine which indeed reflects the notion of the rule of law underlying much of the Convention itself. It is not however persuaded that the application of the doctrine in the present case respects the principle of proportionality.

[39] The Court observes that local authorities inevitably enter into many agreements of a private law nature with ordinary citizens in the pursuance of their functions, not all of which however will concern matters of vital public concern. In the present case, the local authority entered in a lease and was unaware that its powers to do so did not include the possibility of agreeing to an option for renewal of the lease. It nonetheless obtained the agreed rent for the lease and, on exercise of the renewal of the option, had the possibility of negotiating an increase in ground rent. There is no issue that the local authority acted against the public interest in the way in which it disposed of the property under its control or that any third party interests or the pursuit of any other statutory function would have been prejudiced by giving effect to the renewal option.

This analysis—which led to the UK having to pay damages as 'just satisfaction' under Article 41 ECHR—is significant because it treats legal incapacity merely as a factor to be placed in the balance when deciding whether the legitimate expectation may lawfully be frustrated. The implications of *Stretch* for domestic law—which has traditionally treated legal incapacity in precisely the manner condemned by the ECtHR—were confronted in the next case.

Rowland v. *Environment Agency* [2003] EWCA Civ 1885, [2005] Ch 1
Court of Appeal

In 1974, the claimant's husband purchased an estate which included Hedsor Water, a non-tidal stretch of the River Thames, believing the water to be private. This belief was founded partly on the fact that the navigation authority, assuming the stretch of river to be private, had allowed signs to be erected to that effect. However, in 2001, by which time the claimant had succeeded to the estate following the death of her husband, the navigation authority concluded that public rights of navigation (PRN) still existed in relation to Hedsor Water, and ordered the claimant to remove signs giving the contrary impression. The claimant argued that PRN did not exist over Hedsor Water or that, in the alternative, the navigation authority's conduct had given rise to a legitimate expectation that it would treat Hedsor Water as private, thereby preventing it from ordering the removal of the signs. The claimant was unsuccessful at first instance, and appealed to the Court of Appeal. All three Court of Appeal judges agreed that PRN existed over Hedsor Water and that it was beyond the powers of the navigation authority to extinguish those rights. The following excerpts are concerned only with the arguments based on legitimate expectation.

Peter Gibson LJ

[After reviewing the evidence upon which the claimant contended a legitimate expectation could be founded, his Lordship said:]

[78] … [S]ubject to the effect of the rule under English law that a legitimate expectation can only arise on the basis of a lawful promise or practice, I would accept that Mrs. Rowland has a legitimate expectation that she would continue to be entitled to enjoy Hedsor Water as private. However, I share Mance L.J.'s reservations about the scope and strength of that expectation in the particular circumstances (see paras. 157 and 158 of his judgment) …

[81] [However,] [a]s it is accepted by Mrs. Rowland there can only be a legitimate expectation founded on a lawful representation or practice, her claim to a legitimate expectation that she would continue to be entitled to enjoy Hedsor Water as private was bound to fail under English domestic law if taken alone without the Convention in the absence of any statutory basis for the extinction of PRN over Hedsor Water. I therefore turn next to the question whether the Convention has altered the position …

[82] Mrs. Rowland relies on Art. 8, the right to respect for private and family life, and on Art. 1 [of Protocol 1], providing for the protection of property …

[83] … [Counsel for Mrs Rowland] argued that what would be a legitimate expectation under English law, but for being ultra vires the public authority concerned, relating to specific rights connected with a specific property is a possession within the meaning of Art. 1 and so cannot be taken away or interfered with except in accordance with the requirements of Art. 1 as regards the principles of legal certainty and proportionality.

[Having considered *Stretch* v. *United Kingdom* (see earlier), his Lordship agreed that the expectation in the present case constituted a 'possession', and continued:]

[96] In my judgment the judge [at first instance in the present case] was right on this issue for the reasons which he gave. It was inevitable that once the Defendant was aware that it had made

a mistake in allowing Hedsor Water to be treated as a private water, it, as the guardian of navigation in the Thames, should resile from its sprevious stance. Courts should be slow to fix a public
authority permanently with the consequences of a mistake (see *Begbie* [[2000] 1 WLR 1115] at
p. 1127), particularly when it would deprive the public of their rights. The Defendant had no power
to fulfil the expectation of Mrs. Rowland, and it was bound to conclude that it should remove the
misleading signs that Hedsor Water was private, as they were inconsistent with the continued
existence of PRN over that stretch of the Thames. The rights of the public, expressly recognised by s. 1 of the [Thames Preservation Act 1885], now s. 79(1) of the [Thames Conservancy
Act 1932], required nothing less. The Defendant rightly took account of the expectation of Mrs.
Rowland that Hedsor Water was and would continue to be private, of the fact that Hedsor Wharf
was purchased on the understanding that it was private, and of Mrs. Rowland's wish to continue
to enjoy privacy. In consequence ... it gave the assurances not to promote public use of Hedsor
Water and to minimise for her the effect of removing the prohibition on the public using Hedsor
Water. True it is that the details of such minimisation were not spelt out ..., but to respond as the
Defendant did ... was in my judgment neither disproportionate nor unjustified ...

May LJ

[99] I agree that this appeal should be dismissed for the reasons given by Peter Gibson LJ, whose
account of the facts and circumstances of the appeal I gratefully adopt. I also agree with Mance
LJ that it would be appropriate to grant a further declaration in the terms which he suggests.
I agree with the structure of Mance LJ's reasoning which reaches his conclusion. But I would put
a rather different emphasis, more favourable to Mrs Rowland, on the strength of the legitimate
expectation to which in my judgment the facts give rise ...

[100] I reach the conclusion that this appeal should be dismissed, for the reasons given by
Peter Gibson and Mance LJJ, with undisguised reluctance. I say this because I regard the outcome as unjust. It is, in my view, the unjust product of a developing, but at times over complicated, body of related jurisprudence, elements of which need reconsideration. Binding authority
prevents constructive reconsideration in this court. The most unusual facts and circumstances of
this appeal seem to me to illustrate related problems of real importance ...

[102] ... English law recognises that there may be circumstances where fairness and proportionality require that a public body should not be able to resile from a representation which has
resulted in a legitimate expectation in an individual or group of individuals. Unfairness may arise
of the third kind identified by Lord Woolf in *R v North and East Devon Health Authority, ex parte
Coughlan* [2001] QB 213 at paragraphs 57 to 58. This kind of unfairness arises where there is no
overriding interest which would justify the public body in resiling from its representation. But
orthodox English domestic law does not allow the individual to retain the benefit which is the
subject of the legitimate expectation, however strong, if creating or maintaining that benefit is
beyond the power of the public body.

[103] Such is the present case. Hedsor Water was part of the original main stream of the
River Thames. From time immemorial, a public right of navigation has existed over the river.
The public right of navigation now exists by statute going back to the Thames Preservation Act
1885. Successive Navigation Authorities had no power to extinguish that right. A public right of
navigation cannot be extinguished by prescription, even over a period exceeding 100 ... years.
The respondents and their predecessors have acted for a period in excess of 100 years so as to
give rise to the legitimate expectation on which Mrs Rowland relies. But, because the Navigation
Authorities had no power to extinguish the public right of navigation over Hedsor Water, English
domestic law cannot give effect to Mrs Rowland's legitimate expectation. This is unjust and
illustrates a defect in the law. In my view, the just outcome of these proceedings is that Hedsor
Water should remain private. English law cannot at present achieve this.

[104] So resort is had to the Human Rights Convention and jurisprudence under it. This should not be necessary. I agree that Mrs Rowland's legitimate expectation should be seen as a possession within Article 1 of the first Protocol. An intricate process of reasoning is required to reach this conclusion. But, as Peter Gibson LJ has explained in paragraph 96 of his judgment, this conclusion does not take Mrs Rowland very far. The Human Rights Convention does not enable Mrs Rowland to retain Hedsor Water as private, when to achieve this is beyond the statutory power of the respondents. They must not act so as to abuse their power, but I agree that they have not done so. Their letter of 20th February 2001 was not only considerate, but a genuine statement of the respondents' intention to moderate, so far as they were able, the effect on Mrs Rowland of their discovery that Hedsor Water is not private and cannot continue to be so ...

[114] I have already indicated my view that the law is defective and that in consequence this court is obliged to uphold an unjust outcome. A sustained and powerful academic analysis to this end is to be found in Professor Paul Craig's *Administrative Law* ... [See 6.2.4 for discussion of Craig's analysis of this point.]

[115] Professor Craig addresses and disapproves of, as I do, an unmitigated state of the law to the effect that a representation by a public authority, which the public authority has no power to make, is not binding and cannot sustain a legitimate expectation or an estoppel. The logic of the jurisdictional principle is followed through to its inexorable end. But a moment's reflection makes evident the hardship to the individual ...

[120] [After discussing Craig's views on this issue, his Lordship concluded:] I regret that it is not, in my view, open to this court to implement Professor Craig's balancing approach. At this level, it would amount to legislation. I say nothing about whether the House of Lords could or would consider implementing it ...

Mance LJ

[136] ... [I]n *Bibi* [[2001] EWCA Civ 607 [2002] 1 WLR 237] (at paras. 21 and 46) this Court suggested as likely that the 'legitimacy' of any expectation depended upon whether the relevant representation was within the authority's lawful power. In *Stretch v. West Dorset CC* (11th November 1997) this Court, with no enthusiasm, applied the principle that a local authority can rely on the invalidity of its own actions (cf. *Hazell v. Hammersmith and Fulham LBC* [1992] 2 AC 1 and *Credit Suisse v. Allerdale BC* [1997] QB 306), holding invalid an option for a further 21 year term granted to the tenant under a lease for an initial 21 year term. The local authority's only relevant power was to let, and thus did not extend to granting an option. So, in the present case, Lord Lester [for the claimant] recognises that at common law, prior [to] the incorporation of the Convention on Human Rights, the Agency's lack of any power to abrogate or qualify the public's PRN, or therefore to represent that such PRN did not exist, would pose an apparently insuperable obstacle to success in an argument that the Agency by words or conduct had led Mrs Rowland to have a legitimate expectation that a PRN did exist.

[137] Since the incorporation of the Convention, Lord Lester submits, this lacuna has been closed in the context of Article 1 of the First Protocol by decisions in the European Court of Human Rights, which we should now take into account ...

[After considering the decisions of the ECtHR in *Pine Valley Developments Ltd v. Ireland* (1991) 14 EHRR 319 and *Stretch v. United Kingdom* (2004) 38 EHRR 12, his Lordship said:]

[152] ... [I]t can no longer be an automatic answer under English law to a case of legitimate expectation, that the Agency had no power to extinguish the PRN over Hedsor Water or to treat it as private. However, the present case differs significantly from those two cases. In *Pine Valley* and *Stretch*, the European Court was considering claims for relief against states. Those states undoubtedly had the power to pay compensation for any inability of the part of the public authority whose conduct was in issue to fulfil any legitimate expectation which it had created. Here there is before us no claim against the state, and indeed no claim for compensation against

anyone. We are concerned simply and solely with a claim for declaratory relief regarding the conduct of the Agency, which can only act in accordance with its statutory mandate. That mandate involves preserving the PRN, and it is not suggested (nor could it be in the light of the public interest) that the alchemy of s. 3(1) of the Human Rights Act 1998 can affect that mandate. The Agency was therefore bound in law to adjust its attitude, as it did in December 2000, once it became apparent that the PRN had never in law been extinguished. The Court cannot grant relief which would have the effect of obliging the Agency to continue to treat Hedsor Water as private. Lord Lester's submissions recognise this. The argument is that the Agency's mandate confers on it sufficient powers and discretion for it to be able to give effect to Mrs Rowland's legitimate expectation without any need to neglect or affect that mandate. If the Agency created in Mrs Rowland an expectation which should in European Convention terms be regarded as legitimate, but which goes beyond the Agency's discretionary powers to fulfil under domestic law, that might lead to some different claim for compensation against the state. But I understood Lord Lester to accept that this would not lie against the Agency ...

[153] The present case thus resolves itself into issues regarding the nature (including the strength) of any expectation created by the Agency and the extent to which the Court both can and should grant relief requiring the Agency to take that expectation into account in the course of exercising its discretionary powers. For my part, I accept that the Agency's conduct conferred on Mrs Rowland a legitimate expectation to the effect, at least, that, should it transpire that Hedsor Water was not private, the Agency would, in reacting to any such discovery, take into account the previous common assumption of the Rowlands and of the Agency to the contrary and the fact that Hedsor Water has been effectively private (so far as can be judged without any serious public discontent) over many years; and would smooth the position (as far as possible consistently with its duties to preserve the PRN) for Mrs Rowland while she owns and resides at Hedsor Wharf. Considerations which can and should properly be taken into account by the Agency in that regard include the long period of Mrs Rowland's previous residence at Hedsor Wharf with her husband, during which she has foregone any opportunity of moving elsewhere, together with her wish to continue to reside there and to make it into her main English home for the rest of her life. It seems to me very likely that the expectation encouraged in Mrs Rowland would also require the Agency, at least during an initial period, to consult Mrs Rowland, particularly with regard to any steps that might be proposed following the realisation that there was still in law a PRN over Hedsor Water. Since both the Agency (which could have been expected to have a good grasp of the true position) and the Rowlands were under the like misapprehension until December 2000, I cannot regard the Rowlands' failure to investigate or appreciate the true legal position prior to that date as undermining an expectation along these lines ...

[163] I would supplement the declarations granted [at first instance] to the Agency [that PRN existed over Hedsor Water] by a further declaration to the effect that the Agency was obliged to take into account in the exercise of its statutory functions the common assumption prior to November 2000 of the Rowlands and of the Agency to the effect that Hedsor Water was private.

The appeal was allowed only to the extent of granting a declaration in the terms set out in the previous paragraph.

This decision does not fundamentally challenge the orthodoxy that the courts cannot order public bodies to fulfil promises which lie beyond their powers; to that extent, *Rowland* does not embrace the balancing approach to unlawful representations favoured by Craig (see 6.2.4). This orthodoxy has been reinforced since. For example, in the 2011 Court of Appeal decision in *R (Albert Court Residents' Association)* v. *Westminster City Council* [2011] EWCA Civ 430, [2012] PTSR 604, Stanley Burnton LJ, with whom the other judges agreed, said the Court could not 'grant any relief that would have the effect of preventing [the defendant] from complying with its statutory duty … [A]n otherwise legitimate expectation cannot require a public authority to act contrary to statute' (at [34]–[35]). This proposition 'is no more than an incident of the principle of legislative supremacy' (at [36]). In the Privy Council decision in *Rainbow Insurance Company Ltd* v. *The Financial Services Commission (Mauritius)* [2015] UKPC 15, Lord Hodge, giving the judgment of the Board, recalled that there is 'an established line of authority that nobody can have a legitimate expectation that he will be entitled to an ultra vires relaxation of a statutory requirement' and applied that line of authority, observing, 'what is at stake here is the principle of legality' (at [52]). He noted the obiter statements in *Rowland* that fairness might prevail over legality where Convention rights are at stake but considered such approach could only possibly apply in the Convention context (at [53]). He went one step further, endorsing the view in *De Smith's Judicial Review* (2013) at [12.078]–[12.079] that even where Convention rights are in play 'the law should be slow to weaken the principle of legality', and that an unlawful representation could not prevail where third party interests might be compromised (at [53]).

Nonetheless, it is worth considering the viability of a potential middle path between enforcement of *ultra vires* representations (which the courts will not countenance) and completely ignoring such representations (which may result in unfairness and breach of the ECHR). Such a middle way potentially lies in the 'benevolent exercise of powers doctrine'. According to this approach, which enjoys particular prominence in Mance LJ's judgment in *Rowland*, while agencies cannot be required to do the legally impossible, they *can* be required—by court order if necessary—to exercise their powers benevolently, so as to respect, as far as is legally possible, the legitimate expectations they engendered. (So, in *Rowland*, while the navigation authority could not extinguish the PRN, it could be required to exercise its powers so as not to draw attention to the existence of the PRN.)

So what would be the *content* of the benevolent exercise of powers doctrine? Just how benevolently can agencies be required (lawfully) to exercise their powers? This is an important issue which fundamentally affects the capacity of the doctrine to facilitate the striking of a meaningful balance between the public and private interests which are in play. An intriguing possibility arises in this context, the elaboration of which first requires us to consider the role of compensation in this area. Compensation in lieu of the fulfilment of unlawfully created expectations is advanced by some commentators (*eg* Wade and Forsyth, *Administrative Law* (Oxford 2009) at 284–5) as the best means by which to reconcile the tension between public and private interests: the public interest in legality is respected (because the unauthorized representation is not enforced) while fairness to the individual will usually be achieved by the provision of monetary compensation. Others, however, voice concerns about the appropriateness of compensation. For instance, in *Rowland*, May LJ opined (at [121]) that enforcement of unlawfully generated expectations, if acceptable on a balancing test, is 'a fairer and more proportionate outcome … than for the public purse to compensate' the disappointed individual. A further difficulty arises, in that where breach of an expectation implies violation of a Convention right, the use of s 8 of the Human Rights Act 1998—the obvious vehicle for a damages claim in such circumstances—would seem to be barred by s 6(2), which provides that it is not unlawful for a public authority to act in a given way when primary legislation constrains it to do so.

However, the benevolent exercise of power doctrine raises the possibility of an alternative approach to compensation (as distinct from damages). We know from the *Coughlan* case, considered at 6.1.5, that the legitimate expectation principle does not necessarily require the individual to be given that which he expected. Rather, it places the public authority under a duty to strike a fair balance between the interests of the individual (in the fulfilment of the expectation) and of the wider community (in the pursuit of some policy objective that conflicts with the fulfilment of the individual's expectation). The ECHR principle of proportionality also requires such a balance to be struck. Drawing upon the case of *S* v. *France* (1990) DR 250, it is clear that compensating an individual whose legitimate expectation is not to be fulfilled may, in some circumstances, strike the fair balance that is required, thereby avoiding a breach of the relevant Convention right (and, by extension, the *unlawful* frustration of the legitimate expectation as a matter of English law). Since s 6(1) of the Human Rights Act 1998 requires public authorities to act compatibly with the Convention rights whenever possible, it can be argued that compensation should be paid where this is necessary to strike the required fair balance, so as to avoid a breach of such rights. This, in turn, suggests that the benevolent exercise of power doctrine may be given real teeth. It is, moreover, possible to argue that this approach need not be confined to ECHR cases, since it would be open to English courts to hold in appropriate cases that the payment of compensation is a necessary component of the domestic requirement to strike a fair balance between the interests of the wider community and of the individual whose legitimate expectation the decision-maker proposes to frustrate.

Indeed, there are prior cases which could be drawn upon to support such approach. Albeit not in the context of *ultra vires* expectations specifically, the courts have in some legitimate expectation cases made statements which suggest they would be willing to sanction the payment of compensation in lieu of actual enjoyment of the expectation. In this way compensation is viewed as a second-best, alternative way of 'satisfying' the expectation. For example, in *Bibi* [2001] EWCA Civ 607, [2002] 1 WLR 237 at [56], Schiemann LJ said: 'A further element for the authority to bear in mind is the possibility of monetary compensation or assistance. As this court indicated in [*Coughlan* at] para 82, a legitimate expectation may in some cases be appropriately taken into account by such a payment.'

It is clear that a requirement to pay compensation would not be appropriate in every case. The general principle is that the decision-maker should, in frustrating the individual's expectation, act as benevolently as is necessary to meet the fair balance requirement *in the individual case*; in some cases, the degree of benevolence required may extend to the payment of compensation.

6.3 Concluding remarks

The decline of the principle of estoppel in public law, following its Denning-induced high-water mark in the middle of the last century, stands in stark contrast to the increasing enthusiasm of courts for the protection of lawfully issued undertakings through the vehicle of legitimate expectation. In both contexts, a similar dilemma presents itself: how to resolve the tension between those concerns which favour holding defendants to their representations such as legal certainty, individual fairness, and ideas of fair dealing, and countervailing concerns which pull in the opposite direction? Yet this conundrum takes on different forms depending on the legality of the initial representation.

So far as unlawfully created expectations are concerned, the constitutional and public interest concerns highlighted earlier introduce a substantial bias against the protection of the expectation induced by the representation. Although some writers argue that too much weight is presently attached to these concerns, the courts generally find them compelling—a point which remains true today, notwithstanding the shift in this context from 'estoppel' to 'legitimate expectation' analysis.

In contrast, the principle of legitimate expectation has developed along quite different lines in relation to lawful representations. However, even in this context, the manner in which the competing interests should be weighed against each other raises a number of problems. This is most obviously so in relation to substantive legitimate expectations, where protection of the individual's expectation may impact with particular force on the executive's discretionary freedom. In turn the law of substantive expectation reflects a more general debate concerning how judges and decision-makers should relate to one another, and the extent to which judicial review may curtail the executive's freedom to formulate, apply, and change policy. It is to that wider question which we turn in the following two chapters, as we address the principles of reasonableness and proportionality.

FURTHER RESOURCES

Craig, 'Representations by Public Bodies' (1977) 93 *LQR* 398

Elliott, 'From Heresy to Orthodoxy: Substantive Legitimate Expectations in English Public Law' in Groves and Weeks (eds), *Legitimate Expectations in the Common Law World* (Oxford 2017)

Forsyth, 'The Provenance and Protection of Legitimate Expectations' [1988] *CLJ* 238

Forsyth, 'Legitimate Expectations Revisited' (29 May 2011) ALBA Summer Conference 2011 *http://www.adminlaw.org.uk/library/publications.php*

Hannett and Busch, 'Ultra Vires Representations and Illegitimate Expectations' [2005] *PL* 729

Reynolds, 'Legitimate Expectations and the Protection of Trust in Officials' [2011] *PL* 330

Sales, 'Legitimate Expectations' [2006] *JR* 186

Sales and Steyn, 'Legitimate Expectations in English Public Law: An Analysis' [2004] *PL* 564

Schønberg, *Legitimate Expectations in Administrative Law* (Oxford 2000)

Steele, 'Substantive Legitimate Expectations: Striking the Right Balance?' (2005) 121 *LQR* 300

Vanderman, 'Ultra Vires Legitimate Expectations: An Argument for Compensation' [2012] *PL* 85

Varuhas, 'In Search of a Doctrine: Mapping the Law of Legitimate Expectations' in Groves and Weeks (eds), *Legitimate Expectations in the Common Law World* (Oxford 2017)

7 ABUSE OF DISCRETION I

7.1 Introduction

The principles considered in the two preceding chapters regulate the extent to which discretion may be restricted by making representations, entering into contracts, and so on. In this chapter and the next, we consider a further set of principles which regulate how decision-makers should behave when exercising discretion. The overarching idea running throughout the various rules developed by the courts in this field is that there is no such thing as an unfettered discretion, a proposition classically illustrated by the cases of *Anisminic Ltd* v. *Foreign Compensation Commission* [1969] 2 AC 147 (on which see 14.6.2) and *Padfield* v. *Minister of Agrictulture, Fisheries and Food* [1968] AC 997 (considered at 7.3.2).

QUESTION

- Are the courts justified in refusing to countenance unfettered discretion, even if this is apparently contemplated by the statutory scheme?

Discretionary power is today regarded as an unavoidable feature of our administrative system. However, the existence of unlimited or unregulated discretion is considered anathema to the rule of law. It is unsurprising, therefore, that writers such as Allan (in Forsyth (ed), *Judicial Review and the Constitution* (Oxford 2000)) and Jowell regard the subjection of discretionary power to rule-of-law-based constraints as a central function of administrative law.

Jowell, 'The Rule of Law' in Jowell, Oliver, and O'Cinneide (eds), *The Changing Constitution* (Oxford 2015)

[T]he practical implementation of the Rule of Law takes place primarily through judicial review of the actions of public officials. During the first half of the twentieth century, ... the courts rarely interfered with the exercise of discretionary powers. From that time on, however, they began to require that power be exercised in accordance with three 'grounds' of judicial review, each of them resting in large part on the rule of law.

The first ground, 'legality', requires officials to act within the scope of their lawful powers. The courts ensure that the official decisions do not stray beyond the 'four corners' of a statute by failing to take into account 'relevant' considerations (that is, considerations that the law requires), or by taking into account 'irrelevant' considerations (that is, considerations outside the object and purpose that Parliament intended the statute to pursue). This exercise is ... a clear instance of implementation of the rule of law, whereby the courts act as guardians of Parliament's intent and purpose ...

> The second ground of review, that of 'procedural impropriety' [see chs 9–11], requires decision-makers to be unbiased and to grant a fair hearing to claimants before depriving them of a right or significant interest (such as an interest in livelihood or reputation) ...
>
> This kind of procedural protection ... is a concrete expression of the rule of law ...
>
> Over the past few years, the courts have extended the requirement of a fair hearing even where the claimant does not possess a threatened right or even an important interest. A hearing will be required where a 'legitimate expectation' [see ch 6] has been induced by the decision-maker. In such a case the claimant has, expressly or impliedly, been promised either a hearing or the continuation of a benefit. The courts will not sanction the disappointment of such an expectation unless the claimant is permitted to make representations on the matter. The notion of the legitimate expectation is itself rooted in that aspect of the rule of law which requires legal certainty.
>
> The third ground of judicial review, 'irrationality' or 'unreasonableness' [see ch 8], also applies aspects of the rule of law. Suppose the police charge only bearded drivers, or drivers of a particular race, with traffic offences? Suppose an education authority chose to dismiss all teachers with red hair? Suppose a prison officer refused to permit a prisoner to communicate with his lawyer? ... Would these decisions offend the rule of law? If so, the rule of law becomes a substantive doctrine and not merely formal or procedural.

As this excerpt illustrates, many, perhaps all, of the principles applied by courts when testing the validity of purported exercises of discretion may be *related back* to the rule of law, and courts often make this connection; however, that principle provides rather uncertain *guidance* in this context, bearing in mind that there is considerable disagreement (see, *eg* Craig [1997] *PL* 467) about precisely what values the rule of law comprises. It is therefore necessary to acknowledge (see further 1.4) the role of *judges* in developing the principles of judicial review, albeit that they are clearly influenced by the rule of law in this regard. In the remainder of this chapter, we examine two principles of administrative law which reflect the rule-of-law-based view that decision-makers may not enjoy unfettered discretion, and that it is the courts' role to discern and enforce appropriate limits.

7.2 Loyalty to the statutory scheme: the propriety of purpose doctrine

7.2.1 Overlapping principles?

The two key principles with which this chapter is concerned are those which require decision-makers to act *only on the basis of factors which are legally relevant*, and which dictate that statutory powers may be used *only for the purposes for which they were created*. Taylor [1976] *CLJ* 272 at 272 writes that:

> Abuse of discretion is too easily regarded as a 'grab-bag' from which a ground of review can always be found to suit the conclusion sought to be reached on the merits. Judicial review is a flexible tool but each ground has a limited use. 'Improper purposes' and 'irrelevant factors' exist as distinct phrases because each represents a separate mode of analysis which is particularly useful in a given situation.

Taylor argues that the two principles of review serve distinct functions, and should not be used interchangeably. However, as we shall see, the courts often tend to do precisely that, not least because the two modes of analysis can often be applied within the same factual matrix. Moreover, the two doctrines, while conceptually distinct, are interconnected in important ways, not least as application of each is intimately connected to statutory context. For example, the range and type of factors a decision-maker may legitimately take into account in exercising a discretion is constrained by the purpose for which the discretion was granted.

Before going on to consider these doctrines in detail it is important to emphasize that while fashionable debates over reasonableness review, 'rights', and proportionality rage on in the higher courts and in academic commentary (discussed in ch 8), it is longer established and axiomatic administrative law doctrines, such as improper purpose and relevant considerations, which, while they less often catch law journal headlines, continue to form the bread and butter of administrative law and the Administrative Court's work. Furthermore, their importance in maintaining the rule of law cannot be underestimated, and should not be taken for granted. As Lord Rodger observed in *R (GC)* v. *Commissioner of Police for the Metropolis* [2011] UKSC 21, [2011] 1 WLR 1230 at [107], the improper purpose doctrine is 'one of the most important bulwarks which our predecessors so painstakingly erected against arbitrary acts of the executive'. Let us now turn to examine this fundamental doctrine of administrative law.

7.2.2 Express and implied purposes

It is not uncommon for legislation which confers statutory powers expressly to state the purpose or purposes for which those powers are to be used. In such situations the courts (in the absence of discovering additional, implied purposes for which the powers may legitimately be used) will require the decision-maker to act only for the stated purpose or purposes. It is not difficult to locate a justification for this principle. Most straightforwardly it supports the sovereignty of Parliament, ensuring that the legislature's will is executed, rather than frustrated, by requiring the powers it creates to be used for the purposes it intends. The propriety of purpose doctrine also safeguards the rule of law. One of the central strands within any conception of the rule of law is the principle of legality, which directs that the administration must be able to justify its actions by reference to some legal authority (through the existence of statutory or, much more rarely, prerogative power). The principle was explained in the following terms by Sir Thomas Bingham MR in *R* v. *Somerset County Council, ex parte Fewings* [1995] 1 WLR 1037 at 1042, a case in which the defendant council asserted an unfettered discretion to determine how its land could be used:

> To the famous question asked by the owner of the vineyard ('Is it not lawful for me to do what I will with mine own?' St. Matthew, chapter 20, verse 15) the modern answer would be clear: 'Yes, subject to such regulatory and other constraints as the law imposes.' But if the same question were posed by a local authority the answer would be different. It would be: 'No, it is not lawful for you to do anything save what the law expressly or impliedly authorises. You enjoy no unfettered discretions. There are legal limits to every power you have.'

If the position were otherwise, the executive would, in practice, be free to do as it wished, and any meaningful control of its actions would be rendered impossible. The same would be true if the executive could, at whim, deploy powers granted for one purpose so as to achieve something quite different. If the executive is to be constrained by reference to the legal powers conferred upon it, then courts must be permitted to verify that those powers are not being misapplied. The operation of the propriety of purpose doctrine is illustrated by our next case.

Municipal Council of Sydney v. *Campbell* [1925] AC 339
Privy Council

The facts are stated in the judgment. For a fuller statement, see (1924) 24 SR (NSW) 179.

Duff J (delivering the judgment of the Judicial Committee)

By s. 16 of the Sydney Corporation Amendment Act, 1905, the Municipal Council of Sydney is empowered from time to time, with the approval of the Governor, to purchase or 'resume' any land required for 'carrying out improvements in or remodelling any portion of the city.' ... By s. 3 of an amending Act of 1906, the Council is authorized to purchase or 'resume' any lands required for the opening of new public ways or for widening, enlarging or extending any public ways in the city, as well as any lands of which those required for such purposes are a part.

On March 12, 1923, the Lord Mayor prepared a minute relating to the subject of the extension of Martin Place, an important thoroughfare in the centre of Sydney, and in this minute he recommended the extension of Martin Place to Macquarie Street, and the resumption of a considerable area, which embraced property belonging to the respondents. The proposals of the Lord Mayor's minute were adopted by a resolution of the Council on June 28, and the resumption provided for by the resolution was approved by the Governor in Council.

On the application of the respondents, injunctions were granted by the Chief Judge in Equity, restraining the Council from proceeding under this resolution; and subsequently the Lord Mayor presented another minute, and on November 29 another resolution was passed by the Council, authorizing the resumption of the identical area affected by the former resolution. Again proceedings were taken before the Chief Judge in Equity, who granted injunctions restraining the Council from proceeding under the second resolution; and at the hearing of the actions these injunctions were made permanent. Admittedly, the Council had authority (under s. 3 of the amending Act of 1906) to 'resume' lands for the purpose of extending Martin Place. It is also undisputed that the lands of the respondents which the Council proposes to take are not within the limits of any area which could be required for that purpose. The right to resume them is based upon the assertion that they are 'required' for the purpose of remodelling and improving the city within the sense of s. 16 of the Sydney Corporation Amendment Act.

The learned Chief Judge in Equity held that in point of fact these lands were not really 'required' for any such purpose, but that, as in the case of the other parts of the area affected which were not necessary for the extension of the street, the resumption proceedings were taken with the object of enabling the Council to get the benefit of any increment in the value of them arising from the extension, and thus, in some degree at all events, recouping the municipality the cost of it; and that, since the resumption of lands for such a purpose alone was indisputably not within the ambit of the authority committed to the Council, the resolutions of June and November were both invalid ...

The legal principles governing the execution of such powers as that conferred by s. 16, in so far as presently relevant, are not at all in controversy. A body such as the Municipal Council of Sydney, authorized to take land compulsorily for specified purposes, will not be permitted to exercise its powers for different purposes, and if it attempts to do so, the Courts will interfere. As Lord Loreburn said, in *Marquess of Clanricarde v. Congested Districts Board* [79 JP 481]: 'Whether it does so or not is a question of fact.' Where the proceedings of the Council are attacked upon this ground, the party impeaching those proceedings must, of course, prove that the Council, though professing to exercise its powers for the statutory purpose, is in fact employing them in furtherance of some ulterior object.

Their Lordships think that the conclusion of the learned Chief Judge in Equity upon this question of fact is fully sustained by the evidence … [I]t is admitted that no plan of improvement or remodelling was at any time before the Council; and their Lordships think there is great force in the argument that the course of the oral discussion, as disclosed in the shorthand note produced, shows, when the events leading up to the second minute of the Lord Mayor are considered, that in November the Council was applying itself to the purpose of giving a new form to a transaction already decided upon, rather than to the consideration and determination of the question whether the lands to be taken were required for the purpose of remodelling or improvement. Their Lordships think the learned Chief Judge was right in his conclusion, that upon this question there was no real decision or determination by the Council.

Appeal dismissed.

Even if the enabling legislation does not specify the purposes for which discretionary power may be employed, decision-makers are still held to be constrained by the statutory scheme as a whole, and by the purposes *implicit* in that scheme, as Laws J explained in *R* v. *Somerset County Council, ex parte Fewings* [1995] 1 All ER 513 at 525:

[W]here a statute does not by express words define the purposes for which the powers it confers are to be exercised, the decision-maker is bound nevertheless to ascertain and apply the aims intended, since no statute can be purposeless: and therefore unless the Act's true purpose is correctly understood the decision-maker, who is Parliament's delegate, is at risk of using powers to an end for which they were never given him. If he does so, he exceeds his authority as surely as if he transgresses the plainest statutory language.

7.2.3 The purpose doctrine and the intensity of review

There are numerous cases in which administrative action has been set aside because it contravenes implied statutory purposes; for two celebrated examples, see *Bromley London Borough Council* v. *Greater London Council* [1983] 1 AC 768 and *Congreve* v. *Home Office* [1976] QB 629. However, the judicial task of discerning implied statutory purposes from the general thrust of the legislative scheme can be both difficult (the scheme may be opaque, offering little guidance to the judges) and important (the court's determination that a particular power is limited by an implied purpose may have significant implications for the scope of the decision-maker's discretion). These points are illustrated by our next case.

R v. *Secretary of State for Foreign and Commonwealth Affairs, ex parte World Development Movement Ltd* [1995] 1 WLR 386
Queen's Bench Division

Section 1(1) of the Overseas Development and Co-operation Act 1980 provided that '[t]he Secretary of State shall have power, for the purpose of promoting the development or maintaining the economy of a country or territory outside the United Kingdom, or the welfare of its people, to furnish any person or body with assistance, whether financial, technical or of any other nature'. Purporting to act under this power, the Secretary of State approved aid and trade provision (ATP) for the construction of a hydro-electric power station on the Pergau river in Malaysia. Before final approval was given, but after the British government had informally agreed with the Malaysian government that it would contribute to the project, the Overseas Development Administration concluded that the project was economically unviable and a 'very bad buy'. The claimant, a pressure group, felt that the Secretary of State, by going ahead with the project in spite of these problems, was misusing public funds and acting unlawfully. It there-fore sought judicial review. (The standing of the claimant is considered in a separate excerpt at 14.7.4.)

Rose LJ

... The provision of A.T.P. for a purpose known by the Government not to be 'sound economic development,' submitted Mr. Pleming [for the claimant], could not be within section 1 [of the Act of 1980] ... The reason or motive [for funding the project], submitted Mr. Pleming, was polit-ical or diplomatic, namely that the Prime Minister had given an undertaking in March 1989 that Britain would provide A.T.P. support, and to go back on that word would be detrimental to the interests of Britain, British companies and British workers. Section 1, submitted Mr. Pleming, confers no power to make decisions on such a basis ...

Mr. Richards [for the defendant] submitted that this decision was taken by the Secretary of State personally and his thinking is of decisive importance in determining the purpose for which the assistance was furnished. The Secretary of State plainly considered, from the terms of his affidavit, that the assistance was for a developmental purpose, and he also took into account additional considerations. Mr. Richards submitted further that the applicant's argument that an unsound development cannot furnish a purpose within section 1 should be rejected ... because the word 'sound' does not appear in the Act. What the statute requires is a developmental pur-pose within the broad terms of section 1(1), and the statutory power cannot be limited by the adoption of 'soundness' by an A.T.P. scheme or anything else ...

For my part, I am unable to accept Mr. Richards's submission that it is the Secretary of State's thinking which is determinative of whether the purpose was within the statute and that there-fore paragraph 3 of his affidavit is conclusive. Whatever the Secretary of State's intention or purpose may have been, it is, as it seems to me, a matter for the courts and not for the Secretary of State to determine whether, on the evidence before the court, the particular conduct was, or was not, within the statutory purpose.

As to the absence of the word 'sound' from section 1(1), it seems to me that, if Parliament had intended to confer a power to disburse money for unsound developmental purposes, it could have been expected to say so expressly. And I am comforted in this view by the way in which the successive Ministers, guidelines, governments and White Papers, identified by Mr. Pleming, have, over the years and without exception, construed the power as relating to economically sound development ...

The Secretary of State is, of course, generally speaking, fully entitled, when making decisions, to take into account political and economic considerations such as the promotion of regional stability, good government, human rights and British commercial interests. In the present case, the political impossibility of withdrawing the 1989 offer has been recognised since mid-April of that year, and had there, in 1991, been a developmental promotion purpose within section 1 of the Act of 1980, it would have been entirely proper for the Secretary of State to have taken into account, also, the impact which withdrawing the 1989 offer would have had, both on the United Kingdom's credibility as a reliable friend and trading partner and on political and commercial relations with Malaysia. But for the reasons given, I am of the view, on the evidence before this court, that there was, in July 1991, no such purpose within the section. It follows that the July 1991 decision was, in my judgment, unlawful.

Scott Baker J delivered a short, concurring judgment. A declaration was issued to the effect that the Secretary of State's decision was unlawful.

Rose LJ's decision to read the criterion of economic soundness into the enabling provision, thereby limiting the purposes for which aid could be granted, had a major impact on the scope of the Secretary of State's power, and, allied with the Court's view that the project was economically unsound, was fatal to the legality of the decision. This demonstrates the potential potency of the purpose doctrine. Once the court concludes that a statutory power may only be used to further a particular purpose, the freedom of the decision-maker is necessarily limited: unless the court is satisfied that the action undertaken by the administrator was within the purpose, it will be held unlawful. The *Pergau Dam* case—and, in particular, its use of the purpose doctrine to facilitate an intensive mode of judicial review—is roundly condemned by Irvine, *Human Rights, Constitutional Law and the Development of the English Legal System* (Oxford 2003) at 164–5:

[T]he courts [in judicial review cases] have no choice but to exercise self-restraint ... [However,] it is, perhaps, unsurprising that in this sensitive area the courts have occasionally overstepped the mark. For instance, in the *Pergau Dam* case, the issue was whether a grant of aid to help build a dam in Malaysia was 'for the purpose of promoting the development' of that country within the meaning of the relevant legislation. The court held that, properly understood, this meant 'sound development', and concluded that the decision to make the grant was unlawful because, in the view of the court, the grant was economically unsound. By reading an additional requirement into the statute in this way, the court took away from the executive a considerable degree of autonomy. It is this type of judicial activism which begins to blur the boundary between appeal and review, thereby undermining the constitutional foundations on which the courts' supervisory jurisdiction rests.

QUESTION

• How might the decision of the Court be defended against Irvine's criticism?

It is worth noting that, if the criterion of economic soundness had been characterized by the Court as a relevant consideration which the Secretary of State was obliged to take into account, rather than as part of the definition of purpose underlying the discretion, the outcome would most likely have been different since, as we shall see later, it is for the decision-maker, not the court, to determine how much weight (if any) to attach to relevant considerations. This mode of analysis tends to lead to a less intensive standard of review and, in turn, ascribes a wider discretion to the decision-maker. This demonstrates that, although the propriety of purpose and relevancy of considerations doctrines are often regarded interchangeably, they can in fact yield different styles of review and, ultimately, different results. The choice between those two approaches is therefore open to instrumental use by courts seeking to manipulate the standard and outcome of judicial review. The general failure by the judiciary explicitly to address which mode of analysis is appropriate in particular cases makes it difficult to determine whether such instrumentalism actually operates, but certainly leaves room for suspicion that, consciously or otherwise, judges pick and choose in order to produce the 'right' outcome.

7.2.4 Multiple purposes

It is often the case that, when a public authority adopts a particular course of action pursuant to an exercise (or purported exercise) of discretion, it is motivated by more than one purpose. If all of the purposes for which the authority acts are legitimate statutory purposes, no problem arises. But what if an authority is spurred to action by a number of purposes, not all of which are legitimate? This question arose in *Westminster Corporation v. London and North Western Railway Co* [1905] AC 426. The Corporation built public toilets and a subway affording access to them from both sides of the street under which the toilets were situated. The appellant railway company, which owned premises opposite one of the entrances, took exception to this. It argued that while the Corporation was empowered to build public toilets, the real purpose of the scheme was to build a subway—which the Corporation had no power to do. However, this argument failed for reasons set out by Lord Macnaughten (at 432):

> It is not enough to shew that the corporation contemplated that the public might use the subway as a means of crossing the street. That was an obvious possibility. It cannot be otherwise if you have an entrance on each side and the communication is not interrupted by a wall or a barrier of some sort. In order to make out a case of bad faith it must be shewn that the corporation constructed this subway as a means of crossing the street under colour and pretence of providing public conveniences which were not really wanted at that particular place.

The upshot of the approach in the *Westminster* case is that administrative action based upon mixed purposes will be lawful provided that the 'dominant purpose'—as Denning LJ put it in *Earl Fitzwilliam's Wentworth Estates Co v. Minister of Town and Country Planning* [1951] 2 KB 284 at 307—is a legitimate one. The application of this test raises evidential difficulties, particularly if public authorities put forward legitimate purposes in order to mask other, unlawful motives for their action. The courts are, however, alert to this problem; as Lord Denning MR explained in *R v. Governor of Brixton Prison, ex parte Soblen* [1963] 2 QB 243 at 302, the courts will, where necessary, 'go behind' the face of the act in order to determine its true purpose. Indeed, public bodies are required to assist the reviewing court by furnishing it with relevant evidence (see 11.1), but it is important to note that traditionally the capacity of courts to hear oral evidence and order disclosure within review proceedings has been limited (see 13.2).

7.2.5 Parliament's purpose or individual rights?

Since the improper purpose doctrine was recognized, a number of more modern rules or maxims of statutory construction have entered administrative law, which are geared not towards vindicating Parliament's purpose in conferring particular powers but to protecting individual rights which might be compromised where powers are exercised in pursuit of public purposes set by Parliament. In recent years, and especially since the last edition of this book, there has been a glut of important cases in which these newer doctrines have come into direct conflict with the more established proposition that powers should be exercised for their intended purposes.

One such maxim of interpretation, developed by the courts, is the principle of legality, which holds that for a statute to permit executive interference with basic common law rights, that statute must expressly or by necessary implication authorize such interference: *R v. Secretary of State for the Home Department, ex parte Simms* [1999] UKHL 33, [2000] 2 AC 115. Another, which shall be our focus here, is the rule introduced by s 3 of the Human Rights Act 1998 (HRA), that '[s]o far as it is possible to do so, primary legislation and subordinate legislation must be read and given effect in a way which is compatible with the Convention rights'. This interpretive rule tends to be more potent than the legality principle as it requires courts to actively seek, as far it is possible to do so, to adopt rights-consistent interpretations.

Often a power exercised consistently with its underlying purposes will not impermissibly interfere with the rights of individuals subject to exercise of that power, so that there shall be no tension between the demands of the improper purposes doctrine and rights-centred rules of interpretation. In other words, a discretion or power will often be framed broadly enough that there will be rights-compatible ways in which the discretion or power can be exercised which also remain faithful to the purpose for which the power was conferred. However, sometimes there may be no way for the decision-maker to exercise the discretion or power genuinely for its intended purpose, while also acting compatibly with human rights. Such cases pose a conundrum. Should Parliament's purposes prevail or should the courts afford statutory provisions a rights-consistent meaning which, while affording due protection to rights, operates to undermine decision-makers' ability to exercise powers in pursuit of the public purposes for which the powers were conferred?

While some cases through the 2000s suggested courts could go so far as to adopt an interpretation of statutory provisions plainly contrary to Parliament's clear intent (*Ghaidan v. Godin-Mendoza* [2004] UKHL 30, [2004] 2 AC 557), recent cases clearly indicate that an interpretation contrary to the underlying purposes of the legislation is impermissible; in other words, the purpose doctrine must trump principles of rights-consistent interpretation. While it is generally accepted that HRA, s 3 gives courts licence to adopt an interpretation which 'stretches' the plain meaning of a provision, adoption of an interpretation fundamentally at odds with parliamentary purpose now seems a bridge courts refuse to cross: this would be to go beyond what is 'possible', to quote s 3. Thus, in *R v. Waya* [2012] UKSC 51, [2013] 1 AC 294 at [20], the Supreme Court endorsed the proposition that

> the clear limitation on the domestic court's power to read and give effect to the statute in a manner which keeps it Convention-compliant [under s 3 of the HRA] is that the interpretation must recognise and respect the essential purpose, or 'grain' of the statute.

Therefore, if there are a range of rights-consistent interpretations open to a court, it must choose among those which respect the essential grain of the legislation. If all possible rights-consistent interpretations run against the essential purpose of the legislation then those interpretations shall be impermissible, and an interpretation consistent with the statute's underlying purpose must win out.

At first blush such approach clearly prioritizes administrative pursuit of those public purposes for which powers are conferred, ahead of rights protection. Such approach reflects the different roles of Parliament and the courts in the separation of powers: to alter the ordinary meaning of statutory language via some creative word play to protect a fundamental right would be one thing, but to adopt an interpretation at odds with Parliament's clear intent would pose a direct challenge to parliamentary sovereignty as it would involve courts creating a fundamentally different legislative scheme from that which Parliament intended.

However, whether a court reaches the stage of the analysis where the purpose doctrine will trump depends on whether the court identifies an irreconcilable clash between a purposive and a rights-consistent interpretation in the first place; only if there is an irreconcilable clash will a court need to choose between the two. Whether there is a clash hinges on a prior question: what purposes did Parliament intend the relevant statutory discretion or power to be used for? As discussed earlier the reality is that courts may enjoy significant leeway as to how they formulate the relevant purpose. In many cases we find courts adopting a view of Parliament's purpose which enables the court to avoid a direct clash between purpose and rights. This shall allow the courts the leeway to adopt a rights-consistent interpretation, and maintain that their interpretation does not undercut the purposes for which Parliament conferred the relevant statutory powers.

The Supreme Court case of *R (GC)* v *Commissioner of Police for the Metropolis* [2011] UKSC 21, [2011] 1 WLR 1230 provides an excellent illustration of the matters discussed in the previous paragraph. The case concerned, among other matters, the proper interpretation of s 64(1A) of the Police and Criminal Evidence Act 1984, which grants the police a discretion to retain the data obtained from a criminal suspect as part of a 'DNA database'. The provision makes no express provision for any time limit for the retention of the data or any procedure to regulate its destruction. However, the police had adopted guidelines as to how the discretion should be exercised. These provided that the police would not exercise their discretion to remove data from the database or order destruction of DNA or fingerprint samples—for example where the suspect had requested that their data be removed or destroyed—except in an exceptional case, and such cases would be rare. It was clear these guidelines were incompatible with human rights as the ECtHR had previously found the guidelines breached Article 8: operating a blanket policy of indefinite data retention was a disproportionate interference with privacy. For the scheme to be compatible with Article 8 the police would have to exercise their discretion *on a case-by-case basis* and in each case assess whether retention of an individual's data was a proportionate and thus justifiable interference with privacy, given consideration of various factors such as the nature of offence which the individual was suspected of committing and their age. Obviously, the blanket policy in the guidelines in favour of retention was at odds with such a case-sensitive approach.

A core question for the Supreme Court was whether, on its proper interpretation, s 64(1A) necessarily required the blanket approach adopted in the guidelines, or whether that provision afforded sufficient leeway for the discretion to remove data to be exercised more liberally, and therefore consistently with Article 8. The Court split on this issue. At the core of the disagreement between majority and minority was the purpose for which the discretion in s 64(1A) had been conferred.

In the minority, Lord Rodger invoked the purpose doctrine: '[I]n my view the power which was conferred on the police by s 64(1A) had to be exercised in accord with the policy and objects of that enactment'. For his Lordship 'the policy and objects of Parliament in enacting s 64(1A) were plainly that DNA samples and data derived from suspects should be retained indefinitely so that a large and expanding database should be available to aid the detection and prosecution of the perpetrators of crimes'. Given this underlying purpose '[t]he police were therefore bound to exercise the power given to them by s 64(1A) in order to promote that policy and those objects. Adopting a purposive approach this meant, in effect, that, subject to possible very narrow exceptions ... the police had to retain on their database the samples and profiles of all suspects.' In response to the argument that the purposive interpretation should be departed from according to s 3 of the HRA, Lord Rodger argued that retention of data indefinitely was a 'fundamental feature' of the legislation: 'The truth is that Parliament wanted to eliminate the danger, which existed under the pre-existing legislation, that valuable evidence would be lost and potential prosecutions of the guilty based on the latest science would be jeopardised if material had to be removed from the database. Providing for the material to be retained on the database indefinitely was therefore *the* fundamental feature of the amending legislation which inserted s 64(1A) into PACE.' He considered that reinterpreting s 64(1A) so as to afford police greater leeway or flexibility to delete entries on a case-by-case basis would 'negate the defining feature of the legislation. In other words, the court would have crossed the line from interpreting to amending the legislation. Amending section 64(1A) in that way is something which only Parliament can do.' Thus, consistent with other decisions such as *Waya*, the purpose doctrine trumps.

The majority took a different view. However, the point of disagreement between the majority and minority was not over whether the purpose doctrine should trump. Rather, the majority took a different view of the purpose behind s 64(1A), defining the purpose in more general terms than Lord Rodger did, which in turn avoided any irreconcilable clash between a purposive interpretation and a rights-consistent interpretation. Thus, Lord Dyson, in the majority, said that if it was, as Lord Rodger had concluded (at [23], emphasis in original),

> the intention of Parliament that, save in exceptional cases, the data taken from *all* suspects in connection with the investigation of an offence should be retained *indefinitely*' then it 'goes without saying that ... section 64(1A) ... can only be interpreted as conferring a discretion which *must* be exercised so as to give effect to that intention. The conclusion necessarily follows from the premise.

However, Lord Dyson did 'not accept the premise' (at [24]). He considered the purposes underlying the provision to be less prescriptive or specific than the purpose Lord Rodger had imputed to Parliament. While Parliament had clearly intended to create a scheme for retention of data taken from suspects so that that data could be used for certain purposes such as investigation of crime, it did not necessarily follow from this that Parliament intended the data to generally be retained indefinitely barring exceptional circumstances; if Parliament had intended a scheme with such specific features it would have recorded this in the terms of the Act—but it had not. The broad framing of s 64(1A) as a power that police 'may' retain data told against this more specific intention. Because of the majority's more general framing of the purpose underlying s 64(1A), the police would have more leeway as to how they could exercise the discretion under s 64(1)—it was not the case, as Lord Rodger had held, that in order to give effect to Parliament's purpose the police generally had to exercise their discretion in favour of retaining suspects' data indefinitely. All the police had to do to fulfil Parliament's purpose, on the majority's view of that purpose, was to maintain a database of data obtained from suspects, but the terms on which that database was administered, including the criteria governing whether and when data should be removed from the database, was for the police to determine. On this view it would be compatible with Parliament's purpose for the police to depart from the blanket policy of retention and instead exercise their powers to release data on a case-by-case basis and compatibly with Article 8, and the police ought to do so given the interpretive rule in HRA, s 3 that a rights-consistent approach ought to be favoured.

Thus, even in this new line of cases on the improper purpose doctrine we find a familiar story: while the courts may frame their conclusions as to statutory purpose as following inexorably from a dispassionate and objective exercise in statutory interpretation, there is often significant room for disagreement over what the relevant purpose is. Further, there is scope for one's normative preferences to shape the distillation of Parliament's purpose: the strength of one's desire to ensure protection of human rights may (consciously or not) shape one's conclusions as to how purpose is to be framed.

7.3 Inputs into the decision-making process: the relevancy doctrine

7.3.1 Introduction

Although it is of the essence of discretion that the decision-maker can *choose* how to resolve a particular case, it is important that he exercises judgment on the basis of germane matters. The relevancy doctrine exists to this end, and was explained in the following terms by Megaw J in *Hanks* v. *Minister of Housing and Local Government* [1963] 1 QB 999 at 1020:

> [I]f it be shown that an authority exercising a power has taken into account as a relevant factor something which it could not properly take into account in deciding whether or not to exercise the power, then the exercise of the power, normally at least, is bad. Similarly, if the authority fails to take into account as a relevant factor something which is relevant, and which is or ought to be known to it, and which it ought to have taken into account, the exercise of the power is normally bad. I say 'normally' because I can conceive that there may be cases where the factor wrongly taken into account, or omitted, is insignificant, or where the wrong taking into account, or omission, actually operated in favour of the person who later claims to be aggrieved by the decision.

By requiring decision-makers to take account of all those factors which are relevant to the matter in hand, and forbidding the consideration of irrelevant factors, the relevancy doctrine aims to uphold the quality of administrative decisions by regulating the evidence upon which they are based. Other principles of administrative law, which we consider later in the book, address the same problem in different (but complementary) ways. For instance, the principles of procedural fairness, which are addressed in ch 10, confront this issue from a pragmatic perspective; by requiring the decision-maker to listen to the views and evidence of the citizen who will be affected by the decision in question, those principles seek to ensure that the decision-maker is, in the first place, in receipt of all the relevant evidence. Meanwhile, the relevancy doctrine insists that once a fair procedure has yielded such information to the decision-maker, it must actually be taken into account when the decision is finally made. It is important, therefore, to remember that the relevancy doctrine operates not in a vacuum, but as part of a network of administrative law principles which seek to promote good decision-making. The difficulty, as we shall see, lies in drawing a line between matters which are and are not legally relevant.

7.3.2 General principles

The operation of the relevancy doctrine is illustrated by the following case. Note, however, that the propriety of purpose and relevancy doctrines are used somewhat interchangeably—a trait which, as we noted earlier, is often found in the case law.

Padfield v. *Minister of Agrictulture, Fisheries and Food* [1968] AC 997
House of Lords

Section 19(3) of the Agricultural Marketing Act 1958 provides that '[a] committee of investigation shall … *(b)* be charged with the duty, if the Minister in any case so directs, of considering, and reporting to the Minister on … any … complaint made to the Minister as to the operation of any scheme which, in the opinion of the Minister, could not be considered by a Consumers' Committee'. England and Wales were divided into 11 regions for the purpose of the Milk Marketing Board. Producers had to sell their milk to the Board at prices which differed from region to region to reflect the varying costs of transporting milk from the producers to the consumers. Transport costs had altered and the south-eastern region wished the differential to be altered. The constitution of the Board made it impossible for the south-eastern producers to get a majority for their proposals and they asked the Minister to appoint a committee of investigation. When the Minister refused they applied for a mandatory order directing him to refer the complaint to a committee of investigation or to deal with it according to law, *ie* on relevant considerations only, to the exclusion of irrelevant considerations. At first instance this was granted, but the Court of Appeal allowed an appeal by the Minister and the producers appealed to the House of Lords.

Lord Reid

… [The Minister] contends that his only duty is to consider a complaint fairly and that he is given an unfettered discretion with regard to every complaint either to refer it or not to refer it to the committee as he may think fit. The appellants contend that it is his duty to refer every genuine and substantial complaint, or alternatively that his discretion is not unfettered and that in this case he failed to exercise his discretion according to law because his refusal was caused or influenced by his having misdirected himself in law or by his having taken into account extraneous or irrelevant considerations.

In my view, the appellants' first contention goes too far. There are a number of reasons which would justify the Minister in refusing to refer a complaint. For example, he might consider it more suitable for arbitration, or he might consider that in an earlier case the committee of investigation had already rejected a substantially similar complaint, or he might think the complaint to be frivolous or vexatious. So he must have at least some measure of discretion. But is it unfettered?

It is implicit in the argument for the Minister that there are only two possible interpretations of this provision—either he must refer every complaint or he has an unfettered discretion to refuse to refer in any case. I do not think that is right. Parliament must have conferred the discretion with the intention that it should be used to promote the policy and objects of the Act; the policy and objects of the Act must be determined by construing the Act as a whole and construction is always a matter of law for the court. In a matter of this kind it is not possible to draw a hard and fast line, but if the Minister, by reason of his having misconstrued the Act or for any other reason, so uses his discretion as to thwart or run counter to the policy and objects of the Act, then our law would be very defective if persons aggrieved were not entitled to the protection of the court. So it is necessary first to construe the Act.

When these provisions were first enacted in 1931 it was unusual for Parliament to compel people to sell their commodities in a way to which they objected and it was easily foreseeable that any such scheme would cause loss to some producers. Moreover, if the operation of the scheme was put in the hands of the majority of the producers, it was obvious that they might use their power to the detriment of consumers, distributors or a minority of the producers. So it is not surprising that Parliament enacted safeguards.

The approval of Parliament shows that this scheme was thought to be in the public interest, and in so far as it necessarily involved detriment to some persons, it must have been thought to be in the public interest that they should suffer it. But in sections 19 and 20 Parliament drew a line. They provide machinery for investigating and determining whether the scheme is operating or the board is acting in a manner contrary to the public interest.

The effect of these sections is that if, but only if, the Minister and the committee of investigation concur in the view that something is being done contrary to the public interest the Minister can step in. Section 20 enables the Minister to take the initiative. Section 19 deals with complaints by individuals who are aggrieved. I need not deal with the provisions which apply to consumers. We are concerned with other persons who may be distributors or producers. If the Minister directs that a complaint by any of them shall be referred to the committee of investigation, that committee will make a report which must be published. If they report that any provision of this scheme or any act or omission of the board is contrary to the interests of the complainers *and* is not in the public interest, then the Minister is empowered to take action, but not otherwise. He may disagree with the view of the committee as to public interest, and, if he thinks that there are other public interests which outweigh the public interest that justice should be done to the complainers, he would be not only entitled but bound to refuse to take action. Whether he takes action or not, he may be criticised and held accountable in Parliament but the court cannot interfere.

I must now examine the Minister's reasons for refusing to refer the appellants' complaint to the committee …

The first reason which the Minister gave in his letter of March 23, 1965, was that this complaint was unsuitable for investigation because it raised wide issues. Here it appears to me that the Minister has clearly misdirected himself. Section 19(6) contemplates the raising of issues so wide that it may be necessary for the Minister to amend a scheme or even to revoke it. Narrower issues may be suitable for arbitration but section 19 affords the only method of investigating wide issues. In my view it is plainly the intention of the Act that even the widest issues should be investigated if the complaint is genuine and substantial, as this complaint certainly is.

Then it is said that this issue should be 'resolved through the arrangements available to producers and the board within the framework of the scheme itself.' This re-states in a condensed form the reasons given in paragraph 4 of the letter of May 1, 1964, where it is said 'the Minister owes no duty to producers in any particular region,' and reference is made to the 'status of the Milk Marketing Scheme as an instrument for the self-government of the industry,' and to the Minister 'assuming an inappropriate degree of responsibility.' But, as I have already pointed out, the Act imposes on the Minister a responsibility whenever there is a relevant and substantial complaint that the board are acting in a manner inconsistent with the public interest, and that has been relevantly alleged in this case. I can find nothing in the Act to limit this responsibility or to justify the statement that the Minister owes no duty to producers in a particular region. The Minister is, I think, correct in saying that the board is an instrument for the self-government of the industry. So long as it does not act contrary to the public interest the Minister cannot interfere. But if it does act contrary to what both the committee of investigation and the Minister hold to be the public interest the Minister has a duty to act. And if a complaint relevantly alleges that the board has so acted, as this complaint does, then it appears to me that the Act does impose a duty on the Minister to have it investigated. If he does not do that he is rendering nugatory a safeguard provided by the Act and depriving complainers of a remedy which I am satisfied that Parliament intended them to have.

Paragraph 3 of the letter of May 1, 1964 [a letter written by the Ministry, explaining the considerations the Minister would take into account in deciding whether to refer the issue to a committee of investigation] refers to the possibility that, if the complaint were referred and the committee were to uphold it, the Minister 'would be expected to make a statutory Order to give effect to the committee's recommendations.' If this means that he is entitled to refuse to refer a complaint because, if he did so, he might later find himself in an embarrassing situation, that would plainly be a bad reason ...

[After considering the Minister's reasons, his Lordship turned to the argument that the discretion was unfettered, and said:] I have found no authority to support the unreasonable proposition that it must be all or nothing—either no discretion at all or an unfettered discretion. Here the words 'if the Minister in any case so directs' are sufficient to show that he has some discretion but they give no guide as to its nature or extent. That must be inferred from a construction of the Act read as a whole, and for the reasons I have given I would infer that the discretion is not unlimited, and that it has been used by the Minister in a manner which is not in accord with the intention of the statute which conferred it.

As the Minister's discretion has never been properly exercised according to law, I would allow this appeal. It appears to me that the case should now be remitted to the Queen's Bench Division with a direction to require the Minister to consider the complaint of the appellants according to law ...

Lord Upjohn

... The Minister in exercising his powers and duties, conferred upon him by statute, can only be controlled by a prerogative writ which will only issue if he acts unlawfully. Unlawful behaviour by the Minister may be stated with sufficient accuracy for the purposes of the present appeal (and here I adopt the classification of Lord Parker C.J., in the Divisional Court): (a) by an outright refusal to consider the relevant matter, or (b) by misdirecting himself in point of law, or (c) by taking into account some wholly irrelevant or extraneous consideration, or (d) by wholly omitting to take into account a relevant consideration.

There is ample authority for these propositions which were not challenged in argument. In practice they merge into one another and ultimately it becomes a question whether for one reason or another the Minister has acted unlawfully in the sense of misdirecting himself in law, that is, not merely in respect of some point of law but by failing to observe the other headings I have mentioned.

In the circumstances of this case, which I have sufficiently detailed for this purpose, it seems to me quite clear that prima facie there seems a case for investigation by the committee of investigation. As I have said already, it seems just the type of situation for which the machinery of section 19 was set up, but that is a matter for the Minister.

He may have good reasons for refusing an investigation, he may have, indeed, good policy reasons for refusing it, though that policy must not be based on political considerations which as Farwell LJ said in Rex v. Board of Education [1910] 2 K.B. 151 at 181 are pre-eminently extraneous. So I must examine the reasons given by the Minister, including any policy upon which they may be based, to see whether he has acted unlawfully and thereby overstepped the true limits of his discretion, or, as it is frequently said in the prerogative writ cases, exceeded his jurisdiction. Unless he has done so, the court has no jurisdiction to interfere. It is not a Court of Appeal and has no jurisdiction to correct the decision of the Minister acting lawfully within his discretion, however much the court may disagree with its exercise.

[His Lordship then considered the Minister's reasons. In dealing with the argument that the discretion was unfettered he said:] My Lords, I believe that the introduction of the adjective

'unfettered' and its reliance thereon as an answer to the appellants' claim is one of the fundamental matters confounding the Minister's attitude, bona fide though it be. First, the adjective
nowhere appears in section 19, it is an unauthorised gloss by the Minister. Secondly, even if the
section did contain that adjective I doubt if it would make any difference in law to his powers,
save to emphasise what he has already, namely that acting lawfully he has a power of decision
which cannot be controlled by the courts; it is unfettered. But the use of that adjective, even in
an Act of Parliament, can do nothing to unfetter the control which the judiciary have over the
executive, namely that in exercising their powers the latter must act lawfully and that is a matter
to be determined by looking at the Act and its scope and object in conferring a discretion upon
the Minister rather than by the use of adjectives.

*Lords Hodson and Pearce delivered speeches in favour of allowing the appeal. Lord Morris delivered
a speech in favour of dismissing the appeal. The appeal was therefore allowed, and the Minister
was required to reconsider the matter.*

As a result of the case the Minister referred the complaint to the Committee, which reported
that the current prices were contrary to the interests of the south-eastern region and the
public interest. However, the Minister decided not to direct the Milk Marketing Board to
act on the Committee's conclusions since this could precipitate the collapse of the system
for organized milk marketing, and because he had taken into account wider policy matters
that were beyond the scope of the Committee's inquiry.

QUESTIONS

- Even though the Minister was obliged to take into account relevant matters
  and exclude irrelevant factors from consideration, the outcome in *Padfield* was
  ultimately unfavourable to the milk producers. Harlow [1976] *PL* 116 at 120
  concludes that the judicial 'remedy had proved illusory; the same decision could
  be reached with only nominal deference to the court, and the waste of time and
  money entailed is a deterrent to future complainants'. How does this relate to the
  connection, postulated at 7.3.1, between the nature of the decision-making process
  and the quality of its outputs?
- And what light does *Padfield* shed on the distinction between appeal and review?

One of the main difficulties which arises in this context relates to the determination of
relevancy and irrelevancy. How are the courts to decide which, if any, of those categories
a particular factor falls into? Much turns upon close analysis of the legislation (see, *eg R
(Sainsbury's Supermarkets Ltd)* v. *Wolverhampton City Council* [2010] UKSC 20, [2010] 2
WLR 1173), but four particular issues are worth highlighting.

First, as Cooke J explained in *CREEDNZ* v. *Governor-General of New Zealand* [1981] 1
NZLR 172 at 183, '*the more general and the more obviously important the consideration,
the readier the court must be to hold that Parliament must have meant it to be taken into
account*' (emphasis added). For instance, in *R (Corner House Research)* v. *Director of the
Serious Fraud Office* [2008] UKHL 60, [2009] 1 AC 756, the Director of the Serious Fraud
Office decided to stop a criminal investigation into allegations of bribery against a major
British company. He did so in the light of a threat issued by the Saudi Arabian government—members of which were allegedly recipients of the corrupt payments—that it would
cease co-operation with the UK government on counter-terrorism matters. The defendant was advised that this threat, if carried out, would place at risk 'British lives on British

streets'. The House of Lords held that the defendant's decision was lawful, and that he had been entitled to take the Saudi threat into account in making his decision. On that point, Baroness Hale, at [53], said:

> It is common ground that it would not have been lawful for him to take account of threats of harm to himself, threats of the 'we know where you live' variety. That sort of threat would have been an irrelevant consideration. So what makes this sort of threat different? Why should the Director be obliged to ignore threats to his own personal safety (and presumably that of his family) but entitled to take into account threats to the safety of others? The answer must lie in a distinction between the personal and the public interest. The 'public interest' is often invoked but not susceptible of precise definition. But it must mean something of importance to the public as a whole rather than just to a private individual. The withdrawal of Saudi security co-operation would indeed have consequences of importance for the public as a whole.

The relative importance of a consideration, and thus whether it is relevant or irrelevant, may well depend on the importance of *other, competing* interests or considerations and/or *the context* in which the decision falls to be made. Thus, in *R (HSE)* v. *Wolverhampton City Council* [2012] UKSC 34, [2012] 4 All ER 429, Lord Carnwath suggested that how a decision impacts upon public funds may in general be a relevant consideration in exercising public power, if not a mandatory consideration. However, he also thought the relevancy of the consideration may well depend on the context in which the decision was being made; thus, where a national security decision needed to be taken as a matter of urgency, the financial impact of the decision would not necessarily be relevant, or as relevant. Similarly, in *Hayes* v. *Chief Constable of Merseyside Police* [2011] EWCA Civ 911, [2012] 1 WLR 517 at [40], the Court recognized the need to take into account the demands of practical policing in determining how the relevancy doctrine applied to a police officer's decision to effect an arrest. The Court held a police officer does not have to turn his mind to all relevant considerations, exclude every irrelevant matter, and consider all alternatives to arrest when deciding whether to make an arrest. To require officers to do so would impose an unattainable and unrealistic burden on them, especially as officers may have to make urgent decisions in dangerous circumstances.

Second, the *nature of the decision-making function* is important. For instance, in *R* v. *Secretary of State for the Home Department, ex parte Venables* [1998] AC 407, the Home Secretary, when deciding on the minimum period of detention for a child convicted of murder (a function which has since been held inconsistent with Article 5 ECHR: *Stafford* v. *United Kingdom* (2002) 35 EHRR 32), took into account public revulsion in relation to the incident in question. The fact that the Home Secretary was exercising a sentencing power meant that he had acted improperly by considering such factors, as Lord Steyn explained at 526:

> The comparison between the position of the Home Secretary, when he fixes a tariff representing the punitive element of the sentence, and the position of a sentencing judge is correct. In fixing a tariff the Home Secretary is carrying out ... a classic judicial function ... Plainly a sentencing judge must ignore a newspaper campaign designed to encourage him to increase a particular sentence ... Like a judge the Home Secretary ought not to be guided by a disposition to consult how popular a particular decision may be. The power given to him requires, above all, a detached approach. I would therefore hold that public protests about the level of a tariff to be fixed in a particular case are legally irrelevant and may not be taken into account by the Home Secretary in fixing the tariff.

More generally, it seems the courts will not look kindly upon decision-makers who make decisions out of a concern for political expediency. Public power ought to be exercised for the common good, not so as to preserve the government's political popularity and save government blushes. Thus, in *R (Evans)* v. *Lord Chancellor* [2011] EWHC 1146, [2011] 3 All ER 594, the Court considered it was impermissible for government to radically restrict legal aid funding for public interest groups out of a concern that the outcomes of judicial review challenges brought by such groups may be politically damaging for government.

Third, the *statutory scheme* plays an important part in the determination of relevancy. This point is usefully illustrated by *R* v. *Gloucestershire County Council, ex parte Barry* [1997] AC 584 and *R* v. *East Sussex County Council, ex parte Tandy* [1998] AC 714. Both cases concerned the question whether financial implications could be taken into account in determining the level of provision to make in relation to (respectively) domestic assistance for the disabled and educational services; scarcity of resources was held to be a legitimate consideration in the former case, but a prohibited consideration in the latter. The decisions were distinguished on the basis of differences between the two statutory frameworks.

Fourth, where decisions are being made pursuant to a policy or statutory scheme, the *underlying objectives* of the policy or scheme will help to determine what count as relevant and irrelevant considerations. Take, for example, *R (Limbu)* v. *Secretary of State for the Home Department* [2008] EWHC 2261 (Admin), [2008] HRLR 48. The Home Secretary announced a change in the policy concerning the circumstances in which certain former members of the Brigade of Gurkhas—a part of the British Army made up of foreign nationals—were to be permitted to settle in the UK. In making the announcement, the Minister referred to the loyalty and bravery of the Gurkhas and said he was 'very keen to ensure that we recognise their role in the history of our country and the part they have played in protecting us'. Yet the policy was extremely restrictive. For example, it permitted immigration officers to grant entry clearance to Gurkhas who had already spent three years in the UK—a criterion very few could satisfy—and did not provide for account to be taken of such matters as length and distinction of military service. This, it was held, was unlawful: Blake J said at [69] that the policy appeared to have 'excluded material and potentially decisive considerations that the context and the stated purpose of the policy indicate should have been included'.

7.3.3 Relevancy, judicial intervention, and executive autonomy

An underlying tension in the relationship between the judiciary and executive may be discerned in this context. To what extent should the former, by means of the relevancy doctrine, prescribe the nature of the decision-making process and, by possible extension, its outcomes? Two particular issues arise.

The first concerns how prescriptive the courts should be in setting the parameters of the decision-making process. How willing should courts be to determine that a given factor is legally relevant, such that it *must* be taken into consideration, or legally irrelevant, such that it *must not* be? We will see later that there is a good deal to be said for judicial caution in this context, in particular for recognition of an intermediate category of factors which decision-makers should be largely free to *choose* whether to consider. However, in order to demonstrate why this is important, it is first necessary to illustrate the extent to which categorizing factors as legally relevant or irrelevant may allow the courts to prescribe the premises on which decisions are taken—and perhaps (indirectly) the decisions themselves—with a high degree of specificity.

The classic House of Lords decision of *Roberts* v. *Hopwood* [1925] AC 578 provides a striking example of the extent to which the courts can, through application of the relevant considerations doctrine, exert significant influence over both the decision-making process and outcome.

At a time when both the cost of living and trade union scale wage rates had been falling for some time, Poplar Borough Council resolved not to reduce its employees' wages. The Council also continued to pay male and female employees at the same rate. Section 62 of the Metropolis Management Act 1855 gave the Council power to pay employees 'such ... wages as ... [the Council] may think fit'. Under s 247(7) of the Public Health Act 1875 the district auditor had power to 'disallow any item of account contrary to law, and surcharge the same on the person making or authorising the illegal payment'. The auditor, having placed significant emphasis on the cost of living in his calculations of what he considered to be reasonable wages and taken representations from councillors, ultimately decided that the Council had acted contrary to law in setting the wages that it had—the amounts paid were so generous relative to falling wages so as to be gratuities rather than wages—and disallowed £5,000 and surcharged the councillors responsible accordingly. The councillors applied for a quashing order under s 247(8) of the Public Health Act 1875 (which permitted relief for errors of law and fact). The central question for the House of Lords was whether the auditor had been right to conclude the Council's approach to setting employee wages was contrary to law, and specifically contrary to the Council's empowering provision in the 1855 Act. The Law Lords unanimously held the Council had acted contrary to law in setting wages as it did.

Their Lordships' speeches emphasize a reluctance to hold that the Council had acted unlawfully, given that its statutory powers to set wages were broadly framed and it was first and foremost for the Council to weigh different options and choose that which it considered to be optimal. But seemingly in defiance of this self-denying ordinance their Lordships' approach made significant inroads into the Council's freedom to set wages. Their Lordships were generally of the view that it would be perfectly permissible, and indeed proper, for the Council to have been guided, in setting the wages, by 'ordinary economic (and economical) considerations', as Lord Sumner put it (at 609). However, to the extent that the Council had been guided by wider considerations, its approach had been impermissible and unlawful.

Lord Buckmaster considered that by setting wages other than according to economic considerations such as the cost of living and the value of labour the Council had acted unlawfully. By setting a minimum wage below which wages would not fall on the basis that it wanted to act as a 'model employer', and by seeking to standardize the wages of women and men, the Council had not properly calibrated wages to the task performed by individuals, which Lord Buckmaster clearly considered ought to be a primary consideration (at 590).

[T]hey did not base their decision upon the ground that the reward for work is the value of the work reasonably and even generously measured, but ... they took an arbitrary principle and fixed an arbitrary sum, which was not a real exercise of the discretion imposed upon them by the statute.

Lord Atkinson said similarly, 'it does not appear to me that there is any rational proportion between the rates of wages at which the labour of these women is paid and the rates at which they would be reasonably remunerated for their services to the council' (at 600). More generally, he opined (at 594):

> The council would, in my view, fail in their duty if, in administering funds which did not belong to their members alone, they put aside all [the] aids to the ascertainment of what was just and reasonable remuneration to give for the services rendered to them, and allowed themselves to be guided in preference by some eccentric principles of socialistic philanthropy, or by a feminist ambition to secure the equality of the sexes in the matter of wages in the world of labour.

By concluding that the council had taken into account what he considered 'eccentric principles of socialistic philanthropy' and 'a feminist ambition to secure the equality of the sexes', and by holding such considerations to be irrelevant, Lord Atkinson was able to conclude that the council's decision was unlawful. Thus, the doctrine of relevancy allows potentially extensive judicial intervention in the administrative process, permitting the policy preferences of the decision-maker to be swept away if the matters upon which they are founded can be characterized by the court as irrelevant. Although judges naturally present their determinations as to relevancy in terms of statutory interpretation, it is highly likely that their own opinion of the policy issues will to some extent be in play. Indeed, in *Roberts* itself, Lord Atkinson did not seek to disguise his disapproval of the council's progressive views on employment practice and equal treatment, opining (at 591–2) that council members were guilty of 'vanity' in attempting to appear as 'model employers', and had 'become such ardent feminists'—a term which Lord Atkinson appears to have intended pejoratively—'as to bring about, at the expense of the ratepayers whose money they administered, sex equality in the labour market'. More generally, it might be said that their Lordships, by emphasizing that economic considerations were proper and important considerations, were themselves favouring a free market political ideology: wages ought to follow market conditions.

While there must, of course, come a point at which decisions have to be set aside because they are founded upon irrelevant considerations—if this were not possible, then the courts would be denied an important part of their machinery for controlling arbitrary and capricious administration—there are many cases in which the question of relevancy is far from clear-cut. For instance, on the facts of *Roberts*, could it not be argued that the local authority, having discretion to pay its employees such wages as it thought fit, might legitimately have invoked ideological factors in determining their policy in that context? Is it not arguable that there may be room—and, crucially, that Parliament, in creating a very broad discretion for the councillors to set wages as they 'think fit', might have accepted that there was such room—for a range of reasonable views on this question?

These questions, of course, go to the heart of the distinction between appeal and review, and the debate about how judges and decision-makers ought properly to relate to one another. We have already touched upon these issues (at 1.3.1) and explore them in more detail in ch 8. The basic proposition, however, is straightforward—that the court's role is to review the legality of administrative decisions, not to substitute its own view for that of the decision-maker. It is on the basis of this philosophy that the classic doctrine of *Wednesbury* unreasonableness (see *Associated Provincial Picture Houses Ltd*

v. *Wednesbury Corporation* [1948] 1 KB 223, considered at 8.2) held that a substantive administrative decision may be set aside only if it is so unreasonable that no reasonable authority could ever have reached it.

The same philosophy, it has been argued, should inform the courts' approach to questions of relevancy and irrelevancy which, as we have seen, have potentially far-reaching consequences *vis-à-vis* the agency's autonomy. For instance Cooke J, in the New Zealand case of *Ashby* v. *Minister of Immigration* [1981] 1 NZLR 222 at 224, draws a distinction between 'obligatory considerations', which are those 'the Act expressly or impliedly requires the Minister to take account of', and 'permissible considerations', which 'can properly be taken into account but do not have to be'. On this view there exist three types of consideration: at the extremes, there are those which must be taken account of and those which must be disregarded; in between, however, is a category of factors whose relevance is for the decision-maker, rather than the court, to decide. Similar comments by Cooke J in another New Zealand case, *CREEDNZ Inc* v. *Governor General* [1981] 1 NZLR 172 at 183, were subsequently approved by Lord Scarman (with whose judgment the other members of the House of Lords agreed) in *Re Findlay* [1985] AC 318 at 333. Further (implicit) support for this approach was provided by Lord Bingham (whose speech was supported by a majority of the other Law Lords) in *R (Corner House Research)* v. *Director of the Serious Fraud Office* [2008] UKHL 60, [2009] 1 AC 756 at [40], when he said that a 'discretionary decision is not ... vitiated by a failure to take into account a consideration which the decision-maker is not obliged by the law or the facts to take into account, even if he may properly do so'. In *G (AP)* v. *Scottish Ministers* [2013] UKSC 79, 2014 SC (UKSC) 84 at [59], the Supreme Court took a similarly permissive approach, considering that if there was nothing in the relevant statutory provision explicitly or implicitly preventing the public entity from taking into account a given consideration, the entity should be free to consider it (subject of course to the consideration not being one that undermines Parliament's intention) (at [54]). Irvine [1996] *PL* 59 at 67 strongly approves of this approach, and of the underlying relationship between the courts and the administration which it implies:

> The *Wednesbury* principle of relevance is premised upon the view that the decision-maker is in the best position ... to determine the range of factors which bear upon his decision. The statute may expressly, or by necessary implication, provide that some factors *must*, and some *must not* be considered, but there is a margin of appreciation within which the decision-maker may decide for himself which considerations should play a part in his reasoning process. Thus, there are three categories of consideration: those that must, those that must not and those that may, in the decision-maker's discretion, be taken into account. An important part of *Wednesbury* [theory] is the recognition of this free area of optional considerations.

While one might agree that such a 'free area' should be maintained, questions arise as to how great or small this area should be. One answer might be that consonant with moves towards a more flexible, context-sensitive approach to *Wednesbury* (see ch 8) judicial readiness to constrain the decision-maker's powers through the relevancy doctrine—for example by recognizing mandatory considerations or permitting the decision-maker to take account of a wide range of permissible considerations—should vary with various factors relevant to the case at hand. For example, perhaps courts should afford an expert scientific tribunal a significant 'free area' to determine what is relevant to its decision-making, given the tribunal will have far greater knowledge of the relevant subject matter than courts. Some support for such approach appears in Lord Reed's judgment in *AXA General Insurance Ltd v. HM Advocate* [2011] UKSC 46, [2012] 1 AC 868 at [142]–[143], where his Lordship places particular emphasis on the breadth of the decision-maker's discretion as a factor relevant to calibrating the court's approach to review on relevancy grounds:

> The extent of the courts' responsibility in relation to a particular exercise of power by a public authority necessarily depends upon the particular circumstances, including the nature of the public authority in question, the type of power being exercised, the process by which it is exercised, and the extent to which the powers of the authority have limits or purposes which the courts can identify and adjudicate upon.
>
> If, for example, a public authority's powers are so widely drawn that it is in principle free to decide for itself what considerations are relevant to its decision-making, the courts cannot then review its decisions as having been based on irrelevant considerations or as having failed to have regard to relevant considerations, except to the limited extent to which any constraints on its freedom might be implied, for example in order to protect fundamental rights or the rule of law.

QUESTIONS

- Do you agree with Lord Reed's flexible approach?
- What are the pros and cons of this approach?

One further point, which arises from recognition of the distinction between obligatory and permissible considerations, should be considered. The existence of the latter category implies the existence of a preliminary discretion (whether or not to take account of permissible considerations) on the part of the decision-maker. The exercise of that preliminary discretion may have implications for the lawfulness of subsequent exercises of discretion. This point is illustrated by *R (Rogers)* v. *Swindon NHS Primary Care Trust* [2006] EWCA Civ 392, [2006] 1 WLR 2649. The claimant challenged the defendant's decision to refuse to fund her breast cancer treatment with a drug, Herceptin, that had not at that time been approved for use with patients suffering from her particular form of the illness. However, the defendant had a discretion whether to fund the treatment of such patients. It exercised a preliminary discretion by deciding to treat the cost of treatment with Herceptin as an irrelevant consideration. This it could lawfully do because cost was a permissible rather than an obligatory relevant consideration. It then adopted a policy of providing funding only to patients whose circumstances were exceptional (rather than to all patients prescribed the drug by their consultants), pursuant to which it refused to fund the claimant's treatment. The Court of Appeal held that, in doing so, it had acted unlawfully: if cost was to be regarded as irrelevant, there could be no rational basis for refusing to provide funding for any patient who would, in their clinician's view, benefit from the treatment. Sir Anthony Clarke MR, giving the judgment of the Court, said at [79] that

> once financial considerations are ruled out ... then the only concern which the [Primary Care Trust] can have must relate to the legitimate clinical needs of the patient. The non-medical personal situation of a particular patient cannot in these circumstances be relevant to the question whether Herceptin prescribed by the patient's clinician should be funded for the benefit of the patient. Where the clinical needs are equal, and resources are not an issue, discrimination

between patients in the same eligible group cannot be justified on the basis of personal characteristics not based on healthcare.

In *G (AP)*, Lord Reed (at [55]), helpfully explained this sort of problem as one of *consistency*: the decision-maker 'cannot rationally exercise its discretion at stage two on a basis which is inconsistent with its conclusion [at stage one]'.

Another respect in which the intrusiveness of the relevancy doctrine as a principle of review falls for consideration concerns the attribution of weight to relevant factors. If the court concludes that a given factor must be taken into account—an 'obligatory considera-tion'—can the court go on to prescribe how seriously it is to be considered, and how much weight should be attached to it? Or is this a time for judicial control to yield to executive autonomy? Precisely this point was addressed by the House of Lords in *Tesco Stores Ltd v. Secretary of State for the Environment* [1995] 1 WLR 759. The case concerned an applica-tion by Tesco for permission to build a new supermarket. When its application was turned down in favour of a rival bid by another supermarket firm, Tesco sought judicial review, argu-ing that the Secretary of State had unlawfully failed to take into account its offer, in return for planning permission, to fund the construction of a new road intended to relieve traffic congestion in the town concerned. Tesco's judicial review claim failed in the House of Lords, in which a distinction was drawn between *failing to take account of an obligatory relevant consideration* (which, of course, is unlawful) and *choosing to attach little or no weight to such a consideration*. The point was explained by Lord Hoffmann at 780:

> The law has always made a clear distinction between the question of whether something is a material consideration and the weight which it should be given. The former is a question of law and the latter is a question of planning judgment, which is entirely a matter for the planning authority. Provided that the planning authority has regard to all material considerations, it is at lib-erty (provided that it does not lapse into *Wednesbury* irrationality) to give them whatever weight the planning authority thinks fit or no weight at all. The fact that the law regards something as a material consideration therefore involves no view about the part, if any, which it should play in the decision-making process.

There can be no doubt that *Tesco* represents longstanding orthodoxy. However, increas-ingly there are counterexamples of courts adopting a more intrusive approach, and actively prescribing the weight that decision-makers ought to afford particular considerations. Perhaps this is unsurprising given more general trends in substantive review away from the strictures of *Wednesbury* (discussed in ch 8). Given courts are more routinely entering the substance of executive decisions and assessing balances struck by decision-makers between competing concerns in the context of substantive review, it is unsurprising that they would, in applying the relevancy doctrine, feel more comfortable moving beyond an inquiry into relevancy and scrutinizing the weight given to particular factors.

Consider the case of *R (FDA) v. Secretary of State for Work and Pensions* [2012] EWCA Civ 332, [2013] 1 WLR 444. The background to the case is that public sector pensions and various state welfare benefits are uprated each year to keep up with inflation. Under s 150(1) of the Pensions (Increase) Act 1971 the Minister has the power to decide the measure to be applied to determine by how much pensions etc should be uprated. For some time the Retail Price Index had been used to gauge changes in general price levels; however, the Minister then decided to change to the Consumer Price Index. The effect was that pensions and benefits were uprated by less than they would have been under the Retail Price Index. This decision was challenged via judicial review. One of the grounds of challenge was that the Minister had illegitimately taken into account the state of the national economy in preferring the measure which would produce less of an impact on public funds.

The Court concluded that the Minister could take impact on public funds into account. The relevant statutory provision conferred a 'relatively wide discretion', while the Minister's decision under the provision 'has the obvious potential of having a significant effect on the country's finances. It therefore seems to me unrealistic to say that the Secretary of State is required to ignore the wider economic realities, irrespective of the circumstances' (at [58], [61]). However, this was not the end of the matter. The Court went on to qualify its ruling that impact on public funds was a permissible factor, and gave detailed, prescriptive guidance as to the *way* in which this consideration could be factored into the decision process and the *weight* it should be afforded (at [62]–[64]):

> I do not consider that the Secretary of State could opt for an index which was clearly less good [in the sense of less accurate or reliable in gauging changes in general price levels], and more detrimental to the recipients of pensions, than another index, simply because the former index was beneficial to the national exchequer. Indeed, if the Secretary of State thought that one index was significantly less reliable or less accurate than another, I find it very hard to conceive of any circumstances where he could select the former index merely because he thought it was just about acceptable for the estimating exercise required by section 150(1).
>
> While I am not seeking to lay down a firm standard, it seems to me that, before the Secretary of State could invoke the benefit to the national exchequer by selecting an index he considered less good, three requirements would normally have to be met. Those requirements are (i) there would, in the Secretary of State's view have to be little to choose between the indices in terms of reliability and aptness, (ii) the benefit to the national exchequer of choosing the less good index would have to be significant, and (iii) the need to benefit the national exchequer, in terms of the national economy and demands on the public purse, would have to be clear.
>
> In other words, the Secretary of State could only select the less good index if it was proportionate to do so, and, bearing in mind the purpose of the up-rating exercise, the circumstances would normally have to be unusual before it could be proportionate to select an index, or other method, which the Secretary of State considered was less good than another.

This approach is a long way from Lord Hoffmann's approach in *Tesco*, where his Lordship did not consider it the court's role to inquire into how a relevant consideration was taken into account, and scrutinize the weight it was afforded. The *FDA* decision is particularly striking given that the discretion at issue was an exceptionally wide one, the statute providing that the Minister could estimate price levels as he 'thinks fit'; consistently with Lord Reed's dicta in *AXA* (see earlier), the breadth of the discretion tells strongly against the sort of intensive approach to review on relevancy grounds adopted in *FDA*.

QUESTION

- Perhaps Lord Hoffmann's approach in *Tesco* afforded decision-makers too much latitude by allowing them to ascribe whatever weight they wished to relevant considerations (provided they did not act unreasonably in the *Wednesbury* sense), but does the approach in *FDA* go too far in the other direction and entail courts illegitimately trespassing on executive autonomy?

7.3.4 Consequences of taking irrelevant considerations into account

One last point to consider is the legal consequence of a decision-maker taking into account an irrelevant consideration; in other words, will the courts necessarily invalidate an administrative decision based on an irrelevant consideration? The practical consequences of a finding of irrelevancy are crucial in considering the extent to which the irrelevant considerations doctrine impinges upon executive autonomy. For example, if the inevitable result of a decision-maker taking into account an irrelevant consideration was that the decision must be quashed, such strict approach, while providing a strong affirmation of the rule of law, could nonetheless cause a great deal of unnecessary administrative disruption, as the decision-maker may not have placed much weight on the factor and may well have reached the same decision even if they had ignored the impugned consideration. As in the substantive law of relevant considerations, the courts, in their approach to remedies, have sought to strike a balance between vigilance against arbitrary decision-making and preservation of administrative interests.

In *R (FDA)* v. *Secretary of State for Work and Pensions* [2012] EWCA Civ 332, [2013] 1 WLR 444, Lord Neuberger MR helpfully summarized the relevant principles. He said, at [67], that where a decision-maker takes into account an irrelevant consideration the 'normal principle is that the decision is liable to be invalid unless the factor played no significant part in the decision-making exercise'. However, even if the factor did play a significant part in the decision, the decision may nonetheless exceptionally be saved from invalidation where the court is satisfied that the same decision would have been made if the irrelevant consideration had not been taken into account. How certain does the court have to be that the same decision would have resulted anyway? It must be proven that it was 'inevitable' that the same decision would have resulted, and the defendant bears the burden of convincing the court. The Court emphasized that the inevitability standard was a 'high hurdle' that would only be passed relatively rarely. Albeit it is important to note that the threshold may no longer be set so high in light of recent legislative reforms (Senior Courts Act 1981, s 31(2A)–(2C)), which provide that relief *must* be denied if it is 'highly likely' (on its face a lower threshold than inevitability) 'that the outcome for the claimant would not have been substantially different if the conduct complained of had not occurred', though the full effect of these reforms is not yet clear (we discuss these new reforms further at 14.8).

Thus, in practice, the most pertinent question for a court will be whether the irrelevant consideration played a significant or substantial part in the decision: if it did, the decision is likely to be invalidated (albeit invalidation is rendered somewhat less likely given the new statutory test), and if not, the decision will most likely be allowed to stand. The courts' approach is thus a pragmatic one: if the consideration did not have a great bearing on the decision there shall be insufficient justification to invalidate the decision and thus impose on the decision-maker the expense and disruption of having to reopen the matter and take the decision again. Thus, even where a court finds an irrelevant consideration was unlawfully taken into account, this finding of unlawfulness may, in practical terms, nonetheless entail no incursion into executive autonomy.

QUESTION

- Does this approach strike an appropriate balance between the demands of the rule of law and administrative interests?

Lastly, it is informative to compare the judicial approach to legal consequences where a decision is tainted by improper purpose. In general a finding of improper purpose will result in the impugned decision being invalidated, given a decision taken for an improper purpose is one that is fundamentally at odds with the basic reasons why Parliament conferred the power in the first place. This is obviously a stricter approach to remedies than that taken in irrelevant consideration cases, where there is greater leeway for a court to refuse to invalidate the decision. For this reason it may be thought that the purpose doctrine has strategic advantages for claimants over the relevant considerations doctrine. However, one must recall that before we even get to the question of remedies/legal consequences, for the claimant to successfully invoke the improper purpose doctrine to impugn a decision he must show the improper purpose was the decision-maker's *dominant* purpose. This may be difficult to prove where multiple purposes informed the decision. In contrast, for a claimant to succeed in convincing a court to invalidate a decision on irrelevancy grounds the claimant does not need to show the irrelevant consideration was the sole or dominant factor in the decision-maker's decision, only that the consideration was one substantial or significant factor (see *R v. Rochdale Metropolitan Borough Council, ex parte Cromer Ring Mill* [1982] 3 All ER 761 at 770). Thus, overall, it seems that, within some factual matrices at least, it may be easier for claimants to succeed in having a decision invalidated on the basis of an irrelevant factor than an improper purpose, given that the test of 'substantial influence' is likely to be easier to satisfy than that of 'dominant purpose'.

7.4 Concluding remarks

We began this chapter with the notion that there is no such thing as an unfettered discretion, and the requirement, which derives from the rule of law, that discretionary powers must therefore be used within legally-prescribed limits. The propriety of purpose and relevancy doctrines play a central role in this context, by ensuring that discretion is exercised for the purposes for which it was conferred and that decisions are based upon relevant considerations. Together, these principles of administrative law encourage a mode of administration which is faithful to the legislative scheme set out by Parliament, and seek to prevent the use of discretionary power for extraneous reasons. They are, therefore, important mechanisms through which the goal of government limited by law may be realized.

We noted earlier that the courts tend to use the propriety of purpose and relevancy doctrines interchangeably. This is unsurprising, given that many factual situations can comfortably be analysed using either of the two approaches. But, by way of conclusion, we ought to consider whether there is a principled way in which the courts should decide which of the two analyses to adopt and, relatedly, whether there are any important differences between the doctrines. Taylor [1976] *CLJ* 272 argues that the proper mode of review is determined by the empowering provision. When the provision is expressed in broad terms, and gives little guidance as to how the power should be used, a purposive style of interpretation is appropriate; this naturally leads to the application of the propriety of purpose doctrine. In contrast, when the statutory scheme is more specific about the reasons for which decision-makers may act, the relevancy doctrine is apposite. It is fair to say this pattern does not reflect the state of the authorities, and courts continue to use the two doctrines largely interchangeably.

However, there are examples of the more disciplined approach propounded by Taylor in operation. In particular, the recent Supreme Court decision in *G (AP)* v. *Scottish Ministers* [2013] UKSC 79, 2014 SC (UKSC) 84 effectively adopts Taylor's approach. In this case a tribunal was imbued with a broad discretion. Given the breadth of the discretion the Court was very reluctant to intervene on the basis of the relevancy doctrine; because the power was so broadly framed there was no concrete basis in the terms of the statute upon which the Court could hold that certain considerations taken into account by the tribunal were irrelevant. However, while 'the range of matters which [the tribunal] may take into account is not subject to any express restriction, and is necessarily wide ... its discretion must nevertheless be exercised in a manner which is consistent with the intention of Parliament' (at [54]). Thus, we have a clear example of the highest court finding the relevancy doctrine largely inapplicable to a broadly framed power, but nonetheless emphasizing that the purposes doctrine was applicable and did constitute a substantive limit on the power. Perhaps this decision will offer a guiding light in the quest for consistency of judicial approach in this area.

FURTHER RESOURCES

Craig, 'Formal and Substantive Conceptions of the Rule of Law: An Analytical Framework' [1997] *PL* 467

Taylor, 'Judicial Review of Improper Purposes and Irrelevant Considerations' [1976] *CLJ* 272

Wilberg, 'Deference on Relevance and Purpose? Wrestling with the Law/Discretion Divide' in Wilberg and Elliott (eds), *The Scope and Intensity of Substantive Review: Traversing Taggart's Rainbow* (Oxford 2015)

8 ABUSE OF DISCRETION II

8.1 Introduction

It is sometimes said that judicial review is concerned with matters of process as distinct from matters of substance. There is certainly some truth in this. Many of the established grounds of review concentrate on such matters as the fairness of the procedure by which the decision was reached and the quality of the decision-making process. This process-oriented conception of judicial review finds its putative justification in the distinction between appeal and review (see 1.3.1): by confining itself to the decision-making process, the court tends to avoid interference with the merits of the decision, thereby reducing the scope for judicial usurpation of the executive's functions.

However, English administrative law has never wholly eschewed substantive, as distinct from process-oriented, review. Review can be substantive in one or both of two senses. First, it might have the effect of reducing the range of substantive options open to a decision-maker. The duty to act procedurally fairly (see ch 10) does not do this: it regulates only the manner in which the decision is taken. In contrast, review on the ground of jurisdictional error (see ch 2) *is* substantive in our first sense: if a statutory power to provide financial assistance can be exercised only in favour of 'students', and if the reviewing court interprets 'students' narrowly, the range of decisions that can be made—in the sense of the range of potential beneficiaries of the exercise of the power—is narrowed. Second, review can be substantive in the sense that it involves judicial examination not of the quality of the process adopted by the decision-maker—by, for instance, determining whether a 'fair hearing' was given (see ch 10) or irrelevant considerations taken into account (see ch 7)—but of the quality of the reasons for the decision itself.

We are concerned in this chapter with grounds of judicial review that are substantive in both of the senses described above—and which, for that reason, tend to excite the greatest controversy about the proper limits of the judicial role. The chapter is divided into four principal parts. We begin by considering the doctrine of *reasonableness* or *rationality*, which is the form that substantive review of the type presently under consideration has traditionally taken in English law. We then address the doctrine of *proportionality*, which has come increasingly to the fore in recent years, largely—but not exclusively—thanks to the Human Rights Act 1998 (HRA). Third, we examine the notion of *deference*—which, as we will see, serves as a way of modulating the intensity of the court's scrutiny of the quality of the reasons for an administrative decision. Fourth, we take a step back and consider the *trajectory* of the law in this area—in particular, the question whether English courts are heading towards jettisoning the reasonableness doctrine in favour of utilizing proportionality in all relevant cases.

8.2 Reasonableness and rationality

8.2.1 The *Wednesbury* and *GCHQ* cases

The term 'Wednesbury unreasonableness' trips off the tongue of English administrative law-yers. It refers to the classic case of *Associated Provincial Picture Houses Ltd* v. *Wednesbury Corporation* [1948] 1 KB 223, in which the Court of Appeal was asked—but refused—to declare *ultra vires* the defendant local authority's decision that the claimant should be allowed to open its cinema on Sundays only on condition that under-15s would not be admitted to performances. The defendant had imposed the condition pursuant to its statutory power under s 1(1) of the Sunday Entertainments Act 1932, which allowed local authorities to permit Sunday opening of cinemas 'subject to such conditions as the author-ity think fit to impose'. In response to the argument that the condition was 'unreasonable', Lord Greene MR (at 229) acknowledged that 'the discretion must be exercised reasonably' but went on to emphasize that, in administrative law, the notion of reasonableness and the corresponding notion of unreasonableness bear very particular meanings:

> Lawyers familiar with the phraseology commonly used in relation to exercise of statutory discre-tions often use the word 'unreasonable' in a rather comprehensive sense. It has frequently been used and is frequently used as a general description of the things that must not be done. For instance, a person entrusted with a discretion must, so to speak, direct himself properly in law. He must call his own attention to the matters which he is bound to consider. He must exclude from his consideration matters which are irrelevant to what he has to consider. If he does not obey those rules, he may truly be said, and often is said, to be acting 'unreasonably.' Similarly, there may be something so absurd that no sensible person could ever dream that it lay within the powers of the authority. Warrington L.J. in *Short* v. *Poole Corporation* [[1926] Ch 66 at 90–1] gave the example of the red-haired teacher, dismissed because she had red hair. That is unreasonable in one sense. In another sense it is taking into consideration extraneous matters. It is so unreasonable that it might almost be described as being done in bad faith; and, in fact, all these things run into one another.

In this passage Lord Greene recognizes that unreasonableness in its substantive sense bleeds into other grounds of review, including, for instance, taking account of irrelevant considerations. He is, however, clear that there is something exceptional about unreason-ableness *per se*. Lord Greene went on (at 230) to underline that point, and to explain the reasons for it:

> It is clear that the local authority are entrusted by Parliament with the decision on a matter which the knowledge and experience of that authority can best be trusted to deal with. The subject-matter with which the condition deals is one relevant for its consideration. They have considered it and come to a decision upon it. It is true to say that, if a decision on a competent matter is so unreasonable that no reasonable authority could ever have come to it, then the courts can interfere. That, I think, is quite right; but to prove a case of that kind would require something overwhelming, and, in this case, the facts do not come anywhere near anything of that kind ... I think [counsel for the claimant] in the end agreed that his proposition that the decision of the local authority can be upset if it is proved to be unreasonable, really meant that it must be proved

to be unreasonable in the sense that the court considers it to be a decision that no reasonable body could have come to. It is not what the court considers unreasonable, a different thing altogether. If it is what the court considers unreasonable, the court may very well have different views to that of a local authority on matters of high public policy of this kind. Some courts might think that no children ought to be admitted on Sundays at all, some courts might think the reverse, and all over the country I have no doubt on a thing of that sort honest and sincere people hold different views. The effect of the legislation is not to set up the court as an arbiter of the correctness of one view over another.

Lord Greene (at 233–4) concluded his judgment with the following, oft-cited summary of the relevant principles:

In the result, this appeal must be dismissed. I do not wish to repeat myself but I will summarize once again the principle applicable. The court is entitled to investigate the action of the local authority with a view to seeing whether they have taken into account matters which they ought not to take into account, or, conversely, have refused to take into account or neglected to take into account matters which they ought to take into account. Once that question is answered in favour of the local authority, it may be still possible to say that, although the local authority have kept within the four corners of the matters which they ought to consider, they have nevertheless come to a conclusion so unreasonable that no reasonable authority could ever have come to it. In such a case, again, I think the court can interfere. The power of the court to interfere in each case is not as an appellate authority to override a decision of the local authority, but as a judicial authority which is concerned, and concerned only, to see whether the local authority have contravened the law by acting in excess of the powers which Parliament has confided in them.

QUESTIONS

- Do you think that the model of substantive review set out by Lord Greene is appropriate?
- What sort of relationship between judges and decision-makers does it envisage?

It is clear that Lord Greene's central concern was to emphasize that the court's role is not to retake decisions, or to substitute its own view of the merits for that of the decision-maker. A similarly restrictive vision of substantive review was presented by Lord Diplock in his speech in *Council of Civil Service Unions* v. *Minister for the Civil Service* [1985] AC 374 at 410–11—the 'GCHQ case'—in which he replaced the language of 'reasonableness' with that of 'rationality':

By 'irrationality' I mean what can by now be succinctly referred to as '*Wednesbury* unreasonableness' ... It applies to a decision which is so outrageous in its defiance of logic or of accepted moral standards that no sensible person who had applied his mind to the question to be decided could have arrived at it. Whether a decision falls within this category is a question that judges by their training and experience should be well equipped to answer, or else there would be something badly wrong with our judicial system. To justify the court's exercise of this role, resort I think is today no longer needed to Viscount Radcliffe's ingenious explanation in *Edwards* v. *Bairstow* [1956] A.C. 14 of irrationality as a ground for a court's reversal of a decision by ascribing it to an inferred though unidentifiable mistake of law by the decision-maker. 'Irrationality' by now can stand upon its own feet as an accepted ground on which a decision may be attacked by judicial review.

The restrained approach to substantive review which is commended by the *Wednesbury* and *GCHQ* rhetoric has been endorsed strongly by Irvine [1996] *PL* 59 at 60–1, who identifies three reasons for judicial self-restraint in this sphere:

> First, a *constitutional imperative*: public authorities receive their powers from Parliament which intends, for good reason, that a power be exercised by the authority to which it is entrusted. This is because each and every authority has, within its field of influence, a level of knowledge and experience which justifies the decision of Parliament to entrust that authority with decision-making power. Secondly, *lack of judicial expertise*: it follows that the courts are, in relative terms, ill-equipped to take decisions in place of the designated authority. This is all the more true where the decision in question is one of 'policy'; and the further into the realm of policy an issue lies, the more reluctant a court should be to interfere with the authority's decision. Thirdly, the *democratic imperative*: it has long been recognised that elected public authorities, and particularly local authorities, derive their authority in part from their electoral mandate. The electoral system also operates as an important safeguard against the unreasonable exercise of public powers, since elected authorities have to submit themselves, and their decision-making records, to the verdict of the electorate at regular intervals.

QUESTIONS

- Do you find these arguments convincing?
- Do they support a globally restrictive approach to substantive review, or do they demand judicial self-restraint only in particular contexts (and, if so, which ones)?

Taken at face value, the passages above from *Wednesbury* and *GCHQ*—together with arguments such as those of Irvine—paint a relatively simple picture of substantive review, within which the courts scrutinize administrative decisions according to a universally deferential standard. However, as Jowell and Lester [1987] *PL* 368 at 372 observed, the reality—even three decades ago—was somewhat different:

> [The *Wednesbury* test] seeks to prevent review except in cases where the official has behaved absurdly ... In practice, however, the courts are willing to impugn decisions that are far from absurd and are indeed often coldly rational. Were the courts only to interfere with decisions verging on the insane, a zone of immunity would be drawn around many oppressive or improper decisions that are in reality vulnerable to judicial review.

Jowell and Lester's point was that courts tend to interfere more readily than the formulations in *Wednesbury* and *GCHQ* imply. Some judges, however, have sought to realign the the rubric with (what Jowell and Lester, at least, would regard as) the reality of judicial practice. Take, for instance, the version of the test advanced by Lord Cooke in *R v. Chief Constable of Sussex, ex parte International Traders' Ferry Ltd* [1999] 2 AC 418 at 452:

> It seems to me unfortunate that *Wednesbury* and some *Wednesbury* phrases have become established incantations in the courts of the United Kingdom and beyond. *Associated Provincial Picture Houses Ltd. v. Wednesbury Corporation* [1948] 1 K.B. 223, an apparently briefly-considered case, might well not be decided the same way today; and the judgment of Lord Greene M.R. twice uses (at pp. 230 and 234) the tautologous formula 'so unreasonable that no reasonable authority could ever have come to it'. Yet judges are entirely accustomed to respecting the proper scope of

administrative discretions. In my respectful opinion they do not need to be warned off the course by admonitory circumlocutions. When, in *Secretary of State for Education v. Tameside Metropolitan Borough Council* [1977] A.C. 1014, the precise meaning of 'unreasonably' in an administrative context was crucial to the decision, the five speeches in the House of Lords, the three judgments in the Court of Appeal and the two judgments in the Divisional Court all succeeded in avoiding needless complexity. The simple test used throughout was whether the decision in question was one which a reasonable authority could reach. The converse was described by Lord Diplock, at p. 1064, as 'conduct which no sensible authority acting with due appreciation of its responsibilities would have decided to adopt'. These unexaggerated criteria give the administrator ample and rightful rein, consistently with the constitutional separation of powers.

Although this formulation is undeniably question-begging—how do we tell whether a decision is one that a 'reasonable authority' could reach?—it clearly does regularize the concept of unreasonableness by expanding its reach beyond the utterly absurd. This point was amplified by Lord Cooke in *R (Daly)* v. *Secretary of State for the Home Department* [2001] UKHL 26, [2001] 2 AC 532 at [32]:

[T]he day will come when it will be more widely recognised that ... *Wednesbury* ... was an unfortunately retrogressive decision in English administrative law ... in so far as it suggested that there are degrees of unreasonableness and that only a very extreme degree can bring an administrative decision within the legitimate scope of judicial invalidation. The depth of judicial review and the deference due to administrative discretion vary with the subject matter. It may well be, however, that the law can never be satisfied in any administrative field merely by a finding that the decision under review is not capricious or absurd.

We will see as this chapter unfolds that these remarks form the background against which many of the recent developments in this field have taken place. In particular, the ideas that the 'depth of judicial review' can vary, and that different degrees of 'deference' might be due to the administration depending on the context, have firmly taken root.

8.2.2 Deference, reasonableness, and variable intensity review

Laws (in Forsyth and Hare (eds), *The Golden Metwand and the Crooked Cord* (Oxford 1998) at 186–7) writes:

On the surface at least the test of unreasonableness or irrationality ... is monolithic; it leaves no scope for a variable standard of review according to the subject-matter of the case ... But in fact the courts, while broadly adhering to the monolithic language of *Wednesbury*, have to a considerable extent in recent years adopted variable standards of review [to suit the subject matter of the case before them].

In some situations the courts have exhibited a willingness to intervene on substantive grounds only if the decision in question crosses an especially high threshold of unreasonableness, sometimes referred to as 'super-*Wednesbury*'. Some cases which have applied this concept have set the threshold very high indeed; for example, in *Nottinghamshire County Council* v. *Secretary of State for the Environment* [1986] AC 240, Lord Scarman (at 247), said that in the circumstances of the case judicial review would lie only if the Minister had 'acted in bad faith, or for an improper motive, or that the consequences of his guidance were so absurd that he must have taken leave of his senses'.

In setting the bar so high, Lord Scarman set great store by the fact that the Minister's decision—the effect of which was to impose financial penalties upon local authorities which he regarded as profligate—had been endorsed, as required by the relevant legislation, by a resolution of the House of Commons. He said (at 250) that, in such circumstances, 'it is no part of the judges' role to declare that the action proposed is unfair, unless it constitutes an abuse of power in the sense which I have explained; for Parliament has enacted that one of its Houses is responsible'. He went on (at 250–1) to caution that '[j]udicial review is a great weapon in the hands of the judges: but the judges must observe the constitutional limits set by our parliamentary system upon their exercise of this beneficent power'. However, while the House of Commons' involvement was considered to be important, so was the nature and complexity of the issues that the Minister had to address in deciding whether and, if so, how to exercise the power. As Lord Phillips MR subsequently put it in *R (Asif Javed)* v. *Secretary of State for the Home Department* [2001] EWCA Civ 789, [2002] QB 129 at [49], the decision in *Nottinghamshire* 'turned on political and economic considerations to be evaluated by the Minister and Parliament, whose rationality could not be measured by any yardstick available to the court'.

The *Nottinghamshire* case thus illustrates the capacity of both *democratic considerations* and *institutional matters* (*eg* pertaining to the respective expertise of the courts and the executive) to modulate the intensity of judicial review. There is, however, disagreement about the *extent* to which such matters should inhibit judicial evaluation of administrative decisions and about the *relative importance* of those two factors, as the Supreme Court's recent judgment in *R (Rotherham Metropolitan Borough Council)* v. *Secretary of State for Business, Innovation and Skills* [2015] UKSC 6, [2015] PTSR 322 illustrates. The case concerned an unsuccessful challenge to the lawfulness of UK government allocations of EU funds to different parts of the country, the essential argument being that the basis upon which such allocations were made failed to treat like regions alike and unlike regions differently. A number of arguments were made in seeking to attack the lawfulness of the allocations, one of which was characterized by Lord Neuberger (at [55]), giving one of the majority judgments, in terms of unreasonableness.

Lord Sumption, delivering the other majority judgment, considered the case for deference to be compelling on both institutional and democratic grounds. As to the former, he observed (at [22]) that there was no 'right' answer to the question that had faced the Minister, and that 'the Secretary of State was required to make a complex evaluation of a wide range of overlapping criteria, all of which involved difficult and sometimes technical judgments about matters of social and economic policy'. Lord Sumption also considered (at [23]) that judicial deference was apposite on democratic grounds, given that the decision was a 'particularly delicate' one involving 'the distribution of finite resources' between the UK's nations and regions. This involved 'arbitrating between different public interests affecting different parts of our community' and was 'an exercise in which the legitimacy of the decision-making process depends to a high degree on the fact that ministers are answerable politically to Parliament'. Lord Sumption went on to endorse extra-curial remarks made by Lord Hoffmann ((2002) 7 JR 137 at [19]) to the effect that the 'allocation of public expenditure—whether we should spend more or less on defence, health, education, police and so forth, whether at a national or local level—is very much a matter for democratic decision'.

Lord Neuberger agreed with Lord Sumption that deference was appropriate on the ground of relative institutional competence because (as he put it at [62]) the decision

(i) ... involves an allocation of money, a vital and relatively scarce resource, (ii) it could engage a number of different and competing political, economic and social factors, and (iii) it could result in a large number of possible outcomes, none of which would be safe from some telling criticisms or complaints.

However, he saw (at [64]) less merit in Lord Sumption's case for deference on democratic grounds:

To say that the 'allocation of public expenditure ... is very much a matter for democratic decision' takes matters very little further at least in connection with a decision made by the executive. The fact that the legislature assigns such a decision to the executive does not alter the fact that it is the executive's decision and not that of the legislature. In any event, the legislature will obviously have intended the rule of law to apply, so that such a decision, as with any executive decision, must be susceptible to judicial oversight.

We examine the idea of deference in greater depth at 8.4, with particular reference to its role in respect of the proportionality test. It is important, however, to recognize that deference is relevant to reasonableness review as well—not only because, as cases like *Nottinghamshire* and *Rotherham* demonstrate, courts might be moved to apply the reasonableness test in an *especially deferential* way because of particular features of the case, but also because the reasonableness test, at least in its orthodox form, is *inherently deferential*, so as to guard against courts exceeding (a traditional conception of) their proper constitutional role.

QUESTION

- If the reasonableness test is *inherently* deferential, is it ever appropriate for it to be applied in an *especially* deferential way?

The reverse side of the deference coin is that, in some circumstances, courts are willing to evaluate the reasonableness of decisions *more* rigorously than usual. This point assumed particular prominence in the late 1980s and 1990s in cases concerning human rights. Most such cases could now be decided under the HRA; it is, however, necessary to understand something of the courts' pre-HRA jurisprudence in order to contextualize the current position. An early and prominent example of this approach is supplied by the House of Lords' decision in *R v. Secretary of State for the Home Department, ex parte Brind* [1991] 1 AC 696, in which it was (unsuccessfully) contended that executive acts which had the effect of precluding live broadcast interviews with representatives of certain terrorist organizations were unreasonable. Their Lordships refused directly to apply Article 10 of the European Convention on Human Rights, which protects freedom of expression, on the ground that the Convention had not been incorporated into domestic law. However, Lord Bridge (at 748), building on his speech in *R v. Secretary of State for the Home Department, ex parte*

Bugdaycay [1987] AC 514 at 531, said that in deciding whether the restriction imposed by the Minister was reasonable, the court was

perfectly entitled to start from the premise that any restriction of the right to freedom of expression requires to be justified and that nothing less than an important competing public interest will be sufficient to justify it. The primary judgment as to whether the particular competing public interest justifies the particular restriction imposed falls to be made by the Secretary of State to whom Parliament has entrusted the discretion. But we are entitled to exercise a secondary judgment by asking whether a reasonable Secretary of State, on the material before him, could reasonably make that primary judgment.

We noted earlier that one of the hallmarks of substantive review is judicial evaluation not of the decision-making process but of the outputs of that process—and, in particular, of the quality of the *reasons* for the decision. Understood in its traditional sense, the reasonableness doctrine opens the door to some—but very limited—scrutiny of those reasons. In contrast, Lord Bridge's approach in *Brind* provides for more critical scrutiny: the decision will be lawful only if the reason for the decision amounts to the pursuit of 'an important competing public interest'. This implies review that is substantive—in the sense of involving evaluation of the reasons for the decision—to a greater degree than is reasonableness in its conventional form. However, Lord Bridge's caveat—that the court must limit itself to asking whether it is reasonable to think that the public interest justifies a decision that infringes an important right—is a significant one, as the subsequent decision in *R* v. *Ministry of Defence, ex parte Smith* [1996] QB 517 shows.

Pursuant to the policy then in force, which had been debated and supported by both Houses of Parliament and by a select committee, the claimants in *Smith*—gay and lesbian members of the armed forces—were dismissed because of their sexual orientation. The claimants challenged the decisions to dismiss them, and the policy on which those decisions were based, arguing (*inter alia*) that they were irrational. In the Court of Appeal, Sir Thomas Bingham MR (at 554) agreed with counsel for the claimants that

[t]he court may not interfere with the exercise of an administrative discretion on substantive grounds save where the court is satisfied that the decision is unreasonable in the sense that it is beyond the range of responses open to a reasonable decision-maker. But in judging whether the decision-maker has exceeded this margin of appreciation the human rights context is important. The more substantial the interference with human rights, the more the court will require by way of justification before it is satisfied that the decision is reasonable in the sense outlined above.

The Master of the Rolls also said (at 556) that the Court 'has the constitutional role and duty of ensuring that the rights of citizens are not abused by the unlawful exercise of executive power' and that while it 'must properly defer to the expertise of responsible decision-makers, it must not shrink from its fundamental duty to "do right to all manner of people"'. Nevertheless, the claimants' challenges failed in the domestic courts, precisely because—as Lord Bridge had earlier explained in *Brind*—the role of those courts was limited to the making of a 'secondary judgment' about the reasonableness of the decision. As Simon Brown LJ put it in the Divisional Court in *Smith* (at 540), the question was:

[C]an the Secretary of State show an important competing public interest which he could reasonably judge sufficient to justify the restriction? The primary judgment is for him. Only if his purported justification outrageously defies logic or accepted moral standards can the court,

> exercising its secondary judgment, properly strike it down … Only if it were plain beyond sensible argument that no conceivable damage could be done to the armed services as a fighting unit would it be appropriate for this court now to remove the issue entirely from the hands both of the military and of the government.

On this basis, Simon Brown LJ concluded (at 541)

> that, my own view of the evidence notwithstanding, the Minister's stance cannot properly be held unlawful. His suggested justification for the ban may to many seem unconvincing; to say, however, that it is outrageous in its defiance of logic is another thing. There is, I conclude, still room for two views. Similarly it is difficult to regard the policy as wholly incompatible with 'accepted moral standards'. There is no present uniformity of outlook on this issue: not everyone would condemn the ban on moral grounds, morally neutral though the ministry avow their own stance to be.

Much has changed in the 20 or so years since *Smith* was decided. If a century ago it was—as Warrington LJ suggested in *Short* v. *Poole Corporation* [1926] Ch 66 at 90–1—unreasonable to dismiss a teacher because she had red hair, it is doubtless equally unreasonable today to dismiss a soldier because he is gay. But that is not because the nature of the reasonableness doctrine has fundamentally changed. Rather, the policy that the courts upheld in *Smith* today seems unreasonable thanks to the evolution in recent decades of the prevailing 'moral standards' to which the *GCHQ* test refers. For that reason, *Smith*—antiquated though it might seem when viewed in terms of the outcome—remains a vivid and pertinent illustration of the way in which the reasonableness doctrine can limit the judicial role and invest the administrative branch with correspondingly generous discretion. Whether such a deferential approach to substantive review is normatively desirable is a separate matter. So too is the question whether the law in this area is moving towards an approach that rejects the degree of deference with which the reasonableness doctrine is generally associated. We examine those issues in the remainder of this chapter—first in the course of addressing the proportionality test and considering how it differs from reasonableness, and then by examining administrative law's direction of travel in this sphere and, in particular, the extent to which the reasonableness and proportionality tests may be converging.

8.3 Proportionality

8.3.1 What is proportionality?

The precise meaning of proportionality is elaborated in the remainder of this chapter but, to begin with, a working definition is called for. A useful starting-point is provided by Lord Sumption's judgment in *Bank Mellat* v. *HM Treasury (No 2)* [2013] UKSC 39, [2014] AC 700 at [20]. His Lordship said that determining whether an administrative measure is proportionate

> depends on an exacting analysis of the factual case advanced in defence of the measure, in order to determine (i) whether its objective is sufficiently important to justify the limitation of a fundamental right; (ii) whether it is rationally connected to the objective; (iii) whether a less intrusive

measure could have been used; and (iv) whether, having regard to these matters and to the severity of the consequences, a fair balance has been struck between the rights of the individual and the interests of the community.

It is implicit in the first stage of Lord Sumption's test that the measure must, to begin with, involve the limitation of a fundamental right. This suggests that there are in fact five stages:

(i)   Does the measure limit a fundamental right?

(ii) Does the measure pursue an objective that is legitimate in the sense of being important enough to justify limitation of the right?

(iii) Is the measure rationally connected to—in the sense of being capable of securing— that objective?

(iv) Is the adoption of the measure necessary in order to secure that objective, or could the objective have been secured by means of a measure that would have impacted less (or not at all) on the right?

(v)   Does the measure strike a fair balance in the sense that the losses inflicted by it (*eg* in terms of the restriction of human rights) are justified, or outweighed, by the gains which it purchases (*eg* in terms of benefits which flow to the community from securing the legitimate objective)?

We need to unpack the proportionality test in order to understand how it works, and what its strengths and weaknesses are. A good place to start is by considering how it differs from the reasonableness test. Many commentators argue that proportionality is preferable to reasonableness both in *methodological terms* (because it is more structured and transparent) and in *normative terms* (because it enables the court to undertake appropriately searching scrutiny of administrative action). We consider each of these claims in turn, using them as a vehicle to explore the nature and extent of the differences between the two tests.

8.3.2 Methodology

The methodological critique is centrally concerned with transparency. It is argued that *Wednesbury* review lacks this quality, because a finding of unreasonableness (or, for that matter, reasonableness) risks creating the impression of judicial decision-making by intuition since such a conclusion may be unaccompanied by any structured explanation of the judicial reasoning process which yielded it. This, to an extent, is a function of the circularity of the traditional test: if the 'unreasonable' decision is defined simply in terms of that which no reasonable decision-maker would reach, then little scope exists for the elaboration of a structured and transparent judicial decision-making process. The test, viewed in this way, naturally encourages an intuitive adjudicative method. Craig (in Ellis (ed), *The Principle of Proportionality in the Laws of Europe* (Oxford 1999) at 99–100) underscores this point by contrasting *Wednesbury* with the proportionality test:

Proportionality provides a more structured analysis of the kind which is often lacking under the *Wednesbury* formula ... [Its] more structured analysis has a beneficial effect in that it requires the administration to justify its policy choice more specifically than under the traditional *Wednesbury* approach. The structure provided by the proportionality inquiry is also beneficial in relation to the courts themselves. It requires that the courts, when striking down a decision, do so on grounds which are more readily identifiable and ascertainable than is often the case under the *Wednesbury* test.

The transparency problem is particularly acute because of its self-evident capacity to obscure the normative foundation of substantive review. As well as understanding the structure of the courts' reasoning process, we also want to know what substantive norms the court is protecting through a finding of unreasonableness. A mere finding of 'unreasonableness' does not convey anything very particular about *why* the decision in question is objectionable, or about which values it infringes. Adherence to *Wednesbury* therefore permits the courts to vindicate (or not, as the case may be) substantive norms without necessarily identifying them explicitly, as Jowell and Lester [1987] *PL* 368 at 372 explain:

> [T]he *Wednesbury* test is confusing, because it is tautologous. It allows the courts to interfere with decisions that are unreasonable, and then defines an unreasonable decision as one which no reasonable authority would take ... [This test] is unhelpful as a practical guide ... The incantation of the word 'unreasonable' simply does not provide sufficient justification for judicial intervention. Intellectual honesty requires a further and better explanation as to why the act is unreasonable. The reluctance to articulate a principled justification naturally encourages suspicion that prejudice and policy considerations may be hiding underneath *Wednesbury's* ample cloak.

However, reasonableness review need not be—and is not always—as methodologically sloppy as these criticisms imply. For instance, Daly [2011] *PL* 238 argues—on the basis of an analysis of apex court decisions in the UK, the USA, and Canada—that buried within the case law is a mode of analysis that lends greater structure to reasonableness review than it is commonly supposed to possess. In particular, argues Daly, such review essentially boils down to determining whether a suspect aspect of a decision can be justified. On this analysis, a decision will be suspect if the court identifies in the decision an 'indicium of unreasonableness'—such as 'illogicality', 'disproportionality', 'inconsistency with statute', 'differential treatment', or 'unacknowledged or unexplained changes in policy'—and will be unreasonable (and so unlawful) if the presence of the indicium cannot be justified.

The Supreme Court's decision in *R (Rotherham Metropolitan Borough Council) v. Secretary of State for Business, Innovation and Skills* [2015] UKSC 6, [2015] PTSR 322 illustrates such an approach. As explained at 8.2.2, the case involved a challenge to the way in which the UK government had allocated EU funds, including on the ground that there had been unjustified differential treatment of various parts of the country. Lord Sumption (at [26]) observed that the principle that 'comparable situations are not to be treated differently or different situations comparably without objective justification' is 'fundamental to any rational system of law' and 'part of English public law', and referred to Lord Hoffmann's remarks in *Matadeen* v. *Pointu* [1999] 1 AC 98 at 109 to the effect that an absence of 'equality' is a 'ground for holding [an] administrative act to have been irrational'. Viewed thus, the issue for the Court was whether the differential treatment in question had been adequately justified; the majority, influenced in part by the considerations of deference noted at 8.2.2, concluded that it had.

A further illustration of the methodological structure and transparency with which the reasonableness test can be deployed is to be found in Lady Hale's judgment in *Keyu* v. *Secretary of State for Foreign and Commonwealth Affairs* [2015] UKSC 69, [2015] 3 WLR 1665. The pertinent question was whether Ministers had abused their discretion by declining to establish a public inquiry into the killing in 1948 by British troops of 23 unarmed citizens in the Federation of Malaya (now Malaysia), in which the UK was then the colonial power. The majority held that refusal to hold an inquiry was lawful. However, Lady Hale, the sole dissentient, considered the refusal to be unreasonable. In arriving at that conclusion, she was notably explicit as to the factors that a reasonable decision-maker would, in her view, be bound to consider. Having listed no fewer than nine such background factors, she went on to outline six advantages and disadvantages of establishing a public inquiry which, again, she considered that a reasonable decision-maker would have to take into account. Lady Hale concluded (at [312]) that the relevant Ministers 'did not take into account all the possible purposes and benefits of such an inquiry and reached a decision which was not one which a reasonable authority could reach'. This formulation is somewhat opaque, since it is ambiguous as to whether the Ministers fell into error by making a substantive decision that was not open to them (on account of its unreasonableness) or by failing to consider all legally relevant factors. However, the preceding paragraph of Lady Hale's judgment implies an error of the former type:

> The reasons given by the Secretaries of State focussed on what might now be learned of contemporary relevance, either to the organisation and training of the army or to promoting race relations, from conducting an inquiry. They did not seriously consider the most cost-effective form which such an inquiry might take. They did not seriously consider the 'bigger picture': the public interest in properly inquiring into an event of this magnitude; the private interests of the relatives and survivors in knowing the truth and seeing the reputations of their deceased relatives vindicated; the importance of setting the record straight—as counsel put it, balancing the prospect of the truth against the value of the truth.

The implication is that Lady Hale regarded the reasons given for the decision as insufficient for the purpose of justifying it. However, while amounting to an unusually detailed template of what, in the circumstances of the case, is required of a reasonable decision-maker, the transparency of Lady Hale's reasoning still leaves something to be desired. By framing her criticism in terms of the Ministers having failed to 'seriously consider' various matters, Lady Hale implies that they ascribed insufficient importance to them within the calculus of pros and cons that fell to be weighed. There is, however, little attempt in the judgment to explain with any precision what Lady Hale considers the relative importance of the various factors to be within the factual matrix of the case and why, therefore, she considers the Ministers' decision to amount to an unreasonable ordering of those factors.

From our earlier discussion, we can draw a number of conclusions about reasonableness. It does not necessarily, and does not always, live up to the caricature according to which it serves as nothing more than a vehicle for free-wheeling judicial discretion. Courts engaging in reasonableness review can, and sometimes do, articulate either a core normative value (such as equality, as in *Rotherham*) against which the justifiability of the administrative measure falls to be assessed or a set of considerations (as in Lady Hale's judgment in *Keyu*) that a reasonable decision-maker must consider and weigh in relation to each other. At the same time, however, reasonableness review has its limits in this regard. Indeed, Daly [2011] *PL* 238 at 242 acknowledges that

> [t]he case law is (almost) resolutely opaque. Mysterious references by reviewing courts to unreasonableness, multiple factors, judgment, and balancing are commonplace. It was therefore necessary to examine the case-law closely to ascertain what reviewing courts take into account in determining whether or not a decision is unreasonable.

It is clearly the case, then, that while reasonableness review can be operated in a relatively transparent and structured manner, in reality it often takes a more opaque form. This forms one of the central planks in the case advanced by some commentators for abandoning the reasonableness doctrine in favour of an across-the-board proportionality test, the argument being that the *inevitably* structured nature of the proportionality test forces courts to adopt a methodologically more rigorous and transparent approach to review.

That argument invites two questions. One involves asking whether, to the extent that proportionality is more structured than reasonableness, the more structured proportionality test is always appropriate. We examine that matter at 8.5.2. The other question is whether, in the first place, proportionality really is more determinate, structured, and transparent. The answer may seem obvious, given the highly particularized, five-stage account of the test set out at 8.3.1. That account of the test, as already noted, is derived from Lord Sumption's judgment in *Bank Mellat (No 2)*. However, it is significant that that judgment represented the culmination of more than a decade of case law which evidenced a surprising variety of judicial conceptions of the test. Initially, for instance, the leading formulation of the test was considered to be that set out by the Privy Council in *De Freitas* v. *Permanent Secretary of Ministry of Agriculture, Fisheries, Lands and Housing* [1999] 1 AC 69 at 80, which omitted any reference to the need for (as Lord Sumption subsequently put it in *Bank Mellat (No 2)* at [20]) a 'fair balance ... between the rights of the individual and the interests of the community'. That requirement was not cemented as an aspect of the proportionality test to be applied by domestic courts in human rights cases until the House of Lords' decision in *Huang* v. *Secretary of State for the Home Department* [2007] UKHL 11, [2007] 2 AC 167.

All of that might fairly be regarded today as part of the history: even if there was uncertainty about what the structure of proportionality was, there is now, it seems, a settled view. However, the extent to which this yields a cut-and-dried proportionality test that stands in contrast to a blancmange-like reasonableness test is debatable—not only because, as noted earlier, reasonableness is at least capable of more structured and transparent deployment than is commonly assumed, but also because what proportionality requires of reviewing courts is itself to some extent malleable and uncertain. This is so for two reasons.

First, as we will see at 8.4, the reality of proportionality review is significantly influenced by the operation upon it of the doctrine of deference. The existence and application of that doctrine are testament to the fact that the various elements of the proportionality test—and certain of those elements in particular—describe not a rigidly fixed approach to substantive review, but a spectrum of possibilities, the doctrine of deference operating to determine where upon that scale review lies in a given factual matrix.

Second—and to some extent relatedly—the formally expressed requirements of the proportionality test are not rigidly fixed. Sometimes, for instance, the requirement of a 'fair balance' is understood to be a distinct element within the test (as in *Bank Mellat (No 2)*), but sometimes it is taken to be a synonym for what proportionality requires as a whole, so that the structured approach gives way to an open-ended judicial balancing of disparate considerations (see, *eg Kay* v. *Lambeth London Borough Council* [2006] UKHL 10, [2006] 2 AC 465). Meanwhile, the 'necessity' element of the test sometimes means that the least restrictive means must be adopted (as in *Smith* v. *United Kingdom* (2000) 29 EHRR 493, on which see 8.3.3) but sometimes requires only that the measure adopted is 'reasonably' necessary (see, *eg R (Clays Lane Housing Co-operative Ltd)* v. *The Housing Corporation* [2004] EWCA Civ 1658, [2005] 1 WLR 2229).

None of this is to deny that proportionality supplies a relatively structured and transparent methodology for substantive review or that reasonableness can be less unstructured and more opaque. The point remains, however, that the differences between the tests are less stark than is sometimes supposed. Whether that is an argument for or against getting rid of reasonableness altogether is a matter of perspective. On the one hand, if reasonableness review is not as dissimilar to proportionality review as is sometimes assumed, jettisoning reasonableness might simplify the law without sacrificing very much of value. On the other hand, the foregoing analysis suggests that proportionality is not straightforwardly, as is sometimes suggested, methodologically superior to reasonableness—an insight that undermines the case for excising the latter from the courts' judicial review toolbox.

8.3.3 Intensity

Criticism of the *Wednesbury* test is not limited to its perceived *methodological* inadequacies. At a *normative* level, it is contended that *Wednesbury* supplies a standard of review that is too deferential. While deference may be manifestly appropriate in some situations, it is argued that where strict scrutiny is called for—paradigmatically in human rights cases—the reasonableness test is incapable of rising to the challenge. This argument can be illustrated by comparing the domestic courts' decisions in *R* v. *Ministry of Defence, ex parte Smith* [1996] QB 517 with the decision that the European Court of Human Rights (ECtHR) made when the matter was before it in *Smith* v. *United Kingdom* (2000) 29 EHRR 493. As we saw at 8.2.2, although the domestic courts considered that the reasonableness test should be adapted to take account of the fact that the policy banning gay and lesbian service personnel engaged a fundamental right (albeit not one that had, at that time, been given domestic legal effect), they were ultimately prepared to make only a 'secondary judgment' as to the reasonableness of the Minister's view that there was a sufficient public interest justification for the curtailment of the right.

The ECtHR's judgment in *Smith* v. *United Kingdom* shows that proportionality review is fundamentally different because the reviewing court exercises a primary, as distinct from a secondary, judgment. It must therefore decide *for itself* whether the various elements of the proportionality test are satisfied, rather than asking whether someone else could reasonably have come to the view that they were. That point assumes particular significance when combined with the fact that the questions posed by the proportionality test are, other things being equal, more searching than that posed by the reasonableness test. As a result, the intensity of review under the proportionality test has at least the potential to be greater. For instance, in *Smith*, the ECtHR held (at [90]) that the interferences with the applicants' right to respect for private life were 'especially grave'—not least because of the 'exceptionally intrusive character' of the investigations to which they had been subject and the 'profound effect [of the dismissals] on their careers and prospects'—and that 'particularly serious reasons by way of justification' were therefore required.

This laid the foundation for an examination of the quality of the justifications offered by the UK government that went far beyond anything the domestic courts had been prepared to undertake. The centrepiece of the government's argument was its contention that the presence of gay or lesbian members of the armed forces would have a destabilizing effect that would impair operational effectiveness. The ECtHR noted (at [95]) that

[t]he core argument of the Government in support of the policy is that the presence of open or suspected homosexuals in the armed forces would have a substantial and negative effect on morale and, consequently, on the fighting power and operational effectiveness of the armed

forces. The Government rely in this respect on the report of the HPAT [the Homosexuality Policy Assessment Team, established by the Ministry of Defence to assess the policy] ... Although the Court acknowledges the complexity of the study undertaken by the HPAT, it entertains certain doubts as to the value of the HPAT report for present purposes. The independence of the assessment contained in the report is open to question given that it was completed by Ministry of Defence civil servants and service personnel ... and given the approach to the policy outlined in the letter circulated by the Ministry of Defence in August 1995 to management levels in the armed forces [which suggested that the objective of the HPAT report was to furnish evidence for the purposes of defending the policy against attack in the Strasbourg Court] ... In addition, on any reading of the report and the methods used ... only a very small proportion of the armed forces' personnel participated in the assessment. Moreover, many of the methods of assessment (including the consultation with policy-makers in the Ministry of Defence, one-to-one interviews and the focus group discussions) were not anonymous. It also appears that many of the questions in the attitude survey suggested answers in support of the policy.

Alongside those procedural concerns, the Court noted (at [96]) that the risk to operational effectiveness identified in the HPAT report was based 'solely upon the negative attitudes of heterosexual personnel towards those of homosexual orientation'. This meant, in effect, that the government was arguing that gay and lesbian personnel would have destabilized the armed forces, compromising operational effectiveness, because of entrenched homophobia. That argument failed before the Court for two reasons. First, the Court (at [99]) did not consider that it was adequately substantiated:

The Court notes the lack of concrete evidence to substantiate the alleged damage to morale and fighting power that any change in the policy would entail. Thorpe L.J. in the Court of Appeal found that there was no actual or significant evidence of such damage as a result of the presence of homosexuals in the armed forces, and the Court further considers that the subsequent HPAT assessment did not, whatever its value, provide evidence of such damage in the event of the policy changing. Given the number of homosexuals dismissed between 1991 and 1996 [361], the number of homosexuals who were in the armed forces at the relevant time cannot be said to be insignificant. Even if the absence of such evidence can be explained by the consistent application of the policy, as submitted by the Government, this is insufficient to demonstrate to the Court's satisfaction that operational effectiveness problems of the nature and level alleged can be anticipated in the absence of the policy.

Second, to the extent that the presence of gay and lesbian personnel might present any difficulties, the Court did not consider an outright ban to be a necessary way of addressing such difficulties:

[102] The Court considers it important to note, in the first place, the approach already adopted by the armed forces to deal with racial discrimination and with racial and sexual harassment and bullying ... [Measures introduced in 1996], for example, imposed both a strict code of conduct on every soldier together with disciplinary rules to deal with any inappropriate behaviour and conduct. This dual approach was supplemented with information leaflets and training programmes, the army emphasising the need for high standards of personal conduct and for respect for others. The Government, nevertheless, underlined that it is 'the knowledge or suspicion of homosexuality' which would cause the morale problems and not conduct, so that a conduct code would not solve the anticipated difficulties. However, in so far as negative attitudes to homosexuality are insufficient, of themselves, to justify the policy ..., they are equally insufficient to justify the

rejection of a proposed alternative. In any event, the Government themselves recognised during the hearing that the choice between a conduct code and the maintenance of the policy lay at the heart of the judgment to be made in this case. This is also consistent with the Government's direct reliance on Section F of the HPAT's report where the anticipated problems identified as posing a risk to morale were almost exclusively problems related to behaviour and conduct. The Government maintained that homosexuality raised problems of a type and intensity that race and gender did not. However, even if it can be assumed that the integration of homosexuals would give rise to problems not encountered with the integration of women or racial minorities, the Court is not satisfied that the codes and rules which have been found to be effective in the latter case would not equally prove effective in the former. The 'robust indifference' reported by the HPAT of the large number of British armed forces' personnel serving abroad with allied forces to homosexuals serving in those foreign forces, serves to confirm that the perceived problems of integration are not insuperable.

[103] The Government highlighted particular problems which might be posed by the communal accommodation arrangements in the armed forces. Detailed submissions were made during the hearing, the parties disagreeing as to the potential consequences of shared single-sex accommodation and associated facilities. The Court notes that the HPAT itself concluded that separate accommodation for homosexuals would not be warranted or wise and that substantial expenditure would not, therefore, have to be incurred in this respect. Nevertheless, the Court remains of the view that it has not been shown that the conduct codes and disciplinary rules referred to above could not adequately deal with any behavioural issues arising on the part either of homosexuals or of heterosexuals.

On the face of it, the ECtHR's judgment in *Smith* suggests that the proportionality test supplies an intensity of judicial scrutiny that is radically different from—and greater than—that which the reasonableness doctrine furnishes. However, as with the question of methodology, the distinction between the tests is not as stark as it might at first appear. This is so for two reasons. First, the intensity with which courts scrutinize decisions under the proportionality test is itself variable thanks to the doctrine of deference that operates upon it. In circumstances in which the reviewing court considers substantial deference to be warranted, the intensity of review will be commensurately reduced, even sometimes in cases of fundamental rights. We examine this matter in detail at 8.4.

Second, not only does proportionality review entail less intense scrutiny when deference is called for: the reasonableness test sometimes supplies review that is more intense than the default version of the test implies. We have already seen that, before the HRA was at their disposal, courts were prepared to conceive of the reasonableness test in rather more exacting terms when basic rights were at stake—although, as the domestic courts' decisions in *Smith* show, that did not necessarily amount to much in the end. We have also seen, however, that in *Keyu* Lady Hale adopted an approach to reasonableness review that went well beyond merely seeking to discern absurdity of a degree exemplified by the dismissal of a teacher because she has red hair. Indeed, in *Keyu*, Lady Hale's analysis—and, at least implicitly, weighing—of the pros and cons of holding a public inquiry imply a considerable degree of scrutiny of the Ministers' reasons for refusing to establish such an inquiry.

More generally, the level at which the reasonableness test is pitched—in terms of the quality of the justification it demands—is necessarily informed by the context. For instance, in *R (Bradley) v. Secretary of State for Work and Pensions* [2008] EWCA Civ 36, [2009] QB 114 (on which see further at 19.4.4) Sir John Chadwick, giving the leading judgment in the Court of Appeal, held (at [72]) that a Minister had to have 'cogent reasons' for rejecting findings contained in a report of the Parliamentary Ombudsman. He made it clear that this required something more than conventional reasonableness, explaining (at [91]) that it was 'not enough that the Secretary of State has reached his own view on rational grounds', because the 'legislative intention' founded a relationship between public bodies and the Ombudsman that did not accommodate ready dismissal by the former of the latter's findings. Similarly, in *R (Evans)* v. *Information Commissioner* [2015] UKSC 21, [2015] AC 1787, Lord Mance, giving one of the majority judgments, held that particularly searching scrutiny was called for when examining the reasonableness of the use by the executive of a statutory power to override a decision of the Upper Tribunal. Lord Mance considered (at [130]) that if a Minister were to seek to exercise the override power because he disagreed with a finding of fact or law made by the Tribunal, this would require 'the clearest possible justification'—a hurdle that, he indicated, was so high that it would only rarely be cleared.

Whether, examined in normative terms, these decisions involve judicial review that is unduly searching is a contested question; for the time being, however, the essential point is simply that they demonstrate the possibility of relatively searching review without sacrificing the reasonableness test on the altar of the proportionality doctrine. This is not to suggest that such cases show the reasonableness and proportionality doctrines to be more or less the same. They are not: in their default forms, the tests differ, in terms both of methodology and the intensity of review that they supply. At the same time, however, neither test is monolithic: the reasonableness doctrine, as we have seen, can be applied in a relatively structured form and can supply review whose intensity outstrips that envisaged by Lord Greene MR in the *Wednesbury* case itself. Meanwhile, although proportionality—as the ECtHR's *Smith* judgment shows—can provide an intensity of review that goes well beyond that which is traditionally associated with the reasonableness test, proportionality does not—thanks to the doctrine of deference, examined at 8.4—invariably entail such searching scrutiny.

8.3.4 The role of the proportionality test in English law: background

Precisely because proportionality can form a basis for high-intensity review, it was regarded with suspicion by judges, who feared that its adoption might erode the distinction between appeal and review, thereby causing courts to exceed their proper constitutional role under the separation of powers. For instance, in *R* v. *Secretary of State for the Home Department, ex parte Brind* [1991] 1 AC 696 at 766–7, Lord Lowry considered that

> there is *no* authority for saying that proportionality … is part of the English common law and a great deal of authority the other way. This, so far as I am concerned, is not a cause for regret for several reasons: 1. The decision-makers, very often elected, are those to whom Parliament has entrusted the discretion and to interfere with that discretion beyond the limits as hitherto defined would itself be an abuse of the judges' supervisory jurisdiction. 2. The judges are not, generally speaking, equipped by training or experience, or furnished with the requisite knowledge and advice, to decide the answer to an administrative problem where the scales are evenly balanced, but they have a much better chance of reaching the right answer where the question is put in a *Wednesbury* form. The same applies if the judges' decision is appealed. 3. Stability and relative certainty would be jeopardised if the new doctrine held sway, because there is nearly always something to be said against any administrative decision and parties who felt aggrieved would be even more likely than

at present to try their luck with a judicial review application both at first instance and on appeal. 4. The increase in applications for judicial review of administrative action (inevitable if the threshold of unreasonableness is lowered) will lead to the expenditure of time and money by litigants, not to speak of the prolongation of uncertainty for all concerned with the decisions in question, and the taking up of court time which could otherwise be devoted to other matters. The losers in this respect will be members of the public, for whom the courts provide a service ...

It finally occurs to me that there can be very little room for judges to operate an independent judicial review proportionality doctrine in the space which is left between the conventional judicial review doctrine and the admittedly forbidden appellate approach. To introduce an intermediate area of deliberation for the court seems scarcely a practical idea, quite apart from the other disadvantages by which, in my opinion, such a course would be attended.

Such concerns notwithstanding, it is clear that even before the commencement of the HRA—to which we turn shortly—English administrative law was beginning to embrace the concept of proportionality (or something like it). Indeed, English courts have long had to employ the proportionality principle in cases engaging relevant provisions of European Union law, albeit that the version of the test applicable in EU law (on which see generally *R (Lumsdon)* v. *Legal Services Board* [2015] UKSC 41, [2015] 3 WLR 121) differs somewhat from that which applies in ECHR and HRA cases. But even outside the EU context, English courts had begun to inch towards proportionality-style review, as the domestic courts' decisions in *Smith* indicate. While this plainly did not go as far as the ECtHR's application of proportionality *per se*, the pre-HRA domestic approach did exhibit some of the essential characteristics of that test, in terms of both structured analysis and the normative demand for greater justification where important rights are in play.

Consider, for example, the decision of the House of Lords in *R* v. *Secretary of State for the Home Department, ex parte Simms* [2000] 2 AC 115, which concerned a blanket policy prohibiting prisoners from giving interviews to journalists. The legality of that policy was successfully challenged by prisoners who wished to give interviews to investigative journalists in order to contend their innocence. Lord Steyn said (at 125) that the 'starting point' was 'the right of freedom of expression', and (at 127) that because the claimant prisoners wanted to exercise that right for the purpose of challenging the safety of their convictions—and hence the deprivation of liberty to which they were subjected as a result—it was 'not easy to conceive of a more important function which free speech might fulfil'. In the light of that, Lord Steyn said (at 129), echoing language used in the ECtHR, that 'only a pressing social need can defeat freedom of expression' and (echoing the domestic courts' decisions in *Smith*) that 'the more substantial the interference with fundamental rights the more the court will require by way of justification before it can be satisfied that the interference is reasonable in a public law sense'.

Simms is not an isolated example. Several other cases—including *R* v. *Secretary of State for the Home Department, ex parte Leech* [1994] QB 198; *R* v. *Lord Saville of Newdigate, ex parte A* [2000] 1 WLR 1855; *R* v. *Secretary of State for the Home Department, ex parte Pierson* [1998] AC 539; and *R* v. *North and East Devon Health Authority, ex parte Coughlan* [2001] QB 213—suggest that *before* the activation of the HRA English courts were willing, in limited circumstances, to engage in something akin to proportionality review. At one time these observations might have been regarded as a historical footnote bearing in mind that proportionality review—as explained in the next section—now straightforwardly takes place in fundamental rights cases under the auspices of the HRA. However, in ways and for reasons that we chart at 8.5, the question whether the proportionality test has a life at common law, independently of the HRA, is today very much a live issue—to which the fact that elements of proportionality review were apparent in domestic law prior to the HRA is self-evidently pertinent.

8.3.5 The role of the proportionality test in English law: the current position

Although, as we have just seen, elements of proportionality-style review were evident in the pre-HRA case law, that legislation acted as a catalyst for further development in this area by resolving two areas of uncertainty. First, although substantive review—at least in human rights cases—was evidently moving towards the proportionality test, many judgments were at best equivocal. Even cases like *Simms*, which appeared to embrace proportionality, did so in a somewhat qualified fashion: Lords Hobhouse and Steyn invoked both the reasonableness *and* proportionality principles, leaving a question mark over whether proportionality had become a ground of review in its own right. Second, the range of rights or interests which could be protected by means of proportionality-style review was uncertain.

Neither of those uncertainties exist in cases to which the HRA applies. The rights protected by the Act are clearly stated in it (s 1 defines the 'Convention rights' as Articles 2–12 ECHR, Articles 1–3 of the First Protocol to the Convention, and Articles 1–2 of the Sixth Protocol); public authorities are obliged by s 6 to act consistently with the Convention rights; and s 3 requires their statutory powers to be construed, as far as is possible, compatibly with those rights. Administrative action in breach of the Convention rights can therefore be quashed as unlawful (unless such a breach is sanctioned by primary legislation (s 6(2)). Meanwhile, it is clear from the jurisprudence of the ECtHR, which English courts are obliged to take into account (s 2), that the concept of proportionality is inherent in many of the Convention rights. It is therefore unsurprising that English courts have embraced the proportionality test in relevant HRA cases. Against that background, we turn to consider the House of Lords' highly significant judgment in the *Daly* case.

R (Daly) v. *Secretary of State for the Home Department* [2001] UKHL 26, [2001] 2 AC 532
House of Lords

All governors of closed prisons were required by the Home Secretary to operate a standard cell searching policy. Under the policy prisoners were not permitted to remain in their cells during searches, in order to prevent intimidation of those conducting the search and to stop prisoners gaining knowledge of search techniques. Prison officers were permitted to examine, but not read, legal correspondence stored in cells. The claimant, who stored such correspondence in his cell, contended that the policy requiring prisoners to be absent while their legal correspondence was examined was unlawful.

Lord Bingham

[15] It is necessary, first, to ask whether the policy infringes in a significant way Mr Daly's common law right that the confidentiality of privileged legal correspondence be maintained. He submits that it does for two related reasons: first, because knowledge that such correspondence may be

looked at by prison officers in the absence of the prisoner inhibits the prisoner's willingness to communicate with his legal adviser in terms of unreserved candour; and secondly, because there must be a risk, if the prisoner is not present, that the officers will stray beyond their limited role in examining legal correspondence, particularly if, for instance, they see some name or reference familiar to them, as would be the case if the prisoner were bringing or contemplating bringing proceedings against officers in the prison. For the Home Secretary it is argued that the policy involves no infringement of a prisoner's common law right since his privileged correspondence is not read in his absence but only examined.

[16] I have no doubt that the policy infringes Mr Daly's common law right to legal professional privilege ... In an imperfect world there will necessarily be occasions when prison officers will do more than merely examine prisoners' legal documents, and apprehension that they may do so is bound to inhibit a prisoner's willingness to communicate freely with his legal adviser.

[17] The next question is whether there can be any ground for infringing in any way a prisoner's right to maintain the confidentiality of his privileged legal correspondence. Plainly there can. Some examination may well be necessary to establish that privileged legal correspondence is what it appears to be and is not a hiding place for illicit materials or information prejudicial to security or good order.

[18] It is then necessary to ask whether, to the extent that it infringes a prisoner's common law right to privilege, the policy can be justified as a necessary and proper response to the acknowledged need to maintain security, order and discipline in prisons and to prevent crime. Mr Daly's challenge at this point is directed to the blanket nature of the policy, applicable as it is to all prisoners of whatever category in all closed prisons in England and Wales, irrespective of a prisoner's past or present conduct and of any operational emergency or urgent intelligence. The Home Secretary's justification rests firmly on the points already mentioned: the risk of intimidation, the risk that staff may be conditioned by prisoners to relax security and the danger of disclosing searching methods.

[19] In considering these justifications, based as they are on the extensive experience of the prison service, it must be recognised that the prison population includes a core of dangerous, disruptive and manipulative prisoners, hostile to authority and ready to exploit for their own advantage any concession granted to them. Any search policy must accommodate this inescapable fact. I cannot however accept that the reasons put forward justify the policy in its present blanket form. Any prisoner who attempts to intimidate or disrupt a search of his cell, or whose past conduct shows that he is likely to do so, may properly be excluded even while his privileged correspondence is examined so as to ensure the efficacy of the search, but no justification is shown for routinely excluding all prisoners, whether intimidatory or disruptive or not, while that part of the search is conducted. [In the absence of] extraordinary conditions ..., it is hard to regard the conditioning of staff as a problem which could not be met by employing dedicated search teams. It is not suggested that prison officers when examining legal correspondence employ any sophisticated technique which would be revealed to the prisoner if he were present, although he might no doubt be encouraged to secrete illicit materials among his legal papers if the examination were obviously very cursory. The policy cannot in my opinion be justified in its present blanket form. The infringement of prisoners' rights to maintain the confidentiality of their privileged legal correspondence is greater than is shown to be necessary to serve the legitimate public objectives already identified. I accept Mr Daly's submission on this point ... In my opinion the policy provides for a degree of intrusion into the privileged legal correspondence of prisoners which is greater than is justified by the objectives the policy is intended to serve, and so violates the common law rights of prisoners ...

[23] I have reached the conclusions so far expressed on an orthodox application of common law principles derived from the authorities and an orthodox domestic approach to judicial review. But the same result is achieved by reliance on the European Convention. Article 8(1)

gives Mr Daly a right to respect for his correspondence. While interference with that right by a public authority may be permitted if in accordance with the law and necessary in a democratic society in the interests of national security, public safety, the prevention of disorder or crime or for protection of the rights and freedoms of others, the policy interferes with Mr Daly's exercise of his right under article 8(1) to an extent much greater than necessity requires. In this instance, therefore, the common law and the Convention yield the same result. But this need not always be so. In *Smith and Grady* v *United Kingdom* (1999) 29 EHRR 493, the European Court held that the orthodox domestic approach of the English courts had not given the applicants an effective remedy for the breach of their rights under article 8 of the Convention because the threshold of review had been set too high. Now, following the incorporation of the Convention by the Human Rights Act 1998 and the bringing of that Act fully into force, domestic courts must themselves form a judgment whether a Convention right has been breached (conducting such inquiry as is necessary to form that judgment) and, so far as permissible under the Act, grant an effective remedy. On this aspect of the case, I agree with and adopt the observations of my noble and learned Lord Steyn which I have had the opportunity of reading in draft ...

Lord Steyn

[24] My Lords, I am in complete agreement with the reasons given by Lord Bingham of Cornhill in his speech. For the reasons he gives I would also allow the appeal. Except on one narrow but important point I have nothing to add.

[25] There was written and oral argument on the question whether certain observations of Lord Phillips of Worth Matravers MR in *R (Mahmood)* v. *Secretary of State for the Home Department* [2001] 1 WLR 840 were correct. [Lord Phillips said (at [37]) that in cases concerning Convention rights the court should only 'intervene where the decision fell outside the range of responses open to a reasonable decision-maker'.] The context was an immigration case involving a decision of the Secretary of State made before the Human Rights Act 1998 came into effect. The Master of the Rolls nevertheless approached the case as if the Act had been in force when the Secretary of State reached his decision ...

[26] The [relevant part of the judgment] of the Master of the Rolls ... requires clarification. It is couched in language reminiscent of the traditional *Wednesbury* ground of review ... and in particular the adaptation of that test in terms of heightened scrutiny in cases involving fundamental rights as formulated in *R* v. *Ministry of Defence, Ex p Smith* [1996] QB 517, 554E–G per Sir Thomas Bingham MR. There is a material difference between the *Wednesbury* and *Smith* grounds of review and the approach of proportionality applicable in respect of review where Convention rights are at stake.

[27] The contours of the principle of proportionality are familiar. In *de Freitas* v *Permanent Secretary of Ministry of Agriculture, Fisheries, Lands and Housing* [1999] 1 AC 69 the Privy Council adopted a three-stage test ... Clearly, these criteria are more precise and more sophisticated than the traditional grounds of review. What is the difference for the disposal of concrete cases? ... The starting point is that there is an overlap between the traditional grounds of review and the approach of proportionality. Most cases would be decided in the same way whichever approach is adopted. But the intensity of review is somewhat greater under the proportionality approach. Making due allowance for important structural differences between various convention rights, which I do not propose to discuss, a few generalisations are perhaps permissible. I would mention three concrete differences without suggesting that my statement is exhaustive. First, the doctrine of proportionality may require the reviewing court to assess the balance which the decision maker has struck, not merely whether it is within the range of rational or reasonable decisions. Secondly, the proportionality test may go further than the traditional grounds of review inasmuch as it may require attention to be directed to the relative weight

accorded to interests and considerations. Thirdly, even the heightened scrutiny test developed in *R* v *Ministry of Defence, ex parte Smith* [1996] QB 517, 554 is not necessarily appropriate to the protection of human rights. It will be recalled that in *Smith* the Court of Appeal reluctantly felt compelled to reject a limitation on homosexuals in the army. The challenge based on article 8 of the Convention for the Protection of Human Rights and Fundamental Freedoms (the right to respect for private and family life) foundered on the threshold required even by the anxious scrutiny test. The European Court of Human Rights came to the opposite conclusion: *Smith* v *United Kingdom* (1999) 29 EHRR 493 … [Thus] the intensity of the review, in similar cases, is guaranteed by the twin requirements that the limitation of the right was necessary in a democratic society, in the sense of meeting a pressing social need, and the question whether the interference was really proportionate to the legitimate aim being pursued.

[28] The differences in approach between the traditional grounds of review and the proportionality approach may therefore sometimes yield different results. It is therefore important that cases involving Convention rights must be analysed in the correct way. This does not mean that there has been a shift to merits review. On the contrary, as Professor Jowell [2000] PL 671, 681 has pointed out the respective roles of judges and administrators are fundamentally distinct and will remain so. To this extent the general tenor of the observations in *Mahmood* are correct. And Laws LJ rightly emphasised in *Mahmood* … 'that the intensity of review in a public law case will depend on the subject matter in hand'. That is so even in cases involving Convention rights. In law context is everything.

Lord Cooke

[29] My Lords, having had the advantage of reading in draft the speeches of my noble and learned friends, Lord Bingham of Cornhill and Lord Steyn, I am in full agreement with them. I add some brief observations on two matters, less to supplement what they have said than to underline its importance.

[30] First, while this case has arisen in a jurisdiction where the European Convention for the Protection of Human Rights and Fundamental Freedoms applies, and while the case is one in which the Convention and the common law produce the same result, it is of great importance, in my opinion, that the common law by itself is being recognised as a sufficient source of the fundamental right to confidential communication with a legal adviser for the purpose of obtaining legal advice. Thus the decision may prove to be in point in common law jurisdictions not affected by the Convention. Rights similar to those in the Convention are of course to be found in constitutional documents and other formal affirmations of rights elsewhere. The truth is, I think, that some rights are inherent and fundamental to democratic civilised society. Conventions, constitutions, bills of rights and the like respond by recognising rather than creating them.

[31] To essay any list of these fundamental, perhaps ultimately universal, rights is far beyond anything required for the purpose of deciding the present case. It is enough to take the three identified by Lord Bingham: in his words, access to a court; access to legal advice; and the right to communicate confidentially with a legal adviser under the seal of legal professional privilege. As he says authoritatively from the woolsack, such rights may be curtailed only by clear and express words, and then only to the extent reasonably necessary to meet the ends which justify the curtailment. The point that I am emphasising is that the common law goes so deep.

[32] The other matter concerns degrees of judicial review. Lord Steyn illuminates the distinctions between 'traditional' (that is to say in terms of English case law, *Wednesbury*) standards of judicial review and higher standards under the European Convention or the common law of human rights. As he indicates, often the results are the same. But the view that the standards are substantially the same appears to have received its quietus in *Smith* v *United Kingdom* (1999) 29

EHRR 493 and *Lustig-Prean v United Kingdom* (1999) 29 EHRR 548. [Lord Cooke then went on to make the remarks set out at 8.2.1.]

Lords Hutton and Scott agreed with Lords Bingham, Steyn, and Cooke that the cell-searching policy was unlawful.

The House of Lords' judgment in *Daly* is important for four reasons. First, it represents the first unequivocal adoption of the proportionality test in a human rights case at apex court level in the UK.

Second, *Daly* strikes a very different tone in relation to proportionality than that which was adopted in earlier cases such as *Brind*. In the latter case, as noted at 8.3.4, Lord Lowry (along with Lord Ackner) was highly resistant to the possibility of domestic courts applying proportionality for fear that it would cause them to exceed their proper constitutional role. In contrast, in *Daly*, while acknowledging that proportionality and reasonableness are different tests that can yield different results, their Lordships take the view that proportionality can be applied without constitutional impropriety; there is certainly no indication that they consider the HRA to have foisted upon them a function that they should not properly have.

Third, that point is underscored by the fact that, although their Lordships refer to the HRA and the ECHR in *Daly*, the basis of the judgment is in fact the *common law* right to legal professional privilege. As the earlier passage shows, Lord Bingham (with whose judgment all the other Law Lords agreed) treated the proportionality test as applicable to that common law right, asking whether restrictions upon it were 'necessary' in order to secure 'legitimate public objectives' and whether the 'degree of intrusion' into the right was justified by the objectives the policy sought to advance. The willingness of the House of Lords to deploy proportionality in order to analyse the lawfulness of measures impinging upon a common law right is important when it comes to considering—as we do at 8.5—the scope of application of the proportionality test, and the extent to which it has displaced, or may come to displace, reasonableness.

Fourth, Lord Steyn's judgment—including his oft-quoted remark that 'context is everything'—served to highlight the fact that although *Daly* itself represented a turning point due to its acknowledgement of proportionality as a ground of review, a good deal of work remained to be undertaken in terms of mapping the intensity of proportionality review. That work fell to be done by means of developing a doctrine of deference that operates upon the proportionality test so as to modulate it in a way that is sensitive to context. It is to the matter of deference that we now turn.

8.4 Deference

8.4.1 Introduction

Twenty years ago, the term 'deference' was rarely encountered in English administrative law judgments or commentaries. Today, the term—or at least the concept for which it stands: the term itself is deprecated by some judges—is commonplace. This tells us two important things, respectively, concerning *why deference is necessary* and *what deference involves*.

First, deference as a separate idea was not much needed when the boundaries of substantive review were traced by the reasonableness doctrine because that doctrine is (at least in its traditional guise) inherently deferential. It was only as the courts moved towards embracing the potentially more intrusive proportionality doctrine that talk of deference began to take root, the idea being that the application of a doctrine of deference would serve to tone down proportionality review when appropriate.

Second, the fact that deference as a distinct concept was surplus to requirements when the traditional reasonableness test prevailed tells us something about what deference means in practice. The (traditional conception of) reasonableness is deferential in the sense that it involves posing, in respect of administrative decisions, a relatively undemanding question. If, to use the language adopted by Lord Diplock in *GCHQ*, the court limits itself to asking whether the decision is 'outrageous in its defiance of logic or of accepted moral standards', any concerns about deference are automatically taken care of, since there seems little risk of the court exceeding its proper function by asking such a question. However, the fact is that some of the questions that form the proportionality test—such as whether the measure is necessary and whether it strikes a fair balance between the right of the individual and the broader interests of the community—are less inherently deferential. If it is considered that, in the circumstances of a particular case, posing such questions risks causing the reviewing court to exceed its proper role, two ways forward present themselves.

Those two options can be illustrated by reference to *R (Carlile) v. Secretary of State for the Home Department* [2014] UKSC 60, [2015] AC 945. The question was whether the right to freedom of expression had been breached by a refusal to allow a dissident Iranian politician to enter the UK in order to address a group of parliamentarians—a refusal the Home Secretary considered necessary in order to avoid destabilizing UK–Iranian relations and thereby impeding the effective conduct of foreign policy. In these circumstances, Lord Sumption (at [32]) considered that the court's role should be heavily circumscribed:

> [T]here are cases where the rationality of a decision is the only criterion which is capable of judicial assessment. This is particularly likely to be true of predictive and other judgmental assessments, especially those of a political nature. Such cases often involve a judgment or prediction of a kind whose rationality can be assessed but whose correctness cannot in the nature of things be tested empirically.

This amounts to a radical form of deference which effectively substitutes reasonableness for proportionality review because the latter is considered too intrusive in the circumstances. Deference is thus achieved by replacing a more demanding question ('Is the measure proportionate?') with a less demanding one ('Is the measure rational?').

An alternative, and more nuanced, way in which a court can defer is by continuing to ask the questions entailed in proportionality review while ascribing a degree of weight or respect to decision-makers' views on pertinent issues. This means that even if the *question* posed by the court is demanding, the likelihood of the court's being satisfied by the *answer* to it is enhanced by virtue of the store that the court is prepared to set by the public body's view. For instance, in *Carlile*, Lady Hale did not agree with Lord Sumption that the court should do nothing more than ask whether the measure in question was rational: rather, she said (at [89]), the court had to 'go through an orderly process of decision-making, answering a series of questions' (*ie* the proportionality questions). However, she continued (at [98]):

> I have no doubt that it is for the court to make the proportionality assessment; but I have equally no doubt that on some parts of that assessment the court should be very slow indeed to disagree with the assessment made by the Government.

The degree of difference between these two possible ways of securing deference should not be overstated. After all, even if the court still chooses to ask (for example) whether a measure strikes a fair balance between the right of the individual and the interests of the community, that might amount to very little in practice if—as Lady Hale advocated in *Carlile*—the court should be 'very slow indeed' to disagree with the government's view that the balance is a fair one. In effect, asking the fair balance question in that way is not very different from asking a question—such as whether the decision is rational—that is in the first place less demanding. That said, however, there are advantages to the approach favoured by Lady Hale over that preferred by Lord Sumption. In particular, Lady Hale's approach allows for a more targeted form of deference, since it can be applied as appropriate to the various stages of the proportionality inquiry. In contrast, Lord Sumption's approach, by excising some of those stages and substituting them with a less demanding question, amounts to a blunter instrument.

8.4.2 Deference triggers

We have seen so far that a court can adopt a deferential posture either by asking less searching questions of the impugned administrative measure or by ascribing weight to pertinent governmental views. A further—indeed, prior—issue is what, in the first place, ought to trigger deference. When deference was first considered by the courts, the idea took root that it involved demarcating particular areas of decision-making—defined by reference to the subject-matter of the decision—within which courts would necessarily defer to the decision-maker's view. On this analysis, if the subject-matter of the decision is, for instance, national security, then deference is called for. Hunt (in Bamforth and Leyland (eds), *Public Law in a Multi-Layered Constitution* (Oxford 2003) at 345) calls this 'spatial deference'. Such an approach was endorsed in *R v. Director of Public Prosecutions, ex parte Kebilene* [2000] 2 AC 326 at 380, in which Lord Hope spoke of 'an area of [administrative] judgment within which the judiciary will defer, on democratic grounds, to the considered opinion' of an elected decision-maker. Similarly, in *International Transport Roth GmbH v. Secretary of State for the Home Department* [2002] EWCA Civ 158, [2003] QB 728 at [77], Laws LJ said (in a dissenting judgment which has nevertheless been treated as an influential statement of principle) that

> the extent of any deference ... depends in part on the nature and quality of the measure in question: more concretely, whether its content falls within the special responsibility of the executive ... or the special responsibility of the judiciary. A paradigm of the executive's special responsibility is the security of the State's borders. A paradigm of the judiciary's special responsibility is the doing of criminal justice.

The fundamental error which, according to Hunt (at 347), characterizes the spatial approach is the assumption that cases can be 'neatly classified into categories according to the kind of subject matter they raise, and then a particular standard of review applied to them'. Reality is more complex. Cases can, and frequently do, arise which concern areas of administration which, on a spatial approach, would attract cursory or no judicial scrutiny, but which, viewed from another perspective, call for searching judicial review—as, for instance, in cases that implicate both national security and human rights matters.

The foregoing dicta notwithstanding, the case law clearly shows that English courts are not wedded to a spatial approach to deference. One of the clearest illustrations of this is the *Belmarsh* case, in which the House of Lords subjected secondary legislation to intensive scrutiny (and ultimately struck it down) on human rights grounds, notwithstanding that the government sought to justify it by reference to national security considerations. We consider *Belmarsh* at 8.4.5.

'Due deference', which is an alternative version of the concept to 'spatial deference', is to be preferred, both because it is more subtle and because it more accurately captures the reality of contemporary judicial practice. On this view, deference operates in a more granular fashion by requiring the reviewing court self-reflectively to determine the proper intensity of review at each stage of the proportionality inquiry, ascribing such weight or respect to the decision-maker's pertinent views as is appropriate in the light of that reflection. Viewed thus, the trigger for deference is not that the case is concerned with a particular subject-matter. Rather, deference is triggered by the assessment—in relation to each stage of the proportionality inquiry—of whether there are institutional or democratic reasons that require the court to reduce the intensity of review by attaching a suitable degree of weight to a governmental view that is relevant to the stage of the inquiry in question.

The principal sites of deference, on this view, are stages (iv) and (v) of the proportionality test as set out at 8.3.1. At these stages, it will be recalled, the court asks (iv) whether it was *necessary* for the relevant interest (*eg* a human right) to be restricted to the extent that it was restricted, and (v) even if it was, whether the extent of that restriction can be justified by reference to the resulting gains. On point (iv), there may well be disagreement between the claimant and the decision-maker: the claimant may say that the decision-maker could have secured its policy objective (*eg* of upholding national security) without restricting the claimant's rights to the extent that they were actually restricted (*eg* by electronically tagging, rather than locking up, the claimant). Similarly, there may be disagreement on point (v): the government might think that locking up a handful of suspected terrorists is a price worth paying for protecting the public from the risk of a devastating terrorist attack; the suspects may well not share that view. It is ultimately for the court to decide on the answers to the questions: but in arriving at its view, the court may, and in some circumstances should, ascribe appropriate weight to the opinion of the decision-maker, either because the decision-maker has particular expertise or because its democratic credentials mean that its views are worthy of a degree of respect.

This is precisely the approach which the House of Lords articulated in *Huang* v. *Secretary of State for the Home Department* [2007] UKHL 11, [2007] 2 AC 167. The case was concerned with decisions refusing the claimants indefinite leave to remain in the UK—decisions which the claimants challenged, arguing that they breached their right to respect for private and family life under Article 8 ECHR. The key question for the House of Lords was whether the interference with the right could be justified by reference to a legitimate public interest. Lord Bingham, delivering the sole judgment, said (at [16]):

There will, in almost any case, be certain general considerations to bear in mind: the general administrative desirability of applying known rules if a system of immigration control is to be workable, predictable, consistent and fair as between one applicant and another; the damage

to good administration and executive control if a system is perceived by applicants internation-
ally to be unduly porous, unpredictable or perfunctory; the need to discourage non-nationals
admitted to the country temporarily from believing that they can commit serious crimes and yet
be allowed to remain; the need to discourage fraud, deception and deliberate breaches of the
law; and so on. In some cases much more particular reasons will be relied on to justify refusal,
as in *Samaroo* v *Secretary of State for the Home Department* [2002] INLR 55 where attention was
paid to the Secretary of State's judgment that deportation was a valuable deterrent to actual or
prospective drug traffickers, or *R (Farrakhan)* v *Secretary of State for the Home Department* [2002]
QB 1391, an article 10 case [concerning freedom of expression], in which note was taken of the
Home Secretary's judgment that the applicant posed a threat to community relations between
Muslims and Jews and a potential threat to public order for that reason. The giving of weight to
factors such as these is not, in our opinion, aptly described as deference: it is performance of the
ordinary judicial task of weighing up the competing considerations on each side and according
appropriate weight to the judgment of a person with responsibility for a given subject matter and
access to special sources of knowledge and advice.

Like Lord Sumption in *R (Carlile)* v. *Secretary of State for the Home Department* [2014]
UKSC 60, [2015] AC 945 at [22]—who criticized the use of the word 'deference' in the light
of 'its overtones of cringing abstention in the face of superior status'—the Law Lords in
Huang rejected the *language* of deference. Yet the approach they advocated in *substance*
amounts to precisely the approach to deference outlined here. In this chapter, we continue
to use the term deference as a convenient shorthand for that approach.

8.4.3 Is deference a good thing?

Allan [2006] *CLJ* 671 mounts a spirited normative attack on deference, arguing (at 689)
that it

turns out, on close inspection, to be nonjusticiability dressed in pastel colours. ['Due deference'
involves] an abdication of judicial responsibility for the protection of rights, [and] is marked
precisely by reliance on the expertise or experience or public visibility of the decision-maker
as opposed to the apparent quality of the decision itself. Here the judges' reliance on the supposedly superior qualifications of the decision-maker effectively divests the court of its role as
independent scrutineer. An experienced and well-qualified public official can always make an
error of judgment as regards the balance of private rights and public interest; and a similar error
can be made by a body accountable to Parliament or the electorate. Yet a form of deference that
deflects attention from the legislative or administrative act, in order to evaluate the merits of the
actor, is ill-suited to the identification of error. Undermining the impartiality and independence of
judicial review, such deference is no more legitimate when employed as one doctrinal consideration among others than when constituting the sole basis of the court's decision.

Allan's argument, then, is that deference entails the court allowing itself to be persuaded by
a decision-maker's view not because of the intrinsic quality of the reasons in support of the
view but because some external characteristic of the decision-maker (*eg* that it has relevant
expertise) leads the court to accept an argument that it would otherwise (evaluating the
argument purely on its own merits) have rejected. This, Allan contends, amounts to dereliction of judicial duty. What courts should instead be doing, says Allan, is simply deciding

whether the impugned administrative act is lawful or unlawful—a function it ought to discharge by reference to the quality of the arguments, not the characteristics of those advancing them. This view has attracted considerable criticism: Taggart [2008] *NZ L Rev* 423 at 456 calls it 'extreme' and 'utterly implausible'. Two particular issues should be noted.

First, Allan's view appears, as Young (2009) 72 *MLR* 554 at 576 notes, to presuppose that the questions which arise for judicial decision have correct answers. Whether this is so is highly doubtful. Take the sort of question liable to arise at stage (v) of the proportionality analysis. The question might, for example, be as follows: 'Given that (as accepted by the court at stage (iv)) the least restrictive way of protecting national security is to imprison the claimant without charge or trial, does the extent to which such detention benefits national security outweigh, and thereby justify, depriving the claimant of his liberty?' In order to answer this question, the court must, whether consciously or otherwise, decide how much value to attach to the two factors which are in tension with one another—*viz* the public's national security 'gain' and the claimant's human rights 'loss'. This task can only be performed by making a value judgement: as Laws LJ observed in *Miranda v. Secretary of State for the Home Department* [2014] EWHC 255 (Admin), [2014] 1 WLR 3140 at [40], whether a given measure 'fails to strike the right balance between private right and public interest' is a question that cannot easily be distinguished 'from a political question to be decided by the elected arm of government'. None of the leading participants in the debate presently under consideration would contend that courts should simply give the government a completely free hand by allowing it to attach as much weight as it likes to national security and as little as it likes to personal liberty. But it is at least arguable that, in relation to such matters, courts should, on democratic grounds, attach a degree of weight to the views of a democratically accountable decision-maker in recognition of its democratic credentials.

Second, courts may be confronted with questions that are hard to answer not because they involve the making of value judgements but because they involve making predictions. As Lord Sumption put it in *Carlile* (at [32]): '[W]here the justification for a decision depends on a judgment about the future impact of alternative courses of action, there is not necessarily a single "right" answer'. Predictive issues can, for instance, arise in relation to stage (iv) of the proportionality test. Is it necessary to detain the claimant in order to protect national security? To put the question another way, are there less drastic steps which would be equally effective in upholding national security? The claimant might, for instance, contend that something less draconian—electronically tagging him, subjecting him to curfews, or prohibiting him from associating with other suspects—might have been just as effective, but it is impossible to know for sure whether he is right. In practice, then, answering the question becomes an exercise in the evaluation of risk. If the decision-maker has access to special expertise in this regard, it would seem odd, to say the least, if the court did not recognize that and attach appropriate weight to the decision-maker's view.

QUESTIONS

- If the court was to do what has just been described—namely, taking account of the decision-maker's special expertise—this would, on Allan's view, be improper: the court would be allowing itself to be influenced by external considerations (such as the decision-maker's characteristics) rather than by focusing exclusively upon the quality of the arguments themselves. Do you agree with Allan that this would be improper?
- Why (not)?

Is Allan's position, then, that the factors by which proponents of deference set store—such as the expertise of the decision-maker—are wholly irrelevant? He accepts ((2010) 60 *UTLJ* 40) that some factors by which deference-exponents set store, such as the rigour of the decision-maker's procedure, may be relevant *to the extent that they result in better, more defensible decisions*. But, as Allan has explained elsewhere ([2006] *CLJ* 671 at 688–9), this does not mean that he supports deference of the form propounded by its advocates:

> Here is the nub of the case against 'due deference'. It requires a court to set off against its own appraisal of the arguments for and against an infringement of rights a wider range of competing considerations, relating to characteristics of the decision-maker or its procedures rather than the intrinsic quality of its decision. Yet these external considerations are not commensurable with the reasons that determine the justice of the substantive outcome. They operate on different scales of assessment. What criteria should determine when a court ought to accept a doubtful decision on the grounds that, though unjust, it was reached by a fair procedure or by a decision-maker accountable to elected representatives? Can a litigant whose rights have been unjustly infringed be properly informed that his treatment is merely the unfortunate outcome of a fair procedure, operated in good faith by a politically-accountable decision-maker? And if so, would his 'rights' have any independent content, distinct from the procedure that has led to their 'infringement'?
>
> [The] fundamental mistake … of … advocates of judicial deference … is to think that a court must decide the 'degree of deference which is due'. But no such calculations should be made and, accordingly, no criteria are needed. The only proper question for the court is simply whether or not the decision falls within the sphere of decision-making autonomy that the claimant's right, on its correct interpretation, allows. The relative expertise of the decision-maker and the excellence of its procedures are relevant insofar as they generate convincing arguments—good reasons for curtailing rights grounded in reasonable policies and supported by clear evidence. The court must be persuaded by the reasons, however, rather than impressed by expertise or procedural competence. The availability of means of review of policy, making the decision-maker politically accountable, will enhance the likelihood that objectives being pursued have been carefully considered; significant objections may have prompted further thought. Faced with the claim that the individual has been unfairly treated, however, the court must itself appraise the defence presented, in the most cogent form that those responsible can muster.

This passage demonstrates that at the heart of the disagreement between Allan and his critics is the question whether external factors should be invested with any relevance independent of the quality of the arguments they generate. On the one hand, Allan argues that such factors are relevant only 'insofar as they generate convincing arguments'. In other words, if a decision-maker has particular knowledge or expertise, and if that enables it to put an especially convincing argument to the court, then so be it—but that is as far as it must go: the court ought not to attach any *additional* weight to the argument merely because of the decision-maker's expertise. Proponents of deference, on the other hand, contend that external factors may, in appropriate circumstances, carry independent weight: in other words, a court might attach more weight to an argument *because* it is made by an expert decision-maker. The difference ultimately boils down to the question whether courts have one or two jobs in such cases. Allan contends for the former position: the court must simply decide whether the decision-maker's argument in favour of limiting a human right is sufficiently convincing. In contrast, Kavanagh (2010) 126 *LQR* 222 at 231 says that

> [t]here is an alternative understanding of the nature of judicial reasoning in constitutional adjudication, which fits better with contemporary constitutional practice. On this understanding, judges have not one but two obligations. The first (and primary) duty is to carry out the

substantive evaluation, i.e. to evaluate the legal issues on their merits and to uphold rights, scrutinising Parliament and the executive for compliance with them. Their second duty is to consider questions of relative institutional competence, expertise and legitimacy vis-à-vis the elected branches of government. The latter duty engages concerns about the constitutional separation of powers, including judges' views about the extent and limits of their own role. Thus, alongside a consideration of the merits of the substantive legal issue before them, they must also reflect on the constitutional and pragmatic limits of their role.

QUESTION

- Do you prefer Allan's or Kavanagh's view? (Try to justify your answer by reference to your underlying views concerning relevant fundamental principles, such as the rule of law and the separation of powers, which ought to condition the relationship between the courts and the executive.)

8.4.4 The story so far

It is worth pausing at this point to take stock of what has been said thus far. The foregoing discussion demonstrates that those who argue in favour of a doctrine of deference wish to enable decision-makers (in appropriate circumstances) to adopt a view at odds with that of the court, for that view to be capable of surviving judicial scrutiny, and for such survival to be facilitated by means of ascribing special weight to the decision-maker's views because of the particular characteristics it possesses. Deference-advocates do not contend that courts should always accept decision-makers' views—merely that some situations will arise in which it is appropriate to confer latitude upon the decision-maker. Although, as we have just seen, there is lively academic debate as to whether deference, thus conceived, is appropriate, the reality is that English courts do embrace such a doctrine (whether or not they are comfortable with the *language* of 'deference'). In the light of this, it is necessary to turn our attention to the way in which that doctrine works, by examining, in particular, the circumstances in which courts will be prepared to ascribe particular weight to decision-makers' views.

8.4.5 Expertise-based deference

Expertise-based deference is related to, but distinct from, the concept of 'margin of appreciation' which the ECtHR uses. That concept, as Lady Hale explained in *Re G (Adoption: Unmarried Couple)* [2008] UKHL 38, [2009] 1 AC 173 at [118]–[119], was developed by the ECtHR in order to afford national authorities a degree of latitude in relation to the making of judgments about such matters as whether given 'restrictions are necessary in the democratic societies they serve'. The concept thus recognizes what Laws [1998] *PL* 254 at 258 calls the 'cultural distance between [the Strasbourg judges] and the state organs whose decisions are impleaded before them'. While *domestic* judges applying the HRA are not subject to that particular inhibition (as is shown, for instance, by the Supreme Court's decision in *R (Nicklinson)* v. *Ministry of Justice* [2014] UKSC 38, [2015] AC 657), they have recognized that other factors might make it appropriate for national courts to ascribe particular weight to decision-makers' views.

One such factor is the competence or expertise of the decision-maker relative to that of the court. When, thanks to its institutional characteristics or situation, the decision-maker possesses or has access to a degree of expertise that is unavailable to the court, it may be appropriate for the court to attach greater weight to the decision-maker's views. Such considerations are most likely to be relevant at stage (iv) of the proportionality inquiry, as Rivers [2006] *CLJ* 174 at 198–200 explains:

> The test of necessity asks whether the decision, rule or policy limits the relevant right in the least intrusive way compatible with achieving the given level of realisation of the legitimate aim. This implies a comparison with alternative hypothetical acts (decisions, rules, policies, etc.) which may achieve the same aim to the same degree but with less cost to rights …
>
> … A claimant may suggest an alternative policy which all agree would be less onerous, but the public body will typically deny that it achieves the same level of the aim being pursued, that it is as effective. If the public body is correct, the claimant will have failed to show by the example that the decision in question was not necessary. It is at this point that deference to the primary decision-taker potentially comes into play. In order to know how effective a policy might be, the court is reliant on others. Deference on grounds of institutional expertise seems particularly appropriate in the relationship between judiciary and executive bodies. To the extent that there is expertise, judges are correct to rely on the executive as part of 'getting it right.'

The case of *A v. Secretary of State for the Home Department* [2004] UKHL 56, [2005] 2 AC 68—often referred to as the *'Belmarsh Prison'* case—helpfully illustrates both when expertise-based deference is appropriate and when it is not. It therefore also shows that—contrary to the notion of 'spatial deference'—'due deference' involves setting the intensity of judicial scrutiny on an issue-by-issue basis, rather than globally for the case as a whole.

The claimants were detained by the UK government under the Anti-terrorism, Crime and Security Act 2001, which had been enacted in the wake of the terrorist attacks that took place in the USA on 11 September 2001. The legislation established a regime for detaining without criminal charge or trial suspected foreign terrorists whose deportation would be contrary to Article 3 ECHR on the ground that they would face a real risk of torture or ill-treatment in the destination state. Since this regime was plainly incompatible with the right to liberty under Article 5, the UK government sought to derogate from that right. Article 15 allows such derogation provided that there is a 'war or other public emergency threatening the life of the nation' and that the extent of the derogation is no greater than that which is 'strictly required by the exigencies of the situation'. The UK government invoked Article 15 and sought to rule out the possibility of the 2001 Act being the subject of a declaration of incompatibility under s 4 of the HRA by making a 'designated derogation order'—a piece of secondary legislation in effect suspending the right to liberty in respect of the detained suspects. The central issue for the House of Lords was whether the order was valid—a question which, it held, turned upon whether the Article 15 criteria were met—such that the claimants would be unable to obtain the declaration of incompatibility that they sought. This required the House of Lords to confront two key questions: whether there was a 'public emergency' and, if so, whether the steps taken were 'necessary'.

As to the first of those matters, Lord Bingham, giving one of the majority judgments, noted (at [25]) that, on behalf of the government, the Attorney-General had

> submitted that the judgment on this question was pre-eminently one within the discretionary area of judgment reserved to the Secretary of State and his colleagues, exercising their judgment with the benefit of official advice, and to Parliament.

In response, Lord Bingham (at [29]) said:

> I would accept that great weight should be given to the judgment of the Home Secretary, his colleagues and Parliament on this question, because they were called on to exercise a pre-eminently political judgment. It involved making a factual prediction of what various people around the world might or might not do, and when (if at all) they might do it, and what the consequences might be if they did. Any prediction about the future behaviour of human beings (as opposed to the phases of the moon or high water at London Bridge) is necessarily problematical. Reasonable and informed minds may differ, and a judgment is not shown to be wrong or unreasonable because that which is thought likely to happen does not happen. It would have been irresponsible not to err, if at all, on the side of safety. As will become apparent, I do not accept the full breadth of the Attorney General's argument on what is generally called the deference owed by the courts to the political authorities. It is perhaps preferable to approach this question as one of demarcation of functions or what Liberty in its written case called 'relative institutional competence'.

The House of Lords held by an 8–1 majority that the government's conclusion that there was a public emergency threatening the life of the nation should not be overturned. In reaching that conclusion a relatively deferential approach was adopted, as the excerpt above from Lord Bingham's speech indicates, with considerable weight being ascribed to the government's views, bearing in mind its access both to intelligence and to expert analysis thereof.

However, when their Lordships turned to the other question—whether the claimants' indefinite detention without charge or trial was strictly necessary—a different approach prevailed. All but one of the Law Lords who considered this point held that the steps taken by the government were *not* necessary. This meant that the designated derogation order was invalid, that Article 5 remained in force under the HRA, and that a declaration of incompatibility could therefore be issued in respect of the relevant provisions of the 2001 Act. It is striking that, on this question, the majority's approach was far from deferential, notwithstanding that the government played the national security card—a step which, prior to the *Belmarsh* case, almost always resulted in something approaching judicial surrender. For instance, Lord Nicholls observed (at [81]) that

> [t]he subject matter of the legislation is the needs of national security. This subject matter dictates that, in the ordinary course, substantial latitude should be accorded to the legislature. But the human right in question, the right to individual liberty, is one of the most fundamental of human rights.

Similarly, Lord Rodger (at [176]) considered that '[d]ue deference does not mean abasement before [the] views [of the government and Parliament], even in matters relating to national security'. This amounts to a clear rejection of the spatial conception of deference mentioned at 8.4.2. The Law Lords were not prepared to allow this case to be placed in a category labelled 'national security' and thereby to be put beyond meaningful judicial scrutiny. Rather, they recognized that in any given case there may be factors in tension with one another, some pointing towards and some away from deference. Their Lordships also took the view (quite rightly) that the level of deference cannot necessarily be set globally for a given case: it did not follow from the deferential approach adopted in relation to the public emergency question that an equally deferential approach should be applied to the necessity question. Thus, Lord Hope (at [108]) said:

> We are not dealing here with matters of social or economic policy, where opinions may reasonably differ in a democratic society and where choices on behalf of the country as a whole are properly left to government and to the legislature. We are dealing with actions taken on behalf of society as a whole which affect the rights and freedoms of the individual. This is where the courts may legitimately intervene, to ensure that the actions taken are proportionate. It is an essential safeguard, if individual rights and freedoms are to be protected in a democratic society which respects the principle that minorities, however unpopular, have the same rights as the majority. The intensity of the scrutiny will nevertheless vary according to the point that has to be considered at each stage.

Lord Hope was also influenced by the fact that although (as explained earlier) he was willing to accept the government's view that there was an emergency in the Article 15 sense, there are 'emergencies' and there are 'emergencies'. He said, at [119], that the emergency constituted by the *threat* of a terrorist attack was 'of a different kind, or on a different level, from that which would undoubtedly ensue if the threats were ever to materialise'. As he pointed out elsewhere in his speech (at [116]), '[o]ne cannot say what the exigencies of the situation require without having clearly in mind what it is that constitutes the emergency.' This demonstrates that, even on the initial question—whether there was a public emergency—Lord Hope's deference did not reduce to servility. He was prepared to form a view about the nature of the emergency—a view which influenced his subsequent assessment of the necessity of the measures adopted.

That said, the Court's scrutiny of the necessity issue was clearly sharper than that to which the public emergency question was subjected. Why was this? The answer, quite simply, is that the Law Lords took the view that special expertise was not required in order to address the necessity question. For instance, the detention regime, as we have seen, applied only to foreign nationals. This proved fatal to the scheme's compatibility with the ECHR. All of the majority judges who addressed the necessity question were in agreement on this point. It is, in fact, a strikingly simple one, and was expressed succinctly by Lady Hale who, having noted the absence of any power to detain British nationals, observed (at [231]) that

> [t]he conclusion has to be that it is not necessary to lock up the nationals. Other ways must have been found to contain the threat which they present. And if it is not necessary to lock up the nationals it cannot be necessary to lock up the foreigners. It is not strictly required by the exigencies of the situation.

The absence of deference on the necessity question demonstrates that, quite properly, expertise-based deference will be exhibited by a reviewing court only when the matter is one upon which the decision-maker possesses relevant expertise. If the position is as it was in *Belmarsh*, such that the court is able to deduce that the impugned measure is unnecessary without having to evaluate matters upon which the decision-maker has pertinent expertise, there will be no room or need for expertise-based deference.

Against the general background set out here, four further points should be noted. First, *the courts will not blindly defer to a decision-maker which claims to possess relevant expertise*: any such claim can properly influence the court only to the extent that it is a reliable claim. A point along these lines was made in *Belmarsh* itself: in a surprisingly trenchant passage, Lord Scott (at [154]) said:

> The Secretary of State is unfortunate in the timing of the judicial examination in these proceedings of the 'public emergency' that he postulates. It is certainly true that the judiciary must in general defer to the executive's assessment of what constitutes a threat to national security or to 'the life of the nation'. But judicial memories are no shorter than those of the public and the public have not forgotten the faulty intelligence assessments on the basis of which United Kingdom forces were sent to take part, and are still taking part, in the hostilities in Iraq. For my part I do not doubt that there is a terrorist threat to this country and I do not doubt that great vigilance is necessary, not only on the part of the security forces but also on the part of individual members of the public, to guard against terrorist attacks. But I do have very great doubt whether the 'public emergency' is one that justifies the description of 'threatening the life of the nation'. Nonetheless, I would, for my part, be prepared to allow the Secretary of State the benefit of the doubt on this point and accept that the threshold criterion of article 15 is satisfied.

Second, even if the court is prepared to accept that the decision-maker possesses relevant expertise, *the decision-maker's view cannot logically be invested with any special weight on the ground of that expertise if it has failed to use it*. This point was made by Baroness Hale in *Belfast City Council* v. *Miss Behavin' Ltd* [2007] UKHL 19, [2007] 1 WLR 1420 at [37], which involved a challenge, on freedom of expression grounds, to a council's refusal to grant a licence permitting a sex shop to operate:

> The legislation leaves it to the local authority to [balance the conflicting interests at stake] in each individual case. So the court has to decide whether the authority has violated the Convention rights. In doing so, it is bound to acknowledge that the local authority is much better placed than the court to decide whether the right of sex shop owners to sell pornographic literature and images should be restricted—for the prevention of disorder or crime, for the protection of health or morals, or for the protection of the rights of others. But the views of the local authority are bound to carry less weight where the local authority has made no attempt to address that question. Had the Belfast City Council expressly set itself the task of balancing the rights of individuals to sell and buy pornographic literature and images against the interests of the wider community, a court would find it hard to upset the balance which the local authority had struck. But where there is no indication that this has been done, the court has no alternative but to strike the balance for itself.

Although Baroness Hale went on to say that, in striking the balance, the court would give 'due weight to the judgments made by those who are in much closer touch with the people and the places involved than the court could ever be', it stands to reason, as she had already acknowledged, that the scope for doing so will be limited if the decision-maker has failed to consider relevant issues.

Third, the converse proposition also applies: *if an expert decision-maker carefully and thoroughly balances the issues relevant to the proportionality of the measure, the court will be slower to disturb its conclusion*. In *R (SB)* v. *Governors of Denbigh High School* [2006] UKHL 15, [2007] 1 AC 100, the claimant argued that a school's uniform policy—which prohibited the wearing of the jilbab, a strict form of Islamic dress—was inconsistent with her right to freedom of religion under Article 9 ECHR. In ruling in favour of the school, the House of

Lords was strongly influenced by the way in which the governors had gone about formulating the uniform policy. Lord Bingham (at [34]) observed that they

> had taken immense pains to devise a uniform policy which respected Muslim beliefs but did so in an inclusive, unthreatening and uncompetitive way. The rules laid down were as far from being mindless as uniform rules could ever be. The school had enjoyed a period of harmony and success to which the uniform policy was thought to contribute. On further enquiry it still appeared that the rules were acceptable to mainstream Muslim opinion. It was feared that acceding to the respondent's request would or might have significant adverse repercussions. It would in my opinion be irresponsible of any court, lacking the experience, background and detailed knowledge of the head teacher, staff and governors, to overrule their judgment on a matter as sensitive as this. The power of decision has been given to them for the compelling reason that they are best placed to exercise it, and I see no reason to disturb their decision.

Fourth, it would be easy—but mistaken—to conclude from the two previous points that decision-makers must (at least if they want their decisions to stand a reasonable prospect of surviving judicial scrutiny) approach matters in a way that explicitly addresses human rights concerns. Should public bodies, for instance, work through the various stages of the proportionality test, in order to enhance the chances of their decisions withstanding any subsequent judicial review? Surprisingly, the Court of Appeal, when it decided the *Denbigh High School* case in favour of the claimant, did so largely on the ground that the school had failed to consider the human rights issues in a procedurally correct manner. Brooke LJ ([2005] EWCA Civ 199, [2005] 1 WLR 3372 at [76]) said:

> The decision-making structure should therefore go along the following lines. (1) Has the claimant established that she has a relevant Convention right which qualifies for protection under article 9(1)? (2) Subject to any justification that is established under article 9(2), has that Convention right been violated? (3) Was the interference with her Convention right prescribed by law in the Convention sense of that expression? (4) Did the interference have a legitimate aim? (5) What are the considerations that need to be balanced against each other when determining whether the interference was necessary in a democratic society for the purpose of achieving that aim? (6) Was the interference justified under article 9(2)?

This reasoning (like the Court of Appeal's substantive decision) was rightly overturned by the House of Lords. Lord Bingham concluded that the Court of Appeal had elevated form over substance:

> [29] ... [T]he focus at Strasbourg is not and has never been on whether a challenged decision or action is the product of a defective decision-making process, but on whether, in the case under consideration, the applicant's Convention rights have been violated ...
> [31] ... The Court of Appeal's decision-making prescription would be admirable guidance to a lower court or legal tribunal, but cannot be required of a head teacher and governors, even with a solicitor to help them. If, in such a case, it appears that such a body has conscientiously paid attention to all human rights considerations, no doubt a challenger's task will be the harder. But what matters in any case is the practical outcome, not the quality of the decision-making process that led to it.

As Lord Hoffmann later put it in *R (Nasseri)* v. *Secretary of State for the Home Department* [2009] UKHL 23, [2010] 1 AC 1 at [14], 'when breach of a Convention right is in issue, an impeccable decision-making process by the Secretary of State will be of no avail if she actually gets the answer wrong'. The position, then, is that a decision will withstand judicial scrutiny if, having ascribed any appropriate weight to the decision-maker's views, the court concludes that the decision represents a necessary and proportionate restriction upon the human right in play. It is not necessary for the decision-maker to go through the sort of reasoning process set out by Brooke LJ in *Denbigh High School*, but, in line with the comments (set out earlier) of Lord Bingham in *Denbigh* and Baroness Hale in *Miss Behavin'*, there will be greater scope for a court to attach weight to the decision-maker's view if it can demonstrate that it brought its expertise to bear on the relevant issues.

8.4.6 Democracy-based deference

That courts practice expertise-based deference is clear. What of democracy-based deference? By this we mean the ascription of weight or respect to the view of a decision-maker on the ground of its democratic credentials. We begin our examination of this matter by considering the normative arguments for and against democracy-based deference. We then turn to the case law, which reveals that, at least in some circumstances, courts are prepared to exhibit such deference.

Whether deference on democratic grounds is normatively warranted is a contested matter. For example, while Jowell [2003] *PL* 592 at 598 accepts that expertise-based deference may sometimes be appropriate, he doubts whether deference is ever required on democratic grounds. This, he says, is because the HRA ushered in a new sense of democracy under which 'democratic principle' can no longer be equated with 'majority approval'. It follows, he says, that 'the courts have no need to expose their jugular whenever Parliament or its agents speak on the matter of public interest'. Hunt (in Bamforth and Leyland (eds), *Public Law in a Multi-Layered Constitution* (Oxford 2003) at 350) does not agree that considerations of democracy—or 'constitutional competence'—can so readily be dismissed, arguing that Jowell's approach

> excludes from the deference inquiry important normative considerations about what the court's proper role is, by assuming that those normative questions have been settled by the HRA itself … But a rich conception of legality and of the rule of law should not only be able to legitimate a role for courts in enforcing legal standards on public decision-makers; it ought, at the same time, to have space for a proper role for democratic considerations, including a role for the democratic branches in the definition and furtherance of fundamental values.

While Hunt and Jowell are explicitly disagreeing about whether there should be deference on democratic grounds, their underlying disagreement is much deeper: it relates to fundamental questions about the respective roles of the courts and other branches of government. This really boils down to a debate about what constitutes legitimacy for the purpose of making given decisions—in particular, whether *democratic* legitimacy is necessary. This point is drawn out by Feldman [2006] *PL* 364 at 374–5:

> The legitimacy of political bodies stems from representativeness, democratic accountability, tradition, or all three. The House of Commons derives its legitimacy as the body which chooses a Prime Minister, participates in legislation and scrutinises government from its character as a body

of representatives of the people, as well as the democratic elections through which its members are selected. The legitimacy of the House of Lords stems partly from the traditional authority of the institution and partly from the acknowledged expertise of its members. The legitimacy of the government stems from its support in the representative House of Commons, as well as the government's indirect accountability to the people embodied in the two Houses of Parliament.

By contrast, the legitimacy of the judiciary arises from three very different sources: first, the obligation to justify its decisions publicly by means of rational arguments; second, the require-ment that the reasons be formulated with reference to objective, publicly accessible standards with legal authority derived from a source other than the opinions of an individual judge; and third, the independence of the judiciary from the political arms of government, guaranteeing an unbiased and objective assessment of the legality of the acts and decisions of the executive. This independence from political processes is a positive, not negative, characteristic, because of the distinctive role of judges.

The crunch question, then, centres upon the form of legitimacy that is felt to be the most appropriate in relation to any given undertaking. Here, it is necessary to recognize that application of the proportionality test itself requires courts to undertake several distinct tasks. For example, if the court concludes (at stage (i)) that the impugned measure impinges upon a human right, it is hard to see why democracy would require the court to defer to the decision-maker's contrary view that no right is implicated. However, by the time we get to stage (v) of the proportionality analysis, the picture is more complex. Here, the question is whether the measure in question, even though necessary, can be justified in the sense that the public policy gains it is liable to yield outweigh the human rights losses it is liable to occasion. We noted earlier that, in order to answer this question, the court must ascribe value to two sets of factors that are in tension with one another—and that, this being a value judgement, there is no obvious reason why the court's view should necessarily pre-vail. While it would be going too far (not least because it would eviscerate the human rights jurisdiction given to the courts by the HRA) to contend that decision-makers should there-fore have a free hand in this regard, it is certainly arguable that, where the scales are finely balanced on the stage (v) justification question, the decision-maker should enjoy a degree of discretion constituted by judicial deference to its value judgements.

This argument finds a degree of favour with the courts, although judges' receptiveness to it varies. For instance, we have already seen (at 8.2.2) that Lord Sumption was open to the idea of deference on democratic grounds in *R (Rotherham Metropolitan Borough Council)* v. *Secretary of State for Business, Innovation and Skills* [2015] UKSC 6, [2015] PTSR 322. The proportionality doctrine was not itself involved in that case, but Lord Sumption has shown similar receptiveness to arguments about democratic deference in cases in which propor-tionality is in play. Take, for instance, *R v. Secretary of State for the Home Department, ex parte Carlile* [2014] UKSC 60, [2015] AC 945, which, as noted at 8.4.1, concerned the pro-portionality of a refusal to permit Maryam Rajavi, a dissident Iranian politician, to enter the UK to address parliamentarians. The government sought to justify this limitation upon freedom of expression on the ground that permitting Rajavi to enter the UK for the desired purpose would risk destabilizing diplomatic relations between the UK and Iran, and that this would, in turn, prejudice the UK government's capacity to secure its foreign policy objectives in relation to the Middle East.

As already discussed, Lord Sumption was prepared in *Carlile* to conceive of proportion-ality in highly constricted terms which in essence amounted to inquiring only into the rationality of the decision. In adopting such an approach, Lord Sumption (at [28]–[29]) took account of the fact that although 'traditional notions of the constitutional distribution of powers have unquestionably been *modified* by the Human Rights Act 1998', the Act 'did not *abrogate* the constitutional distribution of powers between the organs of the state which the courts had recognised for many years before it was passed' (our emphasis). He noted that '[e]ven in the context of Convention rights, there remain areas which although not immune from scrutiny require a qualified respect for the constitutional functions of decision-makers who are democratically accountable'.

Lady Hale was also prepared, in *Carlile*, to take democratic considerations into account when determining whether a fair balance had been struck between individual rights and the wider public interest. She pointed out (at [104]) that the fair balance question

> involves weighing or balancing values which many may think cannot be weighed against one another. Some will think that our foreign policy interests in the Middle East are so important, not only to the safety and security of this country but to the safety and security of the whole wide world, that nothing should be allowed to put them at risk. Some may think that freedom of political expression, especially where such serious and controversial issues are involved, is such a vital feature of any democracy.

She continued (at [105]) that while determining the fairness of the balance 'is ultimately a task for the court', the court must be 'properly humble about its own capacities'. As well as saying (as noted previously) that the court should be 'slow to interfere' when such reticence is warranted by the decision-maker's relative expertise, Lady Hale said that 'the Government in a democracy such as ours should be at least as mindful of the need to strike the necessary balance between individual rights and the common good as are the courts; and if it does not protect those rights, it is accountable to Parliament in a way which we are not'.

A different approach was adopted—and a different conclusion reached—by Lord Kerr. In his dissenting judgment, he drew a sharp distinction between situations in which he considers deference to be appropriate and inappropriate respectively. He was prepared (at [151]) to countenance deference—in the sense of the according of weight or respect—to the Home Secretary's views as to the extent of any damage likely to be done to the UK's relations with Iran:

> On the matter of the judgment to be made on how foreign relations would be affected by allowing Mrs Rajavi to come to this country, the courts should ... be prepared to give considerable, if not uncritical, respect to what the Home Secretary has said ... Interpretation of historical events and assessment of their impact on relations between countries are not the concern of the courts.

However, Lord Kerr adopted a very different posture in relation to scrutiny of the Home Secretary's views as to the importance of freedom of speech within the factual matrix of the case (the weight to be accorded to the right being directly relevant to the question whether competing policy objectives are, in the context, a sufficient justification for its infraction). Thus, he said (at [152]):

> Whether executive action transgresses a Convention right, however, and, if it does, the importance to be attached to the right interfered with are emphatically matters on which courts are constitutionally suited to make judgments. The courts' competence to make those judgments is secondary, however, to the consideration that the current constitutional order, in the form of the Human Rights Act 1998, requires courts to make those very judgments. And, although it is

trite to say it, one must always remember that they make those judgments on the command of Parliament. The importance given by government to the impact that a particular outcome may have on foreign relations should give courts pause and, undoubtedly, they should be appropriately reticent about questioning the validity of a decision taken on grounds which a government minister considers to be in the national interest. But this should not operate as an inhibition on the discharge of the courts' proper constitutional function. If there has been an interference with Convention rights (and in this case there certainly has been), courts are there to examine whether that interference is justified. That examination must focus on the proffered reasons of the decision-maker but the inquiry necessarily extends beyond that. The courts, charged with the solemn duty by Parliament of deciding whether the political reasons that have actuated the decision to interfere with the particular Convention right justify the interference, have a clear obligation to have proper regard to the importance of the right which has been interfered with. That exercise requires the courts not only to examine the reasons given for the interference but also to decide *for themselves* whether that interference is justified.

QUESTION

- How does the position adopted by Lord Kerr in *Carlile* in respect of deference on democratic grounds relate to the view of Allan that the courts should have no truck with a 'doctrine' of deference?

Of course, not all decision-makers are (equally) 'democratic'. Indeed, what it means to say that a decision-maker is 'democratic'—such that deference to them on democratic grounds might be considered warranted—requires further discussion. At some level of abstraction, all decision-makers exercising statutory powers can argue that they are acting under democratic dispensation, in that an elected legislative body has charged them with making the decision in question. But it is far from clear that a claim to democratic status that can go no further than that ought to elicit deference on that ground. A stronger claim can be made by those decision-makers who are elected or who are clearly accountable for their decisions to an elected body. Ministers in the UK and devolved administrations, for instance, are accountable to their respective legislatures—although, as is well known, the extent and quality of such accountability is open to question.

The case for deference on democratic grounds must be at its zenith, then, when the decision-maker is *itself* an elected legislative body, as the Supreme Court's decision in *AXA General Insurance Ltd v. The Lord Advocate* [2011] UKSC 46, [2012] 1 AC 868 (on which see further at 4.2) illustrates. In concluding that legislation enacted by the Scottish Parliament was not disproportionate with reference to a Convention right, Lord Hope acknowledged (at [32]) the case for 'respecting, on democratic grounds, the considered opinion of the elected body by which [the relevant] choices are made'. And when it came to the question whether, at common law, the Scottish Parliament's enactments could be challenged on the ground of unreasonableness, Lord Hope concluded (at [49]) that democratic considerations (among other things) ruled this out entirely:

The dominant characteristic of the Scottish Parliament is its firm rooting in the traditions of a universal democracy. It draws its strength from the electorate. While the judges, who are not elected, are best placed to protect the rights of the individual, including those who are ignored or despised by the majority, the elected members of a legislature of this kind are best placed to judge what is in the country's best interests as a whole. A sovereign Parliament is, according to the traditional view, immune from judicial scrutiny because it is protected by the principle of sovereignty. But it shares with the devolved legislatures, which are not sovereign, the advantages that flow from the depth and width of the experience of its elected members and the mandate that has been given to them by the electorate. This suggests that the judges should intervene, if at all, only in the most exceptional circumstances.

QUESTION

- In *AXA*, Lord Hope concludes that the proportionality test can be used in order to determine whether legislation enacted by legislative bodies such as the Scottish Parliament is compatible with Convention rights, but that the enactments of such bodies cannot be reviewed by reference to what is generally considered to be the less interventionist rationality test. Can these two views satisfactorily be reconciled?

The notion of democratic deference considered so far in this section rests on the argument that, on certain matters, the ascription of weight to the views of the decision-maker is appropriate either because the decision-maker is *accountable to* a democratic body (such as a representative legislature) or because the decision-maker *is* such a body. The appropriateness of this form of democratic deference is contested, the cases in favour of and against it being ultimately normative in nature. In cases concerning Convention rights, for instance, the position to be adopted turns upon the relative importance that one respectively accords to (on the one hand) allowing decision-makers with democratic credentials to resolve questions about how the public interest is best served and (on the other hand) permitting independent courts to intervene in respect of such matters in the name of protecting fundamental rights. It is precisely because the legislature generally provides no clear steer on the proper extent of the judicial role that the matter falls to be resolved by judges by reference to their underlying conceptions of the judicial function. This is apparent, for instance, from the contrasting positions adopted by Lords Sumption and Kerr in *Carlile*.

It is, however, open to the legislature to provide precisely the sort of steer mentioned earlier by specifying, or at least providing guidance as to, the relative weight to be ascribed to individual rights and competing public interests. The UK Parliament did precisely that when it enacted the Immigration Act 2014, which inserted new provisions in the Nationality, Immigration and Asylum Act 2002. Those provisions—ss 117A–D of the 2002 Act—concern decisions taken under immigration legislation that are challenged on the ground that they breach the right to respect for private and family life under Article 8 ECHR. The new provisions stipulate that courts and tribunals determining such cases must have regard to specified considerations when addressing 'the public interest question'—*ie* 'the question of whether an interference with a person's right to respect for private and family life is justified' by reference to a competing public interest. Among the considerations to which courts and tribunals must have regard are that maintaining effective immigration control is in the public interest, and that those who seek to enter and remain in the UK are 'able to speak English' and 'financially independent'. The legislation is also prescriptive as to the weight to be accorded to certain factors by courts and tribunals examining the public interest question: for instance, 'little weight' is to be given to a private life or relationship established when the person was in the UK unlawfully or subject to a 'precarious immigration status'. Moreover, in relation to 'foreign criminals', the legislation provides that deportation is in the public interest absent certain 'exceptional circumstances', and that, in the case of such criminals sentenced to at least four years' imprisonment, deportation is in the public interest absent 'very compelling circumstances' that go beyond merely 'exceptional' circumstances.

In *Secretary of State for the Home Department* v. *Foreman* [2015] UKUT 412 (IAC), the Upper Tribunal (at [20]) considered the ss 117A–D criteria to be 'rigid' and 'prescriptive'. Nevertheless, it insisted that '[t]he court or tribunal concerned has no choice: it must have regard to the listed considerations', albeit (at [17]) that 'the list of considerations in [the relevant provisions] is not exhaustive'. The Upper Tribunal thus set aside the First-tier Tribunal's judgment on the ground that the judge had failed to address the public interest question in the statutorily required way. In particular, he had failed to acknowledge that the respondent's private life in the UK had been established while his immigration status was precarious. That had led the judge into further error by preventing him from properly conducting the balancing exercise. If he had done what the legislation required, said the Upper Tribunal (at [19]), the judge 'would have been obliged to find unequivocally that the Respondent's private life in the United Kingdom could not be accorded more than slight weight'.

What the Upper Tribunal's judgment in *Foreman* demonstrates is that when courts and tribunals are statutorily required to assign a particular degree of weight either to a right or to a competing public interest, questions of democratic deference essentially fall by the wayside in relation to the relevant matter. If, as it ought to have done, the First-tier Tribunal had assigned no more than 'slight weight' to the private life that the respondent had established in the UK, it would not have been *deferring* either to the Home Secretary's view as decision-maker or to Parliament's view as legislator; rather, it would straightforwardly have been implementing Parliament's will. This conclusion is unsurprising. The extent to which courts defer to administrative judgement amounts to an attempt to wrestle with contestable questions about the proper extent of the judicial role. When Parliament carefully prescribes what that role is to be on a given matter, deference is rendered beside the point, save in the highly general sense that the court is deferring to—in the sense of respecting—Parliament's stated intention, as the court is of course constitutionally required to do. In contrast, where the legislation merely requires the court to have regard to a given consideration—*eg* that it is in the public interest that immigrants are able to speak English—this does not foreclose the issue of deference on democratic grounds, since it leaves open questions about the weight to be accorded to the stipulated factor relative to other relevant matters, and hence about the extent of any respect that the court should attach to the decision-maker's view on that point.

8.5 The future

From what has been said so far in this chapter it should be clear that the law has not stood still since Lord Greene MR delivered his oft-cited judgment in the *Wednesbury* case. That English courts today apply the proportionality test, and that the test can supply a significantly more searching form of scrutiny than that which is traditionally associated with the reasonableness doctrine, cannot be denied. But nor can it be denied that the changes in judicial approach recorded in this chapter have, in large part, been influenced by the enactment of the HRA. This raises some fundamental questions about exactly what has changed and what that might mean for the future direction of the law in this area. This section proceeds in three parts. First, we briefly take stock of where things presently stand. Second, we examine a range of arguments that bite upon the question whether time should be called on the reasonableness doctrine and proportionality relied upon across the piece. Third, we analyse recent case law—focusing particularly on recent Supreme Court jurisprudence—which, while not being determinative of these questions, provides some indications as to possible directions of travel.

8.5.1 Taking stock

We begin by considering the range of circumstances in which the proportionality test is applicable. In doing so, it is helpful to distinguish between three categories.

First, there are cases in which public authorities' decisions are challenged on the ground that they infringe qualified Convention rights or relevant principles of EU law. Within both the ECHR and EU legal regimes, proportionality is the operative test in such cases, and domestic courts—in giving effect to the relevant bodies of European law, as they are required to do by the European Communities Act 1972 and the HRA—must therefore utilize proportionality. In these contexts, then, domestic courts have not taken it upon themselves to rely upon the proportionality doctrine: they do so because they are required to.

Second, however, in two further types of case the (domestic) courts have adopted the proportionality test of their own volition (rather than because of a legislative requirement to do so). This is so in relation both to cases concerning common law constitutional rights (as the *Daly* case, on which see 8.3.5, illustrates) and certain cases concerning substantive legitimate expectations (on which see 6.1.5).

The first two categories are relatively settled. The existence and extent of the third category is far less settled. There are, however, some indications that courts are prepared to engage in proportionality review, or something similar to it, in circumstances that do not involve fundamental rights (whether under the HRA or at common law), substantive legitimate expectations, or EU law. For instance, in *Kennedy* v. *Charity Commission* [2014] UKSC 20, [2015] AC 455, one of the questions for the Supreme Court was whether the Charity Commission was acting lawfully by refusing to disclose certain information. Lord Mance, giving one of the majority judgments, considered (at [47]) that what was in issue was 'the common law presumption in favour of openness', and (at [54]) saw 'no reason' why proportionality—or at least the factors that form the elements of the proportionality test—'should not be relevant in judicial review even outside the scope of Convention and EU law'. Similarly, *Pham* v. *Secretary of State for the Home Department* [2015] UKSC 19, [2015] 1 WLR 1591 concerned a decision to strip the appellant of British citizenship and deport him to Vietnam, where he was born. The appellant argued that in assessing the lawfulness of the decision, the Court should apply the proportionality test because stripping him of British citizenship would also revoke his EU citizenship—thus implicating EU law and requiring recourse to proportionality review. The Court's view, however, was that it did not much matter whether EU law applied, because the proportionality test, or something closely resembling it, would be used anyway given that a 'fundamental status' was at stake.

This third category of cases suggests that the range of circumstances in which proportionality review is applicable goes beyond the circumstances that form our first two categories. However, the scope of the third category—and hence the ultimate reach of the proportionality doctrine—is far from clear, given the developing nature of the case law. It does, however, appear that there is growing judicial receptiveness to the notion that the proportionality test should not necessarily be considered to be limited to cases concerning fundamental rights, EU law, and substantive legitimate expectations. The difficulty then becomes ascertaining how much further the proportionality test should reach, and by reference to what criteria its reach should be contained. And that, inevitably, raises the question whether the reach of proportionality ought to be so great as to squeeze out the reasonableness test altogether.

8.5.2 Should time be called on the reasonableness doctrine?

Some writers argue that the reasonableness test should be jettisoned in favour of reliance upon proportionality across the board in substantive review cases. One of that view's most prominent proponents is Craig (see, *eg* [2010] *NZ L Rev* 265). He argues (at 266) that 'proportionality should become a general head of judicial review', meaning that it should be adopted *in place of* the reasonableness test. In this section, the appropriateness of taking such a step is examined from four perspectives.

First, from a constitutional perspective, Sales (2013) 129 LQR 223 argues that it would be improper to accord to proportionality a role as broad as that favoured by Craig. Relying upon the doctrine of *ultra vires* (on which see 1.4), Sales argues (at 229) that judicial review takes place

> by reference to statutes construed in accordance with a set of presumptions articulated by the judges—yet having a form which it may reasonably be assumed Parliament would itself recognise and accept. Statute can override common law, so it is necessary to accommodate the development of the law in relation to judicial review of the exercise of statutory powers within the meaning to be given to statutes.

Sales goes on to argue that it would be too radical a reconceptualization of Parliament's intention to assume that it was willing to permit judicial review on the ground of proportionality except to the extent that (as through the HRA) it has clearly manifested such an intention. To make such an assumption, Sales argues (at 231), would involve a fundamental redistribution of judicial and administrative power:

> [T]he meaning of a statute is given by the intention of the Parliament which enacts it. Parliament has promulgated legislation on the footing that it is the *Wednesbury*/rationality standard which applies. It is for the courts to interpret the statute, but that does not involve a power to change its meaning.

On this analysis, the province of proportionality review would be limited to circumstances involving EU law or ECHR rights: *ie* situations in which legislation (at least implicitly) licenses judicial recourse to proportionality. Courts should otherwise (on the logic of Sales's argument) go no further than reviewing administrative decisions by reference to the reasonableness test, so as to avoid subverting the intention Parliament is taken to have had when it conferred the discretion in the first place. Whether this argument is convincing is essentially a facet of the question whether (the traditional version of) the *ultra vires* doctrine is convincing—a matter that we addressed at 1.4. Here, we simply note that whether or not Sales's argument is considered to be normatively appealing, it stands in contrast to the reality of contemporary judicial practice, which evidences a willingness to engage in relatively searching review outwith the narrow range of circumstances in which Sales considers such review to be constitutionally appropriate.

Second, the appropriateness of embracing proportionality as a general head of review—in place of reasonableness—turns in part upon whether this would secure substantive review of suitable intensity. Given that proportionality can yield review that is more searching than that which the reasonableness doctrine is generally considered to be capable of delivering, one potential objection is that getting rid of reasonableness might result in high-intensity review across the board, thus causing the courts, in some circumstances, to exert undue control. Craig, however, considers this objection to be misplaced. He argues (*UK, EU and Global Administrative Law: Foundations and Challenges* (Cambridge 2015) at 259–60) that his thesis does not

> connote[] the same test of review being applied in the same way in all types of case. This is not even a straw man. My argument in favour of proportionality becoming a general head of review has always been expressly predicated on its variable application. This variation pertains not only between rights and non-rights cases, but also within the former category. Not all rights are of equal importance. There can, moreover, be significant variance in the importance of the claim when the same right is pleaded, as exemplified by the fact that freedom of speech may be pleaded to protect political speech, and the ability to run a sex shop. The courts take account of these differences in a number of ways, inter alia through varying the intensity of proportionality review.

It is certainty true, as Craig points out, that proportionality is not monolithic in terms of the intensity of review that it supplies. Indeed, the same (as we saw at 8.3.3) goes for the reasonableness doctrine. But if Craig's essential point is that the intensity of proportionality review can be dialled back so as to ensure that review is as hands-off as reasonableness review when that is normatively warranted, the question arises whether this makes or defeats his case. On the one hand, it serves to neutralize the objection that adopting proportionality across the piece would inflict high-intensity review upon decisions to which lower intensity review is appropriate. On the other hand, however, if proportionality can, where necessary, be made to amount—in intensity of review terms—to something akin to reasonableness, this invites the question whether jettisoning reasonableness would amount to anything more than a formal change.

For those who support the adoption of proportionality as a general head of review, the answer to that question may lie in the third of the perspectives from which the appropriateness of getting rid of reasonableness falls to be considered. As discussed earlier in the chapter, one of the factors that is traditionally thought to distinguish reasonableness from proportionality review is the more structured form taken by the latter. However, we have seen that this difference can be overstated, both because proportionality does not invariably live up to its promise in this regard and because reasonableness—as Craig (2013) 66 *CLP* 131 acknowledges—can take a form that is much more structured than is commonly supposed. Nevertheless, for Craig, the structured nature of the proportionality test is a key attraction of it, and is central to his argument that that test should replace reasonableness. He argues ([2010] *NZ L Rev* 265 at 272–3) that

> [t]he structural component of the normative argument rests on the benefits that flow from the three part proportionality inquiry, which focuses the attention of the agency being reviewed and of the court undertaking the review. The agency has to explain why it thought that the challenged action really was necessary and suitable to reach the desired end, and why it felt that the action did not impose an excessive burden on the applicant. If the reviewing court is minded to overturn the agency choice it must do so in a manner consonant with the proportionality inquiry. It will be for the court to explain why it felt that the action was not necessary, et cetera, in the circumstances. It is precisely this more structured analysis which has often been lacking when the 'monolithic' *Wednesbury* test has been applied.

For other writers, however, the structured nature of proportionality, far from being a knock-out argument in favour of allowing it to replace reasonableness, amounts to its Achilles heel. The point is well made by Hickman [2010] *NZ L Rev* 303 at 321:

> The essence of the proportionality methodology is that it assesses the relationship between means and ends. However, some decisions cannot suitably be analysed in this way and some complaints are not about the relationship between means and ends.

Hickman (at 321–2) goes on to give as an example a decision

> to close a waste disposal facility, challenged by a local resident who is concerned but not directly affected by the decision. It is very difficult to see how a proportionality test could sensibly be applied to this type of decision. In the absence of a legitimate expectation that the facility would remain open, the decision would not impact on the claimant's rights or interests in any real or substantial sense. Its impact would be multifaceted—potentially affecting jobs, the environment and the convenience of local residents. Paul Craig nonetheless seems to suggest that the courts should ask in such a case whether the impact was the least injurious means of achieving the objective. It is, however, very difficult to see how one can sensibly ask whether the closure of such a facility is the least onerous decision that could have been taken, because it is not clear what one should identify as the impact to be minimised.

This thinking has been echoed judicially. For instance, in *R (Rotherham Metropolitan Borough Council)* v. *Secretary of State for Business, Innovation and Skills* [2014] EWHC 232 (Admin), Stewart J (at [69]) took the view that proportionality analysis is useful only when 'there is a specific legal standard and a decision by a public body which derogates from that standard. The court then has to address the question as to whether there is a legally justifiable basis for so derogating.' At the very least, it stands to reason that if proportionality is to be applied in all substantive review cases, it would have to mean different things in different contexts. Lord Kerr was alive to this point in *Keyu* v. *Secretary of State for Foreign and Commonwealth Affairs* [2015] UKSC 69 (the facts of which are set out at 8.3.2). Noting (at [131]) the argument that 'the four-stage [proportionality] test identified

by Lord Sumption and Lord Reed in *Bank Mellat* should now be applied in place of rationality in all domestic judicial review cases', Lord Kerr said (at [281]) that he would 'question
its feasibility':

> In the first instance there is no legislative objective and no interference with a fundamental right;
> secondly, it is difficult to see how the 'least intrusive means' dimension could be worked into a
> proportionality exercise where the decision did not involve interfering with a right.

In the light of this, Lord Kerr said (at [282]) that he envisaged

> a more loosely structured proportionality challenge where a fundamental right is not involved.
> As Lord Mance said in *Kennedy*, this involves a testing of the decision in terms of its 'suitability or
> appropriateness, necessity and the balance or imbalance of benefits and disadvantages'.

QUESTION

- If, as Lord Kerr suggests in *Keyu*, proportionality would have to take a looser,
  less structured form in non-rights cases, would there be any point in utilizing
  proportionality in such cases? Would proportionality review, understood
  and applied thus, differ substantially from the form of reasonableness review
  advocated by Daly?

The fourth perspective from which it is worth considering whether time should be called on
the reasonable doctrine is foreshadowed by what has just been said about the appropriateness of shifting to proportionality review in cases that are not about rights. As well as raising
specific questions, such as those noted above, about the suitability of the structure of the
proportionality doctrine in non-rights cases, whether such cases should be subsumed within
the proportionality test—and, in that sense, assimilated to rights cases—raises a far larger
question about the topography of administrative law itself. For some writers—such as Poole
[2009] *CLJ* 142 at 142–4—the distinction between cases that are and are not about rights is
one that is being eroded: administrative law is being 'reconfigure[d]' such that '[r]ights and
substantive review' have taken 'centre stage'. On this analysis, the proportionality doctrine
comes to the fore not because (as, for example, Craig argues) it is suitable in non-rights cases,
but because more and more cases are, in the first place, rights cases. Proportionality thus
displaces reasonableness not because proportionality is malleable enough to occupy the territory that once belonged to reasonableness, but because that territory itself is ceded as the
landscape of administrative law comes to be dominated by the notion of rights.

If administrative law really was undergoing such a form and degree of transformation,
that would certainly alter the terms of the debate concerning the proper reach of the proportionality doctrine. However, the reality is that administrative law is not being transformed in the way that 'righting' theorists like Poole contend. It is certainly the case that the
HRA has resulted in judicial review on rights grounds to a greater extent than previously.
It is also true that the development of the doctrine of 'common law constitutional rights'
means that administrative action is challengeable, to a greater extent than before, on rights
grounds. Nevertheless, it remains the case that many administrative law cases, including
many substantive review cases, self-evidently have nothing whatsoever to do with rights.
Indeed, administrative law has traditionally been conceived of as being concerned primarily

not with the protection of individual rights but with securing good administration. It is for precisely that reason that, as noted at 14.7.7, the approach to standing in non-HRA cases is a generous one that allows judicial review claims to be brought, where appropriate, by those who are not themselves affected by the decision in question.

At one time, Taggart (in Bamforth and Leyland (eds), *Public Law in a Multi-Layered Constitution* (Oxford 2003)) took the view that administrative law was being 'righted', but he stepped back from that position in his later work. In a landmark contribution to the debate ([2008] *NZ L Rev* 423), Taggart argued in favour of what he called a 'rainbow of review' within which the proportionality test applies in cases concerning rights, while in other cases, concerning what he termed 'public wrongs', the reasonableness doctrine remains operative. The arguments advanced by Taggart (at 477–8) in support of his (revised) position were a blend of the normative and the methodological:

1. In the absence of 'rights' there is no compelling normative justification for more searching scrutiny or intensive review than provided by the usual grounds of review and traditional (*Wednesbury*) unreasonableness as residual 'safety net';

2. That without the anchor of 'rights' as a starting point the proportionality methodology loses many of its touted advantages as a transparent and visible tool for ensuring reasonable or proportionate decision-making. It has a 'determinate-looking' structure without the reality of determinacy;

3. That reversion to the traditional conception of *Wednesbury* unreasonableness … is likely to properly balance up the collective and private interests at stake. In other words, in the absence of legal error on the usual grounds or something patent the decision should stand. The placement of the burden on the applicant respects the institutional, functional, and pragmatic limitations on judicial review;

4. The well-established and wide-ranging statutory duties to give reasons and the emerging common law duties apply as well on the 'public wrongs' side, so there is no reason to think that the emerging culture of justification will be fractured;

5. Tradition is not a bad thing in itself. It is a bulwark against unduly privileging individualism under the cloak of proportionality at the expense of effective government;

6. There may be more clarity and certainty, rather than less, if this division is manifest on the rainbow of review;

7. It will constrain somewhat more the exercise of judicial discretion …

It seems to me at this stage of development of our administrative law that to draw a line on the rainbow—even a categorical one—is more likely to encourage lawyers, judges, and jurists to think carefully about where the case actually should be situated and why. On the 'public wrongs' part of the rainbow, the old dichotomies still seem to me to respect the institutional, functional, and pragmatic limitations on judicial review in a small, modern, welfarist state with a mixed economy. What this will mean in practice is that the push-and-pull of proportionality and deference on the 'rights' part of the rainbow will not occur in quite the same way in the 'public wrongs' part because there the architecture of judicial review for unreasonableness (reflecting the dichotomies articulated in the *Wednesbury* case) has deference built into it.

QUESTION

- Should the proportionality test be applied across the 'rainbow of review', so displacing the reasonableness test?

8.5.3 Recent case law: direction(s) of travel

In *R (Association of British Civilian Internees (Far East Region))* v. *Secretary of State for Defence* [2003] EWCA Civ 473, [2003] QB 1397, giving the judgment of the Court of Appeal, Dyson LJ said (at [34]) that the Court had 'difficulty in seeing what justification there now is for retaining the *Wednesbury* test'. However, he concluded (at [35]) that it was 'not for [the Court of Appeal] to perform its burial rites': that would have to wait for (what is now) the Supreme Court. More than a decade later, those 'burial rites' remain to be performed. Indeed, just as the Court of Appeal concluded that it could not perform them in the *Internees* case, so the Supreme Court considers that it ought not to fundamentally alter the law in this area unless sitting as a nine-member panel. In *Keyu* v. *Secretary of State for Foreign and Commonwealth Affairs* [2015] UKSC 69, [2015] 3 WLR 1665, Lord Neuberger said:

> [131] … [T]he appellants contend that the four-stage [proportionality] test identified by Lord Sumption and Lord Reed JJSC in *Bank Mellat v HM Treasury (No 2)* [2014] AC 700, paras 20, 74 should now be applied in place of rationality in all domestic judicial review cases.
>
> [132] It would not be appropriate for a five-justice panel of this court to accept, or indeed to reject, this argument, which potentially has implications which are profound in constitutional terms and very wide in applicable scope. Accordingly, if a proportionality challenge to the refusal to hold an inquiry would succeed, then it would be necessary to have this appeal (or at any rate this aspect of this appeal) re-argued before a panel of nine justices …
>
> [133] The move from rationality to proportionality, as urged by the appellants, would appear to have potentially profound and far reaching consequences, because it would involve the court considering the merits of the decision at issue: in particular, it would require the courts to consider the balance which the decision-maker has struck between competing interests (often a public interest against a private interest) and the weight to be accorded to each such interest—see *R (Daly) v Secretary of State for the Home Department* [2001] 2 AC 532, para 27, per Lord Steyn.

While it is apparent from Lord Neuberger's remarks that he is at least prepared to countenance consideration of proportionality being applied 'in place of rationality in all domestic judicial review cases', it is equally clear that he considers that, as things stand, the rationality, or reasonableness, test remains a part of English administrative law. It is, of course, impossible to be certain what the Supreme Court would do if it were to conduct the sort of thoroughgoing review of the law that Lord Neuberger contemplates. However, a series of recent cases decided by that Court provide some indications of the directions that the law in this area might take. Key among those cases are *Kennedy* v. *Charity Commission* [2014] UKSC 20, [2015] AC 455; *Pham* v. *Secretary of State for the Home Department* [2015] UKSC 19, [2015] 1 WLR 1591; *R (Keyu)* v. *Secretary of State for Foreign and Commonwealth Affairs* [2015] UKSC 69, [2015] 3 WLR 1665; and *R (Youssef)* v. *Secretary of State for Foreign and Commonwealth Affairs* [2016] UKSC 3, [2016] 2 WLR 509.

The general tenor of these cases is that the law in this area is evolving. While we do not speculate about what the reasons for that might be, Lady Hale—giving a lecture entitled 'UK Constitutionalism on the March?' in 2014—identified a number of possible causes. She pointed out to her audience that

> litigants (or more importantly litigators) have been reminded that they should look first to the common law to protect their fundamental rights: radical suggestions have been made about the

power of judicial review to protect them. Whether this trend is developing as a response to the rising tide of anti-European sentiment among parliamentarians, the press and the public, whether it is putting down a marker for what might happen if the 1998 Act were repealed, whether it is a reflection of distinctive judicial philosophies of the judges who are at the forefront of this development, or whether it is simple irritation that our proud traditions of UK constitutionalism seemed to have been forgotten, I leave it to you and to the academics to decide.

That the law may be approaching a turning-point—or at least a milestone—in this area is underlined by the fact that some Justices have endorsed the case for a careful review of the whole area by the Supreme Court. That much is implicit in the earlier passage from Lord Neuberger's judgment in *Keyu*. Giving the only judgment in *Youssef*, Lord Carnwath (at [55]) explicitly called for a root-and-branch re-examination of relevant matters: 'It is to be hoped that an opportunity can be found in the near future for an authoritative review in this court of the judicial and academic learning on the issue, including relevant comparative material from other common law jurisdictions.' The very fact that such a review is considered necessary is consonant with the notion that the traditional position—that reasonableness is the default doctrine, and that proportionality applies only in certain exceptional circumstances—is increasingly open to question. For instance, as Lord Mance put it in *Kennedy* (at [51]): 'The common law no longer insists on the uniform application of the rigid test of irrationality once thought applicable under the so-called *Wednesbury* principle. The nature of judicial review in every case depends upon the context.' It does not, however, inexorably follow from this that the reasonableness, or *Wednesbury*, principle should or must be replaced by proportionality. Against this background, it is necessary to distinguish three broad lines of thinking—three potential directions of travel along which the case law might develop—that are discernible within the Supreme Court's recent jurisprudence. As important as understanding how the three lines of analysis differ is grasping that—in ways we will explain—they also bleed into one another: a point that is underlined by the fact that some judges' dicta disclose aspects of more than one of the approaches.

The first line of thinking—which essentially amounts to a clarification of the position that has already been reached—holds that the range of circumstances in which the proportionality doctrine applies is broader than has, until recently, generally been acknowledged. On this view, proportionality is treated not as an essentially European concept that enters UK law only to the extent that is necessary in respect of EU law or the domestic application of the ECHR under the HRA. Rather, proportionality is treated as something that has taken root in domestic law and which can therefore apply in purely 'domestic' cases, albeit only in certain such cases, reasonableness otherwise remaining the applicable test. For instance, in *Pham*, Lord Mance (at [98]) said:

Removal of British citizenship under the power provided by section 40(2) of the British Nationality Act 1981 is, on any view, a radical step, particularly if the person affected has little real attachment to the country of any other nationality that he possesses and is unlikely to be able to return there. A correspondingly strict standard of judicial review must apply to any exercise of the power contained in section 40(2), and the tool of proportionality is one which would, in my view …, be both available and valuable for the purposes of such a review.

Lord Reed reached a similar conclusion in *Pham*, albeit by reference to rather different reasoning. He took as his starting point the 'principle of legality', according to which legislation impinging upon fundamental rights falls to be construed strictly. Lord Reed said (at [119]) that

> where Parliament authorises significant interferences with important legal rights, the courts may interpret the legislation as requiring that any such interference should be no greater than is objectively established to be necessary to achieve the legitimate aim of the interference: in substance, a requirement of proportionality.

He went on to tentatively conclude (at [120]) that such a requirement of proportionality may apply in circumstances such as those that arose in *Pham* itself which, as already explained, centred upon not a fundamental *right* as such, but a fundamental *status* (*ie* British citizenship):

> Given the fundamental importance of citizenship, it may be arguable that the power to deprive a British citizen of that status should be interpreted as being subject to an implied requirement that its exercise should be justified as being necessary to achieve the legitimate aim pursued. Such an argument has not however been advanced at the hearing of this appeal, and it would be inappropriate to express any view on it.

This approach certainly does not condone the use of proportionality whenever substantive review is undertaken—quite the reverse: it acknowledges that proportionality will be appropriate only in a subset of such circumstances. Nevertheless, Lord Reed's approach opens up the possibility of a greater role for proportionality, the thinking apparently being that reading in a requirement to act proportionately is normatively warranted when the statutory power in question places in jeopardy a sufficiently important right or interest.

If the first line of analysis envisages a greater, but still a distinct, role for proportionality, the second takes as its premise the porousness of the distinction between the respective provinces of the reasonableness and proportionality tests. Such porousness can be conceived of in two respects. In normative terms, the porousness of that distinction is arguably acknowledged—or at least nodded towards—by the first line of thinking, given that it treats the appropriateness of proportionality review as a function of the normative importance of the right or value that is at stake. Only if we consider there to be two crisply demarcated groups of such rights or values—*ie* ones that respectively are and are not important enough to be protected by means of the proportionality test—would we envisage a sharp line demarcating that test's field of application. This is one of the ways in which, as noted earlier, the different lines of analysis evident in the Supreme Court's case law shade into one another.

The porousness of the distinction can also be conceived of in terms of methodology. For instance, in *Kennedy*, Lord Mance (at [54]), relying upon Craig's work, says that 'both reasonableness review and proportionality involve considerations of weight and balance, with the intensity of the scrutiny and the weight to be given to any primary decision maker's view depending on the context'. Meanwhile, Lord Sumption, in *Pham*, states (at [105]) that 'although English law has not adopted the principle of proportionality generally, it has for many years stumbled towards a concept which is in significant respects similar' by 'expand[ing] the scope of rationality review so as to incorporate at common law significant elements of the principle of proportionality'. This, says Lord Sumption, has enabled English courts—'even in the context of rights arising wholly from domestic law'—to 'differentiate between rights of greater or lesser importance and interference with them of greater or lesser degree'. On this view, whether review is described in terms of 'reasonableness' or 'proportionality' is less important than tailoring the nature and intensity of review to the requirements of context. Taken together with the fact that, as Lord Kerr said (at [271]) in *Keyu*, the differences between proportionality and reasonableness 'have been overestimated in the past', this view may suggest (as Lord Kerr went on to argue at [272]) that 'the very notion that one must choose between proportionality and irrationality may be misplaced'.

The third line of thinking holds—or is at least open to the possibility—that the sort of contextualist impulses that animate the second mode of analysis can and should be accommodated by an explicit switch to utilizing proportionality review across the board. There is limited—but arguably some—evidence of judicial appetite for this. For instance, Lord Kerr's position as to the second and third views is ambiguous. Although, as noted previously, he appears to advocate a contextualist approach that is consonant with the second line of thinking, he does not dismiss the possibility that the necessary degree of contextualism might be achieved through sufficiently flexible use of the proportionality doctrine. In *Keyu*, while doubting whether proportionality in its fullest sense can sensibly be applied when a fundamental right is not at stake, Lord Kerr (at [282]) said that he could 'envisage a more loosely structured proportionality challenge where a fundamental right is not involved' and emphasized (at [272]) that constitutional objections to proportionality are wide of the mark because it does not require the court to substitute its opinion for that of the decision-maker, or 'demand that the decision-maker bring the reviewer to the point of conviction that theirs was the right decision in any absolute sense'. (It is worth noting, however, that this view is in tension with that expressed in other cases—see, *eg Belfast City Council* v. *Miss Behavin' Ltd* [2007] UKHL 19, [2007] 1 WLR 1420 at [37]—which emphasize that when the proportionality test is in play, it is for the *court* to strike the balance. This arguably shows that the more broadly the courts seek to deploy proportionality, the less determinate it becomes as a test.) Meanwhile, in *Kennedy*, Lord Mance—having advanced the view that 'both reasonableness review and proportionality involve considerations of weight and balance'—went on (at [54]) to suggest that:

> The advantage of the terminology of proportionality is that it introduces an element of structure into the exercise, by directing attention to factors such as suitability or appropriateness, necessity and the balance or imbalance of benefits and disadvantages. There seems no reason why such factors should not be relevant in judicial review even outside the scope of Convention and EU law. Whatever the context, the court deploying them must be aware that they overlap potentially and that the intensity with which they are applied is heavily dependent on the context.

Lord Mance continues that while in 'the context of fundamental rights' it is 'a truism that the scrutiny [supplied by proportionality] is likely to be more intense than where other interests are involved', 'proportionality itself is not always equated with intense scrutiny'. He noted, for instance, that in *R* v. *Secretary of State for Health, ex parte Eastside Cheese Co* [1999] 3 CMLR 123 at [47]—a case concerned with the application of the proportionality test in an EU context—Lord Bingham had explained that (as Lord Mance put it) 'proportionality review may itself be limited in context to examining whether the exercise of a power involved some manifest error or a clear excess of the bounds of discretion'. The burden of Lord Mance's argument is that proportionality is so flexible a concept as to be capable of accommodating circumstances falling outside those—such as fundamental rights cases—in which high-intensity scrutiny is considered to be normatively warranted.

He returned to this point in *Pham* (at [96]), in which he endorsed the view that the intensity of proportionality review is not a fixed necessary consequence of the structure, but a variable consequence of the degree of judicial restraint that is practised when engaging in such review. If, however, review under the rubric of proportionality really does sometimes amount to nothing more than detecting such matters as 'manifest error', it is hard to see in what sense it meaningfully amounts to proportionality review given that, in such circumstances, review will exhibit *neither* the intensity *nor* the structure classically associated with that doctrine.

How, then, do the three lines of thinking that can be discerned from the case law differ from and relate to one another? They are all contextualist in the sense that they buy into the idea that the intensity of substantive review ought to vary depending on the normative importance of what is placed at stake by the decision under challenge. They differ, however, in the ways in which they seek to concretize such contextualism. The first school of thought does so by retaining distinct spheres of operation for the reasonableness and proportionality tests; in essence this is a categorical approach: different approaches to substantive review will be taken in different categories of case. The second school of thought differs in that it envisages less of a bright-line distinction between those spheres, and more of a shading of lower intensity reasonableness into higher intensity proportionality review. The third school of thought bears some resemblance to the second, but seeks to satisfy the contextualist impulse by conceiving of the proportionality test itself in chameleonic terms in an attempt to enable it to operate across the piece without yielding judicial overreach.

The question, however, is whether the third approach renders proportionality such a malleable doctrine as to make it into little more than a blank canvas upon which the judge's sense of the 'right' approach to substantive review in the given context falls to be projected. Giving the 2013 annual lecture to the Constitutional and Administrative Law Bar Association, Lord Carnwath appeared not only to anticipate but to endorse such an approach:

> In 19 years as a judge of administrative law cases I cannot remember ever deciding a case by simply asking myself whether an administrative decision was 'beyond the range of reasonable responses', still less whether it has caused me logical or moral outrage. Nor do I remember ever asking myself where it came on a sliding scale of intensity. My approach I suspect has been much closer to the characteristically pragmatic approach suggested by Lord Donaldson in [*R* v. *Takeover Panel, ex parte Guinness plc* [1990] 1 QB 146], by way of a rider to what Lord Diplock had said in [*Council of Civil Service Unions* v. *Minister for the Civil Service* [1985] AC 374]: 'the ultimate question would, as always, be whether something had gone wrong of a nature and degree which required the intervention of the court and, if so, what form that intervention should take'. If the answer appears to be yes, then one looks for a legal hook to hang it on. And if there is none suitable, one may need to adapt one ... Generally we [judges] should look to the academics to do the theorising, and to put our efforts into a wider context. That way, we can decide the cases, and then they can tell us what we really meant, so that we can make it sound better next time.

However, Lord Carnwath now appears to have stepped back from this arresting position. In *Youssef* (at [55]), he said, as noted above, that he hoped that there would soon be an opportunity for the Supreme Court to review the law in this area, and suggested that such a review 'might aim for rather more structured guidance for the lower courts than such imprecise concepts as "anxious scrutiny" and "sliding scales".'

The provision of such structured guidance could only be a good thing. But questions remain as to what it would bite upon—and, in particular, whether that should be a highly pliable notion of proportionality that would apply across the board. If it is the case that (as Lord Mance suggests in *Kennedy* at [54]) proportionality can sometimes involve nothing more than looking for 'manifest error' or a clear 'excess of discretion' or (as Lord Sumption said in *R (Carlile)* v. *Secretary of State for the Home Department* [2014] UKSC 60, [2015] AC 945 at [32]) evaluating the rationality of a decision, and if (as Lord Kerr argues in *Keyu* at [282]) proportionality in non-rights cases cannot be applied in its usual, structured form, it is dif- ficult to see what—other than a semantic shift—is achieved by advocating the eclipse of the reasonableness doctrine with an all-embracing proportionality test. Of course, if this really is all just a question of semantics, then saying that courts are engaging in 'proportionality review' when they are really engaging in reasonableness review is no more (but no less) than an obstacle to understanding what is actually going on. The risk, however, is that relying upon an extremely pliable conception of the proportionality test as a panacea may result in the removal of much needed conceptual scaffolding, thereby making more feasible the sort of free-wheeling approach advocated by Lord Carnwath in his lecture. If that were to hap- pen, it would be as unfortunate as it would be ironic, given that one of the central criticisms of the reasonableness test is that (as Jowell and Lester [1987] *PL* 368 at 372 memorably put it) '*Wednesbury*'s ample cloak' is (or was) capable of serving as cover for precisely such an approach.

8.6 Concluding remarks

One of the key foundations upon which English administrative law has been built is the distinction between review and appeal. The notion of substantive review poses a particu- lar challenge in this context. The traditional response was to permit such review only in very limited circumstances—hence the reasonableness test. However, the proportionality doctrine, which potentially involves much closer judicial scrutiny of administrative deci- sions and the reasons underlying them, is now unequivocally part of English law. As a result, questions have arisen concerning whether the distinction between appeal and review remains relevant and, if so, how it should be preserved. Recognizing that the consti- tutional principles underlying the distinction between appeal and review remain relevant, the courts have proceeded on the basis that their function remains distinct from that of primary decision-makers, and have sought to develop the proportionality test in a way that respects that distinction. As this chapter has shown, much has happened in this area in recent years and decades—but it is clear that the law is not yet settled. In particular, the Supreme Court evidently has further work to do in this context, not least in relation to the question whether the reasonableness test should be jettisoned in favour of deploying the proportionality doctrine across the board. At one level, that question is a highly technical one that is concerned with how the law can best be configured in order to secure substantive review of a form and intensity that is appropriate to the subject-matter of any given case. At another level, however, the issue is a fundamentally normative one that goes to the heart of the debate about the proper extent of judicial review of administrative action. For precisely that reason, the law in this area has long been a barometer signifying the courts' perception of how fundamental constitutional principles shape their own role relative to that of the executive government. As the law continues to evolve in this area, as it surely will, much will therefore turn upon the Supreme Court's understanding of where the constitutional parameters of judicial power lie; in an unwritten constitutional order such as that of the United Kingdom, discerning their location is no easy matter.

FURTHER RESOURCES

Allan, 'Human Rights and Judicial Review: A Critique of "Due Deference"' [2006] *CLJ* 671

Bamforth and Leyland (eds), *Public Law in a Multi-Layered Constitution* (Oxford 2003), chs 12 (Taggart: 'Reinventing Administrative Law') and 13 (Hunt: 'Sovereignty's Blight: Why Contemporary Public Law Needs the Concept of "Due Deference"')

Hickman, *Public Law after the Human Rights Act* (Oxford 2010), chs 4–7

Kavanagh, 'Defending Deference in Public Law and Constitutional Theory' (2010) 126 *LQR* 222

Rivers, 'Proportionality and Variable Intensity Review' [2006] *CLJ* 174

Taggart, 'Proportionality, Deference, *Wednesbury*' [2008] *NZ L Rev* 423

Wilberg and Elliott (eds), *The Scope and Intensity of Substantive Review: Traversing Taggart's Rainbow* (Oxford 2015), chs 3 (Jowell, 'Proportionality and Unreasonableness: Neither Merger nor Takeover'), 4 (Elliott, 'From Bifurcation to Calibration: Twin-Track Deference and the Culture of Justification'), and 5 (Varuhas, 'Against Unification')

9 BIAS, IMPARTIALITY, AND INDEPENDENCE

9.1 The rule against bias: its scope and rationale

The notion of procedural fairness is a wide-ranging one, and encompasses a number of distinct principles of administrative law. In chs 10 and 11 we examine various things that administrative decision-makers may be required to *do*—such as provide a hearing or give reasons—under the banner of procedural fairness. In this chapter, however, we are concerned with a prior question regarding not the fairness of the decision-making *process* but the nature of the decision-making *body* itself.

It is not difficult to identify underlying rationales for procedural fairness. It is self-evident that fairness, in some form, is a highly desirable characteristic in any system of public administration. Because it promotes full and fair consideration of the issues and evidence, procedural fairness, as Lord Steyn observed in *Raji* v. *General Medical Council* [2003] UKPC 24, [2003] 1 WLR 1052 at [13], plays 'an instrumental role in promoting just decisions'. It is normatively significant, too, because to accord fair treatment to individuals is to act in a manner which respects their dignity and value as members of the community, rather than characterizing them as the objects of an arbitrary and authoritarian governmental process. It is also important for public confidence in, and co-operation with, the administrative system that it *appears* to be fair, as well as actually being fair. We consider these underlying objectives of procedural fairness in greater detail in ch 10.

However, this chapter is concerned specifically with the notions of impartiality (and bias, which is the flip side of the same coin) and independence (a concept that, as we will see, is related but distinct). If a decision-making system is to lay claim to any degree of fairness, then the provision of unbiased tribunals and decision-makers is a prerequisite. No amount of procedural safeguards (such as the right to legal representation or to cross-examine witnesses) is likely to deliver fairness if the tribunal is, in the first place, biased in the sense of being partial rather than impartial: *ie* inherently predisposed against (or, indeed, for) the individual about whom the decision is being made. The connection between impartiality and fairness is drawn out in the following excerpt. (Although it is concerned with judges, Galligan's argument is applicable to other, including administrative, decision-makers.)

Galligan, *Due Process and Fair Procedures* (Oxford 1996)

To lack impartiality means being willing to decide a matter for reasons which are unrelated to legitimate reasons. The judge who allows his personal feelings towards a party to intrude on his deliberations, or the licensing justice who takes into account his own financial interest in the licence being refused, are both acting out of bias and have surrendered their impartiality. The personal feelings of the judge and the financial interests of the justice are reasons which should be excluded from their decisions. They are improper reasons because they are unrelated to the authoritative standards by which the cases should be decided. The judge is supposed to decide between the two parties according to the principles of civil law, while the justice should determine licensing applications according to the statutory criteria. Where there is discretion so that the judge or the justice has to settle for himself at least some of the standards to apply, it would be equally illegitimate to adopt standards based on personal feelings or financial interest. Any choice which discretion allows does not include the selection of standards based on personal feelings or financial interest.

Once the link is made between loss of impartiality and the process of reasoning which an official is required to follow, the relationship between bias and fairness can be seen. For the official who acts for improper reasons fails to apply authoritative standards correctly or to exercise discretion properly; as a consequence, the person affected is not treated in accordance with those standards and, therefore, is treated unfairly. This does not undermine the idea that reasons do not come ready-made or branded as good or bad; reasons, of course, are constructed out of a social context, guided, but not closely constricted, by given legal standards. The present argument claims merely that whatever reasons are good reasons, those displaying bias will never be amongst their number. We can now see why loss of impartiality is roundly condemned: the unseemliness of prejudice or personal interest influencing the holder of a public office is evidence of the deeper principle rather than the principle itself. We can also see that, being an attack on the idea that in any legal context there are authoritative standards to apply, the absence of impartiality is a fundamental flaw which renders the process illegitimate.

Galligan's explanation helpfully illuminates the connection between the rule against bias—which insists upon impartiality on the part of the decision-maker—and the relevancy of considerations and propriety of purpose doctrines which we considered in ch 7. All of those principles are constituted on the basis that discretion can be exercised properly only on the strength of considerations—or 'standards'—which are legitimate. Whereas the relevancy of considerations and propriety of purpose doctrines tend to focus our attention on those constraints on discretion which are explicit or implicit in the statutory scheme—and whose identification is therefore largely a matter of context—the rule against bias is concerned with a more fundamental, and more obvious, set of factors such as personal animosity and pecuniary interest, the operation of which necessarily calls into question the legitimacy of the decision-making process.

One of the objectives of the rule against bias, therefore, is to deliver a system of decision-making which, at quite a fundamental level, is *actually* fair and legitimate. However, as the following excerpt demonstrates, the rule's rationale is in fact somewhat broader—and so, as a result, is the rule itself.

R v. Sussex Justices, ex parte McCarthy [1924] 1 KB 256
Divisional Court of the King's Bench Division

Whitworth, the driver of a motorbike which was involved in a collision with McCarthy's motorbike, made a claim through his solicitor for damages from McCarthy. In addition, a criminal prosecution was brought for dangerous driving and McCarthy was convicted by a magistrates' court. The person who acted as the clerk to the justices on the day in question—the deputy clerk—was a partner in the firm of solicitors which was acting on Whitworth's behalf. He had retired with the justices, but, according to the justices' affidavit, he had not referred to the case during his retirement with them and he had not been consulted whilst the justices were coming to their decision. McCarthy's solicitor stated that he (the solicitor) had been unaware of the deputy clerk's interest in the case until the justices had retired; however, he brought the matter to their attention when they returned to court. McCarthy later sought a quashing order in respect of his conviction.

Lord Hewart CJ

It is clear that the deputy clerk was a member of the firm of solicitors engaged in the conduct of proceedings for damages against the applicant in respect of the same collision as that which gave rise to the charge that the justices were considering. It is said, and, no doubt, truly, that when that gentleman retired in the usual way with the justices, taking with him the notes of the evidence in case the justices might desire to consult him, the justices came to a conclusion without consulting him, and that he scrupulously abstained from referring to the case in any way. But while that is so, a long line of cases shows that it is not merely of some importance but is of fundamental importance that justice should not only be done, but should manifestly and undoubtedly be seen to be done. The question therefore is not whether in this case the deputy clerk made any observation or offered any criticism which he might not properly have made or offered; the question is whether he was so related to the case in its civil aspect as to be unfit to act as clerk to the justices in the criminal matter. The answer to that question depends not upon what actually was done but upon what might appear to be done. Nothing is to be done which creates even a suspicion that there has been an improper interference with the course of justice. Speaking for myself, I accept the statements contained in the justices' affidavit, but they show very clearly that the deputy clerk was connected with the case in a capacity which made it right that he should scrupulously abstain from referring to the matter in any way, although he retired with the justices; in other words, his one position was such that he could not, if he had been required to do so, discharge the duties which his other position involved. His twofold position was a manifest contradiction. In those circumstances I am satisfied that this conviction must be quashed, unless it can be shown that the applicant or his solicitor was aware of the point that might be taken, refrained from taking it, and took his chance of an acquittal on the facts, and then, on a conviction being recorded, decided to take the point. On the facts I am satisfied that there has been no waiver of the irregularity.

Lush and Sankey JJ agreed. The conviction was quashed.

Lord Hewart's directive that 'justice should not only be done, but should manifestly and undoubtedly be seen to be done' is part of the bedrock of English administrative law. It reveals a view of the rule against bias—and of the policy objectives which underpin and shape that rule—that emphasizes perception as much as reality. The purpose of the rule, on this view, is not merely to promote fairness in decision-making, but to ensure that practices which merely create an *impression* of bias are rendered unlawful. The reason for construct-ing the rule against bias thus is perhaps most readily apparent in relation to decision-making in a judicial context. It is clear, for instance, that the perception that criminal trials are conducted in a fair, impartial, and unbiased manner is one of the foundations upon which public confidence in the criminal justice system rests. Perception is, however, also import-ant in other, including administrative, contexts. Public trust in government—and, hence, the willingness of individuals to co-operate with public authorities in their endeavour to secure effective administration for the public good—requires a conviction on the part of the public that decision-making functions are discharged in an unbiased manner, such that (for instance) applications for licences, asylum, and planning permission are determined on merit, not on grounds of status or favour.

9.2 Automatic disqualification

9.2.1 Financial interests: the general principle

If the circumstances in which a decision is made are such that a fair-minded and informed observer would perceive a real possibility of bias on the part of a given decision-maker, then it is usually unlawful for that decision-maker to participate in the making of the decision. We will call that rule—which we consider in detail at 9.3—the 'fair-minded observer rule'. However, we begin with a second, alternative route—which we will call the 'automatic disqualification rule'—by which a decision-maker can be disqualified. That rule provides that if a decision-maker has a sufficient financial interest in the outcome of the decision-making process, he will be automatically disqualified from taking part. If he takes part in spite of his interest, his decision may be set aside. In fact Jones [1999] *PL* 391 at 399 suggests that the rule

> might be better thought of as a rule of automatic *disclosure*, rather than *disqualification*. The mere fact that a judge feels that he has an interest which needs to be disclosed to the parties to the litigation does not mean that he must automatically disqualify himself. It is open for him to do so, but the normal expectation would be that the decision is one for the parties (and fellow judges, if appropriate) to make. In the absence of adequate disclosure, the disqualification is retrospective, operating on appeal from the original decision.

If full disclosure is made of financial interests (or indeed any other interest that would otherwise disqualify the decision-maker on grounds of bias), it is therefore open to the relevant party to waive his right to object, provided that, as the Court of Appeal put it in *Locabail (UK) Ltd* v. *Bayfield Properties Ltd* [2000] QB 451 at 475, the waiver is 'clear and unequivocal, and made with full knowledge of all the facts relevant to the decision whether to waive or not'. (It should also be noted that the rule against bias yields in the face of both statutory authorization and necessity—that is, where no alternative decision-maker exists—although the ECtHR held in *Kingsley* v. *United Kingdom* (2001) 35 EHRR 10 that the common law doctrine of necessity cannot excuse breaches of Article 6 ECHR, which we discuss at 9.5.) We begin, however, with a classic example of the operation of the rule in circumstances in which the judge failed to disclose his financial interest—and in which, therefore, disqualification followed automatically (albeit, as Jones observes, retrospectively).

> ### *Dimes* v. *The Proprietors of the Grand Junction Canal* (1852) 3 HLC 759
> House of Lords
>
> The respondent company had been involved in proceedings before Lord Cottenham LC and had been granted relief by him. Lord Cottenham, however, held shares in the company (partly on his own account, and partly as a trustee for others), and the validity of his action was in issue in this case.

Lord Campbell

No one can suppose that Lord Cottenham could be, in the remotest degree, influenced by the interests that he had in this concern; but, my Lords, it is of the last importance that the maxim that no man is to be a judge in his own cause should be held sacred. And this is not to be confined to a cause in which he is a party, but applies to a cause in which he has an interest. Since I have had the honour to be Chief Justice of the Court of Queen's Bench, we have again and again set aside proceedings in inferior tribunals because an individual, who had an interest in a cause, took a part in the decision. And it will have a most salutary influence on these tribunals when it is known that this high Court of last resort, in a case in which the Lord Chancellor of England had an interest, considered that his decree was on that account a decree not according to law, and was set aside. This will be a lesson to all inferior tribunals to take care not only that in their decrees they are not influenced by their personal interest, but to avoid the appearance of labouring under such an influence.

Lord St Leonards LC and Lord Brougham agreed that Lord Cottenham had been disqualified from acting as a judge in the proceedings in question on account of his interest.

Lord Campbell's speech raises important questions concerning the *rationale* and *scope* of this limb of the rule against bias. We consider those matters in turn.

9.2.2 Can automatic disqualification be justified?

As we observed earlier, the importance of securing public confidence in judicial and administrative decision-making is such that the rule against bias prohibits not only practices that are *actually* unfair, but also those which may give the *impression* of unfairness. It is unclear, however, where precisely the aspect of the bias rule presently under consideration fits into this framework. Although Lord Campbell's opening remark—that '[n]o one can suppose that Lord Cottenham could be, in the remotest degree, influenced by the interests that he had in this concern'—is questionable (see Olowofoyeku's comments in the next excerpt), the fact that he adopted that premise raises an important question. If Lord Campbell was satisfied that the Lord Chancellor was *not actually influenced* by his financial interest, and that *no one could form the impression that he was so affected*, what purpose did the latter's disqualification serve?

> **QUESTION**
> - Which (if any) part of the rationale underlying the rule against bias is furthered by the decision in *Dimes*, and the principle for which it now stands?

In the following passage, Olowofoyeku, reflecting on, among other decisions, *Dimes*, argues that the automatic disqualification rule is too blunt an instrument that pays insufficient regard to policy considerations which point towards a more subtle approach. (The tests for bias, referred to in the following extract, based variously upon 'danger', 'likelihood', 'suspicion', and 'apprehension' are considered at 9.3; for the time being, the key factor which distinguishes those tests from the automatic disqualification principle is that they require evaluation of the circumstances, and provide for disqualification only if there is a sufficient degree of likelihood that they would give rise to a perception of bias.)

Olowofoyeku, 'The *Nemo Judex* Rule: The Case against Automatic Disqualification' [2000] *PL* 456

There is nothing magical about automatic disqualification (other than expediency) which makes it better at protecting the integrity of the administration of justice than any other principle. The warning of Slade J. in *R* v. *Camborne Justices, ex parte Pearce* [[1955] 1 QB 41 at 51] against the erroneous impression that 'it is more important that justice should appear to be done than that it should in fact be done' is salutary. Indiscriminate application of automatic disqualification, or, treating automatic disqualification as an end in itself, may well imply that such an erroneous impression is correct, and may serve to undermine the integrity of the administration of justice. For, if the purpose of the *nemo judex* rule is to preserve public confidence in the administration of justice, it may be that such confidence would be compromised rather than enhanced if the public go away feeling that justice was not done because of a 'mere technicality', rather than because there was a real risk of injustice having occurred. The famous statement of Lord Denning M.R. in *Metropolitan Properties Ltd* v. *Lannon* [[1969] 1 QB 577 at 599] was to the effect that justice is rooted in confidence, and that confidence is destroyed when right-thinking people go away thinking that the judge was biased.

There is a corollary to this, and it is found in these words of Sackville, Finn and Kenny JJ. of the Australian Federal Court in [*Ebner* v. *Official Trustee in Bankruptcy* [1999] FCA 110 at [37]]:

> It would seem on the authorities (and [counsel for the applicant] said it was settled law) that a failure to disclose, say, a shareholding in a corporate party to litigation will disqualify a judge, even though the shares are worth very little and the prospect of the litigation making a difference to the price of the shares is utterly remote. If this is so, the consequence is that a judgment delivered after many days of hearing is liable to be set aside, notwithstanding that no reasonable person could suggest that there is any suspicion of judicial bias. Why is it to be assumed that the confidence of fair-minded people in the administration of justice would be shaken by the existence of a direct pecuniary interest of no tangible value, but not by the waste of resources and the delays brought about by setting aside a judgment on the ground that the judge is disqualified for having such an interest[?]

Thus, it may be that to ask whether there is any good reason in principle for limiting automatic disqualification to cases of financial interest is to ask the wrong question. [This question was prompted by the decision of the House of Lords in *R* v. *Bow Street Stipendiary Magistrate, ex parte Pinochet Ugarte (No 2)* [2000] AC 119, which, as we will see later, extended the scope of the automatic disqualification principle in English law.] It may be that a better question is whether there is any need [at all] for a rule of automatic disqualification. In *Ebner*, the Full Court of the Australian Federal Court said [at [36]] that it might be 'thought somewhat anomalous that a special rule of automatic disqualification has survived for cases of direct pecuniary interest, especially in Australia where the more stringent 'reasonable suspicion' test [on which see at 9.3.1] has been adopted'. The Court referred to the statement of Lord Hewart C.J. in *R* v. *Sussex Justices, ex p. McCarthy* that justice should not only be done, but should be seen to be done as the principle underlying the Australian 'reasonable suspicion' test, and queried why, if this was the case, it was necessary to have a special rule which disqualifies a judge even where an ordinary reasonable member of the public could not suspect bias on the part of the judge.

... In *Dimes* itself ... [i]t is true that Lord Campbell said that no one could suppose that Lord Cottenham could be, in the remotest degree, influenced by the interest he had in the canal company. But it has been commented [by Sackville, Finn, and Kenny JJ in *Ebner, op cit*] that, 'while lawyers might be prepared to accept that Lord Cottenham could not have been influenced, it is a little difficult to see why Lord Campbell was so confident that *no-one* could reasonably reach a different view'. Lord Cottenham's interest of 'several thousand pounds' in 1852 would probably translate to 'several hundreds of thousands of pounds' today. It would be fairly open to reasonable people to suspect or apprehend that a judge might be influenced by such a substantial shareholding, *a fortiori* if the liability of the shareholders is not limited. A view that there would be a real likelihood or danger that a judge with such a stake in a litigant might be prejudiced in favour of the litigant could not be described in any way as unreasonable or fanciful, notwithstanding the judge's eminence. Therefore *Dimes* could just as easily have been decided on the basis of [a] real likelihood or danger, or reasonable apprehension, of bias ...

... [M]y conclusion is that automatic disqualification is draconian, disproportionate and unnecessary. There is nothing that can be achieved by automatic disqualification that cannot be achieved by an application of the real danger/reasonable apprehension test. On the other hand, application of the automatic disqualification rule may well lead to the disqualification of judges in situations wherein a closer inspection of the circumstances would reveal that there was never any realistic possibility of bias. While it may be expedient for judges to apply a mechanical rule, such mechanistic adjudication smacks of abdication. There may well be cases wherein it is obvious that the judgment should not be allowed to stand. Examples of such may be the ... *Dimes* [case]. Such cases can fit within the apprehended bias rule, for if, in the circumstances, reasonable people would not apprehend bias, then it cannot be said that 'it is obvious' that the judgment should not be allowed to stand.

9.2.3 The scope of automatic financial disqualification

The foregoing illuminates a fundamental tension concerning the rationale for the automatic disqualification rule. One possible rationale is that a simple, bright-line rule is desirable so that officials can easily determine whether their participation in a given decision-making process is appropriate and lawful. Such an understanding of the rule's purpose invites an unsubtle formulation of it which lends it a particularly broad scope. If simplicity is key, then disqualification should be triggered by *any* financial interest, without any need for analysis of (for example) its nature, directness, or extent. Some judicial formulations of the rule reflect this sort of crude—and so broad—conception of it. For instance, in *R v. Rand* (1866) LR 1 QB 230 at 232, Blackburn J said that 'any direct pecuniary interest, however small, in the subject of inquiry, does disqualify a person from acting as a judge in the matter'.

However, such an uncompromising conception of the rule sits in tension with a second possible rationale for it—namely, that it is intended to facilitate identification of circumstances that would result in disqualification even if a closer analysis of the matter were to be conducted. On this view, circumstances that satisfy the automatic disqualification rule are merely a subset of—and therefore do not add quantitatively to—the category of cases that fall foul of the rule considered at 9.3 that is concerned with the apprehension of bias upon close analysis of the factual matrix. This view was taken by Rix LJ giving the only reasoned judgment in *R (Kaur)* v. *Institute of Legal Executives Appeal Tribunal* [2011] EWCA Civ 1168. He said (at [44]) that 'it would seem odd to me if the two [rules] rendered different results'. Rix LJ went on to suggest that the two rules are simply different

strands of a single over-arching requirement: that judges should not sit or should face recusal or disqualification where there is a real possibility on the objective appearances of things, assessed by the fair-minded and informed observer (a role which ultimately, when these matters are challenged, is performed by the court), that the tribunal could be biased.

On this view, only financial interests capable of giving rise to the perception of a real possibility of bias should result in disqualification.

If Rix LJ's view in *Kaur* were taken to its logical conclusion, the automatic disqualification rule would be made redundant: it would not be doing any work that was not already done by the real possibility of bias rule. It is not clear that such a radical view is widely judicially held. However, there is evidence of some movement in this direction. In particular, in the leading case of *Locabail (UK) Ltd v. Bayfield Properties Ltd* [2000] QB 451, the Court of Appeal acknowledged (at [10]) a 'de minimis exception' to the automatic disqualification rule, the effect of which is to shield from automatic disqualification financial interests that are 'incapable of affecting [the] decision one way or the other'. The Court of Appeal went on to apply this more subtle view of the automatic disqualification principle to the facts of the case.

Locabail (UK) Ltd v. Bayfield Properties Ltd [2000] QB 451
Court of Appeal

Locabail (UK) Ltd took legal proceedings, in the latter part of 1998, against two companies which were both controlled by Mr Emmanuel, in order to enforce charges securing the payment of advances made to him. The securities consisted of property owned by the companies: Hans House, Knightsbridge, in the case of Waldorf Investment Corporation, and Hawks Hill in Surrey, in the case of Bayfield Properties Ltd. Mrs Emmanuel, however, who was (or became) a defendant in both actions, claimed, on the basis of representations made to her by her husband, and her reliance thereupon, to be the equitable owner of Hawks Hill and to have a beneficial interest in Hans House. On 27 October 1998, the judge discovered in one of the bundles a press cutting stating that the City law firm Herbert Smith was acting for Sudoexport against Mr Emmanuel and against a company (Howard Holdings Inc, a company controlled by Mr Emmanuel which had money claims against him). Previously unaware of Herbert Smith's involvement, the judge—a deputy High Court judge—immediately drew the parties' attention to the fact that he was a senior partner in the firm. Mrs Emmanuel raised no objection at the time. However, in March 1999, after the judge had rejected Mrs Emmanuel's contentions as to the beneficial ownership of the two properties, she made an application asking him to disqualify himself from further involvement in the case and to direct a rehearing before a different judge. The judge concluded that no conflict of interest arose, and refused Mrs Emmanuel's application; she therefore sought permission to appeal. Three points arose: whether the judge was automatically disqualified; if not, whether an appearance of bias arose on the facts (on which see 9.3), and whether Mrs Emmanuel, by inaction, had waived any right to object.

Lord Bingham of Cornhill CJ, Lord Woolf MR, and Sir Richard Scott V-C

[42] [Miss Williamson, counsel for Mrs Emmanuel] submits that there was a conflict of interest between Mrs. Emmanuel and Herbert Smith's clients, Sudoexport and/or the liquidator of Howard Holdings Inc. The conflict of interest is constructed as follows: Sudoexport has money claims against Mr. Emmanuel. So does Howard Holdings Inc. in liquidation. Locabail is one of Mr. Emmanuel's creditors. If Mrs. Emmanuel's claims to equitable interests in the two properties were to succeed, there would be a reduction in the value to Locabail of its security and an increase in the unsecured debt owing by Mr. Emmanuel to Locabail. This would be detrimental to the ability of Sudoexport and the liquidator of Howard Holdings Inc. to obtain payment of the sums owing to them by Mr. Emmanuel. The deputy judge explained the point in his judgment: 'if [Mrs Emmanuel] failed, [Locabail] would be removed as a creditor in competition with

Sudoexport'. There is, therefore, Miss Williamson submitted, a conflict of interest between Mrs. Emmanuel and Herbert Smith's clients ...

[47] There was an additional issue. When, on Day 8 of the hearing, the deputy judge made the disclosure recorded in the transcript, Mrs. Emmanuel could then have made an objection to the deputy judge continuing to hear the case. Or she could have asked for time to consider the position. She did neither, but allowed the hearing to continue to a conclusion. She could, after the Hawks Hill hearing had come to an end, have objected to the deputy judge hearing the Hans House appeal. She did not do so, and, without objection, he heard the appeal. Thereafter, during the three and half month delay before the reserved judgment was delivered, no bias objection was made. An inference that might be drawn is that Mrs Emmanuel wanted to await the result of the two hearings, and only made her bias objection when she knew she had lost. So the question arises whether she must be taken to have waived any bias objection.

[48] As to this, [Miss] Williamson's response was to submit, first, that the disclosure made by the deputy judge was not complete disclosure, second, that a waiver could only be effective when made by a person with full knowledge of the relevant facts and, third, that in view of Mrs. Emmanuel's incomplete knowledge of the circumstances of Herbert Smith's involvement in the litigation against her husband, she was never put to her election as to what she should do and waiver could not be raised against her.

[49] The 'waiver' issue is one which, logically, falls to be considered after the bias issues have been considered ...

[50] This is not a case in which actual bias on the part of the deputy judge is alleged. Is it a case in which the judge has a sufficient pecuniary or proprietary interest in the outcome of the trial so as to attract the automatic disqualification principle expressed in the *Dimes* case, 3 H.L.Cas. 759? If it is, then the deputy judge is automatically disqualified. If it is not, then it is a case to which the principles expressed in *Reg. v. Gough* [1993] A.C. 646 must be applied. It was suggested by Miss Williamson that this was a case to which the *Dimes* case applied. Her argument went like this. The deputy judge is a partner in Herbert Smith. Herbert Smith was acting for Sudoexport and Howard Holdings Inc. in litigation against Mr. Emmanuel. Success in achieving the maximum possible recovery from Mr. Emmanuel would enhance the goodwill of Herbert Smith and thereby tend to increase its profits. The deputy judge would share in the firm's profits. Miss Williamson suggested, also, the possibility that Herbert Smith might be acting under a conditional fee agreement with fees dependent on the level of recoveries extracted from Mr. Emmanuel. But in order to attract the *Dimes* consequence of automatic disqualification something more must, in our judgment, be present than the tenuous connection between the firm's success in an individual case on the one hand and the firm's goodwill and the level of profits on the other. And if the pecuniary or proprietary interest has to depend upon the existence of a conditional fee agreement of the unusual character suggested by Miss Williamson, there must be at least some evidence to suggest the existence of such an agreement. Here there is none. Miss Williamson's suggestion is wholly speculative and hypothetical. In our judgment this is not a case to which the *Dimes* principle of automatic disqualification applies. The *Gough* test must be applied and the court must ask itself whether 'in the circumstances of the case ... it appears that there was a real likelihood, in the sense of a real possibility, of bias' on the part of the deputy judge: see [1993] A.C. 646, 668, per Lord Goff ... [The Court of Appeal then considered whether the facts gave rise to an appearance—or, using the test which was then applicable and which is discussed later, a 'a real danger'—of bias, and concluded that they did not. The question of waiver was then considered.]

[68] In our judgment, Mrs. Emmanuel and her lawyers had to decide on 28 October what they wanted to do. They could have asked for time to consider the position. They could have asked the deputy judge to recuse himself and order the proceedings to be started again before another judge. They could have told the judge they had no objection to him continuing with the hearing.

In the event they did nothing. In doing nothing they were treating the disclosure as being of no importance. The hearing then continued for a further seven days, judgment was reserved, the Hans House appeal was heard, judgment was reserved, and judgment in both cases was given three and half months later. During all this period Mrs. Emmanuel and her lawyers did nothing about the disclosure that had been made on 28 October. They only sprang into action and began complaining about bias after learning from the deputy judge's judgment that Mrs. Emmanuel had lost.

[69] Mrs. Emmanuel's application for permission to appeal and draft notice of appeal raise a large number of objections to the 9 March judgment expressed over several pages. We are concerned with none of these objections. They may or may not be well founded. The deputy judge may or may not have been unfair to Mrs. Emmanuel in the way in which he dealt with her evidence and that of her witnesses. These are matters which must be raised with another court on another occasion. We are concerned only with the complaint based upon an appearance of bias allegedly produced by Herbert Smith's involvement in the litigation against Mr. Emmanuel. This involvement was, in its essentials, disclosed on 28 October. It was not open to Mrs. Emmanuel to wait and see how her claims in the Locabail litigation turned out before pursuing her complaint of bias. Miss Williamson protests that on 28 October not enough was disclosed to put Mrs. Emmanuel to her election. We disagree. The essentials of the conflict of interest case that is now relied on were to be found in the press cutting. Mrs. Emmanuel wanted to have the best of both worlds. The law will not allow her to do so.

Permission to appeal refused.

The Court adopted a similar approach to the automatic disqualification rule in *R* v. *Bristol Betting and Gaming Licensing Committee, ex parte O'Callaghan*, which was heard with the *Locabail* case. In *O'Callaghan* the claimant was in dispute with Coral Racing Ltd over the validity of a bet which he placed and which, if valid, would have yielded a pay-out of almost £260,000. The claimant wished to attend a hearing of the Bristol Betting and Gaming Licensing Committee at which the renewal of Coral's permit was to be considered; he was, however, certified as medically unfit to attend and sought an adjournment. The Committee refused the adjournment, and made an award of £5,000 costs against Mr O'Callaghan. Since he was out of time for judicial review, the claimant sought an extension before Dyson J. By the time of the hearing, Coral's permit had been extended to three years; Dyson J concluded, therefore, that the only issue on which judicial review could bite was the lawfulness of the costs order and that, in light of the modest sum involved, an extension of time would not be appropriate. It then became apparent, through an article in *The Sunday Times*, that Dyson J was a director of family investment property companies whose tenants included Coral Racing Ltd. Mr O'Callaghan argued that, if Dyson J had disclosed this connection, he would have objected to his involvement in the case. The Court of Appeal concluded (at [108]) that

[i]t cannot be said that this is a case where the strict principle of automatic disqualification laid down in *Dimes* v. *Proprietors of Grand Junction Canal*, 3 H.L.Cas. 759 and *Reg.* v. *Bow Street Metropolitan Stipendiary Magistrate, Ex parte Pinochet Ugarte (No. 2)* [2000] 1 A.C. 119 applies. Miss Jackson [for Mr O'Callaghan] submitted that if the judicial review proceedings had continued they could have had a significant effect upon Corals and in consequence adversely affected that company's ability to meet its obligations to the Dyson family companies. We do not agree. The judicial review proceedings by the time they came before Dyson J. were only concerned with the issue of £5,000 costs. It would be absurd to suggest that recovery or non-recovery of this sum could affect Corals' ability to pay the rent of its shop in Leeds. It was suggested that the court in

326 • BIAS, IMPARTIALITY, AND INDEPENDENCE

> the judicial review proceedings could grant Mr. O'Callaghan a declaration which would be helpful in his dispute with Corals. However, we cannot see any basis for such a declaration. Once Corals' betting permits had been renewed, the judicial review proceedings could only have relevance with regard to costs. It cannot be said that the judge had anything more than a nominal and indirect interest because of his directorship and shares in the company. Such an interest does not establish a bar to the judge sitting.

It is clear from cases such as *Locabail* and *O'Callaghan* that the automatic disqualification rule, as presently conceived, is subtle enough to ensure that not every financial interest—irrespective of how remote it may be—falls within its scope. Constructing the rule in this way goes some distance towards meeting Olowofoyeku's criticism that it is 'draconian' and 'disproportionate'. However, the more subtly it is constructed, the more the rule comes to resemble a substantive evaluation of the circumstances in which the decision is made. It is clearly possible to manipulate the criterion of directness in order to ensure that only financial interests that are likely to raise a reasonable apprehension of bias fall within the rule's prohibitive scope, but this merely raises the question whether the automatic disqualification rule is necessary, given that it would appear that the underlying policy is simply to address situations which give rise to a reasonable apprehension of bias—a matter which is already covered by the fair-minded observer rule, which we discuss at 9.3. This is not to suggest that the presence of a financial interest is insignificant. It is, as a matter of fact, something which is very likely to give rise to an appearance of bias. The key point, however, is that disqualification in the face of financial interests is not an end in itself, but simply a manifestation of the wider underlying principle that judicial and administrative decision-making must not give rise to the perception of bias. It is arguable, therefore, that a single rule, based on disqualification in the face of apprehended bias, is perfectly capable of dealing with the whole range of situations which are of concern in this context—and that a single rule would better capture and reflect the policy of the law in this area.

QUESTIONS

- Do you agree?
- Should the special category of automatic disqualification remain?

9.2.4 Beyond financial interests: *Pinochet*

The scope of the automatic disqualification principle was clarified—in a rather surprising way—by the House of Lords in the following case.

R v. Bow Street Metropolitan Stipendiary Magistrate, ex parte Pinochet Ugarte (No 2) [2000] 1 AC 119
House of Lords

Senator Augusto Pinochet was arrested in the United Kingdom under warrants issued under s 8(1) of the Extradition Act 1989, following the issue of warrants by a Spanish court in respect of crimes against humanity which the senator was alleged to have committed, mainly in Chile. The claimant challenged the validity of the warrants, arguing that, as a former head of state, he was immune from arrest and extradition proceedings in respect of his conduct while in office. The Divisional Court accepted this argument, although the quashing of one of the warrants was stayed pending an appeal to the House of Lords by the prosecuting authorities. The appeal was successful, by a majority of three to two. In the hearing before the House of Lords, Amnesty International (AI)—a charitable organization which campaigns for respect for human rights—was granted permission to intervene, and was represented by counsel at the hearing. After the House of Lords had announced its decision, it came to light that Lord Hoffmann—one of the judges in the majority—was a director of Amnesty International Charity Ltd (AICL), a charity which was intimately related to, and undertook work on behalf of, AI in the United Kingdom. In light of this the claimant took the extraordinary step of petitioning the House of Lords to set aside its previous decision. The application was heard by a panel of five current and retired Law Lords sitting as an Appeal Committee. Lord Browne-Wilkinson, with whom the other four judges agreed, stated (at 132) that the House of Lords, 'as the ultimate court of appeal, [must] have power to correct any injustice caused by an earlier order of this House'. Having established this novel jurisdiction, Lord Browne-Wilkinson went on to consider whether its exercise would be appropriate.

Lord Browne-Wilkinson

… Senator Pinochet does not allege that Lord Hoffmann was in fact biased. The contention is that there was a real danger or reasonable apprehension or suspicion that Lord Hoffmann might have been biased, that is to say, it is alleged that there is an appearance of bias not actual bias.

The fundamental principle is that a man may not be a judge in his own cause. This principle, as developed by the courts, has two very similar but not identical implications. First it may be applied literally: if a judge is in fact a party to the litigation or has a financial or proprietary interest in its outcome then he is indeed sitting as a judge in his own cause. In that case, the mere fact that he is a party to the action or has a financial or proprietary interest in its outcome is sufficient to cause his automatic disqualification. The second application of the principle is where a judge is not a party to the suit and does not have a financial interest in its outcome, but in some other way his conduct or behaviour may give rise to a suspicion that he is not impartial, for example because of his friendship with a party. This second type of case is not strictly speaking an application of the principle that a man must not be judge in his own cause, since the judge will not normally be himself benefiting, but providing a benefit for another by failing to be impartial.

In my judgment, this case falls within the first category of case, *viz* where the judge is disqualified because he is a judge in his own cause. In such a case, once it is shown that the judge is himself a party to the cause, or has a relevant interest in its subject matter, he is disqualified without any investigation into whether there was a likelihood or suspicion of bias. The mere fact of his interest is sufficient to disqualify him unless he has made sufficient disclosure … I will call this 'automatic disqualification'.

In *Dimes v. Proprietors of Grand Junction Canal* (1852) 3 H.L.Cas 759, the then Lord Chancellor, Lord Cottenham, owned a substantial shareholding in the defendant canal which was an incorporated body. In the action the Lord Chancellor sat on appeal from the Vice-Chancellor, whose judgment in favour of the company he affirmed. There was an appeal to your Lordships' House on the grounds that the Lord Chancellor was disqualified. Their Lordships consulted the judges who advised, at p 786, that Lord Cottenham was disqualified from sitting as a judge in the cause because he had an interest in the suit. This advice was unanimously accepted by their Lordships. There was no inquiry by the court as to whether a reasonable man would consider Lord Cottenham to be biased and no inquiry as to the circumstances which led to Lord Cottenham sitting. Lord Campbell said, at p 793:

'No one can suppose that Lord Cottenham could be, in the remotest degree, influenced by the interest he had in this concern; but, my Lords, it is of the last importance that the maxim that no man is to be a judge in his own cause should be held sacred. And that is not to be confined to a cause *in which he is a party*, but applies to a cause in which he has an interest.' (Emphasis added.)

On occasion, this proposition is elided so as to omit all references to the disqualification of a judge who is a party to the suit: see, for example, *R v. Rand* (1866) L.R. 1 Q.B. 230; *R v. Gough* [1993] A.C. 646, 661. This does not mean that a judge who is a party to a suit is not disqualified just because the suit does not involve a financial interest. The authorities cited in the *Dimes* case show how the principle developed. The starting-point was the case in which a judge was indeed purporting to decide a case in which he was a party. This was held to be absolutely prohibited. That absolute prohibition was then extended to cases where, although not nominally a party, the judge had an interest in the outcome.

The importance of this point in the present case is this. Neither A.I., nor A.I.C.L., have any financial interest in the outcome of this litigation. We are here confronted, as was Lord Hoffmann, with a novel situation where the outcome of the litigation did not lead to financial benefit to anyone. The interest of A.I. in the litigation was not financial; it was its interest in achieving the trial and possible conviction of Senator Pinochet for crimes against humanity.

By seeking to intervene in this appeal and being allowed so to intervene, in practice A.I. became a party to the appeal. Therefore if, in the circumstances, it is right to treat Lord Hoffmann as being the alter ego of A.I. and therefore a judge in his own cause, then he must have been automatically disqualified on the grounds that he was a party to the appeal. Alternatively, even if it be not right to say that Lord Hoffmann was a party to the appeal as such, the question then arises whether, in non financial litigation, anything other than a financial or proprietary interest in the outcome is sufficient automatically to disqualify a man from sitting as judge in the cause.

Are the facts such as to require Lord Hoffmann to be treated as being himself a party to this appeal? The facts are striking and unusual. One of the parties to the appeal is an unincorporated association, A.I. One of the constituent parts of that unincorporated association is A.I.C.L. A.I.C.L. was established, for tax purposes, to carry out part of the functions of A.I.—those parts which were charitable—which had previously been carried on either by A.I. itself or by A.I.L. [Amnesty International Ltd, another related registered charity]. Lord Hoffmann is a director and chairman of A.I.C.L., which is wholly controlled by A.I., since its members (who ultimately control it) are all the members of the international executive committee of A.I. A large part of the work of A.I. is, as a matter of strict law, carried on by A.I.C.L. which instructs A.I.L. to do the work on its behalf. In reality, A.I., A.I.C.L. and A.I.L. are a close-knit group carrying on the work of A.I.

However, close as these links are, I do not think it would be right to identify Lord Hoffmann personally as being a party to the appeal. He is closely linked to A.I. but he is not in fact A.I. Although this is an area in which legal technicality is particularly to be avoided, it cannot be ignored that Lord Hoffmann took no part in running A.I. Lord Hoffmann, A.I.C.L. and the executive committee of A.I. are in law separate people.

Then is this a case in which it can be said that Lord Hoffmann had an 'interest' which must lead to his automatic disqualification? Hitherto only pecuniary and proprietary interests have led to automatic disqualification. But, as I have indicated, this litigation is most unusual. It is not civil litigation but criminal litigation. Most unusually, by allowing A.I. to intervene, there is a party to a criminal cause or matter who is neither prosecutor nor accused. That party, A.I., shares with the government of Spain and the C.P.S., not a financial interest but an interest to establish that there is no immunity for ex-heads of state in relation to crimes against humanity. The interest of these parties is to procure Senator Pinochet's extradition and trial a non-pecuniary interest. So far as A.I.C.L. is concerned, clause 3(c) of its memorandum provides that one of its objects is 'to procure the abolition of torture, extra-judicial execution and disappearance.' A.I. has, amongst other objects, the same objects. Although A.I.C.L., as a charity, cannot campaign to change the law, it is concerned by other means to procure the abolition of these crimes against humanity. In my opinion, therefore, A.I.C.L. plainly had a non-pecuniary interest, to establish that Senator Pinochet was not immune.

That being the case, the question is whether in the very unusual circumstances of this case a non-pecuniary interest to achieve a particular result is sufficient to give rise to automatic disqualification and, if so, whether the fact that A.I.C.L. had such an interest necessarily leads to the conclusion that Lord Hoffmann, as a director of A.I.C.L., was automatically disqualified from sitting on the appeal? My Lords, in my judgment, although the cases have all dealt with automatic disqualification on the grounds of pecuniary interest, there is no good reason in principle for so limiting automatic disqualification. The rationale of the whole rule is that a man cannot be a judge in his own cause. In civil litigation the matters in issue will normally have an economic impact; therefore a judge is automatically disqualified if he stands to make a financial gain as a consequence of his own decision of the case. But if, as in the present case, the matter at issue does not relate to money or economic advantage but is concerned with the promotion of the cause, the rationale disqualifying a judge applies just as much if the judge's decision will lead to the promotion of a cause in which the judge is involved together with one of the parties. Thus in my opinion if Lord Hoffmann had been a member of A.I. he would have been automatically disqualified because of his non-pecuniary interest in establishing that Senator Pinochet was not entitled to immunity. Indeed, so much I understood to have been conceded by Mr. Duffy [for AI].

Can it make any difference that, instead of being a direct member of A.I., Lord Hoffmann is a director of A.I.C.L., that is of a company which is wholly controlled by A.I. and is carrying on much of its work? Surely not. The substance of the matter is that A.I., A.I.L. and A.I.C.L. are all various parts of an entity or movement working in different fields towards the same goals. If the absolute impartiality of the judiciary is to be maintained, there must be a rule which automatically disqualifies a judge who is involved, whether personally or as a director of a company, in promoting the same causes in the same organisation as is a party to the suit. There is no room for fine distinctions if Lord Hewart C.J.'s famous dictum is to be observed: it is 'of fundamental importance that justice should not only be done, but should manifestly and undoubtedly be seen to be done:' see *Rex. v. Sussex Justices, Ex parte McCarthy* [1924] 1 K.B. 256, 259.

Since, in my judgment, the relationship between A.I., A.I.C.L. and Lord Hoffmann leads to the automatic disqualification of Lord Hoffmann to sit on the hearing of the appeal, it is unnecessary to consider the other factors which were relied on by Miss Montgomery [for the claimant], viz. the position of Lady Hoffmann as an employee of A.I. and the fact that Lord Hoffmann was involved in the recent appeal for funds for Amnesty. Those factors might have been relevant if Senator Pinochet had been required to show a real danger or reasonable suspicion of bias. But since the disqualification is automatic and does not depend in any way on an implication of bias, it is unnecessary to consider these factors. I do, however, wish to make it clear (if I have not already done so) that my decision is not that Lord Hoffmann has been guilty of bias of any kind: he was disqualified as a matter of law automatically by reason of his directorship of A.I.C.L., a company controlled by a party, A.I. ...

It is important not to overstate what is being decided. It was suggested in argument that a decision setting aside the order of 25 November 1998 would lead to a position where judges would be unable to sit on cases involving charities in whose work they are involved. It is suggested that, because of such involvement, a judge would be disqualified. That is not correct. The facts of this present case are exceptional. The critical elements are (1) that A.I. was a party to the appeal; (2) that A.I. was joined in order to argue for a particular result; (3) the judge was a director of a charity closely allied to A.I. and sharing, in this respect, A.I.'s objects. Only in cases where a judge is taking an active role as trustee or director of a charity which is closely allied to and acting with a party to the litigation should a judge normally be concerned either to recuse himself or disclose the position to the parties. However, there may well be other exceptional cases in which the judge would be well advised to disclose a possible interest.

Their Lordships were unanimous that the petition should be granted, and the earlier decision of the House of Lords was therefore set aside. A panel of seven Law Lords, none of whom had been involved in the original appeal, was convened to reconsider the case. It concluded (by a majority of six to one) that, in respect of a small number of the charges laid against him, Senator Pinochet was not immune from extradition. The Home Secretary subsequently decided that Senator Pinochet should be extradited to Spain. Later, however, the Home Secretary concluded that Senator Pinochet was medically unfit to be tried; he therefore returned to Chile.

Lord Browne-Wilkinson was at pains, in his speech, to emphasize that—in two senses— the application of the automatic disqualification principle to the circumstances of *Pinochet* was less radical than might initially appear. First, he stated that the principle, properly understood, applies (and, in theory, has always applied) to all cases in which the judge is a party, or may be treated as if a party because he has an interest—financial, proprietary, *or otherwise*—in the outcome. Second, Lord Browne-Wilkinson was anxious to point out that the automatic disqualification principle would, in the absence of a financial interest, oper- ate only in the event of a rare concatenation of circumstances, such as that which arose in *Pinochet* itself. Thus, in *Helow* v. *Secretary of State for the Home Department* [2008] UKHL 62, [2008] 1 WLR 2416, there was no question of the *Pinochet* principle applying to a judge who was a member of an organization which had expressed views arguably relevant to the case where the organization was not involved in the proceedings and where the judge had not actively associated herself with the views in question.

One difficulty with *Pinochet* is that it may compromise the efficiency of the automatic disqualification rule. The rule is intended to permit the matter of disqualification to be dealt with straightforwardly, because it is triggered by particular kinds of interest—*viz* those which are financial and proprietary. We have already seen that this hard-edged approach is blunted by the courts' (understandable) willingness to examine the directness of a financial interest. But *Pinochet* further complicates matters by recognizing a new category of non- financial interests which are capable of activating the rule. This adds weight to the argu- ment, advanced earlier, that the more context-sensitive the automatic disqualification rule, the more blurred the distinction between that rule and the apprehended bias rule becomes. This, in turn, further calls into question the need for the former.

That said, the extent of such concerns must turn upon the extent of the circumstances capable, in the first place, of triggering the *Pinochet* limb of the automatic disqualification rule. In *R (Northamptonshire District Council)* v. *Secretary of State for Communities and Local Government* [2012] EWHC 4377 (Admin), Underhill J took *Pinochet* to have given rise to 'an absolute rule that a judge who is a member of an association which is a party is [automatically] disqualified, however inactive his or her role may be'. The position is more complex, however, where—as in *Pinochet* itself—the decision-maker has a relationship with a party that falls short of membership. Lord Browne-Wilkinson indicated in *Pinochet* that, in such circumstances, the automatic disqualification rule was triggered because of a combination on Lord Hoffmann's part of a close relationship with a party and a strong interest in the matters to which the case related. In contrast, Lord Hutton ([2000] 1 AC 119 at 145) appeared to consider that the rule would operate in *either* of these situations—an approach which would extend the ambit of *Pinochet* well beyond the very unusual circum- stances of that case.

Against the background of that disagreement, subsequent cases have taken a relatively narrow view of *Pinochet*. In *Locabail (UK) Ltd* v. *Bayfield Properties Ltd* [2000] QB 451, the Court of Appeal said (at [14]) that the automatic disqualification rule should be narrowly confined because of its capacity to 'limit the power of the judge and any reviewing court to take account of the facts and circumstances of a particular case' and in the light of its 'potential to cause delay and greatly increased cost'. Subsequently, in *Meerabaux* v. *Attorney General of Belize* [2005] UKPC 12, [2005] 2 AC 513, Lord Hope gave further support to the view that *Pinochet* should not be regarded as having effected a major expansion of the automatic disqualification rule. He said (at [21]) that the decision in *Pinochet* 'appears, in retrospect, to have been a highly technical one' which turned upon an unusual combination of factors—viz Lord Hoffmann's close involvement in an organization that was itself closely related to a party. Lord Hope also observed (at [22]) that one of the 'undercurrents' in *Pinochet* was judicial concern about the then-prevailing formulation of (what is now) the fair-minded observer rule (to which we turn at 9.3). Lord Hope thought it unlikely that the House of Lords in *Pinochet* would have found it necessary to invoke the automatic disqualification rule in the absence of such concerns.

QUESTION

- Was the House of Lords right, in *Pinochet*, to extend the scope of the automatic disqualification rule?

9.3 The apprehension of bias

9.3.1 Introduction

The Court of Appeal commented in *Locabail (UK) Ltd* v. *Bayfield Properties Ltd* [2000] QB 451 at [16] that

> [i]n practice, the most effective guarantee of the fundamental right [to a fair hearing by an impartial tribunal] ... is afforded not ... by the rules which provide for disqualification on grounds of actual bias, nor by those which provide for automatic disqualification, because automatic disqualification on grounds of personal interest is extremely rare and judges routinely take care to disqualify themselves, in advance of any hearing, in any case where a personal interest could be thought to arise. The most effective protection of the right is in practice afforded by a rule which provides for the disqualification of a judge, and the setting aside of a decision, if on examination of all the relevant circumstances the court concludes that there was a real danger (or possibility) of bias.

Disqualification on the basis of an apprehension of bias is thus distinct from the automatic disqualification principle, because the former, in contrast to the latter, requires a judgment to be made about how the particular factual situation in question is likely to be perceived. Disqualification is therefore not, on this basis, automatic—there is no inevitable presumption of bias; rather, disqualification follows only if the facts give rise to a sufficient apprehension or perception of bias.

However, for some time, the courts struggled to adopt a consistent position on the matter of what amounts to a sufficient perception of bias. Semantic inconsistency—for instance, it was unclear whether the test to be applied related to a 'reasonable suspicion' or a 'real likelihood' of bias—reflected disagreement about deeper issues. Through whose eyes—the court's or a reasonable person's—must the likelihood of bias be assessed? If the latter, how much knowledge of the circumstances should be imputed to the reasonable person? And what degree of likelihood is required—probability or mere possibility? In *R v. Gough* [1993] AC 646, the House of Lords attempted to lay the confusion to rest. After reviewing the authorities, Lord Goff (at 670) said:

> I think it unnecessary, in formulating the appropriate test, to require that the court should look at the matter through the eyes of a reasonable man, because the court in cases such as these personifies the reasonable man; and in any event the court has first to ascertain the relevant circumstances from the available evidence, knowledge of which would not necessarily be available to an observer in court at the relevant time. Finally, for the avoidance of doubt, I prefer to state the test in terms of real danger rather than real likelihood, to ensure that the court is thinking in terms of possibility rather than probability of bias.

However, while *Gough* brought some clarity by establishing that a possibility—as distinct from a probability—of bias is sufficient to trigger disqualification on the present ground, it also sowed confusion. By holding that the matter was to be decided by reference to the court's evaluation of the circumstances, the impression was given—notwithstanding Lord Goff's insistence that the court personifies the reasonable person—that the test was concerned with the possibility of *actual* bias, rather than with how members of the public might perceive the impartiality or otherwise of the decision-maker. This, in turn, gave rise to the view that the law in this area was no longer concerned with Lord Hewart's guiding principle that justice must be seen to be done. Indeed, in *R v. Inner West London Coroner, ex parte Dallaglio* [1994] 4 All ER 139 at 151, Lord Bingham MR (at 161) said that, in the light of *Gough*, 'if despite the appearance of bias the court is able to examine all relevant material and satisfy itself that there was no danger of the alleged bias having in fact caused injustice, the impugned decision will be allowed to stand'. The High Court of Australia thus refused to follow *Gough* in *Webb* v. *The Queen* (1994) 181 CLR 41. Mason CJ and McHugh J were strongly critical of *Gough*, arguing that it was based on

> the assumption that public confidence in the administration of justice will be maintained because the public will accept the conclusions of the judge. But the premise on which the decisions in this Court are based is that public confidence in the administration of justice is more likely to be maintained if the Court adopts a test that reflects the reaction of the ordinary reasonable member of the public to the irregularity in question.

QUESTIONS

- How should public confidence in the integrity of a decision-making process be secured?
- Is it better, as suggested in *Webb*, to align the perspective of the reviewing court with that of the ordinary person, or to rely upon the ordinary person's preparedness to accept the conclusion of the reviewing court?

9.3.2 The fair-minded and informed observer

In the light of the difficulties caused by the *Gough* test, Lord Browne-Wilkinson, in *Pinochet (No 2)* [2000] 1 AC 119 at 136, indicated that the test may need to be reconsidered. The Court of Appeal did precisely that in *Re Medicaments and Related Classes of Goods (No 2)* [2001] 1 WLR 700. The approach that it favoured was endorsed, with limited modification, by the House of Lords in the following case.

Porter v. Magill [2001] UKHL 67, [2002] 2 AC 357
House of Lords

In the mid-1980s Westminster City Council, under the leadership and deputy leadership of (respectively) Shirley Porter and David Weeks, adopted a policy of selling council houses to tenants in marginal wards in the hope that this would encourage them to vote for the Conservative Party. Legal advisors had indicated that an earlier version of the policy, under which *only* houses in marginal wards would have been offered for sale, was unlawful, and so a revised policy was implemented which permitted the sale of a larger number of homes, while still offering for sale those in the marginal wards. Opposition councillors argued that the policy would inhibit the local authority from discharging its obligations as a housing authority, and notified the auditor under s 17 of the Local Government Finance Act 1972. The auditor investigated the matter and certified, under s 20, that a number of councillors and officers, including Porter and Weeks, were guilty of wilful misconduct, by knowingly adopting and implementing a policy which was unlawful (because it deployed the power to sell council homes for an illegitimate, party political purpose). The councillors and officers were therefore liable to make good the loss of £31 million which they had caused to the council. Porter and Weeks unsuccessfully appealed against the auditor's decision to the Divisional Court. On a further appeal, however, the Court of Appeal quashed the auditor's certificates on the ground that the unlawful objectives of Porter, Weeks, and various others could not be said to have caused the losses which later occurred, because the policy had been implemented following approval by the housing committee—an event which, the Court of Appeal concluded, broke the chain of causation between the conduct of Porter, Weeks, and the other individuals concerned, and the losses. The auditor appealed to the House of Lords, which concluded that the losses could be attributed to the conduct of Porter and Weeks. However, Porter and Weeks argued that, irrespective of the causation issue, the auditor's decision could not stand, because it was tainted by apparent bias, caused by a media conference which the auditor had held.

Lord Hope of Craighead

[100] The 'reasonable likelihood' and 'real danger' tests which Lord Goff described in *R v Gough* have been criticised by the High Court of Australia on the ground that they tend to emphasise the court's view of the facts and to place inadequate emphasis on the public perception of the irregular incident: *Webb v The Queen* (1994) 181 CLR 41, 50 per Mason CJ and McHugh J. There is an uneasy tension between these tests and that which was adopted in Scotland by the High Court of Justiciary in *Bradford v McLeod*, 1986 SLT 244. Following Eve J's reference in *Law v Chartered Institute of Patent Agents* [1919] 2 Ch 276 (which was not referred to in *R v Gough*), the High Court of Justiciary adopted a test which looked at the question whether there was suspicion of bias through the eyes of the reasonable man who was aware of the circumstances: see also *Millar v Dickson* 2001 SLT 988, 1002L–1003B. This approach, which has been described as 'the reasonable apprehension of bias' test, is in line with that adopted in most common law

jurisdictions. It is also in line with that which the Strasbourg court has adopted, which looks at the question whether there was a risk of bias objectively in the light of the circumstances which the court has identified: *Piersack* v *Belgium* (1982) 5 EHRR 169, 179–80, paras 30–31; *De Cubber* v *Belgium* (1984) 7 EHRR 236, 246, para 30; *Pullar* v *United Kingdom* (1996) 22 EHRR 391, 402–3, para 30. In *Hauschildt* v *Denmark* (1989) 12 EHRR 266, 279, para 48 the court also observed that, in considering whether there was a legitimate reason to fear that a judge lacks impartiality, the standpoint of the accused is important but not decisive: 'What is decisive is whether this fear can be held objectively justified.'

[101] The English courts have been reluctant, for obvious reasons, to depart from the test which Lord Goff of Chieveley so carefully formulated in *R* v *Gough*. In *R* v *Bow Street Metropolitan Stipendiary Magistrate, Ex p Pinochet Ugarte (No 2)* [2000] 1 AC 119, 136A–C Lord Browne-Wilkinson said that it was unnecessary in that case to determine whether it needed to be reviewed in the light of subsequent decisions in Canada, New Zealand and Australia. I said, at p 142F–G, that, although the tests in Scotland and England were described differently, their application was likely in practice to lead to results that were so similar as to be indistinguishable. The Court of Appeal, having examined the question whether the 'real danger' test might lead to a different result from that which the informed observer would reach on the same facts, concluded in *Locabail (UK) Ltd* v *Bayfield Properties Ltd* [2000] QB 451, 477 that in the overwhelming majority of cases the application of the two tests would lead to the same outcome.

[102] In my opinion however it is now possible to set this debate to rest. The Court of Appeal took the opportunity in *In re Medicaments and Related Classes of Goods (No 2)* [2001] 1 WLR 700 to reconsider the whole question. Lord Phillips of Worth Matravers MR, giving the judgment of the court, observed, at p 711A–B, that the precise test to be applied when determining whether a decision should be set aside on account of bias had given rise to difficulty, reflected in judicial decisions that had appeared in conflict, and that the attempt to resolve that conflict in *R* v *Gough* had not commanded universal approval. At p 711B–C he said that, as the alternative test had been thought to be more closely in line with Strasbourg jurisprudence which since 2 October 2000 the English courts were required to take into account, the occasion should now be taken to review *R* v *Gough* to see whether the test it lays down is, indeed, in conflict with Strasbourg jurisprudence. Having conducted that review he summarised the court's conclusions, at pp 726H–727C:

> '85 When the Strasbourg jurisprudence is taken into account, we believe that a modest adjustment of the test in *R* v *Gough* is called for, which makes it plain that it is, in effect, no different from the test applied in most of the Commonwealth and in Scotland. The court must first ascertain all the circumstances which have a bearing on the suggestion that the judge was biased. It must then ask whether those circumstances would lead a fair-minded and informed observer to conclude that there was a real possibility, or a real danger, the two being the same, that the tribunal was biased.'

[103] I respectfully suggest that your Lordships should now approve the modest adjustment of the test in *R* v *Gough* set out in that paragraph. It expresses in clear and simple language a test which is in harmony with the objective test which the Strasbourg court applies when it is considering whether the circumstances give rise to a reasonable apprehension of bias. It removes any possible conflict with the test which is now applied in most Commonwealth countries and in Scotland. I would however delete from it the reference to 'a real danger'. Those words no longer serve a useful purpose here, and they are not used in the jurisprudence of the Strasbourg court. The question is whether the fair-minded and informed observer, having considered the facts, would conclude that there was a real possibility that the tribunal was biased.

[104] Turning to the facts, there are two points that need to be made at the outset. The first relates to the auditor's own assertion that he was not biased. The Divisional Court said, at p 174A–B, that it had had particular regard to his reasons for declining to recuse himself in reaching its

conclusion that he had an open mind and was justified in continuing with the subsequent hearings. I would agree that the reasons that he gave were relevant, but an examination of them shows that they consisted largely of assertions that he was unbiased. Looking at the matter from the standpoint of the fair-minded and informed observer, protestations of that kind are unlikely to be helpful. I think that Schiemann LJ adopted the right approach in the Court of Appeal when he said that he would give no weight to the auditor's reasons: [2000] 2 WLR 1420, 1457H. The second point relates to the emphasis which the respondents place on how the auditor's conduct appeared from the standpoint of the complainer. There is, as I have said, some support in the jurisprudence of the Strasbourg court for the proposition that the standpoint of the complainer is important. But in *Hauschildt v Denmark* (1989) 12 EHRR 266, 279, para 48 the court emphasised that what is decisive is whether any fears expressed by the complainer are objectively justified. The complainer's fears are clearly relevant at the initial stage when the court has to decide whether the complaint is one that should be investigated. But they lose their importance once the stage is reached of looking at the matter objectively.

[105] I think that it is plain, as the Divisional Court observed, at p 174B, that the auditor made an error of judgment when he decided to make his statement in public at a press conference. The main impression which this would have conveyed to the fair-minded observer was that the purpose of this exercise was to attract publicity to himself, and perhaps also to his firm. It was an exercise in self-promotion in which he should not have indulged. But it is quite another matter to conclude from this that there was a real possibility that he was biased. Schiemann LJ said, at p 1457D–E, that there was room for a casual observer to form the view after the press conference that the auditor might be biased. Nevertheless he concluded, at p 1457H, having examined the facts more closely, that there was no real danger that this was so. I would take the same view. The question is what the fair-minded and informed observer would have thought, and whether his conclusion would have been that there was real possibility of bias. The auditor's conduct must be seen in the context of the investigation which he was carrying out, which had generated a great deal of public interest. A statement as to his progress would not have been inappropriate. His error was to make it at a press conference. This created the risk of unfair reporting, but there was nothing in the words he used to indicate that there was a real possibility that he was biased. He was at pains to point out to the press that his findings were provisional. There is no reason to doubt his word on this point, as his subsequent conduct demonstrates. I would hold, looking at the matter objectively, that a real possibility that he was biased has not been demonstrated.

Their Lordships unanimously supported Lord Hope's comments on the test for bias, and agreed that the auditor's decision should not be set aside. Their Lordships were also in agreement that the actions of Porter and Weeks had caused the relevant losses. Appeals allowed.

QUESTIONS

- How does the *Porter* v. *Magill* test differ from that advanced in *Gough*?
- Is the former an improvement on the latter?
- Why (not)?

9.3.3 Who is the fair-minded and informed observer?

Porter v. *Magill* placed the ordinary person—in the form of the 'fair-minded and informed observer'—squarely back in the spotlight. In adopting such an approach, the House of Lords conceded that public confidence in the integrity of a decision-making process is best secured by aligning judicial analysis of the matter with the way in which an ordinary person would approach it. However, it is self-evident that the extent of such alignment depends, in the first place, on the notional observer's attributes: if the observer turns out to be the reviewing judge in all but name, then the insertion of the observer between the judge and the facts that fall for examination is likely to serve little if any purpose. The extent to which the fair-minded observer test succeeds in its aim of aligning judicial analysis with public perception thus turns upon questions about the observer that were not specifically answered in *Porter v. Magill*. Such questions have been answered to some extent—but not always consistently—by subsequent cases. Three such questions are particularly worth noting.

First, we know from *Porter v. Magill* that the observer is 'informed'—but *exactly how informed?* In *Medicaments* at [65], Lord Phillips appeared to suggest that the court should have regard only to such information as would be apparent to 'ordinary, reasonably well informed members of the public'. Similarly, in *Gillies v. Secretary of State for Work and Pensions* [2006] UKHL 2, [2006] 1 WLR 781 at [17], Lord Hope said that the observer 'can be assumed to have access to all the facts that are capable of being known by members of the public generally'. However, in some cases, this has been taken to mean that the observer may take steps to equip himself with knowledge that can be *obtained* by members of the public, albeit that the information in question might not normally be *possessed* by such people. As Stanley Burnton LJ put it in *Virdi v. Law Society of England and Wales* [2010] EWCA Civ 100, [2010] 3 All ER 653 at [39], '[a] fair-minded person would not reach a conclusion that a tribunal was biased or appeared to be so, without seeking to obtain the full facts and any explanation put forward by the tribunal'.

In a number of cases, the courts have been prepared to impute to the observer a surprising degree of knowledge that significantly exceeds what the average person is likely to know. For instance, in *Taylor v. Lawrence* [2002] EWCA Civ 90, [2003] QB 528, it transpired that the night before giving judgment in a boundary dispute case, the judge had had his will amended free of charge by the firm of solicitors representing the claimant. Giving the judgment of the Court of Appeal, Lord Woolf CJ said (at [72]) that it was 'unthinkable' that the fair-minded and informed observer would perceive a real possibility of bias in such circumstances. This was so not least because, said Lord Woolf CJ (at [61]), the observer 'can be expected to be aware of the legal traditions and culture of this jurisdiction', including

> the practice of judges and advocates lunching and dining together at the Inns of Court; the Master of the Rolls's involvement in the activities of the Law Society; the fact that it is commonplace, particularly in specialist areas of litigation and on the circuits, for the practitioners to practise together in a small number of chambers and in a small number of firms of solicitors, and for members of the judiciary to be recruited from those chambers and firms.

The majority in *Belize Bank Ltd v. Attorney General of Belize* [2011] UKPC 36 demonstrated a comparable propensity to ascribe technical knowledge to the observer. The case arose against the background of a dispute concerning US$10m which had been transferred from Venezuela to Belize. The Belizean government was concerned that its predecessor had used the money for purposes other than those for which it had been transferred to Belize. The new Prime Minister was quoted as saying that his government would 'continue to pursue justice on behalf of the Belizean people and will leave no stones unturned to bring to account those who have robbed the people of this country'. The Central Bank of Belize then issued a directive requiring the money to be transferred from the appellant bank to the government. The appellant bank appealed. This triggered the establishment of a statutory appeal board chaired by a judge appointed by the Chief Justice and two other members appointed by the Minister for Finance (which office was held by the Prime Minister). All members of the board had to swear an oath undertaking to act impartially, and any majority had to include the judicial chairman. The appellant challenged the lawfulness of the Prime Minister's involvement in the making of the appointments, given his strong statements about the substantive issue.

Lord Kerr, in the majority, was mindful (at [39]) of the need to ensure 'that the objectivity of the notional observer should not be compromised by being drawn too deeply into a familiarity with the procedures, if that would make him or her too ready to overlook an appearance of bias'. However, he endorsed the view advanced by Lord Bingham in *Prince Jefri* v. *The State of Brunei* [2007] UKPC 62 at [16] that the observer 'does not come to the matter as a stranger or complete outsider; he must be taken to have a reasonable working grasp of how things are usually done'. In the light of this, Lord Kerr concluded that the observer would not perceive a real possibility of bias in the circumstances that had arisen in the *Belize* case:

> [40] ... [I]t would be necessary for the informed observer to be aware of the general structure of the system of appeal from the Central Bank's directive; to be conscious that this is a procedure under which the minister is statutorily authorised to appoint members of the Board; to have in mind that there is a limited pool of candidates who might fill the position; to be aware that the appointees are required to take the oath of office; and to take into account that the minister's appointees cannot outvote the chairman and that the appointment of the chairman has nothing to do with the minister.
>
> [41] The concept of apparent bias does not rest on impression based on an incomplete picture but on a fair and reasoned judgment formed as a result of composed and considered appraisal of the relevant facts. Moreover, while the judgment to be made is whether an ordinary, well informed member of the public would consider that there was a real possibility of bias, one should not neglect to take into account that a fair-minded assessment would include the knowledge that those performing the important task of serving on the Appeal Board are themselves professional people against whom no criticism has been levelled.

In contrast, Lord Brown (dissenting) cautioned against the attribution to the observer of such extensive, technical knowledge, and (at [99]) endorsed the following remarks made by Lord Rodger in his 2010 Sultan Azlan Shah Law Lecture:

> The whole point of inventing this fictional character [i.e. the fair-minded and informed observer] is that he or she does not share the viewpoint of a judge. Yet, in the end, it is a judge or judges who decide what the observer would think about any given situation. Moreover, the informed observer is supposed to know quite a lot about judges—about their training, about their professional experience, about their social interaction with other members of the legal profession, about the judicial oath and its significance for them etc. Endowing the informed observer with these pieces of knowledge is designed to ensure that any supposed appearance of bias is assessed on the basis of a proper appreciation of how judges and tribunals actually operate. The risk is that, if this process is taken too far, ... the judge will be holding up a mirror to himself. To put the matter another way, the same process will tend to distance the notional observer from the ordinary man in the street who does not know these things. And yet the whole point of the exercise is to ensure that judges do not sit if to do so would risk bringing the legal system into disrepute with ordinary members of the public.

Other examples of the courts' liberality when it comes to imputing knowledge to the observer are furnished by *R (Royal Brompton and Harefield NHS Foundation Trust)* v. *Joint*

Committee of Primary Care Trusts [2012] EWCA Civ 472 and *Turner* v. *Secretary of State for Communities and Local Government* [2015] EWCA Civ 582.

The second noteworthy matter concerning the fair-minded and informed observer test concerns *the notional observer's attitude*. A particularly trusting person would be far less likely than an especially cynical one to perceive a real possibility of bias: so how suspicious is the notional observer? This point was considered by Lord Steyn in *Lawal* v. *Northern Spirit Ltd* [2003] UKHL 35, [2004] 1 All ER 187 at [14]:

> It is unnecessary to delve into the characteristics to be attributed to the fair-minded and informed observer. What can confidently be said is that one is entitled to conclude that such an observer will adopt a balanced approach. This idea was succinctly expressed in *Johnson* v *Johnson* (2000) 201 CLR 488, 509, para 53, by Kirby J when he stated that 'a reasonable member of the public is neither complacent nor unduly sensitive or suspicious'.

Stated in the abstract, this guidance is not particularly helpful. The extent of the notional observer's tendency to be suspicious is therefore better ascertained by inference from the way in which the test has been applied within particular factual matrices. It may, for instance, be supposed on the basis of *Taylor* v. *Lawrence* that the fair-minded observer is peculiarly trusting. (Further examples, which may shed additional light on this matter, are given in the following paragraphs.)

Third, it is also important to consider *the observer's powers of reasoning*. In fact, this point relates closely to the second. If, for instance, the fair-minded and informed observer is capable of appreciating the existence and significance of subtle distinctions, he may, in particular circumstances, be less likely to perceive a real possibility of bias. Conversely, if his approach is broad-brush—'no smoke without fire!'—then there is a greater likelihood of a perception of bias. Cases like *Gillies* v. *Secretary of State for Work and Pensions* [2006] UKHL 2, [2006] 1 WLR 781, in which the alleged perception of bias emanates from the fact that someone has two potentially conflicting roles, exemplify this point. In *Gillies*, a doctor had for several years acted as an 'examining medical practitioner' (EMP) on behalf of the (now defunct) Benefits Agency by reporting on the medical circumstances of individuals claiming disability and incapacity benefits. The doctor also sat (albeit not in cases in which she had written reports) as the medically-qualified member of the appeal tribunal, the function of which was to determine disputes between benefit claimants and the Agency. The claimant—who had lost a tribunal case concerning entitlement to disability benefit, and in which the doctor had sat—alleged that the doctor's dual role gave rise to the appearance of a real possibility of bias, an argument which failed before the House of Lords. Lord Hope said (at [17]) that

> [i]t is to be assumed ... that [the fair-minded and informed observer] is able to distinguish between what is relevant and what is irrelevant, and that he is able when exercising his judgment to decide what weight should be given to the facts that are relevant.

It followed, said Lord Hope (at [18]), that the fair-minded observer would not make the crude assumption that the doctor 'was to be seen as a Benefits Agency doctor or that she was in some other way aligned with the Benefits Agency':

> Her relationship with the Benefits Agency was as an independent expert adviser. Her advice was sought and given because of the skills that she was able to bring to bear on medical issues in the exercise of her professional judgment. A fair-minded observer who had considered the facts

> properly would appreciate that professional detachment and the ability to exercise her own independent judgment on medical issues lay at the heart of her relationship with the Benefits Agency. He would also appreciate that she was just as capable of exercising those qualities when sitting as the medical member of a disability appeal tribunal.

The observer will thus be taken to be capable of factoring into his evaluation the decision-maker's ability to perform a given function without being improperly influenced by other roles that the decision-maker might have. (The drawing of such relatively subtle distinctions might, in turn, be premised—as Arnold J indicated in *Resolution Chemicals Ltd* v. *H Lundbeck A/S* [2013] EWHC 3160 (Pat) at [66]—upon knowledge imputed to the observer of the training received by the decision-maker so as reduce the likelihood of improper matters being taken into account.)

Having concluded that the observer in *Gillies* would be able to appreciate the doctor's capacity to keep her different roles distinct, Lord Hope said (at [20]) that

> [t]he weakness of the argument that [there] was a real possibility is exposed as soon as the task that [the doctor] was performing as an EMP is compared with the task which she was performing on the tribunal. In each of these two roles she was being called upon to exercise an independent professional judgment, drawing upon her medical knowledge and her experience. The fair-minded observer would understand that there is a crucial difference between approaching the issues which the tribunal had to decide with a predisposition in favour of the views of the EMP, and drawing upon her medical knowledge and experience when testing those views against the other evidence. He would appreciate, looking at the matter objectively, that her knowledge and experience could cut both ways as she would be just as well placed to spot weaknesses in these reports as to spot their strengths. He would have no reason to think, in the absence of any other facts indicating the contrary, that she would not apply her medical knowledge and experience in just the same impartial way when she was sitting as a tribunal member as she would when she was acting as an EMP.

It does not, however, inevitably follow that no real possibility of bias will be perceived in circumstances where the decision-maker has two potentially conflicting roles. For instance, in *R* v. *Secretary of State for the Home Department, ex parte Al-Hasan* [2005] UKHL 13, [2005] 1 WLR 688, a deputy prison governor who had been present when it was decided that all inmates on particular wings should be subjected to intrusive searches was disqualified from later adjudicating in a case in which prisoners challenged the legitimacy of the decision. Lord Brown (at [39]) concluded that 'a fair-minded observer could all too easily think him predisposed to find it lawful. After all, for him to have decided otherwise would have been to acknowledge that the governor ought not to have confirmed the order and that he himself had been wrong to acquiesce in it.'

QUESTIONS

- Was the House of Lords in *Gillies* guilty of ascribing inappropriately sophisticated powers of reasoning to the fair-minded and informed observer?
- Does such an approach risk assimilating the observer to a judge, thereby reinstating by the back door the much-criticized approach which *Gough* was perceived to have introduced?

Some of the cases considered earlier may be thought to give grounds for concern that the courts have failed to characterize the notional observer in terms that are sufficiently distinct from those of reviewing courts, leading to the risk that decisions will be upheld when ordinarily suspicious, averagely informed members of the public would entertain real doubts about the impartiality of the decision-maker—thereby imperilling public confidence in the courts' capacity to hold relevant constitutional actors, including other courts, to account. However, in *Virdi* v. *Law Society of England and Wales* [2010] EWCA Civ 100, [2010] 3 All ER 653 at [38], Stanley Burnton LJ (with whom Lloyd and Jacob LJJ agreed) indicated that the purpose of the fair-minded observer test is not, as might have been thought, to acknowledge that reviewing courts' perceptions may diverge from those of normal people. Rather, the observer is simply

> a construct, a tool, a hypothetical conception posited in order to assist the Court in deciding whether the proceedings in question were and were seen to be fair ... If on examination of all the relevant facts, there was no unfairness or any appearance of unfairness, there is no good reason for the imaginary observer to be used to reach a different conclusion.

It is hard to see, at least on the face of it, how this view can withstand the authority of *Porter* v. *Magill*, given that it endorsed the test laid down in *Medicaments*, which, as we saw at 9.3.2, was formulated on the basis that the previous test laid down in *R* v. *Gough* risked inappropriately conflating the perspectives of the reviewing court and the reasonable person. Indeed, if the view advanced in *Virdi* is accepted, it raises the question what purpose, if any, does and should the observer test serve? None, according to Olowofoyeku [2009] *CLJ* 388 at 406–7:

> Choosing the perspective of a lay person rather than that of the reviewing court might look attractive from the points of view of the avoidance of excessive legalism and of engendering public confidence on a matter in which the public may be suspicious—judges judging judges. However, having seen the kinds of knowledge routinely attributed to the fictitious lay person, it is obvious that the courts are quite unable to resolve convincingly the question of how this matter would appear to a lay person. The best way to ensure that such a fiction becomes reality is to empanel lay juries in bias cases, hence leaving the question of how the matter would appear to a lay person to real lay persons. Unless that is done, then the courts might as well assume the position of the impartial observer. This would not require any significant change to the current principle. It would only involve dispensing with a fictional and theoretical 'middle-man'.

QUESTION

- Olowofoyeku readily acknowledges that he is calling for a return to the *Gough* test. Is he right to do so?

Two further points should briefly be noted. First, where a decision falls to be made by *a multi-member panel*, the fact that the fair-minded and informed observer would perceive a real possibility of bias on the part of one member or some members does not necessarily undermine the lawfulness of the decision of the decision-maker—*ie* the panel—itself. This point was reiterated by Carnwath LJ in *R (Berky)* v. *Newport City Council* [2012] EWCA Civ 378, [2012] 2 CMLR 44 at [30].

Second, the *stage of the decision-making process* that is said to give rise to a perception of bias is relevant to the question whether such a perception makes the decision itself unlawful. For instance, in *R (Royal Brompton and Harefield NHS Foundation Trust)* v. *Joint*

Committee of Primary Care Trusts [2012] EWCA Civ 472, (2012) 126 BMLR 134, it was argued that an advisory process that fed into the decision-making process itself was tainted by an appearance of bias. In holding that the decision need not be set aside, Arden LJ, giving the judgment of the Court of Appeal, said (at [125]) that 'the question has to be whether the observer, knowing the composition and remit of both the advisory body and the deciding body, would perceive a real possibility both of bias in the advice *and of its infecting the decision*' (emphasis added). Arden LJ concluded that any concern the observer might have entertained in the light of the presence of certain individuals on the advisory panel would have been assuaged by the fact that it tendered advice to a distinct and expert decision-making body that was well placed to appreciate and make allowances in respect of any concerns relating to the composition of the advisory body.

9.4 Bias, policy, and politics

The cases considered earlier largely concern the requirement that judges, or others exercising functions similar to those of judges, should be unbiased. To what extent do—and should—the same requirements apply to other decision-makers whose position may be explicitly political? It is helpful, in this context, to distinguish between two types of scenario.

In the first, there is a suspicion that a 'political' decision-maker, such as a Minister or a local councillor, may be influenced by some *improper personal interest* concerning the matter to be decided. For instance, a decision might have to be made about an individual with whom the decision-maker has some sort of association (for example through friendship, family, or business connections). Here, the political context is irrelevant, and there is no good reason for exempting political decision-makers from the same standards as those already considered. This point was recognized by Pill LJ in *R (Lewis)* v. *Redcar and Cleveland Borough Council* [2008] EWCA Civ 746, [2009] 1 WLR 83 at [62]: 'There is no doubt that councillors who have a personal interest, as defined in the authorities, must not participate in council decisions.'

That scenario, however, must be contrasted with a second, in which the allegation is that a political figure is influenced, in the making of a particular decision, by '*political*' *considerations that are unconnected with his personal circumstances*. For example, it might be argued that a particular councillor or Minister is tainted by apparent bias because he is called upon to make a decision in a specific case which touches upon general policy matters on which he has already expressed a view in public debate, or on which his party has already made a commitment via its election manifesto. Here, the complaint is not that the decision-maker has a personal interest as such in the outcome, but that he may, to some extent, be wedded to a position with which he has already associated himself, such that when he comes to exercise discretion he may fail to do so with an open mind.

Should cases falling into this category be treated as lying within the scope of the rule against apparent bias? That depends on the nature and purpose of that rule. To an extent, it is simply a particular manifestation of the relevancy doctrine. We know from ch 7 that decision-makers may not lawfully take into account irrelevant considerations. But we also know that a decision can be set aside on relevancy grounds only if the irrelevant consideration actually influenced the decision-maker. In contrast, the rule against bias is more easily invoked: all that need be established is the perception of a real possibility that some prohibited factor entered into play. What demarcates the respective provinces of the relevancy doctrine and the rule against bias is—or at least ought to be—the notion that there exists a particular subset of considerations which, if taken into account, would be so inimical to good administration that, first, there are *no* circumstances (short of statutory authorization) in which they may legitimately be considered and, second, even the suspicion that they have operated should result in the invalidity of the decision.

It is arguable that the sort of 'political' considerations presently under discussion should not be regarded as falling within the subset of factors with which the rule against bias is properly concerned. Properly understood, the objection in cases of this type is not that the decision-maker took into account the matter in question, but that he accorded it so much importance as to crowd out other relevant considerations. In the light of this, it is arguable that such cases should not be analysed by reference to the rule against bias. Consider, for instance, the following remarks of Sedley J in *R v. Secretary of State for the Environment, ex parte Kirkstall Valley Campaign Ltd* [1996] 3 All ER 304 at 235:

In the case of an elected body the law recognises that members will take up office with publicly stated views on a variety of policy issues … [W]here predetermination of issues or forfeiture of judgment is alleged, the court will be concerned to distinguish, within the statutory framework, legitimate prior stances or experience from illegitimate ones. But such issues will be governed by the separate line of authority on predetermination.

This view was endorsed and amplified by Ouseley J in *R (C (A Child)) v. Camden London Borough Council* [2001] EWHC 1116 (Admin) at [254]:

The first question is whether there was a real danger that a councillor's decision would be influenced by a personal interest, or putting it in what may be a slightly different formulation of the test for bias …: would the fair-minded observer, knowing the background, consider that there was a real danger of bias from, in this context, a personal interest held by a councillor? There is an important distinction between bias from a personal interest and a predisposition, short of predetermination, arising say from prior consideration of the issues or some aspect of a proposal. The decision-making structure, the nature of the functions and the democratic political accountability of Councillors permit, indeed must recognise, the legitimate potential for predisposition towards a particular decision. The source of the potential bias has to be a personal interest for it to be potentially objectionable in law.

However, this view—which treats predetermination as a separate matter from bias, such that the mere appearance of predetermination is insufficient—has not been fully endorsed in more recent cases. Take, for instance, *R (Island Farm Development Ltd) v. Bridgend County Borough Council* [2006] EWHC 2189 (Admin). A local election disrupted negotiations between a company and a council over the purchase by the former of a piece of land owned by the latter. After the election, the new council refused to sell the land. The company unsuccessfully argued that the decision was tainted by apparent bias: some of the councillors had fought the election arguing the land should not be sold, and some had helped local action groups campaigning against the sale of the land. Collins J said:

[30] … Councillors will inevitably be bound to have views on and may well have expressed them about issues of public interest locally. Such may, as here, have been raised as election issues. It would be quite impossible for decisions to be made by the elected members whom the law

requires to make them if their observations could disqualify them because it might appear that they had formed a view in advance ...

[31] ... Councillors must ... approach their decision-making with an open mind in the sense that they must have regard to all material considerations and be prepared to change their views if persuaded that they should.

Collins J adopted the approach outlined here in that he based his decision on the distinction between legitimate predisposition and illegitimate predetermination. However, he went on to incorporate this distinction within the standard bias test, holding that the fair-minded observer would have recognized that the councillors had not gone beyond legitimate pre-disposition. Other cases have adopted the same approach. For instance, in *R (Georgiou)* v. *Enfield London Borough Council* [2004] EWHC 779 (Admin), it was held that members of a planning committee were tainted by apparent bias due to their participation in the work of another committee which had considered the application in question. Richards J, noting that predetermination had been alleged in *Porter* v. *Magill* itself, said at [31] that

in considering the question of apparent bias in accordance with the test in *Porter v Magill*, it is necessary to look beyond pecuniary or personal interests and to consider in addition whether, from the point of view of the fair-minded and informed observer, there was a real possibility that the planning committee or some of its members were biased in the sense of approaching the decision with a closed mind and without impartial consideration of all relevant planning issues.

The dominant view therefore appears to be that if a fair-minded and informed observer perceives a real risk of predetermination, this should be sufficient to make the decision-maker's involvement unlawful. However, the rule against bias, properly understood, is concerned with influences upon the decision-making process which are peculiarly toxic, such that they must not even be permitted to be *seen* to operate. On that view, is it arguably inappropriate to treat predetermination as a form of bias which attracts the application of the fair-minded observer test.

Finally, the position is statutorily modified by s 25 of the Localism Act 2011. It provides:

(1) Subsection (2) applies if—

    (a) as a result of an allegation of bias or predetermination, or otherwise, there is an issue about the validity of a decision of a relevant authority, and

    (b) it is relevant to that issue whether the decision-maker, or any of the decision-makers, had or appeared to have had a closed mind (to any extent) when making the decision.

(2) A decision-maker is not to be taken to have had, or to have appeared to have had, a closed mind when making the decision just because—

    (a) the decision-maker had previously done anything that directly or indirectly indicated what view the decision-maker took, or would or might take, in relation to a matter, and

    (b) the matter was relevant to the decision.

This provision is unlikely to make much difference, since it merely confirms something that is already consistent with the common law position: that a disqualifying perception of bias will not arise simply because the decision-maker has previously indicated his view on a relevant matter. A decision-maker could still be disqualified, however, if he were to go further than doing the kinds of things mentioned in s 25, by, for example, doing something that would be suggestive of an unwillingness to consider arguments in tension with his own previously expressed view. The upshot is that s 25 does little more than tell us that certain things that would not anyway disqualify a decision-maker should not disqualify him.

QUESTIONS

- If the rule against bias was, as suggested above (and by Ouseley J in the *Camden* case mentioned earlier), confined to cases involving personal interests, would there be any scope for its operating in predetermination cases?
- What if, for instance, a councillor staked his reputation on doing something: could it be argued that the rule against bias would be triggered by virtue of the appearance of a personal interest on the councillor's part in protecting his reputation by sticking to his original view?

The foregoing must be read in light of the fact that, as is apparent from the excerpts from the *Alconbury* case at 9.5.1 and 9.5.3, the determination of some planning matters is now (by operation of the Human Rights Act 1998 (HRA)) covered by Article 6 ECHR. When Article 6 applies, further questions arise about the involvement of 'political' decision-makers; these are addressed by Lord Hoffmann in the extract at 9.5.1.

9.5 Article 6

9.5.1 Introduction: Article 6 in an administrative context

Issues of procedural fairness now fall for consideration under Article 6 of the European Convention on Human Rights—which is made effective in domestic law by the HRA—as well as at common law. Article 6(1) provides:

> In the determination of his civil rights and obligations or of any criminal charge against him, everyone is entitled to a fair and public hearing within a reasonable time by an independent and impartial tribunal established by law. Judgment shall be pronounced publicly but the press and public may be excluded from all or part of the trial in the interest of morals, public order or national security in a democratic society, where the interests of juveniles or the protection of the private life of the parties so require, or to the extent strictly necessary in the opinion of the court in special circumstances where publicity would prejudice the interests of justice.

Our concerns in this chapter are with the circumstances in which Article 6(1) applies and what the requirement of an 'independent and impartial tribunal' amounts to. We consider other aspects of Article 6 in chs 10 and 11.

Article 6(1) was originally intended to regulate the conduct only of criminal courts and civil courts in the determination of private law rights: it was explained in the dissenting opinion in *Feldbrugge* v. *The Netherlands* (1986) 8 EHRR 425 at 444 that this much is apparent from the *travaux préparatoires*. However, although some very early cases excluded public law matters from the scope of Article 6(1), the ECtHR decided in Ringeisen v. Austria (No 1) (1971) 1 EHRR 455 that Article 6(1) does apply to administrative proceedings if they are decisive of civil rights and obligations. Given that the requirement of an 'independent' tribunal means a tribunal that is independent of the government, the extension of Article 6(1) to administrative decision-making creates some obvious difficulties. Such matters weighed heavily upon the House of Lords in the following case.

R (Alconbury Developments Ltd) v. Secretary of State for the Environment, Transport and the Regions [2001] UKHL 23, [2003] 2 AC 295
House of Lords

Alconbury Developments agreed with the Ministry of Defence that, if planning permission were granted, it would develop a disused airfield, owned by the Ministry, into a national distribution centre. Applications were made to the relevant planning authorities, but permissions were not granted; Alconbury therefore appealed. Most such appeals—although formally made to the Secretary of State—are actually determined by a planning inspector. However, under the Town and Country Planning Act 1990, sch 6, para 3(1), the Secretary of State may 'recover' an appeal: the effect of this is that the inspector simply makes a recommendation, while the decision is left to the Secretary of State. Alconbury's appeal was recovered in this way. Two groups representing local interests objected to the recovery of the appeal, contending that the Secretary of State was not an independent and impartial tribunal for Article 6(1) purposes. Alconbury therefore sought judicial review in order to clarify the position. The Divisional Court concluded that the Secretary of State did not comply with Article 6(1), and issued a declaration of incompatibility (under HRA, s 4(2)) in respect of the relevant provisions of the planning legislation. The matter then went on appeal to the House of Lords. This excerpt is concerned only with the difficulties arising from the application of Article 6(1) to administrative decision-making.

Lord Hoffmann

[69] In a democratic country, decisions as to what the general interest requires are made by democratically elected bodies or persons accountable to them. Sometimes the subject matter is such that Parliament can itself lay down general rules for enforcement by the courts. Taxation is a good example: Parliament decides on grounds of general interest what taxation is required and the rules according to which it should be levied. The application of those rules, to determine the liability of a particular person, is then a matter for independent and impartial tribunals such as the general or special commissioners or the courts. On the other hand, sometimes one cannot formulate general rules and the question of what the general interest requires has to be determined on a case by case basis. Town and country planning or road construction, in which every decision is in some respects different, are archetypal examples. In such cases Parliament may delegate the decision-making power to local democratically elected bodies or to Ministers of the Crown responsible to Parliament. In that way the democratic principle is preserved.

[70] There is no conflict between human rights and the democratic principle. Respect for human rights requires that certain basic rights of individuals should not be capable in any circumstances of being overridden by the majority, even if they think that the public interest so requires. Other rights should be capable of being overridden only in very restricted circumstances. These are rights which belong to individuals simply by virtue of their humanity, independently of any utilitarian calculation. The protection of these basic rights from majority decision requires that independent and impartial tribunals should have the power to decide whether legislation infringes them and either (as in the United States) to declare such legislation invalid or (as in the United Kingdom) to declare that it is incompatible with the governing human rights instrument. But outside these basic rights, there are many decisions which have to be made every day (for example, about the allocation of resources) in which the only fair method of decision is by some person or body accountable to the electorate.

[71] All democratic societies recognise that while there are certain basic rights which attach to the ownership of property, they are heavily qualified by considerations of the public interest. This is reflected in the terms of article 1 of Protocol 1 to the Convention ...

[72] ... [U]nder the first paragraph, property may be taken by the state, on payment of compensation, if the public interest so requires. And, under the second paragraph, the use of property may be restricted without compensation on similar grounds. Importantly, the question of what the public interest requires for the purpose of article 1 of the First Protocol can, and in my opinion should, be determined according to the democratic principle—by elected local or central bodies or by Ministers accountable to them. There is no principle of human rights which requires such decisions to be made by independent and impartial tribunals.

[73] There is however another relevant principle which must exist in a democratic society. That is the rule of law. When Ministers or officials make decisions affecting the rights of individuals, they must do so in accordance with the law. The legality of what they do must be subject to review by independent and impartial tribunals. This is reflected in the requirement in article 1 of the First Protocol that a taking of property must be 'subject to the conditions provided for by law'. The principles of judicial review give effect to the rule of law. They ensure that administrative decisions will be taken rationally, in accordance with a fair procedure and within the powers conferred by Parliament. But this is not the occasion upon which to discuss the limits of judicial review. The only issue in this case is whether the Secretary of State is disqualified as a decision maker because he will give effect to policies with which, ex hypothesi, the courts will not interfere ...

[74] My Lords, these basic principles are the background to the interpretation of article 6(1) ... Apart from authority, I would have said that a decision as to what the public interest requires is not a 'determination' of civil rights and obligations. It may affect civil rights and obligations but it is not, and ought not to be, a judicial act such as article 6 has in contemplation. The reason is not simply that it involves the exercise of a discretion, taking many factors into account, which does not give any person affected by the decision the right to any particular outcome. There are many such decisions made by courts (especially in family law) of which the same can be said. Such decisions may nevertheless be determinations of an individual's civil rights (such as access to his child: compare *W v United Kingdom* (1987) 10 EHRR 29) and should be made by independent and impartial tribunals. But a decision as to the public interest (what I shall call for short a 'policy decision') is quite different from a determination of right. The administrator may have a duty, in accordance with the rule of law, to behave fairly ('quasi-judicially') in the decision-making procedure. But the decision itself is not a judicial or quasi-judicial act. It does not involve deciding between the rights or interests of particular persons. It is the exercise of a power delegated by the people as a whole to decide what the public interest requires ...

[76] In principle, therefore, and apart from authority, I would say that article 6(1) conferred the right to an independent and impartial tribunal to decide whether a policy decision by an administrator such as the Secretary of State was lawful but not to a tribunal which could substitute its own view of what the public interest required. However, section 2(1) of the Human Rights Act 1998 requires an English court, in determining a question which has arisen in connection with a Convention right, to take into account the judgments of the European Court of Human Rights ('the European court') and the opinions of the Commission. The House is not bound by the decisions of the European court and, if I thought that the Divisional Court was right to hold that they compelled a conclusion fundamentally at odds with the distribution of powers under the British constitution, I would have considerable doubt as to whether they should be followed. But in my opinion the Divisional Court misunderstood the European jurisprudence. Although the route followed by the European court has been a tortuous one and some of its statements require

interpretation, I hope to demonstrate that it has never attempted to undermine the principle that policy decisions within the limits imposed by the principles of judicial review are a matter for democratically accountable institutions and not for the courts ...

[80] The seminal case [on the scope of Article 6(1)] is *Ringeisen v Austria (No 1)* (1971) 1 EHRR 455. This concerned an Austrian statute which required transfers of agricultural land to be approved by a District Land Transactions Commission with a right of appeal to a Regional Commission. In the absence of approval, the contract of sale was void. The purpose of the law was to keep agricultural land in the hands of farmers of small and medium holdings and the District Commission was required to refuse consent to a transfer which appeared to violate this policy. This was a classic regulatory power exercisable by an administrative body. The court nevertheless held that article 6(1) was applicable to its decision on the ground that it was 'decisive' for the enforceability of the private law contract for the sale of land. Thus a decision on a question of public law by an administrative body could attract article 6(1) by virtue of its effect on private law rights. On the facts, the court held that article 6(1) had been satisfied because the Regional Commission was an independent and impartial tribunal.

[81] The full implications of *Ringeisen* were not examined by the court until some years later. It led in *König v Germany* (1978) 2 EHRR 170 to a sharp disagreement between those members of the court who saw it as a means of enforcing minimum standards of judicial review of administrative and domestic tribunals and those who regarded it as a potential Pandora's box and wanted to confine it as narrowly as possible. Dr König was a surgeon charged with unprofessional conduct before a specialist medical tribunal attached to the Frankfurt Administrative Court. It withdrew his right to practice and run a clinic. He appealed to an administrative Court of Appeal and there followed lengthy and complicated proceedings. His complaint to the European court under article 6(1) was that he had been denied the right to a decision 'within a reasonable time'. But this raised the question of whether, in principle, article 6(1) applied to disciplinary proceedings before an administrative court. By a majority, the court held that it did. On the *Ringeisen* principle, it affected private law rights such as his goodwill and his right to sell his services to members of the public.

[82] Judge Matscher delivered a powerful dissent, saying that it was unwise to try to apply the pure judicial model of article 6(1) to the decisions of administrative or domestic tribunals. They might share some characteristics with courts (eg requirements of fairness) but in other respects they were different. For example, one could not apply the imperative of a public hearing to a professional disciplinary body. A private hearing might be more in the public interest. If article 6(1) was going to be applied to administrative law, it would have to be substantially modified ... [T]he dissent of Judge Matscher in *König's* case 2 EHRR 170 has been vindicated in the sense that the application of article 6 to administrative decisions has required substantial modification of the full judicial model.

QUESTIONS

- Why does Article 6(1) need to be 'substantially modified' if it is to be applied to administrative law?
- What sort of modifications might be appropriate?

We return to this judgment at 9.5.3, where we will see exactly how the 'full judicial model' is modified in the administrative context. However, before considering what Article 6(1) requires in relation to administrative decision-making, we must confront a logically prior question.

9.5.2 When does Article 6(1) apply to administrative decision-making?

When will administrative proceedings be found to be decisive of civil rights and obligations, thus triggering Article 6(1)? The ECtHR held in *König* v. *Federal Republic of Germany* (1978) 2 EHRR 170 at [88] that 'civil rights and obligations' is an autonomous European concept; the test to be applied is therefore substantive in nature, and does not turn upon the classification of the right or obligation as a matter of domestic law. In developing this autonomous concept of civil rights and obligations, the ECtHR and the (now defunct) European Commission of Human Rights have concluded that it does not extend to matters such as immigration (*Uppal* v. *United Kingdom* (1981) 3 EHRR 391), deportation (*Maaouia* v. *France* (2001) 33 EHRR 42), taxation (*Ferrazzini* v. *Italy* (2002) 34 EHRR 45), and detention on remand (*Neumeister* v. *Austria* (1979–80) 1 EHRR 91). In contrast, Article 6(1) has been held to apply to disciplinary proceedings which affect the right to pursue a profession (*König* v. *Federal Republic of Germany* (1978) 2 EHRR 170), expropriation of land (*Sporrong* v. *Sweden* (1983) 5 EHRR 35), and access to children (*W* v. *United Kingdom* (1988) 10 EHRR 29).

At one time, the guiding principle—to the extent that any could be discerned at all—was thought to be whether the private law features of the case were predominant. For instance, in *Feldbrugge* v. *The Netherlands* (1986) 8 EHRR 425 and *Deumeland* v. *Germany* (1986) 8 EHRR 448, both of which concerned entitlement to contribution-based social security benefits, the Court was prepared to hold Article 6(1) applicable. Commenting on these cases in *Runa Begum* v. *Tower Hamlets London Borough Council* [2003] UKHL 5, [2003] 2 AC 430 at [63]–[64], Lord Hoffmann noted that the schemes involved 'had certain affinities with private insurance [since] employees paid contributions', thus leading the ECtHR to the conclusion that 'the features of private law were cumulatively predominant'. However, in *Salesi* v. *Italy* (1993) 26 EHRR 187, the ECtHR extended the reach of Article 6(1) beyond that implied by *Feldbrugge* and *Deumeland* by applying it to a *non-contributory* welfare scheme on the ground that what was at stake was an 'individual, economic right flowing from specific rules laid down in a statute'.

The evident reluctance of the ECtHR to define the scope of Article 6(1) in abstract terms has presented English courts with real difficulties when attempting to determine whether a given matter engages that provision. The two leading domestic cases in which this question has been considered are *Runa Begum* v. *Tower Hamlets London Borough Council* [2003] UKHL 5, [2003] 2 AC 430 and *Ali* v. *Birmingham City Council* [2010] UKSC 8, [2010] 2 WLR 471. Both concerned issues arising under the homelessness provisions of the Housing Act 1996. The scheme of the Act is such that local authorities are required to provide accommodation to certain homeless persons. However, an authority ceases to be under such a duty if, *inter alia*, an applicant declines an offer of accommodation that the authority considers to be suitable, having been warned that, if he does so, the authority will regard itself as having discharged its duty. When disputes arise as to whether an authority has ceased, under these provisions, to owe a duty to an applicant, the applicant can seek an internal review under s 202 by a local authority housing officer, from whose decision there is, under s 204, a right of appeal on a point of law to the County Court. In both *Runa Begum* and *Ali*, the claimants alleged that this scheme for resolving disputes was insufficiently independent for Article 6 purposes. This raised the logically prior question whether Article 6(1) applied in the first place—which depended on whether the Housing Act generated 'civil rights'.

In *Runa Begum*, the House of Lords refused to tackle this question head-on: instead, it assumed that Article 6(1) applied but went on to hold (for reasons considered later) that it had not been breached. However, the nettle was grasped in *Ali*. The particular issue that arose for determination in that case centred upon the local authority's duties under s 193 of the Act, the effect of which was summarized by Lord Collins at [72]:

> Section 193 sets out the duties to persons in priority need, in particular the duty to 'secure that accommodation is available for occupation by the applicant' (section 193(2)). The consequence is that the local authority has to investigate whether applicants are homeless, whether they are in priority need, and whether they are intentionally homeless. It is only in relation to applicants with priority need that the local authority comes under the full duty to secure accommodation. By section 193(5) the local authority ceases to be subject to the duty if the applicant [having been informed of the possible consequences of refusal] refuses an offer of accommodation which the authority is satisfied is suitable.

The claimants asserted that they had not been informed of the possible consequences of refusal; that the authority had therefore failed to discharge its duty towards them; and that this factual dispute was concerned with a 'civil right' arising under the Housing Act such that Article 6(1) applied. The Supreme Court unanimously held that a 'civil right' was not in play. Giving the leading judgment, with which Lady Hale and Lord Brown agreed, Lord Hope drew attention (at [43]) to a number of

> straws in the wind since *Runa Begum* that suggest that a distinction can indeed be made between the class of social security and welfare benefits that are of the kind exemplified by *Salesi* v *Italy* whose substance the domestic law defines precisely and those benefits which are, in their essence, dependent upon the exercise of judgment by the relevant authority. The phrase 'civil rights' is, of course, an autonomous concept: eg *Woonbron Volkshuisvestingsgroep* v *The Netherlands* (2002) 35 EHRR CD161. In that case it was held that decisions about state subsidies to housing associations do not raise issues about civil rights. But the phrase does convey the idea of what, in *Stec* v *United Kingdom* (2005) 41 EHRR SE295, para 50, the Grand Chamber referred to as 'an assertable right'. The court's references in *Loiseau* v *France* application no 46809/99, 18 November 2003 (unreported), para 7, to 'a "private right" which can be said, at least on arguable grounds, to be recognised under domestic law' and to 'an individual right of which the applicant may consider himself the holder' are consistent with this approach. So too are the references in *Mennitto* v *Italy* (2000) 34 EHRR 1122, para 23, to 'a "right" which can be said, at least on arguable grounds, to be recognised under domestic law', where the court added: 'The dispute must be genuine and serious; it may relate not only to the actual existence of a right but also to its scope and the manner of its exercise. The outcome of the proceedings must be directly decisive for the right in question.'

Lord Hope thus reached the conclusion (at [49]) that

> cases where the award of services or benefits in kind is not an individual right of which the applicant can consider himself the holder, but is dependent upon a series of evaluative judgments by the provider as to whether the statutory criteria are satisfied and how the need for it ought to be met, do not engage article 6(1). In my opinion they do not give rise to 'civil rights' within the autonomous meaning that is given to that expression for the purposes of that article. The appellants' right to accommodation under section 193 of the 1996 Act falls into that category.

Although Lord Collins agreed that Article 6(1) did not apply, he placed less weight than Lord Hope upon the evaluative nature of the judgements that had to be made by the decision-maker, and instead emphasized the fact that the dispute turned upon a benefit in kind (*ie* accommodation). Lord Collins therefore concluded that no 'economic right' was at stake, such that *Ali* could be distinguished from *Salesi*.

In emphasizing the extent to which the emergence of the 'right' is contingent upon the exercise of evaluative judgment, Lord Hope was affirming views that had been more tentatively expressed by the Supreme Court in *R (A)* v. *Croydon London Borough Council* [2009] UKSC 8, [2009] 1 WLR 2557. The case was decided on another point, but in obiter comments there was consideration of whether local authorities were caught by Article 6 when deciding, under s 20(1) of the Children Act 1989, whether to provide accommodation to children. Section 20(1) provides that

> [e]very local authority shall provide accommodation for any child in need within their area who appears to them to require accommodation as a result of—(a) there being no person who has parental responsibility for him; (b) his being lost or having been abandoned; or (c) the person who has been caring for him being prevented (whether or not permanently, and for whatever reason) from providing him with suitable accommodation or care.

Lady Hale noted (at [35]) that 'once the qualifying criteria are established, the local authority has no discretion under section 20(1): the accommodation must be provided. The existence of the criteria is a matter of judgment, not discretion.' While this might be thought to point towards the existence of a 'civil right', Lady Hale (at [40]) went on to observe that '[a]ny entitlement under section 20(1) does not depend upon discretion, but it does depend upon an evaluation of some very 'soft' criteria rather than specific rules, and it is difficult to say at what point the applicant may consider himself to be the holder of such a right.' She concluded (at [44]) that she 'would be most reluctant to accept, unless driven by Strasbourg authority to do so, that article 6 requires the judicialisation of claims to welfare services of this kind'.

While it would be going too far to suggest that Strasbourg authority now compels precisely the conclusion that Lady Hale resisted in *Croydon*, the ECtHR's judgment in *Ali* v. *United Kingdom* [2015] HLR 46—the epilogue to *Ali* v. *Birmingham City Council*—does move things in that direction. Although, for reasons considered shortly, the ECtHR agreed with the House of Lords that there was no *breach* of Article 6(1), the Strasbourg court, unlike the House of Lords, held that Article 6(1) *applied*:

> [58] It is now well-established that disputes over entitlement to social security or welfare benefits generally fall within the scope of art.6(1) of the Convention ... However, the present case differs from previous cases concerning welfare assistance, as the assistance to be provided under s.193 of the 1996 Act not only was conditional but could not be precisely defined ... It concerns, as the Government noted, a 'benefit in kind' and the court must therefore consider whether a statutory entitlement to such a benefit may be a 'civil right' for the purposes of art.6(1). ...
>
> [59] It is true that accommodation is a 'benefit in kind' and that both the applicant's entitlement to it and the subsequent implementation in practice of that entitlement by the Council were subject to an exercise of discretion. Nonetheless, the Court is not persuaded that all or any of these factors necessarily militate against recognition of such an entitlement as a 'civil right'. For example, in *Schuler-Zgraggen v Switzerland* (A/263) 24 June 1993, in which the applicant's entitlement to an invalidity pension depended upon a finding that she was at least 66.66% incapacitated, the court accepted that art.6(1) applied. In any case, the 'discretion' in the present case had clearly defined limits: once the initial qualifying conditions under s.193(1) had been met, pursuant to

> s.206(1) the Council was required to secure that accommodation was provided by one of three means, namely by providing accommodation itself; by ensuring that the applicant was provided with accommodation by a third party; or by giving the applicant such advice and assistance to ensure that suitable accommodation was available from a third party.

The differing analyses of the Supreme Court and the ECtHR in *Ali* reflect disagreement about two matters. First, Lord Hope (with whom Lord Brown and Lady Hale agreed) and Lord Kerr placed emphasis upon the discretionary nature of the process whereby the decision-maker had to determine *whether there was an entitlement* to accommodation. The ECtHR, in contrast, was unprepared to give any weight to that consideration. Second, all of the Supreme Court Justices set a degree of store by the fact that *the content of the entitlement* was itself discretionary in the sense that no entitlement to a defined sum of money or any particular property arises when the statutory criteria are met. The ECtHR was less dismissive of this consideration, but implied that the Supreme Court had exaggerated the extent to which the content of the entitlement was discretionary. The upshot is that, on the ECtHR's reasoning, civil rights can be in play even if they are conjured into existence only by a decision-making process that is (to borrow the language of Lord Hoffmann in *Runa Begum* at [67]) 'shot through with discretion'. In *Ali*, Lord Collins pejoratively noted the ECtHR's 'reluctance to enunciate principles which will enable a line to be drawn between those rights in public law which are to be regarded as "civil rights" and those which are not to be so regarded'. The Supreme Court's judgment in *Ali* made a significant contribution to the drawing of such a line; the same cannot be said of the ECtHR's decision. The latter decision may therefore have significant ramifications in domestic law, bearing in mind the reliance placed by lower courts on the Supreme Court's judgments in *Ali* and *Croydon* in order to exclude a broad range of matters from Article 6 but which fall within the scope of that provision according to the ECtHR's *Ali* decision.

QUESTIONS

- How should Lord Collins' line between 'rights in public law which are to be regarded as "civil rights" and those which are not to be so regarded' be drawn?
- To what extent should the degree of discretion to be exercised by the decision-maker be relevant?

Finally, the fact that civil rights or obligations are involved is not sufficient: Article 6(1) only applies to proceedings which are *determinative* of such rights or obligations. It is therefore necessary to distinguish decisions that *concern* civil rights and obligations (to which Article 6(1) will generally not apply) and decisions that *determine* such rights and obligations (to which Article 6(1) will apply). The point can be illustrated by reference to the contractual rights of employees. In *Mattu v. The University Hospitals of Coventry and Warwickshire NHS Trust* [2012] EWCA Civ 641, [2012] IRLR 661, the question was whether Article 6(1) applied to the dismissal by a hospital of a doctor. Elias LJ observed (at [102]) that 'plainly contractual rights are in issue and they are civil rights, as is the right to remain in the employment one currently holds'; however, that did not in itself establish the applicability to the dismissal proceedings of Article 6:

> This cannot be because they do not engage civil rights. It is because at that stage there is no dispute which is being determined. In the employment context that comes later once an

> employer asserts and acts on what he believes to be his contractual rights. If the employer's actions are challenged, a dispute arises and the determination of rights will then be made by a court or employment tribunal, as the case may be, which will be Article 6 compliant.

However, while, for the reason given by Elias LJ, Article 6(1) will not normally apply to dismissal proceedings—and, by analogy, other forms of proceedings that are *concerned with* but not *determinative of* civil rights—the position may be different if such proceedings interact with proceedings that *are* determinative. Take, for instance, *R (G) v. X School Governors* [2011] UKSC 30, [2012] 1 AC 167. Here, the question was whether the claimant teacher was, thanks to Article 6(1), entitled to legal representation in dismissal proceedings taken against him on the ground of an inappropriate relationship with a child. A decision to dismiss by the school would trigger a statutory procedure whereby the Secretary of State would decide whether to place the claimant on a register of persons barred from teaching or working with children. Article 6 uncontroversially applies to proceedings of the latter type (since they involve the well-established civil right to pursue one's profession), but did this mean that the prior dismissal proceedings also had to comply with the relevant Article 6 procedural requirements? The Supreme Court endorsed the following test, articulated by Laws LJ in the Court of Appeal ([2010] EWCA Civ 1, [2010] 2 All ER 555 at [37]):

> [W]here an individual is subject to two or more sets of proceedings (or two or more phases of a single proceeding), and a 'civil right or obligation' enjoyed or owed by him will be determined in one of them, he may (not necessarily will) by force of Article 6 enjoy appropriate procedural rights in relation to any of the others if the outcome of that other will have a substantial influence or effect on the determination of the civil right or obligation. I do not mean any influence or effect which is more than *de minimis*: it must play a major part in the civil right's determination.

Applying this test, Laws LJ concluded (at [47]) that Article 6 applied to the dismissal decision because there was 'every likelihood', in the light of the finding of 'abuse of trust by virtue of sexual misconduct', that the school's disciplinary process would have a 'profound influence on the decision-making procedures relating to the barred list'. The Supreme Court, however, disagreed as to the application (as distinct from the content) of the test. Lord Dyson observed (at [79]) that the body responsible for making the barring decision was 'required to make its own findings of fact and bring its own independent judgment to bear as to their seriousness and significance before deciding whether it is appropriate to place the person on the barred list'. The Supreme Court thus concluded that Article 6 did not apply to the initial disciplinary process conducted by the school. This suggests that the greater opportunities for the subsequent decision-maker to form its own view of the facts and exercise independent judgement, the less likely it is that prior proceedings—that would not otherwise be considered determinative of a civil right—will attract the application of Article 6.

9.5.3 What does Article 6(1) require in the administrative sphere?

Article 6(1) imposes a number of obligations on the administrative decision-makers to which it applies. Some of those relate to the way in which the decision-making process is conducted, and therefore fall for consideration in ch 10. We are presently concerned with

Article 6(1)'s requirements of 'independence' and 'impartiality'. The latter need not detain us, since it aligns closely with the common law requirements concerning bias and the perception of bias and therefore adds little, if anything, to them.

However, the 'independence' limb of Article 6(1) has no clear analogue at common law. Whereas the rule against bias (and the 'impartiality' requirement) focuses on *personal* characteristics of the decision-maker, such as a financial interest in the outcome of the case or a pre-existing relationship with a party, the notion of 'independence' pertains to the *institutional* position of the decision-maker. Article 6(1) appears to call for a 'full judicial model', such that decisions to which it applies must be taken by decision-makers possessing judicial-style independence from the political branches of government. To the extent that Article 6(1) applies to some functions that are typically carried out by the executive and which may involve the making of policy choices, its apparent insistence that they be performed by independent judges rather than accountable decision-makers may be thought to be problematic in democratic terms.

However, such concerns are to an extent allayed by the way in which Article 6(1) has been interpreted by the ECtHR. In *Albert and Le Compte* v. *Belgium* (1983) 5 EHRR 533 at [29], the Court set out two means by which Article 6(1) can be complied with:

> [E]ither the jurisdictional organs [*ie* decision-makers] themselves comply with the requirements of article 6(1), or they do not so comply but are subject to subsequent control by a judicial body that has full jurisdiction and does provide the guarantees of article 6(1).

The second of the two routes to compliance means that a breach of Article 6(1) does not necessarily follow even if the original decision-maker lacks independence. In this way, Article 6(1) permits the making by a non-independent decision-maker of decisions to which it applies provided that the decision-maker is subject to control by a judicial body that is itself independent in the Article 6(1) sense and which 'has full jurisdiction'. This gives rise to what is known as the 'curative principle', the implication being that subsequent judicial oversight cures, or makes up for, the original decision-maker's lack of independence.

The crucial issue then becomes what is meant by 'full jurisdiction'. In particular, the question arises whether the subsequent judicial process must amount to a full appeal on the facts, merits, and law, or whether some other form of scrutiny—such as judicial review— will suffice. In *Ali* v. *United Kingdom* [2015] HLR 46 (the facts of which are given at 9.5.2), the ECtHR—affirming positions adopted in its previous case law—held that in general something less than a full rehearing will be sufficient. In particular, the Court said (at [77]) that in applying the curative principle it is mindful of the fact that

> in administrative-law appeals in the Member States of the Council of Europe it is often the case that the scope of judicial review over the facts of a case is limited and that it is the nature of review proceedings that the reviewing authority reviews the previous proceedings rather than taking factual decisions. It can be derived from the relevant case law that it is not the role of art.6 of the Convention to give access to a level of jurisdiction which can substitute its opinion for that of the administrative authorities. In this regard, particular emphasis has been placed on the respect which must be accorded to decisions taken by the administrative authorities on grounds of 'expediency' and which often involve specialised areas of law.

Holding in *Ali* that the curative principle applied, such that no breach of Article 6(1) was disclosed, the ECtHR noted the range of matters that the County Court, when considering a challenge to a local authority's internal review decision, can consider. (The County Court, in the circumstances that arose in *Ali*, has the power to quash unlawful decisions, much as the Administrative Court can quash unlawful decisions on judicial review.) In particular, the ECtHR (at [83]) placed emphasis upon the fact that although the County Court would not 'conduct a full rehearing of the facts', it was able to

> carry out a certain review of both the facts and the procedure by which the factual findings of the officer were arrived at. In particular, the applicant could—and initially did—argue that in reaching the decision the officer had taken into account irrelevant considerations and/or acted under a fundamental mistake of fact; that the Council had failed to make adequate inquiries to enable it to reach a lawful decision; that the decision was one which no rational Council could have made; that it fettered its discretion; and that it acted in breach of natural justice.

In the circumstances of *Ali*, therefore, judicial review-like oversight was sufficient. This does not, however, mean that the availability of judicial review will *always* offset, under the curative principle, any lack of independence on the part of the original decision-maker. The ECtHR said in *Ali* (at [78]) that it would also consider (*inter alia*)

> the subject-matter of the decision appealed against, in particular, whether or not it concerned a specialised issue requiring professional knowledge or experience and whether it involved the exercise of administrative discretion and if so, to what extent ... and the manner in which that decision was arrived at, in particular, the procedural guarantees available in the proceedings before the adjudicatory body.

So far as the 'subject-matter of the decision' is concerned, the domestic and European case law discloses a distinction between decisions that pertain to matters of policy, and those that centrally concern the finding of facts and the determination of individual cases. For reasons set out in the extract from Lord Hoffmann's speech in *R (Alconbury Developments Ltd) v. Secretary of State for the Environment, Transport and the Regions* [2001] UKHL 23, [2003] 2 AC 295 at 9.5.1, insistence upon judicial-style independence in relation to policy-making functions would raise particularly acute democratic concerns. For precisely that reason, the curative principle is invested with particular potency in such circumstances, thereby ensuring that there is ample opportunity for the involvement of accountable decision-makers, provided that there is also the possibility of subsequent judicial oversight. Such considerations underpinned Lord Hoffmann's conclusion in *Alconbury*—which was unanimously shared by the other members of the Appellate Committee—that no breach of Article 6(1) had occurred:

> [123] My Lords, I must now examine the reasoning of the Divisional Court. It considered the way in which decisions are made by the Secretary of State and came to the conclusion that he was not independent or impartial. Even though the department has elaborate procedures to ensure that the decision-making process is not contaminated by reliance on facts which had not been found by the inspector or fairly put to the parties, the decision is bound to be influenced by the departmental view on policy. Mr Kingston, who appeared for the Huntingdonshire District Council, spent a good deal of time making this proposition good by examining the documents showing how the department was, at various levels, involved in the development of policy for Alconbury. But this was entirely what I would have expected. It is the business of the Secretary of State, aided by his civil servants, to develop national planning policies and co-ordinate local policies. These

policies are not airy abstractions. They are intended to be applied to actual cases. It would be absurd for the Secretary of State, in arriving at a decision in a particular case, to ignore his policies and start with a completely open mind.

[124] For these reasons, the Divisional Court said that the Secretary of State was not impartial in the manner required by article 6: 'What is objectionable in terms of article 6 is that he should be the judge in his own cause where his policy is in play.' (see paragraph 86). I do not disagree with the conclusion that the Secretary of State is not an independent and impartial tribunal. He does not claim to be. But the question is not whether he should be a judge in his own cause. It is whether he should be a judge at all.

[125] The Divisional Court then considered whether the requirements of article 6 were satisfied by the right to have an application for judicial review determined by a court. This was rightly described by Tuckey LJ as the crucial question. The answer he gave was that the procedure by which the Secretary of State arrived at his decision did not contain 'sufficient safeguards to justify the High Court's restricted power of review'. The Secretary of State, having complied with the requirements of natural justice, was 'free to make his own decision' and to take account of legal and policy guidance and recommendations from within the department 'which are not seen by the parties'. Therefore, said Tuckey LJ, at paragraph 95:

> 'In terms of article 6 the decision on the merits, which usually involves findings of fact and planning judgment, has not been determined by an independent and impartial tribunal or anyone approaching this, but by someone who is obviously not independent and impartial.'

[126] There are three strands of reasoning here. First, there is the fact that the parties are not privy to the processes of decision-making which go on within the department. These contain, on the one hand, elaborate precautions to ensure that the decision-maker does not take into account any factual matters which have not been found by the inspector at the inquiry or put to the parties and, on the other hand, free communication within the department on questions of law and policy, with a view to preparing a recommendation for submission to the Secretary of State or one of the junior Ministers to whom he has delegated the decision. The latter is standard civil service procedure and takes place, as Lord Greene MR said in *B Johnson & Co (Builders) Ltd v Minister of Health* [1947] 2 All ER 395, after the Secretary of State's quasi-judicial function has been concluded and when he is acting in his capacity as an administrator making a public policy decision ...

[127] ... If the Secretary of State was claiming to be, in his own person, an independent and impartial tribunal, the fact that he received confidential advice and recommendations from civil servants in his department might throw some doubt upon his claim. But, since he not only admits but avers that his constitutional role is to formulate and apply government policy, the fact that both formulation and application require the advice and assistance of his civil servants is no more than one would expect.

[128] The second strand concerns the facts. These are found by the inspector and must be accepted by the Secretary of State unless he has first notified the parties and given them an opportunity to make representations in accordance with rule 17(5) of the Town and Country Planning (Inquiries Procedure) (England) Rules 2000. This is the point upon which, in my opinion, the *Bryan* case 21 EHRR 342 is authority for saying that the independent position of the inspector, together with the control of the fairness of the fact-finding procedure by the court in judicial review, is sufficient to satisfy the requirements of article 6.

[129] Finally, the third strand is that of planning judgment. In this area the principle in the *Zumtobel* case 17 EHRR 116 ... does not require that the court should be able to substitute its decision for that of the administrative authority. Such a requirement would in my opinion not only be contrary to the jurisprudence of the European court but would also be profoundly

undemocratic. The Human Rights Act 1998 was no doubt intended to strengthen the rule of law but not to inaugurate the rule of lawyers.

[130] For these reasons I respectfully disagree with the Divisional Court's conclusion that decisions by the Secretary of State in planning cases are incompatible with Convention rights.

It is important to remember that *Alconbury* concerned a challenge to the Secretary of State's role as a policy-maker. Their Lordships clearly felt that it was appropriate for Ministers to determine matters of planning policy: note Lord Hoffmann's comments at 9.5.1, and Lord Nolan's remark (at [60]) that to hand over such functions to an 'independent and impartial body with no central electoral accountability would not only be a recipe for chaos: it would be profoundly undemocratic'. Heavily influenced by this conclusion that the Secretary of State's role was constitutionally acceptable—indeed, desirable—their Lordships held that it did not matter that the Minister was not an independent and impartial body, since the regime as a whole was Article 6-compliant by virtue of the availability of judicial review. However, a different approach applies in cases concerning fact-finding functions. The next extract demonstrates that, in such cases, much closer attention is paid to the extent of the procedural safeguards at the initial stage.

Bryan v. *United Kingdom* (1996) 21 EHRR 342
European Commission of Human Rights

Vale Royal Borough Council issued an enforcement notice under s 172 of the Town and Country Planning Act 1990 requiring the applicant to demolish buildings which had been erected without planning permission. The applicant appealed to the Secretary of State; a planning inspector was appointed, but he rejected the appeal. The applicant therefore exercised his right under s 289(1) of the 1990 Act to appeal to the High Court on a point of law. That appeal was rejected. The applicant argued before the European Commission of Human Rights that the original decision did not comply with the requirements of Article 6(1), and that the appellate jurisdiction of the High Court was incapable of curing that defect. (The Commission operated as the principal Strasbourg fact-finding organ and determined the admissibility of applications; cases could be referred to the Court for final decision if, during or after the Commission stage, a friendly settlement could not be reached. The ECHR was amended and, in 1998, the Commission was abolished and replaced by a new court.)

Concurring opinion of Mr N Bratza

I share the view of the majority of the Commission that, on the facts of the present case, the only challenge to the enforcement notice which the applicant pursued in the High Court related to matters of planning policy and that, consistently with the Court's reasoning in the *Zumtobel* case [(1993) 17 EHRR 116], Article 6 does not in any event require that a court should have the power to substitute its view for that of the administrative authorities on matters of planning policy or 'expediency' ...

... I also find that there has been no violation of Article 6 in the present case on the broader ground that the powers of review of the High Court under section 289 of the 1990 Act are sufficiently wide to satisfy the requirement held by the Court to be inherent in Article 6 that the judicial body determining the applicant's civil rights and obligations should have 'full jurisdiction'.

It appears to me that the requirement that a court or tribunal should have 'full jurisdiction' cannot be mechanically applied with the result that, in all circumstances and whatever the subject matter of the dispute, the court or tribunal must have full power to substitute its own findings of fact, and its own inferences from those facts, for that of the administrative authority concerned. Whether the power of judicial review is sufficiently wide to satisfy the requirements of Article 6 must in my view depend on a number of considerations, including the subject matter of the dispute, the nature of the decision of the administrative authorities which is in question, the procedure, if any, which exists for review of the decision by a person or body acting independently of the authority concerned and the scope of that power of review.

In my view the powers of review of the High Court, when combined with the statutory arrangements under the 1990 Act for appealing against an enforcement notice, satisfy the requirements of Article 6(1).

So far as the statutory arrangements are concerned, section 174 of the 1990 Act provides that an appeal against an enforcement notice served by a local authority may be made to the Secretary of State on grounds, inter alia, that the matters alleged in the notice do not constitute a breach of planning control. Section 175(3) of the Act provides that if an appellant or the local authority desires, the Secretary of State shall give each of them the opportunity of appearing before and being heard by a person appointed by the Secretary of State ('the inspector') and power is conferred on the inspector to determine the appeal.

In determining planning appeals inspectors act in a quasi-judicial capacity and in accordance with prescribed procedures, full powers being conferred on both parties to appear, with or without legal representation, adduce evidence, both written and oral, and make submissions of both law and fact. Further, the appeal results in a reasoned decision letter.

In paragraph 42 of the Report the Commission, while accepting that the inspector is a 'tribunal' within the substantive sense of the expression as used in Article 6(1) and that such a tribunal is one 'established by law', concludes that an inspector does not satisfy the requirement of independence and impartiality: it is correctly pointed out that inspectors are chosen from salaried staff of the Planning Inspectorate, which serves the Secretary of State in the furtherance of his policies, and that while the Secretary of State and his inspector are not parties to the dispute as such, the fact that those policies can be in issue on appeals means that the inspector cannot have the independence necessary for Article 6 of the Convention.

While this is true, there is equally nothing to suggest that, in finding the primary facts and in drawing conclusions and inferences from those facts, an inspector acts anything other than independently, in the sense that he is in no sense connected with the parties to the dispute or subject to their influence or control; his findings and conclusions are based exclusively on the evidence and submissions before him.

An appeal is from an inspector's decision to the High Court under Section 289 of the Act 'on a point of law'. As appears from the Commission's Report, this does not mean that the inspector's findings of fact or the inferences drawn by him from those facts are free from review by the Court. The Court cannot substitute its own findings of fact or its own inferences from those facts for those of the inspector. However, the Court can set aside a factual finding by an inspector if that finding is unsupported by any evidence before him. The Court can also set aside inferences drawn by the inspector from those facts if those inferences are perverse or irrational in the sense that no inspector properly directing himself could reasonably have drawn such inferences ...

In my view this power of review of the High Court, combined with the statutory procedure for appealing against an enforcement notice, is sufficient to meet the requirement of 'full jurisdiction' inherent in Article 6(1) of the Convention.

The Commission found, by majority, that the possibility of appeal to the High Court on a point of law rendered the process, taken as a whole, consistent with Article 6(1). The same conclusion was reached by the Court.

Commenting with approval on this opinion, Lord Hoffmann said in *Alconbury* [2001] UKHL 23, [2003] 2 AC 295 at [110] that its great strength was its recognition that

> a tribunal may be more or less independent, depending upon the question it is being called upon to decide. On matters of policy, the inspector was no more independent than the Secretary of State himself. But this was a matter on which independence was unnecessary—indeed, on democratic principles, undesirable—and in which the power of judicial review, paying full respect to the views of the inspector or Secretary of State on questions of policy or expediency, was sufficient to satisfy article 6(1). On the other hand, in deciding the questions of primary fact or fact and degree which arose in enforcement notice appeals, the inspector was no mere bureaucrat. He was an expert tribunal acting in a quasi-judicial manner and therefore sufficiently independent to make it unnecessary that the High Court should have a broad jurisdiction to review his decisions on questions of fact.

QUESTIONS

- Do you agree that fact-finding and policy-making functions should be distinguished in this context?
- What difficulties might arise in seeking to draw such a distinction?

It follows that more judicial-style independence is required in relation to fact-finding than policy-making functions. Such independence is to be supplied pre-eminently by the sort of safeguards, operating at first instance, that were mentioned in the *Bryan* opinion. If those safeguards do not secure full compliance with the judicial model, then judicial review or appeal may compensate for this. For instance, in *Bryan* itself, the inspector's lack of institutional separation from the executive branch was 'cured' by the possibility of appeal on a point of law to the High Court. However, the greater the absence of the safeguards at first instance, the more that will be required by way of appeal or judicial review, bearing in mind the high overall degree of adherence to the judicial model that is required where fact-finding is at stake.

So far, we have seen that a distinction is drawn, for the reasons already considered, between fact-finding and policy-making functions. However, a further distinction has been drawn *within* the fact-finding category.

Runa Begum v. *Tower Hamlets London Borough Council* [2003] UKHL 5, [2003] 2 AC 430
House of Lords

This case arose in relation to the homeless provisions in the Housing Act 1996, on which see 9.5.2. Runa Begum complained that a local authority's internal review, under Part VII of the Housing Act 1996, of its determination that she had unreasonably rejected an offer of accommodation failed to comply with Article 6(1), and that in rejecting her reasons for refusing the accommodation the reviewing officer had acted on the basis of mistaken facts. Their Lordships assumed, without deciding, that Article 6(1) applied in these circumstances, but as the following extract shows they concluded that the problems with the internal review could be cured by the possibility of appeal to the County Court under s 204 of the 1996 Act, which was able to exercise the normal judicial review jurisdiction of the High Court.

Lord Hoffmann

[41] *Bryan* was ... a case about the application of article 6 to decisions on fact. In that respect it was distinguishable from *Alconbury*. But when one comes to consider what *Bryan* decided, it is important to notice not only what the question was (whether buildings were designed for the purposes of agriculture) but also the context in which it arose, namely, as a ground of appeal against an enforcement notice. The inspector's decision that Bryan had acted in breach of planning control was binding upon him in any subsequent criminal proceedings for failing to comply with the notice: *R v Wicks* [1998] AC 92. This part of the appeal against the enforcement notice was closely analogous to a criminal trial and, as I noted in *Alconbury*, at pp 1416–1419, paras 89–97, used to come before the magistrates.

[42] A finding of fact in this context seems to me very different from the findings of fact which have to be made by central or local government officials in the course of carrying out regulatory functions (such as licensing or granting planning permission) or administering schemes of social welfare such as Part VII. The rule of law rightly requires that certain decisions, of which the paradigm examples are findings of breaches of the criminal law and adjudications as to private rights, should be entrusted to the judicial branch of government. This basic principle does not yield to utilitarian arguments that it would be cheaper or more efficient to have these matters decided by administrators. Nor is the possibility of an appeal sufficient to compensate for lack of independence and impartiality on the part of the primary decision maker: see *De Cubber* v *Belgium* (1984) 7 EHRR 236.

[43] But utilitarian considerations have their place when it comes to setting up, for example, schemes of regulation or social welfare. I said earlier that in determining the appropriate scope of judicial review of administrative action, regard must be had to democratic accountability, efficient administration and the sovereignty of Parliament. This case raises no question of democratic accountability. As Hale LJ said in *Adan's* case [2002] 1 WLR 2120, 2138, para 57:

> 'The policy decisions were taken by Parliament when it enacted the 1996 Act. Individual eligibility decisions are taken in the first instance by local housing authorities but policy questions of the availability of resources or equity between the homeless and those on the waiting list for social housing are irrelevant to individual eligibility.'

[44] On the other hand, efficient administration and the sovereignty of Parliament are very relevant. Parliament is entitled to take the view that it is not in the public interest that an excessive proportion of the funds available for a welfare scheme should be consumed in administration and legal disputes ...

[46] [His Lordship cited passages from the joint dissenting opinion in *Feldbrugge* v. *The Netherlands* (1986) 8 EHRR 425 and *Matthews* v. *Eldridge* (1976) 424 US 319 in support of this view, and continued:] It therefore seems to me that it would be inappropriate to require that findings of fact for the purposes of administering the homelessness scheme in Part VII should be made by a person or body independent of the authority which has been entrusted with its administration ...

[47] Although I do not think that the exercise of administrative functions requires a mechanism for independent findings of fact or a full appeal, it does need to be lawful and fair. It is at this point that ... arguments ... about the impartiality of Mrs Hayes [the local authority official] and the regulations for the conduct of reviews become relevant. To these safeguards one adds the supervisory powers of the judge on an appeal under section 204 to quash the decision for procedural impropriety or irrationality. In any case, the gap between judicial review and a full right of appeal is seldom in practice very wide. Even with a full right of appeal it is not easy for an appellate tribunal which has not itself seen the witnesses to differ from the decision-maker on questions of primary fact and, more especially relevant to this case, on questions of credibility.

[48] [Counsel] drew attention to the expanding scope of judicial review which, he said, may, in a suitable case allow a court to quash a decision on the grounds of misunderstanding or

ignorance of an established and relevant fact: see the views of Lord Slynn of Hadley in *R* v *Criminal Injuries Compensation Board, Ex p A* [1999] 2 AC 330, 344–345 and in the *Alconbury* case [2001] 2 WLR 1389, 1407, para 53 or, at least in cases in which Convention rights were engaged, on the ground of lack of proportionality: *R (Daly)* v *Secretary of State for the Home Department* [2001] 2 AC 532. He said that this should be taken into account in deciding whether the jurisdiction of the county court was adequate.

[49] I do not think that it is necessary to discuss the implications of these developments. No doubt it is open to a court exercising the review jurisdiction under section 204 to adopt a more intensive scrutiny of the rationality of the reviewing officer's conclusions of fact but this is not the occasion to enter into the question of when it should do so. When one is dealing with a welfare scheme which, in the particular case, does not engage human rights (does not, for example, require consideration of article 8) then the intensity of review must depend upon what one considers to be most consistent with the statutory scheme. In this case, Laws LJ [2002] 1 WLR 2491, 2513, para 44, said that the county court judge was entitled to subject Mrs Hayes's decision to 'a close and rigorous analysis'. On the other hand 17 years ago Lord Brightman, speaking for a unanimous Appellate Committee in *R* v *Hillingdon London Borough Council, ex parte Puhlhofer* [1986] AC 484, 518, made it clear that their Lordships contemplated a fairly low level of judicial interventionism:

> 'Parliament intended the local authority to be the judge of fact. The Act abounds with the formula when, or if, the housing authority are satisfied as to this, or that, or have reason to believe this, or that. Although the action or inaction of a local authority is clearly susceptible to judicial review where they have misconstrued the Act, or abused their powers or otherwise acted perversely, I think that great restraint should be exercised in giving leave to proceed by judicial review.'

[50] All that we are concerned with in this appeal is the requirements of article 6, which I do not think mandates a more intensive approach to judicial review of questions of fact. These nuances are well within the margin of appreciation which the Convention allows to contracting states and which, in a case like this, the courts should concede to Parliament. So I do not propose to say anything about whether a review of fact going beyond conventional principles of judicial review would be either permissible or appropriate. It seems to me sufficient to say that in the case of the normal Part VII decision, engaging no human rights other than article 6, conventional judicial review such as the Strasbourg court considered in the *Bryan* case 21 EHRR 342 is sufficient.

[51] Is this view consistent with the Strasbourg jurisprudence and with *Bryan* in particular? I think it is ...

[52] In this case the subject matter of the decision was the suitability of accommodation for occupation by Runa Begum; the kind of decision which the Strasbourg court has on several occasions called a 'classic exercise of an administrative discretion'. The manner in which the decision was arrived at was by the review process, at a senior level in the authority's administration and subject to rules designed to promote fair decision-making. The content of the dispute is that the authority made its decision on the basis of findings of fact which Runa Begum says were mistaken. In my opinion the Strasbourg court has accepted, on the basis of general state practice and for the reasons of good administration which I have discussed, that in such cases a limited right of review on questions of fact is sufficient ...

[Lord Hoffmann considered the *Bryan* case further, as well as *Kingsley* v. *United Kingdom* (2001) 33 EHRR 13, and continued:]

[56] The key phrases in the judgments of the Strasbourg court which describe the cases in which a limited review of the facts is sufficient are 'specialised areas of the law' (*Bryan's* case 21 EHRR 342, 361, para 47) and 'classic exercise of administrative discretion' (*Kingsley's* case 33 EHRR 288, 302, para 53). What kind of decisions are these phrases referring to? I think that one has to take them together. The notion of a specialised area of the law should not be taken too

literally. After all, I suppose carriage of goods by sea could be said to be a specialised area of the law, but no one would suggest that shipping disputes should be decided otherwise than by normal judicial methods. It seems to me that what the court had in mind was those areas of the law such as regulatory and welfare schemes in which decision-making is customarily entrusted to administrators. And when the court in *Kingsley* spoke of the classic exercise of administrative discretion, it was referring to the ultimate decision as to whether Kingsley was a fit and proper person [to hold a management position in the gaming industry] and not to the particular findings of fact which had to be made on the way to arriving at that decision. In the same way, the decision as to whether the accommodation was suitable for Runa Begum was a classic exercise of administrative discretion, even though it involved preliminary findings of fact.

[57] National traditions as to which matters are suitable for administrative decision and which require to be decided by the judicial branch of government may differ. To that extent, the Strasbourg court will no doubt allow a margin of appreciation to contracting states. The concern of the court, as it has emphasised since *Golder's* case (1975) 1 EHRR 524 is to uphold the rule of law and to insist that decisions which on generally accepted principles are appropriate only for judicial decision should be so decided. In the case of decisions appropriate for administrative decision, its concern, again founded on the rule of law, is that there should be the possibility of adequate judicial review. For this purpose, cases like *Bryan* and *Kingsley* make it clear that limitations on practical grounds on the right to a review of the findings of fact will be acceptable ...

Lords Bingham and Millett similarly concluded that the County Court's jurisdiction was adequate for Article 6(1) purposes. Lords Hope and Walker delivered only short concurring speeches.

According to Lord Hoffmann's analysis, a distinction must be drawn between fact-finding in cases concerning private rights, and those, like *Runa Begum*, involving the administration of welfare or regulatory schemes. In the former category, the requirements of independence and impartiality fall to be enforced strictly (as in *Bryan*). In the latter category, a more general requirement, that the process is 'lawful and fair', obtains.

The scope of the latter category was considered in *Ali* v. *Birmingham City Council* [2010] UKSC 8, [2010] 2 WLR 471. The facts, as noted at 9.5.2, were similar to those of *Runa Begum*: reviewing officers upheld the council's initial decisions, and the claimants then launched Article 6 challenges. They sought to distinguish their cases from that of *Runa Begum* by reference to the precise focus of the dispute. In *Runa Begum*, the question had been about what Article 6 required in relation to the *decision as to suitability*: the House of Lords' conclusion, as we have seen, was that the requirements of Article 6 were to be diluted in recognition of the discretionary aspects of that determination. In contrast, the focus of the dispute in *Ali* was over a *pure finding of fact*: the reviewing officers had held that the councils had complied with a statutory requirement to send a letter explaining the consequences of declining an offer of accommodation, whereas the claimants said that they had not. The claimants argued that their cases fell into the *Bryan* category, rather than the *Runa Begum* category, because the disputed determination did not involve the exercise of discretion. Strictly speaking, the Supreme Court did not need to address this issue, since it concluded—contrary, as we have seen, to the subsequently adopted view of the ECtHR—that Article 6 was not engaged. Nevertheless, in his leading judgment, Lord Hope considered whether, if applicable, Article 6 would be satisfied. Holding that it would be, he said:

[53] ... The question whether or not the letters were received was just one among a number of questions that had to be addressed to determine whether the defendants' duty under section 193 of the 1996 Act had been discharged. They are dealt with together in section 193(5) in a way

that shows that they are all interlinked. The scheme of the Act is that they are to be dealt with together both at the initial stage and, in the event of a review, by the reviewing officer. To separate out questions as to whether the formalities laid down by the subsection were complied with from those as to whether the accommodation was suitable would complicate a scheme which, in the interests of speed and economy, was designed to be simple to administer. Several of the further cases referred to in section 193(6) in which the authority ceases to be subject to the duty also raise issues that require the exercise of judgment. That is inherent in the entire structure of Part VII of the 1996 Act.

[54] … For ease of administration the review is entrusted to a single officer who is equipped to deal with issues as to the suitability of the accommodation that has been declined. An answer to the question whether or not the letters were received was incidental to a more searching and judgmental inquiry into the accommodation's suitability. It was, as Lord Bingham put it in *Runa Begum*, para 9(2), a staging post on the way to the much broader judgment that had to be made … I would hold that the ratio of the decision in *Runa Begum* should be applied and that the absence of a full fact-finding jurisdiction in the court to which an appeal lies … does not deprive it of what it needs to satisfy the requirements of article 6(1).

This suggests that what Article 6 requires has to be determined globally for the purposes of a given administrative scheme. Although, when *Ali* reached the ECtHR, that Court did not consider this particular matter in as much detail as the Supreme Court, the ECtHR's reasoning does not cast doubt on this aspect of the Supreme Court's reasoning.

Finally, it is necessary to consider whether the approach adopted by the English courts is called into question by the following decision of the ECtHR.

Tsfayo v. *United Kingdom* (2009) 48 EHRR 18
European Court of Human Rights

In 1997, the applicant moved into accommodation owned by a housing association, and made a successful application for housing benefit. She did not, however, realize that it was necessary to reapply annually for housing benefit. When she did eventually reapply, the local authority agreed to resume payments, but refused to backdate them to cover the rent arrears which had accrued following the cessation of payments. In light of the applicant's inability to pay the arrears, the housing association sought to evict her. She unsuccessfully appealed to the council's Housing Benefit Review Board (HBRB) against the refusal to backdate the payments, arguing that there had been 'good cause' for her delay in reapplying. (She had a poor command of English and claimed not to have received certain relevant correspondence.) For reasons that are apparent from the judgment below, the applicant contended, *inter alia*, that the HBRB was not independent for Article 6 purposes. At the relevant time, the HRA was not in force, and the applicant's claim in the High Court failed. She therefore pursued the matter before the ECtHR.

Judgment

[40] The Court recalls that disputes over entitlement to social security and welfare benefits generally fall within the scope of art.6(1). It agrees with the parties that the applicant's claim for housing benefit concerned the determination of her civil rights and that art.6(1) applied. The applicant therefore had a right to a fair hearing before an independent and impartial tribunal.

[41] The HBRB was composed of five elected councillors from the same local authority which would have been required to pay a percentage of the housing benefit if awarded, and the Government conceded on these grounds that the Board lacked structural independence. It

contended, however, that the High Court on judicial review had sufficient jurisdiction to ensure that the proceedings as a whole complied with art.6(1).

[42] The Court recalls that even where an adjudicatory body determining disputes over 'civil rights and obligations' does not comply with art.6(1) in some respect, no violation of the Convention can be found if the proceedings before that body are, 'subject to subsequent control by a judicial body that has full jurisdiction and does provide the guarantees of Article [6(1)]'.

[The Court then summarized its decision in *Bryan*, noting that it had been applied in several subsequent ECtHR cases as well as by the House of Lords in *Runa Begum*, and continued:]

[46] The Court considers that the decision-making process in the present case was significantly different. In *Bryan* [and] *Runa Begum* ..., the issues to be determined required a measure of professional knowledge or experience and the exercise of administrative discretion pursuant to wider policy aims. In contrast, in the instant case, the HBRB was deciding a simple question of fact, namely whether there was 'good cause' for the applicant's delay in making a claim. On this question, the applicant had given evidence to the HBRB that the first that she knew that anything was amiss with her claim for housing benefit was the receipt of a notice from her land-lord—the housing association—seeking to repossess her flat because her rent was in arrears. The HBRB found her explanation to be unconvincing and rejected her claim for back-payment of benefit essentially on the basis of their assessment of her credibility. No specialist expertise was required to determine this issue, which is, under the new system, determined by a non-specialist tribunal. Nor, unlike the cases referred to, can the factual findings in the present case be said to be merely incidental to the reaching of broader judgments of policy or expediency which it was for the democratically accountable authority to take.

[47] Secondly, ... the HBRB was not merely lacking in independence from the executive, but was directly connected to one of the parties to the dispute, since it included five councillors from the local authority which would be required to pay the benefit if awarded. As Moses J. observed in [*R (Bewry)* v. *Norwich City Council* [2001] EWHC 657 (Admin)], this connection of the councillors to the party resisting entitlement to housing benefit might infect the independence of judgment in relation to the finding of primary fact in a manner which could not be adequately scrutinised or rectified by judicial review. The safeguards built into the HBRB procedure were not adequate to overcome this fundamental lack of objective impartiality.

[48] The applicant had her claim refused because the HBRB did not find her a credible witness. Whilst the High Court had the power to quash the decision if it considered, inter alia, that there was no evidence to support the HBRB's factual findings, or that its findings were plainly untenable, or that the HBRB had misunderstood or been ignorant of an established and relevant fact, it did not have jurisdiction to rehear the evidence or substitute its own views as to the applicant's credibility. Thus, in this case, there was never the possibility that the central issue would be determined by a tribunal that was independent of one of the parties to the dispute.

[49] It follows that there has been a violation of art.6(1).

What should we make of *Tsfayo*? On the one hand, it serves as a clear reminder that the curative principle is not always a panacea: circumstances can, and will, arise in which judicial review (or something equivalent, such as appeal on a point of law) will not outweigh a lack of independence on the part of the original decision-maker. On the other hand, it would be going much too far to suggest that *Tsfayo* fundamentally calls into question the curative capacity of judicial review. As is apparent from the excerpt above, the facts of *Tsfayo* were substantially different from those of many of the cases considered in this section. The function was characterized as one of pure fact-finding; and the extent of the HBRB's lack of independence was especially striking, given the membership of the councillors and the fact that the council would have had to meet part of the cost if the award had been backdated.

The law in this area is undeniably complicated. It is often unclear whether Article 6 applies at all; and, if it does, what it requires is often uncertain. This state of affairs is unfortunate, but the reasons for it are not hard to fathom. In particular, Article 6(1), rightly or wrongly, has been pressed into service in a very wide range of circumstances. Indeed, it might fairly be said that Article 6(1), as interpreted by the ECtHR, has come to serve not only as a right to the *determination* of certain matters by independent judicial decision-makers, but as a proxy for a (limited) right to administrative justice which ensures that certain categories of almost inevitably executive decision-making are subject to an appropriate degree of *oversight* by independent courts or tribunals.

9.6 Concluding remarks

The absence of bias is fundamental to the notion of fairness. No amount of procedural safeguards—such as the right to be heard, to cross-examine witnesses, or to be represented by a lawyer—can yield fairness if the tribunal is, in the first place, biased. And, as we have seen, even the perception of bias is damaging to an administrative or judicial system, given the importance of ensuring public confidence in the integrity of the decision-making process. English law, on the whole, treats these matters with appropriate seriousness by recognizing the importance of ensuring the appearance—as well as the reality—of fairness. But we have also seen that these issues do not exist in a vacuum, and that other policy concerns—not least effective and efficient decision-making—make competing claims on, and ultimately help to shape, the legal rules which operate in this area. The effect given to Article 6 ECHR by the HRA has added another layer to English law in this context by increasing the scope for challenges based on the institutional position of the decision-maker. In particular, English courts, applying Article 6, are having to confront questions about the legitimacy of Parliament's allocation of decision-making functions to particular institutions which simply would not have arisen only a few years ago.

FURTHER RESOURCES

Atrill, 'Who is the "Fair-Minded and Informed Observer"? Bias after *Magill*' [2003] *CLJ* 279

Craig, 'The Human Rights Act, Article 6 and Procedural Rights' [2003] *PL* 753

Galligan, *Due Process and Fair Procedures* (Oxford 1996)

Hammond, *Judicial Recusal: Principles, Process and Problems* (Oxford 2009)

Malleson, 'Safeguarding Judicial Impartiality' (2002) 22 *LS* 53

Olowofoyeku, 'Bias and the Informed Observer: A Call for a Return to *Gough*' [2009] *CLJ* 388

Woodhouse (ed), *The Pinochet Case: A Legal and Constitutional Analysis* (Oxford 2000)

10 PROCEDURAL FAIRNESS

10.1 The idea of procedural fairness

We saw in ch 9 that if a decision-making system is to adhere to the notion of procedural fairness, then it must operate in an impartial way—hence the rule against bias. That principle is a necessary but not a sufficient condition if procedural fairness is to be realized. Although it is self-evident that the decision-maker must be impartial—meaning free from bias—the overall goals of procedural fairness can be secured only if it goes on to apply a decision-making process which is itself fair. This aspect of procedural fairness is sometimes referred to as the right to a fair hearing, and is said to be summed up by the latin maxim *audi alteram partem*—literally, 'hear the other side'. The fundamentality of this principle was underlined by Fortescue J in *R* v. *The Chancellor of Cambridge* (1723) 1 Stra 557, in which Dr Bentley challenged the University's decision to strip him of his degrees following alleged misconduct, without first giving him an opportunity to respond to those allegations:

> I remember to have heard it observed by a very learned man upon such an occasion, that even God himself did not pass sentence upon Adam, before he was called upon to make his defence. 'Adam' (says God) 'where art thou? Has thou not eaten of the tree whereof I commanded thee that thou shouldest not eat?' And the same question was put to Eve also.

Some of the principal reasons for requiring fairness in decision-making are set out at 9.1. Although the importance of fair treatment may, at a general level, be uncontroversial, it is crucial to articulate *precisely* why fairness is important, since the ethos which underpins a legal system's commitment to procedural fairness necessarily plays a central role in determining the exact shape and reach of the legal rules which operate to secure such fairness. In the following passage, Galligan attempts to provide what he calls 'a general theory of fair treatment' by exploring what it is that legal rules requiring procedural fairness might seek to achieve.

Galligan, 'Procedural Fairness' in Birks (ed), The Frontiers of Liability (volume one) (Oxford 1994)

Consider the distribution of welfare and the case of X applying for a particular benefit. Imagine that the conditions of eligibility are clear, that X, seeking to show his entitlement, presents his case to the tribunal, and that the tribunal, after considering the claim and the relevant facts, awards the benefit. This process can be understood at two levels. At one level it is a matter of officials distributing welfare according to the criteria set by the governing statute. If the law is properly applied, those criteria are met, and the social good in distributing welfare on that basis is satisfied. Correct decisions about whether applicants are entitled to benefits means that the system is working well; mistakes mean it is not, and the social good is to that extent diminished. At this level of understanding, questions of fairness do not arise; the only concern is whether the statutory scheme is working effectively. That is important because society has decided that that is how welfare should be allocated. The role of procedures is to see that the law is applied accurately and, as a consequence, that the social good is realized. Anyone familiar with Bentham's writings will recognize here his theory of procedures [see Bentham, *A Treatise of Judicial Evidence* (London 1825)]. Bentham wrote at length about the civil and criminal trials, but his account can be transposed to other forms of decision-making. He considered accuracy of outcome, or rectitude as he called it, to be the object of the trial, subject only to considerations of delay, vexation and expense. Accurate outcomes serve the ends of utility, in particular the utility in having a stable and reliable system of civil and criminal laws. The task for rules of evidence and procedure is to produce accurate outcomes. Much of Bentham's writings was directed to the reform of those areas of English law in accordance with this view of their rightful purpose.

On this approach, the value of legal procedures is judged according to their contribution to general social goals. The object is to advance certain social goals, whether through administrative processes, or through the civil or criminal trial. The law and its processes are simply instruments for achieving some social good as determined from time to time by the law makers of the society. Each case is an instance in achieving the general goal, and a mistaken decision, whether to the benefit or the detriment of a particular person, is simply a failure to achieve the general good in that case. At this level of understanding, judgments of fairness have no place, for all that matters is whether the social good, as expressed through laws, is effectively achieved.

In order to introduce ideas of fair treatment and in particular fair procedures, we must move to a second level of understanding. For whenever pursuit of the common good involves the distribution of benefits and burdens, advantages and disadvantages to individuals (or groups), questions of fair treatment come into play. The principles of distribution are the subject-matter of fair treatment. So, whenever the state, through its officials, decides how people are to be treated, considerations of fair treatment arise. Welfare decisions can now be seen at two levels: at one, they are elements in the effective distribution of welfare, where the object is the common good; at the other, they are about the fair treatment of those persons whose cases are being considered. But fair treatment is not a kind of optional extra; it is, on the contrary, a fundamental requirement of any justifiable political and legal theory.

It is not appropriate here to attempt to provide a moral foundation for the idea that, in the distribution of advantages and disadvantages, each person should be treated fairly. It is enough to note that the principle is fundamental to liberal and democratic theory, and that it is at the foundation of western law. The underlying idea is that each person should be treated with respect. The idea of respect for each person is open-textured and wide in its reach, but in political philosophy it means at least that each person counts as an individual with interests and concerns. The notion of fair treatment is connected to respect for persons. One aspect of respect is to give a person his due, which is in turn the essential element of fair treatment. Questions of respect and, therefore, fair treatment occur in many contexts, but one of special importance is where the state has power over a person, whether in distributing benefits or imposing burdens, and must decide how that person is to be treated. The community, through its officials, has a basic duty to treat fairly those affected by its laws and legal processes.

In this passage Galligan helpfully identifies two distinct perspectives concerning the value of legal procedures. The first is an instrumental one: it presents legal procedures as a means to an end, the end being the effective and efficient delivery of those social goals which are set by policy-makers. The second perspective, in contrast, is non-instrumental: it requires the adoption of fair procedures because respect for the individual demands that he be treated fairly. On this view, a decision-making process which *involves* the individual—by giving him notice of the issues, allowing him to have his views taken account of and, ultimately, supplying him with reasons for the decision—characterizes him as a participant in the process of decision-making, rather than as the object of a distant and authoritarian administrative regime, and in this way accords respect to him as an individual. These themes are explored further by Galligan in his book *Due Process and Fair Procedures: A Study of Administrative Procedures* (Oxford 1996) in which he concludes that the importance of procedural fairness is primarily instrumental. In the following passage, taken from a review of Galligan's book, Allan critically examines that view, concluding that it is possible—indeed desirable—to recognize *both* the instrumental *and* non-instrumental values served by procedural fairness.

Allan, 'Procedural Fairness and the Duty of Respect' (1998) 18 OJLS 497

Procedural fairness is a topic close to the heart of any lawyer who takes pride in the contribution of the rule of law to good and decent government, properly respectful of the governed. But wherein exactly lies its special importance? Do the rules of natural justice and related principles of procedural fairness serve only to guarantee that legal rules governing matters of substance are accurately applied to the appropriate cases? Or does procedural propriety have an intrinsic, non-instrumental value more directly related to the citizen's dignity? Moreover, if we acknowledge the injustice which consists in a failure to secure for people the rights which the law confers or protects, how can we justify our adoption of imperfect procedures, which we know are likely to generate mistaken decisions?

In the course of his illuminating discussion of the nature and role of procedural fairness, *Due Process and Fair Procedures*, Professor D J Galligan offers thoughtful and interesting answers to such questions. His major theme, which runs throughout the book, is that procedural fairness is fundamentally an instrumental good, in the sense that procedures should be designed to ensure accurate or appropriate outcomes. Legal processes function within a framework of values, some specific to a particular form of process and others reflecting more general moral and political ideas ... 'Dignitarian' theorists, who emphasize the intrinsic value of procedures, have failed to understand that treating a person in accordance with legal standards is itself an important aspect of according him respect, and accordingly they have undervalued the significance of accurate outcomes ...

The important part played by non-outcome values—values independent of the accuracy or soundness of the substantive decision or verdict—in any complete and convincing analysis is readily acknowledged; but Laurence Tribe's suggestion, that the 'rights to interchange' between citizen and official conferred by a fair hearing have intrinsic value, is typical of the dignitarian assertions which attract Galligan's scepticism. According to Tribe, such rights 'express the elementary idea that to be a *person*, rather than a *thing*, is at least to be *consulted* about what is done with one' [*American Constitutional Law* (New York 1988) at 666]. Ronald Dworkin [*A Matter of Principle* (Oxford 1986) at 101–3] has criticized this passage as failing to explain why the absence of a hearing entails an injustice or 'moral harm' which is in some sense distinct from that entailed by an inaccurate substantive decision. Galligan takes similar objection: the alleged link between respect for persons and fair procedures stands in need of explanation, which dignitarian theorists have hitherto failed to provide. The dignitarian approach may serve to remind us that non-outcome values (such as privacy and confidentiality) should not be overlooked; the rules protecting a suspect from being tricked or cajoled into confessing, for example, are based on values which are quite independent of any concern with accuracy of outcome … Although Galligan is right to protest against a view of procedures which belittles their instrumental value in ensuring appropriate outcomes, there are at least aspects of procedural fairness or good practice which may serve an independent function. Moreover, the whole design or character of a hearing may well reflect non-instrumental values of no less importance than those which underlie our concern for accuracy and reliability …

The instrumental value of procedures should not be underestimated; the accurate application of authoritative standards is, as Galligan clearly explains, an important aspect of treating someone with respect. But procedures also have *intrinsic* value in acknowledging a person's right to understand his treatment, and thereby to determine his response as a conscientious citizen, willing to make reasonable sacrifices for the public good. If obedience to law ideally entails a recognition of its morally obligatory character, there must be suitable opportunities to test its moral credentials. Procedures may also be thought to have intrinsic value in so far as they constitute a fair balance between the demands of accuracy and other social needs: where the moral harm entailed by erroneous decisions is reasonably assessed and fairly distributed, procedures express society's commitment to equal concern and respect for all.

Within the constraints of limited resources, the purpose of a fair hearing is to allow the individual citizen to make a genuine contribution to a decision which impinges directly on his freedom and welfare, invoking his sense of justice as much as his self-interest. The value of fair procedures finally consists in the combination of our commitment to substantive justice and our uncertainty about what that means in the circumstances of any particular case, a matter on which the person or persons most closely affected can often cast valuable light, and also, and above all, in our desire to commend the outcome to a fellow-citizen who must suffer for the common good.

Allan's view, according to which procedural fairness is valuable in both instrumental and non-instrumental terms, is highly persuasive. There are, nevertheless, instances when the two perspectives direct different approaches; here, a choice must be made about which underlying conception of fairness is paramount. We encounter an example of this at 10.2.5, where we consider whether the obligation to act procedurally fairly should yield in the face of the argument that, in the circumstances of a given case, engaging in procedural fairness would 'make no difference'.

QUESTION

- Is fairness important because it helps to secure the 'right' outcome, or does its value exist independently of this consideration?

10.2 When must decision-makers act fairly?

Two interlocking questions must be confronted if the notion of procedural fairness is to be understood. First, when are decision-makers required to act fairly? Second, what does 'acting fairly' actually mean? We address the second of those questions at 10.3; for now, our focus is on the first.

10.2.1 A question of function or of impact?

The case law in this sphere evidences a number of highly significant shifts in judicial perspective. Two specific traditions may be identified. One adopts a formal approach by asking whether the power in question is 'judicial' or 'administrative' in nature. The other concentrates on the likely impact of the decision on the individual. Each approach has, at times, been dominant; the following case is a famous illustration of the latter.

Cooper v. *The Board of Works for Wandsworth District* (1863) 14 CBNS 180, (1863) 143 ER 414
Court of Common Pleas

The claimant had started to build a house without giving the required notice to the defendant district board. The board then proceeded to demolish the partially-built house without providing a hearing to the claimant. The claimant sued the defendant for trespass, arguing that a right to such a hearing ought to be implied into the relevant statutory power (s 76 of the Metropolis Local Management Act 1855).

Erle CJ

The district board here say, that no notice was given by the plaintiff of his intention to build the house in question, wherefore they demolished it. The contention on the part of the plaintiff has been, that, although the words of the statute, taken in their literal sense, without any qualification at all, would create a justification for the act which the district board has done, the powers granted by that statute are subject to a qualification which has been repeatedly recognized, that no man is to be deprived of his property without his having an opportunity of being heard. The evidence here shews that the plaintiff and the district board had not been quite on amicable terms. Be that as it may, the district board say that no notice was given, and that consequently they had a right to proceed to demolish the house without delay, and without notice to the party whose house was to be pulled down, and without giving him an opportunity of shewing any reason why the board should delay. I think that the power which is granted by the 76th section is subject to the qualification suggested. It is a power carrying with it enormous consequences. The house in question was built only to a certain extent. But the power claimed would apply to a complete house. It would apply to a house of any value, and completed to any extent; and it seems to me to be a power which may be exercised most perniciously, and that the limitation which we are going to put upon it is one which ought, according to the decided cases, to be put upon it, and one which is required by a due consideration for the public interest. I think the board ought to have given notice to the plaintiff, and to have allowed him to be heard. The default in sending notice to the board of the intention to build, is a default which may be explained. There may be a great many excuses for the apparent default. The party may have intended to conform to the law. He may have actually conformed to all the regulations which they would wish to impose, though by accident his notice may have miscarried; and, under those circumstances, if he explained how it stood, the proceeding to demolish, merely because they had ill-will against the party, is a power that the legislature never intended to confer. I cannot conceive any harm that could happen to the district board from hearing the party before they subjected him to a loss so serious as the demolition of his house; but I can conceive of a great many advantages which might arise in the way of public order, in the way of doing substantial justice, and in the way of fulfilling the purposes of the statute, by the restriction which we put upon them, that they should hear the party before they inflict upon him such a heavy loss. I fully agree that the legislature intended to give the district board very large powers indeed: but the qualification I speak of is one which has been recognized to the full extent. It has been said that the principle that no man shall be deprived of his property without an opportunity of being heard, is limited to a judicial proceeding, and that a district board ordering a house to be pulled down cannot be said to be doing a judicial act. I do not quite agree with that; neither do I undertake to rest my judgment solely upon the ground that the district board is a court exercising judicial discretion upon the point: but the law, I think, has been applied to many exercises of power which in common understanding would not be at all more a judicial proceeding than would be the act of the district board in ordering a house to be pulled down.

Willes, Byles, and Keating JJ agreed that there should have been a hearing.

In deciding that a right to be heard—which, as we shall see at 10.3, is central to any notion of procedural fairness—was implicit in the Wandsworth Board's powers, Erle CJ's focus was on questions of impact; he was centrally concerned with how the exercise of the Board's powers affected the position of the individual. The very grave implications which could follow from an exercise of the power—such as the demolition of a person's house—led Erle CJ to conclude that a duty to comply with natural justice necessarily arose. Traditionally, the term 'judicial' (or 'quasi-judicial') was used as a conclusory label signifying that the holder of the power was under a duty to exercise the power fairly, *as if he were* the holder of a judicial or similar office. The term 'administrative' signified the converse conclusion. Thus it was quite possible to find that an *administrative* body possessed 'judicial' or 'quasi-judicial' powers if the implications of their exercise were sufficient to require adherence to principles of due process. Wade (1951) 67 *LQR* 103 at 106 explained that 'it was not the *power* which was judicial, but the procedure which the courts held must be followed before the power could be properly exercised'.

However, the courts, over time, began to lose sight of the rationale underpinning this distinction between 'judicial' and 'quasi-judicial' powers on the one hand, and 'administrative' powers on the other. This led to the adoption of a more formal analysis which asked whether the decision-maker was discharging a 'judicial' or an 'administrative' *function*, the thinking being that a duty to comply with natural justice would apply only to the former. By shifting their analysis from questions of impact to questions of formal classification, the courts overlooked the fact that the discharge of 'administrative' functions could quite easily have a very serious impact upon the individual—a conclusion which, on an impact-oriented analysis, would activate the duty to comply with natural justice. Thus arose the fallacy that the concept of procedural fairness extended only to decision-makers exercising 'judicial' functions, in turn rendering immune from scrutiny on due process grounds whole swathes of decision-making powers which (on a formal analysis) were 'administrative' in nature. For example, the Privy Council found in *Nakkuda Ali* v. *Jayaratne* [1951] AC 66 that a trading licence could be revoked by an administrative authority without giving the licence-holder a hearing; the same conclusion was reached in *R* v. *Metropolitan Police Commissioner, ex parte Parker* [1953] 1 WLR 1150 concerning a taxi driver's licence. Meanwhile, in *Franklin* v. *Minister of Town and Country Planning* [1948] AC 87, the House of Lords proceeded on the basis that a ministerial decision could not be challenged on apparent bias grounds (on which see generally ch 9) because the Minister was not exercising a 'judicial' function.

Wade (1951) 67 *LQR* 103 castigated this line of reasoning as the product of a distorted understanding of the earlier decisions in which the terms 'judicial' (or 'quasi-judicial') and 'administrative' merely expressed a conclusion as to impact (and hence the appropriate style of procedure). However, the scaling back of procedural fairness effected by the functional dichotomy which the courts embraced must also be located within a broader context. In particular, the courts, during the early part of the twentieth century, adopted a remarkably *laissez-faire* approach when it came to scrutinizing government action, a complacency which, according to Sedley (1994) 110 *LQR* 270 at 279–84, had its roots in judicial confidence that changes to the way in which the executive operated, most notably the emergence of a modern and professional civil service, rendered the need for judicial intervention in administrative affairs less compelling.

Viewed against this background, the retreat from natural justice evidenced by cases such as *Franklin* forms only part of a wider phenomenon. By the same token, the following decision—which is widely regarded as one of the most significant landmarks in the development of our contemporary system of administrative law—must be seen not simply as a reassertion of the importance of procedural fairness, but as part of a broader renaissance in judicial oversight of the executive.

Ridge v. *Baldwin* [1964] AC 40
House of Lords

Ridge, the Chief Constable of Brighton, was suspended from duty after he had been arrested and charged with conspiracy to obstruct the course of justice. At his trial Ridge was acquitted; however, when sentencing two police officers from his force who were charged with him (but who were convicted), the trial judge, Donovan J, was critical of Ridge's leadership of his force. At a later date, when a corruption charge was brought against Ridge, the prosecution offered no evidence. Donovan J directed Ridge's acquittal, but made another comment concerning the leadership of the force. The watch committee met the next day (7 March 1958) and decided that Ridge should be dismissed. Section 191(4) of the Municipal Corporations Act 1882 provided that a watch committee could dismiss 'any borough constable whom they think negligent in the discharge of his duty, or otherwise unfit for the same'. Ridge was not asked to attend the meeting; he was later told that he had been summarily dismissed and was also told of certain resolutions passed at the meeting. At the request of Ridge's solicitor, the watch committee reconvened on 18 March 1958. Having received representations from Ridge's solicitor, the watch committee decided not to change its original decision. Before this second meeting Ridge gave formal notice of appeal against the original decision to the Home Secretary under the Police (Appeals) Act 1927. However, he also stated that this was without prejudice to his right to argue that the procedure adopted by the watch committee was in breach of the relevant statutory provisions and contrary to natural justice, and therefore invalid. The Home Secretary dismissed the appeal and Ridge resorted to the courts. Part of the relief sought was a declaration that the purported termination of his appointment was unlawful. Ridge's action failed before Streatfield J and his appeal was dismissed by the Court of Appeal; he appealed to the House of Lords.

Lord Reid

… The appellant's case is that in proceeding under the Act of 1882 the watch committee were bound to observe what are commonly called the principles of natural justice. Before attempting to reach any decision they were bound to inform him of the grounds on which they proposed to act and give him a fair opportunity of being heard in his own defence. The authorities on the applicability of the principles of natural justice are in some confusion, and so I find it necessary to examine this matter in some detail. The principle audi alteram partem goes back many centuries in our law and appears in a multitude of judgments of judges of the highest authority. In modern times opinions have sometimes been expressed to the effect that natural justice is so vague as to be practically meaningless. But I would regard these as tainted by the perennial fallacy that because something cannot be cut and dried or nicely weighed or measured therefore it does not exist ... It appears to me that one reason why the authorities on natural justice have been found difficult to reconcile is that insufficient attention has been paid to the great difference between various kinds of cases in which it has been sought to apply the principle. What a Minister ought to do in considering objections to a scheme may be very different from what a watch committee ought to do in considering whether to dismiss a chief constable ...

[In cases of the present type, involving dismissal from office for good cause] I find an unbroken line of authority to the effect that an officer cannot lawfully be dismissed without first telling him what is alleged against him and hearing his defence or explanation ...

[Having cited *Bagg's Case* (1615) 11 Co Rep 93b; *R* v. *Gaskin* (1799) 8 Term Rep 209; *R* v. *Smith* (1852) 5 QB 614; *Ex parte Ramshay* (1852) 18 QB 173; *Osgood* v. *Nelson* (1872) LR 5 HL 636; *Fisher* v. *Jackson* (1891) 2 Ch 84; *Cooper* v. *Wilson* [1937] 2 KB 309; and *Hogg* v. *Scott* [1947] KB 759, his Lordship continued:] Stopping there, I would think that authority was wholly in favour of the appellant, but the respondent's argument was mainly based on what has been said in a number of fairly recent cases dealing with different subject-matter. Those cases deal with decisions by Ministers, officials and bodies of various kinds which adversely affected property rights or privileges of persons who had had no opportunity or no proper opportunity of presenting their cases before the decisions were given. And it is necessary to examine those cases for another reason. The question which was or ought to have been considered by the watch committee on March 7, 1958, was not a simple question whether or not the appellant should be dismissed. There were three possible courses open to the watch committee—reinstating the appellant as chief constable, dismissing him, or requiring him to resign. The difference between the latter two is that dismissal involved forfeiture of pension rights, whereas requiring him to resign did not. Indeed, it is now clear that the appellant's real interest in this appeal is to try to save his pension rights ...

I would start an examination of the authorities dealing with property rights and privileges with *Cooper* v. *Wandsworth Board of Works* [(1863) 14 CBNS 180]. Where an owner had failed to give proper notice to the board they had under an Act of 1855 authority to demolish any building he had erected and recover the cost from him. This action was brought against the board because they had used that power without giving the owner an opportunity of being heard. The board maintained that their discretion to order demolition was not a judicial discretion and that any appeal should have been to the Metropolitan Board of Works. But the court decided unanimously in favour of the owner ...

[Lord Reid also referred to *Hopkins* v. *Smethwick Local Board of Health* (1890) 24 QBD 712; *Smith* v. *R* (1878) LR 3 App Cas 614; *De Verteuil* v. *Knaggs* [1918] AC 557; and *Spackman* v. *Plumstead District Board of Works* (1885) 10 App Cas 229, and continued:] I shall now turn to a different class of case—deprivation of membership of a professional or social body. In *Wood* v. *Woad* [(1874) LR 9 Ex 190] the committee purported to expel a member of a mutual insurance society without hearing him, and it was held that their action was void, and so he was still a member. Kelly CB said of audi alteram partem: 'This rule is not confined to the conduct of strictly legal tribunals, but is applicable to every tribunal or body of persons invested with authority to adjudicate upon matters involving civil consequences to individuals.' This was expressly approved by Lord Macnaghten giving the judgment of the Board in *Lapointe* v. *L'Association de Bienfaisance et de Retraite de la Police de Montréal* [[1906] AC 535] ...

Then there are the club cases, *Fisher* v. *Keane* [(1878) 11 Ch 353] and *Dawkins* v. *Antrobus* [(1879) 18 Ch 615]. In the former, Jessel M.R. said of the committee [at 362–3]: 'They ought not, as I understand it, according to the ordinary rules by which justice should be administered by committees of clubs, or by any other body of persons who decide upon the conduct of others, to blast a man's reputation for ever—perhaps to ruin his prospects for life, without giving him an opportunity of either defending or palliating his conduct.' In the latter case it was held that nothing had been done contrary to natural justice ...

It appears to me that if the present case had arisen thirty or forty years ago the courts would have had no difficulty in deciding this issue in favour of the appellant on the authorities which I have cited. So far as I am aware none of these authorities has ever been disapproved or even doubted.

Yet the Court of Appeal have decided this issue against the appellant on more recent authorities which apparently justify that result. How has this come about?

At least three things appear to me to have contributed. In the first place there have been many cases where it has been sought to apply the principles of natural justice to the wider duties imposed on Ministers and other organs of government by modern legislation. For reasons which I shall attempt to state in a moment, it has been held that those principles have a limited application in such cases and those limitations have tended to be reflected in other decisions on matters to which in principle they do not appear to me to apply. Secondly, ..., those principles have been held to have a limited application in cases arising out of war-time legislation; and again such limitations have tended to be reflected in other cases. [Lord Reid observed later in his speech that the wartime decisions were explicable by reference to the courts' appreciation that the 'temporary abandonment of the rules of natural justice was one of the sacrifices which war conditions required.'] And, thirdly, there has, I think, been a misunderstanding of the judgment of Atkin L.J. in *Rex* v. *Electricity Commissioners, Ex parte London Electricity Joint Committee Co.* [[1924] 1 KB 171].

In cases of the kind I have been dealing with the Board of Works or the Governor or the club committee was dealing with a single isolated case. It was not deciding, like a judge in a lawsuit, what were the rights of the person before it. But it was deciding how he should be treated—something analogous to a judge's duty in imposing a penalty. No doubt policy would play some part in the decision—but so it might when a judge is imposing a sentence. So it was easy to say that such a body is performing a quasi-judicial task in considering and deciding such a matter, and to require it to observe the essentials of all proceedings of a judicial character—the principles of natural justice.

Sometimes the functions of a Minister or department may also be of that character, and then the rules of natural justice can apply in much the same way. But more often their functions are of a very different character. If a Minister is considering whether to make a scheme for, say, an important new road, his primary concern will not be with the damage which its construction will do to the rights of individual owners of land. He will have to consider all manner of questions of public interest and, it may be, a number of alternative schemes. He cannot be prevented from attaching more importance to the fulfilment of his policy than to the fate of individual objectors, and it would be quite wrong for the courts to say that the Minister should or could act in the same kind of way as a board of works deciding whether a house should be pulled down. And there is another important difference. As explained in *Local Government Board* v. *Arlidge* [[1915] AC 120] a Minister cannot do everything himself. His officers will have to gather and sift all the facts, including objections by individuals, and no individual can complain if the ordinary accepted methods of carrying on public business do not give him as good protection as would be given by the principles of natural justice in a different kind of case.

We do not have a developed system of administrative law—perhaps because until fairly recently we did not need it. So it is not surprising that in dealing with new types of cases the courts have had to grope for solutions, and have found that old powers, rules and procedure are largely inapplicable to cases which they were never designed or intended to deal with. But I see nothing in that to justify our thinking that our old methods are any less applicable today than ever they were to the older types of case. And if there are any dicta in modern authorities which point in that direction, then, in my judgment, they should not be followed.

Following this review of the authorities, Lord Reid went on to consider the following dictum of Atkin LJ in *R* v. *Electricity Commissioners, ex parte London Electricity Joint Committee Co* [1924] 1 KB 171 at 205:

[T]he operation of the writs [of prohibition and certiorari] has extended to control the proceedings of bodies which do not claim to be, and would not be recognised as, courts of justice. Wherever any body of persons having legal authority to determine questions affecting the rights of subjects, and having the duty to act judicially, act in excess of their legal authority, they are subject to the controlling jurisdiction of the King's Bench Division exercised in these writs.

Lord Reid noted that in subsequent cases, such as *R* v. *Legislative Committee of the Church Assembly, ex parte Haynes-Smith* [1928] 1 KB 411 and *Nakkuda Ali* v. *Jayaratne* [1951] AC 66, a 'gloss' had been put upon Atkin LJ's dictum. In particular, in the former case (at 415), Lord Hewart CJ said (in a passage subsequently quoted with approval by the Privy Council in the latter case) that the effect of the *Electricity Commissioners* dictum was that in order for the rules of natural justice to apply,

it is not enough that it should have legal authority to determine questions affecting the rights of subjects; there must be superadded to that characteristic the further characteristic that the body has the duty to act judicially.

This, said Lord Reid in *Ridge*, was *not* what Atkin LJ had meant in the *Electricity Commissioners* case: such an interpretation—which treated the duty to act judicially as a prerequisite for the application of rules of natural justice, rather than as a consequence of their imposition—was fundamentally inconsistent with earlier authorities. In *Electricity Commissioners*, said Lord Reid (in *Ridge* at 76), Atkin LJ (and Bankes LJ) had 'inferred the judicial element from the nature of the power'. Then Lord Reid moved on to say:

Between 1882 and the making of police regulations in 1920 section 191(4) [of the Municipal Corporations Act 1882] had to be applied to every kind of case. The respondents' contention is that, even where there was a doubtful question whether a constable was guilty of a particular act of misconduct, the watch committee were under no obligation to hear his defence before dismissing him. In my judgment it is abundantly clear from the authorities I have quoted that at that time the courts would have rejected any such contention. In later cases dealing with different subject-matter, opinions have been expressed in wide terms so as to appear to conflict with those earlier authorities. But learned judges who expressed those opinions generally had no power to overrule those authorities, and in any event it is a salutary rule that a judge is not to be assumed to have intended to overrule or disapprove of an authority which has not been cited to him and which he does not even mention. So I would hold that the power of dismissal in the Act of 1882 could not then have been exercised and cannot now be exercised until the watch committee have informed the constable of the grounds on which they propose to proceed and have given him a proper opportunity to present his case in defence.

Lord Reid then considered the meeting of the watch committee on 18 March 1958, but concluded that it could not cure the earlier unfairness. (On appeals, see 10.3.4.) Only Lord

Evershed dissented from their Lordships' view that the appeal in *Ridge* should be allowed. The case thus liberated natural justice from the constraints which had been imposed upon it by earlier cases, placing a renewed emphasis on the impact of administrative decisions on individuals' rights and interests.

> **QUESTIONS**
>
> - If the 'impact' of a decision on an individual is the touchstone in this area, how ought such impact be measured?
> - Is losing one's house (*Cooper*) worse than losing one's pension (*Ridge*)?
> - Is losing a social security benefit the same as losing entitlement to a pension fund to which one has contributed?

10.2.2 Natural justice and acting fairly

Although *Ridge* acknowledged that the exercise of administrative functions could trigger a 'duty to act judicially', it did not precisely define the breadth of the circumstances in which such a duty would apply. A related question that arose was whether, if the requirement to observe some form of fair process were to be applied in circumstances wider than those allowed by some of the pre-*Ridge* cases, it ought to take the form of a 'duty to act judicially'. That matter was considered by Lord Parker CJ in *Re HK (An Infant)* [1967] QB 617 at 630, a case concerning what procedural safeguards, if any, applied to immigration officers' decisions regarding permission to enter the United Kingdom:

> [E]ven if an immigration officer is not in a judicial or quasi-judicial capacity, he must at any rate give the immigrant an opportunity of satisfying him of the matters in the subsection, and for that purpose let the immigrant know what his immediate impression is so that the immigrant can disabuse him. That is not, as I see it, a question of acting or being required to act judicially, but of being required to act fairly. Good administration and an honest or bona fide decision must, as it seems to me, require not merely impartiality, nor merely bringing one's mind to bear on the problem, but acting fairly; and to the limited extent that the circumstances of any particular case allow, and within the legislative framework under which the administrator is working, only to that limited extent do the so-called rules of natural justice apply, which in a case such as this is merely a duty to act fairly. I appreciate that in saying that it may be said that one is going further than is permitted on the decided cases because heretofore at any rate the decisions of the courts do seem to have drawn a strict line in these matters according to whether there is or is not a duty to act judicially or quasi judicially.

On this view, administrative law supplied two distinct obligations to act procedurally fairly: a duty to act *judicially* and a duty to act *fairly*, the latter being less onerous, from the decision-maker's perspective, than the former. For example, the immigration officer in *HK* itself was simply required to give the intending immigrant 'his immediate impression' so that the latter could respond—a procedure which falls some way short of 'acting judicially' in the sense of adhering to the wider trappings of the adversarial model.

Although Lord Parker's approach recognized the existence of a duty to act fairly which operated beyond the confines of the duty to act judicially, it implicitly accepted a distinction between situations attracting the latter and those merely attracting the former. This led some judges, such as Lord Pearson in *Pearlberg* v. *Varty* [1972] 1 WLR 534 at 547, to continue placing considerable weight on the administrative–judicial dichotomy:

> A tribunal to whom judicial or quasi-judicial functions are entrusted is held to be required to apply [natural justice] in performing those functions unless there is a provision to the contrary. But where some person or body is entrusted by Parliament with administrative or executive functions there is no presumption that compliance with the principles of natural justice is required, although, as 'Parliament is not to be presumed to act unfairly', the courts may be able in suitable cases (perhaps always) to imply an obligation to act with fairness. Fairness, however, does not necessarily require a plurality of hearings or representations and counter-representations.

Lord Pearson's reasoning differs from Lord Parker's in that the former conceives of acting fairly as distinct from compliance with natural justice, whereas the latter considered that the duties to act fairly and judicially were both (distinct) parts of natural justice. However, both dicta appear to accept that distinct models of procedural fairness should apply in 'judicial' and 'administrative' contexts. In that respect, they should be contrasted with Megarry V-C's more flexible use of language in *McInnes* v. *Onslow-Fane* [1978] 1 WLR 1520 at 1530:

> I do not think that much help is to be obtained from discussing whether 'natural justice' or 'fairness' is the more appropriate term. If one accepts that 'natural justice' is a flexible term which imposes different requirements in different cases, it is capable of applying appropriately to the whole range of situations indicated by terms such as 'judicial,' 'quasi-judicial' and 'administrative.' Nevertheless, the further the situation is away from anything that resembles a judicial or quasi-judicial situation, and the further the question is removed from what may reasonably be called a justiciable question, the more appropriate it is to reject an expression which includes the word 'justice' and to use instead terms such as 'fairness,' or 'the duty to act fairly'.

On this view, our choice of language is relatively unimportant. 'Fairness' is a broad principle whose precise meaning falls to be determined in context, on a sliding scale which does not require clear distinctions to be drawn between 'judicial', 'quasi-judicial', and 'administrative' powers. The upshot is that whether or not a 'duty to act judicially' arises, the exercise of a given decision-making power is likely to be accompanied by an obligation to respect certain procedural norms. Precisely which of those norms will apply in a given situation is another question, and one to which we turn at 10.3.

10.2.3 Legitimate expectations of fair treatment

The modern approach, according to which the applicability of procedural safeguards falls to be determined by reference to such factors as the impact of a given decision on the individual's rights and interests, is now augmented by the doctrine of legitimate expectation. That doctrine was considered in detail in ch 6, and at this point it is necessary merely to emphasize how it relates to the concept of procedural fairness. Two points should be noted.

First, the doctrine of legitimate expectation can influence the *scope* of the duty to act fairly by triggering it in circumstances in which no such duty would arise on the principles just considered. Thus the representations or conduct of a public authority may entitle an individual to fair treatment when, in the absence of such representations or conduct, he would have no enforceable procedural rights. This is classically demonstrated by the decision of the Privy Council in *Attorney-General of Hong Kong* v. *Ng Yuen Shiu* [1983] 2 AC 629, considered at 6.1.4.

Second, circumstances may arise in which an individual is entitled—by virtue, for instance, of the impact of a decision on his rights or interests—to a certain measure of procedural fairness (*eg* a right to make written representations) but can claim a higher level of procedural protection (*eg* an oral hearing) as a result of representations or conduct on the part of the decision-maker. By thus increasing the level of procedural protection to which an individual is entitled, the doctrine of legitimate expectation is capable of affecting not just the scope but also the *content* of the duty to act fairly in given circumstances.

10.2.4 Article 6: the scope of the right to a fair and public hearing

Any entitlement to fair process at common law may be augmented by Article 6 ECHR provided that, in the first place, that provision applies (on which see 9.5.2). To a large extent, the requirements of fairness flowing from Article 6 merely duplicate those which arise at common law: and since the scope of the common law principles is broader than that of Article 6, it is often unnecessary for claimants to rely on the latter. There are, however, two situations in which it may be necessary or desirable to rely on Article 6 rather than the common law.

First, there are some limited respects in which the former imposes more far-reaching requirements than the latter: we consider this in section 10.3.

Second, if primary legislation lays down a decision-making scheme which is flatly inconsistent with common law principles of fairness, that is the end of the matter: for as long as Parliament is sovereign, such principles cannot be used as the basis of a challenge against an Act of Parliament. However, if it can be shown that Article 6 ECHR applies and is infringed by an Act which provides for an unfair decision-making scheme, this will be grounds for issuing a declaration of incompatibility under s 4 of the Human Rights Act 1998 (HRA); and although this does not affect the validity or enforceability of the legislation, it is likely to result in its amendment. For instance, in *R (Wright)* v. *Secretary of State for Health* [2009] UKHL 3, [2009] 1 AC 739, a declaration was issued in respect of s 82(4)(b) of the Care Standards Act 2000 (since repealed) which had allowed people to be provisionally placed on a list of those considered unsuitable to work with vulnerable adults without first being afforded any kind of hearing.

10.2.5 The limits of procedural fairness

Although the general trend, identified earlier, is to extend the application of procedural fairness to a wider range of situations, there remain cases in which decision-makers are not subject to any obligation to act fairly. First, there exist (now rare) situations in which no factor operates in the first place to trigger the duty to act fairly: if, for instance, the court concludes that the decision in question does not have any relevant impact upon the individual's rights, interests, or legitimate expectations, then no duty of fairness arises. Second, it is possible in principle for legislation expressly to displace the principles of procedural fairness, although the courts will only conclude with great reluctance that this was Parliament's intention (see, *eg Wilkinson* v. *Barking Corporation* [1948] 1 KB 721). Third, although there may exist no *prima facie* inhibition to the applicability of the principles of procedural fairness, the wider context within which the decision-making power is exercised may raise such an obstacle. For instance, in *Council of Civil Service Unions* v. *Minister for the Civil Service* [1985] AC 374—considered, in this regard, at 4.3.3—an expectation that a particular procedural safeguard (consultation) would operate was displaced by countervailing national security concerns. Whether fair procedure, or a particular form thereof, is applicable will also depend upon construction of the statutory scheme and its purpose, a point to which we return at 10.3.1. Fourth, as Lord Reed acknowledged in *R (Bourgass)* v. *Secretary of State for Justice* [2015] UKSC 54, [2015] 3 WLR 457 at [93], where circumstances demand that a decision is taken as a matter of urgency, no hearing or other participative process may be required prior to the taking of an initial decision (albeit that fairness may well demand the *subsequent* following of due process in respect of a final or longer-term decision).

It has also been said that if the provision of a hearing (or some other form of procedural fairness) 'would make no difference'—meaning that a hearing would not change the ultimate conclusion reached by the decision-maker—then no legal duty to supply a hearing arises. Such an approach was endorsed by Lord Wilberforce in *Malloch* v. *Aberdeen Corporation* [1971] 1 WLR 1578 at 1595, who said that a 'breach of procedure ... cannot give [rise to] a remedy in the courts, unless behind it there is something of substance which has been lost by the failure. The court does not act in vain.' Relying on these comments, Brandon LJ opined in *Cinnamond* v. *British Airports Authority* [1980] 1 WLR 582 at 593 that 'no one can complain of not being given an opportunity to make representations if such an opportunity would have availed him nothing'.

However, three objections can be raised against this line of thinking (see generally *R* v. *Chief Constable of Thames Valley Police, ex parte Cotton* [1990] IRLR 344 at 352, *per* Bingham LJ). The first—stated in memorable terms by Megarry J in *John* v. *Rees* [1970] Ch 345 at 402—is concerned with the grave practical difficulties entailed in trying to determine *whether* a fair hearing would make a difference:

> It may be that there are some who would decry the importance which the courts attach to the observance of the rules of natural justice. 'When something is obvious,' they may say, 'why force everybody to go through the tiresome waste of time involved in framing charges and giving an opportunity to be heard? The result is obvious from the start.' Those who take this view do not, I think, do themselves justice. As everybody who has anything to do with the law well knows, the path of the law is strewn with examples of open and shut cases which, somehow, were not; of unanswerable charges which, in the event, were completely answered; of inexplicable conduct which was fully explained; of fixed and unalterable determinations that, by discussion, suffered a change.

Second, we have already seen in relation to bias the importance of ensuring not just a fair decision-making process, but also that citizens perceive it to be fair. The same argument can be applied in the present context. In *Secretary of State for the Home Department* v. *AF (No 3)*

[2009] UKHL 28, [2010] 2 AC 269 [72], Lord Hoffmann—referring to the right to know the opposing case: a particular aspect of procedural fairness that we consider at 10.3.2—said:

> The purpose of the rule is not merely to improve the chances of the tribunal reaching the right decision (by giving the accused an opportunity to explain or contradict any such allegations or material) but to avoid the subjective sense of injustice which an accused may feel if he knows that the tribunal relied upon material of which he was not told.

The third objection relates to the distinction, considered at the beginning of this chapter, between normative and instrumental conceptions of procedural fairness. The former view holds that, even if no practical difficulties would result from withholding fair hearings where their provision would make no difference, such conduct on the part of the administration would nevertheless be improper. Such a view was endorsed by Lord Reed, giving the judgment of the Supreme Court in *R (Osborn)* v. *Parole Board* [2013] UKSC 61, [2014] AC 1115 [69]:

> [J]ustice is intuitively understood to require a procedure which pays due respect to persons whose rights are significantly affected by decisions taken in the exercise of administrative or judicial functions. Respect entails that such persons ought to be able to participate in the procedure by which the decision is made, provided they have something to say which is relevant to the decision to be taken. As Jeremy Waldron has written ('How Law Protects Dignity' [2012] CLJ 200, 210):
>
> > 'Applying a norm to a human individual is not like deciding what to do about a rabid animal or a dilapidated house. It involves paying attention to a point of view and respecting the personality of the entity one is dealing with. As such it embodies a crucial dignitarian idea of respecting the dignity of those to whom the norms are applied as beings capable of explaining themselves.'

Referring to the dictum from *R* v. *The Chancellor of Cambridge* (1723) 1 Stra 557 set out at 10.1, concerning God's willingness to grant Adam a hearing, Lord Reed continued (at [69]):

> The point … is that Adam was allowed a hearing notwithstanding that God, being omniscient, did not require to hear him in order to improve the quality of His decision-making.

On this view, the notion of procedural fairness which would 'make no difference' becomes a contradiction in terms, since it rests on an exclusively outcomes-oriented view which overlooks the much wider role played by procedural fairness in an administrative state that seeks to build constructive relationships between individuals and public bodies by casting the former as participants in the process of governance.

Where, then, does English law presently stand on this question? The leading cases do not adopt an entirely consistent approach. Some, like *Osborn*, are clearly open to the notion that fairness is a non-instrumental (as well as an instrumental) good. In that case, which concerned the question whether the Parole Board should have granted the claimant prisoners oral hearings before deciding whether, *eg* to release them on parole, Lord Reed said (at [2]):

> The board should also bear in mind that the purpose of holding an oral hearing is not only to assist it in its decision-making, but also to reflect the prisoner's legitimate interest in being able to participate in a decision with important implications for him, where he has something useful to contribute.

> ... The question whether fairness requires a prisoner to be given an oral hearing is different from the question whether he has a particular likelihood of being released or transferred to open conditions, and cannot be answered by assessing that likelihood.

Compare Lord Reed's approach with that of Lord Phillips in *Secretary of State for the Home Department* v. *AF (No 3)* [2009] UKHL 28, [2009] 3 WLR 74 at [60]:

> I do not believe that it is possible to draw a clear distinction between a fair procedure and a procedure that produces a fair result. The object of the procedure is to ensure, in so far as this is possible, that the outcome of the process is a result that accords with the law.

On Lord Phillips's view, it is in principle possible for a decision-maker lawfully to refuse to supply a fair hearing on the ground that it would make no difference. However, although willing to countenance that possibility in principle, Lord Phillips went on to cite practical reasons of the type mentioned earlier which mean that a court should be very slow to that a fair hearing would make no difference. The upshot is that while it would be going too far to say that the 'makes no difference' will inevitably be rejected, it is likely to succeed only in very limited circumstances, an example of which is furnished by *R (National Association of Health Stores)* v. *Secretary of State for Health* [2005] EWCA Civ 154. It was argued that the Minister had failed, before deciding to prohibit the sale of a herbal remedy known as kava-kava, to discharge his statutory duty to consult. In fact, consultation had taken place—on both the possibility of banning kava-kava outright, and making it available only on prescription—but the claimant argued that the consultation was flawed by the fact that there had been no consultation on the less drastic option of compulsory labelling of products containing kava-kava. This argument failed at first instance and was not pursued before the Court of Appeal for reasons explained by Sedley LJ:

> [21] ... If after what was accepted as being due consultation it was concluded that placing usage and dosage in the hands of qualified medical practitioners was not a sufficient safeguard, the rule-maker could not rationally have concluded, whatever the input from consultation, that a warning on the label would suffice.
> [22] In spite, therefore, of the important cautions to be borne in mind by the courts against denying relief on the ground that a legally correct approach could have made no difference to the outcome ..., the present case seems to me almost a laboratory example of the proper use of the power. This is because it is not the court's own evaluation—frequently a risky business—but a proper evaluation made by the authorised decision-maker which provides a legal, rather than merely a discretionary, measure of what was possible.

QUESTIONS

- Should courts ever be prepared to accede to the 'makes no difference' argument?
- Is the current state of English law in this area satisfactory?

Finally, it should be noted that whether the *legal requirement* to supply a fair hearing dissolves in the face of the 'makes no difference' argument is a distinct matter from whether *relief can or must be withheld* if the court is satisfied that a fair process would make no difference. Section 31(2A)–(2C) of the Senior Courts Act 1981, inserted by s 84 of the

Criminal Justice and Courts Act 2015, bears upon the latter issue, since it precludes the court—absent 'reasons of exceptional public interest'—from issuing relief if it appears 'highly likely that the outcome for the applicant would not have been substantially different if the conduct complained of had not occurred'. We consider these provisions in more detail at 14.8.

10.3 What is the content of the duty to act fairly?

10.3.1 Context, flexibility, and hearings

Now that the *scope* of the duty to act fairly is so broad, much of the heavy lifting—so far as determining what is actually required of a given decision-maker is concerned—inevitably falls to be done by determining what the *content* of that duty is. In *Bank Mellat v. HM Treasury (No 2)* [2013] UKSC 39, [2014] AC 700 at [35], Lord Sumption explained that '[t]he duty of fairness governing the exercise of a statutory power is a limitation on the discretion of the decision-maker which is implied into the statute', and that even if 'the statute makes some provision for the procedure to be followed' that 'does not of itself impliedly exclude' the implication into the statute of other aspects of the duty to act fairly.

At the core of that duty is the decision-maker's obligation to facilitate meaningful participation by relevant parties—a duty which, as Lord Neuberger made clear in *Bank Mellat (No 2)* at [179], is resistant, albeit not impervious, to displacement:

> In my view, the rule is that, before a statutory power is exercised, any person who foreseeably would be significantly detrimentally affected by the exercise should be given the opportunity to make representations in advance, unless (i) the statutory provisions concerned expressly or impliedly provide otherwise or (ii) the circumstances in which the power is to be exercised would render it impossible, impractical or pointless to afford such an opportunity. I would add that any argument advanced in support of impossibility, impracticality or pointlessness should be very closely examined, as a court will be slow to hold that there is no obligation to give the opportunity, when such an obligation is not dispensed with in the relevant statute.

The devil, however, is in the detail. In any given set of circumstances, what does it mean to afford someone 'the opportunity to make representations in advance'? Here, context is central, as Beatson LJ explained in *R (L) v. West London Mental Health NHS Trust* [2014] EWCA Civ 47, [2014] 1 WLR 3103 at [67]:

> [The] starting point in ascertaining what fairness requires in a case such as this is to consider the commonplace orthodoxy in the modern law that what procedure is required by the common law principles of natural justice or fairness is acutely sensitive to context.

Against this background, Beatson LJ went on to note the competing pulls exerted in this context by two sets of considerations. He noted (at [68]) the concern of some commentators that courts have failed fully to exploit the potential offered by the flexibility of today's 'commonplace orthodoxy':

> Some commentators, notably Professor Loughlin and Professor Cane (respectively in (1978) 28 UTLJ 215 and *Administrative Law*, 5th ed (2011), pp 73–75) have been critical of the courts' approach to [the] flexibility of procedural fairness. Despite the signal in *In re HK* and the other cases that the requirement was for a less formal procedure, in different ways they suggest that the courts have not deployed the flexibility inherent in the notion of fairness of administrative decision-making suffciently. This is because the various requirements of a fair hearing are in essence, in Professor Cane's words … 'a skeletal version of the elaborate rules of judicial procedure' so that the courts' menu of choice tends to be a range of possibilities based on adjudicative methods of decision-making.

At the same time, however, Beatson LJ took the view that there comes a point at which flexibility is itself problematic:

> [69] It is … insufficient to react to the danger of over-formalisation and judicialisation simply by emphasising flexibility and context-sensitivity. There are dangers in concentrating on a flexible notion of overarching fairness …
> [72] [It] may lead to a modern version of Sir William Wade's nightmare of a Tennysonian 'wilderness of single instances' in which all the contextual factors will be relevant in considering what the requirements of procedural fairness are in a given situation without any factor or group of factors having decisive weight in shaping what is in practice required. The consequence may either risk obscuring the overarching principle or stating it at a level of generality which is not of use as a practical tool to decision-making. The result could be undue uncertainty and unpredictability.

Beatson LJ concluded (at [72]) that

> [t]here is a need for principled guidance which is practical and does not constitute either a procedural straitjacket, a 'safe harbour' for longstanding ways of doing things in a particular context, or operate with centripetal force towards an adversarial adjudicative process.

As far as such 'principled guidance' is concerned, the case law shows that the precise level of fairness required in any given context is a function of two key variables: the nature and importance of the matter liable to be affected by the decision, and the practical need for particular forms of procedural safeguard. We consider these two matters in turn.

As to the first, *the general principle is that the more important the matter which is at stake, the more that will be required in terms of procedural fairness.* This idea is reflected by the distinction drawn by Megarry J in *McInnes v. Onslow-Fane* [1978] 1 WLR 1520 at 1529 between 'forfeiture cases' involving 'a decision which takes away some existing right or position' and 'application cases' in which 'the decision merely refuses to grant the applicant the right or position that he seeks'. However, as Laws LJ remarked in *R (Khatun) v. Newham London Borough Council* [2004] EWCA Civ 55, [2005] QB 37 at [31], the distinction between application and forfeiture cases is

> not hard and fast. There may be cases where refusal of the application (for example, the refusal of a passport) will carry adverse implications for other rights or interests which the applicant may expect to enjoy. But in general the distinction possesses much force. In an 'application' case there is likely to be legal space for the decision-maker to exercise a discretion whether or not to

accord a right to be heard. In doing so, he will of course have regard to the practicalities of the statutory scheme's operation. A perceived need in the general interest to process applications speedily, against a background of many applicants and scarce resources, may be a legitimate and important factor.

The point, taken by Laws LJ, that hearings may be necessary in application cases is underlined by *R v. Secretary of State for the Home Department, ex parte Fayed* [1998] 1 WLR 763, in which the Court of Appeal found that the Secretary of State had been wrong to refuse to hear an applicant for British citizenship. Lord Woolf MR drew attention to the very high stakes, including damage to the applicants' reputations and the denial of the benefits of citizenship:

The decisions of the Minister are therefore classically ones which but for [a statutory provision which arguably displaced the duty (on which see generally 10.3.2) to give the individual notice of the case against him, but which on analysis turned out not to have that effect] would involve an obligation on the Minister making the decision to give the Fayeds an opportunity to be heard before that decision was reached ... The days when it used to be said that a person seeking a privilege is not entitled to be heard are long gone ... [T]he mere fact that this is a 'privilege' case did not preclude the application of the rules of natural justice.

That hearings should not be regarded as uniformly unnecessary in application cases is manifestly correct. In application cases, just as in forfeiture cases, the decision-maker may have to confront questions which can only be fairly considered by entering into a form of dialogue with the individual concerned. So while considerations of efficiency and economy may often justify the provision of more limited safeguards in application cases, it will sometimes be apposite for the decision-maker to enter into a dialogue with the applicant, giving him an opportunity to comment upon the veracity and significance of information and the relevance of policy considerations which are adverse to his application. As the *Fayed* case indicates, such dialogue may be particularly necessary when what is at stake is especially great.

Alongside the nature and importance of the matter at stake, *the practical usefulness of particular forms of procedural safeguards is an important determinant of what fairness requires in a given case*. We noted at 10.2.5 that courts are generally resistant to the argument that no duty to act fairly should be imposed because acting fairly would make no difference to the outcome. However, the courts exhibit greater receptiveness to the more granular argument that there is no need to insist upon a *particular* procedural safeguard because, in the circumstances of the case, its provision would not in practice enhance the overall fairness of the process. This point emerges at 10.3.3 when we consider the circumstances in which specific safeguards, such as legal representation and cross-examination, are required. Here, however, we address a more general question: when will fairness require the provision of an oral hearing?

Lloyd v. *McMahon* [1987] AC 625
House of Lords

Liverpool City Council failed to set a lawful rate (a forerunner of council tax) for the year 1985–86 by the required date, causing losses to the Council in excess of £100,000. The district auditor warned councillors on a number of occasions that their failure to set a lawful rate could result in personal liability for any resultant losses. After investigating the matter—in the course of which councillors were invited to submit written representations—the auditor issued a certificate under s 20(1) of the Local Government Finance Act 1982 to the effect that the councillors were jointly and severally liable for the losses caused by their wilful misconduct. Issuing a certificate in respect of members of the local authority for sums in excess of £2,000 also carried the consequence of disqualification from office for five years. The certificate was accompanied by a statement of reasons which addressed in detail the matters raised by the councillors in their written representations. The councillors unsuccessfully appealed, under s 20(3), to the High Court and the Court of Appeal, and thereafter to the House of Lords. They alleged, *inter alia*, that the district auditor's failure to offer an oral hearing constituted a breach of procedural fairness which invalidated the s 20(1) certificate.

Lord Keith

… My Lords, if the district auditor had reached a decision adverse to the appellants without giving them any opportunity at all of making representations to him, there can be no doubt that his procedure would have been contrary to the rules of natural justice and that, subject to the question whether the defect was capable of being cured on appeal to the Divisional Court, the decision would fall to be quashed. In the event, written representations alone were asked for. These were duly furnished, in very considerable detail, and an oral hearing was not requested, though that could very easily have been done, and there is no reason to suppose that the request would not have been granted. None of the appellants stated, in his or her affidavit before the Divisional Court, that they had an expectation that an oral hearing, though not asked for, would be offered. The true question is whether the district auditor acted fairly in all the circumstances. It is easy to envisage cases where an oral hearing would clearly be essential in the interests of fairness, for example where an objector states that he has personal knowledge of some facts indicative of wilful misconduct on the part of a councillor. In that situation justice would demand that the councillor be given an opportunity to depone to his own version of the facts. In the present case the district auditor had arrived at his provisional view upon the basis of the contents of documents, minutes of meetings and reports submitted to the council from the auditor's department and their own officers. All these documents were appended to or referred to in the notice of 26 June sent by the district auditor to the appellants. Their response referred to other documents, which were duly considered by the district auditor, as is shown by his statement of reasons dated 6 September 1985. No facts contradictory of or supplementary to the contents of the documents were or are relied on by either side. If the appellants had attended an oral hearing they would no doubt have reiterated the sincerity of their motives from the point of view of advancing the interests of the inhabitants of Liverpool. It seems unlikely, having regard to the position adopted by their counsel on this matter before the Divisional Court, that they would have been willing to reveal or answer questions about the proceedings of their political caucus. The sincerity of the appellants' motives is not something capable of justifying or excusing failure to carry out a statutory duty, or of making reasonable what is otherwise an unreasonable delay in carrying out such a duty. In all the circumstances I am of opinion that the district auditor did not act unfairly, and that the procedure which he followed did not involve any prejudice to the appellants …

Lord Bridge

… My Lords, the so-called rules of natural justice are not engraved on tablets of stone. To use the phrase which better expresses the underlying concept, what the requirements of fairness demand when any body, domestic, administrative or judicial, has to make a decision which will affect the rights of individuals depends on the character of the decision-making body, the kind of decision it has to make and the statutory or other framework in which it operates. In particular, it is well-established that when a statute has conferred on any body the power to make decisions affecting individuals, the courts will not only require the procedure prescribed by the statute to be followed, but will readily imply so much and no more to be introduced by way of additional procedural safeguards as will ensure the attainment of fairness. It follows that the starting-point for the examination of all the appellants' submissions on this aspect of the case is the Act of 1982 ...

So far as procedure is concerned, section 14 of the Act of 1982 provides for the issue of a code of audit practice to be approved by each House of Parliament. The code currently in force contains detailed provisions relating to objections under section 17, but none relating to the procedure to be followed when an auditor contemplates the issue of a certificate under section 20 of his own motion. The gravity of the consequences of a certificate for the person from whom the amount of a loss is certified to be due, particularly if he is a member of a local authority and the amount exceeds £2,000, are obvious enough. No one doubts that the auditor must give to such a person adequate notice of the case against him and an adequate opportunity to present to the auditor his defence to that case. I followed with interest [counsel's] carefully researched review of the history of local government audit legislation, but I did not find that it threw any light on what, in particular, is required to provide such an opportunity in the circumstances of any particular case under the statute presently in force. Still less do I attach any significance to the fact that since 1972, when provisions substantially to the like effect as those which we find in the Act of 1982 first reached the statute book, auditors have, as a matter of practice, always invited oral representations from members of local authorities before certifying the amount of any loss or deficiency as due from them. When a single individual is thought to have failed to bring a sum into account or by his wilful misconduct to have caused a loss or deficiency, it is no doubt a very appropriate practice to invite his explanation orally. But I fail to understand how that practice can constrain the courts to construe the statute as requiring an auditor proposing to act under section 20 to invite oral representations as a matter of law in every case. In this case the auditor seems to have intelligently anticipated that the Liverpool councillors who constituted the majority group would want to present a united front in their response to his notice of 26 June 1985 as they had done in their conduct of the city council's affairs during the previous year. Councillor Hamilton's letter of 19 July 1985 amply confirmed his expectation. If any councillor had wanted to put forward his own independent and individual grounds in rebuttal of the charge of wilful misconduct against himself, I have no doubt he would have done so. If any had asked to be heard orally and the auditor had refused, there would have been clear ground for a complaint of unfairness. I suppose it is conceivable that the appellants collectively might have wished to appoint a spokesman to present their case orally rather than in writing, though the case they did present, embracing as it did such a large volume of documentary material, clearly lent itself more aptly to written than oral presentation. It has never been suggested that it was unfair that the auditor did not invite the appellants to address arguments to him through solicitor or counsel. The proposition that it was, per se, in breach of the rules of natural justice not to invite oral representations in this case is quite untenable.

Lord Templeman agreed that the auditor's failure to offer an oral hearing did not render the process unfair. Lords Brandon and Griffiths agreed with the other three judges. Appeal dismissed.

It is clear that a number of factors informed their Lordships' view that an oral hearing was unnecessary in the circumstances. Although, as Lord Bridge noted, the consequences for councillors of a s 20(1) certificate were potentially serious—a factor which, taken on its own, would point towards a generous level of procedural protection, probably including an oral hearing—this fell to be balanced against competing considerations. Among these were the facts that the case lent itself better to written representations, given the large amount of documentary evidence upon which it turned, and that an oral hearing would have added nothing: it might have allowed the councillors to emphasize the sincerity of their motives but, as Lord Keith observed, this was irrelevant to their liability. It is also clear that Lord Keith's analysis of what fairness required was fundamentally influenced by the legislation itself.

Lloyd v. *McMahon* can profitably be compared with the Supreme Court's decision in *R (Osborn)* v. *Parole Board* [2013] UKSC 61, [2014] AC 1115. The case concerned challenges to Parole Board decisions not to re-release a prisoner who had been recalled to prison on the ground that he had breached licence conditions whilst on parole, and not to release or transfer to open conditions two life sentence prisoners who had served their minimum detention periods. The Court held that, by not agreeing to supply oral hearings to the three prisoners concerned, the Board had acted unlawfully. In reaching that conclusion, Lord Reed, giving the only judgment, set out the following guidance (at [2]):

(i) In order to comply with common law standards of procedural fairness, the board should hold an oral hearing before determining an application for release, or for a transfer to open conditions, whenever fairness to the prisoner requires such a hearing in the light of the facts of the case and the importance of what is at stake.

(ii) It is impossible to define exhaustively the circumstances in which an oral hearing will be necessary, but such circumstances will often include the following. (a) Where facts which appear to the board to be important are in dispute, or where a significant explanation or mitigation is advanced which needs to be heard orally in order fairly to determine its credibility. The board should guard against any tendency to underestimate the importance of issues of fact which may be disputed or open to explanation or mitigation. (b) Where the board cannot otherwise properly or fairly make an independent assessment of risk, or of the means by which it should be managed and addressed. That is likely to be the position in cases where such an assessment may depend on the view formed by the board (including its members with expertise in psychology or psychiatry) of characteristics of the prisoner which can best be judged by seeing or questioning him in person, or where a psychological assessment produced by the Ministry of Justice is disputed on tenable grounds, or where the board may be materially assisted by hearing evidence, for example from a psychologist or psychiatrist. Cases concerning prisoners who have spent many years in custody are likely to fall into the first of these categories. (c) Where it is maintained on tenable grounds that a face-to-face encounter with the board, or the questioning of those who have dealt with the prisoner, is necessary in order to enable him or his representatives to put their case effectively or to test the views of those who have dealt with him. (d) Where, in the light of the representations made by or on behalf of the prisoner, it would be unfair for a 'paper' decision made by a single member panel of the board to become final without allowing an oral hearing: for example, if the representations raise issues which place in serious question anything in the paper decision which may in practice have a significant impact on the prisoner's future management in prison or on future reviews.

(iii) In order to act fairly, the board should consider whether its independent assessment of risk, and of the means by which it should be managed and addressed, may benefit from the closer examination which an oral hearing can provide.

Against this background, the Court concluded that oral hearings should have been supplied to the three prisoners, not least because a number of significant issues of fact were the subject of controversy. For instance, one of the prisoners, Osborn, was (as Lord Reed explained at [18]–[20])

recalled to custody [on] the same day [as his release from prison], after arriving at the hostel where he was to live 20 minutes after the time when he was required by his licence conditions to be there, having visited an address at a village in Staffordshire en route. His licence was revoked the same day. He was informed by the Ministry of Justice that he had been recalled to prison because it had been reported by the probation service that he had breached a condition of his licence by failing to confine himself to an address approved by his supervising officer during the hours of a curfew ...

[Osborn's] offender manager had also received information that on the day of his release, when reminded that he could not have access to firearms, the appellant had said 'not for another two hours' ... It was also reported that shortly before the appellant had left the address which he had visited en route to the hostel he had telephoned the hostel manager to tell her that he would be late, saying falsely that he was on the A38. On returning to his car he had removed and rearranged items in the boot. This gave rise to concern in view of his comment about access to firearms.

Lord Reed went on (at [98]) to say that

there were several facts which ... were in dispute, or for which a significant explanation or mitigation was advanced: the appellant's attitude to the licence conditions; the basis of the official assessment of the risk which he presented; the events on the date of his release, including his alleged statement about firearms; his claim that the hostel manager had agreed to put back the time when he was due to arrive; and his explanation for the detour to the village. An oral hearing should therefore have been held.

QUESTIONS

- Why did procedural fairness require oral hearings in *Osborn* but not in *Lloyd* v. *McMahon*?
- Can the divergent outcomes in those two cases be accounted for by reference to factual differences, or are there points of principle which distinguish the judgments?

10.3.2 The duty to give notice

In his novel *The Trial*, Kafka described a dystopian society in which people were routinely accused of, tried, and punished for crimes whose nature was never revealed to them. As Lord Hope put it in *Secretary of State for the Home Department* v. *AF (No 3)* [2009] UKHL 28, [2009] 3 WLR 74 at [83], 'denunciation on grounds that are not disclosed is the stuff of nightmares'. Against this background, the common law exhibits a strong commitment to the principle of 'open justice'. This requires that criminal and civil proceedings be conducted in a way that facilitates the participation of both (or all) parties; meaning, among other things, that the parties should have equal access to evidence treated as relevant and admissible by the court. On this basis, in cases such as *Al Rawi* v. *Security Service* [2011] UKSC 34, [2012] 1 AC 531 and *R (B)* v. *Westminster Magistrates' Court* [2014] UKSC 59, [2015] AC 1195, the courts have generally taken the view that unless primary legislation so provides (either explicitly or, as in *Bank Mellat* v. *HM Treasury (No 1)* [2013] UKSC 38, [2014] AC 700, by necessarily implication), they may not adopt procedures enabling them to take account of evidence to which one of the parties is denied access (*eg* on national security grounds).

The open justice principle finds its analogue in the administrative context in 'the duty to give notice'. At its lowest, this means that individuals must know that a matter liable to affect them is going to be decided *before* any final decision is taken. As Lord Sumption put it in *Bank Mellat* v. *HM Treasury (No 2)* [2013] UKSC 39, [2014] AC 700 at [29]:

> The duty to give advance notice and an opportunity to be heard to a person against whom a draconian statutory power is to be exercised is one of the oldest principles of what would now be called public law.

Informing the person concerned of the prospect of a decision is thus necessary if the duty to give notice is to be discharged. But it is not (usually) sufficient. In *Kanda* v. *Government of Malaysia* [1962] AC 322 at 337, in which it was held that the dismissal of a police officer without disclosure of a report which was highly prejudicial to him was void, Lord Denning MR said:

> If the right to be heard is to be a real right which is worth anything, it must carry with it a right in the accused man to know the case which is made against him. He must know what evidence has been given and what statements have been made affecting him: and then he must be given a fair opportunity to correct or contradict them.

Viewed thus, the duty to give notice is part and parcel of the duty to act fairly, permitting the individual to make representations (or otherwise participate) being little more than a sham if he is not equipped to do so in an informed manner.

That much is clear from *R (Bourgass)* v. *Secretary of State for Justice* [2015] UKSC 54, [2015] 3 WLR 457, in which one of the claimant prisoners, Bourgass, had been subjected to solitary confinement, or 'segregation', for unbroken periods of several months because of an allegation that he had been involved in—albeit that he had not directly perpetrated or been present during—an assault on another prisoner. Although the initial decision to impose segregation for 72 hours was lawful—no hearing, and so no notice, being required given the urgency of the matter—the Supreme Court considered that subsequent decisions to continue segregation were unlawful. That conclusion was reached on the ground considered at 5.2.4, but Lord Reed also addressed the question of procedural fairness. Having said (at [98]) that 'a prisoner should normally have a reasonable opportunity to make representations before a decision [to continue segregation] is taken', Lord Reed went on:

> [100] A prisoner's right to make representations is largely valueless unless he knows the substance of the case being advanced in sufficient detail to enable him to respond. He must therefore normally be informed of the substance of the matters on the basis of which the authority of the Secretary of State [for the continuation of segregation] is sought. That will not normally require the disclosure of the primary evidence on which the governor's concerns are based: ... the Secretary of State is not determining what may or may not have happened, but is taking an operational decision concerning the management of risk. It is however important to understand that what is required is genuine and meaningful disclosure of the reasons why authorisation is sought. The reasons for continued segregation which were provided by the prison staff involved in the present cases gave, at best, only the most general idea of the nature of their concerns, and of why those concerns were held. More could and should have been said—and was said, in the witness statements filed in these proceedings—without endangering the legitimate interests which the prison authorities were concerned to protect. The imposition of prolonged periods of solitary confinement on the basis of what are, in substance, secret and unchallengeable allegations is, or should be, unacceptable.

[101] More specifically, in Bourgass's case, although some of the reasons given to him explained that his segregation was based on the assault on [another prisoner], the prison failed to provide any information as to why he was considered to have been involved in an assault which took place in his absence, despite being repeatedly asked to do so. The statement that he was to remain in segregation 'pending an investigation into a serious assault' became particularly egregious when repeated after all investigations had ceased ... Stating that 'you are an unacceptable risk to other prisoners', that 'you are known as a threat to other prisoners', that 'your behaviour is deemed to be unsuitable for normal location', or that 'you would be a disruptive influence on normal loca-tion', told him nothing about the basis on which he was considered to present such a risk or threat or disruptive influence, or about the behaviour which was deemed unsuitable.

It is apparent from these remarks that the duty to give notice does not necessarily require the decision-maker to hand over to the individual concerned every last piece of relevant information held by the decision-maker. Rather, the requirement is that the extent of disclo-sure should be sufficient to enable the individual meaningfully and effectively to participate in the decision-making process by making representations that address those matters that are germane to the issue that falls to be decided. In some situations, that may require dis-closure not of, for instance, primary materials held by the decision-maker, but only of their 'gist'—that is, particularly salient information contained in such materials. In *Bourgass*, however, not even that had been provided: the information that was disclosed plainly failed to reach the level of specificity necessary to equip the claimant to participate in such a way.

This leads on to two questions. First, how do we determine, in any given context, how much disclosure is *sufficient*? Second, is it lawful for the extent of disclosure to fall below that sufficiency threshold if, for instance, competing factors—such as the safety of others or national security—are in play?

As to the first matter, useful guidance is offered by *R (L)* v. *West London Mental Health NHS Trust* [2014] EWCA Civ 47, [2014] 1 WLR 3103. The claimant—who, having been convicted of several criminal offences, was detained in Stockton Hall, a medium security hospital—challenged the lawfulness of a decision to transfer him to Broadmoor, a high security hospital. That decision—taken after a 'triggering incident' in which the claimant had made a weapon with which he said he planned to stab another patient, 'SW'—was made by Broadmoor's admissions panel following a referral by the claimant's responsible clinician, Dr Vandenabeele, and an assessment by Dr Sengupta, a Broadmoor doctor. The relevant circumstances in which the decision was made were described by Beatson LJ (with whose leading judgment, in relevant respects, Patten and Moses LJJ agreed) at [18]:

When the panel met on 2 September 2010 it had before it Dr Vandenabeele's referral letter and the reports by Dr Sengupta and the social worker. It also had some 15 earlier reports about L by psychiatrists, psychologists and other healthcare professionals, the witness statements concern-ing the index offence [concerning the weapons and the stated intention to assault], and [a] deci-sion about L dated 23 July 2009 by the mental health review tribunal. At that time none of those documents had been provided to L or his legal representatives.

This might appear to establish a flagrant breach of the duty to give notice. However, the Court of Appeal in fact held that the decision was lawful. Beatson LJ noted (at [90]) that

L knew very soon after the incident ... that, as a result of it and its aftermath, Stockton Hall was considering whether to refer him to Broadmoor. It is not clear from the material before the court precisely what was said to him by Dr Vandenabeele about the incident, but L had an opportunity to give his side of the incident and his view of the circumstances to Dr Vandenabeele before the reference [to Broadmoor was made]. L and Dr Sengupta met ... over two weeks later after the reference. At that meeting he also appears to have had the opportunity of giving his account of the incident and his motivation, this time to Dr Sengupta.

The key question, said Beatson LJ (at [90]), was

whether ... fairness required that L and his representatives be given the 'gist' of the reports before the decision was made, or whether the information he was given at his meetings with Dr Vandenabeele and Dr Sengupta, and the opportunity at those meetings to comment on whether he should be transferred sufficed to satisfy the requirements of fairness.

The Court of Appeal concluded that those requirements had been satisfied. Beatson LJ said (at [94]) that although 'the documents show that the weapons incident was an important factor in Dr Sengupta's assessment', the point in dispute was very narrow:

It only concerned the accuracy of characterising the triggering incident as one in which staff 'discovered' the weapons and the fact that there was no reference to L's attempts before the incident to be separated from SW. It was not in issue that L had fashioned the weapons ... It was not in issue that he stated that he would stab SW. The question whether this was a 'cry for help' rather than any manifestation of intent to harm and a risk to other patients was primarily a clinical one for the psychiatrists involved to determine. Although the way the triggering incident was characterised was no doubt relevant, even if L's conduct was a cry for help, the fundamental question was whether he could be managed in conditions of medium security without risk to himself or others. This also was principally a question for the clinicians and, to reiterate, what was important for their determination was that L went to some effort to fashion the weapons, hid one of them, and made the statements he did. None of that was at issue.

In the light of this, Beatson LJ concluded (at [92]) that the claimant and his representative had been 'able to participate in the procedure by which the decision was made, albeit not by making representations in the light of the reference and the report or their "gists"'.

The *L* case does not involve the duty to give notice being displaced or traded off against some competing policy interest: rather, the duty was not in the first place breached because the disclosure of the relevant materials was not necessary in order to facilitate participation. However, the question remains whether—outwith circumstances in which legislation displaces the right to notice or the principle of open justice, as the Justice and Security Act 2013 does in certain circumstances in respect of civil litigation—it is ever lawful for a decision-maker to withhold information that *is* necessary for that purpose. On this matter, Lord Reed had the following to say in *Bourgass* (at [103]):

It has to be recognized ... that authority [to continue segregation] ... will often be sought on the basis of information which cannot be disclosed in full without placing at significant risk the safety of others or jeopardising prison security ... In such circumstances, fairness does not require the disclosure of information which could compromise the safety of an informant, the integrity of prison security or other overriding interests. It will be sufficient to inform the prisoner in more or less general terms of the gist of the reasons for seeking the authority of the Secretary of State [to continue segregation].

This implies that what the duty to give notice entails is sensitive not only—as it was in *L*—to what is sufficient in order to facilitate participation, but also to extrinsic considerations such as others' safety. On this view, the duty might be taken to be discharged by a level of disclosure that would not normally be considered insufficient, but which is taken to be sufficient in the light of the compelling nature of competing considerations. This raises some further questions. For instance, what sort of interests might be sufficient to dilute the duty to give notice? And might such interests not merely dilute but wholly displace that duty, raising the prospect of decisions being held to be lawful in the absence of *any* notice, provided that there is a compelling reason for the withholding of notice?

Precisely such issues arose in *Roberts* v. *Parole Board* [2005] UKHL 45, [2005] 2 AC 738. The claimant was a convicted murderer who had become eligible for parole. The Parole Board had to decide whether to release him, and in doing so took into account certain sensitive evidence—'closed material'—which was adverse to the claimant. The Board formed the view that if the *content* of the closed material was disclosed to the claimant or his legal representatives, this would enable the identity of its *source* to be deduced—and that this would pose a risk to the safety of the informant. The Board therefore refused to disclose the sensitive evidence to the claimant or his lawyers, instead appointing a 'special advocate' to represent the claimant's interests in a 'closed' part of the hearing from which he and his lawyers were excluded. (The capacity of a special advocate effectively to represent the person concerned may be limited, bearing in mind that, following receipt of the closed evidence, the special advocate is not permitted to take instructions from the person whose interests he is to represent.) In the end, the Board decided that the claimant should not be released—whereupon the claimant sought judicial review. Although the claim was framed in terms of Article 5(4) ECHR, the Law Lords' remarks are of general application to the duty to give notice at common law.

Lord Woolf CJ (at [80]), a member of the majority, noted that cases like this involve a complex collision between the interests of the claimant (who wants full disclosure), the informant (whose life may be endangered by disclosure), and the wider public (who may be endangered if a prisoner is released when, on the basis of the sensitive evidence, he still constitutes a danger to the public). Against this background, Lord Woolf was willing to countenance a 'triangulation' of interests, whereby those of the claimant could be offset against those of the informant and the general public. This led him to the conclusion that, in certain limited circumstances, the procedure adopted by the Parole Board could be lawful. (He expressed no opinion as to whether the treatment of the claimant had been lawful, however: the House of Lords had been asked to rule on the issue only as a matter of principle.)

Lords Steyn and Bingham dissented, holding that it had been unlawful for the Parole Board to proceed as it had done. Lord Steyn said:

> [88] The Parole Board decided to attenuate Roberts's right to a hearing in a drastic manner by imposing upon him, in place of an advocate, who would be able to represent him in the ordinary way, a special advocate ... Under this procedure the prisoner and his legal representatives are not allowed to know anything of the case made against the prisoner. Once the special advocate becomes aware of the case against the prisoner he may not divulge that information to the prisoner. It is not to the point to say that the special advocate procedure is 'better than nothing'. Taken as a whole, the procedure completely lacks the essential characteristics of a fair hearing. It is important not to pussyfoot about such a fundamental matter: the special

advocate procedure undermines the very essence of elementary justice. It involves a phantom hearing only ...

[97] In my view the outcome of this case [as decided by the majority] is deeply austere ... It is contrary to the rule of law.

Roberts was not, however, the House of Lords' last word on this issue. Two subsequent cases—*Secretary of State for the Home Department* v. *MB* [2007] UKHL 46, [2008] 1 AC 440 and *Secretary of State for the Home Department* v. *AF (No 3)* [2009] UKHL 28, [2010] 2 AC 269—involved the use of a procedural model similar to that which had been considered in *Roberts*, but in the context of 'control order proceedings' under the (now repealed) Prevention of Terrorism Act 2005. Such proceedings involved judicial examination of the legality of control orders imposed upon suspected terrorists; such orders could entail far-reaching consequences, including curfews, that could amount to something 'not far short of house arrest', as Lord Hope put it in *AF* (at [77]). In *MB*, a majority held that the involvement of a special advocate was in principle capable of assuaging any disadvantage flowing from non-disclosure: Lord Brown went so far as to say (at [90]) that such a procedure would be unfair only in 'wholly exceptional' cases.

However, their Lordships substantially rowed back from this position in *AF*. They did so in part because, as Baroness Hale frankly acknowledged in *AF* (at [101]), they had been 'too sanguine' about the usefulness of special advocates. However, it was also acknowledged in *AF* that *MB* had cast doubt upon whether (as Lord Phillips put it in *AF* (at [21])) there is a '"core irreducible minimum" of the allegations against a controlee that [have] to be disclosed'. In *AF*, that question was answered in the affirmative, Lord Phillips stating at [59] that

the controlee must be given sufficient information about the allegations against him to enable him to give effective instructions in relation to those allegations. Provided that this requirement is satisfied there can be a fair trial notwithstanding that the controlee is not provided with the detail or the sources of the evidence forming the basis of the allegations. Where, however, the open material consists purely of general assertions and the case against the controlee is based solely or to a decisive degree on closed materials the requirements of a fair trial will not be satisfied, however cogent the case based on the closed materials may be.

It followed that telling one of the claimants in *AF* that an investigation had 'revealed he has a considerable jihadi pedigree, and that prior to his arrival in the UK he took part in both terrorist training and activities' was insufficient.

MB and *AF* were both concerned with the question whether control order proceedings complied with the fair hearing requirements of Article 6(1) ECHR. What, then, is their relevance to the common law duty to give notice? In addressing that question, it is relevant that the discrepancy between *MB* and *AF* can be accounted for, at least in part, by the supervening case of *A* v. *UK* (2009) 49 EHRR 29, in which the Grand Chamber of the ECtHR adopted a position that the House of Lords in *AF* considered to be irreconcilable with *MB*. It is clear that not all of the Law Lords who decided *AF* would have decided it as they did had it not been for *A* v. *UK*. Indeed, Lord Hoffmann thought (at [70]) that the ECtHR's judgment was 'wrong' and might 'destroy' a 'significant part of this country's defences against terrorism'. The implication is that if Lord Hoffmann had been required to consider the matter at common law, unconstrained by the binding force of the Strasbourg Court's judgments, he may well have arrived at a different conclusion.

In fact, the extent to which the protections afforded by the common law duty to give notice and the ECHR are aligned turns upon two factors. The first concerns the respective contents of the common law duty and the relevant Convention rights, principally Article 6(1). Although the latter was held in *A v. UK* to require substantial disclosure, the ECtHR made clear (at [217]) that its view was informed by the fact that the applicants in that case had been subjected to a 'lengthy' (and potentially indefinite) deprivation of liberty that produced a 'dramatic impact' on their fundamental rights. In *Tariq* v. *Home Office* [2011] UKSC 35, [2012] 1 AC 452, the Supreme Court made clear that the extent of disclosure that must be made to the relevant individual can be less—and the capacity of a closed material procedure to offset any potential unfairness greater—in circumstances in which the balance between the relevant competing interests is different. As we noted previously, *Bourgass* implies that the common law is similarly prepared to countenance dilution of the duty to give notice. Indeed, Lord Hoffmann's remarks in *AF* might be taken to go further and to suggest that the common law duty is more prone to such dilution. However, that view is, at the very least, open to question. Referring to the compatibility with common law standards of closed material procedures in civil litigation, Lord Dyson suggested in *Al Rawi* v. *Security Service* [2011] UKSC 34, [2012] 1 AC 531 at [68] that the common law might go *further* than Article 6, while in *R (Maftah)* v. *Secretary of State for Foreign and Commonwealth Affairs* [2011] EWCA Civ 350, [2012] QB 477 at [32] Lord Judge CJ said he would 'need a great deal of persuasion to accept that the standard of fairness set by the common law ... is any less robust than the standards set by article 6'. Given the common law's longstanding commitment not only to open justice in civil and criminal proceedings, but also to the duty to give notice in administrative proceedings, the foregoing remarks are clearly of relevance to the latter context.

However, even if the content of the common law duty to give notice is analogous to relevant aspects of Article 6(1), it remains to consider whether the common law duty is more vulnerable to legislative displacement than a duty to give notice flowing from the ECHR. A duty of the latter type is highly resistant to legislative displacement because s 3(1) of the Human Rights Act 1998 ensures that the legislation in question is interpreted, if possible, compatibly with the relevant Convention right. The common law duty to give notice, of course, falls outside the HRA regime. However, that does not mean that courts are likely readily to concede that the duty has been limited or displaced by legislation. In *Bank Mellat v. HM Treasury (No 1)* [2013] UKSC 38, [2014] AC 700, the question was whether s 40(2) of the Constitutional Reform Act 2005, which creates a right of appeal to the Supreme Court 'from any order or judgment of the Court of Appeal in England and Wales in civil proceedings', could be read as permitting the Supreme Court to adopt a closed material procedure in circumstances in which a lower court had adopted such a procedure. In his dissenting judgment, Lord Kerr concluded that s 40(2) could not be so read, stating (at [101]) that

> [t]wo principles of absolute clarity govern the law in relation to the manner in which trials should be conducted. The first is that a party to proceedings should be informed of the case against him and should have full opportunity to answer that case in open court. The second principle is that the first principle may not be derogated from except by clear parliamentary authority.

The majority judgments are consistent with that statement of principle, albeit that the majority was prepared to conclude that the Act did authorize closed material procedures in the Supreme Court, given the impractical and undesirable consequences of holding otherwise. *Bank Mellat (No 1)* thus demonstrates that the open justice principle at common law is resistant—but certainly not invulnerable—to legislative displacement. The extent of that resistance is, however, more debatable, as the disagreement between the majority and minority Justices shows. Although *Bank Mellat (No 1)* was concerned with the open justice principle in the context of civil litigation, as distinct from the duty to give notice in administrative proceedings, it would be surprising—given that it lies so close to the core of the concept of natural justice—if the latter were any less resistant to legislative erosion. Thus, in *R v. Secretary of State for the Home Department, ex parte Fayed* [1998] 1 WLR 763, the Court of Appeal refused to countenance the *implied* exclusion of the duty.

QUESTION

- When, if ever, is it (a) acceptable and (b) lawful for information to be withheld if this would make a fair decision less likely?

10.3.3 Particular aspects of the duty to act fairly

We have so far considered two fundamental, and intimately connected, aspects of the duty to act fairly—namely, the requirements that those liable to be affected by administrative decisions must be afforded an opportunity to make representations, and that, in order that they may make proper use of that opportunity, they must be given notice of relevant matters. We have seen that even these requirements, which collectively form the core of the duty, are sensitive to context: the making of representations, for instance, need be facilitated by means of an oral hearing only in particular circumstances. Contextual considerations play at least as crucial a role in relation to other aspects of the duty to act fairly. Indeed, when we consider such questions as whether that duty requires the individual to be allowed legal representation or to engage in the cross-examination of witnesses in oral proceedings, the relevant contextual features might include certain aspects of the process that the decision-maker has chosen to adopt. The more formal that procedure, for instance, the more difficult it might be for an unrepresented person adequately to engage with it.

Before we consider particular issues such as representation and cross-examination, it is worth making a further preliminary point. The adoption of such trappings of procedural fairness are not cost neutral. They may increase the length of time that proceedings take; they may result in a degree of judicialization that is at odds with the need for informal, expeditious decision-making; and they may, as a result, impose financial burdens on the decision-maker and/or others. (For instance, the *Osborn* judgment dramatically increased the number of oral hearings the Parole Board was required to hold, as a result of which it needed an emergency—and substantial—injection of funds from the Ministry of Justice: HC299, *The Parole Board for England and Wales: Annual Report and Accounts 2013/14* (2014).) This raises the general question whether it is legitimate or sensible to approach questions about which aspects of procedural fairness should apply by means of a form of cost–benefit analysis that asks whether the disbenefits (such as delay and expense) of allowing some procedural safeguard would be outweighed by a likelihood that it would bring to light information relevant to the matter in question. On this issue, Powell J had the following to say in the US case of *Mathews v. Eldridge* (1976) 424 US 319 at 335:

[I]dentification of the specific dictates of due process generally requires consideration of three distinct factors: First, the private interest that will be affected by the official action; second, the risk of an erroneous deprivation of such interest through the procedures used, and the probable value, if any, of additional or substitute procedural safeguards; and finally, the Government's interest, including the function involved and the fiscal and administrative burdens that the additional or substitute procedural requirement would entail.

In *R (Refugee Legal Centre)* v. *Secretary of State for the Home Department* [2004] EWCA Civ 1481, [2005] 1 WLR 2219 at [8], Sedley LJ (relying on Craig, *Administrative Law* (London 2003), ch 13) appeared to endorse this sort of thinking, saying that, in deciding whether a duty to act fairly has been discharged, the court has to weigh three factors: '[T]he individual interest at issue, the benefits to be derived from added procedural safeguards, and the costs to the administration of compliance'. The problem, however, is that, as Sedley LJ acknowledged, 'these are not factors of equal weight': at least in the asylum context (which was relevant in *Refugee Legal Centre*), said his Lordship, the government 'is not entitled to sacrifice fairness on the altar of speed and convenience'. Although, for that reason, it is certainly not possible—and the courts do not attempt—to identify with mathematical precision the way in which the various factors fall to be balanced against one another, administrative law frequently involves the striking of a balance between the interests of individuals and the wider public. It is therefore unsurprising that, when determining what procedural fairness requires, courts take into account not only considerations of fairness to the individual, but also broader questions about the implications for the administration itself of requiring this or that additional safeguard. However, as Sedley LJ indicates, the relative weight of the factors will vary according to the context: for example, considerations of fairness to the individual will prove especially compelling in situations in which the stakes for the individual are particularly high. It does not, therefore, follow that reviewing courts will straightforwardly acquiesce in the face of a decision-maker's argument that supplying a given procedural safeguard would be inconvenient, as the following case clearly demonstrates.

R v. Board of Visitors of Hull Prison, ex parte St Germain (No 2)
[1979] 1 WLR 1401
Queen's Bench Division

The claimants, all of whom were inmates at Hull Prison, were charged with disciplinary offences arising from a riot. Under arrangements which no longer apply, the charges were heard by a Board of Visitors which was empowered to make an order for loss of remission, effectively increasing the length of time served in prison. The claimants were found guilty of a number of offences. They sought judicial review, arguing that the procedure had been unfair; in particular, the chairman of the Board had refused to allow the prisoners to call certain witnesses and had admitted the hearsay evidence of witnesses who were not available to give evidence and who could not therefore be cross-examined.

Geoffrey Lane LJ (giving the judgment of the court)

... [Counsel for the claimants suggested] that the chairman should have no discretion to disallow the calling of a witness whose attendance is requested by the prisoner. This suggestion was largely withdrawn in the course of argument and we do not think it had any validity. Those who appear before the board of visitors on charges are, ex hypothesi, those who are serving sentences in prison. Many such offenders might well seek to render the adjudications by the board quite impossible if they had the same liberty to conduct their own defences as they would have in an ordinary criminal trial. In our judgment the chairman's discretion is necessary as part of a proper procedure for dealing with alleged offences against discipline by prisoners.

However, that discretion has to be exercised reasonably, in good faith and on proper grounds. It would clearly be wrong if, as has been alleged in one instance before us, the basis for refusal to allow a prisoner to call witnesses was that the chairman considered that there was ample evidence against the accused. It would equally be an improper exercise of the discretion if the refusal was based upon an erroneous understanding of the prisoner's defence—that an alibi did not cover the material time or day, whereas in truth and in fact it did.

A more serious question was raised as to whether the discretion could be validly exercised where it was based upon considerable administrative inconvenience being caused if the request to call a witness or witnesses was permitted. Clearly in the proper exercise of his discretion a chairman may limit the number of witnesses, either on the basis that he has good reason for considering that the total number sought to be called is an attempt by the prisoner to render the hearing of the charge virtually impracticable or where quite simply it would be quite unnecessary to call so many witnesses to establish the point at issue. But mere administrative difficulties, simpliciter, are not in our view enough. Convenience and justice are often not on speaking terms: see *per* Lord Atkin in *General Medical Council v. Spackman* [1943] A.C. 627, 638.

... In our view a fair chance of exculpation cannot in many cases be given without hearing the accused's witnesses, eg in a case of an alibi defence ...

... [T]he right to be heard will include, in appropriate cases, the right to call evidence. It would in our judgment be wrong to attempt an exhaustive definition as to what are appropriate cases, but they must include proceedings whose function is to establish the guilt or innocence of a person charged with serious misconduct. In the instant cases, what was being considered was alleged serious disciplinary offences, which, if established, could and did result in a very substantial loss of liberty. In such a situation it would be a mockery to say that an accused had been 'given a proper opportunity of presenting his case' (section 47(2) of the Prison Act 1952) or 'a full opportunity ... of presenting his own case' (rule 49(2) [of the Prison Rules 1964]), if he had been denied the opportunity of calling evidence which was likely to assist in establishing the vital facts at issue.

... So much for the calling of witnesses. We now turn to the suggestion that hearsay evidence is not permissible in a hearing before a board of visitors. It is of course common ground that the board of visitors must base their decisions on evidence. But must such evidence be restricted to that which would be admissible in a criminal court of law? Viscount Simon L.C. in *General Medical Council v. Spackman* [1943] A.C. 627, 634, considered there was no such restriction. That was also clearly the view of the Privy Council in the *Ceylon University v. Fernando* [1960] 1 W.L.R. 223, 234. The matter was dealt with in more detail by Diplock L.J. in *Reg v. Deputy Industrial Injuries Commissioner, Ex parte Moore* [1965] 1 Q.B. 456, 488:

> 'These technical rules of evidence, however, form no part of the rules of natural justice. The requirement that a person exercising quasi-judicial functions must base his decision on evidence means no more than it must be based upon material which tends logically to show the existence or non-existence of facts relevant to the issue to be determined, or to show the likelihood or unlikelihood of the occurrence of some future event the occurrence of which would be relevant. It means that he must not spin a coin or consult an astrologer, but he may take into account any material which, as a matter of reason, has some probative value in the sense mentioned above. If it is capable of having any probative value, the weight to be attached to it is a matter for the person to whom Parliament has entrusted the responsibility of deciding the issue. The supervisory jurisdiction of the High Court does not entitle it to usurp this responsibility and to substitute its own view for his.' [See 2.3 on the current scope of the supervisory jurisdiction *vis-à-vis* the evidential basis of decisions.]

However, it is clear that the entitlement of the Board to admit hearsay evidence is subject to the overriding obligation to provide the accused with a fair hearing. Depending upon the facts of the particular case and the nature of the hearsay evidence provided to the board, the obligation to give the accused a fair chance to exculpate himself, or a fair opportunity to controvert the charge … may oblige the board not only to inform the accused of the hearsay evidence but also to give the accused a sufficient opportunity to deal with that evidence. Again, depending upon the nature of that evidence and the particular circumstances of the case, a sufficient opportunity to deal with the hearsay evidence may well involve the cross-examination of the witness whose evidence is initially before the board in the form of hearsay.

We again take by way of example the case in which the defence is an alibi. The prisoner contends that he was not the man identified on the roof. He, the prisoner, was at the material time elsewhere. In short the prisoner has been mistakenly identified. The evidence of identification given by way of hearsay may be of the 'fleeting glance' type as exemplified by the well-known case of *Reg. v. Turnbull* [1977] Q.B. 224. The prisoner may well wish to elicit by way of questions all manner of detail, eg the poorness of the light, the state of confusion, the brevity of the observation, the absence of any contemporaneous record, etc., all designed to show the unreliability of the witness. To deprive him of the opportunity of cross-examination would be tantamount to depriving him of a fair hearing.

We appreciate that there may well be occasions when the burden of calling the witness whose hearsay evidence is readily available may impose a near impossible burden upon the board. However, it has not been suggested that hearsay evidence should be resorted to in the total absence of any first-hand evidence. In the instant cases hearsay evidence was only resorted to to supplement the first-hand evidence and this is the usual practice. Accordingly where a prisoner desires to dispute the hearsay evidence and for this purpose to question the witness, and where there are insuperable or very grave difficulties in arranging for his attendance, the board should refuse to admit that evidence, or, if it has already come to their notice, should expressly dismiss it from their consideration.

Applying these principles, the court quashed findings of guilt in relation to six of the seven claimants.

For two reasons it is unsurprising that the Court took a strict view of what fairness required in this case. First, the impact of the Board's decision on the individual prisoners was potentially very serious, involving further deprivation of liberty. Second, because the case involved the determination of charges against the prisoners, the traditional adversarial model under which competing cases are presented and evidence is tested was of obvious relevance. Other cases have adopted a similar approach. For example, in *R (S) v. Knowsley NHS Primary Care Trust* [2006] EWHC 26 (Admin), the question was whether a doctor should be removed from a medical performers list (and hence prevented from practising in the area concerned). Toulson J said:

[83] In the case of Dr S, the central allegations are that he indecently assaulted four patients. If those allegations are true, he is plainly unsuitable to remain on the [medical] performers list. The core issue is a stark one of credibility. The investigating officer has given his opinion that the complainants are credible.

[84] The panel [deciding whether to remove Dr S from the list] would obviously be in a far better position to reach a fair judgment whether the complaints are true if they hear from the complainants and Dr S, and their stories are tested, than if the panel's evaluation of the witnesses' credibility is based on their untested statements and Dr Roberts's opinion about their credibility.

> The complainants might not be willing to give evidence, and the panel would then have to proceed without them, but that would be from necessity ...
>
> [85] ... Unless there is some obstacle which I cannot at present see, fairness to the public and to the doctor would appear to me to dictate that the panel should hear the complainants and permit cross-examination of them (if they are prepared to give evidence) concentrating on what the complainants have to say about their relationship with Dr S.

In other situations, however, cross-examination may not be necessary or appropriate. For instance, in *R v. Commission for Racial Equality, ex parte Cottrell and Rothon* [1980] 1 WLR 1580, the Commission for Racial Equality investigated a complaint that a firm of estate agents was acting in an unlawful and discriminatory manner. The firm was notified of the investigation and invited to make written and oral submissions, but no cross-examination of witnesses was possible. When the Commission later issued a notice under s 58(5) of the Race Relations Act 1976 requiring the firm not to commit acts of unlawful discrimination, the firm sought judicial review, contending that the process had been unfair. Lord Lane CJ, with whom Woolf J agreed, did not share that view. He said at 1587–8:

> It seems to me that there are degrees of judicial hearing, and those degrees run from the borders of pure administration to the borders of the full hearing of a criminal cause or matter in the Crown Court. It does not profit one to try to pigeon-hole the particular set of circumstances either into the administrative pigeon-hole or into the judicial pigeon-hole. Each case will inevitably differ, and one must ask oneself what is the basic nature of the proceeding which was going on here. It seems to me that, basically, this was an investigation being carried out by the commission. It is true that in the course of the investigation the commission may form a view, but it does not seem to me that that is a proceeding which requires, in the name of fairness, any right in the firm in this case to be able to cross-examine witnesses whom the commission have seen and from whom they have taken statements. I repeat the wording of section 58(2) in emphasis of that point: 'If in the course of a formal investigation the commission become satisfied that a person is committing, ...' and so on. It seems to me that that is so near an administrative function as to make little difference and is the type of investigation or proceeding which does not require the formalities of cross examination ... [I]t seems to me that the decision [in the *St Germain* case] ... was based upon facts widely differing from those in the present case. That was truly a judicial proceeding carried out by the prison visitors, and the complaint there was that there had been no opportunity to cross-examine prison officers in hotly disputed questions of identity. Speaking for myself, I derive little assistance from any dicta in that case.

This usefully illustrates the influence exerted by the courts' perception of whether the proceedings are investigative or adjudicative—although since the issue of a s 58 notice is effectively a public statement to the effect that the Commission believes that the party under investigation has committed unlawful discriminatory acts, it is not obvious that Lord Lane CJ was right to dismiss the possibility of cross-examination out of hand.

We turn now to consider in what circumstances fairness may require that an individual should be allowed legal representation. It would clearly be unfair if (say) the government but not the individual was allowed legal representation: this would infringe the equality of arms principle which holds that, in general, fairness requires a level playing field. But, this consideration aside, it is not held that fairness generally demands that individuals should be permitted representation. Indeed, as Fenton Atkinson LJ noted in *Enderby Town Football Club Ltd* v. *Football Association Ltd* [1971] Ch 591 at 608–9, the absence of legal representation carries certain benefits in terms of speed and cost. Some circumstances, however, give rise to strong policy arguments in favour of representation, as Lord Denning MR recognized in *Pett v. Greyhound Racing Association Ltd* [1969] 1 QB 125 at 132:

> It is not every man who has the ability to defend himself on his own. He cannot bring out the points in his own favour or the weaknesses in the other side. He may be tongue-tied or nervous, confused or wanting in intelligence. He cannot examine or cross-examine witnesses. We see it every day. A magistrate says to a man: 'You can ask any questions you like'; whereupon the man immediately starts to make a speech. If justice is to be done, he ought to have the help of some-one to speak for him. And who better than a lawyer who has been trained for the task? I should have thought, therefore, that when a man's reputation or livelihood is at stake, he not only has a right to speak by his own mouth. He also has a right to speak by counsel or solicitor.

The general principles which apply in this area are helpfully set out by Webster J in the following extract.

R v. Secretary of State for the Home Department, ex parte Tarrant
[1985] QB 251
Divisional Court

The claimants were serving prison sentences and were alleged to have committed disciplinary offences: three were charged with assault or attempted assault on a prison officer, and the other two with the more serious offence of mutiny. Their cases were heard by Boards of Visitors, which were able to impose various penalties including exclusion from associated work, stoppage of earnings, cellular confinement, and loss of remission (for up to 180 days in cases of assault, and for longer in relation to mutiny). The claimants' requests for legal representation or the assistance of a friend or advisor were refused by the Boards on the ground that they were not empowered to allow such representation or assistance. In three cases the charges were found to be proved; the other two were adjourned. The claimants sought judicial review.

Webster J

[His Lordship accepted, on the authority of *Fraser* v. *Mudge* [1975] 1 WLR 1132, that a prisoner has no absolute *right* to legal representation before a Board of Visitors, but concluded that such Boards have a *discretion* to allow representation. It was clear that no such discretion had been exercised in relation to any of the claimants, the assumption having been made that representation was simply not permitted. His Lordship went on to consider the principles which the Boards should have applied.]

   As it seems to me, the following are considerations which every board should take into account when exercising its discretion whether to allow legal representation or to allow the assistance of a friend or adviser. (The list is not, of course, intended to be comprehensive: particular cases may throw up other particular matters.)

   (1) The seriousness of the charge and of the potential penalty.
   (2) Whether any points of law are likely to arise. There is of course a duty to ensure that the prisoner understands the charge, a duty which is reflected in the [Home Office] Guide [on the procedure for the conduct of adjudications by boards of visitors] at p. 12, para. 11: 'Ask the accused whether he understands the charge(s) and explain anything to him about which he is in any doubt.' But the clerks who sit with boards are not legally qualified and there may be cases where a legal point arises with which the prisoner, without legal representation, cannot properly deal ...

(3) The capacity of a particular prisoner to present his own case. In 'Justice in Prison,' a report of a committee of Justice of which Sir Brian McKenna was the chairman and which was before the court, the following passage is quoted (para. 117, p. 57) from a report by the Home Office Research Unit based on an experiment of interviewing a number of prisoners before and after adjudication of their cases:

> 'Some of the prisoners were poorly educated and not very intelligent. Furthermore, a few spoke poor English and a few appeared to have psychiatric problems. Unless they are given considerable assistance, it is unrealistic to expect such men to prepare an adequate written statement or to present their case effectively.' (Smith, Austin and Ditchfield, Board of Visitors Adjudications, Research Unit paper 3, Home Office 1981, p 31).

As I have said, Mr. Brown [counsel for the Boards of Visitors] does not suggest that a board has no right to admit an interpreter and there must be some cases where this is necessary. I have no doubt, moreover, that in very many cases, where assistance is necessary, the chairman of the board is capable of doing it so as to ensure the fair hearing to which the prisoner is entitled. But the standing orders, and the Guide, provide for the giving of an opportunity to a prisoner to make a written reply to the charge; and an illiterate prisoner could not make use of that opportunity without some assistance. Similarly, a board might not always be satisfied that a mentally subnormal prisoner could be assured of a full opportunity of presenting his own case merely by the assistance of the chairman of the board.

(4) Procedural difficulties. An affidavit has been sworn, in support of three of the applications, by Mr. Ivan Henry, a member of a board of visitors, a magistrate and a legal executive. He points out that a prisoner awaiting adjudication is normally kept apart from other prisoners ... pending the adjudication and that this may inhibit the preparation of his defence. He points out that without the capacity to interview potential witnesses, prisoners are often unable to satisfy boards of visitors that it is reasonable to call a witness and that, where a prisoner asks questions through a chairman, there is frequently no effective presentation of a case or effective cross-examination or testing of the evidence. I will consider, in more detail, the questions of calling witnesses and cross-examination later in this judgment. But in my view a board, when considering the exercise of its discretion, should take into account any special difficulties of the kind I have mentioned and should particularly bear in mind the difficulty which some prisoners might have in cross-examining a witness, particularly a witness giving evidence of an expert nature, at short notice without previously having seen that witness's evidence.

(5) The need for reasonable speed in making their adjudication, which is clearly an important consideration.

(6) The need for fairness as between prisoners and as between prisoners and prison officers.

[His Lordship then went on to apply these principles to the circumstances of the claimants. He began with Tarrant and Leyland, the two claimants charged with mutiny:] There is agreement between Mr. Brown and Mr. Collins, on behalf of Leyland, that mutiny means 'an offence of collective insubordination, collective defiance or disregard of authority or refusal to obey authority': see Lord Goddard C.J. in *Reg. v. Grant* [1957] 1 W.L.R. 906, 908. At Tarrant's hearing the word was not explained to him, although at Leyland's hearing the chairman said:

> '[T]he definition of mutiny is a concerted act of indiscipline involving more than one person relating to the overthrow or supplanting of constituted authority.'

It seems to me that in most, if not all, charges of mutiny, and certainly in these two cases, questions are bound to arise as to whether collective action was intended to be collective, *ie* whether it was concerted or not, and as to the distinction between mere disobedience of a particular order on the one hand and disregard or defiance of authority on the other. In my judgment, where such questions arise or are likely to arise, no board of visitors, properly directing itself, could reasonably decide not to allow the prisoner legal representation. If this decision is to have the result that charges of mutiny will more frequently be referred to the criminal courts in some other form, I, personally, would not regard that result as a matter of regret.

The charges against Tangney and Anderson each included one charge of an assault on a prison officer under rule 51. Each of them was, therefore, exposed to the risk of 'an award' of forfeiture of remission for a period not exceeding 180 days ... For my part, I do not think that it can possibly be said that any reasonable board properly directing itself would be bound to grant legal representation or, in the case of Tangney and Anderson who applied for it, would be bound to have allowed the presence of an adviser. I would, therefore, leave the matter to be decided by any board before which it may come, if it does so.

A concurring judgment was delivered by Kerr LJ. Although it was not necessarily unreasonable to deny legal representation or assistance to the claimants charged with assault, the failure of the Boards to consider the possibility of allowing legal representation rendered their decision unlawful. Quashing orders were therefore issued in all five cases.

The approach of Webster J in *Tarrant* was endorsed by the House of Lords in *R v. Board of Visitors of HM Prison, The Maze, ex parte Hone* [1988] AC 379, in which it was held that two prisoners charged with assault were not entitled to legal representation. Lord Goff concluded (at 392) that

it is easy to envisage circumstances in which the rules of natural justice do not call for representation ... as may well happen in the case of a simple assault where no question of law arises, and where the prisoner charged is capable of presenting his own case. To hold otherwise would result in wholly unnecessary delays in many cases, to the detriment of all concerned including the prisoner charged, and to wholly unnecessary waste of time and money, contrary to the public interest.

Finally, in this regard, it is worth mentioning *R (S) v. Knowsley NHS Primary Care Trust* [2006] EWHC 26 (Admin), which, as noted earlier, concerned a decision whether two doctors should be removed from a medical performers list. Toulson J said (at [93]):

On the subject of legal representation, the fundamental question is whether the doctor could fairly be expected to represent himself. In many cases that may be a quite reasonable expectation. In Dr Ghosh's case none of the allegations made against him is individually complicated, but taken together the case is sufficiently complex (with the large number of allegations, their diverse nature and the volume of paperwork) that I would be very surprised if a doctor could do himself justice in trying to handle the case unrepresented. A helper sitting beside him would be of some but limited assistance.

Article 6(3)(c) ECHR requires a more generous approach to the availability of legal representation in cases where an individual is 'charged with a criminal offence'. Although this is, on the face of it, irrelevant to administrative proceedings, whether the criminal aspects of Article 6 apply turns upon a substantive evaluation of the matter in question and not simply on how it is characterized in domestic law. For instance, in *Ezeh v. United Kingdom* (2004) 39 EHRR 1, the ECtHR held that where the violation of prison rules corresponds to a criminal law prohibition (*eg* assault) and the maximum award is additional days in detention, Article 6(3)(c) applies such that legal representation must be permitted. That case did not consider whether legal aid must also be afforded (it is only explicitly mandatory under Article 6 in criminal cases, and then only 'when the interests of justice so require'), but the severity of the potential punishment and financial and educational positions of many prisoners suggest that the 'interests of justice' probably do so require under Article 6(3)(c), especially where the legal issue involved is complex: *Twalib* v. *Greece* (2001) 33 EHRR 24; *Maxwell* v. *United Kingdom* (1995) 19 EHRR 97.

Although Article 6 does not explicitly require publicly-funded legal representation out-with the criminal context, circumstances can arise in which a fair hearing is impossible without such representation: in such circumstances, the state therefore comes under an implied positive obligation to fund representation. This point is most clearly illustrated by *Steele* v. *UK* (2005) 41 EHRR 22, otherwise known as the 'McLibel' case. The applicants were sued for defamation in the English courts in respect of a leaflet, which they had distributed, making certain allegations about the McDonald's fast food chain. McDonald's won, although the damages award was reduced on appeal. The applicants sued the UK in the ECtHR alleging that its failure to provide them with publicly-funded legal representation had deprived them of a fair trial under the civil limb of Article 6. The ECtHR agreed. However, while this case demonstrates that, in principle, publicly-funded representation may be required under the civil limb of Article 6, this does not by any means establish that everyone involved in administrative proceedings is entitled to such representation. First, as we saw in ch 9, Article 6 does not apply to all administrative proceedings. And, second, even if it does apply, fairness will only rarely demand publicly-funded representation. The facts of the McLibel case were highly unusual: the financial consequences for the applicants (that is, the defendants in the libel case) were serious; the litigation was legally and procedurally complex—100 days of legal argument took place, with 38 separate written judgments; and it was factually complex—there were 130 oral witnesses and 40,000 pages of documentary evidence. In those unusual circumstances, the ECtHR concluded (at [72]) that 'the denial of legal aid to the applicants deprived them of the opportunity to present their case effectively before the court and contributed to an unacceptable inequality of arms with McDonald's'.

10.3.4 Appeals

It is sometimes, but by no means always, the case that decisions may be appealed. This raises a number of distinct issues. First, does fairness require the possibility of appeal? The answer to this question is clearly 'no'. As Lord Denning MR explained in *Ward* v. *Bradford Corporation* (1972) 70 LGR 27 at 35, 'Natural justice does not require the provision of an appeal. So long as the party concerned has a fair hearing by a fair-minded body of men that is enough.' A right of appeal will not therefore be implied: it exists only if conferred by statute.

Second, if a right of appeal exists, must it be exercised before judicial review is sought? There are circumstances in which it is held that alternative remedies must be exhausted before invoking the supervisory jurisdiction, and we examine this at 14.3 in the context of a broader discussion of restrictions on judicial review.

Third, can a fair appeal cure unfairness in the original decision-making process? We have already seen (at 9.5.3) that, where there is a breach at first instance of Article 6(1) ECHR, appeal to or review by a court of full jurisdiction may cure such a breach. What, however, of domestic law? There are strong policy reasons in favour of investing fair appeals with a curative effect—a point that was taken in *R (A (A Child))* v. *Kingsmead School Governors* [2002] EWCA Civ 1822, in which it was held that a fair appeal could cure procedural defects in the defendant's decision permanently to exclude the claimant. Simon Brown LJ (at [37]) pointed out:

> Plainly Parliament did not intend either hearing … to be unfair. But that is by no means to say that Parliament intended a pupil aggrieved by the [original] … decision then to invoke the courts' supervisory jurisdiction rather than proceed to appeal. It is, on the contrary, clear that Parliament intended the aggrieved pupil to seek his remedy before the [independent appeal panel]. In one sense, of course, he then obtains no redress for the earlier unfairness. But what he does obtain is a fresh and fair decision on the merits of the case by a statutory body custom-built for the purpose.

Taken in isolation, this might be thought to imply that fair appeals should *always* exert a curative effect. However, the position is more complex, as the Privy Council acknowledged in *Calvin* v. *Carr* [1980] AC 574. The claimant, a racehorse owner, was subjected to disciplinary proceedings by the Australian Jockey Club. It was decided, pursuant to a rudimentary procedure, that the claimant had been party to a breach of the Club's rules, and he was banned from racing his horses for a year. That decision was upheld on appeal following a hearing at which the claimant was legally represented and permitted to cross-examine witnesses. The Privy Council ultimately decided that, to the extent that the original decision was tainted by procedural unfairness, that flaw was cured by the fairness of the appeal.

It is important, however, to note that the legal background to the impugned decision in *Calvin* differed from the model—involving the making of a decision in exercise of statutory authority—with which administrative law is typically concerned. In particular, the relationship between the claimant and the Australian Jockey Club was based in contract. In the light of this, Lord Wilberforce, giving the judgment of the Judicial Committee, noted that circumstances might arise in which an individual who is party to a contractual or otherwise voluntary relationship with a decision-maker may be taken to have *agreed* that any initial hearing is to be 'superseded' by any appeal hearing, such that a fair appeal renders any unfairness at the initial stage of historical significance only. Lord Wilberforce also noted that a more qualified form of such an agreement might, in some circumstances, be inferred, such that a member of an organization or a party to a contract might be taken to have agreed to accept a decision reached on appeal, notwithstanding any procedural defects at an earlier stage, provided that 'in the end' there is a 'fair decision'.

In cases involving the use of statutory, as distinct from contractual, power, there will be no equivalent form of agreement. Nevertheless, in *Lloyd* v. *McMahon* [1987] AC 625, the facts of which are set out at 10.3.1, the view was taken that there could be statutory cases—of which *Lloyd* v. *McMahon* was one—in which a fair appeal could exert a curative effect. In the Court of Appeal, Woolf LJ said (at 669):

> In my view in cases such as this the question the court should ask is whether, taking into account the complainant's rights of appeal, and if those rights have been exercised what happened on the appeal, the complainant, viewing the combined proceedings as a whole, has had a fair hearing? I regard this approach as appropriate because if Parliament makes provision for an initial hearing followed by appeal then what Parliament should be presumed to intend is that the persons affected by those proceedings should be treated fairly in the proceedings as a whole. Where there are shortcomings in the initial proceedings but the appellant has in fact been dealt with fairly when the proceedings as a whole are considered, to regard the proceedings as invalid

404 • PROCEDURAL FAIRNESS

> would be to condemn something as being unfair because of a flaw in a part when if the whole was considered the flaw would be sufficiently insignificant to enable the whole procedure to be regarded as unblemished. Expressing the matter slightly differently, if the whole procedure is properly regarded as being fair, then to strike that procedure down because of a flaw in part will be to apply an unduly technical approach.

A similar approach was adopted in the House of Lords by Lord Bridge, who (at 709) emphasized the relevance of the 'amplitude' of the appellate body's jurisdiction:

> [W]hen the court has, as here, in fact conducted a full hearing on the merits and reached a conclusion that the issue of a certificate was justified, it would be an erroneous exercise of discretion nevertheless to quash the certificate on the ground that, before the matter reached the court, there had been some defect in the procedure followed.

A fairly conducted appeal is therefore likely to bar an attack, by means of judicial review, upon procedural unfairness tainting the original decision only if the appellate body is institutionally equipped to supply the sort of 'full hearing' referred to by Lord Bridge. This appears to be a more exacting requirement than that of scrutiny by an independent tribunal 'of full jurisdiction' that applies under Article 6(1) ECHR (on which see 9.5.3).

10.4 Consultation

Viewed in one way, much of procedural fairness is about consultation. Giving notice to an individual liable to be affected by a decision and affording him an opportunity to make representations—whether in writing, by way of an oral hearing, or otherwise—amounts to 'consulting' the individual in the sense of permitting him to comment in an informed way on relevant matters, and thereby to contribute to the decision-making process.

However, the term 'consultation' is often used—and we use it here—to mean something different: something that is more specific, and yet at the same time broader, than 'acting fairly' as that concept has so far been considered in this chapter. The duty to act fairly, as we have seen, emerged from what has more traditionally been termed the 'duty to act judicially' or (correlatively) the 'right to a hearing'. As we have also seen, the duty to act fairly is today triggered in a relatively broad range of circumstances. In particular, its operation is not limited to situations in which some extant legal right stands to be extinguished or otherwise affected by the decision—hence the possibility, noted earlier, of a duty to act fairly not only in 'revocation' but also in 'application' cases. However, although not limited in the sense of applying only to decisions that impact upon existing *rights*, the duty to act fairly remains anchored to situations in which the decision and/or its impact is in some relevant way *particularized*. In order to illustrate what is meant by this, consider the following situations:

1. A patient with a terminal disease has been taking a drug that could extend her life by several years. The drug is withdrawn on the ground that the patient no longer meets the relevant agency's criteria for funding the provision of the drug.

2. Publicly funded access to a drug that is currently prescribed to several thousands of patients is withdrawn from all patients on cost grounds.

3. The relevant agency determines that a drug to which publicly funded access has never been available should not be funded because doing so would not represent the best use of limited financial resources.

4. The relevant agency decides to undertake large-scale clinical and public education programmes in order to improve survival rates in respect of certain, but not all, types of cancer.

To what extent are these decisions 'particularized'? The first is highly particularized: it affects a single, identifiable individual and has a tangible (and potentially grave) impact. The second decision is less particularized: it amounts to a policy decision that clearly affects one (large) group of individuals (*ie* those who have been taking the drug) in a tangible way and another (amorphous) category of individuals (*ie* those who might in the future have been prescribed the drug) in a less direct manner. The third decision is less particularized still. It affects, in a loose sense, individuals suffering from the relevant disease and who might therefore have been prescribed the drug had a decision been taken to fund it at public expense. However, since no one can know what criteria would have been applied in determining eligibility for the drug if it had been funded, it is difficult to identify any category of individuals who are indisputably affected by the decision whether or not to fund the use of the drug. The fourth decision might be considered the least particularized of all: it affects, in a very loose sense, those who suffer from the forms of cancer included in the new programmes (because they may benefit from those programmes); those who suffer from other forms of cancer (because they will not benefit); those who may in the future suffer from any form of cancer (because, depending on the form of cancer, they may benefit or will not benefit from the programmes); those suffering from diseases other than cancer (because the new programmes may reduce the health budget available for the treatment of other conditions); and anyone else who might be the beneficiary of public spending (if the funding of the programmes causes the enlargement of the health budget at the expense of spending in other areas).

It is plain that if the first of the four hypothetical decisions sketched earlier were to be taken without giving the patient any opportunity to make representations, that would entail a breach of the duty to act fairly. However, it is equally clear that the fourth decision would attract no duty to act fairly. This gives rise to a number of questions. First, when is the impact of a decision insufficiently particularized to trigger the duty to act fairly? Second, if that duty is not triggered, might there sometimes be a different—perhaps lesser—procedural obligation, *eg* to consult those who may be affected or interested in a non-particularized manner? Third, if there is such a further duty, when does it apply? Fourth, to the extent that it applies, what does it require? And, fifth, where does any such duty sit doctrinally in relation to the duty to act fairly? Is it separate from that duty, or an aspect of it, or are there duties to act fairly and to consult that each form aspects of some larger, unifying doctrine of procedural fairness?

QUESTIONS

- As a matter of principle, where should the line be drawn in relation to the four situations set out earlier?
- Should that line demarcate circumstances in which procedural obligations do and do not exist, or should it demarcate spheres in which different procedural obligations apply?

The decision of the Administrative Court in *R (Plantagenet Alliance Ltd)* v. *Secretary of State for Justice* [2014] EWHC 1662 (Admin) is a useful point at which to begin in seeking to answer the earlier questions. Following the improbable discovery of the remains of King Richard III beneath a car park in Leicester, the claimant argued that there should have been a public consultation about where the remains were to be reinterred. In rejecting that argument, the Court (at [98]) set out several general principles, including the following:

1. There is no general duty to consult at Common Law. The government of the country would grind to a halt if every decision-maker were required in every case to consult everyone who might be affected by his decision ...

2. There are four main circumstances where a duty to consult may arise. First, where there is a statutory duty to consult. Second, where there has been a promise to consult. Third, where there has been an established practice of consultation. Fourth, where, in exceptional cases, a failure to consult would lead to conspicuous unfairness. Absent these factors, there will be no obligation on a public body to consult.

(To the four circumstances mentioned by the Court, we would add a fifth: namely, where there is a policy of consultation.) On this view, then, consultation is generally required only because legislation or the doctrine of legitimate expectation imposes a duty to consult. Only the fourth category holds out any prospect of consultation being legally required at common law as a matter of *fairness*. Yet it is clear from the above that the Court envisaged that cases would rarely fall into the fourth category; indeed, it declined (at [156]) to hold that the decision concerning the reinterring of Richard III's remains fell into that category:

Mr Clarke [for the claimant] was pressed by the Court on a number of occasions to clarify the nature, scope and scale of the 'public' consultation which the Claimant submitted should be carried out. He had difficulty in doing so. His fundamental problem was that he was not able to formulate any limit to the generality of the duty to consult. He eschewed the notion that the Secretary of State was obliged to 'seek out' the numerous people who could claim collateral descent from Richard III, as well he might, since this category could potentially amount to millions of people. Mr Clarke nevertheless stuck resolutely to his requirement for there to be a 'public' consultation. He said that the media interest was such that it would be sufficient for the Secretary of State to engage in public consultation by, e.g., inviting representations from the public via a website. We do not think, however, that this is an answer to the need for specificity. In truth, the 'public' consultation regarded by the Claimant is entirely open-ended and not capable of sensible limit or specificity, in the context of potentially millions of collateral descendants of Richard III. Further, in order to articulate how such a complex consultation would be carried out, a detailed process would have to be prescribed in a manner akin to legislation.

Similar concerns were invoked by Sedley LJ in *R (BAPIO Action Ltd)* v. *Secretary of State for the Home Department* [2007] EWCA Civ 1139, in which it was argued that the government had acted unlawfully when, without consultation, it changed the Immigration Rules in a way that made it more difficult for certain foreign doctors lacking a right of abode to take up medical training posts in the UK. Declining to hold that a common law (or implied statutory) duty to consult arose, Sedley LJ said:

[43] The real obstacle which I think stands in the appellants' way is the difficulty of propounding a principle which reconciles fairness to an adversely affected class with the principles of public administration that are also part of the common law. These are not based on administrative

convenience or potential embarrassment. They arise from the separation of powers and the entitlement of executive government to formulate and reformulate policy, albeit subject to such constraints as the law places upon the process and the product. One set of such constraints in modern public law are the doctrines of legitimate expectation, both procedural and substantive. ... The duty to give reasons is another area in which there has been marked growth. It is not unthinkable that the common law could recognise a general duty of consultation in relation to proposed measures which are going to adversely affect an identifiable interest group or sector of society.

[44] But what are its implications? The appellants have not been able to propose any limit to the generality of the duty. Their case must hold good for all such measures, of which the state at national and local level introduces certainly hundreds, possibly thousands, every year. If made good, such a duty would bring a host of litigable issues in its train: is the measure one which is actually going to injure particular interests sufficiently for fairness to require consultation? If so, who is entitled to be consulted? Are there interests which ought not to be consulted? How is the exercise to be publicised and conducted? Are the questions fairly framed? Have the responses been conscientiously taken into account? The consequent industry of legal challenges would generate in its turn defensive forms of public administration. All of this, I accept, will have to be lived with if the obligation exists; but it is at least a reason for being cautious.

[45] The proposed duty is, as I have said, not unthinkable—indeed many people might consider it very desirable—but thinking about it makes it rapidly plain that if it is to be introduced it should be by Parliament and not by the courts. Parliament has the option, which the courts do not have, of extending and configuring an obligation to consult function by function. It can also abandon or modify obligations to consult which experience shows to be unnecessary or unworkable and extend those which seem to work well. The courts, which act on larger principles, can do none of these things. ...

[47] ... I am not prepared to hold that there was at common law an obligation to consult those affected or their representatives before introducing the material changes to the Immigration Rules. I do not seek to elevate this to a general rule that fairness can never require consultation as a condition of the exercise of a statutory function; but in the present context it seems to me that a duty to consult would require a specificity which the courts, concerned as they are with developing principles, cannot furnish without assuming the role of a legislator. We would have, for example, to determine whether the duty contended for ... arises before or after the formation of the policy prompting the rule-change; whether consultation is to be obligatory or discretionary; whether it is to take the form of a limited approach or a public exercise; whether the identity of the consultees should be prescribed or left to the Secretary of State; if the former, who they should be; if the latter, according to what criteria, if any, they should be chosen; and so forth. It is only if BAPIO could show that it would be entitled to be consulted whatever scheme was chosen that it might be able to overcome these obstacles. But, while I readily recognise the strength of its claim to be heard as the main representative of the cohort most directly and adversely affected, I do not think it can make out such a case.

Although Sedley LJ concluded that no common law duty to consult arose on the facts of *BAPIO*, he was, as the excerpt above demonstrates, at least open to the possibility of such a duty. That willingness flowed in part from Sedley LJ's understanding of the relationship between the statute and common law (or implied statutory) administrative law controls. In particular, Sedley LJ rejected the argument that because the legislation specified a particular parliamentary procedure for the making of changes to the Immigration Rules, that was demonstrative of a parliamentary intention to exclude any other procedural protections such as an obligation to consult, pointing out (at [36]) that '[s]uch reasoning would bring down the entire body of adjectival common law constraints on the use of statutory powers'.

However, while agreeing with Sedley LJ that no duty to consult arose, Maurice Kay and Rimer LJJ saw something in the argument that Parliament had impliedly excluded any duty to consult, Maurice Kay LJ (at [58]) concluding that 'where Parliament has conferred a rule-making power on a Minister of the Crown, without including an express duty to consult, but subject to a Parliamentary control mechanism …, it is not generally for the courts to superimpose additional *procedural* safeguards'.

Sedley LJ's view certainly opens the door to a common law duty a little more than the view preferred by Maurice Kay and Rimer LJJ. However, on neither view is the door thrown widely open, thanks to the concern, shared by all three judges, that acknowledging the *existence* of a common law duty to consult might cause courts improperly to take on a legislative role in prescribing the *content* of the duty in the circumstances of any particular case. It is, however, worth considering why that concern is given such prominence in the present context. After all, as is acknowledged by most of the positions adopted in the debate over the constitutional foundations of judicial review (on which see 1.4), courts play key roles in determining the detailed content of the principles of judicial review both in the abstract and as they apply to particular fact situations and legislative schemes. Indeed, we have seen in this chapter that the courts play precisely such a role in relation to many aspects of procedural fairness by making quite precise determinations about whether (for instance) procedural trappings such as an oral hearing, legal representation, and cross-examination must be afforded.

Against this background, the degree of reticence encountered in respect of an obligation to consult may seem incongruous. One explanation might simply be that consultations are very expensive, and that the courts are reluctant to impose substantial costs on decision-makers in this way. A second explanation might be that the issues liable to be encountered by courts in respect of consultation—including those mentioned by Sedley LJ in the earlier excerpt from *BAPIO*—are *especially* open-ended. A third explanation, however, might be that in relation to consultation the courts are more sensitive to concerns about the proper limits of the judicial function because, in the first place, they are more ambivalent about the importance of consultation than they are about (say) fair hearings in situations in which individual rights or interests are clearly at stake. On this analysis, courts may be less inclined to push the *institutional* envelope so far as the judicial role is concerned because they are not (as) convinced of the *normative* case for consultation. This raises some basic questions about where a common law duty to consult sits, or would sit, in relation to the principles of procedural fairness considered earlier in this chapter. In particular, the question arises whether consultation is, or should be, treated as an aspect of procedural fairness or as something distinct. And that, in turn, raises a still more fundamental question about how, in the first place, the normative foundations of procedural fairness are conceived. Although the following case concerned a statutory duty to consult, it provided an opportunity for the Supreme Court to engage with some of these crucial issues, and to address what the duty to consult requires when it arises.

R (Moseley) v. *Haringey London Borough Council* [2014] UKSC 56, [2014] 1 WLR 3947
Supreme Court

A government 'Council Tax benefit scheme' (CTB) under which some people were wholly or partially relieved of their obligation to pay Council Tax was replaced by a 'Council Tax reduction scheme' (CTRS) that local authorities were required to operate. Before introducing a CTRS, local authorities were required by the Local Government Finance Act 1992, sch 1A, para 3(1) to

(a) consult any major precepting authority which has power to issue a precept to it, (b) publish a draft scheme in such manner as it thinks fit, and (c) consult such other persons as it considers are likely to have an interest in the operation of the scheme.

(Council Tax is usually collected by one local authority—*eg* a district council—on behalf of both itself and other bodies—*eg* county councils—that can levy Council Tax. Such other bodies are known as 'precepting authorities'.) The defendant council took the view that a projected shortfall in central government funding would have to be met by reducing the amount of Council Tax relief available under its proposed CTRS, even though it would have been open to the council to absorb any such shortfall and leave the level of Council Tax relief undisturbed. When the council engaged in consultation pursuant to requirement (c) above, the materials it published gave the impression that the transition from the CTB to a CTRS would *necessarily* reduce the levels of Council Tax relief that would be available. As a result, the council did not consult on whether the shortfall in government funding should have been met in ways other than reducing Council Tax relief—*eg* by increasing Council Tax rates (so as to fund a more generous relief scheme) or reducing spending in other areas. The Supreme Court unanimously concluded that the council had acted unlawfully.

Lord Wilson (with whom **Lord Kerr** agreed)

[23] A public authority's duty to consult those interested before taking a decision can arise in a variety of ways. Most commonly, as here, the duty is generated by statute. Not infrequently, however, it is generated by the duty cast by the common law upon a public authority to act fairly. The search for the demands of fairness in this context is often illumined by the doctrine of legitimate expectation … But irrespective of how the duty to consult has been generated, that same common law duty of procedural fairness will inform the manner in which the consultation should be conducted.

[24] Fairness is a protean concept, not susceptible of much generalised enlargement. But its requirements in this context must be linked to the purposes of consultation. In *R (Osborn) v Parole Board* [2014] AC 1115, this court addressed the common law duty of procedural fairness in the determination of a person's legal rights. Nevertheless the first two of the purposes of procedural fairness in that somewhat different context, identified by Lord Reed JSC in paras 67 and 68 of his judgment, equally underlie the requirement that a consultation should be fair. First, the requirement 'is liable to result in better decisions, by ensuring that the decision-maker receives all relevant information and that it is properly tested': para 67. Second, it avoids 'the sense of injustice which the person who is the subject of the decision will otherwise feel': para 68. Such are two valuable practical consequences of fair consultation. But underlying it is also a third purpose, reflective of the democratic principle at the heart of our society. This third purpose is particularly relevant in a case like the present, in which the question was not: 'Yes or no, should we close this particular care home, this particular school etc?' It was: 'Required, as we are, to make a taxation-related scheme for application to all the inhabitants of our borough, should we make one in the terms which we here propose?'

[25] In *R v Brent London Borough Council, Ex p Gunning* (1985) 84 LGR 168 Hodgson J quashed Brent's decision to close two schools on the ground that the manner of its prior consultation, particularly with the parents, had been unlawful. He said, at p 189:

'Mr Sedley submits that these basic requirements are essential if the consultation process is to have a sensible content. First, that consultation must be at a time when proposals are still at a formative stage. Second, that the proposer must give sufficient reasons for any proposal to permit of intelligent consideration and response. Third ... that adequate time must be given for consideration and response and, finally, fourth, that the product of consultation must be conscientiously taken into account in finalising any statutory proposals.'

Clearly Hodgson J accepted Mr Stephen Sedley QC's submission. It is hard to see how any of his four suggested requirements could be rejected or indeed improved. ... The time has come for this court also to endorse the Sedley criteria. They are, as the Court of Appeal said in *R (Royal Brompton and Harefield NHS Foundation Trust) v Joint Committee of Primary Care Trusts* (2012) 126 BMLR 134, para 9, 'a prescription for fairness'.

[26] Two further general points emerge from the authorities. First, the degree of specificity with which, in fairness, the public authority should conduct its consultation exercise may be influenced by the identity of those whom it is consulting. Thus, for example, local authorities who were consulted about the Government's proposed designation of Stevenage as a 'new town' (*Fletcher v Minister of Town and Country Planning* [1947] 2 All ER 496, 501) would be likely to be able to respond satisfactorily to a presentation of less specificity than would members of the public, particularly perhaps the economically disadvantaged. Second, in the words of Simon Brown LJ in *Ex p Baker* [1995] 1 All ER 73, 91, 'the demands of fairness are likely to be somewhat higher when an authority contemplates depriving someone of an existing benefit or advantage than when the claimant is a bare applicant for a future benefit'.

[27] Sometimes, particularly when statute does not limit the subject of the requisite consultation to the preferred option, fairness will require that interested persons be consulted not only upon the preferred option but also upon arguable yet discarded alternative options. For example, in *R (Medway Council) v Secretary of State for Transport, Local Government and the Regions* [2003] JPL 583, the court held that, in consulting about an increase in airport capacity in South East England, the Government had acted unlawfully in consulting upon possible development only at Heathrow, Stansted and the Thames estuary and not also at Gatwick ...

[28] But, even when the subject of the requisite consultation is limited to the preferred option, fairness may nevertheless require passing reference to be made to arguable yet discarded alternative options. In *Nichol v Gateshead Metropolitan Borough Council* (1988) 87 LGR 435 Gateshead, confronted by a falling birth rate and therefore an inability to sustain a viable sixth form in all its secondary schools, decided to set up sixth form colleges instead. Local parents failed to establish that Gateshead's prior consultation had been unlawful. The Court of Appeal held that Gateshead had made clear what the other options were: see pp 455, 456 and 462. In the *Royal Brompton* case 126 BMLR 134, cited above, the defendant, an advisory body, was minded to advise that only two London hospitals should provide paediatric cardiac surgical services, namely Guys and Great Ormond Street. In the Court of Appeal the Royal Brompton Hospital failed to establish that the defendant's exercise in consultation upon its prospective advice was unlawful. In its judgment delivered by Arden LJ, the court, at para 10, cited the Gateshead case as authority for the proposition that 'a decision-maker may properly decide to present his preferred options in the consultation document, provided it is clear what the other options are ...' It held, at para 95, that the defendant had made clear to those consulted that they were at liberty to press the case for the Royal Brompton ...

[29] ... Those whom Haringey was primarily consulting were the most economically disadvantaged of its residents. Their income was already at a basic level and the effect of Haringey's proposed scheme would be to reduce it even below that level and thus in all likelihood to cause real hardship, while sparing its more prosperous residents from making any contribution to the shortfall in government funding. Fairness demanded that in the consultation document brief reference should be made to other ways of absorbing the shortfall and to the reasons why (unlike 58% of local authorities in England ...) Haringey had concluded that they were unacceptable.

[30] It would not have been onerous for Haringey to make brief reference to other ways of absorbing the shortfall. ...

Lord Reed

[34] I am generally in agreement with Lord Wilson JSC, but would prefer to express my analysis of the relevant law in a way which lays less emphasis upon the common law duty to act fairly, and more upon the statutory context and purpose of the particular duty of consultation with which we are concerned.

[35] The common law imposes a general duty of procedural fairness upon public authorities exercising a wide range of functions which affect the interests of individuals, but the content of that duty varies almost infinitely depending upon the circumstances. There is however no general common law duty to consult persons who may be affected by a measure before it is adopted. ... A duty of consultation will however exist in circumstances where there is a legitimate expectation of such consultation, usually arising from an interest which is held to be sufficient to found such an expectation, or from some promise or practice of consultation. ...

[36] This case is not concerned with a situation of that kind. It is concerned with a statutory duty of consultation. Such duties vary greatly depending on the particular provision in question, the particular context, and the purpose for which the consultation is to be carried out. The duty may, for example, arise before or after a proposal has been decided upon; it may be obligatory or may be at the discretion of the public authority; it may be restricted to particular consultees or may involve the general public; the identity of the consultees may be prescribed or may be left to the discretion of the public authority; the consultation may take the form of seeking views in writing, or holding public meetings; and so on and so forth. The content of a duty to consult can therefore vary greatly from one statutory context to another: 'the nature and the object of consultation must be related to the circumstances which call for it' (*Port Louis Corpn v Attorney General of Mauritius* [1965] AC 1111, 1124). A mechanistic approach to the requirements of consultation should therefore be avoided.

[37] Depending on the circumstances, issues of fairness may be relevant to the explication of a duty to consult. But the present case is not in my opinion concerned with circumstances in which a duty of fairness is owed, and the problem with the consultation is not that it was 'unfair' as that term is normally used in administrative law. In the present context, the local authority is discharging an important function in relation to local government finance, which affects its residents generally. ... All residents of the local authority's area could reasonably be regarded as 'likely to have an interest in the operation of the scheme' [Lord Reed was quoting here from the Local Government Finance Act 1992, sch 1A, para 3(1)], and it is on that basis that Haringey proceeded.

[38] Such wide-ranging consultation, in respect of the exercise of a local authority's exercise of a general power in relation to finance, is far removed in context and scope from the situations in which the common law has recognised a duty of procedural fairness. The purpose of public consultation in that context is in my opinion not to ensure procedural fairness in the treatment of persons whose legally protected interests may be adversely affected, as the common law seeks to do. The purpose of this particular statutory duty to consult must, in my opinion, be to ensure public participation in the local authority's decision-making process ...

[40] In the present case, on the other hand, it is difficult to see how ordinary members of the public could express an intelligent view on the proposed scheme, so as to participate in a meaningful way in the decision-making process, unless they had an idea of how the loss of income by the local authority might otherwise be replaced or absorbed.

> In a joint judgment, Baroness Hale and Lord Clarke said that there was 'very little between' Lords Reed and Wilson and that they could therefore 'safely agree with both judgments'. The Court issued a declaration to the effect that the consultation had been conducted unlawfully. However, in view of the fact that the CTRS had been in operation for two years, the Court concluded that it would be disproportionate to require a fresh consultation exercise to be undertaken.

Three points are worth making in relation to *Moseley*. First, by endorsing the 'Sedley criteria' the case provides authoritative confirmation of what is required if a consultation process is to be carried out in a lawful manner.

Second, *Moseley* demonstrates that even when a duty to consult is imposed by statute, the relevant legislation may not say much about what the duty actually entails. Indeed, the relevant provision in *Moseley* did very little to clarify who should be consulted or what form consultation ought to take. It therefore fell to the Court to determine whether the obligation to consult included an obligation to supply certain contextual information, including about alternative means by which the funding shortfall might have been addressed, just as it would also fall to the courts, in the event of a relevant dispute, to determine to whom the statutory duty to consult is owed. This might be thought to cast some doubt on the argument that a common law duty to consult should be resisted because acknowledging such a duty would require the court to discharge a 'legislative' function. The reality, as *Moseley* illustrates, is that even when a duty to consult is supplied by statute, the court may still have to make determinations—with the benefit of little or no legislative steer—about the scope and content of such a duty.

Third, such questions regarding the relationship between statute and common law take us to the heart of the disagreement between Lords Reed and Wilson. For Lord Wilson, the duty to consult is a function of the common law notion of procedural fairness because, in the first place, that notion is animated by normative concerns that relate not only to the fair treatment of individuals in respect of decisions that particularly affect them, but also to the democratic imperative that calls for public participation in the formulation of policy. The implication is that in circumstances in which it would be unfair—in the sense of being inconsistent with democratic principle—for policy formulation to occur without any public participation, the common law may impose a duty to consult. However, Lord Wilson's analysis goes not only to the existence of a common law duty to consult, but also to the content of all—including statutory—duties to consult. This is so because Lord Wilson invokes common law principles of fairness as factors that (along with any relevant express terms of the legislation) shape the content of the duty. In this way, the common law—to borrow Byles J's well-known expression in *Cooper* v. *Wandsworth Board of Works* (1863) 14 CB (NS) 180—'will supply the omission of the legislature' in relation to consultation just as it does in relation to other aspects of procedural fairness.

Lord Reed, however, rejects the premise, implicit in the previous sentence, that the duty to consult is, in the first place, an aspect of the common law principles of procedural fairness. For Lord Reed, the normative concerns that underlie those principles are engaged only when official action has a particularized impact upon specific individuals. That being so, absent a legitimate expectation, questions about the existence and content of duties to consult fall to be resolved straightforwardly as matters of statutory construction. Lord Reed came to the same ultimate conclusion as Lord Wilson, in that he held that the (statutorily required) consultation process had been unlawfully conducted; but he reached that conclusion because the council had frustrated the implied *statutory* objective of securing meaningful public participation, not because of any general common law requirement that such participation should be facilitated on democratic (or other normative) grounds.

The approach adopted by Lord Reed in *Moseley* is consonant with his judgment in *R (Osborn)* v. *Parole Board* [2013] UKSC 61, [2014] AC 1115, in which he placed particular emphasis on procedural fairness as a means of securing respect for the dignity of the individual. We noted at 10.2.5 that such a dignitarian approach can serve to expand the circumstances in which a duty to act fairly arises by, for instance, rendering beside the point the argument that a fair process would 'make no difference' in the circumstances of the particular case. It is, however, clear from *Moseley* that the sort of individualist conception of fairness preferred by Lord Reed may serve not to expand but to constrict the duty to consult.

QUESTIONS

- Do you prefer the approach adopted by Lord Reed or by Lord Wilson in *Moseley* to the relationship between the duty to consult and the common law duty to act fairly?
- To what extent are those two approaches likely to produce different practical results so far as the incidence and content of duties to consult are concerned?

10.5 Concluding remarks

Procedural fairness can seem to be—and to an extent clearly is—a highly technical area of administrative law, albeit that the nature of such technicality has changed over recent decades as old categories (such as 'judicial' and 'administrative') have given way to a subtler, but arguably no less complex, methodology by which the requirements of procedural fairness fall to be determined. Indeed, that shift from an approach based on rigid categories to one that is flexible and contextualist in nature is the narrative that most obviously defines the development of the law in this area over the last half century or so. However, highly significant though those changes have been, they amount, in the final analysis, to structural or doctrinal changes to this area of the law that reflect underlying shifts of a deeper, normative nature.

The application of standards of procedural fairness to 'administrative', as distinct from 'judicial', decision-making demonstrates a normative conviction relating to the breadth of the circumstances in which individuals deserve to be treated fairly at the hands of the state. Equally, the (sometimes differing) positions taken by courts on the question whether due process should be afforded even if it would 'make no difference' reflect underlying disagreement concerning the extent to which dignitarian concerns trump more practical, or instrumental, ones. And, as we have just seen, whether there should be a common law duty to consult, and whether the common law should inform the content of statutory duties to consult, turn upon fundamental questions about the normative purposes of the notion of procedural fairness. None of this is to deny the importance of engaging with the technical detail of this area of administrative law; it does, however, serve to underline the importance of approaching the doctrinal iceberg whilst bearing firmly in mind what is going on beneath the surface.

FURTHER RESOURCES

Allan, 'Procedural Fairness and the Duty of Respect' (1998) 18 *OJLS* 497

Galligan, 'Procedural Fairness' in Birks (ed), *The Frontiers of Liability* (volume one) (Oxford 1994)

Loughlin, 'Procedural Fairness: A Study of the Crisis in Administrative Law Theory' (1978) 28 *UTLJ* 215

Mashaw, 'The Supreme Court's Due Process Calculus for Administrative Adjudication in *Mathews v. Eldridge*: Three Factors in Search of a Theory of Value' (1976) 44 *U Chi LR* 28

Mullan, 'Fairness: The New Natural Justice' (1975) 25 *UTLJ* 281

Varuhas, 'Judicial Review at the Crossroads' [2015] *CLJ* 215

Wade, 'The Twilight of Natural Justice?' (1951) 67 *LQR* 103

11 GIVING REASONS FOR DECISIONS

In *Stefan* v. *General Medical Council* [1999] 1 WLR 1293 at 1300, Lord Clyde noted a clear trend in English law 'towards an increased recognition of the duty upon decision-makers of many kinds to give reasons' for their decisions. Nevertheless, it remains the case that, in the oft-cited words of Lord Mustill in *R* v. *Secretary of State for the Home Department, ex parte Doody* [1994] 1 AC 531 at 564, there exists no 'general duty to give reasons' for administrative decisions. The proposition that everything depends on context therefore applies with at least as much force here as to the aspects of procedural fairness addressed in the two previous chapters.

11.1 Introductory matters

Before embarking on a detailed examination of the content and scope of the duty to give reasons, it is necessary briefly to differentiate that duty from four cognate, but ultimately distinct, matters, the first of which is *the duty to give notice* (on which see 10.3.2). Now, there is clearly a relationship between notice and reasons: as Lord Woolf MR acknowledged in *R* v. *Secretary of State for the Home Department, ex parte Fayed* [1998] 1 WLR 763, requiring the giving of notice may reveal—or at least allow the claimant to deduce—the ultimate reasons for the decision. It is also possible for circumstances to arise in which reasons and notice are indistinguishable: *eg* reasons for a first-instance decision may in practice amount to also constitute notice for the purposes of a right of appeal. Nevertheless, notice and reasons remain conceptually distinct; the duties to supply notice and reasons arising at different stages in the decision-making process. Notice is given *before* the decision is taken. Reasons are supplied *after* (or contemporaneously with) the decision so as to explain why it was reached. Notice is therefore inherently preliminary in nature—it indicates the case which the individual is required to answer—while reasons for the final decision express qualitative conclusions about the merits of the individual's case, and as to why the decision-maker was or was not persuaded that the claimant managed to marshal evidence and arguments sufficient to overcome the case against him.

The second matter that should be distinguished from the duty to give notice is the possibility of *inferring unreasonableness* from an absence of reasons. *Obiter dicta* in *Padfield* v. *Minister of Agriculture* [1968] AC 997 suggest that if a decision-maker fails to advance reasons in support of a decision, the court may infer that no valid reasons exist and that the decision is therefore *Wednesbury* unreasonable (see 8.2.1). For instance, Lord Pearce said at 1053–4:

> I do not regard a Minister's failure or refusal to give any reasons as a sufficient exclusion of the court's surveillance. If all the prima facie reasons seem to point in favour of his taking a certain course to carry out the intentions of Parliament in respect of a power which it has given him in

> that regard, and he gives no reason whatever for taking a contrary course, the court may infer that he has no good reason and that he is not using the power given by Parliament to carry out its intentions.

It is clear, however, that such an inference will be made only rarely. This point was emphasized by Lord Keith in *R v. Secretary of State for Trade and Industry, ex parte Lonrho plc* [1989] 1 WLR 525 at 539–40, who explained that

> [t]he absence of reasons for a decision where there is no duty to give them cannot of itself provide any support for the suggested irrationality of the decision. The only significance of the absence of reasons is that if all other known facts and circumstances appear to point overwhelmingly in favour of a different decision, the decision-maker, who has given no reasons, cannot complain if the court draws the inference that he had no rational reason for his decision.

It is also important to bear in mind that the *Padfield* approach is conceptually distinct from the duty to give reasons: while it may constitute an *incentive* to supply reasons—so as to make findings of substantive unreasonableness less likely—it imposes no positive *duty* upon decision-makers to furnish reasons for their decisions.

Third, if the circumstances are such that the substantive lawfulness of the decision falls to be considered by reference to *the proportionality doctrine*, the existence or non-existence of reasons becomes particularly pertinent. Most obviously, reasons must be supplied if a proportionality challenge is to be survived—although this matter engages a duty owed to the court (considered in the next paragraph) as distinct from the duty to give reasons (which is owed to the relevant individual) *per se*. In addition, where reasons exist which demonstrate serious engagement with the human rights question, the decision-maker's view is likely to be afforded greater weight in the balancing calculus (on which see further 8.4.5).

Fourth, it is necessary to distinguish the duty to give reasons from *the duty of candour*. Whereas the former duty pertains to the relationship between the decision-maker and the individual, the latter concerns the relationship between the decision-maker and the court that is judicially reviewing the lawfulness of the contested decision. A decision-maker that has neglected to give reasons to the individual (either because no duty to give reasons exists or because such a duty has been breached) may nevertheless choose to give reasons to the reviewing court—a choice that, as noted earlier, might be made in order to avoid falling foul of the *Padfield* principle or in an attempt to demonstrate that the decision is proportionate. However, while grounds of review like reasonableness and proportionality might *incentivize* the giving of reasons to the court, the duty of candour amounts to a legal *obligation* to supply reasons where they are relevant to a legal issue that is before the court.

In *R v. Lancashire County Council, ex parte Huddleston* [1986] 2 All ER 941 at 945, Sir John Donaldson MR said that even if a defendant is not legally obliged to give reasons to the individual, 'the position is quite different if and when the applicant can satisfy a judge of the public law court that the facts disclosed by her are sufficient to entitle her to apply for judicial review of the decision. Then it becomes the duty of the respondent to make full and fair disclosure.' Setting out a view that echoes the green light approach to administrative law examined at 1.2.2, he went on (at 945) to say that the duty of candour reflects a 'partnership' between courts and public authorities, which have a 'common aim' to maintain 'the highest standards of public administration'. The duty of candour is, however, limited in scope. In *Marshall v. Deputy Governor of Bermuda* [2010] UKPC 9 at [29], Lord Phillips, giving the judgment of the Judicial Committee of the Privy Council, said that it arises only when 'it is not possible for the court to assess the merits of an issue that has been raised unless the public authority against whom the claim is brought furnishes the court with information which it alone is in a position to provide'.

In conclusion, while each of the matters considered in this section covers some of, or otherwise relates to, the terrain that is occupied by the duty to give reasons, they are all conceptually and practically distinct from the duty to give reasons. It is to that duty itself that we now turn.

11.2 Why require reasons?

11.2.1 The virtues of reason-giving

Fordham [1998] *JR* 158 observes that '[u]nderlying any analysis of the law on reasons is a functional question. To what ends, for what purposes, are public decision-makers (to be) required to give reasons?' In the following passage, he suggests that three dimensions underlie a fully-developed duty to give reasons.

Fordham, 'Reasons: The Third Dimension' [1998] *JR* 158

A first dimension is that the giving of reasons *serves the interests of the court* (or other tribunal) reviewing the decision. This rationale has to do with disclosure, to the court. The approach is illustrated by the comments of the Court of Appeal in *R* v. *Lancashire County Council, ex parte Huddleston* [1986] 2 All ER 941 at 945g and 947e, where reasons were encouraged in a spirit of cooperation by the public authority with the judicial review process.

A second dimension is that the giving of reasons *serves the interests of the person affected* by the decision. This has to do with disclosure, to the 'parties'. It is exemplified by the decision of the House of Lords in *R* v. *Secretary of State for the Home Department, ex parte Doody* [1994] 1 AC 531, where reasons were required because of the prisoner's basic interest in knowing why decisions affecting liberty had been taken.

The third dimension is that the giving of reasons *serves the interests of the decision-maker* in reaching the decision. This has to do not with disclosure, but discipline. The central point is simple. Consciously duty-bound to articulate their reasons, decision-makers' minds are the more focused and their substantive decision-making the better. This was recognised by the Divisional Court in *R* v. *Higher Education Funding Council, ex parte Institute of Dental Surgery* [1994] 1 WLR 242 at 256H (cited with approval in *R* v. *City of London Corporation, ex parte Matson* [1997] 1 WLR 765 (CA) at 783D and in *R* v. *Ministry of Defence, ex parte Murray* [1998] COD 134 (DC)), as the first of a series of factors in favour of requiring reasons, namely that 'the giving of reasons may among other things concentrate the decision-maker's mind on the right questions'.

Some—such as the JUSTICE-All Souls Committee, *Administrative Justice: Some Necessary Reforms* (Oxford 1988) at 70—also point to a fourth dimension: that reason-giving enhances public confidence in decision-making 'by the knowledge that supportable reasons have to be given by those who exercise administrative power'. In any event, Fordham's analysis reveals progressively broader conceptions of the duty to give reasons, culminating in a view which sees the giving of reasons not as an optional extra which is bolted on to the end of the decision-making process, but as something which is integral to the very notion of good administration, providing an incentive to adhere to the principles of good administrative practice considered earlier in this book. Fordham goes on to argue that the way in which we view the purpose behind the giving of reasons, and in particular whether we accept all three of the dimensions which he identifies, fundamentally influences the scope of the duty and helps determine such matters as the level of detail required when giving reasons; whether they must accompany the decision or can be issued after the event; precisely when the duty arises in the first place, and the relief which is appropriate when it is breached. We explore these issues later in this chapter.

For the time being, we emphasize a distinction which is latent within Fordham's analysis of the virtues of reason-giving. His first and third points highlight the capacity of reason-giving to promote the effective operation of the administrative system—in terms both of decision-making and judicial review thereof. In contrast, Fordham's second point captures a rather different aspect of the importance of reasons. The notion that those whose lives are affected by official decisions have a 'basic interest' in knowing the reasons underlying them implies a particular relationship between the government and the governed which recog- nizes the dignity of the latter as a participant in, rather than the object of, decision-making; on this view, reason-giving is a good in itself. (It should, however, be noted that this can be a double-edged sword; treating dignity as the primary concern might extend the scope of the duty to give reasons in some respects—eg by defeating an argument that reasons need not be given because supplying them 'would make no difference'—while shrinking it in others. For instance, reasons would not be required on dignitarian grounds in respect of a decision of public importance that did not particularly affect any given individual.)

In the following passage, Allan (applying to reason-giving his general thesis, incorporat- ing dignitarian concerns, developed in the extract which appears at 10.1) takes issue with the emphasis placed by Galligan, *Due Process and Fair Procedures: A Study of Administrative Procedures* (Oxford 1996) (an excerpt from which also appears at 10.1), on the instrumental benefits of due process.

Allan, 'Procedural Fairness and the Duty of Respect' (1998) 18 *OJLS* 497

Although Galligan is right to protest against a view of procedures which belittles their instrumental value in ensuring appropriate outcomes, there are at least aspects of procedural fairness or good practice which may serve an independent function. Moreover, the whole design or character of a hearing may well reflect non-instrumental values of no less importance than those which underlie our concern for accuracy and reliability. The giving of reasons by officials, in particular, can readily be understood as serving a 'dignitarian' function quite distinct from the arrangements for securing sound decisions. As Galligan notes, an obligation to give reasons may have a beneficial effect on the quality of the decision and in that sense contribute to fairness; but whether or not that is so in any particular case, giving reasons may be regarded as an integral part of treating a disappointed applicant with the respect which his dignity as a citizen demands. Galligan is very cautious here, sceptical of the bare claim that the giving of reasons is in itself an expression of respect; but he rightly accepts that there is value, independent of outcome, in a person being able to judge for himself whether or not an exercise of authority over him is justified. In view of the inevitable imper- fections of decision-processes and the fallibility of decision-makers, the party affected is entitled to the reassurance which an expression of valid reasons, if they exist, supplies.

It is surely not hard to discern good grounds here for Laurence Tribe's suggestion [in *American Constitutional Law* (New York 1978) at 503–4] that such 'rights to interchange' amount to an expression of a person's humanity, for the idea that procedures may have intrinsic value. Giving reasons expresses respect just as a refusal or failure to do so—where the failure evinces disregard for a person's opinion of the justice of his treatment—expresses contempt. As Lucas [*On Justice* (Oxford 1980) at 79–80] explains the point, a requirement to give reasons 'recognizes a party's right to be disappointed by an adverse decision, and the need to assuage it'. A principal purpose of the rules of natural justice, more generally, is to enable a person to *identify* with the decision-making process: by observing them we make it easier for him to accept the result, and 'make it manifest to anyone disappointed at the outcome that we were solicitous of his interests and did not reach an adverse decision lightly or wantonly, but only for good reason and with evident reluctance' [79–80].

Tribe's reference to 'rights of interchange' suggests an important sense in which, if a fair hearing is understood to encompass the giving of reasons, it has a value quite independent of outcome. By responding to the *particular* arguments which the disappointed applicant or claimant has offered, the official attempts to persuade him of the justice of the decision in terms which acknowledge his special (even unique) position and his independence of mind. As Galligan observes, administrative decision-making generally takes place under conditions of uncertainty, complexity and incommensurability, where inquiry, argument, and deliberation are highly desirable; and the duty of respect requires that attention should be paid to the person's special case, where misjudgment is not simply a social cost but an act of injustice. The reasons given should enable a person to see that his case has been given the careful consideration which it may deserve, and thereby more readily accept the outcome as a reasonable accommodation between private and public interests.

However, there is clearly good reason for Galligan's caution. The intrinsic or non-instrumental value of reason-giving by officials depends on the sincerity with which they respond to a person's claim and examine the merits of his arguments. No reassurance is given by the statement of invalid or inadequate reasons; nor is respect shown by meeting a person's arguments, tailored to his own circumstances, with routine official responses, devised for the standard case which may be quite dissimilar. Respect is shown only when there has been a genuine effort to confront the conditions of uncertainty, complexity and incommensurability as they bear on the citizen's case; and his acceptance of the outcome as a legitimate decision is likely to depend on his being given reasons which demonstrate that such an effort has in fact been made, and the interests of justice accordingly served. To that extent, the intrinsic value of procedures is closely tied to their instrumental purpose—the former is dependent on at least moderate success in regard to the latter.

QUESTION

- Do you agree that reason-giving is important in itself, independent of any contribution it may make to the accuracy or correctness of the decision?

11.2.2 A general duty to give reasons?

The clear virtues of reason-giving give rise to an obvious question: why does English law not recognize a general duty on the part of decision-makers to give reasons? We noted at the outset of this chapter that the starting-point of English law is that no such duty exists, albeit that certain circumstances may trigger a requirement to give reasons. The concerns which underlie the reluctance of English law to embrace a general duty were summarized in the following terms by the JUSTICE-All Souls Committee in their report, *Administrative Justice: Some Necessary Reforms* (Oxford 1988) at 70–1:

(a) Efficient administration requires free and uninhibited discussion among decision-makers, unimpeded by considerations of what can or cannot be made public subsequently.

(b) A general requirement of reasons will impose an intolerable burden on the machinery of government.

(c) Delays in the handling of business will inevitably follow and additional expense will be caused. The public at large will suffer. The benefit will not match the cost.

(d) The imposition of a general duty will have far-reaching implications for central government, local government, and for many other bodies of a public or semi-public character. Many more decisions will be opened up to the possibility of legal challenge and a further step down the road of 'judicialization' of affairs will be taken.

(e) The imposition of a [general] duty to give reasons will not necessarily mean that the true or complete reasons will be stated. Decision-makers will adapt to the new regime and acquire the art of stating sufficient by way of reasons to preclude successful challenge, but candour will not always be displayed.

The Committee did not, however, find these arguments compelling, and considered them to be outweighed by the benefits which flow from a general duty to give reasons. It concluded that the creation of a general duty should not be left to judicial development of the common law, and that legislative intervention would be preferable. The Committee was heavily influenced by s 13(1) of the Australian Administrative Decisions (Judicial Review) Act 1977—which entitles individuals to request from the decision-maker 'a statement in writing setting out the findings on material questions of fact, referring to the evidence or other material on which those findings were based and giving reasons for the decision'— and recommended the adoption of a similar approach in English law. The Committee was particularly impressed that the Australian provision went further than a simple duty to state reasons, commenting (at 72) that the additional obligation to furnish details of the material relied upon in arriving at the decision would ensure that 'matters will be decided and justice administered according to facts and law and not upon arbitrary or extra-legal considerations'. Such a requirement also helps to guard against the giving of standard, non-specific reasons which bear little relation to the circumstances of the individual case—a concern highlighted earlier both by Allan (at 11.2.1) and the JUSTICE-All Souls Committee (in paragraph (e) above).

It is important to bear in mind that a *general* duty to give reasons does not amount to a *universal* duty to give reasons. The starting point in a legal system which recognizes a general duty is that reasons must be given, but there will naturally be exceptional circumstances in which reason-giving would be inappropriate. The JUSTICE-All Souls Committee (at 73) tentatively suggested that exceptions may apply in the following areas:

(a) where the giving of reasons would be prejudicial to the interests of national security, defence, or international relations;

(b) where the reasons would involve disclosing material protected by legal privilege;

(c) where the reasons would disclose information made available to government in confidence (this heading would cover such matters as decisions as to the awarding of commercial contracts, licences and other privileges);

(d) where the reasons would reveal professional or trade secrets or otherwise be hurtful to the interests of third parties;

(e) where the decision of which reasons were sought related to the appointment to or promotion in any post or office or to the assignment of any specific task.

QUESTIONS

- Do these exceptions to a general duty to give reasons go too far?
- Or are there other situations in which you would wish to see administrators free from an obligation to justify their decisions?

11.3 The duty to give reasons at common law

11.3.1 The emergence of a common law duty to give reasons

Traditionally, at common law, the requirements of natural justice did not extend to a duty to give reasons (see, *eg McInnes* v. *Onslow-Fane* [1978] 1 WLR 1520 and *R* v. *Gaming Board for Great Britain, ex parte Benaim and Khaida* [1970] 2 QB 417). A breakthrough, however, was made in *R* v. *Civil Service Appeal Board, ex parte Cunningham* [1991] 4 All ER 310. The defendant, a public body established under the royal prerogative, concluded that the claimant, a prison officer, had been unfairly dismissed, but refused to give reasons explaining how it had arrived at a compensation award which, in the words of Leggatt LJ at 325, 'looks as though [it] is less than it should be'. The case is significant for its recognition of the fact that 'the duty to act fairly in this case extends to an obligation to give reasons' (*per* Leggatt LJ at 326). McCowan LJ (at 322–3) identified seven factors that militated in favour of a reason-giving duty in the circumstances:

1. There is no appeal from the Board's determination of the amount of compensation.
2. In making that determination the Board is carrying out a judicial function.
3. The Board is susceptible to judicial review.
4. … [T]he provision of a recommendation without reasons … is insufficient to achieve justice.
5. There is no statute which requires the courts to tolerate that unfairness.
6. The giving of short reasons would not frustrate the apparent purpose of the code [on civil service pay and conditions].
7. It is not a case where the giving of reasons would be harmful to the public interest.

The next important development in the emergence of a common law duty to give reasons was the House of Lords' decision in *R* v. *Secretary of State for the Home Department, ex parte Doody* [1994] 1 AC 531. In accordance with a practice no longer adopted, the Home Secretary had determined the minimum periods for which the claimants—convicted murderers—should be detained in prison. In doing so, the Home Secretary set minimum detention periods (or 'tariffs') in excess of those recommended by the judiciary. The claimants successfully argued, *inter alia*, that the Minister's failure to give reasons for doing so rendered his decision unlawful. In an important speech, Lord Mustill began (at 561) by laying down the following basic propositions:

> [T]he law does not at present recognise a general duty to give reasons for an administrative decision. Nevertheless, it is equally beyond question that such a duty may in appropriate circumstances be implied, and I agree with the analyses by the Court of Appeal in *Reg. v. Civil Service Appeal Board, Ex parte Cunningham* [1991] 4 All E.R. 310 of the factors which will often be material to such an implication.

The question, then, was whether a duty to give reasons applied in the particular circumstances of this case. Lord Mustill answered the question (at 564–5) by saying:

> [T]he Secretary of State ought to implement the scheme [for determining tariff periods] as fairly as he can. The giving of reasons may be inconvenient, but I can see no ground at all why it should be against the public interest: indeed, rather the reverse. This being so, I would ask simply: Is refusal to give reasons fair? I would answer without hesitation that it is not. As soon as the jury returns its verdict the offender knows that he will be locked up for a very long time. For just how long immediately becomes the most important thing in the prisoner's life. When looking at statistics it is easy to fall into the way of thinking that there is not really very much difference between one extremely long sentence and another: and there may not be, in percentage terms. But the percentage reflects a difference of a year or years: a long time for anybody, and longer still for a prisoner. Where a defendant is convicted of, say, several armed robberies he knows that he faces a stiff sentence: he can be advised by reference to a public tariff of the range of sentences he must expect; he hears counsel address the judge on the relationship between his offences and the tariff; he will often hear the judge give an indication during exchanges with counsel of how his mind is working; and when sentence is pronounced he will always be told the reasons for it … Contrast this with the position of the prisoner sentenced for murder. He never sees the Home Secretary; he has no dialogue with him: he cannot fathom how his mind is working. There is no true tariff, or at least no tariff exposed to public view which might give the prisoner an idea of what to expect. The announcement of his first review date arrives out of thin air, wholly without explanation. The distant oracle has spoken, and that is that.
>
> … I … simply ask, is it fair that the mandatory life prisoner should be wholly deprived of the information which all other prisoners receive as a matter of course. I am clearly of the opinion that it is not.
>
> My Lords, I can moreover arrive at the same conclusion by a different and more familiar route, of which *Ex parte Cunningham* [1991] 4 All E.R. 310 provides a recent example. It is not, as I understand it, questioned that the decision of the Home Secretary on the penal element is susceptible to judicial review. To mount an effective attack on the decision, given no more material than the facts of the offence and the length of the penal element, the prisoner has virtually no means of ascertaining whether this is an instance where the decision-making process has gone astray. I think it important that there should be an effective means of detecting the kind of error which would entitle the court to intervene, and in practice I regard it as necessary for this purpose that the reasoning of the Home Secretary should be disclosed. If there is any difference between the penal element recommended by the judges and actually imposed by the Home Secretary, this reasoning is bound to include, either explicitly or implicitly, a reason why the Home Secretary has taken a different view.

QUESTION

- Is the substance of the decision in *Doody* consistent with Lord Mustill's protestation that there is still no general duty to give reasons in English law?

11.3.2 The scope of the common law duty

A particular puzzle—upon which Lord Mustill touches in the passage set out above—concerns the extent to which the availability or unavailability of rights of challenge may bear upon the question whether a duty to give reasons arises. If there is no right of appeal against an administrative decision, then there is a greater likelihood that the individual concerned will simply have to live with that decision, however objectionable and unfathomable he may consider it to be. It might be considered that, in such circumstances, there is a dignitarian argument in favour of a duty to give reasons: if someone is stuck with a decision that might profoundly affect them for some time to come, do they not deserve to know why the decision was made? A different type of argument, however, can be made in favour of the imposition of a duty to give reasons if there *is* a right of appeal, since in those circumstances an absence of reasons for the original decision would impede both the making of an informed choice about whether to exercise the right of appeal and (if the right is exercised) the making of informed arguments about the original decision. There is therefore a strong argument in favour of giving reasons *before* appellate proceedings are launched.

Against this background, Craig [1994] *CLJ* 282 at 287 writes that '[w]hat has always been something of a mystery is why the same reasoning should not be equally applicable to review, as opposed to appeal'. The final paragraph of the earlier excerpt from *Doody* suggests that Lord Mustill may have had some sympathy with this view. If, however, this position were to be pressed to its logical conclusion, it is hard to see how it could be reconciled with the view—endorsed in *Doody* itself—that there is no general duty to give reasons. If, for the reasons considered earlier, such a duty were to arise whenever a decision could be the subject of an appeal or of judicial review proceedings, then virtually every decision would attract such a duty. However, as the following case, decided shortly after *Doody*, makes clear, the possibility of challenging the decision, whether by way of appeal or review, is in fact only one—and not necessarily the decisive—consideration to be taken into account when determining whether a duty to give reasons exists.

R v. Higher Education Funding Council, ex parte Institute of Dental Surgery [1994] 1 WLR 242
Divisional Court

The Higher Education Funding Council (HEFC) for England assessed, by using panels of academics conducting peer reviews, the quality of research produced by various institutions. The Institute of Dental Surgery was graded at point 2 (having previously been graded at point 3) on a 1–5 scale, resulting in a substantial reduction in research funding. The Institute was informed by the HEFC how the assessment had been carried out, but no reasons were given for the final decision as to grading. The Institute sought judicial review.

Sedley J (giving the judgment of the Court)

... We readily accept Mr. Beloff's [counsel for the defendant] submission that Lord Mustill was not holding [in *Doody*] that reasons are called for wherever it is desired to know whether grounds for challenge exist; for to do so would be to create just such a general duty as Lord Mustill . . . was careful to exclude. Rather he was holding that in the situation of near-total ignorance and impotence in which the prisoner found himself about something as vital to him as his prospects of liberty, such a duty arose. It follows nonetheless from Lord Mustill's reasoning that the 'more familiar route' exemplified by *Ex parte Cunningham* [1992] I.C.R. 816 may be broader than the *Cunningham* situation alone and capable of embracing other situations in which 'it is important that there should be an effective means of detecting the kind of error which would entitle the court to intervene.' This being so, it seems both desirable and practical to test by a common standard both the fairness of not telling a person the reasons for a decision affecting him and the desirability of exposing any grounds of legal challenge. There are, moreover, reasons of principle for a unitary test. As the judgments in *Ex parte Cunningham* show, one aspect of unfairness may be precisely the inability to know whether an error of law or of process has occurred. But since the latter is not a freestanding ground for requiring reasons (for if it were, it would apply universally), it can only be on grounds of fairness that it will arise; so that the need to know whether there has been an error of law or of process is rightly seen not as an alternative to the demands of fairness but as an aspect of them. This approach places on an even footing the multiple grounds on which the giving of reasons may in any one case be requisite. The giving of reasons may among other things concentrate the decision-maker's mind on the right questions; demonstrate to the recipient that this is so; show that the issues have been conscientiously addressed and how the result has been reached; or alternatively alert the recipient to a justiciable flaw in the process. On the other side of the argument, it may place an undue burden on decision-makers; demand an appearance of unanimity where there is diversity; call for the articulation of sometimes inexpressible value judgments; and offer an invitation to the captious to comb the reasons for previously unsuspected grounds of challenge. It is the relationship of these and other material considerations to the nature of the particular decision which will determine whether or not fairness demands reasons.

In the light of such factors each case will come to rest between two poles, or possibly at one of them: the decision which cries out for reasons, and the decision for which reasons are entirely inapposite. Somewhere between the two poles comes the dividing line separating those cases in which the balance of factors calls for reasons from those where it does not. At present there is no sure indication of where the division comes ... [and] this court cannot go beyond the proposition that, there being no general obligation to give reasons, there will be decisions for which fairness does not demand reasons ...

[After considering questions of relief and reiterating the point that the interest in knowing whether the decision-making process is flawed cannot, independently of other contextual factors, generate a duty to give reasons, Sedley J, addressing the importance of the decision as a criterion relevant to the existence of a reason-giving duty, continued:] The chief benchmark of significance which we have at present in this setting is the *Doody* case ... There the applicant knew the evidence on which he had been convicted but little else, while a considerable body of highly relevant matter had accumulated in the hands of the decision-maker and was going to affect many years of his liberty. If the Home Secretary were then to depart from the judicial view of tariff, it is not easy to think of a stronger case for the disclosure of reasons not merely to the applicant but to all mandatory life sentence prisoners, to each of whom result of the case will necessarily apply. Equally here the argument, it seems to us, must be good for all applicants, not just disappointed ones, if they want to know why they have been rated as they have been. One would like to be able to hold that for all such applicants, disappointed or not, the importance of the decision alone was enough. But to do so would generalise the duty to give reasons to a point to which this court, at least, cannot go.

We must therefore look also at the other indicia: the openness of the procedure, widely canvassed in advance and published in circular form; the voluntary submission of self-selected examples of work; the judgment of academic peers. These, it seems to us, shift the process substantially away from the pole represented by *Ex parte Doody*, not on mere grounds of dissimilarity (there will be many dissimilar cases in which reasons are nevertheless now required) but because the nature of the exercise was that it was open in all but its critical phase, and its critical phase was one in which, as Professor Davies [chief executive of the Universities Funding Council, HEFC's predecessor] deposes, 'the grade awarded to a particular institution was not determined by a score against specific features.' We … find [this] remarkable, but it is a fact and not one which Mr. Pannick [for the claimant] has been able to assault on legal grounds. In the result, the combination of openness in the run-up with the prescriptively oracular character of the critical decision makes the council's allocation of grades inapt, in our judgment, for the giving of reasons, notwithstanding the undoubted importance of the outcome to the institutions concerned.

From this case-specific conclusion, it is possible to generalise to a certain extent. The only mystery left in the process is precisely why the final grade of 2 was arrived at. As Mr. Pannick points out, the evidence is replete with answers to the question how it was arrived at, but not why. The question 'why,' in isolation as it can now be seen to be, is a question of academic judgment. We would hold that where what is sought to be impugned is on the evidence *no more* than an informed exercise of academic judgment, fairness alone will not require reasons to be given. This is not to say for a moment that academic decisions are beyond challenge. A mark, for example, awarded at an examiners' meeting where irrelevant and damaging personal factors have been allowed to enter into the evaluation of a candidate's written paper is something more than an informed exercise of academic judgment. Where evidence shows that something extraneous has entered into the process of academic judgment, one of two results may follow depending on the nature of the fault: either the decision will fall without more, or the court may require reasons to be given, so that the decision can either be seen to be sound or can be seen or (absent reasons) be inferred to be flawed. But purely academic judgments, in our view, will as a rule not be in the class of case exemplified, though by no means exhausted, by *Ex parte Doody*, where the nature and impact of the decision itself call for reasons as a routine aspect of procedural fairness. They will be in the *Ex parte Cunningham* [1992] I.C.R. 816 class where some trigger factor is required to show, that, in the circumstances of the particular decision, fairness calls for reasons to be given.

Is there then such a trigger factor here? The second limb of Mr. Pannick's submission is that the applicant has been confronted with a decision which, on the evidence, is inexplicable: the applicant's excellence is widely acknowledged and attested; its original rating of 2.6 would have qualified for rounding up to a 3; and the reduction to 2.4 and hence to a rating of 2 followed reconsideration in circumstances which, at the lowest, can be regarded as unsatisfactory. Mr. Beloff responds, and we agree with him, that neither intrinsically nor on the evidence is there a sufficient basis on which this court can hold the eventual rating to be so aberrant as in itself to call for an explanation. We lack precisely the expertise which would permit us to judge whether it is extraordinary or not. It may be misfortune for the applicant that the court, which in *Ex parte Cunningham* [1992] I.C.R. 816 could readily evaluate the contrast between what the board awarded and what an industrial tribunal would have awarded, cannot begin to evaluate the comparative worth of research in clinical dentistry; but it is a fact of life. The applicant's previous grading, the volume and frequency of citation of its research and the high level of peer-reviewed outside funding which it has attracted, to all of which Mr. Pannick points, may well demonstrate that the applicant has been unfortunate in the grading it has received, but such a misfortune can well occur within the four corners of a lawfully conducted evaluation ...

In summary, then: (1) there is no general duty to give reasons for a decision, but there are classes of case where there is such a duty. (2) One such class is where the subject matter is an interest so highly regarded by the law (for example, personal liberty), that fairness requires that reasons, at least for particular decisions, be given as of right. (3) (a) Another such class is where the decision appears aberrant. Here fairness may require reasons so that the recipient may know whether the aberration is in the legal sense real (and so challengeable) or apparent; (b) it follows that this class does not include decisions which are themselves challengeable by reference only to the reasons for them. A pure exercise of academic judgment is such a decision. And (c) procedurally, the grant of leave in such cases will depend upon prima facie evidence that something has gone wrong. The respondent may then seek to demonstrate that it is not so and that the decision is an unalloyed exercise of an intrinsically unchallengeable judgment. If the respondent succeeds, the application fails. If the respondent fails, relief may take the form of an order of mandamus to give reasons, or (if a justiciable flaw has been established) other appropriate relief.

The claimant's challenge was rejected, and the HEFC was not required to supply reasons for its decision.

The deference of the Court to questions of academic judgment assumed particular importance in this case because the Court treated it as a *Cunningham*-type case: only if the decision to award a grade 2 could be characterized as 'aberrant' would the reason-giving duty be triggered, yet the Court felt institutionally incompetent to determine whether the grade was extraordinary. The outcome would presumably have been different if the Court had been willing to acknowledge that the enormous importance to the Institute of the grade—in terms of both its financial position and institutional morale—equated to an impact on an interest more highly regarded by law, thus making the case analogous to *Doody*. Sedley LJ suggested in *R (Wooder)* v. *Feggetter* [2002] EWCA Civ 554, [2003] QB 219 at [41] that *HEFC* 'would [not] necessarily be decided in the same way today'.

Although the summary given in the final paragraph of the *HEFC* excerpt above is helpful, too much emphasis should not be placed on the various categories of cases which Sedley J identifies; as he pointed out in *R* v. *University of Cambridge, ex parte Evans* [1998] ELR 515 at 521, those categories are not closed. Reading the *HEFC* judgment as a whole, it is clear that the Court's intention was to underscore the point made by Lord Mustill in *Doody* that, ultimately, whether reasons must be given turns upon whether fairness so requires. The factors identified in the *HEFC* case are therefore best regarded as useful indicators of what fairness requires, in terms of reasons, in a given situation. This point is usefully illustrated by *R* v. *Ministry of Defence, ex parte Murray* [1998] COD 134. The reviewing court held that a Court Martial was required to give reasons for imposing a severe sentence on an officer of good character and for rejecting his argument that his impugned behaviour was attributable (at least in part) to anti-malarial medication. It is clear that the Court was influenced by both the seriousness of the matter, since the sentence imposed had the effect of ending the claimant's military career, and the (consequent) importance to the claimant of discovering whether any reviewable errors had occurred.

It is also clear that fairness may require the giving of reasons even if the interests affected by the decision are not as fundamental as liberty or livelihood, as the Court of

Appeal's decision in *R v. City of London Corporation, ex parte Matson* [1997] 1 WLR 765 demonstrates. The claimant had been elected—through a procedure recognized as a 'local government election' by the Representation of the People Act 1983, s 191(1)—an alderman of the City of London, but the Court of Aldermen, which has a customary right to decide whether to confirm such elections, refused to do so. The claimant, concerned that the Court had been influenced by allegations of misconduct which he had attempted to rebut, sought judicial review. The Court of Appeal decided that the Court of Aldermen ought to have given reasons for its decision. As is apparent from the following extract from Neill LJ's judgment (at 776–7) the factors underlying this conclusion are varied, and as well as the fact that an important interest (*viz* reputation) was affected, the public character of the matter and the claimant's practical need to know—for purposes both of challenging the original decision and deciding whether to submit himself to election again—also weighed heavily on the Court:

> I am persuaded that fairness and natural justice require that this decision should not be allowed to go unexplained. I have been led to this conclusion by the following considerations. (1) Mr. Matson was standing for public office and wished to serve his constituents and the City of London in that office. (2) Mr. Matson was elected by the voters at a wardmote by a substantial majority and by an electoral process recognised by section 191(1) of the Representation of the People Act 1983. (3) The second stage of the election involved a decision by the Court of Aldermen which is a court of record. (4) The decision of the court was announced in public and is a matter of public record. (5) During the course of the private interview questions were put to Mr. Matson which suggested that he had acted in an inappropriate manner. He has no means of knowing whether the court accepted his explanation. As McCowan L.J. pointed out in *Reg. v. Civil Service Appeal Board, Ex parte Cunningham* [1992] I.C.R. 816, 830H, in the absence of reasons a person in Mr. Matson's position will not know whether his submissions have been rejected or not. (6) The basis for the court's decision *may* have been that Mr. Matson lacked the necessary positive qualities for the office. On the other hand the court, or some members of it, *may* have been dissatisfied with his answers to some particular questions or as to his experience of or commitment to the City. (7) In the absence of any reasons neither Mr. Matson nor the electors can know whether he should stand again or whether, if re-elected ..., he should supply additional information to the court. The cost and time involved in a further election is not inconsiderable. It is also to be remembered that if an alderman-elect is rejected three times in succession the Court of Aldermen is empowered to nominate and elect some other person to the office. (8) The public rejection of Mr. Matson is bound to cast a shadow on his reputation. It may be that through no fault of his he lacks those special qualities which the office of alderman demands. On the other hand his rejection may be interpreted as meaning that there is a black mark against him. (9) The giving of short reasons will not frustrate or impede the exercise by the court of its customary powers. On the contrary the articulation of short reasons will enable the court to ensure that their decisions in every case are sound and manifestly just and in the interests of the city.

A distinct point was dealt with by Swinton Thomas LJ at 783, concerning the suggestion that it would be difficult to articulate reasons for the decision:

> Mr. Sullivan [counsel for the City of London] puts forward as an objection to the giving of reasons the difficulty of articulating them. He says that the reasons may be based on factual matters or an assessment of the character and personality of the alderman-elect, or a combination of the two. When objections are based on character or personality, Mr. Sullivan submits that it may

be difficult to articulate the general view. It may be based on value judgments. There are 24 aldermen engaged in the process. They may have a variety of views, and there may be difficulty in expressing the view of the aldermen as a body … Mr. Sullivan submitted that to require the aldermen to give reasons for their decision would require them to articulate 'inexpressible value judgments.' I do not accept that argument. I do not believe that it would be unduly difficult or arduous for the aldermen to give a collective reason for their decision. True it is that individual members may have considered differing factors. That is likely to apply to any collective decision. There is no difficulty in articulating a factual basis for a decision. If I am right in my conclusion that the aldermen are entitled to take into account their assessment of the alderman-elect's character and personality then, equally, I do not believe that any adverse assessment involves the articulation of inexpressible value judgments. Assessments of that nature are made day in, day out, in every walk of life.

QUESTIONS

- Can the approach of Swinton Thomas LJ in *Matson* be reconciled with that of Sedley J in *HEFC* (though note the later comments of Sedley LJ mentioned above)?
- Why were the value judgements as to character in the former capable of being the subject of reasons, while the academic judgement exercised in the latter case was incapable of being reduced to reasons?

11.3.3 Reason-giving and legitimate expectation

Before leaving the topic of reason-giving at common law, it is necessary briefly to address one further factor which can help to determine whether reasons must be supplied. We have already seen (at 10.2.3) that the doctrine of legitimate expectation is capable of entitling individuals to fair treatment in circumstances where no such entitlement would otherwise arise, or alternatively of enhancing the procedural safeguards which are applicable. It is clear, therefore, that circumstances may arise in which the statements or conduct of a decision-maker may give rise to a legitimate expectation that it will furnish reasons for its decisions—a possibility acknowledged by Jowitt J in *R v. Secretary of State for Transport, ex parte Richmond-upon-Thames London Borough Council (No 4)* [1996] 1 WLR 1005 at 1020 and discussed by Craig [1994] *CLJ* 282 at 292–4.

As well as requiring reasons when an express or implied undertaking is made to the effect that reasons will be given, the doctrine of legitimate expectation may require reason-giving more broadly (see, eg *R (Bibi)* v. *Newham London Borough Council* [2001] EWCA Civ 607, [2002] 1 WLR 237 at [59]). For instance, where a legitimate expectation as to substance has arisen, reasons may need to be furnished either to the individual (in circumstances where it is possible for the authority to frustrate the expectation provided, for example, that the individual has been consulted—something which can only meaningfully occur if reasons are given) or the court (if, as in *R v. North and East Devon Health Authority, ex parte Coughlan* [2001] QB 213 (see 6.1.5), the expectation can only be lawfully frustrated if the court is satisfied as to the necessity of such a course of action).

11.4 Statutory and other duties to give reasons

11.4.1 Introduction

Alongside the common law duty to give reasons sit several statutory duties. A particularly broad statutory duty to give reasons is imposed by s 10 of the Tribunals and Inquiries Act 1992, which applies to the decisions of certain tribunals and certain ministerial decisions made after a statutory inquiry has been held (or in circumstances in which such an inquiry could have been required); for discussion, see 18.3.3. This obligation does not, however, impinge upon decision-making by other public bodies or by Ministers acting outside the context of statutory inquiries. In addition to express statutory duties to give reasons, a duty 'may arise through construction of the statutory provisions as a matter of implied intention' (*Stefan* v. *General Medical Council* [1999] 1 WLR 1293 at 1297, *per* Lord Clyde).

11.4.2 The Freedom of Information Act 2000

The Freedom of Information Act 2000—on which see generally Birkinshaw, *Freedom of Information: The Law, the Practice and the Ideal* (Cambridge 2010)—does not impose a duty to give reasons as such, but it may, in some circumstances, enable individuals to insist upon the provision of reasons. The extent to which the Act may entitle someone to reasons turns upon two key factors. First, the Act is concerned with 'information' as distinct from 'reasons'. It follows that the Act is relevant to the giving of reasons only to the extent that reasons constitute 'information'—and while there is nothing to suggest that reasons for a decision may not constitute 'information', ss 1(4) and 84 respectively provide that the Act only covers information which is 'held [by the public authority] at the time when the request is received' and which is 'recorded in any form'. This means that unless reasons have been formulated and recorded prior to the request for disclosure, no 'information' in the statutory sense exists. This, in turn, means that, while the Act imposes a duty to disclose reasons which have been formulated and recorded, it imposes no duty to formulate or record reasons in the first place. Of course, even if reasons have not been formulated and recorded at the relevant time, the Act does entitle individuals to such (other) information as is held by the public authority, and in some situations the provision of such information may facilitate the drawing of inferences as to what the reasons for a decision might have been.

The second point is that even if relevant 'information' exists, the Act does not necessarily compel its disclosure. In order to develop this point, it is necessary to sketch how the relevant parts of the Act work. Section 1 entitles a person who requests information from a public authority to be told whether it holds the information and, if so, to have the information communicated to him. Importantly, however, this right to information is substantially qualified by several exemptions set out in Part II. Section 2 provides that some of these exemptions are absolute (such as information supplied by, or relating to, bodies dealing with security matters; court records; and matters covered by parliamentary privilege) while other types of information (relating to such matters as defence, international relations, relations between UK national administrations, the economy, and law enforcement) are protected against disclosure only if the public interest in maintaining the exemption outweighs the public interest in disclosure.

This regime can be criticized on a number of grounds. First, the *number of exemptions* is considerable, and heavily circumscribes the right to information conferred by s 1. Second, the *nature of the exemptions* is contentious: many confer absolute exemption on classes of information, without regard to whether disclosure of the specific information in question would be damaging. Third, even in relation to information which is exempt only if its disclosure would cause harm, the operative *test of harm* is relatively weak: it need only be shown that it is likely that prejudice (rather than, say, substantial prejudice) would be caused to the relevant interest. Fourth, although information the disclosure of which meets the prejudice threshold is thereby rendered exempt only on a *prima facie* basis, the *balancing of interests test* that then falls to be applied has been criticized as insufficiently oriented towards transparency. For instance, Cornford [2001] 3 *Web JCLI* observes that while the balancing test permits non-disclosure only if the public interest in maintaining the exemption outweighs the public interest in disclosure, the public interests in maintaining the exemption and in disclosure are presented as equally important; there is, therefore, no presumption in favour of disclosure under this test—a position that seems to sit uncomfortably within a 'freedom of information' regime. Fifth, the *content of some exemptions* is controversial. In particular, ss 35 and 36 confer protection on (*inter alia*) information concerning the formulation and development of government policy and ministerial communications, and information whose disclosure would, or would be likely to, prejudice the maintenance of collective responsibility or the free and frank exchange of views within and the provision of advice to government. These provisions are felt by some writers fundamentally to contradict the spirit of a freedom of information regime by preserving the culture of secrecy which has traditionally been considered a hallmark of governance in the UK.

If a public authority refuses to disclose information which has been requested, s 17 requires it to give reasons for this refusal, and the person who requested the information may ultimately complain to the Information Commissioner under s 50. If the Commissioner, having investigated the matter, finds that information has been withheld contrary to the Act, he issues a decision notice, specifying the steps to be taken by the public authority and the time-frame within which they must be taken. Where the Commissioner becomes satisfied independently of any complaint that information has been improperly withheld, he may issue an enforcement notice under s 52 requiring appropriate steps to be taken by the public body concerned. Failure to comply with a decision or enforcement notice may be referred to the High Court under s 54, and the matter can then be dealt with as if it were a contempt of court. The powers of the Commissioner are in effect limited by s 53, the effect of which is to allow senior government Ministers to cancel decision or enforcement notices issued by the Commissioner in relation to government departments and public authorities designated by the Secretary of State. This is not to suggest, however, that s 53 gives Ministers *carte blanche* to overrule the Commissioner (or a tribunal that may subsequently address the matter on appeal), not least because, as the decision of the Supreme Court in *R (Evans) v. Attorney-General* [2015] UKSC 21, [2015] AC 1787 attests, the exercise of the s 53 power is itself subject to judicial review.

From all of this, it follows that the Freedom of Information Act does not straightforwardly or generally create any entitlement to reasons for administrative decisions, notwithstanding that, in certain circumstances, it may indirectly create such an entitlement provided that relevant 'information' exists.

11.4.3 Article 6 ECHR

In considering the circumstances in which a decision-maker may be required to give reasons it is also necessary to address the impact of the European Convention on Human Rights. It is well-established that Article 6(1) requires the giving of reasons. As the European Court of Human Rights put it in *Hadjianastassiou v. Greece* (1993) 16 EHRR 219 at 237, courts must 'indicate with sufficient clarity the grounds on which they based their decision'. However, as we saw at 9.5.2, Article 6(1) does not only apply to courts: it also applies to administrative decision-makers when they are determining civil rights or obligations. Article 6(1) may therefore appear to supply a surer foundation for the duty to give reasons than the common law. Whereas the scope of the common law duty turns upon a contextual analysis of the circumstances surrounding the making of the decision, Article 6(1) requires reasons to be given in respect of every decision—including every administrative decision—to which it applies.

However, three important qualifications concerning Article 6(1) must be borne in mind. First, we have already seen (at 9.5.2) that the scope of Article 6(1) is itself unclear, and so, therefore, is the scope of the reason-giving duty arising thereunder. Second, and notwithstanding the first point, it *is* clear that Article 6(1)—and hence the duty to give reasons that it imposes—applies only to a relatively limited range of administrative decisions: as Sedley LJ recognized in *R (Wooder) v. Feggetter* [2002] EWCA Civ 554, [2003] QB 219 at [46], 'the common law sets high standards of due process in non-judicial settings to which the European Court of Human Rights at Strasbourg declines to apply article 6' and in which claimants can therefore 'derive better protection from the common law than from the Convention'.

Third, the duty to give reasons under Article 6(1) is qualified by the curative principle. We saw earlier (at 9.5.3) that such breaches of Article 6(1) as a lack of impartiality on the part of the original decision-maker may be cured by appeal to or judicial review by an independent court of full jurisdiction. In *Stefan v. General Medical Council* [1999] 1 WLR 1293 at 1300, Lord Clyde affirmed that this principle extends to a failure to give reasons at first instance:

> [T]he existence of a right of appeal may, if it be sufficient for the purpose, enable the requirement of fairness embodied in article 6(1) to be met. The obligation on the court may remain to state reasons but a breach of the requirement of fairness embodied in article 6(1) may be obviated by the sufficiency of a right of appeal. On this approach a failure to give reasons may not be fatal to the validity of the decision.

However, this conclusion raises a curious paradox. The ECtHR recognizes that it is the giving of reasons 'which makes it possible for the accused to exercise usefully the rights of appeal'—or, by analogy, to exploit the possibility of judicial review—'available to him' (*Hadjianastassiou v. Greece* (1993) 16 EHRR 219 at 237). Yet the application of the curative principle to a failure to give reasons has the effect of sanctioning such a failure by reference to the curative effect of an appeal which, applying the logic of the former argument, will be less valuable to the individual precisely because reasons were not disclosed at first instance. In *Stefan*, Lord Clyde (at 1300) affirmed that, the curative principle notwithstanding, 'the consideration that the reasons are useful to enable the prosecution of the right of appeal still remains valid', and thus appeared to acknowledge the problem raised by this position without seeking to resolve it.

11.5 Discharging a duty to give reasons

If a duty to give reasons exists, the question may then arise whether it has been discharged. The answer to that question necessarily turns upon the *content* of the duty, about which Lord Brown had the following to say in *South Buckinghamshire District Council* v. *Porter* [2004] UKHL 33, [2004] 1 WLR 1953 at [36]:

> The reasons for a decision must be intelligible and they must be adequate. They must enable the reader to understand why the matter was decided as it was and what conclusions were reached on the 'principal important controversial issues' [*Hope* v. *Secretary of State for the Environment* (1975) 31 P & CR 120 at 123, *per* Phillips J], disclosing how any issue of law or fact was resolved. Reasons can be briefly stated, the degree of particularity required depending entirely on the nature of the issues falling for decision. The reasoning must not give rise to a substantial doubt as to whether the decision-maker erred in law, for example by misunderstanding some relevant policy or some other important matter or by failing to reach a rational decision on relevant grounds. But such adverse inference will not readily be drawn. The reasons need refer only to the main issues in the dispute, not to every material consideration. They should enable disappointed developers to assess their prospects of obtaining some alternative development permission, or, as the case may be, their unsuccessful opponents to understand how the policy or approach underlying the grant of permission may impact upon future such applications.

Although useful, Lord Brown's sketch of the content of the duty to give reasons can be no more than a starting point because—like other aspects of the duty to act fairly—what a reason-giving duty amounts to is heavily dependent on context. It follows that whilst in some circumstances the duty might be relatively burdensome, in others it might be very slight indeed. For instance, in *R (Asha Foundation)* v. *Millennium Commission* [2003] EWCA Civ 88, the defendant, in turning down the claimant's application for National Lottery funding for a museum, simply told the claimant that its application had been 'less attractive than others'. Doing this, it was held, discharged the defendant's duty to give reasons. How, then, do courts determine the content of the duty to give reasons in any particular case? Several factors may operate here. First, the *difficulty* of formulating reasons may lead the court to impose a relatively light duty. Thus, in *Asha Foundation* at [29], Lord Woolf CJ said:

> When the Commission is engaged in assessing the qualities of the different applications which were before them in competition with each other, the difficulties which would be involved in giving detailed reasons become clear. First, the preference for a particular application may not be the same in the case of each commissioner. Secondly, in order to evaluate any reasons that are given for preferring one application to another, the full nature and detail of both applications has to be known. If the Commission were to be required to do what [counsel] submits was their obligation

here, the Commission would have had to set out in detail each commissioner's views in relation to each of the applications and to provide the background material to Asha so that they could assess whether those conclusions were appropriate. This would be an undue burden upon any commission. It would make their task almost impossible.

Second, the *more surprising* the decision that has been made, the more the court is likely to require by way of reasons. For example, in *R (Viggers)* v. *Pensions Appeal Tribunal* [2006] EWHC 1066 (Admin), in which the defendant tribunal overturned the view of a first-instance decision-maker, the former's decision was quashed due to inadequate reasons: it was incumbent upon the defendant to acknowledge that—and explain why—it was adopting a different view from that reached at first instance. Meanwhile, in *Dinedor Hill Action Association* v. *Herefordshire District Council* [2008] EWHC 1741 (Admin), the defendant local authority, in its urban development plan, both rejected a planning inspector's view and adopted an approach that it had not previously advocated at a public inquiry. The Court made it clear that the defendant was under a duty (which it had failed to discharge) to explain in some detail why it had reached these (at least superficially) surprising conclusions.

Third, considerations of *public policy* may shape the extent of any reason-giving duty. For instance, in *Uba* v. *Secretary of State for the Home Department* [2014] EWHC 1166 (Admin), Lang J held (at [45]–[46]) that although the reasons given for excluding a foreign national from the UK were

insufficiently detailed to meet the conventional standard, namely, to enable persons to know why they have won or lost, and to assess whether the decision may be invalid and open to challenge ... a decision by the Defendant to exclude a foreign national person from the UK, on the grounds that his presence is not conducive to the public good, does not require the level of detailed reasons expected from public law decision-makers in other areas ... In this context, it will often be justified in the public interest for the Defendant to adopt a more guarded approach.

Lang J's conclusion on this point was doubtless influenced by her view (at [28]), derived from the case law, that the 'Secretary of State's power to exclude a person from the UK is a broad one, with which the Court must be slow to interfere'.

Fourth, if there exists a *relevant statutory duty* to give reasons, this may discourage the court from concluding that any more extensive common law duty applies. For instance, in *R (Hasan)* v. *Secretary of State for Trade and Industry* [2007] EWHC 2630 (Admin), the claimant contended that the Minister had acted unlawfully by failing to publish reasons for granting licences permitting the export of military equipment to Israel. However, Collins J noted at [21] that legislation already provided for a duty to give reasons to unsuccessful applicants for licences, and that this suggested 'that Parliament considered what information should be given and to whom, and argues against a wide common law obligation'. Collins J's conclusions and reasoning were later upheld by Sir Anthony May P, giving the only reasoned judgment of the Court of Appeal ([2008] EWCA Civ 1312).

Fifth, in determining how onerous a duty to give reasons is, the courts will be mindful that while *good administration* may require the giving of reasons, it may also require that the decision-maker is not unreasonably burdened by the imposition of such a duty. For instance, in *Uprichard* v. *Scottish Ministers* [2013] UKSC 21, 2013 SC (UKSC) 219 at [48], the claimant argued that the Scottish Ministers, when determining the final form of a planning strategy for a particular area, had given inadequate reasons for failing to yield to objections that she had made in respect of a draft version of the strategy. The Supreme Court held that the reasons had in fact been adequate, not least, as Lord Reed explained at [48], because of considerations of proportionality:

> It is … important to maintain a sense of proportion when considering the duty to give reasons, and not to impose on decision-makers a burden which is unreasonable having regard to the purpose intended to be served. In the present case, the Ministers received a plethora of objections to the plan and to their proposed modifications. To judge from the objections which the court has seen, many will have raised numerous distinct matters. The matters raised are likely to have been expressed by different objectors in different ways, with different nuances. If the Ministers were to be expected to address, line by line, every nuance of every matter raised in every objection, the burden imposed in such circumstances would be unreasonable.

Sixth, and more generally, it seems logical that the content of the duty to give reasons will reflect the way in which its *underlying purpose* is conceived. For instance, if the court locates the objective of reason-giving in the need to allow the individual to understand why the decision has been made, this may imply a quite straightforward duty to 'tell the parties in broad terms why they lost or, as the case may be, won' (*Union of Construction and Allied Trades Technicians* v. *Brain* [1981] IRLR 225 at 228, *per* Lord Donaldson MR). In contrast, as Fordham [1998] *JR* 158 at 163–4 explains, if the underlying purpose of reason-giving is viewed differently—for example as a discipline to ensure that decision-making occurs thoroughly and lawfully—then the duty to give reasons becomes more onerous and should logically address the decision-making process as well as the conclusions reached by the agency:

> [I]t is surely in conducting the *reasoning* process (e.g. in identifying [relevant considerations]), and not merely in reaching the principal conclusions, that the decision-maker's mind is to be focussed. The decision-maker needs to be disciplined in addressing questions, not just arriving at answers. A word of caution though. The reality may be that the present low threshold of adequacy [of reasons] is the price of easing the passing of a more general, common law duty to give reasons. After all, a general public law obligation to articulate principal conclusions is surely not too much to ask.

QUESTION

- Do you agree that a *light* duty to give reasons is a price worth paying for a relatively *extensive* duty?

11.6 Remedial consequences

Although, as we explain in ch 12, remedies in judicial review proceedings are discretionary, the norm is for administrative action whose legality is successfully challenged to be the subject of a quashing order. The effect of a quashing order is to affirm that the unlawful action is void. What, then, of administrative action in respect of which reasons should have been, but were not, provided? Does a breach of the duty to give reasons render the relevant administrative action void, thereby opening up the possibility of a quashing order (as well as permitting its unlawfulness to be taken account of by way of collateral challenge)?

It might seem that the answer to that question ought to be 'no'. After all, if the point of reason-giving is to inform individuals about why decisions affecting them have been made in a particular way, the obvious remedy in the event of reasons not being given would appear to be a mandatory order—that is, an order directing that reasons be given—rather than an order quashing the decision itself. On this view, a breach of the duty to give reasons is a distinct matter from those matters going to the legality of the decision: the decision itself might be perfectly lawful even if an accompanying, but separate, duty to give reasons has not been discharged. However, Fordham [1998] *JR* 158 at 160 argues that one of the purposes of the duty to give reasons is the encouragement of a disciplined approach to decision-making, and that decisions which are unaccompanied by reasons should therefore be quashed. On this analysis, the provision of reasons in response to a mandatory order may merely constitute *ex post facto* rationalization which does not demonstrably ensure that the decision was taken correctly in the first place.

As to whether breaching the duty to give reasons can be a ground for quashing a decision, Sedley J adopted an equivocal position in the *HEFC* case [1994] 1 WLR 242. At one point in his judgment (at 257–8), he characterized the duty as 'an independent and enforceable legal obligation and hence a ground of nullity where it is violated'. However, elsewhere (at 263) he said that in the event of a breach of the duty, 'relief may take the form of [a mandatory order requiring the decision-maker] to give reasons, or (if a justiciable flaw has been established) other appropriate relief'—the implication being that failing to give reasons is not itself a 'justiciable flaw' that would warrant 'other appropriate relief' such as a quashing order.

Other cases, however, establish more clearly that failing to give reasons can, in and of itself, render a decision unlawful and so vulnerable to being quashed. In *R v. City of London Corporation, ex parte Matson* [1997] 1 WLR 765, a decision was quashed for lack of reasons, not because this led to an inference of irrationality (on which see 11.1), but because the need for reasons constituted an independent legal requirement, breach of which invalidated the decision. And in *Marshall v. Deputy Governor of Bermuda* [2010] UKPC 9 at [28], Lord Phillips, giving the judgment of the Judicial Committee of the Privy Council, took it as read that breach of the duty to give reasons 'can lead to the quashing of the decision without more'.

However, the fact that breaching the duty to give reasons *can* result in the quashing of the decision does not mean that *every* such breach *will* or *should* produce such consequences. As previously noted, remedial discretion can be exercised, and there is clear evidence to suggest that such discretion is particularly likely to be deployed in this context so as to avoid quashing decisions in the event of a breach of the duty to give reasons. Indeed, some judges have indicated that the use of remedial discretion should be the norm in such circumstances: in *Adami v. The Ethical Standards Officer of the Standards Board for England* [2005] EWCA Civ 1754 at [26], Auld LJ said that unless the decision was 'otherwise and plainly invalid', quashing it would be a 'disproportionate and inappropriate response to a failure to give adequate reasons'. It is evident, however, from cases such as *Matson* and *Marshall* that Auld LJ's view is not universally shared.

QUESTION

- What principles do you think courts should apply when deciding whether, following a breach of the duty to give reasons, to issue a mandatory order requiring the provision of reasons, or a quashing order setting the decision aside?

The position is now further complicated by s 31(2A)–(2C) of the Senior Courts Act 1981, which we consider in more detail at 14.8. The effect of those provisions—inserted into the 1981 Act by s 84 of the Criminal Justice and Courts Act 2015—is that the High Court *must* refuse relief if it appears to the Court 'to be highly likely that the outcome for the applicant would not have been substantially different if the conduct complained of had not occurred', unless the granting of relief is appropriate 'for reasons of exceptional public interest'. On the face of it, these provisions have the capacity radically to limit relief in respect of breaches of the duty to give reasons. Indeed, such breaches might be thought to constitute precisely the perceived mischief at which the provisions were aimed—namely, Pyrrhic victories won on the basis of 'technicalities'.

However, for at least three reasons, the position is more complex. The first point pertains to what is meant by 'outcome' in s 31(2A). If the outcome is the substantive decision (*eg* whether the planning consent that was sought is granted) then, subject to the second and third points below, the new provisions will often preclude the issuing of relief (whether in the form of mandatory or quashing orders). If, however, receipt of a reasoned decision is itself treated as part of the outcome—or, putting the matter another way, if the reasons on which a decision is based are treated as part and parcel of the decision itself, such that the two cannot be decoupled—then the outcome is self-evidently affected by the 'conduct complained of', since whether the duty to give reasons is fulfilled is determinative of whether the outcome is a reasoned or an unreasoned decision. It might be objected that interpreting 'outcome' in s 31(2A) in this way would unduly attenuate the effect of the provision. However, it is a well-established principle of construction that legislation is to be interpreted, as far as is possible, in a way that preserves the courts' powers of judicial review, and that principle must logically extend to preserving not only the courts' capacity to assess the legality of administrative action but their power to issue relief in the event of a finding of unlawfulness.

Second, if, contrary to the approach sketched above, 'outcome' is taken to refer exclusively to substantive outcomes, then it might appear that it will always—or at least usually—be 'highly likely' that the outcome would be the same irrespective of whether reasons were given for the decision. However, this analysis may be eroded if reviewing courts are prepared strictly to construe the 'highly likely' requirement *and* to take seriously Fordham's argument, noted at 11.2.1, concerning the 'disciplining' effect of making explicitly reasoned decisions. Indeed, as seen earlier, one of the situations in which a duty to give reasons will be imposed involves decisions that are inexplicable. If such a decision is quashed on the ground that no reasons have been given, thus requiring the decision-maker to reconsider the matter, it is entirely possible that the outcome might be different—not least because the reviewing court may have concluded that the decision was inexplicable on account of its inconsistency with similar decisions. A decision-maker that had overlooked such other decisions might well reach a different conclusion upon reconsideration in the light of them.

Third, even if, in a given case, it *is* highly likely that the outcome would have been the same, it is open to the court to issue relief if there are 'reasons of exceptional public interest'. Under this provision it may, for instance, be argued that there is a sufficiently strong public interest—alongside the obvious private interest of the affected individual—in ensuring the sort of good governance that reason-giving makes more likely in respect of decisions that have a particularly profound impact upon their recipients.

11.7 Concluding remarks

Giving reasons for decisions should be treated as a central facet of procedural fairness in administrative law. This follows both for practical reasons—in order, for instance, that individuals may know whether it is worth appealing or seeking judicial review—and for normative reasons that spring from a conception of the relationship between the individual and the state according to which the latter should treat the former with respect, and as a participant in, rather than an object of, the process of governance. Constructing the relationship in that manner is important not only because it recognizes the dignity of the individual, but also because it promotes a trust between individuals and public authorities that, in turn, acts as a springboard for co-operation between them. Against this background, it is heartening that, as the developing case law mapped in this chapter attests, English law now takes seriously the duty to give reasons for administrative decisions, and views with increasing scepticism the hackneyed and largely specious argument that forcing decision-makers to give reasons imposes an intolerable burden upon them. Of course, there will be some circumstances in which that argument holds water, or in which other factors point towards the inappropriateness of reason-giving. In substance, however, those situations are increasingly the exceptions, even though the formal position remains that there is no 'general duty' to give reasons.

FURTHER RESOURCES

Birkinshaw, *Freedom of Information: The Law, the Practice and the Ideal* (Cambridge 2010)

Craig, 'The Common Law, Reasons and Administrative Justice' [1994] *CLJ* 282

Elliott, 'Has the Common Law Duty to Give Reasons Come of Age Yet?' [2011] *PL* 56

Fordham, 'Reasons: The Third Dimension' [1998] *JR* 158

JUSTICE-All Souls Committee, *Administrative Justice: Some Necessary Reforms* (Oxford 1988), ch 3

Neill, 'The Duty to Give Reasons: The Openness of Decision-Making' in Forsyth and Hare (eds), *The Golden Metwand and the Crooked Cord* (Oxford 1998)

Website of the Information Commissioner *https://ico.org.uk*

12 REMEDIES

12.1 Introduction

Having considered, in earlier chapters, the grounds on which administrative action may be found to be unlawful, it is now necessary to address the relief which may be granted in respect of such action. We begin, in this chapter, with the remedies themselves. We then move on to consider, in chs 13 and 14 respectively, the special procedure which is typically used in order to challenge the legality of administrative action and various restrictions faced by claimants who seek relief in respect of what is contended to be unlawful administrative action. Leaving aside, for the time being, the possibility of money remedies—addressed in ch 15—a number of remedies need to be considered in the present context.

> ### Senior Courts Act 1981
>
> 31—(1) An application to the High Court for one or more of the following forms of relief, namely—
>
> > (a) a mandatory, prohibiting or quashing order;
> > (b) a declaration or injunction under subsection (2); or
> > (c) an injunction under section 30 restraining a person not entitled to do so from acting in an office to which that section applies,
>
> > shall be made in accordance with rules of court by a procedure to be known as an application for judicial review.
>
> (2) A declaration may be made or an injunction granted under this subsection in any case where an application for judicial review, seeking that relief, has been made and the High Court considers that, having regard to—
>
> > (a) the nature of the matters in respect of which relief may be granted by mandatory, prohibiting or quashing orders;
> > (b) the nature of the persons and bodies against whom relief may be granted by such orders; and
> > (c) all the circumstances of the case,
>
> > it would be just and convenient for the declaration to be made or the injunction to be granted, as the case may be.

It should be noted that new terminology (which is used throughout this book) was introduced in 2000 by the Civil Procedure Rules Part 54, r 2. Section 31 of the Senior Courts Act 1981 (formerly known as the Supreme Court Act 1981) was amended to reflect these changes. Thus *'mandamus'* became 'mandatory order', *'prohibition'* became 'prohibiting order', and *'certiorari'* became 'quashing order'. Meanwhile, although the phrase 'application for judicial review'—the special procedure generally used to challenge the legality of administrative action (on which see ch 13)—is still used by the Act, the CPR (and this book) refer to the 'claim for judicial review' (CPR 54.1).

Until 1977, ordinary remedies—that is, injunctions and declarations—and prerogative remedies—mandatory, prohibiting, and quashing orders—could not be sought in the same proceedings. While the former were available in ordinary proceedings, a different procedure applied to the latter; it was therefore impossible to seek both types of relief in the same proceedings. This problem was largely resolved by the procedural reforms of 1977 (considered in detail in ch 13) which introduced the process known as the application for judicial review—the forerunner of the modern judicial review procedure governed by CPR Part 54. That special procedure must be used if prerogative remedies are sought (CPR 54.2), while ordinary remedies are now available both in ordinary proceedings and under the judicial review procedure (CPR 54.3(1)).

12.2 Injunctions

12.2.1 The role of injunctions in public law

Injunctions are used in private law to prevent the commission of unlawful acts, while mandatory injunctions lie to compel the performance of legal duties. Injunctions serve similar functions in public law by preventing public authorities from acting *ultra vires* or, in the case of mandatory injunctions, requiring them to make those decisions or perform those acts which are legally required of them. Although there is significant overlap with the prerogative remedies—indeed in *Re M* [1994] 1 AC 377 at 415 Lord Woolf said that prohibiting and mandatory orders 'are indistinguishable in their effect from final injunctions'—there is one crucial practical difference between the ordinary and prerogative remedies: while the latter are available only in final form, injunctions can also take effect as interlocutory, or interim, relief (see Senior Courts Act 1981, s 37(1) and CPR 25.1(1)(a)). (This is now true of declarations, too: see 12.3.2.) Interim relief permits the court temporarily to stabilize a situation pending final adjudication—a possibility which is particularly valuable if the defendant's proposed (and allegedly unlawful) action would, if actually undertaken, render meaningless final relief (*eg* a final injunction or quashing order) granted after the commission of the act in question. For example, a court may consider granting an interim injunction to prevent the deportation of an asylum seeker pending final determination of the legality of the decision to deport: see *Re M* [1994] AC 377, considered at 12.2.3.

It is convenient at this point to note the role of stays of proceedings. They are usually issued in order to halt proceedings before courts or tribunals, and there has been some uncertainty as to whether the application of stays could be expanded beyond this setting: *Ministry of Foreign Affairs, Trade and Industry v. Vehicle and Supplies Ltd* [1991] 1 WLR 550. However, it is now clear that either in traditional form or in some modified, *sui generis* form stays can be ordered as a type of interim relief in respect of administrative action—*eg* to halt the implementation of an administrative decision pending final determination of its legality.

In *R v. Secretary of State for Education and Science, ex parte Avon County Council* [1991] 1 QB 558 at 561–2 (followed: *R (H) v. Ashworth Hospital Authority* [2002] EWCA Civ 923, [2003]

1 WLR 127 at [38]), Glidewell LJ, with whom the other judges agreed, took the view that stays *can* be issued to prevent the implementation of administrative decisions. In reaching this conclusion the Court had to confront the problem that if a stay were issued against the defendant authority *as a party* to the proceeding the order would resemble an injunction, rather than an order geared to controlling the legal proceedings themselves. The Court dealt with this apparent problem by reasoning that the defendant authority in review proceedings was more in the nature of a representative of the public interest than a traditional party to civil proceedings whose concern was solely to protect his or her own interests. The Court further argued that a stay of proceedings could logically apply to administrative procedure as such decision processes were a form of 'proceedings'. This analysis, while innovative, was not particularly convincing. In reality it was an attempt to get around the difficulties, prior to the House of Lords decision in *M*, of securing an injunction in public law proceedings. However, now that interim relief against public officers has been recognized (see 12.2.2–12.2.3) the debate around the availability of stays to control administrative action has diminished in practical significance. Nonetheless, in recent years stays of administrative action have retained *some* significance, particularly in cases where a claimant, who the Home Secretary has determined should be removed from the country under immigration laws, wishes to avoid deportation while their appeal from a lower court decision to the Court of Appeal is pending. However, the courts, recognizing the unreality of classifying an order against an administrative decision-maker, who is party to the litigation, as an order addressed to proceedings rather than a defendant, have fashioned a wholly new form of order. This order is in the nature of a stay, but is not a stay in the traditional sense—it is explicitly directed to the defendant. Nor is the remedy an interim injunction. In *YD (Turkey)* v. *Secretary of State for the Home Department* [2006] EWCA Civ 52, [2006] 1 WLR 1646, Brooke LJ, with whom the other members of the Court agreed, said (at [24]):

> [The court] has an inherent jurisdiction to protect its proceedings from being set at naught and to exercise that jurisdiction in the present case by requiring the Home Secretary, as a party to the proceedings, to refrain from removing the appellant from the jurisdiction while it considers the application before it. This will not be a stay in the ordinary sense of staying further action within the proceedings (as, for instance, with a stay on the execution of a judgment), but an order in effect preserving the status quo (namely the presence of the appellant within the jurisdiction) until the court makes a determination on the application.

The Court preferred this solution to requiring the claimant to make a fresh application to the High Court for an interim injunction restraining removal until the Court of Appeal had determined his case. While representing the 'conventional solution ... it would be very inconvenient and needlessly expensive' (at [24]). *YD* has been followed subsequently: *eg R (NB (Algeria))* v. *Secretary of State for the Home Department* [2012] EWCA Civ 1050, [2013] 1 WLR 31 at [28]–[30], and see also *R (SG (Iraq))* v. *Secretary of State for the Home Department* [2012] EWCA Civ 940, [2013] 1 WLR 41.

12.2.2 The availability of interim injunctions

Although interim injunctions are highly beneficial from the point of view of claimants, they are very disadvantageous to defendants, whose freedom of action they curtail and to whom inconvenience and even financial loss may be occasioned. In light of this claimants in whose favour interim injunctions are granted are normally required to undertake to compensate the defendant for any losses suffered should the claimant lose at trial, a requirement from which the Crown as claimant is no longer automatically exempt, albeit the Crown is presumptively exempt in certain categories of case (see *Hoffmann-La Roche and Co v. Secretary of State for Trade and Industry* [1975] AC 295; *Financial Services Authority v. Sinaloa Gold plc* [2013] UKSC 11, [2013] 2 AC 28). In spite of the 'insurance' which this type of undertaking provides, the Court, in exercising its discretion (see 3.3.1) must consider carefully whether or not interim relief is appropriate—not least because it adversely affects the defendant before any final conclusion is reached that it is acting or is proposing to act unlawfully—although this certainly does not mean that interim relief can be resisted simply because it would cause difficulties for the defendant. This much was made clear by Lord Denning MR in *Bradbury v. Enfield London Borough Council* [1967] 1 WLR 1311 at 1324, a case in which interim relief was granted to prevent a reorganization of schools contrary to s 13 of the Education Act 1944:

> Ought an injunction to be granted against the council? It has been suggested by the chief education officer that, if an injunction is granted, chaos will supervene. All the arrangements have been made for the next term, the teachers appointed to the new comprehensive schools, the pupils allotted their places, and so forth. It would be next to impossible, he says, to reverse all these arrangements without complete chaos and damage to teachers, pupils and the public.
>
> I must say this: If a local authority does not fulfil the requirements of the law, this court will see that it does fulfil them. It will not listen readily to suggestions of 'chaos.' The Department of Education and the local education authority are subject to the rule of law and must comply with it, just like everyone else. Even if chaos should result, still the law must be obeyed. But I do not think that chaos will result.

The robustness of Lord Denning's view should not, however, be taken to mean that an interim injunction will be issued irrespective of its consequences (for a good example of such relief being refused on the basis of probable consequences, see, *eg R (Public Interest Lawyers Ltd) v. Legal Services Commission* [2010] EWHC 3259 (Admin)). Indeed, the need for a balance to be struck between the interests of the parties lies at the heart of the 'balance of convenience' test classically expounded by Lord Diplock in *American Cyanamid Co v. Ethicon Ltd* [1975] AC 396 at 406:

> My Lords, when an application for an interlocutory injunction to restrain a defendant from doing acts alleged to be in violation of the plaintiff's legal right is made upon contested facts, the decision whether or not to grant an interlocutory injunction has to be taken at a time when ex hypothesi the existence of the right or the violation of it, or both, is uncertain and will remain uncertain until final judgment is given in the action. It was to mitigate the risk of injustice to the plaintiff during the period before that uncertainty could be resolved that the practice arose of granting him relief by way of interlocutory injunction; but since the middle of the 19th century this has been made subject to his undertaking to pay damages to the defendant for any loss sustained by reason of the injunction if it should be held at the trial that the plaintiff had not been entitled to restrain the defendant from doing what he was threatening to do. The object of the interlocutory injunction is to protect the plaintiff against injury by violation of his right for which he could not be adequately compensated in damages recoverable in the action if the uncertainty were resolved in his favour at the trial; but the plaintiff's need for such protection must be weighed against the corresponding need of the defendant to be protected against injury resulting from his having been prevented from exercising his own legal rights for which he could not be adequately compensated

under the plaintiff's undertaking in damages if the uncertainty were resolved in the defendant's favour at the trial. The court must weigh one need against another and determine where 'the balance of convenience' lies.

The general structure of the balance of convenience test and its applicability in a public law context were helpfully summarized by Lord Goff in *R v. Secretary of State for Transport, ex parte Factortame Ltd (No 2)* [1991] 1 AC 603 at 671–2:

[A] prime purpose of the guidelines established in the *Cyanamid* case was to remove a fetter which appeared to have been imposed in certain previous cases, *viz*, that a party seeking an interlocutory injunction had to establish a prima facie case for substantive relief. It is now clear that it is enough if he can show that there is a serious case to be tried. If he can establish that, then he has, so to speak, crossed the threshold; and the court can then address itself to the question whether it is just or convenient to grant an injunction.

... Lord Diplock approached the matter in two stages. First, he considered the relevance of the availability of an adequate remedy in damages, either to the plaintiff seeking the injunction or to the defendant in the event that an injunction is granted against him. As far as the plaintiff is concerned, the availability to him of such a remedy will normally preclude the grant to him of an interim injunction. If that is not so, then the court should consider whether, if an injunction is granted against the defendant, there will be an adequate remedy in damages available to him under the plaintiff's undertaking in damages; if so, there will be no reason on this ground to refuse to grant the plaintiff an interim injunction.

At this stage of the court's consideration of the case (which I will for convenience call the first stage) many applications for interim injunctions can well be decided. But if there is doubt as to the adequacy of either or both of the respective remedies in damages, then the court proceeds to what is usually called the balance of convenience, and for that purpose will consider all the circumstances of the case. I will call this the second stage.

In this case, the claimant sought an interim injunction to prevent the application of part of an Act of Parliament which, it was argued, was contrary to directly effective European Union law. Lord Goff did not feel that the matter could be resolved at the first stage by considering the adequacy of damages, and therefore proceeded to the second stage. In this context he felt (at 673) that 'matters of considerable weight have to be put into the balance to outweigh the desirability of enforcing, in the public interest, what is on its face the law'. Indeed, notwithstanding the general point that *Cyanamid* abolished the need for a *prima facie* case in favour of substantive relief, Lord Goff noted and followed Lord Diplock's view in *Hoffmann-La Roche and Co AG v. Secretary of State for Trade and Industry* [1975] AC 295 at 367 (see 3.2.1–3.2.2) that a party seeking an interim injunction in respect of a *legislative* measure had 'to show a strong *prima facie* case that the statutory instrument is *ultra vires*'. Lord Goff (along with the other four judges) concluded in *Factortame* that the injunction could be granted in light of the cogency of the claimant's case and the obvious and immediate damage which would be caused if, pending determination of its compatibility with EU law, the Act in question was enforced.

Factortame (No 2) was unusual because the disapplication of *primary legislation* was involved, but our next extract demonstrates that public interest considerations may also weigh heavily upon the court when interim relief is sought in respect of *administrative action*; although the next case involved an application for a stay rather than an interim injunction, the *American Cyanamid* principles were applicable.

R v. Ministry of Agriculture, Fisheries and Food, ex parte Monsanto plc
[1999] QB 1161
Queen's Bench Division

Since 1974 the claimant had manufactured a leading herbicide called Roundup, the patent for which expired in 1991. In 1996 the claimant's data became available to other companies wishing to produce similar herbicides. On the basis of that data the intervener, Clayton, sought and was granted permission—known as 'me too' approval—to market its Rhizeup herbicide in the UK. The claimant sought judicial review of the approval, contending that, by virtue of Article 4(1)(b) of Council Directive 91/414/EEC, the defendant had erred by relying on old data rather than examining the matter 'in the light of current scientific and technical knowledge'. As a result of other challenges by the claimant to 'me too' approvals, a preliminary reference had already been made to the Court of Justice of the European Union concerning the meaning of the relevant parts of the Directive. Since it was likely to take the CJEU some time to deal with the matter, the claimant sought a stay suspending the approval in the meantime.

Rose LJ (delivering the judgment of the court)

... It is common ground that this court has power to grant such relief and that it is a matter for the exercise of the court's discretion whether relief should be granted. It is also common ground that, in exercising its discretion, the court must have regard to the principles enunciated by Lord Diplock in *American Cyanamid Co. v. Ethicon Ltd.* [1975] A.C. 396, 408. But it has been a matter of contention before us as to precisely how those principles should be applied in a public law case.

... In our judgment, although *American Cyanamid* principles are to be applied in the present case, this must be in the context of the public law questions to which the judicial review proceedings give rise. Such proceedings are, generally speaking, intended to provide swift relief against abuse of executive power. They are neither intended for nor well suited to inhibiting commercial activity, particularly over an indefinite, substantial period of time. Monsanto's request for interim relief must, as it seems to us, be judged in that context. Plainly there is a serious question to be tried.

As to the adequacy of a remedy in damages, if Monsanto is likely to suffer loss, we accept it has no adequate remedy against Clayton or the respondents. But, in our judgment, the evidence before this court does not establish actual or likely loss. There are 35 other competitors in the market. Monsanto's own report suggests that, if prices fall, increased sales result. In the absence of any relevant figures from Monsanto we reject the suggestion that this principle is inapplicable to the United Kingdom market. Monsanto's evidence provides no detailed calculations. We are unimpressed by vague assertions about what could happen. In any event, Clayton's proffered undertaking as to ceilings would limit its involvement to a small percentage of the market. Monsanto's cross-undertaking in damages is capable of providing a remedy but we doubt whether that remedy would be adequate, because Clayton has no track record to establish likely losses and all the indications are that Clayton, whose resources are limited, would be faced by fierce resistance by Monsanto, whose resources are comparatively limitless, in seeking to establish any loss. In our judgment, therefore, Monsanto has no sustainable claim for relief based on inadequacy of damages and we doubt if damages would provide an adequate remedy for Clayton.

Turning to consider the balance of convenience, there are a number of public interest factors of relevance and significance. First, in *Reg. v. Secretary of State for Health and Norgine Ltd., Ex parte Scotia Pharmaceuticals International Ltd. (No 1)* [1997] Eu.L.R. 625, 643 Evans L.J. said that he began 'with a strong presumption in favour of there being no order by way of interim relief,' because such an order would have the effect of restricting free competition. We respectfully agree. Secondly, there is, in the present case, no suggested hazard to health or the environment from the use of Rhizeup and this is an important objective of the EEC Directive. Thirdly, the 'me too' procedure has cost Clayton a substantial sum; and it seems to us that, if the grant of approval is in the public interest, applications should not be discouraged by the prospect that the costs thereof may be irrecoverable for a period of years if a competitor obtains interim relief: this is of particular significance when the competitor's patent and data protection have expired. Fourthly, although we attach rather less weight to this factor in the circumstances of the present case, it is in the public interest that, until set aside, the decision of a public body should be respected. This is a variant of the argument which favours maintenance of the status quo. Fifthly, the purpose of the licensing provisions is to serve the public interest, not to protect private commercial interests which are catered for by patent and data protection. That being so, we incline to the view (although it is not determinative in the present case for the reasons already given) that, even where damages are not an adequate remedy for an applicant, it may still be appropriate to refuse him interim relief in public law proceedings …

The application to stay the approval of Rhizeup was dismissed.

Although the Court concluded that Monsanto was not likely to suffer losses as a result of the grant of 'me too' approval to Clayton, it also inclined to the view that even though damages would not have been an adequate remedy if any losses were occasioned, interim relief might still have been inappropriate. This suggests that the need for the court to address public interest issues when interim relief is sought in public law proceedings is such that, taken on its own, the inadequacy of damages will rarely, if ever, satisfy the court of the need for such relief: instead, the balance of convenience test will be applied.

In *Monsanto*, countervailing public interest considerations weighed heavily in application of that test. But this will not invariably be so. All will depend on how the balance falls on the facts of the case, and it is certainly not uncommon for claimants in review proceedings to secure interim relief. For a recent example of where the balance of convenience favoured the claimant, see *R (GSTS Pathology LLP)* v. *Revenue and Customs Commissioners* [2013] EWHC 1801 (Admin), [2013] STC 2017.

Indeed, in one recent decision, a default rule in favour of interim relief was adopted. *R (NB (Algeria))* v. *Secretary of State for the Home Department* [2012] EWCA Civ 1050, [2013] 1 WLR 31—again a case concerning stays rather than interim injunctions—concerned the principles governing stays where the Upper Tribunal had refused permission to seek judicial review and the claimant had applied to the Court of Appeal for permission to appeal the refusal, in circumstances where, if a stay were not granted, the claimant could in theory be deported under immigration legislation pursuant to the original, challenged administrative decision. The Court held that albeit every application should be considered on its merits, for this class of case there should be a presumption in favour of granting a stay. The Court adopted this presumption for various reasons including expediency, *ie* a presumption should guard against significant court time being taken up by applications for stays of proceedings, but also because of the importance of what is at stake for claimants in such cases: '[T]he damage to the public interest (represented by the Secretary of State) is, at least in the majority of cases, likely to be less if a stay is wrongly granted and the applicant is not removed when he would otherwise have been, than the damage to the applicant if a stay is wrongly refused, and he is removed before he can successfully appeal the Upper Tribunal's refusal to permit him to seek [judicial review]' (at [39]).

At times courts have queried whether the *American Cyanamid* tests, developed first in civil proceedings, are apt to be applied in the public law context, and whether a distinctive set of tests should be developed to guide grant of interim relief in public law cases: *eg Smith v. Inner London Education Authority* [1978] 1 All ER 411 at 418. However, there are several reasons why this has not come to pass. First, there are difficulties in delineating public and private law cases, as discussed in ch 13. Second, as Lord Wilson said in *Coventry City Council v. O* [2011] EWCA Civ 729, [2012] 3 WLR 208 at [37], it may be that 'the nature of public law proceedings is too varied to have permitted any authoritative reformulation of the principles applicable to them'. This leads to a third point; that the *American Cyanamid* criteria are flexible enough to accommodate distinctive concerns that arise in different contexts, especially via the open-ended balance of convenience test. Thus, as in *Monsanto*, courts in judicial review cases have, for example, stressed the importance of guarding against introducing undue delay into administrative processes by too readily granting interim relief which may stop administration in its tracks, or granting such relief to claimants who have failed to bring their claim promptly. But, importantly, where courts have laid stress on factors such as delay they have done so within the rubric of the orthodox balance of convenience test derived from *American Cyanamid*. In *Coventry*, for example, Lord Wilson set out a series of questions to guide the balance of convenience inquiry in cases where foster parents seek an interim injunction to restrain the defendant public authority from removing foster children from their care, where the legal challenge is based in judicial review grounds. Reflecting the concern for promptness, two of the questions were: 'Have the foster parents brought the proceedings with reasonable promptness and, if not, how does their delay affect whether an injunction would now serve the interests of the children?' and 'Although in form an application only for an interim injunction, might any injunction be likely to continue (or to be continued) for a substantial period of time and, if so, with what likely consequences?' (at [37]).

Albeit there has been no formal deviation from the *American Cyanamid* tests in judicial review proceedings, courts have taken a more *expansive* view of the scope of application of interim relief than in civil proceedings. Typically, if one wishes to preserve one's interests until one's legal claim is finally determined, one must apply for interim relief on one's own behalf, given any injunction issued will relate specifically to one's own interests; this reflects the fact that often in civil proceedings the only interests in play are those of the parties. However, in review proceedings very often the interests at stake will transcend those of the parties, and indeed implicate the wider public interest. Reflecting this fact the Court of Appeal, in *R (HN (Afghanistan)) v. Secretary of State for the Home Department* [2015] EWCA Civ 1043, has held that in certain exceptional cases at least a 'class' interim injunction (our term) may be granted. The Court left open whether the order was technically in the nature of an injunction or a stay. But what was clear was that this was an interim order granted to preserve the interests of a *class* of persons, including those not party to the proceedings in which the order was made. In *HN*, such an order was made to prevent the removal from the UK on immigration grounds of a class of individuals who were to be removed on the same flight, only some of whom were party to the litigation (and who had appeals pending against decisions of the Upper Tribunal). A later case, *R (Majit) v. Secretary of State for the Home Department* [2016] EWHC 741 (Admin), suggests that the key features which marked out *HN* as exceptional, so that the class injunction was warranted, were (i) the presence of a definable group for whose benefit the injunction could be granted; and (ii) the very short time between the application for the order and the date of departure of flight, which meant it may not have been possible for those on the flight, and not party to the litigation, to make their own claims for review and associated claims for interim relief.

Section 12 of the Human Rights Act 1998 makes special provision concerning interim relief which, if granted, might affect the exercise of the right of freedom of expression contained in Article 10 of the European Convention on Human Rights. Under s 12(3), relief must not be granted 'so as to restrain publication before trial unless the court is satisfied that the applicant is likely to establish that publication should not be allowed'. The meaning of this section was considered by the House of Lords in *Cream Holdings Ltd* v. *Banerjee* [2004] UKHL 44, [2005] 1 AC 253. Lord Nicholls, whose speech commanded the unanimous assent of the Appellate Committee, said at [22] that

> [s]ection 12(3) makes the likelihood of success at the trial an essential element in the court's consideration of whether to make an interim order. But in order to achieve the necessary flexibility the degree of likelihood of success at the trial needed to satisfy section 12(3) must depend on the circumstances. There can be no single, rigid standard governing all applications for interim restraint orders. Rather, on its proper construction the effect of section 12(3) is that the court is not to make an interim restraint order unless satisfied the applicant's prospects of success at the trial are sufficiently favourable to justify such an order being made in the particular circumstances of the case. As to what degree of likelihood makes the prospects of success 'sufficiently favourable', the general approach should be that courts will be exceedingly slow to make interim restraint orders where the applicant has not satisfied the court he will probably ('more likely than not') succeed at the trial. In general, that should be the threshold an applicant must cross before the court embarks on exercising its discretion, duly taking into account the relevant jurisprudence on article 10 and any countervailing Convention rights. But there will be cases where it is necessary for a court to depart from this general approach and a lesser degree of likelihood will suffice as a prerequisite. Circumstances where this may be so include ... [the following]: where the potential adverse consequences of disclosure are particularly grave, or where a short-lived injunction is needed to enable the court to hear and give proper consideration to an application for interim relief pending the trial or any relevant appeal.

In the recent significant Supreme Court decision in *PJS* v. *News Group Newspapers Ltd* [2016] UKSC 26, [2016] 2 WLR 1253, the Court approved *Cream Holdings*. It also put beyond doubt that s 12 does not enhance the weight to be afforded to Article 10 rights in deciding whether an interim injunction should be granted. The Supreme Court disagreed with the Court of Appeal's view that it followed from s 12 that where grant of interim relief would impinge upon Article 10, protection of freedom of expression should necessarily be the starting point in considering whether to grant such relief and that the right ought to be afforded 'enhanced' weight in the court's decision-making. The Supreme Court took this view despite s 12(4) providing that '[t]he court must have particular regard to the importance of the Convention right to freedom of expression'. As a result of *PJS*, where the decision whether to grant interim relief implicates a clash between Article 10 and other basic rights, neither Article 10 nor the other rights ought to be accorded priority at the outset. For example, in *PJS* the claimant sought to restrain publication of information which would seriously impinge his Article 8 right to privacy. If the defendant news company were prevented from publishing the story its freedom of expression would be infringed. At full trial a court would resolve such a case by weighing the importance of the privacy interests against the importance of the expression interests on the facts with neither set of interests being accorded necessary priority over the other. The Supreme Court reasoned that given this would be the approach taken at trial it ought to be the approach taken in deciding, for the purposes of interim relief, whether the applicant would be likely to establish, at full trial, that the publication should not be allowed (at [20]). In other words, s 12 did not have the effect of affording freedom of expression greater weight at the interlocutory stage compared to the weight it would be accorded at full trial.

12.2.3 Injunctions and the Crown

Historically, the Crown could not be sued in its own courts, and coercive remedies such as injunctions therefore could not be issued against the Crown. However, as a result of statutory intervention, it *is* now possible to sue the Crown, as we explain in ch 15. Of present concern, however, is the specific question whether injunctive relief may issue against the Crown. In the public law context this question assumed considerable importance for two reasons. On a practical level, the injunction appeared to offer the only prospect of interim relief in this context (although note the possibility, considered at 12.2.1, of issuing stays in respect of administrative action): the prerogative orders cannot take interim form and the interim declaration is a recent invention. In broader terms, the availability of coercive injunctive relief against the Crown is central to what Harlow (1994) 57 *MLR* 620 at 623 terms a 'mandatory model' of public law—a notion which Lord Templeman clearly had in mind when he said, in *Re M* [1994] 1 AC 377 at 395, that

> the argument that there is no power to enforce the law by injunction or contempt proceedings against a Minister in his official capacity would, if upheld, establish the proposition that the executive obey the law as a matter of grace and not as a matter of necessity, a proposition which would reverse the result of the Civil War.

In spite of the existence of these two arguments in favour of (interim) injunctive relief, it took the courts considerable time to arrive at a settled view. Much of the uncertainty derived from differing interpretations of s 21 of the Crown Proceedings Act 1947. The Act was intended to liberalize proceedings against the Crown, yet s 21 was, on a number of occasions, interpreted restrictively.

Crown Proceedings Act 1947

21—(1) In any civil proceedings by or against the Crown the court shall, subject to the provisions of this Act, have power to make all such orders as it has power to make in proceedings between subjects, and otherwise to give such appropriate relief as the case may require: Provided that:

(a) where in any proceedings against the Crown any such relief is sought as might in proceedings between subjects be granted by way of injunction or specific performance, the court shall not grant an injunction or make an order for specific performance, but may in lieu thereof make an order declaratory of the rights of the parties; and

(b) in any proceedings against the Crown for the recovery of land or other property the court shall not make an order for the recovery of the land or the delivery of the property, but may in lieu thereof make an order declaring that the plaintiff is entitled as against the Crown to the land or property or to the possession thereof.

> (2) The court shall not in any civil proceedings grant any injunction or make any order against an officer of the Crown if the effect of granting the injunction or making the order would be to give any relief against the Crown which could not have been obtained in proceedings against the Crown.

The effect of s 21(1) is quite clear: injunctions may not be issued against *the Crown* in 'civil proceedings' (a term whose definition we consider later). However, s 21(2) imposes only a qualified prohibition on issuing injunctions against *officers of the Crown* (which includes Ministers). As Lord Woolf explained in *Re M* [1994] 1 AC 377 at 412, '[t]hat subsection is restricted in its application to situations where the effect of the grant of an injunction or an order against an officer of the Crown will be to give any relief against the Crown which could not have been obtained in proceedings against the Crown prior to the Act.' To understand the effect of s 21(2), regard must therefore be had to the position which obtained prior to the 1947 Act. After reviewing the authorities, Lord Woolf said at 409–10:

> The position so far as civil wrongs are concerned, prior to the Act of 1947, can be summarised … by saying that as long as the plaintiff sued the actual wrongdoer or the person who ordered the wrongdoing he could bring an action against officials personally, in particular as to torts committed by them, and they were not able to hide behind the immunity of the Crown. This was the position even though at the time they committed the alleged tort they were acting in their official capacity. In those proceedings an injunction, including, if appropriate, an interlocutory injunction, could be granted.

In light of this, Lord Woolf concluded the 1947 Act neither extended nor restricted the courts' power to issue injunctions: they may not issue against the Crown; however, before 1947, they could be issued personally against officials and Ministers acting in their official capacity, and the Act did not alter this. In practical terms this should (and now does) mean that injunctions are unavailable in civil proceedings when duties are placed on the Crown in general—because in such circumstances when a claim is made against a Minister or official they defend it in a purely representative capacity (as the nominated representative of the Crown under s 17 of the Act)—but are available when legislation places duties on named Ministers who may then be held liable for breach of their official duty.

However, in *Merricks* v. *Heathcoat-Amory* [1955] Ch 567 at 575–6, Upjohn J took the general view (subject to the possibility of 'special Acts where named persons have special duties to perform which would not be duties normally fulfilled by them in their official capacity') that when a Minister acts he does so either in a purely individual capacity (in which case the enforcement of statutory duties imposed upon him in his official capacity is beside the point) or as a representative of the Crown (in which case an injunction is prohibited by s 21 of the Act). The House of Lords endorsed this reasoning in *R* v. *Secretary of State for Transport, ex parte Factortame* [1990] 2 AC 85—strongly criticized by Wade (1991) 107 *LQR* 4—in which the Court refused to issue an interim injunction to prevent the Secretary of State for Transport from applying part of the Merchant Shipping Act 1988 pending a preliminary ruling by the CJEU as to its compatibility with certain directly effective provisions of EU law. More recently, however, Lord Woolf recognized in *M* at 415 that the mistake made by Upjohn J in *Merricks* was 'to treat a duty placed upon a named Minister as being placed upon the Government as a whole', thus cloaking the Minister with Crown immunity and emasculating the jurisdiction to grant injunctions personally against Ministers acting in official capacity.

Having established the position in relation to 'civil proceedings' under the 1947 Act, the House of Lords in *M* went on to address the availability of injunctive relief in judicial review proceedings under Order 53 of the Rules of the Supreme Court (since replaced by CPR Part 54). In *R v. Secretary of State for the Home Department, ex parte Herbage* [1987] QB 872, Hodgson J had concluded that while the then-accepted *Merricks* interpretation of the 1947 Act precluded injunctive relief against Ministers and Crown officers in 'civil proceedings', the position was different in relation to proceedings brought via a claim for judicial review. Although that view was repudiated by the Law Lords in *Factortame*, their Lordships revisited the matter in *M* (for commentary see Gould [1993] *PL* 568 and Allan [1994] *CLJ* 1).

Re M [1994] AC 377
House of Lords

The claimant, an asylum seeker from Zaire, was told that he would be deported on 1 May 1991. He sought permission for judicial review but was unsuccessful in both the High Court and, on 1 May 1991, the Court of Appeal. After appointing new solicitors he again sought permission in the High Court on allegedly fresh grounds. Garland J wished the claimant's deportation to be postponed, but apparently as a result of a misunderstanding the claimant was deported. Once informed of the situation overnight, the judge issued an interim mandatory injunction against the Home Secretary, Kenneth Baker, requiring him to procure the return of the claimant to the court's jurisdiction. The Home Secretary failed to do so, on the strength of legal advice to the effect that the injunction had been made without jurisdiction. Although the injunction was later discharged, the question arose whether, while the injunction had been in force, the Home Secretary had committed a contempt of court by failing to comply with it. It was therefore necessary to address the logically prior issue of the jurisdiction of the court to issue an injunction against a Minister in judicial review proceedings. At first instance, Simon Brown J concluded that s 21 precluded the issuing of an injunction in such circumstances, while the Court of Appeal held that the Home Secretary could be *personally* guilty of contempt.

Lord Woolf

... The language of section 23 [of the Crown Proceedings Act 1947] makes it clear that Part II of the Act does not generally apply to all proceedings which can take place in the High Court. In particular, it does not apply to the proceedings which at that time would have been brought for prerogative orders. If there is any doubt about this, that doubt is removed by the general interpretation provisions of the Act contained in section 38, section 38(2) providing:

> 'In this Act, except in so far as the context otherwise requires or it is otherwise expressly provided, the following expressions have the meanings hereby respectively assigned to them, that is to say ... "Civil proceedings" includes proceedings in the High Court or the county court for the recovery of fines or penalties, but does not include proceedings on the Crown side of the [Queen's] Bench Division; ...'

Proceedings for the prerogative orders were brought on the Crown side. [Such proceedings now take the form of a claim for judicial review under Part 54 of the Civil Procedure Rules, formerly the application for judicial review under Order 53 of the Rules of the Supreme Court.]

... Prior to the introduction of judicial review, the principal remedies which were available were certiorari, mandamus, prohibition and habeas corpus. As we are primarily concerned with the possible availability of injunction, I will focus on mandamus and prohibition since they are indistinguishable in their effect from final injunctions ...

The prerogative remedies could not be obtained against the Crown directly as was explained by Lord Denman C.J. in *Reg. v. Powell* (1841) 1 Q.B. 352, 361:

'both because there would be an incongruity in the Queen commanding herself to do an act, and also because the disobedience to a writ of mandamus is to be enforced by attachment.'

Originally this difficulty could not be avoided by bringing the proceedings against named ministers of the Crown: *Reg. v. Lords Commissioners of the Treasury* (1872) LR 7 QB 387. But, where a duty was imposed by statute for the benefit of the public upon a particular Minister, so that he was under a duty to perform that duty in his official capacity, then orders of prohibition and mandamus were granted regularly against the Minister. The proceedings were brought against the Minister in his official name and according to the title of the proceedings by the Crown. The title of the proceedings would be *Reg. v. Minister, Ex parte the applicant* ..., so that unless the Minister was treated as being distinct from the Crown the title of the proceedings would disclose the 'incongruity' of the Crown suing the Crown. This did not mean that the Minister was treated as acting other than in his official capacity and the order was made against him in his official name. In accordance with this practice there have been numerous cases where prerogative orders, including orders of prohibition and mandamus, have been made against ministers ...

[Lord Woolf set out s 31 of the Senior Courts Act 1981 (see 12.1) and continued:] In section 31 the jurisdiction to grant declarations and injunctions is directly linked to that which already existed in relation to the prerogative orders. The jurisdiction to award damages by contrast is restricted to those situations where damages are recoverable in an action begun by writ. It has never been suggested that a declaration is not available in proceedings against a Minister in his official capacity and if Order 53 and section 31 apply to a Minister in the case of declarations then, applying ordinary rules of construction, one would expect the position to be precisely the same in the case of injunctions. As an examination of the position prior to the introduction of judicial review indicates, because of the scope of the remedies of mandamus and prohibition the availability of injunctions against ministers would only be of any significance in situations where it would be appropriate to grant interim relief. Even here the significance of the change was reduced by the power of the court to grant a stay under Ord. 53, r. 3(10) [see now CPR 54.10(2).]

...

Lord Bridge of Harwich in *Reg. v. Secretary of State for Transport, Ex parte Factortame Ltd* [1990] 2 A.C. 85 at 143 acknowledged that 'the question at issue depends, first, on the true construction of section 31'. Lord Bridge also accepted, at 149, that if section 31 'were to be construed in isolation' there would be 'great force in the reasoning' that section 31 did enable injunctions to be granted for the first time against ministers of the Crown in judicial review proceedings. Why then did Lord Bridge come to the conclusion that an injunction could not be granted against a Minister in proceedings for judicial review?

A primary cause for Lord Bridge's taking this view was that he concluded that it would be a dramatic departure from what was the position prior to the introduction of judicial review for an injunction to be available against the Crown or a Minister of the Crown, so that the change was one which could be expected to be made only by express legislation. His conclusion was not, however, based on as comprehensive an argument of the history of both civil and prerogative proceedings as was available to your Lordships. In particular he did not have an account of the developments which had taken place in the granting of prerogative orders against ministers, which meant that in practical terms the only consequence of treating section 31 as enabling injunctions to be granted against *ministers* acting in their official capacity would be to provide an alternative in name only to the orders of prohibition and mandamus which were already available and to allow interim relief other than a stay for the first time.

A secondary cause was his reliance upon Upjohn J.'s judgment in *Merricks* v. *Heathcoat-Amory* [1955] Ch. 567, a judgment which as already indicated should be approached with caution. Lord Bridge was also influenced by the fact that the new Order 53 was introduced following the Law Commission's Report on Remedies in Administrative Law (1976) (Law Com. No. 73) (Cmnd. 6407) and that that report drew attention to the problem created by the lack of jurisdiction to grant interim injunctions against the Crown and recommended that the problem should be remedied by amending section 21 of the Act of 1947. The report included a draft of the legislation proposed. This proposal of the Law Commission was never implemented. Instead the decision was taken following the Law Commission's report to proceed by amendment of the Rules of the Supreme Court rather than by primary legislation. Lord Bridge in his speech [in *Factortame, op cit* at 149–50], explains why, in his view, this meant that section 31 of the Act of 1981 should be given a restricted interpretation ... [Lord Bridge's view] deserves very careful attention coming, as it does, from a judge who is acknowledged to have made an outstanding contribution to this area of the law. Nonetheless, I do not regard it as justifying limiting the natural interpretation of section 31 so as to exclude the jurisdiction to grant injunctions, including interim injunctions, on applications for judicial review against ministers of the Crown ...

I am, therefore, of the opinion that the language of section 31 being unqualified in its terms, there is no warrant for restricting its application so that in respect of ministers and other officers of the Crown alone the remedy of an injunction, including an interim injunction, is not available. In my view the history of prerogative proceedings against officers of the Crown supports such a conclusion. So far as interim relief is concerned, which is the practical change which has been made, there is no justification for adopting a different approach to officers of the Crown from that adopted in relation to other respondents in the absence of clear language such as that contained in section 21(2) of the Act of 1947. The fact that in any event a stay could be granted against the Crown under Ord. 53, r. 3(10) emphasises the limits of the change in the situation which is involved. It would be most regrettable if an approach which is inconsistent with that which exists in Community law should be allowed to persist if this is not strictly necessary. The restriction provided for in section 21(2) of the Act of 1947 does, however, remain in relation to civil proceedings.

The fact that, in my view, the court should be regarded as having jurisdiction to grant interim and final injunctions against officers of the Crown does not mean that that jurisdiction should be exercised except in the most limited circumstances. In the majority of situations so far as final relief is concerned, a declaration will continue to be the appropriate remedy on an application for judicial review involving officers of the Crown. As has been the position in the past, the Crown can be relied upon to co-operate fully with such declarations. To avoid having to grant interim injunctions against officers of the Crown, I can see advantages in the courts being able to grant interim declarations.

Lord Woolf, with whom Lords Keith, Templeman, Griffiths, and Browne-Wilkinson agreed, went on to conclude that a contempt of court had occurred. The appeal was therefore dismissed, although the Secretary of State for Home Affairs was substituted for Kenneth Baker personally as the subject of the finding of contempt.

The *M* decision was broadly welcomed (see, eg Law Com No 226, *Administrative Law: Judicial Review and Statutory Appeals* (London 1994), Part VI). There are, however, two areas in which reservation has been expressed. The first relates to enforcement. After concluding in

M that injunctions could lie against Ministers of the Crown, Lord Woolf went on to consider (at 424–6) whether a Minister could be held in contempt of court:

> Nolan L.J. [in the same case in the Court of Appeal: [1992] QB 270], at 311, considered that the fact that proceedings for contempt are 'essentially personal and punitive' meant that it was not open to a court, as a matter of law, to make a finding of contempt against the Home Office or the Home Secretary. While contempt proceedings usually have these characteristics and contempt proceedings against a government department or a Minister in an official capacity would not be either personal or punitive (it would clearly not be appropriate to fine or sequestrate the assets of the Crown or a government department or an officer of the Crown acting in his official capacity), this does not mean that a finding of contempt against a government department or Minister would be pointless. The very fact of making such a finding would vindicate the requirements of justice. In addition an order for costs could be made to underline the significance of a contempt. A purpose of the courts' powers to make findings of contempt is to ensure that the orders of the court are obeyed. This jurisdiction is required to be coextensive with the courts' jurisdiction to make the orders which need the protection which the jurisdiction to make findings of contempt provides. In civil proceedings the court can now make orders (other than injunctions or for specific performance) against authorised government departments or the Attorney-General. On applications for judicial review orders can be made against ministers. In consequence of the developments identified already such orders must be taken not to offend the theory that the Crown can supposedly do no wrong. Equally, if such orders are made and not obeyed, the body against whom the orders were made can be found guilty of contempt without offending that theory, which would be the only justifiable impediment against making a finding of contempt.
>
> In cases not involving a government department or a Minister the ability to *punish* for contempt may be necessary. However, as is reflected in the restrictions on execution against the Crown [see Crown Proceedings Act 1947, s 25(4)], the Crown's relationship with the courts does not depend on coercion and in the exceptional situation when a government department's conduct justifies this, a finding of contempt should suffice. In that exceptional situation, the ability of the court to make a finding of contempt is of great importance. It would demonstrate that a government department has interfered with the administration of justice. It will then be for Parliament to determine what should be the consequences of that finding. In accord with tradition the finding should not be made against the 'Crown' by name but in the name of the authorised department (or the Attorney-General) or the Minister so as to accord with the body against whom the order was made. If the order was made in civil proceedings against an authorised department, the department will be held to be in contempt. On judicial review the order will be against the Minister and so normally should be any finding of contempt in respect of the order.

Lord Woolf concluded that a finding of contempt—in circumstances such as those in *M*— should be against the Minister in his official rather than personal capacity. He went on to say that 'the object of the exercise is not so much to punish an individual as to vindicate the rule of law by a finding of contempt'. Harlow (1994) 57 *MLR* 620 at 623 finds this aspect of *M* disquieting:

> [T]he decision does move our system of judicial review a long way towards the mandatory model for which Lord Woolf argued. A long way but not all the way because, at the end of his lengthy judgment, Lord Woolf is trapped into making a very dangerous concession ... Without considering the alternative of committal, in principle not impossible, though complicated a little by the status of Ministers as Members of Parliament, Lord Woolf deduces that contempt proceedings are

ultimately unenforceable. At the theoretical level, this admission ... surely undercuts the fundamental premise of Lord Woolf's judgment. A mandatory model of judicial review which cannot be enforced must be a contradiction in terms.

QUESTION

- Do you agree with Harlow's criticism of *M*?

The second area of concern relates to the premise which their Lordships adopted as their starting point—that injunctions do not lie against the Crown itself, as distinct from Crown officers. Although Lord Woolf did not consider this impediment to be of great significance, writers have taken issue with this view in two respects. First, Gould [1993] *PL* 568 at 577 argues that the *practical implications* of this restriction may be more important than first appears:

> [U]ncertainties are caused by the confusion ... between the 'Crown' and 'officers of the Crown'. Lord Woolf confesses to having muddied the waters by using the term 'Crown' loosely in [*R v. Licensing Authority Established under the Medicines Act 1968, ex parte Smith, Kline and French Laboratories Ltd (No 2)* [1990] 1 QB 574], but he is not always consistent in his use of the terms in *M*. The clear intention, reading the judgment as a whole, is to separate remedies available against officers of the Crown, which could include injunctions, from those available against the Crown itself, which are very limited and do not include any form of coercive relief. He is of the view that the distinction between the two categories, although very important in theory, has only minimal practical effect, and notes that 'there are likely to be few situations when there will be statutory duties that place a duty on the Crown in general instead of on a named Minister'. However, in those few situations the practical significance of the distinction between a Minister and the Crown becomes very great—to the extent that the remedies available to an applicant for judicial review would be severely curtailed. Whilst it may be true now that statutes predominantly confer duties on ministers, there is nothing to prevent Parliament from adopting a form of words which confers duties directly on the Crown and using that formula more frequently than at present in order to avoid the very remedies made available in *M*.

Sedley goes further, focusing not on the practical consequences of the distinction drawn in *M* between Ministers and the Crown but on whether such a distinction is defensible in terms of *constitutional theory*.

Sedley, 'The Crown in Its Own Courts' in Forsyth and Hare (eds), *The Golden Metwand and the Crooked Cord* (Oxford 1998)

What ... of the theory that the Crown can do no wrong? As a theory it hardly matters if it is now recognized in practice that the ministers and departments through whom the Crown acts are capable of doing wrong. But in theory too the proposition is flawed because it ignores the very thing that makes a democracy possible, the separation of powers. There is reality as well as symbolic force in the proposition that what the Crown in Parliament enacts is the law and in that constitutional sense right; and that what the Queen's courts hold to be the true meaning and effect of the law, whether common law or statute, is equally, in a constitutional sense, right. Neither is beyond change in the future nor beyond criticism in the present, but in both cases the Crown has constitutionally to be taken as doing no wrong if the rule of law is to be effective. In this temporary sense Parliament and the courts can each be accurately said to be a law unto themselves. But it is precisely because these are the two and the only two sovereign functions of the Crown, and because the functioning of executive government is subordinated to the approval of Parliament and the adjudication of the courts, that the Crown in its executive limb *can* in constitutional theory do wrong. It may be that the Crown as monarch is able to do no wrong, though in a constitutional monarchy there seems to be no reason why the sovereign should be—or indeed should want to be—any freer that the rest of us to break the speed limit. But there is no constitutional theory, and no need for one, which elevates ministerial authority to the status of a sovereign power in a democracy. The twentieth-century world has furnished countless reminders that it is precisely when those holding political power are able to administer the state by means of policy and discretion without regard to law or legislation that democracy founders.

The argument advanced to the Court of Appeal and the House of Lords on behalf of the Home Secretary in *M's* case was at base a straightforward syllogism: the Crown can do no wrong and is in any case not a legal entity; it is therefore beyond the reach of the law; the Minister acting in office acts in the name and on behalf of the Crown; he too is therefore beyond the reach of the law, at least in its coercive forms. The House has not directly challenged this reasoning. It has accepted the counter-argument that the Crown is a legal entity and that its inability to do wrong is a fiction; it has held that a Minister is personally liable for wrongs albeit committed in his official capacity; but rather than go the final step of holding that the Crown can therefore properly be impleaded for wrongs done in its name by its ministers, their Lordships have concluded that the law should recognize the capacity in which the Minister has erred, but in a form which avoids impleading the Crown ...

M v. *Home Office* was a powerful case on its facts, not because they were uncomplicated but because they posed a black-and-white issue: was a Minister who defied a court order answerable to the court for it, or did his status furnish him with an immunity enjoyed by the Crown? There is nothing wrong with starting from the conclusion that if the rule of law is to mean anything the latter proposition cannot be right ... If, however, one also accepts the argument that the Crown can do no wrong, one has to find some way of prising the Minister away from the Crown without eclipsing the fact that it is in his official capacity that he has offended. This is the road their Lordships have gone down. But if one asks ... whether it is actually the case that the Crown in its executive capacity can do no wrong, the answer is plainly No, and the whole of modern public law practice is founded upon that answer. Once this corner is turned, the way is relatively clear: the Crown's courts, applying the law laid down by Parliament and by themselves, may in a proper case hold the Crown, acting in its executive limb, to be in breach of the law without violating either the separation of powers or the status of the Crown. The status of the Crown, acknowledged by Magna Carta, the Bill of Rights, the Act of Settlement and a variety of other statutes, is that of an entity known to the law; and its horizontal division into legislative, judicial and executive functions permits ministers to be called to account politically by Parliament and legally by the courts. Once it is appreciated that these separate powers are not those of equal sovereignties within the state but that the executive, although enjoying great autonomy, is ultimately subordinated to the others, the problem of incongruity in the Crown supposedly calling itself to account melts away. In its place one sees a constitutional monarchy whose functions are so distributed that although all are carried out in the name of the Crown, their relationship to one another is the relationship demanded by one of the most fundamental of all our unwritten constitutional principles—that government is to be conducted within the law.

QUESTION

- Bearing in mind the arguments of Gould and Sedley, was the House of Lords right to conclude in *M* that injunctions cannot be issued against the Crown itself?

12.3 Declarations

12.3.1 The role of declarations in public law

Declarations constitute an authoritative judicial statement of a legal position but are a non-coercive form of relief. While those who act contrary to the law as spelled out in the declaration may well incur liability for the simple reason that they have breached the law so declared, no additional liability arises as a result of the existence of the declaration; this may be contrasted with the position in relation to injunctions, breach of which may ultimately result in liability for contempt of court. Declarations are a useful form of relief in a number of respects.

First, the non-coercive nature of the remedy makes it highly attractive, and is the principal reason why the declaration has become one of the most important remedies in review proceedings, in the sense of one of those remedies most often granted. Because declarations do not involve the courts coercing the administration to do particular acts or decide matters one way or the other, they do not raise the types of separation-of-powers concerns that more intrusive remedies do. Further, because the declaration does not invalidate impugned administrative acts, it protects administrative values of certainty and finality: administrative processes that have run their course remain intact and undisturbed. On the other hand, this does not come at a cost to rule-of-law values: the declaration vindicates the rule of law by stating formally and publically that the administration has acted unlawfully, while also serving an 'educative' function, informing the administration of how it ought to act in order to comply with its legal obligations. Of course this 'rosy' picture of declarations as striking an attractive balance between protecting administrative interests and promoting legality rests very much on a view, such as that espoused by Lord Woolf in *Re M* [1994] 1 AC 377 at 423, that it would rarely be necessary to issue final injunctive relief against officers of the Crown, given the high degree of likelihood that they would cooperate fully with a declaration. This view places a great deal of trust in government. Those more sceptical of government's willingness to voluntarily abide by legal rulings and faithfully integrate them into their decision-making may take a different view of the increasing judicial propensity to favour declarations as a principal form of relief in review cases ahead of coercive remedies, such as mandatory orders.

Second, declarations are more apt than injunctions in circumstances where the relevance of the matter under consideration is general rather than confined to the parties before the court. Relief issued in relation to primary legislation which is found to be inconsistent with directly effective EU law usefully illustrates this point. The Law Commission (Law Com No 226, *Administrative Law: Judicial Review and Statutory Appeals* (London 1994) at [6.20]) noted that

> although in *Factortame (No 2)* an interim injunction was ordered in respect of an Act of Parliament, in the case of legislation such an injunction is not entirely appropriate since it is only addressed to the law maker or those who implement or enforce it, whereas the 'law' may be relied on by a wide range of third parties.

Indeed, declarations were issued by the House of Lords in *R* v. *Secretary of State for Employment, ex parte Equal Opportunities Commission* [1995] 1 AC 1 when it was found that UK legislation was incompatible with directly effective prohibitions upon indirect gender discrimination imposed by EU law.

Third, the inherent flexibility of the declaration makes it appropriate in a wide range of situations; in particular, it permits the courts to clarify the legal position in circumstances which do not yet disclose any specific public law wrong. For instance, it is clear from cases such as *Gillick* v. *West Norfolk and Wisbech Area Health Authority* [1986] AC 112 that declarations may be issued in relation to government circulars, to clarify whether the advice which they contain would, if followed, lead to the commission of unlawful conduct, even if the circulars themselves do not purport to be issued pursuant to—and cannot therefore be outside the scope of—any legal authority. There are, however, limits to the extent of courts' willingness to issue so-called advisory declarations, as we explain at 14.5.

12.3.2 Interim declarations

The House of Lords was forced to confront the availability of injunctive relief against officers of the Crown in *Factortame* and *M* because, when those cases were decided, it was the only type of relief—apart from stays, on which see at 12.2.1—available in interim form. As to declarations, Upjohn LJ, in *International General Electric Company of New York Ltd* v. *Commissioners of Customs and Excise* [1962] Ch 784 at 790, could 'not understand how there can be such an animal … as an interim declaratory order', while Diplock LJ considered such a remedy 'would be a contradiction in terms'. Similarly, in *R* v. *Licensing Authority Established under the Medicines Act 1968, ex parte Smith, Kline and French Laboratories Ltd (No 2)* [1990] 1 QB 574 at 601, Woolf LJ thought it 'difficult to envisage that you can have an interim declaration' (although, as the extract at 12.2.3 shows, he later concluded in *Re M* [1994] 1 AC 377 that such a remedy would be practically useful). In the following extract the Law Commission helpfully summarizes the perceived problems associated with interim declarations, while concluding that those difficulties are not insurmountable.

Law Com No 226, *Administrative Law: Judicial Review and Statutory Appeals* (London 1994)

[Our] consultation paper [*Administrative Law: Judicial Review and Statutory Appeals*, Consultation Paper No 126] sought views on the relative merits of the different techniques for granting interim relief; stays, interim injunctions and interim declarations. The last of these is at present unknown to English law. The overall result was not conclusive. Consultees accepted that what was needed was an effective way of preserving the status quo and a rationalisation of the different techniques for doing so but some reservations were expressed about interim declarations. It was said to be illogical to declare one day in interlocutory proceedings that an applicant has certain rights and on a later day that he has not and it was suggested that interim declarations were inconsistent with the presumption of legality [on which see 3.2.1–3.2.2] …

The advantages of [interim declarations] … are that they are not coercive, they specifically address the interim position and are better suited to clarify the position of third parties. There is no reason why they should not be granted on the same basis as interim injunctions. In New Zealand there is provision for interim declaratory relief in judicial review proceedings against the Crown ..., and such relief is more generally available in Canada. Such declarations would refer to a right or obligation that exists prima facie and are not therefore illogical. In making a merely interim declaration, the judge reserves his or her right and admits an obligation to re-examine the question after a substantive hearing at the trial. In our view this consideration also meets the argument that a declaration in an interim form may inappropriately suggest that the court has already made up its mind as to the likely grant of final relief.

We believe that the perceived difficulties arising from the presumption of validity are met by the fact that the burden of proof lies on the party challenging the decision. It was also commented that it might be more difficult to deal with undertakings regarding damages by the applicant where an interim declaration is given. We believe that where it is clear that an activity should be stopped the principles developed in relation to injunctions could be applied or an interim injunction granted ...

We accordingly recommend that there should be provision for ... interim declarations ... in proceedings by way of judicial review.

The force of these arguments has now been recognized, and CPR 25.1(1)(b) permits interim declarations to be granted. Interim declarations are particularly useful in cases where legislation is challenged on the ground of its alleged incompatibility with EU law. This is because references to the CJEU under Article 267 of the Treaty on the Functioning of the European Union, which are often required in such cases, can take a considerable amount of time. There are, however, few examples of interim declarations being sought or granted in judicial review proceedings in respect of allegedly invalid *administrative* action since, as Solomon [2001] *JR* 10 notes, in such proceedings 'it will often be the case that a request for an expedited hearing is more appropriate than pursuing an interim remedy'.

12.4 Relator proceedings

Relator proceedings are brought by the Attorney-General on behalf of a member of the public or an agency in order to obtain an injunction or declaration. One use to which such proceedings may be put is to prevent, by means of an injunction, a breach of the criminal law. However, since the effect of this is to make any subsequent breach into a contempt of court, thus potentially permitting the imposition of a sanction in excess of the statutorily prescribed maximum for the offence in question, it is generally felt this course of action will be appropriate only rarely.

Less controversially, relator proceedings may be brought in order to obtain an injunction to prevent public authorities from acting *ultra vires* or a declaration to establish that a certain policy or decision is unlawful (*eg Attorney-General ex rel Tilley* v. *Wandsworth London Borough Council* [1981] 1 WLR 854). Used in this way, the principal benefit of relator proceedings is that the person wishing to impugn the administrative action need not establish standing (on which see 14.7). Clearly, the importance of relator proceedings thus depends partly upon the liberality of the rules on standing: the more restrictive those rules, the more important relator proceedings become as a means of escaping their strictures. We shall return to this point later.

Let us now turn to *Gouriet*, the seminal decision on relator proceedings. Although the decision concerns relator proceedings for the purpose of enforcing the criminal law by means of injunction, Lord Wilberforce's comments are of more general relevance, in particular the sharp distinction he draws between public and private rights.

Gouriet v. Union of Post Office Workers [1978] AC 435
House of Lords

Gouriet applied to the Attorney-General for his consent to act as claimant in relator proceedings for an injunction against the Union, which was alleged to be about to call on its members not to handle mail between the United Kingdom and South Africa for the week beginning 16 January 1977, as a protest against the apartheid policy then in force in South Africa. Such interference with postal communications constituted an offence under the Post Office Act 1953. The Attorney-General refused to consent and Gouriet then issued a writ in his own name. A judge in chambers refused the application on 14 January, but the Court of Appeal granted him an interim injunction the next day. At a later hearing Gouriet amended his pleadings by adding a claim for a declaration that the Attorney-General, by refusing his consent to the relator action, had wrongfully exercised his discretion. The majority of the Court of Appeal held that the courts had no jurisdiction to review the Attorney-General's decision and that Gouriet was not entitled to a permanent injunction. However, a majority also held that, in spite of the Attorney-General's refusal to give his consent, Gouriet had been entitled to claim a declaration that the Union was proposing to act unlawfully and that an interim injunction (interim declarations being unavailable at that time) could be issued pending determination of whether such a final declaration would be appropriate. Both parties appealed to the House of Lords, although Gouriet no longer claimed that the refusal of consent was wrongful or reviewable.

Lord Wilberforce

... There is now no longer a claim that the Attorney-General's refusal of consent to relator proceedings was improper or that it can be reviewed by the court. This issue, originally presented as one of great constitutional importance, has disappeared from the case. The importance remains, but the issue has vanished. The Attorney-General's decision is accepted as, in the courts, unassailable. The prerogatives of his office are no longer attacked. All that Mr. Gouriet now claims is that the refusal of the Attorney-General to act does not bar him from acting ...

A relator action—a type of action which has existed from the earliest times—is one in which the Attorney-General, on the relation of individuals (who may include local authorities or companies) brings an action to assert a public right. It can properly be said to be a fundamental principle of English law that private rights can be asserted by individuals, but that public rights can only be asserted by the Attorney-General as representing the public. In terms of constitutional law, the rights of the public are vested in the Crown, and the Attorney-General enforces them as an officer of the Crown. And just as the Attorney-General has in general no power to interfere with the assertion of private rights, so in general no private person has the right of representing the public in the assertion of public rights. If he tries to do so his action can be struck out ...

... [T]he Attorney-General's role has never been fictional. His position in relator actions is the same as it is in actions brought without a relator (with the sole exception that the relator is liable for costs: see *Attorney-General v. Cockermouth Local Board* (1874) L.R. 18 Eq. 172, 176, *per* Jessel M.R.). He is entitled to see and approve the statement of claim and any amendment in the pleadings, he is entitled to be consulted on discovery, the suit cannot be compromised without his approval; if the relator dies, the suit does not abate. For the proposition that his only concern is to 'filter out' vexatious and frivolous proceedings there is no authority—indeed there is no need for the Attorney-General to do what is well within the power of the court. On the contrary he has the right, and the duty, to consider the public interest generally and widely.

It was this consideration which led to the well known pronouncement of the Earl of Halsbury L.C. in 1902, for the suggestion was being made that the court could inquire whether, when the Attorney-General had consented to relator proceedings, the public had a material interest in the subject matter of the suit:

' ... the initiation of the litigation, and the determination of the question whether it is a proper case for the Attorney-General to proceed in, is a matter entirely beyond the jurisdiction of this or any other court. It is a question which the law of this country has made to reside exclusively in the Attorney-General': see *London County Council v. Attorney-General* [1902] A.C. 165, *per* Earl of Halsbury L.C. at p. 169 and *per* Lord Macnaghten at p. 170.

To limit this passage to a case where the Attorney-General has given his consent (as opposed to a case where he refuses consent) goes beyond legitimate distinction: it ignores the force of the words 'whether he ought to initiate litigation ... or not': see p. 168 ...

That it is the exclusive right of the Attorney-General to represent the public interest—even where individuals might be interested in a larger view of the matter—is not technical, not procedural, not fictional. It is constitutional ... [I]t is also wise.

From this general consideration of the nature of relator actions, I pass to the special type of relator action with which this appeal is concerned. It is of very special character, and it is one in which the predominant position of the Attorney-General is a fortiori the general case.

This is a right, of comparatively modern use, of the Attorney-General to invoke the assistance of civil courts in aid of the *criminal law*. It is an exceptional power confined, in practice, to cases where an offence is frequently repeated in disregard of a, usually, inadequate penalty see *Attorney-General v. Harris* [1961] 1 Q.B. 74; or to cases of emergency—see *Attorney-General v. Chaudry* [1971] 1 W.L.R. 1614. It is one not without its difficulties and these may call for consideration in the future.

If Parliament has imposed a sanction (e.g., a fine of £1), without an increase in severity for repeated offences, it may seem wrong that the courts—civil courts—should think fit, by granting injunctions, breaches of which may attract unlimited sanctions, including imprisonment, to do what Parliament has not done. Moreover, where Parliament has (as here in the Post Office Act 1953) provided for trial of offences by indictment before a jury, it may seem wrong that the courts, applying a civil standard of proof, should in effect convict a subject without the prescribed trial. What would happen if, after punishment for contempt, the same man were to be prosecuted in a criminal court? That Lord Eldon L.C. was much oppressed by these difficulties is shown by the discussions in *Attorney-General v. Cleaver* (1811) 18 Ves. Jun. 210.

These and other examples which can be given show that this jurisdiction—though proved useful on occasions—is one of great delicacy and is one to be used with caution. Further, to apply to the court for an injunction at all against the threat of a criminal offence, may involve a decision of policy with which conflicting considerations may enter. Will the law best be served by preventive action? Will the grant of an injunction exacerbate the situation? (Very relevant this in industrial disputes.) Is the injunction likely to be effective or may it be futile? Will it be better to make it clear that the law will be enforced by prosecution and to appeal to the law-abiding instinct, negotiations, and moderate leadership, rather than provoke people along the road to martyrdom? All these matters—to which Devlin J. justly drew attention in *Attorney-General v. Bastow* [1957] 1 Q.B. 514, 519, and the exceptional nature of this *civil* remedy, point the matter as one essentially for the Attorney-General's preliminary discretion. Every known case, so far, has been so dealt with: in no case hitherto has it ever been suggested that an individual can act, though relator actions for public nuisance which may also involve a criminal offence, have been known for 200 years.

There are two arguments put forward for permitting individual citizens to take this action.

The first points to the private prosecution. All citizens have sufficient interest in the enforcement of the law to entitle them to take this step. Why then should this same interest not be sufficient to support preventive action by way of injunction—subject it may be, to ultimate control by the Attorney-General? At one time I was attracted by this argument. But I have reached the conclusion that I cannot accept it.

The Attorney-General's right to seek, in the civil courts, anticipatory prevention of a breach of the law, is a part or aspect of his general power to enforce, in the public interest, public rights. The distinction between public rights, which the Attorney-General can and the individual (absent special interest) cannot seek to enforce, and private rights, is fundamental in our law. To break it, as the plaintiff's counsel frankly invited us to do, is not a development of the law, but a destruction of one of its pillars. Nor, in my opinion, at least in this particular field, would removal of the distinction be desirable. More than in any other field of public rights, the decision to be taken before embarking on a claim for injunctive relief, involving as it does the interests of the public over a broad horizon, is a decision which the Attorney-General alone is suited to make: see *Attorney-General v. Bastow* [1957] 1 Q.B. 514.

This brings me to the second argument. Surely, it is said, since the whole matter is discretionary it can be left to the court. The court can prevent vexatious or frivolous, or multiple actions: the court is not obliged to grant an injunction: leave it in the court's hands. I cannot accept this either. The decisions to be made as to the public interest are not such as courts are fitted or equipped to make. The very fact, that, as the present case very well shows, decisions are of the type to attract political criticism and controversy, shows that they are outside the range of discretionary problems which the courts can resolve. Judges are equipped to find legal rights and administer, on well-known principles, discretionary remedies. These matters are widely outside those areas.

Viscount Dilhorne and Lords Diplock, Edmund-Davies, and Fraser also delivered speeches in favour of dismissing the appeal. Appeal dismissed.

Two issues require comment. First, their Lordships took it for granted (because the claimant did not pursue the point) that the Attorney-General's discretion to consent to relator proceedings cannot be reviewed. Since the power to consent to such proceedings is prerogative in nature, it is perhaps unsurprising that this conclusion was reached when *Gouriet* was decided in 1978 (although even then its correctness was questioned: Feldman (1979) 42 *MLR* 369 at 372–3). But it is unclear whether such a conclusion can withstand more recent case law. As we saw in ch 4, the effect of the House of Lords' decision in *Council of Civil Service Unions v. Minister for the Civil Service* [1985] AC 374 is that discretionary powers are no longer immune from judicial review merely because they are sourced in the prerogative. For example, it is today difficult to envisage a court dismissing as non-justiciable a claim brought on irrelevant considerations grounds challenging the Attorney-General's refusal to consent to relator proceedings, where that refusal was clearly motivated by a desire to prevent judicial scrutiny of the relevant matter, as this might expose the government to political embarrassment.

The second point arising from *Gouriet* concerns the vision of public law, and of the individual's position in relation to it, which underpins Lord Wilberforce's speech. For his Lordship the utility of relator proceedings stems from the fact that 'no private person has the right of representing the public in the assertion of public rights'; only by securing the consent to relator proceedings of the Attorney-General—whose exclusive right and duty it is 'to consider the public interest generally and widely'—may an individual litigate such issues. If this conclusion is combined with the view implicit in *Gouriet* that the Attorney-General's consent is a matter of pure (unreviewable) discretion, it ascribes to individuals a very limited capacity to use legal proceedings to vindicate public rights or the public interest. Such approach is inconsistent with the argument that individuals are stakeholders in government who have a legitimate interest in ensuring the executive respects fundamental principles of good administration. On this view, which is now dominant, the prospective claimant's right to enforce those values transcends circumstances in which his own rights are affected by unlawful action. This vision of the individual's position in respect of public law proceedings has given rise to a liberal approach to standing which often allows individuals or interest groups to sustain judicial review claims on public interest grounds in their own names, obviating the need to resort to relator proceedings and, more generally, eschewing Lord Wilberforce's narrow view of the role of individuals in this sphere. (Indeed, even when *Gouriet* was decided, the law of standing in relation to quashing and prohibiting orders (see 12.5) was such that the Attorney-General did not have a monopoly on public interest claims.) It is true, however, that unless standing rules become so liberal as to recognize an *actio popularis*, the utility of relator proceedings will remain.

12.5 Prerogative remedies

We are concerned in this section with the three prerogative remedies mentioned in s 31(1)(a) of the Senior Courts Act 1981 (set out at 12.1), now known as quashing, mandatory, and prohibiting orders. (It should also be remembered that there exists a fourth prerogative remedy, *habeas corpus*, which is used to test the legality of detention and to require the release of those unlawfully detained, but with which we shall not be dealing in this book in detail.) It is important to note that, whereas ordinary remedies may (subject to the principle of procedural exclusivity, discussed in ch 13) be sought in both judicial review proceedings and ordinary proceedings, the prerogative remedies are available only via a claim for judicial review under CPR Part 54. Prerogative remedies do not lie against the Crown itself, since it is the Crown which nominally issues the claim. However, it has long been accepted that prerogative remedies can be issued against officials and Ministers.

12.5.1 Quashing orders

Quashing orders are the most commonly sought remedy in judicial review proceedings. Reflecting this, in *Cocks v. Thanet District Council* [1983] 2 AC 286 at 295, Lord Bridge said 'certiorari to quash remains the primary and most appropriate remedy' where unlawfulness is found on review (albeit this proposition has arguably come under strain since given the increasing judicial propensity to favour declaratory relief). The effect of such orders is to quash, with retrospective effect, administrative action which the reviewing court finds to be unlawful. The retrospectivity of the order reflects the fact that if something is *ultra vires*—which (except to the extent that the doctrine of non-jurisdictional error of law on the face of the record survives: see further 2.2.2) it must be if a quashing order can lie—then it is void *ab initio*, as discussed above in ch 3. This point was considered by the Supreme Court in *Ahmed* v. *HM Treasury (No 2)* [2010] UKSC 5, [2010] 2 WLR 378, in which Lord Phillips said at [4] that unlawful administrative measures 'are *ultra vires* and of no effect in law', the object of quashing them being merely 'to make it quite plain that this is the case'. In some situations, therefore, an individual may choose to ignore unlawful administrative action, raising its invalidity collaterally if necessary in other proceedings rather than challenging it directly by judicial review (on which see further 3.4).

Nevertheless, there remain many good reasons why a quashing order may be sought in respect of action which is thought to be void. Most obviously, the claimant may wish the court to determine authoritatively that the action in question is void, rather than simply assuming this to be the case: waiting to challenge administrative measures collaterally necessarily involves an element of risk because it may turn out (as, for instance, in *Boddington* v. *British Transport Police* [1999] 2 AC 143: see 3.1.2) that the court does not share the defendant's conviction that the measure in question is invalid. Moreover, circumstances may dictate that merely ignoring the invalid action does not advance the claimant's cause: if, for instance, a licence was sought in order to permit a given activity to be lawfully undertaken, a refusal which is *ultra vires*—because, for example, the decision not to confer a licence was preceded by an unfair procedure—does not change the fact that the individual does not possess a licence and therefore may not lawfully undertake the activity in question. In this situation, only by having the unlawful refusal quashed and requiring the decision-maker to reconsider the matter in a lawful manner may it be possible for the individual to achieve the desired outcome. Similarly, a quashing order may be necessary in order to get third parties to accept that the measure in question is unlawful. In *Ahmed (No 2)*, which concerned secondary legislation providing for the freezing of terrorists' assets, Lord Phillips noted at [7] that banks, even if they knew that the legislation was unlawful, might refuse to release frozen assets until the legislation was quashed. It follows that, although a quashing order does not *render* unlawful administrative action invalid, because its invalidity follows *a priori* from its unlawful status, such an order is often practically important because of the need authoritatively to *establish* the unlawfulness of the action.

Two further points should be noted concerning judicial powers attendant upon the issuing of a quashing order. First, under s 31(5)(a) of the Senior Courts Act 1981, the reviewing court, having issued a quashing order, can 'remit the matter to the court, tribunal or authority which made the decision, with a direction to reconsider the matter and reach a decision in accordance with the findings of the High Court'. CPR 54.19(2)(a) makes substantially similar provision. This does not, however, permit the court to instruct the decision-maker to reach a certain conclusion, since this would eviscerate the distinction between appeal and review. Instead, the decision-maker is simply required to consider the matter again in a manner which is lawful and which avoids the errors (*eg* a breach of natural justice) identified by the court. For this reason, it is quite possible that the same decision may be reached when the matter is reconsidered. This, however, is an inevitable concomitant of the principle that reviewing courts are concerned only with the legality of administrative action.

Second, however, having quashed the decision, the reviewing court may, under s 31(5)(b) of the 1981 Act, 'substitute its own decision for the decision in question'. This may seem surprising in the light of what has just been said. However, s 31(5A) provides that the sub-stitution power is exercisable only if:

(a) the decision in question was made by a court or tribunal,

(b) the decision is quashed on the ground that there has been an error of law, and

(c) without the error, there would have been only one decision which the court or tribu-nal could have reached.

The proviso in s 31(5A)(c) makes it clear, then, that the power conferred upon reviewing courts by s 31(5)(b) does not threaten judicial usurpation of the decision-maker's discretion. Further, the courts observe these provisions place 'strict limits' on a court's power to direct a decision, while the courts will not make use of the power in cases where the administra-tive decision rests on evaluation of multiple factors which implicate factual inquiries; in other words, cases which plainly raise matters of judgement which are properly for the executive decision-maker: *R (Hamill)* v. *Chelmsford Justices* [2014] EWHC 2799 (Admin), [2015] 1 WLR 1798 at [75]–[78].

12.5.2 Prohibiting orders

Whereas quashing orders set aside unlawful action which has *already been taken,* pro-hibiting orders preclude administrative acts *yet to be taken* which, if committed, would be unlawful. In this sense a prohibiting order is similar to an injunction: it anticipates and pro-hibits unlawful action which is yet to occur. If an administrative body undertakes action contrary to a prohibiting order then, as with an injunction, a contempt of court is commit-ted. The circumstances in which this remedy is useful are quite limited, since it requires the claimant to know that unlawful action is planned by a public body. The type of situation in which a prohibiting order is valuable is illustrated by the case of *R* v. *Liverpool Corporation, ex parte Liverpool Taxi Fleet Operators' Association* [1972] 2 QB 299, in which the local authority resolved to increase the number of taxi licences granted, contrary to an under-taking that the total number of licences would be capped at 300 until certain proposed legislation was in force. The court considered it appropriate to issue a prohibiting order to prevent the implementation of the new policy without first hearing representations from interested persons.

12.5.3 Mandatory orders

The role of mandatory orders is analogous to that of mandatory injunctions. Unlike prohibiting orders, which serve to *prevent* the commission of unlawful action, mandatory orders operate to *compel* public bodies to do that which is legally required of them. Manda-tory orders are most obviously applicable in circumstances where legislation straightfor-wardly imposes a duty to do something; if the agency upon which the duty is placed fails to discharge it, then a mandatory order is appropriate to require the performance of the duty. For instance, in *Board of Education* v. *Rice* [1911] AC 179 the Board was required by s 7(3) of the Education Act 1902 to determine certain questions in order to resolve disputes between schools and local education authorities. The evidence established that the Board had not addressed the correct questions and had therefore failed to discharge its duty. Its decision was quashed and a mandatory order was issued, requiring the Board to look again at the matter, addressing itself to the correct questions.

However, it is increasingly rare to find courts issuing mandatory orders more generally. Courts generally favour declaratory relief, probably on the basis that, of all possible remedies discussed in this chapter, it is mandatory orders (alongside mandatory injunctions) which most squarely raise separation-of-powers concerns in that they involve courts compelling government to take particular action. We also noted in our discussion of declarations at 12.3 more general reasons why a court may steer clear of coercive relief, including a traditional judicial trust in the administration to faithfully implement judgments. Given this 'partnership' or 'cooperative' view of court–government relations has often guided remedial decisions on review, it is unsurprising that if mandatory orders are to be granted it is most likely to be in cases where the court has good reasons to doubt whether the administration will faithfully implement its judgment.

An excellent illustration of this point is the Supreme Court's decision in *R (ClientEarth) v. Secretary of State for the Environment, Food and Rural Affairs* [2015] UKSC 28. The Court had to determine whether to issue a mandatory order in the face of the continued failure by the government over several years to comply with set limits for atmospheric levels of nitrogen dioxide for certain geographic zones under EU Directive 2008/50/EC (the Air Quality Directive) and to produce legally compliant action plans to reduce levels of nitrogen dioxide in those zones. The government accepted that it had to take action and prepare new action plans, while the Court had previously issued a declaration that the government had acted unlawfully. However, in addition the Court considered that on the facts a mandatory order was warranted. Reflecting the cooperative model, the Court's starting point was that 'where a responsible public authority is in admitted breach of a legal obligation, but is willing to take appropriate steps to comply, the court may think it right to accept a suitable undertaking, rather than impose a mandatory order' (at [31]). However, in this case the government accepted that an undertaking could not be given as there were restrictions on government business in the lead up to the general election. Given the longstanding and serious nature of the breaches and the fact the government could not provide a formal undertaking the Court said: '[W]ithout doubting the good faith of the Secretary of State's intentions, we would … be failing in our duty if we simply accepted her assurances without any legal underpinning' (at [30]). Thus, whichever political party held power following the election, the new government 'should be left in no doubt as to the need for immediate action to address this issue' (at [31]). As such, the government would be mandated to produce new action plans within a defined timetable, set by the Court.

Further important factors which will likely guide the courts in deciding whether to issue a mandatory order include whether the relevant legal duty is framed in narrow or broad terms: the scope for issuing a mandatory order may be severely limited, or even non-existent, if the duty is framed in very broad or vague terms. Courts will be similarly reluctant to issue mandatory relief if the relevant duty is concerned with a matter that raises questions that are non-justiciable (see ch 4) or which provoke judicial deference (see ch 8). This approach reflects the good sense that in decision-making contexts removed from judicial experience and the constitutional responsibilities of courts, the courts should be reluctant to dictate outcomes.

Since the purpose of mandatory orders is to compel the performance of a legal *duty*, their relevance to discretionary powers—the essence of which is that the decision-maker is free to *choose* whether, rather than being duty-bound, to undertake the relevant action—may not seem obvious. It must be recalled, however, that while the decision-maker certainly has discretion over the merits, there are also duties latent within all discretionary powers. For example, a fundamental duty implicit in any discretionary power is that the recipient of such power must use it. This does not mean that the discretion must be exercised one way or the other, merely that the agency must use the power of decision conferred upon it by addressing its mind in each individual case to the question whether or not to exercise its discretion in favour of the applicant. Consequently, a decision-maker which refuses to exercise its discretion may find itself subject to a mandatory order requiring it to discharge the duty to decide, which is implicit within discretionary power.

It is clear, however, from earlier chapters of this book that the latent duties under which decision-makers find themselves extend well beyond this simple duty to decide. Consequently, when a decision-maker has purported to address the question but has failed to do so consistently with the one or more of the various duties of good decision-making imposed by administrative law, a mandatory order may be issued. This point is illustrated by *Padfield* v. *Minister of Agriculture, Fisheries and Food* [1968] AC 997, which was considered more fully at 7.3.2. It will be recalled that the Minister had a statutory discretion whether to refer complaints about a milk marketing scheme to a committee of investigation. The Court concluded that, in refusing to refer the complaint in question to such a committee, the Minister had taken into account irrelevant considerations and/or acted for purposes contrary to those for which Parliament had conferred the power. In so concluding, the House of Lords rejected the Minister's contention that he possessed unfettered discretion, reminding him that he was under a legal duty to exercise it (*inter alia*) consistently with the objectives of the statutory scheme; a mandatory order was issued to compel the Minister to revisit the question in a manner consistent with that duty. In this context, note that a court which has quashed a decision now has the additional option, under s 31(5)(a) of the Senior Courts Act 1981, of remitting the matter to the decision-maker and directing the decision-maker to reconsider the matter and reach a decision in accordance with the findings of the High Court (see further 12.5.1).

12.6 Concluding remarks

In preceding chapters, we have considered the duties imposed, as a matter of public law, on decision-makers. Having established what duties are owed in a particular case, and whether they have been breached, questions of relief become crucial. We have seen in this chapter that the courts have a number of remedies at their disposal. However, a range of other issues fall for consideration. In the following two chapters, we consider the procedural context within which the legality of administrative action is challenged in court proceedings, and certain restrictions on the availability of relief.

FURTHER RESOUCES

Cane, 'The Constitutional Basis of Judicial Remedies in Public Law' in Leyland and Woods (eds), *Administrative Law Facing the Future* (London 1997), 242–70

Civil Procedure Rules *http://www.justice.gov.uk/courts/procedure-rules/civil*

De Smith, 'The Prerogative Writs' (1951) 11 *CLJ* 40

De Smith, 'Wrongs and Remedies in Administrative Law' (1952) 15 *MLR* 189

Harlow, 'Accidental Loss of an Asylum Seeker' (1994) 57 *MLR* 620

Henderson, *Foundations of English Administrative Law: Certiorari and Mandamus in the Seventeenth Century* (Harvard 1963)

Law Com No 226, *Administrative Law: Judicial Review and Statutory Appeals* (London 1994), Part VI

Lewis, *Judicial Remedies in Public Law* (London 2014), chs 6–8

13 THE JUDICIAL REVIEW PROCEDURE

13.1 Introduction

Subject to the principles discussed in ch 15, if an individual wishes to sue a public body for breach of contract, he may simply issue a claim in the ordinary way. The same is true if the individual wishes to issue a claim in tort. These are matters of *private law*. However, what if the individual wishes to institute proceedings in respect of a *public law* matter? He may, for example, wish to have a decision quashed because it was unreasonable in the *Wednesbury* sense, or taken without compliance with operative rules of natural justice.

This raises two questions. First, is the prospective defendant actually subject to the public law duties to act fairly, reasonably, and so on? This falls to be determined by reference to the principles considered in ch 4.

Second, if the prospective defendant is subject to these public law duties, how, procedurally, may they be enforced? The general principle is that such public law matters should be litigated not by issuing a claim in the ordinary way, but through the use of a special 'judicial review procedure'. However, this general principle is subject to a number of significant exceptions, explored in 13.3, which in turn reflect the difficulties in delineating proceedings concerning 'public law' from those concerning 'private law'—concepts which are not easily defined. Importantly, as we shall see through this chapter, the difficulties in maintaining an exclusive and distinctive procedure for public law claims have been exacerbated by the advent of claims under the Human Rights Act 1998 (HRA).

Civil Procedure Rules Part 54: Judicial Review and Statutory Review

1. (2) In this Section—
    - (a) a 'claim for judicial review' means a claim to review the lawfulness of—
        - (i) an enactment; or
        - (ii) a decision, action or failure to act in relation to the exercise of a public function.
2. The judicial review procedure must be used in a claim for judicial review where the claimant is seeking—
    - (a) a mandatory order;
    - (b) a prohibiting order;
    - (c) a quashing order; or
    - (d) an injunction under section 30 of the Senior Courts Act 1981 (restraining a person from acting in any office in which he is not entitled to act).
3. (1) The judicial review procedure may be used in a claim for judicial review where the claimant is seeking—
    - (a) a declaration; or
    - (b) an injunction.

It follows that a claimant wishing to argue that a defendant has contravened applicable public law principles *must* use the judicial review procedure if a prerogative remedy is sought, whereas it appears that a claimant seeking one of the ordinary remedies may *choose* whether to do so under the judicial review procedure (subject to the conditions laid down in s 31(2) of the Senior Courts Act 1981, on which see 12.1) or by issuing a claim in the ordinary way. This raises two issues, upon which we focus in this chapter. First, exactly what is the judicial review procedure which claimants seeking a prerogative remedy are required to use? Second, to what extent may a claimant seeking to raise a public law matter avoid having to use the judicial review procedure by issuing a claim, in the ordinary way, for an injunction or declaration?

13.2 What is the judicial review procedure?

13.2.1 The origins of today's judicial review procedure

The Civil Procedure Rules were introduced, beginning in 1999, in an attempt to improve the way in which civil litigation is conducted in England and Wales. The Rules form a comprehensive code which governs such litigation; their overriding objective, according to CPR 1.1, is to enable courts to deal with cases 'justly'. It is far beyond the scope of this book to address the general content or implications of the Rules. Instead, our interest primarily lies in the distinct procedural rules which collectively comprise the judicial review procedure. What are these rules? To what extent do they differ from those applicable to civil litigation generally? And what justifications exist for the adoption of a distinct procedural approach in this context? The answers to the first two of these questions, which are today found in the CPR, are addressed later. However, in order to understand how we have arrived at the position now set out in the Rules, and to appreciate why it has been felt by legislators that a distinct procedure is required in this area, it is first necessary to set the Rules in their historical context.

Today's judicial review procedure, the nature of which we address in the following section, shares much in common with its predecessor, which came into being as a result of reforms introduced in 1977 and finessed in 1981. Prior to those reforms, prerogative and ordinary remedies were unavailable in the same proceedings, and it was the obvious practical utility of making all remedies available in a single set of proceedings which was the driving force behind the reforms, as the following excerpt from the Law Commission report upon which the reforms were based indicates. (For further explanation of the changes wrought by the 1977–1981 reforms, see the excerpt at 13.3.1 from Lord Diplock's speech in *O'Reilly v. Mackman* [1983] 2 AC 237.)

Law Com No 73, *Remedies in Administrative Law* (London 1976)

The unsatisfactory nature of the present position has been succinctly stated by the late Professor S A de Smith in his evidence to the Franks Committee [Cmnd 218, *Report of the Committee on Administrative Tribunals and Enquiries* (1957), Minutes of Evidence, Appendix I at 10]:—

'Until the Legislature intervenes, therefore, we shall continue to have two sets of remedies against the usurpation or abuse of power by administrative tribunals—remedies which

THE JUDICIAL REVIEW PROCEDURE • 469

overlap but do not coincide, which must be sought in wholly distinct forms of proceedings, which are overlaid with technicalities and fine distinctions, but which would conjointly cover a very substantial area of the existing field of judicial control. This state of affairs bears a striking resemblance to that which obtained when English civil procedure was still bedevilled by the old forms of action.'

... Our basic recommendation is that there should be a form of procedure to be entitled an 'application for judicial review'. Under cover of the application for judicial review a litigant should be able to obtain any of the prerogative orders, or, in appropriate circumstances, a declaration or an injunction. The litigant would have to specify in his application for judicial review which particular remedy or remedies he was seeking, but if he later desired to apply for a remedy for which he had not initially asked he would be able with the leave of the Court to amend his application. The vital difference, however, from the present system under Order 53 [of the Rules of the Supreme Court] would be that the litigant's choice of remedies in the Divisional Court would not be limited to the prerogative orders but would also (as mentioned above) include, in appropriate circumstances, a declaration or an injunction. Broadly speaking, the circumstances when it would be appropriate to ask for a declaration or an injunction under cover of an application for judicial review would be when the case involved an issue comparable to those in respect of which an application may be made for a prerogative order—*i.e.* when an issue of public law is involved. What we are recommending is only a method whereby the different prerogative orders and the declaration and the injunction may be available to the Divisional Court in the public law field.

It was assumed that the implementation of many of the recommendations in the Law Commission's report would be by legislation. However, the bulk of the proposals were in fact brought into being by an amendment in 1977 to Order 53 of the Rules of the Supreme Court, this amendment coming into force in 1978 (SI 1977/1955). Order 53 was further amended in 1980 (SI 1980/2000), and the Senior Courts Act 1981 affirmed and codified certain aspects of the amendments to Order 53. (This is a convenient point at which to explain why 'Rules of the Supreme Court' existed decades before the creation of the United Kingdom Supreme Court. Prior to the creation of that court, the term 'Supreme Court' was used to describe the system of courts comprising the Crown Court, the High Court, and the Court of Appeal. That usage has been dropped in favour of 'senior courts' now that the UK Supreme Court exists. The legislation dealing with those courts used to be known as the Supreme Court Act 1981, but was renamed the Senior Courts Act 1981 when the UK Supreme Court replaced the Appellate Committee of the House of Lords in 2009.)

As a result of the 1977–81 reforms, the application for judicial review—the forerunner of today's judicial review procedure—was introduced, thus making it possible to seek prerogative and ordinary remedies in the same proceedings (*ie* the application for judicial review). Applicants for judicial review under Order 53 had to comply with a number of conditions designed to protect public authorities against litigation which would unduly interfere with the discharge of their public functions. A defining feature of judicial review procedure, as the courts developed it, was that it was peppered with broad judicial discretions; these discretions, especially as to access to the review procedure and remedies, allowed courts to regulate review on a case-by-case basis and ensure that its operation did not unduly burden or interfere with the operation of public administration or wider public interests. For instance, applicants were required to obtain the leave of the court to seek judicial review (Senior Courts Act 1981, s 31(3)) by applying *ex parte* to a Crown Office judge—that is, a judge nominated to hear public law cases (Order 53, r 3(2))—and courts had a broad discretion as to whether to grant leave; applicants had to avoid delay in making applications by seeking leave 'promptly and in any event within three months from the date when grounds for the application first arose' unless there was a 'good reason' for non-compliance with that requirement (Order 53, r 4(1)), and the court had a discretion to refuse to grant leave or relief on certain grounds if there was 'undue delay' in making an application (Senior Courts Act 1981, s 31(6)).

A further obstacle faced by applicants for judicial review related to the somewhat attenuated ability, or perhaps more accurately willingness, of the courts to resolve disputes of fact in judicial review cases. Under RSC Order 53 it was open to applicants to seek discovery of documents and cross-examination on affidavits, but grant of such orders was subject to broad judicial discretion and courts were rarely minded to accede to such requests. For instance, in *R v. Secretary of State for the Environment, ex parte Islington London Borough Council* [1991] NPC 90, McCowan LJ said that 'unless the applicant in judicial review is in a position to assert that the evidence relied on by a Minister is false, or at least inaccurate, it is inappropriate to grant discovery in order to allow the applicant to check the accuracy of the evidence in question'. This type of approach to discovery was criticized by the Law Commission (Law Com No 226, *Administrative Law: Judicial Review and Statutory Appeal* (London 1994), Part VII), which called for a more liberal approach. Similarly, while it was possible for the courts on judicial review to permit cross-examination in order to test the veracity of evidence submitted by affidavit, Lord Diplock stated in *O'Reilly* v. *Mackman* [1983] 2 AC 237 at 282 that 'it will only be upon rare occasions that the interests of justice will require that leave be given for cross-examination of deponents on their affidavits in applications for judicial review'. Lord Diplock sought to justify this position by arguing that factual issues are rarely in dispute in judicial review and the court should be wary of illegitimately substituting its own factual findings for those of the primary decision-maker. These reasons were reinforced in *O'Reilly* and other cases by pragmatic concerns that reflect core justifications for a distinct procedure for review claims: cross-examination and disclosure could be time consuming and costly for authorities. Another reason often given for a cautious approach to ordering cross-examination or disclosure was that authorities are under a duty of candour in drafting affidavits, so that authorities could generally be trusted to accurately set out the relevant facts. However, it is self-evident that some situations will arise when cross-examination and/or disclosure are essential to ensure the just determination of review claims, while there are obvious dangers in courts becoming complacent in their reliance on the candour of authorities. As Smith [2001] *JR* 138 at 140 puts it, '[t]here must be cases'—such as *R* v. *Derbyshire County Council, ex parte The Times Supplements Ltd* (1991) 3 Admin LR 241, in which Watkins LJ concluded (at 252) *after* cross-examination that councillors' evidence as to the propriety of the purpose underlying their actions 'displayed an unworthy lack of candour'—'where insufficient extraneous evidence exists to demonstrate that a deponent is wrong, or dishonest. In such cases, what mechanism is there other than cross-examination to enable the shortcomings of an affidavit to be proved?'

It often suited litigants to initiate ordinary proceedings, for example framing their claim as one in private law, rather than making an application for judicial review, although the House of Lords did their best to close off this means of escape from review procedure in *O'Reilly* v. *Mackman* [1983] 2 AC 237. We turn to the so-called procedural dichotomy thereby established at 13.3; first, however, it remains to address the new judicial review procedure introduced by the CPR, and to consider the extent to which it differs from the position just described.

13.2.2 The nature of the judicial review procedure

Part 54 of the CPR entered into force on 2 October 2000 following Sir Jeffrey Bowman's *Review of the Crown Office List* (London 2000) (hereinafter 'the Bowman Report'), which advocated (with some modifications) the implementation of many of the recommendations made by the Law Commission in its 1994 review of judicial review procedure (Law Com No 226, *Administrative Law: Judicial Review and Statutory Appeals* (London 1994)) (hereinafter 'the Law Commission report'). Part 54 introduced a revised judicial review procedure. At the same time the Administrative Court was established within the Queen's Bench Division (*Practice Direction (Administrative Court: Establishment)* [2000] 1 WLR 1654) in light of Bowman's conclusion (at 19) that 'speed, certainty, efficiency, consistency and quality of decisions in public law cases can only be realised by having a dedicated office to administer cases and dedicated judicial resources to hear them'. Renaming the Crown Office List—that is, the list of Queen's Bench Division judges nominated to hear cases involving public law—the Administrative Court, said Bowman, would 'emphasise that [its] ... main business is public and administrative law and ... make this clear to users who are not familiar with the work at present done by the Crown Office List'. (It should be noted that the Upper Tribunal is also able to exercise powers of judicial review in certain circumstances; most notably in the majority of review cases concerning immigration. When it does so, it is governed by a procedural regime similar to that applicable to the Administrative Court. The Upper Tribunal is considered in ch 18.)

Bowman's review was prompted by growing pressure on the Crown Office List as a result of, *inter alia*, the increasing tendency to challenge public bodies' decisions and the then imminent activation of the Human Rights Act 1998. In light of this, two of Bowman's key objectives were to reduce delays in the Crown Office List and to promote the efficient use of judicial resources, and many of his recommendations related to practical matters concerning the organization of the proposed Administrative Court. Other recommendations, which were taken up, sought to recast the language of judicial review in terms consistent with the CPR: thus (adopting the recommendation in the Law Commission report at [8.3]) the prerogative remedies have lost their Latin names (see 12.1), while 'applicants' have become 'claimants', respondents are now 'defendants', and 'claims' rather than 'applications' for judicial review are now issued.

But what of the judicial review procedure itself? Following Bowman's recommendations, there have been some changes in this area, but much of the old regime remains: the standing requirement (on which see 14.7) set out in the Senior Courts Act 1981, s 31(3) is unchanged under the new system, as is the need to issue the claim promptly and in any event within three months (CPR 54.5(1)) (discussed at 14.4). However, while the requirement that the claimant obtains the leave—or permission, as it is now called—of the court is also still present, the nature of the permission stage is somewhat altered, and a Pre-Action Protocol has been introduced to require interaction between claimant and defendant prior to the issuing of the claim (see 14.2). The details of these conditions with which intending claimants must comply under the new judicial review procedure are addressed in ch 14; for present purposes, it is sufficient to observe that the preconditions which restricted the availability of judicial review under the Order 53 procedure are largely replicated under the Part 54 regime.

Similarly, the notion—implicit in the courts' previous reluctance, noted above, to permit discovery and cross-examination—that the resolution of factual disputes is not usually something to be undertaken in judicial review proceedings is perpetuated under the revised procedure. (In fact, the Bowman Report (at 17) took it as read that one of the hallmarks of the work of the then Crown Office List was that it involved 'matters which can normally be decided without the need to resolve issues of fact'.) Indeed, although it is Part 54 which sets out the distinguishing features of the judicial review procedure, CPR 54.1(2)(e) provides that "the judicial review procedure' means the Part 8 procedure as modified by [the relevant provisions of Part 54]'. Part 8, it should be noted, applies to claims which are 'unlikely to involve a substantial dispute of fact' (CPR 8.1(2)(a)). Thus, for example, in *Sher* v. *Chief Constable of Greater Manchester* [2010] EWHC 1859 (Admin), permission to seek judicial review of the lawfulness of the claimants' arrest and detention was declined because (*inter alia*) the claims raised 'potentially complex disputes of fact' (*per* Coulson J at [80]). It is clear that the new regime does little, if anything, to enhance the availability of disclosure—as discovery is now called—and cross-examination in judicial review proceedings. Thus, while disclosure is possible, it is not required unless the court specifically so orders (CPR Practice Direction 54A, paragraph 12.1) and, as Cornford [2000] 5 *Web JCLI* noted when Part 54 was being introduced, 'it is hardly to be expected that the CPR will encourage greater disclosure of documents in judicial review, when its basic purpose is to save court time and speed up litigation'. On the other hand, authorities may, especially in high profile litigation, come under pressure to voluntarily disclose relevant material: *eg R (Evans)* v. *Lord Chancellor* [2011] EWHC 1146, [2011] 3 All ER 594 at [5]. More importantly, as we shall see in the next section, claims under the HRA have proven a catalyst for greater judicial willingness to order cross-examination and disclosure, at least in claims under the Act.

It is important to note lastly that, despite the success of the Bowman reforms in encouraging early settlement of claims (see 14.2), the volume of judicial review litigation has remained a live issue and point of contention. In particular, litigation brought by 'repeat players' such as political pressure groups has raised the ire of government in recent years, whose plans may be disrupted and/or delayed by such challenges, while there is within government a perception that judicial review is being abused for political purposes. As is discussed at the beginning of ch 14, government responded to these concerns with two consultations, held in 2012 and 2013 respectively, on reform of judicial review, and which threatened major restrictions on judicial review, largely to be achieved through procedural reforms. While certain reforms were enacted, some of the more radical proposals did not make it into law due to a significant backlash from various groups including the higher judiciary. Thus, while some new restrictions have been implemented following the consultations, for example at the permission and remedies stages, the basic procedural framework put in place following Bowman remains largely intact.

13.2.3 The impact of human rights claims on judicial review procedure: alignment of ordinary and review procedures?

For much of the modern judicial review procedure's existence the vast bulk of claims streamed via the procedure have been made on orthodox common law grounds such as procedural fairness, *Wednesbury* unreasonableness, and illegality. However, the entry into force of the HRA added a significant new dimension to judicial review. The law under the HRA has its own distinctive features which arguably mark it out from review on common law grounds. Such claims are explicitly based in individual rights, which in turn requires detailed consideration of the facts of the individual right-holder's case. Scrutiny of the substance of administrative decisions and by association the facts underpinning them is generally more intensive under human rights doctrines such as proportionality than under the orthodox *Wednesbury* standard (see ch 8). These types of important differences have in turn had knock-on effects on how the review procedure applies to such claims.

Thus, while it remains the case that disclosure is not readily ordered in judicial review proceedings, there are clear signs of a rather more liberal approach in human rights cases, justified by reference to the distinctive nature of human rights claims, as evidenced by the important House of Lords decision in *Tweed* v. *Parades Commission for Northern Ireland* [2006] UKHL 53, [2007] 1 AC 650.

Tweed concerned a decision of the Parades Commission of Northern Ireland, made pursuant to its statutory powers to regulate public processions, to impose a much shorter route than that which had been proposed for a parade by a Protestant group through a mainly Catholic area in the town of Dunloy. The claimant sought judicial review on HRA grounds, arguing that the conditions imposed by the Commission constituted disproportionate restrictions upon the freedoms of religion, expression, and assembly. By way of defence, the Chairman of the Commission swore an affidavit summarizing certain documents, including police reports, assessing the likely implications of permitting the parade to take place along the route proposed by the organizers. In *Tweed*, the House of Lords considered the claimant's request that those documents should be disclosed.

Both Lords Carswell and Brown, giving the two leading speeches, recalled the orthodox approach that disclosure is much more tightly confined in judicial review proceedings than in ordinary proceedings. Over time the courts had developed the restrictive rule that disclosure should only be ordered if the party seeking disclosure of material on which written, affidavit evidence is based could show evidence suggesting that that written evidence was inaccurate, misleading, or incomplete in a material respect. However, as Lord Brown observed, the relevant authorities pre-dated the HRA, and the prevailing rule needed reconsideration in the light of this significant development.

Their Lordships recognized that proportionality challenges in particular had brought a new dimension to judicial review, which in turn justified the adoption of what Lord Carswell described as, 'a more flexible and less prescriptive principle, which judges the need for disclosure in accordance with the requirements of the particular case, taking into account the facts and circumstances' (at [32]). Lord Brown elaborated upon the new dimension that proportionality had brought to review, which in turn required a loosening of the approach to disclosure (at [53]):

> There can be no doubt that proportionality challenges have brought a new dimension to judicial review. In times past, when the *Wednesbury* principle ruled, decision-makers had only to have regard to all material considerations (the weight of which was entirely for them), to ignore immaterial ones, and to have reached decisions which were rational (as opposed to perverse) to be immune from challenge. Subject only to rationality, decisions could not be impugned on the ground that a wrong balance had been struck between competing considerations. Now of course, in certain cases at least, a more sophisticated and intensive process of review is required, in particular when investigating alleged violations of the qualified rights protected by the [European] Convention [on Human Rights].

Because of the greater intensity of review associated with proportionality 'a closer factual analysis of the justification for restrictions imposed [on rights], is required than used to be undertaken on judicial review challenges' (at [54]). As such, Lord Brown concurred in Lord Carswell's proposed move towards a more flexible approach, 'leaving the judges to decide upon the need for disclosure depending on the facts of each individual case' (at [56]–[57]):

> On this approach the courts may be expected to show a somewhat greater readiness than hitherto to order disclosure of the main documents underlying proportionality decisions, particularly in cases where only a comparatively narrow margin of discretion falls to be accorded to the decision-maker (a fortiori the main documents underlying decisions challenged on the ground that they violate an unqualified Convention right, for example under article 3).

However, it ought to be noted that both of their Lordships emphasized that disclosure would still remain relatively uncommon on review, and would not be required to be ordered whenever a claim entailed a proportionality challenge; rather, '[t]he proportionality issue forms part of the context in which the court has to consider whether it is necessary for fairly disposing of the case to order disclosure of such documents' (at [38]). Lord Brown in particular recalled the policy concerns underpinning the traditional judicial reluctance to order disclosure on review: '[C]ourts should continue to guard against what appear to be merely "fishing expeditions" for adventitious further grounds of challenge. It is not helpful, and is often both expensive and time-consuming, to flood the court with needless paper' (at [56]). Despite these warnings the case represents a break from the past and, at least in respect of human rights challenges, the courts will now be more willing to order disclosure. This is reflected in the outcome in *Tweed*, where the House of Lords ordered the defendant to provide the relevant documents to the lower court judge, who would then determine whether to order disclosure of the material to Mr Tweed, applying the new flexible approach enunciated by their Lordships.

Like Order 53, the CPR (see r 54.16(1) read with r 8.6(3)) allow cross-examination to be ordered in judicial review proceedings. While there is no suggestion that the new procedural rules generally make it easier to obtain cross-examination, a more liberal approach again applies in certain human rights cases. For instance, in *R (Wilkinson) v. Broadmoor Hospital* [2001] EWCA Civ 1545, [2002] 1 WLR 419, a mental patient sought judicial review of a decision to treat him forcibly against his will, alleging that this breached his rights under Articles 2, 3, and 8 ECHR, cross-examination of doctors was held to be appropriate in order to resolve a dispute of fact. Although in the subsequent case of *R (N) v. M* [2002] EWCA Civ 1789, [2003] 1 WLR 562 at [39], Dyson LJ, giving the judgment of the Court of Appeal, said that *Wilkinson* should not be 'regarded as a charter for routine applications to the court for oral evidence in human rights cases generally', it is clear that some such cases will call for the giving of oral evidence and cross-examination. An excellent example of application of a more liberal approach in human rights claims is provided by *R (Al-Sweady) v. Secretary of State for Defence* [2009] EWHC 2387 (Admin), [2010] HRLR 2, which arose from a judicial review claim concerning the alleged ill-treatment and murder of Iraqi civilians by British troops in Iraq. The allegations centred upon Articles 2, 3, and 5 ECHR and, as Scott Baker LJ, giving the judgment of the court, put it at [7], raised 'complicated legal and factual issues' concerning the death of the person in relation to whom the murder allegation arose and the way in which some of the claimants had been treated while detained by British forces. Given the seriousness of the matters raised and the particular fundamentality of the rights concerned—including the rights to life and not to be subjected to torture or inhuman or degrading treatment—it was, he said at [26], 'incumbent on [the] court to consider with great care and to apply intense scrutiny' to any claim that those rights had been infringed. This made it appropriate to cross-examine witnesses—in turn making it, as the judge explained at [27], 'vital for full disclosure to occur as otherwise the evidence of [the] witnesses could not be effectively challenged and appraised with the consequence that the truth would not have been discovered'.

In similar vein, and continuing this trend, in *R (A) v. Chief Constable of Kent Constabulary* [2013] EWCA Civ 1706 at [58], the Court of Appeal said: 'Hearing live evidence and making findings may ... be necessary when determining whether there has been a breach of one of the rights under the ECHR.' Interestingly this case also suggested such an approach may be necessary where the claim is a common law one concerning jurisdictional facts; suggesting potential at least for the trend towards liberalization in human rights law to spill over to at least some classes of common law claim—not least as there are increasingly warm judicial attitudes to review for factual error at common law: *E v. Secretary of State for the Home Department* [2004] EWCA Civ 49, [2004] QB 1044 (see 2.4).

Further, as moves towards adopting context-sensitive, rights-based substantive review and proportionality at common law intensify (see ch 8), there will be increased need and pressure for the courts to consider extending the more liberal approach to disclosure and cross-examination to these classes of common law case, given that the same sorts of issues and legal questions will be arising at common law as in human rights law. We find early hints at such developments in the Supreme Court decision in *R (Bourgass) v. Secretary of State for Justice* [2015] UKSC 54, [2015] 1 WLR 457. In that case the Court, at [126], emphasized that in the light of decisions such as *Pham v. Secretary of State for the Home Department* [2015] UKSC 19, [2015] 1 WLR 1591 (discussed in 8.5) substantive review at common law now requires 'sensitivity to context', attention to the 'nature of any interests engaged and the gravity of any adverse effects on those interests', and 'cogent justification' for interferences with such interests; in other words, there are close similarities with the structured proportionality method applied in human rights law. Against this background the Court observed, at [126], that while 'judicial review does not usually require the resolution of disputes of fact, or cross-examination, this is not because they lie beyond the scope of the jurisdiction. Judicial review is a sufficiently flexible form of procedure to enable the court to deal with the situation before it as required' (the Court then cited *Wilkinson*). These warmer attitudes to resolving questions of fact within common law review proceedings are seemingly a long way from Lord Diplock's chillier attitudes in *O'Reilly* (discussed earlier). Thus, as the gaps between human rights law and common law review are reduced, at least in a few pockets of common law, such as where basic rights are engaged, so too does it seem the gaps in procedural treatment of claims will also begin to close. This in turn illustrates the intimate connection between substantive law and procedure.

Where does this leave us? If one focuses on the basic procedural framework, and specifically the rules of court, then with the exception of alterations to the permission stage (considered at 14.2) and a number of other 'tweaks' the judicial review procedure that obtains today shares much in common with its predecessor. In particular, the CPR preserve the character of the claim for judicial review as a distinct procedural model which is deliberately different from that which applies to ordinary proceedings. This reflects the conclusion reached by Bowman (at 60) that '[a] separate procedure is necessary ... because of the special nature of judicial review and the need for speed and flexibility'. It is hardly surprising, therefore, that some claimants seek to litigate public law matters by issuing claims for injunctions or declarations in ordinary proceedings to escape the strictures of the review procedure, thereby gaining access to more generous provision for cross-examination and disclosure, and avoiding the need to obtain permission and comply with very short time limits. We consider, in the next section, the extent to which claimants raising 'public law' matters are able to evade the judicial review procedure.

But while the formal procedural framework of review is characterized by a high degree of continuity over time, if one looks to the *practice* of judicial review, emergent trends in disclosure and cross-examination have the potential to bring review procedure, *at least as it applies to human rights claims*, closer to ordinary procedure. As was discussed previously, this reflects the distinctive nature of the law under the HRA. In particular, like private law claims in tort or contract, which are streamed routinely via ordinary procedure, human rights law is based on ideas of individual, personal rights. Further, as was pointed out in *Wilkinson* at [24], [56]–[59], [62] human rights claims may often cover the same terrain as and be made concurrently with claims in tort, meaning it makes sense for the review procedure to mimic ordinary procedure. In *Wilkinson* itself the judges observed that the claim could have been brought as a tortious claim for battery through ordinary procedure, so the claimant should not be disadvantaged procedurally simply because they happened to bring the claim in human rights law. In addition, and importantly, proportionality analysis often requires detailed judicial scrutiny of executive decisions, and the factual premises which underpin them. More generally, one might question why claims concerning the most fundamental of individual rights should be subject to all of the safeguards for the benefit of authorities which characterize the judicial review procedure, and disadvantage claimants.

Though these trends have so far been limited to claims under the HRA, as the higher courts show warmer attitudes towards review for factual error at common law, and seek increasingly to align substantive review across common law and under the HRA where basic interests are at stake, we are likely to witness changes in the procedural treatment of at least some classes of common law review claims, as foreshadowed by *Bourgass*. It is important to emphasize, however, that this is not (yet) a more general trend across common law review claims. For example, the courts have recently emphasized that cross-examination remains rare on review, and declined to allow cross-examination of officials even in cases where the issues included what the relevant officials knew and thought when they exercised their powers: *R (CC)* v. *Commissioner of Police for the Metropolis* [2011] EWHC 3316, [2012] 1 WLR 1913 at [28]. Indeed, many would maintain that courts must be cautious in this respect. If cross-examination and/or disclosure were increasingly ordered in review proceedings on common law grounds this could operate to seriously undermine the policy concerns which underpin and justify a distinct public law procedure. In a contemporary statement of principle Lord Neuberger MR, emphasizing that cross-examination should be confined to the 'most exceptional case', reiterated these very concerns (*R (Z)* v. *Croydon London Borough Council* [2011] EWCA Civ 59, [2011] PTSR 748 at [24]):

[J]udicial review involves a judge reviewing a decision, not making it; if the judge receives evidence so as to make fresh findings of fact for himself, he is likely to make his own decision rather than to review the original decision. Also, if judges regularly allow witnesses and cross-examination in judicial review cases, the court time and legal costs involved in such cases will spiral.

13.3 When must the judicial review procedure be used?

13.3.1 Procedural exclusivity

There was a time when the courts actively endorsed the tactic of seeking ordinary remedies instead of prerogative remedies, so as to avoid the restrictions which obtain when the latter are sought. In *Barnard* v. *National Dock Labour Board* [1953] 2 QB 18 at 41, for example, Denning LJ considered it highly desirable that litigants should adopt such a strategy in order that the capacity of the courts to enforce the law was not circumscribed by the limitations applicable to the prerogative remedies:

> It is axiomatic that when a statutory tribunal sits to administer justice, it must act in accordance with the law. Parliament clearly so intended. If the tribunal does not observe the law, what is to be done? The remedy by certiorari is hedged round by limitations and may not be available. Why then should not the court intervene by declaration and injunction? If it cannot so intervene, it would mean that the tribunal could disregard the law, which is a thing no one can do in this country.

There is, however, an obvious difficulty with this view, at least today. The existence of a distinct judicial review procedure is founded upon particular policy considerations, such as the need to erect safeguards (*eg* permission and strict time limits) to prevent litigation from unduly interfering with agencies' discharge of their public functions and the desirability of swiftly resolving questions as to the legality of administrative action. Yet, if litigants have a free choice between ordinary and judicial review proceedings, they will (for the reasons considered earlier) usually choose the former, in turn preventing the realization of the policy objectives of the latter. The judicial review procedure is specially designed for the resolution of disputes concerning the discharge by public bodies of their public functions, and it seems to follow that the litigation of such matters should be by way of a claim for judicial review.

The House of Lords, in its landmark decision in *O'Reilly* v. *Mackman*, found the logic of this argument compelling, notwithstanding that, as we will see, its implications posed enormous practical difficulties for intending litigants. (Although Lord Diplock refers to the Order 53 procedure in his speech in *O'Reilly*, we have already seen that many of the key features of that procedure are repeated in CPR Part 54. It should also be noted that Lord Diplock refers to the Supreme Court Act 1981; as mentioned earlier, this is now known as the Senior Courts Act 1981.)

O'Reilly v. Mackman [1983] 2 AC 237
House of Lords

The appellants, who were all prisoners at Hull Prison, wished to challenge decisions reached by the Prison's Board of Visitors in relation to allegations that the appellants had committed breaches of the Prison Rules 1964. It was argued that the rules of natural justice had not been

complied with by the Board and the appellants sought declarations that the findings and consequent penalties were therefore null and void. They proceeded not by way of an application for judicial review under Order 53 but, instead, by ordinary proceedings begun by writ (or, in one of the four
cases involved, originating summons). It was argued that the matter ought to have been pursued by
means of an application for judicial review, and an application was made to strike out the statements
of claim (and the originating summons) on the ground that they were an abuse of the process of the
court. The application was refused by Peter Pain J at first instance but the Court of Appeal allowed
an appeal by the Board. An appeal from that decision was made to the House of Lords.

Lord Diplock

... My Lords, it is not contested that if the allegations set out in the originating summons or
statements of claim are true each of the appellants would have had a remedy obtainable by the
procedure of an application for judicial review under R.S.C., Ord. 53; but to obtain that remedy,
whether it took the form of an order of certiorari to quash the board's award or a declaration of
its nullity, would have required the leave of the court under R.S.C., Ord. 53, r. 3 [see now CPR
54.4]. That judicial review lies against an award of the board of visitors of a prison made in the
exercise of their disciplinary functions was established by the judgment of the Court of Appeal
(overruling a Divisional Court) in *Reg. v. Board of Visitors of Hull Prison, Ex parte St. Germain*
[1979] Q. B. 425: a decision that was, in my view, clearly right and has not been challenged in the
instant appeals by the respondents.

In the *St. Germain* case, the only remedy that had been sought was certiorari to quash the
decision of the board of visitors; but the alternative remedy of a declaration of nullity if the court
considered it to be just and convenient would also have been available upon an application for
judicial review under R.S.C., Ord. 53 after the replacement of the old rule by the new rule in 1977.
In the instant cases, which were commenced after the new rule came into effect (but before the
coming into force of section 31 of the Supreme Court Act 1981), certiorari would unquestionably
have been the more appropriate remedy, since rule 5(4) of the Prison Rules 1964, which provides
for remission of sentence up to a maximum of one-third, stipulates that the 'rule shall have effect
subject to any disciplinary award of forfeiture ...'. Prison rule 56, however, expressly empowers the
Secretary of State to remit a disciplinary award and, since he would presumably do so in the case
of a disciplinary award that had been declared by the High Court to be a nullity, such a declaration
would achieve, though less directly, the same result in practice as quashing the award by certiorari.

So no question arises as to the 'jurisdiction' of the High Court to grant to each of the appellants relief by way of a declaration in the terms sought, if they succeeded in establishing the facts
alleged in their respective statements of claim or originating summons and the court considered
a declaration to be an appropriate remedy. All that is at issue in the instant appeal is the procedure by which such relief ought to be sought. Put in a single sentence the question for your
Lordships is: whether in 1980 after R.S.C., Ord. 53 in its new form, adopted in 1977, had come
into operation it was an abuse of the process of the court to apply for such declarations by using
the procedure laid down in the Rules for proceedings begun by writ or by originating summons
instead of using the procedure laid down by Ord. 53 for an application for judicial review of the
awards of forfeiture of remission of sentence made against them by the board which the appellants are seeking to impugn?

Having formulated the question thus, Lord Diplock (at 275) considered whether the matter
raised in the case should be characterized as one of public or private law:

It is not, and it could not be, contended that the decision of the board awarding him forfeiture of
remission had infringed or threatened to infringe any right of the appellant derived from private

law, whether a common law right or one created by a statute. Under the Prison Rules remission of sentence is not a matter of right but of indulgence. So far as private law is concerned all that each appellant had was a legitimate expectation, based upon his knowledge of what is the general practice, that he would be granted the maximum remission, permitted by rule 5(2) of the Prison Rules, of one third of his sentence if by that time no disciplinary award of forfeiture of remission had been made against him. So the second thing to be noted is that none of the appellants had any remedy in private law.

In public law, as distinguished from private law, however, such legitimate expectation gave to each appellant a sufficient interest to challenge the legality of the adverse disciplinary award made against him by the board on the ground that in one way or another the board in reaching its decision had acted outwith the powers conferred upon it by the legislation under which it was acting; and such grounds would include the board's failure to observe the rules of natural justice: which means no more than to act fairly towards him in carrying out their decision-making process, and I prefer so to put it.

Thus, Lord Diplock's view was that the matter was one of public law. Did this mean that it could only be litigated by means of (what is now known as) the claim for judicial review? In addressing this question, his Lordship observed (at 279) that, prior to the 1977–81 reforms, the use of Order 53 entailed 'considerable procedural disadvantage'— in particular the unavailability of disclosure and cross-examination. His Lordship said (at 282) that in those circumstances

it could not be regarded as an abuse of the process of the court, before the amendments made to Order 53 in 1977, to proceed against the authority by an action for a declaration of nullity of the impugned decision with an injunction to prevent the authority from acting on it, instead of applying for an order of certiorari; and this despite the fact that, by adopting this course, the plaintiff evaded the safeguards imposed in the public interest against groundless, unmeritorious or tardy attacks upon the validity of decisions made by public authorities in the field of public law.

But, he said (at 282–3), the position was different following the reforms of 1977–81:

Those disadvantages, which formerly might have resulted in an applicant's being unable to obtain justice in an application for certiorari under Order 53, have all been removed by the new Order introduced in 1977. There is express provision in the new rule 8 for interlocutory applications for discovery of documents, the administration of interrogatories and the cross-examination of deponents to affidavits. Discovery of documents (which may often be a time-consuming process) is not automatic as in an action begun by writ, but otherwise Order 24 applies to it and discovery is obtainable upon application whenever, and to the extent that, the justice of the case requires [see now CPR 54.16 and Practice Direction 54A, para 12.1, on disclosure]; similarly Order 26 applies to applications for interrogatories [see now CPR 18.1 on orders for further information]; and to applications for cross-examination of deponents to affidavits Ord. 28, r. 2(3) applies [see now CPR 8.6(3)]. This is the rule that deals with evidence in actions begun by originating summons and permits oral cross-examination on affidavit evidence wherever the justice of the case requires. It may well be that for the reasons given by Lord Denning M.R. in *George v. Secretary of State for the Environment* (1979) 77 L.G.R. 689, it will only be upon rare occasions that the interests of justice will require that leave be given for cross-examination of deponents on their affidavits in applications for judicial review. This is because of the nature of the issues that normally arise upon judicial review. The facts, except where the claim that a decision was invalid on the ground that the statutory tribunal or public authority that made the decision failed to comply with the procedure prescribed by the legislation under which it was acting or failed to observe the fundamental rules of natural justice or fairness, can seldom be a matter of relevant dispute upon an application for judicial review, since the tribunal or authority's findings of fact, as distinguished from the legal consequences of the facts that they have found, are not open to review by the court in the exercise of its supervisory powers except on the principles laid down in *Edwards v. Bairstow* [1956] A.C. 14, 36; and to allow cross-examination presents the court with a temptation, not always easily resisted, to substitute its own view of the facts for that of the decision-making body upon whom the exclusive jurisdiction to determine facts has been conferred by Parliament. Nevertheless having regard to a possible misunderstanding of what was said by Geoffrey Lane L.J. in *Reg. v. Board of Visitors of Hull Prison, Ex parte St. Germain (No. 2)* [1979] 1 W.L.R 1401, 1410 your Lordships may think this an appropriate occasion on which to emphasise that whatever may have been the position before the rule was altered in 1977 in all proceedings for judicial review that have been started since that date the grant of leave to cross-examine deponents upon applications for judicial review is governed by the same principles as it is in actions begun by originating summons; it should be allowed whenever the justice of the particular case so requires.

Another handicap under which an applicant for a prerogative order under Order 53 formerly laboured (though it would not have affected the appellants in the instant cases even if they had brought their actions before the 1977 alteration to Order 53) was that a claim for damages for breach of a right in private law of the applicant resulting from an invalid decision of a public authority could not be made in an application under Order 53. Damages could only be claimed in a separate action begun by writ; whereas in an action so begun they could be claimed as additional relief as well as a declaration of nullity of the decision from which the damage claimed had flowed. Rule 7 of the new Order 53 [see now CPR 54.3(2)] permits the applicant for judicial review to include in the statement in support of his application for leave a claim for damages and empowers the court to award damages on the hearing of the application if satisfied that such damages could have been awarded to him in an action begun by him by writ at the time of the making of the application.

Finally rule 1 of the new Order 53 [see now CPR 54.3(1)] enables an application for a declaration or an injunction to be included in an application for judicial review. This was not previously the case; only prerogative orders could be obtained in proceedings under Order 53. Declarations or injunctions were obtainable only in actions begun by writ or originating summons.

Lord Diplock concluded by considering whether the effect of the reforms was to make it acceptable or even desirable to require claimants wishing to litigate public law matters to utilize the claim for judicial review:

My Lords, Order 53 does not expressly provide that procedure by application for judicial review shall be the exclusive procedure available by which the remedy of a declaration or injunction may be obtained for infringement of rights that are entitled to protection under public law; nor does section 31 of the Supreme Court Act 1981. There is great variation between individual cases that fall within Order 53 and the Rules Committee and subsequently the legislature were, I think, for this reason content to rely upon the express and the inherent power of the High Court, exercised upon a case to case basis, to prevent abuse of its process whatever might be the form taken by that abuse. Accordingly, I do not think that your Lordships would be wise to use this as an occasion to lay down categories of cases in which it would necessarily always be an abuse to seek in an action begun by writ or originating summons a remedy against infringement of rights of the individual that are entitled to protection in public law.

The position of applicants for judicial review has been drastically ameliorated by the new Order 53. It has removed all those disadvantages, particularly in relation to discovery, that were manifestly unfair to them and had, in many cases, made applications for prerogative orders an inadequate remedy if justice was to be done ...

Now that those disadvantages to applicants have been removed and all remedies for infringements of rights protected by public law can be obtained upon an application for judicial review, as can also remedies for infringements of rights under private law if such infringements should also be involved, it would in my view as a general rule be contrary to public policy, and as such an abuse of the process of the court, to permit a person seeking to establish that a decision of a public authority infringed rights to which he was entitled to protection under public law to proceed by way of an ordinary action and by this means to evade the provisions of Order 53 for the protection of such authorities.

My Lords, I have described this as a general rule; for though it may normally be appropriate to apply it by the summary process of striking out the action, there may be exceptions, particularly where the invalidity of the decision arises as a collateral issue in a claim for infringement of a right of the plaintiff arising under private law, or where none of the parties objects to the adoption of the procedure by writ or originating summons. Whether there should be other exceptions should, in my view, at this stage in the development of procedural public law, be left to be decided on a case to case basis—a process that your Lordships will be continuing in the next case in which judgment is to be delivered today [*Cocks* v. *Thanet District Council* [1983] 2 AC 286].

In the instant cases where the only relief sought is a declaration of nullity of the decisions of a statutory tribunal, the Board of Visitors of Hull Prison, as in any other case in which a similar declaration of nullity in public law is the only relief claimed, I have no hesitation, in agreement with the Court of Appeal, in holding that to allow the actions to proceed would be an abuse of the process of the court. They are blatant attempts to avoid the protections for the defendants for which Order 53 provides.

I would dismiss these appeals.

Lords Fraser, Keith, Bridge, and Brightman agreed with Lord Diplock. Appeal dismissed.

It is noteworthy that Lord Diplock went to considerable lengths in his speech, by tracing the development of the procedural rules applicable when the prerogative orders are sought and, in particular, contrasting the positions which obtained before and after the 1977–81 reforms, to try to justify the principle of procedural exclusivity which he articulated. This was, no doubt, due in part to the fact that, as Lord Diplock himself acknowledged, there was nothing in RSC Order 53—just as there is nothing in CPR Part 54 now—which *required* the application for judicial review to be regarded as an exclusive procedure. Indeed, the Law Commission report on which the 1977 reforms were based had rejected the idea of exclusivity (Law Com No 73, *Remedies in Administrative Law* (London 1976) at [34], [58]), preferring to preserve litigant autonomy. The development of the exclusivity principle in *O'Reilly* therefore amounts to what Forsyth [1985] *CLJ* 415 at 422 calls 'a novel and rather cavalier use of the abuse of process jurisdiction'. However, although Lord Diplock sought to justify the exclusivity principle by reference to the fact that the 1977–81 reforms had 'drastically ameliorated' the position of claimants, it is undeniable that those using the judicial review procedure continue to face disadvantages such as very short time limits and the reluctance, in practice, of courts to resolve factual disputes on judicial review.

QUESTION

- Do you agree with Lord Diplock's argument that the creation of the exclusivity principle was necessary to preserve the integrity of the procedure for judicial review and of the policy objectives underlying that procedure?

Once the exclusivity principle had been set out in *O'Reilly*, the courts were obliged in subsequent decisions to set about the task of deciding how to distinguish between private law issues, which could be litigated in ordinary proceedings, and public law issues, which had to be pursued by issuing (what is now called) a claim for judicial review. Unsurprisingly, this created considerable difficulties not only for the courts but also for intending litigants, who were left unsure as to which procedure they ought to use, and who risked their claims being struck out as an abuse of process if they chose the wrong procedure. This apparent elevation of form over substance led Jolowicz [1983] *CLJ* 15 at 16 (who was far from alone in criticizing *O'Reilly*: for further criticism see, *inter alios*, Wade (1985) 101 *LQR* 180; Forsyth [1985] *CLJ* 415) to comment:

> It is, on the face of things, astonishing that any court, let alone the highest in the land, should spend any time at all on a question [concerning only the procedure by which relief should be sought], and it is still more astonishing that it should receive the answer given by the House of Lords. It is now well over 100 years since the original Judicature Acts were passed and it is all but 100 years since Bowen LJ felt able to say that 'it is a well-established principle that the object of Courts is to decide the rights of the parties, and not to punish them for the mistakes they make in the conduct of their cases by deciding them otherwise than in accordance with their rights': *Cropper* v. *Smith* (1884) 26 Ch D 700 at 710. It appears that the learned Lord Justice was mistaken.

However, others (see, *eg* Law Com No 226, *Administrative Law: Judicial Review and Statutory Appeals* (London 1994) at [3.2]–[3.5], which did not go as far as to recommend the abolition of the exclusivity rule) have emphasized the need to balance the rule's policy objective, of giving effect to the protections afforded to public authorities by the judicial review procedure, against the interest in securing justice in individual cases. The difficulty, of course, lies in determining the extent to which the strictures of *O'Reilly* may be tempered without undermining its purpose, a tension which was adverted to by Laws J in *R* v. *Ministry of Agriculture Fisheries and Food, ex parte Lower Burytown Farms Ltd* [1999] Eu LR 129 at 137:

> *O'Reilly* has been much discussed both in academic writing and in later judicial decisions ... There have been two countervailing interests. On the one hand, the *O'Reilly* principle has given rise to much time-consuming and expensive debate in the courts as to what is and what is not a purely public law case, fit only for judicial review proceedings. On the other, the rule has not only provided necessary protections for bodies making decisions on the public's behalf which often affect many third parties not before the court, but in general terms has released the administration of public law from the usually inappropriate and cumbersome procedures designed for the resolution of private law disputes, enabling the courts to develop the public law jurisdiction in the swift and convenient procedural milieu of Ord 53 of the Rules of the Supreme Court.

In the years since *O'Reilly* was decided the courts have sought to balance these two considerations by articulating exceptions to the principle of procedural exclusivity while continuing to acknowledge the importance of the policy upon which it is founded. In the following sections we address the principal exceptions articulated by the courts, after which we consider to what extent, in light of these exceptions and other recent developments, a principle of procedural exclusivity can still be said to exist.

First, however, it should be noted that circumstances may arise in which claimants wish to use the judicial review procedure but are not allowed to do so. For instance, in *R* v. *East*

Berkshire Health Authority, ex parte Walsh [1985] QB 152 a senior nursing officer sought to impugn the validity of his dismissal in judicial review proceedings. Had he secured a quashing order, he would have kept his job—the voidness of the dismissal meaning that he had never in law been dismissed—whereas, had he relied exclusively upon proceedings before an employment tribunal or for breach of contract, he may have had to settle for compensation in the event of a finding of (respectively) unfair dismissal or breach of contract. Sir John Donaldson MR, expressing a view shared by May and Purchas LJJ, considered that the claim could not be pursued by means of judicial review, explaining (at 165) that:

> The ordinary employer is free to act in breach of his contracts of employment and if he does so his employee will acquire certain private law rights and remedies in damages for wrongful dismissal, compensation for unfair dismissal, an order for reinstatement or re-engagement and so on. Parliament can underpin the position of public authority employees by directly restricting the freedom of the public authority to dismiss, thus giving the employee 'public law' rights and at least making him a potential candidate for administrative law remedies. Alternatively it can require the authority to contract with its employees on specified terms with a view to the employee acquiring 'private law' rights under the terms of the contract of employment. If the authority fails or refuses to thus create 'private law' rights for the employee, the employee will have 'public law' rights to compel compliance, the remedy being mandamus requiring the authority so to contract or a declaration that the employee has those rights. If, however, the authority [as in this case] gives the employee the required contractual protection, a breach of that contract is not a matter of 'public law' and gives rise to no administrative law remedies.

It follows that, in circumstances where the matter is purely one of private law, far from it being an abuse of process to issue a claim against a public authority in ordinary proceedings (see *Davy* v. *Spelthorne Borough Council* [1984] AC 262), the claim *must* be issued in such proceedings. The general question concerning the circumstances in which prospective defendants are subject to public law duties is considered in ch 4.

13.3.2 Waiver

Although, as we have just seen, some claimants may wish, but be unable, to use judicial review proceedings, the obverse problem is more common. It is therefore necessary to consider to what extent, post-*O'Reilly*, claimants may issue claims in ordinary proceedings where their claim relates, in whole or in part, to matters of public law. In fact, the business of articulating exceptions to the exclusivity rule began in *O'Reilly* itself. Lord Diplock considered that there would be no need to enforce the rule in circumstances where 'none of the parties objects' to the use of ordinary proceedings, a view which Lord Bridge appeared to endorse in *Gillick* v. *West Norfolk and Wisbech Area Health Authority* [1986] AC 112 at 192. This reflects the fact that the purpose of exclusivity is to protect public authorities by ensuring that the safeguards inherent in the judicial review procedure operate: if the public authority defendant does not wish to insist on those safeguards, there may seem to be no need to insist upon the use of the judicial review procedure. However it may be argued that the protections conferred by the judicial review procedure are for the benefit not merely of public authorities but also of the public itself, which has an interest in certainty as to the legal status of administrative action which the procedural restrictions—especially the short time limit—promote. On this view, a bilateral agreement between the claimant and the public authority defendant to waive the protection of the judicial review procedure should be regarded as ineffective if it is prejudicial to the interests of the wider public. It is submitted that this is the better view, since it captures the truth that while the *effect* of the procedural restrictions is to protect public authorities, the *purpose* behind this policy is to benefit not those authorities—which as public bodies have no interests of their own—but the general public. This view perhaps receives implicit support from Lord Woolf MR in *Trustees of the Dennis Rye Pension Fund* v. *Sheffield City Council* [1998] 1 WLR 840 at 849, who remarked that '[i]f the choice [of procedure] has no significant disadvantages for the parties, *the public* or the court, then it should not normally be regarded as constituting an abuse' (emphasis added).

13.3.3 Resolution of factual disputes

It is clear that in the *Dennis Rye* case, an excerpt from which appears at 13.3.5, one of the factors which disposed the Court of Appeal towards allowing the use of ordinary proceedings was that factual matters were in dispute which could more easily be resolved through the use of that procedure. This approach recognizes that claimants are, in practice, disadvantaged by the judicial review procedure where factual disputes need to be resolved, Lord Diplock's contrary assertions in *O'Reilly* notwithstanding. As the Supreme Court recognizes, the review procedure is 'not well suited to the determination of disputed questions of fact' (*R (A)* v. *Croydon LBC* [2009] UKSC 8, [2009] 1 WLR 2557 at [33]).

However, the courts have not always been consistent on this point. In *Trim* v. *North Dorset DC* [2010] EWCA Civ 1446, Carnwath LJ, at [24]–[25], did not consider that existence of a factual dispute constituted a reason for deviating from the exclusivity principle, emphasizing that judicial review can accommodate factual disputes when they arise. Perhaps this different attitude reflects the increased willingness, in recent times, to allow for disclosure and/or cross-examination in review proceedings when necessary (albeit it must be recalled that this trend has been limited to a narrow band of cases) (see 13.2.3).

As such, while, in the light of *Trim*, existence of a factual dispute may not in itself be sufficient to convince a court of the need to deviate from the exclusivity principle, it is difficult to view the consideration as irrelevant and cases such as *Dennis Rye* suggest the factor may well, *in combination with other factors*, point away from requiring a claimant to proceed via review. The human rights cases discussed at 13.3.10 tend to reinforce the continued relevance of this factor, *Trim* notwithstanding.

13.3.4 Defensive use of public law arguments

It has never been doubted that the rule of procedural exclusivity should to some extent yield in the face of collateral challenge. Indeed, Lord Diplock recognized as much in his speech in *O'Reilly* v. *Mackman* ([1983] 2 AC 237 at 285) itself. Moreover, in *Boddington* v. *British Transport Police* [1999] 2 AC 143, considered in detail at 3.4, the House of Lords held that, unless the relevant legislation provides expressly or impliedly to the contrary (see, *eg R* v.

Wicks [1998] AC 92), the rule of law itself demands that a defendant should be able to challenge collaterally the validity of the offence with which he is charged. Procedural exclusivity thus gives way to collateral challenge in criminal proceedings.

Earlier, it had been established in *Wandsworth London Borough Council* v. *Winder* [1985] AC 461 that the same principle applies in civil proceedings. The local authority brought proceedings against one of its tenants for arrears of rent. In response, the tenant argued that the council was applying an improper rental rate to the flat, because certain resolutions which had purported to raise the applicable rent were in law invalid. The council argued that, by raising this point, the tenant was committing an abuse of process: the validity of the resolutions was clearly a public law matter, and could be raised only via judicial review. The House of Lords did not agree. Although Lord Fraser (who curiously, and it is submitted wrongly (see further Beatson (1987) 103 *LQR* 34 at 58), did not characterize this challenge as 'collateral') acknowledged the existence of sound policy reasons for the *O'Reilly* principle, he considered (at 509) that

> [i]t would ... be a very strange use of language to describe the respondent's behaviour in relation to this litigation as an abuse or misuse by him of the process of the court. He did not select the procedure to be adopted. He is merely seeking to defend proceedings brought against him by the appellants.

It was held in *Welsh Water* v. *Corus UK Ltd* [2006] EWHC 1183 (Ch) (reversed on a different point by the Court of Appeal: [2007] EWCA Civ 285) that the *Wandsworth* principle is not confined to situations in which a defendant wishes to raise the validity of an administrative act against a claimant public body: it extends to cases between private parties in which one wishes to defend itself by arguing that an administrative act undertaken by a third party is invalid. It has also been accepted that a public authority may—somewhat counter-intuitively—plead its own public law illegality in defence of a private law claim brought against it. Thus, in *Charles Terence Estates* v. *Cornwall Council* [2012] EWCA Civ 1439, [2013] 1 WLR 466, where a private landlord rented property to an authority and brought proceedings against the authority for unpaid rents it was open to the authority, in the course of civil proceedings, to argue that its conclusion of the rental agreements, on which the landlord's claim rested, were *ultra vires* the authority's own powers and thus void.

Although it is well-established that public law decisions and actions may be raised defensively, difficult questions remain about the further circumstances in which the exclusivity principle yields. In considering this matter, it is helpful to draw a broad distinction between two situations, the first concerning circumstances in which the existence of a private law right is dependent upon the exercise of some public law function, the second relating to situations in which action taken under public law powers affects private law rights which are already acknowledged to exist.

13.3.5 Private law rights dependent upon public law

The House of Lords confronted the first of these scenarios on the same day as its decision in *O'Reilly* was handed down. *Cocks* v. *Thanet District Council* [1983] 2 AC 286 concerned a claim for (*inter alia*) a declaration to the effect that a local authority was in breach of its statutory duty under the Housing (Homeless Persons) Act 1977 to provide the claimant with permanent accommodation. Their Lordships considered that, under the statutory scheme, the individual *could* acquire enforceable private law rights to permanent accommodation, but only if the local authority first concluded (*inter alia*) that he was not intentionally homeless—an exercise of public law discretion which, under *O'Reilly*, should have been challenged by way of judicial review. This case, which appeared to indicate a judicial appetite for surgically separating public and private law for procedural purposes, needs reconsideration in light of two subsequent decisions.

O'Rourke v. *Camden London Borough Council* [1988] AC 188 concerned the duty of a local authority under s 63(1) of the Housing Act 1985 to provide temporary accommodation to the claimant if it had reason to believe that he may be homeless and have a priority need. The claimant, having been evicted from accommodation provided pursuant to s 63(1) but not rehoused pending determination of his application for permanent accommodation, argued that the council had a duty to house him, breach of which could lead to liability in damages in private law. Lord Hoffmann, who gave the only reasoned speech, rejected this contention, but in doing so departed from the reasoning of the House of Lords in *Cocks*. In particular, Lord Hoffmann felt that Lord Bridge had been wrong in *Cocks* to conclude that private law rights would arise once the local authority had made a decision in the individual's favour. Lord Hoffmann was of the view that Lord Bridge's reasoning was fatally flawed by his failure to examine whether, as a matter of statutory construction, Parliament had intended to create a duty in private law sounding in damages. Lord Hoffmann concluded that the homelessness provisions in the 1985 Act (which were the same as those in the 1977 Act which were at stake in *Cocks*) were not intended to create such a duty; it followed that no private law right was or ever could have been in issue, and therefore the matter was one exclusively of public law.

The general thrust of Lord Hoffmann's speech in *O'Rourke* is to the effect that courts should reflect carefully before concluding that breaches of statutory provisions imposing duties in public law may give rise to private law rights of action. His Lordship refused to reach this conclusion in relation to the homelessness provisions because, *inter alia*, they formed part of a social welfare scheme which aimed to benefit the public generally, not just the homeless, and because the existence of the duty to provide accommodation was contingent upon the exercise of a considerable amount of discretion by the council. In light of this, Lord Hoffmann considered it unlikely that Parliament intended that errors of judgment should give rise to an obligation, enforceable in private law, to make financial reparation to disappointed individuals. This prompted Lord Woolf MR, in *Trustees of the Dennis Rye Pension Fund* v. *Sheffield City Council* [1998] 1 WLR 840 at 847–8, to remark that 'a private right which only comes into existence in the circumstances the House of Lords imagined they were dealing with in *Cocks* is in the future going to be a rare animal indeed'. (Breach of statutory duty is discussed at 15.3.5.)

However, *O'Rourke* left open the question whether, in situations where rights enforceable in private law *are* capable of being created through the exercise of powers lying in public law, litigation in which their existence falls for determination may be undertaken by means of ordinary proceedings notwithstanding that questions of public law are necessarily involved. That question was addressed by the Court of Appeal in the *Dennis Rye* case, *op cit*, in which Lord Woolf—evidently frustrated that considerable judicial and financial resources had been expended on the litigation without any court ever having got as far as addressing the merits of the claim—said (at 848) that a proper understanding of *O'Reilly* involved recognizing:

> (a) that remedies for protecting both private and public rights can be given in both private law proceedings and on an application for judicial review; (b) that judicial review provides, in the interest of the public, protection for public bodies which are not available in private law proceedings (namely the requirement of leave and the protection against delay). The proceedings will be heard by a High Court judge and will be managed by the Crown Office which has the necessary experience of public law proceedings to ensure that questions, such as expedition, are dealt with in a manner which is appropriate; (c) that for these reasons it is a *general rule* that it is contrary to public policy 'and as such an abuse of the process of the court, to permit a person seeking to establish that a decision of a public authority infringed rights to which he was entitled to protection under public law to proceed by way of an ordinary action and by this means to evade the provisions of Order 53 for the protection of such authorities' [*per* Lord Diplock in *O'Reilly* at 285].

He continued (at 848–9):

> Having established the foundation of the general rule it seems to me that there will be a reduction in the difficulties which are apparently being *experienced* at present by practitioners and the courts, if it is remembered that:
>
> (1) If it is not clear whether judicial review or an ordinary action is the correct procedure it will be safer to make an application for judicial review than commence an ordinary action since there then should be no question of being treated as abusing the process of the court by avoiding the protection provided by judicial review. In the majority of cases it should not be necessary *for purely procedural reasons* to become involved in arid arguments as to whether the issues are correctly treated as involving public or private law or both. (For reasons of substantive law it may be necessary to consider this issue.) If judicial review is used when it should not, the court can protect its resources either by directing that the application should continue as if begun by writ or by directing it should be heard by a judge who is not nominated to hear cases in the Crown Office List. It is difficult to see how a respondent can be prejudiced by the adoption of this course and little risk that anything more damaging could happen than a refusal of leave.
>
> (2) If a case is brought by an ordinary action and there is an application to strike out the case, the court should, at least if it is unclear whether the case should have been brought by judicial review, ask itself whether, if the case had been brought by judicial review when the action was commenced, it is clear leave would have been granted. If it would, then that is at least an indication that there has been no harm to the interests judicial review is designed to protect. In addition the court should consider by which procedure the case could be appropriately tried. If the answer is that an ordinary action is equally or more appropriate than an application for judicial review that again should be an indication the action should not be struck out …
>
> … I hope … that the far from comprehensive pragmatic suggestions made above will be of some assistance. They do involve not only considering the technical questions of the distinctions between public and private rights and bodies but also looking at the practical consequences of the choice of procedure which has been made. If the choice has no significant disadvantages for the parties, the public or the court, then it should not normally be regarded as constituting an abuse. Here it is important to remember that there does not have to be an application to strike out even if it is considered that the wrong procedure has been adopted. Often the interests of justice and the parties will be better served by getting on with the action.

On this approach, ordinary proceedings can certainly be used to enforce private law rights whose existence is dependent upon objective factors which the court can straightforwardly assess; but even if the rights are contingent upon a discretionary decision, the limits of which are traced only by the public law *Wednesbury* principles, this does not necessarily render the use of ordinary proceedings abusive. This follows because Lord Woolf sought to move the focus of the analysis away from the rigid categorization of public and private matters, and towards more substantive questions about the appropriateness or otherwise of ordinary proceedings over judicial review. This approach is evident in the guidelines set out by Lord Woolf above, in which he suggested that claims brought by ordinary proceedings should not be struck out if permission would have been granted had the judicial review procedure been used, and that it would be appropriate to use ordinary proceedings if the claim raised factual disputes which could not readily be resolved on judicial review. Indeed, the latter factor appears to operate in its own right—that is, without reference to whether any private law rights are at stake—as an exception to the exclusivity rule.

QUESTION

- Following *O'Rourke* and *Dennis Rye*, what is the relevance of *Cocks*?

13.3.6 Private law rights affected by public law

What if, instead of arguing that a private law right has arisen as a result of a decision or action which lies in public law, a claimant wishes to argue that conduct lying in public law has impacted upon some private law right whose existence is not in doubt? Precisely this question arose in *Roy* v. *Kensington and Chelsea and Westminster Family Practitioner Committee* [1992] 1 AC 624. The claimant, a general practitioner, had entered into an agreement with the defendant committee to provide medical services to the NHS. The relevant regulations provided that the committee was to make payments to doctors in accordance with the Statement of Fees and Allowances, paragraph 12.1 of which provided that a practitioner 'will be eligible for the full rate of basic practice allowance if', *inter alia*, 'he is in the opinion of the responsible committee devoting a substantial amount of time to general practice under the National Health Service'. Between 1979 and 1987, the claimant had been absent from his practice, on average, for between one-third and one-half of each year (albeit that these absences had been covered by a locum doctor). Against that background, the committee reduced the claimant's basic allowance by 20 per cent with prospective effect. He sued, using ordinary proceedings, for the additional 20 per cent which, he alleged, was still owed to him—an allegation which turned on his contention that the decision to reduce his allowance was unlawful as a matter of public law.

The precise nature of the legal relationship between the claimant and the defendant was unclear; in particular, there was some uncertainty as to whether the relationship was a contractual one. However, Lord Lowry, in his leading speech, said (at 649–50) that the key point was that the claimant

has in my opinion a bundle of rights which should be regarded as his individual private law rights against the committee, arising from the [relevant legislation] and including the very important private law right to be paid for the work that he has done.

His Lordship went on to say (at 653) that this case was different from *Cocks* (upon which doubt was in any event subsequently cast by *O'Rourke*):

> Mr. Cocks was simply a homeless member of the public [until and unless the council determined that he was not intentionally homeless] ..., whereas Dr. Roy had already an established relationship with the committee when his [case] fell to be considered [by the committee].

Lord Lowry concluded (at 653) by noting that counsel for the claimant had differentiated between two possible approaches to the principle laid down in *O'Reilly*:

> The 'broad approach' was that the rule in *O'Reilly v. Mackman* did not apply generally against bringing actions to vindicate private rights in all circumstances in which those actions involved a challenge to a public law act or decision, but that it merely required the aggrieved person to proceed by judicial review only when private law rights were not at stake. The 'narrow approach' assumed that the rule applied generally to *all* proceedings in which public law acts or decisions were challenged, subject to some exceptions when private law rights were involved. There was no need in *O'Reilly v. Mackman* to choose between these approaches, but it seems clear that Lord Diplock considered himself to be stating a general rule with exceptions. For my part, I much prefer the broad approach ... It would ..., if adopted, have the practical merit of getting rid of a procedural minefield. I shall, however, be content for the purpose of this appeal to adopt the narrow approach, which avoids the need to discuss the proper scope of the rule, a point which has not been argued before your Lordships and has hitherto been seriously discussed only by the academic writers.

Even on the narrow approach, however, Lord Lowry, with whom the other Law Lords agreed, held that the claimant had been fully entitled to use ordinary proceedings given that, as his Lordship put it (at 654), the claimant's 'private law rights dominate the proceedings'. (Compare *Jones* v. *Powys Local Health Board* [2008] EWHC 2562 (Admin), in which a private law claim for repayment of monies was made against the background of an allegedly unlawful failure on the part of the defendant to waive the payment of certain fees. Plender J struck out the proceedings as an abuse of process, holding that the primary focus of the claim was the legality of the impugned public law decision, and that judicial review should have been used. Does this imply that the judge preferred the 'narrow approach' set out in *Roy*—and, if so, was he right to do so?)

The decision in *Roy* is of a piece with much of the case law in this area: its focus is on reducing the significance of the distinction between public and private law matters rather than on clarifying the nature of that distinction. As the Law Commission observed (Law Com No 226, *Administrative Law: Judicial Review and Statutory Appeals* (London 1994) at [3.10]), the decision in *Roy*

> does not address the difficult question of *when* a private right is created by statute; that will remain a matter of construction of individual statutes in their particular contexts. What it does is to provide guidance as to the procedural consequences of finding that such a right exists.

Addressing the former issue, Cane [1992] *PL* 193 at 197 wrote:

> Does *Roy* cast any light on the definition of 'private law right'? Contractual and property rights are obviously private law rights, as are rights to obtain monetary awards for private law wrongs or to obtain restitution on some other basis than wrongful conduct (such as mistake of fact).

The really difficult cases are those in which the right in question arises out of a statutory provision. Dr. Roy's right was such: the Court of Appeal held that there was a contract between Dr. Roy and the Committee, but the House of Lords declined to decide this issue and instead treated Dr. Roy's right as a private law statutory one. Are all statutory 'rights' private law rights? Surely not! It is quite clear that not all statutory duties are actionable in private law. We know from *Cocks* v. *Thanet D.C.* that the statutory right of certain homeless persons to be housed by a local authority is a private law right [but now *cf O'Rourke*, discussed at 13.3.5]; and we know from *Roy* that the statutory right of a registered G.P., under certain circumstances, to receive a full basic practice allowance is a private law right. But just as the courts have found it impossible to provide much guidance in general terms on the question of which statutory duties are actionable in the tort of breach of statutory duty, so it seems unlikely that much general guidance will ever be available on the question of which rights are private law rights for present purposes.

QUESTIONS

- Do you share Cane's pessimism on this point?
- Can you suggest any criteria that may provide more certain guidance in this area?

While *Roy* involves the exception to the exclusivity principle based on the existence of 'private law rights', the House of Lords' decision in *Mercury Communications Ltd* v. *Director General of Telecommunications* [1996] 1 WLR 48 goes further by indicating that the exclusivity principle gives way not only when private law rights are at stake as between the two parties to the case, but also when the defendant's decision is capable of affecting the claimant's relations in private law with others.

13.3.7 Procedural exclusivity and the Civil Procedure Rules

In its report, the Law Commission (Law Com No 226, *Administrative Law: Judicial Review and Statutory Appeals* (London 1994) at [3.13]–[3.14]) was satisfied that there were strong policy reasons—including 'the need for speed and certainty in administrative decision-making'—for requiring the use of what is now Part 54 'in purely public law cases'. However, it considered that

where a case involves a properly constituted private law cause of action or where it is necessary to decide whether a person should be prevented from raising a defence in such an action, on the ground that it involves an issue of public law, a more flexible procedural approach is needed to ensure that private law rights are not 'trumped' by public law justifications.

Indeed, we have already seen that some flexibility was introduced through judicial development of various exceptions to the exclusivity principle. That flexibility has been further enhanced, in two respects, by the introduction of the CPR, as we explain in the following two sections.

13.3.8 A more substantive approach

The first point relates not to the new judicial review procedure contained in Part 54, but to the general principles underlying the CPR and, in particular, the new powers of the courts to give summary judgment. The nature and implications of these changes are apparent from the next extract. When the following case was decided, Part 54 had not entered into force. However, the Order 53 procedure had by that time been made subject to the CPR, so that, as Jackson J commented in *Carter Commercial Developments* v. *Bedford Borough Council* [2001] EWHC 669 (Admin) at [28], 'the principles stated by the Court of Appeal in *Clark*'s case are equally applicable now that Part 54 has come into force'.

Clark v. University of Lincolnshire and Humberside [2000] 1 WLR 1988
Court of Appeal

The claimant had been a student at the defendant institution, a university established under the Education Reform Act 1988. The student was accused of plagiarism, as a result of which she failed one of her final examinations; although the finding of plagiarism was later rescinded, a mark of zero was given for the paper concerned. The student challenged this decision by means of ordinary proceedings in which she alleged breaches of contractual rules under the university's student regulations. The defendant contended that this amounted to an abuse of process: the university was a public body and, it was argued, in the absence of a visitor [on which see the *Page* case, discussed at 2.2.5–2.2.6], judicial review proceedings should have been used.

Lord Woolf MR

[26] … [Judicial review] proceedings now have to be initiated by use of a 'claim form,' maintaining the principle that all proceedings under the CPR are to be commenced in the same way … [Judicial review] is part of the new code of civil procedure created by the CPR. It is subject to the general overriding principles contained in Part 1.

[27] In addition, if proceedings involving public law issues are commenced by an ordinary action under Part 7 or Part 8 they are now subject to Part 24. Part 24 is important because it enables the court, either on its own motion or on the application of a party, if it considers that a claimant has no real prospect of succeeding on a claim or an issue, to give summary judgment on the claim or issue. This is a markedly different position from that which existed when *O'Reilly v Mackman* was decided. If a defendant public body or an interested person considers that a claim has no real prospect of success an application can now be made under Part 24. This restricts the inconvenience to third parties and the administration of public bodies caused by a hopeless claim …

[28] The distinction between proceedings under Order 53 and an ordinary claim are now limited. Under Order 53 the claimant has to obtain permission to bring the proceedings so the onus is upon him to establish he has a real prospect of success. In the case of ordinary proceedings the defendant has to establish that the proceedings do not have a real prospect of success.

[29] A university is a public body. This is not in issue on this appeal. Court proceedings would, therefore, normally be expected to be commenced under Order 53. If the university is subject to the supervision of a visitor there is little scope for those proceedings (*Page v Hull University Visitor* [1993] AC 682). Where a claim is brought against a university by one of its students, if because the university is a 'new university' created by statute, it does not have a visitor, the role of the court will frequently amount to performing the reviewing role which would otherwise be performed by the visitor. The court … will not involve itself with issues that involve making

academic judgments. Summary judgment dismissing a claim which, if it were to be entertained, would require the court to make academic judgments should be capable of being obtained in the majority of situations. Similarly, the court has now power to stay the proceedings if it came to the conclusion that … it would be desirable for a student to use an internal disciplinary process before coming to the court. (See CPR 1.4([2])(e))

[30] One of Lord Diplock's reasons which he gave in *O'Reilly v Mackman* for his concern about an ordinary civil action being commenced against public bodies when a more appropriate procedure was under [Order] 53 was the fact that in ordinary civil proceedings the claimant could defer commencing the proceedings until the last day of the limitation period. This compares unfavourably with the requirement that, subject to the court's discretion to extend time, under [Order] 53 proceedings have to be commenced promptly and in any event within three months. If a student could bypass this requirement to bring proceedings promptly by issuing civil proceedings based on a contract, this could have a very adverse [effect] on administration of universities …

[32] … If it is not possible to resolve the dispute internally, and there is no visitor, then the courts may have no alternative but to become involved. If they do so, the preferable procedure would usually be by way of judicial review. If, on the other hand, the proceedings are based on the contract between the student and the university then they do not have to be brought by way of judicial review.

[33] The courts today will be flexible in their approach. Already, prior to the introduction of the CPR the courts were prepared to prevent abuse of their process where there had been an inordinate delay even if the limitation period had not expired. In such a situation, the court could, in appropriate circumstances, stay subsequent proceedings. This is despite the fact that a litigant normally was regarded as having a legal right to commence proceedings at any time prior to the expiry of the limitation period. (See *Birkett v James* [1978] AC 297)

[34] The court's approach to what is an abuse of process has to be considered today in the light of the changes brought about by the CPR. Those changes include a requirement that a party to proceedings should behave reasonably both before and after they have commenced proceedings. Parties are now under an obligation to help the court further the overriding objectives which include ensuring that cases are dealt with expeditiously and fairly. (CPR 1.1(2)(d) and 1.3) They should not allow the choice of procedure to achieve procedural advantages …

[35] While in the past, it would not be appropriate to look at delay of a party commencing proceedings other than by judicial review within the limitation period in deciding whether the proceedings are abusive this is no longer the position. While to commence proceedings within a limitation period is not in itself an abuse, delay in commencing proceedings is a factor which can be taken into account in deciding whether the proceeding[s] are abusive. If proceedings of a type which would normally be brought by judicial review are instead brought by bringing an ordinary claim, the court in deciding whether the commencement of the proceedings is an abuse of process can take into account whether there has been unjustified delay in initiating the proceedings.

[36] When considering whether proceedings can continue the nature of the claim can be relevant. If the court is required to perform a reviewing role or what is being claimed is a discretionary remedy, whether it be a prerogative remedy or an injunction or a declaration the position is different from when the claim is for damages or a sum of money for breach of contract or a tort irrespective of the procedure adopted. Delay in bringing proceedings for a discretionary remedy has always been a factor which a court could take into account in deciding whether it should grant that remedy. Delay can now be taken into account on an application for summary judgment under CPR Part 24 if its effect means that the claim has no real prospect of success.

[37] Similarly if what is being claimed could affect the public generally the approach of the court will be stricter than if the proceedings only affect the immediate parties. It must not be

forgotten that a court can extend time to bring proceedings under [Order] 53. The intention of the CPR is to harmonise procedures as far as possible and to avoid barren procedural disputes which generate satellite litigation.

[38] Where a student has, as here, a claim in contract, the court will not strike out a claim which could more appropriately be made under Order 53 solely because of the procedure which has been adopted. It may however do so, if it comes to the conclusion that in all the circumstances, including the delay in initiating the proceedings, there has been an abuse of the process of the court under the CPR. The same approach will be adopted on an application under Part 24.

[39] The emphasis can therefore be said to have changed since *O'Reilly v Mackman*. What is likely to be important when proceedings are not brought by a student against a new university under Order 53, will not be whether the right procedure has been adopted but whether the protection provided by Order 53 has been flouted in circumstances which are inconsistent with the proceedings being able to be conducted justly in accordance with the general principles contained in Part 1. Those principles are now central to determining what is due process. A visitor is not required to entertain a complaint when there has been undue delay and a court in the absence of a visitor should exercise its jurisdiction in a similar way. The courts are far from being the ideal forum in which to resolve the great majority of disputes between a student and his or her university. The courts should be vigilant to ensure their procedures are not misused. The courts must be equally vigilant to discourage summary applications which have no real prospect of success.

Sedley LJ, with whom Ward LJ agreed, reached the same conclusion as Lord Woolf MR. The appeal was allowed to the extent of restoring the action.

In terms of its outcome, this decision is perhaps unremarkable. Indeed, as Sedley LJ noted at [16], the claimant in *Clark* was if anything in a stronger position than her counterpart in *Roy*: '[W]here in *Roy's* case a statutory relationship happened to include a contractual element, here it is a contractual relationship which happens to possess a public law dimension'. As Cornford [2000] 5 *Web JCLI* observes, 'If the scope of the judgment is confined to litigants who have contractual rights then it breaks no new ground.' However, Lord Woolf's judgment does not seem to be thus confined, and its implications are potentially far-reaching. On Lord Woolf's view, irrespective of whether a claim concerning public law matters is begun via the judicial review procedure or by means of ordinary proceedings, the court will in substance apply the same tests. If the judicial review procedure is used, then of course the safeguards in Part 54 will apply. If, however, the claim is issued in ordinary proceedings, it is still open to the court to look at these issues: if it concludes that, had the case been brought under Part 54, it would have been rejected on, say, grounds of permission or delay, then it is open to the court to give summary judgment under Part 24. The upshot is that the procedure by which a claim is started now matters very little. According to Hickman [2000] *JR* 178 at 182:

Clark ... means that it will be much less important whether or not proceedings are brought within Ord 53. In both cases the courts can consider whether the public body requires protection, and particularly whether there has been delay. At least the focus of argument should now shift from the precise form of the application to the more practical question of the need for protection.

This shift from form to substance is to be welcomed, and it is clearly desirable that claims should be rejected because the policy of protecting public bodies is being undermined rather than on the formal ground that the wrong procedure was used. It must be remembered, however, that it does not follow from *Clark* that the distinction between issues of public and private law has become irrelevant or the exclusivity principle defunct; that would be to put the position too high. It is inherent in the *Clark* approach that, even if the use of the wrong procedure is no longer fatal *per se*, categorization of the issue as public or private may still be important, since if the matter is one of public law (to which none of the exceptions to *O'Reilly* applies) then *either* the claimant must use the judicial review procedure *or*, if ordinary proceedings are instead used, the court must be satisfied that the requirements of permission, promptitude, and so on would have been met had the matter been litigated by means of Part 54.

Thus, as a practical matter it is relatively rare nowadays to find examples of courts finding an abuse of process on the basis of *O'Reilly*. But such cases do crop up now and then, and serve as a reminder of the continuing relevance of *O'Reilly*. Thus, in *Trim v. North Dorset DC* [2010] EWCA Civ 1446, Carnwath LJ found an abuse of process where a claimant sought, via application for a declaration in ordinary procedure, to challenge a 'breach of condition' notice issued by a council; the council had issued the notice as it believed the claimant had breached one of the conditions of his planning permission. Carnwath LJ observed that the experience since *O'Reilly* 'has shown that a clear division between public and private law is often difficult to maintain, and the rigidity of the rule has had to be relaxed accordingly' (at [21]). But this did not undermine the basic principle 'that purely public acts should be challenged by judicial review, and that it is in the public interest that the legality of the formal acts of a public authority should be established without delay' (at [23]), as demonstrated by the promptness requirement on review. He concluded, at [26]:

> The exclusivity principle is in my view directly applicable in the present case. The service of a breach of condition notice is a purely public law act. There is strong public interest in its validity, if in issue, being established promptly, both because of its significance to the planning of the area, and because it turns what was merely unlawful into criminal conduct. It is an archetypal example of the public action which Lord Diplock [in *O'Reilly*] would have had in mind. It does not come within any other [exceptions] requiring a more flexible approach.

13.3.9 Transfer into Part 54

The disadvantage suffered by claimants who choose the wrong procedure is ameliorated by the CPR. Transfer *out of* the judicial review procedure was possible under Order 53, and this remains the case under CPR 54.20. However, transfer *into* the judicial review procedure was not possible under Order 53 (although Lord Woolf suggested otherwise in *Trustees of the Dennis Rye Pension Fund v. Sheffield City Council* [1998] 1 WLR 840 at 849). The desirability of permitting such transfers was, however, widely recognized, and the Law Commission report (at [3.20]–[3.21]) proposed the amendment of Order 53 to this effect. Under the CPR, transfers into the judicial review procedure are now possible. CPR 54.20 provides that Part 30 of the Rules, which permits transfers within the High Court, 'applies to transfers *to* and from the Administrative Court' (emphasis added). Paragraph 14.2 of Practice Direction 54A goes on to explain that, '[i]n deciding whether a claim is suitable for transfer to the Administrative Court, the court will consider whether it raises issues of public law to which Part 54 should apply'.

> **QUESTION**
>
> - If the court concludes that the claimant is attempting to litigate genuinely public law issues by means of ordinary proceedings, but that the Part 54 safeguards have not been compromised, how should it decide whether to allow the ordinary proceedings to continue or to transfer the case to the Administrative Court under Part 54?

13.3.10 Human rights claims: further inroads into the exclusivity principle

O'Reilly asserted a distinction between claims in public law and those concerning private rights. As we have seen, the distinction is by its nature problematic. But the distinction runs into severe difficulties when attempts are made to apply it to claims under the HRA. On the one hand, human rights claims are claims against public authorities or entities carrying out public functions, and are thus commonly thought to be public law claims. But, on the other hand, the obligations under the HRA are similar in nature to rights in private law fields such as tort, that is, individual, personal rights which protect very basic interests; in contrast judicial review claims at common law have traditionally been concerned with supervising the lawful exercise of public power. As Lord Lowry observed in *Roy* v. *Kensington and Chelsea and Westminster Family Practitioner Committee* [1992] 1 AC 624 at 654, '[w]hen individual rights are claimed, there should not be a need for leave or a special time limit, nor should the relief be discretionary': where an individual claims a basic legal entitlement their access to court to secure a remedy should not be impeded. At 13.2.3 we also saw that the individualized nature of human rights adjudication implicates a strong focus on the specific facts of individual cases, and that certain doctrines such as proportionality may require a court to rigorously scrutinize the factual premises of executive decisions. This feature of many human rights claims in turn makes such claims unsuitable for determination in judicial review procedure, at least in its traditional form, in which cross-examination and disclosure have been rare.

For these reasons some considered that the advent of the HRA would constitute the final nail in the coffin of *O'Reilly*, placing the public–private distinction under such pressure that it would disintegrate completely. This has not quite transpired, but the Act has posed a significant challenge to what remains of the exclusivity principle. As we saw earlier (at 13.2.3), where human rights claims are brought via review procedure, that procedure has been modified, at least for certain classes of human rights claim, so that it closely resembles ordinary procedure. In addition, the distinctive nature of human rights claims, coupled with the more flexible procedural approach established in *Clark* [2000] 1 WLR 1988, has led to courts edging towards a practice whereby if a human rights claimant does not claim a prerogative order (for which, under the CPR, they *must* bring their claim via judicial review), they shall often enjoy a genuine choice of procedure, *ie* they may lawfully proceed via ordinary procedure if they wish. This emergent practice is suggestive of a further major inroad into the exclusivity doctrine: claims based in a core field of public law, human rights law, may not uncommonly be initiated via ordinary procedure. Let us consider the types of cases in which litigants may enjoy choice of procedure.

In *ID* v. *Home Office* [2005] EWCA Civ 38, [2006] 1 WLR 1003 at [105], the Court of Appeal went so far as to suggest that because 'contested actions involving a human rights

496 • THE JUDICIAL REVIEW PROCEDURE

element often require cross-examination' it may be preferable that they be streamed via ordinary procedure rather than judicial review procedure. Similarly, in *R (Wilkinson)* v. *Broadmoor Hospital* [2001] EWCA Civ 1545, [2002] 1 WLR 419, Hale LJ said (at [61]–[62]):

> In some cases, for example where delegated legislation or the policy of a public authority is in question, then the appropriate remedies will only be available in judicial review. But in others, where specific invasions of individuals' rights are in question, an ordinary action would be more appropriate.... [I]t cannot and should not matter whether proceedings in respect of forcible treatment of detained patients are brought by way of an ordinary action in tort, an action under section 7(1) of the 1998 Act, or judicial review. If there are relevant disputed issues of fact these will have to be determined, by cross examination if necessary.

These statements suggest that where a human rights claim raises significant factual questions, for example because of proportionality analysis, or because there are significant factual disputes between the parties, a claimant may have a genuine choice of procedure, or indeed may be encouraged to proceed via ordinary procedure. It may be thought significant that these statements were made in cases where concurrent claims in tort and under the HRA were made in respect of similar rights (in respect of liberty in *ID*), or the claim could have been made in tort or under the HRA: for example, in a case of police brutality the claim could either be brought on the basis of Article 3 or battery or both (see the discussion of *Ruddy* later). It seems that where HRA claims are made alongside tort claims, and concern similar matters and protected rights, it will be uncommon for a court to require the claimant to make their HRA claim via ordinary procedure; because the claims are so close in nature it would be difficult to justify requiring different procedural paths for each claim. Further, the Supreme Court, in *Ruddy* v. *Chief Constable Strathclyde Police* [2012] UKSC 57 at [33], said that in such a situation it would be 'inconvenient and, quite possibly unjust, to require [the claimant] to give evidence [about the same matter] twice over in two separate actions on two separate occasions'. As a matter of ordinary practice, many concurrent claims in tort and HRA are made via ordinary procedure routinely without objection.

It is not only in human rights claims with a significant factual dimension or which cover similar ground to tort claims that a claimant may enjoy genuine choice of procedure. Where a human rights claim concerns administrative conduct that has occurred in the past and has since ceased, and the claimant does not seek invalidation of an existing administrative decision, the claimant shall again likely have a choice of procedure. In *A* v. *Essex County Council* [2010] UKSC 33, [2011] 1 AC 280 at [116], Lady Hale observed:

> The judge placed at the forefront of his account of the relevant legal principles that 'there is a significant public interest in public law claims against public bodies being brought expeditiously' ... That is of course true in judicial review, when remedies are sought to quash administrative decisions which may affect large numbers of people or upon which other decisions have depended and action been taken. It is normally a prospective remedy, aiming not only to quash the past but also to put right the future. Expedition is less obviously necessary in a claim for a declaration in vindication of the claimant's human rights, upon which nothing else depends, or of a claim for damages. These are retrospective remedies, aimed at marking or compensating what has happened in the past ... This claim is more akin to a tort claim than to judicial review.

The gist of Lady Hale's argument is that many of the protections associated with judicial review procedure, such as the requirement of promptness and judicial regulation of access to court via the permission stage, are justified on the basis that most claimants in judicial review proceedings will be seeking quashing orders. However, where a claimant seeks a declaration that their human rights were breached through official action in the past, that action now having ceased, the types of concerns associated with quashing orders do not arise, so that there is less justification for requiring the claimant to proceed via judicial review. In this way procedure is tailored to the particular demands of the claim, consonant with the 'substantive approach' in *Clark*.

The type of approach postulated by Lady Hale subsequently found favour in the Supreme Court's unanimous decision in *Ruddy*. In that case Ruddy sought damages under the HRA for alleged breaches of Article 3 by police in the course of arresting him, as well as damages in tort for harm he allegedly suffered through the police conduct. In other words, this was a claim relating to past, completed official acts. The lower court considered that the human rights claim should be brought via judicial review as it raised questions of public law illegality; if illegality was found then any question of damages could be determined separately via ordinary proceedings. The Supreme Court disagreed. It reiterated, at [17], what Sedley LJ had concluded in *Clark*: '[T]he ground has shifted considerably since *Cocks*', the Supreme Court also relying on *Winder* [1985] AC 461 and *Roy* [1992] 1 AC 624 to reinforce that there had been significant moves away from the rigidity of approach that characterized *Cocks* (and *O'Reilly*). Then, echoing Lady Hale's judgment in *A*, Lord Hope observed at [15]:

> The fallacy which undermines the [lower Court's] whole approach to this issue, however, lies in its assumption that the appellant is seeking an exercise of the court's supervisory jurisdiction. That is not so. He is not asking for the review or setting aside of any decision … He is not asking the court to control their actions in that way at all. His case in regard to both craves is based on averments of things done or omitted to be done and actions that were taken or not taken. The allegations are of completed acts or failures to act. He is not seeking to have them corrected in order to provide a foundation for his claim, nor does he need to do so. What he seeks is just satisfaction for the fact that, on his averments, his article 3 Convention rights have been breached. The essence of his claim is simply one of damages.

Thus, if a human rights claim relates to some administrative act or series of acts in the past, and the claim does not require the quashing of any prevailing administrative decision, but rather seeks a declaration that rights were breached and/or damages, the claimant will likely be able to bring their claim via ordinary procedure.

Something further should be said on the topic of damages specifically, which was raised squarely in *Ruddy*. As we shall see in more detail at 15.4, the HRA provides that damages may be awarded for breach of enumerated rights. This adds a new dimension to public law claims. Breaches of the longstanding public law duties of reasonableness, legality, and procedural fairness cannot generate damages liability in themselves; rather the traditional remedies for such breaches are the prerogative orders.

In *Ruddy*, the Court, at [18], considered that 'the process of judicial review would be quite inept for proceedings in which damages are claimed for an isolated act of physical violence which was in breach of the article 3 Convention right'. One of the reasons why the review procedure is inept for determination of damages issues is that they are highly fact-sensitive: the degree of loss suffered varies from one victim to another so that proper determination of such claims demands close examination of the specific factual circumstances of the case, often requiring disclosure and, particularly, oral evidence. The review procedure of course does not generally provide for oral evidence, and one of the reasons why is that it was never intended to be a procedural route for damages claims. It was intended first and foremost as a route for seeking exercise of the courts' supervisory jurisdiction and grant of prerogative orders. Indeed, CPR 54.3(2) provides that where the only remedy sought by the claimant is damages the claim may not be brought via review procedure. The effect of *Ruddy* is that, absent a claim for a prerogative order, HRA claims for damages can and should proceed via ordinary procedure.

We may also add a point touched upon previously: where human rights damages are claimed the claim invariably closely resembles a tort claim, for which damages have long been a standard remedy, thus making it more difficult to justify procedurally disadvantaging human rights claimants by requiring them to use judicial review procedure.

The approach to human rights damages claims in *Ruddy* is a good example of the common sense of the 'substantive approach' in *Clark*: courts should seek to match procedure to the demands of the particular type of claim. Despite good sense ultimately prevailing, the strictures of an approach concerned to maintain strict procedural separation between public law and private law claims had earlier held sway. In *Anufrijeva* v. *Southwark LBC* [2003] EWCA Civ 1406, [2004] QB 1124 at [53], [79]–[81], Lord Woolf, for the Court, sought to confine human rights damages claims to the judicial review procedure as he viewed them as quintessentially 'public law' claims, and considered that they should be determined speedily and at low cost, consistent with the policy of protection of public authorities underlying the review procedure. The Court held such claims must proceed via judicial review, and where such procedural route was barred by the CPR—*ie* where damages were the only remedy sought—the claim should nonetheless be heard in the Administrative Court, albeit via ordinary procedure. This guidance has now been abandoned in principle, in the light of *Ruddy*, and in practice: human rights damages claims are routinely tried via ordinary procedure (see further Varuhas, *Damages and Human Rights* (Oxford 2016) 212–18).

Thus, claims under the HRA have posed a significant new challenge to the principle that public and private claims should each be streamed via distinct procedures. On the one hand, where such claims are brought via review procedure, for example where a quashing or prohibitory order is sought (in which case the judicial review procedure *must* be used), the procedure may be modified so that it more closely resembles ordinary procedure, with the courts more readily ordering disclosure and cross-examination (see 13.2.3). On the other hand, for a significant class of human rights claims, in which claimants do not seek prerogative orders, claimants will enjoy a genuine choice of procedure.

13.4 Concluding remarks

Where does all of this leave the procedural dichotomy, articulated with such vigour by Lord Diplock in *O'Reilly* v. *Mackman* [1983] 2 AC 237? In light of *Clark* and the possibility of transfer into Part 54, the policy of upholding the safeguards for public authorities remains, but it is prosecuted by more subtle means than those envisaged in *O'Reilly*. The procedural dichotomy has now largely been eclipsed in the sense that, following *Clark*, the circumstances in which public law matters may be litigated by means of ordinary proceedings transcend the exceptional categories considered earlier, while emergence of HRA claims has posed a significant new challenge to the exclusivity principle and a striking illustration of the *Clark* approach in action. However, importantly, although the conclusion that the matter is one of public law no longer necessarily prescribes the procedure to be used, it continues to trigger the application of the protections inherent in the judicial review procedure. The departure from the rigid technicality of *O'Reilly* and *Cocks* is to be welcomed, but it is unsurprising that the public–private distinction survives, albeit in a much more subtle form: it logically *must* survive in some sense if the safeguards which Part 54 confers upon public bodies are to have any practical effect. How those safeguards work, and whether they are necessary, are different questions; we address them in the next chapter.

FURTHER RESOURCES

Beatson, '"Public" and "Private" in English Administrative Law' [1987] 103 *LQR* 34

Bowman, *Review of the Crown Office List* (London 2000) *http://webarchive.nationalarchives.gov.uk/+/http://www.dca.gov.uk/civil/bowman2000/summary2000.htm* (in summary form)

Civil Procedure Rules *http://www.justice.gov.uk/courts/procedure-rules/civil*

Cornford, 'The New Rules of Procedure for Judicial Review' [2000] 5 *Web JCLI http://www.bailii.org/uk/other/journals/WebJCLI/2000/issue5/cornford5.html*

Fredman and Morris, 'A Snake or a Ladder? *O'Reilly v Mackman* Reconsidered' [1992] 108 *LQR* 353

Fredman and Morris, 'The Costs of Exclusivity' [1994] *PL* 69

Law Com No 226, *Administrative Law: Judicial Review and Statutory Appeals* (London 1994), Parts II, III, and VII

Lewis, *Judicial Remedies in Public Law* (London 2014), ch 3

Oliver, 'Public Law Procedures and Remedies—Do We Need Them?' [2002] *PL* 91

Supperstone and Knapman (eds), *Administrative Court Practice* (London 2008)

Varuhas, 'The Public Interest Conception of Public Law: Its Procedural Origins and Substantive Implications' in Bell, Elliott, Varuhas, and Murray (eds), *Public Law Adjudication in Common Law Systems* (Oxford 2016)

14 RESTRICTION OF REMEDIES

14.1 Introduction

Our concern in this chapter is with a wide range of factors that may prevent claimants from obtaining relief in respect of unlawful administrative action. Some such restrictions—*eg* statutory provisions which limit or remove the courts' jurisdiction and the courts' general reluctance to intervene in relation to hypothetical matters—can impact on claimants seeking to invoke the courts' supervisory jurisdiction irrespective of the procedure used. Others—*eg* the need to secure permission and to comply with a strict three-month time-limit—bite only when the claim is brought under CPR Part 54.

In this chapter, we explain when and how these restrictions operate, and consider how they impact on intending litigants and public bodies. Our analysis encompasses a range of new restrictions added since the last edition of this book, introduced in the wake of two government consultations on reform of judicial review: *Judicial Review: Proposals for Reform*, Cm 8515 (2012), *Judicial Review: Further Proposals for Reform*, Cm 8703 (2013). A range of concerns were invoked by government to justify these new restrictions including that judicial review has grown rapidly, too many hopeless judicial review cases are making it to court, judicial review is impeding economic growth, and judicial review is being abused for political ends. More prosaically one may view these reforms as instances of government 'clamping down' on judicial review, that is, government changing the rules of the game in its favour (Harlow and Rawlings, '"Striking Back" and "Clamping Down": An Alternative Perspective on Judicial Review' in Bell, Elliott, Varuhas, and Murray (eds), *Public Law Adjudication in Common Law Systems* (Oxford 2016)).

Thus, the judicial review procedure is characterized by a range of restrictions, and more have been added of late. However, at the outset, it is worth noting that some writers question whether it is appropriate—bearing in mind the vast diversity of issues litigated by means of judicial review—to lump all judicial review cases together by means of a common procedure with uniformly applicable safeguards. Oliver [2002] *PL* 91 at 99–100 observes:

> The Bowman Report [*Review of the Crown Office List* (London 2000)] … referred to 'the special nature of judicial review and the need for speed and flexibility'. But this report did not spell out what was special about *all* judicial review cases, or in what circumstances speed and flexibility were required to any greater extent than in private law cases where injunctions are sought. These protections in judicial review are suggestive of state prerogatives of the kind found in civil law systems, which are quite out of keeping with the common law tradition.

Thus, not only should we ask whether *particular procedural safeguards* (from the point of view of public bodies) or obstacles (from the standpoint of intending claimants) are appropriate; we also need to question the assumption that there should be *a uniform set of safeguards* applicable in all judicial review cases.

14.2 Permission

14.2.1 The Pre-Action Protocol

Obtaining the permission of the court marks the beginning of the judicial review process proper. However, the 'Pre-Action Protocol'—adherence to which is not strictly obligatory—provides (in para 7) that 'the court will normally expect all parties to have complied with it in good time before proceedings are issued and will take into account compliance or non-compliance when giving directions for case management of proceedings or when making orders for costs'. In *R (S) v. Hampshire County Council* [2009] EWHC 2537 (Admin), Walker J refused permission for judicial review on a number of grounds, one of which was (at [61]) 'complete failure to comply with the pre-action protocol'—a matter which, in the circumstances, 'warrant[ed] peremptory refusal of permission'. The Protocol codifies good practice by requiring intending claimants to send a 'letter before claim' in good time before the claim to the prospective defendant, outlining the issues in dispute, to which the defendant is expected to reply within 14 days by means of a 'letter of response'. By encouraging interaction between the parties before the matter reaches court, this scheme seeks to promote recourse to alternative dispute resolution, such as negotiation and mediation, thereby relieving pressure on the Administrative Court.

14.2.2 Judicial review: a two-stage process

If the claimant nevertheless wishes to pursue the matter litigiously, then he must secure the 'permission' (or 'leave', as it used to be known) of the court: CPR 54.4. This means that judicial review proceedings fall into two parts: preliminary consideration of the claim at the permission stage and, if the claim progresses, more detailed consideration at the substantive hearing. The two stages can be dealt with simultaneously in a 'rolled up' hearing, for example where the circumstances require the case to be disposed of urgently. Albeit the courts have warned that 'it is … very important that a practice, on occasions, of ordering a so-called rolled up hearing does not blur the important step of the grant of permission, or the distinction between consideration of permission and substantive consideration of all, or any discrete, grounds': *R (Milner) v. South Central SHA* [2011] EWHC 218 (Admin), [2011] PTSR D27 at [67].

The Law Commission (Law Com No 226, *Administrative Law: Judicial Review and Statutory Appeals* (London 1994)) (hereinafter the 'Law Commission report') considered that the permission stage—or 'preliminary consideration', as they preferred to call it—was highly beneficial. First, the existence of such a 'filter' helps to ensure that only serious issues advance as far as the substantive hearing: this is advantageous from the perspective of *public bodies*—and, by extension, *the public*—since it promotes certainty and finality in decision-making by ensuring that administrative bodies are not distracted unnecessarily by the prospect of litigation (at [3.5]–[3.6]) (but now *cf* 14.2.3 on acknowledgement of service). Second, the permission stage is also advantageous from the *courts'* point of view, since it allows for 'the efficient management of the caseload' (at [5.6]), allowing them, at an early stage and without significant consumption of judicial resources, to reject cases with little prospect of success. Third, the Law Commission expressed the view—shared by, *inter alios*, Le Sueur and Sunkin [1992] *PL* 102 at 107—that the permission stage is helpful to *claimants*, since it provides a relatively quick and inexpensive mechanism by which to obtain the opinion of the Administrative Court.

These advantages of the two-stage process notwithstanding, some commentators entertain serious doubts about its appropriateness. Wade and Forsyth, *Administrative Law* (Oxford 2014) at 553–4, for instance, comment that the permission requirement is wrong '[i]n principle' because it involves treating public authorities 'more favourably than other litigants'. Moreover, Bridges, Meszaros, and Sunkin [2000] *PL* 651 at 664–6 question the practical utility of the permission stage, arguing there is little empirical evidence that permission is an effective case-management tool. We will see later that difficulties in applying consistent principles at the permission stage reveal further problems.

14.2.3 Reform of the permission stage

The nature of the permission stage was changed significantly by the introduction of CPR Part 54, which, in this respect, was heavily influenced by Sir Jeffrey Bowman's *Review of the Crown Office List* (London 2000) (the 'Bowman Report') (see further Cornford and Sunkin [2001] *PL* 11). One of the principal problems considered by Bowman was the increasing workload of (what is now) the Administrative Court, and the delays caused thereby. Bowman advanced a number of proposals for increasing the efficiency of the judicial review process and, more fundamentally, reducing recourse to judicial review. Two specific recommendations concerning permission were made, which were largely implemented through Part 54.

First, Bowman (at 72), building upon the Law Commission report (at [4.4] and [5.9]–[5.12]), suggested permission should always (in the first instance) be determined on paper. This is reflected in CPR Practice Direction 54A, which states (at [8.4]) that '[t]he court will generally, in the first instance, consider the question of permission without a hearing'.

Whereas minimizing the use of hearings at the permission stage aids the efficient use of scarce judicial resources once permission is sought, the second important change sought to reduce recourse to judicial review in the first place. Bowman (at 68) identified post-permission settlement as one of the underlying causes of the courts' high workload. This refers to the practice of claimants using up court time by taking matters as far as obtaining permission, and then settling—often using the granting of permission as a bargaining tool—before the substantive hearing. Bowman argued that increasing early interaction between the parties was key to encouraging settlement *before* any court involvement. As well as the use of a Pre-Action Protocol, Bowman recommended—building upon the Law Commission's recommendation (at [4.9]–[4.11]) that judges should be able to request information on paper from defendants at the permission stage—that the permission stage should be changed from an *ex parte* procedure, involving only the claimant, to an *inter partes* procedure. Thus a claimant seeking permission is now required to file a claim form stating, *inter alia*, the question which he wants the court to decide (CPR 8.2(b)(i)) and the remedy which is sought (CPR 54.6(1)(c)). The claim form must be served on, *inter alios*, the defendant (CPR 54.7(a)), who then has an opportunity to respond by an acknowledgement of service (CPR 54.8). The intention is that by making the permission stage *inter partes*, prospective claimants will seek permission less readily than was the case under the *ex parte* procedure: since the claimant must now 'face' (at least on paper) the defendant at the permission stage, the obtaining of permission becomes a more onerous process, thereby reinforcing the Pre-Action Protocol's encouragement of alternative dispute resolution.

The extent to which the reforms introduced following the Bowman Report have succeeded has been addressed in empirical work carried out by Bondy and Sunkin [2009] *PL* 237 (and see by the same authors: *The Dynamics of Judicial Review Litigation* (London 2009)). They found that 62 per cent of judicial review 'threats' are resolved by dialogue between solicitors. This figure, say Bondy and Sunkin, underlines 'the importance of the [letter before claim] in formally indicating the seriousness of the claimant's position, establishing the parameters of the dispute from the claimant's perspective, and encouraging the public authority to consider or reconsider its position'. Meanwhile, of those disputes that get as far as the issue of proceedings, 34 per cent are resolved *before* reaching the permission stage (compared to pre-permission completion rates of 13 and 20 per cent in 1991 and 1994–95: see Bridges *et al* [2000] *PL* 651). This leads Bondy and Sunkin (*op cit* at 245) to conclude that 'there can be little doubt that [the] reforms have been successful in helping to encourage early settlement'. Yet they found that some 56 per cent claims were settled *after* the granting of permission. Similar rates of post-permission settlement could be discerned before the reforms, suggesting that the increase in pre-permission settlement does not reflect a reduction in post-permission settlement: rather, 'settlement activity as a whole has increased' (at 246–7).

14.2.4 Operation of the permission stage

There are a number of specific grounds on which permission may be refused, such as the claimant's absence of recourse to alternative remedies before resorting to judicial review, failure to comply with the strict time limits which apply to judicial review, lack of standing, and that the outcome for the claimant would not have been substantially different absent the claimed illegality. These are all considered in detail later in this chapter. In addition, the courts are concerned at the permission stage with whether the case is arguable, on which Lord Diplock offered the following guidance in *R* v. *Inland Revenue Commissioners, ex parte National Federation of Self-employed and Small Businesses Ltd* [1982] AC 617 at 643–4:

> The whole purpose of requiring that leave should first be obtained to make the application for judicial review would be defeated if the court were to go into the matter in any depth at that stage. If, on a quick perusal of the material then available, the court thinks that it discloses what might on further consideration turn out to be an arguable case in favour of granting to the applicant the relief claimed, it ought, in the exercise of judicial discretion, to give him leave to apply for that relief.

It is hardly surprising that, thus conceived, the permission stage rarely proved an insuper-able obstacle to claimants: Bondy and Sunkin [2008] *PL* 674 at 648 note that in 1981, 71 per cent of claimants who sought leave (as it was then called) obtained it. But they go on to note (at 653) that '[t]hese heady days ... were not to last'. By 1996 the success rate had fallen to 58 per cent, and by 2006 it had reached 22 per cent. They suggest a number of potential reasons for this dramatic fall. First, in the 1990s, the courts began to apply a much more rigorous test than that adopted by Lord Diplock in the *Inland Revenue* case. The modern approach was set out in the following terms by Lords Bingham and Walker in *Sharma v. Brown-Antoine* [2006] UKPC 57, [2007] 1 WLR 780:

> [T]he court will refuse leave to claim judicial review unless satisfied that there is an arguable ground for judicial review having a realistic prospect of success and not subject to a discretionary bar such as delay or an alternative remedy ... but arguability cannot be judged without reference to the nature and gravity of the issue to be argued. It is a test which is flexible in its application ... It is not enough that a case is potentially arguable.

Second, the decline since 2000 may be attributable to the effects of the Bowman reforms. It has always been the case that permission decisions taken on the papers are less likely to result in the granting of permission than those taken following oral argument: it is there-fore significant that, post-Bowman, the vast majority of such decisions are taken on paper. Moreover, Bondy and Sunkin (*op cit* at 656–7) postulate a link between rising settlement and falling permission rates:

> The increased rate of early settlements occurs because the Pre-Action Protocol ... encourage[s] defendants to look more closely at claims before they reach the permission stage. This leads defendants to concede/settle where they accept the essence of the claim, or for other, pragmatic, reasons. This, in turn, may leave the less meritorious, or more contentious, claims to proceed to the permission stage, which may help explain why judges are insufficiently convinced of the merit of a relatively high proportion of these claims.
>
> If this is correct, it indicates that we should not necessarily assume that, just because lower proportions of claimants are obtaining permission, claimants are becoming less successful in their claims for judicial review. On the contrary, it may be more accurate to argue that because greater numbers of cases are being resolved earlier, access to the court is becoming less necessary.

In its 2012 consultation paper on reform of judicial review the government claimed that despite the growth over time in the numbers of judicial review claims very few in fact stood any reasonable prospect of success (*Judicial Review: Proposals for Reform*, Cm 8515 (2012) at 9–10). To support this claim the government pointed to official sta-tistics which showed that in 2011 of 7,600 applications for permission considered by the Administrative Court, only one sixth (1,200) were granted permission. Bondy and Sunkin (*UK Constitutional Law Blog*, 10 January 2013) (*http://ukconstitutionallaw.org*) in response argued that it was overly simplistic to interpret the statistics as supporting the view that many judicial reviews are unmeritorious. In addition to the arguments quoted immediately above, the statistics do not take into account the 3,200 claims that disap-peared between being issued (11,200 were issued in 2011) and the permission stage (7,600 were considered at the permission stage). Bondy and Sunkin argue that it is likely many of these 3,200 cases would have been withdrawn following a settlement but prior to being considered at the permission stage, and that such cases are usually settled in favour of the claimant. In turn this would suggest a much higher success rate for claimants than the government's statistics suggest. Furthermore, if immigration and asylum judicial reviews are excluded from consideration—given such cases have now largely being transferred to the Upper Tribunal—the success rate rises even higher, given success rates are very low for immigration cases.

Thus, when placed in context falling permission rates are perhaps not as serious a cause for concern as might first appear. However, very serious concerns are raised by the apparently inconsistent way that different judges make decisions at the permission stage. Such inconsistency is perhaps unsurprising given that decisions as to permission are subject to very wide judicial discretion rather than clear-cut rules. Bondy and Sunkin (*op cit* at 664–5) found that of the eight judges they looked at who made substantial numbers of permission decisions within the study period, success rates varied dramatically: one judge granted permission in 46 per cent of the (non-immigration/asylum) cases that came before him, while one of his colleagues granted permission in only 11 per cent of cases. Bondy and Sunkin (*op cit* at 667) note that this problem may become more acute now that the Administrative Court has opened several regional centres:

> The present centralised system provides access to a relatively large pool of judges and, while inconsistency affects the relative chances of individual claimants obtaining permission, more systemic biases are likely to be ironed out by the number of judges involved. As a smaller number of judges take responsibility for judicial review in the regional centres, variation in grant and refusal rates may become a greater concern. While it is not suggested that statistics should be used as a management tool by the judiciary, as justice requires that each case be considered individually, there is a clear need to find a way to ensure that inconsistency of approach across these centres does not make access to judicial review a regional lottery.

QUESTION

- The Bowman Report's recommendation that there should be a presumption in favour of granting permission was never implemented. Should it have been?

If, as is usually the case, the permission decision is taken without a hearing, CPR 54.12(3) permits the claimant to request that the decision be reconsidered at a hearing. If permission is refused again, then the claimant may, under CPR 52.15(1), seek permission from the Court of Appeal to appeal to that court which, under CPR 52.15(3), 'may, instead of giving permission to appeal, give permission to apply for judicial review', in which case, according to CPR 52.15(4), 'the case will proceed in the High Court unless the Court of Appeal orders otherwise'.

Perhaps reflecting the lottery-like nature of the permission stage, cases which have been refused permission at first instance have more often than might be expected ultimately resulted in substantive decisions of the Supreme Court. Even where such appeals are ultimately dismissed by the Supreme Court, the fact that significant judgments of the highest court were required to dispose of these cases reflects that these cases raised serious issues to be tried: eg *R (KM)* v. *Cambridgeshire County Council* [2012] UKSC 23, [2012] PTSR 1189; *R (O)* v. *Secretary of State for the Home Department* [2016] UKSC 19, [2016] 1 WLR 1717. In turn this reinforces the importance of provision for renewal of initial permission decisions at oral hearings, and appellate scrutiny of permission decisions, so as to guard against errors—which are all the more likely where decisions are made absent oral argument, and which have the serious consequence of denying citizens access to court.

Despite the importance of provision for error-correction, reforms introduced in 2013 impose further restrictions on procedures for scrutiny of initial permission decisions. If a case is deemed by the judge who considers the original permission application on the papers as 'totally without merit' (in accordance with CPR 23.12), then the right to renew the case at an oral hearing shall be lost (CPR 54.12(7)), and any appeal against the refusal shall be to the Court of Appeal on the papers only (CPR 52.15(1A)). In *R (Grace)* v. *Secretary of State for the Home Department* [2014] EWCA Civ 1091, [2014] 1 WLR 3432, the Court of Appeal rejected the argument that a narrower meaning should be attributed to 'totally without merit' than the plain meaning of those words indicated. It held that this would be to defeat the policy underlying introduction of the provisions, which was to reel in the number of hopeless judicial review claims which cause needless trouble for public authorities, and burden the courts (as we saw earlier, whether the factual premises of these claims are correct is far from clear). As such, the phrase can mean 'no more and no less than "bound to fail"' (at [13]). Maurice Kay LJ, giving the lead judgment, did however point out that certain safeguards protected against these new provisions operating unfairly: a claimant could appeal to the Court of Appeal on the papers, and 'no judge will certify an application as [totally without merit] unless he is confident after careful consideration that the case truly is bound to fail. He or she will no doubt have in mind the seriousness of the issue and the consequences of his decision in the particular case' (at [15]).

14.3   Exhaustion of alternative remedies

14.3.1   The principle and its rationale

It is generally accepted that, at least in principle, '[j]udicial review has always been a remedy of last resort' (*R (Cart)* v. *The Upper Tribunal* [2011] UKSC 28, [2012] 1 AC 663 at [19], [33]). Judicial review may only be invoked when other avenues, such as rights of appeal (if granted by the relevant statute), have been explored; if they have not, then permission may be denied: *Cart* at [33].

In a canonical statement of principle in *R* v. *Inland Revenue Commissioners, ex parte Preston* [1985] AC 835 at 852, Lord Scarman said that

a remedy by way of judicial review is not to be made available where an alternative remedy exists. This is a proposition of great importance. Judicial review is ... not an appeal. Where Parliament has provided by statute appeal procedures, ... it will only be very rarely that the courts will allow the ... process of judicial review to be used to attack an appealable decision.

Indeed, the importance of exhausting alternative remedies is now reflected in the Pre-Action Protocol for Judicial Review, which states:

[5] Judicial review should only be used where no adequate alternative remedy, such as a right of appeal, is available. Even then, judicial review may not be appropriate in every instance ...

[9] The courts take the view that litigation should be a last resort. The parties should consider whether some form of alternative dispute resolution ('ADR') or complaints procedure would be more suitable than litigation, and if so, endeavour to agree which to adopt. Both the claimant and defendant may be required by the court to provide evidence that alternative means of resolving their dispute were considered. Parties are warned that if the protocol is not followed (including this paragraph) then the court must have regard to such conduct when determining costs.

We will see later that the requirement to exhaust alternative remedies admits of a number of exceptions. First, however, what policy arguments may justify having such a requirement at all?

Lewis, 'The Exhaustion of Alternative Remedies in Administrative Law' [1992] *CLJ* 138

The courts have put forward a twofold justification of the exhaustion of remedies principle. First, [it was said in *R* v. *Panel on Take-overs and Mergers, ex parte Guinness plc* [1990] 1 QB 146 at 177 that] if Parliament has provided an appeals procedure, it is not for the court to usurp the functions of the appellate body. The reasoning is applied also to bodies not created by statute which have their own appellate system. Secondly, the public interest dictates that judicial review should be exercised speedily, and to that end it is necessary to limit the number of cases in which judicial review is used [see the *Guinness* case at 177–8].

... There are further advantages in the rule. Appellate bodies may [for reasons considered at 13.2] be better or equally well equipped to handle disputes of fact than a court operating the judicial review mechanisms. ... An appellate body prepared and able to re-hear evidence and witnesses and determine questions of fact may be a better check on inadequate decisions than judicial review.

There may also be gains in expertise to be made by having recourse to alternative remedies. Where the appeal is to the court, that appeal may be to a Division of the High Court particularly familiar with the area of law in question as in tax cases, where the appeal is heard in the Chancery Division. Administrative appeal bodies may also possess relevant expertise. In tax cases, for example, the appellate body, [the Tax Chamber of the First-tier Tribunal, on which see ch 18], [has] wide experience of the complex and detailed tax legislation. In employment cases, the system of [employment] tribunals may be better equipped to deal with industrial issues than the Divisional Court. In the event that the matter is finally brought before the courts by way of judicial review of the decision of an appellate body, the court will enjoy the advantage of a reasoned decision by those familiar with the legislation and the background issues.

In spite of the practical advantages which apparently flow from the exhaustion principle, objections have been raised, most prominently by Wade and Forsyth, *Administrative Law* (Oxford 2014) at 600:

In principle there ought to be no categorical rule requiring the exhaustion of administrative remedies before judicial review can be granted. A vital aspect of the rule of law is that illegal administrative action can be challenged in the court as soon as it is taken or threatened. There should be no need first to pursue any administrative procedure or appeal in order to see whether the action will in the end be taken or not. An administrative appeal on the merits of the case is something quite different from judicial determination of the legality of the whole matter. This is merely to restate the essential difference between review and appeal.

The point concerning appeal and review merits further consideration. Traditionally, they serve distinct roles, looking respectively at merits and legality: the nature of the alleged defect in the relevant administrative decision should therefore determine which is appropriate. However, Lewis [1992] *CLJ* 138 at 141–2 replies that there 'has been a degree of convergence between appeal and review in recent years', and notes, in particular, that the expansion of the concept of error of law (on which see ch 2) means there is often very little difference between judicial review and appeal on a point of law; developments in substantive review reinforce this argument of convergence: see ch 8. He concludes that because 'many errors can now be corrected either by appeal or judicial review, the choice of which mechanism to apply must be settled by reference to other considerations'.

QUESTION

- Do you agree that alternative remedies should, as a general rule, have to be used before permission to seek judicial review is granted?

Recent judgments have strongly emphasized that the question of exhaustion ought to be determined at the permission stage, and should not be put off until the substantive hearing or dealt with in a rolled up hearing. This contrasts with the treatment of other factors that bear on permission, such as standing, which, as we shall see, is not uncommonly dealt with at the substantive hearing, not least because it depends upon consideration of whether the claimant has a meritorious case or not. In contrast, the question of alternative relief can be more easily decoupled from consideration of the substantive merits of the claim, and thus treated as a threshold issue reserved for the permission stage. The reasons for requiring the exhaustion issue to be dealt with at the permission stage echo the general reasons for having a permission stage: avoidance of wasted court and party costs and time spent on a full hearing which is ultimately pointless: *R (Willford)* v. *Financial Services Authority* [2013] EWCA 677 at [37]; *R (Great Yarmouth Port Company Ltd)* v. *Marine Management Organisation* [2013] EWHC 3052 (Admin) at [68]–[70].

14.3.2 Exceptions to the general principle

It is clear from the terms in which he stated the exhaustion rule in *Preston* (see 14.3.1) that Lord Scarman envisaged that it would operate only as a general principle to which exceptions would exist, while the Supreme Court has since endorsed the necessity of recognizing exceptions: *Cart* [2011] UKSC 28, [2012] 1 AC 663 at [21]. Indeed, over time the courts have recognized a number of circumstances in which judicial review may lie irrespective of whether other remedies have been used. However, it is important to note that courts increasingly emphasize that where there is provision for *statutory appeals*, especially into the new integrated *tribunal system*, it will be an 'exceptional case' where the court entertains review proceedings: *Willford* [2013] EWCA 677 at [20], [36]; *Great Yarmouth Port Company* [2013] EWHC 3052 (Admin) at [41]–[56].

It appears that the exhaustion rule will not be applied if the individual concerned is able to demonstrate that his case is different from the type of case for which the appeal procedure was designed. Sir John Donaldson MR endorsed such an approach in *R* v. *Secretary of State for the Home Department, ex parte Swati* [1986] 1 WLR 477 at 485, saying that prospective claimants should be required to use rights of appeal unless they 'can distinguish [their] case from the type of case for which the appeal procedure was provided'.

Thus, for instance, it is clear that the use of a remedy by way of appeal will not be treated as a condition precedent to judicial review if the appellate body lacks the power to deal with the matter which is complained of. In *Leech* v. *Deputy Governor of Parkhurst Prison* [1988] AC 533, two prisoners wished to challenge deputy prison governors' findings that they were each guilty of a disciplinary offence resulting in loss of remission. A remedy existed by way of petition to the Secretary of State, who was empowered to remit the punishment but not (at that time) to quash the findings of guilt. Both claimants petitioned the Secretary of State, one successfully. However, since both wished the findings of guilt to be quashed, both sought judicial review. The question arose whether the claimants could challenge the deputy prison governors' decisions, as distinct from the Secretary of State's decisions. In deciding that they could, Lord Bridge said (at 567):

> One manifest inadequacy of the remedy by petition is the absence of any power in the Secretary of State to quash the adjudication. This may seem of minor significance. If the award has been remitted, it may perhaps be of little consequence that the adjudication of guilt has not been set aside. But when the prisoner's record shows merely that the punishment awarded for an offence has been remitted by the Secretary of State, those who have to take account of the record, as for example when the prisoner's eligibility for parole is under consideration, will not know, in a case such as that of Leech, that the proceedings leading to the award were wholly invalid and it is at least possible that the record may operate to his prejudice. This is a lacuna in the rules which can readily be cured by amendment and it is very desirable that it should be. If the Secretary of State had power to quash the adjudication as well as power to remit the award, it would be difficult to suppose that the court, as a matter of discretion, would be likely to grant judicial review to a prisoner who had not petitioned the Secretary of State, save in a case of urgency where the prisoner's release was imminent but would be delayed by loss of remission ordered by the disputed award.

It is evident from these remarks that Lord Bridge considered that an alternative remedy may be rendered inadequate, such as to obviate the need to have recourse to it, not only by the limited powers of the appellate body but also by the speed with which a remedy may be issued: in urgent cases, judicial review may be appropriate given the speed with which permission may be obtained and interim relief secured. Thus the fact that, compared to judicial review, the alternative remedy in *R* v. *Chief Constable of the Merseyside Police, ex parte Calveley* [1986] QB 424 at 434 was 'not speedy' was apparently one of the factors which persuaded the Court that the exhaustion principle should give way, in addition to the fact that the Court identified clear administrative unlawfulness that called for judicial intervention (at 433, 435). Contrariwise, the principle is more likely to be applied if the court feels that the disputed point lies within the expertise of the appellate body, raises disputed questions of fact which the appellate body is better placed to resolve, and/or the appellate body is able to take a decision on the merits as opposed to merely having a power to refer the matter back to the decision-maker: *Great Yarmouth Port Company* at [47]–[49]; *General Medical Council* v. *Michalak* [2016] EWCA Civ 172, [2016] ICR 628.

What if the complaint falls squarely within the competence of the appellate body but resorting to appeal rather than review would be inconvenient, or even cause grave hardship, to the individual concerned? This issue arose in *R (Lim)* v. *Secretary of State for the Home Department* [2007] EWCA Civ 773, [2008] INLR 60, in which the claimant had leave to remain in the UK subject to certain conditions, one of which was that he could work only at the Lucky Star restaurant in Norwich. After immigration officers found the claimant (collecting food for the Lucky Star, according to him) at another restaurant, directions were issued to remove him to Malaysia. An 'out-of-country' appeal system existed, meaning that the claimant could have exercised his right of appeal only *after* being removed. This, unsurprisingly, prompted the claimant to attempt to proceed via judicial review instead. Sedley LJ (at [27]–[29]), with whom Potter P and Wilson LJ agreed, had sympathy for the claimant's position: the Home Secretary was guilty of a 'colossal overreaction to what, even if proved, was a venial breach of condition'. Ultimately, however, his Lordship felt he had 'no alternative' but to hold that judicial review was unavailable: the claimant had failed to use the appeal system, and his case raised 'precisely the kind of issue for which the legislation ... prescribed an out-of-country appeal'.

It is important to note, lastly, Lord Phillips MR's judgment of the Court in *R (G)* v. *Immigration Appeal Tribunal* [2004] EWCA Civ 1731, [2005] 1 WLR 1445, which counsels against courts comparing *in a vacuum* the relevant alternative procedure and judicial review proceedings to determine whether the alternative procedure affords an adequate remedy. While the courts must remain vigilant in policing the rule of law, the separation of powers requires courts to 'have regard to legislative policy': 'When Parliament enacts a remedy with the clear intention that this should be pursued in place of judicial review, it is appropriate to have regard to the considerations giving rise to that intention' in deciding whether to entertain a claim for judicial review (at [20]; see similarly *Willford* at [38], [54]). In *G*, the relevant statutory context was s 101(2) of the Nationality, Immigration and Asylum Act 2002, which provided for statutory review of decisions by the Immigration Appeal Tribunal refusing permission to appeal to that tribunal. That review procedure differed from judicial review: it was conducted by a single High Court judge and there was no provision for an oral hearing or an appeal. As such, the procedure was much swifter than judicial review, but also not a perfect substitute for full-fledged review proceedings. Lord Phillips considered that while the statutory provision did not oust judicial review, the Court would refuse permission to hear a case which gave rise to issues that could be dealt with via the statutory procedure. To do otherwise would be to undermine Parliament's intention in creating the procedure, which was to ensure immigration cases were dealt with expeditiously. Given this legislative goal the statutory procedure afforded adequate and proportionate protection to the claimant's rights.

QUESTIONS

- Are the decisions in *Lim* and *G* acceptable?
- Should the duty to exhaust alternative remedies yield when its application would cause inconvenience or hardship to the person concerned or confine the claimant to procedures which are significantly inferior to review proceedings in terms of the procedural protection they afford?

14.4 Time limits

14.4.1 Introduction

Those who wish to use the judicial review procedure must usually act very quickly.

Senior Courts Act 1981

31—(6) Where the High Court considers that there has been undue delay in making an application for judicial review, the court may refuse to grant—

    (a) leave for the making of the application; or

    (b) any relief sought on the application,

if it considers that the granting of the relief sought would be likely to cause substantial hardship to, or substantially prejudice the rights of, any person or would be detrimental to good administration.

  (7) Subsection (6) is without prejudice to any enactment or rule of court which has the effect of limiting the time within which an application for judicial review may be made.

Civil Procedure Rules Part 54

5. (1) The claim form must be filed—

    (a) promptly; and

    (b) in any event not later than 3 months after the grounds to make the claim first arose.

  (2) The time limit in this rule may not be extended by agreement between the parties.

  (3) This rule does not apply when any other enactment specifies a shorter time limit for making the claim for judicial review.

Civil Procedure Rules Part 3

1. (2) Except where these Rules provide otherwise, the court may—

    (a) extend or shorten the time for compliance with any rule, practice direction or court order (even if an application for extension is made after the time for compliance has expired).

The interpretation of these provisions has caused considerable difficulties for the courts, not least because it is unclear how those contained in the Act and those found in the CPR (which largely reproduce the rules that were set down by the Rules of the Supreme Court, Ord 53, r 4) relate to one another. However, before turning to that problem, a preliminary matter should be considered. Whatever interpretative difficulties are raised by the above provisions, it is perfectly clear that they create a very narrow window of opportunity for prospective claimants, with a benchmark requirement that litigation should be initiated within three months. The justification for this very short time limit in judicial review cases is said to lie in the need for certainty in public administration: Lord Diplock considered in *O'Reilly* v. *Mackman* [1983] 2 AC 237 at 280–1 that

> public authorities and third parties should not be kept in suspense as to the legal validity of a decision the authority has reached in purported exercise of decision-making powers for any longer period than is absolutely necessary in fairness to the person affected by the decision.

The position in relation to judicial review stands in stark contrast to that which obtains in private law or other rights-based fields, such as human rights law. Shorter time limits used to apply in respect of private law litigation against public authorities, but that is no longer the case. Thus, for instance, most claims in tort against public authorities are now subject to the standard limitation period of six years under the Limitation Act 1980. Albeit claims under the Human Rights Act 1998 (HRA) must be made within three months if brought via judicial review, if initiated via ordinary proceedings the claim may be brought up to one year from the date on which the act complained of took place (HRA, s 7(5)), this one-year limit matching that for some other torts, such as defamation. Recall that in ch 13 we observed that those who bring claims under the HRA will often have a genuine choice between bringing claims via review or ordinary proceedings.

Beloff (in Forsyth and Hare (eds), *The Golden Metwand and the Crooked Cord* (Oxford 1998) at 270) doubts whether a special case can convincingly be made for judicial review:

> A distinction is presumably drawn between the (relatively slight) consequences to a public authority of having its funds depleted for committing a private law wrong and the (relatively significant) consequences of having its actions impeded for committing a public law wrong. And yet some of the arguments (for example, budgetary certainty) which were once relied on to justify the [shorter] private law limitation period [for public authorities] are [now] echoed in the judicial review cases.

A further difficulty concerns the generality of the strict time limit which applies to judicial review. It is self-evident that some situations will arise in which the need for certainty is compelling; but, as Oliver [2002] *PL* 91 at 98–9 comments, it does not follow that this is true across the board:

> Statutory limitation periods may be justifiably imposed in respect of challenges to certain orders, as is the case with compulsory purchase orders and refusals of planning permission. Short statutory time-limits could be imposed in respect of other matters where delay would materially affect the outcome of the case, as in immigration and asylum claims, for instance. Apart from such specific areas the disadvantages for public administration and for third parties if proceedings are brought late can be met effectively in other ways: by the exercise of the power under Part 24 [of the CPR] to give summary judgment, by the exercise of discretion in the award of remedies and by the award of costs against unsuccessful claimants.

Consonant with this contextual approach the CPR have recently been amended so that shorter time periods apply for certain classes of review claim. Thus, reviews of ministerial or local planning authorities' decisions under planning legislation are subject to a limit of six weeks from the time that grounds for review first arose (CPR 54.5(5)). Judicial review of decisions governed by the Public Contracts Regulations 2015, are regulated by the time limit provided for in regulation 92 of those Regulations, generally 30 days from the time when the claimant knew or ought to have known of the grounds for challenge (CPR 54.5(6)). The promptness requirement in CPR 54.1 does not apply to these classes of case, given that the very short time limits guarantee promptness: CPR 54.5(4). One possible criticism of these shorter time limits is that they may in fact have the counterproductive effect of drawing out disputes. Shorter time limits will allow insufficient time for parties to undertake the Pre-Action Protocol procedure, which in turn will greatly reduce the opportunity for early settlement and avoidance of litigation.

While stricter criteria are applied in some contexts, the courts have been willing to more or less do away with the promptness requirement in other classes of case where delay is unlikely to be prejudicial to public administration. For example, in *A* v. *Essex County Council* [2010] UKSC 33, [2011] 1 AC 280 at [116], Lady Hale drew a distinction between claims for different types of relief, observing that expedition is less obviously necessary for certain types of claim. While grant of an order quashing past decisions may seriously prejudice administrative interests in certainty and finality if issued long after the relevant decisions were made, remedies such as declarations or damages do not necessarily affect the validity of past decisions, so that the grant of such relief long after the impugned administrative decisions were made is unlikely to prejudice good public administration.

QUESTIONS

- Is the general requirement that judicial review claims must be issued promptly and in any event within three months of the commission of the administrative action in question an acceptable one?
- Do you agree with the exceptions that have been established to the three-month time limit and the requirement of promptness?
- Can you think of other classes of judicial review cases which might warrant a longer or shorter limitation period than three months?

14.4.2 Interpreting the rules

The provisions on time limits contained in the Senior Courts Act 1981 and CPR do not easily fit together, leading to considerable problems of interpretation. Authoritative guidance was, however, provided by Lord Goff in *R* v. *Dairy Produce Quota Tribunal for England and Wales, ex parte Caswell* [1990] 2 AC 738 at 747, who said:

> [W]hen an application for leave to apply is not made promptly and in any event within three months, the court may refuse leave on the ground of delay unless it considers that there is good reason for extending the period; but, even if it considers that there is such good reason, it may still refuse leave (or, where leave has been granted, substantive relief) if in its opinion the granting of the relief sought would be likely to cause hardship or prejudice (as specified in section 31(6)) or would be detrimental to good administration.

The effect of Lord Goff's analysis is that the question of time limits falls to be approached in three stages.

14.4.3 Stage one: undue delay

The first question is whether there has been 'undue delay' in the s 31(6) sense; although this term is undefined by the statute, it is evident from CPR 54.5(1) that such delay will exist if the permission is not sought promptly and, in any event, within three months. The clock begins to run, according to CPR 54.5(1), when 'the grounds to make the claim first arose'—an objective criterion which takes no account of when the claimant became aware of the grounds. Although this test is generally straightforward, difficulties can arise when the matter to which the claimant wishes to object has been the subject of more than one administrative decision.

This point is illustrated by the House of Lords' decision in *R (Burkett)* v. *Hammersmith and Fulham London Borough Council* [2002] UKHL 23, [2002] 1 WLR 1593. The claimant lived next to land in respect of which outline planning permission was sought. On 15 September 1999, the planning authority resolved to grant outline planning permission subject to, *inter alia*, the developer's entering into a satisfactory agreement under s 106 of the Town and Country Planning Act 1990 concerning the nature of the proposed development. Outline planning permission was granted on 12 May 2000. The legal issue before the House of Lords was whether time began to run on 15 September 1999 or 12 May 2000: if the former, then the claimant would be *prima facie* out of time; if the latter, then no problem regarding time limits would arise. Their Lordships concluded that, although the resolution could have been challenged, this should not (by virtue of time being deemed to have begun to run as at the date of the resolution) prevent the claimant from challenging the later grant of planning permission itself, for reasons explained by Lord Steyn (at [39]):

> As a matter of language it is possible to say in respect of a challenge to an alleged unlawful aspect of the grant of planning permission that 'grounds for the application first arose' when the decision was made. The ground for challenging the resolution is that it is a decision to do an unlawful act in the future; the ground for challenging the actual grant is that an unlawful act has taken place. And the fact that the element of unlawfulness was already foreseeable at earlier stages in the planning process does not detract from this natural and obvious meaning. The context supports this interpretation. Until the actual grant of planning permission the resolution has no legal effect. It is unlawful for the developer to commence any works in reliance on the resolution. And a developer expends money on the project before planning permission is granted at his own risk. The resolution may come to nothing because of a change of circumstances. It may fall to the ground because of conditions which are not fulfilled. It may lapse because negotiations for the conclusion of a section 106 agreement break down. After the resolution is adopted the local authority may come under a duty to reconsider its decision if flaws are brought to its attention: *R v West Oxfordshire District Council, Ex parte C H Pearce Homes Ltd* (1985) 26 R.V.R. 156. Moreover, it is not in doubt that a local authority may in its discretion revoke an outline resolution. In the search for the best contextual interpretation these factors tend to suggest that the date of the resolution does not trigger the three-month time limit in respect of a challenge to the actual grant of planning permission.

It follows that although preliminary acts may be challenged—subject to the possibility, considered at 14.5, that such challenges may be ruled out on the ground of prematurity—their commission should not necessarily start the clock running such that claimants are effectively forced to challenge preliminary measures instead of 'final' measures which may well be taken more than three months later.

It is important to note, however, that the courts have backtracked somewhat on *Burkett*, or at least not fully embraced the spirit of that decision, in certain factual matrices. Thus, there are increasing indications that where the first decision in a decision process is one with 'legal effect' (thus distinguishing this class of case from the facts of *Burkett*), but the claimant seeks to challenge a second, subsequent decision in the same process, which is substantially based on or premised upon the first decision, on grounds on which the first decision could have been challenged—*ie* each decision raises the same legal concern—the court may hold that time started to run from the first decision. For example, in *R (Nash) v. Barnet London Borough Council* [2013] EWCA Civ 1004, [2013] PTSR 1457, the Court held that the grounds for making a claim of a lack of public consultation first arose when the defendant decided to commence a public procurement process, so that the claimant could not wait to challenge the final decision in that process, namely the grant of a contract, on the same ground. Time ran from the earlier decision. A court may alternatively hold, as a matter of discretion, that the failure to challenge the earlier decision in a timely manner bars the grant of permission to challenge the later decision: *R (Champion) v. North Norfolk District Council* [2015] UKSC 52, [2015] 1 WLR 3710 at [63]. In adopting these positions the courts have laid particular emphasis on the importance of certainty and finality, and the interests of good administration generally. We note, however, that these decisions have largely been confined to the planning and procurement contexts, in which courts and the CPR lay especial emphasis on expedition.

Two further points should be noted concerning stage one. First, acting within three months does not conclusively establish that there has been no undue delay. The requirements in CPR 54.5(1) to act promptly and, in any event, within three months are cumulative: as Keene LJ put it in *Hardy v. Pembrokeshire County Council* [2006] EWCA Civ 240, [2006] Env LR 28 at [10], it is 'quite wrong to assume that filing within three months amounts to filing promptly. It may or may not, depending on the circumstances.' Although claims made within three months are rarely ruled out of time on the ground of lack of promptitude, the possibility of doing so constitutes, as Lord Steyn remarked in *Burkett* at [18], 'a useful reserve power in some cases, such as where an application made well within the three month period would cause immense practical difficulties'. For instance, in *R v. Rochdale Metropolitan Borough Council, ex parte Butterworth* [2000] Ed CR 117, permission for judicial review was denied in respect of a challenge to the defendant council's decision not to allocate the claimants to their first-choice secondary schools. The claim was brought just within three months, but just after the beginning of the academic year. David Pannick QC (sitting as a Deputy Judge of the High Court) justified his finding that the claimants had not acted promptly by saying that it was imperative, in the absence of exceptional circumstances, that such decisions should be challenged before the beginning of the school year, so as to avoid disruption to the pupils concerned and to others. Meanwhile, in *Finn-Kelcey v. Milton Keynes Borough Council* [2008] EWCA Civ 1067, [2009] Env LR 17, permission to seek judicial review of a grant of planning permission was denied notwithstanding that it had been brought (just) within three months. The need for particular promptness in such cases arose, said Keene LJ at [22], because once permission has been granted, the developer is entitled to start work immediately; the need for certainty is therefore particularly compelling.

But note also those classes of case discussed at 14.4.1 where the courts have indicated that the promptness criterion adds little to the three-month limit, such as claims for damages under the HRA or for declarations. Further, if the claimant has a good reason for failing to bring their claim as promptly as might otherwise have been expected, their lack of promptness may be forgiven. For example, in *R (MacRae) v. Herefordshire District Council*

[2012] EWCA Civ 457, [2012] JPL 1356, the claimant only just brought their claim within the three-month time limit, yet the Court considered there was no basis for refusing permission for lack of promptness. A principal reason why was that the defendant council had given inadequate reasons for its decision, so that it had been reasonable for the claimant to take time to seek clarification of those reasons before launching proceedings. In terms of wider guidance as to the reasons courts will accept as justifying a lack of promptness, we suggest courts will be guided by factors similar to those which guide decisions whether to extend the three-month time limit: see 14.4.4.

Second, although cases like *Butterworth* and *Finn-Kelcey* demonstrate the evident utility of the discretion to deny permission, within three months, on the ground of lack of promptitude, Lords Steyn and Hope expressed concern in *Burkett* (obiter, at [53] and [59] respectively) that the resulting restriction on the right of access to court within a reasonable time, enshrined in Article 6(1) ECHR, may fall foul of the Convention principle of legality, which requires limitations imposed by national law on Convention rights to be formulated with sufficient certainty. This matter was considered in more depth in *Hardy*. Keene LJ (with whom the other two judges agreed) was not persuaded that the promptness criterion fell foul of the ECHR. He noted that the ECtHR had considered this matter in *Lam* v. *United Kingdom* Application 41671/98 (ECtHR, 5 July 2001)—a case which had not been cited to the House of Lords in *Burkett*—and had concluded that the criterion constituted a 'proportionate measure taken in pursuit of a legitimate aim'.

However, the CJEU had cause to consider this issue in *Uniplex (UK) Ltd* v. *NHS Business Service Authority* (Case C-406/08) [2010] 2 CMLR 47. The Court held that the notion of promptitude is insufficiently certain to meet the requirements of EU law and that the relevant date for the commencement of the time limit should be the date on which the claimant knew or ought to have known of the ground of challenge. For procurement decisions specifically, which *Uniplex* concerned, a standard 30-day time limit now applies, and the promptness requirement no longer applies: CPR 54.5(6) (see 14.4.1). This change directly implements *Uniplex*. However, the decision has a wider ambit than merely EU procurement cases; domestic courts have confirmed that *Uniplex* applies to all review claims with an EU dimension: *R (Buglife)* v. *Medway Council* [2011] EWHC 746 (Admin), [2011] 3 CMLR 39 at [63]; *R (Berky)* v. *Newport City Council* [2012] EWCA Civ 378, [2012] 2 CMLR 44. For as long as the UK remains a member of the EU national courts shall be required by EU law to set aside national procedural rules which are inconsistent with EU law. Thus, in cases concerning EU law, courts will have to grant permission whenever a claim is brought ('promptly' or not) within three months of the relevant date. However, the courts have indicated that where the claimant has not acted in a timeous manner this *may* lead to a discretionary denial of *relief*, including in EU cases, consistent with a more general reassertion of an open-ended discretionary approach to refusal of relief in judicial review and specifically in EU cases: *Walton* v. *Scottish Ministers* [2012] UKSC 44, [2013] PTSR 52 at [102]–[140], [155]–[156]; *R (Champion)* v. *North Norfolk District Council* [2015] UKSC 52, [2015] 1 WLR 3710 at [54]–[61], [63]; *R (The Licensed Taxi Drivers Association)* v. *Transport for London* [2016] EWHC 233 (Admin) at [78], [84]–[85]. But one would imagine that if discretionary refusal of permission on the basis of a promptness criterion violates the EU principle of certainty, discretionary refusal of relief on essentially the same basis and/or an open-ended discretionary approach more generally, will equally be liable to breach the certainty principle, as it will be very difficult to predict in advance whether a delay will lead to denial of relief (while this remedial approach arguably breaches other precepts of EU law: Varuhas [2013] *CLJ* 243). We observe in passing that certainty as to when remedies will be granted is also a requirement of human rights law under Article 13 ECHR, the right to an effective remedy: *eg McFarlane* v. *Ireland* (2011) 52 EHRR 20 at [117], [120].

14.4.4 Stage two: extending time

If there has been undue delay, then the court has a discretion under CPR 3.1(2) to extend time in favour of the claimant. RSC Ord 53, r 4(1) stated that time could be extended if there was a 'good reason' for doing so. That formula is not repeated in CPR 3.1(2), but was assumed to be implicit in it by Jackson J in *R (M)* v. *The School Organisation Committee, Oxfordshire County Council* [2001] EWHC 245 (Admin) at [14]–[26]. Although, as we saw at 14.2.1, the Pre-Action Protocol for Judicial Review requires intending claimants to communicate with potential defendants before seeking permission for judicial review, the courts are not unequivocally required to treat delay caused by compliance with the Protocol as a good reason for extending time. This follows from the first footnote to the Protocol, which provides that

[t]he court has a discretion to extend time. It cannot be taken that compliance with the protocol will of itself be sufficient to excuse delay or justify an extension of time, but it may be a relevant factor.

It has been held that exhausting rights of appeal can constitute a good reason for extending time (see, *eg R* v. *Rochdale Metropolitan Borough Council, ex parte Cromer Ring Mill Ltd* [1982] 3 All ER 761) but the position is unclear in relation to the use of ADR. The empirical work of Bondy and Sunkin [2009] *PL* 237 shows that such uncertainty acts as a disincentive to the use of devices such as mediation and negotiation. However, Supperstone *et al* [2006] *PL* 299 at 315 argue that in light of increased emphasis on the importance of attempting to resolve disputes non-litigously, claimants who seek to do so 'can expect a certain amount of latitude from the court' *vis-à-vis* the enforcement of time limits. They concede, though, that 'there is no certainty that pursuing mediation'—or indeed other alternative remedies—'will give grounds in every case for extending the period for applying for judicial review', and that 'it may [therefore] be that the CPR should be modified' in order to make formal provision for a relaxation of the time limits in such circumstances.

Some guidance as to what will constitute a good reason for extending time can be gleaned from the case law. For instance, it was held by Ackner LJ in *R* v. *Stratford-upon-Avon District Council, ex parte Jackson* [1985] 1 WLR 1319 at 1324 that obtaining legal aid is a good reason for delay. Albeit, in *R (007 Stratford Taxis Ltd)* v. *Stratford-on-Avon District Council* [2011] EWCA Civ 160, [2012] RTR 5, the Court responded to the claimant's explanation that delay was caused by the need to take advice and organize funding by saying: 'Those excuses are not impressive' (at [33]). Note, however, that this was a case where there had already been a long delay before the claimants began to seek out advice and organize funding; in turn this reflects that all relevant factors have to be considered and weighed in making decisions over time extensions, including the length of the delay. It is clear from the cases that courts' attitudes to extending time are also influenced by the context. Thus, for example, in the *M* case at [27], Jackson J concluded that no extension was appropriate in respect of a challenge to a school reorganization programme, bearing in mind that 'prolonged uncertainty is damaging to teachers, to pupils, to parents and to all the schools affected'. It is worth noting that a similar factor influenced the court in the *Butterworth* case, considered later, and could also be taken into account (at stage three) under s 31(6); the divisions between the three stages of the analysis should not, therefore, be taken to be watertight.

Similar considerations apply in the planning context—given the importance of certainty for development projects and third parties reliant on those projects going ahead and to guard against a rerunning of lengthy and costly consultation exercises after the fact—and the procurement context, given the need to avoid the rerunning of time-consuming procurement processes and where certainty for contracting parties is important. In these areas, courts are far more intent on claimants bringing claims as early as possible, just as they will be less willing to grant remedies to claimants who delay: eg *R (Champion)* v. *North Norfolk District Council* [2015] UKSC 52, [2015] 1 WLR 3710 at [63]; *R (The Licensed Taxi Drivers Association)* v. *Transport for London* [2016] EWHC 233 (Admin) at [78], [84]; *R (Nash)* v. *Barnet London Borough Council* [2013] EWCA Civ 1004, [2013] PTSR 1457 at [73]–[74]. Thus, in a case where planning permission has already been granted, 'very special reasons' will be required before a court will consider extending time, and a very strict approach shall be taken so that even where the claimant was delayed because of matters outside his immediate control, such as where delay is due to bad legal advice, he shall still be denied an extension: *R (Gerber)* v. *Wiltshire Council* [2016] EWCA Civ 84, [2016] WLR (D) 112 at [45]–[58]. In contrast, courts may be more willing to extend the limitation period in a human rights case given the importance of the matters at stake (*Rabone* v. *Pennine Care NHS Foundation Trust* [2012] UKSC 2, [2012] 2 AC 72 at [108]; *Gerber* at [54]).

14.4.5 Stage three: refusal of permission or relief

Even if the court concludes, at stage two, that there is a good reason for extending time, permission (or, at the substantive hearing, relief) may be refused under s 31(6) if granting a remedy would 'be likely to cause substantial hardship to, or substantially prejudice the rights of, any person or would be detrimental to good administration'.

In *R (Gerber)* v. *Wiltshire Council* [2016] EWCA Civ 84, [2016] WLR (D) 112 at [59], Sales LJ, with whom the other judges agreed, said that s 31(6)

> requires the court to make an overall evaluative assessment having regard to what, depending on the circumstances, may be a range of relevant considerations, including the extent of the substantial hardship or prejudice likely to be suffered by such other person … if relief is granted as compared with the hardship or prejudice to rights which would be suffered by the claimant … if relief is refused and the extent of the detriment to good administration if relief is granted as compared with the detriment to good administration through letting public law wrongs go without redress if relief is refused.

Sales LJ added that many of the factors that go to whether a court will extend a time limit (considered in the previous section) will also be relevant to determinations as to relief where the claimant has not acted promptly or in compliance with time limits (at [62]). It is also important to note Sales LJ's emphasis on context in the extract, which tends to suggest courts will be less likely to grant relief where the claimant has not acted with due expedition in planning or procurement cases in particular.

Hardship to individuals and detriment to their rights is particularly likely if late challenges to planning decisions are permitted. For instance, in *R* v. *North West Leicestershire District Council, ex parte Moses* [2000] Env LR 443, permission was denied to seek judicial review of planning permission in respect of runway extensions at an airport some years after planning consent had been granted. Simon Brown LJ had no difficulty in concluding that this would cause substantial hardship to third parties, not least the airport which had incurred construction costs approaching £70 million.

The other limb of s 31(6)—detriment to good administration—was addressed in *R v. Dairy Produce Quota Tribunal for England and Wales, ex parte Caswell* [1990] 2 AC 738. The claimants applied to the defendant for a wholesale milk production quota. Although disappointed by the size of the quota allocated to them in 1985, it was not until 1987 that they became aware of the possibility of seeking judicial review. They then did so, alleging that the Tribunal had misconstrued the relevant legislation. The House of Lords held that allowing the claim to be brought so long after the making of the original decision would be detrimental to good administration. Lord Goff explained (at 749–50) that, in the circumstances of the case, the public interest in good administration lay in

a regular flow of consistent decisions, made and published with reasonable dispatch; in citizens knowing where they stand, and how they can order their affairs in the light of the relevant decision. Matters of particular importance, apart from the length of time [that has elapsed since the decision was taken] ..., will be the extent of the effect of the relevant decision, and the impact which would be felt if it were to be re-opened. In the present case, the court was concerned with a decision to allocate part of a finite amount of quota, and with circumstances in which a re-opening of the decision would lead to other applications to re-open similar decisions which, if successful, would lead to re-opening the allocation of quota over a number of years. To me it is plain ... that to grant the appellants the relief they sought in the present case, after such a lapse of time had occurred, would be detrimental to good administration.

Beloff, in Forsyth and Hare (eds), *The Golden Metwand and the Crooked Cord* (Oxford 1998) at 279–80, draws a contrast between *Caswell* and *Patterson v. Greenwich London Borough Council* (1994) 26 HLR 159, in which permission was sought to challenge a local authority's decision concerning the provision of accommodation. Although undue delay was found, it was held that granting relief would not be detrimental to good administration. Evans LJ explained (at 168) that

this case unlike *Caswell* is not one where records or books of account are closed on a regular basis, and have to be reopened if a particular past decision is revised. Rather, the provision of accommodation and the assessing of applications by homeless persons is an ongoing and continuous process ... [T]he need to deal with such cases as they arise can properly be regarded as part of the responsibilities of good administration, and there is no evidence nor any grounds to infer that the burden will be especially or singularly great in the present case.

Cases where quashing one decision would invariably lead to the reopening of many other decisions are fairly clear cases where a court should pause before granting a quashing order. However, outside of this category of case judicial analysis of whether a remedy should be refused on the basis of detriment to administrative interests has been far from consistent. One reason for this is that decisions over remedies have traditionally been characterized by unstructured discretion, to be exercised on a case-by-case basis. Another problem is that judicial determinations of whether quashing will lead to negative administrative effects, and the extent and degree of those negative consequences is not typically disciplined by evidence. It is very common for judges to simply assert that quashing will result in serious negative consequences, while other judges may dismiss such concerns out of hand. For example, in *R (007 Stratford Taxis Ltd) v. Stratford-on-Avon District Council* [2011] EWCA Civ 160, [2012] RTR 5, the Council's decision to require new taxis to provide for wheelchair access was tainted by a serious procedural flaw which the Court accepted would ordinarily warrant relief; however, relief was denied in part on the assertion that '[w]e do, however, think that it would be detrimental to good administration if the cabinet were now required to reconsider the matter given the time that has elapsed' (at [34]). One may reasonably ask: why?

Some progress towards addressing inconsistency would be made if the courts adopted a structured approach with a common, set starting point. For example, in the early 2000s the House of Lords signalled that the starting point in deciding whether to grant or refuse relief is that unlawful decisions should be quashed, and very good reasons would be required to convince a court to depart from the default rule (albeit, regrettably, there has been regress towards a more open-ended approach to remedial discretion since: 14.4.3). A further improvement would be to require the defendant to produce evidence to substantiate claims of administrative hardship. Judicial conclusions that granting of relief will lead to negative administrative consequences are claims as to likely factual outcomes. In a legal process factual determinations ought to be based in evidence; the problem with not so disciplining factual determinations is that they may very well turn out to be wrong.

In any case, even if a court considers a decision should not be quashed so as to prevent administrative chaos, it should still issue a declaration to mark the illegality. This view was recently endorsed by Lord Toulson in *R (Hunt) v. North Somerset Council* [2015] UKSC 51, [2015] 1 WLR 3575 at [12]: '[I]n circumstances where a public body has acted unlawfully but where it is not appropriate to make a mandatory, prohibitory or quashing order, it will usually be appropriate to make some form of declaratory order to reflect the court's finding.'

14.5 Prematurity and ripeness

14.5.1 Introduction

We have already seen that, when a claimant establishes that administrative action is contrary to the principles of public law, relief does not automatically follow; rather, the court has discretion. It may therefore choose to withhold relief on the basis of, for example, the claimant's conduct or the wider public interest. In this context, a further question arises concerning the types of administrative measures in respect of which the courts are prepared to issue relief. The courts' supervisory jurisdiction is most commonly exercised in relation to decisions which have already been taken and are final or actions which have been completed. There are, however, many other forms of administrative action such as government circulars intended to guide exercise of public power into the future; preliminary decisions which are mere staging posts *en route* to some final, legally effective decision; and statements as to intended future action. Should courts be willing to issue remedies in respect of such actions if they disclose error of law or signify an intention to act unlawfully? Should courts go further, by issuing 'advisory declarations' in order to answer purely hypothetical or academic questions? Consideration of these issues raises questions of 'prematurity' and 'ripeness': when should courts refuse to adjudicate, or refuse relief, on the ground that the claimant has moved prematurely? And at what point does an issue mature into something which is ripe and appropriate for judicial review?

14.5.2 Preliminary and interlocutory decisions

The context in which the concept of prematurity is most developed is that of preliminary and interlocutory decisions. Lord Steyn observed in *R (Burkett)* v. *Hammersmith and Fulham London Borough Council* [2002] UKHL 23, [2002] 1 WLR 1593 at [38] that

> [i]n a context where there is a statutory procedure involving preliminary decisions leading to a final decision affecting legal rights, judicial review may lie against a preliminary decision not affecting legal rights. Town planning provides a classic case of this flexibility. Thus it is in principle possible to apply for judicial review in respect of a resolution to grant outline permission and for prohibition even in advance of it.

Thus, in *R* v. *Electricity Commissioners, ex parte London Electricity Joint Committee Company (1920) Ltd* [1924] 1 KB 171, the Attorney-General's contention that the defendant's decision could not be judicially reviewed because it could not take effect until approved by the Minister of Transport and by resolution of both Houses of Parliament was rejected by Atkin LJ at 208:

> I know of no authority which compels me to hold that a proceeding cannot be ... subject to [judicial remedies] because it is subject to confirmation or approval, even where the approval has to be that of the Houses of Parliament. The authorities are to the contrary.

In the *Electricity Commissioners* case there existed what may be called a complete, if not final, decision: a determination had been made on the issues, and a conclusion reached; in this sense, a complete decision, which would potentially have legal consequences if appropriately endorsed, existed. This situation is, however, to be distinguished from that in which a claimant seeks to intervene before any final determination of a substantive issue is made. An example would be a challenge to the jurisdiction of or procedure adopted by a tribunal *before* the hearing is concluded and any decision on the issues reached. A more limited approach to judicial review applies in this context. In *R* v. *Association of Futures Brokers and Dealers Ltd, ex parte Mordens Ltd* (1991) 3 Admin LR 254 at 263–4, McCullough J explained:

> It is ... only in the most exceptional circumstances that the court will grant judicial review of a decision taken during the course of a hearing, by a body amenable to the court's supervisory jurisdiction, before that hearing has been concluded. The practice which this court almost invariably follows is to decline to hear a challenge to an interlocutory decision until the proceedings in which it was taken have been concluded.
>
> ... The reasons for the general rule are obvious. To entertain challenges at the interlocutory stage would play havoc with the conduct of proceedings in courts and tribunals below. Even to make an application to this court will in most cases occasion at least some interruption to the course of those proceedings. If leave to move is given, so that a substantive hearing follows, the

resulting delay will almost inevitably seriously interfere with the course of those proceedings and very likely give rise to a risk of injustice.

Not only is time wasted, relationships are upset. Once the proceedings in this court are over the hearing must resume with the tribunal once more above and between the parties, rather than alongside one and against the other, as here.

Further, to come to this court too soon is in many cases to come unnecessarily. The party aggrieved by an interlocutory decision may nevertheless be satisfied by the outcome of the proceedings. A decision which, when it was made, was thought to be wrong or likely to have a significant effect on the outcome of the proceedings may, in the end, turn out to have been right or immaterial to the result.

The difficulty lies in determining when this general approach should be departed from. One factor is the level of impact of the preliminary decision on the remainder of the proceedings. For instance, in *R v. Secretary of State for the Environment, ex parte the Royal Borough of Kensington and Chelsea* (1987) 19 HLR 161, a public local inquiry was held in order to determine whether a local authority could compulsorily purchase certain property. The authority wished to do so because tenants living in the property complained of harassment, intimidation, and neglect on the part of the landlord; however, the inspector excluded evidence of such misconduct, ruling it irrelevant. The authority successfully sought judicial review of this decision; Taylor J concluded that the inspector had exercised his discretion unlawfully, and explained (at 173) why judicial review of a preliminary decision was appropriate here:

[O]ne is faced here with a most unusual case. Practically the whole and certainly the main thrust of the applicant's case at the inquiry, has by the challenged ruling been blocked as irrelevant, in my judgment, wrongly so. To decline to intervene now would not only postpone redress for a long time, and until much money has been spent, but it would stultify the presentation of the applicant's real case; the inquiry would be a barren exercise, and if it had to be repeated and reconvened, witnesses' memories would be stale and faulty.

Similarly, courts are sometimes prepared to allow challenges to the jurisdiction of a tribunal before it has reached a decision, provided that any factual information likely to be relevant to the decision as to jurisdiction has already emerged. For instance, in *R v. Broadcasting Complaints Commission, ex parte British Broadcasting Corporation* [1994] EMLR 497, the claimant had broadcast a television programme in respect of which a complaint was made to the defendant to the effect that the complainant's research had not been mentioned in the programme and that she had thereby been unfairly treated. The defendant asserted jurisdiction, notwithstanding that, according to s 150 of the Broadcasting Act 1990, the complainant had to have a 'direct interest' in the subject-matter of the allegedly unfair treatment. Before the defendant had reached a decision, the claimant sought judicial review, arguing that the statute had been misconstrued. Laws J agreed, and (at 501) replied in these terms to the defendant's assertion that judicial review had been sought prematurely:

It is … true … that a challenge to … jurisdiction of the kind now before the court should not be brought at least until all the relevant facts are known; if proceedings were launched before that happened, they would very likely be held to be premature. In this case, however, all the facts were made plain on the correspondence before the letter of 16 September 1992 [in which the defendant told the claimant that it considered itself to have jurisdiction]. Where that is the case, I do not consider that proceedings for judicial review concerned solely with the Commission's jurisdiction should necessarily be discouraged. I accept that in many contexts public bodies should in principle be left to carry out their functions, according to their own perceptions of their duties, without judicial interference at interim stages. But the powers of the Commission touch questions of editorial freedom; they represent a measure of supervision over free expression in the broadcasting media. That is not to say that the court should in any sense presume in favour of a restrictive approach to their interpretation, but it means that it is peculiarly important that their reach should be established, and where there exists all along a clean argument as to whether in law the Commission are entitled to entertain a complaint, it will not generally be contrary to the public interest that its merits be determined at an early stage. Certainly, there is in my judgment nothing inappropriate in these proceedings.

Nor does it necessarily follow that the Administrative Court should not intervene prior to the making of an initial decision just because there is a right of appeal against it. In *R (S) v. Knowsley NHS Primary Care Trust* [2006] EWHC 26 (Admin), the claimant doctors were facing proceedings to determine whether, in the light of serious misconduct allegations, they should be removed from the defendants' medical performers lists. The claimants sought judicial review of the defendants' decisions that they would not be allowed to cross-examine witnesses or have legal representation at the forthcoming hearings. Toulson J rejected the defendants' argument that judicial review of these preliminary decisions was inappropriate, which the defendants had sought to bolster by reference to the existence of a right of appeal against the defendants' decisions. His Lordship said (at [57]) the courts should not, for fear of becoming overburdened, 'readily intervene to prevent prospective unfairness'. However, holding that the defendants should reconsider their procedural decisions, his Lordship said (at [68]) that it could not be right that

the court should be powerless to prevent [an anticipated] violation of a right to a fair procedure, merely because of the existence of a later way of remedying the consequences. A stitch in time may save nine.

Lastly, somewhat perplexingly, the courts have recognized that a judicial review claim may be ruled premature even where the challenged administrative decision is *final*. In *R (Unison) v. The Lord Chancellor* [2014] EWHC 218 (Admin), [2014] IRLR 266, the trade union, Unison, challenged on various grounds the Courts and Tribunals Fee Remissions Order 2013 (SI 2013/2302), which required the payment of fees to commence or continue claims in the Employment Tribunal, whereas access had previously been free. Despite the Order being a final, completed administrative act, various challenges to the Order were dismissed by the Court as premature on the basis that more time was required to observe how the new scheme would operate in practice before any conclusion as to legality could be reached. For example one ground of challenge was that the fees system would breach the EU law principle of effectiveness: Unison argued that the imposition of fees, by erecting a barrier to accessing the tribunal system, would make it virtually impossible or excessively difficult for employees to protect their legal rights. The challenge was ruled premature because whether the fees system did in fact have this effect, for example by preventing significant numbers of employees from launching legal proceedings, was only something that could be gauged by observing 'how the system will work in practice' (at [46]). Rather than determining lawfulness on the basis of 'hypothetical examples and detailed, fine disputes as to statistics and figures ... Far better, we suggest, to wait and see whether the fears of Unison prove to be well-founded' (at [46]).

Similar evidentiary issues arose in respect of the claimant's challenge that the fee regime would have disproportionately prejudicial effects on certain groups such as women and the disabled: while the Court suspected the fee regimes would have an indirect discriminatory effect on certain classes of person, it was not possible at present to determine this nor the extent of any prejudice (at [87], [90]). The challenge was again premature.

Unison was followed in *R (Howard League for Penal Reform)* v. *The Lord Chancellor* [2014] EWHC 709 (Admin) at [45]. The claimant challenged on various grounds a new criminal legal aid regime—pursuant to Criminal Legal Aid (General) (Amendment) Regulations 2013 (SI 2013/2790)—which removed funding for certain classes of prisoner claims. The challenge rested on an argument that inherent in the new regime was an unacceptable risk of procedural unfairness; specifically, there was an unacceptable risk that the scheme would operate to prevent prisoners from accessing legal assistance where procedural fairness required provision of legal assistance. The Court denied permission to bring the claim partly on the basis that 'the claimants face the problem of prematurity as did the claimant in [*Unison*]; they are addressing the situation which will operate, as they see it, once criminal legal aid for prison law is withdrawn' (at [45]). On the one hand, it might be that alternative measures would enable prisoners to put across their views despite lack of access to legal representation, while, on the other, there were no doubt drawbacks to alternatives to legal assistance. However '[a]t present' the claim was not arguable (at [45]): much depended on how the scheme would operate in practice.

QUESTION

- One might criticize *Unison* and *Howard League* on the basis that the correct ground for denying the claims was not prematurity—the challenged administrative act was final after all—but because the claims lacked merit, *ie* the claimant was simply unable to prove illegality based on the facts as they stood at the time of the proceedings. Do you agree?

14.5.3 Advice, guidance, recommendations, and views

Preliminary decisions are liable to have legal consequences in that they form part of a decision-making process which will ultimately result in a determination which has legal effects. What, however, of advice, guidance, recommendations, and views promulgated by (for instance) government departments?

Gillick v. West Norfolk and Wisbech Area Health Authority [1986] AC 112
House of Lords

The Department for Health and Social Security (DHSS) circulated guidance to area health authorities to the effect that, although the provision of contraceptive advice or treatment to children under 16 without parental consent would be unusual, such a course was open to a doctor if it was, in his clinical judgment, appropriate. The claimant sought an assurance from her area health authority that no such advice or treatment would be given, without her consent, to her daughters while under 16. No such assurance was forthcoming, the authority taking the view that, according to the circular, this was a matter for individual doctors. The claimant sought a declaration that the guidance in the circular was unlawful. This excerpt is concerned only with the courts' jurisdiction to review non-statutory guidance.

Lord Bridge

... Throughout the hearing of the argument in the appeal and in subsequent reflection on the questions to which it gives rise I have felt doubt and difficulty as to the basis of the jurisdiction which Mrs. Gillick invokes in her claim to a declaration against the D.H.S.S. ... I ask myself what is the nature of the action or decision taken by the D.H.S.S. in the exercise of a power conferred upon it which entitles a court of law to intervene and declare that it has stepped beyond the proper limits of its power. I frame the question in that way because I believe that hitherto, certainly in general terms, the court's supervisory jurisdiction over the conduct of administrative authorities has been confined to ensuring that their actions or decisions were taken within the scope of the power which they purported to exercise or conversely to providing a remedy for an authority's failure to act or to decide in circumstances where some appropriate statutory action or decision was called for.

Now it is true that the Secretary of State for Health and Social Security under section 5(1)(b) of the National Health Service Act 1977 has a general responsibility for the provision within the National Health Service of what may be described shortly as family planning services. But only in a very loose sense could the issue of the memorandum be considered as part of the discharge of that responsibility. The memorandum itself has no statutory force whatever. It is not and does not purport to be issued in the exercise of any statutory power or in the performance of any statutory function. It is purely advisory in character and practitioners in the National Health Service are, as a matter of law, in no way bound by it.

In the light of these considerations I cannot, with all respect, agree that the memorandum is open to review on '*Wednesbury*' principles (*Associated Provincial Picture Houses Ltd. v. Wednesbury Corporation* [1948] 1 K.B. 223) on the ground that it involves an unreasonable exercise of a statutory discretion. Such a review must always begin by examining the nature of the statutory power which the administrative authority whose action is called in question has purported to exercise, and asking, in the light of that examination, what were, and what were not, relevant considerations for the authority to take into account in deciding to exercise that power. It is only against such a specific statutory background that the question whether the authority has acted unreasonably, in the *Wednesbury* sense, can properly be asked and answered. Here there is no specific statutory background by reference to which the appropriate *Wednesbury* questions could be formulated.

The issue by a department of government with administrative responsibility in a particular field of non-statutory guidance to subordinate authorities operating in the same field is a familiar feature of modern administration. The innumerable circulars issued over the years by successive departments responsible in the field of town and country planning spring to the mind as presenting a familiar example. The question whether the advice tendered in such non-statutory guidance is good or bad, reasonable or unreasonable, cannot, as a general rule, be subject to any form of judicial review. But the question arises whether there is any exception to that general rule.

Your Lordships have been referred to the House's decision in *Royal College of Nursing v. Department of Health and Social Security* [1981] A.C. 800. The background to that case was exceptional, as only becomes fully clear when one reads the judgment of Woolf J. at first instance: [1981] 1 All E.R. 545. The Royal College of Nursing ('R.C.N.') and the D.H.S.S. had received conflicting legal advice as to whether or not it was lawful, on the true construction of certain provisions of the Abortion Act 1967, for nurses to perform particular functions in the course of a novel medical procedure for the termination of pregnancy, when acting on the orders and under the general supervision of a registered medical practitioner but not necessarily in his presence. The R.C.N. had issued a memorandum and a later circular to its members to the effect that it was not lawful. The D.H.S.S. had issued a circular advising that it was lawful. The desirability of an authoritative resolution of this dispute on a pure question of law was obvious in the interests both of the nursing profession and of the public. The proceedings took the form of a claim by the R.C.N. against the D.H.S.S. for a suitable declaration and the D.H.S.S. in due course counter-claimed a declaration to the opposite effect. As Woolf J. pointed out, neither side took any point as to the jurisdiction of the court to grant a declaration. Woolf J. himself felt it necessary to raise and examine certain questions as to the locus standi of the R.C.N. to bring the proceedings and as to the propriety of their form. He answered these questions in a favourable sense to enable him to decide the disputed question of law on its merits. No technical question bearing on jurisdiction attracted any mention in the Court of Appeal or in this House. In the litigation the original conflict between the parties was reflected in a conflict of judicial opinion. On a count of judicial heads a majority of five to four favoured the R.C.N. But by a majority of three to two in your Lordships' House the D.H.S.S. carried the day and obtained the declaration they sought.

Against this background it would have been surprising indeed if the courts had declined juris-diction. But I think it must be recognised that the decision (whether or not it was so intended) does effect a significant extension of the court's power of judicial review. We must now say that if a government department, in a field of administration in which it exercises responsibility, prom-ulgates in a public document, albeit non-statutory in form, advice which is erroneous in law, then the court, in proceedings in appropriate form commenced by an applicant or plaintiff who pos-sesses the necessary locus standi, has jurisdiction to correct the error of law by an appropriate declaration. Such an extended jurisdiction is no doubt a salutary and indeed a necessary one in certain circumstances, as the *Royal College of Nursing* case [1981] A.C. 800 itself well illustrates. But the occasions of a departmental non-statutory publication raising, as in that case, a clearly defined issue of law, unclouded by political, social or moral overtones, will be rare. In cases where any proposition of law implicit in a departmental advisory document is interwoven with questions of social and ethical controversy, the court should, in my opinion, exercise its jurisdic-tion with the utmost restraint, confine itself to deciding whether the proposition of law is errone-ous and avoid either expressing ex cathedra opinions in areas of social and ethical controversy in which it has no claim to speak with authority or proferring answers to hypothetical questions of law which do not strictly arise for decision.

Lord Templeman agreed with Lord Bridge on this point. Lords Fraser and Scarman considered that the guidance was issued pursuant to the National Health Service Act 1977, s 5(1)(b), and that there therefore existed an exercise of statutory power capable of judicial review. Lord Brandon expressed no view on this issue.

The effect of Lord Bridge's speech in *Gillick* and the decision in the *RCN* case to which he refers is that limited circumstances exist in which guidance may be subject to judicial review. Several points should be noted.

First, it may be that the guidance in question must have a practical impact on the parties or the public. The House of Lords was clearly influenced by this consideration in *RCN*: Lord Edmund-Davies, for instance, remarked (at 833) that 'several thousand' of the procedures in question were carried out annually, making it obviously important to clarify the legal position. Similarly, in *R v. Secretary of State for Health, ex parte Pfizer Ltd* [1999] 3 CMLR 875, a case concerning the legality of interim advice to doctors that the drug Viagra should be prescribed only in exceptional circumstances, Collins J considered (at [17]) that '[a]dvice or guidance promulgated by a public authority may be the subject of judicial review if it contains an error of law. This is particularly so if it is likely to be acted upon by those it addresses.' Thus the fact that doctors were highly likely to—and, in fact, did—heed the advice was one of the factors which led to the conclusion that judicial review could lie.

Second, although questions arose in *RCN* and *Gillick* as to whether circulars, if followed, would result in the commission of criminal offences, it is clear that judicial review of advice can occur outwith such circumstances. For instance, the case of *R (UK Renderers Association Ltd)* v. *Secretary of State for the Environment, Transport and the Regions* [2001] EWHC 675 (Admin), [2002] Env LR 21 (upheld: [2002] EWCA Civ 749, [2003] Env LR 7) concerned a challenge to guidance issued in relation to the obligation of animal renderers under s 7(1)(a) of the Environmental Protection Act 1990 to use the 'best available techniques not entailing excessive cost' for preventing the release of prescribed substances as part of the rendering process. The claimants argued (ultimately unsuccessfully) that guidance (some of which was non-statutory in form) requiring the use of all due diligence and the taking of all reasonable steps was unlawful, on the ground that it went beyond the duty laid down in the Act. Although there was no suggestion that any unlawful conduct would result from following it, Ouseley J said (at [33]) that the 'guidance, both in its statutory and non-statutory parts, can be challenged by way of judicial review'.

Third, although Lord Bridge suggested in *Gillick* (at 193–4) that courts should review advice or guidance only in relation to 'a clearly defined issue of law, unclouded by political, social or moral overtones', the *Gillick* and *RCN* decisions seem to demonstrate a judicial preparedness to intervene even if the case *does* possess such overtones. Lord Bridge's comments on this point were, however, taken at face value by Hirst LJ, holding in *R* v. *Secretary of State for Employment, ex parte Equal Opportunities Commission* [1993] 1 WLR 872 at 900 that the view expressed by the Secretary of State in a letter to the Equal Opportunities Commission as to the compatibility of UK and EU law on indirect gender discrimination was not reviewable (a conclusion later upheld by the House of Lords [1995] 1 AC 1 for reasons which are not entirely clear) because it raised matters which were 'closely interwoven with questions of social and political controversy'. Hirst LJ emphasized (at 900) that 'the extended jurisdiction applied in *Gillick* ... is the exception rather than the rule'. However, we would submit that the decision should not be given a great deal of weight given courts in recent years have regularly assessed the legality of guidance which raises difficult moral and/or politically charged matters. For example, the courts have recently considered the legality of a non-statutory scheme governing the release of information about child sex offenders (*R (X)* v. *Secretary of State for the Home Department* [2012] EWHC 2954 (Admin), [2013] 1 WLR 2638) and government guidance for security personnel on detention and interviewing of detainees overseas (*R (Equality and Human Rights Commission)* v. *Prime Minister* [2011] EWHC 2401 (Admin), [2012] 1 WLR 1389), albeit a cautious approach to review was adopted in the latter case.

Fourth, courts are reluctant to assess the legality of guidance in contexts where determinations as to legality are heavily fact dependent. Thus, in *Equality and Human Rights Commission*, Sir Anthony May, delivering the judgment of the Court, was reluctant to rule on whether guidance was compatible with the criminal law (at [51]):

> We agree that the Administrative Court, called upon to determine in the abstract the legality of a public document, should be slow to adopt the mantle of the Court of Appeal (Criminal Division), who would only determine such points if it was necessary to do so in a criminal appeal concerning real facts. Mr Eadie [counsel for the defendant] accepts that there have been cases in which the court has decided public law points of criminal law. Examples are [*RCN*] and [*Gillick*], but these involved narrow issues on agreed facts. In the present case, it is now accepted that most of the original grounds raised questions which could not properly be determined without a particular factual context.

He thus considered that the guidance must be 'unlawful on its face' to be impugned (at [51]). This approach is faithful to Lord Bridge's emphasis on courts only ruling on 'pure questions of law' in *Gillick*. Other judges have shown somewhat less caution. For example, in *R (Suppiah)* v. *Secretary of State for the Home Department* [2011] EWHC 2 (Admin) at [137], Wyn Williams J said: 'I am content to accept that as a matter of law a policy which cannot be operated lawfully cannot itself be lawful; further, it seems to me that there is clear and binding authority for the proposition that a policy which is in principle capable of being implemented lawfully but which nonetheless gives rise to an unacceptable risk of unlawful decision-making is itself an unlawful policy' (the principal authority referred to was *R (Refugee Legal Centre)* v. *Secretary of State for the Home Department* [2004] EWCA Civ 1481, [2005] 1 WLR 2219).

Lastly, recognition of a jurisdiction to rule on the legality of guidance in the abstract may give rise to a concern that the courts may exceed their proper judicial role, which is to rule on questions of law, and be tempted to offer general advice or feedback to government on its guidance documents. For example, in *X*, different guidance documents governing release of information about child sex offenders were the responsibility of different public authorities. Delivering the judgment of the Court, the President said (at [50]):

> [T]here would seem a great deal to be said for producing one document dealing with the disclosure of the convictions of and other information about a sex offender. What is needed is practical guidance covering the various schemes. There is much less of a risk of the right process not being applied if there is one document which carefully explains the circumstances in which each scheme should be used and provides for more 'joining up' of the schemes. We would also observe that it should be possible to do this in a much shorter form than the current guidance.

One may question whether it is the proper role of the courts to advise the executive on the form that policy guidance should take, the most effective means of communicating guidance to executive officers, as well as the length of policy documents.

QUESTIONS

- Should courts be deterred from reviewing guidance if it raises controversial social or political questions?
- How does the position adopted in this context relate to the concept of justiciability (considered at 4.3.3)?
- Do you think the Court in *X* went beyond the proper role of a court in review proceedings?

14.5.4 Hypothetical issues and advisory declarations

Similar problems are evident when we consider the courts' approach to hypothetical matters. To what extent should the courts exercise jurisdiction over such issues? The importance of this question is underlined in the following passage.

Laws, 'Judicial Remedies and the Constitution' (1994) 57 *MLR* 213

There has for many years been a strong tradition in the law that the courts will only decide questions on which a live dispute turns; they will not entertain issues which they perceive as being merely hypothetical or academic. I use the word 'tradition' advisedly; it is not a matter of jurisdiction, but of judicial choice. I think that the effects of this tradition are in some respects harmful to the proper development of public law, in which context it needs to be severely modified. I do not consider this theme to be one of merely peripheral importance, so as to command the attention only of specialists who might understandably find interest in any aspect of public law, however dry or marginal. It engages a question going to the very nature of the role which the judicial arm of government is to play in the State: how far should the judges act proactively, rather than merely reactively?

I should first expose a distinction which seems to me to possess some significance. It is between what may be regarded as a 'hypothetical' question and what may be regarded as an 'academic' question. The courts have tended to use these phrases indifferently. I do not think that they have been right to do so. We should understand an academic question to be one which does not need to be answered for any visible practical purpose at all: thus, if I were a legal antiquarian, and interested in the construction of a statute long since repealed and not replaced, I could not bring proceedings to ask the court to construe it for me, so as to satisfy my intellectual curiosity: the court will not deploy its resources so as to provide authoritative backing for one or other view being canvassed in the lecture hall or the tutorial. A hypothetical question is quite different: it is a question which may need to be answered for real practical purposes; it connotes only a situation in which the events have not yet happened which will clothe the answer to the question with immediate practical effects.

Laws' observation that this issue raises fundamental questions about the judicial role is an important one. As far as public law is concerned, the willingness of the courts to review hypothetical matters reflects the extent to which the function of public law extends beyond dispute resolution to embrace the concept of expository justice. We explore these concepts at 14.7.5, in the context of standing.

Three factors underlie the courts' traditional reluctance to review hypothetical questions. First, it was suggested by Viscount Simon LC in *Sun Life Assurance Co of Canada v. Jervis* [1944] AC 111 at 113 that such review—being inconsistent with the adversarial model, paradigmatically concerned with the resolution of concrete issues—would risk courts undertaking tasks which they are ill-equipped to perform. Thus, in *R (Burke) v. General Medical Council* [2005] EWCA Civ 1003, [2006] QB 273, the Court of Appeal was highly critical of the lower court's willingness to address a range of hypothetical legal questions concerning withdrawal of artificial nutrition and hydration from patients no longer capable of making their wishes known. The Court emphasized there were great dangers in courts grappling with legal issues divorced from any factual context, including that principles could be enunciated without full appreciation of how they would work in practice. Lord Phillips MR said (at [21]): 'This danger is particularly acute where the issues raised involve ethical questions that any court should be reluctant to address, unless driven to do so by the need to resolve a practical problem that requires the court's intervention'.

A second objection is that people may be affected by the decision without any opportunity of putting their arguments to the court. However, this objection only holds water if non-parties are bound by such decisions. Simon Brown LJ took it as read in *R (Campaign for Nuclear Disarmament) v. Prime Minister* [2002] EWHC 2777 (Admin) at [46] that advisory declarations are 'binding on all'. However, surely much depends on how the declaration is framed, which is up to the court. As Lords Neuberger and Toulson said, in their joint judgment in *R (Reilly)* v. *Secretary of State for Work and Pensions* [2013] UKSC 68, [2014] AC 4653—a case which concerned matters which were moot—'the precise formulation of any order that is made will have to be carefully considered' (at [41]). Taking a polar opposite view to Simon Brown LJ in the *CND* case, Lord Goff in *R* v. *Secretary of State for the Home Department, ex parte Wynne* [1993] 1 WLR 115 at 120 said that if a court were to consider a hypothetical question, 'any conclusion, and the accompanying reasons, could in their turn constitute no more than *obiter dicta*, expressed without the assistance of a concrete factual situation, and would not constitute a binding precedent for the future'.

Third, it is sometimes said that determination of hypothetical questions is an inappropriate use of scarce judicial resources. This argument holds particular sway where the issue is *academic*, given court time could be far better spent on issues with potential practical implications. In *Reilly*, the Supreme Court was asked to rule on the validity of regulations where a lower court had invalidated those regulations only for Parliament to subsequently retrospectively validate them through statute. As such, the validity of the regulations was moot. Lords Neuberger and Toulson opined that there was 'considerable force' in the argument that 'it is rather unattractive for the executive to be taking up court time and public money to establish that a regulation is valid, when it has already taken up Parliamentary time to enact legislation which retrospectively validates the regulation'; courts are 'normally concerned with stating the law as it is, not as it was' (at [40]). The Court did ultimately rule on the matter as leave to appeal had been given, but it seemingly did so reluctantly.

Despite these strong arguments against courts entertaining hypothetical questions, the courts have recognized a jurisdiction to hear such matters but exercise it with caution. One core benefit of such a jurisdiction is that it provides certainty for those who wish to pursue a stated course of conduct. In this regard, one area where the courts have been more willing to address hypothetical matters and essentially serve an advisory role is in the context of end-of-life care and decision-making. Thus, in *Airedale NHS Trust* v. *Bland* [1993] AC 789, a hospital was able to obtain declarations to the effect that if it terminated the life support of a patient in a persistent vegetative state, this would not amount to unlawful homicide. *R (Nicklinson)* v. *Ministry of Justice* [2014] UKSC 38, [2015] AC 657 concerned claims brought by various claimants who suffered serious medical conditions and considered their quality of life to be so poor that they wished to end their lives. However, because of their medical conditions they were unable to end their lives without the help of others. Among other matters raised in the litigation, the claimants sought a declaration that if a doctor killed them or a doctor or other person assisted them to take their own life those individuals would not be prosecuted for various criminal offences including murder and assisting suicide. The Court heard and determined the case, ultimately refusing the declaration, without squarely addressing the hypothetical nature of the questions raised. That the matter was not even seriously addressed reflects that in the case law since *Bland*, helpfully traced by Lord Neuberger in *Nicklinson* at [21]–[26], it has become well established that the end-of-life context is one in which courts will be more willing to hear cases based on hypothetical facts.

While in a narrow set of contexts the courts have adopted a more permissive approach to hearing claims based upon hypothetical facts, the general starting point is that they will refuse to hear such claims. Thus, Lord Hobhouse in *R (Pretty)* v. *Director of Public Prosecutions* [2001] UKHL 61, [2002] 1 AC 800 at [116] said that '[i]n exceptional circumstances it may be proper for a member of the public to bring proceedings against the Crown for a declaration that certain proposed conduct is lawful and name the Attorney General as the formal defendant to the claim … But the court [has] a discretion which it would normally exercise to refuse to rule upon hypothetical facts' (see similarly, *R v. Attorney General, ex parte Rusbridger* [2003] UKHL 38, [2004] 1 AC 357 at [16]–[25]). What, then, are the factors which will make it more or less likely that a court will hear a judicial review in respect of hypothetical questions? In *R v. Secretary of State for the Home Department, ex parte Salem* [1999] 1 AC 450 at 456–7, Lord Slynn gave the following general guidance:

> [I]n a cause where there is an issue involving a public authority as to a question of public law, your Lordships have a discretion to hear the appeal, even if by the time the appeal reaches the House there is no longer a lis to be decided which will directly affect the rights and obligations of the parties inter se …
>
> The discretion to hear disputes, even in the area of public law, must, however, be exercised with caution and appeals which are academic between the parties should not be heard unless there is a good reason in the public interest for doing so, as for example (but only by way of example) when a discrete point of statutory construction arises which does not involve detailed consideration of facts and where a large number of similar cases exist or are anticipated so that the issue will most likely need to be resolved in the near future.

In *Pryce* v. *Southwark London Borough Council* [2012] EWCA Civ 1572, [2013] 1 WLR 996, the Court of Appeal directly applied Lord Slynn's guidance. The case concerned the scope of application of the statutory rule that an individual 'subject to immigration control' is ineligible for housing assistance (Housing Act 1996, s 185). The question in the litigation was whether a non-British and non-EU national who did not have leave to remain in the UK should nonetheless be considered to have a right to residence—and thus *not* be classified as a person 'subject to immigration control'—by virtue of their being the parent and primary carer of a child of British and EU nationality. The issue had been rendered moot because the defendant council agreed not to oppose the claimant's appeal. Nonetheless, the second defendant, the Secretary of State for the Home Department, sought a hearing so that the Court could rule on the matter. Many other analogous cases had been stayed in anticipation of clarification of the law in *Pryce*, while it was observed that social welfare claimants and public authorities alike had treated *Pryce* as a test case. The Court determined (at [12]) that it should 'proceed to judgment'. It continued:

> The issue is one involving housing authorities and relates to a question of public law of some importance. Having regard to the significance of the point involved and its likely application to many cases, there is a good reason in the public interest for a public hearing at which judgments available to housing authorities and applicants for housing benefit are given.

The Court was also reluctant to allow the appeal to be disposed of according to an agreed statement of reasons prepared by the claimant and defendant council as some of those reasons were contentious yet may nonetheless have been relied upon in other cases if the Court did not issue its own reasoned judgment (at [12]).

An important factor governing whether a court will address a hypothetical matter is whether the case raises an issue of public importance. This factor was enunciated by Lord Slynn in *Salem*, and reinforced by Lord Steyn in *Rusbridger*: Lord Steyn considered it relevant whether there was 'a cogent public or individual interest' that would 'be advanced by the grant of a declaration' (at [24]). The criterion is rather open-ended and the courts have not laid down concrete guidance, nor perhaps is it possible for such guidance to be formulated. However, some examples may illuminate the types of issues which are likely to be considered sufficiently important. In *Rusbridger*, Lord Steyn said (at [24]) that '*Bland* was an example of an overwhelming interest of an individual in the grant of a declaration that the cessation of life-sustaining medical support was lawful. But the jurisdiction [to grant advisory] declarations is in no way limited to life and death issues.' Lord Steyn indicated that the issue that arose in *Rusbridger* itself was one of sufficient importance. The issues were whether a newspaper editor, who conducts a press campaign advocating the peaceful and constitutional replacement of the monarchy by a republican form of government, may be guilty of an offence under s 3 of the Treason Act 1848, which provides, on its face, for a total ban on republican discourse in print, and whether s 3 of the Human Rights Act 1998 required the provision to be given an interpretation which preserved freedom of expression. In concluding that the matter, though hypothetical, was one of such importance that the court should consider it, Lord Steyn observed: 'The Guardian [newspaper] alleges that some 25% of the population supports republicanism. The Guardian wishes to continue the debate ... It may be a matter of constitutional importance. An historic anomaly in our political democracy could be examined by our courts' (at [24]).

In common with Lord Slynn's guidance in *Salem*, in *Rusbridger* Lord Steyn also laid emphasis on 'whether the case is fact sensitive or not. This is a factor of great importance and most claims for a declaration that particular conduct is unlawful will founder on this ground' (at [23]). This factor was determinative in *R (Noor Khan)* v. *Secretary of State for Foreign and Commonwealth Affairs* [2012] EWHC 3728 (Admin). *Inter alia*, the claimant sought a declaration that a GCHQ employee who passes intelligence to the US government on the location of persons in Pakistan, foreseeing that the information will be used by the US authorities to target or kill those persons using drone strikes, shall be guilty of various criminal offences under English law. The Court, applying the *Rusbridger* guidance, said: 'Questions as to whether conduct amounts to a criminal offence are peculiarly sensitive to the facts of the particular case. Applications for an advisory opinion are more likely to be accepted in relation to issues of pure law; they are most likely to be rejected where the answer will depend on the facts' (at [30]). In *Rusbridger*, for example, the key issue was one of pure statutory interpretation; this feature of the case strongly telling in favour of the Court hearing the appeal. In contrast, the question in *Noor Khan*, whether hypothetical conduct would amount to a criminal offence, implicated various factual variables, such as the perpetrator's state of mind. A declaration not grounded in specific, proven factual circumstances, but based in stylized hypothetical facts would risk being inaccurate or misleading, for example unintentionally including lawful activity within the scope of criminal conduct. At the other extreme a highly generalized declaration, while avoiding any mention of hypothetical facts, would likely be pointless: it would merely replicate the elements of the offence, adding nothing to the statute. On this basis and others the Court refused the claimant permission.

QUESTIONS

- When, in your view, should courts rule on hypothetical issues?
- Are the courts unduly cautious in this area?
- Would you characterize their present approach in 'red' or 'green light' terms (see at 1.2)?

14.6 Exclusion of judicial review

14.6.1 The courts' general approach

Preclusive clauses, otherwise known as privative, exclusion, or ouster clauses, are statutory provisions which *prima facie* prohibit judicial review of the exercise of the discretionary powers to which they relate. Such provisions raise a fundamental tension between the rule of law (which strongly favours access to courts—and therefore judicial review) and the constitutional duty of the courts, under the doctrine of legislative supremacy, to give effect to the will of Parliament. Over the years, courts have consistently attempted to reconcile these two imperatives by means of construction—that is, by adopting a strong presumption that Parliament would not wish to exclude judicial review, and interpreting legislation on that basis.

For instance, the legislation at stake in *R v. Medical Appeal Tribunal, ex parte Gilmore* [1957] 1 QB 574 provided that the decision of the relevant tribunal 'shall be final'. To the argument that this deprived the ordinary courts of jurisdiction, Lord Denning MR responded robustly, saying (at 583) that he found it

> very well settled that the remedy by certiorari [that is, a quashing order available upon judicial review] is never to be taken away by any statute except by the most clear and explicit words. The word 'final' is not enough. That only means 'without appeal.' It does not mean 'without recourse to certiorari.' It makes the decision final on the facts, but not final on the law. Notwithstanding that the decision is by a statute made 'final', certiorari can still issue for excess of jurisdiction or for error of law on the face of the record.

A finality clause will not, therefore, bar judicial review of a decision, although it will prevent the decision from being challenged by appeal (on both points of fact and law: *Re Racal Communications Ltd* [1981] AC 374 at 382, *per* Lord Diplock, disagreeing with Lord Denning MR's suggestion in *Pearlman* v. *Keepers and Governors of Harrow School* [1979] QB 56 at 71 that finality clauses bar appeal only on factual issues). The underlying principle is clear; as Lord Denning MR put it in *Tehrani* v. *Rostron* [1972] 1 QB 182 at 187:

> [W]hen Parliament says that a decision of an inferior tribunal is to be 'final', it does so on the assumption that the tribunal will observe the law. Parliament only gives the impress of 'finality' to the decision on the condition that it is reached in accordance with law: and the Queen's courts will see to it that this condition is fulfilled. Accordingly if a tribunal goes wrong in law ..., the High Court will interfere by certiorari to quash the decision.

Provided, therefore, that the supervisory jurisdiction of the High Court remains intact, in order that the legal limits of the tribunal or decision-maker's powers may be enforced, the courts are untroubled by the fact that other avenues, by which the decision might otherwise be challenged, are closed off by the finality clause.

Just as the courts have experienced little difficulty in continuing to assert supervisory jurisdiction in the face of finality clauses, so they have managed to place similarly benign constructions upon a number of other types of ouster clause. For instance, Denning LJ explained in *Gilmore* at 586 that 'no *certiorari*'—in today's language, 'no quashing order'—clauses cannot exclude judicial review for jurisdictional error:

> In contrast to the word 'final' I would like to say a word about the old statutes which used in express words to take away the remedy by certiorari by saying that the decision of the tribunal 'shall not be removed by certiorari'. Those statutes were passed chiefly between 1680 and 1848, in the days when the courts used certiorari too freely and quashed decisions for technical defects of form. In stopping this abuse the statutes proved very beneficial, but the court never allowed those statutes to be used as a cover for wrongdoing by tribunals. If tribunals were to be at liberty to exceed their jurisdiction without any check by the courts, the rule of law would be at an end. Despite express words taking away certiorari, therefore, it was held that certiorari would still lie if some of the members of the tribunal were disqualified from acting: see *Reg. v. Cheltenham Commissioners* [(1841) 1 QB 467], where Lord Denman CJ said [at 474]: 'The statute cannot affect our right and duty to [see] justice executed.' So, also, if the tribunal exceeded its jurisdiction: see *Ex parte Bradlaugh* [(1878) 3 QBD 508]; or if its decision was obtained by fraud: see *Reg. v. Gillyard* [(1848) 12 QB 527], the courts would still grant certiorari.

A 'no *certiorari*' clause would not, therefore, prevent the courts from issuing (what is now referred to as) a quashing order if a jurisdictional defect could be established. Although such clauses (as opposed to finality clauses) did prevent relief from being issued in the case of errors of law which appeared on the face of the record but which did not go to jurisdiction—hence the importance in *Pearlman* v. *Keepers and Governors of Harrow School* [1979] QB 56 (see 2.2.4) of the claimant establishing the jurisdictional nature of the error—this problem is now unlikely to arise, given the general principle established in *R* v. *Lord President of the Privy Council, ex parte Page* [1993] AC 682 that errors of law are jurisdictional.

The courts have similarly narrowly construed statutory provisions which on their face provide for the making of statutory instruments which would oust judicial review. Consider *R (Ignaoua)* v. *Secretary of State for the Home Department* [2013] EWCA Civ 1498, [2014] 1 WLR 651. In that case the Home Secretary had made a direction excluding the claimant from the UK for national security reasons. Under s 15 of the Justice and Security Act 2013 the Home Secretary certified the direction as one, *inter alia*, based on information that should not be made public on certain grounds such as national security. Under the Act, where a direction is so certified, the individual affected by it can apply to the Special Immigration Appeals Commission for the direction to be set aside, that Commission having power to consider sensitive information in closed hearings. The Act also gave the Home Secretary power to make statutory instruments for various purposes, and which could make provision for 'the termination of any judicial review proceedings ... which relate to a direction ... which is ... certified' (s 19; sch 3, para 4(2)(b)). Pursuant to this power, Article 4(3) was included in the Justice and Security Act 2013 (Commencement, Transitional and Saving Provisions) Order 2013, which provided that where a ministerial certificate was issued any existing judicial review proceedings which related to the relevant direction were to be automatically terminated.

The Court considered that if this were the legal result of a ministerial certificate 'it is a truly remarkable result, since it puts in the hands of the Secretary of State, as a party to (indeed, a defendant to) judicial review proceedings, the power to bring about the termination of those proceedings by her own act and without any intervention by the court'. The

Court proceeded to invalidate the statutory instrument as *ultra vires* the empowering statute, reasoning (at [20]):

> The power to make provision for the termination of judicial review proceedings [in schedule 3 of the 2013 Act] is couched in very general terms but that generality does not assist the Secretary of State. If it had been intended to empower the making of provision whereby the Secretary of State, by making a certificate, could cause existing judicial review proceedings against her to terminate automatically and without the intervention of the court, I would have expected specific, express language to that effect; and in the absence of such express language I do not think that paragraph 4(2)(b) should be read as conferring on the Secretary of State so striking a power.

Of course, as the Court observed, a court could itself order the stay of existing proceedings where a certificate had been issued, on the basis that Parliament had provided for an alternative remedy in a more appropriate forum (see 14.3), namely a claim in the Commission. However, the key point was that the Court retained the jurisdiction to decide that matter for itself.

14.6.2 *Anisminic*: a harder case

In the next case the House of Lords was confronted with an ouster provision which appeared to exclude judicial review in very clear terms, and seemed to leave no scope for a contrary interpretation.

Anisminic Ltd v. *Foreign Compensation Commission* [1969] 2 AC 147
House of Lords

For the facts and discussion of the nature of the error made by the Commission, see 2.2.3. These extracts are concerned with the ouster clause in the Foreign Compensation Act 1950, s 4(4), which provided that '[t]he determination by the commission of any application made to them under this Act shall not be called in question in any court of law'.

Lord Reid

... The next argument was that, by reason of the provisions of section 4(4) of the 1950 Act, the courts are precluded from considering whether the respondent's determination was a nullity, and therefore it must be treated as valid whether or not inquiry would disclose that it was a nullity ...

The respondent maintains that these are plain words only capable of having one meaning. Here is a determination which is apparently valid: there is nothing on the face of the document to cast any doubt on its validity. If it is a nullity, that could only be established by raising some kind of proceedings in court. But that would be calling the determination in question, and that is expressly prohibited by the statute. The appellants maintain that that is not the meaning of the words of this provision. They say that 'determination' means a real determination and does not include an apparent or purported determination which in the eyes of the law has no existence because it is a nullity. Or, putting it in another way, if you seek to show that a determination is a nullity you are not questioning the purported determination—you are maintaining that it does not exist as a determination. It is one thing to question a determination which does exist: it is quite another thing to say that there is nothing to be questioned.

Let me illustrate the matter by supposing a simple case. A statute provides that a certain order may be made by a person who holds a specified qualification or appointment, and it contains a provision, similar to section 4(4), that such an order made by such a person shall not be called in question in any court of law. A person aggrieved by an order alleges that it is a forgery or that the person who made the order did not hold that qualification or appointment. Does such a provision require the court to treat that order as a valid order? It is a well established principle that a provision ousting the ordinary jurisdiction of the court must be construed strictly—meaning, I think, that, if such a provision is reasonably capable of having two meanings, that meaning shall be taken which preserves the ordinary jurisdiction of the court.

Statutory provisions which seek to limit the ordinary jurisdiction of the court have a long history. No case has been cited in which any other form of words limiting the jurisdiction of the court has been held to protect a nullity. If the draftsman or Parliament had intended to introduce a new kind of ouster clause so as to prevent any inquiry even as to whether the document relied on was a forgery, I would have expected to find something much more specific than the bald statement that a determination shall not be called in question in any court of law. Undoubtedly such a provision protects every determination which is not a nullity. But I do not think that it is necessary or even reasonable to construe the word 'determination' as including everything which purports to be a determination but which is in fact no determination at all. And there are no degrees of nullity. There are a number of reasons why the law will hold a purported decision to be a nullity. I do not see how it could be said that such a provision protects some kinds of nullity but not others: if that were intended it would be easy to say so.

The case which gives most difficulty is *Smith v. East Elloe Rural District Council* [1956] A.C. 736 where the form of ouster clause was similar to that in the present case. But I cannot regard it as a very satisfactory case. The plaintiff was aggrieved by a compulsory purchase order. After two unsuccessful actions she tried again after six years. As this case never reached the stage of a statement of claim we do not know whether her case was that the clerk of the council had fraudulently misled the council and the Ministry, or whether it was that the council and the Ministry were parties to the fraud. The result would be quite different, in my view, for it is only if the authority which made the order had itself acted in mala fide that the order would be a nullity. I think that the case which it was intended to present must have been that the fraud was only the fraud of the clerk because almost the whole of the argument was on the question whether a time limit in the Act applied where fraud was alleged; there was no citation of the authorities on the question whether a clause ousting the jurisdiction of the court applied when nullity was in question, and there was little about this matter in the speeches. I do not therefore regard this case as a binding authority on this question ... I have come without hesitation to the conclusion that in this case we are not prevented from inquiring whether the order of the commission was a nullity ...

Lord Pearce

... It has been argued that your Lordships should construe 'determination' as meaning anything which is on its face a determination of the commission including even a purported determination which has no jurisdiction. It would seem that on such an argument the court must accept and could not even inquire whether a purported determination was a forged or inaccurate order which did not represent that which the commission had really decided. Moreover, it would mean that however far the commission ranged outside its jurisdiction or that which it was required to do, or however far it departed from natural justice its determination could not be questioned. A more reasonable and logical construction is that by 'determination' Parliament meant a real determination, not a purported determination. On the assumption, however, that either meaning is a possible construction and that therefore the word 'determination' is ambiguous, the latter meaning would accord with a long-established line of cases which adopted that construction ...

In my opinion, the subsequent case of *Smith v. East Elloe Rural District Council* [1956] A.C. 736 does not compel your Lordships to decide otherwise. If it seemed to do so, I would think it necessary to reconsider the case in the light of the powerful dissenting opinions of my noble and learned friends, Lord Reid and Lord Somervell. It might possibly be said that it related to an administrative or executive decision, not a judicial decision, and somewhat different considerations might have applied; certainly none of the authorities relating to absence or excess of jurisdiction were cited to the House. I agree with Browne J [at first instance in this case: [1969] 2 AC 223] that it is not a compelling authority in the present case ...

Lord Wilberforce

... The question, what is the tribunal's proper area, is one which it has always been permissible to ask and to answer, and it must follow that examination of its extent is not precluded by a clause conferring conclusiveness, finality, or unquestionability upon its decisions. These clauses in their nature can only relate to decisions given within the field of operation entrusted to the tribunal. They may, according to the width and emphasis of their formulation, help to ascertain the extent of that field, to narrow it or to enlarge it, but unless one is to deny the statutory origin of the tribunal and of its powers, they cannot preclude examination of that extent.

It is sometimes said, the argument was presented in these terms, that the preclusive clause does not operate on decisions outside the permitted field because they are a nullity. There are dangers in the use of this word if it draws with it the difficult distinction between what is void and what is voidable, and I certainly do not wish to be taken to recognise that this distinction exists or to analyse it if it does. But it may be convenient so long as it is used to describe a decision made outside the permitted field, in other words, as a word of description rather than as in itself a touchstone.

The courts, when they decide that a 'decision' is a 'nullity,' are not disregarding the preclusive clause. For, just as it is their duty to attribute autonomy of decision of action to the tribunal within the designated area, so, as the counterpart of this autonomy, they must ensure that the limits of that area which have been laid down are observed (see the formulation of Lord Sumner in *Rex v. Nat Bell Liquors Ltd* [1922] 2 A.C. 128, 156). In each task they are carrying out the intention of the legislature, and it would be misdescription to state it in terms of a struggle between the courts and the executive. What would be the purpose of defining by statute the limit of a tribunal's powers if, by means of a clause inserted in the instrument of definition, those limits could safely be passed?

... I find myself obliged to state that I cannot regard *Smith* v. *East Elloe Rural District Council* [1956] A.C. 736 as a reliable solvent of this appeal, or of any case where similar questions arise. The preclusive clause was indeed very similar to the present but, however inevitable the particular decision may have been, it was given on too narrow a basis to assist us here. I agree with my noble and learned friends, Lord Reid and Lord Pearce, on this matter.

Lords Morris and Pearson delivered speeches in which they agreed that the ouster clause would not protect a decision if a jurisdictional error could be established.

The implications of this decision are considerable. Its effect is to render 'shall not be questioned' clauses ineffective to prevent judicial review in respect of jurisdictional errors. If the decision-maker falls into such error, then its conclusion is a nullity rather than a valid determination, with the result that the ouster clause—which only prevents the questioning of such determinations—does not bite. By intervening, the court is merely ascertaining that no valid determination exists, rather than entering into the prohibited enterprise of questioning a determination which does exist. The dividing line between a nullity and a valid determination is, of course, traced by the concept of jurisdictional error: whenever such an error is committed, the decision-maker steps outside of its powers and any decision it purports to reach is actually a nullity.

We saw earlier (at 2.2.4) that, although the *Anisminic* case laid the foundation for the emergence of a general principle that errors of law are jurisdictional, this was not confirmed until the House of Lords' decision some years later in *R* v. *Lord President of the Privy Council, ex parte Page* [1993] AC 682. Thus, when *Anisminic* was decided, errors of law on the face of the record were regarded as reviewable but non-jurisdictional forms of error of law. As a result, the interpretation accorded to the ouster clause in *Anisminic* did not entirely deprive it of effect, since it still operated to preclude review for non-jurisdictional errors. However, now that errors of law are almost inevitably jurisdictional, 'shall not be questioned' clauses will nearly always be ineffective: jurisdictional errors are reviewable notwithstanding the ouster provision, while non-jurisdictional errors are not reviewable in any event (unless the possibility of review for error of law on the face of the record survives). With or without the preclusive clause, the position as to reviewability is likely to be the same. The difficulty, therefore, is that even if *Anisminic* could originally be defended as an exercise in creative and bold interpretation, this view is difficult to sustain now that the 'interpretation' placed upon 'shall not be questioned' clauses appears to render them nugatory. This moves Wade and Forsyth, *Administrative Law* (Oxford 2014) at 614, to the conclusion that, '[i]n order to preserve [the] vital policy [of judicial enforcement of legal limits on administrators' powers] the courts have been forced, in effect, to rebel against Parliament'.

QUESTIONS

- Was the House of Lords' decision in *Anisminic* an exercise in interpretation, or something more than that?
- Does it matter which of these it was?

This view of Wade and Forsyth accords, to some extent, with *obiter dicta* in *R (Jackson)* v. *Attorney-General* [2005] UKHL 56, [2006] 1 AC 262 (considered at 1.4.3) and *AXA General Insurance Ltd* v. *The Lord Advocate* [2011] UKSC 46, [2012] 1 AC 868 at [50] (see 4.2) questioning Parliament's capacity to abolish judicial review or to place areas of governmental activity beyond its reach. Similar sentiments were expressed by Laws LJ in *R (Cart)* v. *Upper Tribunal* [2009] EWHC 3052 (Admin), [2010] PTSR 824 at [38]—although, ingeniously, he argued that Parliament cannot exclude judicial resolution of questions of law *because* it is sovereign:

If the meaning of statutory text is not controlled by [an independent] judicial authority, it would at length be degraded to nothing more than a matter of opinion. Its scope and content would become muddied and unclear. Public bodies would not, by means of the judicial review jurisdiction, be kept within the confines of their powers prescribed by statute. The very effectiveness of statute law, Parliament's law, requires that none of these things happen. Accordingly, as it seems to me, the need for such an authoritative judicial source cannot be dispensed with by Parliament. This is not a denial of legislative sovereignty, but an affirmation of it: as is the old rule that Parliament cannot bind itself. The old rule means that successive Parliaments are always free to make what laws they choose; that is one condition of Parliament's sovereignty. The requirement of an authoritative judicial source for the interpretation of law means that Parliament's statutes are always effective; that is another.

The argument is liable to split opinion. For example, Lady Hale, giving the lead judgment in the Supreme Court appeal in *Cart* [2011] UKSC 28, [2012] 1 AC 663 at [30], cited this passage with approval, whereas Lord Phillips in the same case considered it controversial (at [72]–[73]).

QUESTIONS

- Is the availability of judicial review more important that judicial fidelity to Acts of Parliament?
- Are you convinced by Laws LJ's argument that denial of the effectiveness of ouster clauses would uphold, rather than subvert, parliamentary sovereignty?

14.6.3 Factors that may lead to judicial acceptance of ouster

There are, however, certain contexts in which the courts may be more willing than usual to accept that legislation has the effect of excluding judicial review. In this section, we examine three factors which, individually or collectively, may be taken to establish that the exclusion would not constitute a fundamental threat to the constitutional principle of access to courts—and that legislation appearing to exclude review can therefore be given its natural meaning.

Restriction of time frame within which review is possible

A number of statutes preclude judicial review of certain decisions, but go on to provide instead for a statutory remedy which is virtually identical to judicial review, except that the time limit is usually shorter (typically six weeks) and there is presently no permission stage.

Statutory review coupled with a preclusive clause is used in situations where certainty and expedition are of particular importance. For instance, legislation provides that certain public authorities may compulsorily acquire land; in such circumstances, it is imperative that the authority can be certain, before it commits public funds to the development of the land in question, about the validity of its acquisition. Thus, for example, ss 23–25 of the Acquisition of Land Act 1981 provide for a statutory procedure to challenge such decisions, and impose a time limit of six weeks, while simultaneously providing that a compulsory purchase order shall not be questioned in other types of legal proceedings, such as judicial review.

The courts have generally been willing to accept ousters of judicial review in statutory contexts such as the 1981 Act, most notably in the House of Lords' decision in *Smith* v. *East Elloe Rural District Council* [1956] AC 736. But this raises an apparent conundrum. In *Anisminic* the House of Lords went out of its way to preserve judicial review in the face of what was arguably a crystal clear ouster clause: so why, when faced with provisions such as those in the 1981 Act, do the courts readily accept that 'regular' judicial review is excluded? This question was considered by the Court of Appeal in *R v. Secretary of State for the Environment, ex parte Ostler* [1977] QB 122, in which the claimant sought to challenge on grounds of procedural unfairness and bad faith, outwith the specified six-week period, certain orders concerned with the construction of highways; the relevant legislation provided for statutory review only. Although their Lordships were unanimous that *East Elloe* survived *Anisminic*, such that the only possibility was statutory review within six weeks, the judgments disclose some differences in the reasoning which yielded that conclusion. The centrepiece of Goff LJ's analysis (at 139) was the distinction which he drew between jurisdictional and non-jurisdictional errors:

> I think there is a real distinction between the case with which the House was dealing in *Anisminic* and the case of *Smith* v. *East Elloe Rural District Council* on that ground, that in the one case the determination was a purported determination only, because the tribunal, however eminent, having misconceived the effect of the statute, acted outside its jurisdiction, and indeed without any jurisdiction at all, whereas here one is dealing with an actual decision made within jurisdiction though sought to be challenged.

From a modern perspective, this reasoning is unsatisfactory since, under the wide concept of jurisdictional error for which *Anisminic* is now seen to have laid the foundation, no distinction can be drawn between the types of errors established in *Anisminic*, on the one hand, and those alleged in *Ostler*, on the other: all are jurisdictional. Another view was advanced by Lord Denning MR at 135:

> [I]n the *Anisminic* case the Act ousted the jurisdiction of the court altogether. It precluded the court from entertaining any complaint at any time about the determination. Whereas in the *East Elloe* case the statutory provision has given the court jurisdiction to inquire into complaints so long as the applicant comes within six weeks. The provision is more in the nature of a limitation period than of a complete ouster.

This criterion provides a sounder basis upon which to distinguish *Anisminic* and *East Elloe*, since it reflects the underlying policy which drives the judiciary's approach to ouster clauses. That policy is, self-evidently, one of upholding the rule of law by preserving individuals' access to the courts and ensuring that administrative power is subject to principles of legality and good administration. The type of preclusive clause at stake in *Anisminic* would, if applied literally, have absolutely prevented judicial review; this provided the impetus for the robust approach of the House of Lords, in order that the rule of law might be safeguarded. In contrast, as Lord Denning MR acknowledged in *Ostler*, legislation which excludes the normal supervisory jurisdiction while providing for an alternative statutory form of review effectively imposes a limitation period rather than wholly excluding judicial review. It appears that the rule of law is not, in such circumstances, so fundamentally threatened, because review remains possible, albeit within a shorter than usual time frame. Further, as we have seen (see 14.4.1), recent reforms of judicial review have introduced very short time limits for planning and particularly procurement cases, meaning that statutory procedures which provide for six-week time limits look less suspect compared to time limits on review. The difficulty, however, remains that (as Gravells (1978) 41 *MLR* 383 at 389 notes) a person wishing to challenge a decision may not discover and may have no means of discovering the grounds of challenge until the time limit for statutory challenge has expired. Although this is, of course, true of any time limit, the problem is particularly acute in respect of very short limits.

QUESTION

- In the *Ostler* case, Lord Denning MR said that provision for statutory review within a six-week period was 'more in the nature of a limitation period than of a complete ouster'. Yet the Asylum and Immigration (Treatment of Claimants etc) Act 2004, which was enacted as part of a government climbdown following criticism of its proposal completely to oust judicial review of the Asylum and Immigration Tribunal's decisions, gave prospective claimants as little as *five days* to lodge a claim for review. (Note that the relevant parts of the Act have been superseded by different arrangements.) At what point is Lord Denning's line between 'limitation' and 'ouster' crossed—and what should be the courts' reaction when it is?

The characteristics of the decision-maker (and scarce resources)

It is clear from cases like *Anisminic* that courts will strongly resist legislative attempts to exclude their powers of judicial review over *executive* bodies. But what about *judicial* bodies? If the body concerned is itself an independent judicial body, then the normal arguments (based on rule of law and separation-of-powers considerations) in favour of preserving supervision by the High Court may be less compelling. In such circumstances, there is likely to be less concern over accepting either that judicial review is restricted or excluded by means of an ouster clause, or that the body has been assigned a jurisdiction (eg to determine questions of law conclusively) that is broader than normal, such that judicial review lies on only limited grounds.

The latter situation was held to have arisen in *R (Cart)* v. *Upper Tribunal*, which was considered in some detail at 2.2.7. Recall that the question was whether the Upper Tribunal is susceptible to judicial review, and if so on what basis. This issue arose in part because s 3(5) of the Tribunals, Courts and Enforcement Act 2007 says that the Upper Tribunal is a 'superior court of record'. In light of the fact that in *Re Racal Communications* [1981] AC 374 at 392 Lord Scarman justified his conclusion that the High Court itself could not be subject to judicial review by saying that it is a 'superior court of record', it was suggested the Upper Tribunal's designation as such might also exempt it from review.

In the Divisional Court ([2009] EWHC 3052 (Admin), [2010] PTSR 824, Laws LJ concluded that whether a given body constitutes an inferior court or tribunal, on the one hand, or a superior court of record, on the other, is not determinative of its amenability to judicial review. The High Court's immunity from judicial review is attributable not to its technical status as a superior court of record, but to the fact it has unlimited jurisdiction.

The Court of Appeal ([2010] EWCA Civ 859, [2011] QB 120) agreed with this analysis. Both courts, having come to the view that formalistic analysis based on the tribunal's statutory categorization could not resolve the question of whether the tribunal was exempt from judicial review, albeit through different modes of reasoning, nonetheless considered that the characteristics of the decision-maker being reviewed may weigh heavily in deciding upon the permissibility of ousting or limiting access to review. Laws LJ would have limited review to very narrow grounds on the basis that in substance the tribunal was more or less equivalent in nature to the High Court, being the High Court's alter ego. The Court of Appeal similarly would have limited the grounds on which the Tribunal could be reviewed, but did not adopt Laws LJ's reasoning. Nonetheless, in the Court of Appeal, Sedley LJ's preparedness to exempt the Upper Tribunal from the full panoply of the High Court's review powers was heavily influenced by the Tribunal's institutional characteristics and its situation at the apex of the 'newly coherent and comprehensive edifice' constituted by the new tribunals system (on which see further ch 18).

The Supreme Court ([2011] UKSC 28, [2012] 1 AC 663) agreed with Laws LJ that the Tribunal's formal status could not be determinative. However, the Court also considered restrictions ought to be placed on review, though the Justices enunciated restrictions different from those favoured by either of the lower courts—namely, review of the Tribunal should only be available where an important point of practice or principle is raised or there is some other compelling reason for the court to hear the case. The Court's rationale for imposing these restrictions, in common with the lower courts, rested in part on the nature of the Upper Tribunal and reformed tribunal system. For example, Lord Dyson pointed to the 'status, nature and role of the [Upper Tribunal]' (at [123]), the Tribunal being very similar in nature to a court, as one reason for a restrained approach to review, while Lord Phillips saw the new two-tier tribunal system as largely self-sufficient and considered that the presence of judges on the tribunals and appointment of a judge as Tribunals President, would serve to ensure proper judicial scrutiny of first-tier decisions (at [91]). Indeed, Lord Phillips considered this point to be so powerful that he was minded to favour complete ouster of review—albeit he did not ultimately adopt this position.

Thus, the Supreme Court placed weight on the nature of the decision-maker. But in justifying the restrictions the Justices also placed significant emphasis on the importance of guarding against a flood of claims and preservation of scarce resources. Lady Hale said, in opposition to the argument that no restrictions on review should be imposed, that 'the courts' resources are not unlimited' (at [47]), while Lord Phillips reasoned that 'in exercising the power of judicial review, the judges must pay due regard to the fact that, even where the due administration of justice is at stake, resources are limited' (at [89]). Other Justices made similar points (at [100] *per* Lord Brown; at [104] *per* Lord Clarke; at [124], [126]–[127] *per* Lord Dyson).

It is one thing to argue review might be restricted on the basis of the legal expertise of a primary decision-maker and/or because the tribunal system contains its own effective checks through internal appeals. Decisions emanating from a tribunal system with these characteristics are deserving of respect so that the courts are justified in adopting a generally non-interventionist approach to reviewing such decisions, while if courts too readily intervened this would undermine a core intention underpinning creation of the new tribunal system: that it should be largely self-contained. However, it is quite another thing for the courts to limit review on their own motion on the basis that resources should be preserved. Bare distributive questions over allocation of public monies are for Parliament, given that that institution has the democratic legitimacy to decide how to disperse scare public resources on behalf of the community. In addition to lacking constitutional legitimacy to decide on distributive questions, the courts lack access to information relevant to financial planning, and financial expertise. Within the tribunal legislation in issue in *Cart*, Parliament, the ultimate arbiter of how public resources should be distributed, had not considered it necessary to include any limits on review, despite a proposal for statutory ouster having been before it and which was partly premised on a concern to preserve resources: Leggatt, *Tribunals for Users—One System, One Service* (London 2001) at [6.27], [6.34]. Against this backdrop it is difficult to see how the courts could justify doing that which Parliament had chosen not to do, limiting access to review, based on judicial views over how resources should best be marshalled. In this regard, the caution shown by Lord Dyson in *Cart* is to be welcomed; while he did place some emphasis on matters of resource allocation he considered the argument needed to be treated with caution and said: 'If the floodgates argument were the only point militating against unrestricted judicial review, I doubt whether it would be enough' (at [126]–[127]). Lord Dyson's approach more closely aligns with iconic statements of principle such as that in *R* v. *Board of Visitors of Hull Prison, ex parte St Germain* [1979] QB 425 at 445: '[T]o deny jurisdiction on the ground of expediency seems to me ... to be tantamount to abdicating a primary function of the judiciary'.

QUESTION

- What dangers might there be in courts endorsing a general principle that the ouster or limitation of access to court could be justified on the basis of saving money?

The nature of the norms whose protection is at stake

In *R (A)* v. *Director of Establishments of the Security Service* [2009] UKSC 12, [2010] 2 WLR 1, the claimant wished to mount a legal challenge to a decision taken by the intelligence services denying him permission to publish parts of a book which he had written. The question for determination was whether the claimant could mount that challenge in the High Court, or whether he had to mount it before the Investigatory Powers Tribunal—a body established under s 65 of the Regulation of Investigatory Powers Act 2000 (RIPA) to deal with certain types of legal challenges concerning the intelligence services. The question arose because s 65(2)(a) of the 2000 Act says that the jurisdiction of the Tribunal shall be

> the only appropriate tribunal for the purposes of section 7 of the Human Rights Act 1998 in relation to any proceedings under subsection (1)(a) of that section (proceedings for actions incompatible with Convention rights) which fall within subsection (3) of this section.

Section 65(3) of RIPA goes on to provide that proceedings fall within s 65 if 'they are proceedings against any of the intelligence services'. Meanwhile, s 7 of the HRA says that

> (1) A person who claims that a public authority has acted (or proposes to act) in a way which is made unlawful by section 6(1) may—
>
>   (a) bring proceedings against the authority under this Act in the appropriate court or tribunal ...
>
> (2) In subsection (1)(a) 'appropriate court or tribunal' means such court or tribunal as may be determined in accordance with rules.

Rules of the type mentioned in s 7 were made in the form of Part 7.11 of the Civil Procedure Rules, which provide that

> (1) A claim under section 7(1)(a) of the Human Rights Act 1998 in respect of a judicial act may be brought only in the High Court.
>
> (2) Any other claim under section 7(1)(a) of that Act may be brought in any court.

Against this background, was the effect of s 65(2)(a) of the Act of 2000 that the claimant could not bring his claim in the High Court? In other words, did s 65(2)(a) have the effect of ousting the High Court's jurisdiction over the relevant class of claims? Yes, according to the Supreme Court. This conclusion was reached partly because the Investigatory Powers Tribunal (IPT) was felt to be equivalent in standing and authority to the High Court. But Lord Brown, with whom the other four Justices agreed, was also influenced by another factor:

[21] [The claimant argues] that to construe section 65 as conferring exclusive jurisdiction on the IPT constitutes an ouster of the ordinary jurisdiction of the courts and is constitutionally objectionable on that ground. They pray in aid two decisions of high authority: *Pyx Granite Co Ltd v Ministry of Housing and Local Government* [1960] AC 260 and *Anisminic Ltd v Foreign Compensation Commission* [1969] 2 AC 147. To my mind, however, the argument is unsustainable. In the first place, it is evident, as the majority of the Court of Appeal pointed out, that the relevant provisions of RIPA, HRA and the CPR all came into force at the same time as part of a single legislative scheme. With effect from 2 October 2000 section 7(1)(a) HRA jurisdiction came into existence (i) in respect of section 65(3) proceedings in the IPT pursuant to section 65(2)(a), and (ii) in respect of any other section 7(1)(a) HRA proceedings in the courts pursuant to section 7(9) and CPR 7.11. True it is, as Rix LJ observed [in this case in the Court of Appeal: [2009] EWCA Civ 24], that CPR 7.11(2) does not explicitly recognise the exception to its apparent width represented by section 65(2)(a). But that is not to say that section 65(2)(a) ousts some pre-existing right.

[22] This case, in short, falls within the principle recognised by the House of Lords in *Barraclough v Brown* [1897] AC 615—where, as Lord Watson said at p 622: 'The right and the remedy are given uno flatu [with one breath], and the one cannot be dissociated from the other'—rather than the principle [that the courts' jurisdiction can only be excluded by clear words] ... Distinguishing *Barraclough v Brown*, Viscount Simonds [in *Pyx Granite Co Ltd* v. *Ministry of Housing and Local Government* [1960] AC 260 at 286] pointed out that the statute there in question could be construed as merely providing an alternative means of determining whether or not the company had a pre-existing common law right to develop their land; it did not take away 'the inalienable remedy ... to seek redress in [the courts]'. Before 2 October 2000 there was, of course, no pre-existing common law or statutory right to bring a claim based on an asserted breach of the Convention. Section 65(2)(a) takes away no 'inalienable remedy'.

It must be kept in mind that the issue in this case was somewhat different from that which usually arises in relation to ouster clauses: the question was not whether there had been exclusion of the High Court's *jurisdiction to subject the Tribunal's decisions to judicial review*; it was whether the Act excluded the High Court's *jurisdiction over that class of claims assigned to the Tribunal*. It follows that the general point that can be taken from the present case is that when legislation, in effect, contemporaneously creates rights and prevents them from being enforced in ordinary courts, this is unlikely to be viewed as a constitutionally suspect ouster of such courts' jurisdiction. However, given that the norms enforced via judicial review are not (at least in any straightforward sense) statutory creations, the principle applied by the Supreme Court in *Director of Establishments* can have no application to exclusion of judicial review.

QUESTION

- If a claimant, for whatever reason, chose to pursue proceedings against the security services in the Administrative Court rather than in the IPT, he would be limited to raising regular, as opposed to HRA, grounds of review. Why might this be problematic?

Human rights requirements

We saw (at 9.5.2) that Article 6(1) ECHR applies to the administrative process whenever civil rights and obligations fall for determination. Such determinations must be made by tribunals which are impartial and independent. Although many administrative decision-makers are not independent of the executive, this apparent infraction of Article 6(1) may be cured if provision exists for recourse to a court of 'full jurisdiction'—a characteristic which, for most purposes, is possessed by courts with powers of judicial review. An ouster clause may, however, render judicial review impossible or inadequate for Article 6(1) purposes. For instance, in *Tinnelly and Sons Ltd* v. *United Kingdom* (1999) 27 EHRR 249, a Minister issued a certificate which, according to the relevant legislation, constituted 'conclusive evidence' that it was for national security reasons that the applicants had been unsuccessful in securing a government contract. The applicants, however, contended that they had really been turned down on religious grounds. Having been unsuccessful in judicial review proceedings, they applied to the ECtHR, which held (at [74]) that judicial review had inadequately safeguarded the applicants' Article 6(1) right, because the judge's 'hands were tied by the conclusive nature of the certificate and the Secretary of State's invocation of national security considerations'.

Other Articles may also bear on the permissibility of ouster. For example, Article 13, the right to an effective remedy, requires that where human rights are violated victims must be capable of securing a binding legal determination of the violation and legally binding redress from an independent and impartial tribunal. If the courts' jurisdiction to hear rights claims or classes of rights claim were ousted, it is difficult to see how there could be compliance with Article 13. In this regard, it is worth noting that possible alternative routes to redress, outside of the courts, such as the Ombudsman, public inquiries, and internal agency investigations have all been held to be inadequate for the purposes of Article 13 on the basis that they lack independence from government and/or binding legal authority.

14.7 Standing

14.7.1 Introduction: private rights versus public interests

Judicial review proceedings may be initiated only by a party with standing (sometimes referred to as *locus standi*). To this end, s 31(3) of the Senior Courts Act 1981 provides:

> No application for judicial review shall be made unless the leave of the High Court has been obtained in accordance with rules of court; and the court shall not grant leave to make such an application unless it considers that the applicant has a sufficient interest in the matter to which the application relates.

The crucial issue, therefore, is whether the claimant has 'a sufficient interest'; although the text of s 31(3) suggests that this is resolved at the permission stage (or, in the old language used by s 31(3), the leave stage), we will see later that in fact standing may, and often does, fall for consideration at the substantive hearing. However, before addressing the courts' interpretation of 'sufficient interest', we must consider a logically prior issue: what is the purpose of—and what, therefore, is the justification for—the standing requirement? The importance of asking this question, and of finding a satisfactory answer to it, is underlined by the fact that where standing is denied this may be to allow an ongoing illegality to continue or past illegality to go unremedied.

Whether one considers that standing rules ought to exist to limit access to court, and if so, what those rules ought to be will depend on one's view of the principal function of judicial review, and also wider policy arguments. In this regard, it is informative to contrast two different models of judicial review (drawing on Varuhas, 'The Public Interest Conception of Public Law' in Bell, Elliott, Varuhas, and Murray (eds), *Public Law Adjudication in Common Law Systems* (Oxford 2016)). We might term the first the 'rights based' or 'private law' model, and the other, the 'public interest' model.

On a rights-based view the principal concern of judicial review is to ensure protection of, and grant remedies for invasion of, individuals' personal rights and interests. Within this model standing would be limited to the holders of those legal entitlements and interests which are the object of the law's protection, that is, persons would be granted standing only where their personal rights and interests are directly affected by the challenged administrative action. To grant standing to third parties or to pressure groups to challenge administrative action which touches upon another's rights and interests would be impermissible, as this would be for these third parties to exercise control over rights and interests which are the property of another. Some, such as Allan, would argue that a focus on rights also ensures that courts stay within proper constitutional boundaries (*Constitutional Justice* (Oxford 2001) at 194–9). While no one would dispute that protection and adjudication of individual legal rights is the proper role of the judiciary, outside of such cases it may be harder to dispute the claim that courts are trespassing upon matters of ordinary politics or bare policy, which are the proper province of political institutions. Further, one might consider that if we are going to impose limits on access to judicial review we ought to prioritize those cases which allege interference with basic individual rights.

Standing in contrast to the rights-based model is the public interest model. On this view the principal function of judicial review is to ensure that administrators exercise their powers properly in accordance with precepts of good administration and for the public purposes for which Parliament has conferred those powers. Judicial review does not exist principally to protect individual rights and interests—albeit this may be one of its ancillary purposes—but rather to ensure protection of the public interest. Logically, we all, as members of the community, have a shared and legitimate interest in seeing that public powers are properly administered for the good of the community. As such, the courts should be very reluctant to exclude from judicial review any person or group with an arguable claim of unlawful administrative action, whether they are personally affected by that action or not. On this account a rights-based test would be counterproductive and unduly constrain the courts' ability to intervene where an authority had clearly acted unlawfully and deviated from public goals, but in doing so had not happened to infringe any one individual's rights.

Further, to focus exclusively on cases of rights infringement would arguably be to turn judicial review into a field of private law, so that it would add little to existing fields of law; as Lord Scarman observed in *R v. Inland Revenue Commissioners, ex parte National Federation of Self-Employed and Small Businesses Ltd* [1982] AC 617 at 653, if one could only bring a review claim where one's legal rights were interfered with then judicial review would 'lose [its] public law character, being no more than a remedy for a private wrong'.

Indeed, where an individual holds a recognized legal right, and that right is infringed, could they not simply seek enforcement of that right via a claim in ordinary proceedings? It is not clear why they would need to have recourse to the supervisory jurisdiction. As such, to limit judicial review claims to those based in legal rights would be to radically cut down the scope and distinctive value of judicial review.

Beyond these two models, which are ideal types, there are wider arguments that might be made for and against narrowing or broadening standing. So, for example, one may generally adhere to the public interest model, but consider some practical limits ought to be imposed on standing so as to protect against courts being swamped with claims. Equally, one might largely support a rights-based view, but nonetheless consider standing rules should be loosened in some cases, for example where a government decision raises significant matters of public concern but does not directly infringe individual rights. More generally, consideration of these policy arguments may lead us to revise our adherence to particular models, or the models themselves.

Let us first consider arguments in favour of wider standing rules. Opening up access to judicial review would mean that a greater number of unlawful administrative acts would be exposed and remedied. The more unlawful executive action brought to heel, the more closely our constitutional system shall adhere to the rule of law. More frequent judicial review challenges might have a wider deterrence effect: if administrators know there is a high likelihood that any administrative unlawfulness will be called to account in court, they may take their legal responsibilities more seriously in general.

Even if administrative action prejudices individual rights, those individuals affected may not have sufficient motivation or indeed resources to launch legal proceedings. In such circumstances allowance for a publically spirited citizen or an interest group to launch proceedings ensures that vindication of the rule of law does not depend on the happenstance of whether the directly affected individual has sufficient will or pecuniary resources to launch proceedings.

It is beyond doubt that certain duties owed by authorities are not owed to individuals but are free-standing duties or duties owed to the public as a whole, for the benefit of the public as a whole. Examples include duties to ensure certain administrative action is vetted for environmental impacts and the duty under s 1 of the National Health Service Act 2006 that the Secretary of State 'continue the promotion in England of a comprehensive health service'. There are no rights in play here, and the duties are not directed to any specific person or group of people, nor are they owed for the benefit of specific, identifiable individuals. Nor is it the case that their breach would directly and peculiarly affect any one specific individual. As such, adoption of a rights-based standing requirement would render administrative non-compliance with many statutory duties immune from legal challenge.

On the other hand, there are arguments against widening standing rules.

First, there is the potential for abuse. If claimants need not show individual prejudice to bring review claims this could pave the way for political pressure groups to launch review proceedings in order to disrupt or derail administrative processes to which they are politically opposed, and/or for busybodies to meddle in the affairs of those whose interests are directly affected.

Second, and linked to the first point, vested interests, such as powerful corporations or political pressure groups, may take advantage of wider standing rules in order to seek to systematically skew the exercise of public power in favour of their own interests: the political process, where clashes of political interests ought to be resolved, may be short-circuited as these issues will instead be fought out in court.

Third, if administrators increasingly feel their decisions are liable to be challenged they may be guided more by a concern to 'judge proof' their decisions than by what the public interest demands.

Fourth, wider standing is liable to result in more litigation, which will in turn impose greater costs on authorities, who have to defend claims, and the courts, which must dedicate resources to determining claims, while the legal system may be clogged up leading to delays for other litigants. On the other hand, there are many controls on access to review which operate to regulate levels of litigation including judicial regulation of access to review via the permission stage and the three-month limitation period, while certain classes of judicial review claims have been moved out of the courts to the tribunal system, thus easing the case-load in the Administrative Court (see 18.4.5).

Fifth, administration involves making decisions. Whilst such decisions are under legal attack they are in practice, if not necessarily in theory, to a greater or lesser degree in suspense. Such delay can undermine effective public administration, and prejudice the interests of third parties reliant on particular decisions. On the other hand, the three-month time limit and promptness requirement provide a significant degree of protection against delay.

QUESTIONS

- Can you identify any further arguments for or against narrowing or broadening standing rules?
- Do you favour the rights-based or public interest model of standing?
- Whichever model you favour, would you modify it to some degree to take account of policy concerns? If so, how would you alter the models?

14.7.2 The law prior to the *National Federation* case

Up until at least the late 1970s three features characterized the law of standing. First, different rules of standing applied to different remedies. Second, judicial review generally and the law of standing specifically more closely adhered to the rights-based or private law model of review than to the public interest model. Third, the law of standing was characterized by inconsistency; even in respect of the same remedy different tests were asserted and applied.

Particularly restrictive standing rules governed mandatory orders. Wright J, in a test followed many times since, held that the claimant had to show 'a specific legal right to ask for the interference of the Court' (*R v. Guardians of Lewisham* [1897] 1 QB 498 at 500). A somewhat more liberal approach was adopted in respect of quashing orders (and prohibiting orders, to which 'very analogous' standing rules applied: *R v. Surrey Justices* (1870) LR 5 QB 466 at 472). Nonetheless, the test was still one focused on individual detriment: in *R v. Paddington Valuation Officer, ex parte Peachey Property Ltd* [1966] 1 QB 380 at 400–1, Lord Denning MR, with whom the other judges agreed, held the relevant test was that of a 'person aggrieved'. However, despite general agreement that individual prejudice had to be suffered, there was disagreement as to the width of the category of aggrieved persons. Lord Denning himself took the view in *R v. Liverpool Corporation, ex parte Liverpool Taxi Fleet Operators' Association* [1972] 2 QB 299 at 308–9 that the category extended to anyone 'whose interests may be prejudicially affected by what is taking place'. In contrast, in *R v. Thames Magistrates' Court, ex parte Greenbaum* (1957) 55 LGR 129 at 135, Parker LJ adopted a narrower definition: the claimant must have a 'particular grievance of his own beyond some inconvenience suffered by the general public'.

Thus, notwithstanding the variations of view just highlighted, standing, generally speaking, depended on possession of an individual right or the suffering of individual detriment, in accordance with the private law model. However, it is worth recording that various decisions from Lord Denning in particular offered some support for wider standing rules. For example, in *R v. Greater London Council, ex parte Blackburn* [1976] 1 WLR 550 at 559, he stated as a general proposition that ordinary and prerogative remedies could be granted to 'any member of the public', albeit that 'a mere busybody' would be turned away at the court's discretion (see also *R v. Paddington Valuation Officer, ex parte Peachey Property Ltd* [1966] 1 QB 380 at 400).

14.7.3 The *National Federation* case

The procedural reforms of 1977 introduced the concept of 'sufficient interest' as the test for standing in claims (for both ordinary and prerogative remedies) brought under the judicial review procedure. This reform provided the courts with an opportunity to clarify the approach to standing as against the messy state of the jurisprudence described in the previous section. This opportunity was taken in the landmark case of *R v. Inland Revenue Commissioners, ex parte National Federation of Self-Employed and Small Businesses Ltd* [1982] AC 617, the House of Lords laying the foundations for a more straightforward and liberal approach to standing in respect of claims brought under what is now Part 54 of the Civil Procedure Rules. (When the case was decided, the sufficient interest test was found in RSC Ord 53, r 3(5), later r 3(7). The same test is now set out in the Senior Courts Act 1981, s 31(3).)

The background facts are as follows. It was common practice among casual print workers—known informally as the 'Fleet Street Casuals'—to avoid the payment of tax in respect of casual income by falsifying information provided to the Inland Revenue. Having become aware of this practice, which had caused the loss of substantial amounts of tax, the Inland Revenue offered an amnesty: provided that the casual workers registered for tax purposes, no investigations would be made as to tax lost in certain previous years. The Revenue considered that this was the best way to regularize the situation, but the claimant—an association of small businesses and self-employed persons—argued that the Revenue had exceeded its power in granting the amnesty and sought a declaration to that effect. In the alternative, they argued that, if the Revenue did have the necessary power, they had not exercised their powers properly, in particular failing to act fairly as between taxpayers and failing in their duty to ensure tax is duly assessed, charged, and collected; to this end, a mandatory order was sought in order to compel the assessment and collection of the tax arrears owed by the casual workers.

A key question was whether the claimant had standing to bring the claim. As mentioned earlier, the judgments in general signalled a more liberal approach to standing across the board, but there was also disagreement among their Lordships on key points. Let us consider the key issues that arose.

First, their Lordships were unanimous that questions of standing implicate a two-stage process. Standing is to be considered both at the permission stage and full hearing stage—and following on from *National Federation* it is today very common for standing to be determined at the full hearing.

At the permission stage the court is concerned to exclude cases where there is a clear lack of standing, on a preliminary consideration of the issue. However, even if standing is granted at the permission stage, it may ultimately be refused at the full hearing, given a consideration of the merits of the claim. Lord Wilberforce reasoned as follows (at 630):

> In the Divisional Court, when the motion for judicial review came before it, the point as to locus standi was treated as a preliminary point. 'Before we embark on the case itself,' said Lord Widgery C.J., 'we have to decide whether the federation has power to bring it at all.' After hearing argument, the court decided that it had not. The matter went to the Court of Appeal [1980] Q.B. 407, and again argument was concentrated on the preliminary point, though it, and the judgments, did range over the merits. The Court of Appeal by majority reversed the Divisional Court and made a declaration that the applicants have a sufficient interest to apply for judicial review. On final appeal to this House, the two sides concurred in stating that the only ground for decision was whether the applicants have such sufficient interest.
>
> I think that it is unfortunate that this course has been taken. There may be simple cases in which it can be seen at the earliest stage that the person applying for judicial review has no interest at all, or no sufficient interest to support the application: then it would be quite correct at the threshold to refuse him leave to apply. The right to do so is an important safeguard against the courts being flooded and public bodies harassed by irresponsible applications. But in other cases this will not be so. In these it will be necessary to consider the powers or the duties in law of those against whom the relief is asked, the position of the applicant in relation to those powers or duties, and to the breach of those said to have been committed. In other words, the question of sufficient interest cannot, in such cases, be considered in the abstract, or as an isolated point: it must be taken together with the legal and factual context. The rule requires sufficient interest in the matter to which the application relates. This, in the present case, necessarily involves the whole question of the duties of the Inland Revenue and the breaches or failure of those duties of which the respondents complain.

Thus, as Lord Diplock put it, at the permission stage the court shall form 'a prima facie view about [standing] upon the material that is available at the first stage. The *prima facie* view so formed, if favourable to the applicant, may alter on further consideration in the light of further evidence that may be before the court at the second stage, the hearing of the application for judicial review itself' (at 642). He then elaborated (at 643–4):

> The whole purpose of requiring that leave should first be obtained to make the application for judicial review would be defeated if the court were to go into the matter in any depth at that stage. If, on a quick perusal of the material then available, the court thinks that it discloses what might on further consideration turn out to be an arguable case in favour of granting to the applicant the relief claimed, it ought, in the exercise of a judicial discretion, to give him leave to apply for that relief. The discretion that the court is exercising at this stage is not the same as that which it is called upon to exercise when all the evidence is in and the matter has been fully argued at the hearing of the application.

The sort of basis on which the claim might be dismissed for lack of standing at the permission stage would include that the case was hopeless on its merits and/or that the claimant was simply a meddler or busybody. Thus, Lord Scarman considered that the preliminary evaluation of standing at the permission stage 'enables the court to prevent abuse by busy-bodies, cranks, and other mischief-makers' (at 653). Lord Diplock echoed this view saying that the purpose of the permission stage is 'to prevent the time of the court being wasted by busybodies with misguided or trivial complaints of administrative error, and to remove the uncertainty in which public officers and authorities might be left as to whether they could safely proceed with administrative action while proceedings for judicial review of it were actually pending even though misconceived' (at 642–3).

All agreed that on the facts it was right for standing to have been granted to the claimant on a preliminary basis at the permission stage. This is significant in itself given the claimant could not be said to have been directly or personally affected by the deal struck between the Revenue and the casuals.

What, then, is the approach that ought to be taken to the 'sufficient interest' test at the second stage? All agreed that a more flexible approach to standing was now to take hold in the light of the procedural reforms of the late 1970s, which had been driven by a policy of ridding the law of excessive technicality and opening up access to the courts. As Lord Wilberforce observed, the new procedure for judicial review was 'introduced to simplify the procedure of applying for the relief formerly given by prerogative writ or order—so the old technical rules no longer apply' (at 631). Another factor was what Lord Roskill described as 'modern judicial policy' (at 658): through a series of decisions in the years preceding *National Federation* the 'former and stricter rules determining when such orders, or formerly the prerogative writs, might or might not issue, have been greatly relaxed' (at 656). Given these developments it was now clear that a direct interest in the matter at hand was not required. This prompted Lord Fraser to ask (at 646):

> On what principle, then, is the sufficiency of interest to be judged? All are agreed that a direct financial or legal interest is not now required, and that the requirement of a legal specific interest laid down in *Reg.* v. *Lewisham Union Guardians* [1897] 1 Q.B. 488 is no longer applicable. There is also general agreement that a mere busybody does not have a sufficient interest. The difficulty is, in between those extremes, to distinguish between the desire of the busybody to interfere in other people's affairs and the interest of the person affected by or having a reasonable concern with the matter to which the application relates. In the present case that matter is an alleged failure by the appellants to perform the duty imposed upon them by statute.

Thus, the rules had been and ought to be liberalized; however, their Lordships considered that some limits had to remain. Lord Fraser said: '[W]hile the standard of sufficiency has been relaxed in recent years, the need to have an interest has remained and the fact that ... a sufficient interest [is required] undoubtedly shows that not every applicant is entitled to judicial review as of right' (at 645). Lord Roskill saw the need for some limits as neces-sarily connected to the proper limits of the judicial role on review: it is 'important that the courts do not by use or misuse of the weapon of judicial review cross that clear boundary between what is administration, whether it be good or bad administration, and what is an unlawful performance of the statutory duty by a body charged with the performance of that duty' (at 662).

While there was agreement that the approach to standing had to be applied more liber-ally than in the past, but that some limits must remain, there was less agreement as to how liberally the 'sufficient interest' test ought to be applied. Albeit it was made clear by all of their Lordships that whether or not the claimant had a sufficient interest to bring a review challenge was intimately connected to the substantive merits of the claimant's case.

Lord Diplock adopted the most liberal view. Albeit his views were in the minority in *National Federation*, as we shall see in the next section, it was ultimately his views that 'won out' as the law of standing developed in the post-*National Federation* era. It is no exaggeration to say that the following statement of principle has come to underpin the whole of the modern law of standing (at 644):

> It would, in my view, be a grave lacuna in our system of public law if a pressure group, like the federation, or even a single public-spirited taxpayer, were prevented by outdated technical rules of locus standi from bringing the matter to the attention of the court to vindicate the rule of law and get the unlawful conduct stopped. The Attorney-General, although he occasionally applies for prerogative orders against public authorities that do not form part of central government, in practice never does so against government departments. It is not, in my view, a sufficient answer to say that judicial review of the actions of officers or departments of central government is unnecessary because they are accountable to Parliament for the way in which they carry out their functions. They are accountable to Parliament for what they do so far as regards efficiency and policy, and of that Parliament is the only judge; they are responsible to a court of justice for the lawfulness of what they do, and of that the court is the only judge.

This approach entails a wholesale embrace of the public interest model of standing. The rule of law would be undermined if technical rules of *locus standi* prevented a publically spirited individual or interest group with an arguable case of administrative illegality, from bringing a claim. As we saw from the earlier quotations, Lord Diplock would impose some limits, such as excluding busybodies, but those limits should not stand in the way of a person with a good claim. Unsurprisingly Lord Diplock would have, on the basis of his stated approach, granted the Federation standing. Lord Scarman's approach came close to Lord Diplock's, albeit he ultimately denied the Federation standing. As already discussed, he would exclude mischief-makers from review, but otherwise standing more or less depended on whether the claimant had an arguable case (at 654–5, emphasis added):

> The federation, having failed to show any grounds for believing that the revenue has failed to do its statutory duty, have not, in my view, shown an interest sufficient in law to justify any further proceedings by the court on its application. *Had they shown reasonable grounds for believing that the failure to collect tax from the Fleet Street casuals was an abuse of the revenue's managerial discretion or that there was a case to that effect which merited investigation and examination by the court, I would have agreed with the Court of Appeal that they had shown a sufficient interest for the grant of leave to proceed further with their application.* I would, therefore, allow the appeal.

The remaining three Law Lords, Lord Wilberforce, Lord Fraser, and Lord Roskill, all would have denied the Federation standing, and were less willing to broaden standing requirements to the degree that Lord Diplock and Lord Scarman would have. Thus, in comparison with Lord Diplock's warm attitudes to public interest standing, Lord Fraser's views were somewhat cooler: 'It would, I think, be extravagant to suggest that every taxpayer who believes that the Inland Revenue or the Customs and Excise Commissioners are giving an unlawful preference to another taxpayer, and who feels aggrieved thereby, has a sufficient interest to obtain judicial review' (at 647).

The three judges would have set the bar for such a publically spirited challenge—*ie* a case where the claimant was not themselves directly affected—higher than either Lord Diplock or Lord Scarman, who had each signalled that an arguable case of illegality would generally be sufficient to prove a sufficient interest; in contrast the three majority judges would have required the claimant to demonstrate an arguable case of *serious* illegality. Nonetheless, it is very important to note that, despite these differences, at a more general level these three judges shared Lord Diplock and Lord Scarman's view that standing was intimately connected to questions of legality and thus the merits of the claimant's case. Thus, Lord Fraser considered that a publically spirited taxpayer, who sought to challenge a tax deal made between the Revenue and another taxpayer, could only possibly do so 'if he was relying upon some exceptionally grave or widespread illegality … but such cases would be very rare indeed and this is not one of them' (at 647). Similarly, Lord Wilberforce would only have contemplated granting standing to such a claimant in a case of 'sufficient gravity': 'That a case can never arise in which the acts or abstentions of the revenue can be brought before the court I am certainly not prepared to assert, nor that, in a case of sufficient gravity, the court might not be able to hold that another taxpayer or other taxpayers could challenge them. Whether this situation has been reached or not must depend upon an examination, upon evidence, of what breach of duty or illegality is alleged. Upon this, and relating it to the position of the complainant, the court has to make its decision' (at 633). Lord Roskill shared the view that it would be a rare case in which such standing was granted: 'Theoretically, but one trusts only theoretically, it is possible to envisage a case when because of some grossly improper pressure or motive the appellants have failed to perform their statutory duty as respects a particular taxpayer or class of taxpayer. In such a case, which emphatically is not the present, judicial review might be available to other taxpayers. But it would require to be a most extreme case' (at 662).

These statements set the threshold for a public interest challenge by an unaffected citizen or interest group very high. However, it is important to note that the three judges who took this view were very heavily influenced by the statutory context and subject-matter of the case before them, so that it would be wrong to interpret the statements as setting the threshold for public interest challenges so high in every case—and indeed later courts have not interpreted the foregoing statements as general tests to govern all public interest challenges. So in *National Federation* Lords Wilberforce, Fraser, and Roskill, in the light of the relevant tax statutes under consideration, conceptualized the relationship between an individual taxpayer and the Revenue in respect of tax affairs as having an almost 'private law' character, the relationship being a bipolar one between two specific parties, characterized by a relationship of confidentiality and a degree of 'privity', while they saw the statutory duties owed by the Revenue as being ones owed to specific taxpayers. Given the distinctive nature of this relationship—a highly unusual type of relationship in the field of judicial review in the context of which most statutory duties are conceptualized as 'public' in character—their Lordships took the view that the tax affairs of individual taxpayers were only the proper concern of those taxpayers and the Revenue. The corollary of this view was that third parties, such as the Federation, did not have a legitimate interest in the tax arrangements of other taxpayers, other than in exceptional cases. Notably, Lord Scarman, in contrast, considered the Revenue's duty to act fairly to be one owed to the public, breach of which would be a 'public wrong' as opposed to an individual wrong (at 647–55). This different characterization of the duties in play goes a long way towards explaining the difference of approach to public interest standing on the facts as between Lord Scarman, and the other three judges.

There was one further source of significant disagreement among their Lordships in *National Federation*. This concerned the continuing relevance of the older case law according to which the law of standing varied with the remedy sought; for example, recall that very strict standing requirements governed applications for mandatory orders. Thus, albeit the new rules adopted a single standard for standing across all remedies—sufficient interest—Lord Wilberforce nonetheless considered that the old case law had continuing relevance (at 631):

> [T]he fact that the same words [*ie* sufficient interest] are used to cover all the forms of rem-edy allowed by the rule does not mean that the test is the same in all cases. When Lord Parker C.J. said that in cases of mandamus the test may well be stricter (sc. than in certiorari)—the *Beaverbrook Newspapers* case [1969] 1 Q.B. 342 and in *Cook's* case [1970] 1 W.L.R. 450 at 455F, 'on a very strict basis,' he was not stating a technical rule which can now be discarded—but a rule of common sense, reflecting the different character of the relief asked for. It would seem obvious enough that the interest of a person seeking to compel an authority to carry out a duty is different from that of a person complaining that a judicial or administrative body has, to his detri-ment, exceeded its powers. Whether one calls for a stricter rule than the other may be a linguistic point: they are certainly different and we should be unwise in our enthusiasm for liberation from procedural fetters to discard reasoned authorities which illustrate this. It is hardly necessary to add that recognition of the value of guiding authorities does not mean that the process of judicial review must stand still.

Lord Diplock took the polar opposite view, considering that the adoption of the new pro-cedural reforms and unitary sufficient interest test had washed away the technicalities of the past (at 638):

> Your Lordships can take judicial notice of the fact that the main purpose of the [reforms] was to sweep away these procedural differences including, in particular, differences as to locus standi; to substitute for them a single simplified procedure for obtaining all forms of relief.

His 'progressive' approach was reflected in more general observations that '[a]ny judicial statements on matters of public law if made before 1950 are likely to be a misleading guide to what the law is today' (at 640). Indeed, he argued—perhaps slightly exaggerating the position—that even before the new procedural reforms, the law had already moved beyond the 'old law' (at 640–1):

> The process of liberalisation of access to the courts and the progressive discarding of technical limitations upon locus standi is too well known to call for detailed citation of the cases by which it may be demonstrated. They are referred to and discussed in Wade, *Administrative Law*, 4th ed (1977), pp 543–6 (prohibition and certiorari) and pp 610–12 (mandamus). The author points out there that although lip-service continued to be paid to a difference in standing required to entitle an applicant to mandamus on the one hand and prohibition or certiorari on the other, in practice the courts found some way of treating the locus standi for all three remedies as being the same...
>
>   To revert to technical restrictions on locus standi to prevent this that were current 30 years or more [ago] would be to reverse that progress towards a comprehensive system of administrative law that I regard as having been the greatest achievement of the English courts in my judicial lifetime.

Lord Diplock's view ultimately won out. Judges today rarely if ever discuss the remedy claimed in deciding questions of standing. An early example of the embrace of Lord

Diplock's view is Watkins LJ's judgment in *R v. Felixstowe Justices, ex parte Leigh* [1987] QB 582 at 597:

> I do not find it necessary for the purposes of this judgment to decide, as was urged upon us by counsel for the respondents, whether or not a stricter test of sufficient interest still applies for the issue of mandamus, beyond saying that I am inclined to think it does not. The appropriate approach in this case, it seems to me, is for the court, in using what I regard as its undoubted discretion, to decide the question of sufficient interest on each application primarily within its factual context.

Thus, the *National Federation* case was highly significant for a number of reasons. First, it clearly established that standing implicates a two-stage process: (1) at the permission stage the court will undertake a preliminary assessment, but will only deny standing in obvious cases, this approach in turn facilitating access to the review procedure; (2) assuming the case is granted permission an ultimate determination as to standing will be made at the full hearing.

Second, although it may be disguised by the result in the case—the Federation was ultimately denied standing—the case effected a liberalization of the law of standing, marked a shift away from a private law model of standing, and laid the foundations for emergence of a public interest model. Albeit there was marked disagreement between their Lordships as to how far standing should be broadened out, all agreed a more flexible, less technical approach should be taken than had characterized the field in the past. All accepted that public interest challenges were possible, albeit some judges—particularly Lord Diplock— expressed warmer attitudes towards such claims than others. All considered that standing was intimately tied to the merits of the case.

Third, Lord Diplock's views as to the relevance of the old law of standing provided the impetus for later courts to completely liberate the modern law of standing from the strictures of the past.

QUESTIONS

- Cane [1981] *PL* 322 argues that by tying the sufficient interest test so closely to the substantive merits of the claimant's case, *National Federation* marks the 'death of standing as an independent requirement of success in an application for judicial review'. Do you agree?
- In any case, would this be a positive or negative development?

14.7.4 Representative standing

Cane, *Administrative Law* (Oxford 2004) at 68, writes that 'the best test of the liberality of a regime of standing rules is how it deals with what might be called "representative standing"'. Elsewhere ([1995] *PL* 276 at 276) he distinguishes two forms of such standing which are presently of interest: the concept of *associational standing*, which 'most commonly involves an unincorporated group or a corporation claiming on behalf of (the interests of) identifiable individuals who are its members or whom it claims to represent'; and *public interest standing*, which 'involves an individual, corporation or group purporting to represent "the public interest" rather than the interests of any identified or identifiable individuals'.

The desirability of permitting *associational standing* may be traced to three particular policy concerns. First, by allowing one representative claimant to litigate the issue on behalf of a number of interested parties, a multiplicity of legal challenges to the same policy or like set of decisions is avoided. Second, in some circumstances, a representative claimant may be better placed or better funded to bring a claim than an affected individual. Third, embracing associational standing may allow matters to be litigated on behalf of those who may otherwise—by virtue of factors such as social exclusion or educational disadvantage—be unable or unlikely to have recourse to the courts. Although the question of standing was not directly confronted in *R v. Secretary of State for Social Services, ex parte Child Poverty Action Group* [1990] 2 QB 540, the desirability of permitting claims to be brought on behalf of disenfranchised groups can be seen from Woolf LJ's judgment, who pointed out (at 546) that 'the issues raised'—concerning the provision of financial support to families on low incomes—'are agreed to be important in the field of social welfare and not ones which individual claimants for supplementary benefit could be expected to raise'.

Because the concept of *public interest standing* attributes sufficient interest to litigants unconnected with the matter to which the claim relates, the factors which are said to justify it necessarily consist in different, and broader, arguments. Foremost among these is the idea that some issues are so important that they should not go unchecked by the courts simply because no one is peculiarly affected by the decision; this line of thinking has clearly found favour with the courts, as we shall see below. The flip-side of this approach is that when there are persons directly affected by a decision who would have standing, the court will be less inclined to confer public interest standing upon others unconnected with the matter: see, *eg R (Bulger) v. Secretary of State for the Home Department* [2001] EWHC 119 (Admin), [2001] 3 All ER 449 at [20].

It is now beyond doubt that English courts recognize both associational *and* public interest standing. For 30 years after the *National Federation* case neither the House of Lords nor the Supreme Court delivered a significant judgment on standing. It was left to the High Court and Court of Appeal to work out the implications of the *National Federation* case. In general lower courts gave significant weight to Lord Diplock's judgment, emphasizing that technical standing rules should not get in the way of the courts policing illegality, and over time, through a gradual process, standing was broadened out. Of course it would be wrong to think that legal development was linear. Invariably, and perhaps not surprisingly given that Lord Diplock's expansive statements represented a minority position in *National Federation*, the path was not straightforward. For example, in *R v. Secretary of State for the Environment, ex parte Rose Theatre Trust Co* [1990] 1 QB 504, the Court denied standing to the claimant company, formed for the purpose of preserving the remains of the Rose Theatre, which sought judicial review of the Secretary of State's refusal to list the remains under s 1 of the Ancient Monuments and Archaeological Areas Act 1979. Echoing the private law model, the principal concern underpinning the decision seems to have been that the claimant company was not itself directly affected by the Minister's decision, nor could it be said to represent anyone directly affected by the decision.

However, the general trend has been towards an embrace of representative standing. This trend culminated in two important, recent decisions of the Supreme Court (considered later) which have put beyond doubt that representative standing is a defining feature of modern judicial review.

Associational standing is firmly established in the case law. Courts regularly grant representative groups standing without probing in any detail the relationship between the claimant and the class they claim to represent (a matter to which we return in due course). Courts not uncommonly record core characteristics of the claimant in the opening paragraphs of their judgments, but beyond this typically no more is said of standing. So in *R (Children's Rights Alliance for England)* v. *Secretary of State for Justice* [2013] EWCA Civ 34, [2013] 1 WLR 3667, a judicial review claim relating to the interests of children in custody, the Court merely said of the claimant: 'The appellant is a registered charity whose purpose is to protect the rights of children' (at [5]). Nothing more was said of standing, and the Court went on to hear and determine the appeal on its merits.

The distance that the case law has travelled since *Rose Theatre* is demonstrated by *R (Friends of Hethel Ltd)* v. *South Norfolk District Council* [2009] EWHC 2856 (Admin), [2010] Env LR D4, [2010] EWCA Civ 894, [2011] 1 WLR 1216. The facts of that case are materially similar to those in *Rose Theatre*. The Friends of Hethel, a company formed to represent the interests of local residents, challenged via judicial review the grant of planning permission for erection of three wind turbines in Hethel, Norfolk, on the basis that the defendant had failed to consult English Heritage over the proposals, which impacted on the setting of heritage listed buildings. As in *Rose Theatre* it could not be said that the company was directly affected by the grant of planning permission. However, on this occasion, reflecting how far the law had developed on associational standing since and in stark contrast to the decision in *Rose Theatre*, the claim was determined on its merits, and neither the High Court, at first instance, nor the Court of Appeal, on appeal, even mentioned the issue of standing.

In terms of *public interest standing*, the Divisional Court's decision in *R* v. *Secretary of State for Foreign and Commonwealth Affairs, ex parte World Development Movement Ltd* [1995] 1 WLR 386 is emblematic of legal development since *National Federation* and long stood, up until the recent Supreme Court decisions which we consider shortly, as the most important decision on standing since *National Federation*. For the facts of the case see 7.2.3.

The Court considered whether the claimant ought to be afforded standing. Rose LJ set out a number of core facts about World Development Movement. WDM was a venerable, non-partisan pressure group, with an associated charity which received financial support from a range of entities including charities and the EU. WDM had 7,000 full voting members throughout the UK with a total supporter base of some 13,000, and 200 local groups. WDM tended to attract UK citizens concerned about the role of the UK government in relation to overseas development and poverty relief. It conducted research and analysis in relation to aid, had campaigned against aid cuts, and pressed government and banks, with which it was in regular contact, for better trade access for developing countries. It is involved in various ways with international organizations, including enjoying consultative status with UNESCO. Of direct relevance to the case at hand Rose LJ recorded (at 393) that:

Its supporters have a direct interest in ensuring that funds furnished by the United Kingdom are used for genuine purposes, and it seeks to ensure that disbursement of aid budgets is made where that aid is most needed. It seeks, by this application, to represent the interests of people in developing countries who might benefit from funds which otherwise might go elsewhere.

Rose LJ granted the claimants standing. Having considered the core background facts about WDM and the submissions of the parties, he reasoned (at 395–6):

The authorities referred to seem to me to indicate an increasingly liberal approach to standing on the part of the courts during the last 12 years. It is also clear from [*National Federation*] that standing should not be treated as a preliminary issue, but must be taken in the legal and factual context of the whole case ...

> Furthermore, the merits of the challenge are an important, if not dominant, factor when considering standing …
>
> Leaving merits aside for a moment, there seem to me to be a number of factors of significance in the present case: the importance of vindicating the rule of law, as Lord Diplock emphasised [1982] A.C. 617; the importance of the issue raised …; the likely absence of any other responsible challenger …; the nature of the breach of duty against which relief is sought (see *per* Lord Wilberforce, at p. 630D, in [*National Federation*]); and the prominent role of these applicants in giving advice, guidance and assistance with regard to aid … All, in my judgment, point, in the present case, to the conclusion that the applicants here do have a sufficient interest in the matter to which the application relates.

This decision unequivocally recognized that standing may be conferred upon a claimant because it is in the public interest that the matters which it seeks to raise are adjudicated upon by the court, and usefully sets out a series of factors to guide courts in deciding whether to grant public interest standing; we shall come back to these factors later. Since this decision interest groups with similar characteristics to WDM have established standing routinely.

The line of authorities of which *World Development Movement* is emblematic culminated in what are now the two most significant decisions on standing since *National Federation*. Both are decisions of the Supreme Court in appeals from Scotland. Despite emanating from Scotland the decisions entail authoritative guidance as to the law of standing in England. Indeed, the Court considered that the effect of its two decisions was to align Scottish law with English law.

The traditional approach to standing in review proceedings in Scotland was no different in principle from that in private law (though the test was capable of more flexible application on review): the petitioner (the equivalent term for claimant in Scotland) needed to demonstrate 'title and interest'. This test, which generally required possession of a right and direct prejudice to one's personal interests, was synonymous with the private law model of judicial review. In this regard, the test harked back to the general approach taken to standing in England prior to *National Federation*.

In *AXA General Insurance Ltd* v. *The Lord Advocate* [2011] UKSC 46, [2012] 1 AC 868, this approach received its *coup de grâce*. The case concerned challenges on human rights and common law grounds to legislation passed by the Scottish Parliament—the Damages (Asbestos-related Conditions) (Scotland) Act 2009—reversing court decisions which had held that pleural plaques caused by exposure to asbestos were not actionable loss for the purposes of the tort of negligence. The Court's approach to the substantive issues raised is discussed at 4.2 and 8.4.6. Here our focus is on the question of standing. The case was brought by insurance companies who wished to challenge the legislation, the effect of which would be to greatly expand their financial exposure by expanding the scope of negligence liability. The question of standing at common law arose as several individuals who had been diagnosed with pleural plaques, and who had launched or wished to launch negligence claims on the basis of the legislation, sought leave to enter the proceedings as parties so as to defend the legislation from legal attack. The rule governing leave to allow individuals to join proceedings was the same rule governing standing in general. It seems relatively clear that leave to be joined ought to have been granted on the then prevailing title and interest test, given these individuals were obviously directly and personally affected by the matters at stake in the litigation—and indeed the Supreme Court did grant standing. However, the Supreme Court took the opportunity to undertake a more general review of standing in

Scottish judicial review. Lords Hope and Reed gave the leading judgments, and the other Justices concurred unanimously in these judgments as far as they related to standing.

Lord Hope said (at [62]–[63]):

> I think that the time has come to recognise that the private law rule that title and interest has to be shown has no place in applications to the court's supervisory jurisdiction that lie in the field of public law. The word 'standing' provides a more appropriate indication of the approach that should be adopted. I agree with Lord Reed (see para 170, below) that it cannot be based on the concept of rights, but must be based on the concept of interests ... a person may have a sufficient interest to invoke the court's supervisory jurisdiction in the field of public law even although he cannot demonstrate that he has a title, based on some legal relation, to do so ... A personal interest need not be shown if the individual is acting in the public interest and can genuinely say that the issue directly affects the section of the public that he seeks to represent.

There could be no clearer endorsement of public interest standing than the last sentence of this extract from Lord Hope's judgment. Lord Reed echoed this view and Lord Hope's move to clearly delineate rights-based standing rules associated with private law from an interests-based approach appropriate to public law. Lord Reed reasoned (at [169]–[170]) that the title and interest test

> is appropriate to proceedings where the function of the courts is to protect legal rights: in that context, only those who maintain that their legal rights require protection have a good reason to use the procedures established in order for the courts to perform that function. The essential function of the courts is however the preservation of the rule of law, which extends beyond the protection of individuals' legal rights. As Lord Hope of Craighead DPSC, delivering the judgment of the court, said in *Eba v Advocate General for Scotland (Public Law Project intervening) (Note)* [2012] 1 AC 710, para 8:
>
>> 'the rule of law ... is the basis on which the entire system of judicial review rests. Wherever there is an excess or abuse of power or jurisdiction which has been conferred on a decision-maker, the Court of Session has the power to correct it: *West v Secretary of State for Scotland 1992 SC 385*, 395. This favours an unrestricted access to the process of judicial review where no other remedy is available.'
>
> There is thus a public interest involved in judicial review proceedings, whether or not private rights may also be affected. A public authority can violate the rule of law without infringing the rights of any individual: if, for example, the duty which it fails to perform is not owed to any specific person, or the powers which it exceeds do not trespass upon property or other private rights. A rights-based approach to standing is therefore incompatible with the performance of the courts' function of preserving the rule of law, so far as that function requires the court to go beyond the protection of private rights: in particular, so far as it requires the courts to exercise a supervisory jurisdiction. The exercise of that jurisdiction necessarily requires a different approach to standing.
>
> For the reasons I have explained, such an approach cannot be based upon the concept of rights, and must instead be based upon the concept of interests. A requirement that the applicant demonstrate an interest in the matter complained of will not however operate satisfactorily if it is applied in the same way in all contexts. In some contexts, it is appropriate to require an applicant for judicial review to demonstrate that he has a particular interest in the matter complained of: the type of interest which is relevant, and therefore required in order to have standing, will depend upon the particular context. In other situations, such as where the excess or misuse of

power affects the public generally, insistence upon a particular interest could prevent the matter being brought before the court, and that in turn might disable the court from performing its function to protect the rule of law. I say 'might', because the protection of the rule of law does not require that every allegation of unlawful conduct by a public authority must be examined by a court, any more than it requires that every allegation of criminal conduct must be prosecuted. Even in a context of that kind, there must be considerations which lead the court to treat the applicant as having an interest which is sufficient to justify his bringing the application before the court. What is to be regarded as sufficient interest to justify a particular applicant's bringing a particular application before the court, and thus as conferring standing, depends therefore upon the context, and in particular upon what will best serve the purposes of judicial review in that context.

We consider the wider implications of these statements in the next section. For present purposes these statements of principle are significant in that they resoundingly confirm that standing in public law ought not to be conflated with rights-based tests. Because the concerns of public law transcend individual rights and interests, and preservation of the public interest is a fundamental, overarching concern of judicial review, the courts must logically allow standing in at least some cases where the public interest in lawful exercise of public powers is at stake even though a claimant cannot show any of their rights have been infringed. Lord Reed observed that a range of considerations would bear on whether an individual or group would have standing in such a case. In the subsequent decision of *Walton* v. *Scottish Ministers* [2012] UKSC 44, [2013] PTSR 51 (noted Varuhas [2013] *CLJ* 243) the Supreme Court directly addressed the considerations that would guide public interest standing, many of which echo the considerations elaborated by Rose LJ in *World Development Movement*.

Mr Walton challenged the validity of certain schemes and orders made by the Scottish Ministers under the Roads (Scotland) Act 1984 enabling construction of a new road network near Aberdeen. Walton's argument, that Ministers failed to undertake public consultation on one element of the network as required by the Strategic Environment Assessment Directive (EU Directive 2001/42/EC), failed. However, the Court nonetheless considered Walton's standing to bring the claim.

Lord Reed, addressing the lower court's refusal to grant Walton permission, recalled Lord Hope's statements of principle in *AXA* as well as his own. He then offered more specific guidance as to when an individual or group should be afforded public interest standing (at [92]–[95]):

[A] distinction must be drawn between the mere busybody and the person affected by or having a reasonable concern in the matter to which the application relates … A busybody is someone who interferes in something with which he has no legitimate concern. The circumstances which justify the conclusion that a person is affected by the matter to which an application relates, or has a reasonable concern in it, or is on the other hand interfering in a matter with which he has no legitimate concern, will plainly differ from one case to another, depending upon the particular context and the grounds of the application. As Lord Hope DPSC made plain [in *AXA*] there are circumstances in which a personal interest need not be shown.

I also sought to emphasise that what constitutes sufficient interest has to be considered in the context of the issues raised …

In many contexts it will be necessary for a person to demonstrate some particular interest in order to demonstrate that he is not a mere busybody. Not every member of the public can complain of every potential breach of duty by a public body. But there may also be cases in which any individual, simply as a citizen, will have sufficient interest to bring a public authority's violation of the law to the attention of the court, without having to demonstrate any greater impact upon himself than upon other members of the public. The rule of law would not be maintained if, because everyone was equally affected by an unlawful act, no one was able to bring proceedings to challenge it.

Applying these principles, Lord Reed concluded that Walton had standing. Although Walton had suffered neither direct damage to his personal rights and interests nor greater harm than any other person living in the vicinity of the network, he nonetheless had standing *simply as a citizen*. The factors in favour of this conclusion included (at [88], [96]) that Walton had participated in public consultations on the road network; resided in the vicinity of the network, in an area which would incur greater traffic; was chairman of an organization formed to oppose the network; and was active in local environmental issues.

Lord Hope's judgment was critical of the lower court's focus on the fact Walton had not produced material demonstrating that the challenged schemes and orders substantially prejudiced his own interests or property; this focus was particularly inapt given the environmental context. Lord Hope said (at [152]–[154]):

I think, with respect, that this is to take too narrow a view of the situations in which it is permissible for an individual to challenge a scheme or order on grounds relating to the protection of the environment. An individual may be personally affected in his private interests by the environmental issues to which an application for planning permission may give rise. Noise and disturbance to the visual amenity of his property are some obvious examples. But some environmental issues that can properly be raised by an individual are not of that character. Take, for example, the risk that a route used by an osprey as it moves to and from a favourite fishing loch will be impeded by the proposed erection across it of a cluster of wind turbines. Does the fact that this proposal cannot reasonably be said to affect any individual's property rights or interests mean that it is not open to an individual to challenge the proposed development on this ground? That would seem to be contrary to the purpose of environmental law, which proceeds on the basis that the quality of the natural environment is of legitimate concern to everyone. The osprey has no means of taking that step on its own behalf, any more than any other wild creature. If its interests are to be protected someone has to be allowed to speak up on its behalf.

Of course, this must not be seen as an invitation to the busybody to question the validity of a scheme or order under the statute just because he objects to the scheme of the development. Individuals who wish to do this on environmental grounds will have to demonstrate that they have a genuine interest in the aspects of the environment that they seek to protect, and that they have sufficient knowledge of the subject to qualify them to act in the public interest in what is, in essence, a representative capacity. There is, after all, no shortage of well informed bodies that are equipped to raise issues of this kind, such as the Scottish Wildlife Trust and Scottish Natural Heritage in their capacity as the Scottish Ministers' statutory advisers on nature conservation. It would normally be to bodies of that kind that one would look if there were good grounds for objection. But it is well known they do not have the resources to object to every development that might have adverse consequences for the environment. So there has to be some room for individuals who are sufficiently concerned, and sufficiently well informed, to do this too. It will be for the court to judge in each case whether these requirements are satisfied.

For these reasons it would be wrong to reject Mr Walton's entitlement to bring his application on environmental grounds simply because he cannot show that his own interests would be substantially prejudiced. I agree with Lord Reed JSC's conclusion … that he has demonstrated a genuine concern about the legality of a development which is bound to have a significant impact on the environment, and that he is entitled to [standing].

Thus, the Supreme Court has given its blessing to an expansive view of public interest standing. But the decision whether to grant standing is a discretionary one, and where a claimant cannot show any personal prejudice the court will examine a range of considerations in deciding whether to allow a public interest challenge. Drawing together the guidance from *WDM*, *AXA*, and *Walton*, these include:

- Merits of the claim: does the claimant have a *prima facie* arguable case of administrative unlawfulness? Note (recalling the difference of opinion in *National Federation*) that *serious* illegality is not a formal precondition; however, one would expect that the more serious the illegality, the more likely standing will be granted.

- If the claimant is not accorded standing, is another responsible challenger—perhaps a person who is personally affected by the challenged measure—likely to bring a claim? If so, this may tell against standing.

- Is the matter raised one of significant public importance? If so, the challenge will more likely be allowed to proceed.

- Is the claimant motivated by a genuine concern for the public interest? If, alternatively, they are a busybody or driven by bad faith then they may be refused standing.

- Does the claimant have expertise in the relevant subject-matter? If so, the court will be more likely to grant standing.

- Context: is the relevant field one that raises questions that transcend individual interests and implicate wider public interest concerns? Environmental law is clearly an example of such a field, and public interest standing is more likely to be accorded in such contexts.

- Nature of the duty: this factor is closely related to the previous one. The court will be more willing to grant public interest standing if the claim relates to a duty on an authority which is not individualized, but is rather a general or public duty. For example, in *Walton* the duty was one of public consultation, which cannot be conceptualized as a duty owed to anyone in particular.

None of these factors shall be determinative. They must be weighed in each case. However, the practical reality is that if the claimant can show that they have an arguable claim and the court is convinced they are not a busybody or acting out of ill motive, standing will be granted as a matter of course.

Let us consider two factors a little more closely, each of which is linked to the idea of the 'responsible' challenger, which pervades the case law.

First, the case law emphasizes that the claimant should have a genuine concern for the public interest and specifically the public interests in play in the particular case, such as a concern for preservation of the environment in an environmental judicial review case. Generally the claimant will demonstrate a genuine concern through its prior record of involvement in public interest activities, as Mr Walton did in *Walton*. But, barring vexatious litigants, why should it matter what the claimant's subjective motivations are? If a claimant raises a matter of public importance and has an arguable claim of administrative unlawfulness, why should the court resile from investigating the alleged illegality because the claimant cannot demonstrate a prior concern for the matters raised? Indeed, a person who has no particular track record of political campaigning and is in fact disinterested in political issues may be a preferable challenger to an interest group which, while it may have a long track record of involvement in matters of public concern, is more likely to be partisan and driven by political ends. On the other hand, one may argue that if a claimant wishes to represent the public they should have a demonstrable concern for the public interest, and also be able to show that they speak for a section of the public; for example, interest groups often highlight their wide membership in applications for review. But this is perhaps to take 'representative' standing too literally, and allow a phrase to impede pursuit of the common good. If the underlying concern of public interest standing is to ensure protection of the common good, then it would be folly to prevent litigation that would plainly serve the public interest by exposing and remedying administrative unlawfulness.

Second, the courts have held that expertise is a factor. This factor featured particularly prominently in Lord Hope's judgment in *Walton*: his Lordship indicated that he would ordinarily expect interest groups to bring public interest challenges rather than citizens, and that if citizens were to be accorded standing they would be expected to be sufficiently informed about the relevant issues. In contrast, Lord Reed seemed more open to individuals being accorded standing simply as citizens, irrespective of expertise. On one view Lord Hope's emphasis on expertise is inapt. Most obviously it may be criticized as elitist, making review the preserve of the well educated. This factor may also, in common with the 'genuineness' factor, impede otherwise legitimate public interest challenges. Set against these arguments is Otton J's rationale in *R v. HM Inspectorate of Pollution, ex parte Greenpeace (No 2)* [1994] 4 All ER 329 at 350 for taking into account Greenpeace's expertise in deciding upon standing: compared to Greenpeace a challenge brought by an ordinary citizen would be 'less well-informed' and 'would stretch unnecessarily the court's resources and ... not afford the court the assistance it requires in order to do justice between the parties'. This is not a particularly convincing argument. It is not the claimant who will put forward its case but rather its barristers. There is a reason for this: the principal type of expertise required in legal proceedings is legal expertise. As such, there is no reason to think that where the claimant is an interest group court resources will be saved. In any case, if the matters raised called for the hearing of expert testimony it would not be a party to the litigation who would provide that testimony but rather a third party expert, given experts are expected to be non-partisan.

Overall the case for courts taking into account genuineness and expertise in deciding upon standing is far from clear-cut. But perhaps the rationale is more prosaic than we have so far assumed. For example, perhaps the courts expect that those with expertise, a particular status as a responsible organization, and a demonstrated concern for the public interest are more likely to raise arguable and worthwhile claims than the ordinary person off the street. One might respond that rather than using such imperfect proxies for whether a claimant is likely to have an arguable case, the court should simply inquire into whether the claimant's case is meritorious. However, it may be far more expedient for a court to dismiss claims at the permission stage on the basis of a lack of expertise or genuineness without having to engage with the merits of the case, which may lead to full consideration of standing being postponed until a full hearing. In this light perhaps the criteria serve a highly practical purpose as a control device, aimed at addressing the types of policy concerns raised by wide standing rules discussed at 14.7.1.

QUESTION

- If a matter is sufficiently important to be capable of litigation on public interest grounds by a claimant with no private interest, should the subjective motivation or expertise of the claimant who actually comes forward be relevant?

Let us move from factors which courts will consider in determining *public interest standing* to factors which guide whether courts accord a claimant *associational standing*. It might be thought that an important limiting factor would be the relationship between the claimant and the persons or constituency on behalf of which it acts. Cane [1995] *PL* 276 at 278 develops this point:

> A litigant who claims to represent the interests of identifiable individuals cannot do so convincingly unless there is a reasonably effective mechanism by which the representative can ascertain what the represented believe their interests to be. In order to be a legitimate representative, the claimant must be able to convince the court that the views put forward by it are a fair reflection of the views of the represented. In other words, the represented must have some degree of control over or some 'democratic stake' (as I will call it) in the conduct of the representative. Without some such nexus between the represented and the representative, the claimant may simply be expressing a 'well-informed point of view' [*Health Research Group* v. *Kennedy* (1979) 82 FRD 21]. One exception to this general principle must be recognised, however. A claimant who is the beneficiary of a statutory grant of standing to represent the interests of specific individuals may legitimately do so without consulting the represented, unless the statute requires consultation. A statutory grant of representative status [for instance, to the Equal Opportunities Commission, as recognized in *R* v. *Secretary of State for Employment, ex parte Equal Opportunities Commission* [1995] 1 AC 1; see now Equality Act 2006, s 30(1), concerning the Commission for Equality and Human Rights, which replaces the Equal Opportunities Commission] provides the legitimacy which self-appointed representatives may lack.

A strong argument in favour of recognizing the need for a democratic nexus is outlined by Miles [2000] *CLJ* 133 at 148–50, who observes that, on one view, the autonomy of victims of maladministration requires that they should be able to choose whether the matter is litigated. However, this must be set against the competing view that there is a general interest in good administration which may be threatened if representative claimants are barred from litigating in the place of victims unwilling to do so.

In fact as a matter of practice English courts tend not to scrutinize in any great detail the relationship between representative claimants and those for whom they supposedly speak. For instance, in *R* v. *Secretary of State for Social Services, ex parte Child Poverty Action Group* [1990] 2 QB 540, the claimant sought to speak on behalf of families on low incomes who were affected by the administrative arrangements being challenged. Although he was not required to decide standing, Woolf LJ (at 547) largely took for granted that the claimant could represent benefit claimants, without considering whether any sort of relationship existed between the CPAG and its constituency. One reason why this relaxed approach has been sustained over time—see further the discussion of *Friends of Hethel* and *Children's Rights Alliance for England* (earlier in this section)—is the expansion of public interest standing. Because public interest standing is so generous, even if the claimant was unable to demonstrate standing by association, the likelihood is that they could nonetheless be accorded public interest standing if they could show an arguable case of administrative illegality. As such, locating a 'democratic nexus' takes on less significance.

QUESTION

- Is Cane right to argue that a 'democratic nexus' must exist if standing on an associational basis is to be acknowledged?

14.7.5 Conclusions on the law of standing: the triumph of the public interest model

Since the landmark *National Federation* case English courts have embraced representative standing, including both associational and public interest standing; these developments being capped off by the Supreme Court decisions in *AXA* and *Walton*, which confirm representative standing as a defining, iconic feature of modern judicial review.

Furthermore, a strikingly liberal approach has been taken to representative standing. The practical reality of the modern law of standing is that for all of the formal guidance laid down by the courts, they rarely bat an eyelid when interest groups or publically spirited individuals challenge administrative action which does not affect them personally—as long as the claimant has an arguable case of administrative unlawfulness, is not obviously driven by a desire to cause mischief, and there is no other potential challenger directly affected by the challenged decision who would likely bring a claim. As Rawlings observes, '[s]tanding is typically the dog that does not bark' ((2008) 61 *CLP* 95, 101 fn 30). Of course every now and again a court does deny a claimant standing. Such decisions stand out because they are so uncommon. And when appealed they are more often than not overturned: *eg R (The Project Management Institute)* v. *Minister for the Cabinet Office* [2014] EWHC 2438 (Admin), [2016] EWCA Civ 21, [2016] 1 WLR 1737.

At the outset of our discussion of standing we observed that different approaches to standing reflect different models of judicial review and public law adjudication. In this respect we contrasted a rights-based or private law model with a public interest model. It is now clear that while rights-based approaches to standing prevailed in England before *National Federation* (to the extent one predominant approach could be identified) and in Scotland before *AXA*, a public interest model of standing is now dominant. In turn the embrace of the public interest approach tells us something deeper about how judges conceptualize the functions of judicial review more generally.

Perhaps most telling in this regard is Lord Reed's judgment in *AXA* in which he explicitly differentiated rights-based models that prevail in private law fields such as tort or contract with the approach that should be taken in judicial review. He observed (at [163]) an 'essential difference between the nature and purpose of the court's supervisory jurisdiction, on the one hand, and its jurisdiction to adjudicate on disputed questions of right, on the other'. In private law cases individuals bring claims so as to protect their rights, and those rights form the basis of the claim; as such it is logical that standing should depend on whether the individual has suffered a breach of their rights. Given that rights are the property of their holders it is difficult to see how it would be permissible for a third party to be accorded standing to bring a claim in respect of another's legal entitlement, at least without the right-holder's permission; initiation of proceedings by unaffected parties in respect of another's rights would be an illegitimate interference with the right-holder's autonomy. In contrast, judicial review claims, as Lord Reed said (at [159]), are 'not brought to vindicate a right vested in the applicant, but to request the court to supervise the actings of a public authority so as to ensure that it exercises its functions in accordance with the law'. For Lord Reed the 'essential function' of review is to preserve the rule of law, and this necessarily 'extends beyond the protection of individuals' legal rights' (at [169]). In *Walton*, he added (at [90]) that adoption of rights-based standing rules 'presuppose[s] that the only function of the court's supervisory jurisdiction [is] to redress individual grievances, and ignore[s] its constitutional function of maintaining the rule of law'. There is a wider public interest at play in review proceedings—that of ensuring public powers are exercised in accordance with the law and for the public ends for which they are conferred by Parliament—which transcends the special interests of any one individual. Given this primary function of review 'a different approach to standing' is required (*AXA* at [169]). Thus, when a claimant brings a claim in judicial review proceedings, at least in cases of representative standing, they bring a claim on behalf of the public as a whole or a section of it, rather than on their own behalf as a victim who has suffered a violation of their personal rights.

We do note, however, that some vestiges of a rights-based model remain. For example, the principle that public interest standing is less likely to be accorded where another responsible challenger, whose rights are directly affected by the relevant administrative action, is likely to bring a claim preserves right-holder autonomy. However, it only does so to an extent. First, if a right-holder decides not to pursue a claim, this does not preclude a public interest challenger from pursuing the claim. Second, even if there is another potential challenger, this does not necessarily preclude the claimant being accorded public interest standing; the presence of another possible challenger is only one factor in deciding upon standing. For example, if the claimant demonstrates an exceptionally strong *prima facie* case of administrative unlawfulness and has particular expertise in and a genuine concern for the issues raised by the claim they may well be granted standing. In this way the public interest in ensuring lawful exercise of public power may trump concerns over the autonomy of right-holders.

We also see in the case law on standing an appeal to wider policy concerns, of the type discussed at the outset. Some of these reinforce wide standing rules. For example, Lords Hope and Reed argued in *AXA* that broad standing rules ensure the courts hear sufficient review challenges so that they can continue to develop judicial review principles to meet contemporary needs: as Lord Hope put it (at [58]), legal 'development in the public interest risks being inhibited by a strict adherence to the private law requirement that title and interest must be shown before proceedings for judicial review may be brought'. But countervailing policy arguments are also evident. While recognizing that the public interest demands that standing be accorded in review challenges outside of cases where an individual can demonstrate individual prejudice, Lord Reed observed (at [170]) that 'the protection of the rule of law does not require that every allegation of unlawful conduct by a public authority must be examined by a court ... there must be considerations which lead the court to treat the applicant as having an interest which is sufficient to justify his bringing the application before the court'. Thus, there are limits on public interest standing—and these limits operate in the light of policy concerns such as the court being flooded with claims, or authorities being harassed with vexatious review challenges. However, overall, the pull of the public interest model is such that the hurdles which a public interest claimant must leap to be granted access to review are relatively low.

QUESTIONS

- Do you think English law has adopted the correct approach to standing?
- What might be some objections to the prevailing approach?

Let us conclude with two final observations.

First, adoption of public interest standing rules tells us something of the conceptual nature of the administrative law norms of rationality, fairness, and legality. It tends to suggest that these norms are not in the nature of individual rights—*ie* individual rights to fair, rational, or lawful decisions—but rather free-standing standards or duties owed to the public at large, for the benefit of the public. If these norms were in the nature of personal rights akin to rights in private law, then public interest standing would be out of place: it would be for the person directly affected by a decision to claim that their personal right to rational or legal decision-making was breached. On the other hand, if these duties are public duties, it makes sense that public interest standing ought to be adopted, as we each, as members of the public, have an equal and legitimate stake in seeing that these public duties are complied with. Thus, in the *National Federation* case, Lord Scarman spoke of a 'legal duty owed to the general body of taxpayers' *as a collectivity*, and of breach of this duty as a 'public wrong' (at 648, 651–3). Similarly, in *Bourgoin SA v. Ministry of Agriculture, Fisheries and Food* [1986] QB 716 at 761, 763, 767, Oliver LJ considered 'a mere "right" to have the provisions of the law observed, shared as it is by every member of the public whether or not he is likely to suffer by breach is, it seems to me, the antithesis of an "individual" right requiring protection'. In *R v. Somerset County Council, ex parte Dixon* [1998] Env LR 111 at 121, Sedley J explicitly drew together the idea that judicial review concerns public wrongs and a public interest approach to standing:

> Public law is not at base about rights, even though abuses of power may and often do invade private rights; it is about wrongs—that is to say misuses of public power; and the courts have always been alive to the fact that a person or organisation with no particular stake in the issue or outcome may, without in any sense being a mere meddler, wish and be well placed to call the attention of the court to an apparent misuse of public power. If an arguable case of such misuse can be made out on an application for leave, the court's only concern is to ensure that it is not being done for an ill motive. It is if, on a substantive hearing, the abuse of power is made out that everything relevant to the applicant's standing will be weighed up, whether with regard to the grant or simply to the form of relief.

Lord Reed and Lord Hope's judgments in *AXA* are consistent with this view.

Second, rules of standing reflect a particular view about the nature of public law adjudication. According to the *dispositive justice* model, the role of the courts is to resolve disputes between the parties: such a view fits with a narrow doctrine of standing which permits only the victim of maladministration to raise the matter in court. Miles [2000] *CLJ* 133 at 153–5 distinguishes the *expository justice* model, and the wider approach to standing it commends, in the following terms:

> Under this model ... there is no automatic reason to insist that individual victims alone be permitted to invoke the jurisdiction of the court. If the function of the court is not simply to determine disputes brought by victims but generally to expound the law, then there is no *necessary* constitutional reason (certainly not one derived from a view about the limits of the judicial function) to insist on victim standing ... [On this view,] in so far as there is a danger that insistence on victim standing may *impede* sound exposition of the law ... then standing rules *should* be devised in such a way as to permit a broader range of applicants to move the court. It may be that the only acceptable standing rule in this model would be no standing rule at all, or at least a very flexible one, permitting any case to proceed if it raised a serious point which seemed to have substantive merit, despite the lack of close connection between applicant and issue.

As well as impacting upon how the law of standing is constructed, the choice between dispositive and expository models also fundamentally informs the courts' attitude to reviewing moot questions. The higher courts' willingness to countenance judicial review in such circumstances (see 14.5.4), coupled with the prevailing approach to standing, suggests public law adjudication in England is significantly influenced by the expository model.

14.7.6 Intervention

Situations inevitably arise in which someone (or more often a group or organization) who is not a party wishes to have input into judicial review proceedings. Provision is made for this in the Civil Procedure Rules.

Civil Procedure Rules Part 54

7. The claim form must be served on—

   (a) the defendant; and
   (b) unless the court otherwise directs, any person the claimant considers to be an interested party,

   within 7 days after the date of issue.

17. (1) Any person may apply for permission—

   (a) to file evidence; or
   (b) make representations at the hearing of the judicial review.

   (2) An application under paragraph (1) should be made promptly.

The facts that such provision is made and that courts are increasingly willing to permit intervention by third parties are noteworthy against the background of the foregoing discussion. Just as the courts' relatively liberal approach to standing is illuminative of how the purpose of judicial review is conceived, so too is the modern attitude to intervention. Harlow (2002) 65 *MLR* 1 at 3 characterizes these developments as a 'tiny'—but significant— 'procedural revolution'. The effect, she says (at 7–8), is

a shift away from the traditional bipolar and adversarial lawsuit familiar to common lawyers, to something more fluid, less formal and possibly less individualistic in character. By making access easier, judges are subtly changing the rules of the game. A novel public interest action is in the making, with the help of which campaigning groups are gaining entry to the legal process.

Whether this is a good thing depends on one's perspective. Fordham [2007] *PL* 410 at 412 argues that appropriate third-party intervention is to be welcomed, lamenting the fact that, greater liberality in this area notwithstanding, there remains 'a representation-deficit problem': too often, he says, courts find themselves 'being asked to decide important issues on the basis of what is effectively one-sided argument'. He favours a more systematic approach to ensure that courts make such decisions, when appropriate, with the benefit of a range of views, and makes practical suggestions (such as better information, to ensure that potential intervenors know litigation is in the offing) to that end.

Harlow, *op cit* at 2, adopts a different perspective. She contends that too liberal an approach—both to standing and intervention—risks conflating, and confusing the roles of, the legal and political processes. She likens the latter to a 'freeway, to which all citizens of a modern democracy should have access'. But the former, she says, 'is valued for different qualities':

> Its objective being primarily the protection of legal interests, it is appropriate for access to be limited to those who can show such an interest. This is, of course, a stereotype. I am suggesting, however, that, if we move too far away from the stereotype, we may end by stultifying it. If we allow the campaigning style of politics to invade the legal process, we may end by undermining the very qualities of certainty, finality and especially independence for which the legal process is esteemed, thereby undercutting its legitimacy.

Harlow concludes that the courts should row back from the liberality that constitutes modern orthodoxy in this area, and (*op cit* at 18) defends her position thus:

> If this does not sound particularly 'democratic', there is no particular reason why it should. Courts are one of the pillars of a modern democracy, just as representative government is another. The contribution made by each to the democratic process does not have to be identical. Diversity is a key value in our society and a crucial attribute of the informal separation of powers on which our constitution so precariously balances. Politics cannot do everything. Neither can law. Their distinctiveness needs to be recognised.

The increasing prevalence of interventions in review proceedings has raised one further, more prosaic concern, which has now been addressed through legislative reform. That is, interventions may render judicial review proceedings more costly for the parties to the dispute. First, parties may be ordered to pay the intervener's costs or part thereof. Second, additional legal costs may be incurred by the claimant and defendant as a result of issues raised or matters pursued by the intervention, for example because this draws out the length of proceedings.

Given these concerns the government sponsored and Parliament recently passed reforms aimed at ensuring that parties should generally not have to bear extra costs because an intervener chooses to become involved in the litigation. Section 87(3) of the Criminal Justice and Courts Act 2015 sets out a general rule that neither the High Court nor Court of Appeal may order a party to the proceeding to pay the intervener's costs in connection with the proceedings, unless—pursuant to s 87(4)—exceptional circumstances warrant such an order. Section 87(5) provides that the High Court or Court of Appeal, upon an application from a party to the proceedings, *must*, if certain conditions are met, order the intervener to pay any costs specified in the application 'that the court considers have been incurred by the relevant party as a result of the intervener's involvement in [the relevant stage] of the proceedings'. The relevant conditions, which if met will mandate that the court issue such an order, are specified in s 87(6):

> (a) the intervener has acted, in substance, as the sole or principal applicant, defendant, appellant or respondent;
> (b) the intervener's evidence and representations, taken as a whole, have not been of significant assistance to the court;
> (c) a significant part of the intervener's evidence and representations relates to matters that it is not necessary for the court to consider in order to resolve the issues that are the subject of the stage in the proceedings;
> (d) the intervener has behaved unreasonably.

Section 87(7) provides that s 87(5) will not require the court to make an order where a condition in s 87(6) is met if the court 'considers that there are exceptional circumstances that make it inappropriate to do so'. These provisions mark a break from the ordinary position according to which it is only in an 'exceptional' case that a court will make a costs order against a person not party to the claim, costs orders in general being confined to shifting costs between the parties: *Arken* v. *Borchard Lines Ltd* [2005] EWCA 655, [2005] 1 WLR 3055.

QUESTION

- A principal concern raised by those who responded to the government consultation on these reforms was that the reforms 'would prevent interveners from being involved in cases, the point being made that this could be to the detriment of the final outcome of the case as interveners bring expertise from which the court and parties will benefit' (*Judicial Review—Proposals for Further Reform: The Government Response*, Cm 8811 (2014) at [61]). Do you agree with these criticisms or do you consider the reforms are justified?

14.7.7 Standing in human rights cases

Rather different standing rules apply to claims under the Human Rights Act 1998 compared to the position at common law. Pursuant to s 7(1) of the HRA a claimant may only bring a claim alleging a public authority has acted in a way made unlawful by s 6(1)—that is, in contravention of enumerated Convention rights—if they are or would be 'a victim of the unlawful act'. Section 7(7) elaborates on the meaning of 'victim':

> For the purposes of this section, a person is a victim of an unlawful act only if he would be a victim for the purposes of Article 34 of the Convention if proceedings were brought in the European Court of Human Rights in respect of that act.

Thus, it is to Article 34 of the ECHR, and more particularly the jurisprudence under it, that we must look to understand the 'victim' criterion under the HRA. Article 34 provides:

> The Court may receive applications from any person, non-governmental organisation or group of individuals claiming to be the victim of a violation by one of the High Contracting Parties of the rights set forth in the Convention or the protocols thereto. The High Contracting Parties undertake not to hinder in any way the effective exercise of this right.

The notion of a 'victim' in itself suggests an approach to standing far narrower than that at common law. It implies a rights-based model of standing within which only those whose individual rights and interests have been directly affected by administrative action may bring a claim. And indeed this is the general approach that the Strasbourg court, and domestic courts under the HRA, have taken. An illustrative example is *R (Children's Rights Alliance for England)* v. *Secretary of State for Justice* [2013] EWCA Civ 34, [2013] 1 WLR 3667. The background to the case was that there was widespread unlawful use of bodily restraint techniques upon children and young persons detained in Secure Training Centres (STCs), which house children sentenced to custody or on remand. The claimant was a charity whose purpose was to protect children's rights. It sought to establish that the Secretary of State was legally obliged to take steps, specifically to provide information, to enable those who were subject to unlawful physical restraints to discover that they were wronged, so that they could then pursue claims against those who had wronged them. The claimant was accorded standing to bring claims on common law grounds, but was denied standing to bring claims under the HRA. The Court of Appeal did not disturb the conclusion of the lower court that '[i]f the Claimant's case had rested solely on asserting Convention rights of former detainees of the four STCs, I would have been obliged not even to consider the merits of the case before me' (at [48]). It was fatal to the claimant's standing under the HRA that its own rights were not directly affected by the conduct of STC officers; even the fact that the charity existed to represent the interests of those whose rights were directly affected by the STCs' conduct was insufficient to ground standing for an HRA claim. Similarly, in *Application for Judicial Review by the Northern Ireland Commissioner for Children and Young People* [2007] NIQB 115, the claimant Commissioner, a statutory officeholder whose work is to advance the interests of children, was denied standing to bring claims of breaches of children's human rights: 'There is no specific case before me where a child is a victim and I cannot permit a complaint against this law *in abstracto* simply because the Commissioner feels, however sincerely, it contravenes the Convention unless *she* is a victim' (at [15]).

It may be tempting to criticize the narrow standing requirement on the basis that it is inconsistent with the approach at common law and thus creates incoherence across the public law system as a whole, and may prevent claims by public interest groups or publically spirited individuals where the public interest would be served by claims being brought. However, while such criticisms are intuitively appealing they ignore important differences between common law review and human rights law. In particular, the law under the HRA is an individualistic, rights-based field of law, whereas—as we saw earlier—obligations at common law are often in the nature of public duties designed to benefit the public at large. A significant aspect of being the holder of a right is that one has the exclusive liberty to make significant decisions in relation to those rights, including whether to pursue a claim and secure a remedy where they are breached.

While the narrow standing rule is consistent with the rights-based nature of the field the jurisprudence has recognized that standing rules may need to be liberalized where maintenance of a narrow approach would undermine the central goal of the Convention, that is the effective protection of rights.

Thus, an *indirect victim* of a rights violation may, in confined circumstances, be accorded standing. In *Rabone* v. *Pennine Care NHS Foundation Trust* [2012] UKSC 2, [2012] 2 AC 72 (noted Varuhas [2012] *CLJ* 263), the Supreme Court held that the defendant had breached its positive duty under Article 2 to protect an individual from a known, real, and immediate risk to their life when it granted Melanie Rabone, who was in the defendant's care and had a history of attempting suicide, home leave, whereupon she committed suicide. In this tragic scenario it is the deceased who is the *primary victim*, as it was her rights that were directly violated. The question in *Rabone* was whether Melanie's parents could bring a claim as *indirect victims* of the Article 2 violation. The Court unanimously held that they could. Lord Dyson, in the lead judgment, said (at [46]):

> The ECtHR has repeatedly stated that family members of the deceased can bring claims in their own right both in relation to the investigative obligation and the substantive obligations [under Article 2]. Examples of such cases are *Yasa v Turkey* (1999) 28 EHRR 408, para 64; *Edwards v United Kingdom* [(2002) 35 EHRR 19] at para 106; *Renolde v France* (2009) 48 EHRR 42, para 69; and *Kats v Ukraine* (2010) 51 EHRR 44, para 94.

The general rationale given by the ECtHR for allowing indirect victims to sue in cases of deprivation of life rests on the 'nature of the violation alleged and considerations of the effective implementation of one of the most fundamental provisions in the Convention system' (*Nassau Verzekering Maatschappij NV* v. *Netherlands* Application 57602/09, [2011] ECHR 1798 at [19]). As Varuhas explains: 'Life would not be protected effectively if a victim were killed in consequence of breach of the duty to protect, but no legal finding to that effect could ever be secured because the victim were not alive to sue' (*Damages and Human Rights* (Oxford 2016) at 103–4). But it does not follow that any person can sue. The idea of 'indirect victim' still incorporates the notion of 'victim', which suggests that to qualify as an indirect victim an individual must be personally affected by the death in some way. It is therefore no surprise that indirect victim status has most often been confined to the deceased's close family members. Thus, Lady Hale in *Rabone* (at [92]) seemed to suggest that the rationale for recognizing family members as victims in such situations is based in the unique agony a family member would naturally feel at the loss of a close relation, especially where the death was preventable.

One criticism sometimes levelled at the jurisprudence on indirect victims is that it offers no real guidance as to the extent of the class of persons who may count as indirect victims. For example, it is unclear whether a very close friend of the deceased, who would naturally be devastated by their friend's death, could sue despite not being a family member. Thus, in *Savage* v. *South Essex Partnership NHS Foundation Trust* [2008] UKHL 74, [2009] AC 681 at [5], Lord Scott referred, disapprovingly, to 'an undefined, and perhaps undefinable, class composed of persons close to the deceased who have suffered distress and anguish on account of the death'. But equally it may be very difficult to know in advance who might be accorded standing at common law under the very broad standing rules that apply, yet this has not prevented a wholesale embrace of those standing rules by the higher judiciary. Furthermore, no doubt a pattern will emerge over time which provides guidance. The courts will in all likelihood be guided by the parameters discussed in the previous paragraph. For example, one might argue that a distant relation of the deceased—as opposed to a close relation—may nonetheless be accorded standing if no one else is likely to bring proceedings, on the basis that to deny standing would be to prevent judicial examination of an alleged breach of the right to life.

The ECtHR has also recognized that *potential victims* may be accorded standing, specifically in circumstances where a claimant challenges a general measure which may potentially be applied to infringe the rights of a class of persons to which the claimant belongs. In common with the cases on indirect victims, the rationale for recognizing a wider concept of standing in such situations is arguably to ensure effective protection of rights: where there is a significant risk of a general measure being applied so as to violate rights it is better to prevent those violations *ex ante* than to remedy them, necessarily imperfectly, *ex post*. In *AXA General Insurance Ltd* v. *The Lord Advocate* [2011] UKSC 46, [2012] 1 AC 868, the Supreme Court gave effect to this approach in domestic law. The facts were discussed earlier in this chapter (at 14.7.4) and will not be repeated here. Lord Reed stated the relevant principle (at [111]) (see also [24]–[28] *per* Lord Hope, [86]–[90] *per* Lord Mance):

> It is necessary to bear in mind in the first place that the Convention is concerned with the reality of a situation rather than its formal appearance, so as to ensure that it guarantees rights that are practical and effective. The interpretation of the concept of a 'victim' is correspondingly broad: as the Strasbourg court has observed, an excessively formalistic interpretation of that concept would make protection of the rights guaranteed by the Convention ineffectual and illusory (*Lizarraga v*

Spain (2004) 45 EHRR 1039, para 38). It is also well established that a person can claim to be a victim of a violation of the Convention in the absence of an individual measure of implementation: as the Strasbourg court stated in *Burden v United Kingdom* (2008) 47 EHRR 857, para 34, it is open to a person to contend that a law violates his rights, in the absence of an individual measure of implementation, if he is a member of a class of people who risk being directly affected by it. Individuals have been held to be victims by virtue of legal situations which, for example, permitted corporal punishment in schools (*Campbell and Cosans v United Kingdom* (1980) 3 EHRR 531, para 116), conferred on children born out of wedlock inheritance rights inferior to those enjoyed by children born in wedlock (*Marckx v Belgium* (1979) 2 EHRR 330, para 27), restricted the provision of information concerning abortion clinics (*Open Door Counselling and Dublin Well Woman v Ireland* (1992) 15 EHRR 244, para 44), or prevented sisters who lived together from enjoying the same exemption from inheritance tax as married or same-sex couples (*Burden v United Kingdom*), even in the absence of the practical application to those individuals of the laws in question. On the other hand, where a person is not at risk of a violation of a Convention right unless and until a particular decision is taken, for example as to deportation, the person cannot claim to be a victim unless and until such a decision is in fact made (*Vijayanathan and Pusparajah v France* (Application Nos 17550/90 and 17825/91) (unreported) 27 August 1992, para 46).

On the facts of *AXA* the members of the Court considered it clear that the operation of the challenged law would risk interference with insurers' proprietary interests under Article 1 of Protocol 1 by imposing on them financial burdens by significantly broadening the scope of the law of negligence (see facts at 14.7.4). As such, insurance companies were accorded standing to challenge the law on HRA grounds. The objection was raised that it was employers who were responsible for exposing their employees to asbestos and would be the relevant defendants who would pay damages to claimants under the expanded law of negligence. As such, so the argument went, insurers could not be considered potential victims as they were only affected by the legislation *indirectly* rather than *directly*. The argument was rejected. Lord Reed reasoned that one had to look beyond the formal legal position to the practical reality that damages would be funded out of the employers' insurance, so that it was insurers rather than employers who would bear the economic brunt of expanded liability under the legislation (at [112]). Lord Hope considered the key question was 'whether the consequences for the [insurers] of the 2009 Act are too remote or tenuous for them to be directly affected by it' (at [27]). In order to determine whether the potential effect of the challenged measure on the claimant was too remote one had to examine the purpose of the challenged measure. The purpose was to make pleural plaques actionable, and this created a risk, as a matter of practice, that insurance companies would bear the burden of liability, even though employers would be the designated defendants and formally pay damages. In addition, '[t]here is ample material in the record of the proceedings before the Scottish Parliament to show that it was the insurance industry that was expected, and intended, to bear the burden of meeting' the claims (at [27]). As such, the risk could not be dismissed as hypothetical or remote.

Thus, there has been some recognition that the victim requirement should be broadened in confined circumstances where to maintain a strict approach would undermine the purpose of human rights law, to ensure practical and effective protection of rights.

In practice there may be other ways to 'get around' the strictures of the victim requirement. For example, as we saw in ch 8 many of the rights protected by the HRA are increasingly being recognized at common law. As such, a public interest group which wishes to launch proceedings so as to ensure protection of human rights may be able to do so at common law, given the broader standing rules that apply in that context. Indeed, longstanding common law grounds find analogues in human rights law. For example, procedural fairness and Article 6 share much in common. Importantly, it may often be possible to frame one's claim as a simple common law claim of *ultra vires*, so that one may take advantage of broad standing rules, while simultaneously relying on norms under the HRA. The victim requirement will apply—pursuant to HRA, s 7(1)—if one seeks to impugn an individual exercise of power on the basis that that exercise of power was incompatible with one's Convention rights, and thereby unlawful pursuant to s 6(1) of the Act. However, the victim requirement will not apply if one relies on the *common law ground* of illegality and argues that the exercise of power was *ultra vires* the parent Act under which it was exercised. While the claim would be based in common law grounds, one could simultaneously rely on Convention rights by arguing that the relevant administrative act was *ultra vires* the parent Act *on the basis of a rights-consistent interpretation of the parent Act*; put another way, Convention rights could be relied upon as implied statutory restrictions upon the discretionary power. In this regard, s 3(1) of the HRA provides: 'So far as it is possible to do so, primary legislation and subordinate legislation must be read and given effect in a way which is compatible with the Convention rights.' Thus, instead of arguing that an exercise of power was unlawful as directly infringing one's rights, one could instead argue it was *ultra vires* the empowering statute on the basis of a rights-consistent interpretation of that statute. In this way a claimant may rely on HRA norms without needing to fulfil the victim requirement.

Finally, Parliament may enact statutory exceptions to the victim requirement. Section 30(3) of the Equality Act 2006 provides that, without any need to establish victim status, the Equality and Human Rights Commission (EHRC) may in certain circumstances rely on Convention rights in legal proceedings, including as an intervener. Interventions by the EHRC have, for example, allowed HRA matters to be raised in proceedings brought by claimants, such as pressure groups, who themselves lack standing to raise HRA challenges: *eg Children's Rights Alliance for England* at [6], [48].

14.8 The 'no difference' principle

Recent amendments to the Senior Courts Act 1981 (pursuant to s 84 of the Criminal Justice and Courts Act 2015) have introduced a new set of potentially far-reaching restrictions on judicial review. These new reforms may be relied upon to limit access to judicial review proceedings and/or deny remedies in cases where alleged or proven illegalities are considered to make no real difference to the overall outcome of the administrative decision-making process for the claimant. We shall first consider how these new reforms bear on the judicial discretion whether to grant permission, and then go on to consider how they affect the discretion as to relief.

Senior Courts Act 1981

31—(3C) When considering whether to grant leave to make an application for judicial review, the High Court—

    (a) may of its own motion consider whether the outcome for the applicant would have been substantially different if the conduct complained of had not occurred, and

    (b) must consider that question if the defendant asks it to do so.

> (3D) If, on considering that question, it appears to the High Court to be highly likely that the outcome for the applicant would not have been substantially different, the court must refuse to grant leave.
>
> (3E) The court may disregard the requirement in subsection (3D) if it considers that it is appropriate to do so for reasons of exceptional public interest.
>
> (3F) If the court grants leave in reliance on subsection (3E), the court must certify that the condition in subsection (3E) is satisfied.
>
> …
>
> (8) In this section 'the conduct complained of', in relation to an application for judicial review, means the conduct (or alleged conduct) of the defendant that the applicant claims justifies the High Court in granting relief.

These provisions make what we shall describe as the 'no difference' principle—a potentially significant barrier to citizen access to the judicial review procedure.

We note at the outset that this principle or an analogous principle has long characterized judicial review. Courts had, prior to these provisions entering into force, not uncommonly denied *relief* on the basis that the same outcome would have been reached by the decision-maker regardless of the challenged conduct, albeit application of the principle at the *permission* stage was less common. However, judicial invocation and application of this principle has never been particularly consistent. For example, while the test has been more clearly articulated in certain contexts (see, *eg* the discussion in 7.3.4), in general it was never entirely clear how confident a court had to be that the outcome would have been the same or similar but for the challenged conduct before denying permission or relief on the basis of the no difference principle. In this regard, courts seldom articulated the standard of proof to be applied (*eg* balance of probabilities, real possibility, high likelihood, inevitability) nor did courts apply a uniform legal test consistently from one case to the next (albeit the government, in its consultation paper on reform, considered that the pre-existing position was that before relief could be denied the court had to be convinced that it was 'inevitable' that the same outcome would have occurred but for the unlawful conduct: *Judicial Review: Proposals for Further Reform*, Cm 8703 (2013) at [104]). Further, there were inexplicable variations across cases; for example, on materially similar facts some judges would invoke the principle to deny relief, whereas others would not even mention the principle. Thus, if for no other reason, the new provisions of the Senior Courts Act are welcome as they set out a general test, which will hopefully facilitate consistency in judicial decision-making.

Let us now examine those provisions. There is yet to be a significant appellate-level decision interpreting these provisions, therefore we approach them from first principles.

The key principle is set out in s 31(3D): if it appears to the court that it is highly likely that the outcome for the applicant would not have been substantially different had the conduct complained of not occurred the courts *must* refuse permission. This is a mandatory rule: if the conditions precedent arise then the court has no choice but to refuse permission. However, two preliminary points must be borne in mind. First, the no difference principle will only require the court to withhold permission if the court chooses, in the first place, to consider whether the outcome would have been substantially different, or if the defendant raises the point—in which case the court must consider the matter. Second, even if the principle is applied, and the test in s 31(3D) fulfilled, the court may nonetheless disregard the requirement in s 31(3D) if it certifies that there are reasons of exceptional public interest which warrant the grant of permission: s 31(3E)–(3F).

Several factors suggest that a court should take a very cautious approach to denying access to review proceedings based on the no difference principle. These factors ought to colour judicial interpretation and application of s 31. First, as we saw in our discussion of ouster clauses, the principle of access to the courts is classed as a constitutional right at common law, and courts should be very reluctant to cut down this principle. Where *civil rights* are in play this common law right is reinforced by Article 6 ECHR, which requires access to an independent and impartial tribunal for adjudication of civil rights. Where *human rights* under the HRA are at stake, Article 13 ECHR requires access to an impartial and independent tribunal for adjudication of those rights and which has the power to grant legally binding remedies; the ECHR has said that Article 13 is close to an absolute right, so that very few implied limits have been recognized.

Second, in the parliamentary debates on these new provisions the Minister in charge of the Bill in the House of Lords, Lord Faulks, said: 'Our ambition for this clause is relatively modest: it is simply to limit the time and resources spent on judicial reviews brought on grounds highly unlikely to make a substantial difference to the outcome for the applicant' (HL Deb 21 Jan 2015, vol 758, col 1342). Thus, the intention behind the reform is not to drastically cut down access to review. Rather, the reforms are intended to have more modest effects, reflected in the choice of the standard to be applied: the court must consider it *highly likely* that the outcome would not have been different for the claimant before permission is refused. This is a higher standard than the ordinary civil standard of proof, the *balance of probabilities*, which requires only proof that something was *more likely than not* to occur. To conclude that something is highly likely to occur one would require a high degree of confidence, on the evidence, that that outcome would indeed eventuate.

Third, for a court to decide whether it is highly likely that a substantially similar outcome would eventuate if the conduct complained of never occurred, the court must in effect stand in the shoes of the executive decision-maker and decide how their decision-making power would have been exercised absent the conduct complained of. In making such a decision a court must be aware of its constitutional and institutional limits, and proceed with great caution; courts are not well placed to determine how executive powers will be exercised. The courts must acknowledge that their predictions of how powers would be exercised may well be wrong given they do not, for example, have access to all relevant information that the decision-maker would have access to nor equivalent expertise in the relevant subject-matter addressed by the decision.

Fourth, it is important to bear in mind that the inquiry in s 31(3D) takes place at the permission stage, before the court has heard full argument on the merits of the case. Given the court at this stage does not have full information it may simply not be possible for the court to conclude with the requisite confidence what would have transpired if the challenged conduct never took place. Far better to reserve judgment on this matter for the remedies stage, once full argument and facts have been placed before the court, not least because of the very serious consequences for the applicant if permission is refused: they shall be denied access to the court to argue the merits of their case.

Thus, there are good reasons why the courts should take a very cautious approach to denying access to the courts on the basis of the no difference principle. Let us now consider a few specific features of the statutory scheme.

First, the test in s 31(3D) is focused on whether, if the challenged conduct is ignored, the outcome would have nonetheless been substantially different *for the applicant*. Given this focus it is difficult to see how this provision has application outside cases of individuated administrative decision-making. For example, where a pressure group mounts a challenge to guidance issued by the government on the basis that the guidance fails to state accurately a legal position, an inquiry into how the outcome would have been different for the claimant makes no sense. There is no 'outcome' as such, let alone one *for the claimant*. We suggest the new statutory provisions have no bearing on such cases.

Second, there is some ambiguity around the term 'outcome'. As discussed at 11.6, where the ground of challenge is a failure to give reasons for a decision, we might naturally think that the relevant outcome by which the counterfactual inquiry is to be conducted is the substantive decision reached. If one takes this view it may be more likely that a court will conclude that the same substantive decision would have been reached whether reasons were given or not. But it is possible to interpret the relevant outcome as being a *reasoned* decision. On this view the no difference principle would not be made out: a reasoned decision is a different outcome from an unreasoned decision. We suggest the latter strict interpretation should be adopted given that it promotes access to the review procedure. There is similarly ambiguity around other statutory terms including the concept of a 'substantially different' outcome. Again, in light of the fundamental principles engaged in this context, we suggest that if there is some ambiguity over whether the outcome that would have resulted but for the illegality would have been substantially the same or different from the actual outcome, the court should err on the side of allowing access to review so that the claims can be tried on their merits.

Third, the no difference principle is likely to have no or limited application in cases where the grounds of challenge are substantive rather than procedural. That is because where a court impugns a decision on substantive grounds it often does so on the basis that the outcome reached was an unlawful one; for example, it was one that was disproportionate or irrational. A lawful decision would therefore logically entail a different outcome. As such, the provision is much more likely to, and indeed is specifically intended to target (see the Lord Chancellor's remarks quoted later), cases where the grounds of challenge are procedural in nature. But while the provision more naturally applies to such cases, courts should nonetheless be cautious in concluding that the outcome would not have been substantially different even if correct procedures were followed. One key reason for recognizing principles of procedural fairness is that, where abided by, they lead to better decision-making; in this way process and outcome are inherently linked. For example, it is very difficult to conclude with any confidence that a decision that was the outcome of a process which included significant public consultation would be substantially the same as a decision that was the product of a closed decision process with no opportunities for consultation. Similarly, one rationale for requiring reasons to be given for certain classes of decision is that this is likely to concentrate the mind of the decision-maker, and thus produce better decisions.

Fourth, several of the principles already discussed, including the fundamental importance of access to court, would suggest that the 'exceptional public interest' test should be interpreted generously. However, given the open-endedness of the phrase it is difficult to predict how courts will interpret it. Two different views were put forward in the parliamentary debates on these provisions. Lord Faulks, the government Minister sponsoring the bill through the House of Lords, said (HL Deb 21 Jan 2015, vol 758, cols 1342–43):

> First, a high degree of public interest specific to the case is required for the exception to be met. We think that that is a fair compromise in the light of my second observation: we have purposely not defined the term 'exceptional public interest', meaning that the judiciary will apply the term in practice to the facts at hand. For fear of appearing to seek to fetter that discretion, I will forbear from setting out further detail on how the Government would wish to see the term applied in

future. I simply add this: in one regard it could be said that it is always in the public interest for a government body, local authority or anybody amenable to judicial review to follow to the letter the law. One can see the force of that argument. However, that, in a sense, is what public law is all about. It could also be said that simply saying that something is in the public interest is almost tautologous, when we are dealing with a public law remedy. Hence the requirement that there must be 'exceptional public interest'—although, as I have said, we think that is a matter for the judges to decide.

On this view there must be something more than an arguable claim of administrative unlawfulness before the court may rely on the exception. On the other hand, Lord Pannick, speaking from the cross-benches, suggested that the phrase should be interpreted in the light of statutory purpose (HL Deb 21 Jan 2015, vol 758, col 1345). He recalled that the Lord Chancellor, in leading the legislation through the House of Commons, had said (HC Deb 13 Jan 2015, vol 590, col 812) that the no difference provisions were only intended to exclude cases raising 'relatively minor procedural defects'. As such, Lord Pannick argued, the provisions as a whole, including the public interest exception, should not be relied upon to exclude cases outside that narrow band of cases characterized by minor procedural error; in particular, 'those raising allegations of substantial errors of law or of systematic wrong-doing are outside the legislative aim and are therefore ... exceptional'.

QUESTIONS

- What sorts of factors do you think the courts should consider in determining whether the exception is fulfilled?
- Are you convinced by Lord Pannick's analysis?

Thus, we have seen that the no difference principle may be relied upon by a court to deny permission to a claimant to bring review proceedings, and we have observed that access to court should only rarely be denied on the basis of this principle. But the no difference principle may not only 'bite' at the permission stage. It may also bite at the remedies stage, so as to deny a claimant, who has successfully proven administrative unlawfulness, relief.

Section 31(2A) provides that a court 'must refuse to grant relief on an application for judicial review ... if it appears to the court to be highly likely that the outcome for the applicant would not have been substantially different if the conduct complained of had not occurred'. Note that, unlike at the permission stage, it seems the court must always consider the no difference principle in deciding upon relief, and must refuse relief if the principle is fulfilled. Whereas at the permission stage the court has a discretion whether to consider the principle, and is only bound to consider it if the defendant raised the point: s 31(3C). Otherwise, the no difference test at the remedies stage is framed in precisely the same terms as the test that applies at the permission stage. Also, in common with the provisions governing the permission stage, the court may, under s 31(2B), disregard the no difference principle 'if it considers that it is appropriate to do so for reasons of exceptional public interest'; if the court relies on this provision to deny application of the no difference principle it must certify that the test in s 31(2B) is fulfilled: s 31(2C).

The application of the no difference test at the remedies stage raises many of the same issues as it raises at the permission stage, and which suggest the courts should be slow to deny relief for a proven illegality on the basis of the no difference principle. In addition we highlight two points peculiar to application of the no difference principle at the remedies stage.

First, if the no difference principle applies and the public interest exception is not established then the court may not 'grant relief', such as a quashing order, prohibiting order, or declaration. However, it does not necessarily follow from this that the unlawful administrative action remains valid. This is because on one view at least it is not the grant of a quashing order which invalidates unlawful administrative action. As discussed in ch 3, on one view, which has the support of the courts, invalidity is a reflex of unlawfulness. A quashing order only confirms this consequence. Thus, even if the no difference principle disables a court from making an order for relief, this will not necessarily rob the claimant of the fruits of their victory.

Second, fundamental principles reinforce that relief should only rarely be denied on the basis of the no difference principle. The right to a remedy is a core principle of the rule of law: the rule of law is undermined if courts allow unlawful government action to stand, and provide no relief against its effects. This would be to render legal norms, such as procedural fairness, rationality, and legality, hollow commitments, given they could be ignored by government without consequence. It is clear that statutory provisions ought to be interpreted consistently with the requirements of the rule of law if possible: *R v. Secretary of State for the Home Department, ex parte Pierson* [1998] AC 539 at 591. Where human rights under the HRA are at stake, the United Kingdom must abide by the requirements of Article 13 ECHR, which provides for the right to an effective remedy. As already discussed, this is close to an absolute right, so that very few implied restrictions upon it have been recognized. There is thus a very real risk that if domestic courts deny remedies for human rights violations on the basis of the no difference principle, the UK shall eventually be found in breach of the ECHR.

Let us conclude with some more general observations on the no difference principle. We have, in our discussion of standing in the last two sections, distinguished two models of review: an individualistic, private law model and a public interest model. Recall that within the private law model the focus of review is upon protecting individuals from unlawful interference with their interests. It is not difficult to argue in favour of the no difference principle within this model. If the individual's interests would be prejudiced in exactly the same way regardless of the illegality, then the basis for judicial intervention on judicial review—protection from individual prejudice—falls away, so that the claimant is unjustified in troubling the court with his claim. However, as we saw in our discussion of public interest standing, one criticism that can be levelled at the private law model is that it construes the functions of judicial review far too narrowly. Important public interests are also implicated in judicial review proceedings, which transcend the interests of any one individual. For example, regardless of whether illegality causes an individual prejudice, there is a public interest in ensuring lawful decision-making, while successful review proceedings can spur improvements in public administration to the benefit of all people who interact with government, even if the proceedings make no difference in individual cases. These important wider functions of review may be stymied if access to review or remedies are denied on the basis of the no difference principle. Furthermore, the trajectory of legal development in administrative law is firmly towards acknowledging judicial review's wider functions, as demonstrated by the courts' wholesale embrace of public interest standing. The no difference principle is out of step with these developments, and if applied liberally could reverse at least some of the tremendous progress made in judicial review over the last 30 years, to the ultimate detriment of the public interest. However, if the arguments made herein as to how the principle should be applied are followed by the courts then the effect may be to mitigate any negative effects; in particular, the principle should be applied with caution, it should rarely be invoked to deny access to review or relief in human rights cases, it should not apply to public interest challenges, and the public interest exception should be applied liberally. Importantly, such an approach would not undermine Parliament's intent in passing the new provisions, given that—as those government Ministers who guided the reforms through Parliament said—the reforms were intended to be modest in nature and apply principally to cases of minor procedural irregularities.

14.9 Concluding remarks

As this chapter has demonstrated, the restrictions on obtaining relief via judicial review are many and various. Three broad themes, however, may be drawn out. First, there is a strong policy in favour of making judicial review available: witness, for instance, the liberalization of the law of standing and the courts' reluctance to allow legislative displacement of their supervisory jurisdiction. Second, however, there is a concern, reflected in the existence of a permission stage, the no difference principle, strict time limits, and the limits on standing, to ensure that public authorities are afforded protection from, for example, hopeless judicial review claims, delayed claims, and vexatious or meddlesome claims. Third, there is clear recognition—evidenced by, for instance, the introduction of the Pre-Action Protocol, the reform of the permission stage, the exhaustion of alternative remedies principle, and restrictions on judicial review of decisions emanating from the new tribunal system—that it is necessary to relieve pressure on the Administrative Court by encouraging the resolution of disputes otherwise than by recourse to judicial review or simply by restricting access to judicial review. Taken together, these strands reflect the contemporary view that the possibility of judicial review of government action by an independent judiciary is a crucially important constitutional longstop, but that it is important, in the practice of judicial review, to also account for the interests of public administration and the court system, and to recognize that administrative justice can, and should, also be delivered by other means. It is to this final point that we return in chs 17–19, in which we consider how administrative justice may be promoted otherwise than through court proceedings.

FURTHER RESOURCES

Andenas and Fairgreave (eds), *Judicial Review in International Perspective* (The Hague 2000), chs 19 (Wade: 'British Restriction of Judicial Review—Europe to the Rescue'), 20 (Beloff: 'Who Whom? Issues in *Locus Standi* in Public Law'), and 22 (Hare: 'The Law of Standing in Public Interest Adjudication')

Bondy and Sunkin, 'Accessing Judicial Review' [2008] *PL* 647

Bondy and Sunkin, 'Settlement in Judicial Review Proceedings' [2009] *PL* 237

Bowman, *Review of the Crown Office List* (London 2000) *http://webarchive.nationalarchives. gov.uk/+/http://www.dca.gov.uk/civil/bowman2000/bowman2000fr.htm* (in summary form)

Bridges, Meszaros, and Sunkin, 'Regulating the Judicial Review Caseload' [2000] *PL* 651

Civil Procedure Rules *http://www.justice.gov.uk/civil/procrules_fin/index.htm*

Feldman, 'Public Interest Litigation and Constitutional Theory in Comparative Perspective' (1992) 55 *MLR* 44

Forsyth and Hare (eds), *The Golden Metwand and the Crooked Cord* (Oxford 1998) chs 9 (Beatson: 'Prematurity and Ripeness for Review') and 11 (Beloff: "'Time, Time, Time's on My Side, Yes It Is'")

Harlow, 'A Special Relationship? American Influences on Judicial Review in England' in Loveland (ed), *A Special Relationship? American Influences on Public Law in the UK* (Oxford 1996)

Law Com No 226, *Administrative Law: Judicial Review and Statutory Appeals* (London 1994), Parts IV, V, VIII, and XII

Lewis, 'The Exhaustion of Alternative Remedies in Administrative Law' [1992] *CLJ* 138

Lewis, *Judicial Remedies in Public Law* (London 2015), chs 9, 11, and 12

Miles, 'Standing in a Multi-Layered Constitution' in Bamforth and Leyland (eds), *Public Law in a Multi-Layered Constitution* (Oxford 2003)

Ministry of Justice, *Judicial Review: Proposals for Reform*, Cm 8515 (2012) *http://www.justice.gov.uk/digital-communications/judicial-review-reform/supporting_documents/judicialreviewreform.pdf*

Ministry of Justice, *Judicial Review: Proposals for Further Reform*, Cm 8703 (2013) *https://www.gov.uk/government/uploads/system/uploads/attachment_data/file/264091/8703.pdf*

Varuhas, 'Judicial Review: Standing and Remedies' [2013] *CLJ* 243.

Woolf, 'The Rule of Law and a Change in Constitution' [2004] *CLJ* 317

Pre-Action Protocol for Judicial Review *http://www.justice.gov.uk/civil/procrules_fin/contents/protocols/prot_jrv.htm*)

15 LIABILITY OF PUBLIC AUTHORITIES

15.1 Introduction

It is all too easy today to conflate the field of administrative law with judicial review claims made via the public law procedure for orders based on the old prerogative writs, injunctions and declarations. As a result of such conflation one might consider monetary remedies, such as damages, foreign to administrative law. For example, a major textbook on constitutional law states that '[d]amages and compensatory remedies have not traditionally played a major role in British public law' (Turpin and Tomkins, *British Government and the Constitution* (2007) at 276, 340 (2011) at 361). As we shall see, such claims are at worst plain wrong and at best misleading. Yet the error is neither uncommon nor perhaps surprising. The tremendous, exponential growth and development of judicial review in the post-War era has preoccupied public law academics and also judicial thinking about administrative law and public law more generally. As Lord Reed has observed it was the exponential growth in applications for exercise of the courts' supervisory jurisdiction following creation of the distinct judicial review procedure in the late 1970s that 'resulted in the development of public law as an area of practice and academic study. In consequence, an area of the law which had previously been relatively neglected has become the subject of intensive consideration, and legal doctrine has been examined, criticised and refined' (*AXA General Insurance Ltd* v. *The Lord Advocate* [2011] UKSC 46, [2012] 1 AC 868 at [164]).

While the conflation of administrative law with judicial review is perhaps unsurprising and possibly understandable, it is nonetheless an error of the first order. As we shall see in this chapter, it was claims for damages based in ordinary private law fields, especially the law of torts, that for most of English legal history ensured strong protection of basic individual rights in the face of public power. Not only did such claims secure protection of basic rights, but it was through the vehicle of damages actions that many fundamental precepts of English public law were elaborated, maintained, and vindicated, most importantly the rule of law. The law of torts continues to perform these important public law functions today. In addition, new fields of liability which regulate administrative action, some of which are specifically dedicated to regulating administrative action, have emerged or been added over time. These include, as we shall see, damages actions under the Human Rights Act 1998 (HRA) and in EU law, as well as recognition of a novel restitutionary claim for recovery of gains wrongfully made by public authorities at the expense of individuals. As authorities have increasingly sought to utilize contract as a tool of government the law of contract has taken on increased prominence as a major field of law which regulates government conduct. Albeit, regrettably, there is not space to consider such matters here, equity may also give rise to public authority liability for money awards, for example where authorities give undertakings to the court to pay damages in exchange for grant of injunctive relief (see *Financial*

Services Authority v. *Sinaloa Gold plc* [2013] UKSC 11, [2013] 2 AC 28; Varuhas and Turner (2014) 130 *LQR* 33), while, albeit the remedy is still developing, it is in principle possible that an authority may be liable to pay equitable compensation if it were to breach relevant equitable obligations: *AIB Group (UK) plc* v. *Mark Redler & Co Solicitors* [2014] UKSC 58, [2015] AC 1503. Put simply, one cannot have a complete understanding of the law governing administrative action without consideration of these fields of law. Regrettably, the influence of the flawed idea of a fundamental divide between private law and public law has too often obscured this reality, and in consequence full understanding of the field of administrative law.

At the outset it is important to record that thanks to a fundamental precept of English law, known as the *principle of equality*, the same ordinary rules of private law fields such as tort and contract that apply to individuals and corporations in principle apply equally to public authorities. Dicey considered this principle to be of such importance that he elevated it to a principle of the rule of law. There are good reasons why this totemic principle of English law should be adhered to. The great danger in countenancing deviations from it is that this will result in special exceptions for the benefit of authorities. If public authorities were above the ordinary law this could undermine the basic principle of government under law and thus the rule of law—where law ends there is greater scope for tyranny and abuse of power. Further, special exemptions may allow public authorities to interfere with individuals' most basic rights, and cause them significant harm, without justification yet with impunity, leaving those individuals to bear their own losses. This is not only fundamentally unjust, but it may encourage cavalier exercises of public power, whereas in contrast, exposure of authorities to liability where they breach rights may encourage compliance. Not only would special government immunities be bad for the rule of law and for individuals, but they would operate to erode trust in government and undermine its legitimacy. For example, it would surely breed a sense of resentment—'one rule for us, another rule for them'—if individuals were required to pay damages for particular wrongs, but when the government harmed individuals in exactly the same way, it was subject to no equivalent obligation. Thus, the common law has known no special public law of torts or contract. As Lord Denning MR said, '[o]ur English law does not allow a public officer to shelter behind a droit administratif' (*Ministry of Housing and Local Government* v. *Sharp* [1970] 2 QB 223 at 266).

However, this orthodoxy is, in some contexts, under threat, as courts have shown greater receptiveness to arguments that authorities require special protection, while some commentators have pushed strongly for establishment of special protections. Typical policy arguments include that it is important to protect the funding of public services, which serve the greater good, from crippling damages liability; that such liability may result in officials being unduly cautious in their exercises of public power for fear of exposing their public authority employer to damages liability (often known as the chilling effect argument); and that authorities may be exposed to a flood of damages claims. These arguments seem intuitively appealing but they are complex, and it is questionable whether they are apt for consideration by judges. Many of these typical policy arguments, such as the floodgates and chilling effects arguments, rest on factual premises which are highly contested. It is impossible for judges to know whether awarding damages in one case will lead to a flood of claims, or how it will affect administrative behaviour, if it has any effect at all. Other arguments, such as a concern to preserve public funds, seem inapt for judicial consideration: it is not for judges to make decisions as to liability on the basis of how they think public money is best spent as between redressing harms or funding services; such bare questions over distribution of scarce resources are for the political branches not judges. Further, erection of special areas of immunity from ordinary law by judges seems out of step with the opening up of public authority liability by Parliament, for example through establishment of the damages action under the HRA. Ultimately, if government, whose own pecuniary interests are implicated by liability, or Parliament become concerned that the scope or extent of liability is threatening important public interests, then those institutions are perfectly capable of taking action, and have done so in some areas, for example through the creation of statutory immunities for particular authorities or classes of official. If neither government nor Parliament act, it is unclear why the courts should act to preserve government interests, and in doing so risk their own legitimacy: it is for the Chancellor to worry about the government books, not the courts.

In contrast to the view that authorities should be specially protected, others would argue that authorities should be subject to wider liabilities and/or under more stringent obligations than ordinary persons. For example, one might argue that authorities have a special capacity to harm, because they are empowered to do things which ordinary individuals are not empowered to do: police officers may use deadly force, while immigration officers may detain you. Further, in such contexts there is a power imbalance: it is very difficult to resist the commands of an armed police officer, even if one knows them to be unlawful; indeed it may be unlawful to resist, so that one is completely vulnerable. Thus, we may, for example, argue for additional, greater obligations to be placed on public officers to ensure individuals are strongly protected, and award very heavy damages against public officers where power is abused in order to deter such conduct. Of course, however, there are also often great power disparities between private persons, as between an ordinary citizen and a huge multinational corporation. But this may simply mean we should impose greater obligations on more powerful parties wherever power imbalances arise, whether the more powerful party is a public entity or not.

A distinct argument is that because our expectations of public actors may quite legitimately be greater than our expectations of strangers, the law should, at least in certain situations, impose greater obligations on public actors than it does on others. For example, in tort an individual cannot in general be held liable for failing to help another individual who is in danger. While we might hope that a stranger would help us if we were in danger, it would seem harsh to hold them liable for not throwing themselves into a life-threatening situation, which, given they are unlikely to be qualified to deal with such situations, may only make things worse. On the other hand, we may have higher expectations of a police officer or ambulance officer given that protecting and helping citizens is a core aspect of their public functions, while they are empowered and trained specifically to deal with such situations.

These tensions—between the equality principle, a concern that authorities ought to be specially protected, and a concern that authorities ought to be subject to wider and more onerous obligations—lie at the heart of many of the topics that will be discussed herein. Nonetheless, the equality principle remains the default approach, and a defining characteristic of the English legal system.

Before going on we make one observation. This chapter is not intended as a mini-textbook on the fields considered: torts, contract, restitution, EU state liability, human rights damages, etc. It is important to emphasize that our coverage of these topics is not exhaustive, and also that it would be impossible within one chapter to do justice to these highly complex, elaborate, and significant fields of English law. Rather, we consider a number of select topics in order to give a flavor of the nature and operation of these fields of liability, and of some of the issues that arise when they are applied to public authorities. Those whose interest is pricked by the discussion are referred to specialist works on the fields under consideration; some of these works are catalogued in the 'further resources' section at the end of this chapter.

15.2 Relationship with judicial review

There are various aspects to the relationship between the materials in this chapter and actions directly involving the grounds of review that have been explored earlier in this book. First, not uncommonly an action for damages will implicate an inquiry into the legality of government action on the basis of judicial review grounds. For example, if a police officer detains you and you bring a claim against them in false imprisonment, they may be able to defend the claim on the basis that they had statutory power to detain you. However, whether that defence of 'lawful excuse' will be effective for the officer to avoid liability will depend on whether the officer exercised their powers *lawfully*; if the powers were not exercised lawfully their defence of lawful excuse shall fail, they shall not be able to show justification for detaining you, and they shall be liable to you in damages. Of course the legality of exercise of public powers implicates ordinary review doctrines, such as legality, procedural fairness, and rationality. Thus, if the exercise of power was, for example, tainted by procedural unfairness or did not abide by statutory conditions for its exercise or was *Wednesbury* unreasonable, the officer's defence shall fail.

A second point to note is that since 1977 it has been possible for damages, and, since 2004, for restitution and the recovery of a sum due, to be obtained in a claim brought via judicial review procedure (see now s 31(4) of the Senior Courts Act 1981 and CPR 54.3(2)). If a claimant seeks a prerogative order alongside damages or restitution then they *must* use the public law procedure, as the procedure must be used where prerogative orders are sought. Where the claimant seeks damages and a remedy other than a prerogative order such as an injunction or declaration, they *may* be able to use the judicial review procedure, but will not necessarily be required to do so. In such a case it would be in the claimant's interests to proceed via ordinary procedure given it is not characterized by the many procedural safeguards for the benefit of authorities that apply in review proceedings. If the claimant only seeks damages, restitution, or a sum due then they are *barred from* using the judicial review procedure. Often when concurrent claims for damages and other types of relief are made via judicial review, the Administrative Court will determine any judicial review points raised—such as claims of irrationality or procedural unfairness—and then transfer the proceedings to the Queen's Bench Division for the damages claim to be determined via ordinary procedure. One of the reasons for such practice is that damages claims are often very fact-specific so that cross-examination and disclosure will be required for proper determination of the claim, whereas judicial review procedure does not typically make provision for these.

Third, damages are not an available remedy for breach of the common law duties of legality, procedural fairness, or rationality *per se*. Damages may only be recovered where a claimant can make out a private law claim, such as a claim in tort or contract, or a claim for damages under the HRA or in EU law. Of course this does not necessarily mean that an individual who suffers loss through administrative action, but cannot fit their claim within a damages action, shall not be able to recover compensation for their loss. The law, while not requiring the provision of compensation, may encourage it; for example, as we saw in 6.1.5 and 6.2.6, an authority that frustrates a legitimate expectation may escape a finding of illegality or having its decision quashed, if it has afforded the claimant compensation in lieu of satisfaction of the expectation. Importantly, there are 'administrative' routes to compensation. For example, the Parliamentary Ombudsman has the power to and often does recommend that government afford an individual compensation for injustice suffered through maladministration. These recommendations are almost always implemented by government.

More generally, a public authority may, of its own volition—pursuant to third source powers or discretionary statutory powers—decide to make a voluntary payment to an individual, even though no legal wrong which could generate liability has been committed. Such 'administrative compensation' has a venerable tradition, and it would be a mistake to view such payments as playing a marginal role in administrative redress: many such payments are made each year which add up to significant amounts of public expenditure (see Harlow [2010] PL 321). The circumstances where such awards may be made range from a one-off *ex gratia* payment for a particularly bad individual case to establishment of major compensation schemes to compensate a significant class of individuals affected by the same large-scale event, and which may be backed by a pool of public funds in the hundreds of millions. It should be noted that such payments are often made for loss caused by administrative action that is not even *ultra vires*, but where it is nonetheless felt—for reasons of sympathy, social solidarity, fairness, etc—that the individual ought not to have to bear the relevant losses.

We observe in passing here that the Law Commission, several years ago, undertook a major project to investigate, among other things, the possibility of establishing a statutory action for compensation of loss suffered through *ultra vires* administrative action; however, the proposals were ultimately kiboshed by government: Law Com Consultation Paper No 187, *Administrative Redress: Public Bodies and the Citizen* (London 2008); Law Com No 322, *Administrative Redress: Public Bodies and the Citizen* (London 2010) (see further 15.5). As such, establishment of a general system of public authority liability for maladministration 'is not on the cards in the United Kingdom' (*Mohammed* v. *Home Office* [2011] EWCA Civ 351, [2011] 1 WLR 2862 at [24]), while the courts are unlikely to take such a bold move themselves, consistently emphasizing that such a significant step would be for Parliament.

15.3 The law of torts

15.3.1 Constitutional fundamentals

The principle of equality

Although it is commonplace to refer to tort law as a field of private law, it is a defining feature of the English legal tradition that the law of torts applies, in principle, equally to public officials as it does to private individuals. Public officials, in the common law tradition, are not viewed as having some special status, but are merely citizens in uniform; if they infringe the basic rights of others they may be held liable in damages for their wrongs as may anyone else. Because of this principle of equality, which Dicey considered to be a fundamental aspect of the rule of law in England, the law of torts was a significant field of law that regulated the exercise of public power and protected individuals against abuse of power, and did so for centuries before the emergence of the modern law of judicial review. As Lord Denning MR observed, it is 'unthinkable' that an 'injured person would be left without a remedy' simply because the defendant is an official (*Ministry of Housing and Local Government* v. *Sharp* [1970] 2 QB 223 at 266). Thus it was that Dicey recorded with pride (*Introduction to the Study of the Law of the Constitution* (MacMillan 1960) at 193),

> [t]he Reports abound with cases in which officials have been brought before the courts, and made, in their personal capacity, liable to punishment, or to the payment of damages, for acts done in their official character but in excess of their lawful authority.

This tradition continues today; the courts maintaining that there is 'nothing in the slightest bit peculiar about an individual bringing a private law claim for damages against an executive official who has unlawfully infringed his private rights' (*ID* v. *Home Office* [2005] EWCA Civ 38, [2006] 1 WLR 1003 at [57]). Actions continue to be brought against officials including those at the very apex of government, as demonstrated by various tort claims brought against the former Home Secretary, Mr Jack Straw, in relation to his alleged role in the practice of extraordinary rendition: *Belhaj* v. *Straw* [2014] EWCA Civ 1394, [2015] 2 WLR 1105 (on appeal to the Supreme Court).

Of course it was traditionally the case that the Crown was immune from actions in tort. The concept of 'the Crown' is a fraught, anachronistic concept steeped in theoretical disagreement. For present purposes we shall define the Crown as central government. However, notwithstanding Crown immunity the principle of equality ensured there was in general always an individual officer who could be sued personally, while the Crown would often stand behind its officers and pay damages awarded against officers for wrongs committed in their official capacity. In any case, Crown immunity was eventually rolled back, and gave way to the principle of equality. The great piece of reforming legislation, the Crown Proceedings Act 1947, adopted a general principle that 'the Crown shall be subject to all those liabilities in tort to which, if it were a person of full age and capacity, it would be subject ... in respect of torts committed by its servants or agents' (s 2(1)(a)). Through this legislation Parliament chose to prioritize government under law, over governmental interests in immunity. As such, it is most common today for claimants to initiate claims against the Crown, rather than its officers. Nonetheless, it is still in principle possible for a claimant to sue individual officers, albeit there are clear advantages in suing the Crown, in particular that government departments will be well placed to pay significant damages awards whereas individual officers will be of more modest means. It is important to note that the 1947 Act does not work by creating a direct liability of the Crown. Rather, by s 2(1) it provides that the Crown may be liable *vicariously* for the wrongs *of its employees*. As Sedley LJ observed in *Chagos Islanders* v. *Attorney-General* [2004] EWCA Civ 997 at [20]:

> [T]he 1947 Act does not work by making the state a potential tortfeasor: it works by making the Crown vicariously liable for the torts of its servants. It has only been with the enactment of the Human Rights Act 1998 that the Crown, in the form of a 'public authority', has acquired a primary liability for violating certain rights.

We shall come back to the HRA later, which does create a direct liability of the Crown and other public authorities. It is of course possible to sue statutory public bodies in the same way that one may sue anyone else, as statutory bodies were not covered by a special general immunity as the Crown was. However, Parliament may decide to confer statutory immunities from liability upon particular statutory bodies. Thus, pockets of immunity do exist. Nonetheless, the analytical starting point is the principle of equality, and it is well established that any immunities will be construed narrowly, not least as such immunities, given they create a legal 'black hole' within which wrongs may be committed with impunity, are in principle inconsistent with the rule of law.

The constitutional function of the law of torts

The law of torts, given its equal applicability to public officials and authorities, has long been of constitutional importance, serving a similar role to bills of rights in affording strong protection to basic rights, such as rights in liberty, physical integrity, and property, in the face of public power, while through its operation it has served wider constitutional functions.

In particular, torts actionable *per se*, sometimes referred to as 'vindicatory' or 'rights-based' torts, have long played a crucial role in protecting those basic interests fundamental to English civil society from interference by public actors, which we would now describe as human rights. These torts include trespass to land, which protects interests in exclusive possession of land; false imprisonment, which protects liberty; battery, which protects physical integrity; and defamation, which protects one's reputation. The core features of these torts ensure that they afford these most basic interests very strong protection from outside interference:

1. These torts are actionable *per se*, which means that the claimant does not need to demonstrate loss in order to bring a claim; all they need to show to get their claim off the ground is that the defendant interfered with their basic interests. Furthermore, the slightest of interferences may generate liability. That the claimant may potentially prove a wrong and recover substantial damages for a fleeting interference with their liberty or physical integrity reinforces the importance of these interests, that they ought to be maintained inviolate and respected, and demonstrates how strongly they are protected by the law.

2. In addition to these torts being actionable *per se*, liability is generally strict. This means that a claimant may establish the tort and recover damages even if the defendant could not really be blamed for interfering with the claimant's rights. The strictest form of liability is found in trespass to land: the defendant may be liable in trespass for coming onto my land without my consent even if they did not know it was my land, had no reason to know it was my land, and acted in the utmost good faith. This reflects the importance which the law of torts places on such basic interests. As Pollock recorded long ago, speaking of battery, where the 'primary rights to security for a man's person' are at stake 'the knowledge or state of mind of the person violating the right is not material for determining his legal responsibility' (*Law of Torts* (London 1887) at 7, 218). In false imprisonment too, liability may be established even where the imprisonment was down to a simple error on the part of the defendant, the defendant was completely blameless, and had even acted conscientiously; to hold otherwise would be to 'reduce the protection currently

provided by ... false imprisonment' (*R* v. *Governor of Brockhill Prison, ex parte Evans (No 2)* [2001] 2 AC 19 at 35).

3. In addition, defences, by which the defendant may justify their wrong and avoid liability, are construed narrowly, and are limited to protecting only the most important and pressing of public and other interests. Importantly, the defendant bears the onus of justifying their act. The most common defence where a public officer or entity is sued is that they had statutory authorization to do the otherwise wrongful act. However, reflecting the importance placed by the law on the protected interests, the courts have emphasized that they will 'strictly and narrowly construe general statutory powers whose exercise restricts fundamental common law rights and/or constitutes the commission of a tort' (*R (Lumba)* v. *Secretary of State for the Home Department* [2011] UKSC 12, [2012] 1 AC 245 at [53]). The executive cannot justify wrongs by amorphous appeals to expediency or the common good (*Bici* v. *Ministry of Defence* [2004] EWHC 786 at [86]), and any claim of justification will 'be examined with very great care': *Lindley* v. *Rutter* [1981] QB 128 at 134. Thus, the justificatory onus faced by a defendant where they trespass on the most basic of rights may be a heavy one.

In each of these vindicatory torts the law starts from the assumption that one's basic interests ought to be maintained inviolate and should not be interfered with. If the defendant interferes with those interests the law assumes the defendant has acted wrongfully and should be held liable, unless the defendant can justify their act, for example by showing lawful justification or that the claimant consented to the wrongful act. In this way the law affords basic interests strong protection from outside interference and sends a signal as to the importance of the protected interests and that they ought not to be interfered with.

In addition, substantial compensatory damages—damages that compensate for damage and loss—will in general follow proof of a vindicatory tort as a matter of course. For interference with basic rights damages are presumed, so that one may recover substantial sums of compensatory damages without having to prove any particular loss: 'In all such cases the law presumes that some damage will flow in the ordinary course of things from the mere invasion of the plaintiff's rights' (*Ratcliffe* v. *Evans* [1892] 2 QB 524, 528). That significant damages are routinely awarded for the rights violation in and of itself, without the claimant having to show loss, serves to vindicate the importance of the right, and also afford strong protection to the underlying protected interests (see further Varuhas (2014) 34 *OJLS* 253). Thus, in the Australian case of *Plenty* v. *Dillon* (1991) 171 CLR 635, where public officers trespassed on the claimant's land, the High Court awarded substantial damages despite the officers causing no damage to the land through their trespass. Gaudron and McHugh JJ, in their joint judgment, explained the award thus (at 654–5):

> In his judgment, the learned trial judge said that, even if a trespass had occurred, it was 'of such a trifling nature as not to found (sic) in damages'. However, once a plaintiff obtains a verdict in an action of trespass, he or she is entitled to an award of damages. In addition, we would unhesitatingly reject the suggestion that this trespass was of a trifling nature. The first and second respondents deliberately entered the appellant's land against his express wish. True it is that the entry itself caused no damage to the appellant's land. But the purpose of an action for trespass to land is not merely to compensate the plaintiff for damage to the land. That action also serves the purpose of vindicating the plaintiff's right to the exclusive use and occupation of his or her land. Although the first and second respondents were acting honestly in the supposed execution

of their duty, their entry was attended by circumstances of aggravation. They entered as police officers with all the power of the State behind them, knowing that their entry was against the wish of the appellant and in circumstances likely to cause him distress. It is not to the point that the appellant was unco-operative or even unreasonable. The first and second respondents had no right to enter his land. The appellant was entitled to resist their entry. If the occupier of property has a right not to be unlawfully invaded, then, as Mr Geoffrey Samuel has pointed out in another context, the 'right must be supported by an effective sanction otherwise the term will be just meaningless rhetoric': 'The Right Approach?' (1980) 96 *Law Quarterly Review* 12, at p 14, cited by Lord Edmund-Davies in *Morris* v. *Beardmore*, at p 461. If the courts of common law do not uphold the rights of individuals by granting effective remedies, they invite anarchy, for nothing breeds social disorder as quickly as the sense of injustice which is apt to be generated by the unlawful invasion of a person's rights, particularly when the invader is a government official. The appellant is entitled to have his right of property vindicated by a substantial award of damages.

Of course in addition to this type of presumed damages, proven damages suffered in consequence of the wrong, such as mental suffering, physical injury, lost wages, or damage to property will also be recoverable so that the claimant is not left materially worse off by the wrong, but rather restored to the position they would have been in but for the defendant's wrongful conduct. We also ought to note that compensatory damages in tort are recoverable *as of right*; they are not subject to judicial discretion in the way that quashing orders, injunctions, or declarations are.

In addition, other types of damages, beyond compensatory damages, may be awarded against a defendant for a vindicatory tort. The availability of this wide range of damages serves to afford stronger, added protection to the claimant's basic interests in the face of particularly egregious wrongdoing by the defendant. Aggravated damages may be awarded. These are a type of compensatory damages for mental distress which compensate for the *added* injury to the claimant's proper feelings of pride and dignity where their basic interests are interfered with out of malice, arrogance, malevolence, insolence, or spite (*Rookes* v. *Barnard* [1964] AC 1129 at 1221, 1229). Such damages have often been awarded against public defendants. For example, in false imprisonment such damages may be awarded for the aggravated mental suffering the claimant will naturally suffer where they are wrongly arrested or imprisoned by the police in humiliating circumstances or in a 'high handed, insulting, malicious or oppressive manner': *Thompson* v. *Commissioner for the Metropolis* [1998] QB 498 at 516.

A defining characteristic of the common law tradition is the availability of exemplary or punitive damages in the law of torts. Such damages are not designed to compensate for loss, but are instead awarded in addition to compensatory damages, and their explicit function is to punish outrageous wrongdoing. Traditionally such damages have only been available for certain torts, and in particular the vindicatory torts: exemplary damages are 'well established in the torts of defamation, false imprisonment and trespass to property' (McGregor, *McGregor on Damages* (2014) at [13-011]). While they are now in principle available for all torts, their availability remains circumscribed and limited to three categories of case (see *Rookes*). The first category of case is where public officials have acted oppressively, arbitrarily, or unconstitutionally. The availability of exemplary damages in cases of public wrongdoing is a longstanding feature of the law of torts, and a totemic feature of the English constitutional tradition. Thus, for example, Holt CJ in 1703, in the famous case of *Ashby* v. *White* (1703) 2 Lord Raymond 938 at 956, said: 'If publick officers will infringe mens rights, they ought to pay greater damages than other men, to deter and hinder other officers from the like offences.' That the common law takes the exceptional step of punishing an official—punishment generally being a function reserved for the criminal law rather than the civil law—for their egregious wrong, sends a powerful signal that basic rights must be respected by officials, vindicates the rule of law by symbolically reinforcing the importance of legal constraints on the exercise of public power, serves to express societal outrage at the public officer's conduct, and will hopefully deter similar official conduct in future. Note that the availability of exemplary damages specifically against public officers is an example of the common law breaching the equality principle to afford *greater* protection to individuals.

Thus, the law of torts, and especially the vindicatory, rights-based torts, have long performed a fundamental constitutional function, affording strong protection to the most basic of rights in the face of public power. As ECS Wade said in his introduction to the tenth edition of Dicey's famous treatise, *Introduction to the Study of the Law of the Constitution* (London 1960) at cviii:

> Foreign constitutions contain statements of guaranteed rights. Such rights with us proceed from the enforcement of private rights by the courts which are able to punish illegalities. Therefore the constitution, so far as it is concerned with the protection of private rights, comes from the common law.

Thus, when courts adjudicate damages claims in tort they are in essence defining constitutional rights, in liberty, the person, and property, and courts were engaged in such constitutional adjudication long before modern ideas of human rights emerged. For this reason much of Dicey's seminal treatise on the law of the constitution reads as a treatise on the law of civil wrongs; the book offering detailed accounts of false imprisonment and defamation, as these torts have long protected rights constitutional in nature.

As touched upon in our discussion of exemplary damages, in addition to performing the important constitutional function of protecting basic rights, damages actions against public defendants have, through their operation, long served and continue to serve wider constitutional functions. The routine award of substantial sums against public defendants where they infringe the basic rights of citizens symbolically reinforces the first principle of the rule of law, government under law; in Dicey's words, it 'ensure[s] the supremacy of the law of the land' (at 210). Dicey also thought the making of awards would 'curb the arbitrariness of the Crown' (at 210). In other words, if public defendants were faced with substantial damages liability where they infringed basic rights without justification this would help to ensure that public defendants took greater care to abide by the legal constraints on their powers. It is, of course, difficult to know what effects damages have *in fact* had on administrative behaviour, but one cannot doubt that significant awards serve to draw attention to and thus facilitate accountability for legal wrongs, and that they symbolically reinforce rule of law values and respect for basic rights. Having said this, there are significant empirical studies which show that where a glut of significant awards are made against the same authority in respect of a particular type of wrongdoing this can lead to radical administrative reform so as to ensure legal compliance into the future: Epp, *Making Rights Real* (Chicago 2009).

It is important to emphasize that the law of torts, and the vindicatory torts specifically, continue to perform these important constitutional functions. This is despite the emergence of other controls on public power including the growth of judicial review, human rights legislation, alternative paths to compensation such as the Ombudsman, and advances in mechanisms for political accountability. Consider the case of *Muuse* v. *Secretary of State for the Home Department* [2010] EWCA Civ 453 (noted Varuhas [2011] *CLJ* 284). The Court awarded heavy damages, including compensatory, aggravated, and exemplary damages, for a long period of wrongful imprisonment, during which Muuse was subject to poor treatment, and which was the result of officials' 'manifest incompetence', while the overarching system which allowed these events to transpire, for which the Minister and senior officials were responsible, was also flawed. However, despite these serious failings there was no internal nor parliamentary inquiry, no Minister or senior official held accountable, and a 'paucity of measures' taken to prevent recurrence: 'The *only* way in which the misconduct of the Home Office has been exposed to public view and [Muuse's] rights vindicated is by the action in the High Court' (at [75]–[77] (emphasis added)). The case also demonstrates the potential for actions to play wider functions; through the litigation the Minister was held to account in a public forum for systemic failures and a lack of subsequent action, while the Court took the opportunity to entreat that this episode required urgent investigation by the Minister.

15.3.2 The tort of negligence: introduction

Different torts perform different functions. The basic function of torts actionable *per se*, or vindicatory torts, is to afford strong protection from outside interference to fundamental rights, and to vindicate those rights, in the sense of affirming their importance and that they ought to be respected and maintained inviolate. As we have seen, those torts have performed this vital constitutional function through the ages. The tort of negligence is of more recent vintage; the modern tort being established through the coalescence of various disparate actions into one unitary 'mega-tort', this process culminating in 1932 in the famous case of *Donaghue* v. *Stevenson* [1932] AC 562 (the case of the snail in the ginger beer bottle). This modern tort, as it has developed since 1932, is underpinned by a very different concern from the vindicatory torts. Its principal function is not to ensure strong protection of basic interests for their own sake and to reinforce their importance, but rather to afford compensation for harms caused by the fault of another. As the great tort scholar Weir put it, '[t]he tort of trespass vindicates rights', whereas 'the law of negligence offers damages as compensation for harm' (*An Introduction to Tort Law* (Oxford 2006) at 148). Yet another way to capture the difference is to say that negligence is a 'loss-based' tort whereas torts actionable *per se* are 'rights-based'.

We can see this difference in function if we consider the core elements of the tort of negligence. To establish negligence and recover damages for loss the claimant must prove four elements:

1. The claimant must prove that they suffered material loss. Thus, it is commonly said that damage is the 'gist' of the negligence action. But not just any loss will do, it must be a type of loss that is 'actionable' or recognized as recoverable through the tort of negligence. Typically actionable loss is limited to physical damage, to the person or to property, albeit psychological harm and economic loss may in narrowly confined circumstances ground a claim. If the defendant's actions have left the claimant no worse off than they otherwise would have been, there can be no claim.

2. The defendant must have owed the claimant a 'duty of care'. This is a core concept that we will return to later. For the moment it suffices to observe that such duties are

only recognized in certain circumstances. As such, the duty concept operates as a 'control device' delineating the circumstances in which a defendant may be liable for damages where they act carelessly.

3. Not only must a duty be owed, but the defendant must have breached that duty. The typical standard for breach is the objective standard of the reasonable person: all that is required of the defendant is that they take reasonable care not to harm others. Thus, one can only possibly be held liable for causing another loss where one has not taken reasonable care. On the other hand, one cannot be liable, even if one inflicted loss on another, if one took reasonable care.

4. There must be a causal relationship between the breach of the duty and the loss suffered by the claimant. Even if one owed a duty, and breached that duty, one may only be liable if one's lack of care was the cause of the claimant's losses. Various tests are applied to determine causation, however, we need not get into them here.

Thus, as is readily apparent, the 'structure' of the negligence action is rather different from that of the vindicatory torts. In particular, the claimant must prove actual loss in order to mount a claim, whereas vindicatory torts are actionable *per se* and one may recover substantial damages despite not having proven any loss. Another core difference is that liability is strict for torts actionable *per se*—the defendant may be held liable for interfering with basic interests despite being blameless—whereas liability in negligence depends on proof of fault, that is, the claimant must prove the defendant did not take reasonable care; if the defendant was not blameworthy then they cannot be liable. These differences reflect the distinct concerns of the different types of claim: negligence performs a compensatory role, it is concerned to compensate losses caused by another's lack of care, whereas vindicatory torts are concerned to afford strong protection to basic rights regardless of proof of loss or the defendant's blameworthiness.

Thus, negligence is a very different type of tort from vindicatory torts. However, in considering how it applies to public entities, the starting point is, as for the torts actionable *per se*, the principle of equality. In principle negligence applies in the same way to public bodies as it does to private individuals who negligently inflict harm on others. Thus, if a careless driver hits you while you are crossing the street, it shall make no difference for the purposes of recovery that the car was owned by the Ministry of Transport and the driver was carrying out official duties at the time. As Lord Hoffmann observed in *Stovin* v. *Wise* [1996] AC 923 at 946G, 'in the absence of express statutory authority, a public body is in principle liable for torts in the same way as a private person.'

However, tensions and difficulties have arisen where claimants claim that an authority has acted negligently in exercise of statutory discretions, and also where the claimant alleges not that the authority has caused harm through a positive act, but rather that it should be held liable for a negligent failure to act, *ie* an omission. It is to these two 'flashpoints' that we now turn.

15.3.3 Negligence and statutory discretion: preliminaries

One of the most controversial issues across the entire field of public authority liability is whether and in what circumstances courts ought to impose negligence liability on public authorities for harm caused through exercises of statutory discretion.

This issue is characterized by a fundamental clash of competing concerns. On the one hand, is a concern to ensure individual justice, *ie* that those harmed through public authority negligence ought to be compensated for those losses. For example, it has been said that 'the public policy consideration that has the first claim on the loyalty of the law is that wrongs should be remedied and very potent considerations are required to override that policy' (*X v. Bedfordshire CC* [1994] 2 WLR 554 at 571). There are also, of course, wider public interests potentially served by imposing liability on authorities for harm negligently inflicted in the exercise of statutory discretion including that liability may deter careless exercises of discretion and improve the general standard of public administration, while such damages claims may facilitate public accountability for bad decisions.

On the other hand are concerns that tell against imposition of liability. There are three principal types of concern in this regard.

First, courts are cautious about scrutinizing the exercise of statutory discretions for constitutional and institutional reasons. If the court were to recognize that an authority owed a duty of care in the context of exercise of a statutory discretion, it would—in adjudicating any claim of negligence—be required to judge breach. In adjudicating breach the court would be required to determine whether the defendant authority's exercise of discretion was 'reasonable'. In negligence, reasonableness means reasonableness in the ordinary sense of the word. This is obviously a lower threshold than the *Wednesbury* standard of reasonableness which courts have traditionally applied to assess the legality of statutory exercises of discretion in judicial review. This is, *prima facie* at least, problematic because courts are constitutionally and institutionally ill-equipped to judge the substantive merits of executive action. On the other hand, there are reasons why courts should not be so reticent. First, the judgement is one over whether the authority took reasonable *care*, not the merits of an administrative decision *per se*. Second, as we saw in ch 8, the tests governing substantive review are no longer limited to *Wednesbury* irrationality. Courts now, under emergent tests of proportionality, go far further in judging the substance of executive decisions than they used to. Third, it is doubtful whether this sort of concern should ever completely preclude the possibility of negligence liability given courts are capable of deferring to executive judgments, where it is right and proper to defer, as they do in judicial review.

The second consideration that tells against imposition of liability is that courts are concerned not to undermine the statutory scheme in the context of which public powers are exercised. Generally it is the case that Parliament has not, itself, decided to create rights of action within the relevant statute. Rather, Parliament's concern in creating statutory schemes which confer powers of decision upon public officials is typically to fulfil some public goal, such as immigration control, defence of the realm, education, or provision of welfare. Courts worry that if they are to superimpose on such a statutory scheme a set of private duties owed to specific individuals this will create a conflict of duties for the decision-maker: they will be pulled in two different directions, towards ensuring due regard for the individual on the one hand, and on the other pursuing the public interest. It would be contrary to parliamentary intention for the courts to impose duties in direct conflict with the statutory duties Parliament has set for the decision-maker. However, typically these sorts of irreconcilable conflicts do not arise. A more common concern is that imposing duties of care in negligence on decision-makers may unhelpfully distract them or impede them from pursuit of the public goals, as in pursuing public goals they will have to ensure that they give due regard to those who may be harmed through exercises of public power. However, this seems relatively uncontroversial from a judicial review perspective given developments in substantive review; it is relatively common for courts today to hold that decision-makers must give due regard to individual rights and interests in exercising public power, and only trespass upon them if they have good reasons for doing so in the public interest.

Third, imposition of negligence liability in respect of exercises of statutory discretion may give rise to policy concerns of the type discussed at 15.1. These include fears of a flood of claims, draining of public resources, and chilling effects.

This clash of concerns has typically played out at the duty of care stage of the analysis, and, as such, duty of care cases will be our focus. Thus, the court will consider the foregoing array of concerns in determining whether the public defendant owes a duty of care when they exercise particular statutory powers. As such, resolution of this clash of concerns will be of an all or nothing nature. The balance of concerns may come down on the side of recognizing a duty of care, so that damages may in principle be recovered for negligence in the course of exercise of statutory powers (assuming the other elements of the negligence action are fulfilled). Or the balance of factors will come down on the side of excluding a duty of care, in which case there shall be no chance of recovering losses caused by negligent exercise of the relevant power.

Some have argued that an alternative approach is possible and preferable. That is that instead of considering these various considerations at the duty stage, or exclusively at the duty stage, they could be taken into account at the breach stage on a case-by-case basis. This approach has the benefit of nuance. Rather than completely ousting the prospect of negligence liability in the context of particular statutory powers, by refusing to recognize that the authority can ever owe a duty of care in exercise of those powers, the courts could instead take a more liberal approach to recognizing duties and mediate the clash of concerns at the breach stage. For example, when courts judge whether professionals, such as doctors or lawyers, have exercised reasonable care for the purposes of the breach inquiry, they afford a degree of deference to professional judgement: *Bolam* v. *Friern Hospital Management Committee* [1957] 1 WLR 582. It is not clear why the same approach could not be taken to the breach inquiry as it applies to professional exercises of judgement by public officials. Further, many of the policy-type concerns discussed earlier are in general weighed on a case-by-case basis at the breach stage already. For example, in determining whether the reasonable person should have taken a particular precaution or not, the court will often weigh on the one hand the degree and likelihood of harm if the precaution were not taken versus the cost and other burdens of taking the precautionary measure. If the harm likely to result from not taking the relevant precaution is minimal, but the cost of taking the precautionary measure is high, the defendant's failure to take the relevant precaution will not entail a breach of duty.

QUESTION

- What might be the drawbacks of moving the balancing of interests from the duty stage to the breach stage?

15.3.4 Negligence and statutory discretion: the case law

Thus, the courts have principally sought to regulate the bounds of public authority liability in negligence via the duty of care concept. In order to keep liability within what the judges consider to be acceptable limits, given the concerns discussed in the previous section, the courts have adopted two principal techniques for limiting when duties arise in exercise of statutory discretion. First, they may add additional hurdles or control devices to the ordinary tests governing when duties of care arise, so that authorities are afforded a degree of special protection from liability not applicable to other persons. Second, within the ordinary legal framework governing when duties of care arise, the courts might give weight to considerations particular to the context in which the claim is made. Albeit the case law is not characterized by a high degree of coherence or consistency of approach, the general trend is in favour of the second technique. Such approach accords more closely with the principle of equality, as it involves applying the ordinary tests of liability.

Duty of care: the ordinary tests

There is no single general principle governing when duties of care arise: there is no 'universal formula or yardstick', 'single general principle', or 'blueprint' (*Michael* v. *Chief Constable of South Wales* [2015] UKSC 2, [2015] 1 AC 1732 at [103], [106]). Rather, the court will consider a number of relevant considerations, with none of these considerations given *a priori* weight in the calculus. A general test emerges from the seminal House of Lords decision in *Caparo Industries plc* v. *Dickman* [1990] 2 AC 605, which courts will generally apply, albeit even this test is not definitive and only intended as guidance (*Caparo* at 617–18): '[A] set of fairly blunt tools' (*Customs and Excise Commissioners* v. *Barclays Bank plc* [2006] UKHL 28, [2007] 1 AC 181 at [71]).

According to the *Caparo* test, the considerations which a court should consider fall into two broad categories. First, there are considerations relating to the parties. One consideration is whether the type of harm suffered by the claimant was reasonably foreseeable. If it was not then the defendant could not have been expected to take steps to avoid it. A further consideration is proximity. This is a difficult concept to define, however, broadly it implicates an inquiry into the nature and closeness of the relationship between the parties. The closer the relationship then the stronger will be the argument that the defendant was appropriately placed to take care to avoid harm to the claimant; on the other hand it may be more difficult to establish a duty of care where the claimant and defendant have only an arm's length relationship.

Second, the court will ask whether recognizing a duty of care is fair, just, and reasonable. This element implicates a fairly open-ended inquiry. Even the courts have observed that it 'means little more than the court should only impose a duty of care if it considers it right to do so' (*An Informer* v. *A Chief Constable* [2012] EWCA Civ 197, [2013] QB 579 at [58]). Generally the courts will, at this stage of the inquiry, consider a range of wider public policy considerations that go beyond the relationship between the parties. These policy concerns include the types of concerns discussed at 15.1, such as concerns over chilling effects or a flood of claims. The court will also consider policy arguments in favour of liability, including whether imposing a duty of care will promote safety and greater precaution among a class of defendants, so as to reduce the incidence of injuries.

Having taken into account these considerations the courts will decide whether on balance a duty should be recognized. The courts need only undertake this enterprise when a claimant seeks to argue for recognition of a novel duty of care. Once a duty has been established then future claimants will simply be able to invoke that established duty of care. Thus, for example, there are established categories of duty, including the duty one motorist owes to other motorists to drive responsibly, the duty an employer owes their employees to ensure a safe workplace, and the duty a doctor owes their patient to exercise due skill and care.

Additional control devices

Thus, we now have an understanding of the ordinary principles governing whether a duty of care shall arise. Let us then consider those cases where courts have placed additional hurdles in the way of a claimant who seeks to establish that an authority owes a duty of care in exercise of their statutory powers. On such an approach the claimant must not only make out the *Caparo* tests, but must also prove additional elements to establish a duty.

One such extra hurdle erected from the 1970s onwards was that before a duty could possibly arise, and the defendant potentially be held liable in negligence, the claimant would have to prove that the defendant had exercised their statutory discretion unlawfully in public law terms. Put another way, *intra vires* administrative action could not found liability. In this way liability in negligence was subordinated to judicial review concepts. Thus, in the formative decision of *Home Office* v. *Dorset Yacht Co Ltd* [1970] AC 1004 at 1069, Lord Diplock said that it was a 'condition precedent' for a duty to arise in the context of a statutory discretion that the defendant must have exercised that discretion *ultra vires*. He elaborated (at 1067–8):

> Parliament has entrusted to the department or authority charged with the administration of the statute the exclusive right to determine the particular means within the limits laid down by the statute by which its purpose can best be fulfilled. It is not the function of the court, for which it would be ill-suited, to substitute its own view of the appropriate means for that of the department or authority by granting a remedy by way of a civil action at law to a private citizen adversely affected by the way in which the discretion has been exercised. Its function is confined in the first instance to deciding whether the act or omission complained of fell within the statutory limits imposed upon the department's or authority's discretion. Only if it did not would the court have jurisdiction to determine whether or not the act or omission, not being justified by the statute, constituted an actionable infringement of the plaintiff's rights in civil law.

Where a public officer's decision rests on a consideration and weighing of the risks that their decision may cause individual harm and also the general public interests for which their powers must be exercised 'there is no criterion by which a court can assess where the balance lies between the weight to be given to one interest and that to be given to another' (at 1067). It was 'for practical reasons of this kind'—*ie* that the judges were not institutionally well placed to judge such matters—'that over the past century the public law concept of ultra vires has replaced the civil law concept of negligence as the test of the legality, and consequently of the actionability, of acts or omissions of government departments or public authorities done in the exercise of a discretion conferred upon them by Parliament as to the means by which they are to achieve a particular public purpose' (at 1067).

Lord Reid (at 1031) also singled out exercise of statutory discretion as a special case:

> [T]here may, and almost certainly will, be errors of judgment in exercising such a discretion and Parliament cannot have intended that members of the public should be entitled to sue in respect of such errors. But there must come a stage when the discretion is exercised so carelessly or

> unreasonably that there has been no real exercise of the discretion which Parliament has con-
> ferred. The person purporting to exercise his discretion has acted in abuse or excess of his power.
> Parliament cannot be supposed to have granted immunity to persons who do that.

Lord Reid did not endorse Lord Diplock's proposition that the administrative action had to be *ultra vires* before liability in negligence could be imposed. However, he did rest his approach on one ground of *ultra vires*: Lord Reid effectively erected the *Wednesbury* test as a threshold criterion for establishing liability: 'In my view, this decision could only be upheld if it could be said that the failure of those authorities to deal with the situation was so unreasonable as to show that they had been guilty of a breach of their statutory duty and that that had caused the loss suffered by the plaintiff.' In setting this high threshold Lord Reid not only relied on parliamentary intent but also factors which suggested the court should accord the decision-maker leeway: '[R]esponsible authorities have a difficult and delicate task', and 'there is much room here for differences of opinion and errors of judgment' as to how clashes of interests implicated by exercise of a statutory decision-making function should be resolved (at 1031).

  X (Minors) v. *Bedfordshire County Council* [1995] 2 AC 633 involved claims that the defendant public authorities negligently carried out, or failed to perform, statutory duties imposed on them to protect children from child abuse, and claims that authorities failed to carry out statutory duties in relation to children with special educational needs. Lord Browne-Wilkinson, giving the lead speech, endorsed a special threshold for discretion cases, saying (at 736):

> It is clear both in principle and from the decided cases that the local authority cannot be liable in
> damages for doing that which Parliament has authorised. Therefore if the decisions complained
> of fall within the ambit of such statutory discretion they cannot be actionable in common law.
> However if the decision complained of is so unreasonable that it falls outside the ambit of the
> discretion conferred upon the local authority, there is no a priori reason for excluding all common
> law liability.

Thus, of Lord Diplock's and Lord Reid's approaches in *Dorset Yacht*, he preferred Lord Reid's. Of Lord Diplock's general *ultra vires* threshold he said (at 736):

> For myself, I do not believe that it is either helpful or necessary to introduce public law concepts
> as to the validity of a decision into the question of liability at common law for negligence. In public
> law a decision can be ultra vires for reasons other than Wednesbury unreasonableness ... (e.g.
> breach of the rules of natural justice) which have no relevance to the question of negligence.
> Moreover it leads, in my judgment mistakenly, to the contention that claims for damages for neg-
> ligence in the exercise of statutory powers should for procedural purposes be classified as public
> law claims and therefore ... should be brought in judicial review proceedings.

One senses that underpinning the prioritization of Lord Reid's approach is a concern to avoid casting the bounds of public authority liability too wide. If *ultra vires* in general was the relevant condition precedent then a minor procedural error or failure to comply with a technical statutory requirement could open up liability. However, instead to require the claimant to demonstrate that the exercise of discretion was one so unreasonable that no reasonable decision-maker could have come to it, sets the bar for liability exceptionally high. Thus, under the approach in *X* a claimant would, to establish a duty of care, need to prove the exercise of discretion was *Wednesbury* irrational, and then go on to argue that a duty arises under the ordinary *Caparo* tests.

This might be considered a restrictive approach in itself. But Lord Browne-Wilkinson went on to elaborate a further 'justiciability' limit on when a duty could arise in the context of exercise of a statutory discretion, which he rested on a distinction between 'policy' and 'operational' matters (this distinction first being formulated by Lord Wilberforce in *Anns v. Merton London Borough Council* [1978] AC 728 at 754). The more that matters raised by a particular exercise of discretion implicated matters of policy, the less likely the matters would be ones the court could properly adjudicate upon—and no duty could possibly arise if the courts could not adjudicate the relevant matters. On the other hand, the closer the matters raised are to being operational in nature—that is, decisions and acts done to implement a given policy—the more likely the court will be able to adjudicate the claim. (We shall return to this (fraught) distinction later.) Thus, in *X*, Lord Browne-Wilkinson summarized the governing principles as follows (at 738):

> Where Parliament has conferred a statutory discretion on a public authority, it is for that authority, not for the courts, to exercise the discretion: nothing which the authority does within the ambit of the discretion can be actionable at common law. If the decision complained of falls outside the statutory discretion, it *can* (but not necessarily will) give rise to common law liability. However, if the factors relevant to the exercise of the discretion include matters of policy, the court cannot adjudicate on such policy matters and therefore cannot reach the conclusion that the decision was outside the ambit of the statutory discretion. Therefore a common law duty of care in relation to the taking of decisions involving policy matters cannot exist.

Note that even if the matters raised are towards the operational end of the spectrum, so that the court can adjudicate on them, the claimant must still prove that the exercise of discretion was *Wednesbury* unreasonable before a duty may possibly arise—and then go on to argue that the ordinary *Caparo* criteria are fulfilled.

Thus, following *X* it was clearly established in the case law that for a claimant to prove that a duty of care is owed by a public defendant in the exercise of statutory discretions, special control devices, additional to the ordinary *Caparo* tests, applied, and these included that the claimant must prove the defendant had acted outwith the ambit of its statutory powers through a wholly irrational exercise of discretion. This approach came under scrutiny in the following case.

Barrett v. *Enfield London Borough Council* [2001] 2 AC 550
House of Lords

The appellant (claimant) alleged that, while still an infant, he was mistreated by his mother, and was, as a result, placed under the care of the respondent (defendant). The appellant alleged (*inter alia*) that the respondent owed (and had breached) a common law duty of care in the practical implementation of its obligations under various statutes concerning the protection and welfare of children. The common law duty was said to include a duty to act *in loco parentis* and to provide the appellant with the standard of care which could be expected of a reasonable parent. The appellant alleged that this duty had been breached by the respondent's failures (*inter alia*) to consider whether he could be placed with his half-sister on a long-term basis; have regard to his health and hygiene; find a proper home for him (he was accommodated with various foster parents and in children's homes but was not adopted); properly manage his meetings with his mother after 11 years of separation; and to provide him with appropriate psychiatric treatment. The appellant alleged that, if these breaches of duty had not occurred, then he would not 'on the balance of probabilities have left the care of the Local Authority as a young man of eighteen years with no family or attachments whatsoever, who had developed a psychiatric illness causing him to self-harm and who had been involved in criminal activities'. The Court of Appeal had struck out the appellant's claim.

Lord Slynn

[Having referred to certain speeches in *Home Office* v. *Dorset Yacht Co Ltd* [1970] AC 1004 and *Anns* v. *Merton London Borough Council* [1978] AC 728, his Lordship said:] On this basis, if an authority acts wholly within its discretion—i.e. it is doing what Parliament has said it can do, even if it has to choose between several alternatives open to it, then there can be no liability in negligence. It is only if a plaintiff can show that what has been done is outside the discretion and the power, then he can go on to show the authority was negligent. But if that stage is reached, the authority is not exercising a statutory power, but purporting to do so and the statute is no defence.

This, however, does not in my view mean that if an element of discretion is involved in an act being done subject to the exercise of the overriding statutory power, common law negligence is necessarily ruled out. Acts may be done pursuant and subsequent to the exercise of a discretion where a duty of care may exist—as has often been said even knocking a nail into a piece of wood involves the exercise of some choice or discretion and yet there may be a duty of care in the way it is done. Whether there is an element of discretion to do the act is thus not a complete test leading to the result that, if there is, a claim against an authority for what it actually does or fails to do must necessarily be ruled out.

Another distinction which is sometimes drawn between decisions as to 'policy' and as to 'operational acts' sounds more promising. A pure policy decision where Parliament has entrusted the decision to a public authority is not something which a court would normally be expected to review in a claim in negligence. But again this is not an absolute test. Policy and operational acts are closely linked and the decision to do an operational act may easily involve and flow from a policy decision. Conversely, the policy is affected by the result of the operational act (see *Reg v Chief Constable of Sussex, Ex parte International Trader's Ferry Ltd* [1998] 3 WLR 1260).

Where a statutory power is given to a local authority and damage is caused by what it does pursuant to that power, the ultimate question is whether the particular issue is justiciable or whether the court should accept that it has no role to play. The two tests (discretion and policy/ operational) to which I have referred are guides in deciding that question. The greater the element of policy involved, the wider the area of discretion accorded, the more likely it is that the matter is not justiciable so that no action in negligence can be brought. It is true that Lord Reid and Lord Diplock in the *Dorset Yacht* case accepted that before a claim can be brought in negligence, the plaintiffs must show that the authority is behaving so unreasonably that it is not in truth exercising the real discretion given to it. But the passage I have cited was, as I read it, obiter, since Lord Reid made it clear that the case did not concern such a claim, but rather was a claim that Borstal officers had been negligent when they had disobeyed orders given to them. Moreover, I share Lord Browne-Wilkinson's reluctance [expressed in *X (Minors)*] to introduce the concepts of administrative law into the law of negligence, as Lord Diplock appears to have done. But in any case I do not read what either Lord Reid or Lord Wilberforce in the *Anns* case (and in particular Lord Reid) said as to the need to show that there has been an abuse of power before a claim can be brought in negligence in the exercise of a statutory discretion as meaning that an action can never be brought in negligence where an act has been done pursuant to the exercise of the discretion. A claim of negligence in the taking of a decision to exercise a statutory discretion is likely to be barred, unless it is wholly unreasonable so as not to be a real exercise of the discretion, or if it involves the making of a policy decision involving the balancing of different public interests; acts done pursuant to the lawful exercise of the discretion can, however, in my view be subject to a duty of care, even if some element of discretion is involved. Thus accepting that a decision to take a child into care pursuant to a statutory power is not justiciable, it does not in my view follow that, having taken a child into care, an authority cannot be liable for what it or its employees do in relation to the child without it being shown that they have acted in excess of power. It may amount to an excess of power, but that is not in my opinion the test to be adopted: the test is whether the conditions in the *Caparo* case have been satisfied.

In *Rowling v Takaro Properties Ltd* [1988] AC 473 Lord Keith of Kinkel, said at p 501 in giving the opinion of the Privy Council in relation to the policy/operational test:

> 'They incline to the opinion, expressed in the literature, that this distinction does not provide a touchstone of liability, but rather is expressive of the need to exclude altogether those cases in which the decision under attack is of such a kind that a question whether it has been made negligently is unsuitable for judicial resolution, of which notable examples are discretionary decisions on the allocation of scarce resources or the distribution of risks: see especially the discussion in *Craig on Administrative Law* (1983), pp 534–538. If this is right, classification of the relevant decision as a policy or planning decision in this sense may exclude liability; but a conclusion that it does not fall within that category does not, in their Lordships' opinion, mean that a duty of care will necessarily exist.'

Both in deciding whether particular issues are justiciable and whether if a duty of care is owed, it has been broken, the court must have regard to the statutory context and to the nature of the tasks involved. The mere fact that something has gone wrong or that a mistake has been made, or that someone has been inefficient does not mean that there was a duty to be careful or that such duty has been broken. Much of what has to be done in this area involves the balancing of delicate and difficult factors and courts should not be too ready to find in these situations that there has been negligence by staff who largely are skilled and dedicated.

Yet although in my view the staff are entitled to rely mutatis mutandis on the principle stated in *Bolam v Friern Hospital Management Committee* [1957] 1 WLR 582, the jurisdiction to consider whether there is a duty of care in respect of their acts and whether it has been broken is there. I do not see how the interests of the child can be sufficiently protected otherwise ...

... In the present case, the allegations which I have summarised are largely directed to the way in which the powers of the local authority were *exercised*. It is arguable (and that is all we are concerned with in this case at this stage) that if some of the allegations are made out, a duty of care was owed and was broken. Others involve the exercise of a discretion which the court may consider to be not justiciable—e.g. whether it was right to arrange adoption at all, though the question of whether adoption was ever considered and if not, why not, may be a matter for investigation in a claim of negligence. I do not think it right in this case to go through each allegation in detail to assess the chances of it being justiciable. The claim is of an on-going failure of duty and must be seen as a whole. I do not think that it is the right approach to look only at each detailed allegation and to ask whether that in itself could have caused the injury. That must be done but it is appropriate also to consider whether the cumulative effect of the allegations, if true, could have caused the injury.

Nor do I accept that because the court should be slow to hold that a child can sue its parents for negligent decisions in its upbringing that the same should apply necessarily to all acts of a local authority. The latter has to take decisions which parents never or rarely have to take (e.g. as to adoption or as to an appropriate foster parent or institution). In any case, in respect of some matters, parents do have an actionable duty of care.

On the basis that [X (Minors)] does not conclude the present case in my view it is arguable that at least in respect of some matters alleged both individually and cumulatively a duty of care was owed and was broken ...

Lord Hutton

... I do not think that the speech of Lord Browne-Wilkinson in the *Bedfordshire* case precludes a ruling in the present case that although the decisions of the defendant were within the ambit of its statutory discretion, nevertheless those decisions did not involve the balancing of the type of policy considerations which renders the decisions non-justiciable.

... I consider that where a plaintiff claims damages for personal injuries which he alleges have been caused by decisions negligently taken in the exercise of a statutory discretion, and pro-vided that the decisions do not involve issues of policy which the courts are ill-equipped to adjudicate upon, it is preferable for the courts to decide the validity of the plaintiff's claim by applying directly the common law concept of negligence than by applying as a preliminary test the public law concept of *Wednesbury* unreasonableness to determine if the decision fell outside the ambit of the statutory discretion. I further consider that in each case the court's resolution of the question whether the decision or decisions taken by the defendant in exercise of the statu-tory discretion are unsuitable for judicial determination will require ... a careful analysis and weighing of the relevant circumstances.

Lord Browne-Wilkinson delivered a speech in favour of allowing the appeal. Lords Nolan and Steyn agreed with the speeches of Lords Browne-Wilkinson, Slynn, and Hutton. Appeal allowed.

That *ultra vires* as a condition precedent to negligence claims *vis-à-vis* statutory discretions was abandoned in *Barrett* was placed beyond doubt by Lord Slynn (with whose judgment all the other Law Lords agreed) in *Phelps* v. *Hillingdon London Borough Council* [2001] 2 AC 619 at 653 where he stated:

This House decided in *Barrett v. Enfield London Borough Council* [2001] 2 AC 550 that the fact that acts which are claimed to be negligent are carried out within the ambit of a statutory discretion is not in itself a reason why it should be held that no claim for negligence can be brought in respect of them. It is only where what is done has involved the weighing of competing public interests or has been dictated by considerations on which Parliament could not have intended that the courts would substitute their views for the views of Ministers or officials that the courts will hold that the issue is non-justiciable on the ground that the decision was made in the exercise of a statutory discretion.

In *Barrett*, Lord Hutton acknowledged that such an approach might appear inconsistent with that of Lord Browne-Wilkinson in *X*. However, Lord Hutton said that certain dicta of Lord Browne-Wilkinson that could (in isolation) be taken to establish a general rule to the effect that *ultra vires* is a condition precedent had to be viewed within their particular con-text in the *X* case, as dealing with cases where the nature of the issues meant that the court was ill-equipped to adjudicate on matters lying within the discretion of the defendant. This is a polite way of saying that the Law Lords in *Barrett*, and then *Phelps*, effected a departure from—and effectively overruled—the precedent in *X*.

We also note that in *Phelps* the downgrading of the importance of the policy/operational distinction was confirmed. Lord Clyde, for example, said: '[T]his kind of classification does not appear to provide any absolute test for determining whether the case is one which allows or excludes a duty of care. The classification may provide some guide towards identifying some kinds of case where a duty of care may be thought to be inappropriate' (at 673–4). Lord Nicholls stated that he had 'reservations about any attempt to draw a sharp-edged distinction between 'policy' decisions and 'operational' decisions', recalling earlier criticisms of the distinction he had expressed in *Stovin* v. *Wise* [1996] AC 923 at 938–9.

Two observations are pertinent. First, the move in *Barrett* and *Phelps* away from the unitary *Wednesbury* standard as an invariable condition precedent for a duty of care to arise is consonant with contemporary trends within judicial review. It is no longer the case on judicial review that the bounds of executive discretion are necessarily circumscribed by the deferential *Wednesbury* standard. There has been a general move, particularly in the last few years, away from an invariably deferential standard towards a context-sensitive approach, so that the intensity of review may be more or less intense than the traditional *Wednesbury* standard, but in general more intense (see ch 8). Linked to this—and perhaps this is a different way of saying the same thing—the view of justiciability that characterized Lord Browne-Wilkinson's speech in *X* was a product of its time. His view of the judiciary's role in scrutinizing the substance of executive action was a very limited one, which was consistent with the judiciary's approach to assessing the substance of executive action on judicial review. But as judicial review has developed over time the judiciary's role in this respect has greatly expanded. When the courts in judicial review proceedings are routinely assessing the proportionality of executive action, it would seem rather odd for the courts in negligence to maintain that they must be constrained by the high *Wednesbury* standard. Similarly, judicial review of the substance of executive decisions does not necessarily rest on a bright line distinction between policy and operational matters. In certain circumstances—for example where basic rights are at stake—it might be quite legitimate for courts to scrutinize the substance of policy matters, and at other times this may be inapt, depending on the circumstances of the case. Thus, the move in *Barrett* and *Phelps* to only treat the policy/operational divide as one, non-determinative factor in assessing whether it is appropriate for the court to adjudicate on the matters raised in negligence brings the conception of the judicial role in negligence into line with the contemporary conception of the judicial role that prevails in public law.

Second, we see some progress towards moving matters of 'justiciability' away from the duty stage of the analysis to the breach stage. As such, that an executive discretion entails assessment of delicate and complex matters and the striking of difficult balances between conflicting interests does not require the court to completely oust liability. Rather, these considerations can be taken into account in evaluating whether the decision-maker has deviated from accepted standards and thus breached their duty of care; in the language of judicial review, the court can afford the decision-maker 'due deference' in assessing whether they took reasonable care or not.

Consider the approach in *Phelps*. In that case a claimant sought to hold a local council vicariously liable for the allegedly negligent acts of psychologists employed by the council to advise on certain matters. Lord Slynn dismissed justiciability issues in a couple of sentences, and then proceeded to apply the ordinary *Caparo* tests to assess whether a duty arose. However, that justiciability issues did not stand as a bar to recognizing a duty of care did not mean that Lord Slynn did not consider the types of concerns that justiciability tests are concerned to address, only that such matters would be addressed in a more nuanced way at the breach stage. His Lordship drew attention to the fact that, given that the psychologists are professionals, the test for breach would be whether they exercised 'the ordinary skill of an ordinary competent man exercising that particular art' (at 655). He observed, 'recognition of the duty of care does not of itself impose unreasonably high standards' and '[t]he difficulties of the tasks involved and of the circumstances under which people have to work in this area must also be borne fully in mind' (at 655). In other words, the courts will afford professionals exercising specialist judgements a margin of discretion. Lord Clyde expressed similar views (at 672–3). For Lord Bingham in *D* v. *East Berkshire Community NHS Trust* [2005] UKHL 23, [2005] 2 AC 373 at [49], this 'shift [was] welcome, since the concept of duty has proved itself a somewhat blunt instrument for dividing claims which ought reasonably to lead to recovery from claims which ought not'. But note that some scepticism towards moving justiciability-type concerns to the breach stage remains: *D* at [94], [137].

Applying the ordinary tests

Thus, there has been a general retreat from application of additional controls at the duty stage, which may prevent a duty arising without consideration of the ordinary *Caparo* criteria. As such, the law now more closely adheres to the principle of equality. However, it is nonetheless possible that in application of the ordinary *Caparo* tests, considerations particular to public authorities may militate against recognition of a duty. Such considerations tend to arise as an aspect of the 'fair, just and reasonable' inquiry; that is, the third limb of the *Caparo* test. It is open to question whether this practice breaches the equality principle. The better view is that it does not. First, the considerations arise within the ordinary framework of the *Caparo* tests, which apply to private persons. Second, in any context, whether the defendant is private or public, it is possible that considerations specific to that context will be taken into account as part of the fair, just, and reasonable inquiry. If duties are denied it is not merely on the basis that the defendant is 'public', or on the basis of special tests which afford added protection to authorities which do not apply where the parties are private persons. Rather, if a duty is denied it is because the balance of relevant considerations simply tells against imposition of a duty.

One principle which has particular application to authorities is the 'conflict of duty' principle. In the wake of *Barrett* and *Phelps*, and seemingly irreconcilably with the decision in *X*, it has emerged as clear that a local authority can owe a duty of care to a child at danger of abuse (see the litigation in *D* v. *East Berkshire Community NHS Trust* [2003] EWCA Civ 1151, [2004] QB 558, on appeal [2005] UKHL 23, [2005] 2 AC 373)—*though not to the parent in such a case*. The basis for this latter point is to avoid the danger of a conflict between the interests of the child and the parent if a suspect: recognition of a 'duty of care to the parents would cut across the duty of care to the children' (at [110]). A similar principle was applied in *Jain* v. *Trent Strategic Health Authority* [2009] UKHL 4, [2009] 1 AC 853 at [28], Lord Scott (with whose speech the other members of the House agreed) saying:

> [W]here action is taken by a state authority under statutory powers designed for the benefit of or protection of a particular class of persons, a tortious duty of care will not be held to be owed by the state authority to others whose interests may be adversely affected by an exercise of the statutory power. The reason is that the imposition of such a duty would or might inhibit the exercise of the statutory powers and be potentially adverse to the interests of the class of persons

the powers were designed to benefit or protect, thereby putting at risk the achievement of their statutory purpose.

Thus, if imposition of a duty would fundamentally cut across the statutory scheme, it should not be recognized as this would be to frustrate Parliament's intent, and Parliament's intent is sovereign and must be abided by. However, one would expect such cases of irreconcilable conflict to be relatively uncommon.

More common has been the denial of duties of care on the basis of public policy considerations, under the umbrella of the fair, just, and reasonable inquiry. Consideration of public policy concerns within the duty calculus is not unique to public authority cases; policy concerns are typically taken into account in any novel duty claim. However, it may be that the specific policy considerations taken into account vary from context to context, so that policy concerns that arise in public authority cases may differ from those that arise in other types of case—but equally similar types of concerns might arise across cases involving private and public defendants.

The line of cases beginning with *Hill* v. *Chief Constable of West Yorkshire* [1989] AC 53 provide a striking illustration of judicial invocation of policy concerns to deny duties of care, specifically in the context of police investigations. The claimant argued that the police owed a duty of care to potential victims of crimes, to exercise reasonable care in the investigation of crime; the corollary of recognition of such a duty would be that an individual harmed by a criminal could potentially sue the police for their negligent failure to apprehend the criminal earlier and thus prevent the claimant's injuries. Lord Keith, giving the lead speech, considered the factual circumstances were not such that a duty could arise. But in addition he offered more general policy reasons against recognition of such a duty of care (at 63):

[I]n my opinion there is another reason why an action for damages in negligence should not lie against the police in circumstances such as those of the present case, and that is public policy … Application of [the fair, just and reasonable] stage is … capable of constituting a separate and independent ground for holding that the existence of liability in negligence should not be entertained. Potential existence of such liability may in many instances be in the general public interest, as tending towards the observance of a higher standard of care in the carrying on of various different types of activity. I do not, however, consider that this can be said of police activities. The general sense of public duty which motivates police forces is unlikely to be appreciably reinforced by the imposition of such liability so far as concerns their function in the investigation and suppression of crime. From time to time they make mistakes in the exercise of that function, but it is not to be doubted that they apply their best endeavours to the performance of it. In some instances the imposition of liability may lead to the exercise of a function being carried on in a detrimentally defensive frame of mind. The possibility of this happening in relation to the investigative operations of the police cannot be excluded. Further it would be reasonable to expect that if potential liability were to be imposed it would be not uncommon for actions to be raised against police forces on the ground that they had failed to catch some criminal as soon as they might have done, with the result that he went on to commit further crimes. While some such actions might involve allegations of a simple and straightforward type of failure—for example that a police officer negligently tripped and fell while pursuing a burglar—others would be likely to enter deeply into the general nature of a police investigation, as indeed the present action would seek to do. The manner of conduct of such an investigation must necessarily involve a variety of decisions to be made on matters of policy and discretion, for example as to which particular line of inquiry is most advantageously to be pursued and what is the most advantageous way to deploy the available resources. Many such decisions would not be regarded by the courts as appropriate to be called in question, yet elaborate investigation of the facts might be necessary to ascertain whether or not this was so. A great deal of police time, trouble and expense might be expected to have to be put into the preparation of the defence to the action and the attendance of witnesses at the trial. The result would be a significant diversion of police manpower and attention from their most important function, that of the suppression of crime. Closed investigations would require to be reopened and retraversed, not with the object of bringing any criminal to justice but to ascertain whether or not they had been competently conducted. I therefore consider that Glidewell L.J., in his judgment in the Court of Appeal [1988] Q.B. 60, 76 in the present case, was right to take the view that the police were immune from an action of this kind on grounds similar to those which in *Rondel v. Worsley* [1969] 1 A.C. 191 were held to render a barrister immune from actions for negligence in his conduct of proceedings in court.

This 'Hill principle' has been adhered to relatively consistently since: see, *eg Brooks v. Commissioner of Police of the Metropolis* [2005] UKHL 24, [2005] 1 WLR 1495; *Smith v. Chief Constable of Sussex Police* [2008] UKHL 50, [2009] 1 AC 225.

However, one senses a growing degree of scepticism over judicial reliance on policy arguments to deny duties of care.

First, there is a growing, if sporadic, recognition that the public policy which has the first claim upon the law's loyalty is that wrongs should be remedied, and that weighty considerations will be required before departure from this starting point will be countenanced: *X (Minors)* at 663, 749; *Jones v. Kaney* [2011] UKSC 13, [2011] 2 AC 398 at [113]; *Crawford Adjusters v. Sagicor General Insurance (Cayman) Ltd* [2013] UKPC 17, [2014] AC 366 at [73]; *Smith* at [56]; *Gorringe v. Calderdale Metropolitan Borough Council* [2004] UKHL 15, [2004] 1 WLR 1057 at [2]. In *Spring* v. *Guardian Assurance plc* [1995] 2 AC 296 at 326, Lord Lowry said if an otherwise 'perfectly good cause of action' is to be defeated on public policy grounds this may only be in 'clear cases in which the potential harm to the public is incontestable', and whether the harm is likely to occur 'must be determined on tangible grounds instead of on mere generalities', the burden of proof lying with those who seek to evade enforcement of a liability that *prima facie* exists.

Second, there are real doubts as to whether courts are well placed institutionally to assess the strength of policy factors. In turn this suggests courts should focus on what they do best—deciding cases according to legal principle—or at least, consonant with Lord Lowry's approach in *Spring*, courts should approach public policy factors with extreme caution. For example, courts have very little hope of predicting accurately whether recognition of a duty in one case will lead to a flood of claims. Equally, they have little chance of accurately gauging whether imposition of a duty will lead to officials taking greater care in performance of their duties, lead to overly defensive administrative practices, or have no effect whatsoever. Empirical studies of the impacts of liability suggest there is no straightforward interrelationship between imposition of liability, and rates of claiming or impacts on administrative behaviour. Further, courts seldom rely on any evidence in analysing public policy arguments, such as studies of the impacts of liability on administrative behaviour. Rather, judicial assessment of public policy concerns tends to be based more on gut instinct or speculation. As such, it is not uncommon to find in the same case one judge claiming recognition of a duty will have detrimental effects on public administration and another judge claiming the effects will be positive, neither basing their views in evidence. This is not a particularly rigorous approach to decision-making. (On these points see further Varuhas, *Damages and Human Rights* (Oxford 2016) ch 6).

Following on from years of academic criticism of such practice it seems courts are increasingly cognizant of their limitations in this regard. For example, in *Michael* v. *Chief*

Constable of Wales [2015] UKSC 2, [2015] AC 1732, in which the claimant sought to establish a duty of care on the police to protect individuals against known threats of physical harm, Lord Toulson, giving the majority judgment, said (at [121]):

> As to the argument that imposition of … liability … should improve the performance of the police in dealing with cases of actual or threatened domestic violence, the court has no way of judging the likely operational consequences of changing the law of negligence in the way that is proposed. Mr Bowen and Ms Monaghan were critical of statements in the *Hill* case [1989] AC 53 and other cases that the imposition of a duty of care would inevitably lead to an unduly defensive attitude by the police. Those criticisms have force. But the court would risk falling into equal error if it were to accept the proposition, on the basis of intuition, that a change in the civil law would lead to a reduction of domestic violence or an improvement in its investigation. Failures in the proper investigation of reports of violence or threatened violence can have disciplinary consequences … and it is speculative whether the addition of potential liability at common law would make a practical difference at an individual level to the conduct of police officers and support staff. At an institutional level, it is possible to imagine that it might lead to police forces changing their priorities by applying more resources to reports of violence or threatened violence, but if so, it is hard to see that it would be in the public interest for the determination of police priorities to be affected by the risk of being sued.

In a minority judgment, Lord Kerr, invoking Lord Lowry's comments in *Spring*, entreated that the courts should not deny duties of care on the basis of defendant claims of negative consequences unsupported by any evidence (at [182]–[186]).

In respect of the continuing relevance of policy-type concerns it is worth noting the Supreme Court decision in *Smith v. Ministry of Defence* [2013] UKSC 41, [2014] AC 52. The case concerned claims that the Ministry of Defence owed duties of care to military personnel in combat roles, variously to provide them with suitable equipment, and also suitable technology to protect against the risk of 'friendly fire'. The claims were brought by the families of soldiers who had died in the Iraq War or by soldiers injured in the course of duty. The defendant applied to have the claims struck out on the basis that it would not be fair, just, and reasonable to impose a duty of care to protect against loss of life and injury in the circumstances of the case, relying on the types of public policy arguments deployed in the *Hill* line of cases. However, a majority of the Court refused to strike out the claims on this basis (at [97]–[100]). The majority emphasized that duties of care in respect of military activities should not be ruled out in a blanket manner on the basis of the *Hill* public policy considerations because the circumstances of different cases varied greatly. As such, whether public policy considerations militated against recognition of a duty of care must depend on detailed analysis of evidence and thus the facts of the case, which could only take place at full trial.

The refusal to strike out these claims on the basis of public policy considerations is again suggestive of the weakening influence of such concerns, an increased unwillingness to create blanket zones of immunity from challenge, and the growing view that evidence is necessary before ruling out a duty on policy grounds. The decision is particularly striking as the conduct of military operations is, one would think, a far more contentious context in which to impose a duty of care than the investigation of crime by the police. Yet *Hill*-type reasoning was insufficient to convince the Court to rule out that a duty may arise. The boldness of the decision, and the seeming break from the approach in the *Hill* line of cases, is reflected in the strength of the dissents. For example, Lord Mance, dissenting, warned that

the majority approach would likely lead to the 'judicialisation of war' as 'extensive litigation' would become 'almost inevitable after, as well as quite possibly during and even before,
any active service operations undertaken by the British army' (at [150]). The minority considered the *Hill*-type policy arguments were directly engaged by this case and would have
struck out the claims: *eg* at [128]–[136] *per* Lord Mance, at [167]–[170] *per* Lord Carnwath.

On the other hand, it is important to note that the majority did not hold that a duty
would arise on the facts; rather the matter had to be determined at trial on the basis of
evidence. Further, Lord Hope, for the majority, recorded that '[g]reat care needs to be taken
not to subject those responsible for decisions at any level that affect what takes place on the
battlefield, or in operations of the kind that were being conducted in Iraq after the end of
hostilities, to duties that are unrealistic or excessively burdensome' (at [99]). Yet, for the reasons already discussed, the decision not to strike out the claim is highly significant in itself.

Lastly, if a claimant is able to 'fit' their claim within a pre-existing, established duty category then they may be able to avoid proving a duty from scratch and thus the fair, just, and
reasonable inquiry under the *Caparo* tests. For example, it is well established that employers
owe their employees a duty of care to provide a safe work place, including taking reasonable steps to protect their health. The courts have shown a willingness to recognize that
public authorities owe the same duty to their employees, so long as recognition of such
duty does not create a conflict with performance of statutory duties: see *Connor* v. *Surrey
County Council* [2010] EWCA Civ 286, [2011] QB 429 and *Smith* v. *Ministry of Defence*
[2012] EWCA Civ 1365, [2013] 2 WLR 27 (as we have seen, a majority of the Supreme Court,
on appeal from this decision, agreed with the Court of Appeal that the claim should not be
struck out but did not follow the Court of Appeal in explicitly premising its decision on the
employer–employee relationship between the defendant Ministry and claimant military
personnel).

QUESTION

- Do you agree with the argument that courts should not in general deny duties of
  care on the basis of public policy arguments, given the courts lack the institutional
  capacity to rigorously analyse such arguments?

15.3.5 Negligence and omissions

From the foregoing analysis it is apparent that within the law of torts adherence to the equality principle has generally promoted protection of individual interests in the face of public
power, and where that fundamental principle has been deviated from, authorities have been
afforded special protections and the goal of individual protection set back. However, negligence liability for omissions is one field where commentators have argued that strict adherence to the equality principle has held back the goal of individual protection.

The general rule at common law is that there is no liability for mere omissions, that is,
there shall be no liability in situations where harm is caused by an individual failing to
do an act (albeit there are limited situations in which such liability may arise). A classic
example of an omission is standing by and not helping another person who is in danger.
The law of tort generally imposes no liability for such omission. Most negligence cases
involve liability for harm caused through positive acts performed with a lack of due care,

often referred to as misfeasance—to be contrasted with nonfeasance, or omissions. Classic examples of misfeasance, for which liability will be imposed, include driving badly, or performing a surgical procedure poorly.

The principal rationales typically given for not imposing liability for omissions were traversed by Lord Hoffmann in *Stovin* v. *Wise* [1996] AC 923, 943–4. One core reason is the protection of individual liberty; our freedom of action would begin to be seriously eroded if we owed multifarious positive duties to consider the interests of others, under pain of damages. There is also the 'why pick me?' argument: 'A duty to prevent harm to others or to render assistance to a person in danger or distress may apply to a large and indeterminate class of people who happen to be able to do something.' It would seem arbitrary to single out one person of a large class of people who omitted to take any action, and require them to pay damages. Lord Hoffmann also articulates an economic argument: 'In economic terms, the efficient allocation of resources usually requires an activity should bear its own costs. If it benefits from being able to impose some of its costs on other people (what economists call "externalities,") the market is distorted because the activity appears cheaper than it really is. So liability to pay compensation for loss caused by negligent conduct acts as a deterrent against increasing the cost of the activity to the community and reduces externalities. But there is no similar justification for requiring a person who is not doing anything to spend money on behalf of someone else.'

The problem with applying the omissions rule to public authorities in unmodified form is that these rationales either do not apply or lose much of their strength where the defendant is an authority. As to the freedom argument, statutory bodies do not have an intrinsic interest in freedom as ordinary individuals do. Public authorities are created to fulfil specific purposes, and bestowed with power specifically so as to fulfil those purposes, for the benefit of the community. In other words, they very often exist for the very purpose of conferring benefits, and failure to act would often entail dereliction of their duty. This feature of authorities also bears on the 'why pick me?' argument. A police officer who fails to act to protect an individual who is being beaten up on the street does not have this argument open to them; they are specifically conferred with powers so as to act in such situations, so there is a very good reason to pick them out for failing to act. Similarly, we expect an ambulance to come when we ring for help because ambulance services are specifically constituted to help those in need. The economic rationale does not work very well when applied to public authorities because public authorities are often created to provide public goods which, within economic theory, defy analysis according to the precepts of microeconomics. In any case, why should the economic value of wealth maximization trump other values such as protection of important individual interests in health and well-being? More generally, albeit we cannot get into the matter here, it is seriously open to question whether the distinction between acts and omissions is a sound distinction, and if sound whether it is a good basis on which to rest decisions over liability. For example, when one causes a road traffic accident by failing to apply the brakes is the cause of the accident an *omission* to apply the breaks or the *act* of driving badly?

Of course there may be good arguments in a specific context against imposing liability for omissions on public authorities, such as the argument that imposition of such liability may undermine an authority's ability to fulfil its statutory functions. However, this is not an argument specific to cases of omissions liability, nor is it an argument for ruling out omissions liability in general—it is rather one factor that can be weighed in the *Caparo* calculus alongside other relevant factors within the particular context of the case.

In *Stovin* Lord Hoffmann acknowledged at least some of these points, saying (at 946):

It is certainly true that some of the arguments against liability for omissions do not apply to public bodies like a highway authority. There is no 'why pick on me?' argument: as Kennedy L.J. said, [[1994] 1 WLR 1124] at p. 1139, the highway authority alone had the financial and physical resources, as well as the legal powers, to eliminate the hazard [on the highway]. But this does not mean that the distinction between acts and omissions is irrelevant to the duties of a public body or that there are not other arguments, peculiar to public bodies, which may negative the existence of a duty of care.

Despite the rationales for the rule against omissions liability being open to question when applied to public authorities, the courts have tended to set their face against imposing negligence liability for omissions upon public authorities. Thus, in *Stovin* itself (the facts of which are stated, in outline, in our next excerpt) it was argued that a highway authority, in failing to exercise a statutory power, had breached a common law duty of care which, it was argued, the authority owed to the claimant. Lord Hoffmann (with whom a majority agreed) considered no duty could arise and that (at 953)

the minimum preconditions for basing a duty of care upon the existence of a statutory power, if it can be done at all, are, first, that it would in the circumstances have been irrational not to have exercised the power, so that there was in effect a public law duty to act, and secondly, that there are exceptional grounds for holding that the policy of the statute requires compensation to be paid to persons who suffer loss because the power was not exercised.

Against this background, we turn to the next case.

Gorringe v. *Calderdale Metropolitan Borough Council* [2004] UKHL 15, [2004] 1 WLR 1057
House of Lords

Lord Hoffmann

[7] On 15 July 1996, on a country road in Yorkshire, Mrs Denise Gorringe drove her car head-on into a bus. It was hidden behind a sharp crest in the road until just before she reached the top. When she first caught sight of it, a curve on the far side may have given her the impression that it was actually on her side of the road. At any rate, she slammed on the brakes and at 50 miles an hour the wheels locked and the car skidded into the path of the bus. Mrs Gorringe suffered brain injuries severely affecting various bodily functions including speech and movement.

[8] On the face of it, the accident was her own fault. It was certainly not the fault of the bus driver. He was driving with proper care when Mrs Gorringe skidded into him. But she claims in these proceedings that it was the fault of the local authority, the Calderdale Metropolitan Borough Council. She says that the council caused the accident by failing to give her proper warning of the danger involved in driving fast when you could not see what was coming. In particular, the Council should have painted the word 'SLOW' on the road surface at some point before the crest. There had been such a marking in the past, but it disappeared, probably when the road was mended seven or eight years before ...

[His Lordship went on to reject a claim based on s 41 of the Highways Act 1980 (duty to maintain the highway) and continued:]

[17] The alternative claim is for common law negligence. Mr Wingate-Saul QC, who appeared for Mrs Gorringe, accepts that in the absence of the statutory provision to which I shall shortly refer, such a claim would be hopeless ...

[18] ... Mr Wingate-Saul submits that a common law duty has been created by (or 'in parallel' with) section 39(2) and (3) of the Road Traffic Act 1988:

'(2) Each local authority must prepare and carry out a programme of measures designed to promote road safety. ...

(3) Without prejudice to the generality of sub-section (2) above, in pursuance of their duty under that sub-section each local authority—(a) must carry out studies into accidents arising out of the use of vehicles on roads ... within their area, (b) must, in the light of those studies, take such measures as appear to the authority to be appropriate to prevent such accidents, including the dissemination of information and advice relating to the use of roads, the giving of practical training to road users or any class or description of road users, the construction, improvement, maintenance or repair of roads for which they are the highway authority ... and other measures taken in the exercise of their powers for controlling, protecting or assisting the movement of traffic on roads ...'

[19] These provisions, with their repeated use of the word 'must', impose statutory duties. But they are typical public law duties expressed in the widest and most general terms: compare section 1(1) of the National Health Service Act 1977: 'It is the Secretary of State's duty to continue the promotion ... of a comprehensive health service ...'. No one suggests that such duties are enforceable by a private individual in an action for breach of statutory duty [breach of statutory duty is the name given to actions for damages created under statute, either explicitly or by implication from the scheme and terms of the Act; such an action is distinct from the tort of negligence]. They are enforceable, so far as they are justiciable at all, only in proceedings for judicial review.

[20] Nevertheless, Mr Wingate-Saul submits that section 39 casts a common law shadow and creates a duty to users of the highway to take reasonable steps to carry out the necessary studies and take the appropriate measures. At any rate, their conduct in compliance with these duties must not be such as can be described as 'wholly unreasonable'. The judge found that it was unreasonable for the council not to have painted a warning sign on the road and Potter LJ thought that he was entitled to come to this conclusion.

[21] The effect of statutory powers and duties on the common law liability of a highway authority was considered by this House in *Stovin v Wise* [1996] AC 923. Mrs Wise emerged from a side road and ran down Mr Stovin because she was not keeping a proper look-out. When he sued her for damages, she (or rather her insurance company) joined the Norfolk County Council as a third party because the visibility at the intersection was poor and they said that the council should have done something to improve it. The council had statutory powers which would have enabled the necessary work to be done and there was evidence that the relevant officers had decided in principle that it should be done, but they had not got round to doing it.

[22] The decision of the majority was that the council owed no private law duty to road users to do anything to improve the visibility at the intersection. 'Drivers of vehicles must take the highway network as they find it' (p 958). The statutory power could not be converted into a common law duty. I pointed out in my speech that the council had done nothing which, apart from statute, would have attracted a common law duty of care. It had done nothing at all. The only basis on which it was a candidate for liability was that Parliament had entrusted it with general responsibility for the highways and given it the power to improve them and take other measures for the safety of their users.

[23] Since the existence of these statutory powers is the only basis upon which a common law duty was claimed to exist, it seemed to me relevant to ask whether, in conferring such powers, Parliament could be taken to have intended to create such a duty. If a statute actually imposes a duty, it is well settled that the question of whether it was intended to give rise to a private right of action [pursuant to the tort of breach of statutory duty] depends upon the construction of the statute: see *R v Deputy Governor of Parkhurst Prison, Ex parte Hague* [1992] 1 AC 58, 159, 168–171. If the statute does not create a private right of action [which could found an action for breach of statutory duty], it would be, to say the least, unusual if the mere existence of the statutory duty could generate a common law duty of care.

[24] For example, in *O'Rourke v Camden London Borough Council* [1998] AC 188 a homeless person sued for damages on the ground that the council had failed in its statutory duty to provide him with accommodation. The action was struck out on the ground that the statute did not create a private law right of action. ...

[25] In the absence of a right to sue for breach of the statutory duty itself, it would in my opinion have been absurd to hold that the council was nevertheless under a common law duty to take reasonable care to provide accommodation for homeless persons whom it could reasonably foresee would otherwise be reduced to sleeping rough. (Compare *Stovin v Wise* at pp 952–953.) And the argument would in my opinion have been even weaker if the council, instead of being under a duty to provide accommodation, merely had a power to do so.

[26] This was the reasoning by which the majority in *Stovin v Wise* came to the conclusion that the council owed no duty to road users which could in any circumstances have required it to improve the intersection. But misunderstanding seems to have arisen because the majority judgment goes on to discuss, in the alternative, what the nature of such a duty might have been if there had been one. It suggests that it would have given rise to liability only if it would have been irrational in a public law sense not to exercise the statutory power to do the work. And it deals with this alternative argument by concluding that, on the facts, there had been no breach even of such a duty. The suggestion that there might exceptionally be a case in which a breach of a public law duty could found a private law right of action has proved controversial and it may have been ill-advised to speculate upon such matters.

[27] The approach of the minority, in a speech by Lord Nicholls of Birkenhead, was very different. He thought that the statutory powers had invested the highway authority with general responsibilities which could in appropriate circumstances give rise to a common law duty of care. He referred to a number of circumstances which might singly or cumulatively justify the existence of a duty and he said that on the facts there had been such a duty and that the council had been in breach ...

[32] Speaking for myself, I find it difficult to imagine a case in which a common law duty can be founded simply upon the failure (however irrational) to provide some benefit which a public authority has power (or a public law duty) to provide ...

[33] [In a previous case (*Larner* v. *Solihull Metropolitan Borough Council* [2001] LGR 255) to which Lord Hoffmann had referred, the Court of Appeal, relying on *Stovin* v. *Wise*, had accepted that there might be exceptional circumstances where a duty of care could arise out of s 39 of the Road Traffic Act 1988. Lord Hoffmann continued:] The Court of Appeal in *Larner* ... went on to hold that on the facts there had been no breach of duty. But the consequences of the door which it left open can be seen in the present case. The Council was obliged to give discovery of documents relating to its accident studies undertaken pursuant to section 39(3)(a), the decision-making process by which it decided what measures in the light of such studies were appropriate and the steps which had been taken to implement such measures. It was heavily criticised by the judge for the lateness and insufficiency of such discovery. The trial lasted six days, during which the Council called a number of its officers as witnesses and was criticised for not calling enough. The simple facts which I have summarised at the beginning of this speech seem to have disappeared from view in the enthusiasm for a hostile judicial inquiry into the Council's

administration. If section 39 continues to provoke investigations of this nature, much of the road safety budget will be consumed in the cost of litigation. ...

[38] My Lords, I must make it clear that this appeal is concerned only with an attempt to impose upon a local authority a common law duty to act based solely on the existence of a broad public law duty. We are not concerned with cases in which public authorities have actually done acts or entered into relationships or undertaken responsibilities which give rise to a common law duty of care. In such cases the fact that the public authority acted pursuant to a statutory power or public duty does not necessarily negative the existence of a duty. A hospital trust provides medical treatment pursuant to the public law duty in the National Health Service Act 1977, but the existence of its common law duty is based simply upon its acceptance of a professional relationship with the patient no different from that which would be accepted by a doctor in private practice. The duty rests upon a solid, orthodox common law foundation and the question is not whether it is created by the statute but whether the terms of the statute (for example, in requiring a particular thing to be done or conferring a discretion) are sufficient to exclude it. The law in this respect has been well established since *Geddis v Proprietors of the Bann Reservoir* (1878) 3 App Cas 430.

[Lord Hoffmann then explained the *Dorset Yacht* case, *Barrett*, and *Phelps* along the lines of this reasoning, and continued:]

[44] My Lords, in this case the council is not alleged to have done anything to give rise to a duty of care. The complaint is that it did nothing. Section 39 is the sole ground upon which it is alleged to have had a common law duty to act. In my opinion the statute could not have created such a duty. The action must therefore fail. For these reasons and those of my noble and learned friends Lord Scott of Foscote, Lord Rodger of Earlsferry and Lord Brown of Eaton-under-Heywood, I would dismiss the appeal.

Lords Scott, Rodger, and Brown delivered speeches in which they agreed with each other's speeches and with that of Lord Hoffmann. Lord Steyn delivered a speech in which he agreed that there was no duty of care in this case.

With respect, the reasoning in this case is rather odd. The gist of the reasoning seems to be that one needs to find some positive intention to create a duty of care in negligence within the legislation before a duty of care in negligence can be owed. This is confused. The approach taken—searching for a positive intention to create legal rights—is the general approach taken in discerning whether a cause of action for breach of statutory duty arises under an Act. This tort is a distinct tort from negligence. It arises where Parliament explicitly creates a cause of action for damages under a statute, or where a court finds that a cause of action is impliedly created under a statute. It is a fundamental error to conflate that tort with the law of negligence, or at least it is not clear why the absence of an action for breach of a statutory duty should logically lead to the exclusion of a duty of care in negligence. Whether a duty of care arises in negligence is governed by separate tests at common law, principally the *Caparo* tests. To determine whether a duty arises one must follow those tests. It may be that one finds that imposition of a duty of care would create a conflict with performance of a statutory duty or that the statute explicitly or impliedly immunizes the statutory body from liability in negligence. However, it makes no sense to search through the terms of a statute looking for a positive intention to create a duty of care in negligence, when a duty of care is a creature of the *common law*, governed by *common law* tests—namely, those in *Caparo* and associated principles such as the rule against omissions liability. This also reveals the error in Lord Hoffmann's reasoning that a common law duty of care cannot arise simply out of the existence of a statutory duty. This is a strange way to frame the matter. The question, surely, is whether a duty arises given a consideration of established common law principles in negligence. Lord Steyn appeared to make a similar point in *Gorringe* when he said (at [3]):

> [I]n a case founded on breach of statutory duty the central question is whether from the provisions and structure of the statute an intention can be gathered to create a private law remedy? In contradistinction in a case framed in negligence, against the background of a statutory duty or power, a basic question is whether the statute excludes a private law remedy? An assimilation of the two enquiries will sometimes produce wrong results.

Another dubious feature of the approach in *Gorringe* is that Lord Hoffmann endorses his analysis in *Stovin* that before a duty of care could ever arise which requires a statutory body to exercise its statutory powers—*ie* a duty under which an authority may be liable for an omission—the failure to act must have been one which was *Wednesbury* irrational. It is difficult to see how this approach can be reconciled with *Barrett* and *Phelps*.

None of the foregoing critique should be taken to suggest that it would have been right to have recognized a duty of care on the facts of *Gorringe*. The point is that the correct tests ought to have been applied, and that if the true reasons for not imposing a duty related to policy concerns implicated by imposing liability for omissions, or simply the common law rule against imposing liability for omissions, then Lord Hoffmann ought to have focused attention on establishing those arguments as opposed to the curious search for a positive parliamentary intention to recognize a duty of care. Of course Lord Hoffmann did reinforce his reasoning with some ancillary policy arguments, for example that if damages claims in negligence continued to be brought in respect of s 39 of the Road Traffic Act 'much of the road safety budget will be consumed in the cost of litigation'. However, it is highly questionable whether courts should concern themselves with bare questions of the allocation of resources, *ie* whether money is best spent on redressing injury or funding frontline services. As we saw earlier, there is a growing recognition of the institutional and constitutional limits of the courts in this respect. Notwithstanding the shortcomings of the reasoning in *Gorringe*, and the arguments traversed earlier that the rationales for the rule against omissions do not read across well to the public authority context, Lord Hoffmann in *Gorringe* nonetheless asserted: 'I find it difficult to imagine a case in which a common law duty can be founded simply upon the failure (however irrational) to provide some benefit which a public authority has power (or a public law duty) to provide' (at [32]). In light of *Gorringe* it seems public authorities may only potentially be liable in negligence where they make things worse, as opposed to where they fail to make things better. Thus, the net effect of *Gorringe*, putting aside the actual reasoning employed in that case, is that the general rule against imposing liability for omissions applies more or less equally to public defendants as it does to other defendants.

The failure to control the acts of third parties is an aspect of omissions. In common with the general reluctance to impose liability for omissions, it is generally the case—albeit there are some exceptions—that courts will not impose duties of care which require a defendant to control the acts of third parties. In recent years the House of Lords/Supreme Court has had to grapple with claims asserting a duty of care in negligence on the police to take positive steps to protect individuals from threats of harm from third parties where the threat is known to the police and the risk is pressing. In *Van Colle v. Chief Constable of Hertfordshire* [2008] UKHL 50, [2009] 1 AC 225, a majority of the House of Lords declined to recognize such a duty, albeit Lord Bingham, dissenting, would have. Various reasons for denying the duty were given by members of the majority including invocation of the *Hill* principle—no duty should be imposed on the police towards victims in the investigation and prevention of crime—and that imposition of the claimed duty would unduly skew police time and resources towards cases with similar facts to *Van Colle*.

The matter came before the Supreme Court again in *Michael* v. *Chief Constable of South Wales* [2015] UKSC 2, [2015] AC 1732 (noted McBride (2016) 32 *Professional Negligence* 14, and see Tofaris and Steel [2016] *CLJ* 128). The Court, by a majority, again refused to recognize a duty. But this time the majority turned to the rule against imposing liability for omissions as the principal basis for denying a duty.

Michael made a 999 call to the police in the middle of the night. She told the operator that her former partner had found her at her home in bed with another man, that he had assaulted Michael, and taken the other man away, and he had said that he would return to assault her further. She told the operator that she believed her former partner would kill her. Through a series of technological mishaps and human errors the call was wrongly graded as a lower priority meaning the police response time would be longer than it would otherwise be. The police not having arrived, Michael made another 999 call—at a time after the time when the police would have reached her if the call had been properly graded—and screaming could be heard. The call priority was upgraded. However, by the time the police arrived, approximately 16 minutes after they would have arrived if the first call had been properly graded, Michael had been murdered by her former partner.

A majority of the Supreme Court held that the police had not owed Michael a duty of care in these circumstances to take reasonable steps to safeguard her life. Lord Toulson, delivering the majority judgment, rested his conclusion on the orthodox common law rule against imposing liability for omissions. In this regard, the decision steadfastly conforms to the principle of equality, maintaining the same liability principles for private citizen and public authority alike. Lord Toulson said:

> [97] English law does not as a general rule impose liability on a defendant (D) for injury or damage to the person or property of a claimant (C) caused by the conduct of a third party (T): *Smith v Littlewoods Organisation Ltd* [1987] AC 241, 270 (a Scottish appeal in which a large number of English and Scottish cases were reviewed). The fundamental reason, as Lord Goff explained, is that the common law does not generally impose liability for pure omissions. It is one thing to require a person who embarks on action which may harm others to exercise care. It is another matter to hold a person liable in damages for failing to prevent harm caused by someone else ...
>
> [101] These general principles have been worked out for the most part in cases involving private litigants, but they are equally applicable where D is a public body. *Mitchell v Glasgow City Council* [2009] AC 874 is a good example. The victim and T were secure tenants of D and were next door neighbours. On a number of occasions T directed abuse and threats to kill at the victim, which he reported to D. D summoned T to a meeting and threatened him with eviction, without informing the victim. Soon afterwards T attacked the victim, causing fatal injuries. The victim's widow and daughter sued D, alleging negligence in failing to warn him of the meeting with T. The House of Lords held that D was not under a duty to do so, applying the principle in *Smith v Littlewoods Organisation Ltd* [1987] AC 241.

He then observed that the categories of negligence are never closed and it was in principle possible for the courts to make an exception to the general rule against omissions. However, he did not consider there was a good reason for doing so. Having traversed the authorities, and focused particular attention on *Stovin* and *Gorringe*, he concluded that orthodoxy ought to be maintained:

[112] In some areas, such as health care and education, public authorities provide services which involve relationships with individual members of the public giving rise to a recognised duty of care no different from that which would be owed by any other entity providing the same service. A hospital and its medical staff owe the same duty to a patient whether they are operating within the National Health Service or the private sector: *Roe v Minister of Health* [1954] 2 QB 66. A school and its teaching staff owe the same duty to a pupil whether it is a state main-tained school or a private school: *Woodland v Swimming Teachers Association* [2014] AC 537. Educational psychology is a professional service linked to education. An organisation which pro-vides an educational psychology service, and its educational staff, owe the same duty to a pupil whether they are operating in the public or the private sector: *X (Minors) v Bedfordshire County Council* [1995] 2 AC 633.

[113] Besides the provision of such services, which are not peculiarly governmental in their nature, it is a feature of our system of government that many areas of life are subject to forms of state con-trolled licensing, regulation, inspection, intervention and assistance aimed at protecting the general public from physical or economic harm caused by the activities of other members of society (or sometimes from natural disasters). Licensing of firearms, regulation of financial services, inspections of restaurants, factories and children's nurseries, and enforcement of building regulations are ran-dom examples. To compile a comprehensive list would be virtually impossible, because the systems designed to protect the public from harm of one kind or another are so extensive.

[114] It does not follow from the setting up of a protective system from public resources that if it fails to achieve its purpose, through organisational defects or fault on the part of an individual, the public at large should bear the additional burden of compensating a victim for harm caused by the actions of a third party for whose behaviour the state is not responsible. To impose such a burden would be contrary to the ordinary principles of the common law.

[115] The refusal of the courts to impose a private law duty on the police to exercise reasonable care to safeguard victims or potential victims of crime, except in cases where there has been a representation and reliance, does not involve giving special treatment to the police. It is consist-ent with the way in which the common law has been applied to other authorities vested with powers or duties as a matter of public law for the protection of the public. Examples at the highest level include *Yuen Kun Yeu v Attorney General of Hong Kong* [1988] AC 175 and *Davis v Radcliffe* [1990] 1 WLR 821 (no duty of care owed by financial regulators towards investors), *Murphy v Brentwood District Council* [1991] 1 AC 398 (no duty of care owed to the owner of a house with defective foundations by the local authority which passed the plans), *Stovin v Wise* [1996] AC 923 and *Gorringe v Calderdale Metropolitan Borough Council* [2004] 1 WLR 1057 (no duty of care owed by a highway authority to take action to prevent accidents from known hazards).

[116] The question is therefore not whether the police should have a special immunity, but whether an exception should be made to the ordinary application of common law principles which would cover the facts of the present case.

Note that in the last paragraph Lord Toulson emphasizes that the Court, by denying a duty on the basis of the omissions rule, is not affording the police a special exception or immunity from liability, but rather applying the same ordinary rules to the authority as would be applied to an ordinary citizen. It is also worth noting in passing that Lord Toulson did not invoke nor apply the *Wednesbury* irrationality test propounded by Lord Hoffmann in *Stovin* and *Gorringe*.

Lord Kerr and Lady Hale registered strong dissents. They made a number of arguments for why a duty ought to be recognized and against the line of reasoning adopted by the majority. For present purposes the most pertinent aspect of these dissents is Lord Kerr's argument against straightforward application of the rule against omissions liability (see also Lady Hale's judgment at [197]):

[177] In support of [the rule against imposed liability for omissions], Lord Hoffmann in *Stovin v Wise* [1996] AC 923, 943 said that 'it is less of an invasion of an individual's freedom for the law to require him to consider the safety of others in his actions than to impose on him a duty to rescue or protect'. As Tofaris and Steel point out, it is at least questionable that it is particularly valuable to the freedom of a public authority that it should be permitted to negligently fail to assist an identified individual who is at serious risk of physical injury. Whereas it is arguable that a private individual's freedom has an intrinsic value in its contribution to an autonomous life, the value of the state's freedom is instrumental and lies in the contribution that it makes to the fulfilment of its proper functions.

[178] The common law has historically required professional persons carrying out a skill to do so with reasonable care and skill ...

[179] In all manner of fields if the professional fails to act with due care and skill, he or she will be liable for any damage caused by their negligence. This is justified on a number of bases; it attributes loss to the person who caused it, it locates compensation in the private rather than the public sector and, arguably, the risk of litigation improves professional standards. The principle holds true even where professionals are acting in response to the acts of third parties. Other emergency services can be liable for their negligence, provided there is sufficient foreseeability and proximity: *Kent v Griffiths* [2001] QB 36 and *Capital & Counties plc v Hampshire County Council* [1997] QB 1004. Why should the police be an exception?

[180] It is suggested that the police do not constitute an exception but rather that their exemption from liability is soundly based on the general rule that omissions to act (particularly in relation to actions of a third party) do not give rise to liability. I propose, however, that the cases on which this claim rests can be readily distinguished. In none of those cases was there a proximity of relationship such as exists in the present appeal. In *Stovin v Wise* [1996] AC 923, for instance, the failure to improve safety at a road junction affected all who used the particular stretch of road. Likewise in *Gorringe v Calderdale Metropolitan Borough Council* [2004] 1 WLR 1057. Long-standing or pre-existing dangers stemming from actions of third parties such as in *Murphy v Brentwood District Council* [1991] AC 398 or the geography of the local area which lay within the public authority's power to mitigate are of a completely different character from cases where a specific, urgently communicated threat has been imparted to the public agency with the resources and capacity (as well as the public duty) to protect the individual against whom it has been made.

[181] To find that no duty arises on the facts of the present case requires us to squarely confront the consequence of such a finding. If the police force had not negligently downgraded the urgency of Ms Michael's call, on the facts as they are known at present, it is probable that she would still be alive. While the police are not responsible for the actions of her murderer, if the allegations made against them are established, police played a direct, causative role in her death as a result of their negligence. If they were to be found liable for such negligence, would this be so different from the liability of the doctor of a patient who fails to provide life-saving drugs to prevent an aggressive condition in the necessary time? The police have been empowered to protect the public from harm. They should not be exempted from liability on the general common law ground that members of the public are not required to protect others from third party harm; such protection of autonomy for individuals is not appropriate for members of a force whose duty it is to provide precisely the type of protection from the harm that befell Ms Michael. This is the essential and critical obligation of the police force. Any other professional would be liable for inaction with such grievous consequences. So also should be the police.

> **QUESTIONS**
>
> - Do you find the majority or minority reasoning more persuasive?
> - It was taken for granted by the Court that *Michael* was an omissions case. Read over the facts again. Do you think this was an omissions case?

Lastly, for completeness, it is important to record that *Michael* confirms that the recognized *exceptions* to the no liability rule for omissions that apply to private defendants also apply to cases involving public defendants. Liability in respect of omissions may arise where the defendant is responsible for creating a danger; they may then be under a duty to take positive steps to ameliorate that danger, and if they omit to do so they may be liable. Another class of case is 'where D was in a position of control over T and should have foreseen the likelihood of T causing damage to somebody in close proximity if D failed to take reasonable care in the exercise of that control' (*Michael* at [99]). A duty could not arise on this basis in *Michael* as the police did not have control of Michael's former partner. A further category is where the defendant assumes responsibility for the welfare of the claimant. For a duty to arise in such cases there must be a representation by the defendant to the claimant that they will take responsibility for the claimant's well-being, and the claimant must then rely on that representation (albeit the courts have, in some contexts, more or less imputed an assumption of responsibility absent any clear representation). If the defendant then omits to fulfil their assumed responsibility for the claimant they may be liable. In *Michael*, a duty did not arise on this basis as '[t]he only assurance which the call handler gave to Ms Michael was that she would pass on the call to the South Wales Police. She gave no promise how quickly they would respond' (at [138]). In contrast, a duty was held to arise in *Kent v. Griffiths* [2001] QB 36 when an emergency call was placed for an ambulance, and the call handler gave representations that the ambulance would arrive shortly—which it did not. As the reader may surmise, there may be fine margins between cases in which a duty arises and those in which it does not.

15.3.6 Negligence and human rights

An issue which has continued to divide opinion among the Law Lords since the entry into force of the HRA is the interrelationship between negligence and human rights law. This issue has been raised squarely in a number of the cases which we have already discussed in which claimants have argued that the court ought to recognize duties on authorities to take positive steps to protect individuals, such as *Van Colle v. Chief Constable of Hertfordshire* [2008] UKHL 50, [2009] 1 AC 225; *Smith v. Ministry of Defence* [2013] UKSC 41, [2014] AC 52; and *Michael v. Chief Constable of South Wales* [2015] UKSC 2, [2015] AC 1732. An apparent tension arises between the two fields because while the courts have in general been reluctant to recognize duties to protect within the law of negligence, such duties have been recognized in human rights law.

Thus, the European Court of Human Rights' decision in *Osman v. United Kingdom* (2000) 29 EHRR 245 established that, under Article 2 (the right to life), there is a duty on public authorities to take reasonable steps to protect the life of the claimant, where the authority becomes aware or ought to be aware of a real and immediate risk to the life of the claimant from the acts of a third party. This duty was originally recognized in the context of the police, but has since been generalized by the European Court so that it could potentially apply across a range of contexts. This duty has been recognized and often applied by domestic courts under the HRA: see, *eg Rabone* v. *Pennine Care NHS Foundation Trust* [2012] UKSC 2, [2012] 2 AC 72.

In *Van Colle*, Lord Bingham, dissenting, argued that the law of negligence ought, more or less, to be brought into alignment with human rights law, and he would have held that in the law of negligence, 'if a member of the public (A) furnishes a police officer (B) with apparently credible evidence that a third party whose identity and whereabouts are known presents a specific and imminent threat to his life or physical safety, B owes A a duty to take reasonable steps to assess such threat and, if appropriate, take reasonable steps to prevent it being executed' (at [44]). As is obvious this 'liability principle' (as Lord Bingham described it), is analogous to the *Osman* duty. On the interrelationship between human rights law and negligence he said:

[58] Considerable argument was devoted to exploration of the relationship between rights arising under the Convention (in particular, the article 2 right relied on in Van Colle) and rights and duties arising at common law. Should these two regimes remain entirely separate, or should the common law be developed to absorb Convention rights? I do not think that there is a simple, universally applicable answer. It seems to me clear, on the one hand, that the existence of a Convention right cannot call for instant manufacture of a corresponding common law right where none exists: see *Wainwright v Home Office* [2004] 2 AC 406. On the other hand, one would ordinarily be surprised if conduct which violated a fundamental right or freedom of the individual did not find a reflection in a body of law ordinarily as sensitive to human needs as the common law, and it is demonstrable that the common law in some areas has evolved in a direction signalled by the Convention: see the judgment of the Court of Appeal in *D v East Berkshire Community NHS Trust* [2004] QB 558, paras 55–88. There are likely to be persisting differences between the two regimes, in relation (for example) to limitation periods and, probably, compensation. But I agree with Pill LJ in the present case [2008] HRLR 600, para 53, that 'there is a strong case for developing the common law action for negligence in the light of Convention rights' and also with Rimer LJ, at para 45, that 'where a common law duty covers the same ground as a Convention right, it should, so far as practicable, develop in harmony with it'.

Lord Brown, in the majority, held that no such duty of care should be recognized at common law. He gave a number of reasons why he considered that the law of negligence should not be developed so as to bring it into alignment with human rights law:

- Given a claim can be brought directly under the HRA 'it is quite simply unnecessary now to develop the common law to provide a parallel cause of action' (at [136]).

- Lord Brown considered that the public policy considerations of the type recognized in *Hill* militated against recognizing a duty to protect (at [136]). In response to Lord Brown's argument there is an obvious counterargument that the *Hill*-type policy arguments against imposing liability are rendered moot by the fact that a duty to protect is already imposed by human rights law. Lord Brown's response was as follows (at [137]):

True it is that the possibility of a Human Rights Act claim now to some extent weakens the value of the *Hill* principle in so far as that is intended to safeguard the police from the diversion of resources involved in having to contest civil litigation. That, however, is no good reason for mirroring the *Osman* principle by the introduction of a common law duty of care in this very limited class of case, still less for weakening the value of the *Hill* principle yet further by creating a wider duty of care.

- Lord Brown argued that an analogy between negligence and human rights law is false because 'Convention claims have very different objectives from civil actions. Where civil actions are designed essentially to compensate claimants for their losses,

Convention claims are intended rather to uphold minimum human rights standards and to vindicate those rights' (at [138]). His Lordship pointed to various differences between the types of claim to reinforce that an analogy between the fields is inapt including differences in limitation periods and in the approach to compensation as between the two fields (on which see further 15.4).

- Lord Brown considered that recognition of a duty of care in negligence would 'neither add to the vindication of the right nor be likely to deter the police from the action or inaction which risks violating it in the first place. Such deterrence must lie rather in the police's own disciplinary sanctions ... and, in a wholly exceptional case ... in criminal liability' (at [139]).
- Lord Brown also referred to the possibility that the claimant would be awarded an *ex gratia* payment under the Criminal Injuries Compensation Scheme (at [139]).

Overall while Lord Brown acknowledged that there is 'always a price to be paid by individuals denied [compensation] for public policy reasons', 'the wider public interest is best served by maintaining the full width of the *Hill* principle' (at [139]) (see also [81]–[82] *per* Lord Hope, [98]–[99] *per* Lord Phillips). Some of the arguments set out by Lord Brown are more convincing than others. One that is less convincing is the view that it is simply unnecessary to develop the law of negligence because claims can be made under the HRA. As we shall see at 15.4 it is wrong to present the HRA claim as a perfect substitute for a negligence claim, given damages under the HRA are rarely awarded and very low compared to tort standards.

In *Michael*, Lord Toulson rejected a similar argument for human rights and negligence to march hand in hand, placing heavy reliance on the majority views in *Van Colle* and invoking similar types of argument, noting that the development of negligence is simply 'not necessary to comply with articles 2 and 3' and that 'creation of such a statutory cause of action does not itself provide a sufficient reason for the common law to duplicate or extend it' (at [125], [130]). In contrast, in *Smith* (the factual background is set out in 15.3.4), Lord Hope, for the majority, gave as one reason for not striking out the claimed duties in negligence, in circumstances in which an Article 2 duty to protect was held to arise, Lord Bingham's view in *Van Colle* 'that one would ordinarily be surprised if conduct which violated a fundamental right or freedom of the individual under the Convention did not find a reflection in a body of law as sensitive to human needs as the common law' (at [98]). It is rather difficult to reconcile the contrasting views of the relevance of human rights law adopted in *Michael* and *Smith* (for further examples of such inconsistencies see 15.3.8).

QUESTION
- Do you think strict separation ought to be maintained between human rights law and the law of negligence?

15.3.7 Misfeasance in public office: its rationale and elements

Within the common law of torts the tort of misfeasance in public office is unusual in that it may only be committed by those in public office. Thus, it is as close as the common law has come to recognizing a special 'administrative tort'. As such, the tort may also be classed as an example of 'equality-plus': *ie* the common law affording individuals greater protection from loss against the acts of public officers than against the acts of private individuals.

The tort is probably best rationalized as a 'residual' or 'safety net' form of liability, ensuring compensation for someone who is injured through the exceptional act of a public official. That compensation for loss rather than protection of basic rights is the tort's basic concern is reflected in the fact that, as is the case with negligence, 'damage is the gist of the action' (*Watkins* v. *Secretary of State for the Home Department* [2006] UKHL 17, [2006] 2 AC 395 at [15], [79]); in other words, a claimant must prove some actual loss before they may bring a claim. The action is a safety net from the tort perspective, in that it may provide a route to redress against a public official for a claimant who cannot found an alternative private law cause of action for breach of one of their basic rights in physical integrity, liberty, or land. From the judicial review perspective it is a safety net in that the default position is that one cannot recover damages merely for *ultra vires* administrative action; misfeasance in public office does, however, provide a damages remedy for abuses of power in exceptional cases where an official has inflicted loss on a citizen motivated by bad faith. Thus, as Stevens has observed, misfeasance in public office is an 'exceptional form of liability' (*Torts and Rights* (Oxford 2007) 242).

Why should this exceptional form of liability apply to officials but not others? The answer seems to be that we should expect more from officials: 'The rationale of the tort is that in a legal system based on the rule of law executive or administrative power "may be exercised only for the public good" and not for ulterior and improper purposes' (*Jones* v. *Swansea City Council* [1990] 1 WLR 54, 85). We expect officials to use their office purely to serve the public interest. When an officer instead intentionally uses their position to maliciously harm citizens or knowingly acts contrary to law, this is such a shocking deviation from what we expect of public officers, and why we empower them, that the law countenances a departure from the usual rule that compensation is unavailable for maladministration. The tort may, through its operation, also serve valuable wider functions. For example, the tort may facilitate public accountability: 'There is an obvious public interest in bringing public servants guilty of outrageous conduct to book' (*Watkins* at [8]).

With the tort's basic rationale in mind, let us turn to the elements of the tort, which were considered by the House of Lords in the following case.

Three Rivers District Council v. Governor and Company of the Bank of England (No 3) [2001] UKHL 16, [2003] 2 AC 1
House of Lords

BCCI, a deposit-taking institution licensed in the UK and supervised by the Bank of England (and later the Financial Services Authority), went into liquidation in July 1991. Until April 1990, the Bank of England had been unaware of what Lord Steyn, in his speech, called the 'fraud on a vast scale perpetrated at a senior level in BCCI' and which had been the 'principal cause of [its] collapse'. The claimants—6,000 former depositors—sought damages from the Bank of England, alleging (*inter alia*) the tort of misfeasance in public office. As Lord Steyn explained, they claimed that senior officials acted in bad faith '(a) in licensing BCCI in 1979, when they knew that it was unlawful to do so; (b) in shutting their eyes to what was happening at BCCI after the licence was granted; and (c) in failing to take steps to close BCCI when the known facts cried out for action at least by the mid 80s'. On the trial of preliminary issues, it was held by Clarke J at first instance that (*inter alia*) the claim for misfeasance was unsustainable. The claimants' appeal was dismissed, whereupon they appealed to the House of Lords. This excerpt is concerned only with the misfeasance aspects of the appeal.

Lord Steyn

... The ingredients of the tort

It is now possible to consider the ingredients of the tort. That can conveniently be done by stating the requirements of the tort in a logical sequence of numbered paragraphs.

(1) The defendant must be a public officer

It is the office in a relatively wide sense on which everything depends. Thus a local authority exercising private-law functions as a landlord is potentially capable of being sued: *Jones v Swansea City Council*. In the present case it is common ground that the Bank satisfies this requirement.

(2) The second requirement is the exercise of power as a public officer

This ingredient is also not in issue. The conduct of the named senior officials of the Banking Supervision Department of the Bank was in the exercise of public functions. Moreover, it is not disputed that the principles of vicarious liability apply as much to misfeasance in public office as to other torts involving malice, knowledge or intention: *Racz v Home Office* [1994] 2 AC 45.

(3) The third requirement concerns the state of mind of the defendant

The case law reveals two different forms of liability for misfeasance in public office. First there is the case of targeted malice by a public officer i.e. conduct specifically intended to injure a person or persons. This type of case involves bad faith in the sense of the exercise of public power for an improper or ulterior motive. The second form is where a public officer acts knowing that he has no power to do the act complained of and that the act will probably injure the plaintiff. It involves bad faith inasmuch as the public officer does not have an honest belief that his act is lawful.

The distinction, and the availability of an action of the second type, was inherent in the early development of tort. [Having considered various 18th and 19th century cases, his Lordship continued:] These decisions laid the foundation of the modern tort; they established the two different forms of liability; and revealed the unifying element of conduct amounting to an abuse of power accompanied by subjective bad faith. In the most important modern case in England the existence of the two forms of the tort was analysed and affirmed: *Bourgoin SA v Ministry of Agriculture, Fisheries and Food* [1986] QB 716. Clarke J followed this traditional twofold classification. He expressly held that the two forms are alternative ways in which the tort can be committed. The majority in the Court of Appeal commented on 'a rather rigid distinction between the two supposed limbs of the tort' and observed that there was 'the need to establish deliberate and dishonest abuse of power in every case:' [2000] 2 WLR 15 at 67C–D. As a matter of classification it is certainly right to say that there are not two separate torts. On the other hand, the ingredients of the two forms of the tort cannot be exactly the same because if that were so there would be no sense in the twofold classification. Undoubtedly there are unifying features, namely the special nature of the tort, as directed against the conduct of public officers only, and the element of an abuse of public power in bad faith. But there are differences between the alternative forms of the tort and it is conducive to clarity to recognise this.

The present case is not one of targeted malice. If the action in tort is maintainable it must be in the second form of the tort. It is therefore necessary to consider the distinctive features of this form of the tort. The remainder of my judgment will be directed to this form of the tort.

The basis for the action lies in the defendant taking a decision in the knowledge that it is an excess of the powers granted to him and that it is likely to cause damage to an individual or individuals. It is not every act beyond the powers vesting in a public officer which will ground the tort. The alternative form of liability requires an element of bad faith. This leads to what was a disputed issue. Counsel for the Bank pointed out that there was no precedent in England before the present case which held recklessness to be a sufficient state of mind to ground the tort. Counsel argued that recklessness was insufficient. The Australian High Court and the

Court of Appeal of New Zealand have ruled that recklessness is sufficient: *Northern Territory v Mengel* (1995) 69 AJLR 527; *Garrett v Attorney-General* [1997] 2 NZLR 332; *Rawlinson v Rice* [1997] 2 NZLR 651. Clarke J lucidly explained the reason for the inclusion of recklessness [1996] 3 All ER 558, 581:

> 'The reason why recklessness was regarded as sufficient by all members of the High Court in *Mengel* is perhaps most clearly seen in the judgment of Brennan J. It is that misfeasance consists in the purported exercise of a power otherwise than in an honest attempt to perform the relevant duty. It is that lack of honesty which makes the act an abuse of power.'

The Court of Appeal accepted the correctness of this statement of principle: [2000] 2 WLR 15, 61G–62A. This is an organic development, which fits into the structure of our law governing intentional torts. The policy underlying it is sound: reckless indifference to consequences is as blameworthy as deliberately seeking such consequences. It can therefore now be regarded as settled law that an act performed in reckless indifference as to the outcome is sufficient to ground the tort in its second form.

   ... [D]uring the oral hearing ... counsel for the plaintiffs accepted that only reckless indifference in a subjective sense will be sufficient. This concession was rightly made. The plaintiff must prove that the public officer acted with a state of mind of reckless indifference to the illegality of his act: *Rawlinson v Rice* [1997] 2 NZLR 651. Later in this judgment I will discuss the requirement of reckless indifference in relation to the consequences of the act.

(4) Duty to the plaintiff

The question is who can sue in respect of an abuse of power by a public officer. Counsel for the Bank argued that in order to be able to claim in respect of the second form of misfeasance, there must be established 'an antecedent legal right or interest' and an element of 'proximity'. Clarke J did not enunciate a requirement of proximity. ... It would be unwise to make general statements on a subject which may involve many diverse situations. What can be said is that, of course, any plaintiff must have a sufficient interest to found a legal standing to sue. Subject to this qualification, principle does not require the introduction of proximity as a controlling mechanism in this corner of the law. The state of mind required to establish the tort, as already explained, as well as the special rule of remoteness hereafter discussed, keeps the tort within reasonable bounds. There is no reason why such an action cannot be brought by a particular class of persons, such as depositors at a bank, even if their precise identities were not known to the bank. The observations of Clarke J are correct.

   In agreed issue 4 the question is raised whether the Bank is capable of being liable for the tort of misfeasance in public office to plaintiffs who were potentially depositors at the time of any relevant act or omission of misfeasance by the Bank. The majority in the Court of Appeal and Auld LJ held that this issue is unsuitable for summary determination. In my view this ruling was correct.

(5) Causation

Causation is an essential element of the plaintiffs' cause of action. It is a question of fact. The majority in the Court of Appeal and Auld LJ held that it is unsuitable for summary determination. That is plainly correct ...

(6) Damage and remoteness

The claims by the plaintiffs are in respect of financial losses they suffered. These are, of course, claims for recovery of consequential economic losses. The question is when such losses are recoverable. It would have been possible, as a matter of classification, to discuss this question under paragraph 3 in which the required state of mind for this tort was examined. It is, however, convenient to consider it under the traditional heading of remoteness.

... The real choice is ... between the test of knowledge that the decision would probably damage the plaintiff (as enunciated by Clarke J.) and the test of reasonable foreseeability (as contended for by counsel for the plaintiffs) ...

Enough has been said to demonstrate the special nature of the tort, and the strict requirements governing it. This is a legally sound justification for adopting as a starting point that in both forms of the tort the intent required must be directed at the harm complained of, or at least to harm of the type suffered by the plaintiffs. This results in the rule that a plaintiff must establish not only that the defendant acted in the knowledge that the act was beyond his powers but also in the knowledge that his act would probably injure the plaintiff or person of a class of which the plaintiff was a member. In presenting a sustained argument for a rule allowing recovery of all foreseeable losses counsel for the plaintiffs argued that such a more liberal rule is necessary in a democracy as a constraint upon abuse of executive and administrative power. The force of this argument is, however, substantially reduced by the recognition that subjective recklessness on the part of a public officer in acting in excess of his powers is sufficient. Recklessness about the consequences of his act, in the sense of not caring whether the consequences happen or not, is therefore sufficient in law. This justifies the conclusion that the test adopted by Clarke J. represents a satisfactory balance between the two competing policy considerations, namely enlisting tort law to combat executive and administrative abuse of power and not allowing public officers, who must always act for the public good, to be assailed by unmeritorious actions ...

... In the light of my statement of the requirements of the tort of misfeasance in public office I would adjourn this part of the appeal for further argument.

Lords Hope, Hutton, Hobhouse, and Millett delivered speeches in which they agreed with Lord Steyn's order for disposing of this appeal. Lords Hobhouse and Millett agreed with Lord Steyn's speech on the question of the misfeasance tort (and also Lord Hutton's views on that issue). When the striking out issue was further considered, the House of Lords decided that the action should not be struck out.

Aronson, in a recent article, helpfully summarizes the elements that emerge from *Three Rivers*, and the case law more generally, as follows ((2016) 132 *LQR* 427 at 427):

Briefly, misfeasance in public office is a tort remedy for harm caused by acts or omissions that amounted to:

1. an abuse of public power or authority;
2. by a public officer;
3. who either
   (a) knew that he or she was abusing their public power or authority, or
   (b) was recklessly indifferent as to the limits to or restraints upon their public power or authority;
4. and who acted or omitted to act
   (a) with either the intention of harming the claimant (so-called 'targeted malice'), or
   (b) with the knowledge of the probability of harming the claimant, or
   (c) with a conscious and reckless indifference to the probability of harming the claimant.

To these elements we must add a point to which we will return later: the claimant must have suffered material, actionable loss in consequence of the defendant's acts. If no recognized loss is suffered there can be no claim. We may also add that, as noted by Lord Steyn in *Three Rivers*, the defendant does not need to have in mind or be indifferent towards inflicting the exact harm ultimately suffered by the claimant; it is sufficient that the defendant contemplate the broad *type* of harm, such as financial loss.

A question arises over the definition of 'public officer'. The matter has not been conclusively resolved in the case law. However, in *Three Rivers* there were suggestions the concept should be interpreted broadly; the concept obviously included those 'vested with governmental authority and the exercise of executive powers' (at 230). In a later case it was suggested that the test is a functional one: the tort 'may be committed by any person performing a public function notwithstanding that he is not actually employed in the public service' (*Crawford Adjusters (Cayman) Ltd* v. *Sagicor General Insurance (Cayman) Ltd* [2013] UKPC 17, [2014] AC 366 at [134]). It thus may be suggested that private contractors, carrying out public functions, could fall within the scope of the tort. However, the statement was obiter. Further, one must bear in mind the reluctance of the courts to extend the scope of similar functional tests to include contractors, for example under the HRA (see 4.6).

Various other points in the *Three Rivers* case have arisen for interpretation in later cases. For example, Lord Steyn's reference (at 196) to the claimant having to establish that the 'defendant acted ... in the knowledge that his act would probably injure the [claimant] or person of a *class* of which the [claimant] was a member' (emphasis added) was analysed in *Akenzua* v. *Secretary of State for the Home Department* [2002] EWCA Civ 1470, [2003] 1 WLR 741. Sedley LJ at [19]–[20] (with the agreement of Scott Baker and Simon Brown LJJ) took the view that the reference to such an individual or class was not a 'freestanding requirement of the tort'; rather, it followed from the 'antecedent proposition that the intent or recklessness must relate ('be directed') to the kind of harm suffered'. In Sedley LJ's opinion, it is 'an expansive rather than a restrictive element of the tort, allowing the action to be maintained even where the identities of the eventual victims are not known at the time when the tort is committed, so long as it is clear that there will be such victims. So understood, the need for a class is not a special hurdle set by legal doctrine but a practical means, in the kind of case then before the House, of relating and restricting liability to effects in the direct contemplation of the wrongdoer'.

It is important to record that very few misfeasance claims actually succeed, and the courts are generally reluctant to interpret the elements of the tort liberally for fear of exposing public officers to expansive liability. As Aronson records, the bad faith requirement is the main stumbling block (at 427–8):

> Pleading bad faith is difficult. The pleading rules require details, and professional conduct rules forbid practitioners alleging fraud or bad faith except on the basis of available material by which the allegations can properly be supported. Proving bad faith is even more difficult. Where they have a choice, the courts are strongly disposed to believing that bureaucratic error was caused by genuine mistake, even incompetence, rather than by bad faith. The result is that of the hundreds of misfeasance claims that are actually filed, very few make it to trial. Most are filtered out for inadequate pleading of bad faith, or because an allegation of bad faith has no real prospects of success.

15.3.8 Misfeasance in public office: causation and damage

It will have been seen that Lord Steyn referred to causation as a *factual* issue in the *Three Rivers* case. This suggests that causation depends on an orthodox 'but for' analysis. In other words, one must ask whether the claimant would have suffered the relevant damage but for the defendant's wrongful conduct. If they would have suffered the loss even if the defendant had not acted with bad faith then there can be no recovery. It is for the claimant to prove causation.

Causation can pose a particular problem with the misfeasance tort. For example, where the claimant requires some positive exercise of power in his favour (*eg* the grant of a licence), then it may be unclear whether the wrongful denial of the licence has caused him any loss. The court may be unable to say what the result of an exercise of the power without the improper factor would have been. Another causation issue could be raised in respect of this tort—here in the situation where there has been, for example, a withdrawal of a licence—by the view in *Dunlop* v. *Woollahra Municipal Council* [1982] AC 158 at 172 that a person can ignore a purported exercise of power. Despite earlier support for this view in the case law (McBride [1979] *CLJ* 323 at 337–40), it is submitted that it should not, and will not, be followed in English law today (and see 3.2–3.3).

The type of damage alleged in *Three Rivers* was economic loss, but it is clear that the tort also encompasses physical injury, recognized psychiatric illness, and damage to property. However, the suffering of mere distress, indignation, humiliation, or anxiety will not suffice; the loss must be 'material': *Watkins* v. *Secretary of State for the Home Department* [2006] UKHL 17, [2006] 2 AC 395 at [7], [27]; *Hussain* v. *Chief Constable of West Mercia Constabulary* [2008] EWCA Civ 1205. In *Karagozlu* v. *Commissioner of Police of the Metropolis* [2006] EWCA Civ 1691, [2007] 1 WLR 1881, the Court of Appeal 'stretched' the tort to also cover loss of liberty. Whether this view would be met with approval if the issue ever reached the Supreme Court is open to question, especially in light of *Watkins*, to which we now turn. *Watkins* concerned the question whether the claimant was indeed required to prove damage in order to bring a claim of misfeasance, or whether the tort should be redeployed as a vindicatory-type tort which was actionable *per se* and concerned to protect constitutional rights (see 15.3.1).

Watkins v. *Secretary of State for the Home Department* [2006] UKHL 17, [2006] 2 AC 395
House of Lords

The respondent (claimant) alleged that certain prison officers had opened and read his mail in contravention of the Prison Rules. At the trial the judge found bad faith on the part of three of the officers but dismissed the claim on the basis that the claimant had not proved any actionable harm. The Court of Appeal allowed an appeal, taking the view that where a claim involved 'constitutional rights', no special damage had to be proved. On appeal to the House of Lords:

Lord Bingham

[23] [The] authorities present a remarkably consistent body of law on the point now at issue. The proving of special damage has either been expressly recognised as an essential ingredient, or it has been assumed. None of these cases (and no authority, judicial or academic, cited to the House) lends support to the proposition that the tort of misfeasance in public office is actionable per se. . . . I would be very reluctant to disturb a rule which has been understood to represent the law for over 300 years, and which has been adopted elsewhere, unless there were compelling grounds for doing so.

[24] The feature on which the Court of Appeal fastened was the breach in this case of the respondent's constitutional right to protection of the confidentiality of his legal correspondence. . . . The respondent relied on the authority of the Court of Appeal (per Steyn LJ) that the

right of access to a court, closely linked with the right to obtain confidential legal advice, is a constitutional right: *R v Secretary of State for the Home Department, Ex p Leech* [1994] QB 198, 210. In a number of cases rights of this kind have been described as 'constitutional', 'basic' or 'fundamental': see, for instance, *R v Secretary of State for the Home Department, Ex p Pierson* [1998] AC 539, 575; *R v Secretary of State for the Home Department, Ex p Simms* [2000] 2 AC 115, 130–131; *R (Daly) v Secretary of State for the Home Department* [2001] 2 AC 532, para 12; *R v Lord Chancellor, Ex p Witham* [1998] QB 575, 581, 585, 586. In all these cases the importance of the right was directly relevant to the lawfulness of what had been done to interfere with its enjoyment.

[25] In the present context the unlawfulness of what was done to interfere with the respondent's enjoyment of his right to confidential legal correspondence is clear. I see scant warrant for importing this jurisprudence into the definition of the tort of misfeasance in public office. ... It is, I think, entirely novel to treat the character of the right invaded as determinative, in the present context, of whether material damage need be proved.

[26] Novelty is not in itself a fatal objection, and the respondent contends that the importance of the right in question requires or justifies the modification of a rule, if there be such, that material damage must be proved to establish a cause of action. I do not, however, think that the House should take or endorse this novel step, for a number of reasons. The first is that it would open the door to argument whether other rights less obviously fundamental, basic or constitutional than the right to vote and the right to preserve the confidentiality of legal correspondence, were sufficiently close to or analogous with those rights to be treated, for damage purposes, in the same way. Since, in the absence of a codified constitution, these terms are incapable of precise definition, the outcome of such argument in other than clear cases would necessarily be uncertain. My second reason ... is the undesirability of introducing by judicial decision, without consultation, a solution which the consultation and research conducted by the Law Commission may show to be an unsatisfactory solution to what is in truth a small part of a wider problem. [See, however, 15.2 for later developments.] Thirdly, the lack of a remedy in tort for someone in the position of the respondent, who has suffered a legal wrong but no material damage, does not leave him without a legal remedy. Prison officers who breach the rules (even in the absence of bad faith), and the governors of both prisons, would be amenable to judicial review. Errant officers would be susceptible to disciplinary sanctions, and failure to initiate such proceedings could also, on appropriate evidence, be challenged by judicial review. The officers might well be indictable for the common law offence of misconduct in public office: see *Attorney General's Reference (No 3 of 2003)* [2005] QB 73. Breach of a fundamental human or constitutional right would also, in all probability, found a claim under section 7 of the Human Rights Act 1998, as it would in this case where the violation occurred after the Act came into force. I have myself questioned, albeit in a lone dissent, whether development of the law of tort should be stunted, leaving very important problems to be swept up by the European Convention (*D v East Berkshire Community Health NHS Trust* [2005] 2 AC 373, para 50), but the observation was made in a case where, in my opinion, the application of familiar principles supported recognition of a remedy in tort, not a case like the present where the application of settled principle points strongly against one. A fourth reason for not adopting the rule for which the respondent contends is to be found in enactment of the 1998 Act: it may reasonably be inferred that Parliament intended infringements of the core human (and constitutional) rights protected by the Act to be remedied under it and not by development of parallel remedies. It is true, as the respondent pointed out, that section 11 of the 1998 Act contains a safeguard for existing rights, and monetary compensation awarded at Strasbourg tends, in comparison with domestic levels of award, to be ungenerous. But there is, as I have concluded, no existing right to damages where misfeasance in public office has caused no material damage to the victim, and if the evidence showed an egregious and deliberate abuse of power by a public officer one would expect the Strasbourg court to award compensation for non-pecuniary loss even though its practice is not to award exemplary

damages: *BB v United Kingdom* (2004) 39 EHRR 635, para 36. It is, however, a fifth reason for resisting the respondent's argument that what he seeks, for himself and others in a like position in similar actions, is not an award of damages to compensate the claimant but an award to punish the defendant. Such, after all, is the function of exemplary damages. That exemplary damages may be awarded where a compensatory award is insufficient to mark the court's disapproval of proven misfeasance in public office, and deter repetition, is, as already noted, accepted. But the policy of the law is not in general to encourage the award of exemplary damages, and I would not for my part develop the law of tort to make it an instrument of punishment in cases where there is no material damage for which to compensate.

[27] For these reasons, and those given by my noble and learned friends, Lord Hope of Craighead, Lord Rodger of Earlsferry and Lord Carswell, I would accordingly rule that the tort of misfeasance in public office is never actionable without proof of material damage.

Lords Hope, Rodger, Walker, and Carswell delivered speeches in favour of allowing the appeal. Lords Hope, Rodger, and Carswell specifically agreed with Lord Bingham. Appeal allowed.

Two observations are pertinent. First, the House of Lords clearly took the view that the principal function of misfeasance in public office is to provide compensation in exceptional cases of public wrongdoing. It is a loss-based tort. As Lord Hope said, the tort's 'function is to compensate the claimant, not to punish the public officer' (at [32]). As Lord Bingham said, to have removed the material loss prerequisite would have been to turn the tort into an instrument of punishment, as exemplary damages could then be claimed and recovered absent the suffering of any loss whatsoever. But there were more general statements that even in a case where material loss and all of the other elements of the tort were proven, the award of exemplary damages should be 'confine[d] ... very closely indeed' (at [81]). And indeed it is very difficult to find cases in which exemplary damages have been awarded for misfeasance. But this seems inconsistent with the availability of exemplary damages specifically for unconstitutional, oppressive, or arbitrary conduct of public officials (see 15.3.1). One would have thought that the intentional infliction of harm by a public officer in excess of their powers is exactly the sort of case that falls within this category. There might be policy concerns that if a court is ready to award exemplary damages for misfeasance, this could lead to a raft of claims or lead to public officials being over-cautious in the fulfilment of their public tasks. But given misfeasance claims hardly ever succeed, these concerns seem wholly unlikely to materialize.

Second, *Watkins* raises the issue, already discussed in respect of negligence (15.3.6), of the interrelationship between human rights law and the law of torts. *Watkins* is another in a line of cases in which the courts have maintained strict separation between the two fields. For example, Lord Bingham argued (at [26]) that given the passing of the HRA, 'it may reasonably be inferred that Parliament intended infringements of the core human (and constitutional) rights protected by the Act to be remedied under it and not by development of parallel remedies'. But this approach is rather difficult to reconcile with the exact opposite approach taken in other fields. For example, as we saw in ch 8, within the common law of judicial review it is increasingly common for the courts to recognize common law constitutional or fundamental rights equivalent to those human rights under the HRA, to apply methods drawn from human rights law, such as proportionality, and to grant remedies for interference with common law fundamental rights (see *Kennedy* v. *Information Commissioner* [2014] UKSC 20, [2015] AC 455; *Pham* v. *Secretary of State for the Home Department* [2015] UKSC 19, [2015] 1 WLR 1591). It is unclear why the development of parallel remedies in common law judicial review is permissible, but not the development of parallel remedies in the law of torts. In any case, parallel remedies *already* exist in the law of torts, and the courts do not consider this to be problematic. For example, false imprisonment and Article 5 of the ECHR both protect interests in liberty, while Article 3 and battery both protect interests in physical integrity.

QUESTION

- How satisfactory is the misfeasance tort in providing a remedy for someone who suffers loss as a result of *ultra vires* action by a public body?

15.4 Damages under the Human Rights Act 1998

15.4.1 Human rights damages and the principle of equality

The HRA introduced a new statutory action for damages for breaches of those human rights protected by the Act. The liability is not vicarious in nature but rather a direct liability of public authorities. Given human rights duties under the Act only bind public authorities, the liability is one unique to public authorities (as defined under s 6 of the Act). In this way the action differs from damages actions at common law (except for misfeasance in public office), given duties under the common law of torts apply not only to public entities, but to all: police officers and individuals are under the same duties not to falsely imprison others, for example. At first glance, therefore, human rights damages entail a deviation from the equality principle, so as to ensure greater protection of basic interests in the face of public power. However, it is important to record that many of the rights protected under the HRA have also been long protected by the common law, and specifically the vindicatory torts.

It is for this reason that many see bills of rights, far from representing a departure from English constitutional traditions, as building upon the longstanding constitutional tradition in the law of torts, discussed earlier (see 15.3.1)—serving to update the list of protected rights to include those not traditionally protected by tort law but which are now considered of great importance, such as freedom of expression and privacy, and to fill the gaps in protection of basic interests within the law of torts more generally. As such, it has sometimes been said that bills of rights operate to give greater effect to the equality principle, in that they reflect and give effect to a general principle that no one, public or private, should interfere with basic rights without authority. Interestingly ECS Wade, in his introduction to the tenth edition of Dicey's treatise on the Constitution said: 'The progress which has been made towards the recognition of the human rights of individual citizens within their own States approaches more closely to Dicey's conception of equality before the law' (Dicey, *Introduction to the Study of the Law of the Constitution* (London 1960) at xcvii). This might be thought an odd claim to make given Dicey's well-known preference for ordinary common law protections ahead of bills of rights. However, it is not so if one recognizes that one 'purpose of subjecting officials to the ordinary courts, applying primarily the rules of private law, was to make government subservient to principles of justice that protected fundamental interests in personal liberty and security' (Allan, *Constitutional Justice* (Oxford 2003) 19).

Given the law of torts has long served to protect basic constitutional rights in the face of public power through imposition of damages liability, it is unsurprising that early decisions under the HRA drew on damages principles within the law of torts in developing the law of damages for breach of basic, human rights. However, this was not to last. The higher courts, in later decisions, rather than viewing human rights damages claims as a continuation of English constitutional traditions, viewed the new HRA action as a novel type of claim. As such, they drew a bright line between the law of tort and human rights damages. The result has been the marginalization of the damages remedy: there are few claims, damages have not uncommonly been denied by the courts, awards have been relatively rare, and where awards are made they are modest in amount and in general well below the amounts awarded in tort for equivalent heads of loss. As such, fundamental rights under the HRA are afforded far weaker protection than fundamental rights in the law of torts. There can be little doubt that, albeit not always apparent at the surface level, underpinning the marginalization of this remedy are public policy concerns favouring insulation of public authorities from liability.

15.4.2 Human rights damages: statutory provisions and case law

Section 6 of the HRA and its scope have been discussed earlier (see 4.6). For present purposes it suffices to note that that provision makes it unlawful for a public authority to act contrary to protected rights. Section 7 of the Act creates the cause of action for breach of human rights, and sets out various procedural requirements. Section 8 is the key remedial provision that addresses damages.

Human Rights Act 1998

8—(1) In relation to any act (or proposed act) of a public authority which the court finds is (or would be) unlawful, it may grant such relief or remedy, or make such order, within its powers as it considers just and appropriate.

(2) But damages may be awarded only by a court which has power to award damages, or to order the payment of compensation, in civil proceedings.

(3) No award of damages is to be made unless, taking account of all the circumstances of the case, including—

(a) any other relief or remedy granted, or order made, in relation to the act in question (by that or any other court), and

(b) the consequences of any decision (of that or any other court) in respect of that act,

the court is satisfied that the award is necessary to afford just satisfaction to the person in whose favour it is made.

(4) In determining—

(a) whether to award damages, or

(b) the amount of an award,

> the court must take into account the principles applied by the European Court of Human Rights in relation to the award of compensation under Article 41 of the Convention.
>
> (5) A public authority against which damages are awarded is to be treated—...
>
> (b) for the purposes of the Civil Liability (Contribution) Act 1978 as liable in respect of damage suffered by the person to whom the award is made.
>
> (6) In this section—
>
> 'court' includes a tribunal;
>
> 'damages' means damages for an unlawful act of a public authority; and
>
> 'unlawful' means unlawful under section 6(1).

Note that s 9 of the Act sets out certain rules governing human rights breaches by judges.

As already mentioned, early decisions under the Act drew heavily on the law of torts as a guide, not least because the HRA and the law of torts protect many common interests. Thus, in the case of *R (KB)* v. *South London and South and West Region MHRT* [2003] EWHC 193 (Admin), [2004] QB 936, which involved claims for breaches of Article 5, the right to liberty and security, Stanley Burnton J drew on the law of false imprisonment (at [56]):

> I see no justification for an award of damages being lower under the Human Rights Act 1998 than it would be for a comparable tort. For example, the tort of false imprisonment, if committed by a public authority, will normally, if not invariably, coincide with infringement of article 5(1). I see no reason why there should be any difference between the measure of damages for the wrongful detention of an individual under the two causes of action: in both cases, the object of the award is to compensate the individual for the same wrongful detention.

Despite the apparent sense of this approach, the Court of Appeal in the important decision of *Anufrijeva* v. *Southwark LBC* [2003] EWCA Civ 1406, [2004] QB 1124 began to distance the human rights action from the law of torts. Lord Woolf MR, with whom the other judges agreed, asserted: '[D]amages or compensation should play a different role in relation to claims in respect of public law rights from that which it plays in private law proceedings' (at [54]). He said (at [52]–[53]):

> The remedy of damages generally plays a less prominent role in actions based on breaches of the articles of the Convention, than in actions based on breaches of private law obligations where, more often than not, the only remedy claimed is damages. Where an infringement of an individual's human rights has occurred, the concern will usually be to bring the infringement to an end and any question of compensation will be of secondary, if any, importance. This is reflected in the fact that, when it is necessary to resort to the courts to uphold and protect human rights, the remedies that are most frequently sought are the orders which are the descendants of the historic prerogative orders or declaratory judgments. The orders enable the court to order a public body to refrain from or to take action, or to quash an offending administrative decision of a public body. Declaratory judgments usually resolve disputes as to what is the correct answer in law to a dispute.

Thus, given the 'public law' nature of the rights at stake, it was traditional public law remedies such as the prerogative orders and also declarations that ought to take remedial priority in human rights law, with damages of secondary if any importance; later in his judgment Lord Woolf added that damages under the Act are a 'a remedy of "last resort"' (at [56]). Underlying this ordering of remedial priority is a view that public law is principally concerned with ensuring authorities exercise public power properly in the wider public interest, rather than a concern for protection of the individual from harm. This is a tenable view of public law as a matter of theory, but it seems out of place within human rights law, which is specifically concerned with protecting *individuals'* basic rights. Reflecting traditional public policy concerns over imposing liability on public authorities Lord Woolf considered that in making decisions whether to award damages and how much, a balance had to be drawn between the individual victim's interest and the interests of the public as a whole, including those in 'continued funding of a public service' (at [56]). Thus, even where loss is suffered, awards may be denied or reduced in order to protect the public purse.

Lord Woolf considered that the statutory scheme supported his view that human rights damages ought to be treated differently from ordinary damages in English law. For example, damages under the Act are subject to judicial discretion whereas damages in tort are available as of right, HRA claims may only be made against authorities unlike claims in tort, and the court must have regard to the principles applied by the European Court of Human Rights in its own remedial jurisdiction pursuant to s 8(4) of the Act.

Albeit Lord Woolf's approach clearly envisages that damages would be rare—a last resort and of secondary importance—he did nonetheless consider that the view he had espoused in an article written extrajudicially, that awards under the Act should be on the low side relative to tort, should now be ignored (at [73]). Thus, while he emphasized that damages would be discretionary and marginal, where awarded the levels of awards in tort could serve as a guide, alongside awards recommended by the Ombudsman (at [74]).

Thus, Lord Woolf distinguished damages under the Act from those in tort, albeit he did nonetheless consider tort may be a useful source of guidance, at least as to quantum. However, any role for tort rules and principles was eschewed in the subsequent House of Lords decision in *R (Greenfield)* v. *Secretary of State for the Home Department* [2005] UKHL 14, [2005] 1 WLR 673. In that case Lord Bingham, with whom the other Law Lords agreed, concurred in Lord Woolf's view in *Anufrijeva* that damages under the Act are of secondary if any importance, and would thus be rare (at [9]). However, he did not support this view on the same basis as Lord Woolf. Instead of placing emphasis on the remedy being a public law one, he placed significant emphasis on s 8(4) of the Act, and the requirement therein to take into account the principles applied by the ECtHR under Article 41 of the Convention in awarding 'just satisfaction', the term used for money awards made by the European Court.

Article 41 is the provision of the European Convention which governs the European Court's own jurisdiction to award remedies in those cases that come before it. It reads:

> If the Court finds that there has been a violation of the Convention or the Protocols thereto, and if the internal law of the High Contracting Party concerned allows only partial reparation to be made, the Court shall, if necessary, afford just satisfaction to the injured party.

The effect of *Greenfield* is that a 'mirror approach' is to be taken to the award of damages under the HRA. In other words, English courts must seek to mechanistically replicate the Strasbourg court's practice as to making awards and quantum in domestic law. One consequence of this approach is that damages will be uncommon. This is because a defining characteristic of the Article 41 jurisprudence is that the Strasbourg court often holds that the finding of a violation constitutes just satisfaction in itself. As Lord Bingham observed, this remedial approach reflects that the ECtHR's role is to uphold human rights standards rather than afford individual redress: 'The routine treatment of a finding of violation as, in itself, just satisfaction for the violation found reflects the point already made that the focus of the Convention is on the protection of human rights and not the award of compensation' (at [9]). Similarly, in the later case of *DSD* v. *Commissioner for the Metropolis* [2015] EWCA Civ 646, [2016] QB 161 at [65]–[66], Laws LJ said, 'the focus is on the State's compliance, not the claimant's loss', 'compensation for loss' being a 'private law purpose'. In terms of quantum Lord Bingham rejected counsel's submission that English courts should follow domestic comparators as to quantum, such as awards made in discrimination law, and thereby overruled Lord Woolf's view in *Anufrijeva* that courts could have regard to awards in tort. He gave three main reasons for rejecting this argument (at [19]):

> First, the 1998 Act is not a tort statute. Its objects are different and broader. Even in a case where a finding of violation is not judged to afford the applicant just satisfaction, such a finding will be an important part of his remedy and an important vindication of the right he has asserted. Damages need not ordinarily be awarded to encourage high standards of compliance by member states, since they are already bound in international law to perform their duties under the Convention in good faith, although it may be different if there is felt to be a need to encourage compliance by individual officials or classes of official. Secondly, the purpose of incorporating the Convention in domestic law through the 1998 Act was not to give victims better remedies at home than they could recover in Strasbourg but to give them the same remedies without the delay and expense of resort to Strasbourg. This intention was clearly expressed in the White Paper 'Rights Brought Home: The Human Rights Bill' (1997) (Cm 3782), para 2.6:
>
> > 'The Bill provides that, in considering an award of damages on Convention grounds, the courts are to take into account the principles applied by the European Court of Human Rights in awarding compensation, so that people will be able to receive compensation from a domestic court equivalent to what they would have received in Strasbourg.'
>
> Thirdly, section 8(4) requires a domestic court to take into account the principles applied by the European court under article 41 not only in determining whether to award damages but also in determining the amount of an award. There could be no clearer indication that courts in this country should look to Strasbourg and not to domestic precedents. The appellant contended that the levels of Strasbourg awards are not 'principles' applied by the court, but this is a legalistic distinction which is contradicted by the White Paper and the language of section 8 and has no place in a decision on the quantum of an award, to which principle has little application. The court routinely describes its awards as equitable, which I take to mean that they are not precisely calculated but are judged by the court to be fair in the individual case. Judges in England and Wales must also make a similar judgment in the case before them. They are not inflexibly bound by Strasbourg awards in what may be different cases. But they should not aim to be significantly more or less generous than the court might be expected to be, in a case where it was willing to make an award at all.

Thus, in terms of quantum domestic courts must follow Strasbourg. This is highly significant because ECtHR awards under Article 41 are in general far lower than awards in domestic tort law: for a comparison of domestic and Article 41 scales of awards see Varuhas, *Damages and Human Rights* (Oxford 2016) at 104–13. Lord Bingham, in a later case, himself observed that Strasbourg scales are 'ungenerous' by English tort standards (*Watkins* v. *Secretary of State for the Home Department* [2006] UKHL 17, [2006] 2 AC 395 at [26]), while it has been suggested awards will be 'modest' even for deliberate wrongdoing (*Watkins* at [73]). On top of this there is no recognition in Article 41 jurisprudence of aggravated or exemplary damages, strongly suggesting these shall not be available domestically for human rights breaches—Lord Woolf would have ruled out exemplary damages in *Anufrijeva* (at [55]), although the issue has been kept open by the House of Lords: *Kuddus*

v. *Chief Constable of Leicestershire Constabulary* [2001] UKHL 29, [2002] 2 AC 122 at [46], [92]; *cf Watkins* at [32], [64].

This mirror approach was confirmed in the Supreme Court's decision in *R (Faulkner)* v. *Secretary of State for Justice* [2013] UKSC 47, [2013] 2 AC 254. In that case Lord Reed, delivering the lead judgment, interpreted Lord Bingham in *Greenfield* as having construed s 8(3) and (4) of the Act as (at [29])

> introducing into our domestic law an entirely novel remedy, the grant of which is discretionary, and which is described as damages but is not tortious in nature, inspired by article 41 of the Convention. Reflecting the international origins of the remedy and its lack of any native roots, the primary source of the principles which are to guide the courts in its application is said to be the practice of the international court that is its native habitat.

In terms of quantum Lord Reed confirmed that the effect of *Greenfield* had been that '[d]icta in earlier cases, suggesting that awards under section 8 should not be on the low side compared with tortious awards and that English awards should provide the appropriate comparator, were implicitly disapproved' (at [27]). Consonant with this guidance most awards under the Act have been awards of several hundred pounds for distress and anxiety.

It is very difficult to discern a set of worked-out and concrete principles from the human rights damages case law, the field instead being characterized by open-ended judicial discretion. However, some patterns emerge. As a result of the mirror approach damages are very often denied under the Act, subject to the broad discretionary approach that characterizes the Article 41 jurisprudence. As already mentioned, under such an approach the finding of violation itself is often considered sufficient remedy, even where loss has been suffered. The ECtHR has enunciated no clear principles as to when courts should deviate from this default approach and grant awards. Awards have been denied altogether in cases involving serious rights violations. For example, where a prisoner, in violation of his Article 8 rights, was subjected to continuous solitary confinement for an exceptionally long period of 58 months, the Supreme Court, in its discretion, resolved that this was not a case entailing suffering of the sort that warranted compensation, concluding that the finding of violation and award of costs constituted just satisfaction: *Shahid* v. *Scottish Ministers* [2015] UKSC 58, [2016] AC 429 at [87]–[90]. It is not uncommon to find statements in the case law that '[t]here is a factual basis for an award of damage, but that does not mean that an award must follow' (*R (Guntrip)* v. *Secretary of State for Justice* [2010] EWHC 3188 at [53]). It is common practice, following on from the ECtHR jurisprudence, that awards will be denied where the court considers the level of loss suffered is not 'sufficiently serious' or of 'such intensity' to warrant an award. Again, there is very little guidance as to when loss will or will not be sufficiently serious to warrant an award, and inconsistencies of approach and outcome are readily apparent in the Strasbourg case law, and in domestic law. As the ECtHR itself states, whether it considers an award justified depends on an open-ended 'equitable' assessment of 'what is just, fair and reasonable in all the circumstances of the case' (*Al-Jedda* v. *United Kingdom* (2011) 53 EHRR 23 at [114]). It has nonetheless been observed by domestic courts that awards will be more likely to be made in cases of 'severe or permanent injury to ... health': *R (Sturnham)* v. *Secretary of State for Justice* [2012] EWCA Civ 452, [2012] 3 WLR 476 at [21]–[22]; *Shahid* at [89]. As such, awards have been made for breach of Articles 2, the right to life, and 3, the right against torture and inhuman and degrading treatment: *DSD* v. *Commissioner for the Metropolis* [2014] EWHC 2493, [2015] 1 WLR 1833 (*DSD* HC) and *Rabone* v. *Pennine Care NHS Foundation Trust* [2012] UKSC 2, [2012] 2 AC 72 at [85]–[86].

Various factors have been taken into account on an *ad hoc* basis and sporadically, such as concerns to protect public finances (see the earlier discussion of *Anufrijeva*) and concerns to prevent a compensation culture emerging (*DSD* HC at [41]). No clear pattern emerges as to when such concerns will or will not be relied upon.

It is important to note that somewhat worryingly the courts have taken into account how the public would react to awards, and also the moral worthiness of the victim in deciding whether to make awards and how much. Thus, in *Anufrijeva*, Lord Woolf gave as one reason for keeping awards low that '[i]f the impression is created that asylum seekers whether genuine or not are profiting from their status, this could bring the HRA into disrepute' (at [75]). In other cases the courts, inspired by ECtHR practice, have denied awards to prisoners partly on the basis of the seriousness of crimes they had committed in the past: *R (Downing)* v. *Parole Board* [2008] EWHC 3198 (Admin) at [29], [31]; *R (Biggin)* v. *Secretary of State for Justice* [2009] EWHC 1704 (Admin), [2010] 1 Prison LR 269 at [35] (albeit other judges on similar facts have not mentioned such a factor, or doubted its relevance: *R (Degainis)* v. *Secretary of State for Justice* [2010] EWHC 137 at [19]). These are very concerning developments, in that they are directly contrary to the fundamental principle of equal treatment before the law: justice should not depend on populist reaction or whether the court considers the claimant morally worthy.

There is next to no general guidance as to assessment of quantum, other than repeated statements that awards must be kept low, albeit some highly generalized guidance has emerged in respect of awards under Articles 2 and 3: see *Rabone*, DSD HC. However, where greater guidance has been given, it has not necessarily been coherent. For example, in *DSD* HC the judge's efforts to divine some meaningful guidance from Strasbourg was commendable, but aspects of the approach adopted were highly questionable. For example, the judge emphasized that following Article 41 practice awards are limited to compensation and exemplary damages are probably unavailable, but then, in assessing quantum, took into account factors such as whether awards should be enhanced to encourage compliance and whether the violations were of a systemic nature, these factors having nothing to do with the degree of loss suffered and being more at home in the assessment of exemplary damages (see [118] onwards). It has been clearly stated that the courts will take a right-by-right approach, so that there is no general approach to damages, but rather the approach will vary from one type of rights violation to the next. Predictably, given the lack of a 'joined-up' approach, the result has been inexplicable variations in the case law. For example, it has been established that awards for distress will readily be made for breach of the procedural requirement under Article 5(4) of a speedy hearing where one's liberty is at stake (assuming loss is of sufficient severity) (*Faulkner*), but have more or less been ruled out completely for distress suffered due to breach of procedural fairness requirements under Article 6 (*Greenfield*), and violation of procedural safeguards under Article 5(4) other than the requirement for a speedy hearing (*R (Osborn)* v. *Parole Board* [2013] UKSC 61, [2014] 1 AC 1115 at [2](xiii)). There has been no attempt to explain or reconcile these different positions.

Thus far we have been concerned principally with awards for non-economic losses. There has been a greater willingness to countenance claims for economic losses in a few confined contexts, albeit hardly any such awards have been made. A number of very significant awards—including the largest award by far made under the Act to date (£94,393.62 in *R (Infinis plc)* v. *Gas and Electricity Markets Authority* [2011] EWHC 1873, [2013] EWCA Civ 70, [2013] JPL 1037)—have been made to companies that had suffered economic loss consequential upon breaches of the right to peaceful enjoyment of property under Article 1 of

Protocol 1. The Supreme Court in *Faulkner* signalled that economic losses should be readily recoverable where they result from wrongful deprivation of liberty (at [13](8)). But, on the other hand, the House of Lords in *Greenfield* indicated courts should be slow to make pecuniary awards (at [11]), while in *Anufrijeva* Lord Woolf seemed to suggest that only 'significant' economic losses 'clearly caused' (seemingly a more stringent requirement than ordinary 'but for' causation) by the violation could possibly be recovered (at [59]). Again, these variations have neither been recognized by the courts, nor rationalized. More generally, it is rather perplexing that in the field of *human* rights law the most significant award made under the Act to date has been to a company for economic losses, whereas awards are commonly denied to human claimants for interferences, sometimes very serious interferences, with their dignitary interests.

We note that the procedural law governing human rights damages claims has already been discussed at 13.3.10.

Thus, overall, human rights damages are 'sparingly awarded and modest in amount': *R (Calland)* v. *Financial Services Ombudsman Ltd* [2013] EWHC 1327 (Admin) at [37]. In the light of the state of the jurisprudence one has great sympathy for lower court judges required to decide whether to make awards and assess quantum, and who observe: 'There is little guidance in the authorities on the approach to be taken when quantifying an award of damages ... If one looks at the authorities for appropriate comparators again there is relatively little assistance' (*Re H* [2014] EWFC 38 at [84]–[91]).

15.4.3 Issues raised by the human rights damages jurisprudence

The judicial approach to damages under the HRA and the jurisprudence under the Act have been subjected to strong and sustained academic criticism. See in particular, Varuhas, *Damages and Human Rights* (Oxford 2016); (2009) 72 *MLR* 750.

First, one may immediately question whether such a restrictive approach is warranted within a field concerned to afford strong protection to the most fundamental of rights. Human rights law shares the same sort of function as the vindicatory torts (see 15.3.1): to protect and vindicate important interests. This is reflected in the two fields sharing many similar features; for example, human rights claims are also generally actionable *per se* and liability is generally strict for interferences with basic rights. On top of this the two fields protect many of the same basic interests. In light of this it is hard to justify why damages should be rarely awarded and very low in human rights law, but damages presumed and awarded as a matter of course for vindicatory torts, with levels of compensation much higher, and a range of damages including exemplary damages available to ensure strong protection of rights. Why should human rights be treated as second-class rights? One might respond to such arguments for the alignment of tort and human rights on the same basis as Lord Woolf: human rights claims are public law claims. But this argument does not take one far when one considers that claims in tort are a core aspect of the English public law tradition.

The English and Scottish Law Commissions, in their report on damages under the HRA—a report published as the Act was entering into force and which was intended as an authoritative reference point for judges as they developed the jurisprudence under the

Act—were highly critical of the Strasbourg jurisprudence, and preferred an approach to damages based in tort: Law Com 266/Scot Law Com 180 *Damages under the Human Rights Act 1998* (2000). The Commissions considered that the award of damages in tort is the 'obvious comparator in English law' (at [4.14]); while care should be taken in reading across principles developed in tort, 'in the majority of cases under the HRA the courts ... will find it possible and appropriate to apply the rules by which damages in tort are usually assessed to claims under the HRA' (at [4.21], [4.26]). Aside from the early case law under the Act, this advice has fallen on deaf judicial ears.

Second, as should be apparent from the foregoing analysis of the case law under the Act, there are serious problems with the mirror approach (see Varuhas, *Damages and Human Rights* (Oxford 2016) at ch 5). The higher courts have directed that English courts should follow the Strasbourg Article 41 jurisprudence. But that jurisprudence is characterized by a paucity of stated principle, incoherence, inconsistency, and unpredictability. As a result of tying domestic law to the troubled Strasbourg case law, a deeply problematic domestic jurisprudence is emerging, characterized by many of the same problems as the Strasbourg jurisprudence. At a practical level the Strasbourg decisions on compensation are nearly completely unreasoned, so there is no guidance for lower court judges. There are myriad statements from lower court judges that '[i]t is notoriously difficult to deduce clear principles in relation to "just satisfaction" from the Strasbourg jurisprudence' (*R (Hooper) v. Secretary of State for Work and Pensions* [2003] EWCA Civ 813, [2003] WLR 2623 at [147]) and 'it is well known ... that there are no articulated principles, and no discernible tariff, by which [the ECtHR's] awards [under Article 41] are set' (*Faulkner v. Secretary of State for Justice* [2011] EWCA 349 at [6], [15]). Even Lord Reed in *R (Faulkner) v. Secretary of State for Justice* [2013] UKSC 47, [2013] 2 AC 254, despite directing lower courts to follow Strasbourg, struggled to derive any guidance from the Strasbourg material (at [34], [63], [74], [75]). This poses a conundrum for lower courts. On the one hand, the Supreme Court has said that lower courts must apply 'clear and consistent practice of the European Court' (at [13](3)). But given such clear and consistent guidance will typically not be discernible it is unclear what principles should be applied, while through the decisions in *Greenfield* and *Faulkner* the highest court has prohibited lower courts from looking to established principle in tort. The result is a vacuum of principle, and a troubled jurisprudence.

Third, the provisions of the Act do not justify the adoption of the mirror approach, yet the courts have relied solely on the provisions of the Act to justify their approach. Section 8(4) only requires courts to 'take into account' the Strasbourg material, not to follow it as if it were precedent. A duty to take material into account entails a freedom to depart from that material. Further, courts are directed, under s 8(4), to take account of the broad 'principles' that emerge from Strasbourg—which are very few and include very basic ideas of causation and compensation for loss—not to mechanistically follow every decision made under Article 41, a point echoed by Lord Carnwath writing separately in *Faulkner* (at [113]).

Fourth, the ECtHR's practice under Article 41 is that of a supranational court exercising a secondary, supervisory jurisdiction, whereas under the Convention system domestic courts have primary responsibility for provision of redress. Article 41 practice is not and was never intended as a model for domestic courts to follow. Domestic courts are bound in international law not by Article 41 but by Article 13, the right to an effective remedy, and it is that provision which ought to be given effect to and guide damages practice domestically. Importantly, the ECtHR itself has said that under Article 13 domestic courts have a 'discretion' to organize remedies consistently with domestic traditions, and has also said that it would be 'easier for the domestic courts to refer to the amounts awarded at domestic level for other types of damage', including 'personal injury, damage relating to a relative's death or damage in defamation cases': *Scordino* v. *Italy (No 1)* (2007) 45 EHRR 7, [188]–[189]; *Cocchiarella* v. *Italy* Application 64886/01 (ECtHR, 29 March 2006) at [79]–[80]. Thus, there is not even an imperative from Strasbourg for domestic courts to follow Article 41.

QUESTIONS

- Do you find these criticisms convincing?
- Can you think of any counterarguments in defence of the mirror approach?

Lastly, in *Faulkner*, Lord Reed made a number of observations concerning the future development of this field. He said Strasbourg jurisprudence should be the starting point 'at this stage of the development of the remedy' and that over time 'the remedy should become naturalised' (at [29], [39], [96]). Arguably what he meant was that as Strasbourg practice is read across to domestic law a domestic jurisprudence would emerge over time—but nonetheless be one firmly steeped in Strasbourg practice. On the other hand, the observation may signal that there is scope for a change of approach in future, and a refocusing on domestic damages traditions and rules and principles.

15.5 State liability in EU law

EU law may impose liability upon public authorities where they cause individuals loss through breach of EU law. We include discussion of this field because, albeit 'Brexit' looms large, we are here concerned to state the prevailing legal position, and the UK remains a member of the EU for the time being, and may continue to do so for some time to come—the time frame for formal withdrawal from the EU has not yet been determined.

Damages claims founded in EU law may be brought in domestic proceedings against national authorities including the judiciary (*Kobler* v. *Republik Osterrich* [2004] QB 848) and the legislature (*R* v. *Secretary of State for Transport, ex parte Factortame Ltd (No 5)* [2001] 1 AC 524), but are most often brought against central government. This type of liability is a direct liability of the Member State as opposed to a vicarious liability. Such claims most commonly arise where the state fails to transpose into domestic law an EU law Directive or fails to correctly transpose such a Directive. However, claims may be made in respect of breaches of EU law more generally. Thus, for example, in *R (Chester)* v. *Secretary of State for Justice* [2013] UKSC 63, [2014] AC 271, prisoners brought claims for damages, claiming that the UK's blanket ban on prisoners voting in elections under s 3 of the Representation of the People Act 1983 and s 8 of the European Parliamentary Elections Act 2002 directly breached various provisions of the EU treaties, including equal treatment and non-discrimination clauses. However, the claims ultimately failed on their merits, and because the liability principles established under EU were not fulfilled.

The EU principle of state liability was first established by the Court of Justice of the EU in *Francovich and Bonafaci* v. *Italian Republic* [1991] ECR 5357, and is typically referred to as *Francovich* liability. The subsequent decision of the Court in *Brasserie du Pêcheur SA v. Germany* [1996] QB 404 articulates the prevailing principles governing when liability will arise. According to *Brasserie*, in general the breach of EU law in itself shall *not* be sufficient to generate liability. Rather, a three-pronged test must be fulfilled (*Brasserie* at [51]):

1. the rule of law infringed was intended to confer rights on individuals; and

2. the breach was sufficiently serious; and

3. there was a direct causal link between the breach of the obligation and the damages suffered by the individual claimants.

The most significant feature of this test—that feature which in the vast majority of cases determines whether the claim succeeds or fails—is the 'sufficiently serious' element. Breach of a rule of EU law which confers rights on individuals shall not in general be sufficient to generate liability *per se*. Rather, the breach must be one that is sufficiently serious to warrant the imposition of liability. This is in most cases a high hurdle, and requires that the breach be 'grave and manifest' (*Brasserie* at [55]). In *Brasserie*, the Court elaborated a range of factors which a court should consider in determining whether a breach is sufficiently serious:

> [56] The factors which the competent court may take into consideration include the clarity and precision of the rule breached, the measure of discretion left by that rule to the national or Community authorities, whether the infringement and the damage caused was intentional or involuntary, whether any error of law was excusable or inexcusable, the fact that the position taken by a Community institution may have contributed towards the omission, and the adoption or retention of national measures or practices contrary to Community law.

There are a few categories of case in which the fact of breach shall be conclusive of sufficient seriousness, so that recourse to the above factors will be unnecessary, and successful claims have generally been limited to such cases. Two such circumstances were articulated by the Court in *Brasserie*:

> [57] On any view, a breach of Community law will clearly be sufficiently serious if it has persisted despite a judgment finding the infringement in question to be established, or a preliminary ruling or settled case-law of the Court on the matter from which it is clear that the conduct in question constituted an infringement.

A further circumstance is where the measure breached affords the Member State no discretion, a classic example being where a Member State does not transpose a Directive into domestic law within the prescribed time limit for transposition. Thus, in *Dillenkofer* v. *Germany* [1997] QB 259, the Court said:

> [25] On the one hand, a breach of Community law is sufficiently serious if a Community institution or a Member State, in the exercise of its rule-making powers, manifestly and gravely disregards the limits on those powers ... On the other hand, if, at the time when it committed the infringement, the Member State in question was not called upon to make any legislative choices and had only considerably reduced, or even no, discretion, the mere infringement of Community law may be sufficient to establish the existence of a sufficiently serious breach (see [*R* v. *Ministry of Agriculture, Fisheries and Food, ex parte Hedley Lomas* [1997] QB 139 at [28]]).

[26] So where, as in *Francovich*, a Member State fails … to take any of the measures necessary to achieve the result prescribed by a directive within the period it lays down, that Member State manifestly and gravely disregards the limits on its discretion.

Note that while in such cases the fact of breach shall be conclusive of the sufficiently serious inquiry, the other two elements of the test in *Brasserie* must still be fulfilled—that is, the measure in question must be one which confers individual rights, and there must be a causal connection between breach and loss suffered.

As signalled by the decision in *Dillenkofer*, over time the degree of discretion left to a Member State—which implicates an inquiry into the clarity and precision of the rule breached—has emerged as the dominant factor in determining whether the breach is sufficiently serious, with the other factors articulated in *Brasserie* treated as ancillary and of less consequence: *Chester* at [76]–[79]; *Laboratoires Pharmaceutiques Bergaderm SA* v. *Commission* [2000] ECR I-5291 at [43]–[44]. Where the state enjoys no or very limited discretion, say because the norm breached enunciates a clear rule with no exceptions, the court will likely conclude the breach was sufficiently serious. But where the rule breached is other than crystal clear and allows for a margin of judgment, or the case law is not such that the parameters of the rule are clear-cut (*Chester* at [79]), practice shows that it is very unlikely that a court will reach a conclusion of sufficiently serious breach. Put another way, it will be far more difficult to show that the state has gravely and manifested disregarded the limits of its discretion where that discretion is very broad, and characterized by uncertain limits, compared to where the scope of discretion is narrow and the limits clearly delineated.

Three observations are pertinent. First, while the rationale for the EU state liability principle is contested the best explanation is that it is underpinned by a compliance concern. That is, a concern to incentivize Member State compliance with EU norms and to sanction or punish non-compliance by imposing damages liability. At a more general level establishment of the liability principle is part of a long-term and sustained effort by the Court of Justice to ensure the effectiveness of EU law and the penetration of EU norms into the domestic order; put simply, to secure European integration.

This compliance rationale is reflected in core features of the liability principle, particularly the sufficiently serious criterion. A state will almost certainly incur damages liability if it deliberately or recklessly violated a clear norm of EU law, or persists in conduct found to have been unlawful by the Court. On the other hand, if a state makes a genuine attempt to comply with an ambiguous rule but fails or was led into error by erroneous guidance provided by EU institutions, it is unlikely to be held liable. In this way, recalcitrant behaviour is punished whereas genuine attempts at compliance will be rewarded.

Of course, it cannot be ignored that the *Brasserie* test makes reference to individual rights. Some might argue that this suggests that the primary concern of *Francovich* liability is the protection of individuals, rather than compliance, while any damages awarded would, after all, be paid to individuals to compensate personal losses. However, the claim is unconvincing. If individual protection is a goal of *Francovich* liability, it is only given effect to the extent that it carries forward the primary goal of incentivizing compliance. That the individual protection goal is so contingent is made clear by the fact that individuals may suffer extraordinary levels of loss and harm through a state violation of fundamental norms of EU law, but that loss will go uncompensated if the defendant state has shown some commitment to compliance or their non-compliance is excusable, so that the breach is not sufficiently serious. Further, none of the factors elaborated in *Brasserie* which guide judicial consideration of the sufficiently serious inquiry refer to protection of individual rights or the degree of loss suffered by individuals. Thus, while individual protection is no doubt *a* concern of *Francovich* liability, it is not the primary or dominant concern.

Other factors too have undoubtedly influenced the framing of the liability tests. For example, the sufficiently serious criterion operates as a control measure to ensure that the Court of Justice and national courts are able to keep liability in check. While the Court is acutely concerned with ensuring the effectiveness of EU norms, it is also cautious not to undermine its own legitimacy and that of the EU more generally by overly burdening Member States. For further discussion of this point, and consideration of other factors which shape the *Francovich* jurisprudence, see Varuhas, *Damages and Human Rights* (Oxford 2016) 433–46.

Second, it is worth noting, however, that the sufficiently serious criterion has arguably worked too well as a control on liability. As Lock ((2012) 49 *CML Rev* 1675) records, in a valuable empirical study of EU state liability claims, 'the vast majority of claims fail because the national court was unable to establish a sufficiently serious breach'. (For recent examples of claims that have failed on this basis see, eg *Chester*; *Test Claimants in the FII Group Litigation* v. *Revenue and Customs Commissioners* [2010] EWCA Civ 103, [2010] STC 1251 (conclusion on *Francovich* liability not disturbed on appeal: [2012] UKSC 19, [2012] 2 AC 337); *Cooper* v. *Attorney General* [2010] EWCA Civ 464, [2011] QB 976). Lock records that in England there has been, on average, just over one claim decided by English courts per year, and only 36 per cent of claims have been successful. That is just nine successful claims (out of 25) in the 20-year period following *Francovich*. This does not reflect that Member States routinely comply with their legal duties; we know, for example, that Member States regularly violate duties to transpose Directives in time, while the European Commission brings a significant number of public infringement proceedings against Member States for non-compliance each year. As such, 'in the overall picture of enforcement, *Francovich* type cases are only of limited importance' (at 1687). Given this very low number of claims and very low success rate, it is difficult to see how Member States could view *Francovich* liability as a credible threat, which in turn suggests the principle is failing on its own terms as a tool for incentivizing compliance.

Lastly, it has been suggested that if a damages remedy were ever to be established to compensate individuals who had suffered loss through breach of the common law judicial review duties of legality, rationality, and procedural fairness, the sufficiently serious test derived from EU law or an analogous test could be adopted as the governing liability principle. Most prominently, the Law Commission, in its now abandoned proposals for creation of such a special public law damages claim (see 15.2), placed at the centre of its proposed scheme the idea of 'serious fault' (Law Com Consultation Paper No 187, *Administrative Redress: Public Bodies and the Citizen* (London 2008); see also the final report: Law Com No 322 (London 2010)). Thus, on the Commission's proposals a breach of the judicial review duties could not generate liability *per se*; rather, damages could only be awarded where, *inter alia*, the public defendant's conduct was characterized by serious fault. The Commission considered the 'serious fault' test to be 'the key to our proposals': it 'would properly balance the interests of claimants with the competing demands made on public bodies' (at [4.144], [4.152] (all references herein are to the consultation paper)). In adopting this test the Commission explicitly drew on the *Brasserie* criteria. However, under the proposed 'serious fault'—as opposed to the

EU 'sufficiently serious breach' test test—the factors a court would consider would be somewhat wider, though the Commission suggested the *Brasserie* factors could also be drawn upon. The relevant factors included (at [4.146]):

1. The risk or likelihood of harm involved in the conduct of the public body.

2. The seriousness of the harm caused.

3. The knowledge of the public body at the time that the harm occurred that its conduct could cause harm, and whether it knew or should have known about vulnerable potential victims.

4. The cost and practicability of avoiding the harm.

5. The social utility of the activity in which the public body was engaged when it caused the harm; this would include factors such as preventing an undue administrative burden on the public body.

6. The extent and duration of departures from well-established good practice.

7. The extent to which senior administrators had made possible or facilitated the failure or failures in question.

The Commission, clearly concerned to allay government fears that creation of a new type of public law claim could lead to a flood of claims which would cripple public services, was keen to emphasize that it would be an uncommon case where liability was established (at [4.147]):

> Mere fault on the part of a public body is established where it is clear that the public body, having regard to the above factors, should not have acted in the manner that caused harm to the claimant, or should have taken appropriate steps to prevent such harm occurring. However, 'serious fault' would only be established where the behaviour goes beyond mere administrative failure and engages these factors in an aggravated manner. For example, where the potential harm to the citizen was particularly grave or the departure from the principles of good administrative practice clearly blameworthy. As such, 'serious fault' would only be established where the breach of the factors meant that the administrative failure of the public body fell *far* below the standard expected of public bodies.

QUESTIONS

- Is the concept of 'serious fault' materially different from the concept of 'sufficiently serious breach'?
- If you think they are different, which test do you prefer as a test to govern public authority liability, and why?
- Do you think the Law Commission's proposals strike the right balance between individual redress and the public policy concerns raised by creation of a judicial review damages remedy?
- Given the marginal nature of *Francovich* liability under the 'sufficiently serious test', and that the Law Commission considered the 'serious fault' test would only lead to damages being awarded in those uncommon cases where an authority's conduct was *far* below the expected standards, are damages actions based on such principles worthwhile?

15.6 Contract

15.6.1 Introduction

English law, unlike the law of some other jurisdictions, knows no public law of contract. The starting point is, as in the law of torts, the principle of equality: the ordinary law of contract applies to contracts concluded by public bodies as it does to others. The absence of any special body of law of public contracts means that public authorities appear to have the same freedom as the private citizen in deciding with whom to contract and on what terms. This freedom is, however, subject to certain restrictions imposed by (i) the *ultra vires* doctrine, (ii) the laws of the European Union which apply to public contracting in the UK, and (iii) specific statutes. It is also important to note that a significant quantity of 'soft law' such as policy guidance or circulars has been developed within government to guide exercise of contracting powers, and may often constrain contractual freedom, even if these constraints are not sourced in law (albeit it is increasingly the case that such soft law is imbued with legal status (see 5.3.3), and note that such policy guidance is itself amenable to judicial review in principle). Further, there are other, non-legal checks on contracting; for example, the National Audit Office regularly vets government activity, including contracting, for value for money.

A party to an agreement with a public authority which is not incompatible with its public duties will have ordinary contractual rights against the authority. As a general rule contractual *obligations* are not enforceable via judicial review, while as we saw in 4.5.4 the presence of contractual relations within a factual matrix more generally will make it unlikely that judicial review may be sought. This raises serious concerns given the increasing contractualization of government service delivery (discussed at 1.5.5). However, as we shall discuss, review may be available where the question is whether the authority has acted in excess of its powers. If a contract contains terms required by statute or regulations, these may raise issues amenable to judicial review (see in general Beatson (1987) 103 *LQR* 34 at 63; Ewing and Grubb (1987) 16 *ILJ* 145). Also, recall that public law-type principles, in the light of recent Supreme Court authority, now generally govern the exercise of discretion under contracts, whether a party to the contract is public or not: 4.5.5.

15.6.2 (Basic) contractual capacity

The Crown has the power to contract without the need for any specific statutory authority: this is because it has legal personality and the powers of a natural person. Central government departments will typically conclude contracts on the Crown's behalf. In certain cases the powers of individual Ministers have been defined by statute (*eg* s 1 of the Supply Powers Act 1975) or by statutory instruments made under the Ministers of the Crown Act 1975. These may limit the capacity of the Crown itself (*Cugden Rutile (No 2) Ltd* v. *Chalk* [1975] AC 520) or the scope of the authority possessed by Ministers and Crown agents (see 15.6.6).

On a procedural point, at one time it was recognized that the Crown could be liable for breach of contract, but it had a special legal position in that the only remedy for breach was a petition of right. Legislation in 1947 changed this.

Crown Proceedings Act 1947

1 Where any person has a claim against the Crown after the commencement of this Act, and, if this Act had not been passed, the claim might have been enforced, subject to the grant of His Majesty's fiat, by petition of right, or might have been enforced by a proceeding provided by any statutory provision repealed by this Act, then, subject to the provisions of this Act, the claim may be enforced as of right, and without the fiat of His Majesty, by proceedings taken against the Crown for that purpose in accordance with the provisions of this Act.

Broadly, as a result of the 1947 Act, proceedings against the Crown in contract are now similar to those applying between subjects, so that the principle of equality is generally abided by, but there are some differences. For example, no injunctive or specific relief may be given against the Crown in any 'civil proceedings' (see further 12.2.3).

Generally speaking, public bodies other than the Crown, such as local authorities, need statutory authority to contract; this can be express or implied. Thus, if a local authority acts in excess of power any contract so formed shall be void. In such circumstances neither party may sue for breach. The problems that this can cause can be shown by a case such as *Hazell* v. *Hammersmith and Fulham London Borough Council* [1992] 2 AC 1, which involved what was known as a 'swap contract'. The authority had entered into several of these contracts and would make or lose money under them depending on the movement of interest rates. The House of Lords held that the local authority had no power to enter into such swaps contracts. Large sums of money were at stake (other authorities had also entered into these sorts of contracts) but there could be no contractual action to recover money which was owed. Similar types of issues arose in *Credit Suisse* v. *Allerdale Borough Council* [1997] QB 306 and *Credit Suisse* v. *Waltham Forest London Borough Council* [1997] QB 362.

In response to such problems some flexibility in respect of the consequences of an invalid contract is now provided by the Local Government (Contracts) Act 1997 (for commentary see Davies (2006) 122 *LQR* 98 at 115–22). Section 1 increases the capacity of local authorities (as defined) to contract. For example, it provides that '[e]very statutory provision conferring or imposing a function on a local authority confers power on the local authority to enter into a contract with another person for the provision or making available of assets or services, or both, (whether or not together with goods) for the purposes of, or in connection with, the discharge of the function by the local authority'.

Turning to questions of validity, s 2(1) provides:

Where a local authority [as defined] has entered into a contract, the contract shall, if it is a certified contract, have effect (and be deemed always to have had effect) as if the local authority had had power to enter into it (and had exercised that power properly in entering into it).

Certification is dealt with in detail by ss 3 and 4. One particular point to note is that it must be a contract which lasts or is intended to last for five years or more and which the local authority has entered into with another for the provision of services (although assets and goods can be included with the services) in connection with the discharge of any of the authority's functions (s 4(3)). Contracts so certified shall thus have effect as if entered into lawfully. But what if the validity of the contract is challenged via judicial review? Section 5(1) provides that s 2(1) does not prevent the *vires* of the relevant contract being addressed by a review claim. Section 5(2) provides that s 2(1) has effect subject to any order or determination concerning a 'certified contract' made in such proceedings. Thus, the contract can be invalidated if *ultra vires*. However, pursuant to s 5(3), in a claim for judicial review, the court can, if it does find the authority acted *ultra vires* in entering the contract, 'determine that the contract has (and always has had) effect as if the local authority had had power to enter into it (and had exercised that power properly in entering into it)' if it considers this right 'having regard in particular to the likely consequences for the financial provision of the local authority and for the provision of services to the public, of a decision that the contract should not have effect'. Thus, the court has the power to 'save' the contract from invalidity, despite it being *ultra vires*. If the contract made provision for 'discharge terms' then these shall remain operative even if the court does invalidate the contract.

Where there are no discharge terms and the result of judicial review proceedings is that the 'certified contract' is ineffective, s 7(2) comes into play and provides for the local authority to pay the other contractual party

> such sums (if any) as he would have been entitled to be paid by the local authority if the contract—
>
> (a) had had effect until the time when the determination or order was made, but
> (b) had been terminated at that time by acceptance by him of a repudiatory breach by the local authority.

15.6.3 Freedom to contract

Ordinary judicial review norms are a potential control over decisions to contract, and also refusals to contract at all or only on particular terms. One may query why authorities ought to be subject to such controls in their contracting decisions whereas others are not. The reason is simply the rule of law. Authorities must abide by the legal constraints which govern exercises of their public functions, including where this involves decisions over contracts, and judicial review norms are among the relevant legal constraints.

We said that judicial review norms are a *potential* control because there are limits on when judicial review norms apply. As we saw in 4.5.4, where contracts form an aspect of the factual matrix, courts are cautious about exercising the supervisory jurisdiction, for fear of trespassing upon contractual rights. There is a special line of jurisprudence on when decisions or refusals to contract may be subject to judicial review. These cases establish that review norms will only be applicable where the challenged decision has a sufficient public law element: *R v. East Berkshire Health Authority, ex parte Walsh* [1985] QB 152; *R v. Bolsover DC, ex parte Pepper* [2001] BLGR 43. There is no real guidance as to when this element will be fulfilled, but it is clear that under this test it will not be enough for the decision to have been one taken in exercise of statutory powers; something more will be required to imbue the decision with a sufficient degree of 'publicness'. As an illustrative example consider *R (Agnello) v. Hounslow London Borough Council* [2003] EWHC 3112 (Admin), [2004] BLGR 536. The claimant sought to challenge the defendant's refusal to offer tenancies in the council's newly established market. Silber J considered that a number of factors told in favour of the decision being amenable to review on the basis that it was characterized by a sufficient public law element (at [30]–[35]): the council had specific statutory powers in relation to the market; the market was held on publicly owned land; the council could regulate market activity not only via lease but also byelaws; the council had exercised its powers to make byelaws regulating conduct at the market, including provisions for fines for certain prohibited behaviour, which showed the council's functions were different from those of a private landlord; and the public had access to the market, albeit relatively little weight was placed on this last point. As Bailey [2007] *PL* 444 observes, the problem with this reasoning is that it is difficult to see how it is significantly different from saying the council's decision is amenable to review because it was exercising statutory power (at 454).

Bailey has observed that the 'public law element' test is 'inherently unclear'—the courts have struggled to articulate what additional element over and above exercise of statutory power is required to bring the claim within the scope of judicial review—resulting in the waste of much litigation time as authorities do not and cannot provide sufficient guidance. He also points out that some of the distinctions drawn in the case law as to when the test is fulfilled or not 'seem arbitrary and unconvincing', and that the uncertainty of the test has led to 'an excessively narrow view of the amenability of judicial review' (at 451, 462–3). This should not surprise us as we have often through the course of this book discovered that where legal decision-making is based on the idea of 'public law' or 'publicness' such decision-making is characterized by all sorts of problems (see 4.5.6 and 13.3). Bailey suggests that rather than deciding upon the scope of review by reference to the amorphous concept of 'public law' or 'publicness' the courts should follow the approach propounded by Arrowsmith (1990) 106 *LQR* 277 at 291. That is, any statutory exercise of power ought to presumptively fall within the ambit of review, albeit the presumption may be defeated if there are good policy reasons for not bringing the matter within the ambit of review. Another approach that Bailey considers preferable to the prevailing approach, and which is not necessarily inconsistent with Arrowsmith's view, is that of Elias J in *R (Molinaro)* v. *Royal Borough of Kensington and Chelsea* [2001] EWHC 896 (Admin), [2002] BLGR 336. On that approach the scope of review is effectively determined by whether the claimant can identify an abuse of power: the challenged decision will be within the scope of review if it involves the exercise of public power and the claimant is able to ground their complaint in some public law principle. Elias J demonstrates that this would be a meaningful control on the scope of review (at [66]–[67]):

> Of course, in many circumstances the nature of the complaint is one that identifies no public law principle. In such cases the fact that the defendant is acting pursuant to statute is irrelevant. For example, if the Council sues for the rent due from a tenant, no public law issue arises. Indeed, in general questions of construction of the contract or breach will attract no special public law principles, and judicial review is not an appropriate procedure to resolve such disputes. The fact that a public body is a party to the proceedings is, in such cases, irrelevant to the action formulated or to the relief granted. There is no justification then for treating the local authority in any different way to private bodies.
>
> But public bodies are different to private bodies in a major respect. Their powers are given to them to be exercised in the public interest, and the public has an interest in ensuring that the powers are not abused. I see no reason in logic or principle why the power to contract should be treated differently to any other power. It is one that increasingly enables a public body very significantly to affect the lives of individuals, commercial organisations and their employees.

In the later case of *R (A)* v. *Chief Constable of B Constabulary* [2012] EWHC 2141 (Admin) at [37]–[42], Kenneth Parker J cited Bailey's article with approval, as well as Elias J's approach; also in common with Elias J he drew attention to the potentially significant power to affect interests through decisions involving contract, and as such the dangers of allowing authorities to act with impunity where they contract (at [42]). We await to see whether the decision marks the beginning of the turning of the tide away from the public law element test.

In terms of possible grounds of challenge, the full array of grounds will in principle be available, albeit some, such as substantive review, may be applied with greater caution. For example, a blanket refusal to contract may fall foul of the no-fettering principle (considered further at 15.6.5) or involve breach of an individual's legitimate expectation. In *Agnello*, the claimants won on an orthodox claim of procedural unfairness: the Council had not given the claimants an opportunity to comment on the information on the basis of which it intended to select tenants for the market. In *R* v. *Lewisham LBC, ex parte Shell UK Ltd* [1988] 1 All ER 938, a council's refusal to contract with Shell UK as part of a campaign to persuade other local authorities to boycott trade with Shell UK so as to bring pressure on the Shell Group to sever its trading links with South Africa was held *ultra vires* on the ground of improper purpose under the relevant legislation.

As we have seen (1.5.5) contracting out of public functions is pervasive. However, the non-delegation doctrine may pose a significant impediment to the delegation of public functions via the tool of contract. Statutory reform has been implemented to get around this problem. The most significant piece of legislation in this respect is the Deregulation and Contracting Out Act 1994. This empowers a Minister, by order, to authorize any person to exercise a statutory function which may be exercised by one of his or her officials pursuant to the *Carltona* doctrine, such as officials in his department (on this doctrine see 5.2.4). There are limits to which functions may be delegated, however: neither judicial nor legislative functions may be delegated, nor powers which may affect liberty. Such delegations are time-limited: they may not extend more than 10 years. There are other checks including that any ministerial order effecting such a delegation is subject to the parliamentary negative resolution procedure. Further, in the same vein as the *Carltona* doctrine, the Minister remains ultimately responsible as any acts of the delegate are, in general, to be treated as acts of the Minister. Albeit, as discussed in ch 5, whether ministerial responsibility is a particularly effective mechanism for ensuring political accountability for exercises of ministerial power by delegates is open to question.

It is clear that public bodies may, as long as legal constraints are abided by, use their contracting power as an instrument of policy (see generally Arrowsmith (1995) 111 *LQR* 235). This may occur in the allocation of contracts, for example to support certain domestic industries, to support regions that are underdeveloped or have a high level of unemployment by preferring tenders from companies operating in those regions, and to encourage the reorganization of an industry. Policy may also be promoted by insisting on the inclusion of certain terms in contracts, although note that if a standard term excludes or restricts liability, the Unfair Contract Terms Act 1977 will apply (and see the Unfair Terms in Consumer Contracts Regulations 1999).

However, public bodies are by no means unfettered in their ability to use contract as an instrument of policy. In addition to the constraints imposed by ordinary review grounds, EU law imposes a number of restrictions in this area, stemming (*inter alia*) from the principles of non-discrimination enshrined in the EU Treaties; such restrictions bite, for example, if compliance with given contractual standards is liable to be more difficult for other EU, as opposed to domestic, contractors. EU law, driven by a concern for market integration and reducing trade barriers between EU members, prescribes specific and elaborate rules to govern public procurement contracts above a certain value, so that procurement decisions are subject to standards of transparent and procedurally fair decision-making. Thus, these rules deviate from the equality principle by requiring more of authorities than others in their contracting decisions. Albeit interestingly these rules have not necessarily been driven by the distinctive nature of authorities or a sense that our expectations of authorities are greater than our expectations of private parties, but rather by a concern to further market integration within the single market by opening up lucrative government contracts to bidders from across the EU through a transparent and fair process—so as to prevent governments favouring domestic suppliers. The EU Public Procurement Directive (2014/24/EC) sets out the substantive requirements of EU procurement law, and these have been implemented domestically by the Public Contracts Regulations 2015 (SI 2015/102). The substantive and procedural requirements imposed on authorities are elaborate and far-reaching. When the regulations apply the authority is, for example, required to state transparently in advance the selection and award criteria, and the authority must award contracts to the most economically advantageous tenderer (there are different possible measures of this) from the perspective of the authority. Note that these requirements do not apply when services are sourced in-house, or from a separate juridical entity which is in reality an extension of the authority: *Risk Management Partners Ltd* v. *Brent London Borough Council* [2011] UKSC 7, [2011] 2 AC 34.

Myriad other statutory requirements may bear on government contracting. For example, s 17 of the Local Government Act 1988 imposes a general duty on local and many other public authorities to exercise their functions in relation to public works or supply contracts without reference to 'non-commercial matters', such matters including, for example, 'the country or territory of origin of supplies to, or the location in any country or territory of the business activities or interests of, contractors' and 'any political, industrial or sectarian affiliations or interests of contractors or their directors, partners or employees' (s 17(5)(e), (f)). Section 29(6) of the Equality Act 2010 prohibits discrimination on certain grounds by persons exercising 'public functions' (which may include the awarding of certain contracts), while s 149 imposes a general duty on authorities to have due regard, in exercise of their functions, to the need to advance equality of opportunity for certain groups. Section 17(10)(a) of the Local Government Act 1988 states as an exception to the general prohibition on taking into account non-commercial matters, that it is permissible for relevant authorities to take such matters into account to the extent necessary or expedient to enable compliance with s 149 of the 2010 Act.

15.6.4 Is parliamentary appropriation of funds necessary?

Central government expenditure is dependent on the government's spending plans being approved by Parliament; principally by Parliament voting through as legislation the government's annual Budget. This raises an interesting question: can the Crown avoid its contractual obligations, for example to pay for contracted goods and services, on the basis that Parliament has not authorized government expenditure for this purpose?

The State of New South Wales v. *Bardolph* (1934) 52 CLR 455
High Court of Australia

Acting on the authority of the State Premier, and 'as a matter of Government policy', the New South Wales Tourist Bureau contracted for the insertion of advertisements in the claimant's newspaper, *Labor Weekly*, for a period of 12 months in the financial years 1931–32 and 1932–33. Shortly after the making of the contract there was a change of government and the new administration refused to use or to pay for any further advertising space in the newspaper. The claimant (Bardolph) continued to insert the advertisements for the remainder of the contract period and claimed £1,114 10s, the amount outstanding on the contract. The contract had not been expressly authorized by the State legislature or by any Order in Council or executive minute. The Supply and Appropriation Acts for the relevant years included the provision of sums for 'Government advertising'. This provision was for sums much larger than the amount involved in the contract.

Evatt J

... The suggested defence that the contract was not authorized by the Government completely fails. It is only right to add that, although raised in the pleadings, this defence was not seriously pressed at the hearing.

The main, indeed the only real defence relied upon by the State of New South Wales, was that Parliament did not make public moneys available for the express purpose of paying the plaintiff for his advertising services. The defence is, of course, quite unmeritorious, and its success might tend to establish a dangerous precedent in the future. But it raises an interesting question of law, the examination of which shows that the repudiation of subsisting agreements by a new administration can seldom be ventured upon with success ...

[He then considered the facts in relation to the relevant grants of public money by Parliament for the period ending 30 June 1932, and concluded:] The net result is that the total supply which Parliament made available during the year for Government advertising can be reckoned as amounting to eleven-twelfths of £6,600, plus one-twelfth of £9,900, that is, £6,875 in all.

It appears from the statement prepared by Mr. Kelly, Chief Accountant at the Treasury, that if payment had been made to the plaintiff in respect of the advertisements inserted before the end of the financial year, 30th June, 1932, but not paid for, the total expenditure for the service would only have amounted to £4,595 18s, a figure considerably lower than the assumed minimum supply voted by Parliament, that is, £6,875 ...

Before referring to what took place in the financial year 1932–1933, it is convenient to consider the legal position as it existed on and in respect of 30th June, 1932. It was argued for the State that it was a condition of the contracts with the plaintiff that all payments of money thereunder should be authorized by Act of Parliament, and it was said that no person can successfully sue the State of New South Wales in the absence of a precise or specific Parliamentary allocation of public moneys for the purpose of making payments under the contracts. It was further contended that, even in an Appropriation Act, the constitutional condition of such contracts is not fulfilled unless it can be shown that Parliament's intention was directed to the particular payment to the particular contractor ...

In the well-known case of *Churchward* v. *The Queen* [(1865) LR 1 QB 173], Shee J., in a passage often cited, adopted the principle that, in the case of a contract by a subject with the Crown, there should be implied a condition that the providing of funds by Parliament is a condition precedent to the Crown's liability to pay moneys which would otherwise be payable under the contract. In that case the actual promise was to pay a sum 'out of the moneys to be provided by Parliament' (see *Churchward* v. *The Queen*); so that the judgment of Shee J. went beyond the actual point necessary to determine the case. *Churchward's Case* was decided upon demurrer, the third plea alleging that 'no moneys were ever provided by Parliament for the payment to the suppliant for, *or out of which the suppliant could be paid* for the performance of the said contract, for any part of the said period subsequent to the 20th June, 1863, or for the payment to the suppliant for, and in respect of, or *out of which the suppliant could be paid* or *compensated for*, in respect of any damages sustained by the suppliant by reason of any of the breaches of the said contract committed subsequent to the said 20th of June, 1863'. (I italicize certain words.)

Further, the Appropriation Acts referred to in that case expressly provided that Churchward's claim was to be excluded from the large sum of money (£950,000) thereby voted for the general purposes of providing and maintaining the Post Office Packet Service.

The judgment of Shee J. has always been accepted as determining the general constitutional principle. But it should be added that Cockburn C.J. said:

'I agree that, if there had been no question as to the fund being supplied by Parliament, if the condition to pay had been absolute, or if there had been a fund applicable to the purpose, and this difficulty did not stand in the petitioner's way, and he had been throughout ready and willing to perform this contract, and had been prevented and hindered from rendering these services by the default of the Lords of the Admiralty, then he would have been in a position to enforce his right to remuneration.'

It appears clear that the first part of this passage has not been acted upon by the Courts in the cases subsequently determined, and that, even where the contract to pay is in terms 'absolute' and the contract fails to state that the fund has to be 'supplied by Parliament,' the Crown is still entitled to rely upon the implied condition mentioned by Shee J.

The second part of Cockburn's C.J. statement, that, if there is a fund 'applicable to the purpose' of meeting claims under the contract, the contractor may enforce his right to remuneration, has never, so far as I know, been questioned. Moreover, its correctness was assumed by the terms of the Crown's third plea in *Churchward's Case* which denies that moneys were ever provided by Parliament 'out of which the suppliant could be paid for the performance of the said contract.' ...

[After considering the views of Durell, *Parliamentary Grants*, pp 21, 296, and 297, and Maitland, *Constitutional History of England*, pp 445–6, he concluded:] [I]n the absence of some controlling statutory provision, contracts are enforceable against the Crown if *(a)* the contract is entered into in the ordinary or necessary course of Government administration, *(b)* it is authorized by the responsible Ministers of the Crown, and *(c)* the payments which the contractor is seeking to recover are covered by or referable to a parliamentary grant for the class of service to which the contract relates. In my opinion, moreover, the failure of the plaintiff to prove *(c)* does not affect the validity of the contract in the sense that the Crown is regarded as stripped of its authority or capacity to enter into the contract. Under a constitution like that of New South Wales where the legislative and executive authority is not limited by reference to subject matter, the general capacity of the Crown to enter into a contract should be regarded from the same point of view as the capacity of the King would be by the Courts of common law. No doubt the King had special powers, privileges, immunities and prerogatives. But he never seems to have been regarded as being less powerful to enter into contracts than one of his subjects. The enforcement of such contracts is to be distinguished from their inherent validity ...

In the present case, the position as it existed on 30th June, 1932, was that *(a)* the Crown had made contracts with the plaintiff, and *(b)* moneys had been made legally available by the Supply Acts, including that of June, 1932. It is admitted that the advertising service vote, if otherwise sufficient to satisfy the rule in *Churchward's Case*, covered the service called for by the contracts with the plaintiff. On 30th June, therefore, there was *(a)* an existing contract, *(b)* a sufficient compliance with the rule in *Churchward's Case*, *(c)* a proved performance by the plaintiff of the contract on his part, *(d)* proved non-payment for this service for five weeks at £29 12s. 6d. per week, that is, £148 2s. 6d. in all.

It cannot be too strongly emphasized at all points of this case that the plaintiff's contracts were not with the Ministers individually or collectively, but with the Crown ...

... The honour of the Crown demands that, subject to Parliament's having made one or more funds available, all contracts for the Crown's departments and services should be honoured. The position on 30th June, 1932, having been examined, what was the position existing on 1st July, 1932, the first day of the financial year 1932–1933? In my opinion, it was plainly this, that the plaintiff's contract with the Crown was still on foot ... The condition that payments thereunder depended upon moneys being made legally available by Parliament still subsisted, but the contract was not inchoate or suspended but existing ...

The only question therefore, is whether in respect to the year 1932–1933 also the condition of *Churchward's Case* was satisfied ...

In order to secure a judgment declaring the Crown's liability, a person who has a subsisting contract with the Crown satisfies the constitutional doctrine laid down in *Churchward's Case* in respect of payments accruing during the financial year when he completes the performance of his contract if, at the time of such completion, there exists in respect of such financial year sufficient moneys in the vote for the relevant service to enable the payments in question to be lawfully made. I also think that the plaintiff is entitled to say that the constitutional doctrine was satisfied in respect of all payments falling due between 1st July, 1932, and the date of his completing his contract if, at the date of the passing of the Appropriation Act (8th November, 1932), enough moneys to pay him in full could have been lawfully paid or set aside to pay him from moneys then remaining from the parliamentary grant in respect of advertising. From a close consideration of the figures and evidence, I draw the inferences of fact that *(a)* on 8th November, 1932, sufficient moneys were available to pay him what was then owing to him in respect of services rendered in the year 1932–1933, and *(b)* sufficient moneys from the same grant were also available to pay him in full on 31st March, when he finally completed the performance of his contracts ...

The above reasoning shows that the plaintiff is entitled to succeed in the argument based on *Churchward's Case.*

Judgment for the plaintiff. The State appealed to the Full Court.

Dixon J

... It remains to deal with the contention that the contract is unenforceable because no sufficient appropriation of moneys has been made by Parliament to answer the contract. 'The general doctrine is that all obligations to pay money undertaken by the Crown are subject to the implied condition that the funds necessary to satisfy the obligation shall be appropriated by Parliament' *(New South Wales* v. *The Commonwealth [No 1]* [(1930) 44 CLR at 353]). But, in my opinion, that general doctrine does not mean that no contract exposes the Crown to a liability to suit ... unless and until an appropriation of funds to answer the contract has been made by the Parliament concerned, or unless some statutory authorization or recognition of the contract can be found.

... The principles of responsible government impose upon the administration a responsibility to Parliament, or rather to the House which deals with finance, for what the Administration has done. It is a function of the Executive, not of Parliament, to make contracts on behalf of the Crown. The Crown's advisers are answerable politically to Parliament for their acts in making contracts. Parliament is considered to retain the power of enforcing the responsibility of the Administration by means of its control over the expenditure of public moneys. But the principles of responsible government do not disable the Executive from acting without the prior approval of Parliament, nor from contracting for the expenditure of moneys conditionally upon appropriation by Parliament and doing so before funds to answer the expenditure have actually been made legally available. Some confusion has been occasioned by the terms in which the conditional nature of the contracts of the Crown from time to time has been described, terms chosen rather for the sake of emphasis than of technical accuracy. But, in my opinion, the manner in which the doctrine was enunciated by Isaacs C.J., when he last had occasion to state it, gives a correct as well as a clear exposition of it. In *Australian Railways Union* v. *Victorian Railways Commissioners* [(1932) 46 CLR at 176], he said: 'It is true that every contract with any responsible government of His Majesty, whether it be one of a mercantile character or one of service, is subject to the condition that before payment is made out of the Public Consolidated Fund Parliament must appropriate the necessary sum. But subject to that condition, unless some competent statute properly construed makes the appropriation a condition precedent, a contract by the Government otherwise within its authority is binding.' Notwithstanding expressions capable of a contrary interpretation which have occasionally been used, the prior provision of funds by Parliament is not a condition preliminary to the obligation of the contract. If it were so, performance on the part of the subject could not be exacted nor could he, if he did perform, establish a disputed claim to an amount of money under his contract until actual disbursement of the money in dispute was authorised by Parliament.

[He then considered the authorities, including *Churchward* v. *R*, and continued:] [The true position there was that] the provision of funds by Parliament [was] simply ... a contractual condition and ... a condition which must be fulfilled before actual payment by the Crown, but not ... a matter going to the formation, legality, or validity of the contract, and not ... a condition precedent to suit ...

In my opinion, it is not an answer to a suit against a State ... upon a contract, that the moneys necessary to answer the liability have not up to the time of the suit been provided by Parliament. This does not mean that, if Parliament has by an expression of its will in a form which the Court is bound to notice, refused to provide funds for the purposes of the contract, it remains actionable ...

That question does not arise in the present case. Indeed a ground upon which the judgment of Evatt J. is based is that moneys were provided by Parliament out of which the liability to the plaintiff might lawfully be discharged. I do not in any way disagree with this view, but, as I have formed a definite opinion that the contention of the Crown misconceives the doctrine upon which it is founded, I have thought it desirable to place my judgment upon the grounds I have given.

In my opinion the judgment of Evatt J. is right and should be affirmed.

Gavan Duffy CJ agreed with Dixon J. Rich, Starke, and McTiernan JJ delivered judgments in favour of dismissing the appeal. Appeal dismissed.

Street, *Governmental Liability* (Cambridge 1953) at 91–2, argues that without the necessary parliamentary appropriation the contract, although valid, is 'unenforceable' in the sense in which that word is used for contracts which do not comply with formal requirements, such as the requirement of writing formerly specified in the Statute of Frauds (see now, for example, s 2 of the Law of Property (Miscellaneous Provisions) Act 1989). In contrast, Turpin, *Government and Procurement Contracts* (Harlow 1989) at 93–4, points out that in the highly unlikely event that payment was refused because it would exceed the existing appropriation, there is no reason in principle why a contractor should not be able to sue the Crown and obtain judgment. Turpin suggests that a court will normally be justified in assuming that money is or will be made available, and continues:

[T]his inference would be rebutted only by a clear indication ... of Parliament's unwillingness to allow payment of the contractor, or if the court were satisfied that Parliament had not voted money sufficient for this purpose and would not be asked to do so. In these remote contingencies the court would doubtless be obliged to dismiss the suit and the contract would be unenforceable against the Crown.

See further Davies, *The Public Law of Government Contracts* (Oxford 2008) at 98–9.

QUESTIONS

- In *Bardolph*, did Dixon J (with whom Rich and Starke JJ agreed on this point) differ from Evatt J on the effect of a failure to appropriate?
- Whatever the relevance of parliamentary appropriation today, can and should the rule apply beyond central government?

15.6.5 The no-fettering rule

One axiomatic review doctrine with which government contracting may conflict is the no-fettering principle, which we examined in ch 5, as contracts concluded by government may operate to fetter the way in which statutory discretions may be exercised (and also possibly prevent government from doing those acts required to fulfil a statutory duty). Just as administrative law places restrictions upon the freedom of decision-makers to constrain their discretion by the adoption of policies—in order to ensure that discretion is actually exercised on the facts before the decision-maker—so administrators are constrained in the extent to which they may tie their own hands by forming contracts which impact upon their ability to exercise discretionary power given the facts before them and the demands of the public interest. At the same time, however, situations inevitably arise in which the objectives which the conferral of the discretion contemplates can be achieved only—or at least most effectively or efficiently—by means of contractual arrangements which necessarily impact upon the further exercise of the discretion. Davies (2006) 122 *LQR* 98 at 105 explains that

[t]he 'no-fettering' rule has potentially serious implications for government contracts because almost any contract is bound to limit the government's discretion to some extent. For example, a contract with a private firm to run a particular prison effectively precludes the government from contracting with another firm to run the prison or bringing it back into the public sector until the contract can be brought to an end. Thus, if strictly applied, the 'no-fettering' rule would operate to render most contracts ultra vires. This would be unsatisfactory in several respects. From the contractor's perspective, it would be impossible to rely on a contract with the government, since at any time the contract could be struck down as a fetter. As a result, firms might decide not to bid for government work at all, or to do so only at an inflated price to take account of the higher risk. This would impede the government's ability to procure goods and services at a competitive price. Moreover, public services would be under constant threat of disruption.

However, Davies goes on to acknowledge that

it is important that the 'no-fettering' rule be maintained in some form. It reflects the special nature of public power. The government is democratically accountable to the electorate. It needs the ability to change its policies in order to reflect the will of the people (particularly after a change of government) or to reflect new circumstances (such as evidence of a new risk to public health). Although the interests of a private contractor should not be lightly displaced, for the reasons just given they should not be allowed to trump an important public interest in adopting a new policy.

The courts must therefore strike a careful balance between, on the one hand, the preservation of discretion and, on the other hand, affording public authorities that degree of freedom to enter into contracts necessary to the effective discharge of their responsibilities. This issue was considered by the House of Lords in *Ayr Harbour Trustees* v. *Oswald* (1883) 8 App Cas 623. The Harbour Trustees exercised their statutory powers of compulsory purchase—which they held for the management and improvement of the harbour—in respect of Oswald's land, but in order to reduce the compensation payable they undertook not to use the land they acquired in a manner which would impede access from Oswald's remaining land to the harbour. Their Lordships concluded that the undertaking was invalid, Lord Blackburn (at 634) explaining his reasoning thus:

> I think that where the legislature confer powers on any body to take lands compulsorily for a particular purpose, it is on the ground that the using of that land for that purpose will be for the public good. Whether that body be one which is seeking to make a profit for shareholders, or, as in the present case, a body of trustees acting solely for the public good, I think in either case the powers conferred on the body empowered to take the land compulsorily are intrusted to them, and their successors, to be used for the furtherance of that object which the legislature has thought sufficiently for the public good to justify it in intrusting them with such powers; and, consequently, that a contract purporting to bind them and their successors not to use those powers is void.

This seems to imply that the interest in preserving the administrator's discretion will always prevail over the advantages which may flow from allowing contractual arrangements to be put in place; Lord Blackburn does not appear to envisage that any kind of balance needs to be struck between these two interests. In similar vein Rowlett J, in *Rederiaktiebolaget Amphitrite* v. *The King* [1921] 3 KB 500 at 503, considered that 'it is not competent for the Government to fetter its future executive action, which must necessarily be determined by the needs of the community when the question arises. It cannot by contract hamper its freedom of action in matters which concern the welfare of the State.'

However, we find a retreat from the strictures of the position apparently adopted by Lord Blackburn in *Ayr Harbour*. In *Birkdale District Electric Supply Co Ltd* v. *Corporation of Southport* [1926] AC 355, the House of Lords adopted an interpretation of *Ayr Harbour* which allows greater scope for government contracting. Lord Sumner said (at 371):

> On examining the facts in the *Ayr Harbour* case it is plain that, in effect, the trustees did not merely propose to covenant in a manner that committed the business of the harbour to restricted lines in the future; they were to forbear, once and for all, to acquire all that the statute intended them to acquire, for, though technically they acquired the whole of the land, they were to sterilize part of their acquisition, so far as the statutory purpose of their undertaking was concerned. ... The land itself was affected in favour of the former owner in the *Ayr* case just as a towpath is affected in favour of the owner of a dominant tenement, if he is given a personal right of walking along it. If the Ayr trustees had reduced the acquisition price by covenanting with the respondent for a perpetual right to moor his barges, free of tolls, at any wharf they might construct on the water front of the land acquired, the decision might, and I think would, have been different.

Birkdale thus rejects the idea that contracts which impact upon the exercise of discretionary powers are *inevitably* void, and instead adopts a more subtle test based on the compatibility of the contractual arrangements with the statutory scheme. This approach, which has its origin in *R v. Inhabitants of Leake* (1833) 5 B & Ad 469, was endorsed by the House of Lords in *British Transport Commission* v. *Westmorland County Council* [1958] AC 126. The question that arose—which did not involve a contract, but which raised the same issues of principle—was whether it was possible for a bridge to be dedicated to public use. The Commission argued, without success, that it could not, because this would cut across its statutory discretion to 'discontinue' the bridge. Having determined that the incompatibility test should be applied, Viscount Simonds said (at 143–4):

> I must next consider what is the test of incompatibility, which, as I have already said, appears to me to be the real difficulty in the case. This is a question of fact. It can be nothing else and it has been so treated, and expressly so treated, in many of the cases to which I have referred. But to say this does not completely solve the problem. For the jury or tribunal of fact must still be properly directed what is the test, and it is to this point that counsel for the appellants directed his attack. He urged that there could only be incompatibility, or, perhaps I should here say, compatibility, if it could be proved that in no conceivable circumstances could the proposed user at any future time and in any way possibly interfere with the statutory purpose for which the land was acquired ...
>
> My Lords, I am satisfied that this argument is misconceived ... [T]o give to incompatibility such an extended meaning is in effect to reduce the principle to a nullity. For a jury, invited to say that in no conceivable circumstances and at no distance of time could an event possibly happen, could only fold their hands and reply that it was not for them to prophesy what an inscrutable Providence might in all the years to come disclose. I do not disguise from myself that it is difficult to formulate with precision what direction should be given to a jury. But, after all, we live in a world in which our actions are constantly guided by a consideration of reasonable probabilities of risks that can reasonably be foreseen and guarded against, and by a disregard of events of which, even if we think of them as possible, we can fairly say that they are not at all likely to happen. And it is, in my opinion, by such considerations as these, imprecise though they may be, that a tribunal of fact must be guided in determining whether a proposed user of land will interfere with the statutory purpose for which it was acquired.

The *Westmorland* case thus affirms that the incompatibility test is to be used in this context. Further, by rejecting the very strict test of incompatibility proposed by counsel for the appellants, the decision provides greater scope for contracting. It is not the case that for a contract to be compatible with a statutory discretion that there must be no conceivable case in which the contract and exercise of the discretion could come into conflict. The exact test to be applied instead is not completely clear from Viscount Simonds' speech, however, it seems that one must ask whether it is probable that the contract will come into conflict with exercise of the discretion, based on reasonably foreseeable events, rather than those not likely to happen even if possible.

More modern case law has largely maintained this approach. On the one hand, the exponential growth in government contracting renders impractical and implausible a retreat to the former strict approach to fettering by contract. On the other hand, however, the courts have, despite the centrality of contracting to modern government, maintained the compatibility principle and thus the ultimate primacy of statute and the public interest. Consider the following extract from the judgment of Mason J in the Australian High Court decision,

Ansett Transport Industries (Operations) Pty Ltd v. *Commonwealth* (1977) 139 CLR 54 at 75 (references to the Commonwealth are to the federal government):

> Public confidence in government dealings and contracts would be greatly disturbed if all contracts which affect public welfare or fetter future executive action were held not to be binding on the government or on public authorities. And it would be detrimental to the public interest to deny to the government or a public authority power to enter a valid contract merely because the contract affects the public welfare. Yet on the other hand the public interest requires that neither the government nor a public authority can by a contract disable itself or its officer from performing a statutory duty or from exercising a discretionary power conferred by or under a statute by binding itself or its officer not to perform the duty or to exercise the discretion in a particular way in the future. To take an example related to this case: the Commonwealth could not, by making a contract with an airline company whereby it promises that the Secretary of the Department of Transport would not for the next fifteen years issue to other airline companies import permits for aircraft, fetter the future exercise by the Secretary of the discretion conferred upon him by the Customs (Prohibited Imports) Regulations. The Secretary must at all times deal with applications for import permits in accordance with the law; if he considers that, in conformity with government policy, the public interest calls for the importation of the aircraft, he should grant the application notwithstanding that the Commonwealth has entered into a contract which provides to the contrary. To hold otherwise would enable the executive by contract in an anticipatory way to restrict and stultify the ambit of a statutory discretion which is to be exercised at some time in the future in the public interest or for the public good.

More generally, there are contextual reasons not to be overly concerned with the potential fettering of statutory discretion by contract. First, as regards contracts with the Crown, it is important to recall that the Crown is immune from coercive remedies such as injunctions and specific performance where it breaches contracts. Thus, the reality is that if a contractual term stood in the way of the Crown exercising its statutory discretion in a particular way, the Crown could simply exercise its discretion in a way that breached the contract, and the other party to the contract would have no means of requiring the Crown to perform their contractual obligation. Of course damages could be recovered from the Crown, or the Crown could negotiate with the other party for release or to vary the contract terms, but the Crown could not be compelled by a court order to fulfil their contractual obligation. Second, as Turpin (*Government and Procurement Contracts* (Harlow 1989) at 90) observes,

> [I]f the government decides that the public interest requires a government contract to be brought to an end, it will usually (in a contract for the procurement of goods or services) be able to determine the contract under the standard contractual 'break' clause, rather than seek to rely on the rule of government effectiveness. In this event provision is made by the standard clause for the compensation of the contractor, in a measure less than that for contractual damages.

It also worth observing that the fettering doctrine in general is not applied as strictly as it once was (see 5.3.2–5.3.3), so that a particularly strict application of the doctrine to contractual fetters would seem out of place given the modern development of the law of fettering.

Lastly, it is important to note the principle that general contractual terms are not to be interpreted as involving an undertaking by the public party to the contract that powers will be exercised a certain way in future. Thus, in *Commissioners of Crown Lands* v. *Page* [1960] 2 QB 274, Devlin LJ said (at 291):

> When the Crown, or any other person, is entrusted, whether by virtue of the prerogative or by statute, with discretionary powers to be exercised for the public good, it does not, when making a private contract in general terms, undertake (and it may be that it could not even with the use of specific language validly undertake) to fetter itself in the use of those powers, and in the exercise of its discretion.

Mason J in *Ansett* echoed this principle saying, 'in the absence of specific words, an undertaking which would affect the exercise of discretionary powers to be exercised for the public good, should not be imputed to the Commonwealth' (at 79).

15.6.6 Agency and public authorities' contracts

It is officials within government departments who conclude contracts on behalf of the Crown. But what if those officials do not have authorization to conclude such contracts, for example because they are not authorized to do so under the relevant parent statute or have not been authorized by their superiors?

Attorney-General for Ceylon v. *AD Silva* [1953] AC 461
Judicial Committee of the Privy Council

The Principal Collector of Customs of Ceylon, in the mistaken belief that certain steel plates belonging to the Crown which were on customs premises were unclaimed goods, obtained the permission of the Chief Secretary of Ceylon to sell them by public auction in accordance with the provisions of the Ceylon Customs Ordinance (below). The claimant, Silva, purchased the steel plates at the auction on 4 March 1947, but when the Collector refused to deliver them Silva brought an action for damages for breach of contract against the Attorney-General as the representative of the Crown. The Collector had refused to make delivery to Silva when he learned of a prior authorized sale of the steel plates to another purchaser. On 23 January 1947, the Services Disposal Board of Ceylon, which had been appointed by the Ministry of Supply in England to dispose of the steel plates, had contracted to sell them to a firm in Ceylon. The Supreme Court of Ceylon held that there had been a valid contract to sell to the claimant and awarded him substantial damages. On appeal by the Attorney-General:

Mr LMD de Silva (giving the judgment of the Judicial Committee of the Privy Council)

... The precise question which arises for their Lordships' decision is whether the Principal Collector of Customs had authority to enter into a contract binding on the Crown for the sale of the goods in question to the plaintiff. This question can conveniently be dealt with under two heads: had the Principal Collector actual authority to enter into a contract; if not, did he have ostensible authority to do so?

It is argued that the Principal Collector had actual authority to enter into the contract by reason of the provisions of sections 17 and 108 of the Customs Ordinance (chapter 185, Legislative Enactments of Ceylon). Section 17 makes warehouse rent payable in respect of goods left in customs warehouses ...

... Section 108 authorizes the sale of goods left for more than three months in customs ware-houses 'to answer' the charges due thereon.

It is claimed by the plaintiff that the Customs Ordinance was binding on the Crown, that warehouse rent was due under section 17 of the Ordinance on the goods in question, and that as they had been left on the customs premises for a period longer than three months, they were liable to be sold after public advertisement under section 108. This was in fact the basis on which the Principal Collector held the sale, and it would without doubt have been a sound basis if the property had all the time been private property. But it is argued by the Crown that, no matter what the Principal Collector thought or did, the Customs Ordinance was not binding on the Crown; that it, or at any rate the provisions in it relevant to this case, were inapplicable to property belonging to the Crown and that therefore the plaintiff's contention fails.

The first matter which arises for consideration is whether the Ordinance binds the Crown ...

[Their Lordships, having considered the relevant legislation, concluded that the Ordinance did not bind the Crown and continued:] It has been argued that apart from the Ordinance the Principal Collector has actual authority to do what he did, and that this authority was reinforced by the letter written to him by the Chief Secretary. It is a simple and clear proposition that a public officer has not by reason of the fact that he is in the service of the Crown the right to act for and on behalf of the Crown in all matters which concern the Crown. The right to act for the Crown in any particular matter must be established by reference to statute or otherwise. It has not been shown that the Principal Collector had any authority to sell property of the Crown or to enter into a contract on its behalf for its sale: nor has it been shown that the Chief Secretary, who authorized the sale, had any such authority. His functions were defined by the Ceylon (State Council) Order in Council, 1931, and under this Order the most that can be said is that he was authorized to deal with certain Crown property under the direct administration of the Government of Ceylon. It is therefore clear that the Principal Collector of Customs had no actual authority to enter into a contract for the sale of the goods which are the subject matter of this action.

Next comes the question whether the Principal Collector of Customs had ostensible author-ity, such as would bind the Crown, to enter into the contract sued on. All 'ostensible' authority involves a representation by the principal as to the extent of the agent's authority. No repre-sentation by the agent as to the extent of his authority can amount to a 'holding out' by the principal. No public officer, unless he possesses some special power, can hold out on behalf of the Crown that he or some other public officer has the right to enter into a contract in respect of the property of the Crown when in fact no such right exists. Their Lordships think, therefore, that nothing done by the Principal Collector or the Chief Secretary amounted to a holding out by the Crown that the Principal Collector had the right to enter into a contract to sell the goods which are the subject-matter of this action ...

In advertising the goods for sale the Principal Collector no doubt represented to the public that the goods were saleable. But the question is whether this act of the Principal Collector can be said to be an act of the Crown. Their Lordships have considered whether by reason of the fact that the Principal Collector had been appointed to his office under the Customs Ordinance, and was the proper officer to administer it, he must be regarded as having had ostensible author-ity on behalf of the Crown to represent to the public that goods advertised for sale under the Customs Ordinance were in fact saleable under that Ordinance. It is argued that, if so, although the goods were in fact not saleable under the Ordinance because they were Crown property, or property to which the sections of the Ordinance authorizing sale were not applicable, or for some other reason, the contract would be binding on the Crown and the Crown would be liable in damages as it could not fulfil it.

Their Lordships think that the Principal Collector cannot be regarded as having any such authority. He had, no doubt, authority to do acts of a particular class, namely, to enter on behalf of the Crown into sales of certain goods. But that authority was limited because it arose under certain sections of the Ordinance and only when those sections were applicable. It was said by Lord Atkinson in *Russo Chinese Bank* v. *Li Yau Sam* [[1910] AC 174 at 184]: 'If the agent be held out as having only a limited authority to do on behalf of his principal acts of a particular class, then the principal is not bound by an act done outside that authority, even though it be an act of that particular class, because, the authority being thus represented to be limited, the party prejudiced has notice, and should ascertain whether or not the act is authorized.' With that view their Lordships respectfully agree. In that case the authority did not arise under a statute, but in their Lordships' view this fact makes no difference. If there is a difference at all it would lie in the circumstance that in a statute the limits of the authority conferred are fixed rigidly and no recourse to evidence is necessary to ascertain them. The Ordinance could no doubt have made the representation by the Principal Collector binding on the Crown, but it has not done so, and to read into it any such provision would be unduly to extend its meaning.

It may be said that it causes hardship to a purchaser at a sale under the Customs Ordinance if the burden of ascertaining whether or not the Principal Collector has authority to enter into the sale is placed upon him. This undoubtedly is true. But where, as in the case of the Customs Ordinance, the Ordinance does not dispense with that necessity, to hold otherwise would be to hold that public officers had dispensing powers because they then could by unauthorized acts nullify or extend the provisions of the Ordinance. Of the two evils this would be the greater one ...

... Their Lordships will therefore humbly advise Her Majesty that the appeal be allowed.

The position of a person who deals with a *Crown* agent acting outside the scope of his authority is exacerbated by the fact that the agent will not be personally liable on the contract (*MacBeath* v. *Haldimand* (1786) 1 TR 172)—the agent is not in law a party but rather the Crown—or, as other agents are, for breach of an implied warranty of authority, this doctrine holding an agent liable where they act outside authority (*Dunn* v. *MacDonald* [1897] 1 QB 401 and 555; *The Prometheus* (1949) 82 LILR 859); in essence the law holds an implied contract to arise between the agent and other party, the basis of the contract being the giving of a promise by the agent that he is acting on his principal's authority, in consideration of the other party agreeing to deal with the agent. The doctrine of implied warranty of authority was said not to be applicable to Crown agents for reasons of public policy, *viz* that if they were not free of personal liability 'no man would accept any office of trust under Government' (*per* Ashhurst J in *MacBeath* v. *Haldimand* at 181, adopted by Charles J in *Dunn* v. *MacDonald* at 405). But could it not be argued equally that individuals would be deterred from acting as agents for private principals if there was a risk they could end up personally liable, which would in turn be detrimental to the carrying on of commerce? Yet that argument does not work to protect agents in such situations from being sued under the implied warranty of authority doctrine.

Lastly, the jurisdictional principle means that the authority of an agent cannot extend to a contract that is *ultra vires* the agent or *a fortiori* his department. Thus, in Silva's case, quite apart from the ordinary principles of agency, it is difficult to see how the Crown could have been bound by the contract in view of the provisions of the Customs Ordinance.

QUESTION

- Do you agree that officials should be exempted from the implied warranty of authority doctrine?

15.7 Restitution

15.7.1 The '*Woolwich* principle'

Whereas fields such as the law of torts are generally concerned with redressing wrong-fully inflicted *losses*, the developing field of restitution is concerned to reverse wrongful *gains*. Consonant with the principle of equality, broadly speaking, public bodies which have received payments or benefited by services rendered to them can be liable in the same way as private individuals under the principles of restitution.

In this section we focus specifically on the development of the position concerning recovery of money paid by a citizen to a public authority in response to an *ultra vires* demand by an authority. We touch upon the rationale for allowing recovery in such cases, and how recovery in such cases relates to the principle of equality, in the next section. But first let us consider the seminal House of Lords decision in this area.

Woolwich Building Society v. Inland Revenue Commissioners [1993] AC 70
House of Lords

The Woolwich Equitable Building Society had paid certain sums in tax under regulations which were later held in the courts to be *ultra vires* so far as these types of payment were concerned: [1990] 1 WLR 1400. The Revenue repaid the money with interest from the date when the order of invalidity was made in the High Court, but Woolwich claimed interest on the sums from the earlier dates on which they were actually paid. The amount in question was agreed by the parties at £6,730,000 and its recoverability depended upon whether Woolwich had a restitutionary claim to the money from the time it was paid. This was an appeal to the House of Lords by the Crown from a decision of the Court of Appeal allowing Woolwich's claim.

Lord Goff

… Take any tax or duty paid by the citizen pursuant to an unlawful demand. Common justice seems to require that tax to be repaid, unless special circumstances or some principle of policy require otherwise; prima facie, the taxpayer should be entitled to repayment as of right.

… [Mr Glick, counsel for the Crown] asserted that, if your Lordships' House were to accept Woolwich's argument [that there is an immediate restitutionary right to the repayment of money levied under an unlawful demand], it would be impossible for us to set the appropriate limits to the application of the principle. An unbridled right to recover overpaid taxes and duties subject only to the usual six-year time bar was, he suggested, unacceptable in modern society. Some limits had to be set to such claims; and the selection of such limits, being essentially a matter of policy, was one which the legislature alone is equipped to make.

My reaction to this submission of Mr. Glick is to confess (to some extent) and yet to avoid. I agree that there appears to be a widely held view that some limit has to be placed upon the recovery of taxes paid pursuant to an ultra vires demand. I would go further and accept that the armoury of common law defences, such as those which prevent recovery of money paid under a binding compromise or to avoid a threat of litigation, may be either inapposite or inadequate for the purpose; because it is possible to envisage, especially in modern taxation law which tends to be excessively complex, circumstances in which some very substantial sum of money may be held to have been exacted ultra vires from a very large number of taxpayers. It may well therefore be necessary to have recourse to other defences, such as for example short time limits within which such claims have to be advanced ...

In all the circumstances, I do not consider that Mr. Glick's argument, powerful though it is, is persuasive enough to deter me from recognising, in law, the force of the justice underlying Woolwich's case. Furthermore, there are particular reasons which impel me to that conclusion. The first is that this opportunity will never come again. If we do not take it now, it will be gone forever. The second is that I fear that, however compelling the principle of justice may be, it would never be sufficient to persuade a government to propose its legislative recognition by Parliament; caution, otherwise known as the Treasury, would never allow this to happen. The third is that, turning Mr. Glick's argument against him, the immediate practical impact of the recognition of the principle will be limited, for (unlike the present case) most cases will continue for the time being to be regulated by the various statutory règimes now in force. The fourth [related to timing] ... Fifth, it is well established that, if the Crown pays money out of the consolidated fund without authority, such money is ipso facto recoverable if it can be traced: see *Auckland Harbour Board v. The King* [1924] A.C. 318. It is true that the claim in such a case can be distinguished as being proprietary in nature. But the comparison with the position of the citizen, on the law as it stands at present, is most unattractive.

There is a sixth reason which favours this conclusion. I refer to the decision of the European Court of Justice, in *Amministrazione delle Finanze dello Stato v. S.p.A. San Giorgio* (Case 199/82) [1983] E.C.R. 3595, which establishes that a person who pays charges levied by a member state contrary to the rules of Community law is entitled to repayment of the charge, such right being regarded as a consequence of, and an adjunct to, the rights conferred on individuals by the Community provisions prohibiting the relevant charges: see paragraph 12 of the judgment of the court, at p. 3612. The *San Giorgio* case is also of interest for present purposes in that it accepts that Community law does not prevent a national legal system from disallowing repayment of charges where to do so would entail unjust enrichment of the recipient, in particular where the charges have been incorporated into the price of goods and so passed on to the purchaser. I only comment that, at a time when Community law is becoming increasingly important, it would be strange if the right of the citizen to recover overpaid charges were to be more restricted under domestic law than it is under European law.

I would therefore hold that money paid by a citizen to a public authority in the form of taxes or other levies paid pursuant to an ultra vires demand by the authority is prima facie recoverable by the citizen as of right. As at present advised, I incline to the opinion that this principle should extend to embrace cases in which the tax or other levy has been wrongly exacted by the public authority not because the demand was ultra vires but for other reasons, for example because the authority has misconstrued a relevant statute or regulation. It is not however necessary to decide the point in the present case, and in any event cases of this kind are generally the subject of statutory regimes which legislate for the circumstances in which money so paid either must or may be repaid. Nor do I think it necessary to consider for the purposes of the present case to what extent the common law may provide the public authority with a defence to a claim for the repayment of money so paid ... It will be a matter for consideration whether the fact that the plaintiff has passed on the tax or levy so that the burden has fallen on another should provide a defence to his claim. Although this is contemplated by the European Court of Justice in the *San Giorgio* case, it is evident from *Air Canada v. British Columbia*, 59 D.L.R. (4th) 161 that the point is not without its difficulties; and the availability of such a defence may depend upon the nature of the tax or other levy ...

For these reasons, I would dismiss the appeal with costs.

Lords Browne-Wilkinson and Slynn delivered speeches in favour of dismissing the appeal, the former expressly agreeing with Lord Goff's 'Woolwich principle'. Lords Keith and Jauncey delivered speeches in favour of allowing the appeal. Appeal dismissed.

662 • LIABILITY OF PUBLIC AUTHORITIES

> **QUESTIONS**
> - As we saw earlier, a claimant cannot recover damages for losses solely on the basis that those losses were caused by an *ultra vires* act. Is this principle reconcilable with the principle established in *Woolwich* that a claimant can recover moneys paid over to government pursuant to an *ultra vires* demand as of right?
> - Do you find convincing Lord Goff's reasons for the courts taking the lead in this area, rather than leaving legal development to Parliament?

15.7.2 The scope of the *Woolwich* principle

It would seem in principle that all *ultra vires* errors should fall within the *Woolwich* principle and that misconstruction of the relevant statute or regulation—a matter to which Lord Goff referred, but on which he expressed no final decision (in the penultimate paragraph of our excerpt above)—would almost always entail *ultra vires* errors in the light of the evolution of the 'error of law' concept which we charted in ch 2. Support was lent to this view by Sir Richard Scott V-C in *British Steel plc* v. *Customs and Excise Commissioners* [1997] 2 All ER 366 at 375–6. He said that '[a]n unlawful demand for duty must, in a sense, always be an *ultra vires* demand'. This would be so, said his Lordship, whether 'the demand is based on *ultra vires* regulations, or on a mistaken view of the legal effect of valid regulations, or on a mistaken view of the facts of the case'. In all such situations, 'the taxpayer would, prima facie, become entitled, on making payment pursuant to the unlawful demand, to a common law restitutionary right to repayment', unless the legislation may be found, upon proper construction, to exclude that right.

The scope of the *Woolwich* principle would appear to be fairly wide. As Beatson (1993) 109 *LQR* 401 at 417–18 writes:

> To sum up, the *Woolwich* principle clearly applies to taxes and duties levied by governmental bodies which are *ultra vires* because of the invalidity of the relevant subordinate legislation. It almost certainly applies where the *ultra vires* nature of the levy stems from an error of law or an abuse of discretion. The position of levies vitiated by procedural unfairness is less clear but, in principle, should not differ. While the House of Lords did not give explicit guidance on the range of bodies subject to the principle, it has been argued that it should apply to other public bodies whose authority to charge is subject to and limited by public law principles, and to other bodies whose authority to charge is solely the product of statute, and thus limited. While the uncertainties do not, it is submitted, undermine the coherence of the principle laid down in the case, they suggest that further statutory clarification is desirable. Additionally, considerations of policy may indicate that the principle should be limited in scope, for instance to governmental exactions or by the exclusion of the public utilities, or by the operation of prudential safeguards.

For further discussion of these latter issues see (1993) 109 *LQR* at 425–31 and more generally see the Law Commission's report, *Restitution: Mistakes of Law and Ultra Vires Public Authority Receipts and Payments* (Law Com No 227, 1994 at [6.32]–[6.42]).

In *Waikato Regional Airport Ltd* v. *Attorney-General (New Zealand)* [2003] UKPC 50 at [79]–[80], the Privy Council lent support to the view that charges under statutory powers, although not a tax, are within the *Woolwich* principle. The Privy Council further stated:

> Their Lordships also note (without basing their decision on it, since it was not cited or discussed in argument) that one of the cases referred to with apparent approval by Lord Goff of Chieveley in *Woolwich, South of Scotland Electricity Board v British Oxygen Company Ltd* [1959] 1 WLR 587, was a case of a public board overcharging for electricity supplies which were of commercial benefit to the recipient, but the House of Lords did not doubt that excessive charges were recoverable by the company which had paid them.

In the most recent significant decision on the *Woolwich* principle, *Test Claimants in the FII Group Litigation* v. *Revenue and Customs Commissioners* [2012] UKSC 19, [2012] 2 AC 337, the Supreme Court ruled, contrary to prior lower court authority (*Norwich City Council* v. *Stringer* (2001) 33 HLR 158), that restitution based on the *Woolwich* principle does not depend on the Revenue making an official demand for tax. As such, a voluntary payment of tax by a citizen in compliance with rules later found *ultra vires* can ground a claim. The judgments reveal a concern that the principle should not be unduly narrowed, at least in the field of tax, given the weighty rationales which underpin it. Lord Walker considered that one reason for not allowing the principle to be read narrowly so that it would depend on the 'details of the procedure adopted for the levying and payment of any particular tax' went back to the 'high constitutional importance of the principle that there should be no taxation without Parliament' (at [74]–[75]). Lord Walker thus considered '[w]e should restate the *Woolwich* principle so as to cover all sums paid to a public authority in response to (and sufficiently causally connected with) an apparent statutory requirement to pay tax which (in fact and in law) is not lawfully due' (at [79]). Note that this formulation of the *Woolwich* principle suggests that it only applies to payments of tax, albeit it does not seem it was Lord Walker's intention to so limit the operation of the principle. Lord Sumption recalled 'the mischief which justified in Lord Goff's eyes a special rule for unlawful charges by public authorities was (i) that no tax should be collected without parliamentary authority, and (ii) that citizens did not deal on equal terms with the state, and could not be expected to withhold payment when faced with the coercive powers of the revenue, whether those powers were actually exercised or merely held in reserve' (at [173]). These rationales were not such as to depend on whether a demand for tax was made or not. Rules held out as being valid are rules with which a citizen must comply whether or not demands are made of them, and they should not be made to suffer losses for innocently relying on those rules when the rules turn out to be invalid.

Let us digress briefly to consider what the quotations from *FII* tell us about the relationship between the *Woolwich* principle and the principle of equality. Lord Sumption apparently considered the *Woolwich* principle to entail a deviation from the equality principle for the benefit of citizens: *Woolwich* established 'a special rule for unlawful charges by public authorities', and this rule is justified partly on the basis that authorities have a special capacity to demand payments and citizens are not able to resist such demands. But, on the other hand, it is also the case that public authorities may, in certain circumstances recover overpayments from citizens, for example via statutory schemes for recovery: eg *R (Cooper)* v. *Secretary of State for Work and Pensions* [2011] UKSC 60, [2012] 2 AC 1. Importantly, recall that Lord Goff's fifth factor in favour of establishing the *Woolwich* principle was the contrast if the citizen could not claim in *Woolwich*, with the ability of the Crown to recover, according to *Auckland Harbour Board* v. *The King* [1924] AC 318, where it had wrongly paid money out of the consolidated fund. Given an authority can seek restitution from a citizen for *ultra vires* payments made to the citizen, would it not constitute a breach of the equality principle to bar a citizen from recovering sums paid to an authority pursuant to an *ultra vires* demand? In this light *Woolwich* moved the law closer to parity of position as between citizen and public authority.

Returning to the issue of scope, at the time of the decision in *Woolwich*, the general position was that money paid under a mistake of law, a separate ground of restitution from the *Woolwich* ground, was irrecoverable (although Woolwich was not itself mistaken in that case: it had contended throughout that the tax was invalidly demanded). There was some reference to the mistake of law issue in *Woolwich*, but the change in the law came about in *Kleinwort Benson Ltd* v. *Lincoln City Council* [1999] 2 AC 349, where the House of Lords held that there was no such general rule against recovery: one could seek restitution on the ground that one had made a payment on the basis of a mistake of law. A case that falls within the *Woolwich* principle may also be a situation where the payment was made by the claimant under a mistake of law, and the House of Lords in *Deutsche Morgan Grenfell Group plc* v. *IRC* [2006] UKHL 49, [2007] 1 AC 558 decided that the claimant could sue in either or both actions: claiming on the basis of one did not exclude the possibility of also claiming on the basis of the other. There are differences between the different types of claim which mean that one may be more advantageous than the other depending on the facts (see *FII* at [186]). There might be an advantage in terms of the limitation period in the case of a claim for mistake of law: time starts running from the time of discovery of the mistake, which may be some time after the making of the payment, whereas for *Woolwich* claims the time period starts running from the time the relevant payment is made. In the *Woolwich* claim one needs to prove the authority acted *ultra vires* but does not need to show the taxpayer was mistaken as to their tax liabilities, while in the mistake of law claim one is relieved of having to prove the authority acted unlawfully but must show the claimant acted on a mistaken basis.

Lastly, statute may expressly or impliedly oust the *Woolwich* principle: *eg Monro* v. *Revenue and Customs Commissioners* [2008] EWCA Civ 306, [2009] Ch 69. It will often be the case that wrongful payment is covered by statutory schemes for repayment. Provision for such schemes may or may not impliedly oust the common law right of recovery. In every case, whether the common law right is ousted 'is a question of construction of the statute in question': *R (Child Poverty Action Group)* v. *Secretary of State for Work and Pensions* [2010] UKSC 54, [2011] 2 AC 15 at [27]. Thus, for example, in *Deutsche Morgan Grenfell Group*, the House of Lords held that a claim in restitution was not impliedly ousted despite statutory provision for a comprehensive scheme for recovery. The statutory scheme governed overpayments in the case of anyone 'who has paid [income tax or capital gains] tax charged under an assessment' (Taxes Management Act 1970, s 33). Their Lordships reasoned that s 33 did not apply where there was no *valid* assessment, as was the case on the facts, and as such the taxpayer could bring a common law restitution claim. Such a strict approach to ouster is warranted on the basis that Parliament would not lightly extinguish ordinary rights, and especially rights, such as those under the *Woolwich* principle, which—as Lords Walker and Sumption observed in *FII*—give effect to fundamental constitutional principles.

FURTHER RESOURCES

Bailey and Bowman, 'Public Authority Negligence Revisited' [2000] 59 *CLJ* 85

Bishop, 'The Rational Strength of the Private Law Model' (1990) 40 *University of Toronto Law Journal* 633

Cane, 'Damages in Public Law' (1999) 9 *Otago Law Review* 489

Cohen and Smith, 'Entitlement and the Body Politic: Rethinking Negligence in Public Law' (1986) 64 *Canadian Bar Review* 1

Craig, 'Once More unto the Breach: The Community, the State and Damages Liability' (1997) 113 *LQR* 67

Davies, *The Public Law of Government Contracts* (Oxford 2008)

Fairgrieve, *State Liability in Tort* (Oxford 2003)

Fairgrieve, Andenas, and Bell (eds), *Tort Liability of Public Authorities in Comparative Perspective* (London 2002)

Harlow, '"Public" and "Private" Law: Definition without Distinction' (1980) 43 *MLR* 241

Harlow, 'Francovich and the Problem of the Disobedient State' (1996) 2 *European Law Journal* 199

Harlow, *State Liability* (Oxford 2004)

Markesinis, Auby, Coester-Waltjen, and Deakin, *Tortious Liability of Statutory Bodies* (Oxford 1999)

Varuhas, *Damages and Human Rights* (Oxford 2016)

Weir, *An Introduction to Tort Law* (Oxford 2006)

Williams, *Unjust Enrichment and Public Law* (Oxford 2010)

16 DELEGATED LEGISLATION

16.1 General matters

16.1.1 The nature and growth of delegated legislation

Administrative law is concerned with a range of matters relating to administrative action—most obviously its lawfulness. The term 'administrative action' tends to trigger two assumptions: first, that such action involves the making of *decisions* within a framework of legislation bequeathed by Parliament and, second, that administrative action can, at least in part, be defined by distinguishing it from *legislative* action, the latter being the province of the legislature as distinct from the executive. The subject- matter of this chapter subverts those assumptions by highlighting, and considering the legal and constitutional implications of, the *legislative* role of the *administration*.

Our concern in this chapter, then, is with *delegated legislation* (or, as it is sometimes called, secondary, subordinate, executive, or administrative legislation). Such legislation—enacted by the administrative branch of government, usually under powers conferred upon it by the *legislative* branch but occasionally under the royal prerogative—is a well-established feature of the constitutional landscape in the UK. Indeed, such legislation is essential. Parliament lacks the time and resources to legislate comprehensively, and must therefore, in effect, contract out the enactment of much legislation to others. Moreover, delegated legislation is particularly apt in areas in which the law may need to be changed quickly, the enactment of primary legislation typically being a time-consuming business. As Chen, *Parliamentary Opinion of Delegated Legislation* (New York 1933) at 13–14 noted, in the UK the idea of 'legislative monopoly'—a notion derived from a pure conception of the separation of powers doctrine, under which only the legislature enacts legislation and to which the notion of administrative legislation is therefore anathema—has ebbed and flowed, but has 'never [been] complete'.

Against that background, it is indisputable that the tide of delegated legislation is at present—and has for some time been—rising. Indeed, such legislation dwarfs Acts of Parliament in terms of volume. For instance, in the period 2010–15, the UK Parliament passed an average of 32 Acts each year. In contrast, an average of 2,444 statutory instruments (a particular form of delegated legislation) were made annually during the same period (see House of Commons Library, *Acts and Statutory Instruments: The volume of UK legislation 1950 to 2015* (London 2015)). It is true that the average Act of Parliament is longer than the average piece of delegated legislation, but even allowing for this there is far more of the latter than the former, the number of pages of delegated legislation passed each year typically being three to four times greater than the number of pages of Acts of Parliament. Indeed, the volume of delegated legislation has increased dramatically in recent decades: whereas in

1990, 6,550 pages of statutory instruments were made, that figure had climbed to just shy of 12,000 by 2009.

However, it is not just the *amount* of delegated legislation that has increased; the *nature* of such legislation— and the scope of the powers under which it is enacted— have also changed. In a report published by the Hansard Society, Fox and Blackwell, *The Devil is in the Detail: Parliament and Delegated Legislation* (London 2014) observe that delegated legislation now routinely goes beyond addressing merely 'technical' matters and 'operational details', and instead affords the executive opportunities to make major policy choices. The House of Lords Constitution Committee (HL116, *Delegated Legislation and Parliament: A Response to the Strathclyde Review* (2015– 16) at [7]) has expressed similar concerns, noting that:

> Delegated powers in primary legislation have increasingly been drafted in broad and poorly-defined language that has permitted successive governments to use delegated legislation to address issues of policy and principle, rather than points of an administrative or technical nature.

One reaction to the modern reality of delegated legislation in the UK might be to argue that it is an affront to basic constitutional principles—most obviously the separation of powers—and that it ought to be radically reined in. However, while the concerns that arise in this area are understandable and legitimate, a more nuanced—and realistic—response is called for. The extent to which delegated legislation is problematic in constitutional terms turns upon a range of matters, including the *types* of powers that Parliament confers on the executive—and, in particular, the extent to which such powers equip the executive to amend or repeal Acts of Parliament themselves, the *scope* of the powers granted, the extent to which Parliament is capable of remaining in the driving seat by adequately *overseeing* the use of the delegated powers with which it equips the executive, and the extent to which there is sufficient *judicial control* of the exercise of such powers. It is with matters such as these—and so with the overarching question of the extent of the constitutional propriety of delegated legislation in the UK today—that we are concerned in this chapter.

16.1.2 Enabling provisions

Delegated legislation takes a number of forms, and a number of different terms—rules, regulations, byelaws, Orders in Council, circulars, guidance, directions, and codes of practice—are used to describe it. The terminology can seem bewildering; however, of much greater significance than these various labels are the different sorts of provisions in primary legislation which, in the first place, confer the power to enact administrative legislation. Such 'enabling provisions' demarcate the extent of the administrator's legislative power: any executive legislation enacted outwith the terms of the enabling statute will be *ultra vires* and vulnerable to judicial review (on which see 16.4).

It is therefore to the enabling provisions in primary legislation that we must look in order to understand the permitted content and nature of the resultant delegated legislation. Leaving to one side for now so-called Henry VIII powers (on which see 16.1.3), three types of enabling provision are worth sketching.

First, the power conferred by the enabling provision might be *very specific and limited*. For instance, the Consumer Rights Act 2016 provides certain protections to consumers who enter into contracts for (among other things) the supply of services. However, s 48(5) authorizes the Secretary of State to make an order providing that the Act's protections do not apply in respect of contracts concerning specified categories of services.

Second, although still relatively confined, the power conferred by an enabling provision might be *more substantial* in that its exercise may profoundly affect the operation of the relevant statutory regime. For example, the Education and Inspections Act 2006 authorizes the Secretary of State to intervene in respect of schools that are 'coasting' (as opposed to doing well). However, the meaning of the term 'coasting', which is central to the extent of the Secretary of State's intervention powers, is not set out in the Act; instead, s 60AB(3) requires the Secretary of State to make regulations defining the term (and hence the scope of his own powers).

Third, an enabling provision might in effect *delegate to the executive the task of setting out a whole legislative regime* by authorizing the making of detailed rules on some matter. For instance, s 20(1) of the Health and Social Care Act 2008 requires the Secretary of State to make regulations that impose such requirements as he considers necessary to ensure that certain health and social care-related activities are provided in ways that 'cause no avoidable harm to the persons for whom the services are provided'. Section 20(3) goes on to say that such regulations may make provision as to a broad range of matters, including who is a fit person to carry on or manage a relevant activity, how such activities are to be carried on, the state of the premises on which such activities are provided, and the handling of complaints and the learning of lessons from them. This approach is sometimes taken to quite extreme lengths through the enactment of 'framework' or 'skeleton' Acts which themselves have very little to say about the matters they are concerned with, instead delegating to the executive the task of making relevant law. The Childcare Act 2016, for example, requires 30 hours' free-of-charge childcare to be available for certain children, but the Act itself stretches to only four substantive sections, which leave entirely to regulations the details of the scheme. This attracted strong criticism from the House of Lords Delegated Powers and Regulatory Reform Committee (HL12, *2nd Report* (2015– 16) at [8]), which said that the approach to delegated legislation reflected in the Act was 'flawed' because it contained 'virtually nothing of substance beyond the vague "mission statement"' at the beginning of the legislation which set out the 30-hour requirement. The legislation was nevertheless enacted.

The foregoing examples demonstrate that to inquire as to the constitutional appropriateness of the executive's having powers to enact delegated legislation is somewhat meaningless. Closely defined powers to fill in minor gaps in the parent Act are as innocuous as they are inevitable. At the other end of the spectrum, however, there are real grounds for concern about the propriety of Parliament's transferring substantial law-making authority by means of enabling provisions that, in effect, permit the executive to devise entire legislative regimes.

16.1.3 Henry VIII powers

Enabling provisions known as 'Henry VIII clauses' (in reference to that king's autocratic style) have the particular characteristic of authorizing delegated legislation that amends or repeals primary legislation. Henry VIII powers have attracted strong criticism from some quarters. Hewart, *The New Despotism* (London 1929) at 53, considered them 'egregious'; by permitting amendment or repeal of provisions in primary legislation, such clauses may be thought to tip the balance too far in favour of the administrative branch at the expense of Parliament. More recently, former Lord Chief Justice Lord Judge, 'Ceding Power to the Executive; the Resurrection of Henry VIII' (Lecture, King's College London, April 2016) has argued that Henry VIII powers are (except in highly constrained circumstances) anathema to constitutional principle:

> When we speak of the sovereignty of Parliament nowadays we tend, perhaps inevitably, to think of the majority in the Commons having its way, of winning. Sovereign is a word which implies primacy, triumph. Fair enough. But surely we should remember that the sovereignty of Parliament has a less glamorous but no less crucial role in our constitution. At the heart of the development of our constitutional arrangements, Parliament is there to protect us from authoritarianism, from despotism, from an over mighty monarch, but also from an over mighty executive. That responsibility remains undiminished. … Unless strictly incidental to primary legislation, every Henry VIII clause, every vague skeleton bill, is a blow to the sovereignty of Parliament. And each one is a self-inflicted blow, each one boosting the power of the executive.

These general concerns about Henry VIII powers notwithstanding, it is necessary to bear in mind that not all such powers are equally suspect in constitutional terms. Some, for instance, are very modest in scope, and the reasons for them readily comprehensible. Take, for example, the Riot Compensation Act 2016, which establishes a regime for compensation for those whose property has been damaged, destroyed, or stolen in the course of a riot. Section 8(1) provides that such compensation must not exceed £1m. However, s 8(9) authorizes the Secretary of State to make regulations altering that figure. The need for this power is obvious: passing fresh primary legislation so as to amend the compensation cap in the light of inflation would hardly be a good use of Parliament's time.

However, Henry VIII powers can be framed much more broadly. For instance, while the primary legislation upon which a Henry VIII power bites might be the legislation that confers the power in the first place, that is not necessarily the case. Such a power might authorize the amendment or repeal of *any* legislation, including Acts of Parliament enacted subsequently to the Act conferring the Henry VIII power itself. A well-known example is s 10(2) of the Human Rights Act 1998 (HRA), which allows legislation (irrespective of whether it was enacted before or after the HRA) that has been judicially declared incompatible with the ECHR, or which, following a decision of the ECtHR, appears incompatible, to be amended by order if the Minister considers that there are 'compelling reasons' for doing so. The effectiveness of such clauses (for discussion of which see Barber and Young [2003] *PL* 112 at 115 and Marshall (1998) 118 *LQR* 493 at 496– 9) was considered in *Thoburn v. Sunderland City Council* [2002] EWHC 195 (Admin), [2003] QB 151. Counsel argued that generally- worded Henry VIII powers could not be used to enact secondary legislation that was inconsistent with provisions in later primary legislation, because such subsequent legislation would impliedly repeal the Henry VIII power to the extent that the latter had conferred *vires* to enact measures at odds with the former. However, this argument was rejected— and the efficacy of prospective Henry VIII powers vouchsafed— by Laws LJ who, at [50], held that, '[g]enerally, there is no *inconsistency* between a provision conferring a Henry VIII power to amend future legislation and the terms of any such future legislation'.

Barber and Young, *op cit* at 114, find the increasing use of prospective Henry VIII clauses disquieting, ultimately concluding that their use is only (rarely) justified by a need to empower certain institutions, such as the devolved legislatures, to defend themselves (in the name of democracy) against interference by the Westminster Parliament:

> Whereas with retrospective clauses the enacting Parliament could, in theory, gauge the maximum possible extent of the power, with prospective Henry VIII clauses the enacting Parliament must put its trust entirely in the body to whom power is delegated. There is no way of assessing at the time of enactment which future statutes the power will be used against … Prospective Henry VIII clauses thus constitute a fetter on the power of future Parliaments, creating the risk that as yet unthought of statutes will be overturned through the exercise of delegated power.

QUESTIONS

- Are concerns regarding Henry VIII powers well founded?
- If, as seems inevitable, such powers must be accepted as a feature of the modern administrative landscape, how might their misuse be guarded against?

16.1.4 The extent of delegated powers

Henry VIII clauses vividly illustrate that delegated powers may transcend their classical function of simply empowering the administration to supplement statutory schemes. Just as such powers may differ in nature, so their scope may vary dramatically. While some delegated powers are conferred in quite specific terms, other powers are framed much more broadly. Here are three particularly noteworthy examples.

First, we cited s 10(2) of the HRA earlier as an example of a Henry VIII clause; we return to it here in view of the fact that it creates a competence to enact delegated legislation notable for its scope. Not only does s 10(2) permit the amendment of legislation which has been judicially condemned as inconsistent with the ECHR; according to sch 2, para 1(1)(a) of the HRA, a s 10(2) order may also 'contain such incidental, supplemental, consequential or transitional provision as the person making it considers appropriate'. Moreover, sch 2, para 1(1)(b) provides that (except in relation to criminal liability: para 1(4)) a s 10(2) order may be made 'so as to have effect from a date earlier than that on which it is made'. In other words, legislative amendments and supplementary provisions may have retrospective effect, thereby applying to events which have already taken place.

Second, the Civil Contingencies Act 2004 makes provision for emergencies, defined by s 19 as events or situations which threaten serious damage to human welfare in or the environment of part or all of the United Kingdom, or war or terrorism that threatens serious damage to the security of the UK. Section 20(1) provides that 'Her Majesty may by Order in Council make emergency regulations if satisfied that the conditions in section 21'—that it is urgently necessary to make provision to prevent, control, or mitigate an aspect or effect of an emergency that has occurred, is occurring, or is about to occur—'are satisfied'. By s 20(2), senior Ministers may make such regulations subject to the same conditions, and to the additional requirement that an Order in Council could not, without serious delay, be arranged. Emergency regulations lapse after a maximum of 30 days (s 26(1)) (but this does not prevent the making of fresh regulations (s 26(2)(a))) and after seven days if not approved by Parliament (s 27). The range of issues which emergency regulations may cover is extraordinarily wide (s 22). In particular, they 'may make provision of any kind that could be made by Act of Parliament' (s 22(3)), including the creation of criminal offences connected with non-compliance with emergency regulations (s 22(3)(i)) and the disapplication and modification of primary legislation (s 22(3)(j)). However, thanks to political pressure during the enactment of the legislation, emergency regulations can be struck down under the HRA if incompatible with the Convention rights (s 30(2)) and cannot amend the HRA itself (s 23(5)(b)).

Third, the Legislative and Regulatory Reform Act 2006 enables Ministers to enact delegated legislation—which may provide for the amendment or repeal of primary legislation—in order to remove or reduce any 'burden', the latter concept being broadly defined as including administrative inconvenience and financial costs. This is an extremely general and wide-ranging power, the impact of which is potentially very far-reaching. Indeed, when predecessor legislation was enacted in 1994, the House of Lords Select Committee on Delegated Powers (HC60, *Eighth Report* (1993–94) at [1]) commented that the Act conferred powers to make secondary legislation on a scale 'unprecedented in time of peace'. In fact, the government wanted the 2006 Act to confer drastically broader powers than those it actually confers. As originally drafted, the Bill contained a power to make orders (which, subject to very limited exceptions, could make any provision that could be made by Act of Parliament) for the purpose of reforming legislation, including primary legislation. Since 'reform' could be executed for any purpose, this would virtually have amounted to a plenary legislative power being placed in the hands of Ministers. Notwithstanding that the government initially sought to present the Bill as an uncontentious technical measure, enormous controversy ensued, and following excoriating criticism inside and beyond Parliament (on which see Davis [2007] *PL* 677), the Bill was amended so as to cast the powers in the narrower terms, concerned with the removal of 'burdens', described earlier.

QUESTION

- Do you agree that the Bill, in its original form, would have been wholly unacceptable? Why (not)?

16.1.5 Legislative and administrative measures

The examples considered so far in this chapter have unambiguously concerned administrative powers to enact *legislative measures*, in the sense of generally applicable, legally enforceable rules. Such measures can be contrasted with, for instance, *administrative decisions* as to how discretion is to be used in the circumstances of an individual case. However, reality is too complex to be accommodated by a stark dichotomy between administrative decisions and administrative legislation, since many measures emanate from government that do not neatly fall into one or other of those categories. Megarry (1944) 60 *LQR* 125 at 126 used the term 'administrative quasi-legislation' to describe such measures, which— as Ganz, *Quasi Legislation: Recent Developments in Secondary Legislation* (London 1987) at 1 notes— have been the subject of a 'population explosion' since the middle of the last century. Such measures include codes of practice and conduct, guidelines, practice statements, tax concessions, and circulars issued by government departments and other public bodies.

Little purpose would be served by becoming preoccupied with ultimately arid questions of categorization. However, two important practical issues do arise. The first concerns the applicability of procedural safeguards that may attach to the exercise by the executive of a legislative function but not to the exercise of an administrative function. Take, for instance, the Immigration Rules, which exist as a result of the requirement in s 3(2) of the Immigration Act 1971 that the Secretary of State must 'lay before Parliament statements of the rules, or of any changes in the rules, laid down by him as to the practice to be followed in the administration of this Act'. In *R (Alvi)* v. *Secretary of State for the Home Department* [2012] UKSC 33, [2012] 1 WLR 2208, the claimant was the subject of an adverse immigration decision because he had failed to amass sufficient credit under the so-called points-based immigration system. That failure arose because the claimant's job— according to criteria applied by the Secretary of State— fell below the requisite skill level. However, the claimant argued that because the criteria had not been laid before Parliament pursuant to s 3(2), they could not be applied by the Secretary of State. The case therefore turned on the question whether the criteria were 'rules' within the meaning of s 3(2), such that they should have been laid before Parliament, or (as the government contended) merely non-legislative guidance that, as such, did not need to be laid. The Supreme Court held that they were 'rules', and that the failure to adhere to the procedure set out in s 3(2) rendered them inapplicable. In arriving at that view, the Court was influenced by the fact that, as Lord Dyson put it (at [94]), the criterion amounted to a 'requirement which, if not satisfied by the migrant, will lead to an application for leave to enter or remain being refused'. On this approach, the more important the matter addressed by the administrative measure, the more likely it is to be characterized as a legislative measure attracting the democratic scrutiny provided for by the parent Act. The second practical matter concerns the legal effect of administrative measures. Although primary legislation does not invariably do so, the default expectation in respect of it is that it produces legal effects by doing such things as creating, extinguishing, or limiting legal rights, or attaching criminal or civil liability to certain conduct. To what extent, however, does administrative legislation produce legal effects? Or, to put the matter the other way around, how do we know whether administrative action produces effects such as to warrant its characterization as legislative? In seeking to answer this question, a number of considerations arise.

First, and most obviously, *the enabling legislation may indicate the legal status and effects of measures adopted under it.* For example, under s 3(3)(a) of the Terrorism Act 2000, the Secretary of State is empowered to make proscription orders in respect of terrorist organizations. The effect of such an order is readily evident from other provisions in the Act: ss 11–13 make it a criminal offence to be a member of or to support such proscribed organizations, and the legal effect of s 3(3)(a) orders is therefore both substantial and clear.

Second, however, *legislation is sometimes vague, or even wholly silent, about the legal status and effects of measures adopted pursuant to it.* For instance, s 3(2) of the Immigration Act 1971, which, as already noted, authorizes and requires the making of the Immigration Rules, makes no provision as to their legal effect. It has therefore fallen to the courts to determine the legal effect of the Rules. In *Odelola* v. *Secretary of State for the Home Department* [2009] UKHL 25, [2009] 1 WLR 1230, the claimant would have been eligible for leave to remain in the UK under the Rules in force when she applied, but her case was decided under a new version which had entered into force after the application was lodged. This, it was held, was acceptable: the Rules did not straightforwardly constitute law, meaning that the claimant had not acquired an enforceable right from the older version; the newer version could therefore be applied against her interests.

Third, however, even if, as in the case of the Immigration Rules, the enabling legislation is not interpreted as conferring (in any straightforward sense) legal status upon measures adopted pursuant to it, *legislation may confer specific legal relevance upon particular parts of the measures in question.* For example, as Lord Hoffmann noted in *Odelola* at [6], the effect of the relevant legislation was that 'one may appeal against an immigration decision on the ground that it is not in accordance with the immigration rules'. Thus, as Sedley LJ noted in *Secretary of State for the Home Department* v. *Pankina* [2010] EWCA Civ 719 at [16], at the appellate stage, the Rules had 'the force of law', in the sense that departure from them constituted an appeal-able error of law. The law on immigration appeals has changed since *Odelola* and *Pankina* were decided, but the general point that they illustrate remains pertinent: namely, that the existence of rules or other measures made under statutory authority may vary depending on the circum-stances and the perspective from which the question is considered.

Fourth, even if measures like the Immigration Rules are not straightforwardly legally enforceable, *this does not necessarily mean that they are legally irrelevant.* At the very least, if the government has promulgated some formal statement—whether a policy or a set of rules—as to how it proposes to exercise its discretion, this will constitute a policy attract-ing the application of the legitimate expectation doctrine or the principle of consistency (on which see 5.3.3 and ch 6). This limits the ability of the decision-maker to refuse to treat any given individual in line with the policy or rules *in force at the relevant time*—although often, as was held in *Odelola* to be the case in respect of the Immigration Rules, the govern-ment retains its freedom to *change the rules*, even if this disappoints those who would have been treated more favourably under an earlier version.

Fifth, when the enabling legislation provides uncertain (or no) guidance, *contextual factors may play an important role in judicial determinations of the extent, if any, of the legal effects of measures adopted thereunder.* This point is illustrated by the sharp division of opinion in the House of Lords in *R (Munjaz)* v. *Mersey Care NHS Trust* [2005] UKHL 58, [2006] 2 AC 148. Section 118 of the Mental Health Act 1983 required the Minister to draw up a code of practice concerning the admission to hospital and treatment of patients suffering from mental disorders. The Minister duly did so, and, *inter alia*, made detailed provision concerning a practice called 'seclusion', which the code defined as 'the super-vised confinement of a patient in a room, which may be locked to protect others from sig-nificant harm'. It required, *inter alia*, regular and frequent reviews both of the condition of secluded patients and of whether seclusion remained necessary. The claimant was a patient at Ashworth Hosptial—one of three hospitals providing high security accommodation for the mentally disordered—which operated a seclusion policy which provided for less fre-quent reviews than the code stipulated.

The question for the House of Lords was whether it was lawful for the hospital to deviate from the code—which, in turn, required analysis of the code's legal status. The majority con-cluded that the code was not binding and that the hospital had lawfully departed from it. This followed, said Lord Bingham, because the code itself said that it was not binding, and because while the Minister did have powers to issue binding instructions to hospitals, he had chosen not to exercise them in relation to this matter. Lord Bingham thus concluded at [21] that

the Code does not have the binding effect which a statutory provision or a statutory instru-ment would have. It is what it purports to be, guidance and not instruction. But ... the guidance should be given great weight. It is not instruction, but it is much more than mere advice which an addressee is free to follow or not as it chooses. It is guidance which any hospital should consider with great care, and from which it should depart only if it has cogent reasons for doing so.

In this case, the fact that Ashworth was a high security hospital at which seclusion had to be used on a much larger scale than in most institutions was held to constitute sufficient reason for departure from the code. Lord Steyn, however, entered a strong dissent. At [44], he said that the code was

> a very special type of soft law. It derives its status from the legislative context and the extreme vulnerability of the patients which it serves to protect ... [T]he Court of Appeal [2004] QB 395, 418, para 11 explained, and I accept, that the concern about seclusion lies 'in the combination of the potentially harmful or degrading effects of seclusion upon the patient and its potential for misuse by those looking after him'. This is the contextual scene of section 118(1) ... [Counsel for the claimant] pointed out that the preceding white paper of November 1981, *Reform of Mental Health Legislation* (Cmnd 8405), para 38 observed that the Code 'might include reference to treatments such as electroconvulsive therapy when used in particular circumstances, long acting drugs, and behaviour therapies'. These examples reveal that in section 118(1) Parliament had authorised a Code with some minimum safeguards and a modicum of centralised protection for vulnerable patients. This is inconsistent with a free-for-all in which hospitals are at liberty to depart from the published Code as they consider right.

Lord Steyn was not saying that the code could *never* be departed from, but he thought that hospitals' discretion to depart should be very limited indeed. As a result, he concluded that the hospital had acted unlawfully: the code, he said at [46], was 'a corner of mental health law in which a dilution of minimum centrally imposed safeguards, by pragmatic policy decisions from hospital to hospital, is not appropriate'.

16.2 The making of delegated legislation

16.2.1 Publication

It is inherent in the rule of law that individuals should be governed by rules which are openly available, in order that they have the opportunity to comply with them and plan their lives accordingly. It is therefore vital that legislation—including delegated legislation—should be published. The Statutory Instruments Act 1946 requires the publication of any delegated legislation which is classified as a 'statutory instrument'. Delegated legislation is classified as a statutory instrument if the enabling provision so provides. Most enabling provisions do so provide; but if a given enabling provision does not so provide, delegated legislation enacted under it does not count as a statutory instrument and is therefore not subject to the publication requirement in the 1946 Act. That requirement is set out in the following terms by s 2(1) of the Act:

> Immediately after the making of any statutory instrument, it shall be sent to the King's printer of Acts of Parliament and numbered in accordance with regulations made under this Act, and except in such cases as may be provided by any Act passed after the commencement of this Act or prescribed by regulations made under this Act, copies thereof shall as soon as possible be printed and sold by or under the authority of the King's printer of Acts of Parliament.

It appears that, although this requirement is almost always complied with, failure to do so does not render the statutory instrument invalid. This was the view of Streatfield J in *R v. Sheer Metalcraft Ltd* [1954] 1 QB 586 at 590, who opined that requirements as to publication are 'purely procedure for the issue of an instrument [already] validly made'. This conclusion was reached because s 3(2) of the Act provides that it is a defence to a criminal charge of contravening a statutory instrument to prove that the legislation had not been published at the date of the alleged contravention, unless it is proved that 'at that date reasonable steps had been taken for the purpose of bringing the purport of the instrument to the notice of the public, or of persons likely to be affected by it, or of the person charged'. This appears to presuppose that there are some circumstances in which a statutory instrument will be effective in spite of non-publication, and is therefore inconsistent with the view that publication is always essential to validity.

QUESTION

• Should non-publication render statutory instruments ineffective?

The 1946 Act imposes a publication requirement *only* in respect of statutory instruments, raising the prospect of non-publication of other measures, so that—in the words of Scott LJ in *Blackpool Corporation v. Locker* [1948] 1 KB 349 at 362—the citizen

> may remain in complete ignorance of what rights over him and his property have been secretly conferred by the Minister on some authority or other, and what residual rights have been left to himself. For practical purposes, the rule of law, of which the nation is so justly proud, breaks down.

However, an obligation to publish such measures may be imposed by other legislation, such as the Freedom of Information Act 2000, or by general principles of law. For example, in *Salih v. Secretary of State for the Home Department* [2003] EWHC 2273 (Admin), the non-publication of a policy which existed in relation to the provision of support to failed asylum seekers was found to be unlawful. Stanley Burnton J invoked a general constitutional principle rooted in the rule of law to the effect that legislative and analogous measures should be publicly available, explaining, at [48] and [52], that

> the policies of public authorities may have a significance approaching or approximating to a law, and may be equally important to the individual ... [I]t is in general inconsistent with the constitutional imperative that statute law should be made known [on which see *R (L) v. Secretary of State for the Home Department* [2003] EWCA Civ 25, [2003] 1 WLR 1230] for the government to withhold information about its policy relating to the exercise of a power conferred by statute.

This statement of principle was endorsed in *R (WL (Congo)) v. Secretary of State for the Home Department* [2011] UKSC 12, [2012] 1 AC 245 at [36], while in *R (Reilly) v. Secretary of State for Work and Pensions* [2013] UKSC 68, [2014] AC 453 it was held that the Secretary of State was obliged to make available to those subject to an administrative scheme the details of it, albeit that the Court stopped short of insisting upon publication to the world at large. On this view, it would seem to follow ineluctably that even if delegated legislation is not caught by the publication requirement in the Statutory Instruments Act 1946, general principles of public law will require that it is published or otherwise made available to relevant parties.

Finally, although not concerning the publication of delegated legislation, *R (Anufrijeva)* v. *Secretary of State for the Home Department* [2003] UKHL 36, [2004] 1 AC 604 is worthy of note in this context. The case concerned an asylum seeker; from the date on which her asylum claim was turned down, the Home Office treated her claim as 'having been determined' within the meaning of the relevant legislation, thereby disentitling her to further income support. However, the Home Office had not communicated its decision to the individual concerned, and the question therefore arose whether, in the absence of such communication, the claim had been 'determined' such that income support could lawfully be terminated. Their Lordships (by a majority) held that it had not. Lord Steyn, at [28]– [30], considered that the rule of law

> requires that a constitutional state must accord to individuals the right to know of a decision before their rights can be adversely affected. The antithesis of such a state was described by Kafka: a state where the rights of individuals are overridden by hole in the corner decisions or knocks on doors in the early hours. That is not our system ... In our system of law surprise is regarded as the enemy of justice.

It is strongly arguable that if general principles of constitutional law require the communication of administrative decisions, then the same principles must require the publication of legislative measures.

16.2.2 Consultation

Primary legislation authorizing the making of delegated legislation sometimes stipulates that consultation must take place before the delegated legislation is made. What, however, if the primary legislation is silent on this point? Can a duty to consult arise at common law? We considered this matter generally at 10.4, and saw that, in the absence of a statutory obligation to consult or a legitimate expectation of consultation, the courts are generally reluctant to hold that a common law duty to consult arises. We also saw that such judicial reticence is attributable, at least in part, to the prevailing notion— albeit one that was challenged by Lord Wilson's judgment in *R (Moseley)* v. *Haringey London Borough Council* [2014] UKSC 56, [2014] 1 WLR 3947— that the duty to act fairly is triggered only in circumstances in which administrative action has a particularized impact upon specific individuals. In the light of that, it comes as no surprise that the general position is that, in the absence of a statutory duty to consult in respect of the making of delegated legislation, no duty to do so arises at common law. After all, the making of administrative *legislation* is, par excellence, a function that is liable to have a general, as distinct from a particularized, impact. The general principle, therefore, is that in the absence of a statutory obligation to consult in relation to the making of delegated legislation, no duty to do so arises at common law.

However, in applying this general principle, the courts rightly look beyond formal considerations by considering the substantive nature of the executive action being undertaken. For instance, *Bank Mellat* v. *HM Treasury (No 2)* [2013] UKSC 39, [2014] AC 700 concerned the legality of the Financial Restrictions (Iran) Order 2009, a statutory instrument made under sch 7 of the Counter- Terrorism Act 2008 that prohibited all persons operating in the financial sector from doing business with the claimant, a major Iranian bank, and IRISL, a shipping line. The claimant challenged the legality of the Order on various grounds, including the failure to afford it any opportunity to address the allegations underpinning the decision to make the Order. Although three members of the nine- Justice panel that decided the case concluded that no obligation to consult arose, Lord Sumption— advancing the majority view on this point— held that the claimant should have been consulted prior to the making of the Order, notwithstanding its legislative character:

[46] In point of form, a statutory instrument embodying a Schedule 7 direction is legislation. But, as Megarry J observed in *Bates v Lord Hailsham of St Marylebone* [1972] 1 WLR 1373, 1378 the fact that an order takes the form of a statutory instrument is not decisive: 'what is important is not its form but its nature, which is plainly legislative'. The Treasury direction designating Bank Mellat under Schedule 7, paragraph 13, was not legislative in nature. There is a difference between the sovereign's legislation and his commands. The one speaks generally and impersonally, the other specifically and to nominate persons. As David Hume pointed out in his *Treatise of Human Nature* (Book III, Part ii, sec 2–6),

'all civil laws are general, and regard alone some essential circumstances of the case, without taking into consideration the characters, situations, and connexions of the person concerned.'

The Treasury direction in this case was a command. The relevant legislation and the whole legislative policy on which it was based, were contained in the Act itself. The direction, although made by statutory instrument, involved the application of a discretionary legislative power to Bank Mellat and IRISL and nothing else. It was as good an example as one could find of a measure targeted against identifiable individuals. Moreover, ... it singled out Bank Mellat from other Iranian banks on account of the Bank's conduct or, in Hume's words, its 'characteristics, situations and connexions'. It directly affected the Bank's property and business assets. If the direction had not been required to be made by statutory instrument, there would have been every reason in the absence of any practical difficulties to say that the Treasury had a duty to give prior notice to the Bank and to hear what they had to say. In a case like this, is the position any different because a statutory instrument was involved? I think not. That was simply the form which the specific application of this particular legislation was required to take.

The position occupied by the majority in *Bank Mellat (No 2)* should not, however, be taken to signal that an obligation to consult in respect of the making of delegated legislation will readily be found at common law. Indeed, *Bank Mellat (No 2)* entirely buys into the notion that non- particularized legislative decisions attract no consultation duty, albeit that the majority view acknowledges that a measure's characterization as legislative is not determinative as to whether it is sufficiently particularized as to trigger a common law requirement to consult. It therefore remains the case that a significant amount of secondary legislation is made without prior consultation, behind a veil of obscurity, which leads Page, *Governing by Numbers* (Oxford 2001), ch 1 to call executive rule- making 'the politics of seclusion'. Should there therefore be a general requirement— imposed either by statute or common law— of consultation in this context? In the following passage, Cane is unconvinced that a higher level of participation— such as that which obtains in the US— purchases advantages which necessarily outweigh the associated costs.

Cane, *Administrative Law* (Oxford 2011)

The main advantages of a more formal procedure of rule- making are said to be that it gives the citizen a greater chance to participate in decision- making and that it improves the quality of the rules made. However, if the participants object to the rules made, despite extensive involvement, and feel that participation has only 'worked' if the result they favour is reached, then participation by itself is of limited value. The [more formal] procedures used in the United States do not seem to have reduced dissatisfaction with … administrative rule- making. It may be that Americans are much less happy than the British about having their lives regulated by government at all, and that this, rather than the actual content of the regulation, is the main source of the discontent. No amount of formalized procedure can overcome this problem.

As for the second alleged advantage, the concept of increased quality of rule-making is a very difficult one to pin down. If quality refers to technical matters such as drafting, participation of non-experts may not improve quality. On the other hand, consultation of those whose interests will be affected may assist the rule-maker, in designing a rule which will effectively and efficiently achieve the desired policy objectives, by providing detailed information about the circumstances in which the rule will operate. If 'quality' is really a surrogate for political acceptability, then once again there may be a reason to doubt that increased popular participation will make rules more acceptable to those who dislike them.

There are considerable problems associated with more formal participatory forms of rulemaking. They take a lot of time and money; and so groups with the greatest resources tend to have an advantage over less well-endowed interest groups. It is unlikely that statutory obligations to consult would overcome such inequalities in resources. Furthermore, it is not clear that hearing a wide diversity of conflicting views makes it easier to frame a rule; the result may just be that the rule finally formulated fails to satisfy many of those views. On the other hand, consultation at an early stage may at least increase levels of compliance later on and reduce the chance that those dissatisfied with any rules made will seek actively to challenge them.

QUESTIONS

- Do you agree?
- How, other than by generally limiting the extent of consultation, might the problem of powerful interest groups be tackled?

16.2.3 Parliament's role in making delegated legislation

Since the *raison d'être* of delegated legislation is that the executive should be empowered to enact rules, liberating Parliament from the burden of legislative monopoly, it may at first seem surprising that the latter should play any role in the making of delegated legislation. However, basic constitutional principles dictate that the executive should be subject to appropriate forms of scrutiny and control in the exercise of its legislative, just as in relation to its other, functions. Judicial review (discussed at 16.4) plays a part; but it is necessary for delegated legislation to be scrutinized not just in legal, but also in political and policy, terms—a function which Parliament is better placed than the courts to discharge.

Parliament's involvement in the process of making delegated legislation varies considerably, depending on the terms of the enabling legislation. A substantial amount of such legislation—roughly 2,200 statutory instruments each year, according to the House of Lords Delegated Powers and Regulatory Reform Committee (HL119, *Special Report: Response to the Strathclyde Review* (2015–16) at 34)—is not subject to any form of parliamentary involvement. Such instruments tend to concern uncontroversial matters such as the bringing into force of Acts of Parliament or provisions thereof. At the other end of the scale, a very small number of statutory instruments—typically around 10 each year—are subject to one of a variety of particularly rigorous forms of parliamentary oversight and involvement some-times called the 'super-affirmative' process. (We consider an example of this at 16.3.5.)

Most delegated legislation, however, falls to be dealt with by Parliament under either the 'affirmative' or the 'annulment' process. So-called 'affirmative instruments'—of which there are in the region of 225 each year—must be approved by Parliament if they are to take effect (albeit that they may, depending on the terms of the enabling provision, have temporary interim effect pending such approval). This procedure, however, occupies valuable parliamentary time, and is therefore relatively rare. More common are 'negative instruments', of which around 800 are made each year. Rather than requiring parliamentary *approval*, negative instruments take effect in the absence of *disapproval* or annulment (which can be expressed up to 40 days after the instrument is laid before Parliament). The annulment procedure, which is set out in s 5(1) of the Statutory Instruments Act 1946, is much more widely used because it places a far smaller burden upon Parliament. Indeed, securing annulment of negative instruments is very difficult: individual members must attempt to find parliamentary time, and they rarely manage to do so.

Three further, and related, matters should be noted. First, it is not generally possible for Parliament to amend delegated legislation: rather, such legislation must, in the case of affirmative instruments, either be approved or not or, in the case of negative instruments, objected to or not. Second, there is therefore no equivalent in respect of delegated legislation of the so-called ping-pong that can occur in relation to primary legislation. That is, delegated legislation cannot bounce between the House of Commons and the House of Lords until the two chambers reach agreement; instead, each chamber must decide whether to approve (in the case of affirmative instruments) or object to (in the case of negative instruments) each piece of delegated legislation as a whole. Third, some delegated legislation falls to be considered by the Commons alone. Where, however, the House of Lords is also involved, it has a veto: there is no equivalent in relation to delegated legislation to the procedure under the Parliament Acts 1911–49, whereby primary legislation can be forced through by the Commons in the face of opposition in the Lords. It is not, however, the case that the Lords frequently thwarts the enactment of delegated legislation: since 1950, it has done so on only six occasions (although, in what may be a sign of growing assertiveness, five of those occasions have been since 1997).

When the House of Lords refused to approve the Draft Tax Credits (Income Thresholds and Determination of Rates) (Amendment) Regulations 2015, the government asked Lord Strathclyde—a former Leader of the House of Lords—to review the Lords' role in the making of delegated legislation. In his subsequent report (Cm 9177, *Secondary Legislation and the Primacy of the House of Commons* (2015)), Strathclyde concluded that the Lords' involvement should be radically curtailed by investing the Commons with the power immediately to override any attempt by the Lords to block delegated legislation. This, said Strathclyde, would secure the primacy that the Commons, as the elected chamber, ought to enjoy. However, in a highly critical report responding to the Strathclyde Review, the House of Lords Constitution Committee (HL116, *Delegated Legislation and Parliament: A Response to the Strathclyde Review* (2015–16)) argued that the Review was based on an ill-conceived premise that focused unduly upon the balance of power as between the two Houses. The real issue, said the Committee, pertains to the balance of power as between Parliament and the government:

> 51. We recognise the primacy of the House of Commons. But it is essential that any proposals to change the means by which delegated legislation is agreed by Parliament must be evaluated not only in terms of their effect on the balance of power between the two Houses, but between the Executive and Parliament as a whole.
>
> 52. The Government stated that the Review's remit was 'to examine how to protect the ability of elected governments to secure their business in Parliament', and Lord Strathclyde stated in his foreword that he tried to balance parliamentary scrutiny against 'the certainty that government business can be conducted in a reasonable manner and time'. We consider that the starting point for reviewing how Parliament scrutinises the Executive should not be how the Executive can secure its business. The focus should be on how to ensure that the actions of the Executive are scrutinised effectively and that parliamentary approval of delegated legislation—by members of both Houses of Parliament—is not a mere box-ticking exercise.

At the time of writing, the government has not signalled whether it intends to seek to implement Lord Strathclyde's recommendation. However, it is undoubtedly the case that if the House of Lords were largely written out of the picture in the way Strathclyde has proposed, the degree of scrutiny to which delegated legislation is subject would be considerably diminished. That is so because, as we will see in the next section, it is the House of Lords that plays the leading role in relation to the scrutiny of delegated legislation. And while it is true that, under the Strathclyde proposals, scrutiny processes in the Lords could continue to be undertaken, they would be likely to lose much of their bite if the Lords as a chamber were rendered toothless by allowing the Commons immediately to override it.

16.3 Parliamentary scrutiny

16.3.1 The conferral of administrative rule-making powers

It is, of course, open to both the House of Commons and the House of Lords to remove or amend clauses in Bills that confer rule- making powers upon the administration. However, pressures on parliamentary time, coupled with the inevitably technical nature of this issue, mean that such provisions often attract relatively little attention. However, two House of Lords Committees do pay particular attention to provisions in Bills which, if enacted, would authorize the making of delegated legislation. The Constitution Committee, consistently with its remit, examines such clauses from the perspective of general constitutional principles, drawing attention, for instance, to provisions (such as Henry VIII clauses) that may raise separation-of-powers concerns. Meanwhile, provisions authorizing the making of delegated legislation form the central focus of the work of the Delegated Powers and Regulatory Reform Committee. The government provides the Committee with a 'Delegated Powers Memorandum' in respect of any bill conferring such powers. The Committee considers whether proposed grants of delegated powers are appropriate and what level of parliamentary control of the rule- making process (*eg* the negative or affirmative procedure) is desirable, paying special attention to Henry VIII clauses in view of the significant powers which they confer upon the executive. Neither the Constitution Committee nor the

Delegated Powers and Regulatory Reform Committee can itself amend or remove clauses from bills conferring delegated powers, but the committees can issue reports drawing matters to the attention of the House of Lords as a whole, and regularly do so.

16.3.2 The exercise of administrative rule-making powers

As well as scrutinizing the *conferral* of powers to enact subordinate legislation, Parliament also examines their *exercise*. Although a degree of scrutiny is possible through the affirmative and annulment procedures to which much delegated legislation is subject, a number of factors—notably the executive's dominance of Parliament, which makes disapproval or non-approval highly unlikely; the crudeness of these mechanisms, under which approval cannot usually be subject to the amendment of the legislation; and the sheer volume of delegated legislation—conspire to make these forms of control more theoretical than real. Genuine scrutiny is usually possible only through the work of committees. In considering this matter further, it is useful to distinguish between scrutiny on technical and policy grounds.

16.3.3 Technical scrutiny

Nearly all statutory instruments are scrutinized by the Joint Committee on Statutory Instruments. Its role is apparent from its terms of reference, as laid down in the Standing Orders of the House of Commons (No 151) and the House of Lords (No 73), which require it to draw attention to a statutory instrument on any of the following grounds:

(i)   that it imposes a charge on the public revenues or contains provisions requiring payments to be made to the Exchequer or any government department or to any local or public authority in consideration of any licence or consent or of any services to be rendered, or prescribes the amount of any such charge or payment;

(ii)   that it is made in pursuance of any enactment containing specific provisions excluding it from challenge in the courts, either at all times or after the expiration of a specific period;

(iii)   that it purports to have retrospective effect where the parent statute confers no express authority so to provide;

(iv)   that there appears to have been unjustifiable delay in the publication or in the laying of it before Parliament;

(v)   that there appears to have been unjustifiable delay in sending a notification under the proviso to section 4(1) of the Statutory Instruments Act 1946, where an instrument has come into operation before it has been laid before Parliament;

(vi)   that there appears to be a doubt whether it is intra vires or that it appears to make some unusual or unexpected use of the powers conferred by the statute under which it is made;

(vii)   that for any special reason its form or purport calls for elucidation;

(viii) that its drafting appears to be defective;

or on any other ground which does not impinge on its merits or on the policy behind it.

Page, *Governing by Numbers* (Oxford 2001) at 161–8 concludes that the Committee enjoys a 'pervasive influence' because government officials seek to avoid condemnation by the committee, both for reasons of professional pride and because the administration is often willing to amend legislation with which the Committee is dissatisfied on *vires* grounds given the risk that a legal challenge may otherwise ensue. Page's view is affirmed by more recent statistical analysis carried out by the Committee itself, which reports that there is a high level of compliance with its recommendations as to the amendment of defective statutory instruments (HL24, *Scrutinising Statutory Instruments: Departmental Returns, 2009* (2010–12).

16.3.4 Policy scrutiny

While the Joint Committee may supply effective scrutiny of technical and legal matters, consideration of policy issues is outwith its remit. Lack of parliamentary time means that scrutiny of such matters is rarely possible on the floor of either House; when such scrutiny takes place, it is therefore usually by means of a delegated legislation committee. All affirmative instruments are automatically referred to such committees unless, exceptionally, the government agrees that there should be debate on the floor of the House. Meanwhile, negative instruments are only debated in delegated legislation committees if they are 'prayed against' (objected to) and if a Minister agrees to make a motion in the House to the effect that the matter should be referred to a standing committee.

The upshot is that negative instruments are liable to receive very little by way of scrutiny. This would be unproblematic if it were the case that the distinction between affirmative and negative instruments mapped neatly onto the distinction between delegated legislation that does and does not warrant meaningful scrutiny. However, that is not invariably so. Against that background, there have been consistent calls over a substantial period of time for improvements to the way in which delegated legislation is scrutinized—and, in particular, to the way in which instruments requiring more careful scrutiny are singled out. To that end, building upon proposals first made by the Select Committee on Procedure (HC152, *Delegated Legislation* (1995–96)), the Royal Commission on the Reform of the House of Lords (Cm 4534, *A House for the Future* (2000) at 74) proposed the creation of a 'sifting' committee:

> We believe it would strengthen Parliamentary scrutiny of Statutory Instruments if a 'sifting' mechanism could be established. This would be designed to look at the significance of every Statutory Instrument subject to Parliamentary scrutiny; call for further information from Departments where necessary; and draw attention to those Statutory Instruments which are important and those which merit further debate or consideration. Such a mechanism, perhaps in the form of a Committee, could be established by either House, or jointly, as a procedural matter. Its value would lie in focusing Parliamentary attention on those few Statutory Instruments which were of real significance. Its judgement would depend on not only the intrinsic significance of the issue concerned, but also its current political salience (which might vary over time).

This proposal was endorsed by the Procedure Committee (HC48, *Delegated Legislation* (1999–2000))—which, in common with the Royal Commission, recommended that the Statutory Instruments Act 1946 should be amended to extend the time for praying against negative instruments from 40 to 60 days, in order to create sufficient time for scrutiny by a sifting committee and subsequent debate where appropriate.

Although no joint sifting committee has, to date, been established, the House of Lords has established its own committee, which is now known as the Secondary Legislation Scrutiny Committee. Its role, as set out in the terms of reference that appear on its website, is to scrutinize delegated legislation with a view to decide whether to draw it to the attention of the House of Lords on any of several grounds, namely

(a) that it is politically or legally important or gives rise to issues of public policy likely to be of interest to the House;
(b) that it may be inappropriate in view of changed circumstances since the enactment of the parent Act;
(c) that it may inappropriately implement European Union legislation;
(d) that it may imperfectly achieve its policy objectives;
(e) that the explanatory material laid in support provides insufficient information to gain a clear understanding about the instrument's policy objective and intended implementation;
(f) that there appear to be inadequacies in the consultation process which relates to the instrument.

The Committee (see HL73, *Special Report: The Committee's Methods of Working* (2003–04) at [48]) considers that its principal function is to 'improve debate in the House on negative instruments, both in terms of which negative instruments are debated in the House and the focus of debate on specific instruments'. In this way, the Committee seeks to ensure that those negative instruments which warrant greater attention than such instruments would normally receive are subjected to such attention by the House of Lords.

Meanwhile, special arrangements apply in relation to European Union- related matters. A substantial amount of delegated legislation is passed each year in order that the UK may fulfil its obligations under EU law. Although much EU legislation is directly effective, meaning that it takes effect automatically in national legal systems, directives are not. Member States are therefore obliged to enact legislation in order to implement directives, to which end s 2(2) of the European Communities Act 1972 confers wide powers. When the UK government produces delegated legislation implementing EU directives, such delegated legislation can be scrutinized in the usual way, including by the House of Lords Secondary Legislation Scrutiny Committee. However, considerable parliamentary effort is also expended on upstream scrutiny of such matters as legislative proposals emanating from the EU. Such proposals— along with other EU- related matters— are scrutinized by the House of Commons European Scrutiny Committee and the House of Lords European Union Committee. The latter— principally through its six subcommittees, each of which focuses on a particular policy area— undertakes particularly detailed scrutiny of EU- related matters.

16.3.5 Strengthened forms of scrutiny

We noted at 16.2.3 that in very limited circumstances, Parliament's involvement in the making and scrutiny of delegated legislation goes beyond the 'affirmative' process. The approach adopted in such cases is sometimes referred to as the 'super-affirmative' process, although there are in fact a variety of stronger-than-usual scrutiny processes rather than a single model. Indeed, the House of Lords Delegated Powers and Regulatory Reform Committee (HL19, *Strengthened Statutory Procedures for the Scrutiny of Delegated Powers* (2012–13) at [1]) referred to 'a complex patchwork of procedures written into legislation to give Parliament a strengthened scrutiny role over certain legislative powers delegated by Parliament to Ministers', and called for simplification in this area.

Such complexity notwithstanding, strengthened scrutiny generally involves two features—namely, parliamentary involvement at an earlier-than-usual stage (when the proposed delegated legislation is more formative in nature), and enhanced opportunities for Parliament to consider and withhold its consent to the legislation. Strengthened scrutiny may also involve enabling Parliament, on a measure-by-measure basis, to determine the details of the scrutiny process that should apply, thereby permitting Parliament to tailor the level of its involvement and oversight to the significance of the specific legislative measure in question.

These points can be illustrated by reference to the making of legislative reform orders. We explained at 16.1.4 that the Legislative and Regulatory Reform Act 2006 confers broad powers on Ministers to amend or repeal legislation, including primary legislation, in order to remove or reduce administrative, financial, etc burdens. A precondition to the making of a legislative reform order is that the Minister is required (by s 13 of the Act) to consult relevant parties and to lay a draft order and explanatory document before each House (s 14). That document must also recommend the use of one of three procedures for the making of the order (s 15). The recommended procedure will apply unless either House requires a more onerous procedure to apply (s 15(3), (4)).

The least onerous procedure is the *negative resolution procedure* (s 16): an order can be made in the terms of the draft unless (i) either House resolves within 40 days of the laying of the draft that an order in those terms should not be made, or (ii) the committee of either House responsible for scrutinizing the draft order recommends (more than 30 and not more than 40 days after the laying of the draft) that no such order be made. The next most onerous procedure is the *affirmative resolution procedure* (s 17): an order can be made only if, within 40 days of the laying of the draft, both Houses have resolved that this should occur. Moreover, if the responsible committee recommends (within the same timescale as above) that no order be made, the Minister can take no further action in relation to it unless that recommendation is first rejected by resolution of the relevant House. Finally, the *super-affirmative procedure* (s 18) requires the Minister to have regard to, *inter alia*, representations and recommendations from responsible committees made within a 60-day period beginning with the laying of the draft. An order can only be made if, after the expiry of that period, the Minister lays before each House a statement detailing any representations made in relation to the draft; if he wishes to make an order that differs from the draft, the statement must give details of any proposed changes. Thereafter, the order can be made if each House so resolves. Again, however, the responsible committee can recommend (following the making of a statement detailing representations etc) that no order be made, in which case the Minister can proceed only if that recommendation is rejected by resolution of the relevant House.

QUESTIONS

- Is the nature and degree of parliamentary involvement in the making of delegated legislation appropriate?
- Should parliamentary involvement and scrutiny be improved and, if so, how?

16.4 Judicial scrutiny

16.4.1 Introduction

The administration's power to enact delegated legislation is constrained by the terms of the parent Act (or, in the case of legislation made under prerogative power, by the extent of that power). Thus the executive's *vires* are limited in this field just as in relation to administrative decision-making, and judicial review lies if delegated legislation is *ultra vires*. The facts that a parliamentary committee like the Joint Committee on Statutory Instruments has taken the view that a measure is *intra vires* and that delegated legislation may have received the imprimatur of both Houses of Parliament under the affirmative procedure do not preclude judicial review (although the latter may influence the intensity of review, as we explain shortly). Under the separation of powers, it is the courts which bear ultimate responsibility for determining the legality of administrative action—a responsibility that extends to administrative legislation.

16.4.2 Compatibility with primary legislation

As with other forms of executive action, judicial review of delegated legislation frequently involves a close analysis of the enabling provisions, and other relevant Acts, in order to determine whether the administrative branch has exceeded its legal authority. In some instances, the parent Act will make specific provision concerning the way in which delegated legislation is to be enacted. Non- compliance with such requirements may or may not render the subordinate legislation invalid: this will depend on the application of the principles set out at 2.6. The importance attached to consultation in the making of delegated legislation means that non- compliance with statutory consultation requirements is usually fatal to the validity of the legislation (see, *eg R (C)* v. *Secretary of State for Justice* [2008] EWCA Civ 882, [2009] QB 657). However, remedial discretion may be exercised so as to render the delegated legislation inapplicable only against those who were unlawfully not consulted, leaving it intact *vis- à- vis* everyone else (as in *Agricultural, Horticultural and Forestry Industrial Training Board* v. *Aylesbury Mushrooms Ltd* [1972] 1 WLR 190). In contrast, we have already seen (at 16.2.1) that failure to comply with statutory publication requirements does not normally invalidate secondary legislation.

As well as lying on the ground that some straightforward requirement imposed by the enabling legislation— such as a duty to consult— has not been met, judicial review may also lie on the ground that delegated legislation is incompatible, in some more subtle way, with the enabling legislation itself or with other primary legislation that colours the interpretation of the enabling provision. For instance, *R* v. *Secretary of State for Social Security, ex parte Joint Council for the Welfare of Immigrants* [1997] 1 WLR 275 concerned regulations made under the Social Security Contributions and Benefits Act 1992, the effect of which was to preclude subsistence payments to asylum seekers who failed to claim asylum upon arrival in the United Kingdom and to those whose claims had failed but who were in the process of exercising their right of appeal under the Asylum and Immigration Appeals Act 1993. The regulations were struck down by the Court of Appeal because, as Simon Brown LJ explained at 292, they substantially interfered with the ability of asylum seekers to make claims and appeal against adverse decisions— actions which the 1993 Act allowed them to undertake:

> Parliamentary sovereignty is not here in question: the Regulations are subordinate legislation only ... Parliament for its part has clearly demonstrated by the Act of 1993 a full commitment to the United Kingdom's ... obligations [under the Convention Relating to the Status of Refugees]. When the regulation-making power now contained in the Act of 1992 was first conferred, there was no question of asylum seekers being deprived of all benefit and thereby rendered unable to pursue their claims. Although I reject [counsel's] argument that the legislative history of this power (including, in particular, an indication to Parliament in 1986 that the Government was then intending to exercise it in continuing support of asylum seekers) itself serves to limit its present scope, the fact that asylum seekers have hitherto enjoyed benefit payments appears to me not entirely irrelevant. After all, the Act of 1993 confers on asylum seekers fuller rights than they had ever previously enjoyed, the right of appeal in particular. And yet these Regulations for some genuine asylum seekers at least must now be regarded as rendering these rights nugatory. Either that, or the Regulations necessarily contemplate for some a life so destitute that to my mind no civilised nation can tolerate it. So basic are the human rights here at issue that it cannot be necessary to resort to the European Convention on Human Rights to take note of their violation ... I would hold it unlawful to alter the benefit regime so drastically as must inevitably not merely prejudice, but on occasion defeat, the statutory right of asylum seekers to claim refugee status.

16.4.3 General principles of judicial review

While the legality of secondary legislation sometimes falls to be determined, as in the *JCWI* case, by reference to the express terms of relevant primary legislation, general principles of administrative law can also enter into play when it comes to determining the extent of the authority conferred by an enabling provision, and hence the compatibility with such a provision of delegated legislation purportedly made under it. Although we saw earlier, when considering the extent of any common law duty to consult in respect of delegated legislation, that the courts are somewhat reluctant to bring general principles of fairness and participation into play in this sphere, many other of the principles of judicial review which we encountered in earlier chapters are applicable here. For instance, if the administration takes into account irrelevant considerations when making delegated legislation, it is open to the court to conclude that the legislation is *ultra vires*. The presumption against delegation also applies to legislative powers. Indeed, the courts are especially unwilling to conclude that the presumption has been rebutted where legislative powers are concerned: in *King-Emperor v. Benoari Lal Sarma* [1945] AC 14 at 24, Viscount Simon LC assumed, without further discussion, that a power to enact delegated legislation could not itself be delegated. Subordinate legislation made under the influence of an improper purpose is also liable to be quashed. Although, as Mason J explained in *Re Toohey; ex parte Northern Land Council* (1981) 38 ALR 439 at 484, it may be difficult as a matter of evidence to establish whether secondary legislation was in fact made under an improper influence, we have already seen (in the cases considered in ch 7) that the courts will, where possible, deduce purposes from objective evidence; there is no *a priori* reason why this should not occur in relation to legislative measures as well as administrative decisions.

Delegated legislation is also subject to judicial review on substantive grounds such as unreasonableness and (where relevant) proportionality, although—consistently with the judicial reticence in relation to substantive review of administrative decisions later evidenced in the *Wednesbury* case (see 8.2.1)—Lord Russell CJ was of the opinion in *Kruse v. Johnson* [1898] 2 QB 91 at 99–100 that courts should be slow to condemn byelaws on this ground:

> I do not mean to say that there may not be cases in which it would be the duty of the Court to condemn by-laws ... as invalid because unreasonable. But unreasonable in what sense? If, for instance, they were found to be partial and unequal in their operation as between different classes; if they were manifestly unjust; if they disclosed bad faith; if they involved such oppressive or gratuitous interference with the rights of those subject to them as could find no justification in the minds of reasonable men, the Court might well say, 'Parliament never intended to give authority to make such rules; they are unreasonable and ultra vires.' But it is in this sense, and in this sense only, as I conceive, that the question of unreasonableness can properly be regarded. A by-law is not unreasonable merely because particular judges may think that it goes further than is prudent or necessary or convenient, or because it is not accompanied by a qualification or an exception which some judges may think ought to be there. Surely it is not too much to say that in matters which directly and mainly concern the people of the county, who have the right to choose those whom they think best fitted to represent them in their local government bodies, such representatives may be trusted to understand their own requirements better than judges.

Although specifically oriented towards delegated legislation (specifically, byelaws), these remarks do not disclose any concerns that are unique to that context. Rather, Lord Russell's references to those in local government having been chosen (*ie* elected) and to their particular capacity to understand local requirements echo the issues of democratic legitimacy and institutional competence that are pervasive factors which inform the shape and intensity of substantive judicial review. The question therefore arises whether such considerations bite particularly strongly upon delegated legislation, so as to require a degree of judicial restraint in excess of that which applies in respect of administrative action generally.

One reason for thinking that delegated legislation—or at least some delegated legislation—might be a special case is that much of it is in some way approved (or at least not disapproved) by Parliament. For instance, in *Nottinghamshire County Council v. Secretary of State for the Environment* [1986] AC 240 (see 8.2.2), the Appellate Committee of the House of Lords took the view that an administrative measure—albeit not a legislative measure as such—which had been endorsed by the House of Commons was particularly invulnerable to challenge on the ground of unreasonableness. Lord Scarman (at 248) said that such measures could not be struck down as unreasonable unless there was 'perversity or ... absurdity of such proportions' that the targets could not have been set by a 'bona fide exercise of political judgment on the part of the Secretary of State'. That position appeared, at least to some extent, to rest upon the fact that the measure had secured the Commons' approval.

However, subsequent case law has emphasized the particular facts of the *Nottinghamshire* decision. For instance, in *R (Asif Javed) v. Secretary of State for the Home Department* [2001] EWCA Civ 789, [2002] QB 129 at [48] (see 8.2.2), Lord Phillips attributed the extreme judicial deference exhibited in *Nottinghamshire* to the subject- matter (*viz* national economic policy) of the measures in question, not to the fact that they had received parliamentary approval. The Supreme Court's decision in *Bank Mellat v. HM Treasury (No 2)* [2013] UKSC 39, [2014] AC AC 700— considered at 16.2.2 in relation to consultation— conveys a similar message. The statutory instrument prohibiting the doing of business with the claimant bank was successfully challenged on the ground that it was disproportionate. Nothing can be read into the fact that the Court was prepared to consider the question of proportionality, because proportionality was an explicit requirement in the relevant statute. However, what is noteworthy— against the background of the *Nottinghamshire* decision— is that the Court's assessment of the proportionality of the instrument was not discernibly affected by the fact that, pursuant to the affirmative procedure, there had been parliamentary involvement in the making of the instrument.

The position, then, is that the endorsement of delegated legislation by one or both Houses of Parliament certainly does not immunize it against judicial review on substantive or any other grounds, and ought not to trigger such extreme deference as, in effect, to rule out any question of review on the ground of unreasonableness or disproportionality. At the same time, however, the general principles considered in ch 8 apply, so that, for instance, the greater the quality and degree of parliamentary engagement with a given piece of delegated legislation, the greater is the degree of judicial deference that might (other things being equal) be anticipated.

QUESTIONS

- Look back to the discussion of deference in ch 8. Should courts extend greater deference to legislative measures which have been democratically endorsed?
- Should the extent of judicial deference in relation to delegated legislation be informed by the adequacy of parliamentary scrutiny of such measures?

Finally, we should note a further ground of review which is of particular relevance to delegated legislation. By definition, legislation—delegated or otherwise—lays down general rules, compliance or non-compliance with which will have legal consequences. It is important, therefore, that such rules are stated clearly, in order that individuals may act accordingly. Many commentators place this requirement near the heart of the rule of law: Raz, *The Authority of Law* (Oxford 1979) at 214, writes that the law's 'meaning must be clear. An ambiguous, vague, obscure, or imprecise law is likely to mislead or confuse at least some of those who desire to be guided by it.' Some cases indicate a judicial willingness to strike down vague secondary legislation for reasons similar to those advanced by Raz. For instance, in *Kruse* v. *Johnson* [1898] 2 QB 91 at 108, Matthew J said that 'a byelaw to be valid must, among other conditions, ... be certain, that is, it must contain adequate information as to the duties of those who are to obey'. However, more recent authority evidences a narrower approach. Approving a test laid down by Lord Denning in *Fawcett Properties Ltd* v. *Buckingham County Council* [1961] AC 636 at 677–8, Simon Brown LJ in *Percy* v. *Hall* [1997] QB 924 at 941 concluded that secondary legislation should be treated 'as valid unless so uncertain in its language as to have no ascertainable meaning, or so unclear in its effect as to be incapable of certain application in any case'. The Court recognized and accepted that, at the margins, there will often be uncertainty about precisely how a given rule applies to a particular situation, but that this should not be fatal to its validity.

Finally, it should be noted that legal certainty is a core aspect of the requirement under the European Convention on Human Rights that restrictions upon qualified rights must be 'prescribed by law'—meaning, among other things, that legislation (including delegated legislation) which impinges upon such a right must be clear enough to enable the individual to understand the circumstances in which it will apply.

16.4.4 Wider constitutional principles and human rights

As well as being open to challenge if it breaches specific statutory requirements or general principles of administrative law, delegated legislation—like other forms of administrative action—may also be rendered invalid if it conflicts with wider constitutional principles or the rights protected by the Human Rights Act 1998. As is apparent from the following excerpt, the courts apply a general presumption that Parliament, in enacting enabling legislation, would not intend to empower rule-makers to contravene important constitutional principles or rights.

Ahmed v. *HM Treasury (No 1)* [2010] UKSC 2, [2010] 2 WLR 378
United Kingdom Supreme Court

Following terrorist attacks in the United States of America on 11 September 2001, the United Nations Security Council adopted a resolution requiring states to freeze the financial assets of 'persons who commit, or attempt to commit, terrorist acts or participate in or facilitate the commission of terrorist acts'. As a matter of international law, the UK was required, pursuant to its obligations under the United Nations Charter, to implement the resolution. It did so by enacting secondary legislation in purported exercise of powers conferred by s 1(1) of the United Nations Act 1946, which allows the enactment of such Orders in Council as appear to be 'necessary or expedient for enabling [Security Council resolutions] to be effectively applied, including (without prejudice to the generality of the preceding words) provision for the apprehension, trial and punishment of persons offending against the Order'.

This excerpt is concerned only with the legality of the Terrorism (United Nations Measures) Order 2006 (TO) which permitted the freezing of assets if the Treasury had 'reasonable grounds for suspecting' that the person answered the description set out in the resolution and reproduced above. On this basis, the appellants' assets were frozen. The asset- freezing regime was arguably inconsistent with certain of the rights contained in the ECHR and given effect in the UK by the HRA. However, the Supreme Court held (following the House of Lords in *R (Al- Jedda)* v. *Secretary of State for Defence* [2007] UKHL 58, [2008] 1 AC 332) that it was not open to the claimants to attack the lawfulness of the TO by reference to the ECHR, because the effect of Article 103 of the UN Charter is that obligations imposed by Security Council resolutions take priority over those arising from (*inter alia*) the ECHR. However, this left open the question whether the TO was lawful as a matter of domestic law.

Lord Hope (with whom Lord Walker and Lady Hale agreed)

[5] The procedure that section 1 [of the 1946 Act] lays down enables Orders under it to be made by the executive without any kind of Parliamentary scrutiny. This is in sharp contrast to the scheme for the freezing of assets that has been enacted by Parliament in Part 2 of the Anti-terrorism, Crime and Security Act 2001. Orders made under that Act must be kept under review by the Treasury, are time limited and must be approved by both Houses of Parliament … The [effect of] the TO … [is] far more draconian. Yet [it] lie[s] wholly outside the scope of Parliamentary scrutiny. This raises fundamental questions about the relationship between Parliament and the executive and about judicial control over the power of the executive.

[6] The case brings us face to face with the kind of issue that led to Lord Atkin's famously powerful protest in *Liversidge v Anderson* [1942] AC 206, 244 against a construction of a Defence

Regulation which had the effect of giving an absolute and uncontrolled power of imprisonment to the minister ... The consequences of the [TO] ... are so drastic and so oppressive that we must be just as alert to see that the coercive action that the Treasury have taken really is within the powers that the 1946 Act has given them.

[38] The ... regimes ... [established by] the TO and [another Order, with which this excerpt is not concerned, affect] all aspects of [the relevant person's] life, including his ability to move around at will by any means of private or public transport. To enable payments to be made for basic living expenses a system of licensing has been created. It is regulated by the Treasury, whose interpretation of the sanctions regime and of the system of licensing and the conditions that it gives rise to is extremely rigorous. The overall result is very burdensome on all the members of the designated person's family. The impact on normal family life is remorseless and it can be devastating ...

[44] The [language of s 1 of the 1946 Act] leaves the question whether any given measure is 'necessary' or 'expedient' to the judgment of the executive without subjecting it, or any of the terms and conditions which apply to it, to the scrutiny of Parliament. In the context of what was envisaged when the Bill was debated in 1946, which was the use of non-military, diplomatic and economic sanctions as a means of deterring aggression between states, the surrender of power to the executive to ensure the taking of immediate and effective action in the international sphere is unsurprising. The use of the power as a means of imposing restraints or the taking of coercive measures targeted against individuals in domestic law is an entirely different matter ...

[45] ... [T]he phrase 'necessary or expedient for enabling those measures to be effectively applied' does require further examination. The closer those measures come to affecting what, in *R v Secretary of State for the Home Department, Ex p Simms* [2000] 2 AC 115, 131, Lord Hoffmann described as the basic rights of the individual, the more exacting this scrutiny must become ...

[46] [His Lordship went on to set out the following passage from the speech of Lord Browne-Wilkinson in *R v. Secretary of State for the Home Department, ex parte Pierson* [1998] AC 539 at 573:]

> 'I consider first whether there is any principle of construction which requires the court, in certain cases, to construe general words contained in the statute as being impliedly limited. In my judgment there is such a principle. It is well established that Parliament does not legislate in a vacuum: statutes are drafted on the basis that the ordinary rules and principles of the common law will apply to the express statutory provisions.'

At p 575, having examined the authorities, [Lord Browne-Wilkinson] said:

> 'From these authorities I think the following proposition is established. A power conferred by Parliament in general terms is not to be taken to authorise the doing of acts by the donee of the power which adversely affect the legal rights of the citizen or the basic principles on which the law of the United Kingdom is based unless the statute conferring the power makes it clear that such was the intention of Parliament.'

[47] I would approach the language of section 1 of the 1946 Act, therefore, on the basis that Parliament did not surrender its legislative powers to the executive any more than must necessarily follow from the words used by it. The words 'necessary' and 'expedient' both call for the exercise of judgment. But this does not mean that its exercise is unlimited. The wording of the Order must be tested precisely against the words used by the Security Council's resolution ... A provision in the Order which affects the basic rights of the individual but was unavoidable if effect was to be given to the resolution according to its terms may be taken to have been authorised because it was 'necessary'. A provision may be included which is 'expedient' but not

'necessary'. This enables provisions to be included in the Order which differ from those used by the resolution or are unavoidably required by it. But it does not permit interference with the basic rights of the individual any more [than] is necessary and unavoidable to give effect to the [Resolution] and is consistent with the principle of legality. ...

[61] I would hold that, by introducing the reasonable suspicion test as a means of giving effect to [the Resolution], the Treasury exceeded their powers under section 1(1) of the 1946 Act. This is a clear example of an attempt to adversely affect the basic rights of the citizen without the clear authority of Parliament ... In my opinion the TO is ultra vires section 1(1) of the 1946 Act and, subject to what I say about the date when these orders should take effect, it ... must be quashed.

The Justices unanimously agreed that the TO was ultra vires the 1946 Act.

The approach adopted in *Ahmed* is not limited to interference with property rights. Equivalent principles of interpretation have been applied (*inter alia*) to uphold the principle that taxes may be levied only with parliamentary consent (see *Attorney-General* v. *Wilts United Dairies Ltd* (1921) 39 TLR 781), the right of legal professional privilege (see *R (Daly)* v. *Secretary of State for the Home Department* [2001] UKHL 26, [2001] 2 AC 532), freedom of expression (see *R* v. *Secretary of State for the Home Department, ex parte Simms* [2000] 2 AC 115), and access to courts for the resolution of legal disputes (*R* v. *Lord Chancellor, ex parte Witham* [1998] QB 575).

The interpretative model under which common law rights are protected against encroachment by delegated legislation now has a statutory counterpart in the form of the HRA (for discussion of which in this context see *R (Bono)* v. *Harlow District Council* [2002] EWHC 423 (Admin), [2002] 1 WLR 2475). Section 3 obliges the courts, where possible, to read (*inter alia*) legislation that confers rule-making powers consistently with the Convention rights: those rights are therefore read into enabling provisions as implied limits upon them. It follows that ECHR-incompatible delegated legislation will generally be *ultra vires* by operation of s 3.

16.4.5 Prerogative legislation

The vast majority of delegated legislation is enacted under powers conferred by *statute*. It is, however, necessary to address two points concerning *prerogative* legislation.

First, it is possible for the Crown, by exercising the prerogative, to *assign law-making powers*. Here, the position is clear: laws enacted under such powers will constitute delegated legislation. It was famously established in *Council of Civil Service Unions* v. *Minister for the Civil Service* [1985] AC 374 that such prerogative legislation can be judicially reviewed just like delegated legislation purportedly made under statutory powers, provided that the issues thereby raised are justiciable (on which see 4.3.3).

Second, however, what if legislation is *enacted by the Crown itself under a direct exercise of the prerogative*? Will such legislation constitute delegated legislation— and is it subject to judicial review? The key to understanding this point is that these two issues— amenability to judicial review, on the one hand, and characterization as delegated legislation, on the other— are separable. Whether something counts as primary or secondary legislation is a nice semantic question (on which see McHarg [2006] *PL* 539), but the more practically important one is whether, and if so on what grounds, it can be challenged via judicial review. Here, the central issue is whether the authority of the law- maker is unlimited (as is supposedly the case in respect of the UK Parliament) or not. The power of the Crown to enact prerogative legislation is indisputably limited, and the House of Lords confirmed unequivocally in *R (Bancoult)* v. *Secretary of State for Foreign and Commonwealth Affairs (No 2)* [2008] UKHL 61, [2009] AC 453 (on which see further at 4.3.2) that prerogative legislation is therefore subject to judicial review on the normal grounds. (This was notwithstanding the fact that, for the purposes of the HRA, such legislation is characterized as primary legislation such that it can merely be declared incompatible with, but not struck down for, incompatibility with ECHR rights.) It is worth noting in passing that the distinction between how legislation is characterized and whether it is subject to judicial review is also discernible in respect of legislation enacted by the devolved legislatures. For instance, although legislation enacted by the Scottish Parliament is generally considered to be 'primary legislation', it is judicially reviewable, including— according to *AXA General Insurance Ltd* v. *The Lord Advocate* [2011] UKSC 46, [2012] 1 AC 868— on grounds (such as breach of common law constitutional rights) that are extrinsic to the express terms of the devolution legislation. This matter is considered in more detail at 4.2.

16.5 Concluding remarks

Delegated legislation is an inescapable feature of contemporary governance. The enactment of legislative rules by the administrative branch is inevitable, given the volume of regulation that is deemed necessary today. These conclusions should not, however, disguise the fact that vigilance, in two senses, is essential. First, the necessity of a degree of delegation of legislative authority should not blunt critical evaluation of the appropriateness of particular delegations; such evaluation—especially important in view of the tendency to confer increasingly broad legislative powers—is a matter for Parliament. Secondly, delegated legislation should itself be open to critical scrutiny. The difficulty, of course, lies in the highly incomplete implementation in Britain of the separation of powers doctrine. In light of its dominance of Parliament, the administration is very strongly placed to secure the passage of primary legislation that confers wide rule-making powers, and to survive (or even avoid meaningful) parliamentary scrutiny of delegated legislation passed under such powers. Meanwhile, the efficacy of judicial scrutiny of the legality of executive legislation is to an extent compromised by the broad nature of the enabling provisions that administrations are often able to procure. None of this renders political and judicial scrutiny of delegated legislation pointless; much, as we have seen in this chapter, can still be achieved: parliamentary committees are sometimes able to exert sufficient pressure to procure changes, the government's in-built majority in the House of Commons notwithstanding; and the courts do their best, where appropriate, to read enabling provisions subject to relevant principles of constitutional law, administrative justice, and human rights. Nevertheless, it would be naïve to underestimate the impact in this context of the structural features of the British constitution which combine to produce a powerful executive branch that is able, through its effective control of the sovereign legislature, to confer upon itself extensive legislative powers.

FURTHER RESOURCES

Barber and Young, 'The Rise of Prospective Henry VIII Clauses and Their Implications for Sovereignty' [2003] *PL* 112

Cm 4060, *Report of the Committee on Ministers' Powers* (1932)

Daintith and Page, *The Executive in the Constitution* (Oxford 1999)

Ganz, *Quasi-Legislation: Recent Developments in Secondary Legislation* (London 1987)

Hansard Society, *The Devil is in the Detail: Parliament and Delegated Legislation* (London 2014)

House of Commons Library, 'House of Commons Background Paper: Statutory Instruments' (London 2012) *http://researchbriefings.parliament.uk/ResearchBriefing/Summary/SN06509*

McHarg, 'What is Delegated Legislation?' [2006] *PL* 539

Page, *Governing by Numbers* (Oxford 2001)

The websites of the various parliamentary committees referred to in this chapter can be accessed via *http://www.parliament.uk/business/committees/committees-a-z/*

INQUIRIES

17.1 Two types of inquiries

It is not difficult to think of examples of 'inquiries', Sir John Chilcot's inquiry into the Iraq War, Lord Saville's Bloody Sunday inquiry, and the ongoing independent inquiry into historical allegations of child sexual abuse being recent notable examples. These are examples of what we will call in this chapter *ex post*— or after- the- event— inquiries. They take place *after* the occurrence of the event, the making of the decision, or the formulation of the policy that forms the focus of the inquiry. The purposes of such inquiries often include establishing what happened, determining the underlying causes of what it was that went wrong, facilitating the holding to account of those who are responsible for whatever went wrong, and enabling lessons to be learned for the future. We consider such inquiries at 17.3.

While *ex post* inquiries are the ones most likely to grab the headlines, not least because they are often concerned with profoundly controversial matters of grave public concern, the vast majority of inquiries are in fact of a different type. Such inquiries—to which we refer in this chapter as *ex ante*, or before-the-event, inquiries—are concerned not with looking back at something that has already happened. Rather, they are concerned with things that have not yet taken place, their purpose being to inform the making of administrative decisions. Some such decisions—*eg* whether a new nuclear power station should be built in a particular location, or whether a new motorway should follow a given route—might be every bit as significant as and may have a public profile equivalent to the types of controversy with which *ex post* inquiries are concerned. But most *ex ante* inquiries are comparatively mundane, being concerned with such matters as small-scale planning decisions. It is with *ex ante* inquiries that we begin.

17.2 *Ex ante* inquiries

17.2.1 Some examples

In the following sections, we consider why *ex ante* inquiries are held and how they are conducted. However, in order to provide some context, we begin by sketching two of the *ex ante* inquiry models that are encountered in the planning context. The first model involves an inquiry that takes place *before the making of any decision whatever*. For instance, the

Planning Act 2008 sets out the process whereby decisions concerning 'nationally significant infrastructure projects'— such as major transport and energy schemes— are to be
taken. Development consent for such projects is granted by the Secretary of State (s 103),
but the ministerial decision is prefigured and informed by an inquiry process run by the
Planning Inspectorate. Members of the public who register with and make representations
to the Inspectorate are permitted to attend a 'preliminary meeting' chaired by a Planning
Inspector (s 88). After that, further written representations can be made to the Inspectorate
(s 90), and hearings, at which oral representations can be made, must be held on particular
issues in certain circumstances (s 91), while an 'open- floor hearing', enabling all interested
parties (as defined in s 102) to make oral representations, must be held if any such party
requests one (s 93). A report is then made to the Secretary of State (ss 74 and 83), who makes
the final decision.

Second, under the heading of *ex ante* inquiries we place not only inquiries that are taken
in advance of *any* decision on the relevant matter being reached, but also inquiries that are
undertaken *in the course of an appeal that is lodged against a decision*. Inquiries of the latter
type can fairly be characterized as *ex ante* in nature because, although they take place following the taking of the (initial) decision, they nevertheless—by preceding the taking of the
(final) appellate decision—prospectively inform the decision-making process rather than
(as in the case of an after-the-event, *ex post* inquiry) examining a decision that has been
made and which exists as a given. *Ex ante* inquiries of this second type are commonplace in
respect of planning matters that fall outside the regime described above concerning major
infrastructure projects.

For instance, s 57(1) of the Town and Country Planning Act 1990 provides that 'planning
permission is required for the carrying out of any development of land', where 'development' means (according to s 55(1)) 'the carrying out of building, engineering, mining or
other operations in, on, over or under land, or the making of any material change in the use
of any buildings or other land'. It is usually the responsibility of the local planning authority to decide planning applications under s 70 of the 1990 Act, but a right of appeal to the
Secretary of State lies against such authorities' decisions in various circumstances, including outright refusal of planning permission (s 78(1)(a)). Appeals can be decided solely on
the basis of written representations, but, according to s 79(2):

> Before determining an appeal under section 78 the Secretary of State shall, if either the appellant
> or the local planning authority so wish, give each of them an opportunity of appearing before and
> being heard by a person appointed by the Secretary of State for the purpose.

In these circumstances, hearings may be provided by holding a public local inquiry under
s 320. Where the Secretary of State (or his officials) is to determine the appeal, an inquiry—
governed by the Town and Country Planning (Inquiries Procedure) (England) Rules 2000
or the Town and Country Planning (Inquiries Procedure) (Wales) Rules 2003—is held,
the inspector makes a recommendation, and the Secretary of State, who is free to accept
or reject that recommendation, then decides the appeal. However, the Secretary of State
now tends to determine only those appeals which raise particularly complex or sensitive
issues. It is therefore common for the inspector to decide the appeal himself rather than
simply making a recommendation, in which case the inquiry is governed by the Town and
Country Planning Appeals (Determination by Inspectors) (Inquiries Procedure) (England)
Rules 2000 and the Town and Country Planning Appeals (Determination by Inspectors)
(Inquiries Procedure) (Wales) Rules 2003.

With these features of planning inquiries in mind, we turn to consider the nature and role of inquiries.

17.2.2 The nature and purpose of *ex ante* inquiries

We already know that administrative law requires decision-makers not only to take relevant information into account (see ch 7) but also to take procedural steps that may help to bring such information to light (see ch 10). Those procedural steps typically involve permitting relevant parties—such as those who are liable to be affected by an administrative decision—to make informed representations, whether in writing or, via some form of 'hearing', orally. We might regard this as the 'standard' model of administrative decision-making.

Decision-making processes that involve an *ex ante* inquiry differ from the standard model in three key respects. First, *ex ante* inquiries (usually) amount to a *public forum* for the airing of objections and support for proposed administrative action. Such inquiries therefore lend a particular degree of transparency to the decision-making—or at least the initial evidence-gathering—process. Second, precisely because of their publicness, *ex ante* inquiries facilitate a *multilateral form of public input* into the decision-making process that is quite different from the bilateral form that the making of representations—by a given individual to a given public body—usually takes. In this way, inquiries facilitate a form of communal or collective airing of issues that the standard model does not readily accommodate. Third, inquiries often emphasize a distinction—which might exist within the standard model but be hidden under the cloak of departmental decision-making—between *technocratic and political modes of decision-making*. For instance, although a planning inquiry may have a political or 'popular' dimension by dint of public participation, its principal focus will be on questions of a relatively technical nature concerning (for example) the relationship between the planning proposal and relevant planning policies. In contrast, when the Secretary of State comes to decide whether to accept the inquiry's recommendation, he may consider that the issue takes on a different complexion when viewed in a broader political (but still lawful) perspective.

QUESTIONS

- What principles ought to govern the circumstances in which the making of an administrative decision is preceded by the holding of an inquiry?
- Are there types of administrative decisions that are particularly ill-suited to the inquiry model?

It is apparent, then, that inquiries do not straightforwardly adhere to the standard administrative decision-making model. Indeed, as Wade and Forsyth observe (*Administrative Law* (Oxford 2014) at 795), inquiries are 'a hybrid legal-and-administrative process, and for the very reason that they have been made to look as much as possible like judicial proceedings, people grumble at the fact that they fall short of it'. The question whether inquiries ought to be characterized as serving an administrative or a judicial role—an issue which fundamentally affects how inquiries should operate—was considered at length by the Franks Committee in its *Report of the Committee on Administrative Tribunals and Enquiries* (Cmnd 218, 1957). Having considered (with particular reference to planning inquiries) the competing administrative and judicial models—the former casting inquiries as a mere adjunct to the exercise of ministerial discretion, the latter emphasizing the adversarial nature of inquiries and the need for resultant decisions to be founded upon the evidence thereby gathered—the Committee said (at [272]):

> [T]hese procedures cannot be classified as purely administrative or purely judicial. They are not purely administrative because of the provision for a special procedure preliminary to the decision—a feature not to be found in the ordinary course of administration—and because this procedure ... involves the testing of an issue, often partly in public. They are not on the other hand purely judicial, because the final decision cannot be reached by the application of rules and must allow the exercise of a wide discretion in the balancing of public and private interest. Neither view at its extreme is tenable, nor should either be emphasised at the expense of the other.
>
> If the administrative view is dominant the public enquiry cannot play its full part in the total process, and there is a danger that the rights and interests of the individual citizens affected will not be sufficiently protected. In these cases it is idle to argue that Parliament can be relied upon to protect the citizen, save exceptionally. We agree with the following views expressed in the pamphlet entitled *The Rule of Law*: 'Whatever the theoretical validity of this argument, those of us who are Members of Parliament have no hesitation in saying that it bears little relation to reality. Parliament has neither the time nor the knowledge to supervise the Minister and call him to account for his administrative decision.'
>
> If the judicial view is dominant there is a danger that people will regard the person before whom they state their case as a kind of judge provisionally deciding the matter, subject to an appeal to the Minister. This view overlooks the true nature of the proceeding, the form of which is necessitated by the fact that the Minister himself, who is responsible to Parliament for the ultimate decision, cannot conduct the enquiry in person.

The Committee's conclusion that inquiries can be characterized as neither purely judicial nor purely administrative influenced its subsequent proposals for improving inquiries. It sought to apply to inquiries the three principles of openness, fairness, and impartiality, which it had already developed in relation to statutory tribunals (see ch 18), while recognizing (at 61) that, in the quasi-administrative realm of inquiries, the notion of impartiality 'cannot be applied ... without qualification'. Many of the specific recommendations of the Franks Committee were implemented through the adoption of new administrative practices and legal rules (see further the 1963 *Annual Report of the Council on Tribunals* (London 1963), Appendix A), and its legacy is still abundantly evident: the principal piece of legislation in this area, the Tribunals and Inquiries Act 1992, has its origins in the 1958 Act of the same name, which was enacted in the wake of the Franks Report. We refer to the 1992 Act, and to other aspects of Franks's legacy, in the following sections.

17.2.3 The right to know the opposing case

One of the Franks Committee's specific recommendations (at 62) was that '[f]airness requires that those whose individual rights and interests are likely to be adversely affected by the action proposed should know in good time before the enquiry the case which they will have to meet'. The following rules, which apply to inquiries held in relation to appeals against planning permission decisions and which were enacted under s 9 of the 1992 Act, seek to address this issue. They are given here as an example of how the right to know the opposing case is typically delivered in the context of *ex ante* inquiries.

Town and Country Planning (Inquiries Procedure) (England) Rules 2000

Preliminary information to be supplied by local planning authority

4—(1) The local planning authority shall, on receipt of the [relevant notice], forthwith inform the Secretary of State and the applicant in writing of the name and address of any statutory party [*ie* a party whose views the Secretary of State is legally obliged to take into account] who has made representations to them; and the Secretary of State shall, as soon as practicable thereafter, inform the applicant and the local planning authority in writing of the name and address of any statutory party who has made representations to him.

(2) This paragraph applies where—

(a) the Secretary of State has given to the local planning authority a direction restricting the grant of planning permission for which application was made; or

(b) in a case relating to listed building consent, the [Historic Buildings and Monuments] Commission [for England] has given a direction to the local planning authority pursuant to section 14(2) of the Listed Buildings Act as to how the application is to be determined; or

(c) the Secretary of State or any other Minister of the Crown or any government department, or any body falling within rule 11(1)(c), has expressed in writing to the local planning authority the view that the application should not be granted either wholly or in part, or should be granted only subject to conditions; or

(d) any person consulted in pursuance of a development order has made representations to the local planning authority about the application.

(3) Where paragraph (2) applies, the local planning authority shall forthwith after the starting date inform the person concerned of the inquiry and, unless they have already done so, that person shall thereupon give the local planning authority a written statement of the reasons for making the direction, expressing the view or making the representations, as the case may be.

(4) Subject to paragraph (5), the local planning authority shall ensure that within 2 weeks of the starting date—

(a) the Secretary of State and the applicant have received a completed questionnaire and a copy of each of the documents referred to in it;

(b) any—

(i) statutory party; and

(ii) other person who made representations to the local planning authority about the application occasioning the appeal,

has been notified in writing that an appeal has been made and of the address to which and of the period within which they may make representations to the Secretary of State ...

Procedure where Secretary of State causes pre-inquiry meeting to be held

5—(1) The Secretary of State shall hold a pre-inquiry meeting—

(a) if he expects an inquiry to last for 8 days or more, unless he considers it is unnecessary;

(b) in respect of shorter inquiries, if it appears to him necessary.

(2) Where the Secretary of State decides to hold a pre-inquiry meeting the following provisions shall apply—

(a) the Secretary of State shall send with the relevant notice—

(i) notice of his intention to hold a pre-inquiry meeting;

      (ii) a statement of the matters about which he particularly wishes to be informed for the purposes of his consideration of the application or appeal in question and where another Minister of the Crown or a government department has expressed in writing to the Secretary of State a view which is mentioned in rule 4(2)(c), the Secretary of State shall set this out in his statement;

  (b) the Secretary of State shall send a copy of the statement described in the previous paragraph to the Minister or government department concerned;

  (c) the local planning authority shall publish in a newspaper circulating in the locality in which the land is situated a notice of the Secretary of State's intention to hold a pre-inquiry meeting and of the statement sent in accordance with paragraph (2)(a)(ii) above; and

  (d) the applicant and the local planning authority shall ensure that within 8 weeks of the starting date 2 copies of their outline statement have been received by the Secretary of State.

(3) The Secretary of State shall, as soon as practicable after receipt, send a copy of the local planning authority's outline statement to the applicant and a copy of the applicant's outline statement to the local planning authority ...

Receipt of statements of case etc

6—(1) The local planning authority shall ensure that within—

  (a) 6 weeks of the starting date, or

  (b) where a pre-inquiry meeting is held pursuant to rule 5, 4 weeks of the conclusion of that pre-inquiry meeting,

2 copies of their statement of case have been received by the Secretary of State and a copy of their statement of case has been received by any statutory party ...

(3) The applicant shall ensure that within—

  (a) in the case of an appeal or a referred application where no pre-inquiry meeting is held pursuant to rule 5, 6 weeks of the starting date, or

  (b) in any case where a pre-inquiry meeting is held pursuant to rule 5, 4 weeks of the conclusion of that pre-inquiry meeting,

2 copies of their statement of case have been received by the Secretary of State and a copy of their statement of case has been received by any statutory party.

(4) The Secretary of State shall, as soon as practicable after receipt, send a copy of the local planning authority's statement of case to the applicant and a copy of the applicant's statement of case to the local planning authority.

(5) The applicant and the local planning authority may in writing each require the other to send them a copy of any document, or of the relevant part of any document, referred to in the list of documents comprised in the party's statement of case; and any such document, or relevant part, shall be sent, as soon as practicable, to the party who required it.

(6) The Secretary of State may in writing require any other person, who has notified him of an intention or wish to appear at an inquiry, to send within 4 weeks of being so required—

  (a) 3 copies of their statement of case to him; and

  (b) a copy of their statement of case to any statutory party,

and the Secretary of State shall, as soon as practicable after receipt, send a copy of each such statement of case to the local planning authority and to the applicant.

(7) The Secretary of State shall as soon as practicable—

  (a) send to a person from whom he requires a statement of case in accordance with paragraph (6) a copy of the statements of case of the applicant and the local planning authority; and

(b) inform that person of the name and address of every person to whom his statement of case is required to be sent.

(8) The Secretary of State or the inspector may in writing require any person, who has sent to him a statement of case in accordance with this rule, to provide such further information about the matters contained in the statement of case as he may specify and may specify the time within which the information shall be received by him ...

(12) Unless he has already done so, the Secretary of State shall within 12 weeks of the starting date send a written statement of the matters referred to in rule 5(2)(a)(ii) to—

(a) the applicant;

(b) the local planning authority;

(c) any statutory party; and

(d) any person from whom he has required a statement of case.

(13) The local planning authority shall afford to any person who so requests a reasonable opportunity to inspect and, where practicable, take copies of—

(a) any statement of case, information or other document a copy of which has been sent to the local planning authority in accordance with this rule; and

(b) the local planning authority's completed questionnaire and statement of case together with a copy of any document, or of the relevant part of any document, referred to in the list comprised in that statement, and information or other documents sent by the local planning authority pursuant to this rule.

Date and notification of inquiry

10—(1) The date fixed by the Secretary of State for the holding of an inquiry shall be, unless he considers such a date impracticable, not later than—

(a) Subject to paragraph (b), 22 weeks after the starting date; or

(b) in a case where a pre-inquiry meeting is held pursuant to rule 5, 8 weeks after the conclusion of that meeting.

(2) Where the Secretary of State considers it impracticable to fix a date in accordance with paragraph (1), the date fixed shall be the earliest date after the end of the relevant period mentioned in that paragraph which he considers to be practicable.

(3) Unless the Secretary of State agrees a lesser period of notice with the applicant and the local planning authority, he shall give not less than 4 weeks written notice of the date, time and place fixed by him for the holding of an inquiry to every person entitled to appear at the inquiry ...

(4) The Secretary of State may vary the date fixed for the holding of an inquiry, whether or not the date as varied is within the relevant period mentioned in paragraph (1) ...

(5) The Secretary of State may vary the time or place for the holding of an inquiry and shall give such notice of any variation as appears to him to be reasonable.

(6) The Secretary of State may in writing require the local planning authority to take one or more of the following steps—

(a) not less than 2 weeks before the date fixed for the holding of an inquiry, to publish a notice of the inquiry in one or more newspapers circulating in the locality in which the land is situated;

(b) to send a notice of the inquiry to such persons or classes of persons as he may specify, within such period as he may specify; or

(c) to post a notice of the inquiry in a conspicuous place near to the land, within such period as he may specify.

(7) Where the land is under the control of the applicant he shall—

   (a) if so required in writing by the Secretary of State, affix a notice of the inquiry firmly to the land or to some object on or near the land, in such manner as to be readily visible to and legible by members of the public; and

   (b) not remove the notice, or cause or permit it to be removed, for such period before the inquiry as the Secretary of State may specify.

(8) Every notice of inquiry published, sent or posted pursuant to paragraph (6), or affixed pursuant to paragraph (7), shall contain—

   (a) a clear statement of the date, time and place of the inquiry and of the powers enabling the Secretary of State to determine the application or appeal in question;

   (b) a written description of the land sufficient to identify approximately its location;

   (c) a brief description of the subject matter of the application or appeal; and

   (d) details of where and when copies of the local planning authority's completed questionnaire and any documents sent by and copied to the authority pursuant to rule 6 may be inspected.

It can be seen that these rules make detailed provision so as to ensure that the relevant parties are in receipt of one another's cases before the opening of the inquiry. Note, however, that under r 10(3), the minimum four-week notice period can be waived by agreement between the applicant, the Secretary of State, and the local planning authority, to the potential detriment of third parties.

17.2.4 Participation and procedure

We have already seen that one of the difficulties faced by inquiries is the extent to which they should be regarded as—and therefore possess the characteristics of—a judicial, as distinct from an administrative, process. This issue bears clearly upon the procedure which applies at the inquiry, and particularly upon the question of participation. In the absence of rules laying down the procedure to be adopted at an inquiry, the principle of procedural fairness (see ch 10) applies, although in *Bushell* v. *Secretary of State for the Environment* [1981] AC 75 at 95 Lord Diplock cautioned against the unthinking adoption in this context of 'concepts that are appropriate to the conduct of ordinary civil litigation between private parties', preferring to state that an inquiry must be 'be fair to all those who have an interest in the decision that will follow it', but that what constitutes a fair procedure 'will depend upon the nature of its subject matter'. Usually, however, specific provision as to the procedure is made in the relevant legislation, as the following extract illustrates.

Town and Country Planning (Inquiries Procedure) (England) Rules 2000

Appearances at inquiry

11—(1) The persons entitled to appear at an inquiry are—

   (a) the applicant;

   (b) the local planning authority;

(c) any of the following bodies if the land is situated in their area and they are not the local planning authority—

    (i) a county or district council;

    (ii) an enterprise zone authority designated under Schedule 32 to the Local Government, Planning and Land Act 1980;

    (iii) the Broads Authority, within the meaning of the Norfolk and Suffolk Broads Act 1988;

    (iv) a housing action trust specified in an order made under section 67(1) of the Housing Act 1988;

(d) where the land is in an area previously designated as a new town, the Homes and Communities Agency;

(e) any statutory party [*ie* a party whose views the Secretary of State is legally obliged to take into account];

(f) the council of the parish in which the land is situated, if that council made representations to the local planning authority in respect of the application in pursuance of a provision of a development order;

(g) where the application was required to be notified to the Commission under section 14 of the Listed Buildings Act, the [Historic Buildings and Monuments] Commission [for England];

(h) any other person who has sent a statement of case in accordance with rule 6(6) or who has sent an outline statement in accordance with rule 5(5).

(2) Nothing in paragraph (1) shall prevent the inspector from permitting any other person to appear at an inquiry, and such permission shall not be unreasonably withheld.

(3) Any person entitled or permitted to appear may do so on his own behalf or be represented by any other person.

Representatives of government departments and other authorities at inquiry

12—(1) Where—

(a) the Secretary of State or the Commission has given a direction described in rule 4(2) (a) or (b); or

(b) the Secretary of State or any other Minister of the Crown or any government department, or any body falling within rule 11(1)(c), has expressed a view described in rule 4(2)(c) and the local planning authority have included the terms of the expression of view in a statement sent in accordance with rule 5(2) or 6(1); or

(c) another Minister of the Crown or any government department has expressed a view described in rule 4(2)(c) and the Secretary of State has included its terms in a statement sent in accordance with rule 5(2) or 6(12),

the applicant, the local planning authority or a person entitled to appear may, not later than 4 weeks before the date of an inquiry, apply in writing to the Secretary of State for a representative of the Secretary of State or of the other Minister, department or body concerned to be made available at the inquiry.

(2) Where an application is made in accordance with paragraph (1), the Secretary of State shall make a representative available to attend the inquiry or, as the case may be, send the application to the other Minister, department or body concerned, who shall make a representative available to attend the inquiry.

(3) Any person attending an inquiry as a representative in pursuance of this rule shall state the reasons for the direction or expressed view and shall give evidence and be subject to cross-examination to the same extent as any other witness.

(4) Nothing in paragraph (3) shall require a representative of a Minister or a government department to answer any question which in the opinion of the inspector is directed to the merits of government policy.

Proofs of evidence

13—(1) Any person entitled to appear at an inquiry, who proposes to give, or to call another person to give evidence at the inquiry by reading a proof of evidence, shall—

    (a) send 2 copies, in the case of the local planning authority and the applicant, or 3 copies in the case of any other person, of the proof of evidence together with any written summary, to the Secretary of State; and

    (b) simultaneously send copies of these to any statutory party, and the Secretary of State shall, as soon as practicable after receipt, send a copy of each proof of evidence together with any summary to the local planning authority and the applicant ...

(3) The proof of evidence and any summary shall be received by the Secretary of State no later than—

    (a) 4 weeks before the date fixed for the holding of the inquiry, or

    (b) where a timetable has been arranged pursuant to rule 8 which specifies a date by which the proof of evidence and any summary shall be received by the Secretary of State, that date.

(4) The Secretary of State shall send to the inspector, as soon as practicable after receipt, any proof of evidence together with any summary sent to him in accordance with this rule and received by him within the relevant period, if any specified in this rule.

(5) Where a written summary is provided in accordance with paragraph (1), only that summary shall be read at the inquiry, unless the inspector permits or requires otherwise.

(6) Any person, required by this rule to send copies of a proof of evidence to the Secretary of State, shall send with them the same number of copies of the whole, or the relevant part, of any document referred to in the proof of evidence, unless a copy of the document or part of the document in question is already available for inspection pursuant to rule 6(13).

(7) The local planning authority shall afford to any person who so requests a reasonable opportunity to inspect and, where practicable, take copies of any document sent to or by them in accordance with this rule ...

Statement of common ground

14—(1) The local planning authority and the applicant shall—

    (a) together prepare an agreed statement of common ground; and

    (b) ensure that the Secretary of State receives it and that any statutory party receives a copy of it within 6 weeks of the starting date.

(2) The local planning authority shall afford to any person who so requests, a reasonable opportunity to inspect, and where practicable, take copies of the statement of common ground sent to the Secretary of State ...

Procedure at inquiry

15—(1) Except as otherwise provided in these Rules, the inspector shall determine the procedure at an inquiry.

(2) At the start of the inquiry the inspector shall identify what are, in his opinion, the main issues to be considered at the inquiry and any matters on which he requires further explanation from the persons entitled or permitted to appear.

(3) Nothing in paragraph (2) shall preclude any person entitled or permitted to appear from referring to issues which they consider relevant to the consideration of the application or appeal but which were not issues identified by the inspector pursuant to that paragraph.

(4) Unless in any particular case the inspector otherwise determines, the local planning authority shall begin and the applicant shall have the right of final reply; and the other persons entitled or permitted to appear shall be heard in such order as the inspector may determine.

(5) A person entitled to appear at an inquiry shall be entitled to call evidence and the applicant, the local planning authority and any statutory party shall be entitled to cross-examine persons giving evidence, but, subject to the foregoing and paragraphs (6) and (9), the calling of evidence and the cross-examination of persons giving evidence shall otherwise be at the discretion of the inspector.

(6) The inspector may refuse to permit the—

(a) giving or production of evidence;
(b) cross-examination of persons giving evidence; or
(c) presentation of any other matter,

which he considers to be irrelevant or repetitious; but where he refuses to permit the giving of oral evidence, the person wishing to give the evidence may submit to him any evidence or other matter in writing before the close of the inquiry ...

(8) The inspector may direct that facilities shall be afforded to any person appearing at an inquiry to take or obtain copies of documentary evidence open to public inspection.

(9) The inspector may—

(a) require any person appearing or present at an inquiry who, in his opinion, is behaving in a disruptive manner to leave; and
(b) refuse to permit that person to return; or
(c) permit him to return only on such conditions as he may specify,

but any such person may submit to him any evidence or other matter in writing before the close of the inquiry.

(10) The inspector may allow any person to alter or add to a statement of case received by the Secretary of State or him under rule 6 so far as may be necessary for the purposes of the inquiry; but he shall (if necessary by adjourning the inquiry) give every other person entitled to appear who is appearing at the inquiry an adequate opportunity of considering any fresh matter or document.

(11) The inspector may proceed with an inquiry in the absence of any person entitled to appear at it.

(12) The inspector may take into account any written representation or evidence or any other document received by him from any person before an inquiry opens or during the inquiry provided that he discloses it at the inquiry.

(13) The inspector may from time to time adjourn an inquiry ...

Site inspections

16—(1) The inspector may make an unaccompanied inspection of the land before or during an inquiry without giving notice of his intention to the persons entitled to appear at the inquiry.

> (2) During an inquiry or after its close, the inspector—
>
> > (a) may inspect the land in the company of the applicant, the local planning authority and any statutory party; and
> >
> > (b) shall make such an inspection if so requested by the applicant or the local planning authority before or during an inquiry.

These rules form a detailed code for the implementation of procedural fairness in the context of planning inquiries, and reflect many of the recommendations made by the Franks Committee. Two issues arising from these rules merit comment.

First, r 11(1), like the procedural rules governing public inquiries in many other contexts, confers a legal right to appear upon only a limited class of parties. This appears to conflict with the notion of a 'public' inquiry which, as Lord Moulton observed in *Local Government Board* v. *Arlidge* [1915] AC 120 at 147–8, may be thought to imply unrestricted participation. In theory, procedural rules which permit only limited participation may be *ultra vires* parent Acts providing for the holding of 'public' inquiries. In practice, however, inspectors tend generously to exercise discretion, such as that conferred by r 11(2), to permit the participation of parties not *entitled* to appear.

Second, while r 15(1) confers discretion upon the inspector to determine procedure at the inquiry, this discretion is of course bounded both by the rules themselves and by general principles of administrative law. It follows that discretionary power such as that conferred by r 15(6) is not unfettered. In *R* v. *Secretary of State for the Environment, ex parte the Royal Borough of Kensington and Chelsea* (1987) 19 HLR 161 at 172, Taylor J held that, although the inspector at an inquiry into proposed compulsory purchase of property was empowered by the relevant rules to determine the procedure at the inquiry, '[t]otally to exclude evidence on whole issues which are, or may be, relevant is tantamount ... to declining jurisdiction ... [By doing so,] it follows that [the inspector] has not exercised his discretion in accordance with the law.'

17.2.5 Procedure following the inquiry

In his seminal book *The New Despotism* (London 1929), Lord Hewart identified the opaqueness of the inquiry system as one of its fundamental flaws.

> It is sometimes enacted that, before the Minister comes to a decision, he shall hold a public inquiry, at which interested parties are entitled to adduce evidence and be heard. But that provision is no real safeguard, because the person who has the power of deciding is in no way bound by the report or the recommendations of the person who holds the inquiry, and may entirely ignore the evidence which the inquiry brought to light. He can, and in practice, sometimes does, give a decision wholly inconsistent with the report, the recommendations and the evidence, which are not published or disclosed to interested individuals. In any case, as the official [or Minister] who decides has not seen or heard the witnesses, he is as a rule quite incapable of estimating the value of their evidence. So far, therefore, as restraining the arbitrary power of the deciding official is concerned, the requirement of a public inquiry is in practice nugatory.

On this analysis, public inquiries, somewhat paradoxically, failed to advance the cause of transparency because, the public taking of evidence notwithstanding, much of the process was shrouded in obscurity: the report produced by the inquiry might not be published, and the behind-closed-doors ministerial decision—which might contradict both the evidence advanced at and the recommendations made by the inquiry—would be unaccompanied by any form of explanation. In light of these concerns, the Franks Committee suggested that reports should be published and that Ministers should give reasons for decisions reached following inquiries.

As far as reports are concerned, the provision made by r 17(1) of the Town and Country Planning (Inquiries Procedure) (England) Rules 2000 is typical:

> After the close of an inquiry, the inspector shall make a report in writing to the Secretary of State which shall include his conclusions and his recommendations or his reasons for not making any recommendations.

Although this rule, like many other sets of rules governing inquiries, does not require inspectors' reports to be released to the general public, it has been general practice for some time to make such reports available, while access to them is now augmented by the Freedom of Information Act 2000.

Regarding reasons, the general position is laid down in s 10 of the Tribunals and Inquiries Act 1992:

> Subject to the provisions of this section and of section 14 [which restricts the application of the Act to certain bodies], where ...
>
> (b) any Minister notifies any decision taken by him—
>
>   (i) after a statutory inquiry has been held by him or on his behalf, or
>   (ii) in a case in which a person concerned could (whether by objecting or otherwise) have required a statutory inquiry to be so held,
>
> it shall be the duty of the ... Minister to furnish a statement, either written or oral, of the reasons for the decision if requested, on or before the giving or notification of the decision, to state the reasons.

Although the duty to give reasons imposed by s 10 arises only if reasons are requested, rules governing inquiries often impose a duty to give reasons irrespective of whether they are asked for. Take, for instance, r 18(1) of the Town and Country Planning (Inquiries Procedure) (England) Rules 2000:

> The Secretary of State shall, as soon as practicable, notify his decision on an application or appeal, and his reasons for it in writing to—
>
> (a) all persons entitled to appear at the inquiry who did appear, and
> (b) any other person who, having appeared at the inquiry, has asked to be notified of the decision.

The requirement that reasons be given goes some way towards meeting Lord Hewart's criticism that the effect of inquiries upon Ministers is 'in practice nugatory', since the discipline of reason-giving now forces decision-makers demonstrably to confront the evidence gathered at the inquiry and the inspector's recommendations.

A further issue which requires discussion is that of extrinsic evidence. When the Minister (typically after the inquiry has closed) considers, or is invited to consider, additional evidence, difficulties arise, since parties whose interests are affected by evidence submitted outwith the inquiry do not necessarily have an opportunity to respond to it. Rule 17 of the Town and Country Planning (Inquiries Procedure) (England) Rules 2000 makes fairly typical provision in this regard:

> (4) When making his decision the Secretary of State may disregard any written representations, evidence or any other document received after the close of the inquiry.
>
> (5) If, after the close of an inquiry, the Secretary of State—
>
> (a) differs from the inspector on any matter of fact mentioned in, or appearing to him to be material to, a conclusion reached by the inspector; or
>
> (b) takes into consideration any new evidence or new matter of fact (not being a matter of government policy),
>
> and is for that reason disposed to disagree with a recommendation made by the inspector, he shall not come to a decision which is at variance with that recommendation without first notifying in writing the persons entitled to appear at the inquiry who appeared at it of his disagreement and the reasons for it; and affording them an opportunity of making written representations to him or (if the Secretary of State has taken into consideration any new evidence or new matter of fact, not being a matter of government policy) of asking for the reopening of the inquiry ...
>
> (7) The Secretary of State may, as he thinks fit, cause an inquiry to be re-opened, and he shall do so if asked by the applicant or the local planning authority in the circumstances mentioned in paragraph (5).

Rules of this nature are largely the result of the criticism (in Appendix A of its Annual Report for 1963) by the (now abolished) Council on Tribunals of the 'Chalkpit inquiry' of 1961 (see *Buxton* v. *Minister of Housing and Local Government* [1961] 1 QB 278), in which the Minister allowed an appeal against a refusal of planning permission, notwithstanding the inspector's contrary recommendation. The latter was based on a risk of damage to adjoining land and livestock from the proposed use, yet the Minister's decision took account of evidence from another government department which suggested ways of minimizing the risk that had not been before the inquiry and upon which the objectors had had no opportunity of commenting.

Although there are now rules covering this matter (see r 17(5), set out above), their application is not without difficulty. This was apparent in *Lord Luke of Pavenham* v. *Minister of Housing and Local Government* [1968] 1 QB 172, which concerned the application of a rule materially identical to r 17(5). The claimant, having been denied planning permission by the relevant local authority, appealed to the Secretary of State. He appointed an inspector, who recommended that permission should be granted, but the Minister confirmed the local authority's decision. The claimant challenged the Minister's decision, alleging that he had reached it having disagreed with one of the inspector's findings of fact. It was, said the claimant, unfair that the Minister had not notified him of that disagreement and allowed him to make representations as to why the inspector's view should be preferred. The Court of Appeal disagreed. Lord Denning MR said at 191:

> Did the Minister differ from the inspector on a finding of fact? In answering this question it is essential to draw a distinction between findings of fact by the inspector and an expression of opinion by him on the planning merits. If the Minister differs from the inspector on a finding of fact, he must notify the applicant, in accordance with the rules, before coming to his decision. But if the Minister differs from the inspector on the planning merits, he can announce his decision straight away without notifying the applicant beforehand.

Lord Denning went on (at 192) to rule that the only disagreement between the Minister and the inspector was in relation to the passage in the latter's report which stated that:

> A well-designed house within the walled garden would, far from harming the countryside, add to the existing charm of its setting and could not be said to create a precedent for allowing development on farmland to the north or south.

This led Lord Denning to conclude (at 192) that the Minister

> was differing from that expression of opinion by the inspector. The Minister took the view that a house would be 'sporadic development' which would harm the countryside. That was a difference of opinion on a planning matter. The Minister was entitled to come to a different conclusion on such a matter without the necessity of notifying Lord Luke, or giving him an opportunity of making representations.

Alongside Lord Denning's distinction between fact and opinion, two other factors should be noted.

First, disclosure of extrinsic evidence to the affected party may not be sufficient. In *R (Chaston)* v. *Devon County Council* [2007] EWHC 1209 (Admin), the defendant council appointed (on a non-statutory basis) an inspector to investigate and make a recommendation concerning the resolution of a dispute as to the route of a footpath. After the inspector had made a recommendation that was favourable to the claimant, the council received representations from users of the path as to its true route, in the light of which it rejected the inspector's recommendation and decided upon a route less favourable to the claimant. Although the claimant had been told of the further representations, and invited to respond to them, the inspector was not notified of them. This, held Gibbs J, was unlawful: the inspector had been appointed not just to gather evidence, but to make a recommendation— and if evidence came to light that might have affected that recommendation, the council, if it wished to rely on such evidence, should have referred the matter back to the inspector.

Second, *Bushell* v. *Secretary of State for the Environment* [1981] AC 75 suggests that advice given to the Minister after the conclusion of the inquiry may not amount to extrinsic evidence that ought, in fairness, to be disclosed. The case concerned an inquiry into the proposed construction of two stretches of motorway. One of the matters in issue at the inquiry had been whether the new motorway was necessary—a question that turned on assessments of the capacity of the existing road network and future traffic flow. After the inquiry had closed, the government revised its method of assessing such matters—and, in deciding to accept the inspector's recommendation that the green light should be given to the new stretches of motorway, the Minister took account of officials' revised advice concerning capacity and traffic flow. Objectors to the motorway scheme then sought to have it quashed on the ground that natural justice had been breached by the Minister's failure to reopen the inquiry so as to enable them to address matters concerning the revised advice. In holding that the Minister had acted lawfully, Lord Diplock distinguished between different aspects of the decision-making process:

> It is only at one stage in the course of arriving at his decision that there is imposed on [the Minister's] administrative character a character loosely described as being quasi-judicial; and that is: when he is considering the respective representations of the promoting authority and of the objectors made at the local inquiry and the report of the inspector upon them. In doing this he must act fairly as between the promoting authority and the objectors; after the inquiry

has closed he must not hear one side without letting the other know; he must not accept from third parties fresh evidence which supports one side's case without giving the other side an opportunity to answer it. But when he comes to reach his decision, what he does bears little resemblance to adjudicating on a lis between the parties represented at the inquiry. Upon the substantive matter, viz., whether the scheme should be confirmed or not, there is a third party who was not represented at the inquiry, the general public as a whole whose interests it is the Minister's duty to treat as paramount. No one could reasonably suggest that as part of the decision-making process after receipt of the report the Minister ought not to consult with the officials of his department and obtain from them the best informed advice he can to enable him to form a balanced judgment on the strength of the objections and merits of the scheme in the interests of the public as a whole, or that he was bound to communicate the departmental advice that he received to the promoting authority and the objectors.

QUESTION

- Was Lord Diplock right to draw a line—and to place it where he did—between extrinsic information that must be disclosed and matters of internal government policy and advice which do not need to be disclosed?

17.3   *Ex post* inquiries

We have seen so far that *ex ante* inquiries form an integral part of certain decision-making processes, either because such inquiries must be held before any decision is taken (as in the case of the granting of development consent in respect of nationally significant infrastructure projects) or because such inquiries can be triggered as part of an appeal such that they form part of the process whereby a final decision is taken. *Ex post*—or after-the-event—inquiries are entirely different. Whereas *ex ante* inquiries amount to an aspect of the administrative decision-making process itself, *ex post* inquiries amount to an accountability mechanism that serves to scrutinize and facilitate critical reflection upon that process and its fruits.

17.3.1   Why hold an *ex post* inquiry?

Geoffrey Howe—a senior Minister in the Thatcher administration whose interest in inquiries was triggered for reasons explained shortly—identifies six reasons for holding an inquiry. In its *Government by Inquiry* report (HC51-I (2003–04) at [12]), the Public Administration Select Committee (PASC) reproduced the following summary (written by Walshe and Higgins (2002) 325 *British Medical Journal* 896) of those reasons:

- Establishing the facts—providing a full and fair account of what happened, especially in circumstances where the facts are disputed, or the course and causation of events is not clear
- Learning from events—and so helping to prevent their recurrence by synthesising or distilling lessons which can be used to change practice

- Catharsis or therapeutic exposure—providing an opportunity for reconciliation and resolution, by bringing protagonists face to face with each other's perspectives and problems
- Reassurance—rebuilding public confidence after a major failure by showing that the government is making sure it is fully investigated and dealt with
- Accountability, blame, and retribution—holding people and organisations to account, and sometimes indirectly contributing to the assignation of blame and to mechanisms for retribution
- Political considerations—serving a wider political agenda for government either in demonstrating that 'something is being done' or in providing leverage for change.

This accurately captures the wide array of motivations which may lead the government to decide to hold an inquiry; most inquiries are established for a combination of several of the reasons outlined above. Broadly speaking, inquiries usually have both backward-looking and forward-looking facets to them, the intention often being that *past* mistakes should be identified and understood in part so that lessons for the *future* can be learned. However, it is often the case that one or other of those facets predominates.

Some inquiries, for instance, are informed first and foremost by an imperative to establish exactly what happened, albeit that doing so— and, in particular, understanding *why* something happened— might enable the learning of important lessons for the future benefit of others. Take, for example, the inquiry chaired by Lord Saville into an incident on 30 January 1972— 'Bloody Sunday'— in Londonderry or Derry in Northern Ireland, in which the British Army fired shots during a disturbance following a civil rights march, resulting in 14 deaths. The Widgery Inquiry, which reported in 1972, largely exonerated the Army, but was perceived by many, particularly but far from exclusively in the nationalist community, as a whitewash. Bloody Sunday remained a strong point of contention during the subsequent years, and in the context of attempting to broker a peace deal in Northern Ireland, the Blair government in 1998 asked Saville to undertake a fresh inquiry. Saville reported in 2010, concluding, among other things, that the actions of the British Army had been unjustified (HC30, *Principal Conclusions and Overall Assessment of the Bloody Sunday Inquiry* (2010– 11)). Although forward- looking in the sense that it was intended to remove an obstacle to a peace agreement, the Saville Inquiry was principally concerned to establish what happened: it was intended to serve what Howe calls cathartic or therapeutic purposes.

The recently established Independent Inquiry into Child Sexual Abuse also involves a significant backward-looking element. Against the background of large volumes of historical allegations of child sexual abuse that have come to light in recent years, one of the Inquiry's core purposes is simply to establish what happened. Its terms of reference thus require it to 'consider the extent to which State and non- State institutions have failed in their duty of care to protect children from sexual abuse and exploitation'. As is explained on the Inquiry's website, its mode of working will encompass both elements of a 'conventional public inquiry, where witnesses give evidence on oath and are subject to cross examination' and a 'truth project'. The latter will enable survivors of child sexual abuse to provide accounts of their experiences in private; such accounts will not be 'tested, challenged, or contradicted'. The truth project stream of the Inquiry's work will enable it to build up a picture of what happened in a way, and to an extent, that would not otherwise be possible.

However, the Child Sex Abuse Inquiry also has significant forward- looking elements. As well as seeking to establish facts and facilitate cathartic disclosure, it is required to 'consider the steps which it is necessary for State and non- State institutions to take in order to protect children from such abuse in future'. In this regard, it is likely that it will produce wide-ranging recommendations with a view to improving both anticipatory child protection and institutional mechanisms for dealing with allegations of abuse. In this regard, the Goddard Inquiry is likely to have a forward- looking impact comparable to that of Dame Janet Smith's inquiry into the notorious case of Harold Shipman— a family doctor who, Smith concluded, had killed over 200 of his patients. Smith produced a series of reports which were concerned both with establishing what had happened and how, and with what steps should be taken in order to reduce the likelihood of similar events in the future. Her recommendations had far- reaching implications for the regulation of doctors.

Without prejudice to what has already been said, the fact cannot be escaped that decisions to hold inquiries are sometimes animated by intensely political considerations. As former Deputy Prime Minister Michael Heseltine put it (*Government by Inquiry* at [11]): 'No Government wants inquiries; they are usually in circumstances where the government is in trouble ... They are not popular things for governments.' Even if Heseltine overstates the position, there is surely a kernel of truth in what he says— as the circumstances surrounding the establishment of the three principal inquiries relating to the Iraq War amply attest. The first— the Hutton Inquiry (HC247, *Report of the Inquiry into the Circumstances Surrounding the Death of Dr David Kelly CMG* (2003– 04))— was established against the background of an extraordinary row between the government and the BBC. A BBC correspondent claimed that the government's case for military intervention in Iraq had been 'sexed up' by the insertion of claims (which it knew or believed to be false) about Iraq's possession of and capacity to launch weapons of mass destruction (WMD). There was speculation that Dr David Kelly, a government scientist, was the source of the 'sexing up' allegation— a rumour the government subsequently confirmed. When Kelly committed suicide shortly thereafter, the pressure for an inquiry was immense. Tellingly, however, the terms of reference required an investigation only into the circumstances surrounding Kelly's death— not into the broader questions raised by the episode. And although Hutton did end up shedding some light on those questions, there was a perception that the Inquiry— which largely exonerated the government, while accusing the BBC of shoddy journalism— was a whitewash. That— and the fact that in the aftermath of the Iraq War the government's claims about WMD were shown to be false— created pressure for a second inquiry.

Thus, the Butler Inquiry (HC898, *Review of Intelligence on Weapons of Mass Destruction* (2004–05)) was established to look into the intelligence failings which had apparently led the government to form an exaggerated impression of Iraq's military capabilities. Although Butler identified specific failings, its terms of reference confined it to addressing the gathering and analysis of intelligence, and it did not directly consider the political decision-making process that led up to the Iraq War— although some passing criticism was made of the sloppiness of certain aspects of that process.

The third inquiry—the Iraq Inquiry, chaired by Sir John Chilcot—was established in 2009, in the dying days of the 1997–2010 New Labour administrations. Charged with examining how decisions were made in the run-up to, during, and in the aftermath of the Iraq conflict, and identifying lessons to be learned, the Chilcot Inquiry had a much broader remit than Hutton or Butler. Yet it is unlikely in the extreme that there was a strong desire at the top of the Blair and Brown administrations to hold any of these inquiries, given the possibility that they would result in criticism of—or at least unearth evidence damaging to—those administrations. Rather, they were held because it was politically very difficult, perhaps even impossible, not to hold them. It is also worth noting that Chilcot, with its comparatively broad terms of reference, was only established at a time when many of the principal political actors in the Iraq saga had either left office or were destined soon to do so.

17.3.2 The Inquiries Act 2005

Until relatively recently, the ways in which *ex post* inquiries were constituted varied greatly: Blom- Cooper (1993) 46 *CLP* 204 at 208 referred to 'a bewildering variety of statutory and non- statutory inquiries under ministerial or local government aegis, each one adopting different techniques suitable to the topic under scrutiny'. There were in fact three main ways in which inquiries could be established: on an informal, non- statutory basis; under powers, contained in myriad Acts, to set up inquiries on specific subjects; and under the Tribunals of Inquiry (Evidence) Act 1921. The 1921 Act was rarely used, while establishing inquiries under subject- specific statutory powers could be problematic if the issue in question raised cross-cutting issues. Thus, many inquiries were constituted on a non- statutory basis. This had the advantage of great flexibility, but non- statutory inquiries had no legal powers (*eg* to require attendance of witnesses or compel production of documents), while Ministers (legally, if not politically) had an entirely free hand in terms of how such inquiries were set up.

It is against that background that the Inquiries Act 2005 was enacted. It repealed the 1921 Act, along with many provisions in individual statutes providing for the establishment of subject-specific inquiries, replacing them with a new, unified legal basis for inquiries. The intention was that this would remove the need (actual or perceived) to avoid the shortcomings of the old legal framework by resorting to non-statutory inquiries, enabling inquiries in future to be constituted under the 2005 Act as a matter of course. Five aspects of the Act should be noted.

First, it gives *considerable discretion to Ministers*. Ministers— and only Ministers— are able to establish inquiries under the Act (s 1), albeit that they must inform Parliament (or the relevant devolved legislature if the inquiry is established by devolved Ministers) that they have done or intend to do so (s 6). Inquiries can be conducted by a chair alone or with other members (s 3), all members of the panel, including the chair, being selected by the Minister (s 4) subject to requirements that the Minister must have regard to the need to ensure that the panel has adequate expertise (s 8) and that no one must be appointed whose impartiality is in doubt (s 9). Crucially, it is also for the Minister to determine the inquiry's terms of reference (s 5), meaning that Ministers can, if they wish, frame the task with which the panel is charged in a way that is politically convenient. Such discretion places considerable power in ministerial hands, as the concession (prior to the establishment of the Chilcot Inquiry) of only relatively limited inquiries concerning Iraq demonstrates.

Exercises of ministerial discretion under the Act— including the discretion whether to establish an inquiry— are susceptible to judicial review, as *Keyu* v. *Secretary of State for Foreign and Commonwealth Affairs* [2015] UKSC 69, [2015] 3 WLR 1665 illustrates. The case involved a challenge to a ministerial refusal to hold an inquiry into an incident that took place in (what is now) Malaysia in December 1948, when British troops, having been deployed to quell an insurgency, killed 23 unarmed civilians. Although the decision was upheld, the Supreme Court was prepared to examine its lawfulness by reference to the normal grounds of judicial review, including unreasonableness. Indeed, in *R (Litvinenko)* v. *Secretary of State for the Home Department* [2014] EWHC 194 (Admin), [2014] HRLR 6, the Court adopted a surprisingly interventionist approach, holding that several of the reasons given by the Minister for refusing to hold an inquiry into the death of the claimant's husband were inadequate and that the reasons collectively failed to demonstrate a rational basis for the refusal. However, Richards LJ, giving the only reasoned judgment, stopped short (at [75]) of saying that the only rational course open to the Minister was to establish an inquiry, bearing in mind that the 'discretion under s 1(1) of the 2005 Act is a very broad one and the question [whether to hold] an inquiry is ... difficult and nuanced'.

QUESTION

- Monbiot (*The Guardian*, 26 January 2010) said that 'there's a problem with official inquiries in the United Kingdom: the government appoints their members and sets their terms of reference. It's the equivalent of a criminal suspect being allowed to choose what the charges should be, who should judge his case and who should sit on the jury.' Do you agree? If so, how might these problems be resolved?

Second, the Act permits *ministerial intervention in the inquiry process* once it is underway. For example, panel members can be dismissed by the Minister on grounds including misconduct and the emergence of factors calling impartiality into question (s 12), and inquiries can be suspended for a fixed period or indefinitely (s 13) and terminated even if they have not finished their work (s 14). Of course, the fact that it is *legally* possible for a Minister to bury an inquiry that looks as if it might make trouble for the government does not mean that it is *politically* possible to do so—in most circumstances, taking such action would constitute an act of political suicide. (It may be that the enactment of the s 14 deadline-setting power was inspired by the fact that the production of the Bloody Sunday report took 12 years and cost close to £200m.) Similarly, the fact that, as indicated earlier, Ministers can manipulate membership and terms of reference does not mean that they will necessarily do so to their own advantage: if a weak panel is appointed to investigate an issue that is tangential to the real focus of public concern, that is unlikely to have what might be the desired short-term effect of taking the political heat off the government.

Third, the Act makes limited provision about *the procedure to be adopted at inquiries*. Instead, substantial discretion as to such matters is vested in the chair (s 17) subject to any rules made under s 41. Such rules—the Inquiry Rules 2006—have been made, although on some matters they still leave the chair with significant discretion. This is sensible, bearing in mind that the Act provides a general legal basis for a very wide range of inquiries; it does, however, mean that chairs face some difficult choices—an issue we address at 17.3.4. The chair has powers of compulsion: witnesses can be required to attend and produce documents (s 21); failure to comply is a criminal offence (s 35).

Fourth, s 18 imposes upon chairs a duty to take reasonable steps to afford *public (including media) access* to the inquiry itself (or to simultaneous transmission of its proceedings) and to evidence provided to the inquiry. However, s 19 permits the chair or the Minister to restrict public access if, *inter alia*, this is considered to be 'conducive to the inquiry fulfilling its terms of reference' or necessary on public interest grounds including national security, international relations, and the UK's economic interests. Against this background, it is noteworthy that the Chilcot Inquiry into the Iraq War was constituted on a non-statutory basis. Announcing the inquiry, the then Prime Minister, Gordon Brown, said that 'evidence will be heard in private' because the inquiry would be concerned with matters entailing 'a degree of confidentiality that would not suit a public inquiry, where all witnesses give evidence in public' (HC Deb 15 June 2009, vol 494, cols 23– 29). This may explain why the Inquiries Act was not used— and the s 18 duty of openness thereby avoided. But such a furore ensued— the suspicion being that Ministers wanted to spare themselves the embarrassment of giving evidence in public— that Chilcot later announced that hearings would be held in public wherever possible. As a result, senior figures, including Tony Blair and Gordon Brown, gave evidence in public.

Fifth, opportunities for ministerial interference arise at the end of the process, in relation to the *publication of reports*. Under s 25, reports must be published unless the responsible person (who will be the Minister unless he has designated the chair as such) orders otherwise. The power to withhold part or all of a report arises if, *inter alia*, the responsible person considers this necessary in the public interest.

17.3.3 Judges and public inquiries

The following excerpt indicates some of the reasons why politicians may choose to hold inquiries—and, in particular, why they may ask judges to preside over them. The excerpt begins with a passage from an article by Marr, 'Behold the Backlash, Sabres Drawn', *The Independent*, 8 June 1995. (The 'arms to Iraq' affair, mentioned in the excerpt, refers to a political scandal that erupted in the 1990s under John Major's premiership. The collapse of a high-profile prosecution concerning allegedly illegal exports to Iraq of machinery that could be used to manufacture weapons brought to light the fact that the government had in fact granted permission for such exports contrary to its publicly stated position. The scandal was a major aspect of the 'sleaze' allegations that dogged the Major administration.)

Drewry, 'Judicial Inquiries and Public Reassurance' [1996] *PL* 368

'As it became clear that Parliament seemed to have been misled [over the "arms to Iraq" affair], Mr Major [the then Prime Minister] ordered in a judge. He wanted a tough judge, for a very good reason. The administration was so lacking in authority that it was protecting itself, for the time being, with the borrowed authority of Lord Justice Scott. The tougher the judge, the stronger the shield. The judge, in return, would be given a wide remit to investigate what had gone wrong ...'

In [Marr's] notion of borrowed authority lies the main explanation for the frequent choice of senior judges ... to chair major inquiries into political scandals, major public calamities and crises of regime-legitimacy. There are other explanations, too—in particular, a recognition of the professional expertise of judges in conducting hearings, sifting through mountains of evidence and appraising the veracity of witnesses—but the present discussion will be confined to examining the implications of the deployment by politicians of the judges' status and credibility to diffuse matters which those politicians feel they can neither safely ignore nor tackle by normal political and parliamentary methods.

British judges have often been pilloried, especially by left-wing politicians and by feminists and spokesmen for minority groups (these categories are not of course mutually exclusive) as an unrepresentative establishment clique of white middle-class males. But they are also widely recognised, even, albeit grudgingly, by some such critics, as possessing a unique combination of professional skills; and a more positive interpretation of the judges' perceived isolation from the life experiences of mere mortals is that they also display a certain lofty detachment from the rough and tumble of party politics. Herein lies the rationale of judicial inquiries ...

The concept of 'borrowed authority', mentioned earlier resonates with a widely held notion that that there is a qualitative difference, and a functional separation, between law and politics. The Harvard political scientist, Judith Shklar, suggests that this perceived separateness has an ideological basis, rooted in the concept of 'legalism'. Proponents of legalism, she claims, not only emphasise the inherent differences between law and politics but believe also that features of the legal process such as rule-following and the pursuit of certainty and consistency are positive ends in themselves and render law a superior commodity to politics. [Drewry then sets out the following passage from Shklar, *Legalism* (Cambridge, Mass 1964) at 111:]

'There appears to be virtually unanimous agreement that law and politics must be kept apart as much as possible in theory no less than in practice. The divorce of law from politics is, to be sure, designed to prevent arbitrariness, and that is why there is so little argument about its necessity. However, ideologically, legalism does not stop there. Politics is regarded not only as something apart from law, but as inferior to law. Law aims at justice, while politics looks only to expediency. The former is neutral and objective, the latter the uncontrolled child of competing ideologies.'

The ambivalence of our 'legalistic' adherence to the separateness of law and politics is apparent in the eagerness of British politicians to exploit the apolitical credentials of the judges (an image which the judges themselves are anxious to preserve) by employing them as members and chairmen of official inquiries. In particular, whenever something happens that gives rise to a crisis of public confidence, there are calls from all sides for an independent inquiry, to be presided over by the comfortingly apolitical figure of a judge.

While it is clear that judges have many qualities—most obviously independence—which make them attractive chairs of prominent inquiries, a separate—and perhaps more important—question is whether they have the appropriate skills. Jowell *(The Guardian*, 3 February 2004) notes that:

It is true that judges possess special expertise in analysing evidence, assessing the credibility of witnesses, and resolving complex questions of fact. However, this skill is largely confined to the context of a particular set of circumstances, namely, those which surround the issues of guilt and liability. Did A kill B? Was X liable for damage to Y? These 'yes-no' or 'either-or' questions are grist to the judicial mill. And they are determined not in a vacuum, but with the guidance of principle derived from similar previous cases. Political controversies, however narrowly confined, normally involve a wider set of relevant issues than are found in the typical murder trial, and a different set of principles to those found in the law reports.

Jowell goes on to argue that the Hutton Inquiry was substantially undermined by Lord Hutton's tendency to 'confine his attentions to the cut-and-dried matters of personal liability and to avoid the wider political ramifications of his decision'. Blom-Cooper and Drewry [2004] *PL* 472 at 476 also consider that Hutton raised fresh questions in this area:

Perhaps it might be said that the [Hutton] Report reflected absolutely Lord Hutton's qualities as a judge, meticulous and superb in the analysis of details and evidence, but more evidently questionable on matters of wider judgment ... [T]here is ... room to doubt whether a Law Lord's 'borrowed authority' should have been lent to such an inquiry as this. When its subject-matter is considered, the Hutton Inquiry may represent the classic instance of why we should question the public's ready acceptance of asking a senior judge to hold a public inquiry.

Beatson (2005) 121 *LQR* 221 has also expressed concern about the use of the judiciary in this context. He notes (at 235) that simply appointing a judge 'will not depoliticise an inherently controversial matter', and that judicial involvement in inquiries may ultimately compromise (perceptions of) judicial independence. He concludes (at 250) that judges should be asked to lead inquiries with a strong political flavour only where 'the matter is of vital public importance, and where there is really no alternative'. He further argues (at 251) that government should not enjoy uninhibited freedom to choose the judge who is to conduct the inquiry or determine its terms of reference, suggesting that the concurrence of the head of the judiciary should be necessary with respect to the former, and that there should 'be a real opportunity for the head of the judiciary and the individual judge to have some input into the terms of reference'. However, as we have already seen, the Act gives Ministers the ultimate say over terms of reference (albeit that a judge—or anyone else—may refuse to be involved if the terms are inappropriate). Meanwhile, s 10 of the Act does not require the relevant senior judge to consent to the participation of a judge in an inquiry: only consultation with the relevant senior judge is required.

None of this is to suggest that judges ought to play no role in this sphere. However, there are good reasons for checking the sometimes kneejerk reaction that may result in the appointment of judges to chair inquiries. In some circumstances, the skillset, stature, and independence of a senior judge will be imperative both to the success of an inquiry and to the establishment of public trust and confidence in it. There is no clearer example of this than the appointment of Dame Lowell Goddard, a former New Zealand High Court judge, as chair of the Independent Inquiry into Child Sexual Abuse. The need for painstaking forensic work in establishing the scale of the problem of historical child sexual abuse coupled with the fact that the allegations, in certain respects, go to the heart of the British establishment made the appointment of an independent judicial figure as inevitable as it was desirable. Indeed, in the end it proved necessary to appoint not just a judge but a *foreign* judge in order to secure confidence in the independence of the inquiry from some of the individuals and institutions that it will have to examine. It does not, however, follow that judges should always— or even often— be used; the risks *to* judicial independence referred to by Beatson earlier being particularly acute when the subject- matter of the inquiry is an issue of intense political controversy.

QUESTIONS

- Do you share the concerns set out here concerning judicial involvement in inquiries?
- When, if ever, is it appropriate for judges to chair inquiries?

17.3.4 Questions of procedure

One of the most contentious issues concerning *ex post* inquiries is the resolution of what Blom-Cooper (1993) 46 *CLP* 204 at 205 calls the 'tension between the purpose [of the inquiry] of eliciting the truth and the protection of the individual against whom findings of culpability may have to be made'. This issue was examined in detail in the Salmon Report (Cm 3121, *Report of the Royal Commission on Tribunals of Inquiry* (London 1966)) which recommended a number of procedural safeguards: for example, that witnesses should be given advance notice of allegations against them and the evidence on which they are based, that witnesses should have adequate opportunity to prepare their case and to be examined by their own counsel, and that they should be able to test evidence affecting them by cross-examination through counsel. By advancing these recommendations, the Salmon Report displays what Aronson and Franklin, *Review of Administrative Action* (North Ryde, NSW 1987) at 146, identify as the lawyer's instinct to 'turn to the adversary model as providing the greatest measure of procedural protection'.

However, the appropriateness of that model in relation to public inquiries has been seriously doubted. Lord Hutton, giving evidence to the House of Commons Public Administration Select Committee (HC606–i, *Government by Inquiry: Minutes of Evidence* (2003–04)), considered that 'the Salmon principles are not to be applied inflexibly or rigidly and they have to be adapted to the circumstances of the particular inquiry'. Hutton himself chose a partly inquisitorial, partly adversarial style of procedure: witnesses were initially questioned 'neutrally' (as he put it) by counsel to the inquiry, after which some witnesses, having been given notice of 'possible criticisms', were called back to give further evidence, at which point there was cross-examination by interested parties' legal representatives.

The most prominent critic of Salmon is Sir Richard Scott. He refused to apply many of the Salmon principles to his own inquiry into the 'arms to Iraq' affair, arguing (see (1995) 111 *LQR* 596 at 598–9) that:

> In an inquisitorial Inquiry there are no litigants. There are simply witnesses who have, or may have, knowledge of some of the matters under investigation. The witnesses have no 'case' to promote. It is true that they may have an interest in protecting their reputations, and an interest in answering as cogently and comprehensively as possible allegations made against them. But they have no 'case' in the adversarial sense. Similarly, there is no 'case' against any witnesses. There may be damaging factual evidence given by others which the witness disputes. There may be opinion evidence given by others which disparages the witness. In these events the witness may need an opportunity to give his own evidence in refutation. But still he is not answering a case against himself in the adversarial sense. He is simply a witness giving his own evidence in circumstances in which he has a personal interest in being believed.

Scott's refusal to permit legal representation, cross-examination of witnesses (except by the inquiry itself), and many of the other trappings of the adversarial model were roundly condemned by Sir Geoffrey Howe [1996] *PL* 445, who, as a senior Minister at the relevant time, was required to give evidence to Scott. Howe argued that the Scott Inquiry's ability to operate effectively and reach meaningful conclusions was fundamentally undermined by the procedural model it adopted. The Council on Tribunals (*Advice to the Lord Chancellor on the Procedural Issues Arising in the Conduct of Public Inquiries Set Up by Ministers* (London 1996)) also commented that, while 'the infinite variety of circumstances that may give rise to the need for a major public inquiry make it wholly impracticable to devise a single set of model rules or guidelines', systematic restriction of classically 'adversarial' features such as legal representation may be counterproductive. Others, however, share Scott's view that adversarialism is unhelpful in this context. For instance, Blom-Cooper and Munro [2004] *PL* 472 criticize the adversarial procedure adopted at the second stage of Hutton, commenting that such a procedure is 'liable to be inimical to the aims of a process that is essentially inquisitorial'. It is also the case that the adoption of formal procedures risks causing delays that are so substantial as to bring the inquiry into disrepute. For instance, severe delays in the finalization of the Chilcot report on the Iraq War were caused in part by the process whereby those who face criticism are given an opportunity, prior to the publication of the report, to make representations in response.

Finally, and fundamentally, it is worth asking what 'fairness' ought to be taken to mean in this context. Harris [1996] *PL* 508 at 525–7 comments that underlying the discourse in this area is a

> protean idea of 'fairness', a concept which it may now be said underpins Anglo-Australian administrative law in the area of the hearing rule of natural justice. However, the arguments used to support a requirement of detailed 'particularisation' of 'allegations', or of a closer identification [by the inquiry] of 'areas of concern' or of disclosure of 'tentative' views or conclusions [which may be adverse to the witness are] … based squarely upon an *adversarial paradigm* of what [is] connoted by the idea of fairness. An alternative approach is to treat fairness as a more adaptable concept, one which will easily accommodate a shift from an adversarial model of what administrative due process requires to a situation in which what is procedurally 'fair' is defined in terms of what a particular decision-making process demands …
>
> … [T]here is encouraging evidence in Australian cases [eg *Bond* v. *Australian Broadcasting Tribunal* (1988) 84 ALR 646] decided in the context of investigative tribunals of a flexible and nuanced appreciation of what procedural fairness may mean. This approach and, it is submitted, Sir Richard Scott's report, can be seen as providing the occasion for a more general re- appraisal of the sometimes inhibiting and often inappropriate influence of the adversarial paradigm in the wider context of the administrative process. It is, in short, time for lawyers in the common law tradition to break free from the idea that there is no way of viewing fairness in the working of that process except through the prism of adversarialism.

QUESTION

- Harris concludes that the key objective of 'fairness' in this context is that which Lord Diplock identified in *Mahon* v. *Air New Zealand* [1984] AC 808 at 821, of ensuring that witnesses are not 'left in the dark'. How should this be achieved in the context of inquiries?

The Inquiries Act, as already noted, gives inquiry chairs discretion over procedure. However, that discretion is bounded both by the Inquiry Rules 2006 (made under s 41 of the Act) and by the normal principles of administrative law, including the principles of procedural fairness.

In that regard, it should be noted that procedural (and other) decisions made by inquiries are susceptible to judicial review. For example, in *R* v. *Lord Saville of Newdigate, ex parte A* [2000] 1 WLR 1855, soldiers who had fired live rounds on 'Bloody Sunday' and who were required to give evidence to Lord Saville's Inquiry sought judicial review of the Inquiry's general policy that, in the interests of open justice, they should be named. Lord Woolf MR, giving the judgment of the Court at 1865–6, thought that a measure of judicial deference was called for in the circumstances:

> It is accepted on all sides that the [inquiry] is subject to the supervisory role of the courts. The courts have to perform that role even though they are naturally loath to do anything which could in any way interfere with or complicate the extraordinarily difficult task of the [inquiry]. In exercising their role the courts have to bear in mind at all times that the members of the [inquiry] have a much greater understanding of their task than the courts. However, subject to the courts confining themselves to their well-recognised role on applications for judicial review, it is essential that they should be prepared to exercise that role regardless of the distinction of the body concerned and the sensitivity of the issues involved. The court must also bear in mind that it exercises a

discretionary jurisdiction and where this is consistent with the performance of its duty it should avoid interfering with the activities of [an inquiry] of this nature to any greater extent than upholding the rule of law requires.

With this in mind, Lord Woolf continued (at 1867–8):

In *In re Pergamon Press Ltd.* [1971] Ch. 388 Lord Denning M.R. said of Board of Trade inspectors that they must act fairly. He went on to indicate that inspectors have a duty to protect witnesses. He recognised, at p. 400, that inspectors 'must be masters of their own procedure' but subject to the overriding requirement that 'they must be fair'. Although we are here concerned with a very different type of inquiry from that being considered in the *Pergamon Press* case, it can equally be said of this [inquiry] that while it is master of its own procedure and has considerable discretion as to what procedure it wishes to adopt, it must still be fair. Whether a decision reached in the exercise of its discretion is fair or not is ultimately one which will be determined by the courts. This is because there is an implied obligation on the [inquiry] to provide procedural fairness. The [inquiry] is not conducting adversarial litigation and there are no parties for whom it must provide safeguards. However the [inquiry] is under an obligation to achieve for witnesses procedures which will ensure procedural fairness: see *Lloyd v. McMahon* [1987] A.C. 625, 702–703, *per* Lord Bridge of Harwich and *Reg. v. Secretary of State for the Environment, Ex parte Hammersmith and Fulham London Borough Council* [1991] 1 A.C. 521, 598F. As to the content of the requirement of procedural fairness, this will depend upon the circumstances and in particular on the nature of the decision to be taken: see *Council of Civil Service Unions v. Minister for the Civil Service* [1985] A.C. 374, *per* Lord Diplock, at p. 411H, and *per* Lord Roskill, at p. 415A–B ... The requirement of procedural fairness for witnesses is well recognised in the courts by allowing witnesses to give evidence behind screens. A defendant opposing the evidence being given in this way could make this a ground of complaint on appeal. At this inquiry where there are no defendants the requirement of procedural fairness surely involves an obligation to be fair to witnesses, including, for example, protecting them when necessary or giving them notice in a ... letter of proposed findings of improper conduct.

The Court concluded that the general policy of naming the soldiers in question was procedurally unfair.

Judicial review of inquiries extends beyond matters of procedure: indeed, decisions made by the Bloody Sunday Inquiry itself were also quashed on grounds such as unreasonableness (*R v. Lord Saville of Newdigate, ex parte A* [2000] 1 WLR 1855), breach of rights arising under the ECHR (*R (A) v. Lord Saville of Newdigate* [2001] EWCA Civ 2048, [2002] 1 WLR 1249), and failure to take account of relevant considerations (*R v. Lord Saville of Newdigate, ex parte B* The Times, 15 April 1999). In view of the delay and disruption that can be occasioned by judicial review of inquiries, s 38 of the Inquiries Act provides that those seeking review of a decision made by a Minister in relation to an inquiry or of a member of an inquiry panel must act within 14 days of becoming aware of it.

17.3.5 *Ex post* inquiries and the accountability system

It will be apparent from what has already been said that the consequences of inquiries depend very much on the circumstances. In some instances, what is intended—and what is delivered—is a series of very specific recommendations as to how policies, procedures, and so on should be changed to avoid a repeat of past failings. This was the case in relation, for example, to the Smith Inquiry concerning Harold Shipman, the family doctor who killed scores of his own patients. In other instances—particularly where 'big picture' political questions are involved—the inquiry may see its role differently. This is true of the Butler Inquiry into the handling of intelligence in the lead-up to the Iraq War. Speaking to the PASC (HC606–vi, *Government by Inquiry: Minutes of Evidence* (2003–04)) about his *Review of Intelligence on Weapons of Mass Destruction* (London 2004), Lord Butler explained that his main purpose (as he saw it) was to 'tell the story':

> [W]e did try to give a full account of how the policy developed, how the decision came to be taken, but having given a full account of those facts, we left it to Parliament and the public to draw their conclusions about it.

But whether the inquiry's focus is on story-telling or recommendation-making, what stops its output from amounting to nothing more than hot air? Inquiries—whether statutory or not—have no legal power to compel the government to do anything in response to their findings. The extent to which inquiries have a real impact is therefore ultimately a function of the scale of the political pressure which the government finds itself under following publication of the report. The impact may be diffuse but ultimately potent: the findings of the Scott Inquiry may well have contributed to the perceptions of 'sleaze' which afflicted the Major administration in the mid-1990s, which may, in turn, have helped it towards its spectacular defeat at the 1997 general election. In contrast, the impact of an inquiry may be measurable in very specific terms, such as the Shipman Inquiry's detailed recommendations concerning the regulation of medical practitioners and medicines—recommendations which were in due course implemented.

However, the question remains: where do inquiries fit within the system whereby government is held to account? Inquiries clearly do not form part of the legal system for holding the government to account. This is true in the straightforward sense that, as noted earlier, inquiries have no legal power to compel adherence to their recommendations. But this point is arguably of broader relevance, too. An argument to this effect is advanced by Blom-Cooper [2010] *PL* 61 in the course of setting out a detailed critique of the Saville Inquiry. As foreshadowed at 17.3.1, its terms of reference required it to inquire 'into the events of 30 January 1972 which led to the loss of life in connection with the procession in Londonderry on that day, taking account of any information relevant to the events of that day'. Blom-Cooper is highly critical of the adoption by Saville of a legalistic approach in his attempt to discharge these duties. He notes (at 63) that Saville could have sought to comply with the terms of reference by adopting either of two approaches:

1. As a discrete and crucial element in the overall requirement to investigate the events on Bloody Sunday, to ascertain whether victim A (unarmed and engaged in a civil rights march) was killed from a bullet fired from soldier X's rifle, with or without reasonable force; or

2. To assume that the death of each of the 14 victims was the result of direct military action against the victim, without determining precisely how each one had been killed, and which soldier had been directly responsible for firing the fatal shot, but assuming a collective responsibility on the part of the paratroopers, a lesser imposition than findings of individual criminality or serious misconduct by the soldiers. (Whether it would have been publicly acceptable to make such an assumption, or to use it as the basis of the Inquiry, is dealt with hereafter.)

By opting 'decisively for the first alternative', says Blom-Cooper, Saville made a serious error. It led to the inquiry involving itself in the minutiae of what happened on Bloody Sunday, and was the main reason why the inquiry took more than 12 years to report and cost nearly £200 million. Blom-Cooper's criticism, however, goes deeper. He considers (at 78) the *purpose* of public inquiries:

> Far too much legalism has been injected into the process of public inquiries—the inevitable product of ingrained professional practices to seek the 'truth' through independent investigation. Far too little attention, on the other hand, has been paid to the overriding purpose of public inquiries, which is to focus on failures in systems and services. Blameworthiness on the part of individual actors in the public disaster or scandal under inquiry is often unnecessary and frequently distractive from the main thrust of any inquiry. Assessing the responsibility for crime and civil action lies primarily in courts of law. Public inquiries are essentially creatures of public administration; they are not, generally, to be regarded as adjuncts to the forensic process in the traditional courtroom.

Given that public inquiries are not formally part of the judicial system (and should arguably not proceed as if they were), are they, and should they be, part of the parliamentary system for holding government to account instead? They are certainly relevant to that system in the very general sense that inquiries' findings—and the raw material unearthed in the course of arriving at them—equip Parliament more effectively to hold the government to account. This point was made by PASC, in its *Government by Inquiry* report at [170], in the following way:

> Inquiries ... can ... be seen as an adjunct to ministerial responsibility. They are not a substitute for political accountability, which is to, and through, Parliament, but a mechanism which can aid the process. Parliament can hold the minister accountable not only for the inquiry's findings but also for giving effect to any recommendations that are made.

But PASC called, in two key respects, for a much tighter form of integration between Parliament and inquiries. First, it argued for *greater parliamentary involvement in the establishment of inquiries*. In particular, it was concerned that Parliament should be able to cause an inquiry to be held in relation to politically sensitive matters, in order to guard against the possibility of ministerial manipulation of whether inquiries into such issues are held and, if so, on what basis. PASC therefore suggested at [178] that provision should be made in the Inquiries Bill (which was before Parliament at the time) whereby in cases of

> public concern relat[ing] to the conduct, actions or inactions of government—ministers or officials, the Minister will cause an inquiry to be called on the basis of a Resolution of both Houses of Parliament. ... Individual motions for the Resolution could provide for: the form the inquiry should take; its terms of reference; any powers considered necessary; follow-up to the inquiry's report, including a requirement that the report will be debated in Parliament on a substantive motion; and remission, as appropriate, to a select committee for auditing, in due course, of the degree to which an inquiry report's recommendations have been implemented and changes wrought.

Second, PASC took the view that, in relation to certain matters, Parliament should not simply be able to cause *Ministers* to establish an inquiry, but that a system should be put in place under which *Parliament* would establish its own inquiries. It was influenced in this regard by the following comments of Sir Michael Bichard (set out in *Government by Inquiry* at [191]):

> [At one end of the spectrum are] circumstances of fact which are not government- related, and may not even be local government- related, but they are issues of fact. Going a bit further along the continuum, there are issues of fact which also will cover issues of competence, but mostly official competence, whether it is central or local. ... If you go a bit further along the continuum, you will get facts with strong political overtones. If you go to the other end of the continuum, and you are actually talking about politically contentious issues with some facts. I think you should become more cautious about setting up an inquiry the further along that continuum you go. If you get to the far end of the continuum, then my view is it is a matter for Parliament to deal with these issues rather than to set up a public inquiry.

PASC concluded that in relation to highly significant and sensitive political matters, inquiries should be undertaken by 'Parliamentary Commissions of Inquiry'. The precise form which such bodies would take is not entirely clear from PASC's *Government by Inquiry* report (or from its subsequent *Parliamentary Commissions of Inquiry* report (HC473 (2007– 08)), but the basic idea is of an augmented parliamentary select committee: in *Government by Inquiry* at [208], it was intimated that an external inquiry team appointed by the committee might undertake the evidence- gathering process, leaving it to the select committee to interpret and pass political judgment upon such evidence.

Although this model has not been adopted on any systematic basis, a potential blueprint is supplied by the Parliamentary Commission on Banking Standards that was established in 2012 in the wake of a scandal in which some bankers fixed certain interest rates for personal gain—a scandal that came hot on the heels of the global financial crisis which began in 2007 thanks in large part to banks' imprudent lending practices. Members of both Houses of Parliament sat on the Commission, which adopted novel working practices by dividing itself into panels responsible for different aspects of the inquiry, and appointing legal counsel to cross-examine witnesses. The Commission reported relatively swiftly and the government started to implement some of its recommendations less than a year after the Commission was established.

17.4 Concluding remarks

We have seen in this chapter that 'inquiries' take a number of forms, and fulfil diverse roles within the administrative and constitutional system. The hybrid nature of many inquiries, which places them (sometimes uncomfortably) at the interface between administrative and judicial proceedings, raises several questions about how inquiries should be conducted. Straightforward answers to these questions are impossible, not least because the concept of inquiries is itself protean. We have, however, seen that the recommendations of the Franks Committee have played a major role in fashioning the contemporary approach to administrative justice in the context of inquiries. These reforms, by increasing transparency before, during, and after inquiries, have helped to ensure—and to demonstrate—that inquiries serve a genuinely useful role in relation to the gathering of information and opinion, and that their function now transcends that which Lord Hewart attributed to them, of merely creating an *impression* of open-minded decision-makers willing to listen to others' views.

As well as operating as an integral part of the administrative decision-making structure, by facilitating the taking of more informed decisions, inquiries are commonly resorted to for the purposes of investigating matters of public concern. As we have seen, such inquiries raise difficult questions about procedure, forcing administrative lawyers to confront the fact that, while the adversarial model is traditionally viewed as the paradigm of 'fairness', the concept of due process requires considerable re-evaluation in an inquisitorial setting. We have also seen that inquiries into matters of public concern raise important questions about the acceptable extent of ministerial involvement in the establishment and conduct of such inquiries, and about what role, if any, Parliament should play in this sphere.

FURTHER RESOURCES

Beatson, 'Should Judges Conduct Public Inquiries?' (2005) 121 *LQR* 221

Blom-Cooper, 'Public Inquiries' (1993) 46 *CLP* 203

Blom-Cooper, 'What Went Wrong on Bloody Sunday: A Critique of the Saville Inquiry' [2010] *PL* 61

Harlow, 'What Price Inquiries?' (*UK Constitutional Law Blog*, 28 February 2013) *https:// ukconstitutionallaw.org/2013/02/28/carol-harlow-what-price-inquiries/*

Public Administration Select Committee, *Government by Inquiry* HC51-I (2004–05), *http:// www.publications.parliament.uk/pa/cm200405/cmselect/cmpubadm/51/5102.htm*

Scott, 'Procedures at Inquiries—The Duty to be Fair' (1995) 111 *LQR* 596

Steele, 'Judging Judicial Inquiries' [2004] *PL* 738

The reports and websites of the *ex post* inquiries referred to at 17.3 are sources of useful background and context information. See, *eg*:

- Sir Robin Butler's Review of Intelligence on Weapons of Mass Destruction *http://webarchive .nationalarchives.gov.uk/20060105191702/http://www.butlerreview.org.uk/index.html*
- Sir John Chilcot's Iraq Inquiry *http://www.iraqinquiry.org.uk*
- Independent Inquiry into Child Sexual Abuse *https://www.iicsa.org.uk*
- Lord Saville's Inquiry concerning Bloody Sunday *https://www.gov.uk/government/publications/ report-of-the-bloody-sunday-inquiry*

18 STATUTORY TRIBUNALS

18.1 Introduction

18.1.1 The growth of tribunals

Although the work undertaken by the Administrative Court in determining claims for judicial review is of utmost importance, the average person is far more likely to come into contact with a tribunal than with that Court. The number of appeals to tribunals has fluctuated significantly in recent years, but the average annual figure for the main UK tribunals system is in the region of 400,000 to 500,000 (Ministry of Justice, *Tribunals and Gender Recognition Certificate Statistics Quarterly: October to December 2015* (London 2016) at 6). In contrast, just under 4,700 applications for judicial review were lodged at the Administrative Court (Ministry of Justice, *Civil Justice Statistics Quarterly, England and Wales* (London 2016) at 5). As Sir Andrew Leggatt observed (at [1.1]) in his influential Review of Tribunals (*Tribunals for Users: One Service, One System* (London 2001) (hereinafter 'Leggatt' or 'the Leggatt Report')), tribunals' caseload 'alone makes their work of great importance to our society' and '[t]heir collective impact … immense'.

The growth of statutory tribunals mirrors the dramatic expansion of the state itself. As legislation has increasingly conferred benefits on individuals and subjected their everyday lives to growing regulation, so the scope for dispute between the individual and the state has grown. Was the Minister right to conclude that an applicant was not statutorily entitled to a particular benefit? Was a public body correct to hold that an individual was entitled to a given amount of compensation following the imposition upon him of some disadvantage? For successive generations of policy-makers, tribunals have been—and remain—the mechanism of choice for resolving disputes between the individual and the state across 'the whole range of political and social life, including social security benefits, health, education, tax, agriculture, criminal injuries compensation, immigration and asylum, rents, and parking' (Leggatt at [1.16]). Of course, such disputes can, in principle, be resolved by means of judicial review; however, as we saw at 14.3, the Administrative Court rarely entertains claims for judicial review where alternative remedies, such as appeal to a tribunal, are available. A small number of tribunals (for example the Employment Tribunal) are concerned with disputes between individuals. Our focus in this chapter, however, is on tribunals that are concerned with disputes between the individual and the state, covering an enormous swathe of matters including welfare benefits, immigration and asylum, taxation, criminal injuries compensation, the detention of patients on mental health grounds, freedom of information, licensing, and special educational needs.

One final preliminary point is worth making. Whereas, as we have seen in earlier chapters, the 'distinction between appeal and review' limits the role of the reviewing court, it self-evidently does not limit the role of appellate tribunals. Although onward appeals against first-instance tribunals' decisions are often on points of law only, first-instance tribunals can generally examine the merits as well as the legality of administrative decisions, substituting judgement in the event that the tribunal disagrees with the original decision-maker.

18.1.2 What are tribunals—and are they a good thing?

The beginnings of an answer to the question 'what are tribunals?' is implicit in what has just been said. But how are they to be defined more precisely, if not simply by reference to what they do? Cane, *Administrative Tribunals and Adjudication* (Oxford 2009) at 69 suggests that

> [t]he two most distinctive characteristics of administrative tribunals in the UK system are that they are free-standing, mono-functional adjudicatory institutions and that they are understood as being 'court substitutes'.

Indeed, we will see later in this chapter that great efforts have recently been made to emphasize just how court-like—in terms of their independence, for example—tribunals are. But, says Cane, if this is so it becomes necessary to ask why it is that

> since the early 19th century, when confronted with a choice between allocating jurisdiction to review a particular category of government decisions to a court or to some other type of adjudicatory body, UK legislatures have commonly chosen to allocate the jurisdiction to a tribunal rather than a court.

The answer to this question lies (at least partly) in the perception, as Genn (1993) 56 *MLR* 393 at 393 puts it, that tribunals are 'cheap, non-technical substitutes for the ordinary courts for a wide range of grievances and disputes, in which parties can initiate actions without cost or fuss'. However, these are not universally recognized as *positive* characteristics of tribunals. Abel (in Abel (ed), *The Politics of Informal Justice* (New York 1982) at 295–301) argues that tribunals offer a second-rate justice system for poorer members of society (who are more likely to be engaged in disputes with public bodies in areas, such as welfare provision, with which tribunals tend to deal). Meanwhile, Ison (in Harris and Partington (eds), *Administrative Justice in the 21st Century* (Oxford 1999)) is highly sceptical about the notion of 'administrative justice' itself, arguing (at 23) that it places undue weight on *appeals* against administrative decisions, and acts as an apologist for (what he perceives to be) the inadequacies of *first-instance* decision-making (or 'primary adjudication'):

> I know of no evidence ... to demonstrate that there is any substantial correlation between suffering and complaining [about first-instance decisions]. When decisions relate to elderly people, disabled people, single parents, small business people or immigrants, there are large numbers who suffer from erroneous decisions without filing a complaint. Indeed, the total volume of injustice is likely to be much greater among those who accept initial decisions than among those who complain or appeal. For this reason alone, thoroughness and procedural fairness are more important in primary adjudication than they are in appellate processes.

Ison is right to draw our attention to the often low take-up of grievance redress. Empirical research (see, *eg* Cowan and Halliday, *The Appeal of Internal Review* (Oxford 2003)) suggests that take-up may be inhibited by a number of factors, including the perception that the grievance redress mechanism may not be independent of the original decision-maker; lack of awareness of the mechanism in the first place; general perceptions of the bureaucratic system (*eg* a prospective appellant may be deterred from appealing because the original decision was handled badly, thereby giving the impression of systemic problems which would also infect any grievance redress mechanism); and the perception that pursuing the matter is likely to be a trying and time-consuming experience.

The response of policy-makers to these issues should be two-fold. In the first place, as Ison argues, the quality of first-instance decision-making should be high, in order to reduce the need to resort to such bodies as appellate tribunals: it is, after all, to everyone's advantage if the right decision can be made, and be seen to have been made, without further ado. This was recognized in the white paper on administrative justice (Cm 6243, *Transforming Public Services: Complaints, Redress and Tribunals* (2004) (hereinafter 'the 2004 White Paper') at [10.5]), which presaged the far-reaching reforms of the tribunals system described in this chapter. Second, however, the importance of good first-instance decision-making should not obscure the fact that a good appellate structure is also valuable, not least because the latter is capable of buttressing the former. The possibility of appeal can encourage decision-makers to act properly in order to avoid later criticism. Moreover, if the relationship between decision-makers and tribunals is conceived in constructive terms, then it is possible for the latter to work with the former in order to identify and resolve systemic problems of decision-making practice at first instance (see the 2004 White Paper at [6.32]–[6.34]). It is therefore conducive to the existence of a healthy administrative system that an effective appellate structure exists—which, in turn, clearly requires the potential barriers to entry, noted in the preceding paragraph, to be addressed.

18.1.3 The Franks Report and the Leggatt Review

Over the course of the last 60 or so years, two key turning points in the development of tribunals can be discerned: the Franks Report, published in 1957, and the Leggatt Review, published in 2001. The former—the *Report of the Committee on Administrative Tribunals and Enquiries* (Cmnd 218, 1957)—was commissioned in the light of the prominence ascribed to tribunals by the social legislation enacted following the Second World War. Concerns arose, however, that the tribunals regime—by now firmly in the spotlight thanks to its enhanced role—was somewhat chaotic; different tribunals adopted significantly different approaches, and it became apparent that much work needed to be done in order to make the tribunals 'system', such as it was, more coherent.

In its report, the Franks Committee considered why it might be that Parliament singles out certain types of decisions and makes them subject to rights of appeal to tribunals. It concluded that

> [t]his must [be] to promote good administration. Administration must not only be efficient in the sense that the objectives of policy are securely attained without delay. It must also satisfy the general body of citizens that it is proceeding with reasonable regard to the balance between the

> public interest which it promotes and the private interest which it disturbs. Parliament has, we infer, intended in relation to the subject-matter of our terms of reference that the further decisions or, as they may rightly be termed in this context, adjudications must be acceptable as having been properly made. It is natural that Parliament should have taken this view of what constitutes good administration. In this country government rests fundamentally upon the consent of the governed. The general acceptability of these adjudications is one of the vital elements in sustaining that consent.

The Franks Committee went on to argue that 'good administration' should, for these purposes, be conceived of in terms of three key characteristics:

> When we regard our subject in this light, it is clear that there are certain general and closely linked characteristics which should mark these special procedures. We call these characteristics openness, fairness and impartiality.
>
> Here we need only give brief examples of their application. Take openness. If these procedures were wholly secret, the basis of confidence and acceptability would be lacking. Next take fairness. If the objector were not allowed to state his case, there would be nothing to stop oppression. Thirdly, there is impartiality. How can the citizen be satisfied unless he feels that those who decide his case come to their decision with open minds?
>
> To assert that openness, fairness and impartiality are essential characteristics of our subject-matter is not to say that they must be present in the same way and to the same extent in all its parts. Difference in the nature of the issue for adjudication may give good reasons for difference in the degree to which the three general characteristics should be developed and applied. Again, the method by which a Minister arrives at a decision after a hearing or enquiry cannot be the same as that by which a tribunal arrives at a decision ... For the moment it is sufficient to point out that when Parliament sets up a tribunal to decide cases, the adjudication is placed outside the Department concerned. The members of the tribunal are neutral and impartial in relation to the policy of the Minister, except in so far as that policy is contained in the rules which the tribunal has been set up to apply.

In setting out the third of these 'essential characteristics' of tribunals, the Franks Committee nailed its colours firmly to the mast in relation to the then ongoing, but now settled, debate as to whether tribunals ought to be regarded as primarily administrative or primarily adjudicative (or judicial) bodies—a point that we develop at 18.2.1.

If the Franks Report is the first milestone in the development of the modern tribunals system, the Leggatt Report is the second and most recent; many of the recommendations contained in it having been implemented, at least to some extent, via the Tribunals, Courts and Enforcement Act 2007 (TCEA). (Although that Act did not fully enter into force until 2008, we will, for convenience, refer to the changes brought about by the Act as 'the 2007 reforms'.) As well as further enhancing the independence of tribunals—and thereby building upon the foundations laid several decades earlier by the Franks Report—the Leggatt Report recommended, and the 2007 Act brought about, a fundamental refashioning of the tribunals system's architecture. We describe the 2007 reforms in detail later in the chapter. For the time being, it suffices to say (in order to aid understanding of passing references to them in the earlier part of the chapter) that the thrust of those reforms was the replacement of a disparate collection of tribunals with an integrated tribunals regime. Several different tribunals were swept away and replaced with just two: the First-tier Tribunal, which is responsible for hearing first-instance appeals, and the Upper Tribunal, which is principally concerned with hearing appeals against the First-tier Tribunal's decisions. Both tribunals are divided into various chambers, each chamber being concerned with particular subject areas.

The changes introduced by the TCEA following the Leggatt Review relate to the principal UK tribunals system. (We use the expression 'UK tribunals system' to denote that it is established by legislation enacted by the UK Parliament and that it operates in some respects on a UK-wide basis.) It is that system upon which this chapter focuses. It should be noted, however, that not all tribunals operating within the UK are part of that system. In particular, the UK tribunals system operates in only some policy areas outside England, with separate tribunals dealing with certain matters in Scotland, Wales, and Northern Ireland. The Scottish government recently undertook a major review of Scottish tribunals, and a rationalization of those tribunals has now occurred under the Tribunals (Scotland) Act 2014. Among other things, the Act introduces in relation to the Scottish tribunals a two-tier structure comparable to that which applies to UK tribunals under the TCEA.

18.2 The independence of tribunals

18.2.1 Tribunals and government

As already mentioned briefly, when the Franks Committee was carrying out its work in the mid-1950s, there was considerable debate about the very nature of tribunals: *ie* about whether they ought to be regarded as an adjunct of the administration or as independent judicial arbiters of administrative action. This question is a foundational one; many other issues relating to tribunals—including their relationships with government departments, where responsibility should lie for their administration, and the procedural model they adopt—being intimately connected to it. The Franks Report (at [40]) approached the issue in the following terms:

> Tribunals are not ordinary courts, but neither are they appendages of Government departments. Much of the official evidence ... appeared to reflect the view that tribunals should properly be regarded as part of the machinery of administration, for which the Government must retain a close and continuing responsibility. Thus, for example, tribunals in the social service field would be regarded as adjuncts to the administration of the services themselves. We do not accept this view. We consider that tribunals should properly be regarded as machinery provided by Parliament for adjudication rather than as part of the machinery of administration.

The importance of the independence of tribunals was highlighted by the Council on Tribunals—a body established in the light of the Franks Report but abolished in 2013 as part of the government's austerity programme—in its report, Cm 3744, *Tribunals: Their Organisation and Independence* (London 1997) at [2.2]:

> [S]ince tribunals are established to offer a form of redress, mostly in disputes between the citizen and the State, the principal hallmark of any tribunal is that it must be independent. Equally importantly, it must be perceived as such. That means that the tribunal should be enabled to reach decisions according to law without pressure either from the body or person whose decision is being appealed, or from anyone else.

Thus, while it is clearly desirable that a constructive relationship should exist between a tribunal and the government department from whose decisions it hears appeals—*eg* in order that the tribunal may identify and draw to the department's attention systemic problems with its decision-making practice—that relationship must be carefully constituted in order that independence is neither compromised nor seen to be compromised. Leggatt concluded (at [2.20]) that arrangements—which until quite recently were the norm—whereby tribunals were 'sponsored' by and hence financially dependent upon the departments whose work they scrutinized were problematic:

> At best, such arrangements result in tribunals and their departments being, or appearing to be, common enterprises. At worst, they make the members of a tribunal feel that they have become identified with its sponsoring department, and they foster a culture in which the members feel that their prospects of more interesting work, of progression in the tribunal, and of appointments elsewhere depend on the departments against which the cases that they hear are brought.

These concerns were addressed via the 2007 reforms. Administrative responsibility for the tribunals system now rests not with individual government departments, but with the HM Courts and Tribunals Service, an executive agency under the auspices of the Ministry of Justice (MoJ). The MoJ does not itself make the type of decisions that are subject to appeals in tribunals, and it has 'a particular mission to protect judicial independence' (2004 White Paper at [6.14]), meaning that its having responsibility for the tribunals system better reflects—and demonstrates—the independence of that system. Equivalent arrangements apply in Scotland, where devolved tribunals are administered by the Scottish Courts and Tribunals Service.

18.2.2 Judicial leadership of tribunals

While the relationship between tribunals and government is of obvious relevance to the independence of tribunals, the arrangements concerning the organization of and appointments to tribunals are also important. The Council on Tribunals (Cm 3744, *Tribunals: Their Organisation and Independence* (London 1997) at [2.4]) advocated a shift to a 'presidential system', suggesting that 'the independence and integrity of a tribunals system is best served if someone from the judicial side of the tribunal is given a specific role in meeting some or all' of the preconditions for independence which it had identified, such as training and resource-allocation. This suggestion was taken up in the 2007 reforms. Section 2 of the TCEA creates the office of Senior President of Tribunals, whose role was described by Sir Robert Carnwath—the inaugural incumbent of that office—in the following terms ([2009] *PL* 48 at 50):

> The appointment [of the Senior President] is made by the Lord Chancellor with the concurrence of the Lord Chief Justice for England and Wales, and his counterparts in Scotland and Northern Ireland. The statutory functions of the Senior President are modelled in many respects on those of the Lord Chief Justice under the Constitutional Reform Act 2005. They confer wide-ranging responsibility for judicial leadership, including training, welfare and guidance of the tribunal judiciary, and for representing their views to Parliament and to ministers.

Following recent reforms to its devolved system of tribunals, comparable arrangements apply in Scotland; such tribunals fall under the judicial leadership of the Lord President of the Court of Session, who is assisted in this aspect of his work by the President of Scottish Tribunals.

18.2.3 Appointments to tribunals

If tribunals are (actually and apparently) to be independent, then important questions arise concerning the manner in and terms upon which tribunal members are appointed. Prior to the reforms, the system of departmental sponsorship meant that, in a substantial minority of cases, Ministers with responsibility for the very decisions upon which the relevant tribunal adjudicated also had responsibility for appointing tribunal members. The 2007 reforms entailed a very clear and deliberate shift away from this system, and towards one which in many respects assimilates tribunal members to court judges. Those chairing tribunals are therefore now referred to as tribunal judges, and are regarded as members of the 'judiciary' for the purposes, *inter alia*, of the guarantees of judicial independence laid down by s 3 of the Constitutional Reform Act 2005. Moreover, under schs 2 and 3 of the TCEA, all tribunal judges are now appointed by the Lord Chancellor or by the Queen upon his recommendation, and tribunal judges are liable to dismissal only by the Lord Chancellor and only on the ground of inability or misbehaviour. Finally, in this regard, it should be noted that by virtue of ss 4–6 of the TCEA, many court judges—including all Court of Appeal and High Court judges—are *ex officio* tribunal judges.

18.3 Procedure in tribunals

18.3.1 Introduction

Because tribunals deal with a vast range of issues, it is unsurprising that different tribunals adopt different styles of proceedings. In this section, then, we do not attempt to summarize all of the different procedural approaches adopted by tribunals; instead, we seek to draw out some of the key issues and themes which arise in this context. The importance of the procedures adopted by tribunals was recognized in the Franks Report at [62]–[63]:

> Most of the evidence we have received concerning tribunals has placed great emphasis upon procedure, not only at the hearing itself but also before and after it. There has been general agreement on the broad essentials which the procedure, in this wider sense, should contain, for example provision for notice of the right to apply to a tribunal, notice of the case which the appellant has to meet, a reasoned decision by the tribunal and notice of any further right of appeal ... We agree that procedure is of the greatest importance and that it should be clearly laid down in a statute or statutory instrument. Because of the great variety of the purposes for which tribunals are established, however, we do not think it would be appropriate to rely upon either a single code or a small number of codes. We think that there is a case for greater procedural differentiation and prefer that the detailed procedure for each type of tribunal should be designed to meet its particular circumstances.

Although the Franks Committee recommended that the Council on Tribunals should draft tribunals' procedural rules, s 8 of the Tribunals and Inquiries Act 1992 merely required the Council to be consulted. Prior to the 2007 reforms, this meant that, in certain instances, sponsoring departments had a largely free hand when setting the procedural rules for the tribunals that would scrutinize their decisions.

The 2004 White Paper, which heralded the 2007 reforms, recognized that this created a risk that Ministers might fail to strike a proper balance between the interests of the department and the user. The TCEA therefore introduced a new system for the creation of procedural rules for tribunals within the new tribunals system. Section 22(2) provides that such tribunals' rules 'are to be made by the Tribunal Procedure Committee'. That Committee (according to sch 5, part 2) consists of the Senior President (or his nominee), three people appointed by the Lord Chancellor, three people (who must include tribunal judges) appointed by the Lord Chief Justice, and one person appointed by the Lord President of the Court of Session in Scotland. Further appointments may be made at the Senior President's request by a senior judge such as the Lord Chief Justice.

As to content, s 22(4) of the TCEA says that the power to make rules must be exercised with a view to seeing, *inter alia*, that 'justice is done'; that the system is 'accessible and fair'; that proceedings are 'handled quickly and efficiently'; and that the rules are both 'simple and simply expressed'. Sch 5, part 1 goes on to say that rules may, in particular, be made concerning such matters as time limits; the circumstances in which matters can be dealt with without hearings; evidence; and costs. Different rules apply in respect of each of the 'chambers' within the new tribunals system. (We explain the nature of such 'chambers' at 18.4.) However, the general ethos of tribunal proceedings which the various sets of procedural rules attempt to foster is reflected in the 'overriding objective' set out towards the beginning of each chamber's rules. That objective is that cases should be dealt with 'fairly and justly', which means:

(a) dealing with the case in ways which are proportionate to the importance of the case, the complexity of the issues, the anticipated costs and the resources of the parties;
(b) avoiding unnecessary formality and seeking flexibility in the proceedings;
(c) ensuring, so far as practicable, that the parties are able to participate fully in the proceedings;
(d) using any special expertise of the Tribunal effectively; and
(e) avoiding delay, so far as compatible with proper consideration of the issues.

18.3.2 Formality, representation, and the style of tribunal proceedings

While it is crucial to recognize that the diversity of tribunals must be reflected at a procedural level, certain common issues arise. The first concerns the question whether tribunals should adopt formal procedural rules or instead opt for a more informal model. In relation to this dilemma, the Franks Report noted (at [64]) that

[t]here has been considerable emphasis, in much of the evidence we have received, upon the importance of preserving informality of atmosphere in hearings before tribunals, though it is generally conceded that in some tribunals, for example the Lands Tribunal [now the Lands Chamber of the Upper Tribunal], informality is not an overriding necessity. We endorse this view, but we

are convinced that the attempt which has been made to secure informality in the general run of tribunals has in some instances been at the expense of an orderly procedure. Informality without rules of procedure may be positively inimical to right adjudication, since the proceedings may well assume an unordered character which makes it difficult, if not impossible, for the tribunal properly to sift the facts and weigh the evidence. It should here be remembered that by their very nature tribunals may well be less skilled in adjudication than courts of law. None of our witnesses would seek to make tribunals in all respects like courts of law, but there is a wide measure of agreement that in many instances their procedure could be made more orderly without impairing the desired informality of atmosphere. The object to be aimed at in most tribunals is the combination of a formal procedure with an informal atmosphere. We see no reason why this cannot be achieved. On the one hand it means a manifestly sympathetic attitude on the part of the tribunal and the absence of the trappings of a court, but on the other hand such prescription of procedure as makes the proceedings clear and orderly.

One argument in favour of tribunals adopting a less formal procedural style is that individuals who bring cases before tribunals are usually unrepresented: although, under the Legal Aid, Sentencing and Punishment of Offenders Act 2012, legal aid is available in relation to certain types of tribunal proceedings, that is very much the exception rather than the norm. The assumption, then, is that the relative informality of tribunals assuages problems that a lack of legal aid—which implies lack of representation—might otherwise give rise to. However, it is not clear that that assumption is well founded. For instance, research conducted by Baldwin, Wikeley, and Young in relation to social security appeals led them to the conclusion that 'expert representation [is important] in ensuring that an appellant's interests are properly protected' (see *Judging Social Security* (Oxford 1992) at 114). Moreover, Genn (1993) 56 *MLR* 393 at 400 found that

[i]n social security appeals tribunals [now superseded by the Social Entitlement Chamber of the new First-tier Tribunal], the presence of a skilled representative increased the likelihood of success from 30 to 48 per cent. In hearings before immigration adjudicators, the overall likelihood of success was increased by the presence of a representative from 20 to 38 per cent. In mental health review tribunals, the likelihood of a favourable change in conditions rose from 20 to 35 per cent as a result of representation ...

The research indicated clearly that the presence of a representative influences the substantive outcome of hearings, irrespective of the process value that representation may provide. It also showed that the type of representation used by appellants was very important, and that specialist representatives exerted the greatest influence on the outcome of hearings.

In the light of these findings, the question arises whether tribunals should go further than simply adopting a relatively informal version of the traditional adversarial procedural model by, for instance, taking a more inquisitorial approach. In fact, as Leggatt noted (at [7.4]–[7.6]), tribunals have already

developed different ways of assisting unrepresented parties, in particular when the encounter is between citizen and state, and departments are represented by an official or an advocate who is familiar with the law, the tribunal and its procedures. In these circumstances, tribunal chairmen may find it necessary to intervene in the proceedings more than might be thought proper in the courts in order to hold the balance between the parties, and enable citizens to present their cases. All the members of a tribunal must do all they can to understand the point of view, as well as the case, of the citizen. They must be alert for factual or legal aspects of the case which appellants may not bring out, adequately or at all, but which have a bearing on the possible outcomes. It may also be necessary on occasion to intervene to protect a witness or party, to avoid proceedings becoming too confrontational. The balance is a delicate one, and must not go so far on any side that the tribunal's impartiality appears to be endangered ...

We are convinced that the tribunal approach must be an enabling one: supporting the parties in ways which give them confidence in their own abilities to participate in the process, and in the tribunal's capacity to compensate for the appellants' lack of skills or knowledge. The greatest need for that will be during hearings, which are stressful for unrepresented parties.

The extent to which it is necessary and appropriate for tribunals to adopt a more inquisitorial approach (and thus the extent to which tribunals are in practice willing to do so) depends in large part upon the subject-matter of the dispute. Consider, for example, the following comments of Baroness Hale in *Kerr* v. *Department for Social Development* [2004] UKHL 23, [2004] 1 WLR 1372:

[56] The benefits system is necessarily enormously complex. This was true even in the early days, when it was mainly based on flat rate contributory benefits, and means tested benefits were seen as a safety net but not the norm. It has become even more so with increasing attempts to target benefits upon the most needy ...

[61] Ever since the decision of the Divisional Court in *R v Medical Appeal Tribunal (North Midland Region), Ex p Hubble* [1958] 2 QB 228, it has been accepted that the process of benefits adjudication is inquisitorial rather than adversarial. Diplock J said this of an industrial injury benefit claim, at p 240:

'A claim by an insured person to benefit under the Act is not truly analogous to a lis inter partes. A claim to benefit is a claim to receive money out of the insurance funds... Any such claim requires investigation to determine whether any and if so what amount of benefit is payable out of the fund. In such an investigation the minister or the insurance officer is not a party adverse to the claimant. If analogy be sought in the other branches of the law, it is to be found in an inquest rather than in an action.'

However, the adoption of a more inquisitorial approach may be far from a panacea. For instance, Baldwin, Wikeley, and Young, *op cit* at 212, found that the ability of tribunal chairs to ameliorate the position of unrepresented appellants is severely limited. Moreover, the Council on Tribunals, in its *Response to the Consultation Paper on the Report of the Review of Tribunals by Sir Andrew Leggatt* (London 2001), expressed reservations about the appropriateness of tribunals attempting to assist unrepresented appellants, arguing that a risk could arise of compromising tribunals' independence. The Council also doubted whether most people appearing before tribunals would be 'sufficiently capable, confident or knowledgeable to represent themselves'.

This thinking reflects the conclusions of Adler and Gulland, *Tribunal Users' Experiences, Perceptions and Expectations: A Literature Review* (London 2003), who noted (at 11) that most research in this area shows that 'many appellants are confused by the appeal process and have little idea of what will happen at a tribunal hearing. In some cases, they do not even realise that there will be a hearing and they are often confused by the paperwork they are sent.'

Empirical research reported on by Genn (1993) 56 *MLR* 393 also casts doubt on the proposition that the problems of unrepresented individuals may be ameliorated by recourse to such strategies as more informal proceedings. She argues that that view is based upon four misconceptions. First, she points out (at 401) that procedural straight-forwardness cannot ultimately change the often complex nature of the issues which tribunals must determine:

> Although most tribunal hearings are more informal and procedurally more flexible than courts, such informality has been wrongly assumed to extend to all aspects of tribunal processes. The fact that hearings are conducted across a table and that an appellant may choose whether he puts his case first are positive characteristics that should be protected and perhaps extended. However, none of the procedural informality of tribunals can overcome or alter the need for appli-cants to bring their cases within the regulations or statute, and prove their factual situation with evidence. Nor do informal procedures relieve tribunals from the obligation to make reasoned and consistent decisions.

Second, Genn notes (at 401) that procedural informality can constitute a 'trap for the unwary': relying in part on the work of Farmer, *Tribunals and Government* (London 1974) at 108–9, she observes (at 402) that

> [a]pplicants do not succeed with cases for social security benefits because they cannot man-age on their money; immigrants are not permitted to stay in the country because they want to; debtors are not permitted to avoid their debts in small claims courts because they cannot afford to pay. All must assert and establish a legal right, entitlement or defence: 'the assertion of a right is a form of moral criticism: besides the expression of a demand, it involves an appeal to the authority of principle in support of one's claims' [Nonet, *Administrative Justice: Advocacy and Change in Government Agencies* (New York 1969) at 91]. This represents the 'limit' of infor-mality ... Thus, although unrepresented appellants are free to 'speak for themselves' before tribunals, and many value this freedom, it has hidden dangers ... [D]ecision-making processes in tribunals require legally relevant and sufficient accounts. Applicants tell stories which may or may not be relevant. The result is often that they feel satisfied with the process but ultimately lose their case.

Third, Genn found that appellants were less capable of presenting their cases than they themselves had expected to be. Many appellants who were interviewed as part of Genn's research, emboldened by the emphasis on informality in the information published by tri-bunals, made comments such as 'I'm just going to tell the truth' and 'you only need some-one to speak for you if you are telling lies'. Genn found that, particularly in relation to appeals concerning social security benefits, 'many appellants seemed unprepared for the importance of law' and encountered difficulty 'in simply explaining the details of their case' (at 407). Finally, Genn draws attention to a point which we encountered earlier—that rely-ing on the tribunal to ameliorate the position of unrepresented appellants is fraught with difficulty—noting (at 408) that, '[e]ven with the best intentions, tribunals are rarely able to spend the time necessary to elicit relevant information from the undifferentiated stream in which most appellants present their stories'.

QUESTIONS

- Can the problems identified by Genn be overcome only by the provision of legal representation?
- If so, should publicly-funded representation before tribunals become the norm?

18.3.3 Particular issues concerning procedure

In addition to the general issues concerning informality and representation just considered, it is instructive to address a number of more particular issues relating to tribunals' procedures. The concepts of natural justice and fairness are considered in detail in chs 9–11, but here we focus on two specific issues relating to the procedures adopted by tribunals.

First, as noted in passing at 18.1.2, it is self-evident that the tribunals system, as a mechanism for resolving disputes between individuals and administrative decision-makers, can only function effectively if people are aware, in the first place, of how to appeal—and, more fundamentally still, that a right of appeal exists. These matters were noted by Adler and Gulland, *op cit* at 3:

> [One] potential barrier that users encounter in accessing the tribunal system is knowing that they have a right of appeal (or application) in the first place. Most of the research on users' experiences looks at appellants rather than those who do not appeal … This means that most research is based on those who were not deterred by ignorance of their rights. Nevertheless some information can be gained from those who did appeal. There are two types of ignorance which can prevent an appellant from making an appeal—ignorance of the fact that there may be grounds for appealing against the original decision and ignorance of the procedures which need to be followed. The general conclusion, supported by much of the research evidence, is that ignorance about the grounds of appeal is often more important than ignorance of procedures, although some potential appellants may not realise that they have a right of appeal at all.

It is crucial, therefore, that the agency which makes the original adverse decision informs the individual of the possibility of appeal, as well as the potential grounds of appeal.

Second, we have already seen (at 10.3.2) that a hearing can only be 'fair' if the individual is informed beforehand of the case against him. The Franks Report emphasized (at [71]–[72]) the importance of this aspect of natural justice in the tribunals context, observing that

> before the hearing … citizens should know in good time the case which they will have to meet, whether the issue to be heard by the tribunal is one between citizen and administration or between citizen and citizen. This constituent of fairness is one to which much of the evidence we have received has rightly drawn attention …
>
> We do not suggest that the procedure should be formalised to the extent of requiring documents in the nature of legal pleadings. What is needed is that the citizen should receive in good time beforehand a document setting out the main points of the opposing case. It should not be necessary, and indeed in view of the type of persons frequently appearing before tribunals it would in many cases be positively undesirable, to require the parties to adhere rigidly to the case previously set out, provided always that the interests of another party are not prejudiced by such flexibility.

We saw in ch 11 that public authorities are often required to give reasons for their decisions where a right of appeal exists, in order that the individual may exercise an informed judgment about whether to exercise such a right. A detailed statement of such reasons may be adequate to inform the appellant of the case against him for the purposes of fairness at the tribunal stage.

Third, what of reasons for tribunals' decisions (as distinct from reasons for the administrative decisions against which rights of appeal to tribunals may lie)? The Franks Committee emphasized the importance of building a tribunals system in which the public would have confidence. The role of reason-giving (on which see generally ch 11) in this regard is self-evident: as Lord Phillips MR put it (albeit referring to court, rather than tribunal, decisions) in *English* v. *Emery Reimbold and Strick Ltd* [2002] EWCA Civ 605, [2003] 1 WLR 2409 at [16], 'justice will not be done if it is not apparent to the parties why one has won and the other has lost'. It is therefore unsurprising that the Franks Committee (at [98]) was

> convinced that if tribunal proceedings are to be fair to the citizen reasons should be given to the fullest practicable extent. A decision is apt to be better if the reasons for it have to be set out in writing because the reasons are then more likely to have been properly thought out. Further, a reasoned decision is essential in order that where there is a right of appeal [from the first-instance tribunal], the applicant can assess whether he has good grounds of appeal and know the case he will have to meet if he decides to appeal.

Against this background, three issues fall to be addressed. First, *the norm is for tribunals to be under a statutory duty to give reasons*. For most tribunals, that duty will derive from one of two sources. Section 10 of the Tribunals and Inquiries Act 1992 requires tribunals listed in sch 1 of that Act, whenever making a decision, 'to furnish a statement, either written or oral, of the reasons for the decision if requested, on or before the giving or notification of the decision, to state the reasons'. Although wide-ranging, there are some respects in which this duty is limited: it can be displaced by provisions in other legislation (s 10(5)(a)), by national security considerations (s 10(2)), or, in certain circumstances, by order of the Lord Chancellor (s 10(7)). Moreover, the duty to give reasons is a reactive one which does not arise automatically upon the tribunal's determination of the relevant matter: instead, reasons (written *or* oral: cf Franks' recommendation) need only be given 'if requested'. Nevertheless, it is considered best practice for tribunals to give reasons at their own initiative, irrespective of whether a request has been made.

The importance of s 10 of the 1992 Act is now waning: while it continues to apply to those tribunals listed in sch 1, it does not extend to those tribunals that have migrated—in the way set out at 18.4—into the new tribunals system established as a result of the 2007 reforms. However, the procedure rules applying to such tribunals obliges them to give reasons. The following provision—r 38 of the procedural rules for the General Regulatory Chamber of the First-tier Tribunal—is typical of the reason-giving requirements imposed by tribunal procedure rules:

> (1) The Tribunal may give a decision orally at a hearing.
>
> (2) Subject to rule 14(10) (prevention of disclosure or publication of documents and information), the Tribunal must provide to each party as soon as reasonably practicable after making [a decision (other than a decision under Part 4 [concerning correcting, setting aside, reviewing, and appealing Tribunal decisions]) which finally disposes of all issues in the proceedings or a preliminary issue dealt with following a direction under rule 5(3)(e)]—
>
>   (a) a decision notice stating the Tribunal's decision;
>   (b) written reasons for the decision; and
>   (c) notification of any right of appeal against the decision and the time within which, and manner in which, such right of appeal may be exercised.
>
> (3) The Tribunal may provide written reasons for any decision to which paragraph (2) does not apply.

Unlike s 10 of the 1992 Act, the new tribunal procedure rules impose a proactive rather than reactive duty to give reasons. This is now the norm within the new system, although the old approach—whereby the duty is reactive, arising only upon a request for reasons being lodged—has been retained in certain parts of the new system. Thus, the Social Entitlement Chamber of the First-tier Tribunal (other than in relation to asylum support cases) and the War Pensions and Armed Forces Compensation Chamber of the same Tribunal have a *discretion* to give reasons, a *duty* arising only if a party makes a written request for reasons (see rr 34 and 32 of the procedure rules for the respective chambers).

Second, *what is the content of the duty to give reasons* in this sphere? In the explanatory notes to its *Guide to Drafting Tribunal Rules* (London 2003) at 143, the Council on Tribunals suggested that the standard applicable to reason-giving by tribunals is analogous to that which applies to courts' decisions (on which see Ho (2000) 20 *LS* 42). Particular emphasis was placed by the Council on the decision of the Court of Appeal in *English* v. *Emery Reimbold and Strick Ltd* [2002] EWCA Civ 605, [2003] 1 WLR 2409, which considered the duty incumbent upon judges—both at common law and under Article 6 ECHR—to give reasons for their decisions. After referring to a number of Strasbourg judgments—including *Ruiz Torija* v. *Spain* (1994) 19 EHRR 553, *Garcia Ruiz* v. *Spain* (1999) 31 EHRR 589, and *Helle* v. *Finland* (1997) 26 EHRR 159—Lord Phillips MR concluded in *English* that

[12] The Strasbourg court, when considering article 6, is not concerned with the merits of the decision of the domestic court that is under attack. It is concerned to see that the procedure has been fair. It requires that a judgment contains reasons that are sufficient to demonstrate that the essential issues that have been raised by the parties have been addressed by the domestic court and how those issues have been resolved. It does not seem to us that the Strasbourg jurisprudence goes further and requires a judgment to explain why one contention, or piece of evidence, has been preferred to another. The common law countries have developed a tradition of delivering judgments that detail the evidence and explain the findings in much greater detail than is to be found in the judgments of most civil law jurisdictions. We do not believe that the extent of the reasoning that the Strasbourg court requires goes any further than that which is required under our domestic law, which we are about to consider. It remains to consider, however, the nature of the judicial decisions for which reasons are required under the Strasbourg jurisprudence.

[13] All of the Strasbourg decisions to which we have so far referred were considering judgments which determined the substantive dispute between the parties. The critical issue in each case was whether the form of the judgment in question was compatible with a fair trial. Where a judicial decision affects the substantive rights of the parties we consider that the Strasbourg jurisprudence requires that the decision should be reasoned. In contrast, there are some judicial decisions where fairness does not demand that the parties should be informed of the reasoning underlying them. Interlocutory decisions in the course of case management provide an obvious example. Furthermore, the Strasbourg Commission has recognised that there are some circumstances in which the reason for the decision will be implicit from the decision itself. In such circumstances article 6 will not be infringed if the reason for the decision is not expressly spelt out by the judicial tribunal: see *X* v *Federal Republic of Germany* (1981) 25 DR 240 and *Webb* v *United Kingdom* (1997) 24 EHRR CD 73 ...

[17] As to the adequacy of reasons, as has been said many times, this depends on the nature of the case: see for example *Flannery's* case [2000] 1 WLR 377, 382. In *Eagil Trust Co Ltd* v *Pigott Brown* [1985] 3 All ER 119, 122 Griffiths LJ stated that there was no duty on a judge, in giving his reasons, to deal with every argument presented by counsel in support of his case:

'When dealing with an application in chambers to strike out for want of prosecution, a judge should give his reasons in sufficient detail to show the Court of Appeal the principles on which he has acted and the reasons that have led him to his decision. They need not be elaborate. I cannot stress too strongly that there is no duty on a judge, in giving his reasons, to deal with

> every argument presented by counsel in support of his case. It is sufficient if what he says shows the parties and, if need be, the Court of Appeal the basis on which he has acted ... (see Sachs LJ in *Knight* v *Clifton* [1971] Ch 700, 721).'

Third, *what consequences flow from a failure to discharge the duty to give reasons?* We noted at 11.6 that, in relation to the common law duty to give reasons, there is a degree of ambiguity in relation to this question. In relation to tribunals' statutory duties to give reasons, there has also been some uncertainty in this regard. In *Mountview Court Properties Ltd* v. *Devlin* (1970) 21 P & CR 689, in which there had been a failure to discharge the duty to give reasons imposed by a predecessor to the Tribunals and Inquiries Act 1992, Lord Parker CJ said at 694 that he found it 'impossible to say that a failure to provide sufficient reasons of itself gives rise to the right of this court on an appeal to quash the decision', albeit that 'if the very insufficiency of the reason gives rise to a proper inference that there has been an error of law in arriving at the decision, then clearly it would be a case for quashing the decision'. However, in *Crake* v. *Supplementary Benefits Commission* [1982] 1 All ER 498 at 506, Woolf J suggested that the distinction between these two positions may be practically unimportant. While he regarded *Mountview* as 'the main authority to be applied', he noted that

> it has to be applied in the light of the ten years which have elapsed since that case was decided. Over that period of ten years the approach of the courts with regard to the giving of reasons has been much more definite than they were at that time and courts are now much more ready to infer that because of inadequate reasons there has been an error of law, than perhaps they were prepared to at the time that the *Mountview* case was decided ... Therefore in practice I think that there will be few cases where it will not be possible, where the reasons are inadequate, to say one way or another whether the tribunal has gone wrong in law.

This leaves open the question whether failure to give reasons is an error of law in its own right (as opposed to grounds for inferring the commission of a separate error). There is authority—both in the tribunals context (see, *eg Re Poyser and Mills' Arbitration* [1964] 2 QB 467) and more generally—for the proposition that failure to give reasons can be treated as an error of law. This view—which is the better one—is bolstered by the decision of the Privy Council in *Marshall* v. *Deputy Governor of Bermuda* [2010] UKPC 9, on which see 11.6.

18.4 The structure of the tribunals system and its relationship with the courts

18.4.1 Background

We have already adverted to certain aspects of the 2007 reforms, the central plank of which was the creation of a new structure within which tribunals operate. The nature of that structure—which we set out shortly—was informed by two central concerns.

First, Leggatt found one of the defining features of the old system to be its disjointed nature. He observed (at [1.3] of his report) that

the present collection of tribunals has grown up in an almost entirely haphazard way. Individual tribunals were set up, and usually administered by departments, as they developed new statutory schemes and procedures. The result is a collection of tribunals, mostly administered by departments, with wide variations of practice and approach, and almost no coherence. The current arrangements seem to us to have been developed to meet the needs and conveniences of the departments and other bodies which run tribunals, rather than the needs of the user.

Leggatt regarded this as cause for concern. The disjointedness of the old system resulted in incoherence and substantial variations in terms of the quality of decisions, cost efficiency, provision of information to users, and so on. Moreover, he thought that the disparate nature of the system made it bewildering for prospective appellants.

Second, not only were the *entry points* to the old system confusing: once cases entered it, the route by which *appeals* could be pursued by individuals dissatisfied with first-instance tribunals' decisions was also unduly complex and inconsistent.

The solution to these problems, said Leggatt (at [3.8]), lay in the adoption of a new, rationalized structure:

The overriding aim should be to present the citizen with a single, overarching structure. It would give access to all tribunals. Any citizen who wished to appeal to a tribunal would only have to submit the appeal, confident in the knowledge that one system handled all such disputes, and could be relied upon to allocate it to the right tribunal. This would be a considerable advance in clarity and simplicity for users and their advisers. The single system would enable a coherent, user-focussed approach to the provision of information which would enable tribunals to meet the claim that they operate in ways which enable citizens to participate directly in preparing and presenting their own cases.

18.4.2 The two-tier structure

Leggatt's proposals were implemented by way of the 2007 reforms. Under the Tribunals, Courts and Enforcement Act 2007, a new structure—as shown in Figure 18.1—was created consisting of two tribunals: the First-tier Tribunal (FTT) and the Upper Tribunal (UT).

As mentioned briefly at the beginning of the chapter, the role of the former is to act as the first-instance tribunal, hearing appeals against administrative decisions. Meanwhile, the principal role of the UT is to hear appears against the FTT's decisions. In this way the two central concerns pertaining to the old system are addressed: for those areas covered by the new system, there is now a unified entry-point, via the FTT, and a unified appeal route, to the UT.

It should be noted, however, that not all tribunals have been brought within the two-tier structure. Some UK-wide tribunals, such as the Competition Appeal Tribunal, remain outside the two-tier structure, as do a number of tribunals in Northern Ireland, Scotland, and Wales. However, as noted earlier, Scottish tribunals have themselves been reorganized along the lines of the two-tier structure that is embodied in the TCEA.

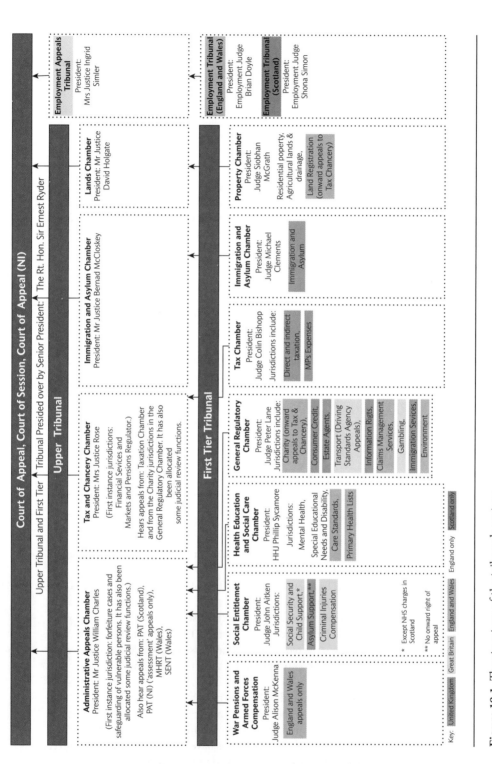

Figure 18.1 The structure of the tribunals system

Source: Senior President of Tribunals' Annual Report 2016

The FTT and the UT are themselves divided into several chambers, as is permitted by s 7 of the TCEA. As Tables 18.1 and 18.2 show, the chambers are organized such that each is able to focus on appeals in specific fields of decision-making.

Under s 7(2) of the TCEA, each chamber has a President and, as noted earlier, the whole system is given judicial leadership by the Senior President of Tribunals. FTT and UT judges are each appointed to a particular chamber, but it is possible for suitably qualified judges to be authorized to sit in cases within other chambers. The structure thus enables specialisms to be demarcated via the chambers system, but the presence of those chambers within a single overarching framework means that judges can be deployed flexibly, across chambers, where appropriate. This is obviously desirable in terms of the efficient use of human resources.

Table 18.1 First-tier Tribunal

Chamber	Deals with appeals against decisions relating to
Asylum Support	Support for asylum seekers
Care Standards	Removal from register of those permitted to work with children or vulnerable adults
Criminal Injuries Compensation	Compensation for victims of violent crime
General Regulatory Chamber	Broad range of matters, including registration and deregistration of charities by the Charity Commission; licensing of driving instructors and estate agents; freedom of information decisions; sanctions imposed by environmental regulators
Immigration and Asylum Chamber	Permission to stay in and deportation from the UK
Mental Health	Discharge of patients detained in psychiatric hospitals
Primary Health Lists	Removal from or refusal to add a doctor, dentist, or ophthalmologist to the relevant medical performers list
Property	Changes to the Land Register; licences for multiple-occupancy houses; right to buy council homes
Social Security and Child Support	A wide variety of benefits, including attendance allowance, child benefit, income support, jobseekers' allowance, and universal credit
Special Educational Needs and Disability	Assessments of children's educational, health, and care needs
Tax	Various tax (*eg* income tax and corporation tax) and tax-related (*eg* National Insurance, statutory sick pay, and statutory maternity pay) matters
War Pensions and Armed Forces	Pensions and compensation payable to current and former servicemen and servicewomen

NB the information in the right-hand column is illustrative of the types of matters with which each chamber deals; it is not an exhaustive description of those matters.

Table 18.2 The Upper Tribunal

Chamber	Deals with appeals against	Other functions
Administrative Appeals	Decisions of several chambers of the FTT, including the Social Security and Child Support, War Pensions and Armed Forces Compenssation, Mental Health, Special Educational Needs and Disability, and General Regulatory Chambers; decisions made by the Disclosure and Barring Service, the Traffic Commissioner; decisions of certain tribunals in Wales and Northern Ireland	Judicial review of decisions of the FTT's Criminal Injuries Compensation Chamber and of other FTT decisions against which there is no right of appeal Judicial review in cases transferred to the UT by the High Court
Immigration and Asylum	Decisions made by the FTT's Immigration and Asylum Chamber concerning visa applications, asylum applications, and the right to enter or stay in the UK	Judicial review of certain immigration and asylum decisions Judicial review in cases transferred to the UT by the High Court
Lands	Certain decisions made by the FTT's Property Chamber; decisions made by certain Welsh tribunals	Deals with certain other matters, including compensation for compulsory purchase of land; valuation of property for certain tax-related purposes; right-to-light disputes; compensation for blighted land Judicial review in cases transferred to the UT by the High Court
Tax and Chancery	Certain decisions made by the FTT's Tax, Property and General Regulatory Chambers, and certain decisions made by regulators such as the Financial Conduct Authority, the Prudential Regulation Authority, the Pensions Regulator, and the Bank of England	Judicial review in cases transferred to the UT by the High Court

NB the information in the second and third columns is illustrative of the types of matters with which each chamber deals; it is not an exhaustive description of those matters.

18.4.3 Routes through the tribunals system

Once the FTT has made a decision, it may be that the parties accept it, and that that is the end of the matter. However, a number of options arise if a party is dissatisfied with the FTT's decision.

First, under s 9 of the TCEA the FTT may be asked (or may on its own initiative decide) to *review its own decision*. The following excerpts from s 9 indicate the nature and potential consequences of such review:

(4) Where the First-tier Tribunal has under subsection (1) reviewed a decision, the First-tier Tribunal may in the light of the review do any of the following—

    (a) correct accidental errors in the decision or in a record of the decision;
    (b) amend reasons given for the decision;
    (c) set the decision aside.

(5) Where under subsection (4)(c) the First-tier Tribunal sets a decision aside, the First-tier Tribunal must either—

    (a) re-decide the matter concerned, or
    (b) refer that matter to the Upper Tribunal.

(6) Where a matter is referred to the Upper Tribunal under subsection (5)(b), the Upper Tribunal must re-decide the matter.

(7) Where the Upper Tribunal is under subsection (6) re-deciding a matter, it may make any decision which the First-tier Tribunal could make if the First-tier Tribunal were re-deciding the matter.

(8) Where a tribunal is acting under subsection (5)(a) or (6), it may make such findings of fact as it considers appropriate.

Under s 10, the Upper Tribunal can also review its own decisions, although the choice which s 9(5) gives the FTT is not open to the UT: the latter must itself re-decide the matter. The virtue of the review system is that it potentially permits rapid correction of errors in original decisions. However, ss 9(3) and 10(3) permit tribunal procedure rules to limit the circumstances in which decisions may be reviewed. Pursuant to those provisions, the procedure rules for the FTT chambers and the UT provide that review may only be carried out when consideration is being given to an application for permission to appeal. In practice, then, the review system allows the appeal system to be short-circuited when the tribunal concerned can see, at the stage of considering permission to appeal, that something is amiss.

Second, as is implicit in what has just been said, provision is made (in s 11 of the TCEA) for any party to *appeal against a decision of the FTT*. The right of appeal arises in respect of all FTT decisions (save those specified in s 11(5) or in an order made thereunder) but can only be exercised with the permission of the FTT or the UT. The appeal is to the UT and lies only on points of law (s 11(1)). The latter restriction means that (for reasons discussed in ch 2) the UT assesses FTT decisions applying the same principles as those which are applicable upon judicial review. However, two points must be borne in mind. First, as seen at 2.4, certain errors of fact can amount to errors of law, and as such can be dealt with by the UT on an appeal on a point of law. Second, as noted at 2.2.9, the distinction between errors of law and fact is malleable, and the Supreme Court in *R (Jones)* v. *First-tier Tribunal* [2013] UKSC 19, [2013] 2 AC 48 explicitly countenanced the possibility of the UT's taking a broad view of what constitutes an error of law so as to enable it to adopt an interventionist stance, thereby allowing the UT to impose a coherent approach across the tribunals system.

The powers of the UT when it hears appeals from the FTT are set out in s 12:

(1) Subsection (2) applies if the Upper Tribunal, in deciding an appeal under section 11, finds that the making of the decision concerned involved the making of an error on a point of law.

(2) The Upper Tribunal—

    (a) may (but need not) set aside the decision of the First-tier Tribunal, and

    (b) if it does, must either—

        (i) remit the case to the First-tier Tribunal with directions for its reconsideration, or

        (ii) re-make the decision.

(3) In acting under subsection (2)(b)(i), the Upper Tribunal may also—

    (a) direct that the members of the First-tier Tribunal who are chosen to reconsider the case are not to be the same as those who made the decision that has been set aside;

    (b) give procedural directions in connection with the reconsideration of the case by the First-tier Tribunal.

(4) In acting under subsection (2)(b)(ii), the Upper Tribunal—

    (a) may make any decision which the First-tier Tribunal could make if the First-tier Tribunal were re-making the decision, and

    (b) may make such findings of fact as it considers appropriate.

Subject to limited exceptions, the UT does not hear appeals arising from decisions other than those taken by the FTT. In relation to tribunals lying outside the two-tier system, then, the position remains as it was before the 2007 reforms. In many instances this means that, under s 11 of the Tribunals and Inquiries Act 1992, there is a right of appeal on points of law to the High Court.

18.4.4 Appeals against tribunal decisions

So far, we have considered ways in which cases may be dealt with within and progress through the tribunals system. But what is the relationship between that system and the courts? In particular, to what extent, if any, may someone who is dissatisfied with the decision of a tribunal choose to challenge that decision before the ordinary courts? Before addressing specific issues raised by these questions, it is necessary to make a general point. A key aspect of the design of the new tribunals system is that it is intended to constitute a counterpart to, rather than a poor relation of, the courts as part of the UK's judicial structure. This is evident in many of the factors mentioned earlier which underpin the independence of the new system, such as its institutional separation from the government departments whose decisions are in question before the new tribunals and its leadership by a member of the senior judiciary. Indeed, in his first annual report (*Tribunals Transformed* (London 2010) at [27]), the Senior President of Tribunals said that

[o]ver time the Upper Tribunal should come to play a central, innovative and defining role in the new system, enjoying a position in the judicial hierarchy at least equivalent to that of the Administrative Court in England and Wales.

The TCEA thus seeks to strike a balance between (on the one hand) affording the tribunals system suitable autonomy by shielding it from undue intervention by regular courts and (on the other hand) permitting an appropriate measure of judicial scrutiny of the UT's decisions.

To that end, there is a right of appeal against such decisions to the 'relevant appellate court' (which in practice means the Court of Appeal in England and Wales, the Northern Ireland Court of Appeal, or the Court of Session: TCEA, s 13(11)–(13)). However, this right of appeal is hedged around with a number of restrictions: it lies only on points of law (s 13(1)), it can be exercised only with the permission of the UT or the relevant appellate court (s 13(4)), and it does not extend to decisions of a type specified in or described in orders made under s 13(8). Most significantly, Article 2 of the Appeals from the Upper Tribunal to the Court of Appeal Order 2008 (made under TCEA, s 13(6)) provides that when the UT has made a decision in an appeal from the FTT, permission to appeal against the UT's decision can only be granted if it would raise 'some important point of principle or practice' or if there is 'some other compelling reason' for the appeal to be heard. These are the same as the 'second-tier appeal criteria' that, by virtue of s 55 of the Access to Justice Act 1999, govern appeals from certain courts to the Court of Appeal. The application of those criteria to appeals against UT decisions underlines the constricted nature of the right of appeal, and hence the fact that, in the vast majority of cases, the decision of the UT will be final. The possibility of appealing against UT decisions directly to the Supreme Court exists under ss 14A–C of the TCEA, but in even narrower circumstances than those which apply to appeals to the Court of Appeal or equivalent.

The question arises whether UT decisions can be challenged not only by means of the exercise of the rights of appeal conferred by the TCEA, but by seeking judicial review of such decisions in the Administrative Court. The short answer to that question is: 'Yes, but only in very limited circumstances.' A longer answer is supplied at 18.4.6. But before considering the possibility of judicial review *of* the UT, it is necessary to explain that judicial review hearings can be conducted *by* the UT.

18.4.5 Judicial review *by* the Upper Tribunal

As well as being (for the most part) subject to appeals to the UT, the FTT's decisions are also, in principle, subject to judicial review. However, as we saw at 14.3, the general principle is that alternative remedies—such as statutory rights of appeal—must be exhausted before permission for judicial review will be granted. In respect of FTT decisions against which such a right of appeal exists, judicial review is therefore a remote possibility at best. There are, though, certain FTT decisions against which no right of appeal exists, and in respect of which judicial review is (subject to the usual limitations considered in ch 14) available. However, rather than taking place in the Administrative Court, such judicial review occurs before the UT. This raises one of the most striking features of the modern tribunals system: the conferral upon the UT of powers of judicial review.

In many respects, judicial review before the UT is identical to judicial review before the Administrative Court: the same remedies can be issued (TCEA, s 15(1)) and have the same effect (s 15(3)), save that the UT cannot grant a declaration of incompatibility under the Human Rights Act 1998; the same principles are applied when deciding whether to grant relief (s 15(4)–(5)); and the position is the same or broadly similar in relation to permission (s 16(2)), standing (s 16(3)), and delay (s 16(4) read with the Tribunal Procedure (Upper Tribunal) Rules 2008, r 28). But there is a crucial difference. Whereas the High Court has an inherent and wide-ranging jurisdiction (see generally ch 4), the UT is a statutory body with jurisdiction over only those matters assigned to it by legislation. In explaining what those matters are, it is helpful to distinguish two points.

First, there are applications for judicial review that can be initiated in the UT and in which the Administrative Court therefore has no involvement whatever. However, an application for judicial review can be initiated in the UT only if all four of the conditions set out in s 18 of the TCEA are fulfilled:

> (4) Condition 1 is that the application does not seek anything other than
>
>   (a) relief under section 15(1) [ie a prerogative order, declaration, or injunction];
>   (b) permission (or, in a case arising under the law of Northern Ireland, leave) to apply for relief under section 15(1);
>   (c) an award [of damages] under section 16(6);
>   (d) interest;
>   (e) costs.
>
> (5) Condition 2 is that the application does not call into question anything done by the Crown Court.
>
> (6) Condition 3 is that the application falls within a class specified for the purposes of this subsection in a direction given in accordance with Part 1 of Schedule 2 to the Constitutional Reform Act 2005 ...
>
> (8) Condition 4 is that the judge presiding at the hearing of the application is either
>
>   (a) a judge of the High Court or the Court of Appeal in England and Wales or Northern Ireland, or a judge of the Court of Session, or
>   (b) such other persons as may be agreed from time to time between the Lord Chief Justice, the Lord President, or the Lord Chief Justice of Northern Ireland, as the case may be, and the Senior President of Tribunals.

The effect of condition 3 is that only cases falling within specified classes can be initiated before the UT. Thus far, two broad classes of cases have been so specified. One such class concerns FTT decisions relating to criminal injuries compensation (against which no right of appeal exists) and certain other FTT decisions against which no right of appeal exists. The other category concerns immigration, the position being that a wide range of such decisions can now be challenged by means of seeking judicial review before the UT.

Second, the implication of what has been said so far is that decisions that can be challenged by way of judicial review before the UT can alternatively be challenged before the Administrative Court—thus implying that claimants have a choice of forum. However, the position is in fact otherwise, thanks to s 31A(2) of the Senior Courts Act 1981, which provides that '[i]f Conditions 1, 2 and 3 [which are equivalent to conditions 1–3 in s 18 of the TCEA, as set out above] are met, the High Court *must* by order transfer the application to the Upper Tribunal' (emphasis added). The upshot is that any application for judicial review that *can be initiated* in the UT *must be transferred* to it if the application is initiated in the Administrative Court. Alongside this duty to transfer cases that fulfil all three conditions to the UT, the Administrative Court is invested by s 31A(3) of the Senior Courts Act with a *discretion* to transfer cases that fulfil only the first two conditions.

Giving the UT powers of judicial review—and, in particular, making it responsible for dealing with a large swathe of immigration judicial review cases—amounts to a significant transformation of the administrative justice landscape. Thomas, 'Immigration Judicial

Reviews' (*UK Constitutional Law Blog*, 12 September 2013 *http://ukconstitutionallaw.org*) observes that the reasons for this change are clear enough:

'Tribunalising' judicial review has clear advantages for the higher courts: off-loading the work elsewhere reduces the pressure on the High Court's caseload and allows it to focus more clearly on the high-end work. The thinking is that it takes non-specialist High Court judges and Deputy High Court judges longer to deal with an immigration judicial review than it would a specialist judge.

However, Thomas also points out that the effect may be to segregate different types of judicial review cases in a way that is unfamiliar given the broad jurisdiction that the High Court has historically exercised:

[These changes have] the effect of institutionalising the distinction between 'constitutional' and 'policy' judicial review challenges and 'bureaucratic' and 'individual' judicial review; the two categories will now, by and large, be streamed into separate forums. This is an important constitutional development. The High Court has, for centuries, provided the forum for legal challenges against executive action affecting personal liberty. Its jurisdiction is based upon common law tradition, the court's own high status, and the quality and independence of High Court judges. By contrast, the Upper Tribunal was established in 2008 and the Immigration and Asylum Chamber has only been in existence since 2010. The Upper Tribunal is not simply another inferior judicial body; it has been designated by the Tribunals, Courts and Enforcement Act 2007 as a superior court of record and part of its role is to provide judicial leadership to the First-tier Tribunal. Nonetheless, it is a relatively new judicial institution and remains untested.

Thomas goes on to argue that while judges in the UT's Immigration and Asylum Chamber may, thanks to their particular expertise, be particularly well placed to determine immigration judicial reviews, the marginalization of generalist senior judges in the Administrative Court may bring problems of its own.

Upper Tribunal judges are accustomed to determining substantive appeals and undertaking an error of law jurisdiction. Many of them will have spent their judicial career solely determining immigration and asylum appeals at tribunal level and might never have heard cases outside of that jurisdiction. This is not to say that Upper Tribunal judges could not with training determine judicial review claims. It does, though, mean that their body of experience in hearing judicial review cases is limited.

More widely, there is a general tension in the tribunal-court structure between specialist tribunals, which are expert in their particular area but lower down the judicial hierarchy, and the higher courts, which are superior though generalist courts. On the one hand, expertise has advantages in terms of allowing specialist judges to conclude matters at an appropriate level of the wider judicial structure. On the other hand, generalist legal expertise is necessary to keep the junior albeit expert judges in check and to ensure that they do not become a law unto themselves.

QUESTION

- The removal of cases from the jurisdiction of the High Court is generally considered to be constitutionally suspect (see, *eg* 14.6 on ouster clauses). Do such concerns arise in relation to the compulsory transfer of certain judicial review cases from the High Court to the Administrative Court? Why (not)?

18.4.6 Judicial review *of* the Upper Tribunal

Having examined the circumstances in which the UT can determine applications for judicial review, it remains to consider whether the UT is itself *subject to* judicial review. The existence of a statutory right of appeal on points of law to the Court of Appeal (or its counterparts in Scotland and Northern Ireland) means that this question will often be moot, given the exhaustion of alternative remedies principle. However, appeal is not always possible: there are limited situations in which no right of appeal *exists*, and there are much wider circumstances in which a right of appeal cannot in practice be *exercised* (most obviously because of the Appeals from the Upper Tribunal to the Court of Appeal Order 2008, which, as we have seen, prohibits the granting of permission unless the restrictive 'second-tier appeal' criteria are satisfied). In such situations, is judicial review of a UT decision possible?

This matter arose in *R (Cart)* v. *Upper Tribunal*. The claimant wished to question the legality of the UT's refusal to grant permission to appeal on a particular ground against an FTT decision. Such UT decisions cannot be the subject of an appeal to the Court of Appeal (TCEA, s 13(8)(c)), and so the claimant sought judicial review (in the High Court: unsurprisingly, the UT has not been given jurisdiction to subject its own decisions to judicial review). We saw at 2.2.7 that neither the Divisional Court ([2009] EWHC 3052 (Admin), [2010] PTSR 824) nor the Court of Appeal ([2010] EWCA Civ 859, [2011] QB 120) was prepared to accept that the UT's designation (by s 3(5) of the TCEA) as a 'superior court of record' was sufficient to immunize it against judicial review. However, the Court of Appeal concluded that although amenable to review, the UT would only be found to act unlawfully relatively rarely on account of what the Court of Appeal considered to be the UT's unusually broad jurisdiction. When *Cart* reached the Supreme Court, the Justices were sympathetic to the notion that the UT should not readily be subject to judicial review. However, they differed substantially from the lower courts in respect of both the nature of the relevant restrictions upon judicial review and the underlying basis of those restrictions.

R (Cart) v. *Upper Tribunal* [2011] UKSC 28, [2012] 1 AC 663
Supreme Court

The Supreme Court considered the appeals of two claimants in this case. The facts relating to only one of the claimants are given here in order to contextualize the legal issues that the Court had to consider. Relevant events occurred around the time of the transition of relevant tribunals into the two-tier tribunals structure. For simplicity, the facts are presented here as if the FTT and the UT had been the relevant tribunals throughout.

The first claimant unsuccessfully appealed to the FTT against an administrative decision concerning the amount of maintenance he was required to pay to his ex-wife in respect of their children. He sought the permission of the UT to appeal against the the FTT's decision on four grounds. The UT granted permission in respect of three grounds but dismissed the appeal on those grounds. It refused to grant permission to appeal in respect of the fourth ground. There is no right of appeal against a decision by the UT to refuse permission to appeal to the UT. The first claimant therefore sought judicial review in the Divisional Court of the UT's refusal. That Court dismissed his claim for judicial review, holding that the UT is subject to judicial review only in limited circumstances. The Court of Appeal dismissed the first claimant's appeal. The first claimant appealed to the Supreme Court.

Baroness Hale

[37] The way in which the argument has developed through the proceedings which are now collected before us enables us to be clear on three points. First, there is nothing in the 2007 Act [the TCEA] which purports to oust or exclude judicial review of the unappealable decisions of the Upper Tribunal. Clear words would be needed to do this and they are not there. The argument that making the Upper Tribunal a superior court of record was sufficient to do this was killed stone dead by Laws LJ [in the Divisional Court] and has not been resurrected. Second, it would be completely inconsistent with the new structure introduced by the 2007 Act to distinguish between the scope of judicial review in the various jurisdictions which have now been gathered together in that new structure. The duties of the Senior President, set out in section 1(2), clearly contemplate that the jurisdictions will retain their specialist expertise, so that one size does not necessarily fit all; but the relationships of its component parts with one another and with the ordinary courts are common to all. So too must be the principles adopted by the High Court in deciding the scope of judicial review. Third, the scope of judicial review is an artefact of the common law whose object is to maintain the rule of law—that is to ensure that, within the bounds of practical possibility, decisions are taken in accordance with the law, and in particular the law which Parliament has enacted, and not otherwise. Both tribunals and the courts are there to do Parliament's bidding. But we all make mistakes. No-one is infallible. The question is, what machinery is necessary and proportionate to keep such mistakes to a minimum? In particular, should there be any jurisdiction in which mistakes of law are, either in theory or in practice, immune from scrutiny in the higher courts? …

[39] The approach of the Divisional Court and Court of Appeal would lead us back to the distinction between jurisdictional and other errors which was effectively abandoned after the *Anisminic* case [1969] 2 AC 147. It is a distinction which lawyers can readily grasp. As Denning LJ put it in *Ex p Shaw* [1952] 1 KB 338, 346: 'A tribunal may often decide a point of law wrongly whilst keeping well within its jurisdiction.' There are, however, several objections to reviving it.

[40] First, we would not in fact be turning the clock back to the days before the *Anisminic* case because, as we have seen, *certiorari* was available to correct errors of law on the face of the record made by tribunals of limited jurisdiction. We would be re-introducing a distinction which had become relevant for the most part only where judicial review was expressly excluded, which it is not here. Secondly, the distinction was given its quietus by the majority in the *Anisminic* case [1969] 2 AC 147 not least because the word 'jurisdiction' has many meanings ranging from the very wide to the very narrow. By the narrow original sense both Lord Reid and Lord Pearson meant that the tribunal had asked itself the wrong question. But, as Lord Reid explained, a tribunal does this if it does any of the things which would ordinarily render its decision susceptible to judicial review: see p 171. And, as Lord Pearson observed, at p 195: 'there has been evolution over the centuries and there have been many technicalities. There have also been many borderline cases.' And Lord Wilberforce did not find the expressions 'asking the wrong question' or 'applying the wrong test' wholly satisfactory, although he agreed that such decisions were a nullity, at p 210 …

[49] Mr Fordham [for the Public Law Project, intervening], in particular, argues that there is no need to introduce further restrictions upon judicial review. The courts have already adopted principles of judicial restraint when considering the decisions of expert tribunals. As long ago as *R v Preston Supplementary Benefits Appeal Tribunal, Ex p Moore* [1975] 1 WLR 624, before the creation of the unified social security appeal tribunals with a common right of appeal to the commissioners, Lord Denning MR observed, at pp 631–632, that the courts should leave the tribunals to interpret the Supplementary Benefit Act 1966 in a broad reasonable way, according to the spirit and not the letter. But it was important that cases raising the same points should be dealt with in the same way, so the courts should be prepared to consider points of law of general application.

Individual cases of particular application should be left to the tribunals. More recently, in *Cooke v Secretary of State for Social Security* [2002] 3 All ER 279, paras 15–17, I (with the agreement of both Clarke LJ and Butterfield J) urged appropriate caution in giving permission to appeal from the Social Security Commissioners, because of their particular expertise in a highly specialised area of the law, where it was 'quite probable that ... the Social Security Commissioner will have got it right' ...

[51] The real question, as all agree, is what level of independent scrutiny outside the tribunal structure is required by the rule of law. The mere fact that something has been taken for granted without causing practical problems in the social security context until now does not mean that it should be taken for granted forever. Equally the fact that the courts have hitherto found it difficult to deter repeated or unmeritorious applications in immigration and asylum cases does not mean that such applications should become virtually impossible. There must be a principled but proportionate approach.

[52] An important innovation in the 2007 Act was the power given to the Lord Chancellor in section 13(6), to prescribe the same criteria for the grant of permission to appeal from the Upper Tribunal to the Court of Appeal as apply to second-tier appeals in the courts of England and Wales. [The second-tier appeals criteria provide that a second appeal should be considered only if 'an important point of principle or practice' is at stake or 'there is some other compelling reason'.] These have now been prescribed for second-tier appeals from the Upper Tribunal in all three jurisdictions. (It was the previous lack of such criteria which led to the remarks about restraint in *Cooke*.) This gives, at the very least, an indication of the circumstances in which Parliament considered that questions of law should be, as Sedley LJ put it [in *Cart*] [2011] QB 120, 169, para 30, 'channelled into the legal system' ...

[55] The claimants accept that if there is to be any restriction on the availability of judicial review, this approach would be far preferable to that of the Court of Appeal in *Cart*. Their main objection is that it would deprive the parties of the second substantive hearing to which they would have been entitled if the Upper Tribunal had spotted the error and given permission to appeal. Another objection is that it would leave uncorrected those errors of law which do not raise an important point of principle or practice and where there is no other compelling reason for the court to hear the case.

[56] But no system of decision-making is perfect or infallible. There is always the possibility that a judge at any level will get it wrong. Clearly there should always be the possibility that another judge can look at the case and check for error. That second judge should always be someone with more experience or expertise than the judge who first heard the case ... But it is not obvious that there should be a right to any particular number of further checks after that. The adoption of the second-tier appeal criteria would lead to a further check, outside the tribunal system, but not one which could be expected to succeed in the great majority of cases.

Lord Phillips

... [91] My initial inclination was to treat the new two-tier tribunal system as wholly self-sufficient. It is under the presidency of a judge who is likely to be a member of the Court of Appeal, and High Court judges can and will sit in the Upper Tribunal. There is considerable flexibility in the system in relation to the administration and composition of the Upper Tribunal. Can it not be left to the Senior President, in consultation with the President of the Queen's Bench Division and other judicial colleagues to ensure that the tribunal judiciary is so deployed as to ensure the appropriate degree of judicial scrutiny of decisions of the lower tier?

[92] Having considered, however, the judgment of Baroness Hale JSC, who has great experience in this field, and those of other members of the court, I have been persuaded that there is, at least until we have experience of how the new tribunal system is working in practice, the

need for some overall judicial supervision of the decisions of the Upper Tribunal, particularly in relation to refusals of permission to appeal to it, in order to guard against the risk that errors of law of real significance slip through the system.

Lord Brown

[99] The very fact that Parliament, by section 13(6) of the Tribunals, Courts and Enforcement Act 2007, has prescribed the same criteria for the grant of permission to appeal from the Upper Tribunal to the Court of Appeal as apply to second-tier appeals in the courts of England and Wales destroys any possibility of an absolutist argument to the effect that the rule of law requires, post-*Anisminic* ..., unrestricted judicial review over all unappealable decisions of courts or tribunals of limited jurisdiction to ensure that they are not permitted, unsupervised by the higher courts, to commit errors of law. The second-tier appeals approach expressly contemplates that some Upper Tribunal decisions, even though erroneous in point of law, will be refused leave to appeal on the basis that they raise no important point of principle or practice and that there is no other compelling reason to hear them. Understandably, it has never been suggested that, following a refusal of leave to appeal on this basis, the underlying decision is nonetheless judicially reviewable for error of law.

[100] If, then, the rule of law allows certain errors of law in substantive decisions of the Upper Tribunal on appeal from the First-tier Tribunal to go uncorrected, why as a matter of principle should it not similarly allow this in respect of decisions of the Upper Tribunal refusing leave to appeal to itself from the First-tier Tribunal? True it is, of course, that the refusal of leave to appeal will have deprived the party refused of a second substantive hearing. Realistically, however, the very fact that he was refused leave to appeal to the Upper Tribunal (by both tribunals) tends to indicate the unlikelihood of there having been a genuinely arguable error of law in the first place. And certainly this situation calls no less for a proportionate answer to the question arising as to the required scope of the court's supervisory jurisdiction to safeguard the rule of law. The rule of law is weakened, not strengthened, if a disproportionate part of the courts' resources is devoted to finding a very occasional grain of wheat on a threshing floor full of chaff.

The Supreme Court unanimously concluded that judicial review of the UT should be available only when the second-tier appeal criteria are met, and that those criteria were not met in the instant case.

The Supreme Court's judgment in *Cart* is very significant—both for what it does and does not do. As to the latter, we observed at 2.2.7 that in *Cart* the Supreme Court declines to engage with underlying questions concerning the scope of the UT's jurisdiction (other than by way of dismissing the lower courts' attempts to demarcate those powers). What the judgment *does* do is adopt a highly pragmatic approach by proceeding on the basis of an assessment of how much oversight of the tribunals system by the senior courts is necessary and appropriate. The conclusion at which the Supreme Court arrives—that judicial review should not lie unless the very narrow second-tier appeal criteria are satisfied—is heavily informed by the notion of 'proportionate dispute resolution'. That notion embodies the idea that the senior courts' limited judicial resources should be used wisely by exercising oversight of the UT only in very particular circumstances. This does not mean that the Supreme Court has turned its back on fundamental constitutional principles such as the rule of law. However, in *Cart*, that principle is refracted by the Supreme Court through the pragmatic prism of proportionate dispute resolution, rather than—as in the Court of Appeal's decision in *Cart*—through the doctrinal lens of jurisdictional error. In this way, the Supreme Court—bearing firmly in mind the limited adjudicative capacity of the senior courts—seeks to tailor the level of oversight of the UT to what the rule of law requires by taking account of the confidence that can be reposed in the tribunals system in the light of its independence and expertise. The Supreme Court's decision in *Cart* is now reflected in the Civil Procedure Rules, which have been amended to provide that in relevant circumstances permission to proceed with judicial review is to be granted only if the second-tier appeal criteria are satisfied (CPR 54.7A).

In *R (G)* v. *Upper Tribunal* [2016] EWHC 239 (Admin), it was argued for the Home Secretary that *Cart* is pertinent not only to the question whether permission for judicial review of the UT should be granted, but also to the nature of such review in cases in which permission is granted. More specifically, it was contended that the rationale of *Cart* required the UT's decisions to be reviewed on grounds that are more limited than usual. Walker J rejected that argument, holding that the reasoning in *Cart* applies only at the stage of deciding whether to grant permission, and not to the reviewing court's role in conducting review once permission has been granted. However, at the same time, it must be borne in mind that (as Walker J acknowledged) the reviewing court will exhibit appropriate deference to the UT in the light of its expertise. Moreover, as *R (Jones)* v. *First-tier Tribunal* [2013] UKSC 19, [2013] 2 AC 48 (on which see 2.2.9) shows, such deference may be heightened by the reviewing court's characterizing a given matter as a question of fact (so as to shield it from the rigours of error-of-law review) even if the same matter would be characterized by the UT as a question of law (so as to enable the UT to exercise sufficient oversight of the tribunals system).

18.5 Concluding remarks

The recent changes to the tribunals system set out in this chapter are far-reaching. It is undeniable that the system which exists today is organized along clearer, more logical, and more readily comprehensible lines than the arrangements which preceded it. The rationalization of tribunals is to be welcomed on a number of counts. Their independence has been enhanced, underlining their status as part of the adjudicative machinery of the state, rather than administrative tools of individual government departments. Meanwhile, the unified approach also creates an opportunity for better public understanding of and easier access to tribunals, through the creation of simple entry points into and clear pathways through the system.

However, as our discussion of the *Cart* case shows, the creation of the new tribunals system has also brought with it certain challenges and complications, raising fundamental questions about the place of tribunals within the wider legal system and, in particular, the relationship between tribunals and the rest of the judicial system. In his judgment in the Court of Appeal in *Cart* ([2010] EWCA Civ 859, [2011] QB 120 at [30]), Sedley LJ said:

> The tribunal system is designed to be so far as possible a self-sufficient structure, dealing internally with errors of law made at first instance and resorting to higher appellate authority only where a legal issue of difficulty or of principle requires it. By this means serious questions of law are channelled into the legal system without the need of post-*Anisminic* judicial review [*ie* judicial review that treats all errors of law as jurisdictional].

In this passage Sedley LJ puts his finger on the challenge that the establishment of the new tribunals system has created: namely, the striking of a suitable balance between according independence to and ensuring adequate oversight of that system. It is perhaps ironic, therefore, that Sedley LJ—in what might be regarded as a Freudian slip—talks of channelling certain cases from the tribunals system 'into the legal system'. The point, of course, is that tribunals now form a key element of the legal—in the sense of the judicial—system. It is perhaps for that reason that the senior courts found *Cart* so difficult, in that it required them to elaborate the nature of a new interface between the judicial system's component parts. What we therefore see in *Cart*, as the courts grapple with this task, is a variety of different attempts to retool or supplement the principles of *administrative* law so as to render them suitable to judicial supervision of *judicial* decision-making.

FURTHER RESOURCES

Cane, *Administrative Tribunals and Adjudication* (Oxford 2009)

Carnwath, 'Tribunal Justice—A New Start' [2009] *PL* 48

Cm 6243, *Transforming Public Services: Complaints, Redress and Tribunals* (2004) *http://webarchive.nationalarchives.gov.uk/+/http://www.dca.gov.uk/pubs/adminjust/transformfull.pdf*

Elliott and Thomas, 'Tribunal Justice and Proportionate Dispute Resolution' [2012] *CLJ* 297

Hickinbottom, 'Tribunal Reform: A New Coherent System' [2010] *JR* 103

Leggatt, *Tribunals for Users: One Service, One System* (London 2001) *http://webarchive.nationalarchives.gov.uk/+/http://www.tribunals-review.org.uk/leggatthtm/leg-00.htm*

Mitchell, 'Judicial Review, But Not As We Know It: Judicial Review in the Upper Tribunal' [2010] *JR* 112

Richardson and Genn, 'Tribunals in Transition: Resolution or Adjudication?' [2007] *PL* 116

Website of HM Courts and Tribunals Service *https://www.gov.uk/government/organisations/hm-courts-and-tribunals-service*

19 OMBUDSMEN

19.1 Introduction

The scale upon which the state—in the form of myriad government and other public bodies—interacts with individuals is immense. Millions of decisions are taken every year, from the issuing of parking tickets to the granting of asylum. Just as the number and variety of such interactions are huge, so is the range of things that can go wrong and which might be the legitimate subject of complaint. The diverse forms that administrative action and administrative failure can and do take mean that no single mechanism can be a panacea when it comes to providing redress and upholding good practice. We have already encountered a number of such mechanisms, including courts, tribunals, and inquiries. There may therefore seem to be little need for yet another mechanism, in the form of ombudsmen. However, as we explain in this chapter, ombudsmen occupy a vital and distinctive place within the administrative justice system, complementing rather than duplicating the work undertaken by other facets of that system.

19.1.1 Ombudsmen in the UK

Although the origins of 'ombudsmen' can be traced to nineteenth-century Sweden, it was not until the 1960s that the concept was embraced by the common law world. A wide range of ombudsman schemes exist in the UK today, including those that deal with complaints against private sector operators such as estate agents, financial services providers, and lawyers. However, our concern in this chapter is with 'public sector ombudsmen'. In seeking to understand what that term means, a useful starting point is supplied by Collcutt and Hourihan, *Review of the Public Sector Ombudsmen in England: A Report by the Cabinet Office* (London 2000) (hereinafter the 'Collcutt Review') at [1.11]:

> Public sector ombudsmen in England were created by statute, are independent from the Government and are impartial in their dealings with complainants and those complained about. They exist to consider complaints by citizens that public organisations (or those acting on their behalf) have caused them injustice by maladministration.

Some of the UK's several public sector ombudsman schemes have a sector-specific remit, such as the Adjudicator's Office (which deals with complaints in relation to HM Revenue and Customs) and the Health Service Ombudsman (who is concerned with complaints concerning health care provided by both the National Health Service and private organizations in England). Other schemes have much broader remits: the Parliamentary Ombudsman investigates complaints of maladministration by UK government departments and a wide range of other UK and English public bodies, while the Local Government Ombudsmen fulfil a similar role in relation to English local authorities.

In addition, there are separate ombudsmen schemes in the devolved nations. Those schemes—to varying extents—adopt an integrated approach, such that a broad range of administrative bodies are swept into the jurisdiction of a single ombudsman, rather than—as in England—retaining separate schemes for different types of public bodies. For instance, the Scottish Public Services Ombudsman and the Public Services Ombudsman for Wales have broad remits covering such matters as local authorities, Scottish and Welsh public bodies, the devolved administrations, and healthcare. In 2016, Northern Ireland adopted a similar model.

Our principal focus in this chapter is on the Parliamentary Ombudsman, although we refer to other schemes for the purpose of comparison. The legislation which establishes some of the ombudsmen schemes uses the term 'commissioner' rather than 'ombudsman': the Parliamentary Ombudsmen is, for instance, formally known as the Parliamentary Commissioner for Administration. However, the term 'commissioner' has largely fallen into disuse in this context, and in this chapter we use the term 'ombudsman' throughout. A final preliminary point that should be noted is that although the Parliamentary and Health Service Ombudsman (PHSO) schemes are rooted in separate pieces of legislation, they are operationally fused, a single individual—served by a single administrative organization—filling both offices.

19.1.2 The need for and role of ombudsmen

The establishment of public sector ombudsmen in the 1960s occurred in a particular legal and political context: as Bradley [1980] *CLJ* 304 at 309 puts it, 'at a time when administrative law was failing to give the individual effective protection, the creation of an Ombudsman was needed to make possible the development of a new equity, suitable for a much governed nation'. Former Parliamentary and Health Service Ombudsman Sir Cecil Clothier [1986] *PL* 204 at 205 notes that concerns relating to Parliament were also part of the impetus for the adoption of an ombudsman system: the former's focus on 'massive and detailed legislation' meant that it could not devote its time to 'those problems of individuals which lack a national or international dimension'.

Against that background, the Parliamentary Ombudsman—the first Ombudsman to be created in the UK—was conceived, as Drewry and Harlow (1990) 53 *MLR* 745 at 753 put it, as 'an adjunct to the MP's traditional and cherished role as grievance-chaser on behalf of constituents'. Richard Crossman MP, the government Minister responsible for piloting what became the Parliamentary Commissioner Act 1967 through the House of Commons, appeared to share this view, stating (HC Deb 18 October 1966, vol 734, col 49) that the Ombudsman would be a 'servant of the House'. However, Crossman also said (col 44) that the Ombudsman's investigations would provide the 'cutting edge of a really impartial and really searching investigation into the workings of Whitehall'. These remarks reveal an ambivalence—shared by many others—about the Ombudsman's role. Is her function to bolster the 'grievance-chasing' role of constituency MPs, securing redress in individual cases of maladministration? Or is her concern principally with oversight of the administration at a general level, identifying problems and recommending changes so as to raise standards?

QUESTIONS

- Which of these roles is more important, in your view?
- Why?

This tension is noted by Seneviratne, *Ombudsmen: Public Services and Administrative Justice* (London 2002), who, building on the work of Heede, *European Ombudsman: Redress and Control at Union Level* (The Hague 2000), distinguishes between 'redress' and 'control' conceptions of ombudsmen's roles. Of the former, Seneviratne writes:

> Redress model ombudsmen are created when the traditional means of redress are perceived to be insufficient. Thus, additional means are sought for the regulation of the relationship between the administration and the individual. This insufficiency could arise because the matters are not justiciable, or because of the obstacles inherent in the court process. Ombudsman schemes adopting this model are often seen as advocates for citizens. Sometimes these ombudsmen are given powers to conduct own-initiative investigations, but this is an adjunct to their redress function. Own-initiative investigations are triggered by complaints, which draw attention to problems that need to be investigated on a large scale.

The control model, Seneviratne goes on, is 'fundamentally different':

> These schemes are created primarily to regulate the way standards are created and understood by a public authority. These ombudsmen therefore supervise the rules and the way they are interpreted. Their concern is with issues of supervision and accountability. For these ombudsmen, the ability to conduct own-initiative investigations is of major importance and complainants are informants only. Nor need there be any suspicion of a wrongful act in order for the ombudsmen to examine the functioning of the administration, as the focus is the prevention of administrative failures. The concern of these ombudsmen is the general protection of fundamental rights and individual liberties.

It does not, however, follow that the Ombudsman's role can or should be conceived of as being wholly concerned with *either* redress *or* control. For instance, Ann Abraham, who was the Parliamentary and Health Service Ombudsman from 2002 to 2011, said (HC9, *Improving Public Service: A Matter of Principle* (2008)):

> My Office has two key strategic objectives. The first is to help individuals who bring their complaints to my Office. I want to provide an independent, high quality and accessible complaint handling service that rights individual wrongs. The second key objective is to offer a wider public benefit. I consider it a fundamental part of my role to use the learning from my Office's 40 years of handling large numbers of complaints to help drive improvements in the delivery of public services and to help inform public policy.

Thus, the redress function, as well as being important in itself, feeds into the control function by enabling the Ombudsman to see where—and why—things have gone wrong at a grass-roots level. Ideally, then, there ought to be a virtuous circle, whereby systemic problems are highlighted by relevant investigations, such that the Ombudsman's reports serve as a basis not just for individual redress but wider service improvement. An example of precisely this is furnished by an investigation into how consular staff failed to provide adequate support to a British woman who was sexually assaulted while in Egypt, and into the subsequent handling by the Foreign and Commonwealth Office (FCO) of complaints relating to the consular response. Upholding the complaint, the Ombudsman concluded that there had been failures to provide the necessary help and advice, and insensitivity to the complainant's needs. The Ombudsman noted ((HC 837, *Sexual Assault Abroad* (2013) at 3) that following the investigation:

> The FCO have changed their approach to helping British nationals who are the victims of sexual assault abroad. As a result of the Ombudsman's investigation the FCO have reviewed the way they handle complaints, putting the needs and feelings of the complainant at the centre of the process. The new culture will focus on encouraging staff to approach complaints as an opportunity for the FCO to improve the service they provide.

Ombudsmen can also use the number of complaints received about a given matter as a barometer, seeking to draw out systemic failures that might account for a particularly high volume of problems. For instance, in 2014–15, the Health Service Ombudsman investigated 221 complaints relating to hospital discharges, upholding over half of them. A catalogue of problems was revealed, including failures to assess patients properly prior to discharge, to tell relatives that (often vulnerable) loved ones had been discharged, and to put in place adequate (or any) home-care plans. The results were often extremely distressing, some patients having been taken home by ambulance and left alone, unable to eat, drink, care for themselves, or get to a toilet. In the light of the individual investigations that were carried out, the Ombudsman published a thematic report in 2016 drawing attention to nine particularly serious cases, using them to identify systemic issues including inadequate co-ordination between acute health and social care organizations and failures by hospitals properly to balance vulnerable patients' interests against the need to free up beds.

A government-commissioned review of public sector ombudsmen (Robert Gordon, *Better to Serve the Public: Proposals to Restructure, Reform, Renew and Reinvigorate Public Services Ombudsmen* (2014) (the Gordon Review)) recently concluded that the control function is vital and should be augmented. In particular, the Review said (at [37]–[38]):

> [C]omplaints can be a powerful tool in identifying public service delivery failures, informing their remedy, and informing more effective future policy and delivery design.
>
> It is for Government to take the lead in making these changes, but the ombudsman can support the development of such an approach, and sustain it over time by drawing attention to good practice at the pinnacle of the complaints structure, demonstrating the benefits of paying close attention to the lessons to be drawn from the [information arising from complaints] and reinforcing culture change wherever necessary and appropriate. I recommend that the reformed ombudsman service should be explicitly provided with a duty to discharge such a role; the extent of its involvement would be for Government to agree and propose to Parliament in bringing forward any modernising legislation.

19.1.3 Ombudsmen in a changing administrative landscape

We have already observed that the Parliamentary Ombudsman was established in the late 1960s in light of concerns about the abilities of the courts and Parliament to safeguard citizens' interests *vis-à-vis* the executive. However, as the developments charted throughout this book indicate, the landscape within which public administration occurs and is regulated has changed almost beyond recognition in the intervening decades.

For instance, the role of judicial review is more prominent today than it was when the Parliamentary Ombudsman was established—although this does not mean that the Ombudsman's role is now less important. While it is true, as Bradley [1980] *CLJ* 304 at 324–9 observes, that there is an overlap between the types of complaints which may be investigated by the Ombudsman and those that can be subjected to judicial review, the two mechanisms differ markedly. First, the Ombudsman (as we explain at 19.3) is able to investigate allegations—of rudeness, delay, and so on—which may not disclose illegality for judicial review purposes. Second, many of the factors which deter recourse to judicial review—in particular, cost—do not apply to the Ombudsman. Third, significant procedural factors distinguish the Ombudsman's approach from that of the Administrative Court: for instance, the Ombudsman adopts an inquisitorial, rather than an adversarial, approach. Meanwhile, outcomes can be different: on the one hand, the Ombudsman cannot compel redress; on the other hand, the Ombudsman can recommend forms of redress—*eg* the setting up of a compensation scheme or the making of an apology—that are broader than those open to courts. Fourth, unlike the courts, the Ombudsman—which, thanks to the informal nature of the processes followed, is able to engage in an ongoing constructive dialogue with government—is sometimes able to negotiate and secure systemic changes to administrative practice. It is perhaps this ability of the ombudsman system to address the wider picture, rather than focusing simply on individual complaints, which distinguishes it most profoundly from curial scrutiny of public administration—and which, in turn, underscores most effectively the usefulness of ombudsmen, the increasing prominence of judicial review notwithstanding.

What of tribunals? It might be thought that the susceptibility of so many administrative decisions to appeal undermines the need for the Ombudsman. However, as we explain at 19.3.2, the Parliamentary Commissioner Act 1967 countenances recourse to the Ombudsman only where there is no possibility of appeal to a tribunal or where it would not be reasonable to expect the individual to exercise a right of appeal. The Ombudsman is therefore intended to complement, not compete with, appellate bodies, filling gaps where the tribunal system is incomplete or inapt. Moreover, tribunals and the Ombudsman are complementary in that the matters over which they have jurisdiction are to some extent distinct, the former often being empowered to examine the merits of decisions, the latter focusing on the quality of the administrative process—although it must be acknowledged (see further at 19.3.1) that this distinction does not, indeed cannot, exist as a bright line.

19.2 Bodies subject to investigation

Only bodies listed in sch 2 of the 1967 Act can be investigated by the Parliamentary Ombudsman. Listed bodies include UK government departments, along with a huge number of other public bodies such as HM Revenue and Customs, the Environment Agency, the Food Standards Agency, the Land Registry, the Information Commissioner, the Civil Aviation Authority, and the Parole Board. Section 4(2) enables the list of public bodies in sch 2 to be adjusted by means of making Orders in Council. This, however, is a cumbersome process; the Public Administration Select Committee (PASC) (HC448, *Ombudsman Issues* (2002–03)), among others, strongly recommended that the legislation should adopt a generic definition of the types of bodies amenable to investigation by the Ombudsman, subject to specific exceptions. In a paper entitled *Review of the Public Sector Ombudsmen in England: A Consultation Paper* (London 2000) at [2.19]–[2.20], the Cabinet Office recognized that such an approach would 'remove the need for regular amendments to the legislation as new bodies are created and existing bodies dissolved' as well as making the 'whole jurisdiction issue more transparent'. It went on to note, however, that, '[i]n order for this to work … the legislation would need to be clear as to the types of public bodies which were within jurisdiction (subject to any specified exclusion). Some types of public body are easy to define generically—*eg* government departments and agencies, NHS Trusts, and local authorities. But others are not.' These concerns are well-founded: in a different context, we saw in ch 4 that trying to define principles which determine what counts as a public body is fraught with difficulty. It is perhaps unsurprising, then, that although the solution adopted in the 1967 Act is rather cumbersome, it is one that the UK's other ombudsman systems—including the integrated schemes in Northern Ireland, Scotland, and Wales—have also adopted. In this way, there can be certainty about which bodies do and do not fall within the remit of the various ombudsmen schemes.

19.3   Matters subject to investigation

Section 5 of the 1967 Act makes provision concerning the matters which may be investigated by the Ombudsman:

(1) Subject to the provisions of this section, the Commissioner may investigate any action taken by or on behalf of a government department or other authority to which this Act applies, being action taken in the exercise of administrative functions of that department or authority, in any case where—

  (a) a written complaint is duly made to a member of the House of Commons by a member of the public who claims to have sustained injustice in consequence of maladministration in connection with the action so taken; and

  (b) the complaint is referred to the Commissioner, with the consent of the person who made it, by a member of that House with a request to conduct an investigation thereon.

(1A) Subsection (1C) of this section applies if—

  (a) a written complaint is duly made to a member of the House of Commons by a member of the public who claims that a person has failed to perform a relevant duty owed by him to the member of the public, and

  (b) the complaint is referred to the Commissioner, with the consent of the person who made it, by a member of the House of Commons with a request to conduct an investigation into it.

(1B) For the purposes of subsection (1A) of this section a relevant duty is a duty imposed by any of these—

  (a) a code of practice issued under section 32 of the Domestic Violence, Crime and Victims Act 2004 (code of practice for victims), or

  (b) sections 35 to 44 of that Act (duties of local probation boards in connection with victims of sexual or violent offences).

(1C) If this subsection applies, the Commissioner may investigate the complaint.

(2) Except as hereinafter provided, the Commissioner shall not conduct an investigation under this Act in respect of any of the following matters, that is to say—

(a) any action in respect of which the person aggrieved has or had a right of appeal, reference or review to or before a tribunal constituted by or under any enactment or by virtue of Her Majesty's prerogative;

(b) any action in respect of which the person aggrieved has or had a remedy by way of proceedings in any court of law:

Provided that the Commissioner may conduct an investigation notwithstanding that the person aggrieved has or had such a right or remedy if satisfied that in the particular circumstances it is not reasonable to expect him to resort or have resorted to it.

(3) Without prejudice to subsection (2) of this section, the Commissioner shall not conduct an investigation under subsection (1) of this section in respect of any such action or matter as is described in Schedule 3 to this Act.

(4) Her Majesty may by Order in Council amend the said Schedule 3 so as to exclude from the provisions of that Schedule such actions or matters as may be described in the Order; and any statutory instrument made by virtue of this subsection shall be subject to annulment in pursuance of a resolution of either House of Parliament.

(4A) Without prejudice to subsection (2) of this section, the Commissioner shall not conduct an investigation pursuant to a complaint under subsection (1A) of this section in respect of—

(a) action taken by or with the authority of the Secretary of State for the purposes of protecting the security of the State, including action so taken with respect to passports, or

(b) any action or matter described in any of paragraphs 1 to 4 and 6A to 11 of Schedule 3 to this Act.

(4B) Her Majesty may by Order in Council amend subsection (4A) of this section so as to exclude from paragraph (a) or (b) of that subsection such actions or matters as may be described in the Order.

(4C) Any statutory instrument made by virtue of subsection (4B) of this section shall be subject to annulment in pursuance of a resolution of either House of Parliament.

(5) In determining whether to initiate, continue or discontinue an investigation under this Act, the Commissioner shall, subject to the foregoing provisions of this section, act in accordance with his own discretion; and any question whether a complaint is duly made under this Act shall be determined by the Commissioner …

These provisions raise three issues that warrant further consideration.

19.3.1 'Maladministration'

Subject to the distinct arrangements set out in s 5(1A)(a) concerning non-performance of certain duties owed to victims of sexual and violent offences, the effect of s 5(1)(a) is to limit the Ombudsman's investigatory powers to claims of injustice sustained in consequence of 'maladministration'. Meanwhile, s 12(3) provides that

nothing in this Act authorises or requires the Commissioner to question the merits of a decision taken without maladministration by a government department or other authority in the exercise of a discretion vested in that department or authority.

Taken together, these provisions appear to envisage a bright-line distinction between the administrative process (which is open to investigation by the Ombudsman) and the substance or merits of decisions and policies which are the fruit of that process (which may not be investigated). This is a familiar distinction which (see chs 1 and 8) has classically shaped the courts' supervisory jurisdiction; but we know from that context that the line between process and merits is difficult, if not impossible, to draw cleanly. Harlow (1978) 41 *MLR* 446 at 453 also doubts whether it is a sensible distinction in the present context, but recognizes that its roots are deep:

> To investigate maladministration without questioning either the policies which underlie the administrator's actions or the legal framework of those actions effectively confines the investigation to questions of procedure. Yet there is in English political theory a well recognised, if furry, boundary between the executive (administrative) functions of government and the prerogative (policy making or political) powers. Responsibility for the second is thought to be vested in the Government, answerable through the doctrine of Ministerial Responsibility to Parliament. Government and Parliament alike watch suspiciously for trespass on political territory.

Today, the Ombudsman judges whether maladministration has occurred by reference to the following 'principles of good administration', which are largely—albeit not exclusively—process-oriented:

1. **Getting it right:** acting in accordance with the law and with regard for the rights of those concerned; acting in accordance with the public body's policy and guidance (published or internal); taking proper account of established good practice; providing effective services, using appropriately trained and competent staff; taking reasonable decisions, based on all relevant considerations.

2. **Being customer focused:** ensuring people can access services easily; informing customers what they can expect and what the public body expects of them; keeping to its commitments, including any published service standards; dealing with people helpfully, promptly and sensitively, bearing in mind their individual circumstances; responding to customers' needs flexibly, including, where appropriate, co-ordinating a response with other service providers.

3. **Being open and accountable:** being open and clear about policies and procedures and ensuring that information, and any advice provided, is clear, accurate and complete; stating its criteria for decision making and giving reasons for decisions; handling information properly and appropriately; keeping proper and appropriate records; taking responsibility for its actions.

4. **Acting fairly and proportionately:** treating people impartially, with respect and courtesy; treating people without unlawful discrimination or prejudice, and ensuring no conflict of interests; dealing with people and issues objectively and consistently; ensuring that decisions and actions are proportionate, appropriate and fair.

5. **Putting things right:** acknowledging mistakes and apologising where appropriate; putting mistakes right quickly and effectively; providing clear and timely information on how and when to appeal or complain; operating an effective complaints procedure, which includes offering a fair and appropriate remedy when a complaint is upheld.

6. **Seeking continuous improvement:** reviewing policies and procedures regularly to ensure they are effective; asking for feedback and using it to improve services and performance; ensuring that the public body learns lessons from complaints and uses these to improve services and performance.

It is apparent from the above that the concept of maladministration encompasses requirements—such as being helpful, sensitive, and polite—breach of which would not be grounds for judicial review. In this sense, then, the Ombudsman is able to address a broader range of administrative failings than that which is relevant in the courts. This point clearly emerges from the 'debt of honour' case (see generally Kirkham (2006) 69 *MLR* 792) in which the government announced the establishment of a compensation scheme for 'British' civilians interned by the Japanese during the Second World War, only to 'clarify' subsequently that the scheme would be limited to those who had been born in the UK or with at least one parent or grandparent who had been born in the UK. In *R (Association of British Civilian Internees: Far East Region)* v. *Secretary of State for Defence* [2003] EWCA Civ 473, [2003] QB 1397, the Court of Appeal held that the original statement did not give rise to a legitimate expectation that restricted the government's capacity subsequently to narrow (or 'clarify') the eligibility criteria. But the Ombudsman later concluded that the way in which the scheme was announced constituted maladministration in that the ministerial statement was so unclear and imprecise as to give rise to confusion and misunderstanding (HC324, 'A Debt of Honour': The Ex Gratia Scheme for British Groups Interned by the Japanese during the Second World War (2005–06) at [199]).

The term 'maladministration' is a relatively broad and flexible one, but two points are worth noting in this regard. First, ombudsmen other than the Parliamentary Ombudsman— including the Health Service, Welsh, and Local Government Ombudsmen—are not restricted to investigating complaints of maladministration, and may also intervene in relation to 'service failure' and 'failure to provide a service'. Second, however flexible the concept of maladministration may be, it is not *infinitely* elastic, since it is ultimately open to the courts to set its limits via judicial review—a matter that we consider at 19.4.4.

Finally, it should be noted that s 5(1)(a) of the Parliamentary Commissioner Act 1967 limits the Ombudsman's jurisdiction to situations in which 'injustice' has resulted from maladministration. Sedley J took a broad approach in *R* v. *Parliamentary Commissioner for Administration, ex parte Balchin (No 1)* [1997] JPL 917 at 926, endorsing the view of De Smith, Woolf, and Jowell, *Judicial Review of Administrative Action* (London 1999) at [1.102], quoting Richard Crossman MP, that the term should cover 'not merely injury redressible in a court of law, but also "the sense of outrage aroused by unfair or incompetent administra-tion, even where the complainant has suffered no actual loss"'—a definition which, Sedley J noted, means that 'the defence familiar in legal proceedings, that because the outcome would have been the same in any event there has been no redressible wrong, does not run in an investigation by the [Ombudsman]'.

19.3.2 Other modes of redress

Section 5(2) indicates that the Ombudsman will generally not entertain complaints in rela-tion to matters that could be the subject of appeal to a tribunal or proceedings in a court. However, the Ombudsman has discretion in this area, and may investigate if satisfied that it would not be reasonable to expect the individual to pursue such forms of redress. As Lord Sumption explained in *Application by JR55 for Judicial Review* [2016] UKSC 22 at [17], the discretion is most likely to be exercisable 'where litigation would not be worth the cost and trouble involved' or where 'the complainant is looking for explanations' rather than the sort of relief that judicial proceedings might offer. The exercise of the discretion is, though, itself subject to judicial review, meaning that if the Ombudsman unreasonably (or otherwise unlawfully) decides to investigate notwithstanding the possibility of a judicial review challenge or the exercise of a right of appeal, such a decision may be quashed: *R v. Commissioner for Local Administration, ex parte Croydon London Borough Council* [1989] 1 All ER 1033.

From the perspective of the aggrieved individual, navigating the administrative justice system and working out how best to pursue a complaint can be a difficult matter. This raises questions about the extent to which the 'system' (such as it is) is sufficiently integrated. For instance, a complaint might initially be pursued by way of a claim for judicial review or a complaint to—triggering an investigation by—the Ombudsman, but it might subsequently become evident that the matter could better be dealt with in some other way. Against this background, Kirkham (HC421, *The Parliamentary Ombudsman: Withstanding the Test of Time* (2006–07) at 11) argues that more thought needs to be given to the relationship between the Ombudsman and the courts, and that a more 'holistic' approach is required:

> [W]hen it becomes clear during legal proceedings that a case could be better dealt with by an ombudsman, it would be helpful if the court could transfer a case without prejudice to the complainant's legal rights. Likewise, when an ombudsman discovers that the outcome of an investigation hinges upon an unresolved legal question, then proceedings could possibly be speeded up were the ombudsman able to refer the issue of law to the courts. Currently, in this area such proportionate redress is reliant upon the common sense of the parties involved and the flexibility of procedural rules. There are limits in both regards, and legislative change could provide a much needed boost to the ease with which complainants receive redress.

In 2011, the Law Commission (Law Com No 329, *Public Services Ombudsmen* (2011) at [3.88] recommended

> that the Administrative Court should have an express power to stay an action before it, in order to allow a public services ombudsman to investigate or otherwise dispose of the matter.

It explained its thinking (at [3.82]–[3.83]) in the following terms:

> We accept that the courts are the primary forum within which to vindicate rights. We see the public services ombudsmen primarily as institutions for administrative justice rather than as human rights defenders. We suggest that this would be a factor that would guide a court's decision whether or not to stay. After the ombudsman has (or has not) conducted an investigation, it would be possible for either party to return to the Administrative Court and ask the court to lift the stay, grant permission (if the stay were granted before permission granted) and allow the application to proceed to a hearing in order to deal with any administrative illegality.
>
> We suggest that it is precisely due to the confusion caused by the complexity of redress mechanisms that our suggested stay procedure should exist. The stay procedure proposed would allow matters to be re-allocated, where it appears to the Administrative Court that a public services ombudsman is the more appropriate forum.

Underlining its vision of an integrated system, the Law Commission also proposed (at [4.95]) that the Ombudsman should be able to refer questions of law to the Administrative Court. The idea is not that the Ombudsman's investigation be transferred to the Court, and so transformed into a legal dispute; rather, the intention is that the Court would have an opportunity authoritatively to determine a point of law relevant to an investigation, and that the Ombudsman would then be able to continue with the investigation, with the benefit of the Administrative Court's ruling on the question of law. However, the Gordon Review did not take up these ideas, and, as a result, they were mentioned nowhere in the consultation that took place in the light of the Review (Cabinet Office, *A Public Service Ombudsman* (London 2015)).

QUESTIONS

- Should a system enabling the Administrative Court to refer matters to a public services ombudsman (PSO) be established?
- What would be the advantages and disadvantages of such an innovation?

19.3.3 Discretion to investigate

The Ombudsman is not obliged to investigate matters which are within her jurisdiction: s 5(1) says that she 'may' do so. There have been judicial suggestions that this discretion is an unfettered one. For instance, in *R (Mencap)* v. *Parliamentary and Health Service Ombudsman* [2011] EWHC 3351 (Admin) at [13], that view was taken by Mitting J in construing s 3(1) of the Health Service Commissioners Act 1993, which, in respect of the Health Service Ombudsman, makes provision equivalent to that which s 5(1) of the 1967 Act makes in relation to the Parliamentary Ombudsman.

The better view, however, is that the discretion of the Ombudsman whether (and if so how) to investigate, while broad, is not unlimited, and that its exercise is therefore—at least in principle—susceptible to judicial review. The leading case is *R v. Parliamentary Commissioner for Administration, ex parte Dyer* [1994] 1 WLR 621. The claimant sought judicial review of the Ombudsman's decision to investigate only certain aspects of her complaint, but it was contended on behalf of the Ombudsman that both the drafting of the 1967 Act and the Ombudsman's accountability to (what is now) the House of Commons Public Administration and Constitutional Affairs Committee (PACAC) rendered judicial review inappropriate. Simon Brown LJ (with whom Buckley J agreed) said (at 625) that he would

> unhesitatingly reject this argument. Many in government are answerable to Parliament and yet answerable also to the supervisory jurisdiction of this court. I see nothing about the Commissioner's role or the statutory framework within which he operates so singular as to take him wholly outside the purview of judicial review.

Nevertheless, Simon Brown LJ conceded (at 626) that successful judicial review of decisions whether and, if so, how to investigate would be rare:

> The intended width of these discretions is made strikingly clear by the legislature: under section 5(5), when determining whether to initiate, continue or discontinue an investigation, the Commissioner shall 'act in accordance with his own discretion;' under section 7(2), 'the procedure for conducting an investigation shall be such as the Commissioner considers appropriate in the circumstances of the case.' Bearing in mind too that the exercise of these particular discretions inevitably involves a high degree of subjective judgment, it follows that it will always be difficult to mount an effective challenge on what may be called the conventional ground of *Wednesbury* unreasonableness.

Applying this approach, it was found that the Ombudsman had not abused his discretion. In *R (Jeremiah) v. Parliamentary and Health Service Ombudsman* [2013] EWHC 1085 (Admin) at [30], Collins J followed *Dyer*—and, in doing so, refused to 'go so far as Mitting J appears to have done in [*Mencap*] in indicating that there is unfettered discretion'—but emphasized that 'such fetters as there are are exceedingly loosely applied' and that the Ombudsman's discretion in this regard is 'very wide'.

19.4 The conduct and consequences of investigations

It is evident from the foregoing discussion that the Ombudsman's investigations are inquisitorial in nature, and adopt an approach which is quite distinct from court proceedings. Moreover, the Ombudsman has considerable discretion in relation to the procedure she adopts, and is not necessarily bound by the usual principles of natural justice (see, *eg Dyer* [1994] 1 WLR 621, in which it was held that natural justice did not require the Ombudsman to show a copy of his draft report to the complainant, notwithstanding that the government department concerned *had* been shown the report). In this section, we focus on a number of specific issues concerning the undertaking and consequences of investigations by the Ombudsman, to which the following provisions of the 1967 Act—along with s 5 of the same Act, which is set out at 19.3—are relevant.

6—(1) A complaint under this Act may be made by any individual, or by any body of persons whether incorporated or not, not being—

    (a) a local authority or other authority or body constituted for purposes of the public service or of local government or for the purposes of carrying on under national ownership any industry or undertaking or part of an industry or undertaking;

    (b) any other authority or body within subsection (1A) below.

(1A) An authority or body is within this subsection if—

    (a) its members are appointed by—

        (i)   Her Majesty;

        (ii) any Minister of the Crown;

        (iii) any government department;

        (iv) the Scottish Ministers;

        (v) the First Minister; or

        (vi) the Lord Advocate, or

    (b) its revenues consist wholly or mainly of—

        (i)   money provided by Parliament; or

        (ii) sums payable out of the Scottish Consolidated Fund (directly or indirectly)...

(3) A complaint shall not be entertained under this Act unless it is made to a member of the House of Commons not later than twelve months from the day on which the person aggrieved first had notice of the matters alleged in the complaint; but the Commissioner may conduct an investigation pursuant to a complaint not made within that period if he considers that there are special circumstances which make it proper to do so...

7—(1) Where the Commissioner proposes to conduct an investigation pursuant to a complaint under section 5(1) of this Act, he shall afford to the principal officer of the department or authority concerned, and to any person who is alleged in the complaint to have taken or authorised the action complained of, an opportunity to comment on any allegations contained in the complaint.

(1A) Where the Commissioner proposes to conduct an investigation pursuant to a complaint under section 5(1A) of this Act, he shall give the person to whom the complaint relates an opportunity to comment on any allegations contained in the complaint.

(2) Every such investigation shall be conducted in private, but except as aforesaid the procedure for conducting an investigation shall be such as the Commissioner considers appropriate in the circumstances of the case; and without prejudice to the generality of the foregoing provision the Commissioner may obtain information from such persons and in such manner, and make such inquiries, as he thinks fit, and may determine whether any person may be represented, by counsel or solicitor or otherwise, in the investigation …

8—(1) For the purposes of an investigation under section 5(1) of this Act the Commissioner may require any Minister, officer or member of the department or authority concerned or any other person who in his opinion is able to furnish information or produce documents relevant to the investigation to furnish any such information or produce any such document.

(1A) For the purposes of an investigation pursuant to a complaint under section 5(1A) of this Act the Commissioner may require any person who in his opinion is able to furnish information or produce documents relevant to the investigation to furnish any such information or produce any such document.

(2) For the purposes of any investigation under this Act the Commissioner shall have the same powers as the Court in respect of the attendance and examination of witnesses (including the administration of oaths or affirmations and the examination of witnesses abroad) and in respect of the production of documents.

(3) No obligation to maintain secrecy or other restriction upon the disclosure of information obtained by or furnished to persons in Her Majesty's service, whether imposed by any enactment or by any rule of law, shall apply to the disclosure of information for the purposes of an investigation under this Act; and the Crown shall not be entitled in relation to any such investigation to any such privilege in respect of the production of documents or the giving of evidence as is allowed by law in legal proceedings.

(4) No person shall be required or authorised by virtue of this Act to furnish any information or answer any question relating to proceedings of the Cabinet or of any committee of the Cabinet or to produce so much of any document as relates to such proceedings; and for the purposes of this subsection a certificate issued by the Secretary of the Cabinet with the approval of the Prime Minister and certifying that any information, question, document or part of a document so relates shall be conclusive.

(5) Subject to subsection (3) of this section, no person shall be compelled for the purposes of an investigation under this Act to give any evidence or produce any document which he could not be compelled to give or produce in civil proceedings before the Court.

9—(1) If any person without lawful excuse obstructs the Commissioner or any officer of the Commissioner in the performance of his functions under this Act, or is guilty of any act or omission in relation to any investigation under this Act which, if that investigation were a proceeding in the Court, would constitute contempt of court, the Commissioner may certify the offence to the Court …

10—(1) In any case where the Commissioner conducts an investigation under this Act or decides not to conduct such an investigation, he shall send to the member of the House of Commons by whom the request for investigation was made (or if he is no longer a member of that House, to such member of that House as the Commissioner thinks appropriate) a report of the results of the investigation or, as the case may be, a statement of his reasons for not conducting an investigation.

(2) In any case where the Commissioner conducts an investigation under section 5(1) of this Act, he shall also send a report of the results of the investigation to the principal officer of the department or authority concerned and to any other person who is alleged in the relevant complaint to have taken or authorised the action complained of.

(2A) In any case where the Commissioner conducts an investigation pursuant to a complaint under section 5(1A) of this Act, he shall also send a report of the results of the investigation to the person to whom the complaint relates.

(3) If, after conducting an investigation under section 5(1) of this Act, it appears to the Commissioner that injustice has been caused to the person aggrieved in consequence of maladministration and that the injustice has not been, or will not be, remedied, he may, if he thinks fit, lay before each House of Parliament a special report upon the case.

(3A) If, after conducting an investigation pursuant to a complaint under section 5(1A) of this Act, it appears to the Commissioner that—

(a) the person to whom the complaint relates has failed to perform a relevant duty owed by him to the person aggrieved, and

(b) the failure has not been, or will not be, remedied,

the Commissioner may, if he thinks fit, lay before each House of Parliament a special report upon the case.

(3B) For the purposes of subsection (3A) of this section 'relevant duty' has the meaning given by section 5(1B) of this Act.

(4) The Commissioner shall annually lay before each House of Parliament a general report on the performance of his functions under this Act and may from time to time lay before each House of Parliament such other reports with respect to those functions as he thinks fit.

19.4.1 Own-initiative investigations

It is clear from s 5(1) and (1A) (set out at 19.3) that the Parliamentary Ombudsman may not investigate on her own initiative, but only upon receiving a complaint. The Collcutt Review (at [6.13]–[6.15]) concluded that this state of affairs was satisfactory:

It has been suggested that the ombudsmen should be given powers to be able to investigate on his own initiative—many overseas ombudsmen are able to do this (though they rarely do) and the argument for it is that it would allow problems to be addressed where no individual has complained. An own-initiative investigation could be a quicker way to tackle a perceived problem. The ombudsmen tell us that they do not feel encumbered by any lack of powers and have generally been able to investigate on the basis of a complaint where they had any concerns. They would be concerned that own-initiative investigations would alter significantly their dealings with bodies under jurisdiction. However, the ombudsmen would value an extension of their powers to allow investigation of maladministration at the request of a public authority under their jurisdiction. We believe that any power for the ombudsmen to initiate an investigation without a complaint will make them vulnerable to external pressure to examine alleged systemic weaknesses. An ombudsman's function must remain grounded in addressing injustice caused to an individual and own-initiative investigation appears inconsistent with impartiality. The landscape is crowded with bodies with regulatory and inspection functions and keeping a clear focus on what the ombudsmen is there to do is essential if clarity is to prevail.

It is unclear why own-initiative investigations would be 'inconsistent with impartiality', given that ombudsmen in any event do not mechanically investigate all complaints, instead exercising discretion in this area. Indeed, many commentators do not share the conclusion reached by the Collcutt Review: a number of expert observers who gave evidence to PASC considered that the possibility of own-initiative investigations may well be beneficial—a view endorsed by the Committee (see HC612, *Review of the Public Sector Ombudsmen in England* (1999–2000) at [11]), as well as by commentators such as Harlow (1978) 41 *MLR* 446 at 453 and Seneviratne, *Ombudsmen: Public Services and Administrative Justice* (London 2002) at 125–7. It is important to remember, however, that the question whether ombudsmen should have the power to initiate investigations without having received a complaint is keyed in to foundational issues about the role of ombudsmen (see 19.1.2): the absence of such a power is indicative of a (perhaps outmoded) view which emphasizes 'redress' over 'control', as well as of the view that the Parliamentary Ombudsman is a 'servant' of the House of Commons.

Thinking in this area is shifting. For instance, from 2018, the recently established Northern Ireland Public Services Ombudsman will be able to undertake own-initiative investigations. Meanwhile in 2015–16 the Finance Committee of the Welsh Assembly consulted on new draft legislation relating to the Public Services Ombudsman for Wales which made provision for own-initiative investigations. However, there appears to be no prospect of own-initiative powers being conferred upon the Parliamentary Ombudsman: although the Gordon Review (at [134]–[139]) was supportive of the idea, the government subsequently dismissed it (Cabinet Office, *A Public Service Ombudsman: Government Response to Consultation* (London 2015) at 18).

When ombudsmen lack the power to undertake own-initative investigations, this has implications for the extent of their powers to undertake investigations in response to complaints. In particular, it means that they cannot use a complaint as a peg on which to hang an investigation into some allied issue that was not actually complained about. This point emerges from *R (Cavanagh)* v. *Health Service Commissioner for England* [2005] EWCA Civ 1578, [2006] 1 WLR 1229 in which the complainant alleged that a hospital was guilty of maladministration by failing to arrange continuing care for his daughter following the closure of the unit primarily responsible for her treatment. To the surprise of the complainant, and of the doctors concerned, the Health Service Ombudsman cleared the hospital but ruled that the doctors had fallen into error by misdiagnosing the girl's condition. Sedley LJ held that the Ombudsman had exceeded her powers by investigating questions of clinical judgement which had not formed part of the subject-matter of the complaint. The Ombudsman, he said (at [16]), 'has no power of investigation at large': her powers 'do not enable her to expand the ambit of a complaint beyond what it contains, nor to expand her investigation of it beyond what the complaint warrants'.

QUESTIONS

- Should the Parliamentary Ombudsman be given the power to conduct own-initative investigations?
- To what extent might the discharge of a 'control' function be inhibited by the absence of such a power?

19.4.2 The MP filter

Section 5(1) and (1A) of the 1967 Act provides that the Parliamentary Ombudsman may only investigate complaints which reach her via an MP (an MP's refusal to refer to the Ombudsman apparently being immune from judicial review: *R (Murray)* v. *Parliamentary Commissioner for Administration* [2002] EWCA Civ 1472 at [17]). This is in contrast to most other countries, where direct access to ombudsmen is the norm, and to other ombudsman systems in the UK: members of the public can complain directly to the Health Service, Local Government, Scottish, Welsh, and Northern Ireland Ombudsmen. In fact, the 'MP filter' was originally envisaged by the Justice report which recommended the creation of an ombudsman (*The Citizen and the Administration* (London 1961) at [157]) as a temporary measure. So why does it still exist?

On a *pragmatic* level, the thinking behind the filter is that it enables MPs to discharge a triage function; as Harlow (1978) 41 *MLR* 446 at 451 puts it, the filter 'allows the MP to settle the trivial administrative muddles', sending only the 'hard nuts' on to the Ombudsman. However, the argument that MPs are effective gatekeepers is undermined by the fact that many MPs (51 per cent, according to the Collcutt Review at [3.45]) automatically refer complaints to the Ombudsman when requested to do so.

On a *constitutional* level, it is sometimes argued that the MP filter is fitting because it renders the Ombudsman an adjunct of the parliamentary process, thereby reflecting the received wisdom that it is MPs who bear primary responsibility for holding the executive to account and resolving constituents' grievances against public bodies. Yet while such thinking was undoubtedly instrumental in the initial inclusion of the filter in the 1967 Act, it has been subjected to sustained criticism ever since. In 2000, the Collcutt Review (at [3.43] and [3.51]) accepted that the relationship between the Ombudsman and MPs is an important one, but questioned whether the MP filter is a necessary component of that relationship:

[It is said that] [t]he MP filter is … an instrument of accountability. An individual MP is able to hold the executive to account through the [Parliamentary Ombudsman's] process—a department is required to respond to a statement of complaint and the report at the end of an investigation is provided to an MP who may wish to take action using it. We agree that in a serious case—where there is serious injustice to an individual or widespread injustice, serious maladministration, refusal by a department to remedy a clear injustice and so on—it is right that this is publicised and steps taken to ensure redress is provided and any systemic problems addressed. The absence of the MP filter does not prevent the MP being involved … in lodging a complaint nor, with the agreement of the complainant, becoming involved after a complaint has been made. For example, if a decision to conduct an investigation is made the [Parliamentary Ombudsman] could, with the agreement of the complainant, contact the relevant MP. Accountability can also be maintained through general oversight and reporting mechanisms to meet concerns of individual MPs about what is happening in their constituencies.

More recently, in a report published in 2014 (HC655, *Time for a People's Ombudsman Service* (2013–14) at [55]), PACAC, reiterating views that its predecessor, PASC, advanced on multiple occasions, issued a clarion call for the abolition of the filter:

> Along with all other informed opinion, we can find no justification for restricting citizens' direct access to the Parliamentary and Health Service Ombudsman for non-NHS complaints. It was intended that the 'MP filter' should be abolished after the first five years of the Parliamentary Ombudsman. Citizens were given direct access for NHS related complaints for good reason. The continuing prohibition of direct access for all complaints is the denial of equal access to administrative justice and is an anachronism which is at odds with the expectations of today's citizens. This defies all logic. It disempowers citizens, obstructs access to their rights, and deters people from making complaints.

Against this background, it is perhaps surprising that Ann Abraham, who served as the Parliamentary and Health Service Ombudsman from 2002 to 2011, saw some merit in the MP filter. Although she called it 'an anachronistic barrier to citizen access' (Abraham (2008) 61 *Parl Aff* 535 at 543), she adopted a nuanced position—in the light of the government's sometimes intransigent stance in the face of the Ombudsman's findings and recommendations, a matter to which we turn later—arguing (at 542–3) that the filter can serve to engage the interest of MPs in the work of the Ombudsman, to 'symbolise the close relationship between the Ombudsman and Parliament', 'to denote the fact that the Ombudsman is ... the 'servant' of Parliament', and to secure MPs' 'buy in ... to the effective operation of the Ombudsman system'.

When it considered the question of the MP filter in 2010–11, the Law Commission was alive to these concerns. It therefore consulted upon what it called a 'dual-track' model, whereby complaints would be able to reach the Ombudsman both directly and via MPs. It explained its thinking in the following terms (Law Commission, Consultation Paper No 196, *Public Services Ombudsmen* (2010)):

> 4.103 We are persuaded that there is value in maintaining a direct link with individual Members of Parliament. ...
>
> 4.104 Given that outright abolition [of the MP filter] could be seen as symbolically ending the direct relationship between individual Members [of Parliament] and the Parliamentary Commissioner, we suggest that the dual-track approach is preferable to outright abolition. This allows for specific provision to be made for the continuing involvement of a Member who referred a complaint to the Parliamentary Commissioner. This is potentially of especial importance where a report is issued.

The government has now signalled that it is 'minded to legislate for dual track access, whereby an individual would be able to approach PSO directly or with the assistance of a representative' (Cabinet Office, *A Public Service Ombudsman: Government Response to Consultation* (London 2015) at 14).

19.4.3 Securing redress

Section 8 of the 1967 Act confers upon the Ombudsman wide-ranging powers to extract information from Ministers and officials and, under s 9, failure to co-operate with the Ombudsman may ultimately be referred to a court and dealt with as if it were contempt of court. However, while the investigation process itself is supported by relatively strong coercive powers, the same is not true of the outputs of that process. In particular, it is apparent from s 10 of the 1967 Act that the Ombudsman cannot *enforce* her recommendations *per se*: she reports and, if she finds injustice occasioned by maladministration, can *recommend* redress. In *Principles for Remedy* (2009) at 1, the Ombudsman explains:

> We aim to secure suitable and proportionate remedies for complainants whose complaints are upheld and, where appropriate, for others who have suffered injustice or hardship as a result of the same maladministration or poor service. We want public bodies to be fair and to take responsibility, to acknowledge failures and apologise for them, to make amends, and to use the opportunity to improve their services.
>
> There is a range of appropriate responses to a complaint that has been upheld. These will include both financial and non-financial remedies. Financial compensation will not be appropriate in every case, but public bodies should not rule it out as a form of remedy for justified complaints. We understand that, for public bodies, there is often a balance between responding appropriately to people's complaints and acting proportionately within available resources. However, finite resources should not be used as an excuse for failing to provide a fair remedy.

The Ombudsman may lay special reports before Parliament where it seems that injustice is unlikely to be remedied. Moreover, the relevant parliamentary committee—currently PACAC—takes an interest in the extent to which the Ombudsman's recommendations are followed, and can apply pressure—by reporting to Parliament—when they are not. The vast majority of the Ombudsman's recommendations are accepted, but in recent years there have been some notable instances of government refusal fully to implement the Ombudsman's recommendations—and, in some cases, refusal even to accept her findings of maladministration and injustice.

A prominent example concerns the case of the Equitable Life Assurance Society, which found itself unable to meet the guarantees it had made to policyholders concerning the level of the pensions they would receive upon retirement. Several policyholders complained to the Ombudsman, alleging that the public bodies responsible for regulating insurers had been guilty of maladministration, and that this had caused injustice to them in the form of loss of anticipated pension income. Following a lengthy investigation, the Ombudsman concluded that there had been 'serial regulatory failure', that there had been a 'series of missed opportunities' for the responsible public bodies to identify and seek to deal with the difficulties which Equitable was getting into, and that the regulators had been 'passive, reactive and complacent' in their approach (HC815, *Equitable Life: A Decade of Regulatory Failure* (2007–08) at 372–5). She went on to recommend that in the light of the injustice occasioned by those failures, the government should, *inter alia*, establish a compensation scheme with the aim of 'put[ting] those people who have suffered a relative loss [that is, a loss compared to the position they would have been in had they invested elsewhere] back into the position that they would have been in had maladministration not occurred' (at 395). Following the publication of the Ombudsman's report, PASC, which at the time was the relevant select committee, said (HC41, *Second Report* (2008–09) at [117] and [49]) that it

> would be deeply concerned if the Government chose to act as judge on its own behalf by refusing to accept that maladministration took place [since this] would undermine the ability to learn lessons from the Equitable Life affair ... It would also be wrong for the Government to refuse compensation on the basis of [the] conclusion [of a separate inquiry] that Equitable Life was

'principally ... the author of its own misfortunes'. This ... must not mask [that inquiry's] further conclusion that it was regulatory failure which permitted Equitable Life's management to carry on undermining the interests of its members for so long.

The Committee's fears were not without foundation. The government rejected several of the Ombudsman's specific findings of maladministration (and of injustice resulting therefrom) and refused to implement her principal recommendation concerning compensation. Instead, it agreed to implement a less generous compensation scheme that would pay out only to those policyholders who had suffered a 'disproportionate impact' (Cm 7538, *The Prudential Regulation of the Equitable Life Assurance Society: The Government's Response to the Report of the Parliamentary Ombudsman's Investigation* (2009)). PASC responded (HC219, *Sixth Report* (2008–09)) in excoriating terms, accusing the government (at [33]) of misrepresenting the views advanced in the Committee's earlier report and asserting (at [9]) that 'the [compensation] scheme proposed by the Government is inadequate as a remedy for injustice'. The Ombudsman herself recognized that it would not necessarily have been improper for the government to refuse to implement as generous a scheme as she would have liked—but, giving evidence to PASC (at Ev 1), took stronger issue with its rejection of her findings:

[The government] might have said, 'We do not see this in the same way as the Ombudsman sees it, but out of respect for the constitutional position of her office, we will accept her findings of maladministration and injustice.' The Government could then have gone on to consider the question of remedy. It could then have brought into play legitimate considerations of public policy and public purse.'

The Ombudsman responded by laying a special report before Parliament under s 10(3) of the 1967 Act indicating: 'it is clear that the injustice I have found to have resulted from maladministration will not be remedied' by the government's proposed compensation scheme (HC435, *Injustice Unremedied: The Government's Response on Equitable Life* (2008–09) at [64]). The government stuck to its guns, refusing fully to implement the Ombudsman's main recommendation and continuing to emphasize that the Ombudsman's report created no *legal* requirement to provide compensation (HC Deb 21 October 2009, vol 497, col 931). MPs from all parties expressed disquiet about the government's treatment of the Ombudsman, but, on a whipped vote, the government defeated an opposition motion calling on it to abide by her recommendations. Following a change of government in 2010, the Equitable Life (Payments) Act 2010 was passed, paving the way for payments to be made to Equitable policyholders, although the extent to which such payments implement the Ombudsman's recommendations has been the subject of controversy: in a debate in the House of Commons in 2016, Sir Edward Leigh MP asserted that '95% of Equitable Life with-profits policyholders have received just 22% of their relative losses' (HC Deb 11 February 2016, vol 605, col 1792).

There have been other cases in which the government, at least initially, has rejected the Ombudsman's findings and refused to implement her recommendations, with acceptance and redress following, if at all, only as a result of political pressure often orchestrated by the relevant select committee. In a report (HC1081, *Sixth Report* (2005–06)) concerning one such affair (the 'pensions promise' case, discussed in the next section), PASC said (at [78]–[79]):

We share the Ombudsman's concern that the Government has been far too ready to dismiss her findings of maladministration. Our investigations have shown that these findings were sound. It would be extremely damaging if Government became accustomed simply to reject findings of maladministration, especially if an investigation by this Committee proved there was indeed a case to answer. It would raise fundamental constitutional issues about the position of the Ombudsman and the relationship between Parliament and the Executive.

We trust that this Report will act as a warning to the Government. We will continue to monitor the Government's responses to the Parliamentary Commissioner's reports. If necessary we will seek a debate on the floor of the House, so that all Members can discuss these issues, and re-establish the Parliamentary Commissioner's role. The Parliamentary Commissioner is Parliament's Ombudsman: Government must respect her.

More recently, PASC concluded (HC655, *Time for a People's Ombudsman Service* (2014) at [88]) that it—and other select committees—should make fuller and more systematic use of the Ombudsman's reports, thereby contributing, at least in a loose sense, to their enforcement:

PASC should have its Standing Orders amended to require it to use the intelligence gathered by the PHSO to hold to account the administration of Government. PASC should also ensure that PHSO's reports are referred to the Departmental Select Committee to which they are most rele-vant. From now on, we will do so. Departmental Select Committees should use PHSO's reports to hold their respective departments to account.

PASC's responsibility in respect of the Ombudsman has now transferred to its successor, the Public Administration and Constitutional Affairs Committee. That Committee's terms of reference, as set out in House of Commons Standing Order No 146, require it 'to examine the reports of the Parliamentary [Ombudsman] and the Health Service [Ombudsman]', but do not contain the specific provision recommended by PASC in the extract set out immediately above.

19.4.4 The role of the courts

It would be tempting to conclude from the foregoing that it is necessary to empower the Ombudsman not just to make findings and recommendations, but to *order* public bodies to put things right—and for such orders to be legally enforceable. This raises some important questions about the extent to which the law does and should intervene in this arena by investing the Ombudsman's conclusions with coercive effect.

The position varies as between different ombudsman schemes. For instance, although the conclusions of the Northern Ireland Public Services Ombudsman are not legally bind-ing *per se*, they can form the basis of court enforcement. If that Ombudsman finds that mal-administration has occasioned injustice, s 53 of the Public Services Ombudsman (Northern Ireland) Act 2016 authorizes the County Court, in certain circumstances, to award dam-ages to the relevant person and to direct the public body in question to take or refrain from taking specified action. Moreover, when the Ombudsman finds 'systematic maladministra-tion' and concludes that it is likely to continue in the absence of intervention by the High Court, s 55 enables that Court to grant an injunction or a mandatory injunction requir-ing the relevant public body to desist from taking or to take certain action. Meanwhile, the Local Government Ombudsmen's findings and recommendations have been held to be binding, such that public bodies are required to abide by them unless they are successfully challenged by way of judicial review: *R* v. *Local Commissioner for Administration, ex parte Eastleigh Borough Council* [1988] QB 855.

The position is different in respect of the Parliamentary Ombudsman, as the so-called pensions promise case illustrates. It concerned complaints about the government's discharge of its responsibilities in respect of the regulation of occupational pensions schemes which, it was alleged, had led to tens of thousands of policyholders finding their pensions to be worth less than they had been led to expect. The Ombudsman (HC984, *Trusting in the Pensions Promise* (2005–06)) found the government guilty of maladministration occasioning injustice by, among other things, deciding on the basis of an inadequate consideration of relevant evidence to cut the minimum amount of assets pension providers were legally required to hold (which resulted in some providers holding insufficient assets to meet policyholders' expectations) and by promulgating information that was potentially misleading as to the extent to which policyholders' interests were protected by the regulatory arrangements. The Ombudsman went on to recommend that the government should consider making arrangements for the restoration of policyholders' benefits 'by whichever means is most appropriate, including if necessary by payment from public funds, to replace the full amount lost by those individuals' (at [6.15]). As in the *Equitable Life* case, the government rejected the Ombudsman's findings of maladministration and refused to implement the principal recommendation set out earlier (although subsequent improvements to the Financial Assistance Scheme went some way towards providing recompense).

In those circumstances, four policyholders sought, in *R (Bradley)* v. *Secretary of State for Work and Pensions* [2007] EWHC 242 (Admin), [2008] EWCA Civ 36, [2009] QB 114, judicial review of the government's decision to reject the Ombudsman's findings and to refuse to implement her recommendations. The Ombudsman, who made submissions to the Court of Appeal as an interested party, argued (at [135]) that

> the Secretary of State must proceed on the basis that the ombudsman's findings of injustice caused by maladministration are correct unless they are quashed in judicial review proceedings. If this is accepted then that is the end of the matter as no application for judicial review has been made seeking to quash the report. The proper, and indeed it is submitted the only, place for the lawfulness of the ombudsman's report to be questioned is in judicial review proceedings aimed at quashing that report.

This view would make it possible for Ministers lawfully to reject the Ombudsman's findings only in very rare circumstances. For precisely that reason, the Court of Appeal held it was an incorrect view that was insensitive to the policy of the 1967 Act. After reviewing the white paper that preceded the Act, Sir John Chadwick, in his leading judgment, endorsed the view of the Royal Institute of Public Administration, *The Parliamentary Ombudsman: A Study in the Control of Administrative Action* (1975) at 503, that

> [i]f he is prepared to take the consequences, and defend his position in Parliament, in the last resort a minister who genuinely believes that he and his department have been unfairly criticised by the [Ombudsman], clearly has the right to say so.

This view reflects the fact that the consequences of the Ombudsman's reports were intended to sound in the political, not the legal, arena. Against this background, the question for the Court, it was held, was neither whether the *Ombudsman's findings* nor the *Minister's preferred view* was irrational. Rather, it was whether the *Minister's decision to reject the Ombudsman's findings* was irrational. Sir John said (at [91]):

> I am not persuaded that the Secretary of State was entitled to reject the ombudsman's finding merely because he preferred another view which could not be characterised as irrational. As I have said, earlier in this judgment, it is not enough that the Secretary of State has reached his own view on rational grounds: it is necessary that his decision to reject the ombudsman's findings in favour of his own view is, itself, not irrational having regard to the legislative intention which underlies the 1967 Act: he must have a reason (other than simply a preference for his own view) for rejecting a finding which the ombudsman has made after an investigation under the powers conferred by the Act.

Superficially, the Court of Appeal's preferred approach gives the government considerable latitude to reject the Ombudsman's findings: any non-irrational rejection will be lawful—and, as we know from ch 8, it is normally hard to show that a decision is irrational. But in fact the Court appeared to adopt a particularly strict form of irrationality review, asking (at [72]) whether the decision to reject the Ombudsman's findings was 'based on cogent reasons'. On that basis, it was held that the Minister *had* acted irrationally in rejecting the Ombudsman's findings that the government's information had been potentially misleading and that the resulting maladministration had caused some injustice. Those decisions were therefore quashed, and the Minister had to think again about the Ombudsman's recommendation to consider full compensation in the light of the findings that had, in effect, been reinstated by the Court. The 'cogent reasons' test was subsequently interpreted in *R (Equitable Members Action Group)* v. *HM Treasury* [2009] EWHC 2495 (Admin) at [66] as requiring the court to engage in a 'careful examination of the facts of the individual case'.

Whether such close judicial scrutiny is appropriate in this context is debatable. It might be argued that it ought not to be open to the government readily to dismiss findings that represent the culmination of a careful (and sometimes lengthy and painstaking) investigation by the Ombudsman. On such an analysis, reduced *judicial deference* to executive dismissals of the Ombudsman's findings might be taken to procure (by placing the executive under a heavier-than-usual justificatory burden) a desirable degree of *executive respect* for those findings and for the Ombudsman's office. Indeed, the Law Commission (Law Com No 329, *Public Services Ombudsmen* (2011) at [5.132]) goes even further:

> Findings are findings of fact and maladministration on complaints made to the ombudsmen and are the result of their investigatory procedure. The ombudsmen's schemes, including the closed nature of their investigations, were designed specifically to facilitate processes leading to such findings. We think, therefore, that it would weaken unnecessarily the ombudsmen's processes if their findings could be dismissed with a mere statement of 'cogent reasons', and that it would undermine an individual's decision to opt for an ombudsman rather than an alternative mechanism for administrative justice.

It therefore recommended (at [5.133]) that findings should be 'binding unless successfully challenged by way of judicial review'. Significantly, this recommendation cuts across the view that the public services ombudsmen themselves submitted to the Law Commission. They argued (at [5.121]):

> The public services ombudsmen's mandate is one of influence not sanction. Much of the distinctive character of the ombudsman process flows from that principle. To deviate

from it so that recommendations became enforceable would potentially undermine that distinctive character. The response to recommendations should remain part of the political process.

To those concerns might be added others, including that judicial intervention—at least to the extent countenanced by the 'cogent reasons' test—risks undermining the essentially political scheme contemplated by the legislation whereby the Ombudsman is intended to augment *Parliament's* capacity to hold government to account. Moreover, judicial intervention in apparent *support* of the Ombudsman's findings might have the paradoxical consequence of *undermining* the Ombudsman scheme. This risk arises because judicial scrutiny of the cogency of the *reasons for executive rejection* of the Ombudsman's findings necessarily requires the court to take a position on the cogency, in the first place, of the *findings themselves*. A judicial finding that there were cogent reasons for rejecting a finding inevitably carries the implication that the finding was, to begin with, unconvincing or otherwise problematic in some respect.

QUESTIONS

- In *Application by JR55 for Judicial Review* [2016] UKSC 22 at [20], Lord Sumption said that *Bradley* 'raises delicate questions about the relationship between judicial and Parliamentary scrutiny of a minister's rejection of the recommendations of the Parliamentary [Ombudsman]'. Do *Bradley* and/or the Law Commission's recommendation risk upsetting that 'delicate relationship'?

The *Equitable Life* case involved a challenge not only to the government's rejection of the Ombudsman's *findings*, but also to its rejection of her *recommendation* concerning the establishment of a compensation scheme. Here, the Court was more reticent. Whether to establish such a scheme—and, if so, on what terms—was, said the Court (at [132])

in general ... a matter for Parliament not us. It is not in dispute, as we understand it, that the question whether to establish a compensation scheme in any particular context, and the limits of such a scheme, is a matter for the Government, reporting to Parliament, and not reviewable in the courts save on conventional irrationality grounds.

The position, therefore, is that even if claimants find themselves in a relatively strong position—by dint of the 'cogent reasons' test—when it comes to challenging rejections of the Ombudsman's findings, they face an uphill struggle if they wish to use judicial review to force the government to implement the Ombudsman's recommendations by having a refusal to do so struck down as irrational. If, on the crunch issue concerning the implementation of recommendations, the courts' role is, as *Equitable Life* suggests, relatively slight, the focus shifts back to the political process. This accords with the position adopted by the Law Commission, which (at [5.130]) sharply distinguished recommendations from findings:

Recommendations allow the ombudsmen to make suggestions as to the manner in which a particular instance of injustice could be remedied and also to suggest improvements that could be undertaken to improve the administration of the public body subject to investigation. Such recommendations may have wide ranging implications, which could be outside the knowledge of the ombudsmen—given their primary focus on the complaints made to them. It is correct, therefore, for recommendations to remain non-binding and questions as to their implementation to remain in the political domain.

QUESTION

- Is the distinction drawn by the case law and by the Law Commission between findings and recommendations a defensible one? Why (not)?

19.4.5 Judicial review of ombudsmen's conclusions

In the previous section we were concerned with the extent to which courts might intervene so as to require public bodies to accept ombudsmen's findings or implement their recommendations. However, to the extent that such 'enforcement' is possible, it can logically bite only upon *lawful* findings and *lawful* recommendations. This raises questions about the legal scope of the discretion of ombudsmen when it comes to making findings and formulating recommendations, and about the extent to which the exercise of that discretion is open to judicial review—either at the instance of a dissatisfied public authority (which might want to argue that an ombudsman has gone too far) or a dissatisfied individual (who might want to argue the converse).

We have already seen that ombudsmen are susceptible to judicial review—hence, for instance, the possibility of judicial review of ombudsmen's decisions whether (and, if so, what) to investigate. But what of ombudsmen's conclusions (by which we mean findings and recommendations)? Can they be judicially reviewed? So far as the Local Government Ombudsmen are concerned, the answer, according to Collins J in *R (Turpin)* v. *Commissioner for Local Administration* [2001] EWHC 503 (Admin) at [36], is 'yes':

[I]f it is clear that the Ombudsman in reaching a decision has misdirected himself as a matter of law, or has failed to have regard to a relevant consideration, or has had regard to an irrelevant consideration, or has given reasons which are so defective that they indicate that his decision is bad in law, then the court can and should intervene. The court will be careful to ensure that it does so only if such errors are clear but, as it seems to me, there is nothing in the legislation to exclude the court's usual power to consider whether a discretion, however widely conferred, has been exercised in accordance with law.

There is no reason why this statement of principle should not apply to other ombudsmen, including the Parliamentary Ombudsman. Indeed, the *Balchin* litigation—*R* v. *Parliamentary Commissioner for Administration, ex parte Balchin (No 1)* [1997] JPL 917; *(No 2)* (2000) 79 P & CR 157; and *(No 3)* [2002] EWHC 1876 (Admin)—places beyond doubt that a finding of maladministration by that Ombudsman can be quashed on judicial review. The cases concerned planning blight caused by a decision to build a new road near to the claimants' home. In the first case, Sedley J struck down the Ombudsman's report—which concluded that no maladministration had occurred—because he had failed to consider whether the Department of Transport ought to have drawn the relevant local authority's attention to new statutory powers which it could have exercised to acquire the claimants' property. A fresh report—in which it was concluded that no maladministration had occurred because the Department had not overlooked the new statutory powers—was quashed by Dyson J in the second case. He concluded (at 168) that

> the finding that the [Department] did not overlook s 246(2A) [of the Highways Act 1980—the new statutory provision in question] was at the heart of the [Ombudsman's] conclusion that there was no maladministration. It was this finding that enabled him to conclude that the decision reached by the [Department] was 'within the reasonable range of responses open to them given their knowledge' and 'one they were entitled to take' ... It is not possible to say what conclusion he would have reached on the issue of maladministration if he had found that those handling the Balchins' case had overlooked s 246(2A). I think that the Commissioner was unwittingly led into error by the rather unspecific evidence of the Permanent Secretary. It is possible that ... there were persons in the [Department] handling the Balchins' case who had not overlooked s 264(2A). But if that is so, there is no trace of them in any of the material that has been placed before me.

Harrison J (see [2002] EWHC 1876 (Admin) at [51]) then quashed the Ombudsman's third report on this matter because internal inconsistencies meant that there had been a 'failure to give adequate reasons for his decision that there was no maladministration' during a particular phase of the process.

The willingness disclosed by these cases to review the Ombudsman's decisions about whether maladministration has occurred was defended by Dyson J in *Balchin (No 2)* (2000) 79 P & CR 157 at 169, who remarked that such review involves judicial scrutiny only of the Ombudsman's reasoning process, not the substance of her decision. Indeed, in *R (Doy)* v. *Commissioner for Local Administration* [2001] EWHC 361 (Admin), [2002] Env LR 11 at [16], Morison J urged particular caution when it comes to examining matters of substance in this context:

> The court's supervisory role is there to ensure that [the Ombudsman] has acted properly and lawfully. However much the court may disagree with the ultimate conclusion, it must not usurp the Ombudsman's statutory function. It is likely to be very rare that the court will feel able to conclude that the Ombudsman's conclusions are perverse, if only because he must make a qualitative judgment based upon his wide experience of having to put mistaken administration onto one side of the line or the other.

However, the Supreme Court's recent judgment in *Application by JR55 for Judicial Review* [2016] UKSC 22 suggests—albeit on the basis of obiter remarks—that the possibility of quashing an ombudsman's decision on substantive grounds is more than a merely theoretical one. The Northern Ireland Commissioner for Complaints (which office has now been superseded by the Northern Ireland Public Services Ombudsman) had concluded that a medical practice was guilty of maladministration in respect of the complainant's deceased husband and recommended that the general practitioner concerned should make a payment of £10,000 to the complainant. The Supreme Court held (for reasons particular to the legislative regime that governed the Commissioner for Complaints) that it was not open to the Commissioner to recommend the payment of money in these circumstances. However, Lord Sumption (giving the only judgment) indicated (at [30]) that even if it had in principle been open to the Commissioner to make such a recommendation, the particular recommendation made in this case would have been unlawful on the ground of irrationality:

> The Commissioner's recommendations, in those cases where he is entitled to make them, are discretionary and he has more latitude in arriving at a figure than a court would have. But a monetary recommendation, like any other, must be rational, and it must be explained. The only explanation proffered is that the £10,000 should be paid 'in respect of the clearly identified failings in the care provided to [the patient] and the events which consequently followed.' The report does not explain why these failings warrant a payment of £10,000 or how that figure has been arrived at. It does not say whether [the complainant or her husband] suffered any loss by the failings for which the £10,000 should be treated as compensation. Some of the failings, notably the failure to take more urgent action ... are found to have made no difference and others, such as the events which followed [the death of the complainant's husband] could not in the nature of things have done so. It is possible that the recommendation was intended as a [form of compensation] for injured feelings, but the report does not say so, and in the absence of explanation £10,000 seems to be an excessive amount to recommend on that basis. On the face of it, the figure has simply been plucked out of the air. If I had concluded that the Complaints Commissioner had power to recommend a payment by the respondent, I would have regarded this particular recommendation as lacking any rational basis.

Whether such judicial oversight of ombudsmen is appropriate is open to question. It might be argued that ombudsmen, as public bodies, should be subject to the same types of judicial control as all other public bodies. However, we already know (see ch 8) that not all public bodies are equal, and that there may be good reasons, for instance on institutional or democratic grounds, for courts to extend particular latitude to certain decision-makers in particular circumstances. As far as ombudsmen are concerned, there are several such reasons. For instance, as Giddings [2000] *PL* 201 at 203 observes, the more that ombudsmen's conclusions are susceptible to judicial scrutiny, the more we

> move towards setting a standard of reasoning on the record for the Ombudsman which could put at risk the essential informality and accessibility of the institution. If judges require the Ombudsman to meet the decision-making standards set for courts, then what was an informal, non-judicial mechanism for complaint-handling will become a formal, judicial one—with consequent costs in time and resources which are likely to deter some potential complainants from pursuing their case.

It is also important to bear in mind that ombudsmen are *themselves* an accountability mechanism—which at least raises questions about the extent to which it is necessary and appropriate for courts to hold ombudsmen to account—and that, as we noted in the previous section, ombudsmen are conceived of as an element of the *political* process for securing good administration. Lord Sumption was careful to note in *JR55* (at [1]) that while the 'various enactments [underpinning the public sector ombudsmen schemes] have a strong family resemblance', 'some of them have distinctive features which mean that considerable caution is required before principles derived from one legislative scheme can be read across to another'. It may therefore be that greater reticence would attach to reviewing the Parliamentary Ombudsman's conclusions on the ground of irrationality than appeared to condition Lord Sumption's consideration of the Northern Ireland Complaints Commissioner's recommendation. An obvious difference between the two schemes is that whereas the Parliamentary Ombudsman is keyed into the parliamentary system for securing accountable government, the Complaints Commission had no equivalent relationship with the Northern Ireland Assembly. Either way, however, it is to be hoped that Lord Sumption's remarks in *JR55* do not prefigure an enhanced judicial preparedness to subject ombudsmen's conclusions to close scrutiny on substantive grounds.

19.5 Institutional matters

The ombudsman system that operates in England is significantly different from those that are found in Northern Ireland, Scotland, and Wales. As noted at 19.1.1, the latter have adopted integrated systems that provide a 'one-stop shop': single ombudsmen thus have jurisdiction over health, local government, social housing, and devolved governmental bodies. In contrast, the arrangements in England are fragmented, with a number of distinct ombudsman jurisdictions. This has long been a source of concern. As long ago as 1998, the ombudsmen themselves called for a 'comprehensive review' of arrangements (see Collcutt Review, Annex A at [1]), arguing that people found it 'difficult to know to which Ombudsman to complain' (at [11]–[13]). Moreover, it is not infrequently the case that a given complaint will raise cross-cutting issues falling within the jurisdiction of more than one ombudsman. The ombudsmen's concerns prompted the Collcutt Review (some aspects of which we have already referred to). Published in 2000, it concluded (at [2.34]) that 'the present fragmented structure of public sector Ombudsmen and complaints systems [is not] able to meet the challenge of handling complaints which cross boundaries'. The Review therefore recommended (at [4.3]–[4.4]) the creation of a single, integrated ombudsman service for England. However, apart from modest legislative changes permitting joint working, reform in this area has been unforthcoming.

Recently, though, the question of institutional reform has risen up the agenda. In 2014, PASC (HC655, *Time for a People's Ombudsman Service* (2014) at [98]) called for 'the creation of a single public services ombudsman for England' which would make for 'a much simpler and more accessible ombudsman service' and would 'allow learning and good practice to be disseminated more easily'. This recommendation was subsequently echoed in the government-commissioned Gordon Review, which (at [51]) drew attention to the problems created by the existing fragmented system and the opportunities likely to be presented by an integrated model:

[A] single structure ensures complaints and complainants are not confined to or restricted by administrative or other jurisdictional boundaries. This provides clarity for the complainant and allows the ombudsman to respond dynamically to complaints. Collcutt wrote in 2000 of the need to ensure that the ombudsman is not 'government shaped' but rather that it has organisational and jurisdictional flexibility to allow it to adapt, recognising the fact that the notion of a single government shape is increasingly fluid. A decade and a half of rapid public service delivery evolution later that argument is stronger. The increasing prevalence of complaints which cross boundaries between agencies and institutions requires action to avoid the need to pursue resolution through multiple complaints processes and multiple complaints handlers. The potential for individuals to have to be passed between ombudsmen remains and even with welcome and positive efforts to ensure sensible joint (but sometimes cumbersome) working between existing organisations, differences in schemes and the simple fact of multiple identities risks confusion and disengagement.

Gordon concluded (at [69]) that a new public services ombudsman embracing the current roles of the Parliamentary, Health Service, Local Government, and Housing Ombudsmen would carry considerable advantages. In 2015, the government signalled that it would 'work to create a single service', but that the Housing Ombudsman would remain separate—albeit that the proposed framework would allow other ombudsmen's jurisdictions to be added 'over time' (Cabinet Office, *A Public Service Ombudsman: Government Response to Consultation* (London 2015) at 8).

One complication that will have to be negotiated when England's new public services ombudsman system is designed is that the system of separate ombudsmen that it will replace does not itself relate exclusively to England. While the Health Service, Local Government, and Housing Ombudsmen's jurisdictions extend only to England, the Parliamentary Ombudsman's does not. Rather, the Parliamentary Ombudsman is constituted on a UK-wide basis. In the light of devolution, it is true that many of the public bodies that the Parliamentary Ombudsman oversees have responsibilities that relate only to England. However, other public bodies about which complaints can be made to the Parliamentary Ombudsman operate beyond England. For instance, HM Revenue and Customs (HMRC) operates across the whole of the UK, and the Parliamentary Ombudsman deals with complaints in relation to HMRC in all four of the UK's constituent nations.

In the light of this, the Parliamentary Ombudsman cannot straightforwardly (along with the (English) Health Service and (English) Local Government Ombudsmen) be folded into an English ombudsman service. Instead, an institutional design will have to be developed which can accommodate the Parliamentary Ombudsman's dual role as a UK ombudsman and a *de facto* English public services ombudsman. The Gordon Review considered this matter only in passing, noting (with apparent approval) the idea that the Parliamentary Ombudsman's England-only functions should shift into a new integrated English ombudsman service, and that a distinct UK ombudsman service should be retained in relation to public functions that are discharged on a UK-wide basis. Meanwhile, although PASC took the view that '[n]on-devolved matters require a UK-wide Ombudsman Service', it was open to the idea of 'a single ombudsman with a dual role as UK and England Ombudsman' (HC655, *Time for a People's Ombudsman Service* (2014) at [104]–[105]). That idea has now found favour with the government, which has indicated (Cabinet Office, *A Public Service Ombudsman: Government Response to Consultation* (London 2015) at 8) that

the new PSO [public services ombudsmen] will cover UK reserved matters [*ie* matters that are delivered on a UK, rather than a devolved or England-only, basis] as well as those public services delivered solely in England. As such it will mirror the accountability of UK reserved matters to the Westminster Parliament, relinquishing jurisdiction over those if and when they transfer to the devolved administrations. At the same time, we will give PSO the ability to build stronger working relationships with its counterparts in the devolved administrations.

While the proposed ombudsman's hybrid nature as both a UK and an England-only ombudsman may seem rather odd, this in fact mirrors legislative and administrative reality in the UK. Indeed, the UK Parliament and the UK government are similarly hybrid in nature, exercising legislative and administrative functions in relation to the whole of the UK so far as reserved matters are concerned, whilst simultaneously operating as the legislature and the executive for England in respect of matters that are devolved elsewhere. The new ombudsman service will simply reflect these governance arrangements.

At the time of writing, although the UK government has signalled its intention to introduce the reforms discussed in this section, no detailed proposals have been brought forward; nor has the primary UK legislation that will have to be enacted been introduced into Parliament or published in draft.

19.6 Concluding remarks

Much of this book has been concerned with legal forms of redress for maladministration, such as those supplied by judicial review and the tribunals system. We have also considered essentially political mechanisms such as *ad hoc* inquiries into matters of public concern. Ombudsmen occupy a somewhat anomalous position. In many respects, the ombudsman system falls on the political, rather than the legal, side of the line (if any such line can be clearly drawn): ombudsmen can address a wider range of concerns than those that would constitute grounds for judicial review; the Parliamentary Ombudsman remains *Parliament's* Ombudsman, in the sense that she reports to Parliament and is (at least for now) linked to it via the MP filter; and the way in which ombudsmen handle complaints bears little resemblance to the formal, adversarial judicial process.

And yet the relationship between the Ombudsman and the judicial system has proven to be an increasingly thorny issue in recent years. In the first chapter of this book, we said that the growth of judicial review has been fuelled, in part, by despair about the capacity of the political process to secure good administration. We conclude by noting that it would be a retrograde step if over-zealous judicial review of government refusals to accept the Ombudsman's findings and recommendations resulted in them becoming, in effect, legally binding. Such an approach would insert courts into an accountability process that is intended to be political in nature, and would risk eroding respect for the Ombudsman scheme by increasingly requiring courts, at least implicitly, to pass judgment on the quality of the Ombudsman's conclusions. At the beginning of the book, we posed the question: 'Is (more) judicial review a good thing?' In the present context, at least, the answer is a resounding 'no'.

FURTHER RESOURCES

Abraham, 'The Ombudsman as Part of the UK Constitution: A Contested Role?' (2008) 61 *Parl Aff* 206; 'The Ombudsman and Individual Rights', at 370; 'The Ombudsman and the Executive: The Road to Accountability', at 535

Buck, Kirkham, and Thomspon, *The Ombudsman Enterprise and Administrative Justice* (London 2010)

Gordon, *Better to Serve the Public* (2014) *http://www.gov.uk/government/uploads/system/ uploads/attachment_data/file/416656/Robert_Gordon_Review.pdf*

Kirkham, 'The Ombudsman, Tribunals and Administrative Justice Section: a 2020 Vision for the Ombudsman Sector' (2016) 38 *Journal of Social Welfare and Family Law* 103

Kirkham and Alt, 'Making Sense of the Case Law on Ombudsman Schemes' (2016) 38 *Journal of Social Welfare and Family Law* 1

Law Commission, Law Com No 329, *Public Services Ombudsmen* (2011) *http://www.lawcom.gov.uk/wp-content/uploads/2015/03/lc329_ombudsmen.pdf*

Public Administration Select Committee, HC655, *Time for a People's Ombudsman Service* (2014) *http://www.publications.parliament.uk/pa/cm201314/cmselect/cmpubadm/655/655.pdf*

Seneviratne, *Ombudsmen: Public Services and Administrative Justice* (London 2002)

Varuhas, 'Judicial Capture of Political Accountability' (London 2016) *http://judicialpowerproject.org.uk/wp-content/uploads/2016/06/Judicial-Capture-of-Political-Accountability-.pdf*

Website of the Ombudsman Association *http://www.ombudsmanassociation.org* (with links to the various ombudsmen's websites)

INDEX